Y0-BSN-096

APA Handbook of

Psychology, Religion, and Spirituality

APA Handbooks in Psychology

APA Handbook of Psychology, Religion, and Spirituality

VOLUME 1

Context, Theory, and Research

Kenneth I. Pargament, *Editor-in-Chief*

Julie J. Exline and James W. Jones, *Associate Editors*

American Psychological Association • Washington, DC

Copyright © 2013 by the American Psychological Association. All rights reserved. Except as permitted under the United States Copyright Act of 1976, no part of this publication may be reproduced or distributed in any form or by any means, including, but not limited to, the process of scanning and digitization, or stored in a database or retrieval system, without the prior written permission of the publisher.

Published by
American Psychological Association
750 First Street, NE
Washington, DC 20002-4242
www.apa.org

To order
APA Order Department
P.O. Box 92984
Washington, DC 20090-2984
Tel: (800) 374-2721; Direct: (202) 336-5510
Fax: (202) 336-5502; TDD/TTY: (202) 336-6123
Online: www.apa.org/pubs/books/
E-mail: order@apa.org

In the U.K., Europe, Africa, and the Middle East, copies may be ordered from
American Psychological Association
3 Henrietta Street
Covent Garden, London
WC2E 8LU England

AMERICAN PSYCHOLOGICAL ASSOCIATION STAFF
Gary R. VandenBos, PhD, *Publisher*
Julia Frank-McNeil, *Senior Director, APA Books*
Theodore J. Baroody, *Director, Reference, APA Books*

Typeset in Berkeley by Cenveo Publisher Services, Columbia, MD

Printer: United Book Press, Baltimore, MD
Cover Designer: Naylor Design, Washington, DC

Library of Congress Cataloging-in-Publication Data

APA handbook of psychology, religion, and spirituality / editor, Kenneth I. Pargament.
v. ; cm. — (APA Handbooks in Psychology)
Includes bibliographical references and index.
ISBN 978-1-4338-1077-0 — ISBN 1-4338-1077-8
1. Psychology and religion. 2. Psychology, Religious. 3. Adjustment (Psychology)—Religious aspects. 4. Spirituality. I. Pargament, Kenneth I. (Kenneth Ira), 1950– II. Title: Handbook of psychology, religion, and spirituality.
BF51.A53 2013
201′.615—dc23
2012015189

British Library Cataloguing-in-Publication Data
A CIP record is available from the British Library.

Printed in the United States of America
First Edition

DOI: 10.1037/14045-000

To psychologists of religion and spirituality,
past, present, and future—
pioneers and partners exploring the deepest dimensions of life.

Contents

Volume 1: Context, Theory, and Research

Editorial Board

EDITOR-IN-CHIEF

Kenneth I. Pargament, PhD, Professor of Clinical Psychology, Department of Psychology, Bowling Green State University, Bowling Green, OH; and Distinguished Scholar at the Institute for Spirituality and Health, Houston, TX

ASSOCIATE EDITORS

Volume 1

Julie J. Exline, PhD, Associate Professor of Psychology, Department of Psychological Sciences, Case Western Reserve University, Cleveland, OH

James W. Jones, PhD, Distinguished Professor of Religion and Adjunct Professor of Clinical Psychology, Department of Religion, Rutgers University, New Brunswick, NJ

Volume 2

Annette Mahoney, PhD, Professor of Clinical Psychology, Department of Psychology, Bowling Green State University, Bowling Green, OH

Edward P. Shafranske, PhD, ABPP, Professor of Psychology and Director of the PsyD Program, Graduate School of Education and Psychology, Pepperdine University, Los Angeles, CA

About the Editor-in-Chief

Kenneth I. Pargament, PhD, is professor of clinical psychology at Bowling Green State University and distinguished scholar at the Institute for Spirituality and Health at the Texas Medical Center. He is an adjunct professor in the Department of Psychiatry and Behavioral Sciences at the Baylor College of Medicine. He has also served as adjunct professor in the School of Theology at Boston University and as distinguished visiting professor at Lackland Air Force Base Medical Center.

Dr. Pargament has been a leading figure in the dramatic resurgence of attention to religion and spirituality by social scientists and practitioners over the past 35 years. Many of his more than 200 published studies have focused on people dealing with trauma. Dr. Pargament has delineated the variety of ways, helpful and harmful, religion expresses itself in times of stress, and his measure of religious coping, the Religious Coping Inventory (RCOPE), is the standard in the field. His 1997 book *The Psychology of Religion and Coping: Theory, Research, Practice* was described by the *Bulletin of the Menninger Clinic* as "the best book on the psychology of religion in a generation or more."

In 1987 Dr. Pargament won the William James Award for excellence in research from Division 36 (Society for Psychology of Religion and Spirituality) of the American Psychological Association. He is coeditor of *Mental Health, Religion, and Culture* and sits on the editorial boards or is editorial consultant to more than 30 journals. In 2009 he received the Oskar Pfitzer Award from the American Psychiatric Association in recognition of his research and practical efforts to understand and enhance the links between religion, spirituality, and mental health. In 2012 he received the National Samaritan Institute Award for his contributions to human health and growth.

A practicing clinical psychologist, Dr. Pargament has long been interested in expanding the field beyond research to practice. He and his colleagues have designed and tested a number of spiritually integrated interventions. This work culminated in his 2007 book *Spiritually Integrated Psychotherapy: Understanding and Addressing the Sacred*, which is unique in the literature.

In addition, Dr. Pargament has been active in mentoring graduate students and colleagues in the field. In recognition of his commitment and contributions to teaching, he received the Virginia Staudt Sexton Mentoring Award from Division 36 of the American Psychological Association in 2000 and the Outstanding Contributor to Graduate Education at Bowling Green State University in 2002. He recently received the Lifetime Contribution Award from the Ohio Psychological Association. Dr. Pargament's research has garnered national and international media attention, including coverage by the *London Times*, *Newsweek*, the *New York Times*, *Scientific American*, and the *Washington Post*.

Contributors

Hisham Abu-Raiya, PhD, Bob Shapell School of Social Work, Tel Aviv University, Tel Aviv, Israel

Amy L. Ai, PhD, College of Social Work; Family Medicine and Rural Health, College of Medicine; and Department of Psychology, College of Arts and Sciences, Florida State University, Tallahassee

Marlyn Allicock, PhD, MPH, Department of Nutrition, Gillings School of Global Public Health, University of North Carolina at Chapel Hill

Hoa B. Appel, PhD, Minority Achievers Program, Snohomish County, Marysville, WA

Elizabeth T. Austin, PsyD, Department of Psychiatry, University of Massachusetts Medical School, Worcester

Justin L. Barrett, PhD, Graduate School of Psychology, Fuller Theological Seminary, Pasadena, CA

Steven R. H. Beach, PhD, Department of Psychology, University of Georgia, Athens

Richard Beck, PhD, Department of Psychology, Abilene Christian University, Abilene, TX

Marvin G. Belzer, PhD, UCLA Mindful Awareness Research Center, Los Angeles, CA

Eric R. Bergemann, PhD, MBA, Mindsight Institute, Los Angeles, CA

Michael E. Berrett, PhD, Center for Change, Orem, UT

Jeffrey P. Bjorck, PhD, Graduate School of Psychology, Fuller Theological Seminary, Pasadena, CA

Andrea K. Blanch, PhD, Center for Religious Tolerance, Sarasota, FL

Chris J. Boyatzis, PhD, Psychology Department, Bucknell University, Lewisburg, PA

Marci K. Campbell, PhD,* Department of Nutrition, Gillings School of Global Public Health, University of North Carolina at Chapel Hill

Robert D. Carlisle, MA, Department of Psychology and Neuroscience, Baylor University, Waco, TX

Stephen T. Carroll, PhD, Department of Education Specialties, Loyola University Maryland, Baltimore

Evan C. Carter, MS, Department of Psychology, University of Miami, Coral Gables, FL

Casey Erin Clardy, PhD, Lawndale Christian Health Center, Chicago, IL

Adam B. Cohen, PhD, Department of Psychology, Arizona State University, Tempe

Lionel Corbett, MD, Pacifica Graduate Institute, Santa Barbara, CA

Sian Cotton, PhD, Department of Family and Community Medicine and Department of Pediatrics, University of Cincinnati College of Medicine, Cincinnati, OH

*deceased

Jeremy P. Cummings, MA, Department of Psychology, Bowling Green State University, Bowling Green, OH
Don E. Davis, PhD, Department of Counseling and Psychological Services, Georgia State University, Atlanta
Simon Dein, PhD, MBBS, MRCPsych, Faculty of Brain Sciences, University College London, London, England
Carrie Doehring, PhD, Department of Pastoral Care and Counseling, Iliff School of Theology, Denver, CO
Kent D. Drescher, PhD, National Center for PTSD, Palo Alto Health Care System, Menlo Park, CA
Donald Edmondson, PhD, Center for Behavioral Cardiovascular Health, Department of Medicine, Columbia University Medical Center, New York, NY
Evonne Edwards, PhD, Rosemead School of Psychology, Biola University, La Mirada, CA
Christopher G. Ellison, PhD, Department of Sociology, University of Texas, San Antonio
Julie J. Exline, PhD, Department of Psychological Sciences, Case Western Reserve University, Cleveland, OH
Roger D. Fallot, PhD, Community Connections, Washington, DC
Margaret Feuille, MA, Department of Psychology, Bowling Green State University, Bowling Green, OH
Frank D. Fincham, PhD, Family Institute, Florida State University, Tallahassee
Amanda M. Fleri, BA, Skidmore College, Saratoga Springs, NY
Edouard Fontenot, PhD, Commonwealth Psychology Associates, Boston, MA
David W. Foy, PhD, Graduate School of Education and Psychology, Pepperdine University, Encino, CA
Leslie J. Francis, PhD, Institute of Education, University of Warwick, Gwynedd, Wales
Annie M. Fujikawa, PhD, Rosemead School of Psychology, Biola University, La Mirada, CA
Marc Galanter, MD, Department of Psychiatry; Director, Division of Alcoholism and Drug Abuse, New York University School of Medicine, New York
Terry Lynn Gall, PhD, Faculty of Human Sciences and Philosophy, Saint Paul University, Ottawa, Ontario, Canada
Aubrey L. Gartner, PhD, Department of Psychology, Virginia Commonwealth University, Richmond
Benjamin J. Gorvine, PhD, Department of Psychology, Northwestern University, Evanston, IL
Harold Gorvine, PhD, Wynnewood, PA
Pehr Granqvist, PhD, Department of Psychology, Stockholm University, Stockholm, Sweden
Nyasha A. Grayman-Simpson, PhD, Department of Psychology, Goucher College, Pikesville, MD
Jeff Greenberg, PhD, Department of Psychology, University of Arizona, Tucson
Manal Guirguis-Younger, PhD, Faculty of Human Sciences and Philosophy, Saint Paul University, Ottawa, Ontario, Canada
Amy Hale-Smith, MA, MCS, Department of Psychology, University of Connecticut, Storrs
Todd W. Hall, PhD, Rosemead School of Psychology, Biola University, La Mirada, CA
William Hathaway, School of Psychology and Counseling, Regent University, Virginia Beach, VA
Andrea D. Haugen, Doctoral Candidate, Department of Psychology, Texas A&M University, College Station

Peter C. Hill, PhD, Rosemead School of Psychology, Biola University, La Mirada, CA
David R. Hodge, PhD, School of Social Work, Arizona State University, Phoenix
Ralph W. Hood Jr., PhD, University of Tennessee at Chattanooga
Joshua N. Hook, PhD, Department of Psychology, University of North Texas, Denton
Elizabeth Gerken Hooten, ScD, Department of Psychiatry and Behavioral Medicine, Duke University Medical Center, Durham, NC
Bu Huang, PhD, Bastyr Research Institute, Bastyr University, Kenmore, WA
Ellen L. Idler, PhD, Department of Sociology, Emory University, Atlanta, GA
David J. Jennings II, MS, MA, Department of Psychology, Virginia Commonwealth University, Richmond
Byron R. Johnson, PhD, Institute for Studies of Religion, Baylor University, Waco, TX
Thomas J. Johnson, PhD, Department of Psychology and Center for the Study of Health, Religion, and Spirituality, Indiana State University, Terre Haute
Veronica Johnson, PsyD, School of Psychology and Counseling, Regent University, Virginia Beach, VA
James W. Jones, PhD, Department of Religion, Rutgers University, New Brunswick, NJ
Julia E. M. Kidwell, PhD, Department of Psychology, University of Saint Thomas, Minneapolis, MN
Jeff King, PhD, Center for Cross-Cultural Research, Department of Psychology, Western Washington University, Bellingham
Pamela Ebstyne King, PhD, School of Psychology, Fuller Theological Seminary, Pasadena, CA
Lee A. Kirkpatrick, PhD, Department of Psychology, College of William and Mary, Williamsburg, VA
Constantin Klein, PhD, Research Center for Biographical Studies in Contemporary Religion, Faculty of History, Philosophy, and Theology, Universität Bielefeld, Bielefeld, Germany
Harold G. Koenig, MD, Department of Psychiatry and Behavioral Sciences, Duke University Medical Center, Durham, NC, and King Abdulaziz University, Jeddah, Saudi Arabia
Joan Koss-Chioino, PhD, Professor Emerita, School of Human Evolution and Social Change, Arizona State University, Tempe, and Research Professor, George Washington University, Washington, DC
Neal Krause, PhD, Department of Health Behavior and Health Education, University of Michigan, Ann Arbor
Jean Kristeller, PhD, Department of Psychology, Indiana State University, Terre Haute
Kevin L. Ladd, PhD, Department of Psychology, Indiana University South Bend
Mark J. Landau, PhD, Department of Psychology, University of Kansas, Lawrence
Kate Miriam Loewenthal, PhD, Department of Psychology, Royal Holloway University of London, London, England; and Glyndwr University, Wrexham, Wales
Annette Mahoney, PhD, Department of Psychology, Bowling Green State University, Bowling Green, OH
Joanna Maselko, ScD, Department of Psychiatry and Behavioral Sciences and Duke Global Health Institute, Duke University, Durham, NC
Kenneth I. Maton, PhD, Department of Psychology, University of Maryland, Baltimore County
Jacqueline S. Mattis, PhD, Department of Applied Psychology, Steinhardt School of Culture, Education, and Human Development, New York University, New York
Michael E. McCullough, PhD, Department of Psychology, University of Miami, Coral Gables, FL

Michael J. McFarland, PhD, Center for Research on Child Well-Being, Office of Population Research, Princeton University, Princeton, NJ
Shane P. Moe, MDiv, MA, Bethel Seminary, St. Paul, MN
Sylvia Mohr, PhD, Department of Mental Health and Psychiatry, University Hospitals of Geneva, Geneva, Switzerland
Aaron Murray-Swank, PhD, Veterans Administration Eastern Colorado Health Care System, Denver
Nichole A. Murray-Swank, PhD, Counseling Department, Regis University, Broomfield, CO
Doug Oman, PhD, School of Public Health, University of California, Berkeley
Kenneth I. Pargament, PhD, Department of Psychology, Bowling Green State University, Bowling Green, OH, and Institute for Spirituality and Health, Houston, TX
Crystal L. Park, PhD, Department of Psychology, University of Connecticut, Storrs
Michelle J. Pearce, PhD, Department of Psychiatry and Behavioral Sciences, Duke University Medical Center, Durham, NC; and Department of Family and Community Medicine, University of Maryland School of Medicine, Baltimore
Ralph L. Piedmont, PhD, Department of Pastoral Counseling and Spiritual Care, Loyola University Maryland, Baltimore
Thomas G. Plante, PhD, ABPP, Department of Psychology, Santa Clara University, Santa Clara, CA
Jenel Sánchez Ramos, PsyD, Private Practice, San Francisco, CA
Lobsang Rapgay, PhD, Department of Psychiatry, University of California, Los Angeles
Ken Resnicow, PhD, Department of Health Behavior and Health Education, School of Public Health, University of Michigan, Ann Arbor
P. Scott Richards, PhD, Department of Counseling Psychology and Special Education, Brigham Young University, Provo, UT
Ana-María Rizzuto, MD, PINE Psychoanalytic Center, Needham, MA
Alyssa Bryant Rockenbach, PhD, Department of Leadership, Policy, and Adult and Higher Education, North Carolina State University, Raleigh
Mark S. Rye, PhD, Department of Psychology, Skidmore College, Saratoga Springs, NY
Steven J. Sandage, PhD, Department of Marriage and Family Therapy, Bethel Seminary, St. Paul, MN
Vassilis Saroglou, PhD, Department of Psychology, Université Catholique de Louvain, Louvain-la-Neuve, Belgium
Edward P. Shafranske, PhD, ABPP, Graduate School of Education and Psychology, Pepperdine University, Los Angeles, CA
Daniel J. Siegel, MD, Mindsight Institute, Los Angeles, CA
Madeleine W. Siegel, UCLA Mindful Awareness Research Center, Los Angeles, CA
Mark W. Smith, CHC, Commander Naval Forces Pacific Fleet, U.S. Navy, San Diego, CA
Melissa Soenke, MA, University of Arizona, Tucson
Len Sperry, MD, PhD, Program in Mental Health Counseling, Florida Atlantic University, Boca Raton, and Department of Psychiatry, Medical College of Wisconsin, Milwaukee
Bernard Spilka, PhD, Professor Emeritus, Department of Psychology, University of Denver, Denver, CO
Mariano R. Sto. Domingo, PhD, Department of Psychology, University of Maryland, Baltimore County
Heinz Streib, PhD, Research Center for Biographical Studies in Contemporary Religion, Faculty of History, Philosophy, and Theology, Universität Bielefeld, Bielefeld, Germany

Sara Susov, EdS, Brigham Young University, Provo, UT
Siang-Yang Tan, PhD, School of Psychology, Fuller Theological Seminary, Pasadena, CA
Nalini Tarakeshwar, PhD, Executive Director, Performance Measurement and Effectiveness, The Children's Investment Fund Foundation, London, England
Tyler Townsend, EdD, Department of Leadership, Policy and Adult and Higher Education, North Carolina State University, Raleigh
Joseph E. Trimble, PhD, Center for Cross-Cultural Research, Department of Psychology, Western Washington University, Bellingham
Jo-Ann Tsang, PhD, Department of Psychology and Neuroscience, Baylor University, Waco, TX
Amy B. Wachholtz, PhD, Department of Psychiatry, University of Massachusetts Medical School, Worcester
Nathaniel G. Wade, PhD, Department of Psychology, Iowa State University, Ames
Lynn C. Waelde, PhD, Pacific Graduate School of Psychology, Palo Alto, CA
James E. Waller, PhD, Keene State College, Keene, NH
Froma Walsh, PhD, Department of Psychiatry and School of Social Service Administration, University of Chicago, and Chicago Center for Family Health, Chicago, IL
Jerren C. Weekes, MA, Department of Psychology, University of Cincinnati, Cincinnati, OH
Sarah L. Weinberger-Litman, PhD, Department of Psychology, Marymount Manhattan College, New York, NY
Anna M. L. Westin, MS, Department of Psychology, University of Maryland, Baltimore County
Teresa A. Wilkins, MS, Department of Pastoral Counseling and Spiritual Care, Loyola University Maryland, Baltimore
Everett L. Worthington Jr., PhD, Department of Psychology, Virginia Commonwealth University, Richmond
Mark A. Yarhouse, PsyD, School of Psychology and Counseling, Regent University, Virginia Beach, VA
Michael S. Yi, MD, MSc, Department of Pediatrics and Division of General Internal Medicine, Department of Internal Medicine, University of Cincinnati College of Medicine, Cincinnati, OH
Bonnie Poon Zahl, Doctoral Candidate, Department of Social and Developmental Psychology, University of Cambridge, Cambridge, England
Brian J. Zinnbauer, PhD, Cincinnati Veterans Affairs Medical Center, Cincinnati, OH

Series Preface

The *APA Handbook of Psychology, Religion, and Spirituality* is the eighth publication to be released in the American Psychological Association's latest reference line, the *APA Handbooks in Psychology*™ series, instituted in 2010. The series primarily comprises multiple two- and three-volume sets focused on core subfields. Some single-volume handbooks on highly focused content areas within core subfields will also be released.

The seven previously released sets are as follows:

- *APA Handbook of Industrial and Organizational Psychology*—three volumes; Sheldon Zedeck, Editor-in-Chief
- *APA Handbook of Ethics in Psychology*—two volumes; Samuel J. Knapp, Editor-in-Chief
- *APA Educational Psychology Handbook*—three volumes; Karen R. Harris, Steve Graham, and Tim Urdan, Editors-in-Chief
- *APA Handbook of Research Methods in Psychology*—three volumes; Harris Cooper, Editor-in-Chief
- *APA Addiction Syndrome Handbook*—two volumes; Howard J. Shaffer, Editor-in-Chief
- *APA Handbook of Counseling Psychology*—two volumes; Nadya A. Fouad, Editor-in-Chief
- *APA Handbook of Behavior Analysis*—two volumes; Gregory J. Madden, Editor-in-Chief

Each set is formulated primarily to address the reference interests and needs of researchers, clinicians, and practitioners in psychology and allied behavioral fields. Each also targets graduate students in psychology who require well-organized, detailed supplementary texts, not only for "filling in" their own specialty areas but also for gaining sound familiarity with other established specialties and emerging trends across the breadth of psychology. Moreover, many of the sets will bear strong interest for professionals in pertinent complementary fields (i.e., depending on content area), be they corporate executives and human resources personnel; doctors, psychiatrists, and other health personnel; teachers and school administrators; cultural diversity and pastoral counselors; legal professionals; and so forth.

Under the direction of small and select editorial boards consisting of top scholars in the field, with chapters authored by both senior and rising researchers and practitioners, each reference set is committed to a steady focus on best science and best practice. Coverage converges on what is currently known in the particular subject area (including basic historical reviews) and the identification of the most pertinent sources of information in both core and evolving literature. Volumes and chapters alike pinpoint practical issues; probe unresolved and controversial topics; and present future theoretical, research, and practice trends. The editors provide clear guidance to the "dialogue" among chapters, with internal cross-referencing that demonstrates a robust integration of topics to lead the user to a clearer understanding of the complex interrelationships within each field.

With the imprimatur of the largest scientific and professional organization representing psychology in the United States and the largest association of psychologists in the world, and with content edited and authored by some of its most respected members, the *APA Handbooks in Psychology* series will be the indispensable and authoritative reference resource to turn to for researchers, instructors, practitioners, and field leaders.

Gary R. VandenBos
APA Publisher

Introduction

Times are changing, especially in the psychology of religion and spirituality. In the 1970s, a psychologist interested in the field could go to the library every few months, spend a leisurely day perusing the journals, and return to his or her office feeling reasonably confident of being on top of recent developments in the field. That is no longer possible. To illustrate the point, a PsycINFO database search for the number of citations for the term *religion* yielded the following results for the past 5 decades: 1,051 (1960s); 2,290 (1970s); 4,205 (1980s); 5,501 (1990s); and 11,629 (2000s). A comparable search for the term *spirituality* revealed an even more striking rise: 5 (1960s); 22 (1970s); 543 (1980s); 2,680 (1990s); and 7,894 (2000s). The number of journals that cover the interface between psychology, religion, and spirituality has also increased sharply. In addition, the psychology of religion and spirituality has become more mainstream in recent years, with several journals featuring special issues or special sections on religion and spirituality, including the *American Psychologist, Psychological Inquiry,* the *Journal of Personality,* the *Journal of Clinical Psychology*, *Personality and Social Psychology Review*, the *Journal of Social Issues,* and the establishment of an American Psychological Association (APA) journal, *Psychology of Religion and Spirituality*. In addition, numerous fine introductory texts on the psychology of religion and spirituality, edited handbooks, and books on the integration of religion and spirituality into psychological interventions have appeared. Indeed, the inclusion of these volumes on religion and spirituality in the *APA Handbooks in Psychology* series (in the major domains of psychology) is a sign that our field has now achieved more mainstream status.

The psychology of religion and spirituality has grown in other ways too. To keep abreast of knowledge in this area, a psychologist cannot afford to stay within his or her disciplinary boundaries. New information that holds direct relevance to the psychology of religion and spirituality is being generated by many disciplines, from the allied social sciences to the medical professions to philosophy and theology. Moreover, the field is moving beyond its research boundaries to encompass practice as well. Indeed, we will assert that it is now possible to talk about an *applied psychology of religion and spirituality.* All of these changes are being accompanied by rapid growth in theory, measurement, and methodology. Finally, the psychology of religion and spirituality is becoming increasingly global, with significant contributions coming out of Asia, South America, and the Middle East as well as North America and Europe. Rapid growth, however, brings with it some challenges. The growth in the field has led to exceptional diversity in concepts, methods, and practices. No single paradigm captures the broad span of psychological interests in and approaches to religion and spirituality.

This state of affairs may be quite appropriate as the psychology of religion and spirituality mirrors the richness and complexity of religious and spiritual life. There is, however, a risk of fragmentation as the field expands, with knowledge becoming isolated into silos of narrow research or practice interests.

The goal of this handbook is to provide thorough coverage of the current state of the field: what we know about religion and spirituality and their roles in human functioning (as well as what we do not know), and how we can apply this knowledge to advance the welfare of people, individually and collectively. In addition, we hope to spur the field forward by encouraging greater coherence and integration in the field. To achieve our first goal of thorough coverage of the psychology of religion and spirituality, we have taken the ambitious approach of creating a two-volume handbook. To achieve our second goal of encouraging greater coherence in the field, we have taken two steps. First, we have developed an integrative paradigm, consisting of several guiding themes for the field. Our integrative paradigm is introduced in the first chapter of Volume 1 and elaborated further in the introduction to Volume 2. Readers are strongly encouraged to read these introductory chapters to provide them with this orienting vision for the field. We also shared the integrative paradigm with the authors of our chapters and asked them to work within this overarching perspective. Second, we have provided a strong organizing framework for these two volumes. Although both volumes integrate research, theory, and practice, the first volume places greater emphasis on research and theory, and the second volume focuses in greater detail on practice. Following is an overview of each part in Volumes 1 and 2.

VOLUME 1: CONTEXT, THEORY, AND RESEARCH

Part I. Setting the Stage: Themes, Contexts, Measures, and Methodology

To set the stage for the handbook, the first part introduces an integrative paradigm for the psychology of religion and spirituality, one that contains several guiding themes that lend greater coherence to a field now encompassing diverse theories, methods, practices, and concepts, including the meanings of the terms *religion* and *spirituality* themselves (see Volume 1, Chapter 1). The chapters in this part also underscore the point that the psychology of religion and spirituality has not grown out of a vacuum; it is instead rooted in a rich social context (Volume 1, Chapter 2). To understand phenomena as intricate and elusive as religion and spirituality, psychologists cannot rely on any single measure or methodology. Setting the stage for things to come in the remainder of the handbook, the chapters in this first part consider the rich diversity of measures and methods that have come to define the field (Volume 1, Chapters 3 and 4).

Part II. Why People Are Religious and Spiritual: Explanatory Models

Among the many questions about religion and spirituality that have long fascinated psychologists, one has received special attention: Why are people religious and spiritual? Psychologists have arrived at a variety of answers to this question. In fact, one way to distinguish among psychologists and other social scientists in the field is by the way they explain religion and spirituality. Freud spoke of religion's role in controlling human impulses and managing anxiety. Durkheim stressed the role of religion in forming a community of believers. Geertz saw religion as a response to the need for meaning and comprehension. The chapters in this part focus on more recent theoretical and empirical developments that speak to the question of why people are religious and spiritual. Each chapter addresses a particular explanation. As a group, they cover a wide expanse of territory, including psychological (Volume 1, Chapters 5, 6, 8, 9, and 12), interpersonal (Volume 1, Chapters 7 and 10), cultural (Volume 1, Chapter 13), and biological (Volume 1, Chapter 11) explanations. And the possibility is raised that spirituality may be a distinctive motivation in and of itself, one that is, at least in part, irreducible (Volume 1, Chapter 14). There is, of course, no reason to pick one explanation alone. Part of the power of religion and spirituality may lie in their ability to respond to diverse human needs and motives. Thus, each chapter in this part may shed important light on the reasons why religion and spirituality become a part of people's lives and lead them toward different destinations.

Part III. How People Are Religious and Spiritual: Expressions and Experiences

In the past, psychologists and other social scientists tended to study religion and spirituality from a distance, relying on global indicators of these processes such as frequency of religious attendance and prayer, religious affiliation, and self-ratings of religiousness and spirituality. These indicators offer a glimpse into the worlds of religion and spirituality, but the resulting picture can also leave people with the mistaken impression that these worlds are uniform, simple, and straightforward. On the contrary, religion and spirituality are anything but simple. They are rich, diverse, and complex processes made up of a tremendous array of expressions and experiences—cognitive, behavioral, affective, and relational. Over the course of their lives, people can follow or construct any number of religious and spiritual pathways. The chapters in this part highlight the progress that has been made and questions that have been raised by psychologists who have moved closer to religious and spiritual life and focused their attention on the specific ways in which people express and experience their faith. They include chapters on God images (Volume 1, Chapter 15), prayer (Volume 1, Chapter 16), meditation (Volume 1, Chapter 17), rituals and practices (Volume 1, Chapter 18), religious and spiritual coping (Volume 1, Chapter 19), relational spirituality (Volume 1, Chapter 20), mystical experience (Volume 1, Chapter 21), conversion (Volume 1, Chapter 22), spiritual virtues (Volume 1, Chapters 23 and 24), religious and spiritual struggles (Volume 1, Chapter 25), and evil (Volume 1, Chapter 26).

Part IV. Who Is Religious and Spiritual: Specific Populations

In Western culture, where great value is placed on personal freedom and autonomy, many people may believe that they have chosen their particular religious and spiritual beliefs, practices, and commitments. Yet, empirical research suggests that religion and spirituality are shaped in part by a larger constellation of personal, social, and cultural factors. It is no accident that a child born in Saudi Arabia will in all likelihood become a Muslim, that a child born to parents who are members of the Church of Jesus Christ of Latter-day Saints will most likely be a Mormon, or that a child born in Sweden will be unlikely to develop a traditional theistic understanding of God. The chapters in this part of the handbook examine how religion and spirituality are manifested within specific populations. Age (Volume 1, Chapters 27–29), ethnicity (Volume 1, Chapters 30–33), and religious identification (Volume 1, Chapters 35–41) play a vital role in determining the form, function, and consequences of religion and spirituality. The chapters highlight the distinctiveness of religious and spiritual subgroups while underscoring the diversity of religion and spirituality that can be found within any particular subgroup. Several of the chapters examine the special religious and spiritual challenges faced by marginalized religious and cultural subgroups (e.g., Volume 1,

Chapter 34). As a group, these chapters emphasize that religion and spirituality cannot be understood apart from a wider set of personal, social, and cultural forces.

VOLUME 2: AN APPLIED PSYCHOLOGY OF RELIGION AND SPIRITUALITY

Part I. Introduction to an Applied Psychology of Religion and Spirituality

The second volume of this handbook shifts the focus from theory and research to practice. Although these chapters place their emphasis on applications of religion and spirituality, they too are informed by theory and research. The chapters in the first part of the second volume introduce readers to the concept of an applied psychology of religion and spirituality. The first chapter (Volume 2, Chapter 1) considers why the time has come for an applied psychology of religion and spirituality and presents a vision for this field that is based on the integrative paradigm introduced in the first volume. As envisioned here, the applied psychology of religion and spirituality is not limited to psychotherapy practiced by clinical and counseling psychologists; instead, it encompasses a variety of efforts to improve the human condition that can be implemented by psychologists from every subdiscipline. Laying the foundation for the contributions that follow, other chapters in this introductory part address the religiousness and spirituality of psychologists themselves (Volume 2, Chapter 2), the challenging ethical issues that arise in the field (Volume 2, Chapter 3), and various models for conceptualizing mature religion and spirituality (Volume 2, Chapter 4).

Part II. Religion and Spirituality From the Perspective of Major Orientations to Change

Spiritually integrated approaches to change are not generally viewed as competitors to other forms of psychological intervention and treatment. Psychologists of religion and spirituality have instead thought carefully about ways to address religion and spirituality within the context of various well-established psychological theories and methods of change. This part of the handbook considers how religious and spiritual problems and resources are assessed (Volume 2, Chapter 5) and approached in practice from the perspective of major orientations to intervention, including psychodynamic (Volume 2, Chapter 6), Jungian (Volume 2, Chapter 7), cognitive behavioral (Volume 2, Chapter 8), family systems (Volume 2, Chapter 9), and mindfulness-based (Volume 2, Chapter 10) approaches. Another chapter considers points of similarity and difference between spiritually integrated therapy, pastoral care, and spiritual direction (Volume 2, Chapter 11). As a group, the chapters highlight how the applied psychology of religion and spirituality can be enriched by contributions from the larger field of psychology, and how the larger field of psychology can be enriched, in turn, by a deeper appreciation for the religious and spiritual character of problems, solutions, and change.

Part III. Religion and Spirituality Applied to Specific Problems

This part of the handbook highlights the significant implications of religion and spirituality for efforts to help people often seen by psychologists in practice, including people with depression and anxiety (Volume 2, Chapter 12), severe mental disorders (Volume 12, Chapter 13), acute and chronic illness (Volume 2, Chapter 14), addiction (Volume 2, Chapter 15), eating disorders (Volume 2, Chapter 16), and sexual trauma (Volume 2, Chapter 17). Each of the chapters underscores the importance of attending to the double-sided nature of religion and spirituality: their capacity to provide people with invaluable resources for solving painful problems and their capacity to exacerbate those problems, making bad matters even worse. Several of the chapters also illustrate how religion and spirituality can be integrated into a wider array of human concerns. Moving beyond individuals as targets for change, religion and spirituality can be involved in attempts to solve social problems, such as political violence (Volume 2, Chapter 18), interpersonal trauma (Volume 2, Chapter 19), prejudice and discrimination (Volume 2, Chapter 20), and family-related problems (Volume 2, Chapter 21). Special attention is given to the ways psychologists can address religious and spiritual problems as significant concerns in and of themselves (Volume 2, Chapter 22). Going beyond the treatment of disorders, religion and spirituality can also be a part of efforts to prevent problems before they develop (Volume 2, Chapters 23 and 24) and to promote positive human qualities and potential (Volume 2, Chapter 25).

Part IV. Religion and Spirituality Applied to Specific Contexts

Much of the practical work involving religion and spirituality has focused on psychotherapy conducted in the context of mental health centers and clinical practices. Exciting advances are now under way in this domain. There are, however, many other settings in which psychologists can address religion and spirituality. The chapters in this part of the handbook highlight the innovative programs and activities that psychologists have developed in recent years in contexts that encompass religious institutions (Volume 2, Chapter 26), health care systems (Volume 2, Chapter 27), correctional settings (Volume 2, Chapter 28), the military (Volume 2, Chapter 29), educational systems (Volume 2, Chapter 30), the workplace (Volume 2, Chapter 31), and communities (Volume 2, Chapter 32). Taken as a whole, these chapters point to the tremendous promise and potential of a more broadly conceived applied psychology of religion and spirituality for individuals, families, institutions, communities, and society as a whole.

Part V. Future Directions for an Applied Psychology of Religion and Spirituality

Although the psychology of religion and spirituality has made great strides in recent years, questions continue to far outnumber answers. The field must address significant challenges if it is to continue to progress as an applied discipline. The final part of the handbook focuses on two areas that call for special attention by researchers and practitioners: graduate education and clinical training (Volume 2, Chapter 33) and evaluative research on the roles of religion and spirituality in psychological interventions (Volume 2, Chapter 34). Both chapters include important recommendations to help advance the applied psychology of religion and spirituality.

ACKNOWLEDGMENTS

We extend our deep appreciation to Theodore (Ted) Baroody and Susan Reynolds from the American Psychological Association for the initiative and vision that helped launch this groundbreaking effort, which places the psychology of religion and spiritually within the mainstream of U.S. psychology. Special thanks go to Ted, our editor, whose constant support and guidance helped shepherd this large and challenging project home to completion.

Kenneth I. Pargament
Editor-in-Chief

Part I

SETTING THE STAGE: THEMES, CONTEXTS, MEASURES, AND METHODOLOGY

CHAPTER 1

ENVISIONING AN INTEGRATIVE PARADIGM FOR THE PSYCHOLOGY OF RELIGION AND SPIRITUALITY

Kenneth I. Pargament, Annette Mahoney, Julie J. Exline, James W. Jones, and Edward P. Shafranske

> China Protests Obama Meeting with Dalai Lama Buddhist . . . Lutheran Church Seeing Fallout over Gay Clergy Issue . . . Meditation Boosts Concentration Skills . . . Thousands Attend Ground Zero Mosque Protest Rally

If current news headlines are any judge, pronouncements about the decline of religion in modern society have been a bit premature. Religious and spiritual issues continue to take center stage in the dramas that are regularly played out among individuals, families, communities, and nations. And it is difficult to ignore the religious dimension that underlies the event that has shaken our globe in the new millennium, the attacks on the World Trade Center and the Pentagon on September 11, 2001.

Newspaper headlines are only the most sensational indicators that religious and spiritual concerns remain alive and well in our times. There is no shortage of less sensational signs. Consider, for instance, the tremendous popularity of recent books, fiction and nonfiction, that address religion and spirituality—*The God Delusion; The Purpose-Driven Life; Eat, Pray, Love*—to name a few. Or, scan the national surveys that continue to show that a majority of Americans attend religious congregations at least once a month, pray at least once a day, state that religion is a very important part of their lives, and believe in heaven, hell, angels, demons, and miracles (e.g., U.S. Religious Landscape Survey, 2008).

What these signs cannot convey are the ways that religion and spirituality are embedded in the greatest hopes and dreams of many people, their deepest disappointments and frustrations, the ways they understand and deal with themselves and the larger world, and their everyday experiences across the life span, from birth to death. Summarizing his survey findings over the years, George Gallup Jr. (1999) concluded that "the depth of religious commitment often has more to do with how Americans act and think than do other key background characteristics, such as level of education, age and political affiliation." In short, religion and spirituality continue to hold tremendous power for large numbers in the world in the 21st century.

With power, however, comes emotion. It is hard to find anyone who is neutral when it comes to religion and spirituality, including those who define themselves as nonreligious and nonspiritual, scientists among them. It is also difficult to engage in calm and dispassionate conversations about this domain. As with politics, people may decide to steer clear of religious and spiritual talk to spare themselves the discomfort of a tense exchange and to preserve and protect their relationships.

The end result has been unfortunate. Instead of conversation and dialogue about such critical and emotionally charged domains, we have either silence or opinion and provocation. The problem is compounded by a lack of education about religion and spirituality within the public school system in the United States as well as religious education programs within many denominations that are limited in depth and scope. Conversations about religious and spiritual matters at home are not an everyday

DOI: 10.1037/14045-001
APA Handbook of Psychology, Religion, and Spirituality: Vol. 1. Context, Theory, and Research, K. I. Pargament (Editor-in-Chief)
Copyright © 2013 by the American Psychological Association. All rights reserved.

occurrence and do not fill this gap (Bartkowski, Xu, & Levin, 2008). All of this adds up to "religious and spiritual neglect"—a type of neglect less publicized than other forms but one that may have equally significant implications for individuals, families, and our culture. In the 21st century, significant numbers of people are left religiously and spiritually uninformed, or to use the stronger language of sociologist Christian Smith, "spiritually illiterate" (cf. Smith & Denton, 2005).

The consequences of this widespread spiritual neglect are not trivial. Take one example. Recently a flight from New York to Louisville was diverted to Philadelphia when crewmembers were alarmed by a young 17-year-old observant Jewish adolescent who was engaged in his regular prayers wearing tefillin (see "Phylacteries Abort Flight," 2010). Tefillin are boxes containing biblical passages and straps that are attached to the head and arm during morning prayers. Uninformed about this religious practice, crewmembers feared that the tefillin might be a bomb. As one Federal Bureau of Investigation agent commented afterward, "It's something that the average person is not going to see very often, if ever." And yet, we might ask, why should the average person be uninformed about a religious practice that is a part of the daily lives of observant Jews around the world? Perhaps the average person might also benefit from more information and knowledge about religion and spirituality and the part that they play in the lives of so many people.

What, if anything, does all of this have to do with psychology? A lot, potentially. A central thesis underlying these two volumes is that the psychology of religion and spirituality has a great deal to offer the effort to understand religion and spirituality and promote health and well-being. With its emphases on skepticism, objectivity, and the scientific method, psychology can shed light on many critical questions: Are religion and spirituality forces for personal wholeness, health and healing, or fragmentation, problems and pathology? Do religion and spirituality encourage social connectedness and compassion or prejudice and condemnation? Why are people religious and spiritual in the first place? How do we explain the troubling links of religion and spirituality with extremist behaviors, on the one hand, and their links with altruistic behaviors, on the other? Are there better ways to address religious and spiritual problems in individual's lives and the world at large? Could we draw more fully on religious and spiritual resources to create more fulfilling lives and relationships? The psychology of religion and spirituality does not offer easy answers to questions such as these. In fact, as this field has advanced, we have learned that we need to replace oversimplified questions with more precise questions. But in spite of the challenges of studying phenomena as rich, complex, and elusive as religion and spirituality, our field is rapidly developing a significant, systematically based body of knowledge about these processes.

Some of this knowledge is profoundly important. For instance, we know that people who attend religious services frequently live considerably longer on average than those who attend less frequently or not at all (McCullough, Hoyt, Larson, Koenig, & Thoresen, 2000). Other knowledge is of great importance but raises as many questions as it answers. For example, Phelps et al. (2009) studied a sample of patients with advanced cancer and found that those who made more use of positive religious and spiritual coping were more likely to receive extremely expensive and intensive life-prolonging care during the last week of life. Were these patients demonstrating their fighting spirit through these coping efforts, or were they demonstrating instead their fear of death and refusal to accept the reality of their plight? Still other knowledge may be less profound or less clear in its practical implications but nonetheless remains fascinating. For example, in one recent study, participants completed a target detection task; God-related words generated attentional shifts in an upward direction of the visual field, whereas devil-related words led to downward shifts in the visual field (Chasteen, Burdzy, & Pratt, 2010). The researchers concluded that terms such as *God* and *devil* are quite strongly tied to the ways we orient ourselves to the physical world. In short, we know a lot more about the links of religion and spirituality to human behavior than we did 25 years ago.

Multiplicity and *diversity* might be the terms that most accurately describe the current status of the psychology of religion and spirituality. No single paradigm dominates the field. No single definition of religion or spirituality has achieved acceptance by most researchers and practitioners. A single methodological approach or a dominant set of measures also does not exist in the discipline, although the field is largely reliant on self-report instruments. Instead, the psychology of religion and spirituality is marked by exceptional diversity in concepts, theories, methods, and measures (see Chapters 3 and 4, this volume). This is, perhaps, as it should be; the multiplicity in the field is an accurate reflection of the richness of religious and spiritual life. As comparative religionist William Paden (1994) noted, the religious world of every individual is in some sense unique, even among individuals identified with the same religious denomination. "Within a single tradition like Christianity," he wrote, "there are thousands of religious worlds" (Paden, 1994, p. viii).

The rapid growth, multiplicity, and diversity in the field, however, is accompanied by the danger of fragmentation—a field that becomes so large, so ill-defined, and so unwieldy that it carries a serious risk of fracture among researchers and practitioners who can pursue their own particular interests while remaining unaware of the relevant work of others. To propel the field forward, we believe that an overarching organizing vision is needed—one that can lend greater coherence to the multiplicity and diversity in the discipline (Reich, 2008).

We have labeled our proposed organizing perspective the *integrative paradigm* for the psychology of religion and spirituality. This paradigm rests on a deep appreciation for both diversity and integration in the field. To grasp the extraordinary breadth and depth of religion and spirituality, psychologists cannot rely exclusively on one set of theoretical, methodological, or practical instruments. Instead, multiple concepts and methods are called for. To create coherence and wholeness, however, it is equally essential at this critical junction in the development of the field that we identify points of connection and interaction, possibilities for convergence and synthesis, and unanticipated questions and challenges that can only come from dialogue and exchange within the field itself.

Our aim for this *APA Handbook of Psychology, Religion, and Spirituality* is to capture the current state of the field, what we know (and do not know) about religion and spirituality in the 21st century, the part they both play in individual and social life, and the ways we can apply this knowledge to advance human welfare. But our interest goes beyond describing what we currently know. We also hope to push the field forward by encouraging greater integration. To bring the meaning of our integrative paradigm to life, we identified five guiding integrative themes. In the remainder of this introductory chapter, we describe these themes that underlie our vision of an integrative paradigm for the psychology of religion and spirituality. The final theme elaborates on the meanings of religion and spirituality that were used to shape and guide this handbook.

THEME 1: INTEGRATING THE MULTIPLE DIMENSIONS AND MULTIPLE LEVELS OF RELIGION AND SPIRITUALITY

Religion and Spirituality as Multidimensional

Donald Capps (1977) once wrote that "the religious is not elusive because it lurks behind ordinary phenomena but because it is woven into the phenomena" (p. 48). We find religion and spirituality in every dimension of life. Theoretical and empirical studies clarify that religion and spirituality are multidimensional constructs, made up of a myriad of thoughts, feelings, actions, experiences, relationships, and physiological responses which serve many purposes and yield a number of consequences (e.g., Glock, 1962; Idler et al., 2003).

But the extraordinary multiplicity and diversity of religion and spirituality make these processes even more difficult to understand. How can we simplify this task? One overarching metaphor is particularly helpful in this regard; this is the metaphor of the journey, one consisting of pathways and destinations (Pargament, 1997, 2007). Think of the individual entering the world and embarking on a religious and spiritual journey that takes him or her on multiple pathways over time. Over the course of the life span, the individual's religious and spiritual travels may be marked by rites of passage, a developing system of beliefs and practices oriented to matters of ultimate importance, critical forks in the journey that lead to greater religious and spiritual involvement in one direction and disengagement in the other, and the merging of the person's travels with those of others. The individual's religious and spiritual pathways say something very important about who that person is; no one person's route in life is identical to that of another.

This is not a farfetched metaphor. Virtually every major religious tradition speaks of life as a journey and provides its adherents with a map for the pathways they should take in life. We hear of the Eightfold Path in Buddhism. The Pillars of Islam describe the central pathway of living as submission to the will of Allah. Within Taoism, the word *Tao* literally means "the Way." It is important to note, however, that although some people may follow the "preconstructed" pathways that have been made available to them through their traditions, others prefer to construct their own paths. Religious and spiritual pathways are constructed out of the raw materials of cognition, affect, behavior, relationship, and biology. To understand religious and spiritual pathways then, we have to take a close look at these ingredients and how they come together to form distinctive paths. In this handbook, we consider many of these vital religious and spiritual raw materials, their place in a larger religious or spiritual way of life, and their implications for health and well-being (see Part III of this volume).

The pathways that mark life journeys also are directed toward particular destinations. Over the years, social scientists have articulated a variety of religious and spiritual destinations, or to put it in more scientific language, religious and spiritual functions. Religion and spirituality have been described as serving functions that range from impulse control and anxiety reduction to meaning making and evolutionary adaptation. And, as we will elaborate later, to those who are most devout, the ultimate destination of religion is spirituality itself. Several chapters in this handbook are devoted to these functional explanations and to the fascinating question of why people are religious and spiritual (see Part II of this volume).

Religion and Spirituality as Multilevel

People do not follow their religious and spiritual paths in isolation. They undertake their journeys within a larger field of social and cultural forces, including religious group, age, ethnicity, family, community, and culture. These forces shape the nature of the individual's religious and spiritual trek over the life span (see Part IV of this volume). Thus, religion and spirituality are not only multidimensional constructs; they are multilevel phenomena as well.

This point deserves special emphasis. Founding father of the field, William James (1902), focused his religious inquiry on "individual men in their solitude," and since that time the psychology of religion and spirituality has been concerned largely with *individual* beliefs, experiences, and behaviors. This body of work has been enriched more recently by studies that have differentiated a more conscious—explicit level of personal belief from a less conscious—implicit level of religious understanding (see Chapter 15 in this volume). Nevertheless, our discipline remains individualistic. This bias is certainly a reflection of larger trends toward what has been described as "self-contained individualism" in Western culture and the larger field of psychology in the United States (Sampson, 1977). It is problematic, however. Commenting on the individualism of research on religion, Barton (1971) wrote:

> Researchers have proceeded to take people out of their actual social contexts and to limit their analysis to individual variables—this is like a biologist putting his experimental animals through a meat grinder and taking every hundredth cell to examine under a microscope; almost all information about anatomy and physiology, about structure and function gets lost. (p. 847)

As important as the individual level of analysis is, other levels of analysis are also relevant foci for religious and spiritual study and practice. In fact, researchers and practitioners have begun to shed fascinating new light on the ways religion and spirituality manifest themselves within intimate relationships, families, organizations, institutions, communities, and cultures. Religion, after all, derives from the idea of "binding," or as Guntrip (1969) put it, "religion is relationship to the *nth* degree" (p. 324).

The chapters in the two volumes of this handbook highlight the tremendous varieties of religiousness and spirituality experienced and expressed at multiple levels. Many of the chapters focus on specific aspects of religion and spirituality within particular levels of analysis. There is no need to pick a winner from among them; each has its own legitimacy. Thus, we have discouraged attempts to reduce religion and spirituality to one primary overarching theory, one primary explanatory framework, or one primary methodology (see Part I of this volume). Given the complexity of religion and spirituality, no single tool is sufficient to the psychologist's task. Bertocci (1972) put it well:

> Especially in the area of the psychology of religion, psychologists may be likened to fishermen throwing their lines into an unexplored lake. What fish they catch depends upon the nature of the hook and of the bait used. It seems clear that a wise psychologist will bring with him a variety of hooks and bait, and try to be aware of his own limitations as a fisherman. (p. 38)

The lake is, however, beginning to get more crowded. To prevent our lines from getting tangled, we have encouraged our contributors to reach beyond their own areas of interest and, where possible, acknowledge and draw on the contributions of other researchers and practitioners in the field. As you will see, this integrative approach makes for some interesting and innovative exchanges between seemingly disparate subareas within the field.

THEME 2: INTEGRATING THE MULTIPLE VALENCES OF RELIGION AND SPIRITUALITY

Are religion and spirituality good or bad for your health and well-being? This is perhaps the most controversial of all questions in the field. Nowadays, we can find many offerings in the popular press that take one position or the other. For instance, Christopher Hitchens (2007) wrote a best-selling book, none-too-subtly entitled, *God Is Not Great: How Religion Poisons Everything*, with chapters equally provocative: "Revelation: The Nightmare of the 'Old' Testament" and "The 'New' Testament Exceeds the Evil of the Old One." This type of rhetoric can certainly stimulate strong passions (and perhaps book sales), but it is not new. Consider some of these "old sayings": "religion is an opiate," "religion is a crutch," "there are no atheists in foxholes," "religion is the root cause of violence in the world," and "religion is a form of denial." Although there may be a grain of truth to each of these stereotypes, they are oversimplified and could prove terribly misleading. Empirical study, in contrast, challenges oversimplifications and may suggest a different set of conclusions (for a review see Pargament, 1997). For example, although stressful situations generally prompt a "quickening" of the religious impulse, significant numbers of individuals are atheists before, during, and after the "foxhole" experiences of their lives. Granted, some people look to their faith as a crutch or a way of avoiding the confrontation with reality; in many cases, however, religion and spirituality encourage active rather than passive forms of coping. It is true that religion can foster denial, but more often than not, it encourages people to place their pain and suffering into a larger, benign framework of meaning. Similarly, we often hear about how religious groups promote terrorism and intergroup conflict, and certainly that can be true (Jones, 2008; Stern, 2003; Chapter 26, this volume; Volume 2, Chapter 18, this handbook); however, religious groups also sponsor movements for peace, reconciliation, and social justice (Silberman, Higgins, & Dweck, 2005).

We believe that debates about whether religion and spirituality are helpful versus harmful ultimately are misdirected, for they rest on the assumption that there is an all-or-none answer; religion and spirituality are either good or bad, in simple, black-and-white terms. To the contrary, the psychology of religion and spirituality makes very clear that these phenomena are multivalent; they can be helpful, but they also can be harmful. The critical question is not *whether* religion and spirituality are good or bad, but rather *when*, *how*, and *why* they take constructive or destructive forms. Or to raise the question in more scientific (and considerably drier) language: "How helpful or harmful are particular religious (and spiritual) expressions for particular people dealing with particular situations in particular social contexts according to particular criteria of helpfulness and harmfulness?" (Pargament, 2002, p. 178). Obviously, this latter question will not be the title of a best-selling book. It does however, come closer to reflecting a basic reality, that religion and spirituality have the capacity for both good and bad. Moreover, this question, complex as it is, points to the need for a massive body of research to disentangle the intricacies of the linkages between religion, spirituality, and human functioning.

The chapters in this handbook steer clear of overgeneralizations, stereotypes, and simplistic evaluations of religion and spirituality. Instead, they treat these phenomena as rich and complex processes, processes that could have constructive or destructive implications for our lives.

THEME 3: INTEGRATING THEORY, RESEARCH, AND PRACTICE

The need for integration is perhaps most apparent in the gap between research and practice that marks the psychology of religion and spirituality. In some respects, our discipline is simply reflecting the split between science and practice in the larger field of psychology (Kazdin, 2008), a split illustrated by the relatively recent rift between the more science-oriented American Psychological Society and more practice-oriented American Psychological Association (APA). The psychology of religion and spirituality, like other disciplines in the field, struggles with the difference in purpose that has come to characterize modern science and practice. Although scientists are especially interested in discovering generalizable rules and principles of human functioning, practitioners are most concerned with the particular case, be it an individual, couple, family, organization, or community. Findings from the nomothetic methods of science are not especially useful to practitioners who may be more interested in ideographically based knowledge that would guide them with specific cases, cases that often represent exceptions to the generalized rule.

The science–practice schism may be especially pronounced in the psychology of religion and spirituality. To establish our discipline as a legitimate area of scientific inquiry, researchers distanced themselves from the field's roots in philosophy, theology, pastoral care, healing, and moral treatment (Shafranske, 2002). Compounding this problem is the fact that much of the research in the field is produced by theorists and researchers who are not themselves involved in application and fail to elaborate on the practical implications of their work. Thus, we find that scientific journals, texts, and handbooks in the psychology of religion and spirituality are generally research oriented; with some important exceptions, relatively few articles and chapters exist that translate research findings into action. To illustrate this point, Bartoli (2007) conducted a review of the psychological literature on religion and spirituality since 1980, discovering that only 10% of the articles on this topic addressed the roles of religion and spirituality in treatment. Practitioners, for their part, often are committed personally to a particular religious or spiritual perspective. Many of them find that theory and research in the discipline overlook topics and concepts of greatest meaning within their theological frame of reference or, even worse, promote reductionist explanations that discount the legitimacy of their religious and spiritual experience. Perhaps not surprisingly then, many practitioners neglect the theoretical and empirical literature in the field. Furthermore, practitioners in the psychology of religion and spirituality do not often contribute to the scholarly literature.

Integrating theory, research, and practice is one of the most critical themes of this handbook. In the tradition of social psychologist Kurt Lewin (1951), who famously remarked that "there is nothing so practical as a good theory" (p. 169), we believe that theory and research have a great deal to offer practice, especially if the scientific enterprise is conducted with an eye toward potential application. In the past 20 years, the psychology of religion and spirituality has opened up to a host of new topics—virtues, attachment, coping, meaning making, modeling, struggles, evil, meditation, relational spirituality, and spiritually integrated interventions, to name just a few. The findings from these studies clarify that religion and spirituality can be potent resources for many people or sources of stress in and of themselves. These findings are not simply of great scientific interest; they also should be of tremendous interest to applied psychologists, both within and outside of religious traditions. Although some psychologists might fear intruding on sacred ground, many people have voiced their interest in more spiritually integrated approaches to psychological care. For instance, in one survey of clients at six mental health centers, 55% reported that they would like to discuss religious or spiritual concerns in counseling (Rose, Westefeld, & Ansley, 2001). Others, psychologists among them, have called for an injection of spiritual concern within our major institutions—educational, correctional, work, and health care (e.g., Astin, 2004). These are good reasons why practitioners should stay abreast of the knowledge that is emerging from research in the field and begin to move from this research to practice.

Applied psychologists can do more than simply consume research. Just as theorists and researchers can contribute to an applied psychology, practitioners can help to advance scientific psychology. By virtue of their closeness to the religious and spiritual experiences of individuals and groups, practitioners have a vital role to play in the process of knowledge generation (Hood, Hill, & Spilka, 2009). Through case studies and qualitative investigations, applied psychologists are well positioned to identify new phenomena and hypotheses that deserve further study. Moreover, they can serve as gatekeepers of scientific information by critically evaluating the degree to which scientific findings speak to and enhance the lived experiences of people.

In the two volumes of the *APA Handbook of Psychology, Religion, and Spirituality*, we strive for greater integration between theory, research, and practice. The emphasis of the first volume is on research and theory. We have asked our contributors, however, to attend to the practical implications of theory and research in their area of interest. The second volume specifically emphasizes applications of the psychology of religion and spirituality from the perspective of different theoretical orientations (see Volume 2, Part II, this handbook), in dealing with different problems (Volume 2, Part III, this handbook), in different applied contexts (Volume 2, Part IV, this handbook). We also have encouraged our authors to draw on the theoretical and empirical foundations of the field, suggesting new research questions that grow out of practice. We are using the term *practice* broadly in both volumes. Practice encompasses not only clinical activities, such as counseling and psychotherapy, but also applications across a variety of settings (e.g., schools, workplace, correctional), problems (physical illness, prejudice, political violence, mental health symptoms, couple distress), and potential times for intervention (e.g., early education, prevention, treatment). Thus, the vision here incorporates clinical interests and concerns within a broader applied psychology of religion and spirituality (Shafranske, 2005).

THEME 4: INTEGRATING THE PSYCHOLOGY OF RELIGION AND SPIRITUALITY WITH THE BROADER FIELD

Even though religion and spirituality were central topics of interest to the founding fathers of psychology, the discipline was marginalized from the mainstream field during much of the past century. Fortunately, this picture has begun to change. The decision of the APA to publish this two-volume handbook as one of a series of handbooks on major disciplines in the field is a sign that our field is coming of age. Nevertheless, we still have a long way to go. In a recent survey of APA leaders, only 40.3% strongly agreed that "religion and spirituality are important topics for psychologists to consider," 36.5% strongly agreed that "religion and spirituality are important to consider when providing professional services," and 30.6% strongly agreed that religion and spirituality can be studied with scientific rigor" (McMinn, Hathaway, Woods, & Snow, 2009). To bring the psychology of religion and spirituality further into the mainstream of psychology, we selected contributors to the handbook who have linked their work to theory, research, and practice within the larger field. For instance, we provide coverage of recent efforts to integrate religion and spirituality within theory and research on topics that include terror management, evolutionary theory, cognitive theory, personality theory, social learning theory, couples and family psychology, and positive psychology. We also link advances in the applied psychology of religion to broader approaches to personal and social change within clinical, industrial–organizational, educational, pastoral, and community psychology.

The psychology of religion and spirituality has much to gain by drawing on advances in the larger field. The converse is also true: The larger field has much to gain by drawing on advances in the psychology of religion and spirituality (Hill & Gibson, 2008). In fact, we would argue that a mainstream psychology that overlooks the religious and spiritual dimension of human functioning remains incomplete. For example, how can we fully understand community life if we overlook the place of religious institutions and individuals within communities? How can we make sense of the major political conflicts of our day if we fail to appreciate the religious and spiritual dimension underlying tensions in the world? How can the core concepts of positive psychology—from forgiveness and gratitude to growth, transformation, and love—be understood without attention to their religious and spiritual roots and expressions? How can we grasp human resilience if we neglect some of the most common ways people deal with major life stressors? To facilitate integration in this domain, we asked our authors to link their topic of interest to developments in the larger field of psychology. We also requested that they highlight the distinctive contributions of the psychology of religion and spirituality to the larger field.

Although the handbook is firmly rooted in psychology, our contributors come from other disciplines, including anthropology, sociology, theology, and medicine. Thus, integration can be envisioned not only among the disciplines within psychology but also between psychology and other disciplines, as Emmons and Paloutzian (2003) noted in their call for a multilevel, interdisciplinary paradigm.

THEME 5: INTEGRATING PERSPECTIVES ON THE MEANINGS OF RELIGION AND SPIRITUALITY

Where do religion and spirituality start and stop? What distinguishes religion and spirituality from other phenomena, such as meaning and purpose, positive psychology, and a sense of community? How do religion and spirituality overlap and differ from each other? These boundary questions are critical to the psychology of religion and spirituality. Without some shared sense of its key parameters, the boundaries of our subdiscipline become so diffuse that we can lose our professional identity. Hill et al. (2000) put it this way: "If any belief or activity that provides individuals with a sense of identity or meaning (e.g., involvement in a social club) is defined as a religious or spiritual endeavor, then this field literally knows no bounds" (p. 71). Because definitional questions about religion and spirituality are so vital to our discipline (and to this handbook), we devote extended attention to this aspect of the integrative paradigm in the remainder of this introductory chapter.

To be fair to the psychology of religion and spirituality, ours is not the only field that struggles to define its parameters. Other disciplines within the social sciences must step carefully around slippery definitional boundaries of their own. Nevertheless, the task of reaching some shared sense of the essential nature of religion and spirituality was and continues to be particularly daunting. In 1958, eminent psychologist of religion, Walter Houston Clark (1958) asked 68 social scientists how they defined religion and concluded that "social scientists may mean very different things by the term 'religion'" (p. 146). Questions about the meanings of religion have only increased over the past 50 years as the distance between members of different faiths and cultures has decreased and people are exposed to greater diversity in religious attitudes and expressions. Hood et al. (2009) have captured a sense of this diversity: "Religion may encompass the supernatural, the non-natural, theism, deism, atheism, monotheism, polytheism, and both finite and infinite deities: it may also include practices, beliefs, and rituals that almost defy circumscription and definition" (p. 7). How do we arrive at a coherent definition of religion in an increasingly multicultural, multifaith world?

Complicating matters even further is the reality that the boundaries of our discipline have been in flux over the past several decades, in large part because of the introduction of a new concept for the field: spirituality. Granted, trying to reach stable definitions of religion and spirituality may be as difficult as trying to capture movement through a few snapshots, and we fully acknowledge this difficulty. Nonetheless, we see it as a worthwhile endeavor. Before presenting the perspective on the meanings of religion and spirituality that we used for this handbook, we will briefly provide some background on the evolving meanings of religion and spirituality.

THE EVOLVING MEANINGS OF RELIGION AND SPIRITUALITY

It is useful to distinguish between classic and contemporary meanings of religion and spirituality (see Zinnbauer, Pargament, & Scott, 1999). For much of the 20th century, religion was seen by psychologists and other social scientists as a broad, multifaceted domain that encompassed both individual and institutional levels of analysis, both constructive and destructive expressions, both traditional and newer forms, both structure and function, and both intrinsic and extrinsic forms of motivation. In fact, some classic definitions of religion would be hard to distinguish from modern-day conceptions of spirituality. Consider, for instance, James's (1902) definition of religion as "the feelings, acts and experiences of individual men in their solitude so far as they apprehend themselves to stand in relation to whatever they may consider divine" (p. 32). In the latter part of the century, the term *spirituality* was introduced and began to appropriate some of the meanings of religiousness. In the process, broad-based views of religion gave way to more constricted perspectives (Wulff, 1997), and the terms *religion* and *spirituality* became increasingly polarized from each other. In the 21st century, social scientists often form striking contrasts between these two terms: religion as institutional versus spirituality as individual, religion as external and objective versus spirituality as internal and subjective, religion as old versus spirituality as new, religion as structural versus spirituality as functional, religion as fixed and frozen versus spirituality as flexible and dynamic, and even religion as bad versus spirituality as good (Zinnbauer et al., 1999).

Judging from studies of the meanings of these terms to the general population, many people have also begun to distinguish religion and spirituality from each other (Mattis, 2000; Schlehofer, Omoto, & Adelman, 2008; Zinnbauer et al., 1997). These studies show that people often associate the term *religion* with predefined belief and rituals along with institutionally based involvement. *Spirituality* more often connotes an individualized, experientially based pursuit of positive values, such as connectedness, meaning, self-actualization, and authenticity. A growing percentage of the population, although still a minority, defines itself as "spiritual not religious." This orientation is reflected in what has become something of a mantra: You don't need to be religious to be spiritual (Marler & Hadaway, 2002).

Some have taken the split even further. Hood (2003) has argued cogently that a subgroup of the "spiritual not religious" might be more accurately described as "spiritual *against* religion." For this group, religion is seen as a defense against spirituality, a form of bondage that must be escaped for personal growth to occur. Spirituality provides the vehicle by which people can free themselves from religious servitude. We can sense undercurrents of this antireligious spirituality in some 21st-century definitions, such as one offered by the president of the World Psychiatric Association: "Spirituality shares with religion the personal belief in ideas of religious significance such as God, the Soul, or Heaven, but rejects the administrative, often bureaucratic and hierarchical, structure and creeds of a particular organized religion" (Maj, 2010, p. xiii).

The reasons behind the shifting meanings of religion and spirituality are far from clear and cannot be reviewed in any detail here. Some implicate the defining events of the 20th century in these changes. Wuthnow (1998) asserted that religious institutions have failed to provide their adherents with "safe homes" and plausible explanations to live securely and deal effectively with the host of problems that have marked the past 100 years—world wars, the Holocaust, nuclear threats, intractable global hunger and poverty, AIDS, racism, and terrorism. Institutional religion also has struggled to adjust to radical changes in modern societies brought about by the women's movement, civil rights movements, biotechnology, and changing norms regarding human sexuality and family life. As a result, the religious tradition "of inhabiting sacred places has given way to a new spirituality of seeking" in which people construct their own distinctive paths toward the sacred (Wuthnow, 1998, p. 3). Others believe that changes in the language of religion and spirituality are reflective of a growing religious pluralization in the United States, particularly the rise of interest in Eastern religions with their emphasis on internal subjective experience rather than institutionalized beliefs and practices (Roof, 2000). Still others have suggested that the trend toward differentiating spirituality from religion is simply one among many manifestations of larger forces at play pushing Western culture toward social fragmentation, deinstitutionalization and the privatization of experience (Bellah, Madsen, Sullivan, Swidler, & Tipton, 1985). Finally, some have described the growing emphasis on spirituality as the latest in a series of religious revitalization movements that have arisen throughout history to inject new energy and fervor into the quest for the sacred and institutions that are perceived as having lost touch with the essential spirit (Roof, 2000).

Regardless of the reasons why, it seems clear that we are witnessing a shift in the meanings of religion and spirituality. How far are these changes likely to go? It is hard to say. Perhaps the term *spirituality* will take on "full independence" from religion. But perhaps not. Even though the number of "spiritual-only" people may be growing, a majority in the United States continue to label themselves as both religious and spiritual (Marler & Hadaway, 2002), and most believe that religiousness and spirituality are overlapping concepts (Zinnbauer et al., 1997). In other words, not all people seem to experience a tension between religion and spirituality. For many, if not most, religion continues to be the home of spirituality; it is their haven, the nest where their spirituality is enhanced and enriched.

OPPORTUNITIES, PROBLEMS, AND CHALLENGES ASSOCIATED WITH THE EVOLVING MEANINGS OF RELIGION AND SPIRITUALITY

The evolving meanings of religion and spirituality raise some opportunities, problems, and challenges for psychologists interested in understanding and addressing these constructs in research and practice. With respect to opportunities, the shifts in meaning alert us to the importance of attending to newer as well as more established forms of religious and spiritual expression. The lion's share of research and practice in the field has focused on religious "dwellers" (cf. Wuthnow, 1998)—that is, people who reside within traditional religious denominations and institutions. The emergence of interest in spirituality opens the door to studies of new movements and a wider range of highly personalized, nontraditional beliefs, practices, and experiences (see Part IV of this volume). Perhaps even more important, the growing interest in spirituality is a reminder that the spiritual dimension is the heart and soul of religious life. As psychologist Paul Johnson once wrote: "It is the ultimate Thou whom the religious person seeks most of all" (1959, p. 70). With some important exceptions, psychologists have tended to overlook the spiritual motivation that lies at the root of many forms of religious expression. Certainly religion works through many mechanisms, including psychological, social and physical. In the effort to explain religion through these factors, however, the most parsimonious explanation has been neglected—that is, the possibility that religion may have direct spiritual effects on human functioning. The contemporary point of view, however, underscores the possibility that spirituality is a significant dimension of life (and religion) in and of itself, one that cannot be explained away (see Chapter 14 in this volume).

We also believe that the growing polarization in the meanings of religion and spirituality is problematic for several reasons (see Pargament, 1999). We will focus on two of the most significant problems here.

Religion as Institutional Versus Spirituality as Individual

This dichotomization creates problems from both the religious and spiritual sides. Focusing on the religious side, the view of religion as purely institutional overlooks the fact that these organizations are concerned with the well-being of their individual members. Of course, some do a better job of caring for their flock than others, but it remains true that they are designed to meet the needs of their members. Toward that end, religious institutions must transmit values, beliefs, and practices to their adherents. This does not mean that most people simply swallow religious teachings hook, line, and sinker. Many are involved in a more active process, selecting, interpreting, and reconstructing institutionally based worldviews and practices. In this sense, religion involves dynamic patterns of exchange between individuals and institutions. When religion is constricted in its definition to a static, institutionalized set of beliefs and practices, we lose sight of the important ways in which individuals form, sustain, and at times transform religious institutions.

Conversely, by treating spirituality as a purely individual phenomena, we lose sight of the rich and varied ways spirituality expresses itself in intimate relationships, marriages, families, friendships, organizations, communities, and cultures. Even personal spiritual expressions unfold in a larger religious, social and cultural milieu. As discussed, many people prefer to practice their spirituality within the context of an established religious tradition. Others seek alternative social outlets for their spirituality, such as healing groups, meditation groups, yoga groups, 12-step groups, and online discussion groups, which may reject traditional religious beliefs and practices but retain a social organization; in essence, these alternative groups become "a religion of no religion" (cf. Spiegelberg, in Kripal, 2007). And many people disengage from religious institutions for a period of time only to seek other like-minded individuals at a later time with whom they can share their spiritual interests. True, there are those who remain disengaged from religious institutions, preferring to construct their own personalized spiritual pathways. It would be a mistake, however, to see their spiritual journeys as context free. Privatized as they are, their spiritual experiences are taking place within a larger system of cultural forces that has helped shape this privatization. The perception that they have removed themselves from the influence of a larger religious context is as illusory as the belief that young adults who have moved out of their family homes are no longer affected by their families. For better or worse, religion is in the air we breathe. In short, defining religion as a purely institutional expression and spirituality as a purely individualistic expression can only lead to a distorted understanding of what we have described in Theme 1 of our integrative paradigm as multilevel phenomena.

Spirituality as Good Versus Religion as Bad

The polarization in the meanings of spirituality and religion has led to a second significant problem—a tendency to view spirituality as the "good guy" and religion as the "bad guy." We have avoided this kind of dichotomization in our integrative paradigm (see Theme 2) and prefer a multivalent perspective for several reasons. First and foremost, this dichotomization does not square with empirical realities. Be it church attendance, beliefs in an afterlife, or religious commitment, traditional religious beliefs and practices in the United States appear to have largely positive implications for health and well-being (Koenig, King, & Carson, 2012). Certainly, we also can identify more harmful forms of religiousness, such as overscrupulosity or unrelenting conflict with the divine (e.g., Exline & Rose, 2005; see Chapter 25 in this volume and Volume 2, Chapter 4, this handbook), and we do not intend to argue that religion is invariably constructive. Rather, we contend that religion can take both constructive and destructive forms. The same point holds true for spirituality. Although many spiritual expressions can be linked to positive outcomes, spirituality also has a darker side: (a) the individual whose ultimate goals in life are marked by narrow self-interest; (b) the animosity, even rage, of spiritual seekers against those who prefer to dwell in established religious homes; and (c) the failure of "spiritual not religious" parents to anticipate and respond to the spiritually related questions, concerns, and needs of their children.

Defining spirituality as good and religion as bad is also poor science. If spirituality and religion are, a priori, good and bad, then we have predetermined the answers to critical questions about the value of these constructs for health and well-being. To put it in more scientific language, defining spirituality and religion as good and bad confounds processes (i.e., the ways in which an individual is spiritual or religious) with outcomes (i.e., the degree to which an individual experiences spiritual or religious benefits or harm), thereby obscuring the distinction between measures of religiousness and spirituality and measures of religious and spiritual well-being. For this reason, Koenig (2008) has called for definitions and indexes of spirituality and religiousness that are uncontaminated by outcomes.

Finally, the polarization of spirituality and religion into "good guy" and "bad guy" is likely to offend many of those who participate in organized religious life (a majority of Americans and citizens of the globe). Psychologists should be especially attentive to this point, for we are "religiously atypical" of the U.S. population at large. As a whole, psychologists are likely to be overrepresented in the group that defines itself as "spiritual only." Although 73% of counseling and clinical psychologists indicate that spirituality is fairly or very important to them, only 48% report that religion is fairly or very important to them (in contrast to 88% of the general population) (Shafranske, 1996; see Volume 2, Chapter 2, this handbook). Even more to the point, psychologists may be overrepresented in the "spiritual against religion" group. It is not hard to find prospiritual–antireligious sentiments in psychological writings. As Hood (2003) noted, "a hostility to religion as thwarting or even falsifying spirituality is evident" (p. 252). Thus, psychologists may be among the vanguard of those who polarize the meanings of religion and spirituality. The "religious mismatch" between psychologists and the majority of people in the United States, however, should provide a warning against overestimating the tensions between religion and spirituality (McMinn et al., 2009) and "declaring in advance the triumph of a spirituality that itself is not religious" (Hood, 2003, p. 261). Moreover, antipathy to organized religion certainly is not compatible with efforts to promote the health and well-being of the large numbers of Americans who affiliate themselves with religious institutions.

We are left then with a definitional challenge. How do we (a) provide definitional boundaries that lend coherence to the field, (b) ensure that these definitions reflect sensitivity to the evolving meanings of religion and spirituality, and (c) sidestep the problems that these shifting meanings pose for scientific study and practice?

DEFINITIONAL BOUNDARIES OF RELIGION AND SPIRITUALITY

Given the evolving nature of meanings of religion and spirituality, we do not believe it is possible to arrive at hard and fast definitions of these terms that would be agreed on by all contributors to this handbook (or much less by the field as a whole). Some definitional clarity is needed, however. Thus, we have taken the more modest approach of offering tentative definitions of religion and spirituality, and then several guiding thoughts about the similarities and dissimilarities between the two constructs. We also have created several guidelines to help the authors in their decisions about whether (and when) to use the language of religion or spirituality in their chapters. A brief description of our perspective on the meanings of these terms follows.

Tentative Definitions

Drawing on the work of Pargament (1999), we define spirituality as "the search for the sacred." There are two important terms here: *search* and *sacred.* Let's start with the meaning of sacred. The term *sacred* is used inclusively here to refer not only to concepts of God and higher powers but also to other aspects of life that are perceived to be manifestations of the divine or imbued with divinelike qualities, such as transcendence, immanence, boundlessness, and ultimacy (Pargament & Mahoney, 2005). Virtually any part of life, positive or negative—including beliefs, practices, experiences, relationships, motivations, art, nature, and war—can be endowed with sacred status (Mahoney, Pargament, & Hernandez, in press). In short, the sacred can be perceived, experienced, and approached in many ways. This may account in part for the multifaced character of spirituality; people can take any number of sacred pathways in search of any number of sacred destinations, from a connection with a loving God, daily transcendent experiences, and a satisfying vocation in life to the creation of a divine kingdom on earth, devotion to an exalted figure, and the avoidance of eternal damnation. The choice of sacred pathways and destinations is not trivial; the chapters of this handbook demonstrate that it makes a great deal of difference which destinations people pursue and which pathways they take toward these destinations.

By *search*, we are referring to an ongoing journey, a process that begins with the discovery of something sacred. Discovery can be experienced as a personal accomplishment (the individual succeeds in finding the sacred) or as a revelation (the sacred reveals itself to the individual; Pargament, 2007). In either case, the search for the sacred does not end there. In response to the discovery of the sacred, the task shifts to building and conserving a connection with it. At times, particularly during periods of stress and turmoil, the searching process also involves the transformation of the individual's tie to what is held to be sacred (Pargament, 1997; see also Chapter 22 in this volume). Following transformation, the task shifts to building and sustaining a reconnection with the sacred as it is now understood and experienced. And the journey, the search for the sacred, continues.

Our definition of spirituality does not specify a particular context in which the journey unfolds. Rather, people can engage in the search for the sacred within any context, traditional or nontraditional: They can follow well-trodden pathways established by traditional institutions, or they can construct their own distinctive pathways that have little if anything to do with established religions.

Building on the work of Hill et al. (2000) and Pargament (1997), we define religion as "the search for significance that occurs within the context of established institutions that are designed to facilitate spirituality." The term *search* refers once again to the ongoing journey of discovery, conservation, and transformation. In this case, however, the destination of the search is "significance": a term that encompasses a full range of potential goals, including those that are psychological (e.g., anxiety reduction, meaning, impulse control), social (e.g., belonging, identity, dominance), and physical (e.g., longevity, evolutionary adaptation, death) as well as those that are spiritual (Mahoney, 2010; Pargament, 1997; see Part II of this volume).

Religion occurs within the larger context of established institutions and traditions that have as their primary goal, the facilitation of spirituality. In contrast to the modern tendency among scholars to dissociate spirituality from religion, our view is that spirituality represents the function most central to institutional religious life. It is the spiritual character of its mission that makes religious institutions distinctive; no other social institution has spirituality as its primary goal (Mahoney, 2010). Toward this end, religious institutions also encourage their members to follow a set of pathways in life that are embedded with sacred character—engaging in religious rituals, attending religious services, studying sacred literature, avoiding religious vices and practicing religious virtues, and participating in the life of the religious community.

Similarities

With these definitions in mind, we can see that spirituality and religion are similar in several respects. First, the sacred lies at the core of both religion and spirituality. We have defined the sacred broadly and by doing so, we open the doors of the psychology of religion and spirituality to a wide range of phenomena of interest, both traditional and nontraditional. By insisting that the sacred is central to both religion and spirituality, however, we also highlight the distinctiveness of these constructs and help to provide clearer boundaries for the subdiscipline. After all, without a sacred substance, religion and spirituality would be indistinguishable from other constructs within the larger field of psychology, such as well-being, community, meaning, hope, and authenticity. Hill et al. (2000) made just this point:

> To say "I find my spirituality in gardening" or "Music is my spirituality" might indeed suggest that a person finds great satisfaction and subjective well-being through gardening or playing music . . . but unless such lifestyles are responses to a perception of the Sacred (e.g., the person gardens because caring for nature is a way of experiencing the creative forces of the universe, the person plays and listens to music because its beauty and the complex mathematical structures underlying music cause the person to contemplate the beauty and order of God or the entire universe) then it is

> inappropriate to refer to gardening or music as "spiritual." (p. 64)

Second, both spirituality and religion are dynamic, searching processes. Neither construct is static; rather, each changes and evolves over time through the processes of discovery, conservation, and transformation. In this sense, we can think of religion and spirituality as developmental phenomena that can be an integral part of the journey over the life span.

Third, both spirituality and religion are multidimensional and multilevel processes, as we noted in Theme 1 of our integrative paradigm. In their spiritual and religious journeys, people can draw on a rich variety of beliefs, practices, experiences, and relationships. To put it another way, people can take a number of pathways in their efforts to reach and realize the significant destinations in their lives. These paths are not necessarily followed in isolation from each other or in isolation from other people. We can understand both religion and spirituality at individual, dyadic, familial, organizational, community, and cultural levels of analysis.

Fourth, both spirituality and religion are multivalent. As we delineated under Theme 2 of our integrative paradigm, each process can express itself in constructive and destructive ways.

Finally, both spirituality and religion matter because they are concerned about issues of great value. Spirituality is directed toward sacred destinations. Religion is directed toward significant goals, goals that may be sacred in nature. In fact, when religion is focused on the sacred, it becomes indistinguishable from spirituality. Religion, however, can focus on other destinations as well and, when it does, it takes on a different appearance.

Dissimilarities

Although religion and spirituality are similar in important respects, they also differ from each other on key two dimensions: function and context. *Function* refers to the destinations or significant goals associated with spirituality and religion. *Context* refers to the larger social milieu in which spirituality and religion unfold. In terms of function, religion is directed toward the pursuit of a broader array of destinations or significant goals than spirituality. Religion serves the important function of facilitating spirituality itself, but it serves other functions as well, including those that are psychological, social, and physical (see Part II of this volume). In contrast, spirituality focuses on the search for one particular significant destination, the sacred. We reiterate: Spirituality is not restricted to an individual's relationship with the sacred understood traditionally as God or a higher power. Seemingly secular functions—psychological, social, and physical—also can be imbued with sacred status. When they are, they also fall beneath the spiritual umbrella (see Chapter 14 in this volume).

With respect to context, religion is more circumscribed than spirituality. Religion is embedded within an established, institutional context. By "established" we are speaking of long-standing organizations and institutions whose mission is to facilitate members' connection with the sacred (see Hill et al., 2000). In contrast, although spirituality can be a vital part of traditional religious life, it also can be embedded in nontraditional contexts.

Guidelines for the Use of the Language of Religion and Spirituality

With these points of similarity and dissimilarity in mind, we offer some general guidelines for when to use the terms *religion* and/or *spirituality* along with a few illustrations. Again, our goal is not to insist on a one-size-fits-all approach to the definition of our key constructs, but rather to encourage greater intentionality in the choice of language to promote clarity, coherence, continuity, and integration within the field.

Our definitions make clear that religion and spirituality have different points of emphasis with respect to the functions they serve and their larger context. Thus, at times, it is appropriate to refer exclusively to religion or spirituality.

1. We recommend using *the language of religion* when emphasizing (a) the search for significant psychological, social, or physical destinations within established institutional contexts designed to facilitate spirituality; or (b) beliefs, practices, experiences, or relationships that are

embedded within established institutional contexts designed to facilitate spirituality. Examples of the use of *religious* include *religiously* based programs to prevent cancer, *religious* conversion as compensation for insecure parental attachment, *religious* beliefs and practices of Hindus, and *religious* support from the church.

2. We recommend using *the language of spirituality* when emphasizing (a) the search for the sacred; or (b) sacred beliefs, practices, experiences, or relationships that are embedded in nontraditional contexts. Examples of the use of *spiritual* include the *spiritual* quest, outdoor *spiritual* retreat, daily *spiritual* experiences, *spiritual* intimacy in marriage, and *spiritual* meditation to attain transcendence.

   Because religion and spirituality are neither totally independent nor opposed to each other, the two constructs can also be used inclusively in a nonpolarized fashion.

3. We recommend using *the language of both religion and spirituality* when referring to (a) the search for the full range of significant destinations, sacred and secular, and (b) beliefs, practices, experiences, or relationships that are embedded within both nontraditional, secular contexts and established institutional contexts designed to facilitate the sacred search. Examples of the use of both terms include links of *religious and spiritual* coping methods to holistic well-being; the psychology of *religion and spirituality*; brief multidimensional measure of religiousness–spirituality; accessing *religious and spiritual* resources to facilitate pastoral and mental health counseling; and *religious and spiritual* healing practices.

CONCLUSION

In this introductory chapter, we have presented our vision of an integrative paradigm for the psychology of religion and spirituality. This is a *psychological* paradigm. It does not offer verification of God's existence, the ontological reality of Biblical accounts, or the truths of fundamental religious and spiritual claims. There is tremendous interest in questions about the ultimate truth and value of religion and spirituality, as even the quickest scan of a bestseller list shows, but the chapters in this handbook do not aim to answer these questions. What they can and will do, however, is to provide some insights into the implications of religion and spirituality for human behavior. The focus here is on the footprints that lead to and are left by faith (cf. Batson, Schoenrade, & Ventis, 1993).

We believe that our readers will be educated, enlightened, and informed by these chapters. As a group, these contributions highlight the tremendous progress that has been made in the psychological study of religion and spirituality. Of course, questions continue to far outnumber answers. The field continues to be marked by mystery. Furthermore, our integrative paradigm for the psychology of religion and spirituality is more of a vision than a reality. In our view, this young field still has a long way to go before it reaches maturity. Nevertheless, it is our hope that this handbook will push the field toward a more coherent, integrated approach to understanding and addressing what may well be the most elusive dimension of human nature.

References

Astin, A. W. (2004). Why spirituality deserves a central place in liberal education. *Liberal Education, 90*(Spring), 34–41.

Bartkowski, J. P., Xu, X., & Levin, M. L. (2008). Religion and child development: Evidence from the Early Childhood Longitudinal Study. *Social Science Research, 37*, 18–36. doi:10.1016/j.ssresearch.2007.02.001

Bartoli, E. (2007). Religious and spiritual issues in psychotherapy practice: Training the trainer. *Psychotherapy: Theory, Research, Practice, Training, 44*, 54–65. doi:10.1037/0033-3204.44.1.54

Barton, A. H. (1971). Selected problems in the study of religious development. In M. Strommen (Ed.), *Research on religious development* (pp. 836–855). New York, NY: Hawthorn.

Batson, C. D., Schoenrade, P. A., & Ventis, W. L. (1993). *Religion and the individual: A social-psychological perspective.* New York, NY: Oxford University Press.

Bellah, R. N., Madsen, R., Sullivan, W. M., Swidler, A., & Tipton, S. M. (1985). *Habits of the heart: Individualism and commitment in American life*. New York, NY: Harper & Row.

Bertocci, P. A. (1972). Psychological interpretations of religious experience. In M. Strommen (Ed.), *Research on religious development: A comprehensive handbook* (pp. 3–41). New York, NY: Hawthorn.

Capps, D. E. (1977). Contemporary psychology of religion: The task of theoretical reconstruction. In H. W. Malony (Ed.), *Current perspectives in the psychology of religion* (pp. 36–52). Grand Rapids, MI: Eerdmans.

Chasteen, A. L., Burdzy, D. C., & Pratt, J. (2010). Thinking of God moves attention. *Neuropsychologia, 48,* 627–630. doi:10.1016/j.neuropsychologia.2009.09.029

Clark, W. H. (1958). How do social scientists define religion? *Journal of Social Psychology, 47,* 143–147. doi:10.1080/00224545.1958.9714350

Emmons, R. A., & Paloutzian, R. F. (2003). The psychology of religion. *Annual Review of Psychology, 54,* 377–402. doi:10.1146/annurev.psych.54.101601.145024

Exline, J. J., & Rose, E. (2005). Religious and spiritual struggles. In R. Paloutzian & C. Park (Eds.), *Handbook of psychology of religion and spirituality* (pp. 315–330). New York, NY: Guilford Press.

Gallup, G., Jr. (1999). *Americans celebrate Easter.* Princeton, NJ: The Gallup Organization. Retrieved from http://www.gallup.com/poll/3958/Easter-Draws-Americans-Back-Church.aspx

Glock, C. Y. (1962). On the study of religious commitment. *Religious Education, 57*(Research Suppl.), S98–S110.

Guntrip, H. (1969). Religion in relation to personal integration. *British Journal of Medical Psychology, 42,* 323–333. doi:10.1111/j.2044-8341.1969.tb02086.x

Hill, P. C., & Gibson, N. J. S. (2008). Whither the roots? Achieving conceptual depth in psychology of religion. *Archive for the Psychology of Religion, 30,* 19–35.

Hill, P. C., Pargament, K. I., Hood, R. W., Jr., McCullough, M. E., Swyers, J. P., Larson, D. B., & Zinnbauer, B. J. (2000). Conceptualizing religion and spirituality: Points of commonality, points of departure. *Journal for the Theory of Social Behaviour, 30,* 51–77.

Hitchens, C. (2007). *God is not great: How religion poisons everything.* New York, NY: Hatchette Books.

Hood, R. W., Jr. (2003). The relationship between religion and spirituality. In A. L. Greil & D. Bromley (Eds.), *Defining religion: Investigating the boundaries between the sacred and secular religion and the social order* (Vol. 10, pp. 241–264). Amsterdam, the Netherlands: Elsevier Science. doi:10.1016/S1061-5210(03)10014-X

Hood, R. W., Jr., Hill, P. C., & Spilka, B. (2009). *The psychology of religion: An empirical approach* (4th ed.). New York, NY: Guilford Press.

Idler, E. L., Musick, M. A., Ellison, C. G., George, L. K., Krause, N., Ory, M. G., . . . Williams, D. R. (2003). Measuring multiple dimensions of religion and spirituality for health research: Conceptual background and findings from the 1998 General Social Survey. *Research on Aging, 25,* 327–365. doi:10.1177/0164027503025004001

James, W. (1902). *The varieties of religious experience: A study in human nature.* New York, NY: Random House. doi:10.1037/10004-000

Johnson, P. E. (1959). *The psychology of religion.* Nashville, TN: Abingdon Press.

Jones, J. (2008). *Blood that cries out from the earth: The psychology of religious terrorism.* New York, NY: Oxford University Press. doi:10.1093/acprof:oso/9780195335972.001.0001

Kazdin, A. E. (2008). Evidence-based treatment and practice: New opportunities to bridge clinical research and practice, enhance the knowledge base, and improve patient care. *American Psychologist, 63,* 146–159. doi:10.1037/0003-066X.63.3.146

Koenig, H. G. (2008). Concerns about measuring "spirituality" in research. *Journal of Nervous and Mental Disease, 196,* 349–355. doi:10.1097/NMD.0b013e31816ff796

Koenig, H. G., King, D., & Carson, V. B. (2012). *Handbook of religion and health* (2nd ed.). Oxford, England: Oxford University Press.

Kripal, J. J. (2007). *Esalen: America and the religion of no religion.* Chicago, IL: University of Chicago Press.

Lewin, K. (1951). *Field theory in social science: Selected theoretical papers* (D. Cartwright, Ed.). New York, NY: Harper & Row.

Mahoney, A. (2010). Religion in families 1999–2009: A relational spirituality framework. *Journal of Marriage and Family, 72,* 805–827. doi:10.1111/j.1741-3737.2010.00732.x

Mahoney, A. M., Pargament, K. I., & Hernandez, K. (in press). Heaven on earth: Beneficial effects of sanctification for individual and interpersonal well-being. In J. Henry (Ed.), *Oxford handbook of happiness.* Oxford, England: Oxford University Press.

Maj, M. (2010). Forward. In P. J. Verhagen, H. M. van Praag, J. J. Lopez-Ibor Jr., J. L. Cox, & D. Moussaoui (Eds.), *Religion and psychiatry: Beyond boundaries* (pp. xiii–xiv). West Sussex, England: Wiley-Blackwell.

Marler, P. L., & Hadaway, C. K. (2002). "Being religious" or "being spiritual" in America: A zero-sum proposition? *Journal for the Scientific Study of Religion, 41,* 289–300. doi:10.1111/1468-5906.00117

Mattis, J. S. (2000). African American women's definitions of spirituality and religiosity. *Journal of Black Psychology, 26,* 101–122. doi:10.1177/0095798400026001006

McCullough, M. E., Hoyt, W. T., Larson, D. B., Koenig, H. G., & Thoresen, C. (2000). Religious involvement and mortality: A meta-analytic review. *Health Psychology, 19*, 211–222. doi:10.1037/0278-6133.19.3.211

McMinn, M. R., Hathaway, W. L., Woods, S. W., & Snow, K. N. (2009). What American Psychologist Association leaders have to say about psychology of religion and spirituality. *Psychology of Religion and Spirituality, 1*, 3–13. doi:10.1037/a0014991

Paden, W. E. (1994). *Religious worlds: The comparative study of religion* (2nd ed.). Boston, MA: Beacon.

Pargament, K. I. (1997). *The psychology of religion and coping: Theory, research, practice.* New York, NY: Guilford Press.

Pargament, K. I. (1999). The psychology of religion and spirituality? Yes and no. *The International Journal for the Psychology of Religion, 9*, 3–16. doi:10.1207/s15327582ijpr0901_2

Pargament, K. I. (2002). The bitter and the sweet: An evaluation of the costs and benefits of religiousness. *Psychological Inquiry, 13*, 168–181. doi:10.1207/S15327965PLI1303_02

Pargament, K. I. (2007). *Spiritually integrated psychotherapy: Understanding and addressing the sacred.* New York, NY: Guilford Press.

Pargament, K. I., & Mahoney, A. (2005). Sacred matters: Sanctification as a vital topic for the psychology of religion. *The International Journal for the Psychology of Religion, 15*, 179–198. doi:10.1207/s15327582ijpr1503_1

Phelps, A. C., Maciejewski, P. K., Nilsson, M., Balboni, T. A., Wright, T. A., Paulk, M. E., . . . Prigerson, H. G. (2009). Religious coping and use of intensive life-prolonging care near death in patients with advanced cancer. *JAMA, 301*, 1140–1147. doi:10.1001/jama.2009.341

Phylacteries abort flight: Jewish prayer ritual item mistaken for bomb; jet lands in Philadelphia (2010, January 21). McClatchey Tribune News Service. Retrieved from http://www.cleveland.com/nation/index.ssf/2010/01/phylacteries_abort_flight_jewi.html

Reich, K. H. (2008). Extending the psychology of religion: A call for exploration of psychological universals, more inclusive approaches, and comprehensive models. *Archive for the Psychology of Religion, 30*, 115–134. doi:10.1163/157361208X316999

Roof, W. C. (2000). *Spiritual marketplace: Baby boomers and the remaking of American religion.* Princeton, NJ: Princeton University Press.

Rose, E. M., Westefeld, J. S., & Ansley, T. N. (2001). Spiritual issues in counseling: Clients' beliefs and preferences. *Journal of Counseling Psychology, 48*, 61–71. doi:10.1037/0022-0167.48.1.61

Sampson, E. E. (1977). Psychology and the American ideal. *Journal of Personality and Social Psychology, 35*, 767–782. doi:10.1037/0022-3514.35.11.767

Schlehofer, M. M., Omoto, A. M., & Adelman, J. R. (2008). How do "religion" and "spirituality" differ? Lay definitions among older adults. *Journal for the Scientific Study of Religion, 47*, 411–425. doi:10.1111/j.1468-5906.2008.00418.x

Shafranske, E. P. (1996). Religious beliefs, practices and affiliations of clinical psychologists. In E. Shafranske (Ed.), *Religion and the clinical practice of psychology* (pp. 149–162). Washington, DC: American Psychological Association. doi:10.1037/10199-005

Shafranske, E. P. (2002). The necessary and sufficient conditions for an applied psychology of religion. *Psychology of Religion Newsletter, 27*(4), 1–12.

Shafranske, E. P. (2005). Psychology of religion in clinical and counseling psychology. In R. Paloutzian & C. Park (Eds.), *The handbook of the psychology of religion and spirituality* (pp. 496–514). New York, NY: Guilford Press.

Silberman, I., Higgins, E., & Dweck, C. (2005). Religion and world change: Violence, terrorism versus peace. *Journal of Social Issues, 61*, 761–784. doi:10.1111/j.1540-4560.2005.00431.x

Smith, C., & Denton, M. L. (2005). *Soul searching: The religious and spiritual lives of American teenagers.* New York, NY: Oxford Press.

Stern, J. (2003). *Terror in the name of God.* New York, NY: Ecco Press.

U.S. Religious Landscape Survey. (2008, February). Washington, DC: Pew Forum on Religion and Public Life.

Wulff, D. (1997). *Psychology of religion: Classic and contemporary views* (2nd ed.). New York, NY: Wiley.

Wuthnow, R. (1998). *After heaven: Spirituality in America since the 1950s.* Berkeley: University of California Press.

Zinnbauer, B. J., Pargament, K. I., Cole, B., Rye, M. S., Butter, E. M., Belavich, T. G., . . . Kadar, J. L. (1997). Religion and spirituality: Unfuzzying the fuzzy. *Journal for the Scientific Study of Religion, 36*, 549–564. doi:10.2307/1387689

Zinnbauer, B. J., Pargament, K. I., & Scott, A. B. (1999). Emerging meanings of religiousness and spirituality: Problems and prospects. *Journal of Personality, 67*, 889–919. doi:10.1111/1467-6494.00077

CHAPTER 2

THE SOCIAL CONTEXT OF RELIGION AND SPIRITUALITY IN THE UNITED STATES

Christopher G. Ellison and Michael J. McFarland

Since the dissemination of the classic theoretical treatises of Marx, Durkheim, and Weber, sociologists—and many other social scientists—have widely assumed that the forces of modernity would erode the social power of religion. In the prevailing secularization narrative, processes such as social differentiation and rationalization would prompt a retreat of religion from the public sphere, resulting in religious privatism and eventual decline (Tschannen, 1991). Such ideas dominated the sociological landscape for most of the 20th century, and secularization theory continues to have its defenders (e.g., Chaves, 1994), especially among many European sociologists (e.g., Bruce, 2002). Beginning in the late 1980s, however, notions of secularization came under harsh scrutiny by a growing number of U.S. sociologists who were increasingly skeptical about the relevance of this perspective to the U.S. experience (Hadden, 1987; Stark, 1999).

Several factors fueled this reconsideration, including (a) evidence regarding continued high rates of religious affiliation, practice, and belief; (b) high rates of financial giving to religious groups and the significant role of faith communities in the nonprofit and voluntary sector; (c) the ongoing emergence of new religious groups, including schismatic movements and so-called cults; and (d) the visibility of religion in social and political movements, including the Christian Right (Hadden, 1987). In light of these and other developments, many U.S. sociologists and other observers have come to view the U.S. religious landscape as a marketplace in which individuals shop and choose their religion and in which religious groups compete for members and other resources (Warner, 1993). Although some scholars employed such concepts loosely, others drew more heavily on economic approaches, notably "rational choice" perspectives (Stark & Finke, 2001).

In the 21st century, contrary to the expectations of some variants of secularization theory, the United States is regarded as one of the most religious societies in the industrial West. Although economic development and national wealth are inversely related to religiousness throughout much of the world, the United States remains a stubborn outlier (Norris & Inglehart, 2004). In contrast to widespread popular and scholarly understandings of the nation's founding, it is now believed that much of the United States was relatively irreligious during the early years of the Republic (Finke & Stark, 1992). The importance of religion increased rapidly in the decades that followed, however, as recognized by Tocqueville during his visit to the United States in the 1840s, and by many observers thereafter. Nevertheless, some observers detect signs of possible secularization on the contemporary scene and looming on the U.S. horizon. Our chapter has three main objectives: (a) to assess patterns and trends in religious affiliation in the contemporary United States, (b) to explore correlates of religious participation and religious and spiritual beliefs, and (c) to identify recent developments and current trends that may reshape the religious and spiritual landscape in the United States over the coming years.

DOI: 10.1037/14045-002
APA Handbook of Psychology, Religion, and Spirituality: Vol. 1. Context, Theory, and Research, K. I. Pargament (Editor-in-Chief)
Copyright © 2013 by the American Psychological Association. All rights reserved.

Three caveats should be noted at this point. First, this chapter necessarily provides a broad and selective overview of these complex phenomena. Many important sociological debates can be presented only in limited fashion. Given the need to restrict our focus, and the fact that a large majority of U.S. adults are Christian or formerly Christian, in the first major sections of the chapter, we concentrate primarily—but not exclusively—on developments within this tradition. In the final section, we return, albeit briefly, to the topic of the growth of non-Christian religions within the United States.

A second issue involves the distinction between *religion* and *spirituality*. Briefly, we should note that there are competing definitions and meanings of these terms that are a perennial source of confusion; on this score, imprecision reigns, and there are important political and value judgments that can underlie this distinction (Zinnbauer et al., 1997; Zinnbauer, Pargament, & Scott, 1999). *Religion* often refers to institutional allegiances and practices. *Spirituality*, on the other hand, often is characterized in terms of engagement with, or experience of, the transcendent. Thus, whereas the meaning of religion is often confined to matters of group identity, organizational participation, and acceptance of doctrines, spirituality frequently takes on a broader meaning, implying interior engagement with the transcendent, including nonorganizational practices and personal experiences (see Chapter 1 in this volume). For a majority of U.S. adults, "religiousness" and "spirituality" are closely linked. To some extent, however, there has clearly been a decoupling of these two phenomena, and it appears that growing numbers of Americans identify themselves as "spiritual, but not religious." In the interests of clarity, the distinction between religion and spirituality will be downplayed until the final section of the chapter, where it will receive closer attention.

A third issue concerns the availability and quality of data on U.S. religion (Sherkat, 2010). In contrast to the situation in many other countries, the U.S. Census Bureau does not collect any information on religion. This was not always the case. Between 1850 and 1936 the U.S. Census Bureau attempted—with varying degrees of breadth and sophistication—to gather data on religious affiliations and congregations across the United States. Following the collapse of these efforts, religious researchers affiliated with several denominations and other organizations—under the auspices of the Glenmary Research Institute—have cooperated in an ongoing initiative to collect data on congregations and religious group membership in the United States (Bradley, Green, Jones, Lynn, & McNeil, 1992; Johnson, Picard, & Quinn, 1974; Jones et al., 2002; Quinn, Anderson, Bradley, Goetting, & Shriver, 1982). Although they remain limited in important ways, the scope and accuracy of these efforts have improved with each iteration. Our estimates of denominational membership are derived from the Glenmary project and correctives thereof (Finke & Scheitle, 2005). On the other hand, data on the religious participation and beliefs of U.S. adults can be obtained only from major surveys on the basis of nationwide probability samples, the best of which are the National Opinion Research Center (NORC) General Social Surveys (GSS; Davis, Smith, & Marsden, 2008) and the American Religious Identification Survey (ARIS; Kosmin, Mayer, & Keysar, 2001). Unless otherwise indicated, figures cited in this chapter are based on these sources.

RELIGIOUS AFFILIATION AND IDENTITY: PATTERNS AND SOCIAL SOURCES

It is estimated that 50% to 60% of U.S. adults report that they are actually members of a religious congregation and that at least 80% maintain a religious identity, preference, or affinity with some religious tradition (Davis et al., 2008; Kosmin et al., 2001). The overwhelming majority of U.S. adults identify with some branch of the Christian faith, even if they are not currently involved in the practice of that faith. On the basis of estimates from these data sources, what follows is a rough breakdown of the religious loyalties of the U.S. adult population: Approximately 30% of U.S. adults self-identify with conservative (i.e., fundamentalist, evangelical, and charismatic) Protestant groups. Although there are significant differences among the various branches of conservative Protestantism, and among specific groups within each branch, in their histories, worship styles, and some specific beliefs, they tend to share several important core tenets, such as biblical inerrancy, original sin, and the imperative of individual salvation through acceptance of divine grace (Hempel & Bartkowski, 2008; Woodberry & Smith, 1998). Official doctrinal statements of most conservative Protestant groups endorse many of the tenets known as "the twelve fundamentals," a set of orthodox Protestant doctrines outlined in the early 20th century (Hunter, 1983).

Among the major conservative Protestant bodies are the Southern Baptist Convention (SBC; the largest Protestant denomination), Lutheran Church–Missouri Synod, Church of Christ, Church of the Nazarene, Wesleyan, Evangelical Free Church, Bible Churches, and numerous other fundamentalist and evangelical groups. This broad category also includes charismatic groups such as the Assemblies of God (the largest Pentecostal body), the Churches of God, the Church of God in Christ, Vineyard Christian Fellowship, all other Pentecostal and Holiness churches, and the many independent charismatic churches (Roof & McKinney, 1987; Smith, 1990; Steensland et al., 2000). High-end estimates of conservative Protestant market share would also include persons who belong to the growing number of nondenominational churches and fellowships, many of which are broadly conservative in theological orientation (Steensland et al., 2000). Furthermore, among predominantly African American denominations and churches, there are signs that the more conservative groups—especially the Church of God in Christ (C.O.G.I.C.), a major Pentecostal body—and sectarian faiths, such as the Jehovah's Witnesses, are gaining members at the expense of more traditional Baptist and Methodist (e.g., African Methodist Episcopal [A.M.E.]) denominations (Ellison & Sherkat, 1990; Sherkat, 2002; see also Chapter 30 in this volume).

According to GSS and ARIS estimates, approximately 12% to 15% of U.S. adults express a preference for mainline (i.e., moderate and liberal) Protestant denominations. Specific groups within this camp include the following: the United Methodist Church, the Episcopal Church, the Presbyterian Church USA (and most other Presbyterian churches, but not the neo-Calvinist Presbyterian Church in America), most variants of Lutheranism (particularly the Evangelical Lutheran Church in America, but not the Missouri or Wisconsin Synod Lutherans, which are conservative Protestant groups), the United Church of Christ (or Congregationalist), and the Disciples of Christ. Although these groups differ from one another in terms of their histories, they generally reject many conservative Protestant teachings, and they also have moved to embrace more moderate or liberal views on many theological and social issues.

Roughly 25% of U.S. adults express a preference for Roman Catholicism; however, many persons who self-identify as Catholics, or who are counted by the Church as members, are not active members. Much smaller proportions report ties to (a) sectarian Christian groups, such as the Latter-day Saints (Mormons) and the Jehovah's Witnesses, as well as (b) various religious groups that are difficult to categorize within most established classification schemes, such as the Unitarian Universalists, various Anabaptist groups (e.g., Friends, Mennonites), and new religious movements. Roughly 5% of U.S. adults now express preferences for non-Christian world faiths, such as Judaism, Islam, Hinduism, and Buddhism, among others. Finally, approximately 15% to 20% of U.S. adults now express no religious preference at all on surveys, although many of these adults continue to hold traditional religious beliefs.

At one time in the early to mid-20th century, nearly all Americans were raised with a religious preference, and although survey data before the 1960s are limited, it is widely believed that most adults retained their religion of origin throughout their lives. This is no longer the case. Indeed, since the 1960s, observers have pointed to considerable fluidity and voluntarism as key features of the U.S. religious marketplace.

Which form of religion or spirituality to identify with, or indeed, whether to identity with one at all, are increasingly matters of choice not ascription. An estimated 40% to 50% of U.S. adults will switch their religious allegiance at least once during their lifetime. Although many persons may switch religions more than once, data on such multiple switchers are scarce and unreliable (Roof, 1989). According to many observers, Americans increasingly employ a market-oriented logic in the arena of religion, shopping for churches much as they might shop for other consumer products.

Regional Factors

One of the key features of the U.S. religious scene is its sheer diversity, at least when viewed in aggregate terms. America is home to several thousand specific religious denominations and faith traditions (Jones et al., 2002). Using economic imagery, one might say that low barriers to entry and limited government regulation in the United States allow for the entry of new religious entrepreneurs and firms with few constraints. Although the Glenmary data and major surveys reveal the existence of many different religious groups within the United States, not all local communities are religiously diverse. To be sure, major metropolitan areas, and especially the leading "gateway cities" for immigration (i.e., New York, Los Angeles, Miami, Washington, Honolulu, San Francisco, Houston), host large numbers of faiths, including non-Judeo-Christian world religions. Furthermore, much of the mid-Atlantic and Midwestern United States is characterized by the presence of (and competition among) numerous Christian denominations. A significant proportion of the more than 3,000 U.S. counties are dominated by adherents of one or a small number of denominations (e.g., Catholic, Southern Baptist, Mormon; Jones et al., 2002). Although religious diversity is slowly coming to many of these areas, these patterns of religious concentration and cultural hegemony at the local and regional levels carry important implications for the texture of social life and public discourse and for the potential for religious prejudice and conflict.

For nearly a century, researchers have observed that religious denominations differ widely in terms of their regional, ethnic, and socioeconomic composition (Niebuhr, 1929; Roof & McKinney, 1987). Although there are signs that these "social sources of denominationalism" may be waning—due to intergenerational mobility, intermarriage, geographic relocation, and other leavening influences—they remain relevant in the 21st century (Park & Reimer, 2002). For example, Catholicism remains the dominant faith in several specific areas of the United States, including the following: (a) New England and much of the Northeast; (b) areas of the upper Midwest; (c) the Southwest, including California and the U.S.–Mexico border states; and (d) areas of Louisiana and Texas along the Gulf Coast. Members of several mainline Protestant denominations—such as the United Church of Christ, Presbyterian Church USA, and Episcopal Church—are disproportionately likely to reside in the Northeast and parts of the Midwest. Although early colonists and planters in the Low Country areas of the Southeast primarily embraced Anglicanism (the Church of England), the South and the lower Midwest are heavily populated by adherents of conservative Protestant religions, which had consolidated social and cultural dominance of these areas by the mid-19th century (Boles, 1985; Finke & Stark, 1989). The Wesleyan tradition, from which the United Methodist Church emerged, competed vigorously with the Baptist faith for adherents in much of the South during the 19th century, but a series of changes in church culture and structure tipped the balance in favor of the Baptists by the early decades of the 20th century (Finke & Stark, 1992). Other conservative Protestant churches, such as the (fundamentalist) Church of Christ and the Assemblies of God, are also disproportionately popular in South Central and lower Midwest regions. One important development since the 1970s has been the spread of conservative Protestantism to areas outside the southern United States (Park & Reimer, 2002).

Other regional patterns are also noteworthy. The Latter-day Saints (Mormons) have been the dominant cultural force in Utah for more than a century; recent decades have seen striking increases in the prevalence of Mormonism in several neighboring areas of the Mountain West (Idaho, Wyoming, and eastern parts of Washington and Oregon; Bradley et al., 1992; Jones et al., 2002; Quinn et al., 1982). Institutional religion has long been weakest in parts of the Mountain West (far northern Idaho) and the Pacific Rim (northern California, Oregon, and Washington), which were among the last-settled areas of the United States. In the 21st century, these locales have low levels of religious participation and a disproportionate shares of unchurched and "spiritual but not religious" residents (Bainbridge, 1990). Jewish Americans also tend to be regionally concentrated. The Jewish population is disproportionately urban and bicoastal. Although there are large Jewish areas in cities like New York, Los Angeles, and San Francisco, among others, Jews have not been the dominant religious group in any U.S. county. The only partial exception to this statement is the case of Palm Beach County, Florida, in which Jews constituted the single largest religious grouping according to the 1990 Glenmary estimates. By 2000, however, increases in the numbers of Catholics (particularly Latinos, but also European American migrants from other parts of the United States) eliminated this Jewish plurality (Bradley et al., 1992; Jones et al., 2002).

Many patterns of geographic concentration closely track the historical immigration of specific ethnic groups (Grammich, 2005). For example, the large percentages of Catholics in the Northeast and Midwest partly reflect the migration histories of Irish and subsequent immigrant streams from southern and eastern Europe (e.g., Italian, Polish, etc.). Catholic dominance elsewhere is bound up with Hispanic (particularly Mexican American), French-speaking Acadian (Cajun), and other ethnic cultures. There are other examples of the lingering confluence of regional religious concentrations and ethnic heritage. Lutheranism continues to prevail in many rural areas of Minnesota, North Dakota, and Montana, reflecting the continuing influence of Scandinavian and German heritage in that region. Pockets of Dutch settlement in western Michigan and Iowa remain home to concentrations of adherents of the Reformed tradition, including the Christian Reformed Church. Despite intergenerational mobility, intermarriage, and other leavening influences, many other examples of the persistent connection between ethnic heritage and religion abound (e.g., Nemeth & Luidens, 1995). Furthermore, perhaps because of the abundance of religious supply in the United States, immigrant groups from some less religious countries of origin have tended to exhibit increases in religiousness across three generations, as part the assimilation process (Stark, 1997).

Socioeconomic Factors

Socioeconomic status (SES) has long varied along denominational lines. Throughout much of U.S. history, adherents of mainline (and especially liberal) Protestant faiths (e.g., Episcopal, Presbyterian Church USA, United Church of Christ) have tended to have higher levels of formal education and wealth and have been disproportionately likely to hold prestigious positions in business and the professions (Niebuhr, 1929; Roof & McKinney, 1987). This has also been the case with Jews (especially Reform Jews) since the mid 20th century. By contrast, as a group, conservative Protestants traditionally have lagged behind most other Americans on these socioeconomic indicators. At least part of this differential may reflect the longstanding concentration of fundamentalists and evangelicals in the South, which was largely rural and economically underdeveloped before the 1960s. Thus, there were minimal education opportunities or incentives for many conservative Protestants of earlier generations, whose prospects were limited by lack of education access, diffusion of resources among numerous siblings, and familial need for agricultural labor. The subsequent industrial and economic boom in the region and the expansion of opportunities for higher education beginning in the 1950s significantly changed these patterns (Massengill, 2008). For example, according to GSS data, among conservative Protestants, the ratio of high school dropouts to college-educated adherents was 10:1 in 1972; by 1996, this figure was 1:1, in large part because of cohort replacement (i.e., older, less educated cohorts died off and were replaced by cohorts with greater access to, and rewards for, education attainment; Davis et al., 2008). Nevertheless, conservative Protestants continue to trail their more moderate and liberal counterparts in education attainment (Massengill, 2008) as well as in other important socioeconomic indicators, including wages, early adult wealth accumulation, and occupational attainment (Keister, 2011; Lehrer, 2008).

Although Catholics tended to have relatively low levels of education and economic standing throughout much of the past 150 years, these patterns have largely reflected the confounding influences of nativity (U.S. born vs. foreign born) and generational status among those of European American ancestry. Whereas first-generation non-Hispanic White Catholic immigrants often arrived with low levels of education and were consigned to low-skill, low-prestige jobs, the upward mobility of recent cohorts has been facilitated by distinctive patterns of education, marriage, and fertility as well as Catholic religious values with regard to work and money (Keister, 2011). Hispanic Catholic immigrants exhibit particularly low average levels of SES; however, given the current constraints imposed by economic and political conditions, it remains to be seen whether they and future generations of Latino Catholics will be able to experience upward mobility in education and earnings.

CHANGE AND CONTINUITY IN RELIGIOUS AFFILIATION AND IDENTITY

The American religious scene is both highly diverse and fluid. Over the past half-century the fortunes of several major religious bodies have shifted dramatically, for a wide range of possible reasons. The sections that follow outline several of these key changes as well as prominent explanations for them.

Conservative Protestant Gains, Mainline Losses

One of the most striking developments over the past several decades has been the strong growth of conservative Protestant and sectarian religious groups, and the concomitant decline of the more liberal mainline Protestant bodies. A few examples, derived from Glenmary data, illustrate these disparate patterns. Between 1970 and 2000, the estimated number of Latter-day Saints (Mormons) adherents increased by a striking 98%. The numbers of Southern Baptists rose by 37.5% during the same period, although there is evidence that membership had started to plateau around 2000 (Lindner, 2011). Between 1980 and 2000, the estimated number of adherents to the Assemblies of God, the largest Pentecostal body, grew by roughly 59% (1970 data were unavailable). The Assemblies of God and other Pentecostal groups have demonstrated robust growth during the early 2000s as well (Lindner, 2011). On the other hand, the estimated number of adherents in the United Church of Christ declined by 24.5%; losses over the same period for two other mainline Protestant churches, the Episcopal Church and the United Methodist Church, were 23% and 10%, respectively. Additional mainline losses have been recorded during the 2000–2010 period (Lindner, 2011). And although these are predominantly (non-Hispanic) White denominations, there are clear indications of a conservative Protestant surge among African Americans and Latinos as well. What factors account for these divergent trends in denominational growth? Several sets of explanations have been proposed, and social scientists remain far from consensus on this issue.

One perspective has focused on differences in the organizational cultures of conservative versus liberal religious groups, emphasizing that conservative Protestant and sectarian churches often are characterized by two key features: (a) strictness, or the inclination to demand doctrinal and behavioral compliance with group norms, and (b) social solidarity, or the tendency to encourage insular networks and shared sacrifice for group objectives (Kelley, 1972). According to Iannaccone (1994), conservative religious communities often impose "sacrifice and stigma," in the form of demands for regular worship attendance and other types of participation, tithing, and perhaps compliance with other lifestyle guidelines. More liberal religions, such as mainline Protestant churches, usually eschew such demands, and are more inclined to accept differences among members in commitment, doctrinal belief, and lifestyle. Iannaccone and others maintain that the strictness of conservative religions has two desirable effects: (a) It weeds out "free riders," or lukewarm members who would otherwise dilute the energy of these groups; and (b) among those who choose to remain, strictness also promotes compliance, monitoring, and informal sanctioning practices against less committed members. The second of these effects allows conservative groups to gain greater volunteer labor and financial donations, two key resources that promote congregational flourishing and achievement of organizational aims (Scheitle & Finke, 2008). The result is thought to be a more satisfying religious product or good, a coherent religious meaning system that is capable of providing compelling answers to religious questions and assurance concerning spiritual salvation. These more rewarding spiritual goods give members a reason to remain in the group; the relative absence of such rewards in liberal groups may lead to spiritual uncertainty and eventual defection (Iannaccone, 1994; Kelley, 1972). Empirically, the strictness thesis has been accorded a major role in explanations of the dramatic rise of the Jehovah's Witnesses, in particular (Stark & Iannaccone, 1997). Although most discussions of the strictness thesis have been pitched at the denominational level, recent research using data on a large sample of congregations from diverse denominations provides considerable evidence of links between strictness, social strength, and church growth (Thomas & Olson, 2010).

One variant of the strictness idea emphasizes the importance of cultural tension with the dominant or surrounding societal order. What is required for this approach to succeed is an optimal level of tension, and given recent increases in education and income levels among many conservative Protestants, this is sometimes a challenging tightrope to negotiate. In one intriguing example, out of displeasure over the policies of the Disney organization regarding lesbian, gay, bisexual, and transgender (LGBT) employees and issues, leaders of the SBC called for members to boycott all Disney products. This attempt to influence Disney—and by extension, other media organizations—was an abject failure and was quickly scuttled. Demands for members to abandon a broad array of desired consumer products aimed precisely at the kinds of middle-class families with children that make up a substantial share of the SBC created too much tension and required too much sacrifice to be viable. Nevertheless, some scholars have argued that the success of evangelicalism as a religious movement has been premised largely on the perception of being "embattled"; that is, evangelicals and their leaders have maintained sufficient tension with society to allow for the construction of a persuasive critique of (what is represented as) the dominant culture (Smith et al., 1998). Mainline Protestantism, by contrast, has experienced greater difficulty in promoting such a critical narrative, in part because it has been so influential in forging the social order of the early to mid-20th-century United States. The vast majority of leaders in business, media, education, and politics have been from mainline Protestant origins.

A second set of explanations has centered on the role of supply-side factors, or mechanisms that affect access or exposure to various types of religious options from which individuals may choose (Finke & Iannaccone, 1993). For example, the cultures of conservative Protestant and sectarian groups are innately more evangelistic in orientation than those of most mainline Protestant denominations. The most striking examples of zealous conversion efforts are found among sectarian religions, such as the Latter-day Saints (Mormons) and Jehovah's Witnesses, for whom door-to-door contacts and mission activities are expected. Vigorous outreach is also an important part of most fundamentalist, evangelical, and charismatic faith communities. Although evangelism receives greater emphasis in conservative and sectarian religious groups, there is also evidence that even modest outreach and recruitment activities (e.g., members inviting friends to visit the congregation, pastors following up with prospective members) can be effective in spurring church growth, even when these efforts are conducted by mainline Protestant denominations (Callahan, 1983; Roozen & Hadaway, 1993).

Another type of supply-side explanation directs attention to the strategic planting of new congregations by conservative religious groups and the near absence of the same by most mainline denominations (Hadaway, 1990). Many of the new churches have been placed in suburbs and exurbs, for example, in areas with relatively homogeneous populations of middle-class families with children. This segment of the religious market may be lured by the promise of active congregations, dynamic youth programs, and family life ministries, and as engaged members of the community, they may be well positioned to recruit others like themselves. Mainline Protestant denominations, by contrast, often are invested heavily in downtown churches, with facilities that are large, expensive to maintain, and difficult to sell. Their members generally have left the urban core and relocated to the suburbs; their closest residential neighbors are now groups to which they may struggle to minister effectively, such as ethnic minorities, new immigrants, and young urban professionals. Taken together, these factors may increase the visibility and appeal of conservative groups to residents of suburban and exurban areas while further diminishing the viability of mainline Protestant denominations.

Finke and Iannaccone (1993) have pointed out yet a third example of supply-side factors at work, this time at the macro level: the potential importance of changes in broadcasting laws and media technologies after the 1960s, such as the rise of cable television and the emergence of religious broadcasting networks. These changes had two effects: (a) They eliminated the monopoly on religious broadcasting that was once enjoyed for free by local, mostly mainline Protestant churches; and (b) they resulted in the ascendancy of paid religious broadcasting—on first a regional and later a national scale—mainly by conservative Protestant clergy and ministries. These developments brought fundamentalist, evangelical, and charismatic doctrines and worship styles to the attention of many viewers outside the traditional southern home base of conservative Protestantism.

Yet another set of explanations for conservative religious growth and liberal religious decline are demographic in nature. One such approach has been offered by Hout, Greeley, and Wilde (2001), who have linked the growth in numbers of conservative Protestant and sectarian adherents to the disproportionately high fertility rates of those groups during the immediate post–World War II period. Others have spotted a broader trend, noting that conservatives and sectarians—especially Mormons, but others as well—have had above-average fertility rates across several cohorts, whereas mainline Protestants have had relatively low fertility rates (Sherkat, 2010). It is also the case that most conservative groups are more successful than their mainline counterparts in retaining offspring raised within the faith (Sherkat, 2001). Over time, this has shifted the age composition of both conservative and mainline faith communities, in ways that suggest greater "demographic potential" for future growth among conservative Protestants, and especially sectarians, as compared with mainline Protestants (Park & Reimer, 2002). Another study has complemented these various findings, showing that there is an interaction or multiplicative effect of fertility rates and switching rates, such that the potential for the growth of a religious group is especially dramatic when switching occurs at high levels among persons of childbearing age (Scheitle, Kane, & Van Hook, 2011).

Yet another type of demographic explanation—this one occurring at the macrolevel—has centered on the importance of migration patterns. Over the past several decades, large numbers of Americans have relocated from the Rustbelt areas of the Northeast and Midwest to the Sunbelt areas of the United States, primarily in search of economic opportunity or retirement. These regional migratory patterns also may have tipped the balance of religious competition and institutional strength further in favor of conservative Protestant groups (Stump, 1998).

Observers seeking to explain the shifting sands of Protestant church membership have also focused on changes within denominations and their seminaries, which may have eroded the appeal and competitive position of mainline Protestantism. Critics have asserted that mainline Protestant seminaries and denominational agencies have been captured by special interest groups focused on social and political issues, such as sexuality and global politics. As early as the 1980s, in mainline Protestant denominations, there was evidence of substantial divisions between clergy and seminarians, on the one hand, and laity, on the other hand, in terms of theological, social, and political matters; such cleavages were not found to the same degree within more conservative groups. Some observers have charged that evangelicals and secular political interests have fueled dissention and disarray within the ranks of mainline Protestant groups by funding theologically and politically conservative "special purpose" groups. These groups, in turn, have spurred opposition to liberal theological tendencies (e.g., ordination of female and gay or lesbian clergy) as well as mainline Protestant support for labor, peace, and antiwar efforts; civil rights, environmentalism; and other left-of-center social causes (Swecker, 2005; Tooley, 2008).

According to critics, mainline Protestant seminaries tended to neglect core training areas, such as preaching, mission activity, and church planning and management, which left new clergy unprepared to assume leadership of local churches. At the congregational level, according to many observers, conservative churches attended more closely to the needs of middle-class families, sponsoring marriage seminars and youth ministries, helping them to deal with the intrusions of new work arrangements into home life, nurturing their spiritual lives through small group experiences and "mix and share" groups, providing dynamic worship services and engaged preaching, and encouraging other practices that fostered religious fulfillment. Consequently, church growth specialists have recommended that mainline congregations emulate some of these programs and innovations (e.g., Hadaway & Roozen, 1995). Indeed, studies of mainline Protestant congregations that have flourished despite the broader negative trends affecting their denominations showed that these successful churches were attempting to incorporate at least some of the lessons from their evangelical counterparts (e.g., Ellingson, 2007).

Catholic Growth

In addition to these dramatic changes within Protestantism, researchers have documented significant growth of Catholicism within the United States. According to estimates derived from the Glenmary data, the number of Catholic adherents rose more than 38% between 1970 and 2000. Steady Catholic growth also has been reported over the ensuing decade (Lindner, 2011). At least some of this increase may reflect more accurate counting of previously undercounted Catholic groups (e.g., Latinos) in more recent iterations of the Glenmary project. Furthermore, the ranks of Catholicism always have gained disproportionately from immigration (Sherkat, 2010), and in recent decades, many new Catholics have arrived from Latin America—particularly Mexico—as well as from parts of Asia and Africa (Massey & Higgins, 2011). Additionally, first-generation immigrants are typically younger than the population at large and have higher average fertility rates. One recent demographic forecasting the religious composition of the U.S. population through 2043 predicted that Catholicism would become the dominant faith in the United States, significantly outstripping its nearest competitors, conservative Protestantism and secularism (Skirbekk, Kaufmann, & Goujon, 2010). This projection, however, is heavily dependent on (a) continued high levels of migration (legal and undocumented) from Mexico, (b) comparatively high levels of fertility among Latino Catholics, and (c) anticipated low levels of religious switching (e.g., to evangelicalism) within the Latino population.

These projections notwithstanding, several important issues and challenges confront U.S. Catholicism as it continues to grow. First, these estimates of numbers of adherents almost certainly include many nonpracticing Catholics. Individuals who were raised as Catholics may have stopped attending mass or participating in other ways for various reasons. For example, researchers have detected sharp declines in mass attendance among certain birth cohorts of Catholics during the 1960s and 1970s, probably reflecting opposition to official Church policies concerning contraception, abortion, and the status of women within the Church (Hout & Greeley, 1987). Some observers also have pointed to growing disagreement among Catholic laity about what it means to be a "good" Catholic (D'Antonio, 1994). There are also signs of broader cohort and generational divisions within U.S. Catholicism. Older Catholics tend to be more supportive of traditional teachings and express greater obedience to the Vatican, whereas baby boomer Catholics have placed greater emphasis on the role of individual conscience in deciding which church teachings and policies to follow; this valorization of personal conscience may have become even stronger among subsequent cohorts of Catholics in the United States (Pogorelc & Davidson, 2000; Williams & Davidson, 1996). Not surprising, there is considerable unease over the long-running clergy sexual abuse scandals and deep discontent over the handling of these issues by church leaders. These trends may signal a loss of confidence in the institutional church and its spiritual leadership among some Catholics.

In addition to these issues, U.S. Catholicism is affected by other significant demographic issues. First and foremost, the Catholic Church faces a well-documented priest shortage that has been developing for decades (Schoenherr & Young, 1993). Estimates from the Glenmary data suggest that there are as many as 10,000 Catholics per parish in some areas (e.g., southern California).

According to some commentators, the priest shortage can be solved only through major changes in Church doctrines and policies, such as allowing married priests and ordaining women (Schoenherr, 2004), which are unlikely to occur in the foreseeable future. Second, the Church is both blessed and challenged by changes in the composition of the Catholic population. In particular, the tremendous growth of Latino Catholics from various national-origin groups (e.g., Mexican Americans, Puerto Ricans) has spurred calls for greater inclusiveness, sensitivity to Latino cultural nuances, and—perhaps especially—the need for Latino priests, who can provide Spanish-language mass while appreciating the backgrounds, experiences, and distinctive needs of Latino parishioners (see Chapter 33 in this volume; Diaz-Stevens, 1993; Fernandez, 2007; Matovina, 2011). Latino priests are in particularly short supply in the United States. Locally, much like mainline Protestant churches, many urban Catholic parishes in the Rustbelt are dealing with the consequences of members' migration (a) to suburbs and exurbs and (b) to the Sunbelt region, in pursuit of economic opportunity or retirement. These developments have led to the consolidation or closure of numerous parishes in cities like Detroit, Cleveland, Chicago, and others (Brand-Williams, 2010; Niedermier, 2009). Finally, declines in the Catholic education infrastructure may have implications for the spiritual formation of current and future generations of Catholics. Such declines may be amplified if large financial settlements to the victims of past clergy abuse degrade the Church's operating resources.

The Rise of Irreligion

Surveys such as the NORC GSS and the ARIS indicate that since the late 1990s, 15% to 20% of U.S. adults claim to have no religious preference (Hout & Fischer, 2002; Kosmin et al., 2001). These figures represent the high-water mark in detachment from institutional religion, at least during the modern period in the United States. Religious nonaffiliation had held steady at 5% to 7% throughout the 1950s and 1960s, and then had risen to 10% to 12% during the 1970s and 1980s (Glenn, 1987). Levels of irreligion are higher among certain segments of the population, such as younger and better educated persons, and recent research on young adults suggests that these figures could continue to rise in the years to come (Smith & Snell, 2009).

What factors may account for the gradual rise in irreligion in the United States? One contributing factor may be the stronger ethos of religious voluntarism, or personal choice, that began with the baby boomer generation and has persisted (and even intensified) among subsequent cohorts (Roof, 2001; Roof & McKinney, 1987). This has led many individuals to be selective about the aspects of religious teaching or practice that one embraces, and by extension, it has made it more acceptable to eschew religion altogether. Furthermore, younger generations express less confidence in religious institutions and their leaders than previous cohorts (Hoffmann, 1998). Overall, declines in confidence in organized religion have been steeper than declines in confidence in other social institutions, such as business, the media, and the various branches of government (Chaves, 2011). Younger cohorts also may be disengaging primarily from more liberal religious groups, such as mainline Protestant denominations that have been less successful than others in socialization and spiritual formation (Sherkat, 2001; Smith & Denton, 2005; Smith & Snell, 2009). Among baby boomers and subsequent generations, the growing ranks of the irreligious also may be swelled by disaffected Catholics, who are relatively unlikely to switch to other denominations, and by secular Jews.

The rejection of institutional religion also may be fueled by social and political developments (Hout & Fischer, 2002; see Chapter 40 in this volume). In particular, many individuals may be expressing antipathy and alienation toward the increased fusion of religion and politics, especially (but not exclusively) on the part of conservatives. This may reflect a rejection of their specific views regarding social issues such as abortion, gay rights, and a host of other topics, or it may imply a broader hostility toward (a) what is perceived as cynical manipulation of the sacred for secular ends and (b) what is seen as an inappropriate thrusting of narrow, group-specific religious views into the realm of public policy. In addition, the growth of the "no religion" category in surveys also may reflect rejection of religious elites for various types of malfeasance (financial, sexual, etc.) and for their maladroit handling of the aftermath of institutional crises, such as the Catholic priest abuse scandals. This current trend may result from the pitched battles waged by some religious groups against what is perceived to be scientific authority and expertise (Hout & Fischer, 2002; Sherkat, 2008). Examples of this would include attempts by religious leaders to challenge the teaching of evolution in public schools; attempts to elevate creationism and its close cousin, intelligent design, to coequal scientific status; and opposition to stem cell research and various forms of contraception.

Individual Religious Affiliation, Denominational Switching, and Apostasy

Studies have shown that 40% to 50% of U.S. adults will alter their religious affiliations at least once during their lifetime, and many numbers will change their religious allegiance multiple times. These individual-level changes may involve switching (moving from one denomination to another) and apostasy (dropping out of organized religion altogether). It is widely suggested that such religious mobility has been heightened in recent decades, heavily influenced by the more voluntaristic religious ethos that prevails among baby boomers and members of subsequent generations. Some also have argued that these apparently elevated rates of religious mobility may have been facilitated by reductions in real or perceived denominational differences, as boundaries among specific groups have been supplanted by broader conservative versus liberal religious divisions (Wuthnow, 1988). Other findings suggest that such a conclusion may be premature (Sherkat, 2001). A number of factors may have lowered boundaries between specific denominations: (a) the rise of ecumenical initiatives among mainline Protestant and Catholic groups, as they joined forces in the 1950s and 1960s against the common enemies of communism, secularism, and materialism; (b) increases in social and geographic mobility; (c) increases in rates of interfaith marriage among persons from most denominations (except for the most conservative and sectarian ones; Sherkat, 2004); and (d) the growth of "special purpose" groups organized around social and political concerns, within and between denominations, which increased within-group heterogeneity as well as contacts among like-minded persons from different denominations (Wuthnow, 1988).

Two types of data have been used to investigate patterns and correlates of religious switching and apostasy. One source of data is panel studies, in which samples of persons from specific birth cohorts have been tracked over time, and data on their religious affiliation have been collected at multiple time points (e.g., Sandomirsky & Wilson, 1990). In some databases, such as the National Survey of Families and Households, which contains detailed information on the timing of major life transitions, it is possible to test fine-grained hypotheses about links between family changes (i.e., cohabitation, marriage, divorce, childbearing) and shifts in religious affiliation and practice. A second type of data involves cross-sectional surveys of U.S. adults, in which respondents are asked about (a) the religion in which they were raised (or their religion at age 16) and (b) their religion at the time of the interview. The latter data often are gathered via replicated cross-sectional survey projects, such as the NORC GSS. Because new samples are drawn every other year, it is possible to monitor switching patterns across "synthetic" birth cohorts, or groups of U.S. adults who were born within specific time intervals, permitting reliable inferences about large-scale trends in switching and apostasy. Thus, these two sources of data can offer complementary insights about changes in religious affiliation and apostasy.

What is known about the individual-level patterns and correlates of religious switching and apostasy? The earliest theoretical perspectives on these phenomena tended to emphasize the role of SES considerations, viewing changes in religious loyalties as either (a) expressions of status or (b) manifestations of status seeking. In other words, individuals who had experienced changes in their social status, in comparison with the social class in which they were raised, were thought to seek religious groups that were consistent with their newly attained status, in which they would encounter religious messages that resonated with their current experiences, and in which they would interact with persons who shared their worldviews and lifestyles. According to this theoretical perspective, persons seeking upward mobility would gravitate to denominations that allowed them to gain information and make contacts that could facilitate social and economic gains. For persons from high-status religious groups (e.g., liberal Protestant denominations), further status ascent (and especially education attainment) could lead to apostasy. Although there is some empirical support for these hypothesized links between SES changes and religious mobility, they provide only partial explanations of the complexity of individual-level religious change in the United States (Sherkat & Wilson, 1995; Wilson, 1966).

Beyond these class-based explanations of individual religious change, how have sociologists and other social scientists broached this topic? One popular approach has involved the use of microeconomic reasoning—often termed *rational choice* theory—to understand individual-level variations in decisions about (a) which to join (if any) and (b) at what level to participate (Sherkat & Ellison, 1999). The cornerstone of this perspective is the maximizing assumption, or the view that individuals make choices with the goal of deriving maximum benefit (e.g., spiritual reward, religious insight, social gains from religious involvement) for minimum cost. Definitions of benefits and costs, as well as other parameters of individual choices, are the focus of much debate and discussion. For example, individuals make decisions on the basis of the best information at hand, which is almost always imperfect and incomplete. Individuals may rule out some potential options at the outset and thus make choices from more constrained lists of possibilities, sometimes termed *feasible sets* (Ellison, 1995).

Although many rational choice analysts accept the notion of "revealed preferences" (i.e., the view that individuals' preferences are demonstrated by the behavioral choices they actually make), others strongly disagree and argue that sociological insights can help to explain the gaps between (a) the religious groups or traditions that individuals themselves might prefer and (b) the religious groups with which they affiliate, if any (Sherkat, 1997; Sherkat & Wilson, 1995). The notion of "adaptive preferences" holds that individuals often come to prefer that with which they have become familiar; in other words, preferences adapt to life circumstances and socialization patterns. This simple idea helps to explain two empirical patterns: (a) An estimated 50% to 60% of U.S. adults will retain their religion of origin throughout much, if not all, of their lifetime; and (b) of those who do switch, many shift to groups that are "close to home" (i.e., similar to their religion of origin in some combination of doctrine, ritual, history, or social values; Sherkat, 2001).

The notion of "adaptive preferences" is in some respects analogous to the concept of "religious human capital," as articulated by the economist Iannaccone (1990). Like other forms of human capital, religious human capital refers to knowledge, skills, and experiences that enhance productivity and efficiency. In the religious arena, individuals learn about doctrines and church teachings, gain experience in religious rituals and worship activities, and become steeped in subgroup cultures through formal religious education classes, informal interactions, and time spent engaged in religious pursuits with family members and others. Iannaccone (1990) has argued that subsequent religious decisions (e.g., about whether to switch, and what other groups to join) are shaped partly by the goal of conserving religious capital, and by avoiding the need to shelve entire stocks of religious training and to learn completely new religious traditions, doctrines, ritual styles, and so on. His work has found some support for this perspective in predicting religious switching behavior, patterns of interfaith marriage and subsequent decisions about religious change, and various other outcomes.

In addition to "adaptive preferences," religious choices may be influenced by such factors as sympathy, antipathy, and example setting (Sherkat, 1997). Briefly, regardless of their own personal religious desires and needs, individuals may choose a religion out of deference to the wishes of others or the desire to emulate others (see Chapter 10 in this volume). Thus, it may be easier to remain in the faith tradition in which one was raised than to risk alienating parents, grandparents, or other family members.

Indeed, among the strongest predictors of such religious retention are having grown up in an intact, two-parent family characterized by a happy marriage and warm parent–child emotional bonds (see Chapter 7 in this volume; Sherkat & Wilson, 1995; Uecker, Regnerus, & Vaaler, 2007). This finding holds true even in samples drawn from members of the baby boomer cohort, as they passed through the tumultuous countercultural and political events of the 1960s and early 1970s (Sherkat, 1998). Conversely, studies of religious nonaffiliation and disaffiliation have found that persons raised by parents with no religious affiliation, and those who attended services rarely or never while growing up, are much more likely to report no religious affiliation in adulthood (Baker & Smith, 2009).

Switching denominations to accommodate the religious loyalties of one's spouse or spouse's family is yet another example of sympathetic religious choice (Waite & Lewin, 2010). Switching for marriage reasons typically occurs when the less religiously committed spouse (often the man) joins the religious faith or denomination of the more religious spouse (Sandomirsky & Wilson, 1990). Religious choices also may be shaped by example-setting motives. This is especially relevant for parents with children, who—regardless of their own religious beliefs, if any—may choose religious communities with strong moral traditions, vigorous youth ministries and family activities, and other mechanisms for socializing young people (e.g., Stolzenberg, Blair-Loy, & Waite, 1995). In the religious arena, women tend to be influenced by family-of-origin factors (i.e., the religious traditions in which they were raised), whereas men are more likely to be influenced by the families they help to form (i.e., the religious traditions of their spouses and the religious needs of their children; Sandomirsky & Wilson, 1990). Religiously unaffiliated persons (sometimes termed *unchurched* in the research literature) are much more likely than others to have religiously unaffiliated spouses and to have no children in the home (Baker & Smith, 2009).

Although sympathetic religious choices have received more attention in the research literature, some religious choices can be made out of antipathy, or the desire to establish distance from family members or one's faith tradition of origin. For some young people, the decision to join certain so-called cults in the 1960s and 1970s partly may have reflected such motives. Some persons may adopt nontraditional forms of spirituality (e.g., Satanism, and perhaps Pagan or Wiccan practices) with an eye toward shocking or scandalizing others, including authority figures (see Chapter 41 in this volume).

Other social factors may lead individuals to make religious choices that do not reflect their own preferences. The norms, conventions, and expectations of surrounding communities may dictate that persons belong to religious groups to sustain respectability or full community membership (Ellison, 1995; Ellison & Sherkat, 1995; Sherkat, 1997). This can lead some persons to maintain their ties to faith traditions that these persons otherwise might abandon. Examples of this phenomenon abound within many ethnic communities, where formally disavowing one's religion of origin also would involve cutting ties with family members, neighbors, and members of one's ethnic group. This can be seen within specific denominations that either (a) overlap significantly with ethnicity (e.g., Catholic; Jewish; to a lesser extent, denominations like Lutheran or Dutch Reformed) or (b) function in ways that are analogous to all-encompassing ethnic groups (e.g., Latter-day Saints or Mormons; Sandomirsky & Wilson, 1990). These various groups are sometimes termed *quasi-ethnic* denominations in the research literature. Because it is more difficult for members to leave these groups than to depart other denominations (e.g., liberal Protestant groups) in which social ties are typically weaker in structure, disaffected members of quasi-ethnic groups are sometimes more likely (a) to abandon religion altogether, as opposed to switching their loyalties to a different denomination, or (b) to defect in place, becoming nominal or inactive members of their denomination of origin.

But the potential role of normative constraints and social expectations is broader than this. In fact, most religious communities are shaped and maintained through social network ties; individuals may be recruited into the group via preexisting social relationships, and congregations are geared toward the establishment of friendships and ongoing social bonds (e.g., Ellison & George, 1994). These social connections offer social support and other rewards, and they also facilitate monitoring and subtle social sanctions when individuals reduce their religious involvement. Thus, events and processes in the lives of individuals that disrupt these relationships may influence religious group membership and practice. For example, studies have repeatedly shown that residential mobility—sometimes within the same community and certainly from one community to another—leads individuals to disaffiliate from their religious group, at least for a time (e.g., Sherkat, 1991). Although some persons join new churches or synagogues as part of the resettlement process, for others, religious involvement is never restored to its previous levels. At the aggregate level, those regions of the United States (e.g., the Mountain and Pacific states) with high levels of population mobility, and those communities in which large percentages of individuals have changed residential addresses within the previous 5 years, tend to have comparatively low levels of religious affiliation and attendance (Bainbridge, 1990).

Finally, the notion of normative constraints may help to explain temporal trends and variations in religious nonaffiliation, disaffiliation, and nonbelief. For example, U.S. adults born between the years 1945 and 1959 are much more prone to be religiously unaffiliated than others; many of these persons were raised with a denominational tie but subsequently abandoned organized religion in adolescence or young adulthood (Schwadel, 2011). These cohort-specific patterns are not replicated among persons born after 1960, perhaps because they were disproportionately raised with no religious affiliation themselves. Much has been written about the evolving religious and spiritual ethos of persons born during the 1945–1959 period, the so-called baby boomers (e.g., Roof, 1993, 2001). Members of this cohort may have left organized religion at comparatively high rates for several reasons, including (a) disaffection over the perceived inauthenticity of spirituality in established churches; (b) rejection of the social and political conservatism of many religious groups (e.g., their embrace or acquiescence vis-à-vis the Vietnam War and domestic social injustices); and (c) broader anti-institutional, antiestablishment sentiments, and recognition of the key role of Judeo–Christian symbols, beliefs, and ethics in legitimating the system of capitalism and republican democracy. In addition, there is an observable tendency for persons, regardless of age, to report having no religion during the post-1990 period (Schwadel, 2010b). This latter pattern is mirrored by declines in self-reports of personal religious faith, measured in terms of "believing in God without doubt" as opposed to believing with varying degrees of doubt or not believing at all (Sherkat, 2008). Some observers have explained such modest but perceptible increases in agnosticism and atheism in terms of diminished normative constraints, which at earlier times might have made it socially costly to acknowledge religious nonbelief, or to abandon organized religious ties entirely (Sherkat, 2008).

Religious Attendance

Perhaps the most common indicator of individual-level religious practice in social science research has been (self-reported) attendance at religious services. There are at least three reasons for the strong focus on this indicator over the years. First, it has been presumed to be a more accurate and "objective" measure of religious involvement than items measuring aspects of private devotional practice (e.g., prayer, meditation, scripture reading), belief, experience, or religious motivation or orientation. As discussed in this section, however, this assumption has come under scrutiny in recent years. Second, although most large-scale nationwide surveys (e.g., the NORC GSS, the National Election Surveys) and most community surveys include at least a few items on religion, very few of these data-collection efforts are focused primarily on religion. Therefore, they tend to incorporate only a handful of generic religious items, one of which inquires about the frequency of attendance at religious services, aside from occasions such as weddings and funerals. Because this has been standard practice for roughly 50 years, we have a wealth of data on attendance patterns over time and from diverse communities across the United States. Furthermore, attendance items are regularly included on international surveys such as the World Values Survey and the International Social Survey Project, thereby facilitating comparisons in religious attendance patterns between the United States and other societies in Western Europe and elsewhere. Third, attendance is thought to be a substantively important indicator of religiousness because it indicates (a) the expenditure of a scarce resource, time, which implies religious commitment; and (b) exposure to religious socialization via exposure to formal moral messages (e.g., sermons), informal reinforcement via social networks, doctrinal training through religious education programs, and other social and institutional processes.

On the basis of self-reported attendance figures, many scholars have concluded that the United States is one of the most religious nations in the Western Hemisphere (e.g., Norris & Inglehart, 2004). Indeed, only Ireland and Italy have higher average levels of self-reported religious attendance than the United States. Although this generalization is almost certainly accurate, over the past 15 to 20 years, a growing body of evidence has raised questions about the accuracy of self-report data on attendance, revealing that significant numbers of Americans exaggerate the frequency with which they attend worship services on surveys. One early study of apparent overreporting was based on data from two sources in a rural county: (a) an effort to monitor attendance on Sundays by visiting congregations and counting cars; and (b) a telephone poll of county residents, inquiring about whether they attended services during the week preceding the survey (Hadaway, Marler, & Chaves, 1993). These investigators concluded that overall rates of overreporting were 30% to 40%; however, because of the study design, it was not feasible to identify which persons or groups were especially prone to misreport their attendance.

Early explanations of this discrepancy attributed it to social desirability bias and interpreted it through the lens of secularization theory (Hadaway et al., 1993; Presser & Stinson, 1998). Critics raised a number of concerns, however. If attendance was being overreported out of social desirability motives, how well would this actually square with notions of secularization? Furthermore, many studies have cast doubt on the view that religious persons are particularly prone to give socially desirable responses to survey items on religious matters or other sensitive topics (Regnerus & Uecker, 2007). And there are other plausible explanations for these exaggerated reports of the frequency of attendance, including various perceptual biases, such as telescoping (i.e., reporting events as taking place more recently than they actually do). Furthermore, while conceding that some overreporting may be occurring, other investigators suggest that the extent of this problem may be exaggerated (Smith, 1998).

More recent research on this topic has compared the responses to survey items on religious attendance with data from time-use diaries. There is some evidence that discrepancies in self-reports and diary data on attendance patterns are strongest among persons with high levels of personal religious identity salience (Brenner, 2011a, 2011b). This finding could be interpreted in several different ways. For example, it is possible that some respondents simply misunderstood the true intent of the survey item and assumed that the goal of the question was to gauge the general religiousness, rather than the actual attendance patterns, of individual survey participants. On the other hand, such findings raise the possibility that social–psychological processes involving identity salience and maintenance may underlie the overreporting of religious attendance in surveys (Brenner, 2011a).

Several studies have examined trends, patterns, and correlates of self-reported religious attendance, primarily using data from the pooled NORC GSS. At the individual level, it is widely recognized that certain segments of the U.S. adult population attend religious services more often than others (Roof & McKinney, 1987; Schwadel, 2010a). On average, women attend services more often than men, southerners attend more often than residents of other regions, and persons living in urban areas attend relatively infrequently, whereas their counterparts in rural settings attend more often than other persons. Average levels of religious attendance are substantially higher among African Americans, as compared with Whites (see Chapter 30 in this volume). Religious attendance levels tend to be higher among married persons than others, particularly their never-married counterparts, and persons with children in the home also are inclined to attend more often than those who are not raising children. In survey data, analysts have observed that age bears a positive association with attendance; however, this relationship appears to be curvilinear, with the age–attendance association diminishing in late life (see Chapter 29 in this volume; Schwadel, 2011). Overall, contrary to many popular stereotypes, there is a modest but persistent positive association between education attainment and religious attendance among U.S. adults, whereas there is no clear association between income and attendance (Schwadel, 2010a).

Moreover, average attendance levels differ widely across religious denominations and faith traditions as well (Schwadel, 2010a). Specifically, members of sectarian groups (e.g., Mormons, Jehovah's Witnesses) and conservative Protestant churches attend services at relatively high levels, followed by members of Black Protestant churches and Catholics. Members of mainline Protestant denominations, on the other hand, report much less frequent attendance at services. Some predictors of individual-level variations in attendance differ by denomination as well (McFarland, Wright, & Weakliem, 2011). For example, attainment of a college degree is positively associated with religious attendance for evangelicals, African American Protestants, and Catholics, suggesting that education may incline the faithful in certain groups into leadership positions or that it may facilitate greater knowledge and understanding of religious doctrines and teachings. By contrast, no such positive link between education and attendance is found among mainline Protestants.

In recent years, sociologists have turned their attention to clarifying temporal trends in religious attendance and other facets of religious practice and belief. Is the overall frequency of attendance at services declining in the United States? Is the percentage of persons who are regular attendees dropping? If yes, do such trends reflect the influence of period effects, such as cultural or political events, that affect the religiousness of wide swaths of the population in similar ways? Might they result from developments that have shaped the worldviews of particular birth cohorts in specific ways? And if there are apparent cohort effects, are they really the result of cohort-specific events or conditions, or do they merely reflect cohort differences in population composition (e.g., more married persons with children in some cohorts as opposed to others)? Furthermore, given the age-related patterning of religious attendance noted thus far, and the fact that birth cohorts are aging as they move through time, how might the influences of age and cohort offset or interact with one another? Recent investigations have been aided by the development and refinement of new and more sophisticated statistical methods with which to explore these complex questions.

Researchers have used two strategies for coding individual responses to items on religious attendance. One of these is an ordinal approach, according to which responses are coded into the following categories: never, less than once a year, once or twice a year, several times a year, once per month, two to three times a month, nearly every week, once per week, and more than once per week. Another strategy has been to focus on those persons who attend services on a weekly basis and to contrast them with all other adults. These distinct approaches have yielded somewhat-divergent findings with respect to age, period, and cohort effects. Specifically, some studies have reported cohort-based declines in the probability of regular religious attendance, even when the potentially confounding effects of aging are taken into account (Schwadel, 2011). On the other hand, the frequency of religious attendance (measured as an ordinal variable) is relatively stable, with a modest period-based decline in the 1990s and little evidence of an overall cohort effect (Schwadel, 2010a).

Despite this apparent stability overall, however, there were substantial shifts across cohorts and periods for specific subgroups of the population (Schwadel, 2010a). For example, on average, in the early 1970s, women attended services approximately 10 days per year more often than men; roughly 30 years later, this gap was reduced to 6 days per year. There also has been some erosion of the regional gaps in religious attendance; although southerners still attend more often than other Americans, on average, this difference diminished noticeably between the early 1970s and the mid-1990s. Shifts in denominational attendance differences were especially noteworthy: Although Catholics attended services an average of 18 days per year more often than mainline Protestants in the early 1970s, the corresponding figure was only 6 days by the early 2000s (Schwadel, 2010a).

These decomposition techniques also have been employed to illuminate changes within single denominations over time. For example, although family income is not a robust predictor of church attendance patterns in the general population, there is fresh evidence from analyses of pooled GSS data of emerging income gaps in attendance among Catholics (Schwadel, McCarthy, & Nelsen, 2009). In particular, low-income White Catholics from younger cohorts are especially prone to disengage from the institutional Church. It is unclear whether such religious distancing results from costs associated with church participation, shame or stigma associated with poverty within religious congregations, or other factors.

Personal Devotion and Religious Belief

Several studies have explored patterns and correlates of personal devotional activities, such as frequency and types of prayer activity. Researchers using data from single cross-sectional surveys of the U.S. adult population have identified a number of reliable correlates of the frequency of prayer (Baker, 2008b; Roof & McKinney, 1987). Women and older adults tend to pray more often than others. Some other demographic groups, such as southerners and parents, also pray more often, but these patterns can be accounted for by the fact that such persons tend to be more religious in general (i.e., they attend services more often, endorse conservative views about the interpretation of the Bible, etc.), and individuals who are more religious by these other indicators also tend to pray relatively often.

One of the most important sets of findings involving the social patterning of prayer frequency is that persons from socially marginal backgrounds, including racial minorities such as African Americans and persons from lower SES backgrounds (i.e., lower income and education), tend to pray more often than other Americans. This latter finding is broadly consistent with classical sociological theories of Marx and Weber. In a famous (or infamous) dictum, Marx characterized religion as an "opiate of the masses," by which was meant that religion was (a) an instrument via which capitalists could pacify workers and (b) a balm capable of dulling the pain caused by oppression. Another classical theorist, Weber, argued that there was an "elective affinity" between social class and religion, not only in the West, but also around the world, throughout history. According to Weber, privileged groups often have gravitated to forms of religion that legitimize and validate the material and status advantages they have accumulated, in their own eyes and those of the surrounding society. By contrast, deprived groups often have embraced religions that valorized and reinterpreted their disadvantaged plight, promising a reversal of fortunes in the world to come.

At least one analysis has attempted to decompose temporal trends in the likelihood of weekly prayer by age, period, and cohort (Schwadel, 2010a). This study has revealed (a) overall age-related increases in weekly prayer that are roughly linear over the life course, and (b) cohort-based declines in weekly prayer that are linear and accelerating for cohorts born during and after the 1940s. Evidence of period effects on weekly prayer, by contrast, is limited.

Individual prayer activity may involve many diverse styles, including, among other forms of prayer, (a) contemplative and meditative forms of prayer, through which individuals seek to draw nearer to a divine other; (b) colloquial prayer, in which individuals engage a divine other in ongoing patterns of communication much like conversation with close friends or other social intimates; (c) ritual prayer activities, in which individuals engage in recitations or other pre-set prayer routines; and (d) petitionary prayer, in which individuals tend to seek specific outcomes (e.g., better health, financial prosperity) or diffuse benefits (e.g., the well-being of others; Baker, 2008b; Poloma & Gallup, 1991). Research has revealed that among persons who pray, the most common foci of prayer are family members and friends, followed by efforts to build and nourish one's relationship with God. Prayers for personal health and material rewards, by contrast, are among the least common types of prayer. Consistent with these arguments, recent studies confirm that the tendency to engage in such prayers—for financial security or personal health—is heavily shaped by social location; for example, African Americans and persons from lower SES backgrounds (i.e., lower levels of income and education) are especially likely to pray for these specific outcomes (see also Chapter 19 in this volume). There are fewer sociodemographic variations in prayers that involve confessing sins or seeking a closer relationship with God (Baker, 2008b).

Next we turn to a small number of specific doctrinal beliefs that have received attention from sociologists. One of these is the belief in an afterlife, which is widely regarded as an important indicator because eternal life is a quintessentially religious phenomenon, a spiritual reward that cannot be obtained through participation in other facets of social life. In the theory of religion outlined by Stark and Bainbridge (1996), the afterlife is "a supernatural otherworldly compensator" (see also Chapter 5 in this volume). Consistent with the classical arguments of Marx, Weber, and others, studies have found that persons from relatively disadvantaged backgrounds (i.e., those with lower SES, racial and ethnic minority groups, aging persons) tend to express greater belief in an afterlife than others in U.S. society. In contrast to some findings from age-period-cohort analyses of other religious indicators, decomposition studies of trends in afterlife belief have demonstrated remarkable stability across periods and birth cohorts (Schwadel, 2011). Thus, although regular religious attendance and prayer, as well as adherence to certain doctrinal tenets, may be waning, belief in an afterlife remains consistently strong among U.S. adults, with no signs of decline on the short-term horizon (Greeley & Hout, 1999).

A second belief that has come in for analytic scrutiny is biblical literalism. Self-described "literalists" believe that the Bible should be interpreted as the literal Word of God and that everything has happened or will happen exactly as the Bible says. Although it may seem that literalism should be treated as a belief that is held by individuals, not everyone agrees with this view. Instead, some scholars have argued that "literalism" is instead a "marker" for a broader array of conservative theological orientations and social values. According to this perspective, there is not (nor can there be) a single "literalist" reading of a complex text such as the Bible. Rather, any interpretation necessarily emphasizes some sections, passages, and elements of the text, while downplaying or ignoring others. Thus, "literalist" readings of scripture are fundamentally social products and are shaped within "interpretive communities," or networks of conservative theologians and pastors who share this common definition of the meaning of the Bible. The meanings of "literalism" are subsequently distilled and disseminated to the faithful through writings, seminars, and sermons (Hempel & Bartkowski, 2008).

Studies have revealed strong associations between biblical literalism and a broad array of conservative social and political attitudes and policy preferences, ranging from family-related attitudes and practices (e.g., regarding gender roles, child discipline, sexuality) to government aid to the poor and support for U.S. foreign policy, among many others (Hempel & Bartkowski, 2008; Woodberry & Smith, 1998). Because biblical literalism is widely and publicly embraced by many conservative Protestant and sectarian churches, it is not surprising that members of these groups are particularly likely to believe that the Bible should be interpreted in this way. Catholics and members of mainline Protestant denominations are, on average, much less inclined to embrace this view (Sherkat, 2010). Individual-level studies have linked biblical literalism with race and ethnicity, as persons from non-White backgrounds are more prone to endorse this tenet; persons with children in the home are also more likely to be literalists (Stroope, 2011). On average, across denominations, more religiously active persons (e.g., regular attenders, particularly those whose spouses and friends belong to the same church) are more prone to endorse literalism (Stroope, 2011). Researchers exploring temporal trends in biblical literalism have found (a) modest positive effects of aging; (b) modest period declines in literalism; and (c) substantial cohort-based declines, which (like some other cohort effects on religious trends) are especially dramatic for cohorts born in the mid-1940s and after (Schwadel, 2011).

Furthermore, education bears an important association with literalism in at least three ways

(Stroope, 2011). First, at the individual level, education attainment is inversely associated with literalism. Second, over and above one's own education, the average education level of one's congregation tends to influence acceptance of biblical literalism, with persons in well-educated congregations being substantially less supportive of this belief. Third, congregational education levels moderate the association between personal education and literalist belief, such that well-educated individuals who belong to congregations with comparatively high mean education levels are especially prone to reject biblical literalism, regardless of denomination. This may reflect the role of education in shaping informal interactions and sermon content among church members. These findings also may be influenced by selection processes, as comparatively well-educated individuals may join congregations composed of similarly educated members, many of whom have access to a broader array of information (about the Bible and about other topics) and greater verbal ability (Sherkat, 2010), and therefore they may find it especially difficult to sustain a literalist worldview. Although the reasons for such complex patterns remain to be investigated, these findings underscore the potentially important role of institutional contexts in shaping matters of belief and doctrinal assent among individuals (Stroope, 2011).

Recent research has underscored the significance of Americans' beliefs about God for a host of outcomes, including childrearing practices; attitudes about morality, civil liberties, and economic policy; views on the nature of the United States as a Christian nation; and attitudes concerning foreign policy (Froese & Bader, 2010). One extensive program of research on this topic has identified four distinct sets of images or beliefs about God, on the basis of the extent to which God is regarded as more or less engaged in human and worldly affairs, and the extent to which God is perceived to be more or less judgmental (Froese & Bader, 2010). According to data from one nationwide probability sample, roughly one third of U.S. adults endorse an authoritative God image (both engaged and judgmental), while an additional one quarter of U.S. adults envision a benevolent deity (engaged but much less judgmental). Another one quarter of the U.S. adult population regards God as critical (judgmental but not very engaged), while approximately one sixth perceive God to be distant (neither engaged nor judgmental, much like the "divine clockmaker" image of the early U.S. Deists). Endorsement of these God images varies substantially across religious and sociodemographic groups. For example, support for an authoritative God image appears strongest among African Americans, women, persons from lower SES backgrounds, residents of the South and Midwest, and members of evangelical and Black Protestant denominations. By contrast, Whites, men, well-educated persons and those with high incomes, and residents of the Northeast and West are more included to endorse a distant image of God, as are Jewish Americans. Benevolent God imagery is comparatively popular among Whites, women, person with a high school degree, and Catholics and mainline Protestants (Froese & Bader, 2010).

Researchers have investigated the social patterning of beliefs concerning religious evil, such as belief in Satan, hell, and demons. The available data indicate that these beliefs are relatively common, with more than 55% of U.S. adults in one poll stating that they "absolutely" believe in Satan and hell, and only slightly less than half reporting that they "absolutely" believe in demons (Baker, 2008a). Such beliefs are more common among African Americans as well as younger adults. Persons who are more religiously engaged (e.g., those who attend services more often) and who endorse the doctrine of biblical literalism are more inclined to believe in Satan, hell, and demons. Furthermore, most other sociodemographic correlates of these beliefs are eliminated when individual-level variations in religious practice, literalism, and affiliation are statistically controlled. Interestingly, belief in religious evil is stronger among persons from low-SES backgrounds, that is, those with lower levels of education and income (Baker, 2008a). This is consistent with arguments that difficult life circumstances, such as racial marginality or economic deprivation, may lead individuals to search for meaning and that religious persons may come to attribute their suffering to negative external spiritual forces. Furthermore, this association between SES and belief is moderated by the frequency of religious attendance: For persons who attend religious services rarely or never, lower SES is linked with greater acceptance of religious evil, whereas among persons who attend services regularly, the effect of SES on such beliefs is neutralized. Thus, individuals who participate regularly in positive worship activities and enjoy the benefits of congregational networks and interactions may be less inclined to focus on such notions of religious evil and spiritual darkness (Baker, 2008a).

THE CHANGING U.S. RELIGIOUS LANDSCAPE

The U.S. religious scene is uncommonly dynamic and fluid, the ongoing product of the interplay of demographic factors, cultural shifts, and endogenous processes within religious organizations and communities. In this final section of the chapter, we identity several of the most important changes currently under way in this domain. Taken together, these changes have the potential to reshape our understanding of religion and spirituality in the American context for decades to come.

Religious Individualism and the Rise of Spirituality

One crucial development over the past 30 to 40 years has been the gradual decoupling of religiousness from spirituality for a significant segment of the population. Clearly, the declines in some forms of conventional religious practice and identification in recent years do not necessarily imply waning interest in the search for meaning or transcendence within the U.S. population. As noted at the outset of this chapter, consensus over the meaning of religion and spirituality remains elusive (Zinnbauer et al., 1997). It has become common, however, to associate the former with organized, institutionalized doctrines and practices, and the latter with personal, noninstitutionalized beliefs, practices, and experiences. It also has become common, in some areas of academic and popular discourse, to imply that the latter is more desirable, and perhaps more authentic, than the former (Zinnbauer et al., 1999). Although it remains the case that most U.S. adults derive their spirituality from religious sources, and thus they identify themselves as both religious and spiritual, a significant minority of U.S. adults (20% to 35%, depending on the data source and the wording of survey questions) now self-identify as "spiritual, but not religious." There is some evidence (from GSS data and other sources) that this percentage has risen over the past 10 to 15 years. This identity is particularly popular among younger cohorts and well-educated persons and among those persons with liberal values on matters of civil liberties and morality (Shahabi et al., 2002; Zinnbauer et al., 1997).

In addition to these emerging trends in self-identification, there are other clear signs of the decoupling of religiousness and spirituality. As historians of U.S. religion remind us, spiritual and philosophical alternatives to Christianity have long flourished (e.g., Fuller, 2001). A wide variety of non-Christian ideas and teachings has risen over the past 20 to 30 years (Roof, 2001). Examples of these alternatives include the widely varied strands of New Age thought and practice, Native American spirituality, Eastern-influenced ideas and practices—those derived from Buddhism, Hinduism, and Taoism—theosophy, astrology, and many others. Some of the most popular emerging alternatives to conventional forms of religious expression involve the integration of spirituality with domains as diverse as art, health, and leisure activities, in ways that are transformative of daily life (Bender, 2010).

These trends may reflect a hunger on the part of many Americans for direct, unmediated experiences of the transcendent. Many individuals who explore alternative modes of spirituality do so without entirely abandoning more traditional denominational identities and loyalties. Viewing such developments from the standpoint of the rational choice (microeconomic) theories discussed earlier, observers have argued that such forays into New Age, Eastern, and other alternatives amount to a "diversification of religious portfolios." Briefly, if established religious groups and traditions cannot provide compelling answers on existential and spiritual matters, then adherents may act rationally by "hedging their bets" (reducing the risk of their spiritual investments) by investigating alternative practices and beliefs (Baker & Draper, 2010; Iannaccone, 1995). Some individuals go even further with spiritual hyperindividualism, melding practices, symbols, and beliefs from a veritable smorgasbord of traditions into unique, highly personal spiritual regimes, a phenomenon sometimes termed *bricolage* (Roof, 2001). Other expressions of spiritual individualism are considerably more idiosyncratic and vacuous, such as Sheilaism, the personal creed ("be good to yourself") expressed by a young adult respondent in the modern classic volume, *Habits of the Heart* (Bellah, Madsen, Sullivan, Swidler, & Tipton, 1985).

Religion Among Adolescents and Young Adults

In recent years, several important programs of research have focused squarely on the religious practices and sensibilities of adolescents and young adults. To be sure, findings from this body of studies may partly reflect life-cycle influences because religious engagement often changes and declines during this period. Nevertheless, researchers have argued persuasively that information on religion among adolescents (ages 13–17) and emerging adults (ages 18–25) may offer vital clues about the future of religion in the United States (Pearce & Denton, 2011; Smith & Denton, 2005; Smith & Snell, 2009). Some of the most impressive results have been based on large-scale longitudinal surveys such as the National Longitudinal Survey of Adolescent Health (or "Add Health") and the National Study of Youth and Religion, supplemented by numerous in-depth interviews with diverse respondents. The findings are complex and defy easy summary, but several patterns warrant specific mention. First, these studies point to apparent declines in religious participation, salience, and other conventional indicators of religiousness within these cohorts. Youth from conservative faith traditions—such as evangelical Protestants, Black Protestants, and members of sectarian groups such as the Mormons—were most resistant to these trends, whereas those from other religious backgrounds were among the most vulnerable. On average, those persons who did not attend college reported greater declines in religiousness than their college-educated counterparts (Uecker et al., 2007). Those who engaged in non-normative behaviors, ranging from early premarital sex or cohabitation to acts of delinquency, also tended to exhibit reduced religiousness over time (Regnerus & Uecker, 2006; Uecker et al., 2007), whereas those who married at relatively young ages were especially unlikely to reduce their religious involvement (Uecker et al., 2007).

It also appears that family background factors may play an important role in shaping religious and spiritual orientations among young adults: According to several recent studies, those persons who experienced parental divorce before age 15, or whose parents were unhappily married, were more likely to abandon organized religion and conventional religious identities between the ages of 18 and 35 than others (Ellison, Walker, Glenn, & Marquardt, 2011; Uecker et al., 2007). A number of factors may contribute to this pattern. It is possible that some divorced parents disengage from congregational life—and thus may limit the religious socialization of children—because of real or perceived marginalization within congregations. Indeed, many observers have noted the cozy, and perhaps exclusivist, connection between religious institutions and "traditional" (nuclear) families, despite the fact that these families are increasingly in the numerical minority. This marginalization has led to calls for greater receptivity and outreach to divorced persons and to alternative family forms more generally. Selectivity may also play a role; divorce may be more likely among persons (and couples) who are less religious to begin with (Lau & Wolfinger, 2011). Another possible explanation, grounded in recent empirical analyses, centers on the lower levels of paternal involvement in religious socialization among children of divorce (Zhai, Ellison, Glenn, & Marquardt, 2007). Further research is clearly needed to clarify the possible role of family demography on changes in young adult religiousness.

Key observers have chronicled the emergence of distinctive religious identities, and an emerging religious ethos, among adolescents and young adults. In one recent analysis of the religious identities of 16- to 21-year-olds (Pearce & Denton, 2011), whereas only a small percentage (5%) of the respondents were declared atheists, roughly one quarter (24%) expressed some belief in a God but placed little emphasis on the role of religion in daily life. By contrast, only one youth in five (20%) reported a high level of religious interest, belief, and participation. Another major study of the religious lives of U.S. teenagers has summed up the dominant ethos of this subpopulation with the term "Moralistic Therapeutic Deism" (Smith & Denton, 2005). According to these researchers, this creed involves a belief in a distant, relatively impersonal God who wants for people to be good, nice, and fair to others. This God intends for people to be happy and to have high self-esteem and remains largely uninvolved in human affairs unless called on to resolve specific personal problems. Good people go to heaven when they die. Except for the minority of youth who take conventional religious orthodoxy seriously, there is little evidence of religious exclusivism, or belief in the superiority of one's own faith, among U.S. youth (Pearce & Denton, 2011). Indeed, one recurrent finding from studies of young people (and their parents) is the lack of familiarity with, and the strong disinterest in, religious orthodoxy or dogma. Even many young people who claim to be strongly religiously committed are strikingly unfamiliar with the teachings of their own faith as well as those of other major religions (Prothero, 2007).

Scholars interested in the religion of younger cohorts have highlighted other issues. For example, focusing on 20- and 30-something adults, one prominent observer has noted with alarm the widespread disinterest in, and perceived irrelevance of, religious institutions and doctrines (Wuthnow, 2007). According to his analysis, religious communities (and other key social institutions in contemporary society) are failing to provide much-needed guidance and support for these young adults as they make momentous decisions regarding marriage and family life, careers and finances, and other major domains. The conventional programming offered at the congregational level (e.g., adolescent Bible study groups, couples ministries), and the canned answers to questions about matters of faith that are offered by clergy and other religious leaders, simply are not attuned to the spiritual and emotional needs of many members of these cohorts.

Changing Forms of Religious Organization

Another important development over the past 10 to 15 years has been the emergence of new forms of religious organization. One particularly significant phenomenon has been the rise of the so-called seeker church (Sargeant, 2000). Many (but certainly not all) seeker churches are also "megachurches," or congregations with an average weekly attendance in excess of 2,000 (Thumma & Bird, 2009; Thumma & Travis, 2007). Megachurches are typically theologically conservative, although in practice, doctrinal issues often are deemphasized. They are most common in suburban areas near major cities and in the Sunbelt region of the United States. Although some megachurches are affiliated with evangelical denominations such as the SBC, many others are independent congregations.

Seeker churches unabashedly capitalize on the market-oriented zeitgeist of the contemporary U.S. religious scene (Sargeant, 2000). They typically attempt to appeal to a wide range of individuals and families by (a) conducting market research to gauge the needs and preferences of potential members and (b) offering targeted, specialized ministries and programs for particular groups, social and spiritual services designed to meet a broad array of personal needs, and small group experiences that stress spiritual intimacy, disclosure, and emotional support. Many of these groups also cultivate highly contemporary worship styles and dynamic preaching that addresses the hurts and hopes of middle-class families (or those that aspire to middle-class status). The seeker church approach allows maximum opportunity for members to choose from a menu of worship options, activities, and services according to their needs, and given their membership numbers in many parts of the United States, this approach clearly appeals to millions of Americans.

Although seeker churches and so-called megachurches have received a great deal of attention from scholars and in the popular media, one recent analysis has documented a crucial, but hitherto neglected, pattern: Although most churches are relatively small in membership, more and more religiously active Americans are attending larger and larger congregations (Chaves, 2006). For at least 2 decades, the average congregation size has been increasing in virtually every Christian denomination. The lone exceptions are sectarian groups, such as the Jehovah's Witnesses and the Mormons

(Latter-day Saints), which place strict limits on the membership size of local congregations. Increases in the number of members per Catholic parish may be driven by financial pressures and the well-documented priest shortage. In most Protestant bodies, this increase appears to be driven by economies of scale, as smaller congregations tend to find it more difficult to produce rewarding spiritual goods and worship experiences in the face of fixed and rising costs, which are led by clergy salaries and compensation. The trend toward increased congregational size may have a number of implications for the experiences of churchgoers. In particular, size tends to undermine social mechanisms that foster intimacy and accountability (Ellison, Krause, Shepherd, & Chaves, 2009). The anonymity of larger groups may make it more difficult to establish friendships, thereby placing greater stress on the role of small group experiences. This may make it more difficult to enforce norms regarding regular attendance, tithing, volunteering, and other activities that produce crucial congregational resources (Scheitle & Finke, 2008; Thomas & Olson, 2010).

Non-Christian Religions in the United States

Because a large majority of U.S. adults are either Christian or post-Christian, this chapter has focused primarily on dynamics involving Christian denominations, practices, and beliefs. Approximately 5% of U.S. adults (estimates are imprecise and vary across surveys), however, are believed to belong to non-Christian world faiths. Over the past decade, the social scientific research community has shown growing interest in the study of various non-Christian groups in the United States. In this brief section, we offer several summary observations about the increasing religious diversity of the American religious scene and its implications.

Although Jews have been present in United States since the 17th century, the largest streams of immigration occurred during the early to mid 19th century (primarily from Germany, Bohemia, and Moravia), the late 19th and early 20th centuries (from Eastern Europe), the mid 20th century (from Germany and environs, in response to the Holocaust), and the post–World War II era (from what was then the Soviet Union; Hertzberg, 1989). Multiple data sources—the GSS, ARIS, and National Jewish Population Survey 2000–2001 (Kotler-Berkowitz et al., 2004)—suggest that the proportion of Jews in the U.S. population has declined significantly in recent decades, from 3% to 4% in the 1960s to an estimated 1.7% in the 21st century. The reasons for this decline are varied, and are likely to include (a) the more rapid growth of other (non-Jewish) groups; (b) declines in Jewish immigration from most regions of the world; (c) relatively high and increasing rates of interfaith marriage among most segments of the Jewish population; (d) relatively high levels of women's education, which is often accompanied by delayed marriage (or no marriage) and reduced fertility; (e) declines in Jewish schooling; and other factors (Kotler-Berkowitz et al., 2004). According to data from the 2001 National Jewish Population Survey, approximately 55% of American Jews are not affiliated with any branch of religious Judaism. In terms of self-identification, however, roughly 38% express a preference for Reform Judaism, the most liberal variant, and 27% indicate ties with Conservative Judaism. Although only 11% embrace Orthodox Judaism, their birth rates are far exceeding those among Conservative and Reform Jews (Klaff, 2006), and it is estimated that the numbers of Orthodox Jews may exceed those of other branches of Judaism within a few decades. The remaining 24% report no religious preference. Levels of religious belief and practice vary widely across the major Jewish denominational categories, with Orthodox Jews exhibiting much higher levels of synagogue attendance as well as most facets of personal piety, doctrinal belief, and home ritual observance than others (see Chapter 37 in this volume). For a significant segment of the U.S. Jewish population, Jewish identity is now constructed primarily in cultural (rather than religious) terms, gauged via commitment to Zionism and domestic Jewish causes and charities, widely shared Jewish values (e.g., tolerance, support for civil liberties and separation of church and state), and the observance of ethnic practices and celebrations (Kotler-Berkowitz et al., 2004).

Although some non-Judeo-Christian world faiths also have a long history in the United States, the visibility of these religions and the numbers of adherents increased sharply following the major revisions to U.S. immigration laws that began in the mid-1960s. These fundamental shifts in U.S. policy opened the door to large numbers of immigrants from non-European nations; although a large majority of entrants came from Latin America and Asia (more than 80% of all immigrants after 1980; see Chapter 33 in this volume), there were also large numbers from the Middle East, Africa, and elsewhere. Consequently, several million Muslims, Buddhists, Hindus, and adherents of other major world religions have made their homes in the United States (Cadge & Ecklund, 2007; Eck, 1997; see also Chapters 35, 36, and 38 in this volume). According to triangulated estimates from the NORC GSS, the ARIS, and several other large-scale nationwide surveys, roughly 0.7% of the U.S. adult population is Muslim, 0.5% is Hindu, and 0.5% is Buddhist (Smith, 2002). Rates of increase for each of these traditions between the 1970s and the 2000s are high, but they begin from quite small baseline membership figures. Although individuals certainly convert from Christianity (or from no religion) to non-Christian world faiths, the precise numbers of such converts are difficult to ascertain. And there are other significant world faiths besides those mentioned here, such as the Sikhs; however, reliable membership estimates for these groups are even more elusive.

At first glance, these estimates of non-Christians in the United States might seem much lower than expected. Why might this be the case? First, many observers may presume that migrants from Asia, the Middle East, and Africa are mainly non-Christians, implying that high levels of immigration may translate into an explosion of Muslims, Hindus, Buddhists, and diverse other faiths. This is an exaggeration, however. According to analyses of data from the National Immigrant Survey, perhaps the most authoritative source of data on recent migrants to the United States, approximately one fifth of the respondents professed a non-Christian faith—a figure that is higher than the current U.S. population but lower than some scholarly and media accounts might imply (Massey & Higgins, 2011). Indeed, surprisingly high percentages from Africa and the Middle East are Christian (Catholic or Orthodox, primarily). Many migrants from Asia are also Christian (Catholic or evangelical Protestant); others convert to Christianity after arriving in the United States (see Chapter 32 in this volume)

A large literature has examined the workings of the religious congregations formed or populated by recent immigrants (Cadge & Ecklund, 2007), including many non-Christian groups. To be sure, religion is often an important source of what Hirschman (2004) termed the three Rs—refuge, respectability, and resources—for immigrants (Connor, 2011). Researchers have demonstrated the significance of religious symbols, practices, and beliefs during the arduous migration process itself (Hagan, 2008). Nevertheless, the empirical links between immigration and religion in the United States are complicated (Alanezi & Sherkat, 2008). Recent research using data from the New Immigrant Survey has indicated that the experience of migration is dislocating, rather than theologizing, for many new immigrants. Overall, immigrants tend to be less religiously active than they were in their countries of origin, and those who join religious communities are typical neither of the broader immigrant population nor of their own faith traditions (Massey & Higgins, 2011).

Observers have suggested several other reasons why perceptions of non-Christians in the United States may be somewhat inflated. These faith traditions have become much more visible in recent years, through popular culture, celebrity conversions, and other developments (Smith, 2002). Many persons who are religious dabblers, tinkerers, and bricoleurs may appropriate elements of non-Christian practice (e.g., Hindu worship techniques, Buddhist home altars) as part of their highly individualized spiritual pursuits, without becoming faithful adherents of the broader tradition (Roof, 2001). Moreover, as we noted, until recently many (perhaps most) non-Christian immigrants remained in major cities, especially the key destination points for immigrants, or in specific areas such as university communities. Consequently, few Islamic mosques, Buddhist and Hindu temples, and other non-Christian religious centers were seen outside these areas. In recent years practice, of non-Christian faiths has become more geographically dispersed, and especially amid the cultural tensions of the post—September 11 environment, this new visibility has sometimes been met with public animosity, especially from proponents of the doctrine of American exceptionalism, who typically believe that the United States is (or should be) a Christian nation (Wuthnow, 2004).

CONCLUSION

Returning to themes raised at the outset of this chapter, our guiding objectives have been threefold: (a) to review evidence regarding religious affiliation and nonaffiliation in the contemporary United States, (b) to explore patterns and correlates of religious practices and beliefs, and (c) to identify and discuss—very selectively—several trends that are reshaping the U.S. religious configuration. To be sure, this has meant that complex issues have been depicted with a broad brush, whereas many worthy issues and important developments have gone unremarked. Nevertheless, it is hoped that this chapter has provided a useful overview of key landmarks and topographical features of the contemporary U.S. scene.

We began this chapter by observing that notions of secularization are central to the works of classical sociological theorists, including Marx, Weber, Durkheim, and others. Consequently, secularization is embedded in the DNA of sociology and other social science disciplines. The assumption that the forces of modernity would chase religion from the public sphere, undermine the persuasiveness of religious ideas and narratives, and eventually erode individual religious practices and beliefs was rarely challenged during much of the 20th century. Despite the appeal of secularization theory among many European sociologists, however, circumstances in the United States had led scholars to question the relevance of these ideas to the U.S. context by the late 20th century. In their eyes, the U.S. religious system functioned much like a market, with minimal regulation, low barriers to entry, and vigorous competition for adherents among a plethora of religious firms and entrepreneurs offering diverse religious goods. In the 21st century, although there are clear signs of secularity within some segments of the U.S. population, the United States remains one of the most religious nations in the industrial West. Barring unforeseen developments, this is likely to remain the case for some time.

References

Alanezi, F., & Sherkat, D. E. (2008). The religious participation of U.S. immigrants: Exploring contextual and individual influences. *Social Science Research, 37*, 844–855. doi:10.1016/j.ssresearch.2008.03.005

Bainbridge, W. S. (1990). Explaining the church member rate. *Social Forces, 68*, 1287–1295.

Baker, J. O. (2008a). An investigation of the sociological patterns of prayer frequency and content. *Sociology of Religion, 69*, 169–185. doi:10.1093/socrel/69.2.169

Baker, J. O. (2008b). Who believes in religious evil? An investigation of sociological patterns of belief in Satan, hell, and demons. *Review of Religious Research, 50*, 206–220.

Baker, J. O., & Draper, S. (2010). Diverse supernatural portfolios: Certitude, exclusivity, and the curvilinear relationship between religiosity and paranormal beliefs. *Journal for the Scientific Study of Religion, 49*, 413–424. doi:10.1111/j.1468-5906.2010.01519.x

Baker, J. O., & Smith, B. G. (2009). The nones: Social characteristics of the religiously unaffiliated. *Social Forces, 87*, 1251–1263. doi:10.1353/sof.0.0181

Bellah, R. N., Madsen, R., Sullivan, W. M., Swidler, A., & Tipton, S. M. (1985). *Habits of the heart: Individualism and commitment in American life*. Berkeley: University of California Press.

Bender, C. (2010). *The new metaphysicals: Spirituality and the American religious imagination*. Chicago, IL: University of Chicago Press.

Boles, J. B. (1985). Evangelical Protestantism in the old south: From religious dissent to cultural dominance. In C. R. Wilson (Ed.), *Religion in the old south* (pp. 13–34). Jackson: University Press of Mississippi.

Bradley, M. B., Green, N. M., Jones, D. E., Lynn, M., & McNeil, L. (1992). *Churches and church membership in the United States, 1990*. Atlanta, GA: Glenmary Research Center.

Brand-Williams, O. (2010). *More Catholic parishes in Detroit to be shuttered*. Retrieved from http://detnews.com/article/20101215/LIFESTYLE04/12150363

Brenner, P. S. (2011a). Exceptional behavior or exceptional identity? Over-reporting of church attendance in the United States. *Public Opinion Quarterly, 75*, 19–41. doi:10.1093/poq/nfq068

Brenner, P. S. (2011b). Identity importance and the over-reporting of religious service attendance: Multiple imputation of religious attendance using the American Time Use Study and the General Social Surveys. *Journal for the Scientific Study of Religion, 50*, 103–115. doi:10.1111/j.1468-5906.2010.01554.x

Bruce, S. (2002). *God is dead: Secularization in the West*. London, England: Blackwell.

Cadge, W., & Ecklund, E. H. (2007). Immigration and religion. *Annual Review of Sociology, 33*, 359–379. doi:10.1146/annurev.soc.33.040406.131707

Callahan, K. (1983). *Twelve keys to an effective congregation*. San Francisco, CA: Jossey-Bass.

Chaves, M. (1994). Secularization as declining religious authority. *Social Forces, 72*, 749–774.

Chaves, M. (2006). All creatures great and small: Megachurches in context. *Review of Religious Research, 47*, 329–346.

Chaves, M. (2011). *American religion: Contemporary trends*. Princeton, NJ: Princeton University Press.

Connor, P. (2011). Religion as resource: Religion and immigrant economic incorporation. *Social Science Research, 40*, 1350–1361. doi:10.1016/j.ssresearch.2010.10.006

D'Antonio, W. V. (1994). Autonomy and democracy in an autocratic organization: The case of the Roman Catholic church. *Sociology of Religion, 55*, 379–396. doi:10.2307/3711978

Davis, J. A., Smith, T. W., & Marsden, P. V. (2008). *The General Social Surveys: Cumulative codebook, 1972–2008*. Chicago, IL: National Opinion Research Center. (Machine-readable data file [MRDF] available via Inter-university Consortium for Political and Social Research [ICPSR], Ann Arbor, MI)

Diaz-Stevens, A. M. (1993). *Oxcart Catholicism on Fifth Avenue: The impact of the Puerto Rican migration on the Archdiocese of New York*. Notre Dame, IN: University of Notre Dame Press.

Eck, D. (1997). *A new religious America: How a "Christian nation" became the world's most religiously diverse nation*. San Francisco, CA: HarperSanFrancisco.

Ellingson, S. (2007). *The megachurch and the mainline: Remaking religious tradition in the twenty-first century*. Chicago, IL: University of Chicago Press.

Ellison, C. G. (1995). Rational choice explanations for individual religious behavior: Notes on the problem of social embeddedness. *Journal for the Scientific Study of Religion, 34*, 89–97. doi:10.2307/1386525

Ellison, C. G., & George, L. K. (1994). Religious involvement, social ties, and social support in a southeastern community. *Journal for the Scientific Study of Religion, 33*, 46–61. doi:10.2307/1386636

Ellison, C. G., Krause, N., Shepherd, B. C., & Chaves, M. (2009). Size, conflict, and opportunities for interaction: Congregational effects on members' anticipated support and negative interaction. *Journal for the Scientific Study of Religion, 48*, 1–15. doi:10.1111/j.1468-5906.2009.01426.x

Ellison, C. G., & Sherkat, D. E. (1990). Patterns of religious mobility among Black Americans. *Sociological Quarterly, 31*, 551–568. doi:10.1111/j.1533-8525.1990.tb00728.x

Ellison, C. G., & Sherkat, D. E. (1995). The semi-involuntary institution revisited: Regional differences in church participation among Black Americans. *Social Forces, 73*, 1415–1437.

Ellison, C. G., Walker, B. A., Glenn, N. D., & Marquardt, E. (2011). The effects of parental divorce and marital discord on the religious and spiritual lives of young adults. *Social Science Research, 40*, 538–551. doi:10.1016/j.ssresearch.2010.10.010

Fernandez, E. C. (2007). *Mexican American Catholics*. New York, NY: Paulist Press.

Finke, R., & Iannaccone, L. (1993). Supply-side explanations for religious change. *Annals of the American Academy of Political and Social Science, 527*, 27–39. doi:10.1177/0002716293527001003

Finke, R., & Scheitle, C. (2005). Accounting for the uncounted: Computing correctives for the 2000 RCMS data. *Review of Religious Research, 47*, 5–22. doi:10.2307/4148278

Finke, R., & Stark, R. (1989). How the upstart sects won America: 1776–1850. *Journal for the Scientific Study of Religion, 28*, 27–44. doi:10.2307/1387250

Finke, R., & Stark, R. (1992). *The churching of America, 1776–1992*. New Brunswick, NJ: Rutgers University Press.

Froese, P., & Bader, C. (2010). *America's four gods: What we say about God—and what that says about us*. New York, NY: Oxford University Press.

Fuller, R. C. (2001). *Spiritual but not religious: Understanding unchurched America*. New York, NY: Oxford University Press. doi:10.1093/0195146808.001.0001

Glenn, N. D. (1987). The trend in no religion respondents to national surveys, late 1950s to early 1980s. *Public Opinion Quarterly, 51*, 293–314. doi:10.1086/269037

Grammich, C. (2005). *Many faiths of many regions: Continuities and changes among religious adherents across U.S. counties* (Working Paper WR-211). Santa Monica, CA: RAND Corporation. Retrieved from http://www.rand.org/pubs/working_papers/WR211

Greeley, A., & Hout, M. (1999). Americans' increasing belief in life after death: Religious competition and acculturation. *American Sociological Review, 64*, 813–835. doi:10.2307/2657404

Hadaway, C. K. (1990). The impact of new church development on Southern Baptist growth. *Review of Religious Research, 31*, 370–379. doi:10.2307/3511562

Hadaway, C. K., Marler, P. L., & Chaves, M. (1993). What the polls don't show: A closer look at U.S. church attendance. *American Sociological Review, 58*, 741–752. doi:10.2307/2095948

Hadaway, C. K., & Roozen, D. A. (1995). *Rerouting the Protestant mainstream: Sources of growth and opportunities for change.* Nashville, TN: Abingdon.

Hadden, J. K. (1987). Toward desacralizing secularization theory. *Social Forces, 65*, 587–611.

Hagan, J. M. (2008). *Migration miracle: Faith, hope, and meaning on the undocumented journey*. Cambridge, MA: Harvard University Press.

Hempel, L. M., & Bartkowski, J. P. (2008). Scripture, sin, and salvation: Theological conservatism reconsidered. *Social Forces, 86*, 1647–1674. doi:10.1353/sof.0.0055

Hertzberg, A. (1989). *The Jews in America.* New York, NY: Simon & Schuster.

Hirschman, C. (2004). The role of religion in the origins and adaptation of immigrant groups in the United States. *International Migration Review, 28*, 1206–1234.

Hoffmann, J. P. (1998). Confidence in religious institutions and secularization: Trends and implications. *Review of Religious Research, 39*, 321–343. doi:10.2307/3512442

Hout, M., & Fischer, C. S. (2002). Why more Americans have no religious preference: Politics and generations. *American Sociological Review, 67*, 165–190. doi:10.2307/3088891

Hout, M., & Greeley, A. (1987). The center doesn't hold: Church attendance in the United States, 1940–1984. *American Sociological Review, 52*, 325–345. doi:10.2307/2095353

Hout, M., Greeley, A., & Wilde, M. (2001). The demographic imperative in religious change. *American Journal of Sociology, 107*, 468–500. doi:10.1086/324189

Hunter, J. D. (1983). *American evangelicalism: Conservative religion and the quandary of modernity*. New Brunswick, NJ: Rutgers University Press.

Iannaccone, L. (1990). Religious practice: A human capital approach. *Journal for the Scientific Study of Religion, 29*, 297–314. doi:10.2307/1386460

Iannaccone, L. (1994). Why strict churches are strong. *American Journal of Sociology, 99*, 1180–1211. doi:10.1086/230409

Iannaccone, L. (1995). Risk, rationality, and religious portfolios. *Economic Inquiry, 33*, 285–295. doi:10.1111/j.1465-7295.1995.tb01863.x

Johnson, D. W., Picard, P. R., & Quinn, B. (1974). *Churches and church membership in the United States, 1971.* Washington, DC: Glenmary Research Center.

Jones, D. E., Doty, S., Grammich, C., Horsch, J. E., Houseal, R., Lynn, M., . . . Taylor, R. H. (2002). *Religious congregations and membership in the United States, 2000.* Nashville, TN: Glenmary Research Center.

Keister, L. A. (2011). *Faith and money: How religion contributes to wealth and poverty.* New York, NY: Cambridge University Press.

Kelley, D. (1972). *Why conservative churches are growing.* San Francisco, CA: Harper & Row.

Klaff, V. (2006). Defining American Jewry from religious and ethnic perspectives: The transitions to greater heterogeneity. *Sociology of Religion, 67*, 415–438. doi:10.1093/socrel/67.4.415

Kosmin, B. A., Mayer, E., & Keysar, A. (2001). *American religious identification survey, 2001.* New York, NY: Graduate Center of the City University of New York.

Kotler-Berkowitz, L., Cohen, S. M., Ament, J., Klaff, V., Mott, F., & Peckerman-Neuman, D. (2004). *The National Jewish Population Survey 2000–2001: Strength, challenge, and diversity in the American Jewish population* (Rev. ed.). New York, NY: United Jewish Committee.

Lau, H.-H., & Wolfinger, N. H. (2011). Parents' divorce and adult religiosity: Evidence from the General Social Survey. *Review of Religious Research, 53*, 85–103. doi:10.1007/s13644-011-0004-7

Lehrer, E. L. (2008). *Religion, economics, and demography: The effects of religion on education, work, and the family.* New York, NY: Routledge.

Lindner, E. (Ed.). (2011). *Yearbook of American and Canadian Churches 2011.* Nashville, TN: Abingdon Press and National Council of Churches of Christ in the U.S.

Massengill, R. P. (2008). Educational attainment and cohort change among conservative Protestants, 1972–2004. *Journal for the Scientific Study of Religion, 47*, 545–562. doi:10.1111/j.1468-5906.2008.00426.x

Massey, D. S., & Higgins, M. E. (2011). The effect of immigration on religious belief and practice: A theologizing or alienating experience? *Social Science Research, 40*, 1371–1389. doi:10.1016/j.ssresearch.2010.04.012

Matovina, T. (2011). *Latino Catholicism: Transformation of America's Largest Church.* Princeton, NJ: Princeton University Press.

McFarland, M. J., Wright, B. E., & Weakliem, D. L. (2011). Educational attainment and religiosity: Exploring variations by religious tradition. *Sociology of Religion, 72*, 166–188. doi:10.1093/socrel/srq065

Nemeth, R. J., & Luidens, D. A. (1995). The persistence of ethnic descent: Dutch clergy in the Reformed Church in America. *Journal for the Scientific Study of Religion, 34*, 200–213. doi:10.2307/1386765

Niebuhr, H. R. (1929). *The social sources of denominationalism.* Gloucester, MA: Henry Holt.

Niedermier, B. (2009). *Cleveland Catholic Diocese announces church closings and mergers.* Retrieved from http://www.wksu.org/news/story/23125

Norris, P., & Inglehart, R. (2004). *Sacred and secular: Religion and politics worldwide.* New York, NY: Cambridge University Press. doi:10.1017/CBO9780511791017

Park, J. Z., & Reimer, S. H. (2002). Revisiting the social sources of American Christianity, 1972–1998. *Journal for the Scientific Study of Religion, 41*, 733–746. doi:10.1111/1468-5906.00158

Pearce, L. D., & Denton, M. L. (2011). *A faith of their own: Stability and change in the religiosity of America's adolescents.* New York, NY: Oxford University Press.

Pogorelc, A. J., & Davidson, J. D. (2000). One church, two cultures? *Review of Religious Research, 42*, 146–158. doi:10.2307/3512526

Poloma, M. M., & Gallup, G. H., Jr. (1991). *Varieties of prayer: A survey report.* Philadelphia, PA: Trinity Press.

Presser, S., & Stinson, L. (1998). Data collection mode and social desirability bias in self-reported religious attendance. *American Sociological Review, 63*, 137–145. doi:10.2307/2657486

Prothero, S. (2007). *Religious literacy: What every American needs to know—and doesn't.* New York, NY: HarperOne.

Quinn, B., Anderson, H., Bradley, M., Goetting, P., & Shriver, P. (1982). *Churches and church membership in the United States, 1980.* Atlanta, GA: Glenmary Research Center.

Regnerus, M. D., & Uecker, J. E. (2006). Finding faith, losing faith: The prevalence and context of religious transformations during adolescence. *Review of Religious Research, 47*, 217–237.

Regnerus, M. D., & Uecker, J. E. (2007). Religious influences on sensitive self-reported behaviors: The product of social desirability, deceit, or embarrassment? *Sociology of Religion, 68*, 145–163. doi:10.1093/socrel/68.2.145

Roof, W. C. (1989). Multiple religious switching: A research note. *Journal for the Scientific Study of Religion, 28*, 530–535. doi:10.2307/1386582

Roof, W. C. (1993). *A generation of seekers: The spiritual journeys of the baby boom generation.* San Francisco, CA: Harper & Row.

Roof, W. C. (2001). *Spiritual marketplace: Baby boomers and the remaking of American religion.* Princeton, NJ: Princeton University Press.

Roof, W. C., & McKinney, W. (1987). *American mainline religion.* New Brunswick, NJ: Rutgers University Press.

Roozen, D. A., & Hadaway, C. K. (Eds.). (1993). *Church and denominational growth: What does (and does not) cause growth and decline.* Nashville, TN: Abingdon.

Sandomirsky, S., & Wilson, J. (1990). Processes of disaffiliation: Religious mobility among men and women. *Social Forces, 68*, 1211–1230.

Sargeant, K. (2000). *Seeker churches: Promoting traditional religion in a nontraditional way.* New Brunswick, NJ: Rutgers University Press.

Scheitle, C. P., & Finke, R. (2008). Measuring congregational resources: Selection versus production. *Social Science Research, 37*, 815–827. doi:10.1016/j.ssresearch.2007.10.001

Scheitle, C. P., Kane, J. B., & Van Hook, J. (2011). Demographic imperatives and religious markets: Considering the individual and interactive roles of fertility and switching in group growth. *Journal for the Scientific Study of Religion, 50*, 470–482. doi:10.1111/j.1468-5906.2011.01580.x

Schoenherr, R. (2004). *Goodbye Father: The celibate male priesthood and the future of the Catholic Church.* New York, NY: Oxford University Press.

Schoenherr, R., & Young, L. (1993). *Full pews and empty altars: Demographics of the priest shortage in U.S. Dioceses.* Madison: University of Wisconsin Press.

Schwadel, P. (2010a). Age, period, and cohort effects on U.S. religious service attendance: The declining impact of sex, southern residence, and Catholic affiliation. *Sociology of Religion, 71*, 2–24. doi:10.1093/socrel/srq005

Schwadel, P. (2010b). Period and cohort effects on religious nonaffiliation and religious disaffiliation: A research note. *Journal for the Scientific Study of Religion, 49*, 311–319. doi:10.1111/j.1468-5906.2010.01511.x

Schwadel, P. (2011). Age, period, and cohort effects on religious activities and beliefs. *Social Science Research, 40*, 181–192. doi:10.1016/j.ssresearch.2010.09.006

Schwadel, P., McCarthy, J. D., & Nelsen, H. M. (2009). The continuing relevance of family income for religious participation: U.S. White Catholic church attendance in the late 20th century. *Social Forces, 87*, 1997–2030. doi:10.1353/sof.0.0220

Shahabi, L., Powell, L. H., Musick, M. A., Pargament, K. I., Thoresen, C. E., Williams, D., . . . Ory, M. A. (2002). Correlates of self-perceived spirituality in American adults. *Annals of Behavioral Medicine, 24*, 59–68. doi:10.1207/S15324796ABM2401_07

Sherkat, D. E. (1991). Leaving the faith: Testing theories of religious switching using survival models. *Social*

Science Research, 20, 171–187. doi:10.1016/0049-089X(91)90015-U

Sherkat, D. E. (1997). Embedding religious choices: Integrating preferences and social constraints into rational choice theories of religious behavior. In L. A. Young (Ed.), *Rational choice theory and religion: Summary and assessment* (pp. 65–86). New York, NY: Routledge.

Sherkat, D. E. (1998). Counterculture or continuity? Competing influences on baby boomers' religious orientations and participation. *Social Forces, 76*, 1087–1114.

Sherkat, D. E. (2001). Tracking the restructuring of American religion: Religious affiliation and patterns of religious mobility, 1973–1998. *Social Forces, 79*, 1459–1493. doi:10.1353/sof.2001.0052

Sherkat, D. E. (2002). African American religious affiliation in the late 20th century: Cohort variations and patterns of switching, 1973–1998. *Journal for the Scientific Study of Religion, 41*, 485–493. doi:10.1111/1468-5906.00132

Sherkat, D. E. (2004). Religious intermarriage in the United States: Trends, patterns, and predictors. *Social Science Research, 33*, 606–625. doi:10.1016/j.ssresearch.2003.11.001

Sherkat, D. E. (2008). Beyond belief: Atheism, agnosticism, and theistic certainty in the United States. *Sociological Spectrum, 28*, 438–459. doi:10.1080/02732170802205932

Sherkat, D. E. (2010). The religious demography of the contemporary United States. In C. G. Ellison & R. A. Hummer (Eds.), *Religion, families, and health: Population-based research in the United States* (pp. 403–430). New Brunswick, NJ: Rutgers University Press.

Sherkat, D. E., & Ellison, C. G. (1999). Recent developments and current controversies in the sociology of religion. *Annual Review of Sociology, 25*, 363–394. doi:10.1146/annurev.soc.25.1.363

Sherkat, D. E., & Wilson, J. (1995). Preferences, constraints, and choices in religious markets: An examination of religious switching and apostasy. *Social Forces, 73*, 993–1026.

Skirbekk, V., Kaufmann, E., & Goujon, A. (2010). Secularism, fundamentalism, or Catholicism? The religious composition of the United States to 2043. *Journal for the Scientific Study of Religion, 49*, 293–310. doi:10.1111/j.1468-5906.2010.01510.x

Smith, C. S. (with Emerson, M., Gallagher, S., Kennedy, P., & Sikkink, D.). (1998). *American evangelicalism: Embattled and thriving*. Chicago, IL: University of Chicago Press.

Smith, C. S., & Denton, M. L. (2005). *Soul searching: The religious and spiritual lives of American teenagers*. New York, NY: Oxford University Press.

Smith, C. S., & Snell, P. (2009). *Souls in transition: The religious and spiritual lives of emerging adults*. New York, NY: Oxford University Press.

Smith, T. W. (1990). Classifying Protestant denominations. *Review of Religious Research, 31*, 225–246. doi:10.2307/3511614

Smith, T. W. (1998). A review of church attendance measures. *American Sociological Review, 63*, 131–136. doi:10.2307/2657485

Smith, T. W. (2002). Religious diversity in America: The emergence of Muslims, Buddhists, Hindus, and others. *Journal for the Scientific Study of Religion, 41*, 577–585. doi:10.1111/1468-5906.00138

Stark, R. (1997). German and German American religiousness: Approximating a crucial experiment. *Journal for the Scientific Study of Religion, 36*, 182–193. doi:10.2307/1387551

Stark, R. (1999). Secularization, R. I. P. *Sociology of Religion, 60*, 249–273. doi:10.2307/3711936

Stark, R., & Bainbridge, W. S. (1996). *A theory of religion* (Rev. ed.). New Brunswick, NJ: Rutgers University Press.

Stark, R., & Finke, R. (2001). *Acts of faith: Explaining the human side of religion*. Berkeley: University of California Press.

Stark, R., & Iannaccone, L. (1997). Why the Jehovah's Witnesses grew so rapidly: A theoretical application. *Journal of Contemporary Religion, 12*, 133–157. doi:10.1080/13537909708580796

Steensland, B., Park, J. Z., Regnerus, M. D., Robinson, L. D., Wilcox, W. B., & Woodberry, R. D. (2000). The measure of American religion: Toward improving the state of the art. *Social Forces, 79*, 291–318.

Stolzenberg, R. M., Blair-Loy, M., & Waite, L. J. (1995). Religious participation in early adulthood: Age and life-cycle effects on church membership. *American Sociological Review, 60*, 84–103. doi:10.2307/2096347

Stroope, S. (2011). Education and religion: Individual, congregational, and cross-level interaction effects on biblical literalism. *Social Science Research, 40*, 1478–1493. doi:10.1016/j.ssresearch.2011.05.001

Stump, R. W. (1998). The effects of geographical variability on Protestant church membership trends, 1980–1990. *Journal for the Scientific Study of Religion, 37*, 636–651. doi:10.2307/1388146

Swecker, S. (Ed.). (2005). *Hard ball on holy ground: The religious right vs. the mainline for the church's soul*. North Berwick, ME: BW Press.

Thomas, J. N., & Olson, D. V. A. (2010). Testing the strictness thesis and competing theories of congregational growth. *Journal for the Scientific Study of Religion, 49*, 619–639.

Thumma, S., & Bird, W. (2009). *Not who you think they are: A profile of people who attend America's megachurches.* Hartford, CT: Hartford Institute for Religion Research; Dallas: Leadership Network.

Thumma, S., & Travis, D. (2007). *Beyond megachurch myths: What we can learn from America's largest churches.* San Francisco, CA: Jossey-Bass.

Tooley, M. (2008). *Taking back the United Methodist Church.* Anderson, IN: Bristol House.

Tschannen, O. (1991). The secularization paradigm: A systematization. *Journal for the Scientific Study of Religion, 30,* 395–415. doi:10.2307/1387276

Uecker, J. E., Regnerus, M. D., & Vaaler, M. L. (2007). Losing my religion: The social sources of religious decline in early adulthood. *Social Forces, 85,* 1667–1692. doi:10.1353/sof.2007.0083

Waite, L. J., & Lewin, A. C. (2010). Religious intermarriage and conversion in the United States: Patterns and changes over time. In C. G. Ellison & R. A. Hummer (Eds.), *Religion, families, and health: Population-based research in the United States* (pp. 148–164). New Brunswick, NJ: Rutgers University Press.

Warner, R. S. (1993). Work in progress toward a new paradigm for the sociological study of religion in the United States. *American Journal of Sociology, 98,* 1044–1093. doi:10.1086/230139

Williams, A. S., & Davidson, J. D. (1996). Catholic conceptions of faith: A generational analysis. *Sociology of Religion, 57,* 273–289. doi:10.2307/3712157

Wilson, B. (1966). *Religion in secular society.* London, England: C. A. Watts.

Woodberry, R. D., & Smith, C. S. (1998). Fundamentalists et al.: Conservative Protestantism in America. *Annual Review of Sociology, 24,* 25–56. doi:10.1146/annurev.soc.24.1.25

Wuthnow, R. (1988). *The restructuring of American religion.* Princeton, NJ: Princeton University Press.

Wuthnow, R. (2004). *America and the challenges of religious diversity.* Princeton, NJ: Princeton University Press.

Wuthnow, R. (2007). *After the baby boomers: How twenty- and thirty-somethings are shaping the future of American religion.* Princeton, NJ: Princeton University Press.

Zhai, J. E., Ellison, C. G., Glenn, N. D., & Marquardt, E. (2007). Parental divorce and religious involvement among young adults. *Sociology of Religion, 68,* 125–149. doi:10.1093/socrel/68.2.125

Zinnbauer, B. J., Pargament, K. I., Cole, B., Rye, M. S., Butler, E. M., Belavich, T. G., . . . Kadar, J. L. (1997). Religion and spirituality: Unfuzzying the fuzzy. *Journal for the Scientific Study of Religion, 36,* 549–564. doi:10.2307/1387689

Zinnbauer, B. J., Pargament, K. I., & Scott, A. B. (1999). The emerging meanings of religiousness and spirituality: Problems and prospects. *Journal of Personality, 67,* 889–919. doi:10.1111/1467-6494.00077

CHAPTER 3

MEASUREMENT IN THE PSYCHOLOGY OF RELIGIOUSNESS AND SPIRITUALITY: EXISTING MEASURES AND NEW FRONTIERS

Peter C. Hill and Evonne Edwards

To paraphrase a well-known credit card advertisement, good measurement is "priceless." Perhaps the value of precise, valid, and reliable measurement is most appreciated when faced with the costs of mismeasurement. In 1999, the price of mismeasurement was $125 million for NASA. While an engineering team used English standard units in their navigational command programming, NASA used the metric system, which led the Mars Climate Orbiter to miss its intended target and hurtle off into space. Yet the cost of inaccurate measurement is not always measured in dollars. In 1981, Alberto Salazar ran the New York City Marathon in what was thought to be a record-setting 2:08:13. His celebration was short-lived, however, when it was discovered that the course was inaccurately measured; the course was 148 meters short of the requisite 42.195 km, meaning that his record-setting time was not record-setting after all.

Recognizing that accurate assessment is foundational to the development of a scientific discipline, psychologists of religion have long been concerned with issues of measurement. Over a quarter century ago, Gorsuch (1984) declared that the dominant paradigm in the psychology of religion was one of measurement, something he considered to be both a "boon" and a "bane" to the field. The measurement paradigm was necessary and beneficial to the psychology of religion as it helped establish scientific credibility; indeed, measurement sophistication is a sure sign of the maturity and health of a scientific field of study. But Gorsuch also warned that the emphasis on measurement could mistakenly become the goal of a discipline rather than an important tool for the substantive study of the discipline's true object—thus even slowing the field's progression. Regardless of whether the measurement paradigm was a boon or bane to the field, it is clear that 21st-century researchers have a vast arsenal of measures "available in sufficient variety for most any task in the psychology of religion" (Gorsuch, 1984, p. 234). Given the sufficiency of available measures, Gorsuch (1990) later explicated the following four criteria for which new measure development would be necessary rather than a detriment or distraction to the field: (a) Existing measures are not psychometrically adequate to the task, (b) there are no measures available for particular constructs, (c) conceptual or theoretical issues demand modification of existing measures, or (d) no existing measure appears useable with a specific clinical population.

Despite these cautions, we have seen a proliferation of measures since Gorsuch's (1984) seminal article. In fact, Hill and Hood (1999) identified and discussed 125 measures of different aspects of religiousness and spirituality published through 1996 and, on the basis of our literature search, we conservatively estimate that another 100 measures have been developed in the past 15 years. Many of the new measures are necessary in that they meet one of Gorsuch's (1990) four criteria. Indeed, there are several measures in the literature, mostly not reported here, that are psychometrically suspect (sometimes because psychometric data are not reported), the first criterion mentioned by Gorsuch. Furthermore, several new theoretical developments in the past

DOI: 10.1037/14045-003
APA Handbook of Psychology, Religion, and Spirituality: Vol. 1. Context, Theory, and Research, K. I. Pargament (Editor-in-Chief)
Copyright © 2013 by the American Psychological Association. All rights reserved.

2 decades have resulted in particular constructs in the field for which no measure currently exists, the second criterion. To be sure, modification of existing measures, the third criterion, is sometimes necessary in this young and developing field, often because of changes in the religious landscape. Furthermore, religious and spiritual measures designed for clinical populations, the fourth criterion, are rare. New or revised measures for such populations may be necessary. For example, the use of religious or spiritual experience as a coping mechanism may differ greatly between someone afflicted with a life-threatening disease and a student who received a poor grade on an exam. It is also true that many of the measures in the psychology of religion have been tested primarily on Christian populations. Therefore, new measures that extend beyond Christianity are needed. To decide whether to invest the resources necessary for developing a new measure, however, it is important to know what instruments are currently available. A primary purpose of this chapter is to provide brief reviews of reliable and valid measures of various aspects of religiousness and spirituality. Given the complexity of religiousness and spirituality, we classify the measures by several categories that fall under two general headings: substantive measures and functional measures. The chapter's other purposes are covered by material that bookend the reviews. At the front end, the reader will find a consideration of general measurement issues as they relate specifically to religiousness and spirituality. There is a special focus on the need for cultural sensitivity, particularly as measures outside of the Judeo–Christian context are being developed. At the back end, suggestions on how to improve measures are provided.

We use both the terms *religiousness* and *spirituality* in this chapter. Our choice of term depends largely on the particular construct that represents the focus of measurement.

GENERAL ISSUES RELATED TO MEASUREMENT

Later in this chapter we discuss "good" measures of religiousness and spirituality on the basis of Hill's (2005) criteria. First, however, we review some basic measurement issues as they apply to the study of religiousness and spirituality. Although the issues are relevant to virtually any domain in psychology, here we are also concerned about the unique aspects of religious and spiritual experience that may clarify the criteria for a good measure. Three major issues must be considered: theoretical considerations, psychometric issues, and sample representativeness.

Theoretical Considerations

The significance and meaning of research findings are undermined if the research itself, including the crucial element of measurement, lacks conceptual clarity. During what Gorsuch (1984) called the measurement paradigm, the pull toward establishing a strong empirical framework often led to measures that, while psychometrically sound, were often without a clear theoretical grounding. Systematic top-down research programs are difficult to maintain without well-defined conceptual frameworks. Even the most dominant theoretical framework in the psychology of religion, Allport's (1950) distinction between intrinsic and extrinsic religious orientation, was subject to theoretical neglect. Despite initial promise as a guiding theoretical framework, the study of religious orientation soon became enmeshed in measurement issues to the point that it lost sight of its theoretical groundings. The failure of subsequent research to systematically examine these orientations in light of underlying theory caused Kirkpatrick and Hood (1990) to conclude that Allport's model was "theoretically impoverished and has really taught us little about the psychology of religion" (p. 442).

An often-overlooked liability of such lack of theoretical coherence involves validity. It is hard to predict how a scale will correlate with other measures if it was not developed with a clear conceptual understanding of the measured construct at hand. In contrast, a strong theoretical base should yield measures with frequent use across a broader range of populations, thus providing ample testing of reliability and validity. Fortunately, the field is starting to see the emergence of systematic research programs that are well grounded in conceptual and theoretical terms Examples include religious questing (Batson,

Schoenrade, & Ventis, 1993), mysticism (Hood, 1975; see also Chapter 21 in this volume), religious coping (Pargament, 1997), and attachment processes (Granqvist & Kirkpatrick, 2004; see also Chapter 7 in this volume), to name but a few. It is not surprising that measures developed in these domains are among the most robust measures in the psychology of religion. Good theory and good measurement go hand in hand.

Psychologists of religion also should be well grounded in the object of their study: religion and spirituality. A concern particularly relevant to many measures of contemporary spirituality is the preference to study spirituality free of any religious or even social context, with the goal of developing a construct and its corresponding measure to be as generalizable as possible. If spirituality is conceptualized so broadly that it loses many of its distinguishing characteristics and is assessed by indicators of good mental health or character (e.g., meaning or purpose in life, general well-being, forgiveness), then it is hardly surprising that spirituality and measures of mental health are correlated and may render such associations "meaningless and tautological" (Koenig, 2008, p. 349). It is thus important, for the purposes of clear and precise measurement, to have operational definitions of religiousness and spirituality that are well conceptualized and theoretically grounded (D. E. Hall, Meador, & Koenig, 2008). This approach calls for serious attention to the substantive aspects of the object of study—that is, *what* a person believes or accepts as part of a religious or spiritual tradition is a major consideration.

Theoretical clarity cannot be overemphasized when looking for a measure. No single scale will be most appropriate for every study, and the focal concept should be well represented in the measure. Of course, one can be certain of this only if clear conceptual frameworks were used to design both the scale itself and the research to which the scale is applied.

Psychometric Considerations

The two most important psychometric considerations, validity and reliability, apply to the study of religious and spiritual experience much as they apply to any other psychological topic of interest (American Educational Research Association, American Psychological Association, & National Council on Measurement in Education, 1999). *Validity* refers to whether a scale is measuring the thing it is trying to measure. Of the many types of measurement validity, those most common in the psychology of religion fit in the general category of *construct validity*. Construct validity is especially important given that religiousness and spirituality are highly complex phenomena that require intricate theoretical constructs. Construct validity within the psychology of religion is most often tested through *criterion* (the correlation between a given scale and some other standard or measure of the construct) and *content* (the degree to which a given scale includes all the facets of the construct) validity. Also commonly emphasized is *convergent validity*, the extent to which a given scale correlates with measures of related constructs. For example, a measure of orthodoxy should be associated with the type of religious institution with which one is a member, identifies with, or attends. Less commonly used in the psychology of religion is *discriminant validity*, the degree to which a given scale is not correlated with measures with which it should be independent.

The extent to which a scale is consistent or *reliable* is also assessed similarly in the psychology of religion as it is in other applied areas of interest to psychologists: *internal consistency* and *consistency over time*. Reliability of measures in the psychology of religion or spirituality usually is assessed by only one of these two criteria. Internal consistency, the degree to which all of the items on the scale are measuring the same thing, is the most commonly used method and often is measured by Cronbach's alpha (α). Measurement efforts using *test–retest reliability* frequently use approximately 2-week intervals, although intervals ranging anywhere from 30 minutes to 1 year have been used. After a review of the psychology of religion measurement literature, Hill (2005) proposed that measures in this field demonstrate reliability above .70 in at least two studies to be considered good measures. With few exceptions, the studies reviewed in this chapter demonstrate adequate reliability and validity.

Sample Representativeness

Perhaps the most serious problem facing the psychological study of religiousness and spirituality is the use of nonrepresentative samples, at least in terms of generalizing findings to broad populations. We know much about the religiousness and spirituality of young, well-educated, middle-class European American individuals who are products of a Judeo-Christian heritage, but significantly less about anyone else (Hill & Pargament, 2003). Using samples of convenience (e.g., undergraduate students) is especially problematic because age, socioeconomic status (SES), and education are three variables clearly correlated with religious experience (Hill, 2005).

Cultural sensitivity. The problem of biased representation is compounded by the fact that the vast majority of religious and spiritual measures have been developed until recently within a Judeo-Christian context, further heightened by a disproportionate focus on European American Protestants (Hill, 2005; Hill & Hood, 1999). For example, some characteristics of religious experience, such as community service (C. G. Ellison & Taylor, 1996) and the notion of reciprocal blessings with God (Black, 1999), are common among perhaps the most religiously oriented and Protestant of all ethnic groups in the United States: African Americans. Yet they are not well captured in any current measure of religiousness. Researchers need to be culturally sensitive (see Chatters, Taylor, & Lincoln, 2002), particularly when selecting a scale for populations with different demographics or different religious contexts than the population upon which the scale was originally developed.

The lack of cultural sensitivity also may be reflected in more subtle ways. For example, as noted, some researchers seek a measure of spirituality that is free from the constraints of a traditional religious system, especially when attempting to study experiences or motivations that may be universal in nature. However, as Cohen (2009; see also Chapter 37 in this volume) has pointed out, both religion and spirituality are cultural variables. When researchers, although purporting to measure a transreligious construct, develop a scale but fail to recognize its culturally loaded assumptions, the scale itself may be culturally insensitive or even irrelevant outside the culture and religious traditions from which it was originally created. For example, Cohen and Hill (2007) found that religious and spiritual experiences, motivations, and identities of U.S. Protestants are construed more individualistically than they are for the more socially and community-oriented U.S. Catholics and U.S. Jews. They found that the expected negative relationship of Allport's (1950; Allport & Ross, 1967) intrinsic (the more mature religious sentiment, according to Allport) and extrinsic (the less mature religious sentiment) religious orientation, which has been well documented in numerous studies over the years among Protestants, did not hold among Catholics and especially among Jews (for which there was a moderately *positive* correlation). The authors concluded by recognizing the futility of developing a single definition or a single measure of religiousness and spirituality independent of a broader religious, cultural, and social context. It remains a challenge for future research to generate ways of measuring religious and spiritual identity and motivation that recognize how cultures differ without explicitly or implicitly privileging certain motivations (Cohen & Hill, 2007).

To more tangibly demonstrate Cohen and Hill's (2007) point, consider the efforts of Hill and Dwiwardani (2010) to apply Allport's (1950) religious orientation concept to an Indonesian Muslim population. Not only did the language of the Religious Orientation Scale (ROS; Allport & Ross, 1967) need revising (e.g., changing church to mosque), but also the concept of extrinsic–social religious orientation (as a motivation to participate in religious services) took on a different meaning in a collectivistic culture in which Islam is a strong pillar. Hill and Dwiwardani (2010) discovered that the extrinsic social dimension should be understood in relation to the broader community and culture rather than specifically to the mosque, as it typically has been conceptualized in the religious orientation literature. Such cultural variation has been captured by the Muslim–Christian Religious Orientation Scale (MCROS; Ghorbani, Watson, Ghramaleki, Morris, & Hood, 2002), a measure that has demonstrated incremental validity among Iranian and Iranian American Muslims beyond the Allport and Ross (1967) measure (Ghorbani, Watson, & Mirhasani, 2007).

With some rewording, certain measures may be generalizable across religious traditions and cultures. For example, Tapanya, Nicki, and Jarusawad (1997) found that the Age Universal I–E scale could be applied to cultures as diverse as Canadian Christians and Thai Buddhists. Also, Piedmont's Spiritual Transcendence Scale has now been validated on samples from the Philippines (Piedmont, 2007) and India (Piedmont & Leach, 2002).

Most measures will probably require significant modifications when exported to other cultures. For example, although Ai, Peterson, and Huang (2003) were able to use a simple translation of the most widely used measure of religious coping, the Brief Religious Coping Inventory (RCOPE; Pargament, Smith, Koenig, & Perez, 1998), into Albanian and Bosnian–Serbian languages for administration to Kosovar and Bosnian Muslim refugees in the United States, other attempts have required significant modifications of the scale. Currently, parallel versions of the RCOPE have been developed for Hindu (Tarakeshwar, Pargament, & Mahoney, 2003a), Jewish (Rosmarin, Pargament, Krumrei, & Flannelly, 2009), and Pakistani Muslim (Khan & Watson, 2006) cultures, but in each case, the new scale had to allow for major religious and cultural variations.

Consider the issue of different religious understandings of the term God. The common Western monotheistic concept of God as a transcendent spiritual being is quite different than the notion, common in many Eastern religious traditions (such as Buddhism, Confucianism, and Daoism), of God as a humanized or philosophical higher power. Such variation in conceptualizations of God was just one of several issues encountered by the developers of the Chinese version of Underwood and Teresi's (2002) 16-item Daily Spiritual Experiences Scale (DSES; Ng, Fong, Tsui, Au-Yeung, & Law, 2009).

The authors detailed the numerous steps they took to ensure that the DSES applied to the religious and spiritual practices of Chinese. Their efforts are an example of the requisite care necessary to successfully apply a measure to another culture (see also Ghorbani, Watson, & Khan, 2007).

We suggest that researchers first be open to the idea that measures (and even the concepts upon which the measures are based) may require revision before they are implemented in cultures beyond which they were originally tested. To do this, it is important that researchers work toward an understanding of the religious and spiritual beliefs, practices, and experiences from *within* the culture to fully understand the phenomenon they wish to investigate (Cohen, 2009). From there, researchers should make a careful and informed judgment, perhaps on the basis of pilot testing, about whether a measure and its underlying construct apply across cultures.

Measures beyond the Judeo-Christian tradition. It may be advisable that researchers develop entirely new measures of religiousness and spirituality that reflect the culture to which they are applied. To maintain content validity, such efforts may require careful consultation with theological and cultural experts. Examples of such a newly developed indigenous measure of religiousness and spirituality outside the Judeo-Christian tradition include the Measures of Hindu Pathway Scales (Tarakeshwar, Pargament, & Mahoney, 2003b; see also Chapter 36 in this volume), in which individual items were created on the basis of interviews with 15 Hindus living in the United States. After themes were coded, a thematic framework was established and reviewed by the Hindu participants. Only then were items generated and eventually selected on the basis of traditional scale development procedures. The result was a 37-item scale measuring four religious pathways consistent with Hindu theology: path of devotion (i.e., devotional practices, participation in religious festivals, and ritual performance), path of ethical action, path of knowledge, and path of physical restraint/yoga. The four subscales were reliable (alphas near or above .80) and moderately intercorrelated (.15 to .44), suggesting that the four paths are distinct yet related.

Another example of an indigenous cultural measure outside the Judeo-Christian tradition is the Religiosity of Islam Scale (RoIS; Jana-Masri & Priester, 2007), a 19-item measure of Islamic beliefs and behavioral practices. To demonstrate the religious cultural particularity of the measure, consider the following items, hardly measures of religiousness or spirituality from a Western European perspective: "I believe that men can shake hands with women" (reverse scored) or "I believe that a man can marry up to four wives" (*not* reverse scored). Other items, such as "I believe that the Qur'an is the final word of Allah," are better matches with Western conceptions of religiousness and spirituality. The scale has good psychometric properties.

Another psychometrically validated measure of Islamic religiousness is the Psychological Measure of Islamic Religiousness (PMIR; Raiya, Pargament, Stein, & Mahoney, 2007). Details of this measure can be found in the primary article. The authors identified several important challenges faced and lessons learned in developing this measure, including the following: (a) Islam is a multidimensional religion, (b) Islam is similar to yet different from other religions, and (c) some types of Islamic religiousness are constructive whereas others are destructive. Challenges faced in the process of developing the PMIR include (a) the dearth of empirical research; (b) antipathy, mistrust, and suspicion among some Muslims about psychology; (c) stigma toward mental health topics; (d) the social–political atmosphere in the post–September 11 era; (e) unwillingness to admit negative consequences of Islam; (f) cultural differences among Muslims in the world; (g) language subtleties; and (h) gender issues.

SUBSTANTIVE MEASURES OF RELIGIOUSNESS AND SPIRITUALITY

Given the criteria of good measurement and the cautions in applying those criteria to the study of religiousness and spirituality, the distinction between substantive and functional approaches is offered as an organizing framework from which to understand available measures. Substantive measures, which will be considered in this section, focus on individuals' religious tendencies, beliefs, behaviors, or other individual traits or actions; in contrast, functional measures, which will be the focus later in this chapter, assess how religious activities and characteristics function in individuals' lives. Full copies of many of the measures published before 1996 that are discussed in this section, whether substantive or functional, can be found in Hill and Hood (1999). This review is selective in that all of the measures reviewed meet or surpass Hill's (2005) criteria of "good" measures in terms of theoretical grounding, sample representativeness, reliability, and validity. Also, all of the measures reviewed here have been used in subsequent research, thus further establishing scale validity and generalization. The number of scales reviewed is far from exhaustive, however. Other resources (Hill, 2005; Hill & Hood, 1999) describe and review additional measures.

Drawing partly from distinctions made by Tsang and McCullough (2003), substantive measures can be further divided into dispositional and behavioral categories. The first six categories of reviewed measures (general religiousness, beliefs or religious preferences, religious or spiritual commitment, religious motivation, relational spirituality, and religious or spiritual development) are dispositional measures designed to quantify or describe the degree to which a person is "religious" or "spiritual." We then review some behavioral measures as the expression of such dispositional characteristics within the confines of specific situations. Common behavioral measures assess the frequency or manner in which individuals engage in various religious or spiritual activities (including involvement in religious communities), frequency of individual or communal religious practices, and participation in organized religious traditions.

General Religiousness or Spirituality

Is there a religious or spiritual personality? Piedmont (1999; see Chapter 9 of this volume) has contended that spirituality could be considered a dimension of personality comparable to the Big Five factors of the five-factor model. With samples of undergraduates and peer raters, Piedmont found that spirituality is (a) independent of the other five factors, (b) at a level of comparable generality as the other five factors, and (c) able to predict a wide range of psychologically salient outcomes over and above the other factors. Piedmont's notion of spirituality is what he calls *spiritual transcendence,* understood as "the capacity of individuals to stand outside of their immediate sense of time and place to view life from a larger, more objective perspective" (1999, p. 988). Such capacity provides "an encompassing vision of life that satisfies more fundamental urges of our nature" (p. 988). Piedmont has maintained that this capacity is inherent within all religious traditions and outside the bounds of traditional religion. Piedmont's findings were based on the 24-item Spiritual Transcendence Scale, designed to assess individuals' search for a connection with the sacred. Results indicated a three-factor structure corresponding to Piedmont's identified subscales: universality, prayer fulfillment, and connectedness. Convergent validity was supported when the standard self-report version was compared with a corresponding observer rating version. The Spiritual Transcendence Scale also was able to uniquely predict a number of psychological outcomes (e.g., positive affect, prosocial behavior, interpersonal orientation, perceived social support, vulnerability to stress, internal health locus of control) beyond the Five-Factor Model of Personality.

Mysticism reflects intense spiritual experiences and felt connection or unity with either the outside world, something beyond oneself (be it God, Ultimate Reality, or some other transcendent notion), or "nothingness" (Stace, 1960). Such experiences may or may not involve religious interpretation. Hood's (1975; see Chapter 21 in this volume) 32-item mysticism measure (the M Scale), originally designed to measure Stace's (1960) eight phenomenological criteria of mystical experience (Ego Quality, Unifying Quality, Inner Subjective Quality, Temporal/Spatial Quality, Noetic Quality, Ineffability, Positive Affect, and Religious Quality), resulted in a two-factor structure (Hood, 1975). The 20-item first factor, denoted general mysticism, was understood by Hood as "an indicator of intense experience [with unity], not interpreted religiously and not necessarily positive" (p. 34). Hood identified this factor as perhaps the "single core" (p. 34) of mystical experience. The 12-item second factor was conceived by Hood as "an indicator of a joyful expression of more traditionally defined religious experiences which may or may not be mystical but which are interpreted to indicate a firm source of objective knowledge" (p. 34). Later factor analyses, however, indicate that a three-component structure may better fit the data (Caird, 1988). Hood et al. (2009) recommended that future research use a modified structure that divides Factor 1 into two factors, unity with the external world (extrovertive mysticism) and unity with "nothingness" (introvertive mysticism). The third factor continues to reflect a religious interpretation. The M Scale demonstrates good internal consistency and validity; it is not strongly related to pathology indexes but is related to such positive characteristics as tolerance and creativity. It also correlates with other measures of spiritual experience, including intrinsic religiosity, openness to experience, and intense religious experiences (Burris, 1999b; T. W. Hall, Tisdale, & Brokaw, 1994).

One of the most widely used measures of spirituality over the past three decades is Paloutzian and Ellison's (1982) 20-item Spiritual Well-Being Scale (SWBS; also see C. W. Ellison, 1983). Developed to assess a need for transcendence (T. W. Hall et al., 1994), the SWBS provides an overall spiritual well-being score and scores on two subscales that moderately correlate with each other: Religious (RWB) and Existential (EWB). Paloutzian and Ellison (1982) interpreted the RWB subscale as a "vertical" dimension reflecting spiritual well-being (with specific reference to God), whereas the EWB is understood as a "horizontal" dimension reflecting a sense of purpose, life satisfaction, and adjustment in relation to self and others. Although the RWB demonstrates the expected unitary factor structure, the EWB loads onto two or more factors, suggesting a possible need for item reorganization or theory revision (Ledbetter, Smith, Fischer, & Vosler-Hunter, 1991). The scale shows high reliability but may produce ceiling effects in some samples (e.g., religiously conservative groups). The SWBS shows convergent and discriminant validity, as revealed by links with other measures of spirituality (e.g., sense of purpose, seeing God as a causal agent, engagement in spiritual practices) and psychological health (C. W. Ellison & Smith, 1991). Such indicators of validity should be viewed with caution, however. The correlation with these other measures is likely a function of the SWBS itself in that many of the EWB items simply assess positive psychological characteristics (Koenig, 2008). The SWBS has been used in populations that are diverse in terms of age (e.g., high school and college students; older adults), religious beliefs (e.g., various Christian denominations, non-Christian traditions, and nonreligious individuals), various communities (e.g., urban, suburban, and rural), prisoners, clinical populations, and populations with health difficulties (e.g., terminally ill patients and those with AIDs). Although some normative data have been compiled (Bufford, Paloutzian, & Ellison, 1991) and a manual developed (Paloutzian & Ellison, 1991), means vary by population. Its repeated reference to God limits it use to monotheistic worldviews and religions. Although the SWBS should not be interpreted as an indicator of spiritual health or maturity, the wide use of the SWBS within various populations (including clinical populations) led T. W. Hall et al. (1994) to conclude that low scores on the SWBS may reflect clinically meaningful impairments in spiritual functioning.

Beliefs and Religious Preferences

There are more measures of religious belief than any other category of religiousness or spirituality, in part because an earlier generation of scales developed mostly before the 1980s focused primarily on this component of religiousness. Most of those scales were thoroughly reviewed in the Hill and Hood (1999) volume. Therefore, our review is brief and selective, with discussions of scales limited to those that are psychometrically sound and that have been used frequently in research. Furthermore, religious belief is an inherent component of many of the scales discussed in other sections of this paper, so it is a topic to which we return frequently.

Measures of religious orthodoxy have largely been limited to the Christian tradition. Fullerton and Hunsberger's (1982) 24-item Christian Orthodoxy (CO) Scale was originally tested among almost 2,300 respondents representing 10 Christian believer groups, mostly in Canada and Australia. Internal consistency on this Likert-type measure (-3 to $+3$; *strongly disagree* to *strongly agree*) is very high ($\alpha = .97$ and .98 among the 10 groups) with total scores ranging from 24 to 168 (a constant of 4 was added to each item's raw score). High mean interitem correlation coefficients ranging from .57 to .70 suggest considerable redundancy among some items and that the operationalization of the concept may be quite narrow. A shortened six-item measure that correlates highly with the longer measure was later developed (Hunsberger, 1989). The scale's validity is well documented in that it correlates highly with measures of trust in the guidance of the Bible (.77) and the church (.68), overall religious behavior (.75), church attendance (.62), frequency of prayer (.70), and scriptural–devotional reading (.57). "Known groups" validity was also demonstrated with the apostate group (people who self-identify as having once believed but no longer do) scoring considerably lower ($M = 61.8$) than any of the other nine groups (*M*s between 111.9 and 130.4).

Several other scales reviewed in Hill and Hood (1999) assess belief in traditional Christian teachings. Examples include Brown and Lowe's (1951) Inventory of Religious Belief, which contains 15 five-point Likert items about agreement with such Christian beliefs as inspiration of scripture, the Trinity, the divinity of Christ, and the reality of heaven and hell. Reliability is acceptable and "known groups" validity was established with Bible college students scoring significantly higher than students at a liberal seminary. Kaldestad and Stifoss-Hanssen's (1993) Humanistic Morality Scale and Liberal Belief Scale (with eight Likert items each) were developed in Norway to measure what seem to be increasingly liberal religious views in Scandinavian countries. Both show adequate reliability and convergent validity. Both scales also have been tested on psychiatric populations, with patients scoring higher than nonpatients (see Wulff, 1999b, for a review). Stellway's (1973) seven-item Christian Conservatism Scale and six-item Christian Liberalism Scale are other brief measures to consider. Although no reliability data were reported by Stellway, an alpha of .86 was found in subsequent research on the Conservatism Scale. Both scales moderately correlated in expected directions with political orientations and, as expected, negatively correlated ($-.48$) with each other.

Few measures of religious belief have been established outside of Christianity. The Student Religiosity Questionnaire (Katz, 1988), developed for use with student populations, assesses Jewish beliefs and practices. Factor analyses on this five-point Likert scale indicate a two-factor structure tapping religious principles and religious practices. Alphas from .83 to .96 were shown in samples of white South

African teacher trainees, teacher trainees at Bar-Ilan University, and Israeli 11th graders at various schools, including administration of a Hebrew translation of the measure. Face validity was established by a panel of 10 Jewish theologians.

Emavardhana and Tori (1997) developed the 11-item Buddhist Beliefs and Practices Scale to assess Buddhist beliefs and practices, such as the importance of Buddhist teachings, observation of the five precepts of Buddhism, the practice of meditation, affirmation of the theory of karma and rebirth, and agreement with the doctrine of *anatta* (the lack of souls). This scale has adequate psychometric properties and correlates with some measures of psychological health (e.g., high self-esteem and low self-criticism). Participants showed a significant increase in scores after a 2-day Vipassana meditation retreat, supporting the scale's validity.

Religious or Spiritual Commitment

A person's level of religious or spiritual commitment could reflect both a religious or spiritual disposition and how religiousness or spirituality function in an individual's life. On balance, most measures seem to assess this construct in dispositional terms.

Plante and Boccaccini (1997) developed the10-item Santa Clara Strength of Religious Faith Questionnaire (SCSRFQ), which should be used only with populations for which the term *faith* is appropriate. High reliability (alphas of .94 to .97; split half-reliabilities of .90 to .96) and validity (correlations from .64 to .92 with related measures) were found in three different samples. Plante, Vallaeys, Sherman, and Wallston (2002) also developed a five-item short form (SCSFQ-SF) with similarly strong psychometric properties. Pending replication with more diverse populations, this brief measure may be extremely useful to researchers.

The 10-item Religious Commitment Inventory (RCI-10; Worthington et al., 2003) shows good internal consistency (alphas above .88), test–retest reliability (.83 and up at a 3-week interval), and discriminant validity. The authors reported six studies with diverse samples, including students from secular and Christian universities, community samples of adults, and therapists and clients at religious and secular counseling agencies. Samples (total *N* of almost 2000) were mainly Christian but included some Hindus, Muslims, and Buddhists. Although analyses have indicated two factors (intrapersonal and interpersonal), the factors correlate highly; thus the measure may be most useful as a full-scale assessment. Each item is rated on a 5-point scale (*not at all true of me* to *totally true of me*). This carefully developed instrument is highly recommended for researchers and clinicians on several counts: solid psychometric qualities, brevity, and potential use in non-Christian traditions.

Relational Measures

Although perhaps most applicable within monotheistic contexts, the understanding of spiritual experiences as interactions with a higher power provides an opportunity to investigate religiousness and spirituality from a relational theoretical framework (see also Chapter 20 in this volume). Reviewed measures may assess underlying interactional dynamics (e.g., attachment-to-God scales), emotional or experiential understanding of God (e.g., God image scales), or cognitive understanding or beliefs regarding God's attributes or characteristics (e.g., God concept scales; see Hill & Hood, 1999).

Attachment to God. Based within attachment theory, a growing body of research uses measures that explore spirituality within monotheistic (generally Christian) religions by framing God as an attachment figure (e.g., Beck, 2006; Kirkpatrick, 1998; see also Chapter 7 in this volume). Within this framework, individual differences in the security of this emotional bond between individuals and God can be assessed. Such measures have shown links with (a) theological exploration, rejection of doctrinal beliefs, and orthodoxy (Beck, 2006); (b) Big Five personality factors, religious orientation, views of God, manifest anxiety, positive and negative affect, avoidance, and self-deception (Rowatt & Kirkpatrick, 2002); and (c) spiritual coping and general mental health as well as religious outcomes (Belavich & Pargament, 2002).

Measures of attachment to God have been developed on the basis of corresponding measures of adult attachment. Modeled after Hazan and Shaver's (1987) attachment-style vignettes, which ask participants to identify which of three paragraphs best describes their experiences in close interpersonal relationships, the Attachment-to-God Scale (Kirkpatrick & Shaver, 1992) asks participants to indicate which of three prototypical paragraphs (one each describing secure, avoidant, and anxious/ambivalent attachment patterns) best describes their relationship with God. Although some studies have successfully used this categorical measure of God attachment, Rowatt and Kirkpatrick (2002) converted the paragraph measure into a nine-item Attachment-to-God Scale to address the psychometric problems presented by categorical measures (e.g., a person may agree with only some aspects of a categorical statement; problems assessing reliability). Although items were derived from all three categories, both a one-factor and two-factor model emerged with satisfactory fits. The authors favored the two-factor model (avoidance and anxiety, with three secure items negatively loading on the avoidant factor), in part because it was consistent with prevailing two-dimensional models of adult romantic attachment (e.g., Brennan, Clark, & Shaver, 1998). The two factors correlate moderately with each other (r = .56), with anxious but not avoidant adult romantic attachments, and with Big Five factors—positively with Neuroticism, negatively with Agreeableness, "minimally" (p. 647) with Conscientiousness, and "negligibly" (p. 647) with Extraversion and Openness to Experience. Also, after controlling for social desirability and such measures as intrinsic religiousness, doctrinal orthodoxy, and loving images of God, avoidant attachment significantly predicted religious symbolic immortality, whereas anxious attachment predicted both negative and positive affect.

Beck and McDonald (2004) also developed a 28-item Attachment-to-God Inventory (AGI) to provide dimensional measures of anxious and avoidant attachment to God. Modeled on the Experiences in Close Relationships Scale (ECR; Brennan, Clark, & Shaver, 1998), a common measure of adult attachment, the AGI has demonstrated a stable two-factor structure: avoidance (lack of intimacy with God and strong self-reliance) and anxiety (lack of intrinsic lovability and concern of potential abandonment). The scales have shown good internal consistency (alphas above .80) and construct validity, as evidenced by strong negative correlations with both facets of spiritual well-being (Paloutzian & Ellison, 1982) and moderately positive correlations with ECR attachment measures in samples of both undergraduate and Christian community samples. As with other measures of attachment to God, however, the AGI remains limited in being utilized primarily within a Judeo-Christian population.

God concept and God image. Gorsuch's (1968) 91-item Adjective Ratings of God Scale was designed as an alternative to the single-item measures of religiousness (e.g., church attendance, self-rated religiousness) often used in research at that time. Respondents rate a series of adjectives as either not describing God (a score of 1), describing God (a score of 2), or describing God particularly well (a score of 3). Scores are summed on five dimensions: Traditional Christian, Deisticness, Wrathfulness, Omni-ness (i.e., omnipresence, omniscience, omnipotence, and infinite nature of God), and Irrelevancy. The resulting five-factor structure has been supported by two unpublished studies conducted in the 1990s that Ladd and Spilka (1999) reported as finding a similar factor structure. Reliability coefficients are above .70 for all subscales except Irrelevancy (α = .49).

A more frequently used measure of God concept is Benson and Spilka's (1973) 10-item Loving and Controlling God Scales. Each scale consists of five semantic differential dimensions measured on a seven-point (0 to 6) response format: Loving God (rejecting-accepting, loving-hating, unforgiving-forgiving, approving-disappointing) and Controlling God (demanding-not demanding, freeing-restricting, controlling-uncontrolling, strict-lenient, permissive-rigid). The scales have shown associations with a number of pertinent religious variables (e.g., spiritual coping) and clinically relevant constructs (e.g., self-esteem, locus of control, differing God images between dissociative identity disorder alters), particularly those within an object relations conceptualization (e.g., attachment and level of object relations development). Yet reliability coefficients, particularly for the Controlling God Scale, have been marginal (.60 to .70 range).

In contrast to measures of God concept, which connote a largely cognitive representation of God, measures of God image assess affectively laden experience of God and often are rooted conceptually in psychodynamic theory. The God Image Inventory (Lawrence, 1997) is one such measure, where ratings of 156 items provide six scales of participants' experience of God (Influence, Providence, Presence, Challenge, Acceptance, and Benevolence) and two control scales (Faith and Salience). All scales are reliable (alpha greater than .84), and evidence has been provided in terms of convergent and discriminant validity. Subsequent use of the scale has been restricted primarily to dissertations, which is likely due to the length of the measure.

Distinct from the other measures reviewed thus far, Rizzuto's God/Family Questionnaires (Rizzuto, 1979) use an open-ended sentence stem structure to assess and compare representations of God with internal representations of family members. Although the lack of quantitative analyses or norms may limit utility in research settings, data from this measure may help clinicians understand a person's religious experiences and beliefs about God through internalized images of God, others, and self. The measure may be especially useful in psychodynamic contexts.

To address the need for an objective, multidimensional relational measure of spiritual development with clinical utility, T. W. Hall and Edwards (1996, 2002; see Chapter 15 in this volume) developed the 49-item self-report Spiritual Assessment Inventory (SAI). This instrument was developed on the basis of object-relations and attachment theories and consists of five subscales: Awareness of God, Realistic Acceptance (of God), Disappointment (with God), Grandiosity (excessive self-importance), and Instability (in one's relationship to God). All five subscales have shown good internal consistency (.73 to .95), and the overall scale shows incremental validity beyond religious orientation or motivation. Exploratory and confirmatory factor analyses support the use and coherence of the five subscales and two stable second-order factors, Quality of Relationship with God and Awareness of God (T. W. Hall & Edwards, 2002). Item response theory (IRT) analyses further support the scale's psychometric qualities (T. W. Hall, Reise, & Haviland, 2007, p. 175).

Religious or Spiritual Development

Religiousness and spirituality may develop over time. Furthermore, the concept of religious development or maturity is value laden: There is an inherent implication that some forms of religiousness or spirituality are superior to others, making this a controversial construct (see Zinnbauer, Volume 2). As already discussed with regard to the intrinsic–extrinsic distinction, what may be considered mature or more highly developed in one context may not apply in other contexts. For this reason, some researchers prefer to define maturity only within specific religious traditions.

The Faith Maturity Scale (FMS) was developed by Benson, Donahue, and Erickson (1993) to assess values, behaviors, commitments, and viewpoints that were deemed "characteristics of vibrant and life transforming faith, as these have been understood in 'mainline' Protestant traditions" (p. 3). The measure seeks to assess both vertical (one's relationship with God) and horizontal (one's relationship with others) dimensions. Developed through a national study of Protestant congregations, this 38-item measure has demonstrated utility within a number of samples, including numerous Protestant denominations, Catholic parishes, and Australian Seventh-Day Adventists. The FMS boasts a number of strengths, including strong reliabilities, ease of administration, convergent validity (e.g., positive correlations with intrinsic religiosity and age, clergy scoring higher than lay persons), and a criterion-based approach to measure development that sought to minimize potential confounding effects of such factors as SES status, ethnicity, church denomination, or church involvement.

Recognizing the need for measures assessing lifelong religious and spiritual experiences and involvement, Hays, Meador, Branch, and George (2001) developed the 23-item Spiritual History Scale in Four Dimensions (SHS-4) using a large sample of Protestant, Catholic, and Jewish older adults. The SHS-4 has four dimensions: God Helped (past help-seeking behavior; received instrumental support), Family History of Religiousness (childhood religious experiences; religiosity of family-of-origin), Lifetime Religious Social Support (religious involvement in adulthood), and Cost of Religiousness (experienced loss or difficulties within health, emotional, or interpersonal domains). The overall measure and subscales show adequate reliability and correlate with religious practices (frequency and duration) and social support. It may be particularly useful in understanding protective impacts of religiosity in health psychology contexts, as SHS-4 scores correlate with measures of health behaviors as well as physical and mental health after accounting for other measures of religious involvement and social support.

Several measures have been developed using James Fowler's (1981) process-oriented (versus content-focused) model of faith development, where faith is understood as a meaning-making process through commitment to a set of organizing principles or values. Faith development, according to Fowler, progresses through a sequence of stages ranging from concrete systems in the early stages to more complex, abstract, and autonomous processes in later stages. Fowler also developed the *Faith Development Interview Guide*, a semistructured interview format (also see Burris, 1999a). Scoring the interview and assigning faith development stage ratings to each of the seven dimensions is a time-intensive process that requires a co-rater. The complexity of the construct caused Burris (1999a) to conclude that the measure may be best understood as a starting point; additional interviewing with clinical acumen may be needed to determine a person's faith development stage. Despite these limitations, studies have shown high inter-rater reliabilities and internal consistency. The measure's validity has been shown in its differentiation of various populations and positive correlations with ego development measures.

The Faith Development Scale (Leak, Loucks, & Bowlin, 1999) is a paper-and-pencil measure that is based on Fowler's (1981) theory. This eight-item forced-choice measure is supported by a variety of findings, including adequate reliability, significant positive correlations with other self-report and peer ratings of faith development, expected cross-sectional and longitudinal patterns in faith development, and expected relationships (both positive and negative) with both religious and personality variables (Leak, 2002). Of possible concern is the measure's questionable factor structure; although many considerations support a unidimensional interpretation, factor analyses in one study indicated that a two-factor solution would best fit the data (Leak, 2002).

Religious Social Participation

The social support provided through involvement in religious practices, such as attending synagogue, mosque, or church, often yields benefits. Yet few measures have been developed to explore various aspects of such participation. In fact, many studies have used a single-item behavior measure (the most common being church attendance) as an overall indication of religiousness. Two people can attend church equally frequently for entirely different reasons. Single-item measures also fail to account for the large number of extenuating factors affecting individuals' church attendance that extend beyond religious variables, such as impacts of health conditions, job requirements, family obligations, locations of churches, social anxieties, and relationships with specific congregation members. Thus, although behavioral measures may be beneficial, emphasizing single behaviors without accounting for underlying factors may obscure the impact and role of religious participation in individuals' lives. Social participation is often one dimension measured in multidimensional scales, which are discussed in a later section. One such example is the 14-item Church Involvement subscale of Hilty, Morgan, and Burns's (1984) Religious Involvement Inventory.

An early measure widely used in the years initially following its development was Thurstone and Chave's (1929) 45-item Attitude Toward the Church Scale. Wulff (1999a) reported that the scale demonstrates exceptional reliability. A key strength of this measure is that it was used in more than 30 studies and correlates with various facets of religiosity and personality (e.g., conservativeness, authoritarianism, and prejudice), all of which contribute to the scale's validity (Wulff, 1999a). A search of literature published within the past 10 years, however, indicates that the measure is now seldom used. Although the wording of the measure may need to be modestly updated, researchers are encouraged to consider using this measure because of its assessment of many attitudes that remain pertinent to the psychology of religion.

Useful to congregational leaders are two related measures of institutional religion: the Congregation Climate Scales (CCS; Pargament, Silverman, Johnson, Echemendia, & Snyder, 1983) and the Congregation Satisfaction Questionnaire (CSQ; Silverman, Pargament, Johnson, Echemendia, & Snyder, 1983). Both measures were normed within 13 Christian congregations, although each measure was designed for use within both Christian churches and Jewish synagogues. The CCS is a 50-item measure designed to assess the psychosocial climate or "personality" of a church along five dimensions (Sense of Community, Activity, Openness to Change, Stability, and Organization and Clarity). The CSQ measures satisfaction with one's church or synagogue through ratings of the degree to which 70 words or short phrases describe one's experience in the congregation. The measure taps seven dimensions (Religious Services, Fellow Members, Leaders, Special Programs and Activities, Religious Education for Children, Religious Education for Adults, and Church Facilities). Both measures show high internal reliability and acceptable test–retest reliability as well as documented convergent validity.

Religious or Spiritual Private Practices

To assess such private practices as prayer, meditation, religious contemplation, worship attendance, and experience of God, Connors, Tonigan, and Miller (1996) developed the Religious Background and Behavior Scale (RBB). The 13-item scale assesses religious practices in the last year and over the life span (six items each). Although use of the complete scale is recommended, either half of the measure can be used depending on research or clinical needs. The full measure also provides scores for two subscales: God Consciousness and Formal Practices. Both the full scale and subscales show solid internal consistency and test–retest reliability. This measure was developed within a multisite trial of alcoholism treatment, and normative data are available for this population. Although references to God may limit usage to monotheistic faiths, this measure is not restricted to Christian populations. Validity is supported through positive correlations with several religious variables and involvement in substance abuse treatment programs (particularly faith-based programs such as Alcoholics Anonymous). In part because of its strong psychometric properties and clinical utility, the scale often has been used for research purposes.

Other measures assess specific spiritual practices such as prayer. On the basis of a conceptual model by Foster (1992), the Inward, Outward, Upward Prayer Scale (Ladd & Spilka, 2002, 2006, Vol. 1) has 29 items (with a six-point Likert response format) designed to assess engagement in different types of prayer; an exploratory factor analysis suggested eight subscales. Each of the eight factors indicated a directionality that helped to define the three second-order factors in accordance with Foster's model (*inward* prayers that stress self-examination, *upward* prayers that focus on the human-divine relationship, and *outward* prayers that emphasize human connections). In turn, the three second-order factors were represented in terms of intentionality (e.g., the intention of an inward directed prayer of examination is to assess one's own spiritual status) and accounted for 62% of the variance. The best fitting model in a confirmatory factor analysis fit not only with the conceptual model of the researchers (eight subscales with three second-order factors) but also with the presence of a single general prayer factor (Ladd & Spilka, 2006).

The overall scale and its subscales demonstrate adequate reliabilities (Ladd & Spilka, 2006). Relationships with other measures of religiosity (e.g., intrinsic religious orientation, extrinsic religious orientation, questing) and personality correlates (e.g., need for structure, coping styles, attitudes toward death) provide evidence for convergent and divergent validity. Engagement in prayer, as assessed by this measure, is related to various demographic variables as well, including years of prayer (those who have prayed for more years indicated a greater variety in use of prayer types), gender (women indicated praying more frequently and at greater lengths than men), and years of education (linked with lower prayer frequency and less confrontational prayers). The measure can be expanded to use in a variety of contexts through altering instructions, such as asking participants to assess their prayer usage after traumatic events. Use of the measure has been restricted to primarily Christian populations.

FUNCTIONAL MEASURES OF RELIGIOUSNESS AND SPIRITUALITY

Functional approaches assess how religion operates within individuals' lives. Tsang and McCullough (2003) have suggested that dispositional variables should be controlled when examining differences at the functional level, as the role of religion and religious practice in individuals' lives may partly reflect deeper, underlying religious tendencies tapped by dispositional measures.

Religious Motivation

No single topic has generated more interest among psychologists of religion than the underlying motivation behind religious experiences, largely because of the dominance of Allport's (1950) theory of religious orientation. Indeed, the fact that much of our measurement discussion has centered on religious orientation suggests how influential this concept has been.

Intrinsic–extrinsic religious orientation. According to Allport (1950), people differ in the motivations that underlie religious experience and behavior. An *intrinsic* orientation is framed as a master motive, a supreme value to address life's most important questions. Others may approach religion from an *extrinsic* orientation, a starkly utilitarian approach focusing on the personal benefits that religion can provide (e.g., a sense of belonging or security, personal fulfillment, or community status). Religion, for the extrinsically motivated person, is called on only when needed and may not be well integrated in the person's life.

Of the 11 measures of religious orientation reviewed by Hill and Hood (1999), all but one owe their heritage to Allport. The original Allport and Ross (1967) measure remains widely used, although the many scales subsequently developed have the benefit of the voluminous research findings and efforts devoted to this topic. For example, Gorsuch and McPherson's (1989) 14-item revision of the Allport and Ross scale took into account Kirkpatrick's (1989) uncovering of two categories in the extrinsic scale: a personally oriented (Ep) and a socially oriented (Es) extrinsic orientation. Their revised scale, the I/E-R, shows sufficient reliability for the eight-item intrinsic measure (.83 in the original study) but lower reliability (.65) for the six-item extrinsic measure. An earlier version of this scale, the Age Universal Religious Orientation Scale (Gorsuch & Venable, 1983), is the only religious orientation measure designed for use with both adults and children. The authors maintained that the scale's brevity allow it to be used with larger samples, thereby retaining its statistical power despite reliability problems (Gorsuch & McPherson, 1989). If brevity is key and one is interested only in measuring intrinsic religious orientation, then the three-item intrinsic religion subscale of the Duke University Religion Index (DUREL; Koenig, Patterson, & Meador, 1997) is recommended. The authors report sufficient reliability ($\alpha = .75$), and the three-item scale correlates strongly with Hoge's (1972) 10-item scale, from which the three items were drawn.

Quest religious orientation. In the years since publication of Allport's 1950 classic *The Individual and His Religion,* the religious landscape has changed dramatically from what has been described as a *dwelling* to a *seeking* orientation (Wuthnow, 1998). A dwelling spirituality emphasizes a spiritual home that promotes a sense of community and interrelatedness, providing clear distinctions between the sacred and the profane. In contrast, a seeking spirituality stresses the journey-like characterization of interiority, thereby valuing the inquisitive and even questing nature of faith. A seeking orientation makes fewer distinctions between the sacred and the ordinary and offers individuals' greater freedom from the constraints of community expectations.

Perhaps reflecting this shift, Batson and his colleagues (Batson & Schoenrade, 1991a, 1991b; Burris, Jackson, Tarpley, & Smith, 1996) proposed an alternative orientation that involves "honestly facing existential questions in all their complexity, while at the same time resisting clear-cut, pat answers" (Batson et al., 1993, p. 166). On the basis of concerns that intrinsic orientation measures may reflect only a devout endorsement of religious teachings at the expense of a fuller, richer conceptualization, the *quest* construct was designed to address three factors from Allport's original ideas about mature religion that were neglected in subsequent measures and research: (a) acknowledging complexity of existential questions, (b) ascribing doubts as healthy, and (c) holding religious views tentatively with openness to change. Numerous quest scales have been developed and refined, which is not surprising given the complexity of the construct. Among the more advanced is the 12-item Quest Scale developed by Batson and Schoenrade (1991b), in which each of the three original factors is measured via four items on a 9-point scale from *strongly agree* to *strongly disagree*. Alphas range from approximately .70 to .80. The scale has been shown to be distinct not only from both intrinsic and extrinsic motivational measures (Batson & Schoenrade, 1991a) but also from measures of antiorthodoxy, religious liberalism, and agnosticism (Burris et al., 1996).

Although moderately correlated with quest (r = .55), the 10-item Spiritual Openness (SO) subscale of Genia's revised Spiritual Experience Index (SEI-R; 1997) provides a distinct measure of spiritual openness. Example items include "One should not marry someone of a different faith" (reverse-scored) and "Ideas from faiths different from my own may increase my understanding of spiritual truth." The SO subscale demonstrates adequate reliability (α = .75; Reinert & Bloomingdale, 2000), and construct validity is supported by negative correlations with fundamentalism, intolerance of ambiguity, and dogmatism. Surprisingly, SO also correlates negatively with other measures of spirituality, such as God consciousness, participation in formal religious practices, and intrinsic religious orientation. Despite moderate correlations with quest, SO appears to be measuring a distinct construct, as evidenced by significant correlations with religious and spiritual well-being when controlling for intrinsic and quest scores.

Fundamentalism as religious motivation. The motivational nature of a fundamentalist religious orientation is captured well by the following definition:

> the belief that there is one set of religious teachings that clearly contains the fundamental, basic, intrinsic, essential, inerrant truth about humanity and deity; that this essential truth is fundamentally opposed by forces of evil which must be vigorously fought; that this truth must be followed today according to the fundamental, unchangeable practices of the past; and that those who believe and follow these fundamental teachings have a special relationship with the deity. (Altemeyer & Hunsberger, 1992, p. 118)

On the basis of this conceptualization, Altemeyer and Hunsberger developed a 20-item Religious Fundamentalism Scale (RFS) that has been tested in Western Christian samples and also with Hindus, Jews, and Muslims. Reliability coefficients ranged from .85 to .94. The authors later made a 12-item version (reliability coefficients above .90) using a sample of predominantly Christian university students and their parents (Altemeyer & Hunsberger, 2004). As the psychometric properties of the short version match or exceed those of the longer version, the short version is now recommended.

An alternative measure, the Intratextualism Fundamentalism Scale (IFS), has been developed (Williamson, Hood, Ahmad, Sadiq, & Hill, 2010) on the basis of the intratextual theory of fundamentalism (Hood, Hill, & Williamson, 2005). The intratextual theory suggests that fundamentalist motivation is less characterized by militancy or right-wing authoritarianism than by an allegiance to a sacred text (usually written but sometimes oral) through which objective truth is defined and the interpretive process for finding such truth is derived. The scale contains five 6-point Likert items and is suitable for testing (with minor wording changes) across religious traditions, with one item each measuring the text as inerrant, authoritative, divine, unchanging, and privileged above all other texts. Internal consistency with a U.S. Christian sample was good (α = .83) but was only marginally acceptable with a Pakistani Muslim sample (α = .65). The scale demonstrates good convergent and divergent validity, at least among Christians, for whom the measure positively correlated with church attendance as well as intrinsic– and extrinsic–personal religious orientations; it also negatively (but weakly) correlated with need for cognition. Among the Pakistani sample, the measure correlated with being male but was unrelated to religious orientations as well as other measures of religiousness. The lack of association with other measures of religiousness in the Pakistani sample may be due to the lack of portability of the IFS or of the other measures used, or both. Regardless of which measure of fundamentalism is used (including four other measures of Christian fundamentalism reviewed in Hill & Hood, 1999), it is important that fundamentalism not be confused with orthodoxy or, in the case of Christianity, evangelicalism (Hood et al., 2005). Although fundamentalists and evangelicals do hold similar foundational beliefs, unique characteristics of fundamentalists center on their views of how sacred texts are to be treated and their tendency to view the surrounding culture in a negative (and sometimes hostile) way.

Religion as a Source of Meaning and Values

Many psychologists of religion (e.g., Hood et al., 2005, 2009; Park, 2005) agree with Paloutzian and Park's (2005) position that the human need for meaning "holds much promise as a unifying construct in psychology" (p. 13). In fact, in 2005 an entire special issue of the *Journal of Social Issues* was devoted to the psychological study of religion as a meaning system. There is also an emerging body of literature (e.g., Krause, 2008, 2009) demonstrating the importance of a sense of meaning in life (including religion's contribution to that sense of meaning) to physical and mental health. Religion is capable of providing a source of meaning; yet, curiously, there is a paucity of measures that frame religion as a meaning system—perhaps because this is a relatively new integrative framework for studying religiousness and spirituality.

Instead, empirical research in the psychology of religion has framed meaning as a dependent or a mediating variable and thus has used measures that are relatively free of religious content: the Purpose in Life scale (PIL; Crumbaugh & Maholick, 1964), a measure of a sense of meaning in one's life; the Seeking of Noetic Goals scale (SONG; Crumbaugh, 1977), which taps a desire or commitment to find meaning in life; the Life Attitude Profile (LAP; Reker, 1992); the Sense of Coherence scale (SOC; Antonovsky, 1987); and Krause's (2009) eight-item measure.

Sometimes meaning is operationally defined as a component of spirituality (e.g., Fetzer Institute/National Institute of Aging Working Group, 1999). Consider, for example, the eight-item Meaning/Peace subscale of the Functional Assessment of Chronic Illness Therapy—Spiritual Well-Being Scale (FACIT-Sp; Peterman, Fitchett, Brady, Hernandez, & Cella, 2002), which includes items such as "I feel peaceful" or "I have a reason for living." Designed for use with a chronically ill population, the FACIT-Sp measures spirituality independent of specific religious or spiritual identification. Both the meaning subscale and a four-item subscale that measure the role of faith in illness show alphas above .80. The overall measure correlates positively with 10 different measures of religion and spirituality; yet these links are almost entirely a function of the faith subscale. The Meaning/Peace subscale failed to correlate significantly with most of the same religious and spiritual measures, leading the scale developers to conclude that the subscale measures "a unique concept not assessed by the other [religious] instruments" (Peterman et al., 2002, p. 56). We offer another possible explanation, however. This subscale may be too broad to discriminate well between the person who ascribes meaning and purpose to his or her spirituality or religiousness and the person who experiences meaning and purpose in relation to some other aspect of life.

A measure that does specifically consider religion in meaning making is Krause's (2008) six-item scale (sample item: "God put me in this life for a purpose"). Although no estimate of reliability was reported, all items load greater than .76 on one factor, suggesting good internal consistency. Validity was supported by findings that as expected, older African Americans derive a greater sense of religious meaning in life than older European Americans. This measure is quite new and has not been used often in research, but it warrants further consideration.

Religious Support

Fiala, Bjorck, and Gorsuch's (2002) 21-item Religious Support Scale is grounded in the social support literature. Its three subscales assess experienced support from God, congregation members, and church leaders (e.g., lay counselors, pastors, clergy). Although its strong psychometric properties (alphas .75–.91) are based on African American and European American Protestant samples, the scale can be used outside Christian contexts. The scale also shows predictive validity beyond measures of attendance and general social support. Also relevant is the 13-item Spiritual Support subscale of Genia's SEI-R (1997), which has good psychometric properties and correlates positively with measures of worship attendance, intrinsic religiosity, fundamentalism, and religious and spiritual well-being.

Spiritual Experiences

Underwood's 16-item DSES (Underwood & Teresi, 2002) was developed to assess subjective experiences (e.g., feelings and awareness) of interactions or involvement with the transcendent in daily life. Developed through interviews with Christians, Jews, Muslims, agnostics, and atheists, the DSES attempts to extend beyond Judeo-Christian populations. To this end, the measure includes both items accessing connection to God (reflective of Western religious traditions) and connection to "all of life" or "a greater whole" (reflective of Eastern and Native American religious traditions; Underwood & Teresi, 2002, p. 24). Caution should be exercised in using the normative data provided by the authors for comparison purposes, as the original sample was primarily Christian and later findings among a Jewish population indicate that norms may differ within other traditions (Kalkstein & Tower, 2009). The measure shows sound psychometric properties, including high internal and test–retest reliability, but factor analyses indicate that two items may load on a second factor (Kalkstein & Tower, 2009; Underwood & Teresi, 2002). The DSES has been used in more than 65 studies of psychological well-being (e.g., quality of life, perceived social support, positive affect, anxiety, depression, caregiver burnout, perceived stress) and health-related outcomes (e.g., alcohol use, epilepsy, arthritis) conducted with participants ranging from adolescents to adults (Ng et al., 2009; Underwood & Teresi, 2002). As of May 2010, the scale's website (http://www.dsescale.org/translations) reported that translations are completed or are being developed in Spanish, Hebrew, Chinese (Mandarin), French, Greek, German, Korean, Portuguese (both Portugal and Brazil), and Vietnamese. The 16-item Chinese version (DSES-C; Ng et al., 2009) demonstrates psychometric properties comparable to the original measure and encompasses both a "humanized and philosophical higher power" (p. 93) for usage within Confucianism, Buddhism, and Daoism. A six-item brief version was also developed for the Fetzer Multidimensional Measure (Fetzer Institute/National Institute of Aging Working Group, 1999).

Religious Coping

An important function of religiousness or spirituality is its ability to help people cope with physical, psychological, and social stressors. One multidimensional measure of religious coping (RCOPE; Pargament, Koenig, & Perez, 2000) is theoretically grounded with 21 subscales of five items each, rated on 4-point Likert scales. What emerged after exploratory (college student sample) and confirmatory (hospital sample) factor analyses was a 17-factor solution that closely approximated the theoretical structure of the scale and accounted for 63% of the variance. The strengths of this measure include its comprehensiveness, a strong theoretical base, strong psychometric properties (including evidence of incremental validity after controlling for gender and global religious measures), and its links with a variety of adjustment indexes.

One difficulty with the full RCOPE is its length (105 items). Therefore, a brief religious coping measure (Brief RCOPE) also was developed (Pargament, Smith, Koenig, & Perez, 1998) and has become the religious coping measure of choice. Recognizing that some of the items of the different subscales of the RCOPE could be classified as positive and some as negative, a two-factor solution was forced on the more comprehensive RCOPE measure. The first factor consists of seven positive coping items (e.g., "sought God's love and care"), each representing a different subscale of the more comprehensive RCOPE measure (spiritual connection, seeking spiritual support, religious forgiveness, collaborative religious coping, benevolent religious reappraisal, religious purification, and religious focus). The second factor consists of seven negative coping items (e.g., "wondered whether God had abandoned me") representing five of the original subscales (spiritual discontent, punishing God reappraisal, interpersonal religious discontent, demonic reappraisal, and reappraisal of God's power). These items also tap into the dimension of religious struggle and strain, which is described in the section Religious Struggle and Strain. Both the positive and negative subscales showed moderate to high alphas (.69 and up) in a college student and an older adult (age 55 and up) hospital population (Pargament et al., 1998). Validity has been established through confirmatory factor analysis (Pargament et al., 1998) and its predictive capability in a number of studies (e.g., McConnell, Pargament, Ellison, & Flannelly, 2006; Sherman, Simonton, Latif, Spohn, & Tricot, 2005). Ano and Vasconcelles (2005) conducted a meta-analysis of 49 studies of religious coping and stress. Most of the studies in their meta-analysis used either the Brief RCOPE, all or some of the subscales of the RCOPE, or an independent measure consisting of items that conceptually fit with RCOPE subscales. They found that positive and negative forms of religious coping are modestly to moderately related to positive and negative psychological adjustment to stress, respectively.

Religious Struggle and Strain

Suffering is part of the human condition and is often addressed by religion, yet the empirical psychology of religion has neglected the study of suffering. The only measure developed specifically around this construct is the Views of Suffering Scale (VOSS; Hale-Smith, Park, & Edmondson, 2012). The VOSS is a 30-item scale with 10 subscales tapping religious beliefs about suffering, including beliefs about randomness, karma, unorthodox theistic views, and various Christian perspectives. Reliability for the overall measure and subscales exceeds .70, and it shows good convergent and divergent validity.

Recognizing that religion can be both personally beneficial and stressful, Exline, Yali, and Sanderson (2000; see Chapter 25 in this volume) developed a 20-item Religious Comfort and Strain (RCS) measure. In addition to a seven-item religious comfort subscale, the measure includes three religious strain subscales (Alienation from God, Fear and Guilt, and Religious Rifts) that can be averaged for a 13-item religious strain subscale. Internal consistency is adequate (alphas from .67 to .77 for the three subscales, .71 for the whole scale). As expected, the strain and comfort scales are negatively correlated. Construct validity has been supported in nonclinical and clinical samples by positive correlations between depression and the Religious Rifts and Alienation from God subscales as well as by positive correlations between suicidality and the Fear and Guilt subscale.

The recently developed nine-item Attitudes Toward God Scale (ATGS-9; Wood et al., 2010), like the RCS measure, recognizes that one's relationship with God can have positive and negative elements, with the latter involving distress, strain, and struggle. The five-item Positive Attitudes toward God factor is positively correlated with such measures of religiosity as religious participation, belief salience, and positive religious coping. The four-item Disappointment and Anger toward God factor correlates negatively with many of those same religious measures and correlates positively with both negative religious coping and maladaptive psychological variables (e.g., depression, distress, neuroticism, entitlement). Surprisingly, the two factors did not correlate significantly with each other in two of the original three samples reported and were only weakly to moderately negatively correlated (−.15) in the third sample. Both factors demonstrate high internal consistency and 2-week temporal stability. The ATGS-9 was validated across samples that were diverse in terms of ethnicity and religious preference (e.g., Christianity, Judaism, Islam, Hinduism, Buddhism, and atheism). There are indications that the factor structure may differ between a general population (assessed in the validation study) and samples consisting only of religiously committed individuals. Given the scale's novelty, brevity, psychometric properties, and demonstrated relationships with both religious and clinically relevant variables (e.g., depression, coping, neuroticism), the ATGS-9 shows promise in both psychological research and clinical practice.

Multidimensional Measures

The 38-item Brief Multidimensional Measure of Religiousness/Spirituality (BMMRS) was developed by Fetzer Institute/National Institute of Aging Working Group (1999) to assess 10 theoretically based religious and spiritual domains (Daily Spiritual Experiences, Values/Beliefs, Forgiveness, Private Religious Practices, Religious/Spiritual Coping, Religious Support, Religious/Spiritual History, Commitment, Organizational Religiousness, Religious Preference) thought to be related to mental and physical health as well as two items assessing overall ratings of oneself as a "religious" or "spiritual" person. Normative data, including percentage distributions, are available for the BMMRS because of its inclusion in the 1997–1998 General Social Survey (GSS), a random national survey. Unfortunately, the inclusion of the measure in the GSS limited the number of items included for each domain. The working group also compiled a number of longer scales for many of these religious and spiritual dimensions from which items in the BMMRS were selected.

Although several studies support the construct validity of the overall measure, there is a lack of consensus regarding factor structure, with none of the structures matching the 10 theoretically based categories. Exploratory factor analysis by Masters et al. (2009) in an undergraduate sample revealed a seven-factor structure onto which 23 items loaded, which was supported in subsequent confirmatory factor analyses. In contrast, Johnstone, Yoon, Franklin, Schopp, and Hinkebein's (2009) analyses of BMMRS data from hospital outpatient settings suggested a six-factor solution. Despite these caveats, the BMMRS has shown utility in studies exploring links between religiousness and spirituality and mental and physical health.

Another multidimensional measure of spirituality and religiousness is the 25-item Ironson–Woods Spirituality/Religiosity Index (Ironson et al., 2002). This measure consists of four subscales: Sense of Peace, Faith in God, Religious Behavior, and Compassionate View of Others, all with alphas greater than .84. The validity of the overall measure was shown in an HIV/AIDS sample by a correlation of .50 with a composite measure of three measures of religiousness. The index also correlates with self-report and physiological measures of hope, good health behaviors, and (low) distress.

The 82-item Religious Involvement Inventory (Hilty et al., 1984) taps seven dimensions of religiousness (Personal Faith, Intolerance of Ambiguity, Orthodoxy, Social Conscience, Knowledge of Religious History, Life Purpose, and Church Involvement). Participants rate agreement with statements or indicate frequency of religious practices on a four-point scale. Alphas range from .79 to .87 for all scales. Although the authors stated concerns with the seven-factor structure, the measure has been used in many studies (Sorenson & Hall, 1999).

HOW MIGHT MEASURES OF RELIGIOUSNESS AND SPIRITUALITY BE IMPROVED?

As impressive as measurement efforts in the psychology of religiousness and spirituality have been, there remains room for growth. Here we identify five areas for which measurement progress has been made but for which continued growth is still necessary.

Further Development of Theoretically Driven Measures

As noted earlier, the strides made in recent decades in the psychological study of religion and spirituality largely reflect the development of stronger theoretical bases that are capable of sustaining robust empirical research programs. Many of the most promising measures reviewed in this chapter are products of such programs. It is clear that the study of religion and spirituality should no longer be simply an "add-on" variable to some other research program. Given the importance and complexity of religiousness and spirituality, however, theoretical frameworks that provide empirical guidance remain relatively sparse. Measures developed within a sound theoretical framework likely will demonstrate greater validity than measures developed without a strong theoretic rationale. Research priority, including funding for research, should be given to those programs with strong theoretical models. Measurement quality will follow.

Further Development of Alternative Measures to Self-Reports

Problems of self-report are not unique to the study of religiousness and spirituality. Yet the validity of self-reports may be easily challenged when the topic being investigated involves personal investment, which religion and spirituality often do. In most cases, attempts to control for social desirability bias do not change the links that emerge between religiousness, spirituality, and other phenomena. Furthermore, the structures and rating scores of some measures (e.g., Piedmont's 1999 Spiritual Transcendence Scale) do not significantly differ whether using self-reports or observer ratings, suggesting that the measure itself may be less subject to personal bias than might be expected. Nevertheless, self-report bias remains a legitimate concern. One response may be to develop alternative measurement techniques. Indeed, researchers should explore all options. Yet it is doubtful that alternative measures, in and of themselves, will be able to capture the full richness and complexity of religious and spiritual experience. We can thus expect that the field will continue to rely heavily on self-report measures.

This does not imply that we should abandon efforts to develop other types of measures (Hill & Pargament, 2003). The psychology of religion is beginning to use implicit measures of religiousness or spirituality, for example. Some of these measures (e.g., Bassett et al., 2005; Ventis, Ball, & Viggiano, 2010) are an adaptation of the Implicit Association Test (IAT), first developed as an implicit measure of racial attitudes. Other measures (e.g., Cohen, Shariff, & Hill, 2008; Wenger, 2004) have used response latency as an index of attitude accessibility, perhaps an indication of the importance or centrality of religion in a person's life. The development of implicit measures is still in its earliest stages, and further research will be necessary before any judgment of their utility can be made. Other possible alternative measures include physiological indicators, such as computerized tomography and positron-emission tomography scans, observer reports, and (especially with children) picture-drawing methods. Realistically, however, given the complexity of our subject matter, we should expect such methodologies to complement and not supplant our reliance on self-reports.

Further Development of Culturally Sensitive Measures

Religion is a cultural variable (Belzen, 2010; Cohen, 2009; see Chapter 13 in this volume). Researchers must seriously consider the extent to which a given measure, and even the concept on which the measure is based, can transcend cultural boundaries—a point reiterated throughout this chapter. The issue of measure generalizability thus may be more complex and more crucial for the psychology of religion than for some other areas of psychological investigation.

Sometimes, of course, measures are designed to assess the particularities of a specific religious tradition. Such measures are necessary if research is to be sensitive to the unique cultural elements of religiousness and spirituality (Belzen, 2010; Cohen, 2009). Sometimes specific traditions will have such unique elements that they will require development of completely new measures, and these measures may not be portable to other traditions or cultures. At other times, the development of parallel measures for different traditions, such as what has been reported in this chapter on religious coping, may be a possibility.

Clearly, there are times when it is desirable to have a measure that can apply to the broadest possible population. The more global a measure is, however, the more it may overlook important characteristics of religious and spiritual experiences. At the very least, researchers are cautioned not to expect global measures of spirituality to always be most appropriate, especially when applied to those who identify strongly with a specific religion.

A common scenario is one in which researchers seek to use a measure for a broad population (e.g., all religious persons) or a population that differs from the one used for the original validation of a measure (e.g., evangelicals). This problem should be partly alleviated over time as the measure is used in further research, evaluating its level of applicability to other populations. This message is simply a reminder that researchers must use caution in selecting measures that have not yet been generalized beyond certain populations.

Further Development of Clinically Relevant Measures

Most measures discussed in this chapter were designed for research purposes, a reflection of the discipline. Although religious and spiritual experiences can be centrally important to clinical concerns, most measures that we found in the literature, whether reviewed in this chapter or not, were not designed for nor specifically tested on clinical populations. The main exception is in health research, for which some measures were developed for a specific population (e.g., Peterman's et al., 2002, FACIT-Sp with critically ill patients). Yet even in this case, measures are designed primarily for research. Their utility for clinicians is limited largely because normative data have not been established. On some of the more developed measures (e.g., religious coping; spiritual well-being), however, for which measures are well grounded in theory, normative data are being established. This is a lead well worth taking, providing an opportunity for the psychology of religion to give back to the broader discipline and to contribute to applied psychology.

Further Development of Measures in New Domains

The psychological study of religiousness and spirituality does not appear to be slowing anytime soon. New ideas will abound and measurement must keep up. Hill and Pargament (2003) reported that measures in such domains as religious and spiritual outcomes, change, or transformation were currently lagging at that time, and since then, little in terms of measurement has been conducted in these areas. For example, as pointed out in Hill and Pargament (2003), researchers might be interested in how religiousness or spirituality predict mental or physical health, but the spiritually minded person might think that such concerns are of secondary importance to their spiritual health. Some measures, such as the SWBS (Paloutzian & Ellison, 1982) or the SAI (T. W. Hall & Edwards, 1996, 2002), may provide useful avenues of assessing spiritual outcomes; however, spiritual outcomes remain a largely undeveloped research area, in part because solid measurement tools are not yet available.

CONCLUSION

Can we, in response to the fictional character Colonel Jessup, played by Jack Nicholson in the movie *A Few Good Men*, handle the truth? We contend that social scientists interested in religion and spirituality do want answers and can handle the truth about their complex and difficult subject matter; but they need a sufficient measurement literature to do so. Fortunately, the long-standing emphasis on measurement should continue to serve the psychological study of religiousness and spirituality well.

References

Ai, A. L., Peterson, C., & Huang, B. (2003). The effects of religious-spiritual coping on positive attitudes of adult Muslim refugees from Kosovo and Bosnia. *The International Journal for the Psychology of Religion, 13*, 29–47. doi:10.1207/S15327582IJPR1301_04

Allport, G. W. (1950). *The individual and his religion.* New York, NY: MacMillan.

Allport, G. W., & Ross, J. M. (1967). Personal religious orientation and prejudice. *Journal of Personality and Social Psychology, 5*, 432–443. doi:10.1037/h0021212

Altemeyer, B., & Hunsberger, B. (1992). Authoritarianism, religious fundamentalism, quest, and prejudice. *The International Journal for the Psychology of Religion, 2*, 113–133. doi:10.1207/s15327582ijpr0202_5

Altemeyer, B., & Hunsberger, B. (2004). A revised Religious Fundamentalism Scale: The short and sweet of it. *The International Journal for the Psychology of Religion, 14*, 47–54. doi:10.1207/s15327582ijpr1401_4

American Educational Research Association, American Psychological Association, & National Council on Measurement in Education. (1999). *Standards for educational and psychological testing.* Washington, DC: American Educational Research Association.

Ano, G. G., & Vasconcelles, E. B. (2005). Religious coping and psychological adjustment to stress: A meta-analysis. *Journal of Clinical Psychology, 61*, 461–480. doi:10.1002/jclp.20049

Antonovsky, A. (1987). *Unraveling the mystery of health.* San Francisco, CA: Jossey-Bass.

Bassett, R. L., Thrower, J., Barclay, J., Powers, C., Smith, A., Tindall, M., . . . Monroe, J. (2005). One effort to measure implicit attitudes toward spirituality and religion. *Journal of Psychology and Christianity, 24*, 210–218.

Batson, C. D., & Schoenrade, P. A. (1991a). Measuring religion as quest: I. Validity concerns. *Journal for the Scientific Study of Religion, 30*, 416–429. doi:10.2307/1387277

Batson, C. D., & Schoenrade, P. A. (1991b). Measuring religion as quest: II. Reliability concerns. *Journal for the Scientific Study of Religion, 30*, 430–447. doi:10.2307/1387278

Batson, C. D., Schoenrade, P., & Ventis, W. L. (1993). *Religion and the individual: A social-psychological perspective* (Rev. ed.). New York, NY: Oxford University Press.

Beck, R. (2006). God as a secure base: Attachment to God and theological exploration. *Journal of Psychology and Theology, 34*, 125–132.

Beck, R., & McDonald, A. (2004). Attachment to God: The Attachment to God Inventory, tests of working model correspondence, and an exploration of faith group differences. *Journal of Psychology and Theology, 32*, 92–103.

Belavich, T. G., & Pargament, K. I. (2002). The role of attachment in predicting spiritual coping with a loved one in surgery. *Journal of Adult Development, Spirituality and Adult Development, 9*, 13–29. doi:10.1023/A:1013873100466

Belzen, J. A. (2010). *Towards cultural psychology of religion: Principles, approaches, applications.* Dordrecht, the Netherlands: Springer. doi:10.1007/978-90-481-3491-5

Benson, P. L., Donahue, M. J., & Erickson, J. A. (1993). The Faith Maturity Scale: Conceptualization, measurement, and empirical validation. In M. L. Lynn & D. O. Moberg (Eds.), *Research in the social scientific study of religion* (Vol. 5, pp. 1–26). Greenwich, CT: JAI Press.

Benson, P., & Spilka, B. (1973). God image as a function of self-esteem and locus of control. *Journal for the Scientific Study of Religion, 12*, 297–310. doi:10.2307/1384430

Black, H. K. (1999). Poverty and prayer: Spiritual narratives of elderly African-American women. *Review of Religious Research, 40*, 359–374. doi:10.2307/3512122

Brennan, K. A., Clark, C. L., & Shaver, P. R. (1998). Self-report measurement of adult romantic attachment: An integrative overview. In J. A. Simpson & W. S. Rholes (Eds.), *Attachment theory and close relationships* (pp. 46–76). New York, NY: Guilford Press.

Brown, D. G., & Lowe, W. L. (1951). Religious beliefs and personality characteristics of college students. *Journal of Social Psychology, 33*, 103–129. doi:10.1080/00224545.1951.9921803

Bufford, R. K., Paloutzian, R. F., & Ellison, C. W. (1991). Norms for the Spiritual Well-Being Scale. *Journal of Psychology and Theology, 19*, 56–70.

Burris, C. T. (1999a). Faith Development Interview Guide. In P. C. Hill & R. W. Hood Jr. (Eds.), *Measures of religiosity* (pp. 163–168). Birmingham, AL: Religious Education Press.

Burris, C. T. (1999b). The Mysticism Scale: Research Form D (M Scale). In P. C. Hill & R. W. Hood Jr. (Eds.), *Measures of religiosity* (pp. 363–367). Birmingham, AL: Religious Education Press.

Burris, C. T., Jackson, L. M., Tarpley, W. R., & Smith, G. (1996). Religion as quest: The self-directed pursuit of meaning. *Personality and Social Psychology Bulletin, 22*, 1068–1076. doi:10.1177/01461672962210010

Caird, D. (1988). The structure of Hood's mysticism scale: A factor-analytic study. *Journal for the Scientific Study of Religion, 27*, 122–127. doi:10.2307/1387407

Chatters, L. M., Taylor, R. J., & Lincoln, K. D. (2002). Advances in the measurement of religiosity among older African Americans: Implications for health and mental health researchers. In J. H. Skinner & J. A. Teresi (Eds.), *Multicultural measurement in older populations* (pp. 199–220). New York, NY: Springer.

Cohen, A. B. (2009). Many forms of culture. *American Psychologist, 64*, 194–204. doi:10.1037/a0015308

Cohen, A. B., & Hill, P. C. (2007). Religion as culture: Religious individualism and collectivism among American Catholics, Jews, and Protestants. *Journal of Personality, 75*, 709–742. doi:10.1111/j.1467-6494.2007.00454.x

Cohen, A. B., Shariff, A. F., & Hill, P. C. (2008). The accessibility of religious beliefs. *Journal of Research in Personality, 42*, 1408–1417. doi:10.1016/j.jrp.2008.06.001

Connors, G. J., Tonigan, J. S., & Miller, W. R. (1996). A measure of religious background and behavior for use in behavior change research. *Psychology of Addictive Behaviors, 10*, 90–96. doi:10.1037/0893-164X.10.2.90

Crumbaugh, J. C. (1977). The Seeking of Noetic Goals test (SONG): A complementary scale to the Purpose in Life Test (PIL). *Journal of Clinical Psychology, 33*, 900–907. doi:10.1002/1097-4679(197707)33:3<900::AID-JCLP2270330362>3.0.CO;2-8

Crumbaugh, J. C., & Maholick, L. T. (1964). An experimental study in existentialism: The psychometric approach to Frankl's concept of noogenic neurosis. *Journal of Clinical Psychology, 20*, 200–207. doi:10.1002/1097-4679(196404)20:2<200::AID-JCLP2270200203>3.0.CO;2-U

Ellison, C. G., & Taylor, R. J. (1996). Turning to prayer: Social and situational antecedents of religious coping among African-Americans. *Review of Religious Research, 38*, 111–131. doi:10.2307/3512336

Ellison, C. W. (1983). Spiritual well-being: Conceptualization and measurement. *Journal of Psychology and Theology, 11*, 330–340.

Ellison, C. W., & Smith, J. (1991). Toward an integrative measure of health and well-being. *Journal of Psychology and Theology, 19*, 35–48.

Emavardhana, T., & Tori, C. D. (1997). Changes in self-concept, ego defense mechanisms, and religiosity following seven-day Vipassana meditation retreats. *Journal for the Scientific Study of Religion, 36*, 194–206. doi:10.2307/1387552

Exline, J. J., Yali, A. M., & Sanderson, W. C. (2000). Guilt, discord, and alienation: The role of religious strain in depression and suicidality. *Journal of Clinical Psychology, 56*, 1481–1496. doi:10.1002/1097-4679(200012)56:12<1481::AID-1>3.0.CO;2-A

Fetzer Institute/National Institute of Aging Working Group. (1999, October). *Multidimensional measurement of religiousness/spirituality for use in health research: A report of the Fetzer Institute/National Institute on Aging Working Group.* Kalamazoo, MI: The John E. Fetzer Institute.

Fiala, W. E., Bjorck, J. P., & Gorsuch, R. L. (2002). The Religious Support Scale: Construction, validation, and cross-validation. *American Journal of Community Psychology, 30*, 761–786. doi:10.1023/A:1020264718397

Foster, R. (1992). *Prayer: Finding the heart's true home.* New York, NY: HarperCollins.

Fowler, J. W. (1981). *Stages of faith: The psychology of human development and the quest for meaning.* San Francisco, CA: Harper & Row.

Fullerton, J. T., & Hunsberger, B. (1982). A unidimensional measure of Christian orthodoxy. *Journal for the Scientific Study of Religion, 21*, 317–326. doi:10.2307/1385521

Genia, V. (1997). The Spiritual Experience Index: Revision and reformulation. *Review of Religious Research, 38*, 344–361. doi:10.2307/3512195

Ghorbani, N., Watson, P. J., Ghramaleki, A. F., Morris, R. J., & Hood, R. W., Jr. (2002). Muslim-Christian Religious Orientation Scales: Distinctions, correlations, and cross-cultural analysis in Iran and the United States. *The International Journal for the Psychology of Religion, 12*, 69–91. doi:10.1207/S15327582IJPR1202_01

Ghorbani, N., Watson, P. J., & Khan, Z. H. (2007). Theoretical, empirical, and potential ideological dimensions of using Western conceptualizations to measure Muslim religious commitments. *Journal of Muslim Mental Health, 2*, 113–131. doi:10.1080/15564900701613041

Ghorbani, N., Watson, P. J., & Mirhasani, V. S. (2007). Religious commitment in Iran: Correlates and factors of quest religious orientations. *Archive for the Psychology of Religions, 29*, 245–257. doi:10.1163/008467207X188847

Gorsuch, R. L. (1968). The conceptualization of God as seen in adjective ratings. *Journal for the Scientific Study of Religion, 7*, 56–64. doi:10.2307/1385110

Gorsuch, R. L. (1984). Measurement: The boon and bane of investigating religion. *American Psychologist, 39*, 228–236. doi:10.1037/0003-066X.39.3.228

Gorsuch, R. L. (1990). Measurement in psychology of religion revisited. *Journal of Psychology and Christianity, 9*, 82–92.

Gorsuch, R. L., & McPherson, S. E. (1989). Intrinsic/extrinsic measurement: I/E-revised and single-item scales. *Journal for the Scientific Study of Religion, 28*, 348–354. doi:10.2307/1386745

Gorsuch, R. L., & Venable, D. G. (1983). Development of an "Age Universal" I-E scale. *Journal for the Scientific Study of Religion, 22*, 181–187. doi:10.2307/1385677

Granqvist, P., & Kirkpatrick, L. A. (2004). Religious conversion and perceived childhood attachment: A meta-analysis. *The International Journal for the Psychology of Religion, 14*, 223–250. doi:10.1207/s15327582ijpr1404_1

Hale-Smith, A., Park, C. L., & Edmondson, D. F. (2012). Measuring religious beliefs: Development of the Views of Suffering Scale. *Psychological Assessment.* Advance online publication. doi:10.1037/a0027399

Hall, D. E., Meador, K. G., & Koenig, H. G. (2008). Measuring religiousness in health research: Review and critique. *Journal of Religion and Health, 47*, 134–163. doi:10.1007/s10943-008-9165-2

Hall, T. W., & Edwards, K. J. (1996). Initial development and factor analysis of the Spiritual Assessment Inventory. *Journal of Psychology and Theology, 24*, 233–246.

Hall, T. W., & Edwards, K. J. (2002). The Spiritual Assessment Inventory: A theistic model and measure for assessing spiritual development. *Journal for the Scientific Study of Religion, 41*, 341–357. doi:10.1111/1468-5906.00121

Hall, T. W., Reise, S. P., & Haviland, M. G. (2007). An Item response theory analysis of the Spiritual Assessment Inventory. *The International Journal for the Psychology of Religion, 17*, 157–178. doi:10.1080/10508610701244197

Hall, T. W., Tisdale, T. C., & Brokaw, B. F. (1994). Assessment of religious dimensions in Christian clients: A review of selected instruments for research and clinical use. *Journal of Psychology and Theology, 22*, 395–421.

Hays, J. C., Meador, K. G., Branch, P. S., & George, L. K. (2001). The Spiritual History Scale in four dimensions (SHS-4): Validity and reliability. *The Gerontologist, 41*, 239–249. doi:10.1093/geront/41.2.239

Hazan, C., & Shaver, P. (1987). Romantic love conceptualized as an attachment process. *Journal of Personality and Social Psychology, 52*, 511–524. doi:10.1037/0022-3514.52.3.511

Hill, P. C. (2005). Measurement assessment and issues in the psychology of religion and spirituality. In R. F. Paloutzian & C. L. Park (Eds.), *Handbook of the psychology of religion and spirituality* (pp. 43–61). New York, NY: Guilford Press.

Hill, P. C., & Dwiwardani, C. (2010). Measurement at the interface of psychiatry and religion: Issues and existing measures. In P. J. Verhagen, H. M. van Praag, J. J. Lopez-Ibor, J. L. Cox, & D. Moussaoui (Eds.), *Psychiatry and religion: Beyond boundaries* (pp. 319–339). New York, NY: Wiley.

Hill, P. C., & Hood, R. W., Jr. (1999). *Measures of religiosity*. Birmingham, AL: Religious Education Press.

Hill, P. C., & Pargament, K. I. (2003). Advances in the conceptualization and measurement of religion and spirituality. *American Psychologist, 58*, 64–74. doi:10.1037/0003-066X.58.1.64

Hilty, D. M., Morgan, R. L., & Burns, J. E. (1984). King and Hunt revisited: Dimensions of religious involvement. *Journal for the Scientific Study of Religion, 23*, 252–266. doi:10.2307/1386040

Hoge, D. R. (1972). A validated intrinsic religious motivation scale. *Journal for the Scientific Study of Religion, 11*, 369–376. doi:10.2307/1384677

Hood, R. W., Jr. (1975). The construction and preliminary validation of a measure of reported mystical experience. *Journal for the Scientific Study of Religion, 14*, 29–41. doi:10.2307/1384454

Hood, R. W., Jr., Hill, P. C., & Spilka, B. (2009). *The psychology of religion: An empirical approach* (4th ed.). New York, NY: Guilford Press.

Hood, R. W., Jr., Hill, P. C., & Williamson, W. P. (2005). *The psychology of religious fundamentalism*. New York, NY: Guilford Press.

Hunsberger, B. (1989). A short version of the Christian Orthodoxy Scale. *Journal for the Scientific Study of Religion, 28*, 360–365. doi:10.2307/1386747

Ironson, G., Solomon, G. F., Balbin, E. G., O'Cleirigh, C. O., George, A., Kumar, M., . . . Woods, T. E. (2002). The Ironson-Woods Spirituality/ Religiousness Index is associated with long survival, health behaviors, less distress, and low cortisol in people with HIV/AIDS. *Annals of Behavioral Medicine, 24*, 34–48. doi:10.1207/S15324796ABM2401_05

Jana-Masri, A., & Priester, P. E. (2007). The development and validation of a Qur'an-based instrument to assess Islamic religiosity: The Religiosity of Islam Scale. *Journal of Muslim Mental Health, 2*, 177–188. doi:10.1080/15564900701624436

Johnstone, B., Yoon, D. P., Franklin, K. L., Schopp, L., & Hinkebein, J. (2009). Re-conceptualizing the factor structure of the Brief Multidimensional Measure of Religiousness/Spirituality. *Journal of Religion and Health, 48*, 146–163. doi:10.1007/s10943-008-9179-9

Kaldestad, E., & Stifoss-Hanssen, H. (1993). Standardizing measures of religiosity for Norwegians. *The International Journal for the Psychology of Religion, 3*, 111–124. doi:10.1207/s15327582ijpr0302_5

Kalkstein, S., & Tower, R. B. (2009). The Daily Spiritual Experiences Scale and well-being: Demographic comparisons and scale validation with older Jewish adults and a diverse Internet sample. *Journal of Religion and Health, 48*, 402–417. doi:10.1007/s10943-008-9203-0

Katz, Y. J. (1988). The relationship between intelligence and attitudes in a bilingual society: The case of White South Africa. *Journal of Social Psychology, 128*, 65–74. doi:10.1080/00224545.1988.9711685

Khan, Z. H., & Watson, P. J. (2006). Construction of the Pakistani Religious Coping Practices Scale: Correlations with religious coping, religious orientation, and reactions to stress among Muslim university students. *The International Journal for the Psychology of Religion, 16*, 101–112. doi:10.1207/s15327582ijpr1602_2

Kirkpatrick, L. A. (1989). A psychometric analysis of the Allport-Ross and Feagin measures of intrinsic-extrinsic religious orientation. In D. O. Moberg & M. L. Lynn (Eds.), *Research in the social scientific study of religion* (Vol. 1, pp. 1–31). Greenwich, CT: JAI Press.

Kirkpatrick, L. A. (1998). God as a substitute attachment figure: A longitudinal study of adult attachment style and religious change in college students. *Personality and Social Psychology Bulletin, 24*, 961–973. doi:10.1177/0146167298249004

Kirkpatrick, L. A., & Hood, R. W., Jr. (1990). Intrinsic-extrinsic religious orientation: The boon or bane of contemporary psychology of religion. *Journal for the Scientific Study of Religion, 29*, 442–462. doi:10.2307/1387311

Kirkpatrick, L. A., & Shaver, P. R. (1992). An attachment-theoretical approach to romantic love and religious belief. *Personality and Social Psychology Bulletin, 18*, 266–275. doi:10.1177/0146167292183002

Koenig, H. G. (2008). Concerns about measuring "spirituality" in research. *Journal of Nervous and Mental Disease, 196*, 349–355. doi:10.1097/NMD.0b013e31816ff796

Koenig, H., Patterson, G. R., & Meador, K. G. (1997). Religion index for psychiatric research: A 5-item measure for use in health outcome studies. *American Journal of Psychiatry, 154*, 885–886.

Krause, N. (2008). The social foundations of religious meaning in life. *Research on Aging, 30*, 395–427. doi:10.1177/0164027508316619

Krause, N. (2009). Meaning in life and mortality. *The Journals of Gerontology, Series B: Social Sciences, 64*, 517–527. doi:10.1093/geronb/gbp047

Ladd, K. L., & Spilka, B. (1999). Loving and Controlling God Scales. In P. C. Hill & R. W. Hood Jr. (Eds.), *Measures of religiosity* (pp. 405–407). Birmingham, AL: Religious Education Press.

Ladd, K. L., & Spilka, B. (2002). Inward, outward, and upward: Cognitive aspects of prayer. *Journal for the Scientific Study of Religion, 41*, 475–484. doi:10.1111/1468-5906.00131

Ladd, K. L., & Spilka, B. (2006). Inward, outward, upward prayer: Scale reliability and validation. *Journal for the Scientific Study of Religion, 45*, 233–251. doi:10.1111/j.1468-5906.2006.00303.x

Lawrence, R. T. (1997). Measuring the image of God: The God Image Inventory and the God Image Scales. *Journal of Psychology and Theology, 25*, 214–226.

Leak, G. K. (2002). Exploratory factor analysis of the Religious Maturity Scale. *Social Behavior and Personality, 30*, 533–538. doi:10.2224/sbp.2002.30.6.533

Leak, G. K., Loucks, A. A., & Bowlin, P. (1999). Development and initial validation of an objective measure of faith development. *The International Journal for the Psychology of Religion, 9*, 105–124. doi:10.1207/s15327582ijpr0902_2

Ledbetter, M. F., Smith, L. A., Fischer, J. D., & Vosler-Hunter, W. L. (1991). An evaluation of the construct validity of the Spiritual Well-Being Scale: A confirmatory factor analytic approach. *Journal of Psychology and Theology, 19*, 94–102.

Ledbetter, M. F., Smith, L. A., Vosler-Hunter, W. L., & Fischer, J. D. (1991). An evaluation of the research and clinical usefulness of the Spiritual Well-Being Scale. *Journal of Psychology and Theology, 19*, 49–55.

Masters, K. S., Carey, K. B., Maisto, S. A., Caldwell, P. E., Wolfe, T. V., Hackney, H. L., . . . Himawan, L. (2009). Psychometric examination of the Brief Multidimensional Measure of Religiousness/Spirituality among college students. *The International Journal for the Psychology of Religion, 19*, 106–120. doi:10.1080/10508610802711194

McConnell, K. M., Pargament, K. I., Ellison, C. G., & Flannelly, K. J. (2006). Examining the links between spiritual struggles and symptoms of psychopathology in a national sample. *Journal of Clinical Psychology, 62*, 1469–1484. doi:10.1002/jclp.20325

Ng, S.-M., Fong, T. C. T., Tsui, E. Y. L., Au-Yeung, F. S. W., & Law, S. K. W. (2009). Validation of the Chinese version of Underwood's Daily Spiritual Experience Scale—Transcending cultural boundaries? *International Journal of Behavioral Medicine, 16*, 91–97. doi:10.1007/s12529-009-9045-5

Paloutzian, R. F., & Ellison, C. W. (1982). Loneliness, spiritual well-being, and quality of life. In L. A. Peplau & D. Perlman (Eds.), *Loneliness: A sourcebook of current theory, research, and therapy* (pp. 224–237). New York, NY: Wiley Interscience.

Paloutzian, R. F., & Ellison, C. W. (1991). *Manual for the Spiritual Well-Being Scale.* Nyack, NY: Life Advance.

Paloutzian, R. F., & Park, C. L. (2005). Integrative themes in the current science of the psychology of religion. In R. F. Paloutzian & C. L. Park (Eds.), *Handbook of the psychology of religion and spirituality* (pp. 3–20). New York, NY: Guilford Press.

Pargament, K. I. (1997). *The psychology of religion and coping.* New York, NY: Guilford Press.

Pargament, K. I., Koenig, H. G., & Perez, L. M. (2000). The many methods of religious coping: Development and initial validation of the RCOPE. *Journal of Clinical Psychology, 56*, 519–543. doi:10.1002/(SICI)1097-4679(200004)56:4<519::AID-JCLP6>3.0.CO;2-1

Pargament, K. I., Silverman, W., Johnson, S., Echemendia, R., & Snyder, S. (1983). The psychosocial climate of religious congregations. *American Journal of Community Psychology, 11*, 351–381. doi:10.1007/BF00894054

Pargament, K. I., Smith, B. W., Koenig, H. G., & Perez, L. (1998). Patterns of positive and negative religious coping with major life stressors. *Journal for the Scientific Study of Religion, 37*, 710–724. doi:10.2307/1388152

Park, C. L. (2005). Religion as a meaning-making framework in coping with life stress. *Journal of Social Issues, 61*, 707–729. doi:10.1111/j.1540-4560.2005.00428.x

Peterman, A. H., Fitchett, G., Brady, M. J., Hernandez, L., & Cella, D. (2002). Measuring spiritual well-being in people with cancer: The Functional Assessment of Chronic Illness-Spiritual Well-Being Scale (FACIT-Sp). *Annals of Behavioral Medicine, 24*, 49–58. doi:10.1207/S15324796ABM2401_06

Piedmont, R. L. (1999). Does spirituality represent the sixth factor of personality? Spiritual transcendence and the five-factor model. *Journal of Personality, 67*, 985–1013. doi:10.1111/1467-6494.00080

Piedmont, R. L. (2007). Cross-cultural generalizability of the Spiritual Transcendence Scale to the Philippines: Spirituality as a human universal. *Mental Health, Religion, and Culture, 10*, 89–107. doi:10.1080/13694670500275494

Piedmont, R. L., & Leach, M. M. (2002). Cross-cultural generalizability of the Spiritual Transcendence Scale in India: Spirituality as a universal aspect of human experience. *American Behavioral Scientist, 45*, 1888–1901. doi:10.1177/0002764202045012011

Plante, T. G., & Boccaccini, M. (1997). Reliability and validity of the Santa Clara Strength of Religious Faith Questionnaire. *Pastoral Psychology, 45*, 429–437. doi:10.1007/BF02310643

Plante, T. G., Vallaeys, C. L., Sherman, A. C., & Wallston, K. A. (2002). The development of a brief version of the Santa Clara Strength of Religious Faith Questionnaire. *Pastoral Psychology, 50*, 359–368. doi:10.1023/A:1014413720710

Raiya, H. A., Pargament, K. I., Stein, C., & Mahoney, A. (2007). Lessons learned and challenges faced in developing the psychological measure of Islamic religiousness. *Journal of Muslim Mental Health, 2*, 133–154. doi:10.1080/15564900701613058

Reinert, D. F., & Bloomingdale, J. R. (2000). Spiritual experience, religious orientation, and self-reported behavior. *The International Journal for the Psychology of Religion, 10*, 173–180. doi:10.1207/S15327582IJPR1003_03

Reker, G. T. (1992). *The Life Attitude Profile–Revised (NAP-R)*. Peterborough, Ontario, Canada: Student Psychologists Press.

Rizzuto, A. (1979). *The birth of the living God: A psychoanalytic study*. Chicago, IL: University of Chicago Press.

Rosmarin, D. H., Pargament, K. I., Krumrei, E. J., & Flannelly, K. J. (2009). Religious coping among Jews: Development and initial validation of the JCOPE. *Journal of Clinical Psychology, 65*, 670–683. doi:10.1002/jclp.20574

Rowatt, W. C., & Kirkpatrick, L. A. (2002). Two dimensions of attachment to God and their relation to affect, religiosity, and personality constructs. *Journal for the Scientific Study of Religion, 41*, 637–651. doi:10.1111/1468-5906.00143

Sherman, A. C., Simonton, S., Latif, U., Spohn, R., & Tricot, G. (2005). Religious struggle and religious comfort in response to illness: Health outcomes among stem cell transplant patients. *Journal of Behavioral Medicine, 28*, 359–367. doi:10.1007/s10865-005-9006-7

Silverman, W. H., Pargament, K. I., Johnson, S. M., Echemendia, R. J., & Snyder, S. (1983). Measuring member satisfaction with the church. *Journal of Applied Psychology, 68*, 664–677. doi:10.1037/0021-9010.68.4.664

Sorenson, R. L., & Hall, T. W. (1999). Religious Involvement Inventory. In P. C. Hill & R. W. Hood Jr. (Eds.), *Measures of religiosity* (pp. 326–330). Birmingham, AL: Religious Education Press.

Stace, W. T. (1960). *Mysticism and philosophy*. Philadelphia, PA: Lippincott.

Stellway, R. I. (1973). The correspondence between religious orientation and sociopolitical liberalism and conservatism. *Sociological Quarterly, 14*, 430–439. doi:10.1111/j.1533-8525.1973.tb00871.x

Tapanya, S., Nicki, R., & Jarusawad, O. (1997). Worry and intrinsic/extrinsic religious orientation among Buddhist (Thai) and Christian (Canadian) elderly persons. *International Journal of Aging and Human Development, 44*, 73–83. doi:10.2190/ENQG-HNV4-5G0D-CQ88

Tarakeshwar, N., Pargament, K. I., & Mahoney, A. (2003a). Initial development of a measure of religious coping among Hindus. *Journal of Community Psychology, 31*, 607–628. doi:10.1002/jcop.10071

Tarakeshwar, N., Pargament, K. I., & Mahoney, A. (2003b). Measures of Hindu pathways: Development and preliminary evidence of reliability and validity. *Cultural Diversity and Ethnic Minority Psychology, 9*, 316–332. doi:10.1037/1099-9809.9.4.316

Thurstone, L. L., & Chave, E. J. (1929). *The measurement of attitude: A psychophysical method and some experiments with a scale for measuring attitude toward the church*. Chicago, IL: University of Chicago Press. doi:10.1037/11574-000

Tsang, J., & McCullough, M. E. (2003). Measuring religious constructs: A hierarchical approach to construct organization and scale selection. In S. J. Lopez & C. R. Snyder (Eds.), *Positive psychological assessment: A handbook of models and measures* (pp. 345–360). Washington, DC: American Psychological Association. doi:10.1037/10612-022

Underwood, L. G., & Teresi, J. A. (2002). The Daily Spiritual Experience Scale: Development, theoretical description, reliability, exploratory factor analysis, and preliminary construct validity using health-related data. *Annals of Behavioral Medicine, 24*, 22–33. doi:10.1207/S15324796ABM2401_04

Ventis, W. L., Ball, C. T., & Viggiano, C. (2010). A Christian Humanist Implicit Association Test: Validity and test–retest reliability. *Psychology of Religion and Spirituality, 2*, 181–189. doi:10.1037/a0018456

Wenger, J. L. (2004). The automatic activation of religious concepts: Implications for religious orientations. *The International Journal for the Psychology of Religion, 14*, 109–123. doi:10.1207/s15327582ijpr1402_3

Williamson, W. P., Hood, R. W., Jr., Ahmad, A., Sadiq, M., & Hill, P. C. (2010). The Intratextual Fundamentalism Scale: Cross-cultural application, validity evidence, and relationship with religious orientation and the Big Five Factor markers. *Mental Health, Religion, and Culture, 13*, 721–747.

Wood, B. T., Worthington, E. L., Jr., Exline, J. J., Yali, A. M., Aten, J. D., & McMinn, M. R. (2010). Development, refinement, and psychometric properties of the Attitudes Toward God Scale (ATGS-9). *Psychology of Religion and Spirituality, 2*, 148–167. doi:10.1037/a0018753

Worthington, E. L., Jr., Wade, N. G., Hight, T. L., Ripley, J. S., McCullough, M. E., Berry, J. W., . . . O'Connor, L. (2003). The Religious Commitment Inventory—10: Development, refinement, and validation of a brief scale for research and counseling. *Journal of Counseling Psychology, 50*, 84–96. doi:10.1037/0022-0167.50.1.84

Wulff, D. M. (1999a). Attitude Toward the Church Scale. In P. C. Hill & R. W. Hood Jr. (Eds.), *Measures of religiosity* (pp. 467–471). Birmingham, AL: Religious Education Press.

Wulff, D. M. (1999b). Humanistic Morality/Liberal Belief Scale. In P. C. Hill & R. W. Hood Jr. (Eds.), *Measures of religiosity* (pp. 19–22). Birmingham, AL: Religious Education Press.

Wuthnow, R. (1998). *After heaven: Spirituality in America since the 1950s*. Berkeley: University of California Press.

CHAPTER 4

METHODOLOGICAL DIVERSITY IN THE PSYCHOLOGY OF RELIGION AND SPIRITUALITY

Ralph W. Hood Jr.

The concern with methodology often characterizes disciplines seeking some recognition within a larger community. It is not clear that disciplines advance through the use of methods as blueprints for discovery. We need but cite the title of the debate between Imre Lakatos and Paul Feyerabend, *For and Against Method* (1999), to recognize that there is no methodological commitment that cannot be made problematic. Any method is at least an implicit epistemology, and any epistemology assumes at least an implicit ontology. Simply put, how we seek to know assumes what we believe to be real.

Because this chapter focuses on methodology, it reflects the guidance of this handbook's editorial team and aims to contribute to an integrative paradigm for the study of the psychology of religion and spirituality. There is no commitment to a single methodology or a single ontological perspective. Thus, one cannot rest comfortably with any declaration presented as if it defined a discipline or required a priori ontological assumptions. For example, commitments to such restrictions as the methodical exclusion of the transcendent (Flournoy, 1903) can carry no absolute authority as a necessary methodological principle. The discussion will assume methodological pluralism (Roth, 1987) in the belief that religion and spirituality are best illuminated by a variety of methods, each of which contributes something to our understanding. More controversially, the chapter will also assume the stance of methodological agnosticism in which transcendent realities remain as possible contributors to a full understanding of at least religious and spiritual experiences (Hood, 2012; Newberg & Newberg, 2010; Popora, 2006). The discussion of methodology in most contemporary psychology textbooks lacks a sophisticated philosophical treatment of various assumptions that are involved in a commitment to any given methodology (Belzen & Hood, 2006; Miles, 2007). This can be illustrated by the fact that the contemporary psychology of religion and spirituality is repeating the scenario that characterized the emergence of the discipline. To note this will frame the nature of how the chapter will explore the methodological options available within an integrative paradigm.

METHODOLOGICAL APPROACHES AND THEIR RELEVANCE TO THE INTEGRATIVE PARADIGM

A bit of history is relevant to help frame our methodological analysis of various options for the psychology of religion and spirituality. The editors of this handbook are committed to clarifying a distinction between religion and spirituality that will facilitate a shared perspective for authors of this handbook and for researchers. As we shall see, methodologically this distinction is crucial. James's (1902/1985) definition of religion for his Gifford lectures is indicative of the methodological confusion that can arise from treating *religion* and *spirituality* as if they were identical terms. James defined religion as "*the feelings, acts, and experiences of individual men, in their solitude, so far as they apprehend themselves to stand in relation to whatever they may*

DOI: 10.1037/14045-004
APA Handbook of Psychology, Religion, and Spirituality: Vol. 1. Context, Theory, and Research, K. I. Pargament (Editor-in-Chief)
Copyright © 2013 by the American Psychological Association. All rights reserved.

consider the divine" (James, 1902/1985, p. 34). This operational move allowed him to ignore the specific religious framing of beliefs about experience. Thus, as Gorsuch and Miller (1999) have noted, if James were writing his classic text in the 21st century, it would be the varieties of spiritual experience—not religious experience. Methodologically, the issue is complex, especially in light of the distinction between religion and spirituality in terms of self-identification. Many persons self-identified as spiritual are not religious. Most persons self-identified as religious also self-identify as spiritual, however (Hood, 2003; Zinnbauer & Pargament, 2005). Thus, many individuals have specific beliefs that may shape not only how they interpret experience but also facilitate the experience itself. Many individuals who are self-identified as spiritual but not religious, however, may have experiences of a similar or identical nature to those religiously framed by others. A methodology that simply equates experience with its interpretation cannot identify commonalities between similar experiences differently interpreted. Even more important, if one commits to a methodological atheism, it is blind to ontological possibilities such as the role of transcendence in producing experience (Porpora, 2006; Shafranske, 2010).

The methodological issue was integral to the concerns and disputes of the founding psychologists. For example, Coon (1992) has documented the role methodology played in the emergence of the American Psychological Association (APA). The earliest psychologists saw themselves as scientists in the natural science tradition and modeled their methods after classical Newtonian physics. They fought against the popular cultural view that psychology was heavily involved in the study of spirituality, where the linkage in popular culture was between *psychic* and *spiritualism*. Funds often were accepted by benefactors seeking a sympathetic study of spiritualism by psychologists such as G. Stanley Hall, who used the funds to expose spiritualism as fraud, deception, or error. A sister association to the APA was the American equivalent of the Society for Psychical Research (SPR), and many psychologists were members of both associations. Unlike APA, SPR was not a priori committed to a natural reductive position, allowing for the possible ontological reality of the phenomena studied and seeking methodologies that were compatible with this possibility. William James remained a member of both associations. Most psychologists, however, abandoned SPR for the epistemological and ontological assumptions implicit in the emerging discipline, as psychology modeled itself after the natural sciences. James was the exception, and his openness to a range of ontological options for psychology represents the stance of methodological pluralism that will be adopted here (Hood, 2008).

James's other undisputed classic text in psychology preceded the *Varieties of Religious Experience* (1902/1985) by more than 20 years. His *Principles of Psychology* (James, 1890/1981) adopted the assumptions of natural science and helped create modern psychology as a natural science. We have noted, however, that James's *Varieties* can best be read as advancing beyond the methodological limits of the *Principles. Varieties* adopted an empirical openness to human experience, suggesting that there is more to reality than the natural science assumptions adopted by psychology following the *Principles* would allow (Hood, 2008). In the abridgment to the *Principles*, James (affectionately called "Jimmy" by his students) appealed to the science of physics and noted that psychology lacked its Galileo but that he [she] would surely come:

> Meanwhile the best way in which we can facilitate their advent is to understand how great is the darkness in which we grope, and never to forget that *the natural science assumptions with which we started are provisional and reversible things* [emphasis added]. (James, 1892, p. 468)

The abandonment of a narrowly conceived natural science assumption allowed for new methodologies and explorations in the *Varieties* and for James's life-long concern with spiritualism. Although most other psychologists abandoned SPR, James remained, refusing to yield to what Coons (1992) has identified as a field that has yet to live down the claim that its methods remain "mired in a metaphysical morass" (p. 143). To the extent that we accept this as a current and not simply a historical description of our discipline, we need not commit to a premature closure on any epistemological or ontological front. Instead, in the spirit of the integrative paradigm, this chapter will explore the rich range of methodological options available to the psychology of religion and spirituality, whether within the limits of natural science or beyond (Miller, 2010; Shafranske, 2010). The metaphysical options are less a morass than a kaleidoscope of options, which in terms of methodological agnosticism remain best conceived as human responses to the transcendent (Hick, 1989; Hood, 2010, 2012; Porpora, 2006).

FOUR METHODOLOGICAL OPTIONS FOR THE PSYCHOLOGY OF RELIGION

A question the integrative paradigm for psychology and spirituality must face is the issue of *what* is to be integrated. The perpetual issue for psychology has been to what extent, if any, it can include religious or spiritual constructs that explicitly involve transcendence. In what remains a useful discussion (Dittes, 1969) in the only social psychology handbook to have a chapter on religion, Dittes provided four possible options. Each has methodological implications, two that maintain the possibility of including transcendence and two that necessarily exclude transcendence. The issue is relevant insofar as some have argued that for the psychology of religion to gain respectability, it must court mainstream psychological methods (Batson, 1977, 1979). In contrast, others have argued that mainstream psychology can be enhanced by adapting methods and topics unique to the psychology of religion (Hood, 2010; James, 1892).

Two of Dittes's (1969) options support methods that allow the psychology of religion to integrate with mainstream psychology. Dittes's first option is the claim that the only variables operating in religion are the same variables that operate in mainstream psychology. Therefore, the psychology of religion need have no unique methodologies because its subject matter is not unique. The second option is that although the variables operating in religion are not unique, they may be more salient in religious contexts; thus, their effect is greater within rather than outside of religion. They remain purely psychological variables, however. By definition, these two options adopt the principle of the exclusion of the transcendent.

Dittes's (1969) second two options allow for the possibility of the inclusion of the transcendent, especially in the study of spiritual experience. The least controversial position is that psychological variables uniquely interact in religious contexts,
and thus the psychology of religion must acknowledge religion as a cultural phenomenon and study psychological processes that interact with religion (Belzen, 2010; Hood, 2012). The final option is that there are unique variables operating in religion that either do not operate in or are ignored by mainstream psychologists. This can include acknowledging the transcendent as an additional causal factor in spiritual experience (Hood, 2012; Porpora, 2006). Obviously, Dittes's second set of options is most compatible with a nonreductive integrative paradigm for the psychology of religion and spirituality that seeks to integrate theological and psychological constructs in meaningful research designs. It is compatible with the claim that at least some forms of science and some forms of spiritual experience are epistemologically similar (James, 1902/1985; Miles, 2007; Walach, Kohls, von Stillfried, Hinterberger, & Schmidt, 2009).

Given Dittes's (1969) four options, we can integrate our discussion of methodology in terms of designs that can be identified with the various options discussed thus far. Assuming that we remain open to methodological (epistemological) and ontological plurality, we can begin with a discussion of what for many psychologists is a privileged methodology, the experiment, and how it actually can hamper as well as foster the integrative paradigm.

EXPERIMENTAL METHODS AND THE QUESTION OF INTEGRATION

My commitment to an integrative paradigm occurs in the shadow of the failure of past efforts. Perhaps most instructive is U.S. social psychology, which began as an explicit integration of two sister disciplines, sociology and psychology. The integration was more conceptual than actual. In one of the most widely adopted social psychology textbooks of the 1960s, a team including a psychologist (Paul F. Secord) and a sociologist (Carl W. Backman) was instrumental in creating an interdisciplinary social psychology, noting that "social psychology can no longer be adequately surveyed by a person trained in only one of its parent disciplines" (Secord & Backman, 1964, p. vii). Because psychologists who identified themselves as social psychologists favored the experimental method, however, this quickly precluded any true integration. Stryker (1977) has identified two social psychologies: psychological social psychology (PSP), which emphasizes experimental methods with concomitant quantitative evaluation of results, and sociological social psychology (SSP), which emphasizes qualitative methods, such as symbolic interactionism and ethnomethodology. House (1977) identified a third SSP that is quantitative but focused on data derived from survey studies rather than experimentation. If historical studies are also acknowledged (Gergen, 1992), then we have four social psychologies, each linked to a most typical methodology. Even within this single area, however, the literatures of one social psychology seldom reference the other. Experimental research came to define empirical research for PSP in a curious restriction of the term (Belzen & Hood, 2006). As SSP became increasingly critical of experimental methods, the percentage of experimental studies in the flagship journal for PSP, the *Journal of Personality and Social Psychology*, continued to increase (Moghadam, Taylor, & Wright, 1993, p. 26). In the decade before Gorsuch's (1984) identification of a measurement paradigm that dominated the psychology of religion, Capps, Ransohoff, and Rambo (1976) noted that only 5% of the 2,800 articles in the psychology of religion were empirical studies, and at least 90% of these were correlational. Dittes (1969) noted the same dominance of correlational studies in empirical research in the psychology of religion. In the 21st century, the same plea for experimental research abounds among psychologist of religion committed to Dittes's more reductive options and opposed to the integration of the transcendent into research. The dominance of a singular ideal methodology, the laboratory experiment, sets a limit to the possibilities of integration and to the development of a nonreductive psychology of religion (Belzen & Hood, 2006). In reviewing the history of social psychology, Allport (1968) noted that social psychology had become a subdiscipline of general psychology, and he warned of the limits of reliance on experimental methodologies. He identified the obvious *disadvantage* that one can seldom generalize beyond the laboratory setting. In Allport's (1968) words, "Even if the experiment is successfully repeated there is no proof that the discovery has wider validity. It is for this reason that some current investigations seem to end up in elegantly polished triviality—snippets of empiricism, but nothing more" (p. 68). Although experimental methods are useful in answering some psychological questions, not all psychological questions can be answered by experimental methods. To restrict available options in terms of experimental control of extraneous variables may in fact mask processes operating in real-world contexts. In this sense, experimental methods must be sensitive to both external validity and to subtle forms of reductionism that experimental methods can entail (Belzen & Hood, 2006).

EXPERIMENTAL METHODS

Contemporary methodologists have worried less about generalization (external) and instead have defended the focus on internal validity as the major criterion by which an experiment is to be judged. Aronson, Wilson, and Brewer (1998, pp. 118–124) identified four steps to the true experiment that ensure its internal validity: (a) setting the stage for the experiment, (b) constructing an independent variable, (c) measuring the dependent variable, and (d) planning the postexperimental follow-up. Because many experiments utilize deception, included in the postexperimental follow-up are items to ascertain whether participants accepted the "cover story" of the experiment and to debrief them if necessary. Deception, although guided by APA ethical codes and university institutional review boards, nevertheless raises serious ethical issues (Kelman, 1967, 1968). It is by no means unproblematic that much of modern social psychology simply assumes deception is a methodological necessity despite the availability of long-recognized alternatives, such as role-playing (Mixon, 1971, 1972).

Experimental psychologists used to speak of internal and external validity; however, with the sense that laboratory phenomena require controls and settings unavailable in a nonlaboratory environment, external validity waned as a concern. Internal validity became (and now is) regarded as the "sine qua non of good experimental research" (Aronson et al., 1998, p. 129). Whatever reality exists in laboratory settings, it is specific to the situation or context. Extrapolating from Belzen and Hood (2006), this chapter refers to laboratory studies as focusing on *contextual realism*. This term subsumes such terms as *mundane realism*, the extent to which the experimental task is similar to one that occurs in everyday life; *experimental realism*, the extent to which participants take the experiment seriously; and *psychological realism*, the extent to which the processes that occur in the experimental situation are assumed to be similar to those that occur in everyday life (Aronson & Carlsmith, 1968; Aronson, Wilson, & Akert, 1994).

Given this justification for experimental methods, we can document their increasing use, primarily in the psychological study of spirituality. The focus on psychological realism necessarily places an emphasis on individual psychological process assumed to be involved in spirituality and religion. Two major areas of experimental research are the study of entheogens, formally commonly identified as psychedelics, a group of drugs noted for their ability to produce altered states of consciousness (see also Chapter 21, this volume), and the rapidly increasing studies in the cognitive psychology of spiritual experience (see also Chapter 12, this volume).

Experimental Research Employing Entheogens

One of the most widely cited experimental studies in the psychology of religion is the doctoral dissertation by Pahnke published in 1966. Twenty graduate students at Andover-Newton Theological Seminary met to hear a Good Friday service after they had been given either psilocybin (a known entheogen) or a placebo control (nicotinic acid). Participants met in groups of four, with two experimental and two controls all matched for compatibility. Each group had two leaders, one who had been given psilocybin. Immediately after the service and 6 months later, the participants were assessed on a questionnaire that included all of Stace's common core criteria of mysticism. Results were impressive in that the experimental participants scored high on all of Stace's common core criteria, whereas the controls did not. It was readily concluded that with appropriate set and setting, psilocybin did facilitate the report of mystical experiences. Smith (2000, pp. 99–105) has revealed an unfortunate fact: Pahnke failed to report that one experimental subject had a psychological disruptive experience that had to be handled by administration of thorazine.

Despite serious critiques of the Good Friday study (Doblin, 1991; Nichols & Chemel, 2006, pp. 10–11), it has until recently been the most significant experimental study attempting to facilitate mystical experience in a religious setting. Now the benchmark study in the tradition of the Good Friday experiment is the study by Griffiths, Richards, McCann, and Jesse (2006). They replicated Pahnke's (1966) original experiment with individual rather than group sessions, using a more rigorous experimental control and a more appropriate placebo (methylphenidate hydrochloride). The double-blind study was effective at two levels: First, the double blind was not broken in a sophisticated between-group crossover design that involved two or three 8-hour drug sessions conducted at 2-month intervals. Of the 30 adult volunteers, half received the entheogen first, followed by the placebo control; the other half received the placebo control first, followed by the entheogen. Six additional volunteers received the placebo in the first two sessions and unblinded psilocybin in the third session. This was done to obscure the study design and protect the double blind. Unlike the Good Friday experiment, the double blind in this John Hopkins study was successful (Griffiths et al., 2006, p. 274). Although the Good Friday participants took psilocybin in a specifically religious setting, volunteers in the John Hopkins study had all sessions in an aesthetically pleasant living-room-like setting. Although the volunteers had spiritual interests, the setting itself did not contain religious artifacts or cues. An experienced male guide who had extensive experience with entheogens monitored all sessions. Unlike the Good Friday experiment, however, neither the entheogenic-experienced male guide nor the companion female guide took psilocybin while serving as guides. Second, numerous measures and observations were involved in this study, including Pahnke's original questionnaire and Hood's Mysticism Scale (M Scale), an operationalized measure of Stace's (1960) common core criteria (Hood, 1975).

The major results of the study indicated that 7 hours after drug ingestion, participants in the experimental group had significantly higher scores on the modified Pahnke (1966) questionnaire than those of the methylphenidate controls. Likewise, 2 months after the experiment, psilocybin participants had higher scores on the M Scale than the methylphenidate controls. Scores on the M Scale *after* psilocybin predicted the spiritual significance of the experience ($r = .77$) in a 12- to 14-month follow-up (Griffiths, Richards, Johnson, McCann, & Jesse, 2008). The majority of psilocybin participants rated their experience in the study as one of the five most spiritually significant in their lives at follow-up appointments several months later.

The experimental study of entheogen-facilitated spiritual experiences is significant for an integrative paradigm in several ways. First, it shows consistent results using standard measures and demonstrates that spiritual experiences can be facilitated under specific conditions and within specific settings. Second, the use of a chemical is significant precisely to the extent that participants do not attribute the experience to the drug. The drug facilitates a sense of ontological wonder that is congruent with identical experiences that occur spontaneously or with other religiously sanctioned practices such as fasting, prayer, or mediation. In this sense, the implications for the inclusion of the transcendent in the understanding of experience are crucial. Third, follow-up measures suggest that individual spiritual experiences have meaning and value on the basis of how such experiences are culturally embedded and accepted. This can be explored only in longitudinal studies of individual experience over time within specific cultures (see Chapter 16 in this volume).

Extending the Implications of Experimental Research

Perhaps no more intriguing possibility for integration exists than the current interest in the return to a classic problem in the social scientific study of religion, the origin of religion. Indeed, many early psychologists sought to legitimate psychology as a science by explaining the psychological origins of religion. Sociologists and anthropologists did the same (Glock & Hammond, 1973).

Psychologists are once again continuing efforts to explain the origin of religion (Baumeister, Bauer, & Lloyd, 2010). There is much contemporary interest among both evolutionary psychology and the emerging discipline of cognitive science in the origins of religion (see Chapters 7 and 12 in this volume). Both have argued that persons have evolved cognitive mechanisms to distinguish animate from merely material objects. In ambiguous situations, it is safest (has survival value) to assume an object is animate until further information disconfirms it. Thus, as Guthrie (1993, 1996) noted, the tendency to anthropomorphism is part of our evolutionary make-up and is the process by which nonexistent spiritual beings are created. In this view, spiritual beings have no independent ontological status. Others such as Boyer (1994, 2001) have argued that counterintuitiveness characterizes imagined spiritual beings. There are a limited number of "supernatural templates" (Boyer, 2001, pp. 77–78) that produce the imaginary beings assumed by some to be given unwarranted ontological validity by religions. Thus, using experimental methods, the claim is to identify the "naturalness of religious ideas" in terms of an overarching appeal to evolutionary theory (Boyer, 1994).

Closely related to evolutionary psychology's concern with the origin of religious ideas are acheopsychopharmacological researchers, who argue that the origin of religion is in altered states of consciousness facilitated (unwittingly or not) by the use of naturally occurring entheogens (Kramrisch, Otto, Ruck, & Wasson, 1986). Both James (1902/1985) and LaBarre (1972) located the origins of religion in individual spiritual experiences. This is perhaps the closest realm in which experimental methods have true religious importance, insofar as spiritual experiences can be facilitated under a wide variety of experimental conditions.

Although many of the researchers influenced by evolutionary theory clearly offer reductive explanations of religion, many do so by assuming that the identification of cognitive processes involved in erroneous attributions of intentionality to inanimate objects can be generalized to all or most religious ideas. This is unwarranted, because intentionality may be an essential aspect of both persons and gods insofar as they are individuals who act intentionally and not simply objects that are moved by causal forces (Strawson, 1959). Furthermore, the assumed naturalness of anthropomorphic tendencies to erroneous attributions must be conceptually balanced by studies that show that even children recognize that God is unique and must be understood in non-anthromorphic terms (Barrett & Richard, 2003). Likewise, Heller (1986) has shown that even Hindu children attribute both personal and impersonal characteristics to God in various complex ways that defy a simple reductionism (see also Chapter 27 in this volume). Hence, it might be a preparedness to accept mature religious ideas in fact is masked by a simple assumption of the naturalness of religious ideas (Barrett & Richard, 2003). The integration of experimental psychology of religion thus works at two levels. The study of individual spirituality, capable of experimental investigation (as well as other methods), is integrated with other approaches that focus on religion, for which experimental investigation may be of limited relevance (Belzen, 2010; Belzen & Hood, 2006).

QUASI-EXPERIMENTAL METHODS

Whether true experimental designs are possible in the psychology of religion remains controversial. Random assignment is possible but only by continually redefining the relevant population as one from which samples are actually drawn. True randomness is seldom possible when consideration is given to all who are excluded from any sampling procedure, including people who simple refuse to be studied or participate in experiments or treatments. Likewise, the manipulation of independent variables seldom can include religion or spirituality, in part because of ethical issues. One cannot assign individuals to groups in which some are to become religious and others not. To cite a clinical example, however, persons can be randomly assigned to different types of religious and spiritual interventions but only among those seeking treatment and willing to be randomly assigned to groups. These issues are not unique to the psychology of religion. In his presidential address to the APA, Campbell (1975) noted that in some areas we are "unable to experiment" (p. 1193). If one is precluded from random assignment of participants to groups, or the ability to manipulate independent variables, however, one can do quasi-experimental studies (Campbell & Stanley, 1963; Deconchy, 1985).

Three examples from psychology of religion research can illustrate the usefulness of quasi-experimental designs. The first is from a field study in which I capitalized on Rosegrant's (1976) finding that mystical experiences were associated with stress experiences in a solitary nature setting. I reasoned that it was unlikely that stress per se should elicit mystical experience. Rather, I hypothesized that the incongruity between anticipatory stress and setting stress would be a likely trigger of mysticism. In a study to test this hypothesis specifically in a nature setting (Hood, 1977), I measured anticipated stress before individuals participated in various experiences in nature over a full week period. Experiences varied in stressfulness, such as canoeing a quiet stretch of river, whitewater rafting in dangerous waters, quiet nature hikes, and a solo experience overnight, alone, without a tent. Students assessed the perceived stressfulness of each activity before participating in it and the actual stress experienced just after completing the activity. As predicted, events anticipated as stressful but actually experienced as nonstressful resulted in higher mysticism scores than those for which anticipated stress and experienced stress were congruent. The full scope of the incongruity hypothesis could not be tested, however, because no student anticipated highly stressful events such as white-water rafting to be nonstressful.

In a second study, I tested the full scope of the incongruity hypothesis using an anticipated natural occurrence, thunderstorms (Hood, 1978). I had established that the solo experience had the widest range of differential ratings on anticipatory stress; some feared it, whereas others were minimally concerned. In the solo experience, I took each student alone into a wilderness area, issued minimal equipment (a tarp, water, and a mixture of nuts and candy for food), and then left the student to spend the night in solitude. Various students were taken out over a 5-night period, regardless of weather conditions. As some indication of the power of this experience, 29 of the 93 participants "broke solo," meaning that they returned to camp before dawn. Before each outing, anticipatory stress was measured by having the students fill out a measure of subjective stress. In addition, setting stress was fortuitously varied by the fact that some students soloed on nights when there were strong rain and thunderstorms. Thus, accepting that being alone in a thunderstorm at night with minimal shelter is more stressful than soling on a pleasant summer eve, we had a natural quasi-experimental design in which we could test the full range of the incongruity hypothesis. Anticipatory stress and experienced stress incongruity elicited higher mysticism scores than congruent conditions. There was no difference between whether the incongruity was between high anticipatory stress and low experienced stress or low anticipatory stress and high experienced stress.

A second area in which quasi-experimental designs approach true experimental designs is evident in the assessment of the efficacy of intercessory prayer. The debate on whether intercessory prayer can be studied using a true experimental design is confounded by ontological issues concerning the nature of God. Gorsuch (2008) has noted that if there is a nomothetic or lawful regularity between prayer and healing, then the implications are profound for an ideothetic or unique role for a personal God. Assuming that one can identify the purpose of prayer in terms of medical benefits, there have been mixed results from studies using large *N*s and double-blind procedures and hence approaching a true experimental design (depending on one's ontological commitment relative to God). Gorsuch has identified only five studies that fulfill these two major criteria. Two of the studies failed to find significant effects when differential medical outcome was assessed as the effect of a double-blind prayer procedure (Aviles et al., 2001; Benson et al., 2006). Two studies found small but statistically significant effects (Byrd, 1988; Harris, Thoresen, McCullough, & Larson, 1999). The small but significant effects (typically $p < .02$) are consistent with Hodge's (2007) meta-analysis of 17 intercessory prayer studies. Gorsuch (2008) concluded that "it appears that when the studies are limited to only the better ones, there is limited support for a positive, though small prayer effect" (pp. 201–202). To assess prayer for its medical effects, however, is seen by some as a distortion of prayer's spiritual efficacy (Shuman & Meador, 2003).

Perhaps the most interesting study in terms of innovative methodology was done by Leibovici (2001). Not only did he find significant medical advantages from intercessory prayer for patients in a double-blind study of more than 3,000 patients with bloodstream infection, but his research design also was novel. The focus was on retroactive effects of remote intercessory prayer. Leibovici assumed that God is not constrained by time or space and hence can act in a manner in which cause need not precede effect. A random number generator was used to create two groups, and then a coin toss determined which was to be the experimental group. A remote intercessory prayer was said for the well-being and full recovery of the intervention group but not the control group. Dependent variables included mortality, duration of fever, and length of stay in hospital. Significant effects were obtained for length of stay in the hospital and duration of fever, both of which were lower in the group that received prayer. Mortality, however, did not differ and actually was higher (514 of 1,702 or 30.2%) in the experimental than in the control (475 of 1,691 or 28.1%) group, but this difference was not significant.

Methodologically, the study of the effects of intercessory prayer can do the most to advance the psychology of religion and spirituality in light of Dittes's (1969) two nonreductive methodological options. For instance, although many assume a cause must precede its effect, this assumption may not always apply. Intercessory prayer research approaches the same methodological dilemmas that have plagued parapsychological research and with some of the same empirical outcomes (Henry, 2005). A serious confound ignored in intercessory prayer studies is the possibility of direct mental effects on human physiological processes (Henry, 2005, pp. 51–52; Schlitz & Braud, 1997). For instance, the issues raised by the apparently small but reliable effects obtained in *ganzfeld* studies, in which individuals stare into a featureless field of vision, have radical implications (Bem & Honorton, 1994). The ganzfeld effect, easily produced by using half of a Ping-Pong ball to cover each eye, is thought by some to facilitate access to internal images by blocking out external sensations. This process, in turn, is assumed to facilitate parapsychological phenomena, especially telepathy (the perception of information directly from another mind) and clairvoyance (the reception of information directly from the environment). The empirical quality of ganzfeld research is impeccable and recognized even by its harshest critics (Milton & Wiseman, 1999). Meta-analyses, effect size, and file drawer analyses have long characterized this research and still are relatively rare in the psychology of religion. Most significant are the theoretical advances that must be considered on the basis of studies in which small but persistent effect sizes exist and yet seem conceptually incomprehensible. Likely researchers in intercessory prayer can lead the way to conceptual advancement in the psychology of religion and spirituality by following the lead of ganzfeld researchers. That is, they could agree on a set of methodological guidelines, ones that a broad range of investigators could use to produce data that would theoretically integrate psychology with other disciplines, such as theology and perhaps even quantum physics (Hyman & Honorton, 1986). As Walach et al. (2009) have argued, the legacy of parapsychological research is a psychology of spirituality that can use concepts from quantum physics (e.g., generalized entanglement) that will demand novel research methods to accommodate an evolving understanding of natural science.

CORRELATIONAL RESEARCH

In the first *Annual Review of Psychology* article devoted to the psychology of religion, Gorsuch (1984) noted that psychology of religion had scales as sophisticated and reliable as in other areas of psychological research and that the field would advance by more systematic research using already established scales. Although many demean merely correlational research, it is arguably the case that the resurgence of psychology of religion in the United States, starting in the 1960s, was based largely on correlational research. Furthermore, it remains true that correlational research continues to play a significant part in advancing the field, as current researchers correlate measures of religion and spirituality with established measures in mainstream psychology. In addition, the use of sophisticated statistical techniques, such as structural equation modeling, allows for correlational research to be suggestive of possible causal factors even in nonexperimental designs (Tomarken & Waller, 2005). Several illustrative correlational studies emphasizing religion and personality will be described next.

Several researchers have related religion to the five-factor model (FFM) of personality (see also Chapter 9, this volume). Saroglou (2002) did a meta-analytic review of eight studies using at least one measure of religion or spirituality and at least one measure of the FFM (NEO Personality Inventory, NEO Five-Factor Inventory, or adjective checklists). He found religiosity (variously measured in the eight studies) to be correlated with conscientiousness and agreeableness. Fundamentalist religion negatively correlated with openness. Inferring an open or mature religiosity from various measures used in the different studies, Saroglou (2002, p. 20) found a stronger relationship to openness (effect size .22) and the same consistent positive but small correlations with conscientiousness and agreeableness. He also found a consistent relationship to extraversion for both religion and inferred mature religiosity but not for fundamentalism.

Saroglou's (2002) data can be interpreted in terms of a higher order factor solution for the FFM. The possibility of a higher order two-factor solution for the FFM makes it more directly relevant to psychology of religion. Agreeableness, conscientiousness, and emotional stability (neuroticism reverse scored) form one factor associated with stability, and openness and extraversion form another factor associated with plasticity (DeYoung, 2006; DeYoung, Peterson, & Higgins, 2002; Digman, 1997). In a recent study of deconversion, Streib, Hood, Keller, Csöff, and Silver (2008) identified the factors as traditionalism and transformation. These two factors mesh nicely with the correlational literature, in that religion as a commitment to a given tradition is essentially mildly correlated with traditionalism (agreeableness, conscientiousness, and emotional stability), whereas spirituality is related to extraversion and openness. The balance between traditionalism and transformation illuminate why some people stay with a given tradition (traditionalists) and others seek alternatives (transformation). The latter are spiritual but not religious, whereas the former can be both religious and spiritual or, if fundamentalist, religious but not spiritual (Hood, 2003; Saucier & Skrzypińska, 2006; Streib et al., 2008).

Finally, the FFM is a complex instrument that in addition to the commonly employed five domains or factors, allows the identification of six facets to each domain. These six facets, in turn, are related to eight basic behavioral, affective, and cognitive tendencies. Future research can benefit from seeking differential correlates for various facets, as recommended by Saroglou (2002) and demonstrated by Aguilar-Vafaie and Moghanloo (2008) in a sample of Shiite Muslims.

The Neurophysiology of Prayer

Advances in technology have allowed minimally invasive procedures for the study of neurophysiological correlates of prayer and meditation (see also Chapter 11 in this volume). Yoga and Zen meditation are associated with the production of alpha brain waves, which also occur with feelings of well-being (Benson, 1975). One effect of prayer at the purely physiological level may be to elicit a general relaxation response, which is associated with lowered rates of carbon dioxide and oxygen exchange. This relaxation pattern has been observed in meditation prayer and is perhaps a common physiological consequence of meditation and prayer (Benson & Stark, 1996).

Another use of correlational methods with the new technology available to neurophysiological researchers is to locate those areas of the brain that are active during prayer, meditation, or other religious experiences. Among the neuroimaging techniques are functional magnetic resonance imagery (fMRI), positron emission tomography (PET), and single-photon emission computer tomography (SPECT). The discussion of these techniques is beyond the scope of this review (see McNamara, 2006; see also Chapter 11 in this volume). Regardless of the sophistication of the technologies used, however, Azari (2006) has cautioned that the majority of this research is correlational and cannot establish with any certainty causal claims, including that a given brain state produces a specific religious experience. Even if certain practices have identical neurophysiological correlates, it does not mean the practices are experienced as the same. They also may differ in other important ways not captured by their neurophysiological correlates.

Ideological Surround

One persistent problem with correlational studies involves the extent to which measurement scales contain conceptually overlapping items, thus creating built-in correlations that are actually due to redundant material. For instance, Koenig (2008) has noted that measures of spirituality often include items consistent with secular views of mental health, ensuring a positive correlation between measures. This has been elevated into a general methodological issue in the psychology of religion by Watson and colleagues (2003) and identified by the term *ideological surround.*

Watson and colleagues utilized empirical measures corrected for their ideological content, thus producing measures acceptable to the internal definition of the group to which they are applied (Watson et al., 2003). Watson's ideological surround method is an empirical procedure that permits identification of different meanings for identical scale items. For instance, the fact that intrinsic religiosity often correlates positively with social desirability measures is not interpreted to mean that intrinsically religious people only wish to appear socially desirable (Batson, Schoenrade, & Ventis, 1993). This interpretation of the empirical data fails to account for the meaning of social desirability items within the ideological surround of an intrinsically religious person. An alternative explanation can readily be derived from simply having individuals rate the various items on social desirability scales for their religious relevance. For instance, among intrinsically religious persons, positive endorsement of social desirability items reflects the ideological surround of their religious tradition, which defines such items as desirable social behaviors (Watson,

Morris, Foster, & Hood, 1986). Thus, intrinsic religiosity correlates with social desirability on items that intrinsically religious persons see as socially desirable. In a similar vein, correcting scales to measure self-actualization for their different ideological surround reveals different meanings of the term for religiously and secularly committed persons (Watson, Morris, & Hood, 1987, 1990). Whether people describe themselves as self-actualized depends on the meaning of any measure of self-actualization within a given tradition.

SURVEY STUDIES

Survey research continues to be useful in providing a sense of the broader context for understanding psychological phenomena. The most commonly used survey question was first asked by Greeley (1974) and was used in several subsequent General Social Surveys (GSS). The question read, "Have your ever felt as though you were close to a powerful spiritual force that seemed to lift you out of yourself?" This question was included in the GSS in 1983–1984, 1988, and 1989. Analysis of these data (Fox, 1992; Yamane & Polzer, 1994) revealed a slight decline (about 10%) in the percentage answering "yes" to the Greeley question during the years specified.

A second value of survey research is in what O'Connor and Vandenberg (2010) have referred to as the exclusionary clause in various editions of the *Diagnostic and Statistical Manual of Mental Disorders*. The most recent edition of this manual (American Psychiatric Association, 2000) simply cautions that "a clinician who is unfamiliar with the nuances of an individual's cultural frame of reference may incorrectly judge as psychopathology those normal variations in behavior, belief, or experience that are particular to the individual's culture" (p. xxxiv). Thus, survey research is essential in documenting variations in belief and experience within U.S. culture. Even behaviors such as handling poisonous serpents and drinking poison can be seen as normal variations of beliefs in Appalachia and hence are not pathological (Hood & Williamson, 2008).

A third contribution of survey research is to empirically test competing models of determinants of religion and spirituality. For instance, Saroglou and Muñoz-García (2008) have noted that values often have been found to be more predictive of religion and spirituality than personality. Saroglou, Delpierre, and Dernelle (2002) conducted a meta-analysis of Schwartz's (1992) model based on 21 samples from 15 countries with an $N = 8{,}551$. Schwartz's Value Survey included 56 single-value items representing 10 motivationally distinct value constructs. Religious persons tended to prefer values linked to tradition, conformity, and security and to not favor openness to change, autonomy, or hedonism. Despite the number of countries sampled, many participants were Catholic and all were from monotheistic traditions in Western societies. Still, the authors noted that the overall effect size for values and religion is greater than the overall effect size for the FFM of personality and religion. Although survey data make causal claims difficult, they provide suggestive data that can help with the design of studies to address causal questions.

QUALITATIVE METHODS

Many psychologists assume that quantification is essential to psychology as a natural science, with experimentation, measurement, and quantification forming a necessary triangle (see also Chapter 3 in this volume). Under the general rubric of qualitative methods, however, one can discuss a variety of methods that do not privilege quantitative data. These might be studies in which the data are words, narratives, or reports that individuals use to convey the meaning of their experiences. In this section, we focus on research that can reveal incongruities between qualitative and quantitative research on the same topic.

As I did with the privileging of the experiment, those who would privilege qualitative methods have assumptions that must be acknowledged. In particular, the focus here is on methods that do not seek to quantify behavior, thoughts, or feelings, but rather seek to interpret human action. Belzen and Hood (2006) have summarized a method of interpretation based on the work of Gadamer (1960/1986) as follows:

> (1) Interpretation begins on the basis of preliminary, intuitive understanding

of the whole, that is open to continual reflection and re-interpretation.

(2) One looks for meaningful relationships within actions and occurrences. External relationships (like correlations or law-like relationships sought in empirical research) are insufficient to reveal meaning.

(3) Emphasis is on the understanding of individual cases, whether this understanding can be generalized or not. The unique is sought, as well as generalized tendencies across cases.

(4) There is a difference between the knowledge/understanding of the researcher/interpreter and the subject of study. When understanding increases, the discrepancy between the two is diminished insofar as the researcher seeks to understand the subject's meaning.

(5). Written texts and human narratives are taken seriously in their claim to truth. (Belzen & Hood, 2006, p. 15)

As the philosophical defense of qualitative methods continues, psychologists can ill afford to simply assert an untenable definition of psychology as an empirical, causal discipline (Belzen & Hood, 2006; Brinkmann, 2006). Neither can they assert that nonlaboratory studies are nonempirical. Psychology has more ecological validity the more it is involved with real-world, nonlaboratory studies (Belzen & Hood, 2006; Neisser, 1976). There is no assumption that psychological processes studied under laboratory conditions generalize to nonlaboratory conditions. This has been demonstrated impressively in two research traditions influenced by cognitive dissonance theory that have produced startling different claims on the basis of different research methodologies.

When Jones wrote a summary of cognitive dissonance theory, he noted that that there were in excess of 1,200 experimental, laboratory-based studies and that the basic theory was so strongly supported that little additional research was needed (Jones, 1998, p. 69). Psychologists of religion, however, can learn a methodological lesson from the parallel research traditions with cognitive dissonance theory, one from psychologically oriented social psychologists (i.e., PSP) and the other from sociologically oriented social psychologists (i.e., SSP). This is crucial, because Festinger's theory requires that beliefs be proven false in a way that is "unequivocal and undeniable" (Festinger, Riecken, & Schachter, 1956, p. 3). Such an objectivist stance is naïve with respect to how beliefs actually operate in real-life contexts. Field studies based on participant observation and ethnographic research, such as is common in SSP, document that failed prophecy entails hermeneutical considerations that make claims to "unequivocal and undeniable" falsification perpetually problematic. As R. P. Carroll (1979, p. 184) noted when applying cognitive dissonance theory to biblical prophecy, there are no simple objective criteria by which one can identify failed prophesy. What outsiders (especially researchers) see as failed prophesy is seldom seen that way by insiders. Tumminia (1998) noted that "what appears to be seemingly irrefutable evidence of irreconcilable contradictions to outsiders, like Festinger, can instead be evidence of the truth of prophecy to insiders" (p. 165).

Sociologically oriented social psychologists have tended to take an insider's perspective, focusing on interpersonal processes that maintain a socially constructed reality incapable of any simple falsification. *Failed prophecy* is thus a negotiated term and depends on negotiated claims to reality and meaning that are masked by measurement-based assessment in laboratory studies (Berger & Luckmann, 1967; R. P. Carroll, 1979; Hood, 2011; Pollner, 1987). Furthermore, among prophetic groups, prophecy is less central than outsiders assume. The exclusive focus upon prophecy leads outsiders to assume that the major concern of the group is prophecy, ignoring the complex cosmology that serves to integrate the group (Melton, 1985). Participant observation studies of prophetic groups have begun to show how rare increased proselytization is as a reaction to what is only apparently failed prophecy (Stone, 2000). The denial of failure of prophecy is the most common response from within prophetic groups, as members struggle to stay within the group and to seek a proper interpretation of what must be only an apparent failure (R. P. Carroll, 1979; Dein, 1997,

2001; Melton, 1985; Stone, 2000; Tumminia, 1998). As Dein (2001) noted, dissonance theory too often is used to persuade outsiders that those who stay within prophetic groups are irrational and driven by forces they do not understand. Such claims are common among PSP, which seeks to use methods that assume individuals are not consciously aware of the determinants of their actions. Hermeneutical and phenomenological methods, however, do not assume that participants are unable to render accurate reports of their engagements and activities (Keen, 1975). They are concerned with obtaining descriptions detailing the "what" of an experience rather than its "why" (Pollio et al., 1997). They seek to understand the reasons people act as they do, and not to understand the causes of their behavior (Brinkmann, 2006). The research goal is to reveal what is currently meaningful about that experience to the participant.

Interestingly, when Festinger was creating his cognitive dissonance theory, he applied it in a participant observation study well known to psychologists of religion as an apparent study of failed prophecy (Festinger, Riecken, & Schachter, 1956). Difficulties in the complexity of interpreting events outside the laboratory quickly created problems. For instance, Melton (1985) noted that the Millerites were not simply focused on prophecy. They also did not disband in the manner that Festinger claimed, thus raising some questions about his idea that "within religious groups prophecy seldom fails" (Melton, 1985, p. 20). Likewise, Van Fossen (1988) noted that despite the continual citation of Festinger's classic study by PSP, it provides a deficient guide to the study of prophetic groups. Finally, Bader (1999), after critically reviewing his own research and Festinger's classic study, concluded that "no study of a failed prophecy, the current research included, has provided support for the cognitive dissonance hypothesis" (p. 120).

Toward the end of his career, at a symposium at the 95th Annual Convention of the APA on dissonance theory, Festinger noted that dissonance theory produced a massive and dominating experimental literature from PSP that relied almost entirely on experimental laboratory methods. He stated, "One thing that I think has to be done is for more research to go on dissonance producing situations and dissonance reduction processes as they occur in the 'real world'" (Festinger, 1999, p. 384).

PHENOMENOLOGY AND HERMENEUTICAL METHODS

Pollio and his colleagues have systematized a qualitative method that combines phenomenological and hermeneutical methods as a complement to quantitative methods that reflect a natural science perspective (Pollio, Henley, & Thompson, 1997). Their method relies heavily on similar methods developed by Giorgi (1970, 1971). The method includes a phenomenological interview followed by hermeneutically based textual analysis that seeks to understand the meaningfulness of lived experience. Not only interview data but also any data that can be translated into text can be used, such as the words of songs or spontaneous sermons (Hood & Williamson, 2008).

Phenomenological Interview

The phenomenological interview is an open-ended exploration of an individual's experience of the topic being investigated. The first concern involves an attempt to formulate an appropriate opening question for the interview (which is actually a dialogue). The initial question chosen will direct the ensuing conversation, so it is important to ensure that this question is sufficiently open to allow for multiple ways of taking it up in the interview. Van Manen (1990) has suggested that the process of coming to terms with this question begins with wondering "what something is really like" (p. 42) and must be based on the passionate interest of the interviewer in what is being investigated. Because "why" questions have been found to lead the participant away from the phenomenon toward an explanation of its origins or mode of operation, phenomenological interviewing is based on the use of "what" questions—that is, with a concern for what the experience was like for the participant (Pollio et al., 1997). In the case of the phenomenon of fear, for example, one possible question might be, "Can you tell me about a specific time that was fearful for you?" Responses to such a question might focus on describing a significant personal event in which fear was experienced in a meaningful way. The opening question, phrased in terms of a specific episode, not only begins the interview but also serves as a constant point of reference in talking about the phenomenon of interest. To be aware of his or her own biases, the interviewer undergoes a bracketing interview in which the interview question is posed to the researcher (Pollio et al., 1997; Williamson & Pollio, 1999).

In a phenomenological study, there are relatively few restrictions on the selection of participants. Because the goal of investigating lived experience is not generalizability but interpretive clarity, random samples are not a consideration (Polkinghorne, 1989). Two criteria for selecting participants are as follows: (a) They must have experienced the phenomenon under investigation, and (b) they must be able to provide an articulate description of the experience. Aside from these requirements, the number of participants chosen is determined by the richness of descriptions obtained during the interviews (Pollio et al., 1997). Interviews continue until the process ceases to render further variation of the phenomenon—typically from 10 to 15 interviews—although no specific restrictions apply, as is common in grounded theory (Glasser & Strauss, 2009; Hood & Williamson, 2008, pp. 247–256).

Hermeneutical Analyses

An essential tool of textual interpretation involves an ongoing attempt to relate parts of the text to its overall meaning—the so-called *hermeneutic circle* (Belzen & Hood, 2006; Kvale, 1996; Williamson & Pollio, 1999). As an interpretation for a single passage or remark is proposed, reflections on meaning derived from earlier passages are considered simultaneously for consistency of understanding. The analysis of any text invariably involves a circular pattern of determining the meaning of a part that affects the meaning of the whole, which, in turn, bears on the meaning of the individual part. This process of going back and forth strengthens internal consistency and the interdependency of emerging themes as they lead toward an overall meaning for the text.

The use of hermeneutic interpretation extends beyond an idiographic description for a single participant to other protocols describing the same phenomenon to produce a "global meaning" or a "homothetic thematic description" (Pollio et al., 1997). At this level, the process includes interpreting the meaning of each text in the context of all others; such extension is not made for purposes of generalization but rather to improve the researcher's understanding of the phenomenon as described in different contexts. In considering all protocols, a particular pattern of themes tends to emerge and constitute the meaning of the phenomenon as experienced. Valle, King, and Halling (1989) have compared such a consistency of themes across contexts to a melody of music transposed to different keys: Although the piece can be played in a variety of keys, the melody is immediately recognized by the familiar sound of its note structure regardless of key. This does not mean, however, that the interpretation of an experience has been exhausted or closed in any way by the structure of nomothetic meaning described, because the meaning of a phenomenon is always open to reinterpretation as unique variations emerge from specific participants and contexts of experience. As Belzen and Hood (2006, p. 19) have observed of hermeneutical methods, in general, that they are open ended and ultimately depend on human judgment. From the standpoint of hermeneutical analysis, psychology is best understood as a human rather than a natural science. It is of constant concern to psychology that a study renders "valid" results. In agreement with Giorgi (1970, 1971), Pollio et al. (1997) have argued that validity for research of this type depends primarily on the degree to which a reader may take up the findings of a study and see what the researcher saw from his or her investigation. Belzen and Hood have noted that although one can speak of inter-researcher reliability insofar as different researchers using similar methods reach similar conclusions (interpretations), ultimately, "certainty is not achieved but is replaced as an aim by the acceptance of the best possible interpretation, which ultimately remains a human judgment" (p. 19).

Belzen (1997) has provided several models and empirical examples of hermeneutical approaches in the psychology of religion. Data culled both from phenomenological interviews and hermeneutical analyses can be archived and made available for other researchers to independently assess (Hood & Williamson, 2008). Furthermore, there are several computer programs for analyzing qualitative data. For example, Weitzman and Miles (1995) provided detailed information on 24 different programs.

N OF 1 STUDIES

It has long been assumed that *N* of 1 studies are of minimal value for developing psychological theory. Both qualitative and quantitative possibilities, however, have suggested reevaluation of the usefulness of N of 1 studies. This is especially the case in what I have referred to as *confessional research* (Hood, 2008), which is becoming increasingly common in research on the psychology of spiritual experience in which the researcher relies on her or his own experience as well as the experience of others.

Confessional methodologists applaud the value of returning psychology to the stance of researcher-as-subject, which characterized psychological research at its inception as a laboratory science (Danziger, 1994). One example comes from the confessional scholars of mysticism, who have used their own experiences to assess the claim that despite different descriptions of mystical experiences, an underlying commonality nevertheless exists (Barnard, 1997; Forman, 1999). The researcher then uses his or her own experience as a basis to investigate others reporting similar experiences. For example, Shanon's (2002) lifelong study of *ayahuasca* includes his own active participation and detailed report on the phenomenology of the experience. He is able to compare his own experience with those of other participants in a fashion similar to the method developed by Pollio et al. (1997). Similarly, the success of the psilocybin studies at Johns Hopkins is likely due to the experienced guide's previous experience with the same entheogen (W. A. Richards, 2009). It has long been the case in some schools of psychology (notably psychoanalysis) that the therapist must be analyzed. Confessional research is committed to a similar view, namely, that the researchers must also be participants. Along these lines, Merkur (2010) has documented the role of personal experience among psychoanalytic mystics. Belzen and Geels (1994) have reintroduced the use of autobiography into the psychology of religion, attesting once again to the importance of personal documents that early researchers such as William James found so valuable. Most autobiographical research, however, links with narrative psychology, which has found a strong footing in personality research that is not restricted to purely experimental or measurement-based approaches (McAdams, 2006).

N of 1 studies can combine qualitative and quantitative analyses. Sophisticated statistics such as auto-regressive–integrated–moving-average (ARIMA) can be applied to observations or measurements on a single subject over time (McCleary & Hay, 1980). Although such studies are rare in the psychology of religion, Murray-Swank and Pargament (2005) used an ARIMA (Box, Jenkins, & Reinsel, 1994) to evaluate the effectiveness of an eight-session spiritually integrated intervention for two female survivors of sexual abuse. Researchers have used a Brunswikian lens model (Brunswik, 1955) that allows a combination of empirical and phenomenological methods to assess individual decisions and to compare judgments across groups. Zinnbauer and Pargament (2002) applied a Brunswikian model to clarify the different meanings of spirituality and religiousness among both clergy and students. As confessional research with *N* of 1 becomes more common, such methods can be applied as well. Thus, N of 1 studies can be both qualitatively and quantitatively rigorous.

PSYCHOANALYSIS

Psychoanalysis remains a rich source of theory for many psychologists of religion and has recently been championed by M. P. Carroll (1983, 1986) in a variety of methodologically innovative studies. He used classical Freudian Oedipal theory to make predictions about apparitions of the Virgin Mary, which Carroll treated as hallucinations, staying clearly with the two reductionist possibilities outlined by Dittes (1969). His empirical efforts focus on retrospective predictions concerning characteristics of Marian apparitions that have occurred historically. In an exemplary example of the integrative paradigm, Carroll marshaled anthropological and ethnographic data to show that in areas where the Mary cult and the *machismo* complex are strongest, males come from father-ineffective families, which allows the assumption of a strong and delayed attachment to the mother on the part of her male children. The inference from Oedipal theory is that males strongly attached to their mothers have intense erotic repressions that can be expressed effectively in attraction to the cult of the Virgin Mary. The idealized Virgin Mary represents the denial of sexual attraction to one's mother; the machismo complex displaces eroticism onto other women, who are treated primarily as sex objects; guilt is assuaged by attraction to the passion of Christ, in which the male identifies with the need for punishment. Thus, sexual sublimation accounts for the appeal of the cult of the Virgin Mary.

M. P. Carroll's (1983, 1986) provocative thesis is rare in the psychology of religion because it incorporates historical, anthropological, ethnographic, and social–historical facts into a single, coherent theoretical framework. It also has led to several empirical studies. For instance, Carroll utilized Walsh's (1906) extensive identification of Marian apparitions associated with the Catholic Church that included those officially recognized by the church as well as those not legitimated. All apparitions from the years 1100 to 1896 for which three empirical criteria could be documented resulted in a sample of 50 (for a list, see M. P. Carroll, 1986, pp. 225–226). The three empirical criteria were as follows: (a) The seer was in a waking state, (b) the seer both heard and saw Mary, and (c) the image of Mary was not provided by an identifiable physical stimulus. Assuming sexual sublimation to foster susceptibility to Marian hallucinations (apparitions), Carroll predicted that the seer would be unmarried (and hence likely to be celibate). The historical data confirmed this.

In a second study using the same Marian apparitions discussed above, M. P. Carroll (1983, 1986) predicted that the gender of the seer would relate to whether apparitions of Mary would contain additional male figures (such as Jesus or adult male saints). He based this prediction on the idea that males desire exclusive possession of the mother and do not want father figures present. Because females identify with the mother to obtain access to the father, they should want father figures present. Carroll found differential gender effects, and most important for his thesis, females were much more likely to report Marian apparitions with males present than were males (M. P. Carroll, 1986, p. 145).

A laboratory-based study tested M. P. Carroll's (1983, 1986) basic theory among Protestant males. From a series of independently related images of Jesus (crucifixes), Hood, Morris, and Watson (1991) selected those that varied in degree of expressed suffering. They also included ambivalent images of the Virgin Mary, culled from artists who had painted images of varying erotic and nurturing quality. Males were previously assessed on a measure of maternal bonding. Males most strongly bonded to their mothers preferred a suffering Christ and an erotic or nurturing Virgin Mary. Thus, insofar as one seeks an integrative paradigm, M. P. Carroll's work models how empirical methods can be used to shed light on both religion in the cultural sense and on psychological processes that may sustain a particular cultural expression of religion.

OBJECT RELATIONS–ATTACHMENT THEORY

If M. P. Carroll's (1983, 1986) work provides exemplary methods congruent with the new integrative paradigm, the sister to classical psychoanalysis, object relations theory can provide reciprocal guidance for attachment theory. Despite efforts to clearly differentiate object relations theory from attachment theory (Granqvist, 2006a, 2006b), their roots are intertwined (Rizzuto, 2006). In terms of the new paradigm, the methodological strengths complement one another. For example, Luyten and Corveleyn (2007) have persuasively made the case for the reciprocal exploration of the findings of object relations and attachment theorists. Much of the distancing is due to philosophical differences in appropriate methodologies, with attachment theory grounded initially in correlational (Kirkpatrick, 1992) and now increasingly in experimental research (Granqvist, 2010), whereas object relations theory is largely fueled by clinically based *N* of 1 studies (Rizzuto, 2006). Roehlkepartain, Benson, King, and Wagener (2006) have argued that "the contrast between the call for deep, multidimensional theoretical frameworks and the 'shallow' measures often used in this domain [attachment theory] represents one of the major challenges for the future of research in child and adolescent spiritual development" (p. 9). Likewise, critics have cautioned that attachment theory reflects a general Western cultural bias in which divinity is more likely to be conceived in personal rather than impersonal terms (Rothbaum, Weisz, Pott, Miyake, & Morelli, 2000). Thus, empirical data remain perpetually problematic if we are unmindful of the precarious relationship between measurement and meaning, numbers and nouns.

Conversely, attachment theorists have been able to tease out two predictions, which can appear to resist falsification. That is, religious commitment can result either from anxious or secure attachment (see Chapter 7 in this volume). Although the compensation hypothesis predicts that persons with insecure attachments will seek religion as a compensation, the socialization hypothesis predicts that person with secure attachment are likely to retain the religion into which they are socialized (Granqvist & Kirkpatrick, 2008).

SPIRITUAL–INTERVENTIONIST STRATEGIES

Perhaps the clearest area in which an integrative paradigm can emerge is in an assessment of the efficacy of therapy. Shafranske's (1996) groundbreaking text raised the issue of inclusion of religion in the clinical practice of psychology. Recently Pargament (2007) has called for what he has termed a spiritually integrative psychotherapy, much of it based on his programmatic research on coping (1997). The methodological issues cover the full range of concerns, both quantitative and qualitative. It may be that religion and psychological health are orthogonal concepts (Hood & Byrom, 2010). If so, adopting a psychological model for spiritually integrated therapy is inherently a secular move (Helminiak, 2010). On the other hand, one can have explicit faith-based therapies (R. C. Richards & Bergin, 1997), and they can be rigorously assessed in terms of therapeutic outcome strategies (Wise, 2004). The issue then becomes what religion? What concept of health? There is a long history of sectarian forms of religion, such as Christian Science, being at odds with a cultural commitment to secular medicine (Hood, Hill, & Spilka, 2009, Chapter 9).Conversely, the inclusion of qualitative and quantitative assessment of therapeutic progress requires the full range of methodological considerations raised in this chapter. There are established methods for assessing the effectiveness of interventions long used in medical research (Koenig, McCullough, & Larson, 2001), although those linking medicine and religion or spirituality often have serious problems with ruling out confounding variables (Sloan, Bagiella, & Powell, 1999). The requirement that secular and religious or spiritual forms of intervention be compared for relative efficacy is not unreasonable, however, although it is fraught with many conceptual difficulties (Shuman & Meador, 2003). Once the considerable conceptual issues are addressed, the comparisons can be methodologically addressed. For instance, Rye et al. (2005) compared religious and secular forgiveness interventions with divorced individuals and found that they did not differ in effectiveness. One methodological issue that must be noted is that Rye found that both secular and religious participants used religious strategies (Rye, 2005, p. 212). Thus, merely placing individuals in a group that does not have explicit spiritual interventions does not mean that members of that group will not use religious or spiritual strategies. This is a crucial issue when evaluating the differential effectiveness of interventionist strategies.

LONGITUDINAL STUDIES

Longitudinal studies are relatively uncommon, partly due to the investment required to sustain a project over many years. Perhaps the most rigorous longitudinal research is associated with researchers using the database provided by the merger in the 1960s of the Oakland Growth Study (consisting of 10- to 12-year-olds from Oakland, California, born in 1920 and 1921) and the Berkeley Guidance Study (initiated in 1928–1929, using a sample of newborn children from Berkeley, California; Block, 1971). Dillon and his colleagues have used this data set to explore issues of concern to the psychology of religion, including personality factors and their relationship to spirituality and religion (Wink & Dillon, 2002, 2003).

McCullough, Enders, Brion, and Jain (2005) creatively used growth mixture models from data in the well-known Terman study to identify three discrete religious development trajectories among adults (ages 27 to 80). Other longitudinal studies have used much shorter time spans. For example, Kirkpatrick (1997) examined how attachment styles changed religious categorizations of spiritual experiences in a sample of 177 females, all of whom responded to an initial newspaper ad and completed a questionnaire mailed 51 months later. Poloma and Hood (2008) spent almost the same amount of time in their participant observation of a religious sect in Atlanta, Georgia, documenting its change and internal dynamics over a 4-year period (Poloma & Hood, 2008). Likewise, by their very nature, clinicians from psychoanalytic and object relations perspectives are involved in longitudinal *N* of 1 studies and have produced significant theoretical works (Rizzuto, 1979). Longitudinal strategies are also common in the all-too-neglected psychohistorical studies (Belzen, 2001).

Innovative effort at analogues to longitudinal research has been made by investigators in the psychology of religion who have relocated participants from early studies and reassessed them at a much later date. In what is also a widely quoted study, Doblin (1991) followed the adventures of the original Good Friday participants. He was able to locate and interview nine of the participants in original experimental group and seven of the participants in the original control group. He also administered Pahnke's original questionnaire. In most cases, comparison of Doblin's results with those of Pahnke (immediately after the service and 6 months later) revealed that participants in the experimental group showed increases on most of Stace's common core criteria of mysticism after almost a quarter of a century.

Another example of a similar effort is the readministering of the adjective checklist (Gough & Heilbrun, 1983) used in the study of a Jesus commune formed in the 1970s called Shiloh. Seventeen years after the initial group was studied, Taslimi, Hood, and Watson (1991) administered the same adjective checklist to 128 former members of the sect. Their aim was to test the prediction that because the group was believed to consist of alienated youth who had "maladaptive" and "addictive" tendencies, they would suffer psychologically if they ever left what was identified by the researchers as "Christ commune" and returned to mainstream society (Richardson, Stewart, & Simmonds, 1972). Results indicated that the former Shiloh members indeed had adapted successfully to mainstream society and were similar to the normative control samples—something not found in the original study. Thus, even though individual subjects were not followed or assessed repeatedly, group effects could be assessed in terms of whether members who left the commune could adjust successfully to mainstream society.

CONCLUSION

This review is far from exhaustive, given the range and scope of not only psychology in general but also the psychology of religion and spirituality in particular. If one accepts that there is no single methodology that is privileged or an ontological stance that can be ruled out a priori, then how questions are asked will dictate what kinds of answers are acceptable. Only then can one select a reasonable methodology that is likely to reveal some truths even as it masks others.

References

Aguilar-Vafaie, M. E., & Moghanloo, M. (2008). Domain and facet correlates of religiosity among Iranian college students. *Mental Health, Religion, and Culture, 11*, 461–483. doi:10.1080/13674670701539114

Allport, G. W. (1968). The historical background of social psychology. In G. Lindzey & E. Aronson (Eds.), *The handbook of social psychology* (2nd ed., Vol. 1, pp. 1–80). Reading, MA: Addison-Wesley.

American Psychiatric Association. (2000). *Diagnostic and statistical manual of mental disorders* (4th ed., text revision). Washington, DC: Author.

Aronson, E., & Carlsmith, J. M. (1968). Experimentation in social psychology. In G. Lindzey & E. Aronson (Eds.), *The handbook of social psychology* (2nd ed., Vol. 2, pp. 1–79). Reading, MA: Addison-Wesley.

Aronson, E., Wilson, T. D., & Akert, R. M. (1994). *Social psychology: The heart and the mind.* New York, NY: HarperCollins.

Aronson, E., Wilson, T. D., & Brewer, M.B. (1998). Experimentation in social psychology. In S. T. Fiske, D. T. Gilbert, & G. Lindzey (Eds.), *The handbook of social psychology* (4th ed., Vol. 2, pp. 99–142). New York, NY: McGraw-Hill.

Aviles, J. M., Whelan, E., Hernke, D. A., Williams, B. A., Kenny, K. E., O'Fallon, W. M., & Kopecky, S. L. (2001). Intercessory prayer and cardiovascular disease progression in coronary care unit population: A randomized controlled trial. *Mayo Clinic Proceedings, 76*, 1192–1198. doi:10.4065/76.12.1192

Azari, N. P. (2006). Neuroimaging studies of religious experience: A critical review. In P. McNamara (Ed.), *Where God and science meet: Vol. 2. The neurology of religious experience* (pp. 33–54). Westport, CT: Praeger.

Bader, C. (1999). New perspectives on failed prophecy. *Journal for the Scientific Study of Religion, 38*, 119–131. doi:10.2307/1387588

Barnard, G. W. (1997). *Exploring unseen worlds: William James and the philosophy of mysticism*. Albany: State University of New York Press.

Barrett, J. L., & Richard, R. A. (2003). Anthropomorphism or preparedness? Exploring children's God concepts. *Review of Religious Research, 44*, 300–312. doi:10.2307/3512389

Batson, C. D. (1977). Experimentation in psychology of religion: An impossible dream? *Journal for the Scientific Study of Religion, 16*, 413–418. doi:10.2307/1386228

Batson, C. D. (1979). Experimentation in the psychology of religion: Living with or in a dream? *Journal for the Scientific Study of Religion, 18*, 90–93. doi:10.2307/1385384

Batson, C. D., Schoenrade, P. A., & Ventis, W. L. (1993). *Religion and the individual: A social-psychological perspective*. New York, NY: Oxford University Press.

Baumeister, R. F., Bauer, I. M., & Lloyd, S. A. (2010). Choice, free will, and religion. *Psychology of Religion and Spirituality, 2*, 67–82. doi:10.1037/a0018455

Belzen, J. A. (Ed.). (1997). *Hermeneutical approaches in the psychology of religion*. New York, NY: Rodopi.

Belzen, J. A. (2001). *Psychohistory in the psychology of religion: Interdisciplinary studies*. New York, NY: Rodopi.

Belzen, J. A. (2010). *Towards cultural psychology of religion: Principles, approaches, and applications*. New York, NY: Springer. doi:10.1007/978-90-481-3491-5

Belzen, J. A., & Geels, A. (1994). *Autobiography and the psychological study of religious lives*. New York, NY: Rodopi.

Belzen, J. A., & Hood, R. W., Jr. (2006). Methodological issues in the psychology of religion:Toward another paradigm? *Journal of Psychology: Interdisciplinary and Applied, 140*, 5–28. doi:10.3200/JRLP.140.1.5-28

Bem, D. J., & Honorton, C. (1994). Does psi exist? Replicable evidence for an anomalous process of information transfer. *Psychological Bulletin, 115*, 4–18. doi:10.1037/0033-2909.115.1.4

Benson, H. (1975). *The relaxation response*. New York, NY: William Morrow.

Benson, H., Dusek, J. A., Sherwood, J. B., Lam, P., Bethea, C. G., Carpenter, C., . . . Hibberd, P. L. (2006). Study of the therapeutic effects of intercessory prayer (STEP) in cardiac bypass patients: A multi-center randomized trial of uncertainty of receiving intercessory prayer. *American Heart Journal, 151*, 934–942. doi:10.1016/j.ahj.2005.05.028

Benson, H., & Stark, M. (1996). *Timeless healing: The power and biology of belief*. New York, NY: Scribner.

Berger, P., & Luckmann, T. (1967). *The social construction of reality: A treatise on the sociology of knowledge*. Garden City, NY: Doubleday.

Block, J. (1971). *Lives through time*. Berkeley, CA: Bancroft.

Box, G. E. P., Jenkins, G. M., & Reinsel, G. C. (1994). *Time series analysis: Forecasting and control* (3rd ed.). Englewood Cliffs, NJ: Prentice-Hall.

Boyer, P. (1994). The naturalness of religious ideas. Berkeley, CA: University of California Press.

Boyer, P. (2001). *Religion explained: The evolutionary origins of religious thought*. New York, NY: Basic Books.

Brinkmann, S. (2006). Mental life in the space of reasons. *Journal for the Theory of Social Behaviour, 36*, 1–16. doi:10.1111/j.1468-5914.2006.00293.x

Brunswik, E. (1955). Representative design and probabilistic theory in functional psychology. *Psychological Review, 62*, 236–242. doi:10.1037/h0040198

Byrd, R. C. (1988). Positive therapeutic effects of intercessory prayer in a coronary care unit population. *Southern Medical Journal, 81*, 826–829.

Campbell, D. T. (1975). On the conflicts between biological and social evolution and between psychology and moral tradition. *American Psychologist, 30*, 1103–1126.

Campbell, D. T., & Stanley, J. C. (1963). *Experimental and quasi-experimental designs for research*. Chicago, IL: Rand McNally.

Capps, D., Ransohoff, R., & Rambo, L. (1976). Publication trends in the psychology of religion to 1974. *Journal for the Scientific Study of Religion, 15*, 15–28.

Carroll, M. P. (1983). Vision of the Virgin Mary: The effects of family structures on Marian apparitions. *Journal for the Scientific Study of Religion, 22*, 205–221. doi:10.2307/1385966

Carroll, M. P. (1986). *The cult of the Virgin Mary: Psychological origins*. Princeton, NJ: Princeton University Press.

Carroll, R. P. (1979). *When prophecy failed: Cognitive dissonance in the prophetic traditions of the Old Testament*. New York, NY: Seabury Press.

Coon, D. J. (1992). Testing the limits of sense and science: American experimental psychologists combat spiritualism, 1880–1920. *American Psychologist, 47*, 143–151. doi:10.1037/0003-066X.47.2.143

Danziger, K. (1994). *Constructing the subject: Historical origins of psychological research.* Cambridge, England: Cambridge University Press.

Deconchy, J.-P. (1985). Non-experimental and experimental methods in the psychology of religion: A few thoughts on their implication and limits. In L. B. Brown (Ed.), *Advances in the psychology of religion* (pp. 76–112). Oxford, England: Pergamon.

Dein, S. (1997). Lubavitch: A contemporary messianic movement. *Journal of Contemporary Religion, 12*, 191–204. doi:10.1080/13537909708580799

Dein, S. (2001). What really happens when prophecy fails: The case of Lubavitch. *Sociology of Religion, 62*, 383–401. doi:10.2307/3712356

DeYoung, C. G. (2006). Higher-order factors of the Big Five in a multiinformant sample. *Journal of Personality and Social Psychology, 91*, 1138–1151.

DeYoung, C. G., Peterson, J. B., & Higgins, D. M. (2002). Higher order factors of the Big Five predict conformity: Are there neuroses of health? *Personality and Individual Differences, 33*, 533–552. doi:10.1016/S0191-8869(01)00171-4

Digman, J. M. (1997). Higher order factors of the Big Five. *Journal of Personality and Social Psychology, 73*, 1246–1256. doi:10.1037/0022-3514.73.6.1246

Dittes, J. E. (1969). Psychology of religion. In G. Lindzey & E. Aronson (Eds.), *The handbook of social psychology* (3rd ed., Vol. 5, pp. 602–659). Reading, MA: Addison-Wesley.

Doblin, R. (1991). Pahnke's "Good Friday" experiment: A long-term follow-up and methodological critique. *Journal of Transpersonal Psychology, 23*, 1–28.

Festinger, L. (1999). Appendix A. Social communication and cognition: A very preliminary and highly tentative draft. In E. H. Jones & J. Mills (Eds.), *Cognitive dissonance: Progress on a pivotal theory in social psychology* (pp. 355–379). Washington, DC: American Psychological Association.

Festinger, L., Riecken, H. W., & Schachter, S. (1956). *When prophecy fails.* Minneapolis: University of Minnesota Press.

Flournoy, T. (1903). Les principles de la psychologie religieuse. *Archives de Psychologie, 2*, 33–57.

Forman, R. K. C. (1999). *Mysticism, mind, consciousness.* Albany: State University of New York Press.

Fox, J. W. (1992). The structure, stability, and social antecedents of reported paranormal experiences. *Sociological Analysis, 53*, 417–431. doi:10.2307/3711436

Gadamer, H. G. (1960/1986). *Truth and method.* New York, NY: Crossroad.

Gergen, K. J. (1992). Toward a postmodern psychology. In S. Kvale (Ed.), *Psychology and postmodernism* (pp. 17–30). London, England: Sage.

Giorgi, A. (1970). *Psychology as a human science: A phenomenologically based approach.* New York, NY: Harper & Row.

Giorgi, A. (1971). Phenomenology and experimental psychology: II. In A. Giorgi, W. F. Fischer, & R. von Eckartsberg (Eds.), *Duquesne studies in phenomenological psychology* (Vol. 1, pp. 17–29). Pittsburgh, PA: Duquesne University Press.

Glasser, B. G., & Strauss, A. L. (2009). *The discovery of grounded theory: Strategies for qualitative research* (4th ed.). Rutgers, NJ: Aldine Transaction.

Glock, C. Y., & Hammond, P. E. (Eds.). (1973). *Beyond the classics? Essays in the scientific study of religion.* New York, NY: Harper & Row.

Gorsuch, R. L. (1984). Measurement: The boon and bane of investigating religion. *American Psychologist, 39*, 228–236. doi:10.1037/0003-066X.39.3.228

Gorsuch, R. L. (2008). On the limits of scientific investigation: Miracles and intercessory prayer. In J. H. Ellens (Ed.), *Miracles: God science and psychology in the paranormal: Vol. 1. Religious and spiritual events* (pp. 280–299). Westport, CT: Praeger.

Gorsuch, R. L., & Miller, W. R. (1999). Assessing spirituality. In W. R. Miller (Ed.), *Integrating spirituality into treatment* (pp. 47–64). Washington, DC: American Psychological Association. doi:10.1037/10327-003

Gough, H., & Helibrun, A. (1983). *The adjective checklist manual.* Palo Alto, CA: Consulting Psychologists Press.

Granqvist, P. (2006a). In the interests of intellectual humility: A rejoinder to Rizzuto and Wulff. *The International Journal for the Psychology of Religion, 16*, 37–49. doi:10.1207/s15327582ijpr1601_4

Granqvist, P. (2006b). On the relation between secular and divine relationships: An emerging attachment perspective and a critique of the "depth" approaches. *The International Journal for the Psychology of Religion, 16*, 1–18. doi:10.1207/s15327582ijpr1601_1

Granqvist, P. (2010). Religion as attachment: The Godwin Award Lecture. *Archive for the Psychology of Religion, 32*, 5–24.

Granqvist, P., & Kirkpatrick, L. A. (2008). Attachment and religious representations and behavior. In J. Cassidy & P. R. Shaver (Eds.), *Handbook of attachment: Theory, research, and clinical application* (2nd ed., pp. 906–933). New York, NY: Guilford Press.

Greeley, A. M. (1974). *Ecstasy: A way of knowing.* Englewood Cliffs, NJ: Prentice-Hall.

Griffiths, R. R., Richards, W. A., Johnson, M. W., McCann, U. D., & Jesse, R. (2008). Mystical-type experiences occasioned by psilocybin mediate the attribution of personal meaning and spiritual significance 14 months later. *Journal of Psychopharmacology*, 22, 621–632. doi:10.1177/0269881108094300

Griffiths, R. R., Richards, W. A., McCann, U. D., & Jesse, R. (2006). Psilocybin can occasion mystical experiences having substantial and sustained personal meaning and spiritual significance. *Psychopharmacology, 187*, 268–283. doi:10.1007/s00213-006-0457-5

Guthrie, S. E. (1993). *Faces in the clouds: A new theory of religion*. New York, NY: Oxford University Press.

Guthrie, S. E. (1996). Religion: What is it? *Journal for the Scientific Study of Religion, 35*, 412–419.

Harris, A. H., Thoresen, C. E., McCullough, M. E., & Larson, D. B. (1999). Spirituality and religiously oriented health interventions. *Journal of Health Psychology, 4*, 413–433. doi:10.1177/135910539900400309

Heller, D. (1986). *The children's God.* Chicago, IL: University of Chicago Press.

Helminiak, D. A. (2010). "Theistic psychology and psychotherapy": A theological and scientific critique. *Zygon, 45*, 47–74. doi:10.1111/j.1467-9744.2010.01058.x

Henry, J. (Ed.). (2005). *Parapsychology: Research on exceptional experiences.* New York, NY: Routledge. doi:10.4324/9780203334492

Hick, J. (1989). *An interpretation of religion.* New Haven, CT: Yale University Press. doi:10.1057/9780230371286

Hodge, D. R. (2007). A systematic review of the empirical literature on intercessory prayer. *Research on Social Work Practice, 17*, 174–187. doi:10.1177/1049731506296170

Hood, R. W., Jr. (1975). The construction and preliminary validation of a measure of reported religious experience. *Journal for the Scientific Study of Religion, 14*, 29–41.

Hood, R. W., Jr. (1977). Eliciting mystical states of consciousness with semi-structured nature experiences. *Journal for the Scientific Study of Religion, 16*, 155–163. doi:10.2307/1385746

Hood, R. W., Jr. (1978). Anticipatory set and setting stress incongruities as elicitors of mystical experiences in solitary nature settings. *Journal for the Scientific Study of Religion, 17*, 279–287. doi:10.2307/1386322

Hood, R. W., Jr. (2003). The relationship between religion and spirituality. In D. Bromley (Series Ed.) & A. L. Greil & D. Bromley (Vol. Eds.), *Defining religion: Investigating the boundaries between the sacred and the secular: Vol. 10. Religion and the social order* (pp. 241–265). Amsterdam, the Netherlands: Elsevier Science.

Hood, R. W., Jr. (2008). Theoretical fruits from the empirical study of mysticism: A Jamesian perspective. *Journal für Psychologie, 16*, Jfp-3.

Hood, R. W., Jr. (2010). Another epistemic evaluation of Freud's Oedipal theory of religion. In B. Beit-Hallahmi (Ed.), *Psychoanalysis and theism: Critical reflections on the Grünbaum thesis* (pp. 135–154). Lanham, MD: Jason Aronson.

Hood, R. W., Jr. (2011). Where prophecy lives: Psychological and sociological studies of cognitive dissonance. In D. Tumminia & W. H. Swatos (Eds.), *How prophecy lives: The Festinger thesis and beyond* (pp. 21–40). Leiden, the Netherlands: Brill.

Hood, R. W., Jr. (2012). Methodological agnosticism for the social sciences? Lessons from Sorokin's and James's allusions to psychoanalysis, mysticism, and Godly love. In M. T. Lee & A. Yong (Eds.), *Godly love: Impediments and possibilities* (pp. 21–40). Lanham, MD: Lexington Books.

Hood, R. W., Jr., & Byrom, G. (2010). Mysticism, madness, and mental health. In R. W. Hood Jr., P. C. Hill, & B. Spilka (Eds.), *The psychology of religion: An empirical approach* (4th ed.). New York, NY: Guilford Press.

Hood, R. W., Jr., Morris, R. J., & Watson, P. J. (1991). Male commitment to the cult of the Virgin Mary and the passion of Christ as a function of early maternal bonding. *The International Journal for the Psychology of Religion, 1*, 221–231. doi:10.1207/s15327582ijpr0104_4

Hood, R. W., Jr., & Williamson, P. W. (2008). *Them that believe: The power and meaning of the Christian serpent-handling tradition.* Berkeley: University of California Press.

House, J. (1977). The three faces of social psychology. *Sociometry, 40*, 161–170.

Hyman, R., & Honorton, C. (1986). A joint communiqué: The psi ganzfeld controversy. *Journal of Parapsychology, 50*, 350–364.

James, W. (1892). *Psychology: The briefer course.* New York, NY: Holt. doi:10.1037/11630-000

James, W. (1981). *The principles of psychology.* Cambridge, MA: Harvard University Press. (Original work published 1890)

James, W. (1985). *The varieties of religious experience: A study in human nature.* Cambridge, MA: Harvard University Press. (Original work published 1902)

Jones, E. E. (1998). Major developments in five decades of social psychology. In D. T. Gilbert, S. T. Fiske, & G. Lindzey (Eds.), The *handbook of social psychology* (4th ed., Vol. 1, pp. 3–47). Boston, MA: McGraw-Hill.

Keen, E. (1975). *A primer in phenemenological psychology*. Lanham, MD: University Press of America.

Kelman, H. C. (1967). Human use of human subjects: The problem of deception in social psychological experiments. *Psychological Bulletin, 67*, 1–11. doi:10.1037/h0024072

Kelman, H. C. (1968). *A time to speak*. San Francisco, CA: Jossey-Bass.

Kirkpatrick, L. A. (1992). An attachment-theory approach to the psychology of religion. *The International Journal for the Psychology of Religion, 2*, 3–28. doi:10.1207/s15327582ijpr0201_2

Kirkpatrick, L. A. (1997). A longitudinal study of changes in religious belief and behavior as a function of individual differences in attachment style. *Journal for the Scientific Study of Religion, 36*, 207–217. doi:10.2307/1387553

Koenig, H. G. (2008). Concerns about measuring "spirituality" in research. *Journal of Nervous and Mental Disease, 196*, 349–355. doi:10.1097/NMD.0b013e31816ff796

Koenig, H. G., McCullough, M. E., & Larson, D. B. (2001). *Handbook of religion and health*. New York, NY: Oxford University Press. doi:10.1093/acprof:oso/9780195118667.001.0001

Kramrisch, S., Otto, J., Ruck, C., & Wasson, R. (1986). *Persephone's quest: Entheogens and the origin of religion*. New Haven, CT: Yale University Press.

Kvale, S. (1996). *Interviews: An introduction to qualitative research interviewing*. Thousand Oaks, CA: Sage.

LaBarre, W. (1972). *The ghost dance: The origins of religion* (Rev. ed.). New York, NY: Delta.

Lakatos, I., & Feyerabend, P. (1999). *For and against method: Including Lakatos's lectures on the scientific method and the Lakatos–Feyerabend correspondence* (M. Motterlini, Ed.). Chicago, IL: University of Chicago Press.

Leibovici, L. (2001). Effects of remote, retroactive intercessory prayer on outcomes with patients with bloodstream infection: Randomized controlled trial. *BMJ, 323*, 1450–1451. doi:10.1136/bmj.323.7327.1450

Luyten, P., & Corveleyn, J. (2007). Attachment and religion: The need to leave our secure base: A comment on the discussion between Granqvist, Rizzuto, and Wulff. *The International Journal for the Psychology of Religion, 17*, 81–97. doi:10.1080/10508610701244114

McAdams, D. P. (2006). *The redemptive self: Stories Americans live by*. New York, NY: Oxford University Press.

McCleary, R., & Hay, R. (1980). *Applied time series analysis for the social sciences*. Beverly Hills, CA: Sage.

McCullough, M. E., Enders, C. K., Brion, S. L., & Jain, A. R. (2005). The varieties of religious development in adulthood: A longitudinal investigation of religion and rational choice. *Journal of Personality and Social Psychology, 89*, 78–89. doi:10.1037/0022-3514.89.1.78

McNamara, P. (Ed.). (2006). *Where God and science meet: How brain and evolutionary studies alter our understanding of religion* (3 vols.). Westport, CT: Praeger.

Melton, J. G. (1985). Spiritualization and reaffirmation: What really happens when prophecy fails? *American Studies, 26*, 17–29.

Miles, G. (2007). *Science and religious experience: Are they similar forms of knowledge?* Portland, OR; Sussex, England: Academic Press.

Miller, L. (2010). Watching for the light: Spiritual psychology beyond materialism. *Psychology of Religion and Spirituality, 2*, 35–36. doi:10.1037/a0018554

Milton, J., & Wiseman, R. (1999). Does psi exist? Lack of replication of an anomalous process of information transfer. *Psychological Bulletin, 125*, 387–391. doi:10.1037/0033-2909.125.4.387

Mixon, D. (1971). Behaviour analysis treating subjects as actors rather than organisms. *Journal for the Theory of Social Behaviour, 1*, 19–31. doi:10.1111/j.1468-5914.1971.tb00164.x

Mixon, D. (1972). Instead of deception. *Journal for the Theory of Social Behaviour, 2*, 145–178. doi:10.1111/j.1468-5914.1972.tb00309.x

Moghadam, F. M., Taylor, D. M., & Wright, C. S. (1993). *Social psychology in cross-cultural perspective*. New York, NY: Freeman.

Merkur, D. (2010). *Explorations of the psychoanalytic mystics*. New York, NY: Rodopi.

Murray-Swank, N. A., & Pargament, K. I. (2005). God, where are you? Evaluating a spiritually integrated intervention for sexual abuse. *Mental Health, Religion, and Culture, 8*, 191–203. doi:10.1080/13694670500138866

Neisser, U. (1976). *Cognition and reality*. San Francisco, CA: Freeman.

Newberg, A., & Newberg, S. (2010). Psychology and neurobiology in a postmaterialist world. *Psychology of Religion and Spirituality, 2*, 119–121. doi:10.1037/a0019264

Nichols, D. E., & Chemel, B. R. (2006). The neurophysiology of religious experience: Hallucinogens and the experience of the divine. In P. McNamara (Ed.), *Where God and science meet: Vol. 3. The psychology of religious experience* (pp. 1–34). Westport, CT: Praeger.

O'Connor, S., & Vandenberg, B. (2010). Differentiating psychosis and faith: The role of social norms and religious fundamentalism. *Mental*

Health, Religion, and Culture, 13, 171–186. doi:10.1080/13674670903277984

Pahnke, W. N. (1966). Drugs and mysticism. *International Journal of Parapsychology, 8*, 295–314.

Pargament, K. I. (1997). *The psychology of religion and coping: Theory, research, practice*. New York, NY: Guilford Press.

Pargament, K. I. (2007). *Spiritually integrated psychotherapy: Understanding and addressing the sacred*. New York, NY: Guilford Press.

Polkinghorne, D. E. (1989). Phenomenological research methods. In R. S. Valle & S. Halling (Eds.), *Existential–phenomenological perspectives in psychology: Exploring the breadth of human experience* (pp. 41–60). New York, NY: Plenum Press.

Pollio, H. R., Henley, T. B., & Thompson, C. J. (1997). *The phenomenology of everyday life*. New York, NY: Cambridge University Press. doi:10.1017/CBO9780511752919

Pollner, M. (1987). *Mundane reason: Reality in everyday and sociological discourse*. New York, NY: Cambridge University Press.

Poloma, M., & Hood, R. W., Jr. (2008). *Blood and fire: Godly love in a Pentecostal emerging church*. New York, NY: New York University Press.

Porpora, D. V. (2006). Methodological atheism, methodological agnosticism and religious experience. *Journal for the Theory of Social Behaviour, 36*, 57–75. doi:10.1111/j.1468-5914.2006.00296.x

Richards, R. C., & Bergin, A. E. (1997). *A spiritual strategy for counseling and psychotherapy*. Washington, DC: American Psychological Association. doi:10.1037/10241-000

Richards, W. A. (2009). The rebirth of research with entheogens: Lessons from the past and hypotheses for the future. *Journal of Transpersonal Psychology, 42*, 139–150.

Richardson, J. T., Stewart, M., & Simmonds, R. (1972). *Organized miracles: A study of a communal youth fundamentalist group*. Brunswick, NJ: Transaction.

Rizzuto, A.-M. (1979). *The birth of the living God: A psychoanalytic study*. Chicago, IL: University of Chicago Press.

Rizzuto, A.-M. (2006). Discussion on Granqvist's article "On the relation between secular and divine relationships: An emerging attachment perspective and a critique of the 'depth' approaches." *The International Journal for the Psychology of Religion, 16*, 19–28. doi:10.1207/s15327582ijpr1601_2

Roehlkepartain, E. C., Benson, P. L., King, P. E., & Wagener, L. (2006). Spiritual development in childhood and adolescence: Moving to the scientific mainstream. In E. C. Roehlkepartain, P. E. King, L. Wagener, & P. L. Benson (Eds.), *The handbook of spiritual development in childhood and adolescence* (pp. 1–16). Thousand Oaks, CA: Sage.

Rosegrant, J. (1976). The impact of set and setting on religious experience in nature. *Journal for the Scientific Study of Religion, 15*, 301–310. doi:10.2307/1385633

Roth, P. A. (1987). *Meaning and method in the social sciences: The case for methodological pluralism*. Ithaca, NY: Cornell University Press.

Rothbaum, F., Weisz, J., Pott, M., Miyake, K., & Morelli, G. (2000). Attachment and culture: Security in the United States and Japan. *American Psychologist, 55*, 1093–1104. doi:10.1037/0003-066X.55.10.1093

Rye, M. S. (2005). The religious path to forgiveness. *Mental Health, Religion, and Culture, 8*, 205–215. doi:10.1080/13694670500138882

Rye, M. S., Pargament, K. I., Wei, P., Yingling, D. W., Shogren, K. A., & Ito, M. (2005). Can group interventions facilitate forgiveness of ex-spouse? A randomized clinical trial. *Journal of Consulting and Clinical Psychology, 73*, 880–892

Saroglou, V. (2002). Religion and the five factors of personality: A meta-analytic review. *Personality and Individual Differences, 32*, 15–25. doi:10.1016/S0191-8869(00)00233-6

Saroglou, V., Delpierre, V., & Dernelle, R. (2002). Values and religiosity: A meta-analysis of studies using Schwartz's model. *Personality and Individual Differences, 32*, 15–25. doi:10.1016/S0191-8869(00)00233-6

Saroglou, V., & Muñoz-García, A. (2008). Individual differences in religion and spirituality: An issue of personality traits and/or values. *Journal for the Scientific Study of Religion, 47*, 83–101. doi:10.1111/j.1468-5906.2008.00393.x

Saucier, G., & Skrzypińska, K. (2006). Spiritual but not religious? Evidence for two independent dispositions. *Journal of Personality, 74*, 1257–1292. doi:10.1111/j.1467-6494.2006.00409.x

Schlitz, M., & Braud, W. (1997). Distant intentionality and healing: Assessing the evidence. *Alternative Therapies in Health and Medicine, 3*, 62–73.

Schwartz, S. H. (1992). Universals in the content of the structure of values: Theoretical advances and empirical test in 20 countries. In M. Zanna (Ed.), *Advances in experimental social psychology* (Vol. 25, pp. 1–65). Orlando, FL: Academic Press.

Secord, P. F., & Backman, C. W. (1964). *Social psychology*. New York, NY: McGraw-Hill.

Shafranske, E. (2010). Advancing "The boldest model yet": A commentary on psychology, religion, and spirituality. *Psychology of Religion and Spirituality, 2*, 124–125. doi:10.1037/a0019624

Shafranske, E. (Ed.). (1996). *Religion and the clinical practice of psychology*. Washington, DC: American Psychological Association. doi:10.1037/10199-000

Shanon, B. (2002). *Antipodes of the mind: Charting the phenomenology of the ayahuasca experience.* New York, NY: Oxford University Press.

Shuman, J. J., & Meador, K. G. (2003). *Heal thyself: Spirituality, medicine, and the distortion of Christianity.* New York, NY: Oxford University Press.

Sloan, R. P., Bagiella, E., & Powell, T. (1999). Religion, spirituality, and medicine. *Lancet, 353,* 664–667. doi:10.1016/S0140-6736(98)07376-0

Smith, H. (2000). *Cleansing the doors of perception: The religious significance of entheogenic plants.* New York, NY: Tarcher/Putnam.

Stace, W. T. (1960). *Mysticism and philosophy.* Philadelphia, PA: Lippincott.

Stone, J. R. (2000). *Expecting Armageddon: Essential readings in failed prophecy.* New York, NY: Routledge.

Strawson, P. F. (1959). *Individuals: An essay in descriptive metaphysics.* London, England: Methuen. doi:10.4324/9780203221303

Streib, H., Hood, R. W., Jr., Keller, B., Csöff, R.-M., & Silver, C. (2008). *Deconversion: Qualitative and quantitative results from cross-cultural research in Germany and the United States: Vol. 4. Research in contemporary religion.* Göttingham, Germany: Vandenhoeck & Ruprecht.

Stryker, S. (1977). Developments in "two social psychologies": Toward an appreciation of mutual relevance. *Sociometry, 40,* 145–160.

Taslimi, C. R., Hood, R. W., Jr., & Watson, P. J. (1991). Assessment of former members of Shiloh: The adjective checklist 17 years later. *Journal for the Scientific Study of Religion, 30,* 306–311. doi:10.2307/1386975

Tomarken, A. J., & Waller, N. G. (2005). Structural equation modeling: Strengths, limitations, and misconceptions. *Annual Review of Clinical Psychology, 1,* 31–65. doi:10.1146/annurev.clinpsy.1.102803.144239

Tumminia, D. (1998). How prophecy never fails: Interpretative reason in a flying saucer group. *Sociology of Religion, 59,* 157–170. doi:10.2307/3712078

Valle, R. S., King, M., & Halling, S. (1989). An introduction to phenomenological thought in psychology. In R. S. Valle & S. Halling (Eds.), *Existential–phenomenological perspectives in psychology: Exploring the breadth of human experience* (pp. 3–16). New York, NY: Plenum Press.

Van Fossen, A. B. (1988). How do movements survive failures of prophecy? In *Research in social movements, culture, and change* (Vol. 10, pp. 193–202). Greenwich, CT: JAI Press.

Van Manen, M. (1990). *Researching lived experience: Human science for an action sensitive pedagogy.* Albany: State University of New York Press.

Walach, H., Kohls, N., von Stillfried, N., Hinterberger, T., & Schmidt, S. (2009). Spirituality: The legacy of parapsychology. *Archive for the Psychology of Religion, 31,* 277–308.

Walsh, W. J. (1906). *The apparitions of the shrines of heaven's bright queen* (4 vols.). New York, NY: Cary-Stafford.

Watson, P. J., Morris, R. J., Foster, J. E., & Hood, R. W., Jr. (1986). Religiosity and social desirability. *Journal for the Scientific Study of Religion, 25,* 215–232.

Watson, P. J., Morris, R. J., & Hood, R. W., Jr. (1987). Antireligious humanistic values, guilt, and self esteem. *Journal for the Scientific Study of Religion, 26,* 535–546. doi:10.2307/1387103

Watson, P. J., Morris, R. J., & Hood, R. W., Jr. (1990). Intrinsicness, religious self-love, and narcissism. *Journal of Psychology and Christianity, 9,* 40–46.

Watson, P. J., Sawyers, P., Morris, R. J., Carpenter, M. L., Jimenez, R. S., Jonas, K. A., & Robinson, D. L. (2003). Reanalysis within a Christian ideological surround: Relationship of intrinsic religious orientation with fundamentalism and right-wing authoritarianism. *Journal of Psychology and Theology, 31,* 315–332.

Weitzman, E. A., & Miles, M. B. (1995). *Computer programs for qualitative data.* Thousands Oaks, CA: Sage.

Williamson, W. P., & Pollio, H. R. (1999). The phenomenology of religious serpent handling: A rationale and thematic study of spontaneous sermons. *Journal for the Scientific Study of Religion, 38,* 203–218. doi:10.2307/1387790

Wink, P., & Dillon, M. (2002). Spiritual development across the adult life course: Findings from a longitudinal study. *Journal of Adult Development, 9,* 79–94. doi:10.1023/A:1013833419122

Wink, P., & Dillon, M. (2003). Religiousness, spirituality, and psychosocial functioning in late adulthood: Findings from a longitudinal study. *Psychology and Aging, 18,* 916–924. doi:10.1037/0882-7974.18.4.916

Wise, E. A. (2004). Methods for analyzing psychotherapy outcomes: A review of clinical significance, reliable change, and recommendations for future directions. *Journal of Personality Assessment, 82,* 50–59. doi:10.1207/s15327752jpa8201_10

Yamane, D., & Polzer, M. (1994). Ways of seeing ecstasy in modern society: Experimental–expressive and cultural–linguistic views. *Sociology of Religion, 55,* 1–25. doi:10.2307/3712173

Zinnbauer, B. J., & Pargament, K. I. (2002). Capturing the meaning of religiousness and spirituality: One way down from a definitional tower of babel. *Research in the Social Scientific Study of Religion, 13,* 23–54.

Zinnbauer, B. J., & Pargament, K. I. (2005). Religiousness and spirituality. In R. F. Paloutzian & C. L. Park (Eds.), *Handbook of religion and spirituality* (pp. 21–42). New York, NY: Guilford Press.

Part II

WHY PEOPLE ARE RELIGIOUS AND SPIRITUAL: EXPLANATORY MODELS

Chapter 5

SACRED ARMOR: RELIGION'S ROLE AS A BUFFER AGAINST THE ANXIETIES OF LIFE AND THE FEAR OF DEATH

Melissa Soenke, Mark J. Landau, and Jeff Greenberg

Religiousness, psychological investment in institutionalized sacred beliefs and practices, is central to the lives of individuals and societies. In his classic treatise, Allport (1950) equated religion to sex as an almost universal human interest. In every human group that exists today, or is known to have existed, people create and communicate shared representations of supernatural worlds (e.g., Atran, 2002; Burkert, 1960). Even in the modern era, with atheism widespread in many countries, 85% of people worldwide report having religious beliefs (Zuckerman, 2005).

Furthermore, for most people, religion is not an occasional or incidental interest: About 82% of people worldwide state that religion constitutes an important part of their everyday life (Crabtree, 2009). Indeed, many people invest substantial material resources and emotional energy into their religion and religiousness permeates major aspects of their lives, from birth celebrations to rites of passage to memorial occasions. Moreover, throughout history, clashes between competing religious ideologies have fueled bitter conflict and bloodshed.

Given religion's central significance, we begin with a basic question: What psychological functions does religion serve for people? Classic and contemporary scholars in philosophy, psychology, and the social sciences have proposed a number of factors that may contribute to the psychological appeal and value of religion. Amid this diversity of viewpoints, we can identify a recurring theme that forms the central thesis of this chapter: A primary function of religiousness is to buffer the individual against anxiety.

In elaborating on this claim, we first discuss how classic theorists such as William James (1902) and Sigmund Freud (1913/1919, 1927/1961) each, in his own way, highlighted religion's anxiety-buffering function. We then present a brief overview of perspectives that focuses on how adherence to religious ideologies may buffer anxiety by providing people with attachment, structure, and hope, particularly when people have doubts about having the internal or external resources to obtain desired outcomes and avoid undesired ones. Next we focus on a core source of anxiety—the awareness that the self will inevitably die—and provide an account of religion's anxiety-buffering function derived from terror management theory (TMT; Greenberg, Pyszczynski, & Solomon, 1986; Solomon, Greenberg, & Pyszczynski, 2004). According to this theory, people manage the potential anxiety stemming from their awareness of mortality by subscribing to *cultural worldviews*, which afford opportunities to view life as valuable and continuing on in some way after death. From this perspective, religiousness serves to buffer anxiety about mortality by offering opportunities to attain immortality, thereby making death less threatening.

We buttress our theoretical analysis with historical, correlational, and experimental evidence for the role of terror management processes in motivating adherence to religion. Also, we review research showing that motivated adherence to religion shapes people's attitudes and behaviors regarding a range of domains, including intergroup relations and medical decision making. In these ways, we

DOI: 10.1037/14045-005
APA Handbook of Psychology, Religion, and Spirituality: Vol. 1. Context, Theory, and Research, K. I. Pargament (Editor-in-Chief)
Copyright © 2013 by the American Psychological Association. All rights reserved.

show that TMT provides a unique and empirically substantiated account of religion's significance in human affairs that can be used to organize diverse evidence regarding religion's social and personal import.

CLASSIC PERSPECTIVES ON RELIGION'S ANXIETY-BUFFERING FUNCTION

Fear, first of all, produced gods in the world.
—Statius (AD 45–96, quoted in Burkert, 1960, p. 31)

James (1902) and Freud (1913/1919, 1927/1961), two of the most influential architects of modern psychology, put forward accounts of religion that, at first glance, completely contradict each other. Whereas James viewed religion sympathetically as a powerful tool for improving well-being, Freud dismissed it as an infantile neurosis and an illusion that humankind may hope someday to outgrow in favor of a rational and scientific worldview. Despite their differences, both theorists recognized that religion often serves as a defense mechanism that keeps anxiety at bay.

James brought the topic of religion into psychology with his lecture series published in 1902 under the title *The Varieties of Religious Experience.* James emphasized religion's power to foster individual growth and happiness. James presented a multifaceted view of religion that explored both religion's growth-oriented and defensive aspects. James recognized that religion is able to promote positive psychological engagement in large part by providing the individual with relief from "evils" in the world. He ultimately concluded that religious experience is on the whole a useful tool for coping with anxiety-provoking stimuli in the natural and social world.

Freud's (1927/1961, 1930/1961, 1939/1961) views were also complex and changed in important ways over his career. Freud's early theory posited that God, like parents, serves psychologically protective functions for the believer (Freud, 1913/1919). While acknowledging this protective function, Freud (1927/1961) ultimately viewed religious belief as a form of psychopathology similar to a delusion. This latter view held that religion arose out of the need to defend oneself against "the superior force of nature" (Freud, 1927/1961, p. 17). He described the function of religion as threefold: to exorcise the terrors of nature, reconcile man to the cruelty of fate and mortality, and compensate the individual for society's restrictions on his or her freedom.

This psychodynamic approach to religion emphasizes the importance of early representations of parents and self in determining the development of the individual's religiosity and representations of God (see Volume 2, Chapter 6, this handbook). Because people's relationship with God is largely modeled after childhood experiences with their father, they differ in the extent to which they rely on God for support and care in adulthood. Although Freud's original idea focused narrowly on the relationship between father and son, later psychodynamic theorists such as Erickson (1959, 1963) broadened the focus to include representations of both parents as they relate to individual images of God.

Broadly consistent with the psychodynamic view, Brown and Cullen (2006) found that religious individuals most frequently described their motivation for engaging in religious activities as arising out of a desire to fulfill their needs for love. In addition, correlational evidence shows that people's representation of their parents predicts their conception of God (Birky & Ball, 1988; Godin & Hallez, 1965; M. O. Nelson, 1971; Tamayo & Desjardins, 1976; Vergote & Tamayo, 1981). In some cases the image of God is correlated with the mother rather than with the father (M. O. Nelson & Jones, 1957), in others with both parental images (Birky & Ball, 1988; Justice & Lambert, 1986; Strunk, 1959), and still others with only the parent of the same sex as the individual (Godin & Hallez, 1965) or the preferred parent (M. O. Nelson, 1971).

CONTEMPORARY PERSPECTIVES ON THE ROLE OF RELIGION IN MANAGING ANXIETIES OF LIFE

Psychodynamic theories essentially view religion as serving the same anxiety-buffering function for adults that the parents serve for children; it provides comfort, protection, answers, and hope when people are distressed or anxious either because good things they want may not happen or bad things they do not want may. A set of precepts and higher powers provides a way to enhance one's chances for attaining good outcomes (e.g., that job one applied for) and for escaping bad outcomes (e.g., the loss of a child to a potentially fatal illness). This perspective is supported by research programs that are based either specifically on the idea that God is a security-providing attachment figure or on the general idea that threats to other psychological resources in people's lives lead to greater reliance on religion.

One influential contemporary approach to religion comes from John Bowlby's (1969) attachment theory. Combining insights from psychoanalysis and evolutionary biology, Bowlby emphasized that as a consequence of their mammalian heritage, human offspring innately respond to threatening stimuli by seeking proximity to attachment figures who regularly provide care. Bowlby then posited that people can regulate distress by bringing to mind mental representations of attachment figures even when those individuals are not physically present.

Kirkpatrick (2005) proposed that the same attachment system that drives the child to seek security from physical proximity to her parents drives the adult to seek security from symbolic proximity to an all-powerful God. In this way, attachment theory explains commonalities in religiousness across individuals and cultures. This perspective suggests that relationships with spiritual figures are modeled after relationships with security-providing parents.

Indeed, most people conceptualize their faith as an intimate relationship with a benevolent caregiver (Birgegard & Granqvist, 2004; Kirkpatrick, 2005). As individuals describe their lives in terms of relationships, religion is also viewed as a relationship between believer and deity (see Chapter 7, this volume). In a poll of Americans, when asked about what best defines their own view of religious faith, 51% indicated that "a relationship with God" was most descriptive (Gallup & Jones, 1989). This may be less true, however, of proponents of certain religions, such as those based on the Buddhist tradition.

Findings obtained in attachment and religion studies support the neo-Freudian emphasis on the protective function of religion, particularly among individuals with insecure attachment style (see Chapter 7, this volume). Just as infants seek proximity to caregivers, individuals seek proximity to God (Kirkpatrick, 2005). Birgegard and Granqvist (2004) found that activating attachment insecurity by subliminal exposure to such phrases as "mother is gone" led to increased desire to be close to God in securely attached individuals. Although physical proximity to supernatural deities is impossible, beliefs in an omnipresent God, prayer, and symbols of God facilitate psychological proximity (Kirkpatrick, 2005).

Further support for the link between views of one's parents and God comes from factor-analytic research indicating that just as there are individual differences in parental images, similar differences are seen in God images (Kirkpatrick, 2005). In nearly all of these studies, the largest factor to emerge reflects God as a benevolent caregiver. This view of God fits well with the notion of God as serving an anxiety-buffering function. The second-largest factor to emerge, however, characterizes God as a controlling and punishing deity (Kirkpatrick, 2005). Generally, individuals with secure attachment characteristics tend to have a more loving God image than individuals with insecure attachment styles, who view God as more distant (Granqvist, 2006). We will further discuss why God is not necessarily viewed as a benevolent caregiver later in this chapter.

In addition to providing a potent attachment figure who can substitute for other security-providing attachments, religion provides the belief in a higher power who will help people attain positive outcomes and avert negative outcomes as long as they stay in the good graces of that power, such as by being a righteous follower or appealing to deities via prayer. They also provide rules and authorities that one can lean on for support and guidance. These features can reduce anxieties people have about getting the good things in life and avoiding the bad things.

Recent research has supported this idea by showing that when you threaten the psychological resources that provide people with feelings of security and hope for good outcomes, such as their self-worth, their close relationships, and faith in the stability of their culture, they increase their faith in and defense of their belief in God, confidence in their beliefs, and negativity toward ideas and people who question their religious beliefs (e.g., Kay, Gaucher, McGregor, & Nash, 2010; McGregor, Haji, Nash, & Teper, 2008). In addition, two studies have implicated anxiety as a mediator of increased investment in religious beliefs (Kay et al., 2010).

Religion as a Buffer Against the Fear of Death

The perspectives we have reviewed so far view religion as a resource people rely on to manage general anxieties. But there is one anxiety that religion seems especially suited to quell. As Freud (1927/1961) noted, individuals turn to religion to cope with threats that even their parents cannot vanquish, namely, the cruelties of fate and the inevitability of death.

Terror management theory built on this psychodynamic tradition, particularly as synthesized by Becker (1971, 1973). The theory posits that over childhood, people eventually become aware of the fragility of life and the inevitability of death as well as of their parents limited ability to provide protection. These realizations conflict with people's desire to continue living, and in this way, create the potential to experience debilitating terror. People consequently transfer their primary basis of security to bigger, more compellingly protective constructs, such as the nation, humanity, noble causes, and for many if not most people, God.

According to TMT, this transference of protective power allows people to buffer themselves from threatening cognitions about death. This is accomplished by investing in two interrelated psychological structures. The first is a *cultural worldview*: a set of socially constructed beliefs about reality that provides a meaningful account of the origin and nature of the universe, a set of principles and standards of value by which to live, and the promise of immortality to those who fulfill those standards. The second structure is *self-esteem*: the perception that one is indeed fulfilling those standards and is therefore a being whose soul or identity will transcend physical death in some form.

TMT views both secular and religious worldviews as offering meaningful conceptions of reality that provide avenues for attaining immortality (indeed, Becker, 1975, viewed even explicitly atheistic cultural worldviews as essentially "religious" in their provision of culturally constructed bases of death transcendence). Both religious and secular worldviews offer standards to uphold in order to attain *symbolic immortality* or to have some aspect of the self "live on" beyond death. For example, academics follow the "publish or perish" maxim in the hopes of leaving some trace of their existence on dusty bookshelves. Additionally, some branches of Judaism place less emphasis on literal immortality and more on living through good deeds and adhering to the Mitzvot, the commandments outlined in the Torah. Religious worldviews typically, although perhaps not always, offer standards by means of which people can also attain *literal immortality*. For example, Christians adhere to the teachings of Jesus to gain entrance to Heaven. Because both secular and religious systems of meaning and personal value are fragile social constructions, however, people must continually strive to buttress the validity of their cultural worldview—and live up to culturally derived standards of value—to avoid the threatening awareness that death may signal the absolute end of their existence.

From the TMT perspective, religions that offer hope of literal immortality are particularly well-suited to buffer people from the terror of inevitable death because they provide socially validated assurance that death does not represent the absolute annihilation of the self; rather, it is merely a transition to eternal life. In this sense (in contrast to personal abilities, science, philosophy, the government or other cultural bases of power and security), such religious belief systems are uniquely suited to handle the problem of death. This TMT view of religion's function illuminates why the earliest known religions focused so much on mortality and immortality. As early as the Upper Paleolithic Era, humans used artistic forms to represent a division of the person into a mortal body and an intangible essence that persists after death (Hauser, 1951), and they adorned burial sites with intricately fashioned goods presumably to equip the deceased for their passage into the afterlife (Tattersall, 1998).

If we fast-forward some millennia, we find the Epic of Gilgamesh—an ancient Sumerian written narrative believed to have originated around 3000 B.C.—describing the titular hero's confrontation with mortality and his quest for immortality. Gilgamesh, king of Uruk, embarks on a journey in search of immortality after his friend and companion Enkidu dies. Gilgamesh campaigns with the gods for immortality, but in the end, his pleas are denied and he is left with the inevitability of death. This earliest known self-referential narrative is believed to have been the basis for the recounting of the Fall in Genesis, the first book of the Bible, which describes early man being expelled from his earthly paradise. Becker (1973) described how this paradise represents man's ignorant and animal-like state. When man reaches awareness of his condition, he is forced to face his corporeal nature and reconcile the duality of his being both divine and mortal. Abrahamic traditions (Christianity, Judaism, and Islam) propose a solution to this problem in the promise of life everlasting in a heaven where people are free from the constraints of their earthly bodies. Ancient Egyptian and Chinese religious beliefs similarly focused on routes to the afterlife. Beliefs in souls extending beyond physical death were also prominent in Western Mayan and Aztec religions as well as in most known tribal cultures.

More recent Eastern religions, like Hinduism and Buddhism, also offer routes to immortality through the belief in the existence of an eternal soul, or atman, which is connected to all other life energies. This soul transcends the physical world and lives on in separate lives throughout a cycle of rebirth (samsara) that ends only upon the achievement of enlightenment (nirvana). Death is an integral part of this process and contemplation of death is encouraged. Both Western religious traditions (which promise immortality in heaven) and Eastern traditions (which provide guidance regarding the experience of death and process of rebirth) offer comfort from the terror of inevitable death by providing assurance that the end of this life is not *our* end.

A wide breadth of literature supports the idea that at the core of religion's appeal is management of anxiety surrounding death. Initial studies utilized unidimensional definitions of both religion and death anxiety. The majority of these studies found that religious individuals express lower levels of death anxiety (e.g., Feifel, 195; Kahoe & Dunn, 1976). More recent investigations utilizing a multidimensional approach and exploring the nature and strength of various religious beliefs have provided more insight into the relationship between religion and death anxiety. One variable showing particular importance in protecting individuals from anxiety about death is the belief in an afterlife (Alvarado, Templer, Bresler, & Thomas-Dobson, 1995; Harding, Flannelly, Weaver, & Costa, 2005). Active commitment and practice also has been repeatedly associated with lower levels of death anxiety (Feifel, 1977; Feifel & Nagy, 1981; Schulz, 1978). Similarly, an inverse relationship between strength and conviction of religious beliefs and death anxiety was found by Triplett et al. (1995).

Although many of these studies have been conducted using Christian participants, studies of other religious orientations using a variety of measures of religiosity are becoming more prevalent and yield similar results. Using a scale of religiousness designed specifically for Muslims, Suhail and Akram (2002) found that among Pakistani Muslims, more religious participants showed significantly lower concerns about death. Similarly, Roshdieh, Templer, Cannon, and Canfield (1998) used a scale developed by Templer and Dotson (1970) modified for Muslims and found a negative correlation between death anxiety and religious involvement among Iranian Muslims. In a study of Israeli Jews using the Jewish Religiosity Index (Ben-Meir & Kadem, 1979), Florian and Kravets (1983) found differences between highly and moderately religious individuals with regard to their specific concerns about death. The highly religious individuals expressed significantly more fear about punishment in the afterlife and less fear about self-annihilation, whereas the moderately religious individuals expressed significantly more fear of death's consequences to loved ones (Florian & Kravets, 1983).

Evidence also shows that events that increase awareness of death often precede spikes in religious activity. For example, following the murder of 3,000 civilians by terrorists on September 11, 2001, people around the world showed a surge in church attendance (Lampman, 2001), Bible sales (Rice, 2001), and visits to religious websites (Lampman, 2001).

Additionally, studies show that among the different components of religious ideology, belief in an afterlife is a particularly strong predictor of low death anxiety (Alvarado et al., 1995; Harding et al., 2005) and more positive associations with death (Schoenrade, 1989).

Experimental Research Supporting the Terror Management Role of Religiousness

These findings are consistent with our claim that religion quells terror, but because they are based on correlations, we cannot be sure that religiousness is causing the lower levels of death anxiety. A growing body of experimental research guided by TMT, however, provides converging evidence for the role of religiousness in coping with mortality concerns. Before describing this evidence, we need to provide a brief overview of the primary methods used to assess TMT hypotheses. Beginning in the late 1980s, researchers developed three broad approaches to testing hypotheses based on TMT that more recently have been used to assess the role of religion in terror management. The first approach is to make mortality salient (MS) and assess whether this motivates greater adherence to and defense of the individual's cultural worldview. The most common MS induction involves responding to two open-ended prompts that are embedded among a series of personality questionnaires: (a) "Please briefly describe the emotions that the thought of your own death arouses in you"; and (b) "Jot down, as specifically as you can, what you think will happen to *you* as you physically die." Participants' proximity to a funeral home, writing a single sentence about death, subliminal primes of the word "death," and completing word-searches containing death-related words have also been used to induce MS. More than one hundred studies have shown that MS does indeed bolster faith in one's worldview and negativity toward those who challenge one's worldview (Greenberg, Solomon, & Arndt, 2008).

The second approach is to assess whether threatening terror management resources increases the accessibility of death-related thought. If faith in the worldview and self-worth protect people from death-related concerns, then threatening these constructs should bring death thoughts closer to consciousness. When death thoughts are highly accessible, lingering outside conscious awareness, we call this high death thought accessibility (DTA). This broad hypothesis has been supported in a variety of ways (Hayes, Schimel, Arndt, & Faucher, 2010). The third approach is to assess whether calling to mind psychological resources posited to serve terror management reduces anxiety and defensive reactions to death-related thought. Substantial research has supported this idea as well (see Greenberg et al., 2008).

In recent years, these three approaches have been used to examine the role of religion in terror management. Like much of the TMT research showing that MS increases positive reactions to people who share one's worldview and negative reactions to those who violate one's worldview (for a review, see Greenberg, Solomon, & Pyszczynski, 1997), early research on religion found that MS leads religious individuals to bolster the legitimacy of their religious beliefs and defend their religious worldview. In one study, Greenberg et al. (1990, Study 1) had Christian participants rate Christian and Jewish targets (who were portrayed as quite similar except for religious background) after an MS or control induction. In the control condition, there were no differences in participants' evaluations of the targets; however, MS increased affection for the fellow Christian target and exaggerated hostility toward the Jewish target. Similar findings have been shown among Islamic students in Iran, who responded to MS with greater approval for a fellow student who endorsed religiously motivated martyrdom attacks against the United States as well as greater willingness to join the martyr's cause (Pyszczynski et al., 2006).

In addition to affecting reactions to people who do and do not share one's religious beliefs, MS has been shown to increase reluctance to use sacred objects in an inappropriate manner. Greenberg, Simon, Porteus, Pyszczynski, and Solomon (1995) presented participants with an ostensible creative problem-solving task that entailed using different objects to hang a crucifix on the wall. Half the participants were given a block of wood with which to hang the crucifix, whereas for the other half, the most effective way of completing the task was to use the crucifix itself as a hammer. As predicted, MS participants reported experiencing more difficulty and tension using the crucifix inappropriately compared with control participants, suggesting that terror management motivation heightens reverence for objects that embody cherished religious beliefs.

Research has assessed the effect of mortality reminders on explicit endorsement of religious beliefs. Before TMT, Osarchuk and Tatz (1973) found that among individuals confident in the existence of an afterlife, exposure to disturbing images of death combined with information suggesting a high likelihood of an early death led to an increased belief in an afterlife. In a set of more recent studies, Norenzayan and Hansen (2006) found among Christians but not atheists that MS increased religiosity, belief in God and divine intervention, and belief in higher powers in general. Even more recently, Vail, Abdollahi, and Arndt (2010) conducted two studies, one in the United States and one in Iran. The first found that for Christians but not atheists, MS, relative to a threat to meaning, increased faith in the Christian God while reducing belief in Buddha and Allah. The second study conducted in Iran, in parallel fashion, found that for Iranian Muslims, MS increased faith in Allah while reducing belief in the Christian God and Buddha.

According to the second approach, if adherence to religious worldviews indeed serves to buffer the individual against mortality concerns, then threatening religious beliefs should unleash those concerns. Indeed, Schimel, Hayes, Williams, and Jahrig (2007) found that when participants who subscribe to the Judeo-Christian account of creation read a scientific article arguing against creationism and in favor of evolution, they exhibited heightened DTA, whereas the same article had no such effect on participants who subscribed to an evolutionary account of the origins of life. DTA was measured using a word completion task (Greenberg, Pyszczynski, Solomon, Simon, & Breus, 1994; Harmon-Jones et al., 1997) in which participants were instructed to complete word fragments with the first word that came to mind. Some of the fragments are designed so that they can be completed with either neutral or death-related words. For instance, "coff__" could be completed as "coffee or "coffin."

Related research shows that because religious belief can serve such an important terror management function for its followers, when individuals feel that they are being punished or abandoned by God, a form of what has been called religious struggle (see Exline & Rose, 2005; Pargament, Murray-Swank, Magyar, & Ano, 2005; see also Chapter 25, this volume), a breakdown of the terror management system occurs. In their study with terminally ill patients, Edmondson, Park, Chaudoir, and Wortman (2008) found that the relationship between this kind of religious struggle and depression was mediated by an increase in personal death concerns. Without the protection of a firm belief in their worldview, people experience an increase in anxiety about death.

The third empirical approach used to test the TMT view of religion is to assess whether affirming an afterlife strengthens the individual's buffer against terror and thus attenuates defensive responses to MS. In one relevant set of studies, Dechesne et al. (2003) had participants read an article that attributed near-death experiences to either the existence of an afterlife or a mere by-product of oxygen deprivation. Among participants primed with mortality, those who read the deflationary account of near-death experiences subsequently showed increased self-esteem striving and defense of nonreligious aspects of their cultural worldview, whereas those who read the proafterlife article did not exhibit increased worldview defense. In other words, when individuals receive evidence confirming the possibility of attaining literal immortality, they have less need to pursue symbolic forms of immortality; but when literal immortality beliefs are undermined, it heightens individuals' need to defend their symbolic worldview. This research did not measure defense of religious aspects of worldviews.

Similarly, a recent study found that after MS, people who do not believe in the existence of an immortal soul exhibited increased DTA but people who do hold this belief did not (Weise & Greenberg, 2010). Follow-up research (Heflick & Goldenberg, 2010) showed that this is only true of positive depictions of an afterlife: Affirming beliefs in a negative afterlife (e.g., hell) do not attenuate defensive responses to MS. Other relevant research shows that making salient the death of religious out-group members—those who challenge the validity of one's own religious beliefs—eliminates defensive responses to MS (Hayes, Schimel, & Williams, 2008).

Research using the three approaches to assessing TMT hypotheses supports the terror management function of religion. Reminders of death increase defense of and commitment to religious belief. Threats to religious beliefs increase death thought accessibility. And belief that existence extends beyond death and a reminder of misfortune to religious out-groups reduces MS-induced DTA and defensiveness. Taken together, these results indicate that religious worldviews serve a unique function in keeping death-related anxieties at bay.

Individual Differences in Religiosity and Terror Management

The research reviewed so far has taken a normative view, focusing on the terror management function of religion for most people. Complementary work looks at how individual differences in religiosity moderate terror management processes. One such individual difference is Allport and Ross's (1967) distinction between intrinsic and extrinsic religiosity. Individuals high in intrinsic religiosity turn to religion to establish the meaning and significance of their lives, whereas those high in extrinsic religiosity use religion instrumentally as a means of obtaining other ends, such as gaining belonging or social status.

From a TMT perspective, intrinsic religiosity provides strong, internalized faith in a death-transcending ideology and therefore should help individuals to cope with mortality and other existential concerns more so than extrinsic religiosity. Correlational support for this possibility is provided by evidence that high levels of intrinsic religiosity are associated with lower levels of death anxiety (Roff, Butkeviciene, & Klemmack, 2002; Thorson & Powell, 1990) as well as more accepting attitudes toward death (Ardelt & Koenig, 2006; Cohen, Pierce, et al., 2005), whereas variations in extrinsic religiosity do not appear to predict these outcomes. We should acknowledge that some authors have questioned the validity of measures of extrinsic religious motivation (Cohen, Hall, Koenig, & Meador, 2005; Kirkpatrick & Hood, 1990).

More direct evidence for the protective role of intrinsic religiosity comes from a series of experiments conducted by Jonas and Fischer (2006). In one study, they grouped participants as either high or low in intrinsic religiosity, provided half the participants with an opportunity to affirm their religious beliefs by completing a German version of Feagin's (1964) Religious Orientation Scale, manipulated MS, and measured worldview defense (specifically, championing one's home city). MS increased worldview defense among individuals low in intrinsic religiosity as well as those high in intrinsic religiosity who were not given an opportunity to affirm their religious beliefs; however, people high in intrinsic religiosity who were allowed to affirm their religious beliefs did not exhibit an intensified worldview defense in response to MS. Interestingly, this effect did not occur for people high in extrinsic religiosity.

A follow-up study found that following a MS prime, participants high in intrinsic religiosity who had just affirmed their religious beliefs did not show an increase in DTA, whereas individuals low in intrinsic religiosity and high in extrinsic religiosity did. These findings show that, after affirming their religious beliefs, those high in intrinsic (but not extrinsic) religiosity are able to react to MS without worldview defense or heightened DTA.

In addition to examining intrinsic versus extrinsic religiosity, researchers have studied individual differences in religious fundamentalism. Altemeyer and Hunsberger (1992) defined fundamentalism as a belief that there is only one set of religious teachings that embodies the inerrant truth about humans and God and that this truth must be followed according to longstanding practices and rules. Individuals high in fundamentalism are afforded well-defined conceptions of the meaning and purpose of their life as well as clear prescriptions for how to conduct themselves across situations. Fundamentalists believe that by following the traditions and laws set forth by their religion, they can enjoy a special relationship with God and transcend death. They are especially adamant about their belief in a literal afterlife.

This ideological certainty comes with a price, however. Because fundamentalist belief systems emphasize the literal truth of sacred texts and absolute notions of good and evil, they are particularly vulnerable to any information that contradicts them. It is this proneness to threat that helps explain why fundamentalist individuals display strong aversion to people with dissimilar lifestyles or beliefs (e.g., Altemeyer, 2003; L. L. Nelson & Milburn, 1999; Saucier & Cawman, 2004). A multitude of studies have found that religious fundamentalism and the authoritarian attitudes that tend to be associated with it are positively associated with racial prejudice (Altemeyer, 2003; Altemeyer & Hunsberger, 1992; Laythe, Finkel, & Kirkpatrick, 2001), prejudice against homosexuals (Fisher, Derison, Polley, Cadman, & Johnston, 1994; Saucier & Cawman, 2004), and support for militarism (Rothschild, Abdollahi, & Pyszczynski, 2009; see also Volume 2, Chapter 20, this handbook). Relevant TMT research shows that Christians who are high (vs. low) in religious fundamentalism demonstrated an increase in DTA when exposed to even subtle inconsistencies in the Bible (Friedman & Rholes, 2007).

In addition to influencing sensitivity to threatening information, individual differences in fundamentalism interact with mortality salience to influence attitudes about modern medicine and health. Vess, Arndt, Cox, Routledge, and Goldenberg (2009) reported a series of studies examining whether MS would lead fundamentalist individuals to adhere to their religious beliefs even if it meant foregoing medical treatment. In one study, Christians high in fundamentalism responded to MS with a decreased desire to inform another individual that prayer is not a substitute for medical treatment. A second study showed that these high fundamentalist participants perceive prayer as more effective after MS (Vess et al., 2009). Three additional studies found that MS led fundamentalist Christians to show increased support for the refusal of medical treatment for religious reasons, increased reliance on faith to treat a medical illness, and greater belief in divine intervention as an alternative to medicine. These studies provide strong evidence that terror management processes can motivate reliance on religious beliefs at the risk of physical health, at least among those individuals disposed to fundamentalism.

Most recently, terror management research has begun examining individual differences in religiousness itself—that is, testing how terror management processes differentially manifest in the responses of individuals who self-identify as religious versus atheist. On the basis of TMT, Hayes, Schimel, Dalton, Webber, and Faucher (2010) reasoned that purely secular worldviews serve a terror management function for atheists, just as religious worldviews do for those of the faith. Supporting this claim, they showed that when atheists read an essay arguing in favor of intelligent design (thereby contradicting evolutionary accounts of the origins of life), they exhibited significantly higher levels of DTA, greater efforts to reconcile the new information with their atheist worldview, and more derogation of the author than their control peers.

These findings fit the idea that even allegedly "secular" worldviews function equivalently to religious worldviews in providing bases of meaning and value that protect individuals against mortality-related concerns. But this finding is far from alone in this regard. In fact, the majority of the research into TMT has explored the role of secular worldviews in quelling death-related concerns. For example, Greenberg et al. (1995) found that following MS, participants experienced difficulty and distress in completing a task that required using a U.S. flag in an inappropriate way just as participants were reluctant to use the crucifix as a hammer. Put simply, both religion and secular or atheistic worldviews serve a terror management function by embedding the individual in a symbolic conception of reality that explains where we as humans come from; our present place in the universe; how we may be valuable contributors to our symbolic reality; and how, through our valued status, we can survive in some way after physical death (for further discussion of this point, see Greenberg, Landau, Solomon, & Pyszczynski, in press). The primary distinction between these worldviews is that religions offer literal as well as symbolic immortality, whereas secular belief systems offer only symbolic bases of immortality.

EXPLAINING THE DARK SIDE OF RELIGIOUS WORLDVIEWS

If a core psychological function of religion is buffering anxiety, why have religious belief systems often portrayed punitive or vengeful deities, fire and brimstone spewing authorities, strict taboos in domains like sexuality, harsh admonitions against various sins, human sacrifice, ghosts, devils, and hellish afterlives? These concepts certainly do not seem psychologically comforting. A complete answer to this question would take up at least a chapter, if not a book series, of its own, but we can briefly offer a few viable explanations here.

First, some of the reasons for these features may relate to other functions of religious belief. A particularly likely candidate is social control (e.g., see Raven, 1999). As religious conceptions of reality developed, community leaders undoubtedly saw the value of including prescriptions for behaviors that would promote group cohesion, harmony, and success. Admonitions like "Thou shalt not kill" make a lot of sense in this regard, and what better way to promote adherence to such commandments than with a deity who will reign down hard upon violators? More cynically, corrupt leaders given the power of conveying what deities want have often used that power to promote control over others to serve their own self-interest. Cult leaders who convince their followers to turn over all worldly processions or even their own lives to perform God's will provide extreme examples, but we also see more subtle illustrations in prominent political figures who claim that God has chosen them to lead a nation.

Although such other factors undoubtedly play a role in the more fearful and controlling aspects of religions, the harsher features of religions also make sense if they are going to be effective anxiety-buffering ideologies. A primary requirement of a worldview that effectively provides psychological security is that it be believable. It must make sense of the events that occur in the world for people to maintain faith in it. If people are struck down by lightning, eaten by lions, drowned by tidal waves, starved by droughts, and so forth, the religious worldviews must offer plausible explanations for such horrors and tragedies of life. Righteous deities striking down the wicked, evil spirits, and avenging ancestors have long been convenient explanations for such things; explanations that help make compelling the overarching conceptualization of spirit, souls, and afterlives that provide hope and comfort to those who are deserving and devout. After all, if there are evil spirits, there must be benevolent ones as well.

We think it is no coincidence that enduring religions typically convey that the bad acts that spirits commit are for those who do not do what is right. Such beliefs in a just world (Lerner, 1980; Lerner & Miller, 1978) set up the transference of the security base from the parents to God by extending the childhood formula for security equating goodness with safety and badness with loss of protection and punishment (e.g., see Solomon, Greenberg, & Pyszczynski, 1991). Furthermore, many religious taboos focus on controlling people's more animal-like impulses, thereby facilitating the anxiety-buffering notion that we are more than just corporeal creatures fated only to extinction upon death (e.g., see Goldenberg, 2005). And rituals like human sacrifice typically served to appease the gods for the luckier group members (Becker, 1975).

The overall point is that although on the surface potentially anxiety-producing aspects of religion seem antithetical to its anxiety-buffering function, we would argue quite the opposite. Believing the tragedies of life are punishments from deities and potentially avoidable by doing the right things is far more comforting than believing that they are random, uncontrollable events that could happen to any of us at any time, regardless of our morality and virtue, or any currying favor with the gods. Better to be anxious because I may not be living up to my religious precepts than because this is an arbitrarily dangerous world in which nothing ends well.

REMAINING QUESTIONS AND ISSUES

The empirical research just reviewed provides strong support for the conclusion that religiousness protects people from anxiety in general and fear of death in particular. This work also points to a number of unanswered questions that could be addressed in future research.

Anxieties of Life Versus the Fear of Death

One question concerns how much the appeal of religion is based on its value in helping with day-to-day threats, such as losing one's job or having a sick child, as opposed to the existential threat of the awareness of mortality. There is no easy way to answer this question because religiousness clearly can help with both kinds of threats. Conceptually, one could argue that religions are most compelling in handling the threat of death because the promise of an afterlife cannot be definitively disconfirmed. In contrast, if religions promise good fortune to those who pray or follow its precepts, life events can call the efficacy of these practices into question. Furthermore, many threats that engender anxiety, such as crime, economic woes, political instability, illness, and environmental contamination involve the potential threat of death.

Further complicating matters, research shows that threats to sources of terror management, such as self-esteem, cherished beliefs, and close relationships all increase the accessibility of death-related thought (Hayes, Schimel, Arndt, et al., 2010), making this question difficult to address for both conceptual and empirical reasons. Perhaps it is enough to simply conclude that research shows that religiousness helps with anxieties regarding both the vicissitudes of life and the inevitability of death; the relative value of religiousness for coping with each type of threat will vary from situation to situation and person to person.

How Does the Anxiety-Buffering Function Interact With Self-Growth in Shaping Religiousness?

We have argued that a primary function of religiousness is to buffer anxiety, but is that in itself a complete explanation of religiousness in all its richness and complexity? Perhaps people turn to religion not only to assuage fears but also to satisfy their urge to explore the world, experience joy and discovery, and expand their sense of self—strivings that lie at the core of both classic (e.g., Maslow, 1943) and contemporary (Deci & Ryan, 1995) humanistic perspectives on the human quest for self-growth. As an anecdotal illustration, one of us recently saw someone staring at the sky and heard them exclaim, "How can anybody look at that beautiful sunset and not believe that there is a God?" Does this person's sentiment reflect a child-like clinging to security, or is it more indicative of something like awe or gratitude—reaching out to the world rather than shielding the self from danger?

Even Becker (1975)—who observed so clearly how fear drives religiousness—acknowledged that religion and spirituality can provide the bases for expressions of freedom and self-reliance. In forming a personal, spiritual connection with the divine, the individual can move away from conventional perspectives on God and experience the relationship in a personal way, James (1902) similarly advocated an approach to religion that is both personal and experiential—one that provides both intimacy and meaning (Pawelski, 2007). And Becker saw this view as similar to that expressed by theologian Paul Tillich:

> Religion opens up the depth of man's spiritual life which is usually covered by the dust of our daily life and the noise of our secular work. It gives us the experience of the Holy, of something which is awe-inspiring, an ultimate meaning, the source of ultimate courage. (1959/1964, p. 9)

How can we characterize the interplay of anxiety-buffering and growth-oriented motives in driving religiousness? One possibility is that religiousness can serve both types of motives at different times, or for different people and cultures (see Chapter 14, this volume). Indeed, Batson and Stocks (2004) proposed that religion addresses all the needs that Maslow (1943) proposed in his need hierarchy, from the needs for security (as TMT would emphasize) to the need for self-actualization. Maslow's theorizing implies that people cannot employ religion as a means of actualizing their potential until they satisfy more basic security needs, either through religion or other sources of meaning and value (for a more complete discussion of the interplay of defensive and growth-oriented needs in adherence to worldviews, see Pyszczynski, Greenberg, & Goldenberg, 2003).

Religious Versus Secular Worldviews: Is One Better at Promoting Individual and Collective Well-Being?

Religiousness certainly has its "upsides" for the well-being of individuals and groups. Anecdotally, individuals often find religion or renew their faith to cope with distressing life events. For example, after being abducted and held captive in Afghanistan by members of the Taliban, American journalist David

Rohde (2009) reported, "For the first time in my life I began praying several times a day, and I found that it centered me" (p. 7). Empirical research confirms that religion is one of the most popular and effective mechanisms for coping with traumatic life events (e.g., McCrae, 1984; Pargament, 1997; see also Chapter 19, this volume). Furthermore, religiosity is positively correlated with various indicators of positive psychological functioning, including hope, a sense of purpose and meaning in life, and perceived self-efficacy (Koenig, McCullough, & Larson, 2001). Also, religious (vs. nonreligious) individuals are less likely to abuse alcohol and drugs; experience less hypertension, heart disease, stroke, cancer, and disability (Koenig et al., 2001); and live longer (Smith, McCullough, & Poll, 2003).

Lifton (1979) argued that symbolic bases of immortality are more mature and constructive than the literal immortality offered by most religions. He noted that religions offer bases of symbolic as well as literal immortality, by offering a place within a longstanding tradition that may continue indefinitely into the future. But it is difficult to deny that hope of literal immortality, when held strongly, can be a unique psychological resource.

Partly on the basis of Kierkegaard, Becker (1971, 1973) argued that worldviews that include a sacred element, some personal spiritual faith, best serve to manage the terror of being mortal. If we all need to believe that we in some way have a significance that transcends our own physical death, than the most compelling belief in that would come from serving some enduring higher power and literally continuing in some form beyond death. Carl Jung proposed that it is in our nature to believe we will in some way last beyond our physical death:

> Mythological and religious imagery of life beyond death, that is, constitutes an "archetype," a primordial, inherited, instinctual structure that is worthy of one's "faith." . . . I therefore consider the religious teaching of a life hereafter consonant with the standpoint of psychic hygiene. When I live in a house that I know will fall about my head in the next two weeks, all of my vital functions will be impaired by this thought; but, if on the contrary, I feel myself to be safe, I can dwell there in a normal comfortable way. (quoted in Lifton, 1979)

Similarly, Otto Rank (1941/1958), who greatly influenced Becker and TMT, concluded that the problem with traditional psychoanalysis was that it deconstructed people's motives and actions, leaving them devoid of bases for viewing their lives as meaningful. He argued that this is precisely the opposite of what people need; people need something to believe in, some basis of significance. Rank posited that the most reliable basis of significance was some form of religiousness

Religion may be helpful in ameliorating anxiety because of its collective nature. Religion helps to strengthen social connections and feelings of group belonging. Individuals participating in religious activities report larger social support networks and are more satisfied with their relationships (Koenig et al., 2001). As to intergroup relations, a growing body of research shows that focusing people on their religion's prescriptions for peace and compassion decreases their negative attitudes and aggressive intentions toward out-group members, particularly when their adherence to their religion is increased by mortality salience (Jonas & Fischer, 2006; Norenzayan, Dar-Nimrod, Hansen, & Proulx, 2009; Rothschild et al., 2009).

But even a cursory glance at history and current events shows that religion is implicated in seemingly intractable national conflicts, intergroup terrorism, and other forms of inhumanity. It would be wrong, however, to blame religion as the foremost cause of human discord, as popular writers have done recently (e.g., Hitchens, 2007). Consider that the explicitly atheist and antireligious reigns of Stalin, Mao, the Khmer Rouge, and Hitler inflicted more death and suffering on the human race in 60 years than all the religion-influenced conflicts in recorded history combined. Bigotry and violence can result from faith in any cause or belief system.

These observations suggest that, in itself, religion represents neither the saving grace nor the scourge of humankind. A TMT analysis points out that people are fundamentally motivated to sustain faith that their lives have meaning and significance beyond mere biological existence. Religion directly serves that need, but secular worldviews do as well. Just as a Christian would be likely to lash out at others who spit on an image of Jesus, a new Mercedes-Benz owner would also lash out at someone who spits on their new vehicle. A more reasonable conclusion, and one that fits best with the research we have reviewed, is that the problem lies in clinging too rigidly onto one's worldview and taking its conceptions of reality and its guidelines for living as absolute truths (see Volume 2, Chapter 4, this handbook). We saw, for example, that individuals who take religious teachings as unerring literal truths showed heightened activation of death-related cognitions in response to intimations that their holy texts are not logically watertight (Friedman & Rholes, 2007) and responded to mortality reminders by taking what might be reasonably considered unhealthy and even fatal attitudes toward modern medicine (Vess et al., 2009).

Perhaps, then, improving the human lot does not require encouraging people to adopt religious or secular worldviews at the expense of the other. Rather, we should encourage people to adopt a more tolerant, relativistic approach to their religious or secular worldview with which they can appreciate that their conceptions of what is and what should be represent only one way to apprehend reality, and that no such conception has a monopoly on truth. The unanswered empirical questions then surround what makes some people particularly prone to developing and relying on rigid narrow worldviews as opposed to tolerant and accepting ones?

Why "Religiousness"?

The editors of this handbook have distinguished between *religiousness*—beliefs, practices, relationships, or experiences having to do with the sacred that are explicitly and historically rooted in established institutionalized systems—and *spirituality*, or beliefs and so on having to do with the sacred not necessarily linked to established systems (see Chapter 1, this volume). We have chosen to focus our discussion on religiousness because we feel that most of the relevant theorizing and research concerning the anxiety-buffering function has focused on conventional socially validated belief in religion rather than more individualized forms of spirituality.

Our analysis, however, may also illuminate aspects of spirituality so defined, including people's efforts to break free from convention and seek out more personally satisfying answers to the "big" existential questions—what Batson, Schoenrade, and Ventis (1993) have referred to as a "quest orientation." Although research has not addressed this possibility to the extent it has focused on religiousness, future attempts to fill this gap can rely on a wealth of sophisticated theorizing, including the works of Becker (1975), Tillich (1959/1964), Lifton (1979/1983), and especially Rank (1941/1958) and May (1953).

CONCLUSION

Concepts of deities and religious ideologies supporting them may very well have originated because of our ancient ancestors' inferences of supernatural agency (e.g., Boyer, 2002; see also Chapter 14, this volume) to explain events in the world and their desires to appeal to such higher powers to maximize good events (e.g., rain) and minimize bad ones (e.g., volcanic eruptions). Many of these functions are now served by scientific knowledge and technological advances. And atheism and a focus on symbolic immortality are surely more widespread now than at any time in human history (Davie, 2000; Zuckerman, 2005). But religiosity persists. It is fashionable for evolutionary speculators to try to explain this persistence in terms of the adaptive value of group cohesion, order, and subjugation to leaders. But all sorts of groups and ideologies can serve and have served these functions. We believe that religiousness continues to thrive and serve humans well because a central function, among its numerous ones, is to help people manage the potential anxiety that would result from viewing one's existence as just a pointless exercise, always in peril, and inevitably terminated. The research we have reviewed provides ample support for this central role of religiousness.

As the knight Antonius Block put it in Bergman's classic 1957 film *The Seventh Seal*, if there is no God, "then life is a senseless terror. No one can live with death, knowing that all is nothing." This may not be the only way to look at life, but it is a persuasive one in a world that every day is full of seemingly senseless tragedies and miseries. Religion can offer hope regarding one's own fate and that of loved ones as well. What other comfort really is there for the person faced with an inoperable brain tumor? Or for an acquaintance of one of ours who, during the writing of this chapter, lost his child weeks before his 13th birthday? So beneath all of religion's complexities, death, the worm at the core, keeps the appeal of religion very much alive.

References

Allport, G. W. (1950). *The individual and his religion.* New York, NY: Macmillan.

Allport, G. W., & Ross, J. M. (1967). Personal religious orientation and prejudice. *Journal of Personality and Social Psychology, 5*, 432–443. doi:10.1037/h0021212

Altemeyer, B. (2003). Why do religious fundamentalists tend to be prejudiced? *The International Journal for the Psychology of Religion, 13*, 17–28. doi:10.1207/S15327582IJPR1301_03

Altemeyer, B., & Hunsberger, B. (1992). Authoritarianism, religious fundamentalism, quest, and prejudice. *The International Journal for the Psychology of Religion, 2*, 113–133. doi:10.1207/s15327582ijpr0202_5

Alvarado, K. A., Templer, D. I., Bresler, C., & Thomas-Dobson, S. (1995). The relationship of religious variables to death depression and death anxiety. *Journal of Clinical Psychology, 51*, 202–204. doi:10.1002/1097-4679(199503)51:2<202::AID-JCLP2270510209>3.0.CO;2-M

Ardelt, M., & Koenig, C. S. (2006). The role of religion for hospice patients and relatively healthy older adults. *Research on Aging, 28*, 184–215. doi:10.1177/0164027505284165

Atran, S. (2002). *In gods we trust: The evolutionary landscape of religion.* New York, NY: Oxford University Press.

Batson, C. D., Schoenrade, P., & Ventis, L. W. (1993). *Religion and the individual: A social psychological perspective* (pp. 141–155). New York, NY: Oxford University Press.

Batson, C. D., & Stocks, E. L. (2004). Religion: Its core psychological functions. In J. Greenberg, S. Koole, & T. Pyszczynski (Eds.), *Handbook of experimental existential psychology* (pp. 141–155). New York, NY: Guilford Press.

Becker, E. (1971). *The birth and death of meaning* (2nd ed.). New York, NY: Free Press.

Becker, E. (1973). *The denial of death.* New York, NY: Free Press.

Becker, E. (1975). *Escape from evil.* New York, NY: Free Press.

Ben-Meir, Y., & Kadem, P. (1979). Index of religiosity of the Jewish population of Israel. *Megamot, 24*, 353–362.

Birgegard, A., & Granqvist, P. (2004). The correspondence between attachment to parents and God: Three experiments using subliminal separation cues. *Personality and Social Psychology Bulletin, 30*, 1122–1135. doi:10.1177/0146167204264266

Birky, I. T., & Ball, S. (1988). Parental trait influence on God as an object representation. *Journal of Psychology: Interdisciplinary and Applied, 122*, 133–137. doi:10.1080/00223980.1988.9712698

Bowlby, J. (1969). *Attachment and loss: Vol. 1. Attachment.* New York, NY: Basic Books.

Boyer, P. (2002). *Religion explained.* New York, NY: Basic Books.

Brown, K., & Cullen, C. (2006). Maslow's hierarchy of needs used to measure motivation for religious behavior. *Mental Health, Religion, and Culture, 9*, 99–108. doi:10.1080/13694670500071695

Burkert, W. (1960). *Creation of the sacred: Tracks of biology in early religions.* Cambridge, MA: Harvard University Press.

Cohen, A. B., Hall, D. E., Koenig, H. G., & Meador, K. G. (2005). Social versus individual motivation: Implications for normative definitions of religious orientation. *Personality and Social Psychology Review, 9*, 48–61. doi:10.1207/s15327957pspr0901_4

Cohen, A. B., Pierce, J. D., Chambers, J., Meade, R., Gorvine, B. J., & Koenig, H. G. (2005). Intrinsic and extrinsic religiosity, belief in the afterlife, death anxiety, and life satisfaction in young Catholics and Protestants. *Journal of Research in Personality, 39*, 307–324. doi:10.1016/j.jrp.2004.02.005

Crabtree, S. (2009). *Analyst insights: Religiosity around the world.* Retrieved from http://www.gallup.com/video/114694/Analyst-Insights-Religiosity-Around-World.aspx

Davie, G. (2000). *Religion in modern Europe.* New York, NY: Oxford University Press.

Deci, E. L., & Ryan, R. M. (1995). Human autonomy: The basis for true self-esteem. In M. H. Kernis (Ed.), *Efficacy, agency, and self-esteem* (pp. 31–49). New York, NY: Plenum Press.

Dechesne, M., Pyszczynski, T., Arndt, J., Ransom, S., Sheldon, K. M., van Knippenberg, A., & Janssen, J. (2003). Literal and symbolic immortality: The effect of evidence of literal immortality on self-esteem striving in response to mortality salience. *Journal of Personality and Social Psychology, 84*, 722–737. doi:10.1037/0022-3514.84.4.722

Edmondson, D., Park, C. L., Chaudoir, S. R., & Wortman, J. H. (2008). Death without God: Religious struggle, death concerns, and depression in the terminally ill. *Psychological Science, 19*, 754–758. doi:10.1111/j.1467-9280.2008.02152.x

Erickson, E. H. (1959). *Identity and the life cycle*. New York, NY: International Universities Press.

Erickson, E. H. (1963). *Childhood and society* (2nd ed.). New York, NY: Norton.

Exline, J. J., & Rose, E. (2005). Religious and spiritual struggles. In R. F. Paloutzian & C. L. Park (Eds.), *Handbook of the psychology of religion and spirituality* (pp. 315–330). New York, NY: Guilford Press.

Feagin, J. R. (1964). Prejudice and religious types: A focused study of Southern fundamentalists. *Journal for the Scientific Study of Religion, 4*, 3–13. doi:10.2307/1385200

Feifel, H. (1977). Death and dying in modern America. *Death Education, 1*, 5–14. doi:10.1080/07481187708252874

Feifel, H. (Ed.). (1959). *The meaning of death*. New York, NY: McGraw-Hill.

Feifel, H., & Nagy, V. T. (1981). Another look at fear of death. *Journal of Consulting and Clinical Psychology, 49*, 278–286. doi:10.1037/0022-006X.49.2.278

Fisher, R. D., Derison, D., Polley, C. F., Cadman, J., & Johnston, D. (1994). Religiousness, religious orientation, and attitudes toward gays and lesbians. *Journal of Applied Social Psychology, 24*, 614–630. doi:10.1111/j.1559-1816.1994.tb00603.x

Florian, V., & Kravets, S. (1983). Fear of personal death: Attribution, structure, and relation to religious belief. *Journal of Personality and Social Psychology, 44*, 600–607. doi:10.1037/0022-3514.44.3.600

Freud, S. (1919). *Totem and taboo*. New York, NY: Dodd, Mead, & Company. (Original work published 1913)

Freud, S. (1961). *The future of an illusion*. New York, NY: Norton. (Original work published 1927)

Freud, S. (1961). *Civilization and its discontents* (Standard ed., Vol. XXI). New York, NY: Basic Books. (Original work published 1930)

Freud, S. (1961). *Moses and monotheism* (Standard ed., Vol. XXIII). New York, NY: Basic Books. (Original work published 1939)

Friedman, M., & Rholes, W. S. (2007). Successfully challenging fundamentalist beliefs results in increased death awareness. *Journal of Experimental Social Psychology, 43*, 794–801. doi:10.1016/j.jesp.2006.07.008

Gallup, G., & Jones, S. (1989). *One hundred questions and answers: Religion in America*. Princeton, NJ: Princeton Religious Research Center.

Godin, A., & Hallez, M. (1965). Parental images and divine paternity. In A. Godin (Ed.), *From religious experience to a religious attitude* (pp. 65–96). Chicago, IL: Loyola University Press.

Goldenberg, J. L. (2005). The body stripped down: An existential account of the threat posed by the physical body. *Current Directions in Psychological Science, 14*, 224–228. doi:10.1111/j.0963-7214.2005.00369.x

Granqvist, P. (2006). On the relation between secular and divine relationships: An emerging attachment perspective and critique of the "depth" approaches. *The International Journal for the Psychology of Religion, 16*, 1–18. doi:10.1207/s15327582ijpr1601_1

Greenberg, J., Landau, M. J., Solomon, S., & Pyszczynski, T. (in press). What is the primary psychological function of religion? In D. Wulff (Ed.), *Handbook of the psychology of religion*. London, England: Oxford University Press.

Greenberg, J., Pyszczynski, T., & Solomon, S. (1986). The causes and consequences of a need for self-esteem: A terror management theory. In R. F. Baumeister (Ed.), *Public self and private self* (pp. 189–212). New York, NY: Springer-Verlag. doi:10.1007/978-1-4613-9564-5_10

Greenberg, J., Pyszczynski, T., Solomon, S., Rosenblatt, A., Veeder, M., Kirkland, S., & Lyon, D. (1990). Evidence for terror management theory II: The effects of mortality salience on reactions to those who threaten or bolster the cultural worldview. *Journal of Personality and Social Psychology, 58*, 308–318. doi:10.1037/0022-3514.58.2.308

Greenberg, J., Pyszczynski, T., Solomon, S., Simon, L., & Breus, M. (1994). Role of consciousness and accessibility of death related thoughts in mortality salience effects. *Journal of Personality and Social Psychology, 67*, 627–637. doi:10.1037/0022-3514.67.4.627

Greenberg, J., Simon, L., Porteus, J., Pyszczynski, T., & Solomon, S. (1995). Evidence of a terror management function of cultural icons: The effects of mortality salience on the inappropriate use of cherished cultural symbols. *Personality and Social Psychology Bulletin, 21*, 1221–1228. doi:10.1177/01461672952111010

Greenberg, J., Solomon, S., & Arndt, J. (2008). A basic but uniquely human motivation: Terror management. In J. Y. Shah & W. L. Gardner (Eds.), *Handbook of motivation science* (pp. 114–134). New York, NY: Guilford Press.

Greenberg, J., Solomon, S., & Pyszczynski, T. (1997). Terror management theory of self-esteem and cultural worldviews: Empirical assessments and conceptual refinements. In M. Zanna (Ed.), *Advances in experimental social psychology* (Vol. 29, pp. 61–139). Orlando, FL: Academic Press.

Harding, S. R., Flannelly, K. J., Weaver, A. J., & Costa, K. G. (2005). The influence of religion on death anxiety and death acceptance. *Mental Health, Religion, and Culture, 8*, 253–261. doi:10.1080/13674670412331304311

Harmon-Jones, E., Simon, L., Greenberg, J., Pyszczynski, T., Solomon, S., & McGregor, H. (1997). Terror management theory and self-esteem: Evidence that increased self-esteem reduces mortality salience effects. *Journal of Personality and Social Psychology, 72*, 24–36. doi:10.1037/0022-3514.72.1.24

Hauser, A. (1951). *The social history of art*. New York, NY: Knopf.

Hayes, J., Schimel, J., Arndt, J., & Faucher, E. (2010). A theoretical and empirical review of the death-thought accessibility concept in terror management research. *Psychological Bulletin, 136*, 699–739.

Hayes, J., Schimel, J., Dalton, A. L., Webber, D., & Faucher, E. H. (2010). *When worldviews change and when they stay the same: Exploring accommodation vs. derogation in response to worldview threat*. Unpublished manuscript, University of Alberta, Edmonton, Alberta, Canada.

Hayes, J., Schimel, J., & Williams, T. J. (2008). Fighting death with death: The buffering effects of learning that worldview violators have died. *Psychological Science, 19*, 501–507. doi:10.1111/j.1467-9280.2008.02115.x

Heflick, N. A., & Goldenberg, J. L. (2010). *Suffering or death? Evidence that "Hellish" afterlives do not buffer mortality salience effects*. Unpublished manuscript, University of South Florida, Tampa.

Hitchens, C. (2007). *God is not great: How religion poisons everything*. New York, NY: Hatchette.

James, W. (1902). *The varieties of religious experience: A study in human nature*. New York, NY: Modern Library. doi:10.1037/10004-000

Jonas, E., & Fischer, P. (2006). Terror management and religion: Evidence that intrinsic religiousness mitigates worldview defense following mortality salience. *Journal of Personality and Social Psychology, 91*, 553–567. doi:10.1037/0022-3514.91.3.553

Justice, W. G., & Lambert, W. (1986). A comparative study of the language people use to describe the personalities of God and their earthly parents. *Journal of Pastoral Care, 40*, 166–172.

Kahoe, R. D., & Dunn, R. F. (1976). The fear of death and religious attitudes and behavior. *Journal for the Scientific Study of Religion, 14*, 379–382. doi:10.2307/1384409

Kay, A. C., Gaucher, D., McGregor, I., & Nash, K. (2010). Religious belief as compensatory control. *Personality and Social Psychology Review, 14*, 37–48. doi:10.1177/1088868309353750

Kirkpatrick, L. A. (2005). *Attachment, evolution, and the psychology of religion*. New York, NY: Guilford Press.

Kirkpatrick, L. A., & Hood, R. W. (1990). Intrinsic–extrinsic religious orientation: The boon or bane of contemporary psychology of religion? *Journal for the Scientific Study of Religion, 29*, 442–462. doi:10.2307/1387311

Koenig, H. G., McCullough, M. E., & Larson, D. B. (2001). *Handbook of religion and health*. New York, NY: Oxford University Press. doi:10.1093/acprof:oso/9780195118667.001.0001

Lampman, J. (2001). Spiritual resurgence rises, falls in U. S.; more in Europe identify as religious. *Christian Science Monitor*, p. 14.

Laythe, B., Finkel, D., & Kirkpatrick, L. A. (2001). Predicting prejudice from religious fundamentalism and right-wing authoritarianism: A multiple-regression approach. *Journal for the Scientific Study of Religion, 40*, 1–10. doi:10.1111/0021-8294.00033

Lerner, M. J. (1980). *The belief in a just world: A fundamental delusion*. New York, NY: Plenum Press.

Lerner, M. J., & Miller, D. T. (1978). Just world research and the attribution process: Looking back and ahead. *Psychological Bulletin, 85*, 1030–1051. doi:10.1037/0033-2909.85.5.1030

Lifton, R. (1979). *The broken connection: On death and the continuity of life*. New York, NY: Simon & Schuster.

Maslow, A. (1943). A theory of human motivation. *Psychological Review, 50*, 370–396.

May, R. (1953). *Man's search for himself*. New York, NY: Norton.

McCrae, R. R. (1984). Situational determinants of coping response: Loss, threat, and challenge. *Journal of Personality and Social Psychology, 46*, 919–928. doi:10.1037/0022-3514.46.4.919

McGregor, I., Haji, R., Nash, K. A., & Teper, R. (2008). Religious zeal and the uncertain self. *Basic and Applied Social Psychology, 30*, 183–188. doi:10.1080/01973530802209251

Nelson, L. L., & Milburn, T. W. (1999). Relationships between problem-solving competencies and militaristic attitudes: Implications for peace education. *Peace and Conflict, 5*, 149–168. doi:10.1207/s15327949pac0502_4

Nelson, M. O. (1971). The concept of God and feelings toward parents. *Journal of Individual Psychology, 27*, 46–49.

Nelson, M. O., & Jones, E. M. (1957). An application of the Q-technique to the study of religious concepts. *Psychological Reports, 3*, 293–297. doi:10.2466/pr0.1957.3.3.293

Norenzayan, A., Dar-Nimrod, I., Hansen, I. G., & Proulx, T. (2009). Mortality salience and religion: Divergent effects on the defense of cultural worldview for the religious and the non-religious. *European Journal of Social Psychology, 39*, 101–113. doi:10.1002/ejsp.482

Norenzayan, A., & Hansen, I. G. (2006). Belief in supernatural agents in the face of death. *Personality and Social Psychology Bulletin, 32*, 174–187. doi:10.1177/0146167205280251

Osarchuk, M., & Tatz, S. J. (1973). Effect of induced fear of death on belief in afterlife. *Journal of Personality and Social Psychology, 27*, 256–260. doi:10.1037/h0034769

Pargament, K. I. (1997). *The psychology of religion and coping: Theory, research, practice.* New York, NY: Guilford Press.

Pargament, K. I., Murray-Swank, N. A., Magyar, G. M., & Ano, G. G. (2005). Spiritual struggle: A phenomenon of interest to psychology and religion. In W. R. Miller & H. D. Delaney (Eds.), *Judeo-Christian perspectives on psychology: Human nature, motivation, and change* (pp. 245–268). Washington, DC: American Psychological Association. doi:10.1037/10859-013

Pawelski, J. O. (2007). *The dynamic individualism of William James.* Albany: State University of New York Press.

Pyszczynski, T., Abdollahi, A., Solomon, S., Greenberg, J., Cohen, F., & Weise, D. (2006). Morality salience, martyrdom, and military might: The Great Satan versus the Axis of Evil. *Personality and Social Psychology Bulletin, 32*, 525–537.

Pyszczynski, T., Greenberg, J., & Goldenberg, J. (2003). Freedom versus fear: On the defense, growth, and expansion of the self. In M. R. Leary & J. P. Tangney (Eds.), *Handbook of self and identity* (pp. 314–343). New York, NY: Guilford Press.

Rank, O. (1958). *Beyond psychology*. New York, NY: Dover (Original work published 1941).

Raven, B. H. (1999). Kurt Lewin address: Influence, power, religion, and the mechanisms of social control. *Journal of Social Issues, 55*, 161–186. doi:10.1111/0022-4537.00111

Rice, P. (2001, December 22). Religious books are rising to the occasion. *St. Louis Post-Dispatch*, Religion section, p. 16.

Roff, L. L., Butkeviciene, R., & Klemmack, D. L. (2002). Death anxiety and religiosity among Lithuanian health and social service professionals. *Death Studies, 26*, 731–742. doi:10.1080/07481180290106517

Rohde, D. (2009, October 17). Held by the Taliban. *New York Times*, p. A1.

Roshdieh, S., Templer, D. I., Cannon, W. G., & Canfield, M. (1998). The relationships of death anxiety and death depression to religion and civilian war-related experiences in Iranians. *Omega: Journal of Death and Dying, 38*, 201–210. doi:10.2190/UB6T-QF51-AF5J-MLCD

Rothschild, Z. K., Abdollahi, A., & Pyszczynski, T. (2009). Does peace have a prayer? The effect of mortality salience, compassionate values, and religious fundamentalism on hostility toward outgroups. *Journal of Experimental Social Psychology, 45*, 816–827. doi:10.1016/j.jesp.2009.05.016

Saucier, D. A., & Cawman, A. J. (2004). Civil unions in Vermont: Political attitudes, religious fundamentalism, and sexual prejudice. *Journal of Homosexuality, 48*, 1–18. doi:10.1300/J082v48n01_01

Schimel, J., Hayes, J., Williams, T. J., & Jahrig, J. (2007). Is death really the worm at the core? Converging evidence that worldview threat increases death-thought accessibility. *Journal of Personality and Social Psychology, 92*, 789–803. doi:10.1037/0022-3514.92.5.789

Schoenrade, P. A. (1989). When I die . . . : Belief in afterlife as a response to mortality. *Personality and Social Psychology Bulletin, 15*, 91–100. doi:10.1177/0146167289151009

Schulz, R. (1978). *The psychology of death, dying, and bereavement.* Reading, MA: Addison-Wesley.

Smith, T. B., McCullough, M. E., & Poll, J. (2003). Religiousness and depression: Evidence for a main effect and the moderating influence of stressful life events. *Psychological Bulletin, 129*, 614–636. doi:10.1037/0033-2909.129.4.614

Solomon, S., Greenberg, J., & Pyszczynski, T. (1991). Terror management theory of self-esteem. In C. R. Snyder & D. R. Forsyth (Eds.), *Handbook of social and clinical psychology: The health perspective* (pp. 21–40). Elmsford, NY: Pergamon.

Solomon, S., Greenberg, J., & Pyszczynski, T. (2004). The cultural animal: Twenty years of terror management theory and research. In J. Greenberg, S. Koole, & T. Pyszczynski (Eds.), *Handbook of experimental existential psychology* (pp. 13–34). New York, NY: Guilford Press.

Strunk, O. (1959). Perceived relationships between parental and deity concepts. *Psychological Newsletter, New York University, 10*, 222–226.

Suhail, K., & Akram, S. (2002). Correlates of death anxiety in Pakistan. *Death Studies, 26*, 39–50. doi:10.1080/07481180210146

Tamayo, A., & Desjardins, L. (1976). Belief systems and conceptual images of parents and God. *Journal of Psychology: Interdisciplinary and Applied, 92*, 131–140. doi:10.1080/00223980.1976.9921346

Tattersall, I. (1998). *Becoming human: Evolution and human uniqueness.* Orlando, FL: Harvest Books.

Templer, D. I., & Dotson, E. (1970). Religious correlates of death anxiety. *Psychological Reports, 26*, 895–897. doi:10.2466/pr0.1970.26.3.895

Thorson, J. A., & Powell, F. C. (1990). Meanings of death and intrinsic religiosity. *Journal of Clinical Psychology, 46*, 379–391. doi:10.1002/1097-4679(199007)46:4<379::AID-JCLP2270460402>3.0.CO;2-A

Tillich, P. (1959/1964). *Theology of culture* (R. Kimball, Ed.). New York, NY: Oxford University Press.

Triplett, G., Cohen, D., Reimer, W., Rinaldi, S., Hill, C., Roshdieh, S., . . . Templer, D. I. (1995). Death discomfort differential. *Omega: Journal of Death and Dying, 31*, 295–304. doi:10.2190/DQCP-PM99-UHHW-B1P7

Vail, K., Abdollahi, A., & Arndt, J. (2010). *Terror management and religious belief in two cultures.* Unpublished manuscript, University of Missouri, Columbia.

Vergote, A., & Tamayo, A. (Eds.). (1981). *The parental figures and the representation of God.* The Hague, the Netherlands: Mouton.

Vess, M., Arndt, J., Cox, C. R., Routledge, C., & Goldenberg, J. L. (2009). Exploring the existential function of religion: The effect of religious fundamentalism and mortality salience on faith-based medical refusals. *Journal of Personality and Social Psychology, 97*, 334–350. doi:10.1037/a0015545

Weise, D., & Greenberg, J. (2010). *Soul belief and death thought accessibility.* Unpublished manuscript, University of Arizona, Tucson.

Zuckerman, P. (2005). Atheism: Contemporary rates and patterns. In M. Martin (Ed.), *The Cambridge companion to atheism* (pp. 47–67). Cambridge, England: Cambridge University Press.

Chapter 6

RELIGION, SELF-CONTROL, AND SELF-REGULATION: HOW AND WHY ARE THEY RELATED?

Michael E. McCullough and Evan C. Carter

Following James (1958), Pratt (1934), and Atran and Norenzayan (2004), we define religion as a broad cultural complex, one characterized by deeply held beliefs as well as the emotions and behaviors that accompany such beliefs. In the case of religion, the beliefs in question arise from awareness of, or perceived interaction with, supernatural agents such as gods and spirits that are presumed to play an important role in human affairs. Individual differences in religiosity are related to a bewilderingly wide array of behaviors and outcomes, including longer life (McCullough, Hoyt, Larson, Koenig, & Thoresen, 2000); fewer depressive symptoms (Smith, McCullough, & Poll, 2003); higher levels of prosocial behavior (Pichon, Boccato, & Saroglou, 2007; Randolph-Seng & Nielsen, 2007; Shariff & Norenzayan, 2007); better marital functioning (Mahoney et al., 1999); less crime, delinquency, and drug use (Baier & Wright, 2001); higher school achievement (Jeynes, 2002); and even more frequent engagement in health behaviors, such as visiting the dentist, using seat belts, and taking vitamins (Hill, Burdette, Ellison, & Musick, 2006; Islam & Johnson, 2003; Shmueli & Tamir, 2007; Wallace & Forman, 1998). These associations are robust and have been replicated with people from many religions and many nations.

In this chapter, we will offer an answer to a "how" question and a "why" question about these associations. The "how" question is straightforward: How does religion obtain its associations with these diverse outcomes? We hypothesize that religion fosters the development and exercise of self-control and self-regulation, which lead to beneficial outcomes in a variety of behavioral and psychological domains. In this chapter, we survey the evidence that is relevant to this "how" hypothesis. We define *self-regulation*, like many other scientists (Baumeister & Vohs, 2004; Carver & Scheier, 1998), as the process by which a system uses information about its present state to change that state toward greater conformity with a desired end state or goal. Self-regulation need not be a deliberative, effortful process: Much of self-regulation occurs in a relatively effortless and automatic fashion (Fitzsimmons & Bargh, 2004), and for that reason, we also wish to understand how religion might be related to automatic or implicit self-regulation (Koole, McCullough, Kuhl, & Roelofsma, 2010).

We reserve the term *self-control* for situations in which people work to override a prepotent response (e.g., a behavioral tendency, an emotion, or a motivation), such as a craving for alcohol, a desire to retaliate against an aggressor, or the temptation to chase a hare instead of remaining with one's hunting group to stalk a stag (Baumeister, Vohs, & Tice, 2007). In other words, when people exert self-control, they modify their response tendencies by suppressing one goal so as to pursue another one that is more highly valued—especially when one is not actively within the thrall of that prepotent motivation to action. For example, when we are setting

Preparation of this chapter was supported by a grant from the John Templeton Foundation.

DOI: 10.1037/14045-006
APA Handbook of Psychology, Religion, and Spirituality: Vol. 1. Context, Theory, and Research, K. I. Pargament (Editor-in-Chief)
Copyright © 2013 by the American Psychological Association. All rights reserved.

an alarm clock in the evening for the next day, we value getting up early the next morning to a greater extent than we value staying in bed, but our preferences can shift when that alarm goes off at 5:30 the next morning. Applying self-control at 5:30 helps us to behave according to the valuations of the various behavioral options that caused us set the alarm the night before, even if our valuations of those behavioral options are different at 5:30 in the morning. Self-control is therefore a more specific concept than self-regulation, and not all psychological states that are self-regulated involve self-control as we use the term here.

The "why" question about religion and self-control is a bit more involved: Why are religious belief and behavior structured in such a way as to be reliably associated with self-regulation and self-control? Of the many variables with which religious belief and practice might be related, why self-control in particular instead of, say, extraversion, or neuroticism (Saroglou, 2010)? The only ultimate answers to such "why" questions are questions about design, and to ask design questions, one must ask questions about *function* (Richerson & Boyd, 2005; Williams, 1966). We hypothesize that many complexes of religious beliefs and behaviors take their current forms (at least as expressed in the Abrahamic traditions) in part because of cultural selection (Richerson & Boyd, 2005). In other words, we propose that religious beliefs and behaviors produced beneficial consequences for the individuals who adopted them, refined them, and passed them on to their neighbors and offspring as human societies were becoming modern. In other words, we hypothesize that many religious beliefs and behaviors take their contemporary forms in part because evolved psychological mechanisms for cultural learning and transmission caused people to acquire, modify, and retain and (perhaps) transmit those beliefs and behaviors to others in light of their beneficial consequences for self-control (Richerson & Boyd, 2005).

We begin this chapter by addressing the "why" question first. We set out to describe the selection pressures in recent human cultural evolution that might have given rise to religious beliefs and behaviors that were well-suited to boosting humans' self-control. Next, we review the evidence for the links of religion to self-regulation and self-control. Finally, we address some implications of our hypotheses for understanding religion's effects more broadly and applying these insights in the real world.

THE "WHY" QUESTION: SELECTION PRESSURES FOR CULTURAL INNOVATIONS TO BOOST SELF-CONTROL

The "why" question first: Why did religion evolve into its current form? Simply put, we think many of the modern features of the world's religions have evolved as they have to prop up humans' abilities to exert control over their appetites, emotions, and desires. These are all forms of control that became acutely important as human societies become sedentary and reliant on agriculture and animal cultivation as an economic base. Consider one historical illustration of how this cultural–evolutionary process might have worked. On the Eastern side of the Mediterranean in what is now modern-day Syria, Israel, Palestine, and Jordan, a society called the Natufians existed from 15,000 to 11,500 years ago. The Natufians were one of the very first societies to adopt a sedentary lifestyle in which people lived in groups including large numbers of non-kin. They were one of the first societies to begin the transition from foraging to agriculture—harvesting wild cereals such as wheat and barley using sickles with stone blades and wooden handles. They were also the first society to bury their dead in large, concentrated numbers near their own settlements (Bar-Yosef, 1998).

Most important for our purposes here, the remnants of Natufian culture include the first known burial site of a shaman in the Near East. Several years ago, anthropologists discovered a 12,000-year-old gravesite in a cave called Hilazon Tachtit, halfway between the Mediterranean and the Sea of Galilee in Northern Israel. The grave contained the body of a 45-year-old woman whose pelvic and spinal deformities would have caused her to drag a leg or limp when she walked (Grosman, Munro, & Belfer-Cohen, 2008). The gravesite was prepared with care; the body was positioned deliberately and held in position by a series of large stones. The grave goods included the types of artifacts that characterize shamans' toolkits worldwide: an ox's tail, the forearm of a wild boar, the wing of an eagle, fragments from a basalt bowl, the horn core from a gazelle in association with the bowl fragments, the pelvis of a leopard, the skulls of two stone martens, 50 tortoise shells, and a fully articulated human foot (someone else's; not the shaman's). The burial—a 10-kilometer walk and a 150-meter climb up a steep escarpment from the nearest Natufian settlement—would have been time-consuming and effortful for the community. Clearly, this shaman woman was a person of great importance to her group.

Shamans were the world's first religious professionals, and they are still found almost universally in the world's extant hunter–gatherer societies (Winkelman, 1990). The Natufian shaman's grave is by no means the world's only prehistoric shaman grave, or even the oldest one (Porr & Alt, 2006). It is tempting, however, to view the care with which this particular shaman was treated (and the fact that she was found in association with *this* Near-Eastern society, and not an earlier Near-Eastern society, nor a later one) as related to the unique characteristics of the Natufian society in which she lived and the dramatic social and economic changes it was experiencing. In part because of climate changes, populations were growing. Thus the former lifestyle of seminomadic foraging, with seasonal moves in pursuit of more plentiful food, was giving way to a lifestyle characterized by permanent settlements in which wild cereals could be exploited and animals could be domesticated for their meat, their milk, and their labor.

To gain benefits from their new semipermanent lifestyle and to cope with their growing population base, the Natufians would have experienced pressure to develop new ways of regulating group life, as is often the case when politically autonomous band-level societies are superseded by larger, more complex societies. Specifically, there would have been novel problems related to *cooperating, tolerating,* and *waiting*. In terms of cooperation, for example, the Natufians would have needed to engage in personally costly and trust-intensive interactions with nonrelatives to create new public and private assets such as kilns for producing lime, fences to pen livestock, or the simple gains of trade. Additionally, conflicts of interest are inevitable, and the emotional effects of these conflicts are less easily salved when the psychological affordances shaped by selection pressures for kin altruism are not activated by cues of genetic relatedness (Lieberman, Tooby, & Cosmides, 2007). Therefore, this transition to large, sedentary societies would also have required an increase in the ability to tolerate. Finally, for their descendants—who would specialize almost exclusively in animal domestication and plant cultivation (Bar-Yosef, 1998)—a willingness to wait would have been particularly valuable. Cereal cultivation requires several months between initial preparation and planting to harvest, unlike economies based on hunting and gathering, in which the time between the onset of acquisition and consumption is measured in seconds to days. And problems like these would only get more intense as societies grew larger, and food economies came to involve more and more waiting. Mithen (2007) put some of the novel problems that agriculture, animal husbandry, and sedentism introduce this way:

> The mobile hunter-gatherer lifestyle always looks far more attractive than sedentism, which creates problems of refuse disposal, hygiene and social conflict within [*sic*] one's neighbours—hunter-gatherers solve these problems by simply moving away, whether from their rubbish or other people. That is no longer an option after one has invested in field clearance, irrigation ditches, stock fences and so forth. (p. 710)

We posit that the waiting, tolerating, and cooperating that sedentary lifestyles and agrarian economic activity require draw on specific cognitive abilities that go together under the label *self-control*. Reyes-García et al. (2007) made a similar argument for how self-control (which they called *patience*) facilitates acquisition of forms of human capital (e.g., formal schooling). These forms of human capital enable people to transition from the economic activities that characterize life in self-sufficient societies (e.g., hunting, foraging, small-scale agriculture) to those that characterize market-based economies (e.g., wage-earning). Consider the following facts about how self-control relates to the sorts of behavioral challenges that we are outlining here.

First, the link between animals' levels of self-control and the specific food ecologies can be viewed as something like an iron law of behavioral ecology: Animals simply cannot exploit food sources that require more waiting than they are capable of enduring, so the ability to exploit food sources that require self-control can exert selective pressure on organisms to attain higher and higher levels of self-control (Stevens, Hallinan, & Hauser, 2005). Second, unfair behavior from others is inevitable in a world in which people's interests never align perfectly. People need to tolerate such unfairness without lashing out against their offenders—a process that draws on cortical areas associated with the top-down suppression of anger and other negative emotions (Jensen-Campbell, Knack, Waldrip, & Campbell, 2007; Tabibnia, Satpute, & Lieberman, 2008). Finally, biologists and psychologists have recently argued that self-control is a cognitive prerequisite both for the evolution of reciprocal altruism (Stevens, Cushman, & Hauser, 2005) and also for its production in real time (Curry, Price, & Price, 2008; Rachlin, 2000; Yi, Buchhalter, Gatchalian, & Bickel, 2007).

Our answer to the "why" question about religion and self-control, then, is this: Changes in religion (particularly, an increasing focus on supernatural entities that possess preferences about modes of human conduct, that monitor human behavior, and that administer punishments and rewards) over the past 10,000 years—in particular, the increasing focus on supernatural agents—reflect the efficacy of belief in these agents to increase self-control. Modern problems related to waiting, tolerating, and cooperating could thus be resolved without exclusive reliance on social or expensive institutional monitoring and policing. Indirect support for this contention comes from Johnson (2005). Johnson documented how the world's distribution of "high gods"—that is, gods with moral preferences that monitor and punish human behavior—correlates positively with various indexes of societal complexity: community size, use of money and credit, police forces, jurisdictional hierarchies, taxation, and—importantly—individual compliance with community norms. These findings suggest that the advent of moralizing gods coincided with increasing concern about the social and emotional challenges that arise when people begin to live in large groups (see also Henrich et al., 2010; Roes & Raymond, 2003).

Our thesis is quite consistent with Johnson's (2005) thesis—and with Norenzayan's and Shariff's, who argued that religious cognition is particularly good at facilitating prosocial behavior that is costly in the short term (Norenzayan & Shariff, 2008; Shariff & Norenzayan, 2007). We think our proposal is also congenial to Robert Wright's (2009) recent description of the connections between the social evolution of economies and the social evolution of religion, and it shares a few similarities with Freud's (1930/2005) notion that humans' religious sentiments function in part to help people stave off undesirable sexual and aggressive urges.

But here is where our thesis departs dramatically from previous ideas: We wish to describe the interplay of (a) an evolved human psychology designed to promote the regulation of impulses and desires and (b) culturally evolved religious beliefs such as belief in moralizing gods and in the afterlife (Bering, 2006). It is at this nexus of adaptively designed psychological mechanisms for self-control and culturally evolved religious innovations that people's capacities for waiting, tolerating, and cooperating might be modified by particular forms of religion. We believe that religious cognitions (especially those involving moralizing gods or the afterlife) have been refined through cultural selection (Richerson & Boyd, 2005) for their ability to promote self-control. Self-control is at a premium in the large, complex, sedentary, agriculturally based societies in which most humans increasingly have been living for the past 8,000 years (Carneiro, 1978).

Human capacities for the control of appetites, impulses, and desires were, we presume, put in place by natural selection acting on neural tissue over many generations in ancestral human populations. The operation of those evolved mechanisms, however, can be influenced by cultural inputs such as religious parental influences (Bartkowski, Xu, & Levin, 2008) or personal involvement in religious institutions (Kenrick, McCreath, Govern, King, &

Bordin, 1990) and practices (Wenger, 2007). This particular aspect of our thesis—that cultural inputs can influence the operation of evolved mental mechanisms—is not particularly controversial (Tooby & Cosmides, 1992, see pp. 114–116).

THE "HOW" QUESTION: RELIGION'S LINKS TO SELF-CONTROL AND SELF-REGULATION

Empirical research on the links of religion to self-control—which addresses our question of how religion affects health and behavior—is in its infancy (McCullough & Willoughby, 2009). Thus, we will limit ourselves here to describing what is currently known about those links. Much of this research is correlational and therefore unable to shed definitive light on religion's ability to foster self-control or self-regulation more broadly. Nevertheless, this research shows that religion as experienced and practiced by many people in the 21st century is associated with higher self-control and specific elements of self-regulation more generally.

The General Connection of Religiosity With Self-Control

Evidence from personality research suggests that religious people tend to score higher on measures of self-control, and measures of personality that subsume self-control, such as conscientiousness and agreeableness, than do their less religious counterparts (Lodi-Smith & Roberts, 2007; Saroglou, 2010). In Eysenck's model of personality, it is psychoticism, which can be thought of as the opposite of Big Five agreeableness and conscientiousness (Costa & McCrae, 1995), that shows consistent negative links with religiosity. This association between psychoticism and low religiosity has been found using a variety of measures and across samples that are diverse in terms of age, religious denomination, and culture (Francis, 1997; Francis & Katz, 1992; Hills, Francis, Argyle, & Jackson, 2004; Lodi-Smith & Roberts, 2007; Wilde & Joseph, 1997). With respect to Cattell's personality system, McCullough and Willoughby (2009) cited studies revealing that scale "G"—known variously as "Conformity," "Superego," and "Expedient Versus Conscientiousness"—is positively associated with church attendance, attitudes toward Christianity, and traditional Christian religious belief.

McCullough and Willoughby (2009) also described 12 studies that reported associations of measures of religiosity with measures of general self-control (e.g., Bouchard, McGue, Lykken, & Tellegen, 1999; Desmond, Ulmer, & Bader, 2008; French, Eisenberg, Vaughan, Purwono, & Suryanti, 2008; Walker, Ainette, Wills, & Mendoza, 2007). Of these 12 studies, 11 reported positive associations between self-report measures of religiosity and self-control, with effect size *r*s ranging from .21 to .38. Since that publication, several additional articles have indicated that some aspects of religiousness (including general measures of religiosity and intrinsic religious motivation) are associated with better self-control or self-regulation (Abar, Carter, & Winsler, 2009; Ahmed, 2009; Vitell et al., 2009). Links of religion with global self-report measures of self-control and self-regulation have been shown not only in studies of U.S. Christians but also in samples of Muslims (e.g., Ahmed, 2009; French et al., 2008).

It is also important to consider the role of *extrinsic religiosity*, a religious orientation characterized by treating religion as a means (as opposed to *intrinsic religiosity*, in which religion is treated as an end; Allport & Ross, 1967). In three of the published studies (Bergin, Masters, & Richards, 1987; Bouchard et al., 1999; Vitell et al., 2009), researchers found extrinsic religious motivation to be negatively associated with self-control. The distinction between intrinsic and extrinsic religion may be an important one to keep in mind as this research area develops, because intrinsic religious motivation is apparently associated with more self-control, whereas extrinsic religious motivation is associated with less self-control.

In the United States, religious families also tend to have children with more self-control (Bartkowski et al., 2008; Brody & Flor, 1998; Brody, Stoneman, & Flor, 1996; Gunnoe, Hetherington, & Reiss, 1999). Parental religiosity, which is variously measured in terms of church attendance, reports of the extent to which religion is discussed in the home, and self-rated importance of religion, is associated with higher parent and teacher ratings of children's self-control and lower impulsivity. These associations do not appear to result from the confounding effects of gender, age, race, socioeconomic status, education, or religious denomination.

Our confidence that the links between religion and self-control are causally related is limited, in part, by the lack of appropriate longitudinal data—as well as by the limited support for the hypothesis that those available longitudinal data provide. McCullough and Willoughby (2009) found six longitudinal studies that reported evidence bearing on the causal nature of this relationship between religion and self-control or self-control-related personality traits (see also Chapter 9 in this volume). Only one of them (Wink, Ciciolla, Dillon, & Tracy, 2007) revealed that religiousness was associated with increases in a personality trait related to self-control—agreeableness—over the life course. Moreover, this finding held only for women, and no connection between religiosity and later increases in conscientiousness was found. In contrast, five studies found that measures of self-control and relevant personality traits predicted religiosity later in life. In one study, conscientious children reliably became more religious adults, even after controlling for confounds such as gender and religious upbringing (McCullough, Tsang, & Brion, 2003). In a second study, children low in agreeableness tended to become less religious adults (McCullough, Enders, Brion, & Jain, 2005). In a third study, conscientious adolescents and agreeable female adolescents showed increases in religiousness through late adulthood, measured nearly 50 years later (Wink et al., 2007). In a fourth study, religious youths who reported making decisions deliberatively and avoided risk-taking remained more religious a year later than did their less religious and less controlled counterparts (Regnerus & Smith, 2005). In a fifth study, high school boys whose psychoticism declined over two time points, and high school girls with increasing conscientiousness at the same two time points, reported more religiosity at a third time point (Heaven & Ciarrochi, 2007).

Taken together, this body of research suggests that religion and self-control are indeed related at the level of personality. The longitudinal evidence that religion can cause increases or reductions in self-control is currently quite limited, however. The evidence that changes in conscientiousness and similar constructs leads to increases in religiosity over time enjoys quite a bit more empirical support. For this reason, experimental data investigating whether religion can create increases in self-control (whether transient or long-term) would be highly desirable from a scientific point of view. To date, experimental work has shown that religious primes slow people's recognition of temptation-related words (i.e., words related to substance use and premarital sex; Fishbach, Friedman, & Kruglanski, 2003). Religious primes also have been shown to increase persistence on a word search task (Toburen & Meier, 2010). Both of these findings implicate religion as a causal factor in self-regulation. The field would benefit greatly from more experimental research of this nature.

Religion and the Cybernetic Model of Self-Regulation

Aside from religion's general connections to personality-level or behavioral measurements of general self-control, it is instructive to consider how religion might influence self-regulation via basic processes that are necessary for systems to effectively self-regulate. Carver and Scheier (1998) conceptualized self-regulation as a dynamic process by which people bring their behavior into conformity with standards through the operation of integrated negative feedback loops. These negative feedback loops consist of several integrated functions. The *input* function detects the system's state. In human terms, this is equivalent to one's perceptions of the self and the environment. The *comparator* function compares the system's state to a *reference value*. Reference values can be conceptualized as goals or standards. When a comparator indicates that the system's state matches its reference value, nothing changes and the existing state is maintained. When the comparator notes a discrepancy between the system's state and its reference value, an *output* function is activated to reduce the discrepancy. Self-regulating systems continuously self-monitor for goal-behavior discrepancies; when discrepancies are noticed, the systems respond by trying to minimize them via outputs.

According to Carver and Scheier (1998), self-regulation relies on at least three processes. First, it requires clear *goals* that are organized to permit effective management of conflict among them (Fitzsimmons & Bargh, 2004). Second, it requires *self-monitoring* or self-directed attention so that one can detect discrepancies between one's goals and one's current behavior. Third, it requires effective mechanisms, or *outputs*, for effecting behavioral change (Schmeichel & Baumeister, 2004). Presently, we consider how religion might influence some of these processes and describe some of the research relevant to these concepts.

Religion and Goals

Religious belief encourages people to acquire specific goals and values that differ from those of nonreligious people (Roberts & Robins, 2000; Saroglou, Delpierre, & Dernelle, 2004). For instance, consider these results from a meta-analysis of 12 studies conducted in primarily Christian, primarily Muslim, and primarily Jewish nations (e.g., the United States, Turkey, and Israel). Results showed that religiosity was reliably and positively correlated with the values from the Schwartz Value Survey called Tradition (including traits such as "responsible" and "helpful"; $r = .45$) and Conformity (including qualities such as "self-discipline" and "politeness"; $r = .23$). Conversely, religiosity was negatively correlated with the values measured on scales known as Hedonism ("self-indulgent," "pleasure"; $r = -.30$), Stimulation ("exciting life"; $r = -.26$), and Self-Direction ("freedom," "independent"; $r = -.24$). These results were obtained in all three types of religious nations. Taken together, these results suggest that Jewish, Christian, and Muslim religiosity promote goals related to respect and concern for others, while they discourage goals related to personal gratification and individuality. It seems to us no accident that religiosity is particularly good at increasing people's valuation of Tradition and Conformity-related values if what religion has evolved to do is increase people's ability to wait, tolerate, and cooperate.

One way in which religious thought may encourage the pursuit of certain goals is by "sanctifying" them, or defining the source of those goals as sacred, thereby making them more important (Emmons, 1999). For example, Mahoney et al. (1999) found that husbands and wives who characterized their marriages as "sacred" and "manifestations of God" reported healthier marriages (better adjustment, better conflict resolution). Mahoney et al. (2005) also showed that college students who sanctified their bodies, believing them to be gifts from God, tended to get more sleep, wear their seatbelts, and disapprove of illicit drug use. It seems that religion can be used to sanctify almost any goal, from getting enough exercise to killing civilians. We anticipate, however, that many of the goals that people commonly sanctify through religion will be relevant to waiting (e.g., being patient), tolerating (e.g., being forgiving), and cooperating (e.g., helping the members of one's group or honoring one's obligations).

Religiosity and Self-Monitoring

Awareness of an evaluative audience increases people's self-awareness. When made self-aware, people then compare their behavior to relevant behavioral standards (Carver & Scheier, 1998). Many religious belief systems posit gods or spirits that observe humans' behavior, pass judgment, and then administer rewards or sanctions (Bering & Johnson, 2005). In many of these religions, these beings can also read thoughts and are not fooled by people's attempts to deceive them. Several studies suggest that priming religious concepts produces behavioral effects on measures such as cooperation, generosity, and honesty that can be construed as prosocial in nature (Pichon et al., 2007; Randolph-Seng & Nielsen, 2007; Shariff & Norenzayan, 2007). Such effects could conceivably be mediated by religious cognition's effects on self-monitoring, although this remains an open question.

Such speculation is also consistent with the finding that exposure to images of eyes (i.e., stimuli indicative of the fact that one is being monitored) increases generosity and honesty (Haley & Fessler, 2005). Religion could also promote self-monitoring through introspective religious rituals (e.g., prayer, meditation, reflecting on scripture) during which people monitor for discrepancies between their goal states and their behavior (Wenger, 2007). Correlational evidence that religious people engage in more self-monitoring than do less religious people is limited and mixed, and direct experimental work on the topic is virtually nonexistent. We believe that this particular question is ripe for research (McCullough & Willoughby, 2009).

Religiosity and Outputs for Self-Change

A final requirement for effective self-regulation is the possession of a suite of effective psychological and behavioral tools for self-change. As discussed, such tools for self-change are called *outputs* (Carver & Scheier, 1998). Religious belief systems, although they do offer uniquely religious outputs, may also encourage effective outputs that are not specifically religious. For example, a person might avoid contact with tempting stimuli, perhaps by avoiding an attractive person with whom a relationship is morally off-limits (Worthington et al., 2001).

Prayer and meditation may have important regulatory effects (Galton, 1872; McNamara, 2002). In one study, Brefczynski-Lewis, Lutz, Schaefer, Levinson, and Davidson (2007) discovered that regions in the brain associated with attention and response inhibition saw more activation in experienced meditators. Also, Chan and Woollacott (2007) found that experienced meditators had less interference during a Stroop task, suggesting that they had more effective regulation of attentional processes. In addition, Koole (2007) conducted five experiments that revealed that when people (particularly religious people) were exposed to a person in need and then instructed to pray for that person, they experienced more reductions in negative affect than did people who were instructed (a) simply to think about the person or (b) to positively reappraise the person's plight.

Other religious behaviors that may be effective outputs for self-change, especially for religious people, include evoking religious imagery (Weisbuch-Remington, Mendes, Seery, & Blascovich, 2005; Wiech et al., 2008) and consulting one's religious scriptures (Wenger, 2007). Rachlin (2000) proposed that behavioral guidance gleaned from religious scripture might be a particularly effective tool for change because of its sacred nature. Wenger's (2007) experiment provided some support for this claim. Participants who were led to focus on religious shortcomings spent longer reading a passage called "How can I know when it is God who is speaking to me?" This finding might illustrate how a self-regulating system can note a discrepancy in behavior relative to a goal state (i.e., not following religious tenets when a goal is to be a good follower of a religious system) and then reduce the discrepancy using a religiously prescribed output function (i.e., reading religious material).

Religion and Implicit Self-Regulation

Recognizing that self-control can occur through automatic mechanisms (Fitzsimmons & Bargh, 2004), Koole, McCullough, Kuhl, and Roelofsma (2010) recently advanced a parallel view of religion's connection to self-regulation that relies on implicit or automatic routes for cognitive processing rather than conscious ones. Implicit self-regulation, as they conceptualized it, operates in three ways that might be influenced by religious cognition. First, religion might help people to form appropriate intentions that can then be translated into effective action (also known as *volitional efficiency*). Second, religion might facilitate *emotion regulation*. Third, religion might help people reconcile new experiences with what has come previously, thereby helping to create and preserve *meaning in life* (see Chapter 8 in this volume).

Many studies in which religious cognition has been primed outside of conscious awareness do indeed suggest that religious cognition can foster self-regulation through implicit processes. As noted, one experiment showed that subliminally presented religious mental content suppressed goals related to temptation (Fishbach et al., 2003). College students were subliminally primed for 50 minutes with either a temptation or sin-related concept (e.g., drugs, temptation, premarital sex), a religion-related concept (e.g., prayer, the Bible, religion, and God), or a neutral word. After each prime, participants were instructed to identify religion-related words or temptation or sin-related words as either words or nonwords as quickly as possible. Fishbach et al. (2003) found that the subliminal presentation of temptation or sin-related primes led to faster recognition of religion-relevant words than did the subliminal presentation of neutral primes. Conversely, subliminally presented religion-relevant primes slowed recognition of temptation or sin-related words in comparison with the neutral primes. These results suggest that people recruit religious concepts to facilitate self-control in the face of temptation, and conversely, that activating religious mental content can suppress temptation or sin-related content. Interestingly, these regulatory processes took place automatically, implying that regulation occurred on the basis of implicit goals that had been internalized through a religious belief system.

One important effect of implicit regulation is to stabilize people's moment-to-moment responses to emotion-inducing stimuli (Koole, 2009). As described previously, Koole (2007) reported the results of five experiments supporting the hypothesis that prayer can reduce negative affect. Weisbuch-Remington, Mendes, Seery, and Blascovich (2005) also found similar effects in two experiments that evaluated whether religious imagery facilitates emotion regulation. These studies revealed that subliminally exposing Christian participants to positive religious imagery (e.g., images of Christ ascending to heaven; Jesus as an infant) before they completed a stressful task caused physiological responses characterized by greater cardiac output (termed a *challenge* response; Blascovich, Mendes, Tomaka, Salomon, & Seery, 2003). In contrast, Christians exposed to negative religious imagery (e.g., demons; satanic symbols) evinced greater total peripheral resistance (termed a *threat* response). A threat response is thought to occur when resources are evaluated as not meeting situational demands, whereas a challenge response indicates that situational demands have been evaluated as surmountable (Blascovich et al., 2003).

Finally, a more recent study showed that religious people who were primed with thoughts about their religious faith had lower defensive neural responses to errors in the Stroop test (Inzlicht & Tullett, 2010). This finding suggests that religious beliefs may have provided a sense of meaning and security that protected participants from negative affective responses to errors. Taken together, these results remind us that even though self-control has traditionally been considered a conscious, effortful process, we know better now. Therefore, we should expect that many of religion's potential self-regulatory effects will occur through automatic processes and not only through conscious cognitive ones. Research in the future should examine religion's effects on self-regulation through both of these possible routes.

Can religion's links to self-control and self-regulation help to explain religion's associations with behavior? Self-regulation and self-control may help to explain religion's well-established associations with measures of health, well-being, and social behavior such as longevity (McCullough et al., 2000), decreased depression (Smith et al., 2003), improved marital functioning (Mahoney et al., 1999), less crime and delinquency (Baier & Wright, 2001), and higher school achievement (Jeynes, 2002)—outcomes that other research has consistently linked to high self-control (for a comprehensive review, see Vohs & Baumeister, 2011).

For instance, six studies have addressed the proposition that religion's associations with measures of substance use and delinquency are due in part to religion's ability to foster self-regulation or self-control and restraint (Bjarnason, Thorlindsson, Sigfusdottir, & Welch, 2005; Desmond et al., 2008; Walker et al., 2007; Welch, Tittle, & Grasmick, 2006; Wills, Gibbons, Gerrard, Murry, & Brody, 2003). Five of these studies found that self-control partially mediated the associations of religiousness with these outcome variables. In one representative study, Walker, Ainette, Wills, and Mendoza (2007) found that religiousness was negatively associated with self-reported substance use in two different cross-sectional data sets: a sample of 1,273 middle school students and a sample of 812 high school students. The negative association of religiousness with substance use in both samples was significantly mediated by a latent variable measuring good self-control. Also, Desmond, Ulmer, and Bader (2008) found that self-control partially mediated the cross-sectional associations of a three-item self-report measure of religiousness with alcohol use and marijuana use in the Add Health data set (a study of students from a nationally representative sample of 132 middle schools and high schools in the United States). These mediational effects obtained even when controlling for participants' sex, age, race, parental education, socioeconomic status, family structure, students' grades, associations with delinquent peers, attachment to their schools, religious denomination, and several other variables.

We have speculated that self-control or self-regulation might mediate religion's associations on many domains, including longevity, psychological symptoms, marital and family functioning, school achievement, and prosocial behavior. However, studies have not been conducted on most of these domains. Moreover, all of the extant research on this proposition is correlational (and cross-sectional). Stronger tests of causality, using a broader array of outcomes, would advance this line of research.

Does religion ever lead to self-control failures?

We are occasionally asked whether religious belief and behavior can lead to self-control failures. We think the answer to this question is a qualified "no." The "no" is qualified for three reasons. First, it is possible that extended exertion in the religious domain (e.g., sustained periods of fasting, meditation, or other forms of religious devotion) sometimes temporarily reduces people's willingness to persist in the pursuit of other goals–a state that might be accompanied by a felt sense of fatigue or boredom. This fatigue, however, might be the result of mental and physical exertion more generally instead of indicating anything special about the religious domain. Second, certain forms of religious belief may more readily lead to failures of self-control. As mentioned, extrinsically motivated religious belief is correlated with lower self-control (Bergin et al., 1987; Bouchard et al., 1999; Vitell et al., 2009). This correlation could mean that extrinsic religious motivation reflects an impulsive, poorly controlled approach to life overall such that more impulsive people, if they are religious, tend to be extrinsically motivated (Vitell et al., 2009). It could also reflect the generally unprincipled quality of extrinsic religiousness: When religious involvement is not based on principles (i.e., high-level goals related to the kind of person one is trying to become), low-level life goals may become uncoordinated (Carver & Scheier, 1998). Finally, it is also possible that some ecstatic religious rituals reduce people's self-control or self-regulation for ritual reasons (e.g., to facilitate the experience of spirit possession, speaking in tongues, or ecstatic joy). However, it is unclear that such changes of consciousness are due to failures of self-control or self-regulation. The term *failure* suggests that something has gone wrong; ritual loss of self-control implies that the loss of self-control is deliberate.

It is obvious that not all of religion's effects—even those that are predicated on religion's ability to foster self-control—are beneficial for society. As a matter of fact, we think the links of religion to self-control and self-regulation can explain some of religion's negative effects—not because religion sometimes reduces self-control, but rather, because it is so good at encouraging people to pursue particular goals and to behave nonimpulsively.

Consider religious violence. Religious stimuli can motivate aggression (Bushman, Ridge, Das, Key, & Busath, 2007) and prejudice (Altemeyer & Hunsberger, 2005) at least as effectively as they facilitate cooperation (Shariff & Norenzayan, 2007) and other forms of prosocial behavior (Saroglou, Pichon, Trompette, Verschueren, & Dernelle, 2005)—perhaps especially when the religion is of a fundamentalist, authoritarian variety (Altemeyer & Hunsberger, 2005; Rowatt et al., 2006). Moreover, the religious sanctification of goals such as dying for one's religion or one's ethnic group, or loyalty to one's small group are highly effective tools for recruiting suicide terrorists (Atran, 2003; see also Chapter 26 in this volume and Volume 2, Chapter 18, this handbook). Means-end analysis of terrorism (Kruglanski & Fishman, 2006) implies a role for cultural (including religious) factors that can influence the many facets of self-regulation, including (a) the goals people select, (b) the motivation that becomes attached to those goals, (c) the psychological processes that influence error monitoring as people set out plans for making progress toward their goals, and (d) the outputs at people's disposal for modifying their behavior to create progress toward goal attainment. In other words, a self-regulation analysis of religion suggests that religion is well-suited to motivate any behavior that is predicated on self-control and self-regulation. Such behaviors might range from studying for exams or avoiding drugs to donning a bomb belt and detonating it on a crowded city bus. For example, even after one has decided to become a suicide terrorist, detonating a bomb must surely involve overcoming some impulse to save oneself. Here again religious socialization may bring about a higher level of self-control that allows people to execute their destructive choices.

POTENTIAL REAL-WORLD APPLICATIONS

We see at least five directions for research that might lead to real-world applications. First, many people wish they had more control over their emotions, appetites, and impulses. Religious rituals such as prayer, meditation, religious imagery, and reading religious scriptures evidently influence the self-control of attention and emotion (McCullough & Willoughby, 2009; see Chapter 18 in this volume). Such rituals might thus be useful to people who want to increase their self-control. Meditation is of special interest here because it might be more broadly applicable (i.e., even to nonreligious people) than prayer. It would be useful to know whether all of these religious rituals could be adapted for use in both religious and nonreligious populations (see Volume 2, Chapter 10, this handbook).

Second, it would be useful to know whether—and if so, how—use of religious beliefs in coping might affect downstream self-control. Pargament, Koenig, and Perez (2000), for example, developed the Religious Coping Inventory (RCOPE), a 17-factor self-report scale of religious coping. This measure taps a wide variety of religious strategies that people use to cope with negative life events. These strategies include (a) taking a religious focus (i.e., engaging in religious activities such as prayer to distract oneself from a stressor), (b) using collaborative religious coping (i.e., seeking control over a stressor through a problem-solving partnership with God), and (c) seeking support from clergy or members of one's religious group. This scale also measures several forms of negative religious coping (e.g., attributing one's problems to demonic influences or God's punishment). It is possible that some of these techniques lead to good short-term responses to stressors but to negative long-term effects on the self-control of emotions or attention. If we knew more about which aspects of religious coping led to better or worse self-control, we could make better predictions (and recommendations) regarding how people under stress might use religious beliefs for coping without encountering unintended negative consequences for self-regulation.

Third, we think there is a potential real-world application that comes from research on subtle environmental primes. Research suggests that priming people with subtle stimuli such as geometric configurations that resemble eyes or faces (Bateson, Nettle, & Roberts, 2006; Haley & Fessler, 2005; Rigdon, Ishii, Watabe, & Kitayama, 2009), reminders of God or religion (Pichon et al., 2007; Shariff & Norenzayan, 2007), and even secular institutions such as contracts and police that regulate prosocial behavior can increase generosity, cooperation, and charitable giving. These effects have been obtained in both laboratory and field experiments, raising the idea that some of the lowest hanging fruit in professionals' efforts to increase prosocial behavior in the real world might be achieved through subtle, non-preachy stimuli that activate religious cognition without conscious awareness (Pichon et al., 2007; Shariff & Norenzayan, 2007).

Fourth, we view the links of religion and self-control as potentially providing new angles for understanding self-control and self-regulation more generally. Can researchers do a better job of explaining the psychological and behavioral processes by which religious families end up with more self-controlled first graders (Bartkowski et al., 2008), or how people who are religious end up with more self-control by the time they reach adulthood? Can they explain these religion and self-control links in terms of the distinct elements of the parenting that religious people receive as children or the social interactions with adults and peers that they experience in their religious congregations? Can they explain them in terms of the goals that religious adolescents set for themselves? Do religious people end up with more self-control through the accumulation of small, daily choices to exert self-control (e.g., waking up the first time the alarm goes off)? Or is it more important to exercise self-control in high-stakes situations (e.g., resisting peer pressure to experiment with drugs)? The sooner we know how religious people acquire higher self-control over the life course, the sooner such insights might be applied to efforts to improve human well-being for religious and nonreligious people alike.

CONCLUSION

Research shows that religion is related to many domains of life—so many, in fact, that one can easily get lost in the details. Here, we have tried to focus on a single mechanistic explanation—self-regulation and self-control—for how religion obtains its associations with so many of these life domains. As important, however, we have tried to offer a cultural–evolutionary explanation for why (we think) religion has evolved to be so good at affecting human functioning through this particular mechanism. By focusing on the "how" and the "why," we hope we can generate research on these ideas that will not only help us to understand religion and self-control more generally but also to generate insights that can improve the lives of individuals and the well-being of their relationships and societies.

References

Abar, B., Carter, K. L., & Winsler, A. (2009). The effects of maternal parenting style and religious commitment on self-regulation, academic achievement, and risk behavior among African-American parochial college students. *Journal of Adolescence, 32*, 259–273. doi:10.1016/j.adolescence.2008.03.008

Ahmed, S. (2009). Religiosity and presence of character strengths in American Muslim youth. *Journal of Muslim Mental Health, 4*, 104–123. doi:10.1080/15564900903245642

Allport, G. W., & Ross, M. J. (1967). Personal religious orientation and prejudice. *Journal of Personality and Social Psychology, 5*, 432–443. doi:10.1037/h0021212

Altemeyer, B., & Hunsberger, B. (2005). Fundamentalism and authoritarianism. In R. F. Paloutzian & C. L. Park (Eds.), *Handbook of the psychology of religion and spirituality* (pp. 378–393). New York, NY: Guilford Press.

Atran, S. (2003). Genesis of suicide terrorism. *Science, 299*, 1534–1539. doi:10.1126/science.1078854

Atran, S., & Norenzayan, A. (2004). Religion's evolutionary landscape: Counterintuition, commitment, compassion, communion. *Behavioral and Brain Sciences, 27*, 713–770. doi:10.1017/S0140525X04000172

Baier, C., & Wright, B. R. E. (2001). "If you love me, keep my commandments": A meta-analysis of the effect of religion on crime. *Journal of Research in Crime and Delinquency, 38*, 3–21. doi:10.1177/0022427801038001001

Bartkowski, J. P., Xu, X., & Levin, M. L. (2008). Religion and child development: Evidence from the early childhood longitudinal study. *Social Science Research, 37*, 18–36. doi:10.1016/j.ssresearch.2007.02.001

Bar-Yosef, O. (1998). The Natufian culture in the Levant, threshold to the origins of agriculture. *Evolutionary Anthropology, 6*, 159–177. doi:10.1002/(SICI)1520-6505(1998)6:5<159::AID-EVAN4>3.0.CO;2-7

Bateson, M., Nettle, D., & Roberts, G. (2006). Cues of being watched enhance cooperation in a real-world setting. *Biology Letters, 2*, 412–414. doi:10.1098/rsbl.2006.0509

Baumeister, R. F., & Vohs, K. D. (2004). Self-regulation. In C. Peterson & M. E. P. Seligman (Eds.), *Character strengths and virtues: A handbook and classification* (pp. 499–516). Washington, DC and New York, NY: American Psychological Association and Oxford University Press.

Baumeister, R. F., Vohs, K. D., & Tice, D. M. (2007). The strength model of self-control. *Current Directions in Psychological Science, 16*, 351–355. doi:10.1111/j.1467-8721.2007.00534.x

Bergin, A. E., Masters, K. S., & Richards, P. S. (1987). Religiousness and mental health reconsidered: A study of an intrinsically religious sample. *Journal of Counseling Psychology, 34*, 197–204. doi:10.1037/0022-0167.34.2.197

Bering, J. M. (2006). The folk psychology of souls. *Behavioral and Brain Sciences, 29*, 453–462. doi:10.1017/S0140525X06009101

Bering, J. M., & Johnson, D. D. P. (2005). "O Lord . . . You perceive my thoughts from afar": Recursiveness and the evolution of supernatural agency. *Journal of Cognition and Culture, 5*, 118–142. doi:10.1163/1568537054068679

Bjarnason, T., Thorlindsson, T., Sigfusdottir, I. D., & Welch, M. R. (2005). Familial and religious influences on adolescent alcohol use: A multi-level study of students and school communities. *Social Forces, 84*, 375–390. doi:10.1353/sof.2005.0088

Blascovich, J., Mendes, W. B., Tomaka, J., Salomon, K., & Seery, M. D. (2003). The robust nature of the biopsychosocial model of challenge and threat: A reply to Wright and Kirby. *Personality and Social Psychology Review, 7*, 234–243. doi:10.1207/S15327957PSPR0703_03

Bouchard, T. J., McGue, M., Lykken, D., & Tellegen, A. (1999). Intrinsic and extrinsic religiousness: Genetic and environmental influences and personality correlates. *Twin Research, 2*, 88–98. doi:10.1375/136905299320565951

Brefczynski-Lewis, J. A., Lutz, A., Schaefer, H. S., Levinson, D. B., & Davidson, R. J. (2007). Neural correlates of attentional expertise in long-term meditation practitioners. *Proceedings of the National*

Academy of Sciences of the United States of America, 104, 11483–11488. doi:10.1073/pnas.0606552104

Brody, G. H., & Flor, D. (1998). Maternal resources, parenting practices, and child competence in rural, single-parent African American families. *Child Development, 69*, 803–816.

Brody, G. H., Stoneman, Z., & Flor, D. (1996). Parental religiosity, family processes, and youth competence in rural, two-parent African American families. *Developmental Psychology, 32*, 696–706. doi:10.1037/0012-1649.32.4.696

Bushman, B. J., Ridge, R. D., Das, E., Key, C. W., & Busath, G. M. (2007). When God sanctions killing: Effect of scriptural violence on aggression. *Psychological Science, 18*, 204–207. doi:10.1111/j.1467-9280.2007.01873.x

Carneiro, R. L. (1978). Political expansion of the principle of competitive exclusion. In R. Cohen & E. R. Service (Eds.), *Origins of the state: The anthropology of political evolution* (pp. 205–223). Philadelphia, PA: Institute for the Study of Human Issues.

Carver, C. S., & Scheier, M. F. (1998). *On the self-regulation of behavior*. New York, NY: Cambridge University Press.

Chan, D., & Woollacott, M. (2007). Effects of level of meditation experience on attentional focus: Is the efficiency of executive or orientation networks improved? *Journal of Alternative and Complementary Medicine, 13*, 651–658. doi:10.1089/acm.2007.7022

Costa, P. T., & McCrae, R. R. (1995). Primary traits of Eysenck's P-E-N system: Three- and five-factor solutions. *Journal of Personality and Social Psychology, 69*, 308–317. doi:10.1037/0022-3514.69.2.308

Curry, O. S., Price, M. E., & Price, J. G. (2008). Patience is a virtue: Cooperative people have lower discount rates. *Personality and Individual Differences, 44*, 780–785. doi:10.1016/j.paid.2007.09.023

Desmond, S. A., Ulmer, J. T., & Bader, C. D. (2008). *Religion, prosocial learning, self control, and delinquency*. Manuscript submitted for publication.

Emmons, R. A. (1999). *The psychology of ultimate concerns: Motivation and spirituality in personality*. New York, NY: Guilford Press.

Fishbach, A., Friedman, R. S., & Kruglanski, A. W. (2003). Leading us not into temptation: Momentary allurements elicit overriding goal activation. *Journal of Personality and Social Psychology, 84*, 296–309. doi:10.1037/0022-3514.84.2.296

Fitzsimmons, G. M., & Bargh, J. A. (2004). Automatic self-regulation. In R. F. Baumeister & K. D. Vohs (Eds.), *Handbook of self-regulation: Research, theory, and applications* (pp. 151–170). New York, NY: Guilford Press.

Francis, L. J. (1997). Personality, prayer, and church attendance among undergraduate students. *The International Journal for the Psychology of Religion, 7*, 127–132. doi:10.1207/s15327582ijpr0702_7

Francis, L. J., & Katz, Y. J. (1992). The relationship between personality and religiosity in an Israeli sample. *Journal for the Scientific Study of Religion, 31*, 153–162. doi:10.2307/1387005

French, D. C., Eisenberg, N., Vaughan, J., Purwono, U., & Suryanti, T. A. (2008). Religious involvement and the social competence and adjustment of Indonesian Muslim adolescents. *Developmental Psychology, 44*, 597–611. doi:10.1037/0012-1649.44.2.597

Freud, S. (2005). *Civilization and its discontents* (J. Strachey, Trans.). New York, NY: Norton. (Original work published 1930)

Galton, F. (1872). Statistical inquiries into the efficacy of prayer. *Fortnightly Review, 12*, 125–135.

Grosman, L., Munro, N. D., & Belfer-Cohen, A. (2008). A 12,000-year-old Shaman burial from the Levant (Israel). *Proceedings of the National Academy of Sciences of the United States of America, 105*, 17665–17669. doi:10.1073/pnas.0806030105

Gunnoe, M. L., Hetherington, E. M., & Reiss, D. (1999). Parental religiosity, parenting style, and adolescent social responsibility. *Journal of Early Adolescence, 19*, 199–225. doi:10.1177/0272431699019002004

Haley, K. J., & Fessler, D. M. T. (2005). Nobody's watching? Subtle cues affect generosity in an anonymous economic game. *Evolution and Human Behavior, 26*, 245–256. doi:10.1016/j.evolhumbehav.2005.01.002

Heaven, P. C. L., & Ciarrochi, J. (2007). Personality and religious values among adolescents: A three-wave longitudinal analysis. *British Journal of Psychology, 98*, 681–694. doi:10.1348/000712607X187777

Henrich, J., Ensminger, J., McElreath, R., Barr, A., Barrett, C., Bolyanatz, A., . . . Ziker, J. (2010). Markets, religion, community size, and the evolution of fairness and punishment. *Science, 327*, 1480–1484. doi:10.1126/science.1182238

Hill, T. D., Burdette, A. M., Ellison, C. G., & Musick, M. A. (2006). Religious attendance and the health behaviors of Texas adults. *Preventive Medicine, 42*, 309–312. doi:10.1016/j.ypmed.2005.12.005

Hills, P., Francis, L. J., Argyle, M., & Jackson, C. J. (2004). Primary personality trait correlates of religious practice and orientation. *Personality and Individual Differences, 36*, 61–73. doi:10.1016/S0191-8869(03)00051-5

Inzlicht, M., & Tullett, A. M. (2010). Reflecting on God: Religious primes can reduce neurophysiological responses to errors. *Psychological Science, 21*, 1184–1190. doi:10.1177/0956797610375451

Islam, S. M. S., & Johnson, C. A. (2003). Correlates of smoking behavior among Muslim Arab-American adolescents. *Ethnicity and Health, 8*, 319–337. doi:10.1080/13557850310001631722

James, W. (1958). *The varieties of religious experience.* New York, NY: Penguin.

Jensen-Campbell, L. A., Knack, J. M., Waldrip, A. M., & Campbell, S. D. (2007). Do Big Five personality traits associated with self-control influence the regulation of anger and aggression? *Journal of Research in Personality, 41*, 403–424. doi:10.1016/j.jrp.2006.05.001

Jeynes, W. H. (2002). A meta-analysis of the effects of attending religious schools and religiosity on Black and Hispanic academic achievement. *Education and Urban Society, 35*, 27–49. doi:10.1177/001312402237213

Johnson, D. D. P. (2005). God's punishment and public goods. *Human Nature, 16*, 410–446. doi:10.1007/s12110-005-1017-0

Kenrick, D. T., McCreath, H. E., Govern, J., King, R., & Bordin, J. (1990). Person–environment intersections: Everyday settings and common trait dimensions. *Journal of Personality and Social Psychology, 58*, 685–698. doi:10.1037/0022-3514.58.4.685

Koole, S. L. (2007). *Raising spirits: An experimental analysis of the affect regulation functions of prayer.* Amsterdam, the Netherlands: Vrije Universiteit.

Koole, S. L. (2009). The psychology of emotion regulation: An integrative review. *Cognition and Emotion, 23*, 4–41. doi:10.1080/02699930802619031

Koole, S. L., McCullough, M. E., Kuhl, J., & Roelofsma, P. H. M. P. (2010). Why religion's burdens are light: From religiosity to implicit self-regulation. *Personality and Social Psychology Review, 14*, 95–107. doi:10.1177/1088868309351109

Kruglanski, A. W., & Fishman, S. (2006). Terrorism between "syndrome" and "tool." *Current Directions in Psychological Science, 15*, 45–48. doi:10.1111/j.0963-7214.2006.00404.x

Lieberman, D., Tooby, J., & Cosmides, L. (2007). The architecture of human kin detection. *Nature, 445*, 727–731. doi:10.1038/nature05510

Lodi-Smith, J., & Roberts, B. W. (2007). Social investment and personality: A meta-analysis of the relationship of personality traits to investment in work, family, religion, and volunteerism. *Personality and Social Psychology Review, 11*, 1–19. doi:10.1177/1088868306294590

Mahoney, A., Carels, R. A., Pargament, K. I., Wachholtz, A., Leeper, L. E., Kaplar, M., & Frutchey, R. (2005). The sanctification of the body and behavioral health patterns of college students. *The International Journal for the Psychology of Religion, 15*, 221–238. doi:10.1207/s15327582ijpr1503_3

Mahoney, A., Pargament, K. I., Jewell, T., Swank, A. B., Scott, E., Emery, E., & Rye, M. S. (1999). Marriage and the spiritual realm: The role of proximal and distal religious constructs in marital functioning. *Journal of Family Psychology, 13*, 321–338. doi:10.1037/0893-3200.13.3.321

McCullough, M. E., Enders, C. K., Brion, S. L., & Jain, A. R. (2005). The varieties of religious development in adulthood: A longitudinal investigation of religion and rational choice. *Journal of Personality and Social Psychology, 89*, 78–89. doi:10.1037/0022-3514.89.1.78

McCullough, M. E., Hoyt, W. T., Larson, D. B., Koenig, H. G., & Thoresen, C. E. (2000). Religious involvement and mortality: A meta-analytic review. *Health Psychology, 19*, 211–222. doi:10.1037/0278-6133.19.3.211

McCullough, M. E., Tsang, J., & Brion, S. L. (2003). Personality traits in adolescence as predictors of religiousness on early adulthood: Findings from the Terman Longitudinal Study. *Personality and Social Psychology Bulletin, 29*, 980–991. doi:10.1177/0146167203253210

McCullough, M. E., & Willoughby, B. L. B. (2009). Religion, self-regulation, and self-control: Associations, explanations, and implications. *Psychological Bulletin, 135*, 69–93. doi:10.1037/a0014213

McNamara, P. (2002). The motivational origins of religious practices. *Zygon, 37*, 143–160. doi:10.1111/1467-9744.00418

Mithen, S. (2007). Did farming arise from a misapplication of social intelligence? *Philosophical Transactions of the Royal Society of London. Series B, Biological Sciences, 362*, 705–718. doi:10.1098/rstb.2006.2005

Norenzayan, A., & Shariff, A. F. (2008). The origin and evolution of religious prosociality. *Science, 322*, 58–62. doi:10.1126/science.1158757

Pargament, K. I., Koenig, H. G., & Perez, L. M. (2000). The many methods of religious coping: Development and initial validation of the RCOPE. *Journal of Clinical Psychology, 56*, 519–543. doi:10.1002/(SICI)1097-4679(200004)56:4<519::AID-JCLP6>3.0.CO;2-1

Pichon, I., Boccato, G., & Saroglou, V. (2007). Nonconscious influences of religion on prosociality: A priming study. *European Journal of Social Psychology, 37*, 1032–1045. doi:10.1002/ejsp.416

Porr, M., & Alt, K. W. (2006). The burial of Bad Dürrenberg, central Germany: Osteopathology and osteoarchaeology of a Late Mesolithic shaman's grave. *International Journal of Osteoarchaeology, 16*, 395–406. doi:10.1002/oa.839

Pratt, J. B. (1934). *The religious consciousness: A psychological study.* New York, NY: Macmillan.

Rachlin, H. (2000). *The science of self-control.* Cambridge, MA: Harvard University Press.

Randolph-Seng, B., & Nielsen, M. E. (2007). Honesty: One effect of primed religious representations. *The International Journal for the Psychology of Religion, 17*, 303–315. doi:10.1080/10508610701572812

Regnerus, M. D., & Smith, C. (2005). Selection effects in studies of religious influences. *Review of Religious Research, 47*, 23–50. doi:10.2307/4148279

Reyes-García, V., Godoy, R., Huanca, T., Leonard, W. R., McDade, T., Tanner, S., & Vadez, V. (2007). The origins of monetary income inequality: Patience, human capital, and division of labor. *Evolution and Human Behavior, 28*, 37–47.

Richerson, P. J., & Boyd, R. (2005). *Not by genes alone: How culture transformed human evolution*. Chicago, IL: University of Chicago Press.

Rigdon, M., Ishii, K., Watabe, M., & Kitayama, S. (2009). Minimal social cues in the dictator game. *Journal of Economic Psychology, 30*, 358–367. doi:10.1016/j.joep.2009.02.002

Roberts, B. W., & Robins, R. W. (2000). Broad dispositions, broad aspirations: The intersection of personality traits and major life goals. *Personality and Social Psychology Bulletin, 26*, 1284–1296. doi:10.1177/0146167200262009

Roes, F. L., & Raymond, M. (2003). Belief in moralizing gods. *Evolution and Human Behavior, 24*, 126–135. doi:10.1016/S1090-5138(02)00134-4

Rowatt, W. C., Tsang, J., Kelly, J., La Martina, B., McCullers, M., & McKinley, A. (2006). Associations between religious personality dimensions and implicit homosexual prejudice. *Journal for the Scientific Study of Religion, 45*, 397–406. doi:10.1111/j.1468-5906.2006.00314.x

Saroglou, V. (2010). Religiousness as a cultural adaptation of basic traits: A five-factor model perspective. *Personality and Social Psychology Review, 14*, 108–125. doi:10.1177/1088868309352322

Saroglou, V., Delpierre, V., & Dernelle, R. (2004). Values and religiosity: A meta-analysis of studies using Schwartz's model. *Personality and Individual Differences, 37*, 721–734. doi:10.1016/j.paid.2003.10.005

Saroglou, V., Pichon, I., Trompette, L., Verschueren, M., & Dernelle, R. (2005). Prosocial behavior and religion: New evidence based on projective measures and peer ratings. *Journal for the Scientific Study of Religion, 44*, 323–348. doi:10.1111/j.1468-5906.2005.00289.x

Schmeichel, B. J., & Baumeister, R. F. (2004). Self-regulatory strength. In R. F. Baumeister & K. D. Vohs (Eds.), *Handbook of self-regulation: Research, theory, and applications* (pp. 84–98). New York, NY: Guilford Press.

Shariff, A. F., & Norenzayan, A. (2007). God is watching you: Supernatural agent concepts increase prosocial behavior in an anonymous economic game. *Psychological Science, 18*, 803–809. doi:10.1111/j.1467-9280.2007.01983.x

Shmueli, A., & Tamir, D. (2007). Health behavior and religiosity among Israeli Jews. *Israeli Medical Association Journal, 9*, 703–707.

Smith, T. B., McCullough, M. E., & Poll, J. (2003). Religiousness and depression: Evidence for a main effect and the moderating influence of stressful life events. *Psychological Bulletin, 129*, 614–636. doi:10.1037/0033-2909.129.4.614

Stevens, J. R., Cushman, F. A., & Hauser, M. D. (2005). Evolving the psychological mechanisms for cooperation. *Annual Review of Ecology Evolution and Systematics, 36*, 499–518. doi:10.1146/annurev.ecolsys.36.113004.083814

Stevens, J. R., Hallinan, E. V., & Hauser, M. D. (2005). The ecology and evolution of patience in two New World monkeys. *Biology Letters, 1*, 223–226. doi:10.1098/rsbl.2004.0285

Tabibnia, G., Satpute, A. B., & Lieberman, M. D. (2008). The sunny side of fairness: Preference for fairness activates reward circuitry (and disregarding unfairness activates self-control circuitry). *Psychological Science, 19*, 339–347. doi:10.1111/j.1467-9280.2008.02091.x

Toburen, T., & Meier, B. P. (2010). Priming god-related concepts increases anxiety and task performance. *Journal of Social and Clinical Psychology, 29*, 127–143. doi:10.1521/jscp.2010.29.2.127

Tooby, J., & Cosmides, L. (1992). Psychological foundations of culture. In J. Barkow, L. Cosmides, & J. Tooby (Eds.), *The adapted mind: Evolutionary psychology and the generation of culture* (pp. 19–136). New York, NY: Oxford University Press.

Vitell, S. J., Bing, M. N., Davison, H. K., Ammeter, A. P., Gamer, B. L., & Novicevic, M. M. (2009). Religiosity and moral identity: The mediating role of self-control. *Journal of Business Ethics, 88*, 601–613. doi:10.1007/s10551-008-9980-0

Vohs, K. D., & Baumeister, R. F. (Eds.). (2011). *Handbook of self-regulation: Research, theory, and applications* (2nd ed.). New York, NY: Guilford Press.

Walker, C., Ainette, M. G., Wills, T. A., & Mendoza, D. (2007). Religiosity and substance use: Test of an indirect-effect model in early and middle adolescence. *Psychology of Addictive Behaviors, 21*, 84–96. doi:10.1037/0893-164X.21.1.84

Wallace, J. M., Jr., & Forman, R. A. (1998). Religion's role in promoting health and reducing risk among American youth. *Health Education and Behavior, 25*, 721–741. doi:10.1177/109019819802500604

Weisbuch-Remington, M., Mendes, W. B., Seery, M. D., & Blascovich, J. (2005). The nonconscious influence of religious symbols in motivated performance situations. *Personality and Social Psychology Bulletin, 31*, 1203–1216. doi:10.1177/0146167205274448

Welch, M. R., Tittle, C. R., & Grasmick, H. G. (2006). Christian religiosity, self-control and social conformity. *Social Forces, 84*, 1605–1623. doi:10.1353/sof.2006.0075

Wenger, J. L. (2007). The implicit nature of intrinsic religious pursuit. *The International Journal for the Psychology of Religion, 17*, 47–60.

Wiech, K., Farias, M., Kahane, G., Shackel, N., Tiede, W., & Tracey, I. (2008). An fMRI study measuring analgesia enhanced by religion as a belief system. *Pain, 139*, 467–476. doi:10.1016/j.pain.2008.07.030

Wilde, A., & Joseph, S. (1997). Religiosity and personality in a Moslem context. *Personality and Individual Differences, 23*, 899–900. doi:10.1016/S0191-8869(97)00098-6

Williams, G. C. (1966). *Adaptation and natural selection: A critique of some current evolutionary thought.* Princeton, NJ: Princeton University Press.

Wills, T. A., Gibbons, F. X., Gerrard, M., Murry, V. M., & Brody, G. H. (2003). Family communication and religiosity related to substance use and sexual behavior in early adolescence: A test for pathways through self-control and prototype perceptions. *Psychology of Addictive Behaviors, 17*, 312–323. doi:10.1037/0893-164X.17.4.312

Wink, P., Ciciolla, L., Dillon, M., & Tracy, A. (2007). Religiousness, spiritual seeking and personality: Findings from a longitudinal study. *Journal of Personality, 75*, 1051–1070. doi:10.1111/j.1467-6494.2007.00466.x

Winkelman, M. J. (1990). Shamans and other "magico-religious" healers: A cross-cultural study of their origins, nature, and social transformations. *Ethos, 18*, 308–352. doi:10.1525/eth.1990.18.3.02a00040

Worthington, E. L., Bursley, K., Berry, J. T., McCullough, M. E., Baier, S. N., Berry, J. W., Wade, N. G., & Canter, D. E. (2001). Religious commitment, religious experiences, and ways of coping with sexual attraction. *Marriage and Family: A Christian Journal, 4*, 411–423.

Wright, R. (2009). *The evolution of God.* New York, NY: Little, Brown.

Yi, R., Buchhalter, A. R., Gatchalian, K. M., & Bickel, W. K. (2007). The relationship between temporal discounting and the prisoner's dilemma game in intranasal abusers of prescription opioids. *Drug and Alcohol Dependence, 87*, 94–97. doi:10.1016/j.drugalcdep.2006.07.007

Chapter 7

RELIGION, SPIRITUALITY, AND ATTACHMENT

Pehr Granqvist and Lee A. Kirkpatrick

> An individual who has been fortunate in having grown up in an ordinary good home with ordinarily affectionate parents has always known people from whom he can seek support, comfort, and protection, and where they are to be found. So deeply established are his expectations and so repeatedly have they been confirmed that, as an adult, he finds it difficult to imagine any other kind of world. (Bowlby, 1973, p. 208)

In this chapter, we summarize the contribution of attachment theory and research to the psychology of religion and spirituality. Much of the research on which the review is based was originally undertaken to test the basic applicability of attachment theory to aspects of religion and spirituality. As this research progressed, however, it became apparent that some key findings may have considerable practical and clinical implications, which also are highlighted. The bulk of the chapter is thematically organized according to six central theoretical propositions that have come to guide the research on religion and spirituality from an attachment perspective. Each proposition contains an introduction to the relevant constructs and ideas behind the proposition as well as a necessarily selective review of research findings that have tested the proposition.

First, we argue that religion and spirituality capitalize on the operation of the attachment system and that believers' perceived relationships with God can be characterized as symbolic attachment relationships. Second, we describe how the generalization of attachment-related mental representations may be expressed in the context of religion and spirituality. Third, we suggest that care-giving quality and attachment security influence the individual's receptivity to parental religious standards. Fourth, we argue that religion provides surrogate attachment figures (most notably gods) that may be used to regulate distress and gain a sense of "felt security" also in the wake of experiences with insensitive caregivers and insecure attachment. Fifth, we review research suggesting that individual differences in attachment to God may affect psychosocial adjustment as well as attachment in the secular domain. Finally, we argue that, via carefully selected mediating variables, attachment may be indirectly linked to aspects of nontheistic spirituality that in themselves are not captured by the central parameters of an attachment framework. We end by discussing limitations and future directions for the attachment–religion/spirituality connection.

RELIGION AND SPIRITUALITY CAPITALIZE ON THE OPERATION OF THE ATTACHMENT SYSTEM

Attachment refers to a strong disposition on the part of offspring in many mammalian species to seek proximity to and contact with a specific figure (i.e.,

Preparation of this chapter was facilitated by a grant to Pehr Granqvist from the Swedish Research Council.

DOI: 10.1037/14045-007
APA Handbook of Psychology, Religion, and Spirituality: Vol. 1. Context, Theory, and Research, K. I. Pargament (Editor-in-Chief)
Copyright © 2013 by the American Psychological Association. All rights reserved.

to display attachment behaviors) and to do so particularly in certain situations such as when he or she is frightened, ill, or tired. John Bowlby (1969/1982), the founder of attachment theory, sought to understand this mammalian phenomenon, by drawing mainly on principles from control systems theory and the theory of evolution by natural selection. Bowlby argued that attachment behaviors have been naturally selected by mammalian species' ancestral environments (i.e., environments of evolutionary adaptedness [EEA]) by keeping offspring in physical proximity to their caregivers and thus protected from natural dangers, such as predation.

According to Bowlby (1969/1982), attachment behaviors are governed by an attachment behavioral system. This system is believed to be universal and to work similarly to mechanical systems, such as thermostats and goal-directed missiles, but to have been programmed by natural selection rather than humans. Like other control systems, the attachment system is activated by certain conditions and deactivated by others. The attachment system is held to be activated by natural clues to danger, which can have both external (e.g., physical separation, predators approaching) and internal (e.g., fear, illness) sources. The system is held to be deactivated by natural clues to safety, most notably physical contact with or proximity to the figure selected as a source of security and safety (i.e., the attachment figure).

During infancy, the offspring typically develops one or a few attachment relationships, usually with their primary caregiver(s). Although the term *attachment* has broad connotations in everyday language, attachment relationships differ from other relationships (including close relationships in general) in important ways. Bowlby (1969/1982) and his close collaborator Mary Ainsworth (1985) used the term *attachment relationship* to denote a strong affectional bond between two individuals, in which no one is interchangeable with others. The *attachment figure* accomplishes two important functions for the attached person: (a) provides a safe haven in times of threat or stress and (b) serves as a secure base from which to explore the environment and develop new mental and physical skills. The attached person also resists separation from the attachment figure and experiences anxiety when involuntarily separated. Moreover, loss of the attachment figure leads to grief and mourning. Finally, the attachment figure is, at least implicitly, viewed as stronger and wiser by the attached person.

In Bowlby's view (1969/1982, 1980), the attachment system is active from cradle to grave, as manifested, for example, in the principal attachments of adulthood, romantic pair-bonds. Thus, unlike some of his psychoanalytic predecessors, Bowlby did not view displays of attachment behaviors later in life as a sign of regression or dependency but rather as markers of healthy development throughout the life cycle (see also Granqvist, 2006). Experientially linked cognitive maturations during early childhood, however—such as a capacity for symbolic thinking, mentalizing abilities, and an increased reliance on mental representations—notably transform the expression of attachment from then on. First, such cognitive maturations enable children to "read" their caregiver's mind, withstand longer separations, and utilize an internalization of the caregiver as a secure base and safe haven to explore the surrounding environment and regulate mild-moderate distress. Thus, "felt security" (i.e., a psychological construct) rather than physical proximity becomes a progressively more viable set-goal (or predictable outcome) of attachment as children mature (Sroufe & Waters, 1977). Relatedly, their attachment relationships develop into goal-corrected partnerships (Bowlby, 1969/1982), marked by a more flexible coordination of joint plans than possible at earlier stages in development.

Second, mentalizing abilities and a capacity for symbolic thinking enable children to elaborate on the existence and agency of unseen figures (e.g., imaginary companions and ghosts; Barrett, Richert, & Driesenga, 2001). As children move farther from parents' immediate physical care, certain unseen figures may also become targets of their attachment systems (i.e., as attachment surrogates). For example, children who experience low levels of psychological well-being and difficulties with peer acceptance are especially prone to turn to imaginary companions (Hoff, 2005). Notably, most unseen figures are not taken seriously by adults, and eventually lose their significance for children (Rizzuto, 1979). As the topic of this chapter illustrates, however, deities are a clear exception of unseen others who have been treated with adult respect throughout history and within most cultures known to mankind (D. E. Brown, 1991). In addition, deities supposedly possess special powers (e.g., omniscience, omnipotence, omnipresence) and dispositions (e.g., benevolence) that may add to their suitability as symbolic attachment figures.

As a central tenet of the religion-as-attachment model, we argue that God (and other divine figures) function like symbolic attachment figures to whom believers actively strive to obtain or maintain a sense of being connected. From an attachment perspective, it is thus not surprising that the term religion (from the Latin *religare*) literally means "being bound" or "connected" (Ferm, 1945). Viewed this way, *religion* refers to the institutionalized pillars erected around people's sense of "spiritual connection" (from this handbook's definition; see Chapter 1, this volume), whereas *spirituality* refers to the private or personal components of this connection.

Kirkpatrick (e.g., 2005; see also Granqvist & Kirkpatrick, 2008) has reviewed more than a hundred years of research and thinking in the psychology of religion and spirituality, showing that many important findings accord well with an attachment-theory perspective. More specifically, he has demonstrated that the perceived relationships between believers and God often tend to meet the established criteria for characterizing attachment relationships (Ainsworth, 1985). For example, the perceived bond between believer and God, as in other attachment relationships, has "love" as its dominant emotional theme; thus, this is a strongly affectional bond. God is also noninterchangeable with others: as declared in the first Commandment, "You shall have no other gods before me." In addition, believers strive to establish and maintain a sense of proximity or closeness to God, most notably through prayer, which not coincidentally is also "the most often practiced form of religiosity" (Trier & Shupe, 1991, p. 354; see also Chapter 16 in this volume).

Furthermore, regarding the safe haven function of attachment, people do indeed turn to God as a safe haven when distressed (e.g., in "religious coping" or sudden religious conversions). Bowlby (1969/1982) discussed three kinds of situations that activate the attachment system and thus elicit attachment behavior: (a) illness, injury, or fatigue; (b) separation or threat of separation from attachment figures; and (c) frightening or alarming environmental events. This list bears an almost uncanny resemblance to the list of potential triggers for people to turn to God: "[a] illness, disability, and other negative life events that cause both mental and physical distress; [b] the anticipated or actual death of friends and relatives; and [c] dealing with an adverse life situation." (Hood, Spilka, Hunsberger, & Gorsuch, 1996, pp. 386–387).

Moreover, religious people often use God as a secure base (i.e., a caring, guiding, loving other) when exploring other aspects of the world. As the 23rd Psalm declares: "Yea, though I walk through the valley of the shadow of death, I will fear no evil: for thou art with me; thy rod and thy staff, they comfort me." In describing the psychological significance of a secure base, Bowlby (1969/1982) noted that

> when an individual is confident that an attachment figure will be available to him whenever he desires it, that person will be much less prone to either intense or chronic fear than will an individual who for any reason has no such confidence. (p. 202)

Therefore, we should not be surprised if the perceived accessibility of God as a symbolic secure base would offer the same sorts of psychological advantages. On the basis of a review of empirical research on religion and mental health, intrinsic religiousness (i.e., religion as an "end" to itself, a "master-motive" in the individual's life) was indeed found to be positively correlated with two secure-base-resembling conceptualizations of mental health, "freedom from worry and guilt" and "a sense of personal competence and control" (Batson, Schoenrade, & Ventis, 1993).

Whether believers also experience anxiety when involuntarily separated from God and grieve the loss through death of God remains disputable. Notably, however, an ideal attachment figure would prevent such pains of separation and loss from ever being experienced. Tellingly, God is generally believed to be available always (i.e., eternal and omnipresent). The potential for true separation from God is usually seen by believers to come only in the hereafter, at which time one spends eternity either with God or separated from God: In most Christian belief systems, separation from God is the very essence of hell. Nevertheless, there are instances in religious life when believers are unable to experience a previously felt and much-desired communion with God (see Chapter 25 in this volume). In religious and mystical literature, such states are often referred to as a "wilderness experience" or a "dark night of the soul" (St. John of the Cross, 1990). Finally, that God is viewed as stronger and wiser by believers goes without saying; after all, this particular attachment figure is held to be omnipotent and omniscient.

This review draws largely on theological conceptions, religious phenomenology, and psychology of religion findings that accrued before attachment theory was first applied to religion. Thus, the conclusion that believers tend to form symbolic attachment relationships with the divine could be criticized as reflecting a selective reading of the literature. Therefore, a body of novel research that has been explicitly designed to test the religion-as-attachment model, from early to late ages in the life cycle, has now accrued in the literature. For example, in a study of children ages 5 to 7 years, participating children were told stories about fictional, visually represented children who were in attachment-activating (i.e., sick, hurt, or alone) and attachment-neutral situations (i.e., bad, good, or neutral mood; Granqvist, Ljungdahl, & Dickie, 2007; cf. Eshleman, Dickie, Merasco, Shepard, & Johnson, 1999). Participating children also selected a symbol fashioned out of felt that could represent God. After each story, participating children placed their God symbol at any location on a felt board, which also bore a representation of the fictional child. As predicted, the God symbol was placed significantly closer to the child when he or she was depicted in the attachment-activating rather than in the attachment-neutral situations. These results have now been replicated across four cross-national samples (in Italy, Sweden, and the United States; see Cassibba, Granqvist, & Costantini, in press; Granqvist & Kirkpatrick, 2008). These studies show that God is already viewed as a safe haven in the late preschool and early school years.

In a set of experimental studies on adults, Birgegard and Granqvist (2004) subliminally exposed theistic (mostly Christian) believers either with a separation-prime targeting their God relation ("God has abandoned me") or with attachment-neutral control primes ("People are walking," "God has many names") and examined whether the wish to be close to God would increase as expected from pre- to postexposure as a result of the separation-from-God priming. Across the two experiments, participants in the separation-prime condition did indeed increase more in their wish to be close to God than participants in the attachment-neutral conditions. Similarly, in an experimental study with a Jewish sample of Israeli college students, participants showed increased mental access to the concept of God following subliminal exposure to threats (the words *failure* and *death*) compared with neutral exposures (Granqvist, Mikulincer, Gurwitz, & Shaver, 2012). These experiments show that even at the level of unconscious processing, threatening primes increase believers' motivation to experience God's closeness as well as their psychological accessibility of God.

Finally, in a prospective survey study of elderly Americans, the importance of religious and spiritual beliefs (but not church attendance) increased for the recently widowed (i.e., who had lost their principal adult attachment figure) as compared with a matched group of nonwidowed elders (S. L. Brown, Nesse, House, & Utz, 2004; for conceptually similar findings, see Cicirelli, 2004). In S. L. Brown et al.'s (2004) study, grief over the loss prospectively decreased specifically as a function of the increased significance of the bereaved individual's religious beliefs, indicating that it may be the attachment component of the individual's religiousness that is activated in such situations and contributes to a more favorable outcome.

Thus, novel research designed to test the religion-as-attachment model has produced supportive findings. Attachment relationships, however, typically develop over time as a function of a visible, physically concrete interaction history between the attached person and the attachment figure. Whether believers actually have an interaction history with God is debatable. Many believers believe that they do (i.e., as an inherent part of their theistic beliefs and related experiences), whereas others view God as a figment of believers' imaginations (i.e., an expression of atheism). Naturally, as scientific psychologists of religion and spirituality, we reserve the right not to take a stand on this metaphysical question but simply to study the beliefs and experiences of religious and spiritual people. Even within their beliefs and experiences, however, it may be exceptional that believers experience their relationship with God as physically concrete more than on rare occasions (e.g., in the context of some mystical experiences). Therefore, to prevent semantic dilution of the attachment construct, we encourage the use of *symbolic* as a prefix to the terms *attachment figure* and *relationship* when referring to God and the perceived believer–God relationship, respectively.

RELIGION AND SPIRITUALITY REFLECT THE GENERALIZATION OF ATTACHMENT-RELATED MENTAL REPRESENTATIONS

Bowlby (1973) noted that parameters of the attachment system tend to be adjusted on the basis of interactions with particular attachment figures, especially (but not exclusively) early in life (e.g., Ainsworth, Blehar, Waters, & Wall, 1978). The theory conceptualizes these relatively stable parameter adjustments in terms of *internal working models* (IWMs) of self and other (i.e., relationship partners). Such IWMs are believed to underlie individual differences in attachment security.

As illustrated in the opening quotation, offspring who have received reliably sensitive and responsive care giving will come to develop secure attachment via a positive and coherent (or singular) set of IWMs; the self is perceived as worthy of care, and the attachment figure is assessed as a likely provider of care (Bowlby, 1973; de Wolff & van IJzendoorn, 1997). Thus, securely attached children will direct their attentional and behavioral focus to attachment (i.e., engage in various forms of attachment behaviors) following attachment system activation, but they will shift their attentional and behavioral focus when this system is not activated.

In contrast, children who have received insensitive care giving will develop some form of insecure attachment via a negative and incoherent (or multiple) set of IWMs. Following attachment activation and repeated experiences of rejecting care giving, they may rigidly shift their attention away from attachment through a defensive exclusion of attachment-related information (i.e., avoidant attachment, indicating a minimizing attachment strategy; Bowlby, 1973; Main, 1991). Avoidant children exposed to attachment activation may, for example, shift their attention to explore toys rather than approach the attachment figure. In other words, avoidant children (and later dismissing adults) implicitly or procedurally view themselves as unworthy of care and others as unavailable to provide care. As is particularly evident in their attachment-related discourse (typically identified via the semistructured Adult Attachment Interview [AAI]; Main, Goldwyn, & Hesse, 2003), at an explicit or declarative level, they tend to emphasize personal strength (e.g., "I get by on my own") and provide idealized representations of caregivers (e.g., "my mother was very loving," without substantiating this portrayal by the recall of supportive episodic memories).

Ambivalent or preoccupied attachment, in contrast, is viewed as a maximizing attachment strategy often stemming from inconsistent sensitivity (e.g., the caregiver is occasionally sensitive but oftentimes neglecting; Main, 1991). The individual views the self as helpless or incompetent and remains attentionally fixated on the caregiver's inability to provide sufficient and reliable care, even in situations that normally should not activate the attachment system. For example, ambivalent children may cling to the attachment figure while fussing when there is no external sign of alarm. Finally, in line with Bowlby's (1980) notion of "segregated systems" (cf. dissociation), disorganized attachment is thought to represent attentional and behavioral breakdown in lieu of repeated experiences with an abusive, frightening, or frightened attachment figure (Hesse & Main, 2006). For example, following attachment activation, the child shows sequential or simultaneous displays of opposing behaviors (e.g., on reunion after a brief separation, the child starts to approach the caregiver, but before the approach is concluded, heads in another direction and cries in a corner of the room without facing the attachment figure).

Internal working models tend to display temporal continuity due to environmental or care-giving stability as well as assimilation, automatization, and self-verification processes (Bretherton & Munholland, 2008). Moreover, IWMs are believed to generalize across relationships such that the attachment pattern established early in life will spill over into a characteristic set of expectations and behavioral inclinations in future relationships, such as in romantic pair-bond attachment (Mikulincer & Shaver, 2007; Roisman, Collins, Sroufe, & Egeland, 2005). Not surprisingly, then, early attachment security is an important predictor of later socioemotional development in general and relationship-related functioning in particular, with secure attachment as a protective factor and insecure (especially disorganized) attachment as a risk factor in development (e.g., Weinfield, Sroufe, Egeland, & Carlson, 2008).

The continuity and generalizing nature of IWMs leads to a set of predictions regarding religion and spirituality, which we refer to as the IWM-aspect of the *correspondence hypothesis*: Individual differences in relevant aspects of religiosity and spirituality correspond with individual differences in IWM and attachment history (i.e., the quality of care received). Individuals who have received sensitive care giving and possess "secure" working models of self and others are expected to view God and other religious entities or agencies as security supporting. Likewise, avoidant or dismissing attachment is expected to manifest itself in a view of God as remote and inaccessible. Ambivalent or preoccupied attachment may find expression in a deeply emotional, all-consuming, and clingy relationship with God. Finally, disorganized attachment may manifest itself in expressions of spirituality characterized by dissociation, such as marked alterations in consciousness (this is discussed in the section Nontheistic Spirituality May Be Linked to Attachment via Mediators later in this chapter).

Considerable evidence for IWM correspondence has now accrued in relation to attachment history, romantic attachment, and AAI classifications alike. Regarding attachment history, a Swedish AAI study revealed that independently coded estimates of probable experiences with loving (cf. sensitive) parents in childhood were associated with participants' reports of a loving, as opposed to a distant, God image (Granqvist, Ivarsson, Broberg, & Hagekull, 2007). Conversely, inferred experiences with parents who were judged highly rejecting or role-reversing (i.e., drawing the child's attention and care to themselves, rather than providing adequate care of the child) were associated positively with a distant God image and negatively with a loving image of God.

Similar findings have been reported from an Italian AAI study (Cassibba, Granqvist, Costantini, & Gatto, 2008). This study examined a group of Catholic priests and other religious professionals (novices, seminarians) and a comparison group of lay Catholic believers. The study is especially important theoretically because members of the former group are likely to experience a *principal* attachment to God (because their lives are to be "lived in Christ," and they are required to abstain from "earthly" attachments). In further support of IWM correspondence, the group of Catholic priests and religious professionals was coded significantly higher than lay believers on loving experiences with mother in childhood. Moreover, across study groups, AAI-based maternal loving scores were positively linked to a loving God image, whereas corresponding scores of parental rejection were correlated in the opposite direction.

Regarding romantic attachment, Kirkpatrick and Shaver (1992) found that people with a secure romantic attachment displayed a higher personal belief in and relationship with God as well as perceptions of God as loving, whereas people reporting avoidant romantic attachment were agnostic or atheist to a larger extent. These findings have since been replicated in a number of studies (for reviews, see Granqvist & Kirkpatrick, 2008; Kirkpatrick, 2005).

Although religiosity tends to be comparatively stable across time for individuals who have experienced sensitive care giving or who currently report secure romantic attachment, religious transformations sometimes do occur (see also Chapter 22 in this volume). In such cases, the religious changes tend to be gradual and to occur within a life context pointing to a positive influence of other relationships, again possibly indicating generalizing positive IWMs. For example, in a prospective study, participants who reported sensitive parenting or secure romantic attachment experienced increases in religiousness over time, but only insofar as they had experienced the formation of a new intimate relationship between assessments (Granqvist & Hagekull, 2003).

IWM correspondence in relation to current AAI-assessed attachment organization was also supported in the Italian study by Cassibba et al. (2008). The group of individuals likely to experience a principal attachment to God (i.e., the Catholic priests and seminarists) had an unusually high percentage (77%) of secure or autonomous "attachment state of mind" classifications as compared with both the matched Catholic lay group (60%) and the normative nonclinical meta-analytic distribution (55%; Bakermans-Kranenburg & van IJzendoorn, 2009). In addition, across the two study groups, Cassibba et al. (2008) found a positive association between a secure or autonomous state of mind and loving-God imagery.

In addition to the correlational studies just reviewed, several sets of experimental and quasi-experimental studies involving direct attempts to activate study participants' attachment systems have been conducted (Birgegard & Granqvist, 2004; Cassibba et al., in press; Granqvist, Ljungdahl, & Dickie, 2007; Granqvist et al., 2012). The main effects of attachment activation observed in these studies have already been described. The main effects, however, were moderated by individual differences in perceived attachment history or current attachment security in a manner that supports the idea of IWM correspondence.

Across the three experiments conducted by Birgegard and Granqvist (2004), an increase in the use of God to regulate distress was observed following subliminal separation primes among adult believers who had reported sensitive experiences with parents. Thus, individuals with more sensitive experiences with caregivers drew on God in this situation, or turned their attention to attachment, presumably via automatic activation of IWMs. These observations tie in with Bowlby's (1973, 1980), and later Main's (1991), proposal that a singular set of IWMs underlies secure attachment. The key point in this context is that God was viewed as an available safe haven also at implicit or procedural levels of operation. In contrast, participants who had reported insensitive experiences with parents decreased in their distress regulatory use of God following the subliminal separation primes. Thus, at an implicit or procedural level of operation, and just like avoidant infants, they (defensively) shifted their attention away from attachment (e.g., Main, 1991). In a later section of this chapter, we will see that such individuals act very differently at explicit or declarative levels, suggesting that the structural incoherence (or multiplicity) of their IWMs spills over also to the religious and spiritual domains.

This moderator effect was also conceptually replicated in the Swedish child study of 5- to 7-year-old children who were asked to place a God symbol at chosen distance from a fictional child (Granqvist, Ljungdahl, & Dickie, 2007). Children who had been judged secure on the basis of the semiprojective Separation Anxiety Test (Kaplan, 1987) placed the God symbol closer to the fictional child when he or she was in attachment-activating situations. This pattern was reversed when the fictional child was in attachment-neutral situations (i.e., insecure children placed God closer). Overall, the discrepancy in God proximity between the two types of situations was much larger in secure than in insecure children. Our interpretation of this interaction is that secure children's attention shifted to God following attachment-system activation, whereas insecure children's attention to God did not shift as a function of attachment activation.

Cassibba et al. (in press) recently extended parts of these findings in an Italian sample, showing that—just as attachment security tends to be transmitted across generations from mother to child (van IJzendoorn, 1995)—maternal security on the AAI predicted a higher degree of proximity in their children's God symbol placements vis-à-vis the fictional child. These findings are theoretically important in illustrating, probably for the first time, that experiences with secure versus insecure mothers generalize to the next generation's perceptions of the availability of another (symbolic) attachment figure besides the mother.

Finally, the increase in psychological accessibility of God concepts following subliminal threat primes, observed by Granqvist et al. (2012), was particularly notable in participants with a secure romantic attachment orientation. In a second experiment, Granqvist et al. showed that participants with a secure romantic attachment orientation implicitly reacted with more positive affect following subliminal exposure to religion-related pictures (compared with neutral pictures).

To summarize, substantial empirical support has been obtained for the idea that religion and spirituality reflect the generalization of attachment-related mental representations (i.e., IWMs). The review in support of this proposal has been selective, drawing entirely on studies explicitly informed by attachment theory. We hasten to add, therefore, that several additional studies have further corroborated this idea (also see Granqvist & Kirkpatrick, 2008; Kirkpatrick, 2005). As one notable example, cross-cultural research indicates that God is construed as more loving in cultures in which parenting is warm and accepting and as more distant in cultures marked by harsh, rejecting parenting (Lambert, Triandis, & Wolf, 1959; Rohner, 1986).

Care-Giving Quality and Attachment Security Influence the Human Offspring's Receptivity to Parental Religious Standards

Research has consistently documented that parental religiousness is an important moderator variable in the attachment-religion connection (Granqvist, 1998, 2002, 2005; Granqvist & Hagekull, 1999; Granqvist, Ivarsson, et al., 2007; Kirkpatrick & Shaver, 1990; Pirutinsky, 2009; Reinert & Edwards, 2009; Wright, 2008). More specifically, memories of a secure attachment history as well as current secure attachment are linked to a high degree of parent–offspring similarity in many aspects of religiousness and spirituality. In contrast, memories of an insecure attachment history as well as current insecure attachment are linked to a virtual absence of associations between parental and offspring religiousness or spirituality. Thus, we have hypothesized that secure attachment and related care-giving experiences increase the offspring's receptivity to parental religious standards (i.e., "social correspondence"; see Granqvist & Kirkpatrick, 2008). This contention converges with conclusions in the developmental attachment literature that caregiver sensitivity and offspring attachment security facilitate the offspring's internalization of parental standards in general (e.g., Ainsworth, Bell, & Stayton, 1974; Kochanska, Aksan, Knaack, & Rhines, 2004; Richters & Waters, 1991). In addition, the idea of social correspondence ties in with previous psychology of religion findings that repeatedly have shown warm, high-quality care giving to be linked to high parent–offspring similarity in religiousness (see Hood, Hill, & Spilka, 2009).

These findings are important to the psychology of religion because they indicate that although parental religiousness is generally the single best predictor of offspring religiousness (Hood et al., 2009), attributes of parental insensitivity constitute an important constraint on its predictive power. An implication of these findings for religious parents who wish their children to embrace their own religion is that religious teaching is not enough and, in fact, may be entirely unsuccessful unless combined with placing a high priority on sensitive care giving that meets the children's needs for protection and security.

By adding the notion of social correspondence to the idea of IWM correspondence (described in the section Religion and Spirituality Reflect the Generalization of Attachment-Related Mental Representations), we can expect securely attached individuals to become actively religious insofar as their parents were (i.e., social correspondence), and in this case, their perceived relations with God are expected to exhibit the attributes of security through IWM correspondence. This combined correspondence hypothesis may be seen, then, as delineating a distinct developmental pathway to religion and spirituality that grows via an interaction history with sensitive, religious caregivers.

Religion Provides Surrogate Attachment Figures (e.g., God) That May Be Used in a Controlled Effort to Regulate Distress and Gain Felt Security

The founding figures of attachment theory discussed the possibility that individuals who have been inadequately cared for or whose principal attachment figures are currently unavailable may select certain other persons or objects as surrogate targets for their attachment systems (Ainsworth, 1985; Bowlby, 1969/1982). Bowlby noted that

> whenever the "natural" object of attachment behavior is unavailable, the behavior can become directed towards some substitute object. Even though it is inanimate, such an object frequently appears capable of filling the role of an important, though subsidiary, attachment "figure." Like the principal attachment figure, the inanimate substitute is sought especially when a child is tired, ill, or distressed. (1969/1982, p. 313)

Regrettably, subsequent students of attachment largely neglected to further pursue the use of attachment surrogates in their research, and instead they remained busy studying principal attachments and their socioemotional correlates in later development (i.e., via presumed continuity and generalization of IWMs). Recall, however, that insecure attachment is believed to reflect a developmentally secondary (or conditional) attachment strategy stemming from defensive processes (e.g., exclusion of attachment-related information and diversion of attention) in the face of a failed primary strategy of obtaining sufficient care from the attachment figure (Main, 1991). The use of surrogate attachments may provide a unique opportunity to observe the presumed remnants of such a primary (or secure) attachment strategy. In other words, although the defensive layer (or filter) thought to characterize insecure attachment becomes automatized and habitual over the course of development, it may constitute a surface aspect of functioning that does not fully override the primary strategy. For example, deeply held wishes to be able to act and relate differently may remain. Moreover, the use of attachment surrogates may inform us about the possibly self-therapeutic behaviors that people initiate when their secondary or insecure strategies actually break down. For example, the minimizing or avoidant strategy is likely to be fragile and crumble during intense stress (cf. Mikulincer & Shaver, 2007). As proposed by the poet and singer Leonard Cohen (1993), "There is a crack, a crack, in everything, that's how the light gets in."

Although neither Bowlby nor Ainsworth explicitly mentioned God (or other divine figures) in their lists of potential attachment surrogates, we argue that God may be particularly appealing as an attachment surrogate. We noted several reasons for this in the first major section of this chapter. In addition to the arguments offered there, God's suitability as an attachment surrogate derives in part from the inherent ambiguity in interpreting a noncorporeal figures' behavior; for example, it is impossible to disconfirm that God actually answered one's prayers. Moreover, for people who view themselves as unworthy of love and care (i.e., who harbor a negative self-model), turning to God might be possible because God's love is supposedly either unconditional—so one need not be "worthy" of love to receive it—or available through particular courses of action (e.g., good deeds, prayer), which allow an otherwise-"unworthy" person to "earn" God's love and forgiveness. In summary, because of the human mind's general proclivity to imagine the existence of and attribute agency to unobservable others from early childhood on, God may eventually come to figure as a principal character in the cast of surrogates that are used to regulate attachment-related distress, which is especially likely in the case of insecure attachment (i.e., the compensation hypothesis).

Considerable empirical support has accrued for the compensation hypothesis. For example, sudden religious conversions, the most dramatic of religious experiences, are associated with parental insensitivity. This connection was reported in the first study of attachment and religion (Kirkpatrick & Shaver, 1990). Since then, the findings have been supported by a meta-analysis of all studies conducted up to 2004, including almost 1,500 participants (Granqvist & Kirkpatrick, 2004), and in a later study of converts to orthodox Judaism (Pirutinsky, 2009). Also, in a more recent AAI study, participants whose parents were estimated to have been relatively less loving reported more sudden and intense increases in religiousness (Granqvist, Ivarsson, et al., 2007).

Several studies have shown that the increases in religiousness reported by individuals whose parents were estimated as low in sensitivity were precipitated by significant emotional turmoil ("themes of compensation"), which was often relationship related (e.g., Granqvist & Hagekull, 1999; Granqvist, Ivarsson, et al., 2007). These studies assessed religious changes retrospectively, but Granqvist and Hagekull (2003) showed that reports of parental insensitivity also prospectively predicted increased importance of the perceived relationship with God following the break up of a romantic relationship.

Insecure romantic attachment predicts essentially the same kinds of religious changes. For example, Kirkpatrick (1997) found that over a 4-year period, women with ambivalent or preoccupied romantic attachments (i.e., who harbor a negative self-model) established a new relationship with God and reported religious experiences more often than securely attached women. These findings were replicated by Kirkpatrick (1998), this time over a 5-month period, and in both males and females. Although the effect sizes were modest in the latter study, when a romantic relationship breakup was considered in another sample, insecure romantic attachment prospectively predicted increases in aspects of religiousness more strongly (Granqvist & Hagekull, 2003).

It is notable that support for the compensation hypothesis may be limited to situations involving a controlled or explicit usage of God to regulate distress. As reviewed in the section on generalizing IWMs, when attachment-related distress is activated at implicit levels, insecure individuals tend to withdraw from God, possibly indicating an incoherent or multiple God representation.

Individual Differences in "Attachment to God" May Affect Psychosocial Adjustment and Attachment in the Secular Domain

If believers' perceived relationships with God do qualify as attachments (symbolic or not), then something analogous to security versus insecurity of attachment to God should be present and should be linked to psychosocial adjustment in ways that are similar to the security–insecurity of attachment to parents and romantic partners. As part of the first study of adult, romantic attachment style and religion described earlier in this chapter, Kirkpatrick and Shaver (1992) found that of many religion variables included in the study, only one evinced significant and strong associations with measures of psychological well-being: "attachment style" with respect to God. Adults who described their perceived relationship with God as secure (God was seen as warm and responsive to the respondent), as opposed to avoidant (God as distant and rejecting) or ambivalent (God as inconsistent), scored lower on measures of loneliness, depression, anxiety, and physical illness and scored higher on general life satisfaction. Belavich and Pargament (2002) similarly documented associations between this measure of attachment to God and styles of religious coping, suggesting that individuals who believe they have a secure attachment to God use more "positive" religious coping strategies to cope with a loved one who is undergoing surgery.

These studies used a very simple measure of attachment to God consisting of three brief forced-choice paragraphs (similar to Hazan & Shaver's, 1987, early measure of romantic attachment style). More recently, researchers have developed somewhat more advanced multidimensional self-report instruments to assess attachment to God, focusing either on individual differences in avoidance and anxiety as these relate to attachment to God (Beck & McDonald, 2004; Rowatt & Kirkpatrick, 2002) or the extent to which an attachment relationship with God is present (Sim & Loh, 2003). In these studies, lower attachment anxiety and avoidant attachment, as well as higher perceptions of having an attachment to God, were correlated with psychological adjustment, such as optimism, positive affect, agreeableness, and (low) neuroticism, again after controlling for potential confounds such as romantic attachment, attachment to parents, and social desirability.

In sum, correlates of attachment to God suggest, as in the case of attachment in general, that attachment security promotes psychological well-being and alleviates distress. In the case of attachment to God, however, this relatively straightforward conclusion seems applicable particularly when other attachments are insufficient or other attachment figures are unavailable. For example, in the study by Kirkpatrick and Shaver (1992), the "effects" of attachment to God on psychological outcomes were moderated by perceived attachment history with the mother. Respondents who remembered their mothers as relatively insensitive but still had perceptions of a secure attachment to God appeared to benefit the most from their perceived relationship with God. In line with these findings, S. L. Brown et al. (2004) found that increased importance of religious beliefs following bereavement was associated with attenuated grief, particularly for individuals whose "secular" attachment orientation was judged insecure. Similarly, the positive effects of religion variables more generally, such as those of religious coping and "intrinsic" religiousness, on mental health outcomes typically are moderated by levels of stress, such that religion confers its most beneficial effects in times of real trouble (e.g., Pargament, 1997; Smith, McCullough, & Poll, 2003).

Findings indicating a positive effect of religion and spirituality on psychosocial adjustment in general are paralleled by two sets of findings, suggesting that religion and spirituality may have positive effects also on attachment. First, self-reported insecure attachment history and romantic attachment (in the latter case, particularly a negative self-model or a high degree of attachment anxiety) have been linked to increasing religiousness and spirituality over time (longitudinal compensation), and yet secure attachment has been linked to higher religiousness and spirituality at a given time (contemporaneous correspondence; see Kirkpatrick, 2005). One interpretation of this pattern is that increasing religiousness somehow helps the individual to gain attachment security. Second, AAI-based estimates of parental insensitivity in the past have predicted a history of using religion as compensation for inadequate attachments, but current insecurity (incoherent attachment discourse) has been unrelated to religion as compensation (Cassibba et al., 2008; Granqvist, Ivarsson, et al., 2007). Thus, similarly, religion-as-compensation may increase attachment security (i.e., lead to a certain degree of "earned security"; Main et al., 2003).

Thus, it is possible that a process of positive change in IWMs of relatively insecure individuals might be initiated by experiencing God's love and forgiveness, which would be comparable to the idea of reparative effects from other relationship experiences, such as with a good therapist or a secure romantic partner (e.g., Bowlby, 1988; Main et al., 2003). In particular, repair of a negative self-model might be one avenue through which earned security via religion or spirituality plays itself out. Although speculative at this point, this interpretation would make theoretical sense if the individual's perceived relationship with God actually functions as a compensatory attachment relationship. It also would be theologically plausible, given the portrayal of God as a sensitive secure base and haven of safety, which we have described in this chapter. An important research question to address in this context—theoretically, clinically, and pastorally alike—is whether people who have earned a certain degree of attachment security via their surrogate attachment to God also come to view God as increasingly accessible at implicit levels of processing or, put differently, in their "ways of being" with God (cf. Hall, Fujikawa, Halcrow, Hill, & Delaney, 2009; see Chapter 15 in this volume).

A special situation in which religion may offer a protective function for adjustment concerns the experience of loss through death of loved ones. Bowlby (1980) noted that to proceed favorably in terms of promoting adaptation to a life without the loved one's physical accessibility, the mourning process requires that bereaved individuals eventually accommodate information regarding the permanence of the person's death into their representational world. Otherwise, the individual is at risk of remaining unresolved or disorganized with respect to the loss, for example, they may display continued searching for the lost person and slip into dissociated states of disbelief regarding the person's physical death (Main et al., 2003). Available evidence indicates that the proportion of unresolved or disorganized loss is somewhat lower in religious samples (3%–12%; Cassibba et al., 2008; Granqvist, Ivarsson, et al., 2007) than in the nonclinical meta-analytic sample (16%; Bakermans-Kranenburg & van IJzendoorn, 2009). As noted by Cassibba et al. (2008), religion may promote mental resolution of loss via offering a prospect of reunion with deceased loved ones in the hereafter. In addition, the bereaved individual's attachment to God may serve as a surrogate bond assisting the individual in distress regulation (e.g., grief work) in lieu of the inaccessibility of a lost attachment figure (S. L. Brown et al., 2004; Granqvist & Kirkpatrick, 2008).

So far, we have dealt primarily with the potentially adjustment-promoting or "constructive" aspects of attachment to God. Just as with religion and spirituality in general, however, attachment to God is a multivalent phenomenon that is likely to include maladaptive or destructive aspects. For example, as implied in the review thus far, reports of insecure attachment to God are linked with "negative" religious coping; higher loneliness, depression, anxiety, neuroticism, and physical illness; and lower general life satisfaction. In particular, we speculate (see also Granqvist, Hagekull, & Ivarsson, in press) that characteristics of disorganized attachment might generalize to the religious and spiritual realm to a view of God as aberrant and frightening and a disposition to have dissociative and fearful spiritual experiences (e.g., ideas of evil spirit possession and mystical experiences marked by fright, as in Rudolph Otto's, 1923, "tremendum"), some of which may be especially compromising for psychological adjustment. However, the available self-reports of religious attachment have not attempted to identify disorganized attachment to God.

Unfortunately, interpretation of the data collected so far on the adjustment effects of attachment to God is limited by several methodological problems. First, and perhaps most obvious, the causal direction of cross-sectional correlation between religion and various outcomes remains open to question. Second, the (self-report) mode of measuring attachment to God and psychosocial adjustment in the studies reviewed here leaves us unable to exclude the possibility that (any combination of) self-deception, impression management, shared method variance, semantic overlap, and so on may be, at least partly, responsible for the associations obtained. Therefore, it is imperative to construct less explicit methods for evaluating individual differences in believers' perceived relationship with God. A longitudinal follow-up of the Swedish AAI-based study (Granqvist, Ivarsson, et al., 2007) addressed this issue by using an interview (Granqvist & Main, 2003) concerning each individual's relationship with God, which was adapted from the AAI protocol. One aim in developing this interview was to undermine some of the potential validity threats to the self-reports of attachment to God (cf. Cassibba et al., 2008).

NONTHEISTIC SPIRITUALITY MAY BE LINKED TO ATTACHMENT VIA MEDIATORS

Attachment theory has a relatively narrow conceptual focus. Another way to say this is that it is reasonably specific. It deals with our proclivity to develop close and enduring affectional bonds as well as the implications of these for relationship-related mental representations and distress regulation. In contrast, religion and spirituality are highly complex, multifaceted realm of phenomena that involve many aspects orthogonal to the attachment construct. Thus, attachment theory is not a comprehensive theory of religion and spirituality; it is applicable primarily to the relational, representational, and distress-regulating aspects of religion and spirituality.

Attachment, however, may still be indirectly linked to certain religious or spiritual outcomes that fall outside of the theory's conceptual framework. Such a relationship may arise, for example, when a mediating variable explains the association between attachment and some aspect of religion or spirituality (Granqvist, Mikulincer, & Shaver, 2010). For example, as will be discussed in more detail, disorganized attachment appears related to certain "unconventional" forms of spirituality by way of their mutual associations with dissociative inclinations (i.e., dissociation acts as the mediator).

As noted earlier in this chapter, disorganized attachment is thought to represent attentional and behavioral breakdown in lieu of repeated experiences with a frightening or frightened attachment figure (Hesse & Main, 2006). Such experiences are believed to place the offspring in an approach-avoidance conflict, or a dissociative state marked by fright without solution. Disorganized behaviors, such as sequential or simultaneous displays of opposing behaviors, are akin to the conflict behaviors (e.g., "freezing") described in the ethological literature (e.g., Hinde, 1966) in animals who can neither fight (e.g., a larger enemy) nor flee (e.g., because the animal is surrounded).

Disorganized attachment foreshadows a propensity to enter dissociated states later in life, and especially when confronted by stress (Carlson, 1998; Hesse & van IJzendoorn, 1999). Dissociation is characterized by a disruption in the usually integrated functions of consciousness, memory, identity, and perception (American Psychiatric Association, 2000). Examples of dissociated states range from ordinary dream sleep, via somewhat more unusual states of absorption (i.e., "episodes of 'total' attention that fully engage one's representational 'resources'"; Tellegen & Atkinson, 1974, p. 268), hypnosis, and trance, to highly pathological states of hallucination and derealization.

Naturally, dissociated states may find expression in the context of religion and spirituality. For example, New Age spirituality coincides with out-of-body experiences, trance states, and susceptibility to hypnosis, all defined as dissociated states in the literature (Granqvist et al., 2005). As another example, Hood et al. (2009; Chapter 21, this volume) have suggested that the common denominator of a long list of triggers of mystical experiences is that they lend themselves as likely objects of absorption. Like New Age spirituality, mystical experiences may well be present in the absence of a felt connection with a symbolic attachment figure such as God (e.g., in nature mysticism or introvertive states of "nothingness"; Hood et al., 2009).

Consequently, a mediating model linking disorganized attachment to New Age spirituality and mystical experiences via a propensity for absorption has been proposed and empirically supported (Granqvist et al., 2009; Granqvist, Hagekull, & Ivarsson, in press). Notably, such a mediating model has *not* proved serviceable in relation to conventional, mainstream expressions of faith or religion, showing some specificity or discriminant validity for the model. For example, both disorganized attachment and absorption are unrelated to theistic beliefs and general degree of religiousness (Granqvist et al., in press).

Of course, New Age spirituality and mystical experiences are but two examples of spiritual or religious outcomes that are indirectly linked to attachment—in this case, disorganized attachment. Other researchers may explore the possibility of indirect relations between other aspects of attachment and other features of religiousness and spirituality, such as religious and spiritual struggles (see Chapter 25 in this volume, presumably by way of other mediators or moderators.

CONCLUSION

The religion-as-attachment model has made important contributions both to the psychology of religion and spirituality and to attachment theory. First, it has benefited the psychology of religion and spirituality by integrating important findings in the field within a well-established conceptual framework. In addition, attachment theory has been of heuristic value in spurring empirical research on why and how people relate to God and why they embrace some less conventional forms of spirituality. Regarding its importance for attachment theory, this model and its associated body of research has highlighted the propensity among human beings to develop symbolic attachments to unseen, imaginary others. We maintain that no model of interpersonal relationships in general, or attachment relationships in particular, will be complete without explicit acknowledgment of the role of God and other imaginary figures in people's relationship networks. Incorporating religious and spiritual phenomena into research on attachment may be useful in addressing lingering questions in the field of attachment concerning such issues as the content, structure, and generality of internal working models, and the dynamic processes underlying change in attachment patterns and working models over time.

Notwithstanding these contributions, extant attachment-religion research has several notable limitations. In particular, potential progress in the field has been suppressed by an absence of long-term longitudinal research and studies conducted outside of the Western world as well as by the preponderance of explicit (self-report) assessments of religion and spirituality. These limitations should be remedied in future research endeavors. We especially encourage studies of attachment-related religious and spiritual expressions in non-Western faith traditions, the use of more implicit methods for studying religion and spirituality, and research that tests the possibility of earned security effects via religion.

Regarding practical implications of the attachment–religion connection, clinical and pastoral work with religious clients should focus on aspects of their perceived relationship with God as a potential resource, or in some cases, a barrier, for promoting positive change in other domains. For example, working with the client's perception of the self in relation to God may facilitate the development of a positive self-model and may be associated with earned security of attachment. If so, the treatment process would not only have beneficial effects in the religious realm but conceivably also would have a favorable impact on other important relationships in the client's life.

As we noted, we make no claim that attachment theory offers a comprehensive theory of religion or spirituality. Attachment theory probably can tell us little, for example, about why some forms of religiousness are associated with prejudice, why religions typically promote particular ethical and moral principles, or why people observe particular rituals or offer sacrifices to gods. Perhaps the most important "future direction" for the field, then, is to identify the other psychological systems and mechanisms that explain these and other aspects of religious belief—specifically, however, within a coherent, broader framework within which attachment and other systems are conceptually integrated.

As Kirkpatrick (1999, 2005) has argued extensively, Bowlby's (1969/1982) original conceptualization of attachment theory suggests that an evolutionary approach provides an ideal conceptual framework for this purpose. Modern evolutionary psychology is based on the premise that humans possess an evolved psychological architecture comprising numerous, functionally domain specific mechanisms and systems, each of which was designed by natural selection to solve particular adaptive problems—much like the many organs and systems of the body. From this perspective, attachment is only one among many evolved psychological systems potentially relevant for understanding religion and spirituality. For example, numerous scholars have converged on the idea that people's tendency to attribute agency to inanimate objects, and to ascribe desires, intentions, and goals to these objects, is understandable in terms of the functioning of evolved psychological systems designed for detecting agency and for understanding other people's minds (e.g., Atran, 2002; Barrett, 2004; Boyer, 2001). Kirkpatrick (1999, 2005) has argued that once these systems give rise to beliefs about supernatural agents, other social–psychological systems come into play to identify the (functionally specific) kind of relationship one might have with these agents and guide further thinking and action accordingly. For example, gods or other supernatural agents might be perceived as attachment figures (who are deeply invested in one's welfare)—as discussed in the present chapter—or alternatively as social exchange partners (to whom one offers sacrifices or engages in particular behaviors in exchange for some benefit), or as a dominant competitor (toward which one must behave submissively to avoid punishment). Adopting such an approach promises to strengthen the psychology of religion and spirituality field not only by providing an organizational framework for conceptually integrating attachment theory with other (equally important) theories in a coherent, systematic way, but also by providing a framework within which to explore the diversity of religious beliefs across cultures and time.

References

Ainsworth, M. D. S. (1985). Attachments across the life span. *Bulletin of the New York Academy of Medicine, 61*, 792–812.

Ainsworth, M. D. S., Bell, S. M., & Stayton, D. J. (1974). Infant-mother attachment and social development: "Socialization" as a product of reciprocal responsiveness to signals. In M. P. M. Richards (Ed.), *The integration of a child into a social world* (pp. 99–135). Cambridge, England: Cambridge University Press.

Ainsworth, M. D. S., Blehar, M. C., Waters, E., & Wall, S. (1978). *Patterns of attachment: A psychological study of the strange situation.* Hillsdale, NJ: Erlbaum.

American Psychiatric Association. (2000). *Diagnostic and statistical manual of mental disorders* (4th ed., text revision). Washington, DC: Author.

Atran, S. (2002). *In gods we trust: The evolutionary landscape of religion.* New York, NY: Oxford University Press.

Bakermans-Kranenburg, M. J., & van IJzendoorn, M. H. (2009). The first 10,000 Adult Attachment

Interviews: Distributions of attachment representations in clinical and non-clinical groups. *Attachment and Human Development, 11*, 223–263. doi:10.1080/14616730902814762

Barrett, J. L. (2004). *Why would anyone believe in God?* Lanham, MD: AltaMira Press.

Barrett, J. L., Richert, R. A., & Driesenga, A. (2001). God's beliefs versus mother's: The development of nonhuman agent concepts. *Child Development, 72*, 50–65. doi:10.1111/1467-8624.00265

Batson, C. D., Schoenrade, P., & Ventis, W. L. (1993). *Religion and the individual: A social psychological perspective.* New York, NY: Oxford University Press.

Beck, R., & McDonald, A. (2004). Attachment to God: The Attachment to God Inventory, tests of working model correspondence, and an exploration of faith group differences. *Journal of Psychology and Theology, 32*, 92–103.

Belavich, T. G., & Pargament, K. I. (2002). The role of attachment in predicting spiritual coping with a loved one in surgery. *Journal of Adult Development, 9*, 13–29. doi:10.1023/A:1013873100466

Birgegard, A., & Granqvist, P. (2004). The correspondence between attachment to parents and God: Three experiments using subliminal separation cues. *Personality and Social Psychology Bulletin, 30*, 1122–1135. doi:10.1177/0146167204264266

Bowlby, J. (1973). *Attachment and loss: Vol. 2. Separation.* New York, NY: Basic Books.

Bowlby, J. (1980). *Attachment and loss: Vol. 3. Loss.* New York, NY: Basic Books.

Bowlby, J. (1982). *Attachment and loss: Vol. 1. Attachment* (2nd ed.). New York, NY: Basic Books. (Original work published 1969)

Bowlby, J. (1988). *A secure base: Parent-child attachment and healthy human development.* NY: Basic Books.

Boyer, P. (2001). *Religion explained: The evolutionary origins of religious thought.* New York, NY: Basic Books.

Bretherton, I., & Munholland, K. A. (2008). Internal working models in attachment relationships: Elaborating a central construct in attachment theory. In J. Cassidy & P. R. Shaver (Eds.), *Handbook of attachment: Theory, research, and clinical applications* (2nd ed., pp. 102–127). New York, NY: Guilford Press.

Brown, D. E. (1991). *Human Universals.* New York, NY: McGraw-Hill.

Brown, S. L., Nesse, R. M., House, J. S., & Utz, R. L. (2004). Religion and emotional compensation: Results from a prospective study of widowhood. *Personality and Social Psychology Bulletin, 30*, 1165–1174. doi:10.1177/0146167204263752

Carlson, E. A. (1998). A prospective longitudinal study of attachment disorganization/disorientation. *Child Development, 69*, 1107–1128.

Cassibba, R., Granqvist, P., & Costantini, A. (in press). Maternal security on the Adult Attachment Interview predicts their children's perception of God's closeness. *Attachment and Human Development.*

Cassibba, R., Granqvist, P., Costantini, A., & Gatto, S. (2008). Attachment and God representations among lay Catholics, priests, and religious: A matched comparison study based on the Adult Attachment Interview. *Developmental Psychology, 44*, 1753–1763. doi:10.1037/a0013772

Cicirelli, V. G. (2004). God as the ultimate attachment figure for older adults. *Attachment and Human Development, 6*, 371–388. doi:10.1080/146167304 2000303091

Cohen, L. (1993). Anthem. On *The future* [CD]. New York, NY: Columbia Records.

de Wolff, M. S., & van IJzendoorn, M. H. (1997). Sensitivity and attachment: A meta-analysis on parental antecedents of infant attachment. *Child Development, 68*, 571–591. doi:10.2307/1132107

Eshleman, A. K., Dickie, J. R., Merasco, D. M., Shepard, A., & Johnson, M. (1999). Mother God, father God: Children's perceptions of God's distance. *The International Journal for the Psychology of Religion, 9*, 139–146. doi:10.1207/s15327582ijpr0902_4

Ferm, V. (1945). *The encyclopedia of religion.* Secaucus, NJ: Poplar.

Granqvist, P. (1998). Religiousness and perceived childhood attachment: On the question of compensation or correspondence. *Journal for the Scientific Study of Religion, 37*, 350-367. doi:10.2307/1387533

Granqvist, P. (2002). Attachment and religiosity in adolescence: Cross-sectional and longitudinal evaluations. *Personality and Social Psychology Bulletin, 28*, 260–270. doi:10.1177/0146167202282011

Granqvist, P. (2005). Building a bridge between attachment and religious coping: Tests of moderators and mediators. *Mental Health, Religion, and Culture, 8*, 35–47. doi:10.1080/13674670410001666598

Granqvist, P. (2006). On the relation between secular and divine relationships: An emerging attachment perspective and a critique of the depth approaches. *The International Journal for the Psychology of Religion, 16*, 1–18. doi:10.1207/s15327582ijpr1601_1

Granqvist, P., Fransson, M., & Hagekull, B. (2009). Disorganized attachment, absorption, and New Age spirituality—A mediational model. *Attachment and Human Development, 11*, 385–403. doi:10.1080/14616730903016995

Granqvist, P., Fredrikson, M., Unge, P., Hagenfeldt, A., Valind, S., Larhammar, D., & Larsson, M. (2005). Sensed presence and mystical experiences are predicted by suggestibility, not by the application of weak complex transcranial magnetic fields.

Neuroscience Letters, *379*, 1–6. doi:10.1016/j.neulet.2004.10.057

Granqvist, P., & Hagekull, B. (1999). Religiousness and perceived childhood attachment: Profiling socialized correspondence and emotional compensation. *Journal for the Scientific Study of Religion*, *38*, 254–273. doi:10.2307/1387793

Granqvist, P., & Hagekull, B. (2003). Longitudinal predictions of religious change in adolescence: Contributions from the interaction of attachment and relationship status. *Journal of Social and Personal Relationships*, *20*, 793–817. doi:10.1177/0265407503206005

Granqvist, P., Hagekull, B., & Ivarsson, T. (2011). *Disorganized attachment promotes mystical experiences via a propensity for alterations in consciousness (absorption)*. Manuscript submitted for publication.

Granqvist, P., Ivarsson, T., Broberg, A. G., & Hagekull, B. (2007). Examining relations between attachment, religiosity, and New Age spirituality using the Adult Attachment Interview. *Developmental Psychology*, *43*, 590–601. doi:10.1037/0012-1649.43.3.590

Granqvist, P., & Kirkpatrick, L. A. (2004). Religious conversion and perceived childhood attachment: A meta-analysis. *The International Journal for the Psychology of Religion*, *14*, 223–250. doi:10.1207/s15327582ijpr1404_1

Granqvist, P., & Kirkpatrick, L. A. (2008). Attachment and religious representations and behavior. In J. Cassidy & P. R. Shaver (Eds.), *Handbook of attachment: Theory, research, and clinical applications* (2nd ed., pp. 906–933). New York, NY: Guilford Press.

Granqvist, P., Ljungdahl, C., & Dickie, J. (2007). God is nowhere, God is now here: Attachment activation, security of attachment, and God proximity among 5- to 7-year-old children. *Attachment and Human Development*, *9*, 55–71. doi:10.1080/14616730601151458

Granqvist, P., & Main, M. (2003). *The Attachment to God Interview*. Unpublished manuscript, Department of Psychology, Uppsala University, Sweden.

Granqvist, P., Mikulincer, M., Gurwitz, V., & Shaver, P. R. (2010). *Experimental findings on the use of God as an attachment figure—Normative process and generalizing working models*. Manuscript submitted for publication.

Granqvist, P., Mikulincer, M., & Shaver, P. R. (2010). Religion as attachment: Normative processes and individual differences. *Personality and Social Psychology Review*, *14*, 49–59. doi:10.1177/1088868309348618

Hall, T. W., Fujikawa, A., Halcrow, S. R., Hill, P. C., & Delaney, H. (2009). Attachment to God and implicit spirituality: Clarifying correspondence and compensation models. *Journal of Psychology and Theology*, *37*, 227–242.

Hazan, C., & Shaver, P. (1987). Romantic love conceptualized as an attachment process. *Journal of Personality and Social Psychology*, *52*, 511–524. doi:10.1037/0022-3514.52.3.511

Hesse, E., & Main, M. (2006). Frightened, threatening, and dissociative (FR) parental behavior as related to infant D attachment in low-risk samples: Description, discussion, and interpretations. *Development and Psychopathology*, *18*, 309–343.

Hesse, E., & van IJzendoorn, M. H. (1999). Propensities towards absorption are related to lapses in the monitoring of reasoning or discourse during the Adult Attachment Interview: A preliminary investigation. *Attachment and Human Development*, *1*, 67–91. doi:10.1080/14616739900134031

Hinde, R. A. (1966). *Animal behaviour: A synthesis of ethology and comparative psychology*. New York, NY: McGraw-Hill.

Hoff, E. V. (2005). Imaginary companions, creativity, and self-image in middle childhood. *Creativity Research Journal*, *17*, 167–180.

Hood, R. W., Jr., Hill, P. C., & Spilka, B. (2009). *The psychology of religion: An empirical approach* (4th ed.). New York, NY: Guilford Press.

Hood, R. W., Jr., Spilka, B., Hunsberger, B., & Gorsuch, R. (1996). *The psychology of religion: An empirical approach* (2nd ed.). New York, NY: Guilford Press.

Kaplan, N. (1987). *The sixth year Separation Anxiety Test classification system*. Unpublished manuscript, University of California, Berkeley.

Kirkpatrick, L. A. (1997). A longitudinal study of changes in religious belief and behavior as a function of individual differences in adult attachment style. *Journal for the Scientific Study of Religion*, *36*, 207–217. doi:10.2307/1387553

Kirkpatrick, L. A. (1998). God as a substitute attachment figure: A longitudinal study of adult attachment style and religious change in college students. *Personality and Social Psychology Bulletin*, *24*, 961–973. doi:10.1177/0146167298249004

Kirkpatrick, L. A. (1999). Toward an evolutionary psychology of religion. *Journal of Personality*, *67*, 921–952. doi:10.1111/1467-6494.00078

Kirkpatrick, L. A. (2005). *Attachment, evolution, and the psychology of religion*. New York, NY: Guilford Press.

Kirkpatrick, L. A., & Shaver, P. R. (1990). Attachment theory and religion: Childhood attachments, religious beliefs, and conversion. *Journal for the Scientific Study of Religion*, *29*, 315–334. doi:10.2307/1386461

Kirkpatrick, L. A., & Shaver, P. R. (1992). An attachment theoretical approach to romantic love and religious belief. *Personality and Social Psychology Bulletin, 18*, 266–275. doi:10.1177/0146167292183002

Kochanska, G., Aksan, N., Knaack, A., & Rhines, H. M. (2004). Maternal parenting and children's conscience: Early security as moderator. *Child Development, 75*, 1229–1242. doi:10.1111/j.1467-8624.2004.00735.x

Lambert, W. W., Triandis, L. M., & Wolf, M. (1959). Some correlates of beliefs in the malevolence and benevolence of supernatural beings: A cross-societal study. *Journal of Abnormal and Social Psychology, 58*, 162–169. doi:10.1037/h0041462

Main, M. (1991). Metacognitive knowledge, metacognitive monitoring, and singular (coherent) vs. multiple (incoherent) models of attachment: Findings and directions for future research. In C. M. Parkes & J. Stevenson-Hinde (Eds.), *Attachment across the life cycle* (pp. 127–159). London, England; New York, NY: Tavistock/Routledge.

Main, M., Goldwyn, R., & Hesse, E. (2003). *Adult attachment scoring and classification systems.* Unpublished manuscript, University of California at Berkeley.

Mikulincer, M., & Shaver, P. R. (2007). *Attachment patterns in adulthood: Structure, dynamics, and change.* New York, NY: Guilford Press.

Otto, R. (1923). *The idea of the Holy.* London, England: Oxford University Press.

Pargament, K. (1997). *The psychology of religion and coping.* New York, NY: Guilford Press.

Pirutinsky, S. (2009). Conversion and attachment insecurity among Orthodox Jews. *The International Journal for the Psychology of Religion, 19*, 200–206. doi:10.1080/10508610902889163

Reinert, D. F., & Edwards, C. E. (2009). Attachment theory, childhood mistreatment, and religiosity. *Psychology of Religion and Spirituality, 1*, 25–34. doi:10.1037/a0014894

Richters, J. E., & Waters, E. (1991). Attachment and socialization: The positive side of social influence. In M. Lewis & S. Feinman (Eds.), *Social influences and socialization in infancy: Genesis of behavior series* (Vol. 6, pp. 185–213). New York, NY: Plenum Press.

Rizzuto, A. M. (1979). *The birth of the living God: A psychoanalytical study.* Chicago, IL: Chicago University Press.

Rohner, R. P. (1986). *The warmth dimension: Foundations of parental acceptance-rejection theory.* Newbury Park, CA: Sage.

Roisman, G. I., Collins, W. A., Sroufe, L. A., & Egeland, B. (2005). Predictors of young adults' representations of and behaviours in their current romantic relationship: Prospective tests of the prototype hypothesis. *Attachment and Human Development, 7*, 105–121. doi:10.1080/14616730500134928

Rowatt, W. C., & Kirkpatrick, L. A. (2002). Two dimensions of attachment to God and their relation to affect, religiosity, and personality constructs. *Journal for the Scientific Study of Religion, 41*, 637–651. doi:10.1111/1468-5906.00143

Sim, T. N., & Loh, B. S. M. (2003). Attachment to God: Measurement and dynamics. *Journal of Social and Personal Relationships, 20*, 373–389. doi:10.1177/0265407503020003006

Smith, T. B., McCullough, M. E., & Poll, J. (2003). Religiousness and depression: Evidence for a main-effect and the moderating influence of stressful life-events. *Psychological Bulletin, 129*, 614–636. doi:10.1037/0033-2909.129.4.614

Sroufe, L. A., & Waters, E. (1977). Attachment as an organizational construct. *Child Development, 48*, 1184–1199. doi:10.2307/1128475

St. John of the Cross. (1990). *Dark night of the soul.* New York, NY: Doubleday.

Tellegen, A., & Atkinson, G. (1974). Openness to absorbing and self-altering experiences ("absorption"), a trait related to hypnotic susceptibility. *Journal of Abnormal Psychology, 83*, 268–277. doi:10.1037/h0036681

Trier, K. K., & Shupe, A. (1991). Prayer, religiosity, and healing in the heartland, USA: A research note. *Review of Religious Research, 32*, 351–358. doi:10.2307/3511681

van IJzendoorn, M. H. (1995). Adult attachment representations, parental responsiveness, and infant attachment: A meta-analysis on the predictive validity of the Adult Attachment Interview. *Psychological Bulletin, 117*, 387–403. doi:10.1037/0033-2909.117.3.387

Weinfield, N. S., Sroufe, L. A., Egeland, B., & Carlson, E. (2008). Individual differences in infant–caregiver attachment: Conceptual and empirical aspects of security. In J. Cassidy & P. R. Shaver (Eds.), *Handbook of attachment: Theory, research, and clinical applications* (2nd ed., pp. 78–101). New York, NY: Guilford Press.

Wright, P. J. (2008). Predicting reaction to a message of ministry: An audience analysis. *Journal for the Scientific Study of Religion, 47*, 63–81. doi:10.1111/j.1468-5906.2008.00392.x

CHAPTER 8

WHY RELIGION? MEANING AS MOTIVATION

Crystal L. Park, Donald Edmondson, and Amy Hale-Smith

> Humans strive to create and maintain order, certainty, and value in light of challenges and abruptions in their endeavours to do so. (Heine, Proulx, & Vohs, 2006, p. 89)

In this chapter, we present the view that a deeply rooted need for a functional meaning system underlies the highly prevalent embrace of religion across time and place. The need for a meaning system is thought to be continuously and pervasively present in everyday life and to be particularly acute in times of severe stress (Park, 2005b). We argue that religion, defined here as a "search for significance in ways related to the sacred" that occurs within the context of religious traditions (Pargament, 1997, p. 37; see Chapter 1 in this volume), is generally a highly functional way to satisfy the need for a meaning system—that is, it usually works well. Because of this functionality, religion is central to the meaning systems of many people in virtually every culture. In particular, it has been suggested that given their versatility, religious beliefs are uniquely capable of meeting the demands for meaning that arise in life such as those for coherence, mastery and control, the reduction of uncertainty, identity, existential answers, and behavioral guidance (Pargament, 2002; Pargament, Magyar-Russell, & Murray-Swank, 2005; Park, 2005b). We begin with a brief overview of the literature regarding the demands for meaning both in daily life and in times of crisis. We then describe how religiousness informs global meaning systems and provides meaning under both normal and highly stressful circumstances. We present and critique literature relevant to these points, concluding with clinical implications and suggestions for future research.

THE "NEED FOR MEANING"

That human beings possess a strong and inherent need for meaning is a widely accepted notion in psychology and many other disciplines (for reviews, see Baumeister, 1991; Proulx & Heine, 2006; Steger, 2009). This need is generally described as a drive to understand one's experience and to feel that one's life has significance and purpose (Steger, 2009). Viktor Frankl (1963) was an early proponent of this notion of a universal human will to meaning. Subsequent generations of researchers have elaborated on this concept, expanding and broadening its reach (Newberg & Waldman, 2006; Stillman & Baumeister, 2009), yet the specific definition of "the need for meaning" remains vague. In fact, in his classic overview, Baumeister described four needs for meaning: a sense of purpose, value/justification, efficacy or control, and self-worth; he referred to these needs as "an existential shopping list" (1991, p. 29).

To bring some clarity to this notion, the approach we take in this chapter is that the diverse array of human motives subsumed under the term "need for meaning" is better considered the need for a coherent and well-functioning meaning system. That is, humans have many pervasive and urgent demands or needs, such as those outlined by Baumeister. To meet these demands, humans construct

DOI: 10.1037/14045-008
APA Handbook of Psychology, Religion, and Spirituality: Vol. 1. Context, Theory, and Research, K. I. Pargament (Editor-in-Chief)
Copyright © 2013 by the American Psychological Association. All rights reserved.

complex internal systems of meaning, which include integrated networks of diverse beliefs, values, and goals. Formed through normative developmental processes as well as idiosyncratic life experiences, meaning systems serve as the filter through which people attend to and perceive stimuli; organize their behavior; conceptualize themselves, others, and interpersonal relationships; remember their past; and anticipate their future. These systems of meaning carry many different labels, including orienting systems (Pargament, 1997), assumptive worlds (Janoff-Bulman, 1992), worldviews (Koltko-Rivera, 2004), and meaning systems (Mischel & Morf, 2003), but all essentially refer to these broad, core frameworks of understanding (for a review, see Koltko-Rivera, 2004).

Because of its essential role in meeting a number of specific demands, including those for coherence, mastery and control, the reduction of uncertainty, identity, existential answers, and behavioral guidance, a well-functional meaning system is likely to be necessary for healthy human functioning (Greenberg, Pyszcznski, & Solomon, 1986; Heine et al., 2006; Swann, Rentfrow, & Guinn, 2003). Indeed, one could argue that at the center of all of the universally experienced, existentially themed threats that trouble or terrorize humanity, such as mortality threats, uncertainty, absurdity, and purposelessness, lie meaning systems that are temporarily weakened (e.g., Hayes, Schimel, Faucher, & Williams, 2008; Schimel, Hayes, Williams, & Jahrig, 2007) or structurally deficient (Edmondson, Park, Chaudoir, & Wortmann, 2008).

Because these demands are continuously present in human existence, people require a strong and functional meaning system that successfully meets these basic challenges. In the following sections, we briefly describe these demands of human existence and the ways that meaning systems help individuals to satisfy them. We then describe the particularly salient role of meaning systems in the context of high stress.

Life's Many Demands for a Meaning System

Psychologists have long recognized the importance of possessing an underlying cognitive structure that helps make sense of the world by organizing experience into a coherent worldview. The need for coherent meaning systems appears to be present at the very earliest stages of processing of sensation and perception (Koltko-Rivera, 2000, 2004). This long-held social constructivist model argues for the collaboration of subject and object in mental representations of the world (e.g., Berger & Luckmann, 1966; Gergen, 1985) and suggests that perception without a meaning system as a mediating influence would be chaotic in the way that the mental life of infants is sometimes described (e.g., Bruner, 1990).

Meaning systems are essential in the way that they provide a sense of mastery or control over one's future and life circumstances. This need for control is well-documented (e.g., Pudrovska, Schieman, Pearlin, & Nguyen, 2005) and strongly related to well-being (Lachman & Firth, 2004). The ubiquitous desire to retain perceptions of control has been conceptualized by some as a subgoal of the larger and more inclusive motivation to defend against perceptions of randomness and chaos in the social environment (Kay, Gaucher, Napier, Callan, & Laurin, 2008). Others, however, consider control or mastery to be distinct (Rotter, 1966; Skinner, 2007). Clearly, people go to great lengths to maintain a sense of control over their current and future life situations (for a review, see Thompson & Schlehofer, 2007).

A strong meaning system is also important for adaptive functioning in the face of the many uncertainties life presents. In particular, beliefs about fairness and justice appear to affect people's emotional reactions when they are dealing with uncertainty (van den Bos, 2001). This notion has been elaborated in the uncertainty management model (Lind & van den Bos, 2002; van den Bos & Lind, 2002), which holds that people have a fundamental need to feel certain about their world, that uncertainty is threatening, and that people rely on their meaning systems to eliminate or manage these distressing feelings of uncertainty.

Meaning systems are also important in addressing the human motive to maintain a sense of identity or self-concept (Janoff-Bulman & Frantz, 1997). The unique human ability to be self-reflective gives rise to individuals' desire to know who they are—and who they are not—known as *self-identity* (Leary & Tangney, 2003). This self is a set of beliefs "defining what it means to be who one is" (Burke, 1991, p. 837) and is at least partly defined in the context of other people and the world (McAdams, 2001). In their sense of self and identity, people define themselves and construe their individuality as well as their relations to others in their social worlds (Leary & Tangney, 2003; Mischel & Morf, 2003). Individuals hold a multitude of different situational, personal, and social identities that collectively comprise the self (Vryan, Adler, & Adler, 2003).

Much of the theorizing regarding meaning systems involves its importance in addressing existential concerns. For instance, the need for a functional meaning system appears to be at least partially rooted in the human awareness of death (Becker, 1973), and it can be observed in everyday cognition, such as negative psychological responses to stimuli that appear meaningless like abstract art (Landau, Greenberg, Solomon, Pyszcznski, & Martens, 2006). Predominant theories of the genesis of meaning systems in humans have pointed to the uniquely human ability to recognize and project the self in temporal–spatial terms, forcing a cognitive–affective confrontation with certain mortality (e.g., Becker, 1973; terror management theory, Greenberg et al., 1986; see also Chapter 5 in this volume). In addition, the uniquely human ability to generate counterfactual past states, as in thinking about how a traumatic event would have been avoided by a slight alteration in an individual's behavior before the event (Dalgleish, 2004), may generate a need for meaning systems that are able to explain why the actual present exists, rather than some other, equally plausible outcome of nearly identical past circumstances.

This sort of counterfactual, or "might-have-been," thinking is a universal human response to negative affect that serves to make an individual feel better or worse about the actual outcome of some set of circumstances, depending on its content, and may facilitate more effective future planning (Mandel & Lehman, 1996; Roese, 1994). The awareness, however, of the existence of wildly disparate alternative outcomes on the basis of seemingly unimportant behavioral determinants (e.g., taking a different route than normal for one's morning jog; Roese, 1997) implies a degree of randomness with which humans are uncomfortable. This discomfort may provide further motivation for the construction and maintenance of meaning systems that provide explanation and certainty. Religion, for many, provides a sense that circumstances are the way that they are for good reason, such as God's will (Park, 2005a).

In addition to needing a coherent meaning system that renders the world relatively predictable, understandable, certain, and controllable, and that provides satisfactory answers to questions of identity and existence, humans require a system of goals (desired future states) to guide them in structuring their lives. A goal hierarchy, directing behavior from the most mundane to the most profound (Austin & Vancouver, 1996), is a core aspect of meaning systems. These goals are essential for providing an overarching purpose and direction to an individual's life as well as determining the smaller intermediate steps needed to attain those ultimate goals. Goal structures also include values, which enable individuals to evaluate the relative importance of various potential outcomes and to judge the morality of the means used in pursuing their goals (Emmons, 1999).

The sense of meaning derived from having a comprehensive belief system and feeling that one is on track in the pursuit of one's goals has been termed *meaning in life* (e.g., Wong, 1998), although it is clear from its operationalization that it more accurately reflects a subjective *sense* of meaning (Park, 2005a). Research suggests that searching for meaning can be a vague and uncomfortable experience (Steger, 2009); in contrast, actually possessing a sense of meaning or life purpose is related to greater well-being, including less anxiety, better mental and physical health, and even lower mortality (e.g., Edmondson, Park, Blank, Fenster, & Mills, 2008; Skrabski, Kopp, Rózsa, Réthelyi, & Rahe, 2005).

In summary, humans possess a general need for a well-functioning meaning system that is motivated by myriad meaning-related demands. Although these various demands for meaning may become more or less salient during various developmental stages or life circumstances, all are met by corresponding, interconnected facets of a single, coherent meaning system. Each of these motivations, and the workings (or failings) of meaning systems in response to them, are most visible in times of heightened stress.

The Need for Meaning Systems in the Context of High Stress

Highly stressful situations typically prompt individuals to more explicitly consider and rely on their global meaning systems (Janoff-Bulman & Frantz, 1997; Park & Folkman, 1997). Global meaning systems are composed of global beliefs (e.g., about the nature of the self, the world, and the self-in-the-world) and goals, which are conceptualized as one's ultimate strivings (Park, 2010). People experience situations as highly stressful when they appraise them as violating their global meaning systems. That is, stress arises when beliefs such as those regarding control or a just world are substantially violated, or when the situation is radically at variance with one's global goals (Park & Folkman, 1997). When people encounter such highly stressful situations, their need for a functioning meaning system is heightened: Individuals must somehow reduce the discrepancy between their global meanings (beliefs and goals) and their understanding of the current stressful or traumatic event. People struggle to understand what is happening to them and why as well as to regain a sense of control, to restore their sense that the world is good and that they are protected and safe. This cognitive–emotional processing, termed *meaning making* (Janoff-Bulman, 1992; Park, Edmondson, Fenster, & Blank, 2008; Thompson & Janigian, 1988), is very common in the aftermath of trauma and loss (Park, 2010). Individuals eventually make meaning by changing either their understanding of the event (assimilation) or their global meaning system (accommodation; Joseph & Linley, 2005; Park & Folkman, 1997).

In sum, there appears to be ample evidence for the proposition that meaning systems are essential and that they serve a number of critical functions in meeting specific demands for coherence, mastery and control, the reduction of uncertainty, identity, existential answers, and behavioral guidance. These demands are present in both everyday life and times of crisis. As we will discuss next, although alternate frameworks of meaning are available, religion serves as the basis of the meaning system for many people.

Religion Meets the Need for a Meaning System

Given that the scientific worldview seems to be the primary competition for religious meaning systems (Gould, 1999; Hefner, 1997), why do most people maintain religiousness rather than adhering to a purely scientific meaning system? Understanding the various religious meaning systems across cultures and tribal groups, as well as the cognitive flexibility often required to maintain those religious meaning systems in the face of logical or experiential evidence to the contrary (Purzycki & Sosis, 2009), has long been a goal of empirical and theological endeavor (e.g., Leuba, 1916; see Paloutzian & Park, 2005). Religion may remain pervasive in humans across time and culture because people find it generally helpful—or perhaps even essential—for maintaining a coherent, organized view of the world and themselves and a clear sense of where they are going and why (Park, 2005a).

Religion is an important part of life for people around the globe. Worldwide, about 85% of people report having some form of religious belief, with only 15% describing themselves as atheist, agnostic, or nonreligious (Zuckerman, 2005). Within North America, eight out of 10 Americans have reported that religion is at least fairly important in their daily lives, and 56% have indicated that it is very important (Newport, 2007). Given its prevalence, religion is perhaps the strongest influence on meaning systems through its impact on myriad aspects of global beliefs, goals, and values.

In fact, for many people, religion is at the core of their meaning systems, informing their beliefs about the self, the world, and their interaction (McIntosh, 1995; Ozorak, 2005). Religion provides a framework through which knowledge and experience can be interpreted (Hefner, 1997; Silberman, 2005), and it can bring meaning to a variety of mundane secular activities (Mahoney et al., 2005; Schweiker, 1969). Religious or spiritual strivings may serve as a central goal or motive for many individuals (Allport, 1950), infusing other goals in their lives with purpose (Baumeister, 1991; Pargament, 1997), and can provide people with motivation for living (Krause, 2003) as well as prescriptions and guidelines for achieving their goals (Park & Slattery, 2009).

In situations of crisis, meaning is created and maintained within and through underlying philosophical or religious belief systems (Janoff-Bulman, 1992). Religion thus provides ways to understand pain and loss (Kotarba, 1983), and it often makes reality and suffering understandable and bearable (Pargament, 1997). By providing a sense of purpose and coherence, religion may help individuals in crisis to increase their sense of control and reduce ambiguity (Hinde, 1999).

Religion Provides a System of Meaning in Daily Life

Although parents and the broader culture typically instill religious meaning systems in childhood, these religious meaning systems are elaborated and reinforced throughout life (McCullough, Enders, Brion, & Jain, 2005; Wink & Dillon, 2002). Religion is almost certainly unique to the human animal. It may therefore arise to meet the need for meaning that comes from uniquely human attributes, such as intense self-reflection, temporal-spatial projection, and counterfactual thinking (Becker, 1973). Many questions about the natural world that enhance individuals' ability to survive, thrive, predict future outcomes, and reproduce can be answered with alternative meaning systems that are objectively verifiable (e.g., scientific worldviews). Meaning systems rooted in naturalistic explanations of sensory data are, for most people, minimally useful for the larger existential questions with which human beings must grapple, such as the following: "Does the self exist as a *real* entity?" "Why do I exist rather than not exist?" "What is the purpose of my life?" "Will I exist after my physical death?" (Allport, 1950; Kaufmann, 1989; Sire, 1997; Tillich, 1961). A different set of rules is needed to answer existential questions. That is, neither objective sensory data nor theories lacking supernatural agency or metaphysical assumptions can address these questions because they lie outside the realm of scientific inquiry. Human nature seems inimically tied to these existential (and therefore religious) needs for meaning.

Religious meaning systems, on the other hand, are capable of addressing both the existential and mundane aspects of life, and they do so in an emotionally and intellectually satisfying way for many. Religious meaning systems may be inherently comforting (e.g., belief in a loving, personal deity). Even those religious meanings that are not inherently comforting (e.g., belief in a strict or punitive god or gods), however, can still provide a consistent and coherent way through the bewildering array of life options and circumstances confronting people (Park & Slattery, 2009), albeit perhaps at some cost to well-being. In ordinary circumstances, religiousness can be highly functional in orienting people by providing a framework for their understanding of the world, natural phenomena, and interpersonal encounters and by giving direction to their personal projects and long-term strivings (McIntosh, 1995). Research has documented the strong and consistent relationships between religious beliefs and goals and higher levels of life satisfaction and functioning (Mahoney et al., 2005). Religions seem to be particularly capable of meeting the motives noted, including coherence, mastery and control, uncertainty reduction, identity, existential answers, and behavioral guidance.

Religious meaning systems seem to be particularly well-suited to provide a sense of coherence (Korotkov, 1998). That is, religions provide adherents with a comprehensive system for synthesizing their understanding of the world and their place within it. Religion helps individuals to create narratives that weave together "the tone, character, and quality of their life, its moral and aesthetic style and mood—and their worldview—the picture they have of the way things in sheer actuality are, their most comprehensive ideas of order" (Geertz, 1966/1973, p. 89). Most religious belief systems can also account for many seemingly disparate aspects of belief and experience, such as a loving, all-powerful God and the suffering that exists in the world (Hall & Johnson, 2001), although some religious explanations that promote coherence may also negatively affect adherents' perceptions of self-worth (Edmondson, Park, Blank, et al., 2008).

Religion provides a sense of agency and control, regardless of the objective controllability of any particular situation (Newton & McIntosh, 2009; Rothbaum, Weisz, & Snyder, 1982). Sometimes individuals perceive a collaborative working relationship with God, (Krause, 2005; Pargament et al., 1988), whereas at other times they may feel relief and comfort in putting their fate in "the hands of God" (Abraído-Lanza, Vasquez, & Echeverria, 2004). In fact, recent experimental research shows that belief in a God who is in control increases when perceptions of personal control are threatened, presumably indirectly bolstering their sense of control (Kay et al., 2008). Further evidence suggests that increased belief in God in response to lowered perceptions of control is an anxiety-driven strategy to restore belief in a nonrandom world (Laurin, Kay, & Moscovitch, 2008). Similarly, Norenzayan and Hansen (2006) found that reminders of mortality increased religiosity, belief in God, and belief in divine intervention in human affairs. The introduction of supernatural control over the physical world by a benevolent deity may open the door to beliefs in malevolent supernatural powers in the world, such as seen in demonic reappraisals, which may be detrimental to psychological adjustment (e.g., Pargament, Smith, Koenig, & Perez, 1998).

As might be expected from a major source of coherence and control, religion is well-situated to reduce uncertainty. For some religions this is an obvious function. One example of religion reducing uncertainty is the belief that God controls every minor fact and detail in the world, as in a mechanical view of Providence (Klooster, 2001). The reduction in uncertainty, however, holds true even in religions that provide fewer promises about certain outcomes. Even in cases in which religion portrays the world as somewhat unpredictable, such as ancient polytheistic religions, followers use religion to manipulate the world around them, thus providing them with a sense of control and efficacy (Segal, 1980). Although reduced uncertainty can benefit the believer, group-level certainty about how the world works may inhibit social or education advances, as some might argue regarding fundamentalist obstruction of education on the theory of evolution (e.g., Paterson & Rossow, 1999).

Religion is a major source of individual and social identity (E. P. King, 2003). Identity is formed as people develop and reflect on the question, "Who am I?" (Burke, 1991). In the context of a religious family or culture, most individuals naturally incorporate some of this religious content into their sense of self (Furrow, King, & White, 2004). The salience of one's multiple identities varies across time and situation, but for many, religious and spiritual orientations and affiliations form a core part of who they are and how they think about themselves (Furrow et al., 2004). Furthermore, religion is reinforced socially (Krause, 2008): The need for meaning that leads to embracing religion also produces community, because meaning systems are strengthened in the context of consensual validation (Becker, 1973). The creation and maintenance of in-groups, however, on the basis of objectively unverifiable beliefs has often set the stage for intergroup violence between conflicting meaning systems, as they adopt different social and political goals (e.g., Arifianto, 2010; Karpov & Lisovskaya, 2008).

Religion is also well-suited to address existential concerns (see Chapter 5 in this volume). Humans' cognitive ability to generate near-infinite alternate pasts on the basis of infinitesimal situational alterations, each of which could have resulted in an alternate present, implies a potentially terrifying degree of randomness and meaninglessness. Religious worldviews, however, seem to be uniquely capable of resolving the existential threats implied by counterfactual thinking through explanations that invoke supernatural agency (for reviews of religion's cognitive evolutionary roots with regard to supernatural agency, see Atran & Norenzayan, 2004; Bloom, 2007). Not only do religious explanations that imply supernatural agency typically provide a sense of comfort (cf. Exline & Rose, 2005; Edmondson, Park, Blank, et al., 2008) that a given outcome was preordained by God or serves God's grander purpose (e.g., Park & Cohen, 1993), but also they are by nature unassailable by logical arguments to the contrary (Atran & Norenzayan, 2004). Thus, the present is "meant to be" because God has a plan, and momentary perceptions of randomness are an illusory reminder that we only perceive reality as "through a glass, darkly" (1 Cor. 13:12, King James Version). One negative outcome of this phenomenon, however, may be a reduction in efforts to change individual circumstances and a passive approach to the world even when known solutions to problems exist. For example, some religious groups refuse medical treatment on the basis of a belief that illness is part of God's plan (Bottoms, Shaver, Goodman, & Qin, 1995).

Religion is not only a prototypic source of coherence, control, certainty, identity, and existential answers but also frequently prescribes individuals' ultimate life goals (e.g., living ethically, reaching heaven or paradise, gaining enlightenment) for which individuals strive (Emmons, 1999; Slattery & Park, 2011). Other commonly reported ultimate goals, such as family and service to one's country, often are imbued with religious motivation, a process called *sanctification* (Mahoney et al., 2005; see also Chapters 14 and 20 in this volume). These ultimate goals then inform the more specific low-level goals, values, and strivings (e.g., the relative value of gathering material goods or worldly and spiritual knowledge, the performance of good works; Slattery & Park, 2011). All major religions provide adherents with a detailed set of guidelines for how to live their lives, including major and minor goals and methods for accomplishing them (Geertz, 1966/1973; Spilka et al., 2003). Unfortunately, the sanctification of social structures can be a means for denying access to those social structures to others who disagree with the belief systems by which adherents sanctify them. For example, both California Proposition 8 and the Defense of Marriage Act of 1996 (both legal actions against homosexual marriage) have strong religious underpinnings (Ruskay-Kidd, 1997; Sherkat, de Vries, & Creek, 2010).

The unique attributes of religion as a meaning system can even be observed at the neurophysiological level. Recent research has found that greater religious zeal (Study 1) and belief in God (Study 2) were related to less activity in the anterior cingulate cortex (ACC) in response to Stroop naming errors (Inzlicht, McGregor, Hirsch, & Nash, 2009). The ACC is a brain region that acts as a "cortical alarm bell" in response to anxiety-provoking events such as the commission of errors, detection of conflict, and experience of uncertainty. The authors interpreted their findings as consistent with Heine et al.'s (2006) assertion; they proposed that religion "buffers against anxiety by providing meaning systems that specify standards for behavior and serve as guides that inform predictions about the self and the world" (Inzlicht et al., 2009, p. 390).

Religion is usually learned early in life, but its unique ability to successfully serve the critically important functions of providing a meaning system of satisfactory beliefs and goals likely leads to a continuous refinement and reinforcement across the life span, perhaps accounting for the gradual increase in religiousness observed across the life span (e.g., McCullough et al., 2005). Part of this reinforcement may be provided by the increased positive affect that people experience when these functions are adequately met; positive affect has been shown experimentally to lead to increased religious or spiritual meaning (L. A. King, Hicks, Krull, & Del Gaiso, 2006; Saroglou, Buxant, & Tilquin, 2008).

Religion Provides a Reliable Meaning System in Stressful Circumstances

Under highly stressful circumstances, religion often becomes even more relevant and useful, providing acceptable and emotionally satisfying means for interpreting and dealing with those circumstances (Aldwin, 2007; Mattlin, Wethington, & Kessler, 1990; Pargament, 1997). In fact, it has been noted that *all* religions have a "vocabulary of suffering" and a "repertoire of methods for their relief" (Wilson, 1982, cited in Pudrovska et al., 2005, p. 550). Research suggests that religion-based meaning systems may be more able to absorb stressful occurrences without shattering than can other types of meaning systems (Inzlicht et al., 2009). That is, religion may equip people to more easily appraise situations as consistent with their global meaning. For example, the extent to which individuals hold such beliefs as "All things happen for a reason, which is beyond human understanding" or "I may not have control over this situation, but I know that God is in control" may allow them to overlook potential discrepancies (Inzlicht et al., 2009; Park, 2005a), averting the crisis of discrepancy and alleviating a need to search for meaning (Park, 2010).

When a stressful event is appraised as discrepant with one's global beliefs and goals and is not amenable to simple problem solving, religion provides many coping options, particularly meaning-based coping strategies that help individuals to restore harmony between their global meanings and their understanding of the stressor (Park, 2005b). Religious meaning-based coping can involve religious attributions to better understand *why* the event occurred as well as ways to think about the situation in less painful or disturbing ways (Spilka, Shaver, & Kirkpatrick, 1985), and it may also exert a potentially powerful type of secondary control (e.g., through prayer; Pargament et al., 1999). These religious meaning-making strategies are effective in alleviating distress by changing the very meaning of the situation.

Religious attributions are usually comforting and help to preserve existing global meaning and to transform appraisals of stressful situations into more benign appraisals that are consistent with global meaning (Spilka, Hood, Hunsberger, & Gorsuch, 2003). For example, religious interpretations of death often involve seeing the death as having occurred for a reason, even if it is beyond human understanding (Park, 2005b), and envisioning the deceased residing in a better place. Religious interpretations of death also may include opportunities for being reunited with the lost love one in the future (Wortmann & Park, 2008), buffering the pain of separation. These religious attributions and appraisals, which mitigate the negativity and permanence of the loss, change the meaning of the death and thereby ease the distress that individuals might otherwise experience (Park & Folkman, 1997).

Many studies demonstrate the effectiveness of religion in minimizing distress (Ano & Vasconcelles, 2005), and people generally regard religion as one of the most helpful resources for them in dealing with crises (Ano & Vasconcelles, 2005; Wortmann & Park, 2008). Religious meaning making not only seems to be the most potent way to successfully cope with crisis and trauma but also seems to be the most likely way to experience posttraumatic growth as well (Park, Edmondson, & Blank, 2009; Shaw, Joseph, & Linley, 2005).

This functionality of religious meaning making in times of crisis likely serves as a powerful reinforcement for most individuals to embrace their religion; people tend to report deepened spirituality following crises such as cancer (e.g., Gall & Cornblat, 2002) and other stressful and traumatic experiences (e.g., Ironson, Stuetzle, & Fletcher, 2006; Schuster et al., 2001). Some types of negative religious interpretations (variously described as spiritual struggle or religious strain) also occur, such as making demonic attributions or feeling abandoned by God (Pargament, Koenig, Tarakeshwar, & Hahn, 2001). Indeed, one recent study of college students exposed to traumatic events found that religious struggle was related to greater subsequent post-traumatic stress disorder symptoms (Wortmann, Park, & Edmondson, in press). Religious struggle has been shown to be strongly related to negative psychological and physical well-being, and even mortality (Edmondson, Park, Chaudoir, et al., 2008; Pargament et al., 2001; Wortmann et al., in press; see also Chapter 25 in this volume). Although religious struggle typically occurs much less frequently than the more positively toned aspects of religious meaning making (Exline & Rose, 2005), it is an important counterpoint to the generally comforting aspects of religious meaning making. Religious struggle is not the breakdown of the meaning system itself; indeed, the behaviors attributed to God, including those that are seen as punishing or abandoning, are consistent with some religious texts (e.g., Qur'an 29:21, Deuteronomy 8:19–20). Rather, religious struggles may arise when discrepancies between personal experience (or observation) and one's meaning system become too large to ignore or incorporate into the believer's extant meaning system. Other struggles may arise when aspects of the meaning system become conflictual, such as when one's goals and desires clash with one's beliefs about right and wrong. For example, guilt over one's behavior may lead to substantial spiritual distress but ultimately help an individual to behave in ways more aligned with his or her spiritual strivings. Thus, over the long term, the distress could help rather than impede the achievement of more mature spirituality (Watts, 2007). Although painful, these spiritual struggles, if successfully resolved, may be an important avenue for spiritual and personal growth (Exline, 2002; see also Chapters 14 and 25 in this volume). We know of no empirical evidence of religious struggle remission over time or long-term benefits. Future research should work to identify those individuals likely to suffer religious struggle, perhaps identifying a time course for religious struggle using longitudinal research designs.

Religion as a Response to the Need for a Meaning System: Clinical Implications

From the standpoint of a meaning system perspective on religion, accurate evaluations and effective clinical work will depend on a thorough understanding of the extent to which religion informs clients' global meanings and their appraisals of presenting problems. Specifically, from a meaning approach, clinicians would focus on clients' global meaning systems, including the ways in which religious meaning imbues clients' views of themselves and the world, such as their images of and relationships with God, their identity, and their goals and values. In addition, clinicians should ask clients about how religion is involved in the appraisal of any precipitating events that brought them to therapy and the extent to which current life events are discrepant with their global meaning (for a more detailed treatment of religious meaning-centered assessment, see Park & Slattery, 2009). In general, religious meaning systems that remain functional are self-reinforcing. When religious meaning systems fail to function properly, however, the process of therapy may focus on helping clients to restore a functional religious meaning system. This process may involve changing the meaning assigned to specific situations to a more benign perspective, or it may involve revising religious beliefs, values, or life goals in light of life experiences that may challenge religious meaning systems. This work would need to be done in ethical ways that are respectful of client's religious worldviews (see Volume 2, Chapter 3, this handbook). Therapists should remain particularly attuned to maladaptive meanings drawn by their clients, such as negative emotions centering on religious aspects of meaning. When people fail to have satisfactory explanations for suffering, or when they have poorly articulated values and beliefs, the stage can be set for increased struggle (Pargament et al., 2005). In addition, therapists may home in on issues of ultimate meaning with their clients (Yalom, 1980), helping them to identify their core purpose and to align their lives with their ultimate systems of meaning.

IMPORTANT UNANSWERED QUESTIONS AND FUTURE DIRECTIONS

"Why are people religious?" Many answers to this question have been put forward, including the management of anxiety (see Chapter 5 in this volume), self-regulation (see Chapter 6 in this volume), or the provision of agency (Gray & Wegner, 2010), control (Kay, Gaucher, McGregor, & Nash, 2010), certainty (Hogg, Adelman, & Blagg, 2010), and identity (Ysseldyk, Matheson, & Anisman, 2010). The notion that meaning is key to these other human motivations is persuasive, however, and it is clear that meaning is implicated in many of these alternatives, particularly when noting the specific meaning-related demands that are well met through religious meaning systems. That is, religious meaning systems serve as the source for these essential functions. In addition to these important functions, religious meaning serves other purposes as well, including providing a sense that one matters to others (Lewis & Taylor, 2009) and helping to maintain beliefs in a fair and just world (Hunt, 2000).

Although we have argued that people may be religious because of deeply held needs that are met by a coherent meaning system, there are limitations to this view. First, many people are not religious. Granted, the fact that nonreligious individuals exist does not necessarily mean that religious worldviews do not meet the needs we have described. It does suggest, however, that these needs may not be as deep or universal as we have argued, or that religious worldviews are not as good at addressing these needs as we have argued. Another possibility is that even secular worldviews are religious in character, in that they are also unverifiable and can provide many of the same meaning provision functions (for a review, see Solomon, Greenberg, Pyszcznski, & Koole, 2004), in which case our definition of religion itself is at fault. Indeed, we have observed previously, in a study of cancer survivors, that possessing a sense of meaning and peace was more beneficial for psychological equanimity than was the possession of faith per se (Edmondson, Park, Blank, Fenster, & Mills, 2008), although the two were related. The completion of this theory, and the answer to its most profound limitation, lies in the circumstances under which an individual adopts or discards a religious worldview. Although we tend to cast such circumstances as cognitive crossroads, it is doubtful that cognition alone is capable of accounting for those circumstances (Paloutzian, 2005). The degree to which religious narratives are perceived as adequate to explain some meaning-discrepant event likely involves a complex interplay between archetypal cultural narratives, the accumulation of idiosyncratic life experiences, current affective state, recent exposure to and internalization of cultural messages, community standards, and a multitude of other internal and external influences. Because it is exceedingly difficult to measure all of these influences, for the time being, the cognitive approach seems to be a useful one for explaining the data we observe.

One particularly intriguing future research direction is religion's role in providing meaning in the face of existential threats. This work should build on previous research showing that certain types of religiousness buffer individuals against death anxiety (Jonas & Fischer, 2006). Although many sources of meaning, such as political ideologies, are theorized to defend individuals against existential threats, we propose that religion is unique in that it informs lower order meaning structures and is (for many individuals) less assailable by logical argument. Future research should focus on the relative strength of religious worldviews as compared with lower level meaning structures for combating existential threats as well as the relative ease of cognitive recruitment of religious versus lower order meaning structures in the face of such threats.

Finally, a particularly promising direction for future research may be to map specific aspects of religion (particularly religious beliefs but also personal and social religious behaviors) on to the functions served by meaning systems. Although much has been written from theological and theoretical perspectives, many of these functions have received minimal empirical attention. For example, there is much to learn about the links between religion and identity or the provision of existential answers. Knowing more about how religion informs various aspects of individuals' meaning systems through meeting demands for coherence, control, comfort, structure, purpose, escape, connection, belongingness, and peace may then lead to greater understanding of the patterns among these demands. Future research is also needed to more explicitly document how these aspects of meaning operate in both day-to-day life and in times of high stress and how these two levels of functioning are interrelated.

References

Abraído-Lanza, A. F., Vasquez, E., & Echeverria, S. E. (2004). En las Manos de Dios: Religious and other forms of coping among Latinos with arthritis. *Journal of Consulting and Clinical Psychology, 72*, 91–102. doi:10.1037/0022-006X.72.1.91

Aldwin, C. (2007). *Stress, coping, and development: An integrative perspective* (2nd ed.). New York, NY: Guilford Press.

Allport, G. W. (1950). *The individual and his religion.* New York, NY: Macmillan.

Ano, G. G., & Vasconcelles, E. B. (2005). Religious coping and psychological adjustment to stress: A meta-analysis. *Journal of Clinical Psychology, 61*, 461–480. doi:10.1002/jclp.20049

Arifianto, A. R. (2010). Explaining the cause of Muslim–Christian conflicts in Indonesia: Tracing the origins of *Kristenisasi* and *Islamisasi*. *Islam and Christian-Muslim Relations, 20*, 73–89. doi:10.1080/09596410802542144

Atran, S., & Norenzayan, A. (2004). Religion's evolutionary landscape: Counterintuition, commitment, compassion, communion. *Behavioral and Brain Sciences, 27*, 713–770. doi:10.1017/S0140525X04000172

Austin, J. T., & Vancouver, J. B. (1996). Goal constructs in psychology: Structure, process, and content. *Psychological Bulletin, 120*, 338–375. doi:10.1037/0033-2909.120.3.338

Baumeister, R. F. (1991). *Meanings in life.* New York, NY: Guilford Press.

Becker, E. (1973). *The denial of death.* New York, NY: Free Press.

Berger, P. L., & Luckmann, T. (1966). *The social construction of reality.* Garden City, NY: Anchor Publishing.

Bloom, P. (2007). Religion is natural. *Developmental Science, 10*, 147–151. doi:10.1111/j.1467-7687.2007.00577.x

Bottoms, B., Shaver, P., Goodman, G., & Qin, J. (1995). In the name of God: A profile of religion-related child abuse. *Journal of Social Issues, 51*, 85–111. doi:10.1111/j.1540-4560.1995.tb01325.x

Bruner, J. (1990). *Acts of meaning.* Cambridge, MA: Harvard University Press.

Burke, P. J. (1991). Identity processes and social stress. *American Sociological Review, 56*, 836–849. doi:10.2307/2096259

Dalgleish, T. (2004). What might not have been: An investigation of the nature of counterfactual thinking in survivors of trauma. *Psychological Medicine, 34*, 1215–1225. doi:10.1017/S003329170400193X

Edmondson, D., Park, C. L., Blank, T. O., Fenster, J. R., & Mills, M. A. (2008). Deconstructing spiritual well-being: Existential well-being and HRQOL in cancer survivors. *Psycho-Oncology, 17*, 161–169. doi:10.1002/pon.1197

Edmondson, D., Park, C. L., Chaudoir, S. R., & Wortmann, J. H. (2008). Death without God: Religious struggle, death concerns, and depression in the terminally ill. *Psychological Science, 19*, 754–758. doi:10.1111/j.1467-9280.2008.02152.x

Emmons, R. A. (1999). *The psychology of ultimate concerns: Motivation and spirituality in personality*. New York, NY: Guilford Press.

Exline, J. J. (2002). The picture is getting clearer, but is the scope too limited? Three overlooked questions in the psychology of religion. *Psychological Inquiry, 13*, 245–247. doi:10.1207/S15327965PLI1303_07

Exline, J. J., & Rose, E. (2005). Religious and spiritual struggles. In R. E. Paloutzian & C. L. Park (Eds.), *Handbook of the psychology of religion and spirituality* (pp. 315–330). New York, NY: Guilford Press.

Frankl, V. E. (1963). *Man's search for meaning: An introduction to logotherapy*. New York, NY: Washington Square Press.

Furrow, J. L., King, P. E., & White, K. (2004). Religion and positive youth development: Identity, meaning, and prosocial concerns. *Applied Developmental Science, 8*, 17–26. doi:10.1207/S1532480XADS0801_3

Gall, T. L., & Cornblat, M. W. (2002). Breast cancer survivors give voice: A qualitative analysis of spiritual factors in long-term adjustment. *Psycho-Oncology, 11*, 524–535. doi:10.1002/pon.613

Geertz, C. (1973). *Interpretation of cultures: Selected essays*. New York, NY: Basic Books.

Gergen, K. J. (1985). The social constructionist movement in modern psychology. *American Psychologist, 40*, 266–275. doi:10.1037/0003-066X.40.3.266

Gould, S. J. (1999). Non-overlapping magisteria. *Skeptical Inquirer, 23*, 55–61.

Gray, K., & Wegner, D. (2010). Blaming God for our pain: Human suffering and the divine mind. *Personality and Social Psychology Review, 14*, 7–16. doi:10.1177/1088868309350299

Greenberg, J., Pyszcznski, T., & Solomon, S. (1986). The causes and consequences of a need for self-esteem: A terror management theory. In R. F. Baumeister (Ed.), *Self, efficacy, and agency* (pp. 189–212). New York, NY: Plenum Press.

Hall, M. E. L., & Johnson, E. L. (2001). Theodicy and therapy: Philosophical/theological contributions to the problem of suffering. *Journal of Psychology and Christianity, 20*, 5–17.

Hayes, J., Schimel, J., Faucher, E. H., & Williams, T. J. (2008). Evidence for the DTA hypothesis II: Threatening self-esteem increases death-thought accessibility. *Journal of Experimental Social Psychology, 44*, 600–613. doi:10.1016/j.jesp.2008.01.004

Hefner, P. (1997). The science-religion relation: Controversy, convergence, and search for meaning. *The International Journal for the Psychology of Religion, 7*, 143–158. doi:10.1207/s15327582ijpr0703_1

Heine, S. J., Proulx, T., & Vohs, K. D. (2006). The meaning maintenance model: On the coherence of social motivations. *Personality and Social Psychology Review, 10*, 88–110. doi:10.1207/s15327957pspr1002_1

Hinde, R. A. (1999). *Why gods persist: A scientific approach to religion*. New York, NY: Routledge.

Hogg, M. A., Adelman, J., & Blagg, R. (2010). Religion in the face of uncertainty: An uncertainty-identity theory account of religiousness. *Personality and Social Psychology Review, 14*, 72–83. doi:10.1177/1088868309349692

Hunt, M. O. (2000). Status, religion, and the belief in a just world: Comparing African Americans, Latinos, and Whites. *Social Science Quarterly, 81*, 325–343.

Inzlicht, M., McGregor, I., Hirsch, J., & Nash, K. (2009). Neural markers of religious conviction. *Psychological Science, 20*, 385–392. doi:10.1111/j.1467-9280.2009.02305.x

Ironson, G., Stuetzle, R., & Fletcher, M. A. (2006). An increase in religiousness/ spirituality occurs after HIV diagnosis and predicts slower disease progression over 4 years in people with HIV. *Journal of General Internal Medicine, 21*, S62–S68. doi:10.1111/j.1525-1497.2006.00648.x

Janoff-Bulman, R. (1992). *Shattered assumptions: Towards a new psychology of trauma*. New York, NY: Free Press.

Janoff-Bulman, R., & Frantz, C. M. (1997). The impact of trauma on meaning: From meaningless world to meaningful life. In M. Power & C. Brewin (Eds.), *The transformation of meaning in psychological therapies: Integrating theory and practice* (pp. 91–106). Chichester, England: Wiley.

Jonas, E., & Fischer, P. (2006). Terror management and religion: Evidence that intrinsic religiousness mitigates worldview defense following mortality salience. *Journal of Personality and Social Psychology, 91*, 553–567. doi:10.1037/0022-3514.91.3.553

Joseph, S., & Linley, P. A. (2005). Positive adjustment to threatening events: An organismic valuing theory of growth through adversity. *Review of*

General Psychology, 9, 262–280. doi:10.1037/1089-2680.9.3.262

Karpov, V., & Lisovskaya, E. (2008). Religious intolerance among Orthodox Christians and Muslims in Russia. *Religion, State, and Society, 36*, 361–377. doi:10.1080/09637490802442975

Kaufmann, W. (Ed.). (1989). *Existentialism: From Dostoevsky to Sartre.* New York, NY: Meridian.

Kay, A. C., Gaucher, D., McGregor, I., & Nash, K. (2010). Religious belief as compensatory control. *Personality and Social Psychology Review, 14*, 37–48. doi:10.1177/1088868309353750

Kay, A. C., Gaucher, D., Napier, J. L., Callan, M. J., & Laurin, K. (2008). God and the government: Testing a compensatory control mechanism for the support of external systems. *Journal of Personality and Social Psychology, 95*, 18–35. doi:10.1037/0022-3514.95.1.18

King, L. A., Hicks, J. A., Krull, J. L., & Del Gaiso, A. K. (2006). Positive affect and the experience of meaning in life. *Journal of Personality and Social Psychology, 90*, 179–196. doi:10.1037/0022-3514.90.1.179

King, P. E. (2003). Religion and identity: The role of ideological, social, and spiritual contexts. *Applied Developmental Science, 7*, 197–204. doi:10.1207/S1532480XADS0703_11

Klooster, F. H. (2001). Decrees of God. In W. A. Elwell (Ed.), *Evangelical dictionary of theology* (2nd ed., p. 303). Grand Rapids, MI: Baker Academic.

Koltko-Rivera, M. E. (2000). The Worldview Assessment Instrument (WAI): The development and preliminary validation of an instrument to assess worldview components relevant to counseling and psychotherapy. *Dissertation Abstracts International: Dissertations and Theses, Full Text* (AAT 9968433).

Koltko-Rivera, M. E. (2004). The psychology of worldviews. *Review of General Psychology, 8*, 3–58. doi:10.1037/1089-2680.8.1.3

Korotkov, D. (1998). The sense of coherence: Making sense out of chaos. In P. T. P. Wong & P. S. Fry (Eds.), *The human quest for meaning: A handbook of psychological research and clinical applications* (pp. 51–70). New York, NY: Erlbaum.

Kotarba, J. A. (1983). Perceptions of death, belief systems and the process of coping with chronic pain. *Social Science and Medicine, 17*, 681–689. doi:10.1016/0277-9536(83)90374-X

Krause, N. (2003). Religious meaning and subjective well-being in late life. *The Journals of Gerontology, Series B: Psychological Sciences and Social Sciences, 58*, S160–S170. doi:10.1093/geronb/58.3.S160

Krause, N. (2005). God-mediated control and psychological well-being in late life. *Research on Aging, 27*, 136–164. doi:10.1177/0164027504270475

Krause, N. (2008). The social foundation of religious meaning in life. *Research on Aging, 30*, 395–427. doi:10.1177/0164027508316619

Lachman, M. E., & Firth, K. M. P. (2004). The adaptive value of feeling in control during midlife. In O. G. Brim, C. D. Ryff, & R. C. Kessler (Eds.), *How healthy are we? A national study on well-being at midlife* (pp. 320–349). Chicago, IL: University of Chicago Press.

Landau, M. J., Greenberg, J., Solomon, S., Pyszczynski, T., & Martens, A. (2006). Windows into nothingness: Terror management, meaninglessness, and negative reactions to modern art. *Journal of Personality and Social Psychology, 90*, 879–892. doi:10.1037/0022-3514.90.6.879

Laurin, K., Kay, A. C., & Moscovitch, D. A. (2008). On the belief in God: Towards an understanding of the emotional substrates of compensatory control. *Journal of Experimental Social Psychology, 44*, 1559–1562. doi:10.1016/j.jesp.2008.07.007

Leary, M. R., & Tangney, J. P. (2003). The self as an organizing construct in the social and behavioral sciences. In M. R. Leary & J. P. Tangney (Eds.), *Handbook of self and identity* (pp. 3–14). New York, NY: Guilford Press.

Leuba, J. H. (1916). *The belief in God and immortality: A psychological, anthropological and statistical study.* Chicago, IL: Open Court.

Lewis, R., & Taylor, J. (2009). The social significance of religious resources in the prediction of mattering to others: African American and White contrasts. *Sociological Spectrum, 29*, 273–294. doi:10.1080/02732170802584484

Lind, E. A., & van den Bos, K. (2002). When fairness works: Toward a general theory of uncertainty management. *Research in Organizational Behavior, 24*, 181–223. doi:10.1016/S0191-3085(02)24006-X

Mahoney, A., Pargament, K. I., Cole, B., Jewell, T., Magyar, G. M., Tarakeshwar, N., . . . Phillips, R. (2005). A higher purpose: The sanctification of strivings. *The International Journal for the Psychology of Religion, 15*, 239–262. doi:10.1207/s15327582ijpr1503_4

Mandel, D. R., & Lehman, D. R. (1996). Counterfactual thinking and ascriptions of cause and preventability. *Journal of Personality and Social Psychology, 71*, 450–463. doi:10.1037/0022-3514.71.3.450

Mattlin, J. A., Wethington, E., & Kessler, R. C. (1990). Situational determinants of coping and coping effectiveness. *Journal of Health and Social Behavior, 31*, 103–122. doi:10.2307/2137048

McAdams, D. P. (2001). The psychology of life stories. *Review of General Psychology, 5*, 100–122. doi:10.1037/1089-2680.5.2.100

McCullough, M. E., Enders, C. K., Brion, S. L., & Jain, A. R. (2005). The varieties of religious development in adulthood: A longitudinal investigation of religion and rational choice. *Journal of Personality and Social Psychology, 89*, 78–89. doi:10.1037/0022-3514.89.1.78

McIntosh, D. N. (1995). Religion-as-schema, with implications for the relation between religion and coping. *The International Journal for the Psychology of Religion, 5*, 1–16. doi:10.1207/s15327582ijpr0501_1

Mischel, W., & Morf, C. C. (2003). The self as a psychosocial dynamic processing system: A meta-perspective on a century of the self in psychology. In M. R. Leary & J. P. Tangney (Eds.), *Handbook of self and identity* (pp. 15–43). New York, NY: Guilford Press.

Newberg, A., & Waldman, M. (2006). *Why we believe what we believe: Uncovering our biological need for meaning, spirituality, and truth*. New York, NY: Free Press.

Newport, F. (2007). *Questions and answers about Americans' religion*. Retrieved from http://www.gallup.com/poll/103459/Questions-Answers-About-Americans-Religion.aspx

Newton, A. T., & McIntosh, D. N. (2009). Associations of general religiousness and specific religious beliefs with coping appraisals in response to Hurricanes Katrina and Rita. *Mental Health, Religion, and Culture, 12*, 129–146. doi:10.1080/13674670802380400

Norenzayan, A., & Hansen, I. G. (2006). Belief in supernatural agents in the face of death. *Personality and Social Psychology Bulletin, 32*, 174–187. doi:10.1177/0146167205280251

Ozorak, E. (2005). Cognitive approaches to religion. In R. F. Paloutzian & C. L. Park (Eds.), *Handbook of the psychology of religion and spirituality* (pp. 216–234). New York, NY: Guilford Press.

Paloutzian, R. F. (2005). Religious conversion and spiritual transformation: A meaning-system analysis. In R. F. Paloutzian & C. L. Park (Eds.), *Handbook of the psychology of religion and spirituality* (pp. 331–347). New York, NY: Guilford Press.

Paloutzian, R. F., & Park, C. L. (2005). Integrative themes in the current science of the psychology of religion. In R. F. Paloutzian & C. L. Park (Eds.), *Handbook of the psychology of religion and spirituality* (pp. 3–20). New York, NY: Guilford Press.

Pargament, K. I. (1997). *The psychology of religion and coping*. New York, NY: Guilford Press.

Pargament, K. I. (2002). Is religion nothing but . . . ? Explaining religion versus explaining religion away. *Psychological Inquiry, 13*, 239–244. doi:10.1207/S15327965PLI1303_06

Pargament, K. I., Cole, B., Vandecreek, L., Belavich, T., Brant, C., & Perez, L. (1999). The vigil: Religion and the search for control in the hospital waiting room. *Journal of Health Psychology, 4*, 327–341. doi:10.1177/135910539900400303

Pargament, K. I., Kennell, J., Hathaway, W., Grevengoed, N., Newman, J., & Jones, W. (1988). Religion and the problem-solving process: Three styles of coping. *Journal for the Scientific Study of Religion, 27*, 90–104. doi:10.2307/1387404

Pargament, K. I., Koenig, H. G., Tarakeshwar, N., & Hahn, J. (2001). Religious struggle as a predictor of mortality among medically ill elderly patients: A 2-year longitudinal study. *Archives of Internal Medicine, 161*, 1881–1885. doi:10.1001/archinte.161.15.1881

Pargament, K. I., Magyar-Russell, G. M., & Murray-Swank, N. A. (2005). The sacred and the search for significance: Religion as a unique process. *Journal of Social Issues, 61*, 665–687. doi:10.1111/j.1540-4560.2005.00426.x

Pargament, K. I., Smith, B. W., Koenig, H. G., & Perez, L. (1998). Patterns of positive and negative religious coping with major life stressors. *Journal for the Scientific Study of Religion, 37*, 710–724. doi:10.2307/1388152

Park, C. L. (2005a). Religion and meaning. In R. F. Paloutzian & C. L. Park (Eds.), *Handbook of the psychology of religion and spirituality* (pp. 295–314). New York, NY: Guilford Press.

Park, C. L. (2005b). Religion as a meaning-making framework in coping with life stress. *Journal of Social Issues, 61*, 707–729. doi:10.1111/j.1540-4560.2005.00428.x

Park, C. L. (2010). Making sense of the meaning literature: An integrative review of meaning making and its effects on adjustment to stressful life events. *Psychological Bulletin, 136*, 257–301. doi:10.1037/a0018301

Park, C. L., & Cohen, L. (1993). Religious and nonreligious coping with the death of a friend. *Cognitive Therapy and Research, 17*, 561–577. doi:10.1007/BF01176079

Park, C. L., Edmondson, D., & Blank, T. O. (2009). Religious and non-religious pathways to stress-related growth in cancer survivors. *Applied Psychology: Health and Well-Being, 1*, 321–335. doi:10.1111/j.1758-0854.2009.01009.x

Park, C. L., Edmondson, D., Fenster, J. R., & Blank, T. O. (2008). Meaning making and psychological adjustment following cancer: The mediating roles of growth, life meaning, and restored just world beliefs. *Journal of Consulting and Clinical Psychology, 76*, 863–875. doi:10.1037/a0013348

Park, C. L., & Folkman, S. (1997). Meaning in the context of stress and coping. *Review of General Psychology, 1*, 115–144. doi:10.1037/1089-2680.1.2.115

Park, C. L., & Slattery, J. M. (2009). Spirituality and case conceptualizations: A meaning system approach. In J. Aten & M. Leach (Eds.), *Spirituality and the therapeutic process: A guide for mental health professionals* (pp. 121–142). Washington, DC: American Psychological Association.

Paterson, F., & Rossow, L. (1999). "Chained to the Devil's throne": Evolution and science as a religio-political issue. *American Biology Teacher, 61*, 358–364.

Proulx, T., & Heine, S. J. (2006). Death and black diamonds: Meaning, mortality, and the meaning maintenance model. *Psychological Inquiry, 17*, 309–318. doi:10.1080/10478400701366985

Pudrovska, T., Schieman, S., Pearlin, L. I., & Nguyen, K. (2005). The sense of mastery as a mediator and moderator in the association between economic hardship and health in late life. *Journal of Aging and Health, 17*, 634–660. doi:10.1177/0898264305279874

Purzycki, B. G., & Sosis, R. (2009). The religious system as adaptive: Cognitive flexibility, public displays, and acceptance. In E. Voland & W. Schiefenhuvel (Eds.), *The biological evolution of religious mind and behavior* (pp. 243–256). New York, NY: Springer.

Roese, N. J. (1994). The functional basis of counterfactual thinking. *Journal of Personality and Social Psychology, 66*, 805–818. doi:10.1037/0022-3514.66.5.805

Roese, N. J. (1997). Counterfactual thinking. *Psychological Bulletin, 121*, 133–148. doi:10.1037/0033-2909.121.1.133

Rothbaum, F., Weisz, J. R., & Snyder, S. S. (1982). Changing the world and changing the self: A two-process model of perceived control. *Journal of Personality and Social Psychology, 42*, 5–37. doi:10.1037/0022-3514.42.1.5

Rotter, J. B. (1966). Generalized expectancies for internal versus external control of reinforcement. *Psychological Monographs: General and Applied, 80*, 1–28. doi:10.1037/h0092976

Ruskay-Kidd, S. (1997). The Defense of Marriage Act and the overextension of congressional authority. *Columbia Law Review, 97*, 1435–1482. doi:10.2307/1123440

Saroglou, V., Buxant, C., & Tilquin, J. (2008). Positive emotions as leading to religion and spirituality. *Journal of Positive Psychology, 3*, 165–173. doi:10.1080/17439760801998737

Schimel, J., Hayes, J., Williams, T., & Jahrig, J. (2007). Is death really the worm at the core? Converging evidence that worldview threat increases death-thought accessibility. *Journal of Personality and Social Psychology, 92*, 789–803. doi:10.1037/0022-3514.92.5.789

Schuster, M. A., Stein, B. D., Jaycox, L. H., Collins, R. L., Marshall, G. N., Elliott, M. N., . . . Berry, S. H. (2001). A national survey of stress reactions after the September 11, 2001, terrorist attacks. *New England Journal of Medicine, 345*, 1507–1512. doi:10.1056/NEJM200111153452024

Schweiker, W. F. (1969). Religion as a superordinate meaning system and sociopsychological integration. *Journal for the Scientific Study of Religion, 8*, 300–307. doi:10.2307/1384341

Segal, R. A. (1980). The myth-ritualist theory of religion. *Journal for the Scientific Study of Religion, 19*, 173–185. doi:10.2307/1386251

Shaw, A., Joseph, S., & Linley, P. A. (2005). Religion, spirituality, and posttraumatic growth: A systematic review. *Mental Health, Religion, and Culture, 8*, 1–11. doi:10.1080/1367467032000157981

Sherkat, D., de Vries, K., & Creek, S. (2010). Race, religion, and opposition to same-sex marriage. *Social Science Quarterly, 91*, 80–98. doi:10.1111/j.1540-6237.2010.00682.x

Silberman, I. (2005). Religion as a meaning system: Implications for the new millennium. *Journal of Social Issues, 61*, 641–663. doi:10.1111/j.1540-4560.2005.00425.x

Sire, J. W. (1997). *The universe next door: A Basic Worldview catalog* (3rd ed.). Downers Grove, IL: InterVarsity Press.

Skinner, E. A. (2007). A secondary control critique: Is it secondary? Is it control? Comment on Morling and Evered. *Psychological Bulletin, 133*, 911–916. doi:10.1037/0033-2909.133.6.911

Skrabski, A., Kopp, M., Rózsa, S., Réthelyi, J., & Rahe, R. H. (2005). Life meaning: An important correlate of health in the Hungarian population. *International Journal of Behavioral Medicine, 12*, 78–85. doi:10.1207/s15327558ijbm1202_5

Slattery, J. M., & Park, C. L. (2011). Meaning making and spiritually oriented interventions. In J. Aten, M. R. McMinn, & E. V. Worthington (Eds.), *Spiritually oriented interventions for counseling and psychotherapy* (pp. 15–40). Washington, DC: American Psychological Association.

Solomon, S., Greenberg, J., Pyszczynski, T., & Koole, S. L. (2004). The cultural animal: Twenty years of terror management theory and research. In J. Greenberg, S. Koole, & T. Pyszczynski (Eds.), *Handbook of experimental existential psychology* (pp. 13–34). New York, NY: Guilford Press.

Spilka, B., Hood, R. W., Jr., Hunsberger, B., & Gorsuch, R. (2003). *The psychology of religion: An empirical approach* (3rd ed.). New York, NY: Guilford Press.

Spilka, B., Shaver, P., & Kirkpatrick, L. (1985). A general attribution theory for the psychology of religion. *Journal for the Scientific Study of Religion, 24*, 1–20. doi:10.2307/1386272

Steger, M. F. (2009). Meaning in life. In S. J. Lopez (Ed.), *Oxford handbook of positive psychology* (2nd ed., pp. 679–687). Oxford, England: Oxford University Press.

Stillman, T., & Baumeister, R. (2009). Uncertainty, belongingness, and four needs for meaning. *Psychological Inquiry, 20*, 249–251. doi:10.1080/10478400903333544

Swann, W. B., Jr., Rentfrow, P. J., & Guinn, J. S. (2003). Self-verification: The search for coherence. In M. R. Leary & J. P. Tangney (Eds.), *Handbook of self and identity* (pp. 367–383). New York, NY: Guilford Press.

Thompson, S. C., & Janigian, A. S. (1988). Life schemes: A framework for understanding the search for meaning. *Journal of Social and Clinical Psychology, 7*, 260–280. doi:10.1521/jscp.1988.7.2-3.260

Thompson, S. C., & Schlehofer, M. M. (2007). The many sides of control: Motives for high, low and illusory control. In J. Y. Shah & W. L. Gardner (Eds.), *Handbook of motivation science* (pp. 41–56). New York, NY: Guilford Press.

Tillich, P. (1961). *Systematic theology* (Vol. 1). Chicago, IL: University of Chicago Press.

van den Bos, K. (2001). Uncertainty management: The influence of uncertainty salience on reactions to perceived procedural fairness. *Journal of Personality and Social Psychology, 80*, 931–941. doi:10.1037/0022-3514.80.6.931

van den Bos, K., & Lind, E. (2002). Uncertainty management by means of fairness judgments. In M. P. Zanna (Ed.), *Advances in experimental social psychology* (Vol. 34, pp. 1–60). San Diego, CA: Academic Press.

Vryan, K. D., Adler, P. A., & Adler, P. (2003). Identity. In L. T. Reynolds & N. J. Herman-Kinney (Eds.), *Handbook of symbolic interactionism* (pp. 367–390). New York, NY: AltaMira Press.

Watts, F. (2007). Emotion regulation and religion. In J. J. Gross (Ed.), *Handbook of emotion regulation* (pp. 504–520). New York, NY: Guilford Press.

Wink, P., & Dillon, M. (2002). Spiritual development across the adult life course: Findings from a longitudinal study. *Journal of Adult Development, 9*, 79–94. doi:10.1023/A:1013833419122

Wong, P. T. P. (1998). Implicit theories of meaningful life and the development of the Personal Meaning Profile. In P. T. P. Wong & P. S. Fry (Eds.), *The human quest for meaning: A handbook of psychological research and clinical applications* (pp. 111–140). New York, NY: Erlbaum.

Wortmann, J., Park, C. L., & Edmondson, D. (in press). Trauma and PTSD symptoms: Does spiritual struggle mediate the link? *Psychological Trauma: Theory, Research, Practice, and Policy.*

Wortmann, J. H., & Park, C. L. (2008). Religion and spirituality in adjustment following bereavement: An integrative review. *Death Studies, 32*, 703–736. doi:10.1080/07481180802289507

Yalom, I. (1980). *Existential psychotherapy*. New York, NY: Basic Books.

Ysseldyk, R., Matheson, K., & Anisman, H. (2010). Religiosity as identity: Toward an understanding of religion from a social identity perspective. *Personality and Social Psychology Review, 14*, 60–71.

Zuckerman, P. (2005). Atheism: Contemporary rates and patterns. In M. Martin (Ed.), *The Cambridge companion to atheism* (pp. 47–67). Cambridge, England: Cambridge University Press.

CHAPTER 9

SPIRITUALITY, RELIGIOUSNESS, AND PERSONALITY: THEORETICAL FOUNDATIONS AND EMPIRICAL APPLICATIONS

Ralph L. Piedmont and Teresa A. Wilkins

Spirituality and religiousness constitute fundamental aspects of who we are as people. The prevalence of these constructs in all societies across the historical record, and their impact on every facet of society, demonstrates the value and importance of these variables. It has been argued that these variables constitute qualities that are unique to the human experience. Sperry (2001) emphasized the centrality of the spiritual dimension and asserted that it "reflects the beliefs, effects, and behaviors associated with the basic spiritual hunger or desire for self-transcendence that all individuals experience" (p. 25). One of the guiding themes of this handbook is to outline the growing scientific awareness that for any model of human functioning to be comprehensive, it will have to include spiritual and religious constructs.

Science can examine spiritual and religious constructs from three different perspectives: as a *demographic variable* (a descriptive, actuarial index of what people do and the types of life outcomes they experience); as a *cultural variable* (reflecting specific patterns, styles, and philosophies of living that characterize different spiritual and religious groups); and as an *organismic variable* (an intrinsic characteristic of an individual that influences the direction and tempo of one's life). It will be the last perspective that will be the focus of this chapter. Our goal is to outline the theoretical linkages between spirituality, religiousness, and personality and the empirical evidence that describes the connections between these constructs. Do they represent constructs that directly affect the course and texture of our mental world and personalities, or are they merely by-products of more basic psychological processes? The answer to this question has profound implications for how we view the scientific value of these constructs and understand their role in the human experience.

THEORETICAL FOUNDATIONS TO SPIRITUALITY AND RELIGIOUSNESS

While interest in religious and spiritual constructs across both the social and medical sciences has exploded over the past 20 years, this short history belies a much longer scientific past. In fact, the psychological study of religion begins with the emergence of the field of psychology itself, and many major philosophers and theoreticians have addressed this topic from both positive and negative perspectives. Although this chapter is not intended as a thorough review of these positions, the following sections provide a brief historical sketch of how ideas of the spiritual and the religious have emerged.

Early Personological Approaches

Although these concepts originate from within the realm of theology, psychologists have long realized that spirituality and religiousness are appropriate objects of analysis for the field and need to be included when studying the human mind (see Volume 2, Chapter 33, this handbook). Consequently, an extensive body of literature links personality with

The authors thank Rose Piedmont for her editorial comments.

DOI: 10.1037/14045-009
APA Handbook of Psychology, Religion, and Spirituality: Vol. 1. Context, Theory, and Research, K. I. Pargament (Editor-in-Chief)
Copyright © 2013 by the American Psychological Association. All rights reserved.

spirituality and religiousness. Beginning with William James (1902/1982), psychologists have pondered which elements constitute the characteristics of a religious temperament. James examined religious experiences from multiple angles, including neurology, conversion, and mysticism. He noted that "religious thought is carried on in terms of personality, this being, in the world of religion, the one fundamental fact" (p. 491) and averred that "to the psychologist, the religious propensities of man must be at least as interesting as any other of the facts pertaining to his mental constitution" (p. 2).

Freud (1913/1950; 1927/1961), an atheist, had little use for what he considered the prohibitory and guilt-laden aspects of religion but spent considerable time analyzing religiousness. He proclaimed religion to be an illusion, springing from defenses against helplessness, and images of God to be introjections of father figures. He equated religiousness with wish fulfillment and saw it as the realm of the neurotic. See Rizzuto's (1998, Volume 2, Chapter 6, this handbook) work for a detailed examination of Freud's rejection of God. Recent psychoanalytic work takes a more favorable view of religiousness, however. For example, Rizzuto (1979; Volume 2, Chapter 6, this handbook) differed from Freud and asserted that the image of God is a transitional object that is never outgrown and that sustains people throughout the life span.

Others in the psychodynamic tradition understood spirituality and religiousness in broader terms with larger significance for psychological functioning. Jung (1938/1966) saw religion as the "fruit and the culmination of the completeness of life" (p. 50). He delineated personality into conscious and unconscious components and spoke of the religious nature of the human psyche. He identified archetypes, themes that repeat throughout time and throughout culture, and placed the image of the Deity among them. Jung asserted that religion acted as a "spontaneous expression of a certain predominant psychological condition" (1938/1966, p. 108), and he saw dogma as a regulating force that helped shield against the intensity of "immediate religious experience" (1938/1966, p. 53). Jung (1921/1971) stressed that Freud had overlooked the healthy aspect of devotion and noted that instead of being regressive, the symbolization of parental figures into God-images constituted psychological growth.

Adler (1927/1998) also examined pathways toward character development and spoke of *social interest* as an important component of a healthy lifestyle. He valued participation in some religious activities, but he cautioned against striving toward "Godlikeness" in the pursuit of perfection (Adler, 1927/1998, p. 117). He noted that ambition and vanity could be the catalysts behind people's attraction to religion and acknowledged that some could become overzealous in manifesting certain character traits. Adler emphasized that a healthy lifestyle revolved around a balanced outlook and involvement in community activities.

Maslow (1970a, 1970b) also stressed balance. He examined what he called *peak-* and *plateau-experiences* and suggested that the path to self-actualization included an integration of both Apollonian and Dionysian personality elements. He saw the Apollonian as rational and behavior-oriented, whereas the more atavistic Dionysian had the capacity for experiencing the transcendent and mystical. He encouraged the cultivation of humanity's *higher nature* and emphasized that although organized religious communities could become oppressive, people still need to live and learn in community. Finally, he examined how *self-actualization* developed via *being-values*. Maslow (1970b) identified 15 being-values: truth, goodness, beauty, wholeness, dichotomy-transcendence, aliveness, uniqueness, perfection and necessity, completion, justice and order, simplicity, richness, effortlessness, playfulness, and self-sufficiency (pp. 92–94). He asserted that spiritual values "do not need supernatural concepts to validate them, that they are well within the jurisdiction of a suitably enlarged science, and that, therefore, they are the general responsibility of *all* mankind" (1970b, p. 4).

Frankl (1959, 1964, 1969) took a different approach and examined an internal motive to find meaning in life. When explaining possible applications of logotherapy, he emphasized that clinicians could draw on patients' spiritual resources, which he labeled the "nöological dimension—in contradistinction to the biological and psychological ones. It is that dimension in which the uniquely human phenomena are located" (1969, p. 17). He insisted that people have an innate yearning for finding meaning and stressed that the will to meaning undergirds their capability to suffer and to endure life's negative experiences.

Most of the aforementioned psychologists framed spirituality and religiousness as positive forces that need to be acknowledged and accounted for in psychological theories. In most of the previously mentioned literature, however, religiousness and spirituality were not examined as separate from one another. Could they actually represent highly correlated but distinct constructs that are mediated by different psychological systems? Could spirituality be part of a process that motivates, directs, and organizes an individual? Allport's trait approach underscored that spirituality was a psychological variable that could be measured and assessed in its own right.

Conceptualizing Spirituality and Religiousness Within Trait Models of Personality

Allport (1950) was one of the first psychologists to assert that the religious aspects of the individual represented an organizing praxis of the personality that had implications for all other aspects of psychological functioning. As he noted, "the developed religious sentiment is the synthesis of these and many other factors, all of which form a comprehensive attitude whose function is to relate the individual meaningfully to the whole of Being" (1955, p. 94). For Allport, religiousness and spirituality served as a cardinal trait, a quality by which the operation of one's personality system is guided and directed. It enjoys this important status because of its seemingly singular place within the mental system. For Allport, the religious sentiment

> is the portion of personality that arises at the core of the life and is directed toward the infinite. It is the region of mental life that has the longest-range intentions, and for this reason is capable of conferring marked integration upon personality, engendering meaning and peace in the face of tragedy and confusion of life. (1950, p. 142)

Working from this perspective, Allport devised one of the first standardized trait measures of religiousness: the Religious Orientation Scale (ROS). The ROS captured both an intrinsic orientation (which represents an internalization of religious concepts that are used to define and direct behavior) and an extrinsic orientation (which represents a utilitarian approach to religious activities, with religion serving as a vehicle for satisfying other needs). A tremendous amount of research has been done employing this scale. Donahue (1985) noted that the intrinsic scale related to being ideologically tolerant and unprejudiced, better levels of mental health, regular church attendance, and being more mature. The extrinsic scale was related to prejudice, dogmatism, trait anxiety, and fear of death. Although infrequently found in the current research literature, the scale's initial wide usage helped to establish the empirical value of religiousness as a predictor of an array of psychosocially relevant outcomes. These findings supported Allport's contention of the centrality of religiousness in the human personality.

With the passage of time, Allport's trait approach to personality became further developed and refined. The major focus of this work was to identify the basic, core dimensions that would summarize and organize the plethora of identified traits. One of the pioneers in this effort was Hans Eysenck (1951, 1978, 1990), who identified three major dimensions that he believed characterized the universe of trait terms: *neuroticism, extraversion,* and *psychoticism.* Neuroticism (N) is the tendency toward negative affect, extraversion (E) is the tendency toward positive affect, and psychoticism (P) is the tendency toward antagonism and hostility. These three domains represented the broadest level of abstraction for the many lower order traits that have been identified. The value of this model was that it provided very clear descriptions of the personological implications associated with various behaviors. In other words, understanding how specific behaviors and traits linked to these larger dimensions would provide insights into the motivations (both psychological and neurobiological) underlying the activities.

Research has noted that neuroticism was mostly independent of spirituality and religiousness, extraversion and psychoticism were negatively related to these constructs, and a positive relationship existed with the Lie scale of the Eysenck Personality Inventory (e.g., Francis, 1991, 1992, 1993, 2005; Francis & Jackson, 2003; Francis & Pearson, 1985). Given that these personality dimensions have specific neurobiological associations, the pattern of these findings provides evidence that religiousness is associated with higher levels of conditionability and tender-minded attitudes (White, Joseph, & Neil, 1995).

Although certainly an important start to understanding how spiritual and religious constructs relate to trait-based dimensions of personality, Eysenck's three-factor model has been overtaken by more recent models that challenge both its structure and comprehensiveness. Specifically, the five-factor model (FFM) of personality has emerged as a more comprehensive and robust taxonomy of personality traits (Costa & McCrae, 1995; McCrae & Costa, 1997). The five dimensions include neuroticism and extraversion, which are similar to those used in the Eysenck model. The other dimensions include *agreeableness* (A, which assesses the quality of one's interactions along a continuum from compassion to antagonism), *conscientiousness* (C, which assesses the persistence, organization, and motivation exhibited in goal-directed behaviors), and finally, *openness to experience* (O, which measures the proactive seeking and appreciation of new experiences). A very large and expanding research literature has demonstrated that these qualities represent personality as traditionally defined and that the FFM captures genotypic qualities that are universal across cultures, robustly stable through adulthood, and predictive of many important physical and mental health outcomes (e.g., Haslam, Whelan, & Bastian, 2009; Kern & Friedman, 2008).

Piedmont (1999b) outlined four ways that the FFM could be fruitfully applied to research on spiritual or religious constructs. One recommendation was to correlate such scales with the FFM domains to "illuminate the larger motivations and anticipated outcomes of [such] scales" (p. 344). Collating data from three different studies (involving 251, 492, and 534 individuals, respectively), Piedmont presented correlations between the FFM domains and 12 spiritual and religiousness scales. Many associations were found, although most were less than $r = .35$. All five personality factors correlated with these scales. For example, Existential Well-Being correlated $r(490) = -.51$, $p < .001$ with Neuroticism, while the Collaborative facet of the Religious Problem Solving scale correlated $r(249) = .34$, $p < .01$ with Conscientiousness. Of the 12 spirituality scales, 10 evidenced significant correlations with multiple personality domains. To better understand the relations between personality and the spiritual inventories, each of the spiritual or religious scales was individually regressed on the five factors. The resulting R^2 values ranged from .02 (for Extrinsic Religious Orientation) to .35 (for Existential Well-Being). More intermediate values were found for Intrinsic Religious Orientation ($R^2 = .03$), Religious Well-Being ($R^2 = .05$), Mysticism, Faith Maturity, and Self-Directed Religious Problem Solving (R^2s = .06). Slightly larger effects were found for the Collaborative ($R^2 = .16$) and Deferring ($R^2 = .20$) Religious Problem-Solving scales. Piedmont concluded, "Scores on these religious scales contain much information about people that is not accounted for by the FFM . . . it is ultimately what religious constructs do *not* [emphasis in original] have in common with the FFM that is of the most importance" (1999b, p. 346).

Saroglou (2002) conducted a meta-analysis of research linking the FFM domains to measures of religiousness and spirituality. Across the 13 reviewed studies, systematic relations with the FFM domains were found; A and C were the major positive correlates. Expanding on this work, Saroglou (2010) conducted an updated meta-analysis of more than 70 studies linking personality to the religious constructs. This international sample of more than 21,000 subjects replicated earlier findings and clearly noted the role of A and C as central correlates of spiritual and religious constructs. Two important conclusions were drawn from these data. First, the linkage with agreeableness and conscientiousness helps to put into context many observed findings using religious constructs, such as the effects of religiousness on physical and mental health (outcomes also linked to C) and relations with social support and prosocial behavior (correlates of A). Second, Saroglou argued, these associations also suggested that spiritual and religious motivations represent characteristic adaptations of A and C. In other words, religious motivations may be culturally conditioned phenomena that develop from people high on A and C who also live in an environment in which religion is present. Being caring, compassionate, and dutiful was hypothesized to predispose individuals to turn to religion and spirituality because of their natural appeal to such motivations. The support for this assertion was based on findings from longitudinal research studies that found similar associations.

Wink and Dillon (2002, 2008) provided a major source of longitudinal data examining the role of religiousness and spirituality across a 60-plus-year life span. Evaluating more than 200 individuals born in the 1920s, Wink and Dillon examined how spirituality and religiousness developed and was expressed from young adulthood until old age. Their findings noted that for their cohort, levels of spirituality increased significantly over the course of adulthood, especially from middle to late adulthood, and more for women than men. Men's spirituality increased significantly more than women's from early to middle adulthood. For women, rises in spirituality in later adulthood were also related to the number of negative life events experienced in middle adulthood, especially financial strain and conflicts with spouses and parents. Using the same sample, Wink, Ciciolla, Dillon, and Tracy (2007) examined the role of personality in predicting levels of religiousness in adulthood. Findings indicated that levels of A, C, and O in adolescence predicted spiritual seeking and religiousness in late life. They concluded that "personality plays an important role in shaping religious and spiritual engagement, and, therefore, personality needs to be considered in any effort to understand how religion affects psychological functioning over the life course" (Wink et al., 2007, pp. 1067–1068).

Heaven and Ciarrochi (2007) examined personality's impact on religious values in a more time-delimited longitudinal study employing Australian high school students over a 3-year period. Using a measure of Eysenck's P scale (this dimension combines both low A and low C) and a marker scale of C, these authors examined how changes in levels of these variables from freshman to sophomore year in high school were related to religious values in the junior year. They found that for boys, decreases in P were related to increased levels of religious values, whereas increases in C for girls were related to increased religiousness. Although it seemed that some elements of C were involved in predicting religious values later in adolescence, the authors argued that among males, the P scale was much more related to "maleness" with high scores related to delinquency, antisocial behavior, and illicit drug use. Thus, decreases on this dimension for boys were related to higher religious values. Although the P scale contained elements of both A and C, the marker scale for C was not a significant predictor of shifts in religious values. This finding suggested that for boys, A may be the key personality predictor of religious values. Thus, gender may be an important moderator for understanding how personality affects religious values.

McCullough, Tsang, and Brion (2003) examined the associations between markers of the FFM personality domains assessed in adolescence with levels of religiousness in adulthood. Using data from the Terman Longitudinal Study of high-ability children, McCullough et al. demonstrated that ratings of personality, specifically C, obtained from parents when their children were between 12 and 18 years old correlated significantly with adult self-ratings of religiousness in 1940–1941. Gender emerged as a significant predictor of religiousness, with women scoring higher on this outcome than men. C emerged as the sole significant personality predictor.

Working further with these data, McCullough, Enders, Brion, and Jain (2005) were able to identify three reliable types of religious individuals, each with its own trajectory through time. There were those who scored low on religiousness in youth and remained low throughout their lives. A second group scored high on religiousness in youth and remained so longitudinally. Finally, one group had a moderate level of religiousness in youth that increased into middle age and then decreased again in old age. In identifying which personality and demographic variables predicted membership in these three groups, A was the only personality factor to emerge, being positively related to levels of religiousness. Thus, across all four of these longitudinal studies, the personality dimensions of A and C appeared to be most closely related to individual differences in religiousness.

A major limitation to these longitudinal studies by Wink et al. (2002, 2007, 2008) and McCullough et al. (2003, 2005) was that no standardized measures of spirituality or religiousness were used. Rather, hybrid indexes were developed from available surveys and interview data at each assessment time point, with no consistent measure being used throughout the studies. With no clear validity established for scores on these indexes, the meaning of these associations across time cannot be clearly determined. Also, for all of the longitudinal studies, the effect sizes linking the religiousness measures and the personality scales were low to moderate (e.g., beta weights less than .25). Finally, because Time 1 spirituality was not partialled from these correlations, it is possible that these cross-lagged associations merely reflect the artifactual covariance among all these measures present at Time 1. For a complete examination of personality's effect on spirituality, a full cross-lagged design would need to be implemented in which the effects of Time 1 personality and spirituality could be examined on their cross-lagged Time 2 counterparts (for reviews of this type of design, see Marmor & Montemayor, 1977; Oud, 2007).

Despite limitations in the research to date, three important issues can be discerned from this review. First, psychological theorists have been formulating the role and importance of religious and spiritual constructs within the psychic system from the beginning of the field. For these individuals, whether existentialists, humanists, or trait psychologists, religious and spiritual variables serve important psychological functions that promote growth and resiliency. Second, correlations with trait models reveal some essential linkages that help to expand our understanding of how religious and spiritual constructs are experienced by individuals, and they partially explain why these variables correlate with outcomes such as prosocial behavior, mental and physical health, and psychological maturity. Third, the causal role of spirituality and religiousness in the mental life of the individual has not been clearly delineated. Some theorists (e.g., Allport) see these constructs as being central to the entire psychic system, impacting all other motivations. Some (e.g., Maslow or Frankl) see religious and spiritual variables as operating at only specific levels of development or in concert with other processes of adaptation. The empirical results found with the trait approach have some researchers (e.g., Wink and Saroglou) interpreting the findings as indicating that spirituality and religiousness are outcomes, or adaptations, of these basic trait dimensions. We, however, believe that religiousness and spirituality represent independent psychological dimensions not contained by other constructs, such as those represented in the FFM. As basic motivational constructs, religiousness and spirituality have their own causal influence on behavior. The next sections will outline the rationale and data that support this contention.

Why Spirituality and Religiousness Are Not Personality Outcomes

Given that spirituality and religiousness are individual difference variables, it is appropriate to correlate them with other measures of personality and with the domains of the FFM. From a personological perspective, such associations help to identify the larger psychological qualities that these constructs represent. It would be inaccurate, however, to conclude from these relations that spirituality and religiousness are mere by-products or adaptations of these other personality domains. There are four reasons for this.

First, correlations between spirituality and religiousness with the FFM show association but not direction. After all, correlation does not imply causation. Although the direction of association is an essential question to be addressed (which we will touch on), the data presented so far are not able to answer this issue. Second, the magnitude of correlations between personality and spirituality or religiousness, although consistent across multiple samples, is relatively small. From individual studies through meta-analyses, the linkages between measures of the FFM and spirituality or religiousness are consistently found to be less than $r = .25$. Such low values are hardly informative interpretively, and they are even less useful when presented as evidence for spirituality and religiousness being products of personality. Associations of this low magnitude may reflect methodological artifacts (e.g., singular reliance on self-report questionnaires) or error (e.g., there is no correction being made for the natural overlap among the FFM domains). With personality explaining less than 7% of the variance in religiousness and spirituality, the larger question is, "What is contributing the other 93%?"

Third, while viewing spirituality and religiousness as outcomes of the FFM domains of A, O, and C may reflect individuals' perceptions of "spiritual" and "religious" people, those qualities do not always match well with the personality styles of individuals who are orthodox or conservative in their religious beliefs. Furthermore, any quick perusal through the Bible presents numerous spiritual people who do not follow this pattern of personality styles. For example, the prophet Jonah, with his insistent prejudiced attitude toward the Ninevites, seems not to reflect the high O and A found in the research. Additional examples suggest themselves, such as Kings Saul and David, Eli the High Priest, and many others. Although variously lacking in the qualities of O, A, and C, those individuals nonetheless had strong, direct relationships with God. Clearly, some other personal quality needs to account for this high level of spirituality. Judeo-Christian scripture itself proclaims that spirituality is an innate quality all its own endowed to us directly from God: "For the truth about God is known to them instinctively; God has put that knowledge in their hearts" (Romans 1: 19–20; see also Ecclesiastes 3:10). Rather than being a by-product of some other process, our ability to connect with the sacred may well be a nonreducible aspect of our humanity.

Fourth, from a philosophical perspective, if spirituality and religiousness are merely cultural adaptations working out of one's personality structure, what interest do they hold for psychology? Why study these constructs if they are merely the by-products or outcomes of other processes? Would it not be of greater interest to study those processes that are causing them? Ultimately, the field of psychology is concerned with identifying and affecting those psychological qualities, processes, and mechanisms that drive our behavior and direct the course of our lives. Without any causal precedence, spirituality and religiousness have less relevance and value as scientific constructs. The next section will provide a different perspective on religiousness and spirituality, seeing both as unique sources of motivation.

UNDERSTANDING SPIRITUALITY AND RELIGIOUSNESS AS INDEPENDENT SOURCES OF MOTIVATION

Rather than relying on simple zero-order correlations, the case for religiousness and spirituality as individual difference dimensions independent of the FFM begins with the factor analysis of trait descriptions adjectives. Goldberg (1990) encountered across multiple samples a factor he labeled "religiosity," which was defined by terms such as *religious versus nonreligious* and *reverent versus irreverent*. Saucier and Goldberg (1998) noted that this dimension has a moderately strong presence in the lexicon and may qualify as an individual difference dimension of some value beyond the traditional FFM domains. Ashton, Lee, and Goldberg (2004) also found evidence for religiosity being an additional, independent factor beyond the FFM. Finally, Saucier and Skrzypinska (2006) provided an extensive and systematic analysis of spiritual and religious constructs and noted that both (a) are independent of the FFM; (b) represent two distinct, nonreducible dimensions having different correlates; and (c) fall within the domain of personality, broadly construed.

Research using questionnaire-based measures of spirituality and religion has shown similar results. For example, MacDonald (2000) factor analyzed a number of spiritually based inventories and derived a measure that captured the resulting dimensions. When this new scale was jointly factor analyzed along with a measure of the FFM domains, he found that the spirituality measure formed an independent dimension from the FFM.

Piedmont (1999a, 2001) used the FFM as an empirical reference point for developing measures of spirituality and religiousness that were independent of the FFM. This research led to the development of the Assessment of Spirituality and Religious

Sentiments (ASPIRES) scale (Piedmont, 2010, in press). The ASPIRES provides measures of spirituality across three correlated facets: Prayer Fulfillment (an experienced feeling of joy and contentment that results from prayer and/or meditation; e.g., "I find inner strength and/or peace from my prayers and/or meditations"), Universality (a belief in the unity and purpose of life; e.g., "All life is interconnected"), and Connectedness (a sense of personal responsibility and connection to others; e.g., "Although dead, memories and thoughts of some of my relatives continue to influence my current life"). There are also two measures of religiousness: Religious Involvement (which assesses the frequency and extent of involvement in performing various rituals and activities; e.g., "How often do you pray?"), and Religious Crisis (RC; which examines whether an individual may be experiencing problems, difficulties, or conflicts with the numinous; e.g., "I feel that God is punishing me").

The ASPIRES scales were designed to operationalize aspects of spirituality that are nondenominational and universal. A growing research literature documents the independence of these two dimensions from the domains of the FFM and demonstrates the incremental validity of the ASPIRES scales to predict a wide range of psychosocially and clinically salient outcomes across samples, cultures, languages, and religious affiliations (for an overview of this research, see Piedmont, 2010). When factor analysis is employed to cluster variables sharing substantive common variance, religiousness and spirituality consistently form an independent sixth factor from the FFM domains (Piedmont, 1999a; Piedmont, Mapa, & Williams, 2006; Rican & Janosova, 2010).

One immediate value of the ASPIRES scale is that it provides empirically sustainable, trait-based definitions of spirituality and religiousness that are generalizable across cultures and religions (e.g., Piedmont, 2007; Piedmont & Leach, 2002; Rican & Janosova, 2010). As such, it provides a common language that can be used for developing more sophisticated models that can be linked to established psychological paradigms. The ASPIRES scales also provide clear, empirically developed definitions for both spirituality and religiousness. This is particularly critical for the field given the need for a rationally developed, consensual definition for these constructs (e.g., Hill et al., 2000; Miller & Thoresen, 2003; see also Chapter 1 in this volume). Spirituality is hypothesized to represent a fundamental, inherent quality of the individual. Such a construct is referred to as a *motive*. Motives are nonspecific affect forces that drive, direct, and select behavior. As an intrinsic source of motivation, motives influence the basic adaptive orientation of individuals to their environments. Motives represent universal aspects of human behavior and are found in all human cultures. The Spiritual Transcendence Scale (STS) of the ASPIRES captures a basic motivation for people to create a durable sense of personal meaning within an eschatological context. In other words, knowing that we are going to die, how do we find meaning, purpose, and direction to the life we are living (cf. Chapter 5 in this volume)? At the heart of this motivation is an effort to connect with a larger sacred reality, what has been described as a search for the sacred (see Chapter 1 in this volume).

Religiousness, on the other hand, represents what we will term a *sentiment*. As defined in this handbook (see Chapter 1 in this volume), religion refers to beliefs, practices, relationships, or experiences involving the sacred that are explicitly and historically rooted in established institutionalized systems. *Sentiment* is an old term in psychology and reflects emotional tendencies that develop out of social traditions and educational experiences (Ruckmick, 1920; Woodworth, 1940), including those related to religion. Sentiments can be very powerful motivators for individuals and have very direct effects on behavior. Sentiments, however, like love, gratitude, and patriotism, do not represent innate, genotypic qualities such as spirituality. That is why the expression of sentiments can and do vary across cultures and time periods. Sentiments may also be more amenable to change and modification.

Religiousness is operationalized through the aforementioned two scales. The first, Religious Involvement (RI), reflects how actively involved a person is in performing various religious rituals and activities (e.g., frequency of attending religious services). Also contained in this domain is the level of importance these activities represent to the person. The second domain, Religious Crisis (RC), examines whether a person may be experiencing problems, difficulties, or conflicts with the God of one's understanding or faith community, akin to the notion of religious struggles (see Chapter 25 in this volume). Both domains examine the value an individual attaches to his or her involvement in specific, ritual-oriented, religious activities. As noted, research has supported the structural validity of this scale as well as the independence of these constructs from the domains of the FFM. Most important, these scales evidence significant incremental validity in predicting psychosocially salient criteria over the predictive effects of the FFM (Piedmont, 2010, in press).

Understanding religiousness and spirituality as a separate dimension of personality has important implications. For example, decoupling spirituality and religiousness from personality is conceptually consistent with how spiritual growth and transformation is thought to occur, especially in adulthood. If spirituality were an outcome of personality, then any spiritual growth would need to be predicated on changes in the underlying levels of personality (e.g., O, A, and C). Those personality dimensions have been shown to be very stable in adulthood (e.g., Costa & McCrae, 1994), however, thus making changes in spirituality unlikely. But spiritual change does happen, and there are theoretical and empirical models that indicate individuals do experience systematic changes in their spiritual levels (e.g., Dalby, 2006; Wink & Dillon, 2002, 2008). These changes occur without any corresponding shifts in personality levels.

An excellent literary example of this process is the case of Ebenezer Scrooge: an ambitious, industrious, hard-nosed, politically conservative, successful entrepreneur (Dickens, 1843/2010). Yet after his nocturnal mystical encounters that forced him to face his mortality, he still awoke to find himself a businessman. He did not give up his work or give away his wealth. Much of his personality was the same, except his spirituality had undergone a transformation. He now recognized a larger sacred reality that he honored by "keeping the Christmas spirit" all year long. He learned that there was a larger, unitive process unfolding in life, and he was an important active agent in that process. He had responsibilities and connections to others who orbited his world: his employees, his nephew, his neighbors. The example of Scrooge is interesting to consider because it does force a critical examination of the exact type of transformation that he experienced. Although it may seem that Scrooge's levels of A and C changed, did they? Or instead, was there an increase in his level of spirituality, especially aspects of Universality and Connectedness? The latter seems more likely given that his nocturnal experience was more focused on his spiritual sensibilities than on improving his tender-mindedness and dutifulness. The timbre of his life had changed, but much of who he was remained stable (see Paloutzian, Richardson, & Rambo, 1999; for a review of research on spiritual transformation, see Chapter 22 in this volume).

The ASPIRES scales also provide an opportunity to examine empirically key conceptual issues surrounding the nature and influence of spirituality and religiousness. Piedmont, Ciarrocchi, Dy-Liacco, and Williams (2009) examined two sets of conceptually important models using structural equation modeling (SEM). SEM is a multivariate technique that examines the value of causal models by testing the extent to which the correlations implied by the model are found in actual data. SEM also allows one to compare several different competing models and to determine which is superior. The first series of models examined how spirituality and religiousness related to each other: Were they independent predictors of psychological growth (Model 1) or were they correlated predictors of growth (Model 2)? If they were correlated, should they be collapsed to form a single predictor dimension (Model 3)? The results showed that Model 2 was superior; spirituality and religiousness were highly correlated ($\Phi = .71$) but not redundant. Each retained sufficient unique variance to warrant separate interpretation.

The next series of analyses evaluated models that examined whether spirituality and religiousness were predictors or consequences of psychological growth and, if predictors, which of the two was more fundamental. Were spirituality and religiousness the products of psychological growth (Model 4)? If not, was spirituality the predictor of both growth and religiousness (Model 5), or was religiousness the predictor of both growth and spirituality (Model 6)? Model 5 was found to be superior to the others. This model presented spirituality, the underlying motivation, as a cause of both religiousness and psychological growth. This is an important finding for two reasons. First, if this model is correct, it suggests that a perceived relationship with a transcendent reality could have positive consequences for a person's emotional health and stability. The predictive roles of spirituality and religiousness occurred *over and above* any predictive roles of the personality dimensions of the FFM (Piedmont, 1999a, 2010). Thus, we contend that for any model of psychological functioning to be comprehensive, it needs to include some measure of spirituality. Second, it opens the door to the possibility of a whole new class of therapeutic interventions that are based on personal meaning, sacredness, and transcendence. These constructs may provide windows into emotional healing and transformation that complement existing treatment modalities (e.g., Murray-Swank & Pargament, 2005).

SPIRITUALITY, RELIGIOUSNESS, AND PERSONALITY DYSFUNCTION

Research has shown that spirituality and religiousness are related to a wide array of important mental and physical outcomes, such as well-being (Piedmont, 2009), quality of life (Sawatzky, Ratner, & Chiu, 2005), psychological maturity (Piedmont et al., 2009), coping ability (Pargament, Smith, Koenig, & Perez, 1998; see Chapter 19 in this volume), wellness (Powell, Shahabi, & Thoresen, 2003), responsiveness to treatment for substance abuse (Piedmont, 2004; see also Volume 2, Chapter 15, this handbook), and burnout (Golden, Piedmont, Ciarrocchi, & Rodgerson, 2004). The current research raises the possibility that religiousness and spirituality could serve as underlying forces influencing personal growth and wellness.

Recognizing that being spiritual and religious may promote positive psychosocial outcomes raises other important questions. For example, could the absence of a relationship with the transcendent lead to psychosocial difficulties? Although Spiritual Transcendence and RI were designed to capture active engagement with the sacred and the potential benefits that may ensue, the lack of these qualities was not conceptualized as leading to negative personal outcomes. Certainly there are individuals who have decided that there is no transcendent reality or larger plan that governs the universe; this physical world represents the sum total of reality. These individuals do not necessarily become "stunted" in terms of emotional growth and maturity because of this perspective. Rather, it was believed that any negative psychological consequences to spirituality and religiousness would be found not in their absence but in disturbances people encountered in their relationship with the transcendent. The RC scale was developed to capture aspects of distress, alienation, and avoidance in our involvement with a transcendent reality. Those negative forces could have adverse consequences for other areas of psychological functioning (e.g., Johnson & Hayes, 2003; see also Chapter 25 in this volume).

To test those assumptions, Piedmont et al. (2007) examined the relations between the ASPIRES scales and Axis II pathology in two independent samples. The aim was to determine whether spirituality and religiousness were negatively related to the experience of psychopathology. Using measures of Axis II dysfunction as the criterion variables, hierarchical multiple regression analyses were employed to examine the incremental predictive power of the ASPIRES scales over the FFM personality domains. In both samples, which used different measures of psychopathology, the results were the same: Only the RC scale emerged as the single, significant predictor over personality. Thus, any associations found between spirituality and pathology appear to be artificial and are most likely a function of the spirituality scales' overlap with either personality or RC.

Using SEM, the causal precedence of RC was modeled. Of the various models tested, the one positing personality and RC as causes of Axis II functioning was best supported by the data. If this model is correct, then perceived disturbances in our relationship with a Transcendent reality could have important implications for one's psychological stability. RC appears to be a significant predictor of psychological distress and may represent an important clinical construct, as suggested in other work on religious or spiritual struggle (for reviews, see Chapter 25, this volume and Volume 2, Chapter 22, this handbook). The findings suggest that the lack of spirituality does not lead to impairment; rather, the independence of the ST scales from measures of characterological pathology indicates that spirituality may serve as a useful therapeutic resource for treating psychopathology (for examples on how spiritual interventions can be employed with clients with Axis II issues, see Keks & D'Souza, 2003; Khalsa, 2005). These findings suggest that it is important to address RC as a potential impediment to health and well-being (see Volume 2, Chapter 22, this handbook).

CONCLUSION

From the very beginning of American psychology in the latter part of the 19th century, spirituality and religiousness have been seen as constructs having important implications for personality and psychological functioning. Over the years, many theorists outlined how and why our search for the sacred through both personal and organizational efforts was so influential in terms of directing behavior, organizing the sense of self, and contributing to ongoing growth and development. Although interest in these variables may have ebbed and flowed over the years, there is no doubt that spirituality and religiousness have experienced a scientific renaissance in the past 20 years (Emmons & Paloutzian, 2003). One reason for this renewed interest is that research has shown that these constructs have numerous behavioral, cognitive, social, emotional, genetic, and neurobiological correlates, underscoring their value as key psychological qualities.

Although this chapter examined only the relations of spirituality and religiousness with personality traits and functioning, we see the findings presented here as clear and compelling. The constructs of religiousness and spirituality provide unique insights into human motivation not contained by other personality dimensions, and we hypothesize that they may even operate as causal agents influencing levels of well-being, resilience, and adaptiveness. But perhaps the most interesting aspect of spirituality and religiousness is that they represent what we believe to be a *uniquely* human quality (Frankl, 1969; Maslow, 1970b; Sperry, 2001; see also Chapter 14 in this volume). No other species shares our capacity for creating such a broad sense of personal meaning, for understanding our lives against an eternal time frame. As Baumeister, Bauer, and Lloyd (2010) noted:

> The capacity to think about the future and orient behavior toward it, beyond the press of the immediate stimulus environment, is arguably one of the most important advances in human cognition, and it may be an essential step in making culture and civilization possible. (p. 76)

Thus, when studying spirituality and religiousness, we are really exploring qualities that create our experience of the universe and represent our quintessential nature.

References

Adler, A. (1998). *Understanding human nature: The psychology of personality*. Center City, MN: Hazelden. (Original work published 1927)

Allport, G. W. (1950). *The individual and his religion*. New York, NY: Macmillan.

Allport, G. W. (1955). *Becoming: Basic considerations for a psychology of personality*. New Haven, CT: Yale University Press.

Ashton, M. C., Lee, K., & Goldberg, L. R. (2004). A hierarchical analysis of 1, 710 English personality-descriptive adjectives. *Journal of Personality and Social Psychology, 87*, 707–721. doi:10.1037/0022-3514.87.5.707

Baumeister, R. F., Bauer, I. M., & Lloyd, S. A. (2010). Choice, free will, and religion. *Psychology of Religion and Spirituality, 2*, 67–82. doi:10.1037/a0018455

Costa, P. T., Jr., & McCrae, R. R. (1994). "Set like plaster"? Evidence for the stability of adult personality. In T. F. Heatherton & J. L. Weinberger (Eds.), *Can personality change?* (pp. 21–40). Washington, DC: American Psychological Association. doi:10.1037/10143-002

Costa, P. T., Jr., & McCrae, R. R. (1995). Primary traits of Eysenck's P-E-N system: Three- and five-factor solutions. *Journal of Personality and Social Psychology, 69*, 308–317. doi:10.1037/0022-3514.69.2.308

Dalby, P. (2006). Is there a process of spiritual change or development associated with ageing? A critical review of research. *Aging and Mental Health, 10*, 4–12. doi:10.1080/13607860500307969

Dickens, C. (2010). *A Christmas carol*. Lexington, KY: Tribeca Books. (Original work published 1843)

Donahue, M. J. (1985). Intrinsic and extrinsic religiousness: Review and meta-analysis. *Journal of Personality and Social Psychology, 48*, 400–419. doi:10.1037/0022-3514.48.2.400

Emmons, R. A., & Paloutzian, R. F. (2003). The psychology of religion. *Annual Review of Psychology, 54*, 377–402. doi:10.1146/annurev.psych.54.101601.145024

Eysenck, H. (1951). The organization of personality. *Journal of Personality, 20*, 101–117. doi:10.1111/j.1467-6494.1951.tb01515.x

Eysenck, H. (1978). Superfactors P, E and N in a comprehensive factor space. *Multivariate Behavioral Research, 13*, 475–481. doi:10.1207/s15327906mbr1304_7

Eysenck, H. (1990). Genetic and environmental contributions to individual differences: The three major dimensions of personality. *Journal of Personality, 58*, 245–261. doi:10.1111/j.1467-6494.1990.tb00915.x

Francis, L. J. (1991). personality attitude towards religion among adult churchgoers in England. *Psychological Reports, 69*, 791–794.

Francis, L. J. (1992). Is psychoticism really a dimension of personality fundamental to religiosity? *Personality and Individual Differences, 13*, 645–652. doi:10.1016/0191-8869(92)90235-H

Francis, L. J. (1993). Personality and religion among college students in the UK. *Personality and Individual Differences, 14*, 619–622. doi:10.1016/0191-8869(93)90159-Z

Francis, L. J. (2005). *Faith and psychology: Personality, religion, and the individual*. London, England: Darton, Longman & Todd.

Francis, L. J., & Jackson, C. (2003). Eysenck's dimensional model of personality and religion: Are religious people more neurotic? *Mental Health, Religion, and Culture, 6*, 87–100. doi:10.1080/1367467031000086279

Francis, L. J., & Pearson, P. R. (1985). Psychoticism and religiosity among 15-year olds. *Personality and Individual Differences, 6*, 397–398. doi:10.1016/0191-8869(85)90066-2

Frankl, V. (1959). *Man's search for meaning*. Boston, MA: Beacon.

Frankl, V. (1964). The will to meaning. *Christian Century, 81*(17), 515–517.

Frankl, V. (1969). *The will to meaning: Foundations and applications of logotherapy*. New York, NY: Meridian.

Freud, S. (1950). *Totem and taboo*. New York, NY: Norton. (Original work published 1913)

Freud, S. (1961). *The future of an illusion*. New York, NY: Norton. (Original work published 1927)

Goldberg, L. R. (1990). An alternative "description of personality": The Big Five structure. *Journal of Personality and Social Psychology, 59*, 1216–1229. doi:10.1037/0022-3514.59.6.1216

Golden, J., Piedmont, R. L., Ciarrocchi, J. W., & Rodgerson, T. (2004). Spirituality and burnout: An incremental validity study. *Journal of Psychology and Theology, 32*, 115–125.

Haslam, N., Whelan, J., & Bastian, B. (2009). Big Five traits mediate associations between values and subjective well-being. *Personality and Individual Differences, 46*, 40–42. doi:10.1016/j.paid.2008.09.001

Heaven, P. C. L., & Ciarrochi, J. (2007). Personality and religious values among adolescents: A three-wave longitudinal analysis. *British Journal of Psychology, 98*, 681–694. doi:10.1348/000712607X187777

Hill, P. C., Pargament, K. I., Hood, R. W., McCullough, M. E., Swyers, J. P., Larson, D. B., & Zinnbauer, B. J. (2000). Conceptualizing religion and spirituality: Points of commonality, points of departure. *Journal for the Theory of Social Behaviour, 30*, 51–77. doi:10.1111/1468-5914.00119

James, W. (1982). *The varieties of religious experience*. New York, NY: Penguin Books. (Original work published 1902)

Johnson, C. V., & Hayes, J. A. (2003). Troubled spirits: Prevalence and prediction of religious and spiritual concerns among university students and counseling center clients. *Journal of Counseling Psychology, 50*, 409–419. doi:10.1037/0022-0167.50.4.409

Jung, C. G. (1966). *Psychology and religion*. New Haven, CT: Yale University Press. (Original work published 1938)

Jung, C. G. (1971). *Psychological types*. Princeton, NJ: Princeton University Press. (Original work published 1921)

Keks, N., & D'Souza, R. (2003). Spirituality and psychosis. *Australasian Psychiatry, 11*, 170–171. doi:10.1046/j.1039-8562.2003.00510.x

Kern, M. L., & Friedman, H. S. (2008). Do conscientious individuals live longer? A quantitative review. *Health Psychology, 27*, 505–512. doi:10.1037/0278-6133.27.5.505

Khalsa, M. K. (2005). Alternative treatments for borderline and Narcissistic personality disorders. In S. G. Kijares & G. S. Khalsa (Eds.), *The psychospiritual clinician's handbook: Alternative methods for understanding and treating mental disorders* (pp. 163–181). New York, NY: Haworth Press.

MacDonald, D. A. (2000). Spirituality: Description, measurement and relation to the Five-Factor Model of personality. *Journal of Personality, 68*, 153–197. doi:10.1111/1467-6494.t01-1-00094

Marmor, G. S., & Montemayor, R. (1977). The cross-lagged panel design: A review. *Perceptual and Motor Skills, 45*, 883–893. doi:10.2466/pms.1977.45.3.883

Maslow, A. H. (1970a). *Motivation and personality* (3rd ed.). New York, NY: Longman.

Maslow, A. H. (1970b). *Religions, values, and peak-experiences.* New York, NY: Penguin Books.

McCrae, R. R., & Costa, P. T., Jr. (1997). Personality trait structure as a human universal. *American Psychologist, 52*, 509–516. doi:10.1037/0003-066X.52.5.509

McCullough, M. E., Enders, C. K., Brion, S. L., & Jain, A. R. (2005). The varieties of religious development in adulthood: A longitudinal investigation of religion and rational choice. *Journal of Personality and Social Psychology, 89*, 78–89. doi:10.1037/0022-3514.89.1.78

McCullough, M. E., Tsang, J., & Brion, S. (2003). Personality traits in adolescence as predictors of religiousness in early adulthood: Findings from the Terman longitudinal study. *Personality and Social Psychology Bulletin, 29*, 980–991. doi:10.1177/0146167203253210

Miller, W. R., & Thoresen, C. E. (2003). Spirituality, religion, and health: An emerging research field. *American Psychologist, 58*, 24–35. doi:10.1037/0003-066X.58.1.24

Murray-Swank, N., & Pargament, K. I. (2005). God, where are you? Evaluating a spiritually-integrated intervention for sexual abuse. *Mental Health, Religion, and Culture, 8*, 191–203. doi:10.1080/13694670500138866

Oud, J. H. L. (2007). Continuous time modeling of reciprocal relationships in the cross-lagged panel design. In S. Boker & M. Wenger (Eds.), *Data analytic techniques for dynamical systems* (pp. 87–129). Mahwah, NJ: Erlbaum.

Paloutzian, R. F., Richardson, J. T., & Rambo, L. R. (1999). Religious conversion and personality change. *Journal of Personality, 67*, 1047–1079. doi:10.1111/1467-6494.00082

Pargament, K. I., Smith, B. W., Koenig, H. G., & Perez, L. (1998). Patterns of positive and negative religious coping with major life stressors. *Journal for the Scientific Study of Religion, 37*, 710–724. doi:10.2307/1388152

Piedmont, R. L. (1999a). Does spirituality represent the sixth factor of personality? Spiritual transcendence and the five-factor model. *Journal of Personality, 67*, 985–1013. doi:10.1111/1467-6494.00080

Piedmont, R. L. (1999b). Strategies for using the five-factor model of personality in religious research. *Journal of Psychology and Theology, 27*, 338–350.

Piedmont, R. L. (2001). Spiritual transcendence and the scientific study of spirituality. *Journal of Rehabilitation, 67*, 4–14.

Piedmont, R. L. (2004). Spiritual transcendence as a predictor of psychosocial outcome from an outpatient substance abuse program. *Psychology of Addictive Behaviors, 18*, 213–222. doi:10.1037/0893-164X.18.3.213

Piedmont, R. L. (2007). Cross-cultural generalizability of the Spiritual Transcendence Scale to the Philippines: Spirituality as a human universal. *Mental Health, Religion, and Culture, 10*, 89–107. doi:10.1080/13694670500275494

Piedmont, R. L. (2009). The contribution of religiousness and spirituality to subjective well-being and satisfaction with life. In L. J. Francis (Ed.), *International handbook of education for spirituality, care and well-being* (pp. 89–105). New York, NY: Springer. doi:10.1007/978-1-4020-9018-9_6

Piedmont, R. L. (2010). *Assessment of spirituality and religious sentiments, technical manual* (2nd ed.). Timonium, MD: Author.

Piedmont, R. L. (in press). Overview and development of a trait-based measure of numinous constructs: The Assessment of Spirituality and Religious Sentiments (ASPIRES) scale. In L. Miller (Ed.), *Oxford handbook of psychology of spirituality and consciousness.* New York, NY: Oxford University Press.

Piedmont, R. L., Ciarrocchi, J. W., Dy-Liacco, G. S., & Williams, J. E. G. (2009). The empirical and conceptual value of the Spiritual Transcendence and Religious Involvement scales for personality research. *Psychology of Religion and Spirituality, 1*, 162–179. doi:10.1037/a0015883

Piedmont, R. L., Hassinger, C. J., Rhorer, J., Sherman, M. F., Sherman, N. C., & Williams, J. E. G. (2007). The relations among spirituality and religiosity and Axis II functioning in two college samples. *Research in the Social Scientific Study of Religion, 18*, 53–73. doi:10.1163/ej.9789004158511.i-301.24

Piedmont, R. L., & Leach, M. M. (2002). Cross-cultural generalizability of the Spiritual Transcendence Scale in India: Spirituality as a universal aspect of human experience. *American Behavioral Scientist, 45*, 1888–1901. doi:10.1177/0002764202045012011

Piedmont, R. L., Mapa, A. T., & Williams, J. E. G. (2006). A factor analysis of the Fetzer/NIA Brief Multidimensional Measure of Religiousness/Spirituality (MMRS). *Research in the Social Scientific Study of Religion, 17*, 177–196.

Powell, L. H., Shahabi, L., & Thoresen, C. E. (2003). Religion and spirituality: Linkages to physical health. *American Psychologist, 58*, 36–52. doi:10.1037/0003-066X.58.1.36

Rican, P., & Janosova, P. (2010). Spirituality as a basic aspect of personality: A cross-cultural verification of Piedmont's model. *The International Journal for the Psychology of Religion, 20*, 2–13. doi:10.1080/10508610903418053

Rizzuto, A. (1979). *The birth of the living God: A psychoanalytic study*. Chicago, IL: University of Chicago Press.

Rizzuto, A. (1998). *Why did Freud reject God? A psychodynamic interpretation*. New Haven, CT: Yale University Press.

Ruckmick, C. A. (1920). *The Brevity book on psychology*. Chicago, IL: Brevity.

Saroglou, V. (2002). Religion and the five factors of personality: A meta-analytic review. *Personality and Individual Differences, 32*, 15–25. doi:10.1016/S0191-8869(00)00233-6

Saroglou, V. (2010). Religiousness as a cultural adaptation of basic traits: A five-factor model perspective. *Personality and Social Psychology Review, 14*, 108–125. doi:10.1177/1088868309352322

Saucier, G., & Goldberg, L. R. (1998). What is beyond the Big Five? *Journal of Personality, 66*, 495–524. doi:10.1111/1467-6494.00022

Saucier, G., & Skrzypinska, K. (2006). Spiritual but not religious? Evidence for two independent dimensions. *Journal of Personality, 74*, 1257–1292. doi:10.1111/j.1467-6494.2006.00409.x

Sawatzky, R., Ratner, P. A., & Chiu, L. (2005). A meta-analysis of the relationship between spirituality and quality of life. *Social Indicators Research, 72*, 153–188. doi:10.1007/s11205-004-5577-x

Sperry, L. (2001). *Spirituality in clinical practice: Incorporating the spiritual dimension in psychotherapy and counseling*. New York, NY: Routledge.

White, J., Joseph, S., & Neil, A. (1995). Religiosity, psychoticism and schizotypal traits. *Personality and Individual Differences, 19*, 847–851. doi:10.1016/S0191-8869(95)00129-8

Wink, P., Ciciolla, L., Dillon, M., & Tracy, A. (2007). Religiousness, spiritual seeking, and personality: Findings from a longitudinal study. *Journal of Personality, 75*, 1051–1070. doi:10.1111/j.1467-6494.2007.00466.x

Wink, P., & Dillon, M. (2002). Spiritual development across the adult life course: Findings from a longitudinal study. *Journal of Adult Development, 9*, 79–94. doi:10.1023/A:1013833419122

Wink, P., & Dillon, M. (2008). Religiousness, spirituality, and psychosocial functioning in late adulthood: Findings from a longitudinal study. *Psychology of Religion and Spirituality*, (1), 102–115. doi:10.1037/1941-1022.S.1.102

Woodworth, R. S. (1940). *Psychology* (4th ed.). New York, NY: Holt.

CHAPTER 10

SPIRITUAL MODELING AND THE SOCIAL LEARNING OF SPIRITUALITY AND RELIGION

Doug Oman

What the outstanding person does, others will try to do. The standards such people create will be followed by the whole world.

—Bhagavad Gita (3:21)

Let us preach [God] without preaching, not by words but by our example, by the catching force, the sympathetic influence of what we do.

—John Henry Newman (quoted in Oman, Flinders, & Thoresen, 2008, p. 90)

Throughout history, religious traditions have emphasized the value of keeping company and attending to the example of good or holy persons, arguing that people tend to become more like those with whom they associate. The power of example has been recognized in modern scientific psychology, and its ability to activate and channel behavior has been documented abundantly. Bandura (1986) summarized existing evidence as indicating that

> one can get people to behave altruistically, to volunteer their services, to delay or to seek gratification, to show affection, to behave punitively, to prefer certain foods and apparel, to converse on particular topics, to be inquisitive or passive, to think innovatively or conventionally, and to engage in almost any course or action by having such conduct exemplified. (p. 206)

Social learning must be considered among the major candidates for explaining why and how people become spiritual or religious, and why their spirituality or religion assumes a particular form. A social learning view of spiritual and religious engagement is also amenable to many practical applications. It may be used by people who seek to deepen their own learning of spirituality or religion as well as by human service professionals who have identified spiritual or religious factors as relevant to client well-being (Oman et al., 2009). And for millennia, social learning has been of interest to religious and spiritual teachers and educators (see epigraphs). Religious educators often place high value on the power of example, saying that religion and spirituality are "caught, not taught." A social learning perspective therefore represents important common ground shared by scientific and religious communities.

Put another way, social learning perspectives are compatible not only with scientific explanations of religion and spirituality from the outside (known as *etic* explanations) but also with many understandings from within religious traditions of how religion and spirituality are learned (*emic* perspectives). Social learning perspectives therefore may represent an important resource for dialogue between scientific and religious communities and for attempts to constructively integrate scientific, religious, and spiritual insights (Jones, 1994; Watts & Dutton, 2006). Nor need social learning explanations be regarded as necessarily competing with most other scientific explanations of religion and spirituality (Rossano, 2010). Rather, social learning perspectives, which tend to emphasize immediate (proximate) causes, are often complementary to other explanations on the basis of more distal factors. As

DOI: 10.1037/14045-010
APA Handbook of Psychology, Religion, and Spirituality: Vol. 1. Context, Theory, and Research, K. I. Pargament (Editor-in-Chief)
Copyright © 2013 by the American Psychological Association. All rights reserved.

Pargament, Koenig, and Perez (2000, p. 521) suggested, there is often "no need to choose" between explanations.

Recently, the term *spiritual modeling* has emerged to characterize the social learning of spiritual or religious beliefs, attitudes, and practices (Bandura, 2003; Oman & Thoresen, 2003b; Oman et al., 2009). A spiritual modeling perspective can potentially be applied to almost any definition of religion and spirituality (Oman & Thoresen, 2003b). This is important, because spirituality and religion have been defined in many ways, some wider and some narrower, as discussed in the introduction (see Chapter 1 in this volume; see also Oman & Thoresen, 2003b). In particular, a spiritual modeling perspective can be applied to the integrative paradigm used in this volume, which views religion and spirituality as related to a search for the sacred.

The added value of a spiritual modeling perspective is most apparent when it is recognized that religion and spirituality do not merely represent compendia of dogmas and codes of behavior ("Thou shalts"). Rather, a central component is often an attempt to exercise virtues and other high-level learned skills related to wise living and effective self-regulation. Such high-level and complex skills frequently involve what philosophers have called a *tacit* dimension, that is, components that cannot be successfully reduced to a collection of explicit rational rules (Oman & Thoresen, 2003b). For example, religious and spiritual wisdom traditions often appear to endorse contradictory principles (e.g., "Answer not a fool according to his folly, lest thou also be like unto him. Answer a fool according to his folly, lest he be wise in his own conceit," Proverbs 26:4–5). But as Clements noted,

> nothing irrational or false is implied by setting side by side two contrasting instructions. . . . The discerning hearer and reader must learn when to apply one guideline or the other, since each may be true in a specific situation. . . . The goal is to create a wise person, rather than to define the rules of what wisdom dictates should be done on particular occasions. (quoted in Oman & Thoresen, 2003b, p. 151)

In this chapter, we will review key elements of social learning theory as applied to spiritual modeling, discussing evidence for spiritual modeling processes in religious traditions. Next, we review recent empirical and theoretical work on spiritual modeling. We close by suggesting implications, limits, and future directions.

SOCIAL LEARNING: THEORY AND APPLICATION TO SPIRITUALITY

As developed in recent psychological research, primarily by Oman and Thoresen (2003b) and their colleagues, spiritual modeling as a research field has extensively employed Bandura's (1986, 1997) social cognitive theory (SCT), viewed as offering "perhaps the most fully developed account of social learning" (Oman et al., 2009, p. 427). Bandura's approach has been extraordinarily influential both theoretically and in generating effective practical applications in fields ranging from education and health care to athletics and organizational functioning.

SCT recognizes a wide range of influences from models on behavior and learning. According to Bandura, "modeling influences can serve as instructors, inhibitors, disinhibitors, facilitators, stimulus enhancers, and emotion arousers" (1986, p. 50). The process of learning from models—referred to as *observational learning*—is seen as enabling people to learn many behaviors and skills much more efficiently or safely than would be possible through painful trial and error or even through direct instruction and reinforcement. Indeed, in Bandura's view, "most human behavior is learned by observation through modeling" (1986, p. 47). Furthermore, modeling influences "operate principally through their informative function," that is, by providing information that is assimilated by the observer (Bandura, 1986, p. 51). People assimilate information about models through observing, which takes place in a variety of ways: conscious or unconscious, ad hoc, or systematically pursued within a community context.

Bandura's (1986) SCT describes four main processes that govern observational learning: attention, retention, reproduction, and motivation. In Bandura's words,

> *Attentional processes* regulate exploration and perception of modeled activities; through *retention processes*, transitory experiences are converted for memory representation into symbolic conceptions that serve as internal models for response production and standards for response correction; *production processes* govern the organization of constituent subskills into new response patterns; and *motivation processes* determine whether or not observationally acquired competencies will be put to use. (p. 51)

Importantly, Bandura (1986) noted that "a special virtue of modeling is that it can transmit simultaneously knowledge of wide applicability to vast numbers of people . . . by drawing on conceptions of behavior portrayed in words and images" (p. 47). SCT thus offers a unified view of observational learning that encompasses not only learning from face-to-face models in the community but also learning from models who are apprehended through visual, written, or even oral media, such as representations of spiritual figures encountered in sermons or dharma talks.

Beyond these four foundational processes, Bandura's (1986) SCT describes a wide range of secondary principles, too numerous to summarize, that in particular circumstances may influence how observational learning occurs. Most prominently, SCT views motivation as often strongly affected by perceptions of *self-efficacy*—that is, one's perceived ability to organize and execute the types of actions needed in a particular area of human functioning. Self-efficacy is a "pivotal" construct in SCT that is widely used in practical applications (Bandura, 1997, p. 35). Motivation is also influenced by knowledge about the likely risks and benefits of different courses of action that is gained "vicariously," by observing models' attitudes and experiences (Bandura, 1986, p. 283). Other less prominent SCT principles of potential relevance include the idea that motivation and self-efficacy can be undermined by hypocrisy that lowers a model's attractiveness and fosters rejection of the standards they propagate (p. 344). SCT also affirms that a major determinant of human lives can be providential or "fortuitous" events. Although such events are unpredictable, SCT sees a role for personal effort in preparing to respond wisely. Paraphrasing Pasteur, Bandura (1986) asserted that "chance favors the prepared mind" (p. 30)—an idea parallel to traditional religious teachings on the value of effort in preparing for providential grace (*kripa*, in Sanskrit).

Oman and Thoresen (2003b) articulated how these SCT processes and principles apply to spirituality and religion, and conveyed the scope of the phenomenon with several examples (adapted as Table 10.1). They and their colleagues have distinguished between *community-based models* and *prominent models*, the latter being widely known human beings who might be encountered through tradition (e.g., scriptural figures or saints) or media (e.g., Mother Teresa, Mahatma Gandhi, Nelson Mandela). They speculated that community-based and prominent models might perform "identifiable and complementary functions" in creating an optimal context for spiritual growth (Oman & Thoresen, 2003a, p. 207). For a more refined typology, one might disaggregate prominent models into subtypes or incorporate supplemental categories for God (whose interactive personality appears in scriptures), animals, fictional characters, and other agents (see Oman et al., 2009; Silberman, 2003).

Oman and Thoresen (2003b, p. 55) argued that "with greater or lesser sagacity," religious traditions often have attempted systematically to facilitate each of the four major observational learning processes for promoting spiritual growth. For example, worship services often include scriptural readings that direct attention to the words and deeds of major spiritual figures such as Jesus, Moses, or the Buddha. Over time, many scriptural passages are read repeatedly, fostering retention. Religious traditions encourage supportive communal fellowship with others who can function as positive spiritual models, and emphasize important spiritual qualities, such as charity, truthfulness, and humility, to be reproduced in daily life. Finally, motivation to persist over time in a religious or spiritual search is supported by worshipping together regularly, music, encouraging

TABLE 10.1

Illustrative Examples of Spiritual Modeling (Observational Spiritual Learning)

Model	Information medium	Description of observational spiritual learning
Fellow congregants	Informal conversation and fellowship	A young man struggling with newfound family responsibilities uses older members of the same synagogue as models for how to balance work responsibilities with marital responsibilities that are perceived as sacred.
Spiritual director	Structured relationship	A middle-aged man striving to make service to God a "master motive" in life finds that fellow congregants offer insufficient models, but that within the confines of a structured relationship, a local spiritual director can effectively model attitudes that promote spiritual growth.
Anonymous 19th-century mystic	Reading	An elderly retired woman, dwelling in a small town and attempting to follow the apostolic injunction to "pray without ceasing," finds that she learns more from the spiritual search chronicled in an anonymous 19th-century autobiographical work, *The Way of a Pilgrim*, than she learns from any living person that she knows.
Scriptural figures	Meditation and meditative reading	A middle-aged woman, trained to be a minister but subsequently having left her church, continues her practice of *Lectio Divina* (prayerful and deliberate sacred reading) as a way to deepen her assimilation of scriptural wisdom narratives and maxims.
Scriptural figures	Verbal rituals	A teenage girl learns to forgive her dysfunctional family by frequently attending religious services, drawing inspiration from the repeated liturgical retelling of gospel narratives of forgiveness.

Note. From "Spiritual Modeling: A Key to Spiritual and Religious Growth?" by D. Oman and C. E. Thoresen, 2003, *The International Journal for the Psychology of Religion, 13*, p. 157. Copyright 2003 by Taylor & Francis. Adapted with permission.

testimonials, and celebrating benefits obtained in this life and perhaps after death. Religious figures, especially the founders and mystics within major traditions, offer repeated testimony to the great peace ("which passeth all understanding," Philippians 4:7) and happiness ("that never leaves," Dhammapada 1:2) that come to persons who persist in the spiritual quest. Religious traditions also endorse practices that appear to improve the quality of attention itself, such as meditation, a practice that has been characterized as "in essence, the effort to retrain attention" (Goleman, 1988, p. 169; Lutz et al., 2009). Oman (2010) noted that meditative and contemplative practices across many traditions include exposure to spiritual modeling information.

Furthermore, as noted, religious traditions themselves contain affirmations of the importance of spiritual modeling. Scriptures sometimes explicitly urge emulation, as when Jesus recounted the story of the Good Samaritan and told his listeners to "go and do likewise" (Luke 10:30–37). Also in Christianity, spiritual modeling is affirmed in the teachings and title of *The Imitation of Christ*, a 15th-century devotional book widely read by Protestants, Catholics, and Orthodox alike, and by slogans in popular culture, such as "What Would Jesus Do?" Islam celebrates Muhammad as a "beautiful exemplar" (*uswa hasana*, Qur'an 33:21). Because of the importance of his example, a central place in Islamic culture is given to *hadith*, the science of the authenticated narratives of the Prophet's sayings and actions (Schimmel, 1985, p. 26). Ancient Hindu scriptures explicitly affirm the power of spiritual modeling (see epigraph). In some forms of Buddhism, "bodhisattvas and buddhas are humanized figures, more to be emulated as models of behavior, than to be worshipped for miraculous efficacy" (Zhiru, 2000, p. 86). In Judaism,

> the Torah's instruction to "cleave unto God" [Deut. 11:22] can be done, according to interpretations, through cleaving to sages. . . . When spiritual role models can't be observed, the same function of learning can be achieved by hearing or reading stories about their lives. (Silberman, 2003, p. 177)

As discussed later, Oman et al. (2009) introduced the term *spiritual modeling metabeliefs* to describe an individual's or group's beliefs about the value or workings of spiritual models.

The cross-cultural pervasiveness of spiritual modeling awareness and practices suggests that, with greater or lesser sagacity, many religious adherents throughout history have intentionally sought to use the power of spiritual modeling to assist them in a spiritual quest. But intentionality may not always be at work because vicarious modeling influences can powerfully operate through exposure, even without engaging a person's conscious intention (Hassin, Uleman, & Bargh, 2005). Indeed, Wuthnow (1998) has suggested that before the 1960s, a more "taken for granted" spirituality allowed many Americans to unconsciously—but nevertheless observationally—learn important patterns of spiritual behavior. Wuthnow argued, however, that such a taken-for-granted or "dwelling" spirituality is becoming increasingly difficult in modern society, as traditional forms of family and community break down, partly because of economic forces.

Learning from spiritual models does not constitute the whole of religion or spirituality. Oman and Thoresen (2007b) argued for a *spiritual modeling perspective* that sensitizes an observer to how spiritual modeling dynamically interacts with other components of spirituality and religion. For example, beliefs, practices, and spiritual models make up three important facets of most religious and spiritual traditions, and they mutually interact over time. As summarized in Figure 10.1, one's beliefs (e.g., Catholic vs. Protestant) generally influence who one is most likely to view as a spiritual model (e.g., Ignatius of Loyola vs. Martin Luther). Beliefs also influence how strongly one may be motivated to engage in various spiritual practices (e.g., priest-mediated confession vs. scriptural reading). Similarly, one's experiences with spiritual practices (e.g., prayer, meditation, or spiritual reading) may influence one's beliefs as well as facilitate identifying and learning from spiritual models. Finally, even though major faiths revere similar character strengths and virtues (Peterson & Seligman, 2004), the precise identities of an individual's primary spiritual models (e.g., the Pope vs. Muhammad) may powerfully shape a multitude of details about beliefs and practices that are worthy of emulation (e.g., attending confession vs. praying toward Mecca).

Spiritual modeling also dynamically interacts with religious coping. In Figure 10.1, religious and spiritual coping is represented as a form of practice. On the one hand, spiritual models may influence one's *choice* of coping strategies. Conversely, *turning to a specific spiritual model,* and giving his or her example extra effort and attention, may sometimes be a component of a religious coping strategy. For example, Pargament (1997, p. 265) has noted that a family in turmoil can follow the example of Joseph or the victim of a crime can try to follow the example of Jesus. A small number of studies have assessed the attempt to learn from spiritual models as a coping strategy (see Abu Raiya, Pargament, Mahoney, & Trevino, 2008).

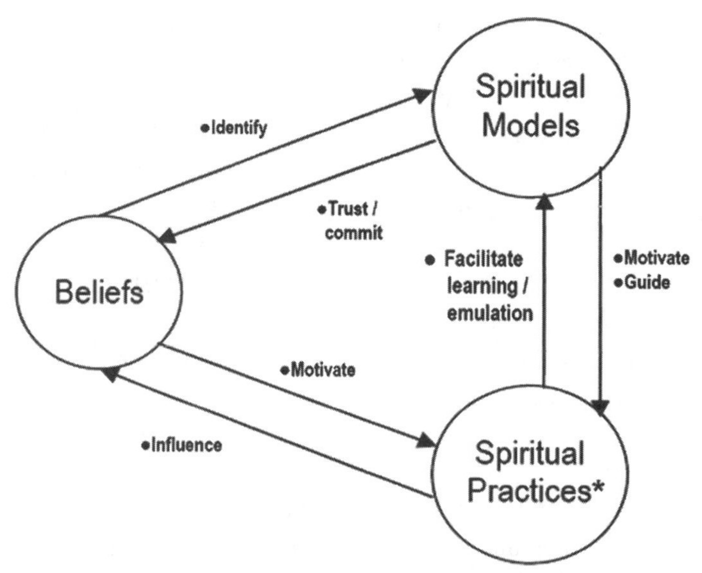

FIGURE 10.1. How spiritual models reciprocally interact with other components of spirituality. From *Spirit, Science, and Health: How the Spiritual Mind Fuels Physical Wellness* (p. 45), by T. G. Plante and C. E. Thoresen (Eds.), 2007, Westport, CT: Praeger. Copyright 2007 by ABC-CLIO, Inc. Adapted with permission.

EMPIRICAL STUDIES OF SPIRITUAL MODELING PROCESSES AND OUTCOMES

Evidence for the social learning of religion and spirituality has long been accumulating in studies of childhood and adolescent spiritual and religious development. In a recent review of family influences, Boyatzis, Dollahite, and Marks (2006; see also Chapters 20, 27, and 28 in this volume) characterized the family as "probably the most potent influence—for better or for worse—on children's spiritual and religious development" (p. 305). The authors noted many studies indicating that children's religiosity appears consistent with their parents' religiosity on various behavioral measures, such as attendance at services and prayer (e.g., Francis & Brown, 1991; Regnerus, Smith, & Smith, 2004). *Beliefs* about religion also display some intergenerational consistency. Okagaki, Hammond, and Seamon (1999) reported that young adults' (18–25 years) perceptions of their parents religious beliefs mediated the relation between parents' beliefs and young adults' beliefs, a finding consistent with SCT's emphasis on the role of information mediation (see Table 10.1, column 2).

Some studies have examined how parents seek to transmit spirituality and religion. A qualitative study reported that deeply religious parents in diverse faith traditions regarded "practicing [and parenting] what you preach" as the single most important way to properly raise their children (Marks, 2004). A number of other studies have examined parent–child dialogue about religion and spirituality, which may provide the child with a wider and more dynamic view of parent religious and spiritual attitudes, perhaps yielding richer modeling information (see Chapters 10 and 27 in this volume). Such dialogue has been found to predict increased concordance between parent–child religiosity (Boyatzis et al., 2006), and dialogue may support the encoding that facilitates psychological retention of observed modeling information (Oman & Thoresen, 2003b).

Evidence suggests that parents' influence on child spirituality and religiousness takes place first in the family but later operates in part through "channeling" of children into settings that support similar norms and practices, such as religious organizations or like-minded peer groups. Schwartz (2006) recently gathered self-report questionnaire data from 4,600 adolescents (mean age 16 years) regarding interactions with peers as well as parents. Factor analyses revealed two identical influences from each source (peers, parents): (a) faith modeling, or "demonstrated authenticity and consistency" of faith, and (b) faith dialogue, or "dyadic sharing and accountability" (Schwartz, 2006, p. 317). Both parent and peer faith modeling predicted adolescent religiosity. Furthermore, consistent with the channeling perspective, combined peer influences (modeling plus discussion) mediated combined parent influences on adolescent religiosity. Others have reported evidence for socialization influences not only from parent and peers but also from the school environment, suggesting a need for even wider ecological analyses of religiosity (Regnerus et al., 2004).

Mentoring by adults outside the family, another source of modeling influences, has also been examined. Evidence indicates that the work of Christian youth ministers supports numerous spiritual outcomes for youth. Youth commonly endorse strength of religious example (e.g., rated "strength of Christian example") as an important quality among youth ministers, indicating that spiritual modeling is a significant factor in youths' perceptions of their own spiritual development (Schwartz, Bukowski, & Aoki, 2006, p. 318). Schwartz et al. (2006) argued that similar spiritual modeling processes are likely to apply to non-Christian mentor figures, such as Jewish sages and Hindu gurus, although spiritual outcomes from these relations have received little study.

Although these studies reveal a good deal of information about the role of spiritual models in religious and spiritual development, few have sought to examine modeling influences in detail, or explored the implications of major social learning theories. Levenson, Aldwin, and D'Mello (2005) expressed concern that "granted the influence of socialization from a kind of 'black box' analysis, we remain in the dark about the process by which it occurs" (p. 150). However, a few recent studies, to which we now turn, have been more systematic in applying comprehensive social learning theories, especially SCT.

Measures and Surveys

A primary need in any scientific field is instruments to measure the phenomena of interest. Psychometric properties of two spiritual modeling instruments have been reported, both relying on data from the same geographically and ethnically diverse sample of college students ($N > 1{,}000$; Oman et al., 2009, 2012). Oman et al. (2009) reported on the Spiritual Modeling Index of Life Environments (SMILE), a detailed and wide-ranging self-report measure of perceptions concerning spiritual models. The SMILE defines spiritual models as everyday and prominent people who have functioned for respondents as exemplars of spiritual qualities, such as compassion, self-control, or faith. Several SMILE questions target efficacy perceptions and indicators of the four spiritual modeling processes identified in SCT. It is intended as a tool for going beyond a "black box" analysis, to probe more deeply into the psychological processes underlying spiritual modeling.

A detailed consideration of the SMILE conveys some of the challenges and opportunities in measuring spiritual models. The SMILE contains three parts, structured to allow earlier questions to set a context for later questions, somewhat analogously to a semistructured interview (Oman et al., 2009). The SMILE seeks to assess spirituality defined along the lines of theologian Paul Tillich's concept of ultimate concerns (Emmons, 1999). To discourage idiosyncratic respondent definitions of *spiritual*, the SMILE's introductory section uses ordinary language to introduce the idea that many people have beliefs about "skills or qualities viewed as 'helpful for what's most important/consequential in life" (Oman et al., 2009, p. 431). The term *spirituality* is then defined with reference to those skills. Slightly later in Part I of the SMILE, respondents are asked to rate their opinion of the degree of helpfulness for spirituality (i.e., for attaining ultimate concerns) of 14 character strengths and virtues, such as compassion, forgiveness, and faith (Peterson & Seligman, 2004). After terms are defined in this manner, Part II of the SMILE assesses respondents' perceived spiritual models in several *life environments* (e.g., family, school). Part III of the SMILE contains numerous "global assessments" that elicit spiritual modeling metabeliefs and other generalized perceptions about spiritual modeling.

Oman et al. (2009) reported the demographic, spiritual, and personality correlates of the SMILE (Parts I and II; full psychometrics and correlates of Part III are not yet available). The SMILE was well received, with about one third of college student respondents indicating that it made them reflect on their beliefs or on their life. For each respondent, Oman et al. (2009) computed a summary measure of perceived "overall spiritual model availability . . . conceived as a summary representation of (substantiated and important) spiritual modeling influences as shaped by both individual and environmental factors" (p. 442). This summary measure was constructed from responses about perceived models within family, school, and religious organization and among prominent individuals from both tradition and media. The summary measure demonstrated good 7-week test–retest reliability (r = .83) and patterns of correlation supporting convergent, divergent, and criterion-related validity. Summary model availability related in expected ways with demographic characteristics—for example, more models were reported by younger students, females, and those at religious rather than public universities.

Who is perceived most often as a spiritual model? Oman et al. (2009) reported that in the family environment, mothers (41%) were most commonly named, more often than fathers (20%) or grandmothers (18%); at school, friends (52%) were named more often than teachers (20%); and in religious organizations, clergy (48%) were named more often than fellow congregants (29%). The identities of the most highly cited models were generally unrelated to covariates, except for a few readily explainable exceptions (e.g., males were more likely to name fathers as models, and younger students were more likely to name teachers as models). Among prominent spiritual models, the six most commonly named were not restricted to Judeo-Christian traditions: Jesus (53%), the Buddha (10%), and Moses (6%; from before 1900), and Mother Teresa (32%), Mahatma Gandhi (24%), and Rev. Martin Luther King Jr. (16%; from after 1900). Surprisingly, participants self-identified as "neither spiritual nor religious," although citing significantly *fewer* prominent models, cited almost the *same* set of prominent models, and in similar proportions, as other participants. Oman et al. (2009) suggested that such similarity may reflect shared influences from schooling and mass media, or perhaps a paucity of highly regarded nonreligious models.

The Spiritual Modeling Self-Efficacy (SMSE) measure is a second spiritual modeling scale that was administered to the same college student cohort. Consisting of 10 items, the SMSE measures a respondent's perceived efficacy for learning from community-based and prominent models. Oman et al. (2012) reported that the SMSE's 10 items load on two strongly correlated subfactors (r = .64), corresponding to perceived efficacy for learning from spiritual models who are community based (five items) and prominent (five items). Total and subscale scores had good internal and 7-week test–retest reliability (αs > .85, rs > .70) and correlated with other constructs that support convergent, divergent, and criterion-related validity. Females scored significantly higher for learning from community-based models, but no gender differences were observed for prominent models. Conversely, younger students scored significantly higher for learning from prominent models, but no age differences existed for community-based models. A variety of other significant demographic differences were observed (e.g., high scores among Blacks), although it is unclear whether such findings generalize to all college students or to the larger adult population (Oman et al., 2012).

Finally, preliminary empirical work in this same college cohort has revealed small but statistically significant associations between the SMILE's summary spiritual modeling measure and a variety of health outcomes. Independent of demographics and socially desirable responding, favorable associations ($.08 \leq r \leq .13$, $p < .05$) were found with physical exercise, diet, adequate sleep, seatbelt use, lack of smoking, self-rated health, and life satisfaction. Compared with similar analyses of the frequency of attending religious services, a variable strongly linked to adult longevity, summary spiritual models in this cohort demonstrated stronger associations for all outcomes except smoking and diet (Oman & Thoresen, 2007b; Oman et al., 2005).

Interventions

Several SMILE and SMSE subscales have been used to evaluate spiritual modeling impacts of widely used meditation-based stress management interventions. Oman et al. (2007) used the SMILE and SMSE in a randomized trial that compared a wait-listed control group ($n = 15$) with two 8-week, 12-hr meditation interventions: (a) Mindfulness-Based Stress Reduction (MBSR, $n = 15$, Kabat-Zinn, 1990), and (b) Passage Meditation (PM, $n = 14$, Easwaran, 1978/2008). MBSR and PM each are based on a form of sitting meditation, and each includes several ancillary practices for integrating meditative states into the remainder of the day. To illustrate and support meditative states of mind, MBSR sessions often incorporate texts from spiritually oriented poets such as Rumi, Whitman, or Rilke, but MBSR does not otherwise systematically support learning from prominent or traditional spiritual models (see Volume 2, Chapter 10, this handbook). In contrast, the PM method of sitting meditation involves focusing directly on spiritual modeling information in the form of a memorized self-chosen text from a scripture or a major spiritual figure. Examples of meditation passages include the 23rd Psalm, the Prayer of Saint Francis, Saint Paul's Epistle on Love, and the Buddha's Discourse on Good Will. Oman et al. (2007) argued that the PM program's meditation method plus ancillary practices supports all four major spiritual modeling processes:

> Memorizing and meditating upon the Psalmist's expressions of faith in the 23rd Psalm, for example, fosters *attention* and *retention* of his beliefs and attitudes . . . . *Motivation*, a third process, is fostered by the positive experiential testimonies contained in many meditation passages (e.g., "my cup runneth over"). The fourth process, *reproduction in behavior* of spiritual qualities, is fostered by ancillary PM program practices . . . such as focused attention and putting others first. (p. 476; emphasis in original)

All participants were assessed at baseline, immediately after meditation training, and 8 weeks later. Results revealed gains in PM group participants on several measures of spiritual modeling. In comparison with the MBSR and control groups, the PM group showed significantly larger increases in the perceived availability of pre-1900 spiritual models ($d = .78$, $p < .05$, Q7 of SMILE). Significantly larger comparative increases were also observed in self-efficacy for learning from prominent or traditional spiritual models ($d = .92$, $p < .05$, prominent model subscale of SMSE) and in the perceived influence of prominent or traditional spiritual models ($d = .81$, $p < .05$, Q9 of SMILE). Changes in control group and MBSR participants did not differ from each other on any spiritual modeling outcomes (although both PM and MBSR groups showed reduced stress and increased forgiveness, compared with controls). Oman et al. (2007) noted that other spiritual modeling influences could potentially emerge with continued practice of either PM or MBSR, but they speculated that the PM group's initial measured advantages in spiritual modeling might plausibly translate into steadier and more sustained spiritual growth over time.

Other Studies

Spiritual modeling variables have occasionally been empirically studied outside of the contexts noted in this chapter. For example, an item on perceptions of having learned from Muslim spiritual models was included in a study of anti-Muslim prejudice among Christians (Abu Raiya et al., 2008). Findings confirmed that learning from Muslim spiritual models, viewed as a form of religious coping, was associated with lower levels of perceived conflict with Muslims.

Some qualitative studies have examined spiritual models. For example, Danzig and Sands (2007) reported that new converts to Orthodox Judaism often use orthodox families and rabbis as spiritual models. Perhaps more dramatically, Steen, Kachorek, and Peterson (2003) reported that U.S. high school students, when asked to cite exemplars of various character strengths were "more likely to name biblical figures or civil rights leaders from the 1960s rather than exemplars from contemporary society" (p. 11). One student stated: "We just don't see many people today who are wise or honest or whatever because those sorts of things aren't valued as much in our society" (Steen et al., 2003, p. 11). More broadly, the topic of youths' perceived heroes, many of whom exemplify virtues related to spirituality, has generated research interest in countries ranging from China and Ireland to Norway and the United States (see Oman et al., 2008).

THEORETICAL WORK ON SPIRITUAL MODELING

Oman et al. (2009) extended spiritual modeling theory in several ways. Perhaps most important, they introduced the concept of *spiritual modeling metabeliefs*, defined as metacognitive beliefs regarding how and why people learn from spiritual models. Such beliefs may be implicitly or explicitly embedded in environments as well as within individuals. They help guide investments of attention and behavior by both individuals and groups and may either facilitate or impede spiritual modeling learning processes. Their relation to social learning processes, life environments, and behavioral outcomes is depicted in Figure 10.2. In this figure, intra-individual factors are represented within the center oval (labeled "Focal Individual"), are viewed as potentially changeable and evolving, and include the social learning processes of attention, retention, and motivation. Life environments, such as family and religious organizations, are represented by the outer semicircle. Spiritual modeling metabeliefs are depicted as implicitly or explicitly embedded in environments (outer ovals) as well as within the focal individual (central circle).

Nonbelievers may have few spiritual modeling metabeliefs if spirituality is defined theistically, rather than according to the integrative paradigm emphasized in this volume (Oman et al., 2009). Regardless of how spirituality is defined, however, metabeliefs may influence spiritual modeling processes of both believers and nonbelievers. Influential metabeliefs may concern *criteria* for recognizing a worthwhile spiritual model (e.g., qualities such as compassion or faith), the *value and function* of learning from spiritual models (e.g., spiritual, social, or physical benefits), *aids* for learning (e.g., devotional reading, meditation, fellowship), observable *signs or conditions* for learning (e.g., born-again experiences), and one's *efficacy perceptions* about one's current capacity to learn from spiritual models. Such efficacy perceptions may pertain to "*personal agency* [emphasis in original] exercised individually" or to "divine proxy agency," one's capacity to influence the divine to act on one's behalf (Bandura, 2003, p. 172). The SMSE makes no attempt to disaggregate how various perceived sources of influence blend together to yield one's total sense of individual efficacy (Oman et al., 2012). Modeling-related efficacy perceptions may pertain to acting in *collaboration* with other people or the divine (Oman & Thoresen, 2003a).

Chances for spiritual learning may be constrained by a paucity of suitable spiritual models, but also by other features of social environments, such as norms and embedded metabeliefs that facilitate or impede attending to a spiritual model's actions and behaviors. The character and valence of embedded metabeliefs—whether proreligious or -spiritual, antireligious or -spiritual, or neutral—may sometimes be a topic of disagreement. For example, thoughtful observers disagree about whether public education institutions in the United States are truly neutral in their attitude toward religion and spirituality, or whether they may unintentionally but systematically convey an antireligious perspective (Oman et al., 2009).

Of the spiritual modeling metabeliefs and processes identified in Figure 10.2, some are measured by the SMILE or SMSE, but many others are not. For example, the SMSE separately assesses perceived efficacy for learning from prominent versus community-based models, but community-based model efficacy is not disaggregated into separate items for family, school, and other life environments. Similarly, the SMILE (Part III, unpublished) assesses selected facets of motivation to learn from spiritual models (e.g., perceived values and functions) but not of signs or conditions (e.g., born again). And the SMILE measures only the respondent-perceived but not other-perceived presence of spiritual models in various life environments, and it does not assess how metabeliefs may be embedded in various environments. Some facets of the process model in Figure 10.2 might be measured with existing instruments (e.g., born-again beliefs, spiritual or mystical experiences). Thus, although the SMILE and SMSE measure some central components of the model in Figure 10.2, its fuller exploration and testing will require a range of other existing and yet-to-be-developed measures.

Negative Effects

Like other fundamental elements of spirituality and religion, spiritual modeling processes may contribute to the negative outcomes that at times come from specific forms of spirituality or religion. Silberman (2003) identified several negative processes that at times are linked to poor spiritual modeling and unhealthy religion, including encouraging negative coping strategies or negative

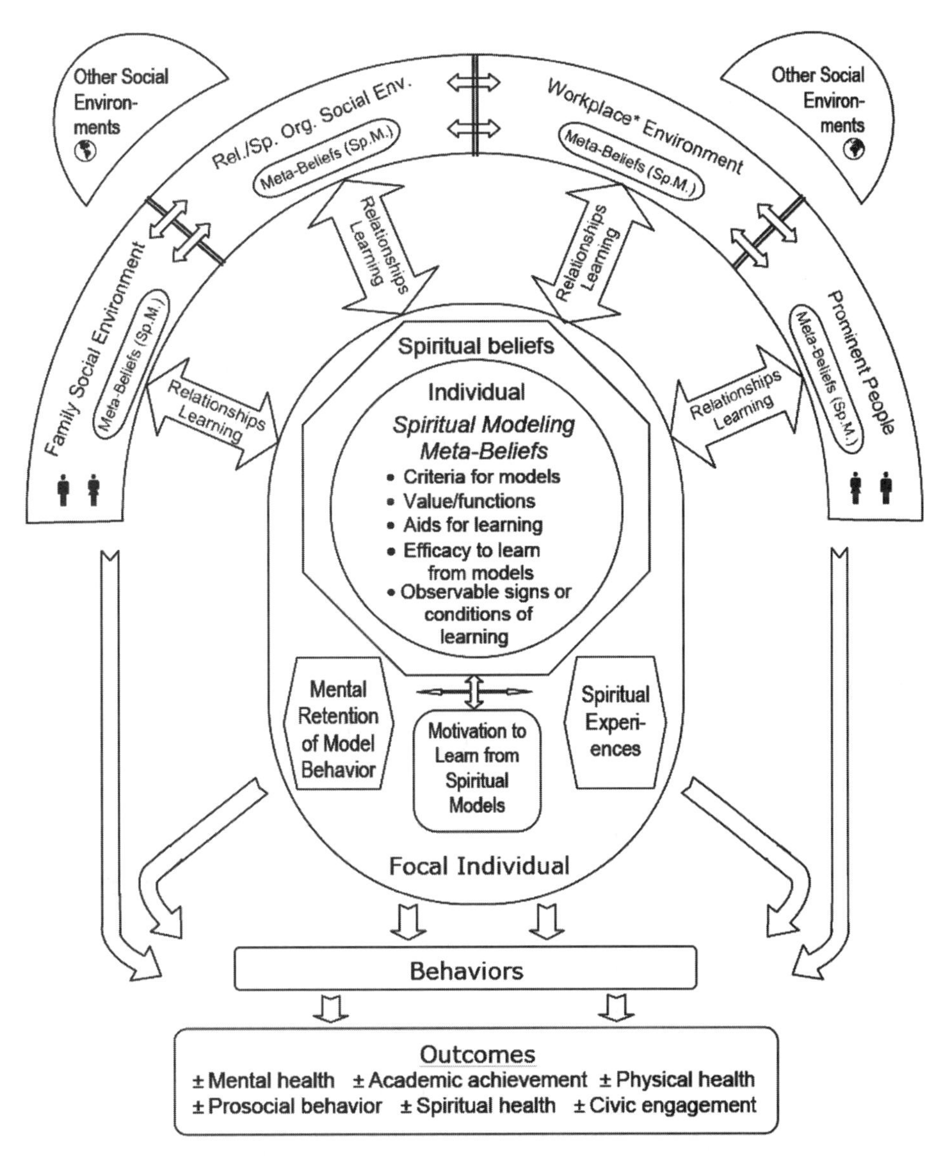

FIGURE 10.2. Conceptual framework of ways in which spiritual modeling processes affect a focal individual through social environments. From "How Does One Become Spiritual? The Spiritual Modeling Inventory of Life Environments (SMILE)," by D. Oman, C. E. Thoresen, C. L. Park, P. R. Shaver, R. W. Hood, and T. G. Plante, 2009, *Mental Health, Religion, and Culture*, *12*, p. 429. Copyright 2009 by Routledge. Adapted with permission.

beliefs about the self (e.g., unrecoverable sinner), prescribing unwise or risky modes of living, acting hypocritically or manipulatively, and, in extreme cases, encouraging violence in the name of religion. More generally, as Parker Palmer noted, "there are real dangers involved when the sacred gets attached to the wrong things" (1998, quoted in Magyar-Russell & Pargament, 2006, p. 94). In extreme cases, leaders of new religious movements may function as malevolently controlling and destructive spiritual models.

Magyar-Russell and Pargament (2006) have also described a variety of ways that negative effects could flow from religion and spirituality, and hence from spiritual modeling (see Chapter 14, this volume, and Volume 2, Chapter 4, this handbook). They suggest that the efficacy of religion for producing positive outcomes often may depend less on specific beliefs or practices than on whether an individual's religion is *well integrated* or *poorly integrated.* For example, studies have distinguished between religious motivation on the basis of personal choice (*identification*) versus religious motivation on the basis of guilt, anxiety, and external pressures (*introjection*) (Ryan, Rigby, & King, 1993). Evidence indicates that poorer outcomes are associated with religiousness undertaken in response to external pressures or other introjective motives. This suggests the possibility that spiritual models who are freely chosen, rather than passively or coercively accepted, often may be more conducive to favorable individual outcomes.

Multiple Levels for Intervention

Oman and Thoresen (2003b) suggested that one strategy for intervening to support spiritual modeling is "to give people the tools to establish effective relationships with individually appropriate spiritual models whose lives facilitate the observational learning of important spiritual skills" (p. 158). This was the primary strategy used in the meditation study by Oman et al. (2007). More recently, Oman et al. (2009) offered an expanded typology of intervention strategies on the basis of the framework in Figure 10.2:

- Supporting an individual in identifying and developing relationships with positive spiritual models in various social environments, such as appropriate mentors, coaches, or faith leaders (see Lerner, 2008);
- Providing individuals with metabeliefs and tools (aids) for learning more effectively from spiritual models, for example, by improving attentional regulation and retention of experiences of spiritual models;
- Modifying social environments to enhance exposure to positive spiritual models; and
- Modifying social environments, especially those dismissive of spiritual concerns, to project spiritual modeling metabeliefs that are more accurate and supportive.

Oman et al. (2009) described these intervention strategies as complementary rather than competing. They noted that the Institute of Medicine—a U.S. National Academy that publishes influential reports on health issues—has recommended that interventions on social and behavioral factors "should link multiple levels of influence [such as] individual, interpersonal, institutional, community, and policy levels" (Smedley & Syme, 2000, p. 9). They also cautioned that to maintain ethical grounding, each mode of intervention must respect individual beliefs, professional codes of conduct, and institutional constraints (including, in the United States, separation of church and state). An important challenge, depending on community context, may sometimes be to include committed *atheistic* models of character strengths and virtues (Oman et al., 2009).

APPLICATION PRINCIPLES

Applications of spiritual modeling to psychotherapy, health promotion, and more general forms of education have been theorized and explored in several ways. Plante (2009, p. 96) highlighted spiritual modeling as one of 13 spiritual tools for a psychotherapeutic toolbox. He suggested that therapists can ask clients who they look to as spiritual models, what qualities these models have that are so appealing, and then help clients to nurture those qualities. Others have argued that diversity training for psychotherapists can benefit by including material about prominent spiritual models from diverse traditions (Oman & Thoresen, 2003a).

Physical and mental health consequences from spiritual models have been theorized more systematically in a conceptual model, the Spiritual Modeling Health Framework (SMHF; Oman & Thoresen, 2007b). The SMHF draws on the spiritual modeling perspective described earlier (see Figure 10.1), postulating contextually influenced reciprocal interactions between beliefs, models, and practices. Spiritual models, beliefs, and practices are viewed as interacting and mutually supportive, somewhat akin to different food groups within a balanced diet. The SMHF describes how spiritual models contribute to a variety of healing processes, even if health interventions do not always make the role explicit. The SMHF is intended to complement and extend well-supported theories that spirituality and religion may causally influence health through such variables as health behaviors, social support, coping strategies, and psychological states. Preliminary empirical support for the SMHF is provided by observed associations between spiritual models and numerous health outcomes, as described in the section Measures and Surveys earlier in this chapter (Oman et al., 2005). Oman and Thoresen (2007b) offered five examples of how the SMHF and a spiritual modeling perspective may deepen understanding of the operation of empirically studied health interventions. Their examples included meditation on a spiritual holy name or mantram, spiritually supportive assessment, mindfulness meditation, passage meditation, and repetition of a spiritual mantram or holy name on occasions throughout the day, a practice that has been theorized as facilitating mental activation of modeled behaviors.

Educational implications of spiritual modeling theory have been discussed by Oman et al. (2008), who argued the value of the carefully designed inclusion of spiritual models into mainstream curricula. They noted that information about spiritual models can perform a variety of pedagogical functions across the curriculum, in subjects such as history and literature, and can support efforts to cultivate character strengths and virtues. They described the design, pedagogy, and outcomes from a college course that included not only standard academic content but also a practical component, analogous to a laboratory section or to training in applied professional skills. The practical component can be seen in part "as enhancing meta-attentional control . . . a student's overall ability to control his or her attention to facilitate learning from spiritual models" (Oman et al., 2008, p. 83). The approach appears adaptable to many academic and applied settings, and Oman et al. (2008, p. 103) suggested that most if not all of their arguments for the importance of their approach apply equally to public and private universities. Recently, Dreher has described an English literature course, focusing on the European Renaissance, that offers another instantiation of the same general approach, including both academic and applied components (Flinders, Oman, Flinders, & Dreher, 2010). Lerner (2008) concurred that this pedagogical model is supported by current theory and research about adolescent and youth development.

IMPLICATIONS FOR THEORY, RESEARCH, AND PRACTICE

The importance of social learning from spiritual models for the transmission of spirituality and religion seems hard to dispute. Their importance is widely affirmed within religious traditions, and the pervasiveness of social learning is supported by an immense scientific literature. In this chapter, we have reviewed evidence for spiritual modeling derived from developmental studies, as well as from recent applications of Bandura's (1986, 1997) approaches, and have noted observational studies, interventions, and measures.

Enormous practical applications have flowed from Bandura's theories, and practical applications have always been the primary concern of religious interest in spiritual modeling. A beneficial practical synergy between these two powerful approaches clearly merits exploration, as there may be "mutual benefits of an integrative approach" (Bandura, 2007, p. viii). For fostering improved applications, spiritual modeling theory has identified numerous intervention points. It has begun to test the corresponding interventions and to validate the measures needed to evaluate them. More immediately, a spiritual modeling perspective can sensitize health professionals, educators, and other human service professionals to the importance of spiritual models and to the value of taking them into account in particular programs and interventions. In all these ways, a spiritual modeling perspective holds promise for contributing substantial added value to psychology and to society.

Our review also shows clearly that empirical research focused directly on spiritual models is still in its early stages. Limitations of work to date include few easily usable measures and an overreliance on young Judeo-Christian study populations. Furthermore, SCT, although comprehensive in many ways, may need to be supplemented by other social cognitive perspectives (e.g., SCT appears to lack a "comparative sense that some goals may be less good for [an] individual than other goals" [Ryan, 1998, p. 120; see also Silberman, 2003]).

Future Directions

This section lists several areas in which additional empirical research and theory development could provide much-needed knowledge concerning fundamental processes and effective applications.

Additional measures. Additional midlength and short spiritual modeling measures are needed for diverse populations. Apart from the SMSE, current measures are either quite long (e.g., the SMILE; Oman et al., 2009) or very short and adapted to specific populations (e.g., Abu Raiya et al., 2008; Schwartz, 2006).

Neural and emotional correlates and substrates. What are the neural and emotional correlates of spiritual modeling, and do they differ from the correlates of other types of social learning? How do they relate to neural correlates of intense spiritual or mystical experiences (e.g., Beauregard & Paquette, 2006)? When is spiritual modeling accompanied by *elevation*, a newly identified emotion that arises in response to witnessing virtue and that "gives rise to a specific motivation or action tendency: emulation" (Algoe & Haidt, 2009, p. 106)?

Health and well-being. Further study is needed of links between spiritual models and health, well-being, and developmental outcomes as well as further elaboration and testing of theoretical models such as the SMHF.

Education. Further exploration is needed of the appropriate settings and optimal methods for integrating spiritual modeling into education (Flinders et al., 2010; Oman, 2010; Oman et al., 2008).

Religious and spiritual outcomes. Study is needed of how spiritual models influence outcomes of interest in pastoral psychology, such as spiritual growth and functioning. Spiritual and religious functioning is also an outcome of interest in psychotherapy (Hathaway, Scott, & Garver, 2004).

Contextual effects. We need to understand individual and environmental factors that impede or facilitate the fundamental SCT-based spiritual learning processes of attention, retention, reproduction in behavior, and motivation (Bandura, 1986). Such factors are a perennial concern of religious and spiritual educators, and their conceptualization might benefit from science–religion dialogue (Oman & Thoresen, 2003b; Watts & Dutton, 2006).

Perceived religious and spiritual efficacy. In Bandura's SCT, many of the benefits of social learning are mediated by gains in perceived self-efficacy. To what extent is this also true in the spiritual domain? Oman and Thoresen (2007a) have argued the viability and productiveness of constructing self-efficacy measures for a wide range of spiritual and religious skills (the SMSE measures efficacy only for learning from models). To what extent may various learnings from spiritual models be mediated by gains in perceived divine willingness to help, or by perceived efficacy in collaboration with the divine, rather than by gains in perceptions of autonomous personal efficacy (Bandura, 2003; Oman & Thoresen, 2003a)?

Spiritual mentoring. What are the varieties and dynamics of spiritual mentoring? Most major faith traditions identify spiritual leadership roles that include some degree of expectation that the individual has comparatively high spiritual attainments and is capable of serving as a spiritual model. Examples include the *guru* (in Hinduism), the *staretz* (in Russian Orthodox Christianity), and the *rebbe* (in Hasidic Judaism; Silberman, 2003). To a lesser degree, such expectations are sometimes held for modern U.S.-based spiritual directors and meditation instructors. Although, according to Moon, "much disparity exists . . . in the role of the spiritual director" (2002, pp. 269–70), the underlying spiritual modeling processes and metabeliefs could be studied and characterized. A question of interest is the ways in which beneficial spiritual modeling is supported or hindered by each tradition's theological understanding of the spiritual mentoring role as well as other role-related norms, expectations, and social relationships. Also of interest are ways that various cultural metabeliefs may foster psychological attachment processes and whether psychological attachment may in turn foster the conditions for assimilation of the mentor's spiritual example (Shaver & Mikulincer, 2008).

Mindfulness contribution. How do meditative practices that foster mindfulness contribute to the deeper assimilation of modeling information? Do breath-focused meditative methods produce different results than methods that focus attention directly on modeling information, as in the *meditatio scripturarum* (meditation on scripture) that predominates in traditional Western contemplative practices (Flinders, Oman, & Flinders, 2009)?

Effects of nominally nonspiritual interventions. Could a spiritual modeling ingredient be responsible for some of the effects of nominally nonspiritual interventions? For example, how many of the empirically documented benefits of psychosocial support groups, or of social support in general, are mediated by various forms of spiritual modeling support? Research that addresses this question could help bridge research on spirituality with other types of health and clinical psychology and could foster their integration.

Group-level spiritual modeling processes. Spirituality and religion are usually measured at the individual level, but they also can be assessed at the level of dyads, groups, organizations, or entire societies. Group-level spiritual modeling measures could facilitate evaluation of appropriately constructed environment-focused spiritual modeling interventions.

Policy implications. Much policy making is concerned with identifying and managing various types of human and natural resources. By exemplifying and thereby facilitating the learning of needed skills and virtues, spiritual models can be viewed as important human resources. In fact, spiritual models might be said to function as *spiritual capital* (Lybbert, 2008), conceived in ways parallel to social capital, human capital, and psychological capital (for concepts of "spiritual capital" going back to the 19th century, see Guest, 2007; see also Luthans, Vogelgesang, & Lester, 2006; Oman & Thoresen, 2007b). Can social learning and spiritual modeling theory contribute to an unbiased and improved policymaking understanding of religion and spirituality?

CONCLUSION

Spiritual modeling, an application of social learning theory, represents a newly developed and flexible approach for understanding how people learn spiritual and religious beliefs and practices. Grounded in an enormous body of empirical work on social learning, it aims to understand how such processes manifest themselves in relation to spirituality and religion, and how they can be harnessed by ethically grounded interventions. Initial empirical studies suggest that spiritual modeling influences can be measured, can show coherent patterning across populations, and can be affected by interventions. Occasionally, spiritual modeling and social learning explanations may contradict and compete with other explanations for spiritual and religious behaviors and beliefs. Perhaps more often, spiritual modeling explanations appear to complement other major explanatory approaches. On the basis of the fruitfulness of social learning approaches in other domains of application (Bandura, 1997), spiritual modeling approaches hold much promise for fostering integrated understanding and effective and beneficial interventions.

References

Abu Raiya, H., Pargament, K. I., Mahoney, A., & Trevino, K. (2008). When Muslims are perceived as a religious threat: Examining the connection between desecration, religious coping, and anti-Muslim attitudes. *Basic and Applied Social Psychology, 30*, 311–325. doi:10.1080/01973530802502234

Algoe, S. B., & Haidt, J. (2009). Witnessing excellence in action: The "other-praising" emotions of elevation, gratitude, and admiration. *Journal of Positive Psychology, 4*, 105–127. doi:10.1080/17439760802650519

Bandura, A. (1986). *Social foundations of thought and action*. Englewood Cliffs, NJ: Prentice-Hall.

Bandura, A. (1997). *Self-efficacy: The exercise of control*. New York, NY: Freeman.

Bandura, A. (2003). On the psychosocial impact and mechanisms of spiritual modeling. *The International Journal for the Psychology of Religion, 13*, 167–173. doi:10.1207/S15327582IJPR1303_02

Bandura, A. (2007). Foreword. In T. G. Plante & C. E. Thoresen (Eds.), *Spirit, science, and health: How the spiritual mind fuels physical wellness* (pp. vii—viii). Westport, CT: Praeger.

Beauregard, M., & Paquette, V. (2006). Neural correlates of a mystical experience in Carmelite nuns. *Neuroscience Letters, 405*, 186–190. doi:10.1016/j.neulet.2006.06.060

Boyatzis, C. J., Dollahite, D. C., & Marks, L. D. (2006). The family as a context for religious and spiritual development in children and youth. In E. C. Roehlkepartain, P. E. King, L. Wagener, & P. L. Benson (Eds.), *The handbook of spiritual development in childhood and adolescence* (pp. 297–309). Thousand Oaks, CA: Sage.

Danzig, R. A., & Sands, R. G. (2007). A model of spiritual transformation of Baalei Teshuvah. *Journal of Religion and Spirituality in Social Work, 26*, 23–48. doi:10.1300/J377v26n02_02

Easwaran, E. (2008). *Passage meditation*. Tomales, CA: Nilgiri Press. (Original work published 1978)

Emmons, R. A. (1999). *The psychology of ultimate concerns*. New York, NY: Guilford Press.

Flinders, T., Oman, D., & Flinders, C. L. (2009). Meditation as empowerment for healing. In J. H. Ellens (Ed.), *The healing power of spirituality* (Vol. 1, pp. 213–240). Santa Barbara, CA: Praeger.

Flinders, T., Oman, D., Flinders, C. L., & Dreher, D. (2010). Translating spiritual ideals into daily life: The eight point program of passage meditation. In T. G. Plante (Ed.), *Contemplative practices in action: Spirituality, meditation, and health* (pp. 35–59). Santa Barbara, CA: Praeger.

Francis, L. J., & Brown, L. B. (1991). The influence of home, church and school on prayer among sixteen-year-old adolescents in England. *Review of Religious Research, 33*, 112–122. doi:10.2307/3511908

Goleman, D. (1988). *The meditative mind*. New York, NY: Tarcher.

Guest, M. (2007). In search of spiritual capital: The spiritual as a cultural resource. In K. Flanagan & P. C. Jupp (Eds.), *A sociology of spirituality* (pp. 181–200). Burlington, VT: Ashgate.

Hassin, R. R., Uleman, J. S., & Bargh, J. A. (Eds.). (2005). *The new unconscious*. New York, NY: Oxford University Press.

Hathaway, W. L., Scott, S. Y., & Garver, S. A. (2004). Assessing religious/spiritual functioning: A neglected domain in clinical practice? *Professional Psychology: Research and Practice, 35*, 97–104. doi:10.1037/0735-7028.35.1.97

Jones, S. L. (1994). A constructive relationship for religion with the science and profession of psychology: Perhaps the boldest model yet. *American Psychologist, 49*, 184–199. doi:10.1037/0003-066X.49.3.184

Kabat-Zinn, J. (1990). *Full catastrophe living*. New York, NY: Delacorte Press.

Lerner, R. M. (2008). Spirituality, positive purpose, wisdom, and positive development in adolescence: Comments on Oman, Flinders, and Thoresen's ideas about "integrating spiritual modeling into education." *The International Journal for the Psychology of Religion, 18*, 108–118. doi:10.1080/1050861070 1879340

Levenson, M. R., Aldwin, C. M., & D'Mello, M. (2005). Religious development from adolescence to middle adulthood. In R. F. Paloutzian & C. L. Park (Eds.), *Handbook of the psychology of religion and spirituality* (pp. 144–161). New York, NY: Guilford Press.

Luthans, F., Vogelgesang, G. R., & Lester, P. B. (2006). Developing the psychological capital of resiliency. *Human Resource Development Review, 5*, 25–44. doi:10.1177/1534484305285335

Lutz, A., Slagter, H. A., Rawlings, N. B., Francis, A. D., Greischar, L. L., & Davidson, R. J. (2009). Mental training enhances attentional stability: Neural and behavioral evidence. *Journal of Neuroscience, 29*, 13418–13427. doi:10.1523/JNEUROSCI.1614-09.2009

Lybbert, T. J. (2008). Exploring the role of spiritual capital in poverty traps and microfinance. *Faith and Economics, 51*, 57–79.

Magyar-Russell, G., & Pargament, K. (2006). The darker side of religion: Risk factors for poorer health and well-being. In P. McNamara (Ed.), *Where God and science meet: How brain and evolutionary studies alter our understanding of religion* (pp. 105–131). Westport, CT: Praeger.

Marks, L. (2004). Sacred practices in highly religious families: Christian, Jewish, Mormon, and Muslim perspectives. *Family Process, 43*, 217–231. doi:10.1111/j.1545-5300.2004.04302007.x

Moon, G. W. (2002). Spiritual direction: Meaning, purpose, and implications for mental health professionals. *Journal of Psychology and Theology, 30*, 264–275.

Okagaki, L., Hammond, K. A., & Seamon, L. (1999). Socialization of religious beliefs. *Journal of Applied Developmental Psychology, 20*, 273–294. doi:10.1016/S0193-3973(99)00017-9

Oman, D. (2010). Similarity in diversity? Four shared functions of integrative contemplative practice systems. In T. G. Plante (Ed.), *Contemplative practices in action: Spirituality, meditation, and health* (pp. 7–16). Santa Barbara, CA: Praeger.

Oman, D., Flinders, T., & Thoresen, C. E. (2008). Integrating spiritual modeling into education: A college course for stress management and spiritual growth. *The International Journal for the Psychology of Religion, 18*, 79–107. doi:10.1080/10508610701879316

Oman, D., Shapiro, S. L., Thoresen, C. E., Flinders, T., Driskill, J. D., & Plante, T. G. (2007). Learning from spiritual models and meditation: A randomized evaluation of a college course. *Pastoral Psychology, 55*, 473–493. doi:10.1007/s11089-006-0062-x

Oman, D., & Thoresen, C. E. (2003a). The many frontiers of spiritual modeling. *The International Journal for the Psychology of Religion, 13*, 197–213. doi:10.1207/S15327582IJPR1303_04

Oman, D., & Thoresen, C. E. (2003b). Spiritual modeling: A key to spiritual and religious growth? *The International Journal for the Psychology of Religion, 13*, 149–165. doi:10.1207/S15327582IJPR1303_01

Oman, D., & Thoresen, C. E. (2007a, August). *Applying self-efficacy theory to spirituality: Achievements, challenges and prospects.* Paper presented at the 115th Annual Convention of the American Psychological Association, San Francisco, CA.

Oman, D., & Thoresen, C. E. (2007b). How does one learn to be spiritual? The neglected role of spiritual modeling in health. In T. G. Plante & C. E. Thoresen (Eds.), *Spirit, science, and health: How the spiritual mind fuels physical wellness* (pp. 39–54). Westport, CT: Praeger.

Oman, D., Thoresen, C. E., Park, C. L., Shaver, P. R., Hood, R. W., & Plante, T. G. (2009). How does one become spiritual? The Spiritual Modeling Inventory of Life Environments (SMILE). *Mental Health, Religion, and Culture, 12*, 427–456. doi:10.1080/13674670902758257

Oman, D., Thoresen, C. E., Park, C. L., Shaver, P. R., Hood, R. W., & Plante, T. G. (2012). Spiritual modeling self-efficacy. *Psychology of Religion and Spirituality*. Advance online publication. doi:10.1037/a0027941

Oman, D., Thoresen, C. E., Park, C. L., Shaver, P. R., Plante, T. G., & Hood, R. W. (2005, April). *Spiritual models predict health behaviors in college undergraduates.* Poster presented at the 26th Annual Meeting of the Society of Behavioral Medicine, Boston, MA.

Pargament, K. I. (1997). *The psychology of religion and coping.* New York, NY: Guilford Press.

Pargament, K. I., Koenig, H. G., & Perez, L. M. (2000). The many methods of religious coping: Development and initial validation of the RCOPE. *Journal of Clinical Psychology, 56*, 519–543. doi:10.1002/(SICI)1097-4679(200004)56:4<519::AID-JCLP6>3.0.CO;2-1

Peterson, C., & Seligman, M. E. P. (2004). *Character strengths and virtues: A handbook and classification.* Washington, DC: American Psychological Association.

Plante, T. G. (2009). *Spiritual practices in psychotherapy: Thirteen tools for enhancing psychological health.* Washington, DC: American Psychological Association. doi:10.1037/11872-000

Regnerus, M. D., Smith, C., & Smith, B. (2004). Social context in the development of adolescent religiosity. *Applied Developmental Science, 8*, 27–38. doi:10.1207/S1532480XADS0801_4

Rossano, M. J. (2010). *Supernatural selection: How religion evolved.* New York, NY: Oxford University Press. doi:10.1093/acprof:oso/9780195385816.001.0001

Ryan, R. M. (1998). Commentary: Human psychological needs and the issues of volition, control, and outcome focus. In J. Heckhausen & C. S. Dweck (Eds.), *Motivation and self-regulation across the life span* (pp. 114–133). New York, NY: Cambridge University Press. doi:10.1017/CBO9780511527869.006

Ryan, R. M., Rigby, S., & King, K. (1993). Two types of religious internalization and their relations to religious orientations and mental health. *Journal of Personality and Social Psychology, 65*, 586–596. doi:10.1037/0022-3514.65.3.586

Schimmel, A. (1985). *And Muhammad is his messenger: The veneration of the Prophet in Islamic piety.* Chapel Hill: University of North Carolina Press.

Schwartz, K. D. (2006). Transformations in parent and friend faith support predicting adolescents' religious faith. *The International Journal for the Psychology of Religion, 16*, 311–326. doi:10.1207/s15327582ijpr1604_5

Schwartz, K. D., Bukowski, W. M., & Aoki, W. T. (2006). Mentors, friends, and gurus: Peer and nonparent influences on spiritual development. In E. C. Roehlkepartain, P. E. King, L. Wagener, & P. L. Benson (Eds.), *The handbook of spiritual development in childhood and adolescence* (pp. 310–323). Thousand Oaks, CA: Sage.

Shaver, P. R., & Mikulincer, M. (2008). Augmenting the sense of security in romantic, leader-follower, therapeutic, and group relationships: A relational model of psychological change. In J. P. Forgas & J. Fitness (Eds.), *Social relationships: Cognitive, affective, and motivational processes* (pp. 55–73). New York, NY: Psychology Press.

Silberman, I. (2003). Spiritual role modeling: The teaching of meaning systems. *The International Journal for the Psychology of Religion, 13*, 175–195. doi:10.1207/S15327582IJPR1303_03

Smedley, B. D., & Syme, S. L. (Eds.). (2000). *Promoting health: Intervention strategies from social and behavioral research*. Washington, DC: National Academy Press.

Steen, T. A., Kachorek, L. V., & Peterson, C. (2003). Character strengths among youth. *Journal of Youth and Adolescence, 32*, 5–16. doi:10.1023/A:1021024205483

Watts, F. N., & Dutton, K. (2006). *Why the science and religion dialogue matters: Voices from the International Society for Science and Religion*. Philadelphia, PA: Templeton Foundation Press.

Wuthnow, R. (1998). *After heaven: Spirituality in America since the 1950s*. Berkeley: University of California Press.

Zhiru. (2000). The emergence of the Sahā Triad in contemporary Taiwan: Iconic representation and humanistic Buddhism. *Asia Major 13*(2), 83–105.

CHAPTER 11

THE NEUROPHYSIOLOGY OF RELIGIOUS EXPERIENCE

Joanna Maselko

This chapter provides an overview of the current state of knowledge of the neuroscience of religion and religious experience. It also touches on what is known about physiological correlates of religious experience. The most elemental definition of the "neuroscience of religion and religious experience" is the study of what happens in the brain when someone engages in an activity or has an experience that is labeled religious or spiritual; it is the study of the neural underpinnings of these experiences. A main motivation for many scholars in this field has been to establish whether human beings are "wired for God." This language has stirred considerable debate. The universality of religiosity across cultures suggests some innateness of the phenomena, and the obvious place that such innateness could be physically located is somewhere in the brain. Although the overall theme of this area of study has been to locate religious and spiritual experiences physically in the brain, there is enormous heterogeneity in approaches partly because of the diversity of these experiences as well as the relatively nascent nature of the field. Even though some researchers have focused on a single region of the brain (especially the studies of temporal lobe epilepsy), this strategy has been criticized by those who are pushing for a more complex approach to the brain than trying to identify a "god module" (Albright, 2000).

In this context, two overarching approaches have emerged: The first has emphasized the mystical-type experiences, including states of deep meditation, and has explored the neural correlates of this type of experience. These studies usually report that quite specific brain regions are involved in these types of experiences. The second approach has focused on the more common religious behaviors and their perceived prosocial outcomes; the research from this perspective has proposed a different, and more varied, set of neural correlates. This chapter discusses both of these approaches.

THE CAUSALITY PROBLEM

A key reason why some of the research in this area has been controversial is that even though it may seem obvious once explicitly stated, the establishment of a correlation between a religious experience and specific neural activity does not actually inform any theological questions about the existence of God (or anything else for that matter). From a scientific perspective, we do not know whether any observed neural activity during a religious experience is the actual cause of the experience, a marker of it, or a consequence. The researcher as well as the reader must be vigilant about potential bias that may creep into the design, analysis, and interpretation of study findings depending on one's own belief system. Hence, taking the perspective that the research on the neurophysiology of religious experience can only *describe* and not *explain* religious phenomena seems prudent (Fingelkurts & Fingelkurts, 2009).

Throughout this chapter, the terms *religiosity* and *religious experience* are used to represent the collection of experiences, activities, and beliefs having to do with the sacred. Although *spirituality* would be appropriate in several instances, *religiosity*

DOI: 10.1037/14045-011
APA Handbook of Psychology, Religion, and Spirituality: Vol. 1. Context, Theory, and Research, K. I. Pargament (Editor-in-Chief)
Copyright © 2013 by the American Psychological Association. All rights reserved.

was chosen for this chapter both to reflect the language most commonly used by the neuroscientists working in this area and the nature of the phenomena that they study (which is often explicitly religious in nature). For an in-depth discussion of the definitions of the terms religiosity and spirituality the reader is encouraged to refer to Chapter 1 in this volume. This chapter is organized as follows: The first section provides a very brief introduction to the methodology used in the neurophysiological study of religious experiences. This introduction is important because it orients the reader to the specific lens through which research approaches religious experiences. The main part of the chapter describes different types of religious experience—namely, starting with extraordinary or mystical type of experiences and moving onto the more common experiences associated with meditation and prayer. The main theories that are rooted in each of these types of experiences are discussed, although the categories are not meant to be completely exclusive. The chapter concludes with some thoughts about ways to advance research in this area.

A QUICK NOTE ON METHODOLOGY

The study of the neural correlates of religious experience described in this chapter has been made possible largely through the development of brain imaging technology. Very crudely, through methods such as single-photon emission computed tomography (SPECT), positron emission tomography (PET) and functional magnetic resonance imaging (fMRI), researchers can track which parts of the brain exhibit an increase in metabolic (blood flow and oxygen) or electrical activity. For SPECT and PET studies, a radioactive dye is injected into the participants' blood stream, which enables the observation of blood blow in the brain in real time.

In the majority of studies, research participants are asked to perform a specific task, such as praying, meditating, or attempting to relive a mystical experience, while ensconced in the appropriate imaging machine without moving their heads. An image is taken, recorded, and compared to a "baseline" or some other control measure in which the participant is asked to engage in another mental task. Unfortunately, choosing an appropriate control measure has been a matter of debate, leading to divergent results (Schjoedt, 2009). As is readily acknowledged, these are crude methods and only measure one small slice of a religious phenomenon. Furthermore, the context itself is somewhat contrived in that participants are likely to be in a hospital (where the scanners are), may have been injected with a tracer, and are very aware of the fact that they are being studied. For an fMRI analysis, the participant has to be lying down (vs. the more natural position of sitting or kneeling), and the machine itself is somewhat loud (potentially more than 100 decibels). The ecological validity of the findings is hard to determine at best and completely invalid at worst (Schjoedt, 2009). To add to these troubles, there is an inherent positive bias in these methodologies in that people are experiencing the positive aspects of religiosity—for example, participants are asked to remember when they felt the most connected to God and not when they felt the most alienated from God, both of which are components of real religious life. All this is to say that the findings must be considered preliminary and that as imaging technology advances together with neuroscience in general, considerable progress in the study of the neurophysiology of religious experience is expected.

MYSTICAL OR EXTRAORDINARY EXPERIENCES

Scientists and medical professionals first came across descriptions of mystical or extraordinary experiences through the case studies of patients with brain disorders, such as temporal lobe epilepsy (TLE; Devinsky & Lai, 2008; Dewhurst & Beard, 1970). Hence, seizures with religious content constituted the first type of "data" for the scientific study of the neurological underpinnings of religious experience (McNamara, 2009). Given that these seizures occur in the temporal lobes, this seemed like a natural place to "locate" religious experience. The studies that focused on TLE and overall limbic system activation in the context of intense religious experiences can be thought of as the first wave of studies on the neurology of religiosity and religious experience. They established a correlation between out-of-the-ordinary religious experiences and out-of-the-ordinary brain function (TLE).

Although there is no shortage of eloquent and detailed descriptions of mystical experiences in the literature, researchers interested in the neurophysiology of these extraordinary religious experiences are forced to take what may seem like a reductionist approach to study them. McNamara has referred to them as *ultimacy experiences*, which are discrete events and include "sensory alterations, self-alterations, a sense of supernatural presence, and cognitive and emotional changes" (2002, p. 145; see also Wildman & McNamara, 2008). Saver and Rabin described "numinous experiences," which include "an awareness of being guided by a presence of God, or experiencing in an extraordinary way that all things are 'one'" (1997, p. 499). What is common among these and other descriptions is that they are extraordinary; intense; feel very real (even more real than everyday life); and at their core, include a connection with what is interpreted by the person having the experience as divine or sacred. Although from the outsider's perspective, these encounters and experiences may look like auditory or visual hallucinations, the profound intensity of such experiences separates them from other supernatural experiences, such as seeing ghosts or spirits, which may also have a religious or spiritual content (Boyer, 2003). Furthermore, intense religious or mystical experiences (Fingelkurts & Fingelkurts, 2009) are distinct from the more common components of religious life, which include beliefs as well as religious activities and behaviors such as praying, participating in rituals, and attending group religious services. How common such experiences are is difficult to ascertain, although the percent of Americans who report having had a "religious or mystical experience" (e.g., "a moment of sudden religious insight or awakening") was 47% in 2006 (up from 22% in 1962; Pew Forum on Religion & Public Life, 2009).

RELIGIOUS EXPERIENCES AND TEMPORAL LOBE EPILEPSY

The first recorded connection between extraordinary religious experiences and brain anatomy came from the observation of epileptic seizures (Gloor, Olivier, Quesney, Andermann, & Horowitz, 1982; Persinger, 1983, 1984, 2001; Saver & Rabin, 1997). In TLE, abnormal electrical activity causes seizures that range from simple to complex (with a loss of consciousness and memory). Depending on the specific location of the seizure, it can cause a diversity of symptoms, including olfactory, auditory and visual hallucinations, feelings of dissociations, and the experience of strong emotions. Seizures in the temporal lobes have also been described as experiences of ecstatic states, out-of-body experiences, and auditory or visual hallucinations of God or other religious figures (Asheim Hansen & Brodtkorb, 2003; Devinsky & Lai, 2008; Saver & Rabin, 1997). The subjective experience can be either explicitly religious (meeting God) or can be interpreted through a religious lens (seeing light and a feelings of unlimited love; Joseph, 2001). Furthermore, seizures may include auras of various types of out-of-body-type experiences (depersonalization, derealization, and double consciousness, i.e., the experience of one's own consciousness simultaneously with another "consciousness with different perception of reality") and such experiences are especially likely to be perceived as religious or mystical (Saver & Rabin, 1997). Only between 0.4% and 3.1% of epileptic patients report religious experiences during a seizure (Devinsky & Lai, 2008), with seizures in the right temporal lobe having a higher likelihood of religious content. An intense religious experience may continue after the seizure as well, such as in the case of a religious conversion (Dewhurst & Beard, 1970). Consequently, patients with TLE (or temporal lobe vulnerability) are more likely to express intense levels of religiosity, as well as beliefs in paranormal phenomena, than the general population (Persinger, 1993, 1997). Given this description, Persinger has agreed with the hypothesis that the mystical experiences of many prominent historical religious figures (including Jesus, Buddha, and Mohammed) may have been epileptic seizures (summaries included in Devinsky & Lai, 2008; Saver & Rabin, 1997).

Given knowledge of the localized nature of TLE seizures, several researchers have hypothesized that the temporal lobes are the "source" of religion in the brain and, furthermore, that experimental stimulation of specific regions of the temporal lobes would induce a mystical or extraordinary-type experience. Persinger famously presented his "God helmet," which, when used to stimulate the temporal (and parietal) lobes, can evoke a "sensed presence" or even a mystical experience (e.g., Cook & Persinger, 1997; Persinger, Tiller, & Koren, 2000). The helmet is literally a motorcycle helmet with attached electrodes that uses weak magnetic fields to stimulate specific temporal–parietal lobe regions. Depending on the nature of the weak complex magnetic fields used and one's "temporal lobe sensitivity," the experience of the individual wearing the helmet ranges from nothing, to the feeling of "someone standing by," to a mystical experience (e.g., see Booth & Persinger, 2009; Munro & Persinger, 1992; Persinger, 1984). The engagement of other parts of the limbic system, such as the amygdale, is hypothesized to add salience and emotion to the experience, making it especially profound and otherworldly. On the basis of these experiments, Persinger (1983) proposed that microseizures deep in the temporal lobes in otherwise healthy individuals (i.e., those without TLE) are responsible for, and form the basis of, religious experiences and religion itself. Although provocative, Persinger's experiments have not been replicated, and there is some evidence that suggestibility cues in the non-double-blind design may be responsible for reports of a sensed presence during his experiments (Granqvist et al., 2005; Persinger & Koren, 2005).

THE LIMBIC SYSTEM AND RELIGIOUS EXPERIENCES

Even though the majority of researchers have rejected the idea that God can be located in a specific location within the temporal lobes (Albright, 2000), the temporal lobes and the limbic system of which they are a part do hold a prominent role in the understanding of the neurology of religion. The temporal lobes are part of a group of brain structures often referred to as the limbic system. The structures of the limbic system are considered the most ancient from an evolutionary perspective, are involved in the emotional processing of stimuli, and have many downstream influences on autonomic nervous system functions as well as endocrine, appetite, sexuality, and other processes. Relevant structures include the amygdale, which is thought to be responsible for attaching positive or negative emotional salience to a stimulus. For example, the amygdale is thought to be overactive in people with anxiety disorders through an overactive fear response to otherwise normal stimuli. The temporal lobes include the hippocampus and are involved with auditory and visual processing, language, and memory. Limbic system structures are traditionally activated during any emotionally intense experience as well as when "dreamlike" mental phenomena occur. For example, increased activity in the temporal lobes, hippocampus, or the amygdale is associated with a sensation of unreality, a sensed presence (Persinger, 2001), sensation of an out-of-body experience (Saver & Rabin, 1997), and sexual ecstasy as well as intense fear (Joseph, 2001). Emotions such as intense, unconditional love and experiences of "religious ecstasy" have also been linked with limbic system activation (Joseph, 2001).

THE LIMBIC SYSTEM AND THE ANGRY GOD

The intensity of emotions processed by structures of the limbic system includes both positive emotions such as "love" as well as negative ones such as "fear." Overstimulation of the amygdale, for example, is associated with experiences of terror and extreme fear (Davis, 1992). The implication is that the fearful and violent God "originates" in this part of the brain. One interesting study found that a subset of religiously active men with higher scores on a measure of partial epileptic-like signs (history of experiences such as feeling that things are not real, experiencing intense smells without obvious source, dreams of floating or flying; Persinger & Makarec, 1987) were more likely to state that they would "kill another person if God told them to do so" when compared with religiously active men without the epileptic signs (Persinger, 1997). This finding supports observations that the intense religiosity often associated with limbic system activation (including TLE) has a tinge of violence in it (Joseph, 2001). This link, however, between limbic system activation and violent behavior is far from established.

CERTAINTY OF RELIGIOUS EXPERIENCES AND BELIEFS

Religious experiences are often described as "more real" than normal experiences (Newberg & Lee, 2005). Persinger (2001) has suggested that the involvement of limbic system structures in religious experiences is thought to transform what could otherwise be a relatively normal experience (e.g., feeling connected to and supported by one's community) to one that is infused with intensity and certainty (e.g., feeling connected on a much deeper, spiritual level). The connection to the limbic system goes beyond TLE-like microseizures and is based on findings that even among healthy individuals, those with temporal lobe sensitivity are more likely to report paranormal activity and infuse odd experiences with deep and ultimate meaning (Makarec & Persinger, 1990). Temporal lobe sensitivity was assessed with a scale inquiring about history of experiences such as "blanking out while talking," sleepwalking, being bothered by smells, hearing voices, or sensing another presence. The scores on the scale are reported to be correlated with a higher level of alpha activity in the temporal lobes (Makarec & Persinger, 1990). The argument is that a profound experience that is "marked" by the limbic system results in strong convictions about the reality of the religious experience and, in turn, of the religious beliefs that interpret that experience (Saver & Rabin, 1997). Although largely theoretical, there is indirect support to this hypothesis in the study of the religious men with TLE who were more willing to admit they would kill "in God's name" than religious men without TLE (Persinger, 1997). Presumably, the willingness to engage in a violent act that is otherwise considered immoral reflects a very high degree of conviction in the certainty of one's beliefs about God. Indeed, certainty of the truthfulness of one's religious beliefs is one of the common hallmarks of religious belief systems. Toward this end, Persinger (1997) has suggested that there is a normal variation in temporal lobe sensitivity, which could explain some of the population variation in religious convictions. The existence and nature of this population variation in temporal lobe sensitivity still needs empirical confirmation.

Many of these papers reflect the historical tension between science and religion by explicitly linking religious experience (a) to a brain disease (i.e., TLE) and (b) to the most primal, reptilian part of the human brain (i.e., the limbic system). These perspectives made religious experience appear primitive and something that can be overcome with higher level processing. Persinger (1987) and others explicitly interpret temporal lobe activation in religious experience as an explanation of religiosity among humans, an artifact of human evolution and a cognitive virus. As methodological and theoretical advances are being made, however, it has become clear that religious experience is more complex than the involvement of the temporal lobes or the limbic system (Devinsky & Lai, 2008).

MORE COMMON RELIGIOUS EXPERIENCE: MEDITATION AND PRAYER

Although extraordinary mystical experiences are a good starting point in the exploration of the neurophysiology of religiosity, they represent only a small percent of the actual religious experience of the majority of people. We thus move on to studies of meditation and prayer, religious experiences that are arguably more accessible to the average individual. Meditation can be completely secular in nature, however, and there is a very large body of literature on the neurophysiological effects of deep meditation without a religious context that are not covered in any depth in this chapter. Here, the focus is on meditation studies that make an explicit link with religiosity or use meditation in an effort to say something about the religious experience more generally. For example, the extensive work on Herbert Benson's Relaxation Response and the parasympathetic processes involved are not covered because this work is mostly devoid of any reference to religion per se (Benson, 1976). Readers who are interested in a more in-depth coverage of meditation specifically are encouraged to read Chapter 17 in this volume as well as several excellent recent studies and reviews on this topic (e.g., Cahn & Polich, 2006; Davidson et al., 2003; Lutz, Greischar, Perlman, & Davidson, 2009).

Newberg's extensive writings on neurotheology have arguably made the greatest contribution to the current understanding of the neural correlates of the meditative type of religious experience. Using SPECT imagining methods, his team was able to identify areas of activation and deactivation in the brain through observed changes in glucose metabolism at a specific point in time (usually in the middle of a meditative experience). Conceptualizing meditation as a complex neurocognitive task, Newberg then extrapolated what was observed from these experiments to develop his neurotheology theory. The main conclusions are that during meditation (a) the parts of the brain that are involved in concentration and attention become more active and (b) there is a decrease of activity in the part of the brain that is involved with our orientation of ourselves in space. This hypothesis comes largely from studies of Buddhist meditators in whom Newberg and others have observed the increase in activity in the dorsolateral prefrontal areas, which are associated with increased focus and attention, and a decrease in the posterior superior parietal lobule (PSPL), which is hypothesized to be associated with orienting the self in physical space (Herzog et al., 1990–1991; Newberg et al., 2001). The overall findings were also supported in a study of Franciscan nuns engaged in a "verbal meditation" (Newberg, Pourdehnad, Alavi, & d'Aquili, 2003). The subjective experience of "being one with God" (Christian nuns) or of "infinity" (Buddhist meditators) is what is hypothesized to be reflected in the decreased activity in the superior parietal areas. The hypothesis is that strong stimulation of the prefrontal cortex (PFC) blocks input to the PSPL, leading to its deactivation and the subjective experience of the loss of orientation of oneself in space and the self–other boundary. Although such a process has not been empirically demonstrated, two recent studies offer some complementary support. In the first, traumatic brain injury associated with diminished right parietal lobe functioning was correlated with lower scores on a spirituality measure (Johnstone & Glass, 2008). In the second study, selective cortical lesions (surgery to remove tumors) in the inferior posterior parietal regions induced a significant increase in a measure of self-transcendance (Urgesi, Aglioti, Skrap, & Fabbro, 2010). In other words, decreased activity in the parietal regions increased an individual's sense of being interconnected to the larger universe in a way that is consistent with Newberg's theory.

Although Newberg hypothesized that numerous distinct meditative and prayer practices reflecting diverse religious traditions could ultimately result in this combination of activation or deactivation of these specific brain regions, it is difficult to generalize from these findings. For example, the reliance on experienced meditators represents a single type of religious activity, one presumably characterized by controlled concentration and a reduction in the perceived self–other boundary, but would not apply to other behaviors such as glossolalia (speaking in tongues), which is characterized by a perceived loss of control. Indeed, Newberg and colleagues have reported a decrease in activity in the frontal lobes during glossolalia (Newberg, Wintering, Morgan, & Waldman, 2006). Specific types of meditation, such as loving-kindness meditations, might be expected to illuminate other parts of the brain as well. For example, Lazar and her team's findings differed somewhat when using fMRI to observe changes during Kundalini meditation, which consists of a focus on breathing and repeating a simple mantra (Lazar et al., 2000). She found increases in the frontal and parietal cortex (involved in focus and attention) as well as in limbic region structures such as the amygdale and the hypothalamus which are related to arousal. These observed limbic increases were somewhat contrary to expectations, but Lazar suggested that their activation potentially reflects the modulation of the autonomic nervous system, given the focus on breathing in the meditation.

A somewhat different approach was taken by Beauregard and Paquette (2006), who studied Carmelite nuns while they were "in a state of union with God" (p. 187). The activity resembled meditation in that the nuns were instructed to practice the attempt to reexperience a past mystical experience, which they would then focus on during the fMRI assessment. The results showed the expected increased activity in such areas as the PFC, along with increases in multiple other areas (temporal cortex, left caudate, among others). These changes were then theoretically linked with the nuns' experiences by, for example, suggesting that the pleasant feelings of unconditional love experienced by the nuns were represented by increased activity in the insula and caudate nucleus. Interestingly, activity in the superior parietal cortex increased contrary to what Newberg's theory might predict when experiencing "union with God"—that is, dissolution of the self–God boundary. Of course, an exercise in remembering and attempting to reexperience a mystical experience is not the same as actually experiencing one.

In more recent work (Newberg & Waldman, 2009), Newberg explicitly incorporated the idea that religious experience is extremely diverse and described detailed hypothesized connections between many features of deep meditation (such as slowed breathing and heart rate) and their neural correlates. The potential connections are explicitly based on the understanding that because religiosity and spirituality are such complex and diverse experiences, the neurological correlates of these experiences are also expected to involve multiple circuits and regions of the brain. He delineated how various circuits and brain structures could be involved during religious experiences and proposed a vast number of connections that provided fodder for experimental studies for years to come. For example, activation of the thalamus was hypothesized to be linked with a sense and experience of a different reality that is common during some religious experiences. Furthermore, the superior parietal cortex is also one of several areas thought to be involved in an individuals' orientation in space and more fine-tuned studies are needed to support Newberg's hypothesis. Although many of the hypothesized connections make logical sense, ultimately, the theory is based on a few studies of expert meditators, with all the inherent limitations. The other difficulty with such an all-encompassing theory is that by trying to explain too much of such a complex experience, the theory fails to narrow our focus of attention.

An important critique of these studies is that by focusing on special populations such as monks, nuns, and other expert meditators, the findings have limited generalizability beyond these arguably unique groups. Studying the neural correlates of even more common behaviors, such as praying, has yielded important insights into the neurophysiology of religious experience in the average person. The activity of prayer usually is defined as the act of communicating with a deity, a saint, or other object of worship. Although seemingly more well defined than something like meditation, prayer exhibits significant diversity, varying by content (e.g., petitionary vs. thanksgiving), context (group vs. alone), structure (formal vs. spontaneous), and method (sung, spoken, or thought silently with or without corresponding bodily movement; see Chapter 16 in this volume). The few prayer studies published to date have explored the affective versus cognitive nature of religiosity as well as its social relational nature.

For example, Azari and colleagues used a prayer experiment to argue that religious experiences are primarily cognitively—and not emotionally—mediated (Azari, 2004; Azari, Missimer, & Seitz, 2005). In her main experiment, Azari compared differences in PET-measured brain activity during a religious condition of reciting a Christian prayer (reading Psalm 23) with the "happy emotional condition" of reading a well-known nursery rhyme. The study participants were lay religious individuals belonging to a single denomination and nonreligious individuals in Germany. The religious condition showed increased activity in the frontal–parietal circuit areas that are involved in social–relational cognition (Azari et al., 2005). In contrast, only the nursery rhyme condition was associated with increased activity in the limbic system (left amygdale), which would be expected during an emotional activation. The findings thus support the hypothesis that the fairly common religious experience of reading a biblical psalm is more likely to be a complex cognitive phenomenon versus an emotional one, with beliefs and thoughts being especially important. Furthermore, the involvement of social–relational areas (frontal cortex) corresponds nicely to the Christian (and the specific Free Evangelical Fundamentalist Community members under study) emphasis on one's relationship with Jesus or God. The link of frontal lobe activity to the subjective experience of a relationship with a deity is an interesting contrast to McNamara's (2009) emphasis on relationships with other individuals (as discussed in the section Religious Experiences, the Prefrontal Cortex, and Executive Cognitive Functions later in this chapter). Azari's study stands out as an excellent example of the potential of prayer studies. As with many experiments in this area, however, the question of the appropriate control condition complicates the interpretability of the findings. One can argue that reading a happy nursery rhyme is not an appropriate control condition to the reading of Psalm 23. The experiment may accurately reflect differences between that particular psalm and that particular nursery rhyme but may not be generalizable beyond that. For example, a prayer of rejoicing might show significantly more limbic system activation than what was observed in the psalm condition, as might a petitionary prayer. Ultimately, a wider repertoire of prayer conditions is needed to validate Azari's claim that religiosity is more cognitively than emotionally mediated.

In the second group of prayer studies, Schjoedt (2009; Schjoedt, Stodkilde-Jorgensen, Geertz, & Roepstorff, 2009) approached religion primarily as a complex cultural phenomena and hypothesized that the neural regions involved in prayer should map onto established cognitive networks appropriate to the given content and context of the prayer. He drew on an understanding of different types of prayers (Geertz, 2008) to hypothesize that improvised prayers (where individuals converse with God in their own way) would reveal different activation patterns from that of a recitation of a formal prayer (The Lord's Prayer). He theorized that for a Christian study participant, improvised praying is similar to having a mental conversation with a "real" individual, with analogous brain activity. If this is the case, there should be an increase of activity in what are referred to as theory of mind areas (anterior medial prefrontal cortex [MPFC], temporopolar region, and temporopareiteal junction; Gallagher & Frith, 2003) in the improvised prayer condition as compared with the formal prayer condition. Using fMRI technology with a sample of Danish Christian study participants, the results do support the hypothesis that during a common experience of improvised, personal prayer, the brain "processed" God more as another social person than as something otherworldly, unbound by space or time. This is in stark contrast to the descriptions by Persinger (1983) and even Newberg et al. (2001), who have focused on religious experiences that are characterized by the loss of self-other boundaries. A second finding of Schjoedt's experiment is that the religious condition was associated with increased activity in the dopamine receptor–rich right caudate nucleus (Schjoedt, Stodkilde-Jorgensen, Geertz, & Roepstorff, 2008). Activation in the dopaminergic system is associated with reward feedback loops and habit formation, and this may help explain why people find behaviors such as prayer intrinsically rewarding (see Exhibit 11.1; McNamara, 2002).

Exhibit 11.1
A Little Molecule Called Dopamine

The neurotransmitter dopamine has emerged as a key molecule in the neuropsychology of religion. Dopamine is a catecholamine that is active throughout the cerebral cortex and the limbic system. Two of the four major dopamine pathways connect structures in the limbic system (including the amygdale and hippocampus) through the ventral tagmental area to the frontal cortex. Dopamine is thus important in several important behavioral and cognitive tasks, such as those having to do with volitional movement, motivation, salience, reward, error processing, and attention and learning. Dopamine is thought to be associated with reward and reinforcement systems by creating pleasurable feelings that are tied to a specific behavior or thought. This engagement of dopamine in reinforcing behavior has been noted both in the reinforcement of religious behaviors such as praying and also in addiction formation. A related effect is that dopaminergic engagement adds "salience" to a particular experience, making it more meaningful and important. Deficits of dopamine are associated with varied problems, depending on where in the brain the deficit lies. In the frontal cortex, low dopamine levels result in problems with attention (attention deficit disorder) and problem solving. The symptoms of Parkinson's disease are a result of decreased dopamine activity in the motor cortex, which is caused by insufficient dopamine production in the basal ganglia. On the other hand, symptoms of mania in bipolar disorder are thought to be caused by an overabundance of dopamine.

Although the mystical experiences and deep meditation studies point to the temporal lobes and other limbic structures that are linked with experiences such as the perceived dissolution of the self–other boundary, a sensed presence, and profound emotion such as unconditional love, studies of prayer suggest that it is the social–cognitive areas of the brain that are more likely to be engaged during the more common religious experiences.

RELIGIOUS EXPERIENCES, THE PREFRONTAL CORTEX, AND EXECUTIVE COGNITIVE FUNCTIONS

The neurological support for the relational nature of prayer described in the previous section provides important empirical support for McNamara's (2002) theory about religion and the development of executive cognitive functions (ECFs). ECFs refer to a set of "higher order" cognitive processes that are activated during novel and complex cognitive tasks, including ones requiring the resolution of potentially conflicting desires (such as short- vs. long-term goals), and negotiating social interactions. ECFs are most closely linked with activity in the PFC, and it has been theorized that a chief role of the PFC is cognitive control, including the ability to control one's actions and emotions (Miller & Cohen, 2001). The PFC becomes activated during tasks requiring sustained concentration, abstract thinking, and behavioral control, such as the inhibition of inappropriate actions. The orbital and medial sections of the PFC have been observed to be activated during situations involving moral reactions, including guilt and shame (together with other structures such as the amygdale and thalamus; Moll et al., 2002). Furthermore, damage to the PFC is linked with a lack of moral and social reasoning (Anderson, Bechara, Damasio, Tranel, & Damasio, 1999). ECFs are thought to play a crucial role in the human ability to understand what another individual is thinking and feeling (theory of mind; Stuss, Gallup, & Alexander, 2001) and hence are important in personality and social functioning. It has been well documented that dysfunction or injury in the PFC causes dramatic changes in personality, loss of impulse control, increase in violent behavior, and decrease overall social functioning (Brower & Price, 2001; Macmillan, 2000). In sum, the PFC and the ECFs that it enables are extremely important to an individual's ability to function successfully in society.

McNamara's (2002) approach to religion is anchored in the belief that the benefits of religion must outweigh its detriments for religion to survive, and so in this way he takes a very functionalist approach. He has drawn on theories of religion as a social system, which encourages individual socialization, integration, and autonomy, such as Allport (1950) and Hartmann (1958) among others. In contrast to Newberg et al. (2001), Newberg and Lee (2005), Persinger (1993), and others, McNamara has downplayed the potential role of the temporal or parietal lobes as important aspects of religious experience.

In short, McNamara (2002, 2009) believes that religious practices, such as prayer, activate the frontal lobes, an activation that is intrinsically rewarding through dopamine pathways. In turn, the activation of frontal lobes in the context of a social religious community helps build executive cognitive functions, further reinforcing engagement in religious practices. He has laid out how specific religious activities can build ECFs—for example, involvement in communal worship services builds "sensitivity to social context" and meditation and contemplation build "resistance to interference, working memory and attentional control" (McNamara, 2002). McNamara has suggested that religion has been the traditional method through which cultures encourage the development of ECFs. Although it is possible to develop ECFs without religion, religion is the most culturally common "package." Although he acknowledged that empirical support for this hypothesis is as yet scarce, he pointed to his team's studies of patients with Parkinson's disease as providing partial support for the dopamine portion of his hypothesis. McNamara, Durso, Brown, and Harris (2006) made the case that a key function of the mesocortical dopaminergic system is to moderate activity level in the frontal lobes, and hence, dysfunction in the system would lead to a "frontal system dysfunction on religiosity" (p. 2). The main feature of the pathology of Parkinson's disease is the progressive dysfunction of dopamine-producing cells and ensuing lower levels of dopamine activity in the central and forebrain regions (see Exhibit 11.1). McNamara and colleagues presented evidence that disease severity is correlated with decreased subjective religiosity and religious salience (Butler, McNamara, & Durso, 2010; McNamara, Durso, & Brown, 2006). The results further suggested that the lack of interest in religiosity is especially linked with dopaminergic dysfunction in right-sided prefrontal networks (Butler et al., 2010).

Although McNamara's theory is plausible, his extrapolation of the meaning of frontal lobe activation goes far beyond what others suggest—namely, that the activation of PFC areas is a reflection of the focus and concentration involved in prayer and meditation activities. For example, as noted, experiments involving glossolalia revealed a deactivation of the prefrontal areas, and this was interpreted as the experience of "letting go" and not controlling one's actions (Newberg et al., 2006). Furthermore, although McNamara acknowledged the need for a theory that can incorporate both the positive and negative aspects of religion, his theory seems overly positive. In his own words, religions "promote development of individuals who are characterized by compassionate service to others as well as individual wholeness, integrity, and autonomy" (McNamara, 2002, p. 144). The single nod to the addictive consequences of the dopamine pathway overactivation fails to fully address some of the potential negative aspects of religious engagement. He started with the position that religion is more "good" than "bad"; identified the parts of the brain associated with these positive characteristics, such as being prosocial, moral, and so on; and then linked them to ECFs and prefrontal lobe activation during religious activities.

Muramoto (2004) has provided another theory of the role of the PFC in religiosity. Focusing on the error detection, self-reflection, and theory of mind processes of the medial PFC, Muramoto extrapolated from reports of PFC dysfunction to create a representation of hyperfunction, balanced function, and hypofunction in terms of religiosity. In terms of error detection, for example, hyperfunction of the medial PFC might be associated with rigid conformity to religious rules, balanced function with expected level of compliance with religious rules, and hypofunction with disregard for religious rules. Similarly, hyperfunction in the theory of mind function would result in grandiose interpretation of God's mind; balanced function with sympathy, empathy, and compassion; and hypofunction with apathy and aloofness. In sum, he proposed that future experimental studies might be able to demonstrate that overactivity in the MPFC area would be correlated with hyperreligiosity, whereas low levels of activity with hyporeligiosity. There is no direct empirical evidence of this hypothesis yet.

The ECF theory hypothesizes that religious engagement would have (mostly positive) spillover effects onto other neural and physiological systems, such as those related with stress and stress reactivity. The subjective reports of the stress and anxiety-reducing effects of religious experiences are now being formally examined at the neural level. In a recent article, Inzlicht, McGregor, Hirsh, and Nash (2009) showed that individuals who were more religious demonstrated less reactivity in the anterior cingulated cortex (ACC), which is a cortical system involved in the stress response and self-regulation. Although the ACC is not part of the limbic system, it modulates both emotional and cognitive processes and is connected with several limbic structures, such as the amygdale, hypothalamus, and anterior insula. Inzlicht et al. tested the hypothesis that religious conviction would reduce the anxiety (as measured by ACC activity) caused by making an error during a Stroop task.[1] The ACC usually becomes activated when another part of the brain detects a conflict, realizes an error has been made, or is uncertain about what to do next. In the study Inzlicht et al. conducted, religious zeal and strength of belief in God were associated with lower ACC reactivity in response to an error in the Stroop task. In a

[1] A Stroop task is used to measure attention. A common example of a Stroop task is a test during which the participant is shown a series of words naming a color, written in ink that may or may not match the written word (e.g., "red" written in green ink). The time it takes for a participant to determine whether it is a match, together with the error rate, is then recorded, with the underlying assumption being that a mismatch takes longer to identify.

"Xanax of the people" kind of interpretation, Inzlicht et al. suggested that "religious conviction curbs ACC activity because conviction acts very much like an anxiolytic and buffers the affective consequences of errors and uncertainty" (p. 386). The findings suggest that religious belief is not necessarily inflexible because, presumably, a certain rigidity would lead to more anxiety in the face of errors. Instead, Inzlicht et al. argued, religious beliefs provide a flexible framework within which to interpret one's environment, including potentially anxiety-producing errors and other situations. Exactly how a religious framework for meaning of presumably larger, existential type of questions would influence ACC reactivity to something as context specific and concrete as a Stroop task is not clear. Inzlicht et al.'s argument implies that religious people should be, on average, "cooler" in the face of uncertainty and stressors. It is not clear whether there is empirical support for such a claim independent of when individuals engage positive religious coping strategies, which have demonstrated stress-reducing effects in (Anastasi & Newberg, 2008; Hogg, Adelman, & Blagg, 2010; see also Chapter 14 in this volume). Furthermore, it is not clear whether more or less ACC activity is ideal as prior studies have linked lower ACC activity to higher rates of error in tasks such as the Stroop task, suggesting that a higher level of ACC activation may increase focus and attention in a given activity (Amodio, Jost, Master, & Yee, 2007).

Focusing on neurotransmitters, Borg, Andree, Soderstrom, and Farde (2003) found that a measure of spiritual acceptance was highly correlated with the density of serotonin receptors in several brain regions, suggesting that serotonin is somehow involved in a person's openness to spiritual experiences or even "spiritual zeal." The serotonin system is also implicated in the mystical-type experiences that are reported to be induced through the use of *entheogens* (psychoactive substances used in religious rituals). Although the use of usually plant-derived substances in religious ceremonies is not uncommon among world religious traditions, recent experimental work has confirmed the enthoegenic properties of specific substances. In a recent, well-controlled experiment, psilocybin administration appears to have induced spiritual-type experiences in study participants (Griffiths et al., 2006). Beyond mimicking the role of serotonin in the brain, the mechanisms underlying psilocybin's effects remain unknown.

Examining other physiological processes, there is also some evidence that religious individuals have healthier levels of allostatic load (an overall indicator of physiological dysregulation measured by summing up the number of "out-of-normal range" values for physiological indicators such as blood pressure, cholesterol, body mass index, etc.), immune function markers, and other physiological markers, such as pulmonary function (Koenig et al., 1997; Maselko, Kubzansky, Kawachi, Seeman, & Berkman, 2007; Maselko, Kubzansky, Kawachi, Staudenmayer, & Berkman, 2006; Woods, Antoni, Ironson, & Kling, 1999), although it is unclear which aspects of being religious are specifically involved. Evidence of an association between religiosity and other physiological factors such as blood pressure have been mixed (Buck, Williams, Musick, & Sternthal, 2009). By far the largest number of studies on other physiological factors have been specific to the activity of meditation (Davidson et al., 2003; Seeman, Dubin, & Seeman, 2003), which may or may not have a religious or spiritual component.

CONCLUSION

The two overarching sets of theories presented in this chapter, reflecting either extraordinary religious experiences or a more common prayer and meditative experiences, are in fact quite complementary. For the majority of people, religiosity occurs in the context of regular rituals, often in social settings, where the PFC and associated areas are more involved. For some, however, religiosity is based on what they experience as more direct encounters with the sacred, which are characterized by parietal and temporal lobe activation. In this regard, the debate on which neural correlates are at the "core" of religiosity appears misplaced as the exact neural correlates would be expected to vary according the nature of any given individual's actual religious experience.

Although the search for the neural underpinnings of religious experience has made great strides in the past 2 decades, many challenges exist, as would be expected in any relatively nascent field (Fingelkurts & Fingelkurts, 2009; Newberg & Lee, 2005; Wildman & McNamara, 2008). These challenges fall into two broad categories, one conceptual and one methodological.

First, both defining and then operationalizing "religious experience" in a way that lends itself to neurological study has been extremely difficult. Measurable aspects such as behaviors, beliefs, and cognitions are all different manifestations of what most researchers agree is a unique phenomenon. Indeed, even the discussion of the neurophysiology of religion in a single chapter makes the assumption that there is an underlying religious phenomenon on which we could agree. However, whether this underlying phenomena is at its core (a) a complex, ultimately social, system (think soccer, with its rituals, commitments, rules, and devotion); or (b) a unique individual trait related to either the ability to connect with the divine, like vision, or a neurological artifact, will influence which regions of the brain or neural pathways will be studied. Researchers like McNamara (2009) approach the neurology of religion from the perspective of a social system that builds executive cognitive functions, whereas Persinger (1983) sees religion originating as a result of microseizures in the temporal lobes. A signal originating in any particular brain region is therefore likely to be interpreted very differently by these two researchers. The researcher's own worldview unfortunately also often influences their research, and this can be observed in the seeming bias in the literature toward positive aspects of religious experience. Of all the empirical findings reviewed in this chapter, only one directly focused on a negative religious domain: willingness to "kill in God's name" in the context of TLE (Persinger, 1997). The experience of religious struggles (see Chapter 25 in this volume), for example, represents one area in which neurological research could make a significant contribution. Related to the problem of causality, defining, and hence measuring, only the positive aspects of religious experience leaves out crucial information about the actual brain processes involved. Furthermore, focusing on religious experiences that are a result of years of practice is likely to yield only limited insight into the neurophysiology of religious experience among most individuals (Schjoedt, 2009). Complicating matters from a methodological view, the more normal religious experiences are more likely to map onto existing neural networks (vs. having their own special networks or nodes), making it much more difficult to discern meaningful differences between a religious and control condition of an experiment (Harris et al., 2009). A related critique is that many of the discussed approaches, including the focus on temporal lobes, lack a strong link to social cognitive psychological theory (Kapogiannis et al., 2009; Schjoedt, 2009). Thoughtful collaborations between neuroscientists and scholars of religion have the potential to prevent this problem by taking a careful theoretical approach to defining which religiosity variables should be measured in the particular context.

The second related challenge is that the use of technologies such as PET or fMRI rest on a number of strong assumptions about brain anatomy, functioning, and the relation between what is measured and actual neural activity in that particular location. The interpretation of the meaning of an increase or decrease in activity in a certain brain region or neural pathway is problematic as all areas of the brain engage in multiple functions, and often do so with complex and little-understood interactions with proximal and distal areas through multiple neural pathways. Even the seemingly concrete religious activity or reading a biblical psalm is a complex cognitive task, and any interpretation of changes in activity in a specific brain region is somewhat strained. This complexity is reflected in the greatly varying interpretations of the engagement of the PFC in religious activities. Additionally, although the link to TLE and Parkinson's disease (with an increase and decrease in religiosity respectively) is very promising, there is no evidence that a well-defined lesion or surgical removal of any section of the temporal lobe results in a significant change in religiosity per se (Muramoto, 2004).

The conceptual and empirical challenges described in this chapter also represent fertile areas of research to inform our understanding of the neurophysiology of religiosity. Many of the key research studies described in this chapter represent doctoral dissertations, suggesting the influx of new researchers interested in this area of research. This new influx of researchers from a variety of disciplines focusing on the relationship between neural activity and religious experiences is very promising. Being such a nascent field, there are several key areas of investment that might be especially fruitful toward establishing a high-quality body of research in this area.

For example, research on TLE and Parkinson's disease has revealed the high potential of studying pathological processes to gain insights about religious experience. The fact that many neurological disorders involve relatively specific regions or neural pathways can be further exploited. New research is needed that combines an understanding of specific disease pathology both at the neural and symptomatic level with an examination of concrete and specific religiosity variable correlates. A recent study on changes in self-transcendence following brain surgery (Urgesi et al., 2010) is an example of fruitful opportunity for interdisciplinary collaboration. The inclusion of religiosity variables in follow-up studies of patients with specific brain lesions could be a relatively low-cost data-collection strategy used to generate new hypotheses. Thoughtful efforts at neurological studies of other religious phenomena commonly described in the psychology of religion literature, such as religious coping or religious and spiritual struggles might also be especially productive. There is a great need for replication of the research described in this chapter by other research teams, teams that are multidisciplinary in nature. Collaboration between social and cognitive psychologists, neurologists, and religion scholars could be especially fruitful.

Although the focus on specific populations, such as nuns or expert meditators, is understandable, more diverse samples as well as controlled experimental conditions are needed. More diverse samples and methods can address selection and reporting bias issues: We need to address the possibility that highly developed dopamine pathways increase the likelihood of becoming a nun or a monk. Alternatively, a nun or a monk who volunteers for a study may have such a strong motivation to produce "strong results" that it is the difference in motivation that is actually detected and not any reflection of the religious experience per se. Attention to these methodological issues will contribute significantly to research quality and standing in the scientific community. Using cross-cultural and multiple religious tradition perspectives and study participants will add another important comparative dimension; at the same time, the inclusion of people representing diverse religious traditions may make some skeptical members within the scientific community a little more comfortable studying this topic.

The main implication for practice from the reviewed studies stems from the realization that religiosity may be affected by neurological changes, either resulting from disease or by natural genetic variation in the population. The research also sheds light on how specific religious activities (such as meditation) may potentially be used to strengthen specific neural pathways (related to dopamine or serotonin, e.g.) when warranted. Clinicians might benefit from understanding expected changes in religiosity that accompany disease progress. For example, knowledge of the effects of disease on religiosity, such as decreased religiosity observed in Parkinson's disease patients, informs treatment options: the loss of interest in religion in a previously religious individual might be distressing in its own right and religiously based coping strategies are unlikely to be effective in this context. The loss of one's innate religiosity may lead to religious struggles and a desire for help. These implications illustrate how an improved understanding of the neurophysiological correlates of religiosity and religious experience can have wide applications within and beyond the field of psychology. And, although our current understanding of the neurophysiology of religion is in its infancy, continuing theoretical and empirical efforts are likely to significantly refine and develop our understanding of the phenomenon of religiosity overall.

References

Albright, C. R. (2000). The "God module" and the complexifying brain. *Zygon*, *35*, 735–744. doi:10.1111/1467-9744.00311

Allport, G. (1950). *The individual and his religion.* New York, NY: Macmillan.

Amodio, D. M., Jost, J. T., Master, S. L., & Yee, C. M. (2007). Neurocognitive correlates of liberalism and conservatism. *Nature Neuroscience, 10*, 1246–1247. doi:10.1038/nn1979

Anastasi, M. W., & Newberg, A. B. (2008). A preliminary study of the acute effects of religious ritual on anxiety. *Journal of Alternative and Complementary Medicine, 14*, 163–165. doi:10.1089/acm.2007.0675

Anderson, S. W., Bechara, A., Damasio, H., Tranel, D., & Damasio, A. R. (1999). Impairment of social and moral behavior related to early damage in human prefrontal cortex. *Nature Neuroscience, 2*, 1032–1037.

Asheim Hansen, B., & Brodtkorb, E. (2003). Partial epilepsy with "ecstatic" seizures. *Epilepsy and Behavior, 4*, 667–673. doi:10.1016/j.yebeh.2003.09.009

Azari, N. P. (2004). The role of cognition and feeling in religious experience. *Zygon, 39*, 901–918. doi:10.1111/j.1467-9744.2004.00627.x

Azari, N. P., Missimer, J., & Seitz, R. J. (2005). Religious experience and emotion: Evidence for distinctive cognitive neural patterns. *The International Journal for the Psychology of Religion, 15*, 263–281. doi:10.1207/s15327582ijpr1504_1

Beauregard, M., & Paquette, V. (2006). Neural correlates of a mystical experience in Carmelite nuns. *Neuroscience Letters, 405*, 186–190. doi:10.1016/j.neulet.2006.06.060

Benson, H. (1976). *The relaxation response.* New York, NY: Morrow.

Booth, J. N., & Persinger, M. A. (2009). Discrete shifts within the theta band between the frontal and parietal regions of the right hemisphere and the experiences of a sensed presence. *Journal of Neuropsychiatry and Clinical Neurosciences, 21*, 279–283. doi:10.1176/appi.neuropsych.21.3.279

Borg, J., Andree, B., Soderstrom, H., & Farde, L. (2003). The serotonin system and spiritual experiences. *American Journal of Psychiatry, 160*, 1965–1969. doi:10.1176/appi.ajp.160.11.1965

Boyer, P. (2003). Religious thought and behaviour as by-products of brain function. *Trends in Cognitive Sciences, 7*, 119–124. doi:10.1016/S1364-6613(03)00031-7

Brower, M. C., & Price, B. (2001). Neuropsychiatry of frontal lobe dysfunction in violent and criminal behavior: A critical review. *Journal of Neurology, Neurosurgery, and Psychiatry, 71*, 720–726. doi:10.1136/jnnp.71.6.720

Buck, A. C., Williams, D. R., Musick, M. A., & Sternthal, M. J. (2009). An examination of the relationship between multiple dimensions of religiosity, blood pressure, and hypertension. *Social Science and Medicine, 68*, 314–322. doi:10.1016/j.socscimed.2008.10.010

Butler, P. M., McNamara, P., & Durso, R. (2010). Deficits in the automatic activation of religious concepts in patients with Parkinson's disease. *Journal of the International Neuropsychological Society, 16*, 252–261. doi:10.1017/S1355617709991202

Cahn, B. R., & Polich, J. (2006). Meditation states and traits: EEG, ERP, and neuroimaging studies. *Psychological Bulletin, 132*, 180–211. doi:10.1037/0033-2909.132.2.180

Cook, C. M., & Persinger, M. A. (1997). Experimental induction of the "sensed presence" in normal subjects and an exceptional subject. *Perceptual and Motor Skills, 85*, 683–693. doi:10.2466/pms.1997.85.2.683

Davidson, R. J., Kabat-Zinn, J., Schumacher, J., Rosenkranz, M., Muller, D., Santorelli, S. F., . . . Sheridan, J. F. (2003). Alterations in brain and immune function produced by mindfulness meditation. *Psychosomatic Medicine, 65*, 564–570. doi:10.1097/01.PSY.0000077505.67574.E3

Davis, M. (1992). The role of the amygdala in fear and anxiety. *Annual Review of Neuroscience, 15*, 353–375. doi:10.1146/annurev.ne.15.030192.002033

Devinsky, O., & Lai, G. (2008). Spirituality and religion in epilepsy. *Epilepsy and Behavior, 12*, 636–643. doi:10.1016/j.yebeh.2007.11.011

Dewhurst, K., & Beard, A. W. (1970). Sudden religious conversions in temporal lobe epilepsy. *British Journal of Psychiatry, 117*, 497–507. doi:10.1192/bjp.117.540.497

Fingelkurts, A. A., & Fingelkurts, A. (2009). Is our brain hardwired to produce God, or is our brain hardwired to perceive God? A systematic review on the role of the brain in mediating religious experience. *Cognitive Processing, 10*, 293–326. doi:10.1007/s10339-009-0261-3

Gallagher, H. L., & Frith, C. D. (2003). Functional imaging of "theory of mind." *Trends in Cognitive Sciences, 7*, 77–83. doi:10.1016/S1364-6613(02)00025-6

Geertz, A. (2008). Comparing prayer: On science, universals, and the human condition. In W. Braun & R. McCutcheon (Eds.), *Introducing religion: Essays in honor of Jonathan Z. Smith* (pp. 113–139). London, England: Equinox.

Gloor, P., Olivier, A., Quesney, L. F., Andermann, F., & Horowitz, S. (1982). The role of the limbic system in experiential phenomena of temporal-lobe epilepsy. *Annals of Neurology, 12*, 129–144. doi:10.1002/ana.410120203

Granqvist, P., Fredrikson, M., Unge, P., Hagenfeldt, A., Valind, S., Larhammar, D., & Larsson, M. (2005). Sensed presence and mystical experiences are predicted by suggestibility, not by the application of transcranial weak complex magnetic fields. *Neuroscience Letters, 379*, 1–6. doi:10.1016/j.neulet.2004.10.057

Griffiths, R. R., Richards, W. A., McCann, U., & Jesse, R. (2006). Psilocybin can occasion mystical-type experiences having substantial and sustained personal meaning and spiritual significance.

Psychopharmacology, 187, 268–283. doi:10.1007/s00213-006-0457-5

Harris, S., Kaplan, J. T., Curiel, A., Bookheimer, S. Y., Iacoboni, M., & Cohen, M. S. (2009). The neural correlates of religious and nonreligious belief. *PLoS ONE, 4*(10), e7272. doi:10.1371/journal.pone.0007272

Hartmann, H. (1958). *Ego psychology and the problem of adaptation.* New York, NY: International University Press. doi:10.1037/13180-000

Herzog, H., Lele, V. R., Kuwert, T., Langen, K. J., Rota Kops, E., & Feinendegen, L. E. (1990–1991). Changed pattern of regional glucose metabolism during yoga meditative relaxation. *Neuropsychobiology, 23*, 182–187. doi:10.1159/000119450

Hogg, M. A., Adelman, J. R., & Blagg, R. D. (2010). Religion in the face of uncertainty: An uncertainty-identity theory account of religiousness. *Personality and Social Psychology Review, 14*, 72–83. doi:10.1177/1088868309349692

Inzlicht, M., McGregor, I., Hirsh, J. B., & Nash, K. (2009). Neural markers of religious conviction. *Psychological Science, 20*, 385–392. doi:10.1111/j.1467-9280.2009.02305.x

Johnstone, B., & Glass, B. A. (2008). Support for a neuropsychological model of spirituality in persons with traumatic brain injury. *Zygon, 43*, 861–874. doi:10.1111/j.1467-9744.2008.00964.x

Joseph, R. (2001). The limbic system and the soul: Evolution and the neuroanatomy of religious experience. *Zygon, 36*, 105–136. doi:10.1111/0591-2385.00343

Kapogiannis, D., Barbey, A. K., Su, M., Zamboni, G., Krueger, F., & Grafman, J. (2009). Cognitive and neural foundations of religious belief. *Proceedings of the National Academy of Sciences of the United States of America, 106*, 4876–4881. doi:10.1073/pnas.0811717106

Koenig, H. G., Cohen, H. J., George, L. K., Hays, J. C., Larson, D. B., & Blazer, D. G. (1997). Attendance at religious service, interleukin-6, and other biological parameters of immune function in older adults. *International Journal of Psychiatry in Medicine, 27*, 233–250. doi:10.2190/40NF-Q9Y2-0GG7-4WH6

Lazar, S. W., Bush, G., Gollub, R. L., Fricchione, G. L., Khalsa, G., & Benson, H. (2000). Functional brain mapping of the relaxation response and meditation. *NeuroReport, 11*, 1581–1585. doi:10.1097/00001756-200005150-00041

Lutz, A., Greischar, L. L., Perlman, D. M., & Davidson, R. J. (2009). BOLD signal in insula is differentially related to cardiac function during compassion meditation in experts vs. novices. *NeuroImage, 47*, 1038–1046. doi:10.1016/j.neuroimage.2009.04.081

Macmillan, M. (2000). *An odd kind of fame: Stories of Phineas Gage.* Cambridge, MA: MIT Press.

Makarec, K., & Persinger, M. A. (1990). Electroencephalographic validation of a temporal-lobe signs inventory in a normal population. *Journal of Research in Personality, 24*, 323–337. doi:10.1016/0092-6566(90)90024-Z

Maselko, J., Kubzansky, L., Kawachi, I., Seeman, T., & Berkman, L. (2007). Religious service attendance and physiological dysregulation among high functioning elderly. *Psychosomatic Medicine, 69*, 464–472. doi:10.1097/PSY.0b013e31806c7c57

Maselko, J., Kubzansky, L., Kawachi, I., Staudenmayer, J., & Berkman, L. (2006). Religious service attendance and changes in pulmonary function in a high functioning elderly cohort. *Annals of Behavioral Medicine, 32*, 245–253. doi:10.1207/s15324796abm3203_11

McNamara, P. (2002). The motivational origins of religious practices. *Zygon, 37*, 143–160. doi:10.1111/1467-9744.00418

McNamara, P. (2009). Neurology of religious experiences. In *The neuroscience of religious experience* (pp. 80–130). Cambridge, England: Cambridge University Press. doi:10.1017/CBO9780511605529.006

McNamara, P., Durso, R., & Brown, A. (2006). Religiosity in patients with Parkinson's disease. *Neuropsychiatric Disease and Treatment*, 2, 341–348. doi:10.2147/nedt.2006.2.3.341

McNamara, P., Durso, R., Brown, A., & Harris, E. (2006). The chemistry of religiosity: Evidence from patients with Parkinson's disease. In P. McNamara (Ed.), *Where God and science meet: How brain and evolutionary studies alter our understanding of religion* (Vol. 2, pp. 1–14). Westport, CT: Praeger.

Miller, E. K., & Cohen, J. D. (2001). An integrative theory of prefrontal cortex function. *Annual Review of Neuroscience, 24*, 167–202. doi:10.1146/annurev.neuro.24.1.167

Moll, J., de Oliveira-Souza, R., Eslinger, P. J., Bramati, I. E., Mourao-Miranda, J., Andreiuolo, P. A., & Pessoa, L. (2002). The neural correlates of moral sensitivity: A functional magnetic resonance imaging investigation of basic and moral emotions. *Journal of Neuroscience, 22*, 2730–2736.

Munro, C., & Persinger, M. A. (1992). Relative right temporal lobe theta activity correlates with Vingiano's hemispheric quotient and the sensed presence. *Perceptual and Motor Skills, 75*, 899–903. doi:10.2466/PMS.75.7.899-903

Muramoto, O. (2004). The role of the medial prefrontal cortex in human religious activity. *Medical Hypotheses, 62*, 479–485. doi:10.1016/j.mehy.2003.10.010

Newberg, A. B., Alavi, A., Baime, M., Pourdehnad, M., Santanna, J., & d'Aquili, E. (2001). The measurement of regional cerebral blood flow during the complex cognitive task of meditation: A preliminary

SPECT study. *Psychiatry Research: Neuroimaging, 106*, 113–122. doi:10.1016/S0925-4927(01)00074-9

Newberg, A. B., & Lee, B. Y. (2005). The neuroscientific study of religious and spiritual phenomena: Or why God doesn't use biostatistics. *Zygon, 40*, 469–490. doi:10.1111/j.1467-9744.2005.00675.x

Newberg, A. B., Pourdehnad, M., Alavi, A., & d'Aquili, E. G. (2003). Cerebral blood flow during meditative prayer: Preliminary findings and methodological issues. *Perceptual and Motor Skills, 97*, 625–630. doi:10.2466/pms.2003.97.2.625

Newberg, A. B., & Waldman, M. R. (2009). *How God changes your brain: Breakthrough findings from a leading neuroscientist.* New York, NY: Ballantine Books.

Newberg, A. B., Wintering, N. A., Morgan, D., & Waldman, M. R. (2006). The measurement of regional cerebral blood flow during glossolalia: A preliminary SPECT study. *Psychiatry Research: Neuroimaging, 148*, 67–71. doi:10.1016/j.pscychresns.2006.07.001

Persinger, M. A. (1983). Religious and mystical experiences as artifacts of temporal lobe function: A general hypothesis. *Perceptual and Motor Skills, 57*, 1255–1262. doi:10.2466/pms.1983.57.3f.1255

Persinger, M. A. (1984). Striking EEG profiles from single episodes of glossolalia and transcendental meditation. *Perceptual and Motor Skills, 58*, 127–133. doi:10.2466/pms.1984.58.1.127

Persinger, M. A. (1987). *Neuropsychological bases of God beliefs*. New York, NY: Praeger.

Persinger, M. A. (1993). Paranormal and religious beliefs may be mediated differentially by subcortical and cortical phenomenological processes of the temporal (limbic) lobes. *Perceptual and Motor Skills, 76*, 247–251. doi:10.2466/pms.1993.76.1.247

Persinger, M. A. (1997). "I would kill in God's name": The role of sex, weekly church attendance, report of a religious experience, and limbic lability. *Perceptual and Motor Skills, 85*, 128–130. doi:10.2466/pms.1997.85.1.128

Persinger, M. A. (2001). The neuropsychiatry of paranormal experiences. *Journal of Neuropsychiatry and Clinical Neurosciences, 13*, 515–523. doi:10.1176/appi.neuropsych.13.4.515

Persinger, M. A., & Koren, S. A. (2005). A response to Granqvist et al., "Sensed presence and mystical experiences are predicted by suggestibility, not by the application of transcranial weak magnetic fields." *Neuroscience Letters, 380*, 346–347, author reply 348–350. doi:10.1016/j.neulet.2005.03.060

Persinger, M. A., & Makarec, K. (1987). Temporal-lobe epileptic signs and correlative behaviors displayed by normal-populations. *Journal of General Psychology, 114*, 179–195. doi:10.1080/00221309.1987.9711068

Persinger, M. A., Tiller, S. G., & Koren, S. A. (2000). Experimental simulation of a haunt experience and elicitation of paroxysmal electroencephalographic activity by transcerebral complex magnetic fields: Induction of a synthetic "ghost"? *Perceptual and Motor Skills, 90*, 659–674. doi:10.2466/pms.2000.90.2.659

Pew Forum on Religion and Public Life. (2009). *Eastern, New Age beliefs widespread: Many Americans mix multiple faiths.* Washington, DC: Pew Research Center.

Saver, J. L., & Rabin, J. (1997). The neural substrates of religious experience. *Journal of Neuropsychiatry and Clinical Neurosciences, 9*, 498–510.

Schjoedt, U. (2009). The religious brain: A general introduction to the experimental neuroscience of religion. *Method and Theory in the Study of Religion, 21*, 310–339. doi:10.1163/157006809X460347

Schjoedt, U., Stodkilde-Jorgensen, H., Geertz, A. W., & Roepstorff, A. (2008). Rewarding prayers. *Neuroscience Letters, 443*, 165–168. doi:10.1016/j.neulet.2008.07.068

Schjoedt, U., Stodkilde-Jorgensen, H., Geertz, A. W., & Roepstorff, A. (2009). Highly religious participants recruit areas of social cognition in personal prayer. *Social Cognitive and Affective Neuroscience, 4*, 199–207. doi:10.1093/scan/nsn050

Seeman, T. E., Dubin, L., & Seeman, M. (2003). Religiosity/spirituality and health: A critical review of the evidence for biological pathways. *American Psychologist, 58*, 53–63. doi:10.1037/0003-066X.58.1.53

Stuss, D. T., Gallup, G., & Alexander, M. (2001). The frontal lobes are necessary for "theory of mind." *Brain: A Journal of Neurology, 124*, 279–286. doi:10.1093/brain/124.2.279

Urgesi, C., Aglioti, S. M., Skrap, M., & Fabbro, F. (2010). The spiritual brain: Selective cortical lesions modulate human self-transcendence. *Neuron, 65*, 309–319. doi:10.1016/j.neuron.2010.01.026

Wildman, W. J., & McNamara, P. (2008). Challenges facing the neurological study of religious behavior, belief, and experience. *Method and Theory in the Study of Religion, 20*, 212–242. doi:10.1163/157006808X317455

Woods, T. E., Antoni, M. H., Ironson, G. H., & Kling, D. W. (1999). Religiosity is associated with affective and immune status in symptomatic HIV-infected gay men. *Journal of Psychosomatic Research, 46*, 165–176. doi:10.1016/S0022-3999(98)00078-6

Chapter 12

COGNITION, EVOLUTION, AND RELIGION

Justin L. Barrett and Bonnie Poon Zahl

In this chapter, we introduce cognitive and evolutionary approaches to the study of religion as relatively new areas in the broader psychological study of religion and spirituality. This chapter has four sections. We begin by providing an overview of what a cognitive account of religion would entail. In the second section we review cognitive and evolutionary accounts of the cross-cultural recurrence of religious beliefs and practices. In the third section we discuss individual variations in religious cognition that give rise to differences in religious belief and experience, and in the last section we suggest implications for the rational justification of religious beliefs and future research.

OVERVIEW OF COGNITIVE APPROACHES TO THE STUDY OF RELIGION

Cognitive accounts of religion draw on the cognitive sciences for insights and methods in developing causal explanations for the occurrence and recurrence of religious expression. These approaches assume that religious belief and experience can be productively explained by ordinary (i.e., not unique to religion) cognitive structures and processes that are shared by all humans. Individual differences in religious belief and expression may be accounted for by variations in processing styles (i.e., nonreflective vs. reflective) and representational content (i.e., affective content in concepts and schemas) within these more universal constraints in cognition.

Propositional Versus Affective Representations

Emotion plays a central and organizing role in social cognition (Forgas, 2001) and religious experience (Watts, 1996), but to date, cognitive science of religion (CSR) accounts have spent little time on the specific role of emotion in people's religious representations (Gibson, 2008). Various authors have argued for applying multilevel theories to the study of religious representations and processing to account for differences in how representations are organized (Hall, 2003; Hill & Gibson, 2008; Hill & Hood, 1999; Watson, Morris, Hood, Miller, & Waddell, 1999; Watts, 2006). Although it is too early to tell which particular theory is the definitive framework for religious cognition, these theories converge in assuming that religious representations stored at the propositional level are explicit, intellectual, rational, affect-free, verbal, and doctrinal (i.e., knowing something "in the head"), whereas religious representations stored at the implicational level are implicit, affect-laden, nonverbal, and experiential (i.e., knowing something "in the heart"). These two types of representations can be congruent, but they also can be in conflict with one another (Rizzuto, 1979; Watts & Williams, 1988). Zahl and Gibson (2008, 2009) found, in a sample of U.S. and British Christian young adults of various denominations and in a sample primarily of British self-identified Christians from many denominations, that respondents professed to believe in a God who was more loving, more responsive, less distant, and more severe than the God they personally experienced,

DOI: 10.1037/14045-012
APA Handbook of Psychology, Religion, and Spirituality: Vol. 1. Context, Theory, and Research, K. I. Pargament (Editor-in-Chief)
Copyright © 2013 by the American Psychological Association. All rights reserved.

and greater discrepancy between professed and experiential concepts was predictive of feeling less positive emotions and more negative emotions in relation to God. These preliminary findings suggest that the two types of representations differ in their influence over people's religious experience and that discrepancies between these representations may lead to specific emotions in relation to God. Despite the interest in individual religious experiences, psychologists of religion have not consistently delineated between these two levels of meaning in their measurement and operationalization of religious representations (Gibson, 2008).

Reflective Versus Automatic Processing

One assumption tacit in much of CSR that generally has been overlooked in the psychology of religion is that human thought can be characterized by a "two-system" or "dual-processing" approach (Stanovich & West, 2000; Tremlin, 2006). The intuitive or nonreflective system is characterized by rapid, automatic, reflexive, seemingly effortless, and often relatively emotional processing. The reflective, reasoning system is slower, deliberate, reflective, effortful, and relatively affect-light. These two systems are not wholly independent. Rather, the automatic deliverances of the intuitive system serve as default presumptions for the reflective system. Unless sufficient reason exists for the reflective system to modify or override the intuitive system, it drives our thinking. Our understanding of the psychology of religion will be enhanced by understanding how religious representations derived from our intuitive, nonreflective system inform and constrain reflective level thought and consequent behaviors.

One consequence of the two-system structure is that there can be contradictory representations of the same thing. In many religious contexts, there would be explicit, doctrinal beliefs that produce certain types of inferences in the offline reflective mode and different inferences in the online nonreflective mode. The gap between the stated, reflective beliefs and the online, automatic representation has been termed *theological correctness* (TC): analogous to political correctness (PC), people know the right thing to say even if their thoughts and feelings are not consistently in line with it. Through a series of experiments with religious believers and nonbelievers in the United States and in India, Barrett and colleagues demonstrated that adults' God concepts can function in markedly divergent ways depending on the conceptual demands of the context (Barrett, 1998, 1999; Barrett & Keil, 1996; Barrett & VanOrman, 1996). Participants answered comprehension questions about a number of short stories that included God (or Vishnu, Kishna, and others for Hindu participants). Similar to studies on the impact of schemata on memory for narratives (Bransford & McCarrell, 1974), "intrusion errors" revealed that participants used a more anthropomorphic conception of God than what they affirmed in direct questioning. For instance, instead of remembering God attending to any number of things at the same time, they remembered that the story specified God acting in serial and being able to be distracted. Control conditions ruled out that these results were only an artifact of the narratives or the comprehension questions. It appears that some divine attributes are too difficult or counterintuitive to easily generate inferences in real-time, cognitive load tasks. Slone (2004) has argued that not only are some theologically correct concepts difficult to understand during on-the-fly processing, but also they are so counterintuitive that they are difficult to understand even during disinterested reflection leading to distortion of the theology—a problem Slone has dubbed "theological incorrectness." For instance, Slone noted systematic distortions in Buddhist representations of karma and in Calvinist understandings of predestination.

It would be a mistake, however, to suggest that the propositional–affective and reflective–intuitive distinctions are identical distinctions. Barrett's studies, for example, used nonaffective material and did not call for affective representations of God, yet individuals used representations that were contrary to their stated doctrinal beliefs. Thus, religious representations lacking affective content can be processed automatically, just as affective religious representations can be processed reflectively and elaborated on with great detail. Individuals may possess highly emotional and theologically correct representations of God, just as they can also process nonaffective religious information in a theologically incorrect manner.

Although CSR accounts of religion tend also to take an evolutionary approach, cognitive approaches to the study of religion need not be evolutionary. They may simply concern how human cognitive systems inform and constrain particular forms of religious expression. Such accounts often do have evolutionary features, however. The particulars of these cognitive systems are often grounded in evolutionary perspectives. Certain cognitive factors, discussed in the next section, might make certain ideas that we might regard as "religious" more likely to be adopted and hence influence cultural evolution. Furthermore, some of these cognitive dynamics give rise to behaviors that then prove adaptive. In these ways, the lines between cognitive and evolutionary approaches are often blurred in the primary literature.

ACCOUNTING FOR THE COGNITIVE ORIGINS AND RECURRENCE OF RELIGIOUS BELIEFS AND PRACTICES

If some ideas are readily acquired in childhood, they may be easy to pass on to the next generation. Furthermore, they may become adopted early in life, become integrated into intuitive, automatic reasoning, and thus serve as default assumptions for later learning and reasoning throughout life. Research from cognitive developmental psychology has long provided evidence that children are naturally receptive to religious ideas; these theories and research are addressed in detail in Chapter 27 of this volume and are described here as they pertain to cognitive approaches to religion.

Theomorphism Versus Anthropomorphism of Superattributes

The Freudian, object-relations, and Piagetian approaches to the development of god concepts all assume anthropomorphism to be the best characterization of young children's ideas—that is, gods are just human beings that might live in the clouds or something similar (Elkind, 1970; Goldman, 1965; Piaget, 1929). More recent cognitive developmental research, however, at least raises the possibility that on some dimensions, children attribute superproperties to humans and gods and then pare back those properties through development until they arrive at adultlike understandings of humans and gods.

Barrett and his collaborators replicated previous findings that children presume others' beliefs and perceptions are reliable reflections of what the child knows to be the case, even in contexts when an adult would recognize the fallibility of thought and perception. For instance, once children were told the meaning of a secret code or rules of a novel game, 3- and 4-year-olds assumed their mother, a dog, and God would all know the meaning of the code or the rules of the game at first presentation. By age 5, they understood that the dog and their mother would not understand a secret code or the game; however, across all ages, these children from Protestant homes did regard God as likely to understand the code or the game (Barrett, Newman, & Richert, 2003). Indeed, even the 3-year-olds were significantly more likely to attribute understanding to God than to a dog. Similarly, if a 3-year-old knows that a cracker box contains rocks, he answers that his mother, a bear, God, or anyone else would know about the surprising contents as well (Barrett, Richert, & Driesenga, 2001). By age 5, children generally know that beliefs are fallible and, for instance, mother would likely believe a cracker box to contain crackers even if the child knows that there are rocks in the box. Knight, Sousa, Barrett, and Atran (2004) replicated this finding with Yukatek-speaking Maya children living in Mexico. Knight (2008) also found that once children understood the fallibility of beliefs, these 4- to 7-year-olds differentiated among various deities in a way similar to adults, more frequently attributing accurate knowledge to the Catholic God than the forest spirits or sun God and these more frequently than animals, people, or household spooks. Importantly, the youngest children tended to treat all of these agents similarly: as superknowing (Knight, 2008). Richert and Barrett (2005) also investigated whether children thought God, a human, and a variety of animals would be able to see an object in the dark, hear a currently inaudible sound, or smell something not currently detected. As in the other tasks, 5-year-olds can successfully discriminate various agents' properties once they outgrow the tendency to overattribute perceptual access to all and learn specific limitations on humans, animals, and some gods.

These studies suggest that it is the limitation of natural minds that take children longer to learn. Theological ideas about superknowing and superperceiving gods may be closer to the early developing default assumptions (Barrett & Richert, 2003). It is possible that these cognitive biases are in part a product of social regularities in children's environments (e.g., most children in the world have powerful and caring mothers, which may predispose them to intuit gods in a similar manner). It may be that such developmental biases (social and cognitive) make the ideas of superknowing, superperceiving creator beings largely intuitive. Concepts of deities that fit the conceptual space relatively well may be more likely to be generated, entertained, communicated, remembered, and affirmed as existent.

Bodies, Spirits, and the Afterlife

One area in which CSR is breaking new ground on the study of religious phenomena as well as raising new issues for psychology generally focuses on how the physical and nonphysical aspects of personhood are conceptualized, and how, in turn, these conceptualizations underpin widespread cultural ideas such as belief in some kind of afterlife and ideas about ghosts, ancestor spirits, and spirit possession (Cohen & Barrett, 2011).

Intuitive dualism. Psychologist Paul Bloom (2004) has argued that humans are naturally "intuitive dualists," regarding minds and bodies as separable entities because of representational conflicts between two different conceptual systems that generate inferences regarding the properties of humans (Bloom, 2004). One system, naive physics, deals with solid, bounded physical objects and is present in the first few months of life (Spelke & Kinzler, 2007). This system registers human bodies as objects with certain physical properties, such as having to be contacted to be moved, moving continuously through space, and the like. The second system, dealing with minded agents, allows considerably more latitude. Agents, after all, can act at a distance. Bloom has argued that these two systems with their different developmental schedules, different evolutionary histories, and different input–output conditions, are only ever tenuously united in reasoning about humans. For this reason, they easily accommodate thinking about disembodied minds and something of us persisting after death, such as ghosts or spirits (Bloom, 2007, 2009).

Afterlife beliefs. Although afterlife beliefs sometimes play a very small role in religious thought, no notion that something of a person persists after death is unusual (see Chapter 5 in this volume). Why so? CSR scholars debate whether such beliefs are intuitive versus counterintuitive (and how counterintuitive) and just which cognitive predilections undergird such beliefs. The common human tendency to seek existential meaning in events after the death of a loved one (such as surprising sights or sounds or dreams) may be taken as evidence of the persistence of the other after death (Bering, 2002, 2006). In one set of experiments Bering and collaborators showed that U.S. children have stronger commitments to an afterlife earlier in childhood suggesting being enculturated out of instead of in to such beliefs (Bering & Bjorkland, 2004; Bering, Hernández-Blasi, & Bjorkland, 2005). Bering further argued that such a strong predisposition to have afterlife beliefs was encouraged in the course of evolution by selective pressure because holding such a belief can promote reputation-enhancing behavior. If you believe ghosts or ancestor spirits might be around and watching, you are more inclined to behave in ways good for your social reputation, thereby making you a more attractive exchange partner (Bering & Johnson, 2005; Bering, McLeod, & Shackelford, 2005). Bloom, likewise, sees some kind of afterlife as a natural extension of intuitive dualism, and as such, intuitive (Bloom, 2004). Other scholars hold that although ordinary cognition may be configured in such a way as to make afterlife reasoning easy and attractive, it still is not fully "intuitive," and they have presented evidence that its prevalence may increase instead of decrease with maturation (Astuti & Harris, 2008).

Spirit possession. The idea that spirits can enter bodies and exert control over them is common across cultures and presents some interesting conceptual challenges for observers of such events, such as "Who am I interacting with at this moment (the spirit or a human)?" and "Who is responsible for the actions I am watching?" (Cohen, 2007). Yet even with its additional conceptual difficulties over ordinary actions, spirit possession is widely conceptualized in similar ways. In a study of Afro-Brazilian spiritual practitioners, Cohen (2007) found that despite explicit and exclusive teaching that spirit possession is an act of two spirits fusing together in one body, it is in practice conceptualized as one intentional agent (the external spirit) displacing another agency (the host's). Perhaps conceptualizing spirit possession capitalizes on an already present conceptual arrangement that favors dualistic thinking (akin to Bloom's intuitive dualism) and further imports a one-mind/one-body principle that governs normal mind–body reasoning. In addition to Cohen's ethnographic evidence, she has begun to produce experimental evidence that something like a one-mind/one-body principle could be a cross-culturally recurrent assumption (Cohen & Barrett, 2008a, 2008b).

Promiscuous Teleology, Creationism, and Intelligent Design

Through numerous experiments, Kelemen and colleagues have produced considerable evidence that children exercise what she has called *promiscuous teleology*: a tendency to find design and purpose in the natural world beyond what parents license (Kelemen, 1999a). For instance, children are inclined to say rocks are "pointy" not because of some physical processes but because being pointy keeps them from being sat on and crushed (Kelemen, 1999b). Using teleological reasoning to account for the origins or causes of things extends to living things, such as plants and animals and nonliving natural things such as rocks and rivers, but it is less applicable to natural events such as thunderstorms (DiYanni & Kelemen, 2005; Kelemen & DiYanni, 2005). Interestingly, Kelemen has recently produced evidence that adults that have not been formally educated show similar preference for teleological explanations as do even scientifically educated adults under conditions of hurried response (Kelemen & Rosset, 2009). These results suggest that promiscuous teleology is not simply outgrown but is only tamped down in some cultural contexts. Perhaps not surprisingly, this teleological reasoning often finds a comfortable fit with the idea that the purpose was brought about by an intentional agent or creator (Kelemen & DiYanni, 2005). This conceptual space seems to invite a god or gods to fill the gap (Kelemen, 2004). Replicating Piaget's investigations into children's ideas about who should be credited with the natural world's apparent design and purpose, contemporary researchers have found that preschoolers show no confusion: Humans make pencils and chairs, but God makes animals and stars (Gelman & Kremer, 1991; Petrovich, 1997, 1999).

This assumption that an intentional being brings about natural order may make it difficult to teach evolution by natural selection as an alternative to direct creation. Evans has found that even children from families and schools that endorse evolutionary explanations for features of animals do not begin to endorse such accounts at rates comparable to their parents until after age 10 (Evans, 2001).

By-Product of a Unitary Cognitive System and Disposition

Although the various developmental biases sketched thus far may encourage particular aspects of god concepts, one theory purports to identify a single factor that leads to belief in gods generally: Guthrie's anthropomorphism theory (1980, 1993). Guthrie argued that humans have a perceptual bias to attend to humanlike forms or other information that might be caused by humanlike beings. He cast the arguments in terms of an evolved tendency that produces false positives for the sake of survival. Humans and other agents usefully regarded as minded, such as predatory mammals, represented our greatest threats and promises for survival and reproduction in our evolutionary environment. Hence, it would be better to "detect" agents even given fragmentary or ambiguous information than to miss their presence. It is better to assume that the rustling in the brush is an intentional agent such as a tiger than to assume it is just the wind and risk becoming the tiger's lunch. Guthrie has argued that we evolved a bias to overdetect evidence of humanlike agency around us and so we attribute natural forces and events to humanlike beings or gods. The special cultural elaborations that we call "religion" are the upshot of an ordinary, panhuman information-processing tendency that can be seen in many different domains of cultural expression. To distinguish this tendency to find intentional agency around us from other treatments of "anthropomorphism" and to remain neutral with regard to whether the bias is best characterized as a tendency to pick out humanlike agency or intentional agency generally, Barrett dubbed the cognitive system responsible for detecting intentional agency the Hypersensitive Agency Detection Device (HADD; Barrett, 2004).

HADD is regarded as part of our automatic, reflexive, intuitive processing system and subject to being overridden by our reflective system. We do, perhaps often, decide that detections of agency were erroneous (hence the "H" in HADD). But if HADD's outputs are easily overridden as mistakes, why would they generate beliefs in gods (Atran, 2002; Boyer, 2001)? Perhaps HADD only provides experiences that might be used in affirming already existing beliefs: People who regard a form in the graveyard mist as a ghost already have a concept of ghosts consonant with the experience; people who see the hand of God in a natural event already have a representation of God. Perhaps, then, HADD is insufficient to generate belief in gods but may be an extra factor encouraging their spread. As Guthrie suggested, occasionally a HADD experience might be pondered later and not overridden and perhaps combined with other's experiences in postulating a suitable agent. Alternatively, people with a god concept may have a HADD experience that either strengthens their belief or motivates them to transmit the concept. Either way, occasionally, HADD experiences could add motivation to generate or transmit god concepts.

By-Product of Multiple Systems: Epidemiological Approaches

Guthrie (1980, 1993) set out to identify a single cognitive factor that might account for the prevalence of belief in invisible agents (gods). Even if critics are correct that Guthrie's account (or the HADD derivative) fails to be sufficient because it does not consider the persistence of some such agent concepts over others (e.g., see Atran, 2002; Boyer, 2001), it may be one of a number of factors that cumulatively encourage belief in gods (and other religious ideas).

From an epidemiological approach (Sperber, 1996), the more factors that encourage the generation or transmission of an idea, the more likely it is to spread and become believed. Ideas that are encountered repeatedly and that resonate with many different intuitions and evidence are more likely to become accepted as true. We have sketched some of the factors that might contribute to the idea of a god being widespread. If the god can account for perceived natural order and purpose, if it has superperception and superknowledge, and if it acts in the world in ways that our HADD might "detect" evidence of its action, the god is likely to be understood, discussed, affirmed, and successfully communicated to others. Following are a number of additional factors that have been suggested.

Cognitive optimum or minimally counterintuitive theory. The most prominent cognitive theory stressing an epidemiological approach to the study of religion is Boyer's (1993, 1994, 1996, 2001, 2003). Boyer suggested that religious concepts transmit particularly effectively because they fall within a "cognitive optimum" of being easy to represent and communicate but also counterintuitive enough to be attention-grabbing. Concepts that are highly intuitive are easy to understand and communicate, but they might not always be all that interesting. Ideas with just one or two tweaks, on the other hand, may enjoy the benefits of good intuitive fit while also being attention-grabbing, thereby leading to more investment and deeper processing. That is, if religious ideas are not radically counterintuitive or wholly intuitive, but instead are minimally counterintuitive (MCI), they will spread well (other dynamics aside).

Boyer's predictions were supported by initial experimental studies that showed MCI ideas were remembered and transmitted more effectively than either intuitive (Barrett & Nyhof, 2001), more massively counterintuitive (Boyer & Ramble, 2001), or intuitive but bizarre concepts (Barrett & Nyhof, 2001). Subsequent studies, however, have provided mixed results (Gonce, Upal, Slone, & Tweney, 2006; Norenzayan, Atran, Faulkner, & Schaller, 2006; Tweney, Upal, Gonce, Slone, & Edwards, 2006; Upal, Owsianiecki, Slone, & Tweney, 2007). Barrett (2008) has suggested that these alleged "failures to replicate" may be the result of ambiguities in how to operationalize counterintutiveness and addressed this problem by developing a formal scheme for coding and quantifying counterintuitive concepts. He then demonstrated the utility of this scheme in analyzing folktales from around the world (Barrett, Burdett, & Porter, 2009). Consonant with Boyer's predictions, when these tales had counterintuitive objects in them, they tended to include only one counterintuitive feature as previous text-coding studies had likewise found (Lisdorf, 2004).

Nevertheless, the first published experimental study using Barrett's coding scheme did not yield simple confirming or disconfirming evidence but found an age effect (Gregory & Barrett, 2009). Participants under 25 years old forgot fewer MCI items than intuitive items over a 1-week delay, whereas those older than 25 forgot significantly more MCI items than intuitive items. It may be that the mnemonic advantage for MCI concepts is unfounded, is limited to the young, requires narrative elaboration, or is mediated by another property of the concepts in question.

Additional selection factors. In his 2001 book, Boyer explicitly recognized that being an MCI concept was insufficient to be a religious concept (Boyer, 2001). Religious concepts—particularly gods—must be able to readily generate inferences, predictions, and explanations in domains broadly meaningful and important to humans—what Boyer has termed "inferential potential." For instance, a tree that vanishes whenever anyone is near it may be counterintuitive but only generates confused or unimportant inferences. A tree that listens to people's conversations, however, gets one thinking about whether the tree might hear and tell secrets or otherwise change life around it. Likewise, the idea of a person who can taste words (e.g., a synthestete) may be MCI, and it may be attention getting, but not much follows from it that will change the way I think and act in many domains. An invisible person, however, may be listening to my secrets or those of my enemy, may work for or against me, and may modify my actions. Boyer argued that intentional agents generally have greater inferential potential than nonagents and so counterintuitive properties that either make a nonagent an agent (e.g., a tree that listens) or augment the normal agency of an intentional agent (an invisible person) are strong candidates for cultural beliefs.

One particular class of agents that Boyer (2001) stressed are those possessing what he termed "strategic information"—that is, information broadly relevant to human survival and reproduction, often of the sort that occupies gossips of any culture: who has lost or gained remarkable wealth, who is cheating on whom, and the like. Possessing strategic information guarantees the inferential potential of the god but also makes the god more likely to factor in emotionally charged concerns over life, death, surviving, and thriving, and morally charged decision making. So, properties of being all-knowing, all-seeing, all-hearing, invisible, mind-reading, and the like are cross-culturally more common than failing to exist on Wednesdays, experiencing time backward, or giving birth to young of a different species.

By virtue of having strategic information, these counterintuitive agents also may serve as moral arbitrators. They know who is naughty and nice and, presumably, can do something about it if they do not like it, even if they only leak the information to someone in the community. Those agents, then, that we typically call gods that become central players in religious systems tend to be minimally counterintuitive in such a way that they have great inferential potential, possess strategic information, have the ability to act in the world (e.g., in ways detectable by HADD), and are morally relevant. By virtue of these properties, they are likely to motivate propitiatory religious actions as well.

ACCOUNTING FOR INDIVIDUAL VARIATIONS IN RELIGIOUS EXPRESSION

That general cognitive foundations incline people toward religious ideas does not mean that there are no important interpersonal differences in religious expression. In the sections that follow, we consider how relational dynamics shape how gods are represented and how life experiences impact religious expression.

Representation of Gods and Relationships With God

Earlier in this chapter we discussed the need for cognitive accounts of religion to distinguish between propositional and affective representations of gods and other religious concepts. Although this distinction has not been made explicitly in CSR literature, the concepts of powerful, knowledgeable, and morally concerned gods are not purely propositional concepts; by being concerned with matters of survival and invoking fear of punishment for wrongdoing, they are affect-laden concepts that motivate how believers think, feel, and behave. In addition to being morally concerned, gods are also represented as agents to whom believers ascribe personality characteristics (Benson & Spilka, 1973; Gorsuch, 1968) and with whom believers report (sometimes intimate) relationships.

Psychodynamic and object relations theorists consider people's parental images to be the root of their god representations (e.g., Erikson, 1959; Freud, 1913/1962; Rizzuto, 1979). One point of similarity between these theories and CSR accounts of religious cognition is that they propose parallel mental representations and processes that can be in conflict with each other and that some processes occur below awareness. Despite this key similarity, empirical support for traditional psychodynamic theories of religion, as Granqvist (2006) critiqued, has been "unsystematic, relying on a few, mostly unrepresentative cases of biographies, often drawn from clinical contexts" (p. 10). This has led some theorists to favor the more empirically grounded attachment theory (Bowlby, 1969/1997, 1973/2004, 1979/2005) to account for individual differences in religious beliefs, behaviors, and experiences.

Attachment theory proposes that through repeated interactions with primary caregivers, an infant develops internal working models (IWMs) of self and others that subsequently become templates for cognitive, emotional, and behavioral responses in other close relationships. Kirkpatrick extended this theory to include relationships with God (Kirkpatrick, 1992, 1994), and two contrasting hypotheses concerning the linkage between attachment and religiosity have subsequently been proposed. The *correspondence hypothesis* predicts continuity between the believer's attachment relationships and their experience of God (IWM correspondence), and the *compensation hypothesis* predicts that individuals with insecure attachment relationships turn to God as a surrogate attachment figure to compensate for their negative attachment experiences. Evidence supporting each hypothesis has been found (a thorough discussion of religion and attachment can be found in Chapter 7 of this volume). Hall, Fujikawa, Halcrow, and Hill (2009; see also Chapter 15 in this volume) have argued that the inconsistency in findings may be due in part to different studies focusing on explicit religious behaviors versus implicit motivations underlying religious behavior. Their argument highlights the key theme underlying this chapter: that people possess multiple religious representations that are processed with varying degrees of efficiency, which may influence religious belief, experience, and expression under different contextual demands, and that a comprehensive account of religion (including religious attachments) must bear in mind the constraints on religious cognition imposed by our cognitive architecture.

As in other relationships, believers report experiencing both positive and negative emotions toward God. Feelings toward God have been found to cluster into three general groups: positive feelings, such as gratitude; negative feelings in relation to the self, such as anxiety and fear; and negative feelings in relation to God, such as anger and frustration (Exline & Martin, 2005; Jonker, Eurelings-Bontekoe, Zock, & Jonker, 2008; Murken, Möschl, Müller, & Appel, 2011). Although theories of emotion vary, there is considerable agreement among theorists that emotions include cognitive appraisals and interpretations of events and experiences (Scherer, Schorr, & Johnstone, 2001). Shame and inadequacy, for example, result from seeing the self as not being good enough, whereas anger and frustration are often directed at the agent perceived to be responsible for blocking core goals or causing significant harm. Emotions toward God appear to follow a similar pattern of appraisal: Exline Park, Smyth, and Carey (2011) found anger at God to be predicted by attributing a significant harmful event to God and perceiving God as having negative intentions for causing the event.

Religious Cognition and Life Experiences

Whatever the precise nature of religious representations, these representations are likely to function similarly to cognitive schemas by exerting top-down influence over how information and experiences are processed, stored, and organized. For example, Lechner (1989) has found that individuals with well-delineated god concepts were more likely to integrate their religious beliefs into their daily lives, and McIntosh, Silver, and Wortman (1993) have found that individuals who considered religion as personally important to them were more likely to engage in cognitive processing of a traumatic event in a schema-congruent manner that was associated with better coping with the event. Thus, the sorts of religious representations held by individuals are likely to influence how life events are interpreted and the sorts of responses that are made (Pargament, 1997).

Attributing events to supernatural agents. In addition to information about the personality of gods, representations of gods also include information about their superattributes: what gods *could* do as well as what gods *would* do. These representations inform how people interpret causal relations between gods, their own experiences, and even their own behaviors.

An initial theoretical account of religious attributions was offered by Proudfoot and Shaver (1975) and subsequently developed by Spilka, Shaver, and Kirkpatrick (1985), and a small body of empirical research has explored factors that influence the making of religious attributions. Religious attributions were more likely to be made by individuals who are religious (Lupfer, Brock, & DePaola, 1992), when the event was important (Spilka & Schmidt, 1983) or life-altering (Lupfer, Tolliver, & Jackson, 1996), when the event was related to medical or health-related needs (Spilka & Schmidt, 1983), when the event was religiously salient (Lupfer & Layman, 1996, although no effect was found for priming the salience of religion to the attributor), when the event concerned moral harm (Gray & Wegner, 2010), when there were no salient alternative explanations to the event (Lupfer et al., 1996), and when God was perceived to be a concurrent cause (Weeks & Lupfer, 2000). Although many of these findings are consistent with CSR predictions concerning conditions under which supernatural agents would be invoked as causes, they should be qualified by the fact that in most studies, religious attributions were the minority; even under conditions that favored religious attributions, the most religious individuals still preferred naturalistic explanations over supernatural ones. One possibility is that the use of experimenter-devised vignettes provided little motivation for individuals to engage in any meaningful attribution search. Vignette-based studies that keep personal salience and involvement at low levels may not engage the participant in the type of processing and use of the sorts of representations they may otherwise use in real life and in more personally salient situations. Even when participants were asked to imagine themselves in the vignettes, the effect was minimal (Spilka & Schmidt, 1983).

When making causal attributions for highly personal and emotionally arousing experiences, individuals also draw on their representations of God's personality. In several studies of anger toward God, Exline et al. (2011) focused on individuals' appraisals of the cause and God's intention for incidents of significant harm or wrongdoing to the self or to a loved one. Individuals for whom religion was more salient were more likely to perceive God as responsible for the incident, but the strongest predictor of anger at God was attributing negative intention to God's involvement—that is, appraising God's involvement as intending to harm or hurt the individual. Thus, in these highly personal and emotionally arousing experiences, individuals were making attributions not only about whether God *could* cause or fail to prevent the harmful event (representations of God's counterintuitive properties) but also about God's intentions behind causing or failing to prevent the harmful event (representations of God's personality). Although these researchers did not explicitly address God representations, their findings are consistent with the idea that individuals'

God representations, self-representations, and God-in-relation-to-self representations could predict anger toward God.

Prayer. Verbally communicating with gods, spirits, and ancestors is a cross-culturally recurrent phenomenon but has received very little attention so far by cognitive scientists of religion (see Chapter 16 in this volume). Following on the idea that nonreflective, automatic god concepts may be more anthropomorphic than explicit theologies profess, Barrett investigated how nonreflective representations of God might shape petitionary prayer practices among U.S. Protestants (Barrett, 2001, 2002). Protestants are encouraged to make requests of God, but they are not typically told that God is more likely to use one type of causation (e.g., psychological, biological, or mechanistic) over another. When I lose my keys, I could ask God to act psychologically (e.g., remind me where I left them or help me see where they are) or I could ask God to act physically (e.g., have them materialize on my desk). Either course of action is possible for an all-powerful God, but through analyses of prayer journals and by asking to judge their most likely prayer strategy in a number of hypothetical situations (controlling for gravity of the situation, goodness of the solution, etc.), Barrett found a tendency for his young adult participants to pray for God to act through psychological or social causation more than through biological or physical causation. Barrett's findings provide a second plausible explanation for the low frequency of religious attributions observed in studies of religious attributions: It may be that individuals' nonreflective representations of God do not include any well-elaborated representations about God's causal role in the world.

Belief (and nonbelief) in supernatural agency. Belief in supernatural agents appears to be widespread across cultures because of the relative intuitiveness and inferential richness of these concepts, leading CSR theorists to advocate the view that belief in supernatural agency is a by-product of naturally evolved cognitive propensities as a result of evolutionary pressures (Boyer, 1994, 2001). As "natural" as supernaturalism might be, CSR also needs to account for the widespread and continual growing presence of nonbelief. Although researchers have begun to attend to the psychology of atheism and nonbelief (Streib, Hood, Keller, Csöff, & Silver, 2009; see also Chapter 40 in this volume), CSR research in nonbelief has been scarce (Geertz & Markússon, 2010). Barrett (2004) suggested that atheism and nonbelief requires extracultural scaffolding to be acquired, and he proposed various environmental factors that may suppress intuitive belief in the supernatural. One factor is urbanized societies that, in the grand scheme of human history, have been the exception rather than the rule. Such manmade environments make it easier for individuals to interpret the events through human (or human-related) causes. Second, the advancement of science and widespread nature of scientific knowledge means that some causes for events that previously were unknown are now known; individuals no longer need to appeal to supernatural causes to explain events like earthquakes and hurricanes, but instead they can turn to scientific explanations as alternatives. Indeed, in some societies, atheism appears to correlate with education level (Beit-Hallahmi, 2007). Third, the paucity of survival threats in the environment means that fewer experiences would activate HADD and leave ambiguous the detected agency. Even when HADD is activated, more alternative nonreligious explanations for interpreting the experiences may be available. In other words, contemporary urban settings have created contexts in which it is easier to suppress supernatural explanations with more reflective, humanistic explanations.

Although many atheists cite rational and scientific reasons for their nonbelief, researchers have suggested the nonbelief of some atheists may be based primarily on emotional experiences rather than reflective, rational explanations. Novotni and Petersen (2001) proposed that some believers ultimately become atheists because they are unable to reconcile the experience of personal disappointments or suffering with belief in an omnibenevolent God. Their anger and disillusionment at God causes them to disassociate from belief altogether. Data from a study of undergraduates by Exline and colleagues supports this theory (Exline, Fisher, Rose, & Kampani, 2006; see also Exline & Martin, 2005):

When asked why they did not believe in God, most nonbelievers cited rational and intellectual reasons; however, closer examination of the data revealed a group of "slipping believers" whose previous belief in God had decreased after experiencing anger at God. Individuals who said they turned away from or rejected God after that experience were more likely to become nonbelievers. Of course, this is not a claim that all atheism is emotional; it does, however, suggest that some atheists are choosing to disbelieve in a negative representation of God.

IMPLICATIONS OF COGNITIVE ACCOUNTS

What then are the implications of current cognitive approaches for whether religious beliefs are warranted? What is the needed future research? We explore these questions in the sections that follow.

Implications for the Truth and Justification of Religious Beliefs

Much like Freudian or Marxist explanations of religion, cognitive explanations of religion have sometimes been considered as a threat to religious beliefs. Do cognitive and evolutionary explanations "explain away" religion? Philosophers and others are beginning to discuss such questions (Barrett, 2007; Clark & Barrett, 2010; Murray, 2008, 2009; Murray & Goldberg, 2009; Van Inwagen, 2009). The general idea of religious beliefs being threatened by CSR explanations has at least two distinct subproblems: whether CSR renders religious beliefs more likely to be false, and whether CSR renders religious beliefs rationally justified. It is easy to see that whether a scientific, naturalistic account of believing something to be the case does not bear on whether the belief is true or false. As Bloom wrote: "Psychologists who study why people believe there is intelligent life on Mars would be very confused if they thought their findings would bear on the debate over the actual existence of extraterrestrial life" (2009, p. 125). Psychologists can study why people have true beliefs (e.g., that 1 + 2 = 3), false beliefs (e.g., why we might believe raccoons are more biologically similar to opossums than to cows), and indeterminate beliefs (why we think others have minds). Cognitive scientists of religion may arrive at a naturalistic explanation of why some people believe the proposition "God exists" and why some people believe "God does not exist." Clearly, just having a naturalistic explanation for a belief is not relevant to the truth or falsehood of the belief, as observed by James (1902). Those who have other reasons to reject belief in one or many gods may find such explanations commensurate with their worldview, but they do not constitute evidence by themselves.

A more interesting problem is whether a scientific explanation of why people generally believe in the existence of gods (for instance) bears on whether such beliefs are rationally justified (whether or not they are true). Most concerns that have been considered on this point fall into one of three different types: whether the origins of religious beliefs in cognitive dynamics or selection pressures undermines their warrant, whether such accounts of religious beliefs entail that people would believe whether the beliefs in question are true or false and thereby undercut justification, and whether such accounts are commensurate with a given theological tradition or with the character of the divine. Published treatments have converged (so far) on such accounts not being a threat to justified religious beliefs, at least not for the first two types of reasons (Barrett, 2007; Murray, 2008). Whether such accounts are commensurate with a particular theology, for instance whether God would use such a process to encourage devotion, is necessarily relative to the particular theology in question (Van Inwagen, 2009).

Implications for Future Research

In this chapter we have reviewed various evolutionary and cognitive accounts of religion from CSR and psychology of religion research. CSR has primarily been concerned with broadly recurrent dimensions of religious belief and experiences (e.g., belief in invisible, superpowerful, superknowing agents; belief in the afterlife or continued existence of a spirit or essence after physical death), whereas the psychology of religion has primarily been concerned with individual differences in religious belief and experiences (e.g., relationships with God, religiosity, and well-being). Rather than continuing these two streams of research without regard for each other, integration of these two disciplines could be mutually beneficial in the following ways.

Theoretical integration. Even as people find it "natural" to believe in supernatural agents with particularly counterintuitive characteristics irrespective of their particular cultures and religious beliefs, this is hardly a full picture of what people would consider as "religion." It is individual differences in religious schemas that shape how individuals think, feel, and behave in relation to their religious beliefs. Significant differences can exist between one believer's religious experience and the experience of another believer of the same religion. Whereas CSR accounts might be able to explain belief in an all-powerful, all-knowing, and all-present God, it is not able to explain why one believer would experience this God as loving and responsive while another believer would experience this God as distant and cruel. Even as CSR can explain why two believers of the same religion believe that God works primarily through psychological causation, it does not explain why one believer is more likely to engage in petitionary prayer while the other is more likely to engage in liturgical prayer. Likewise, although CSR can explain why individuals are likely to make attributions to a supernatural agent, it does not explain why some believers can attribute significant personal suffering to God's activity (or culpable inactivity) and yet experience positive emotions toward God, whereas other believers can make the same causal attribution and experience negative emotions toward God, even to the point of abandoning their religious beliefs altogether. Thus, whereas CSR accounts of religious belief and experience can explain universal characteristics of religious belief and experience, it does not account for individual differences in the affective and motivational dimensions of religiosity or differences in cognitive, emotional, and behavioral outcomes that result from such differences. Theoretical integration would allow for both cognitive and traditional approaches to arrive at more comprehensive pictures of the universal and the idiosyncratic dimensions of religious belief and experiences. As we have mentioned, a promising point of theoretical integration would be to consider the interaction between people's representations of gods' counterintuitive properties with their affective representations of gods' personality. How must a god be conceptualized to make it a vehicle for emotional and relational investment? Could gods be represented as benevolent but "weak" (e.g., a loving god who cannot intervene in the believers personal affairs)? These types of deities appear in mythologies, but do they actually appear in the world's religions as objects of commitment? What might motivate individuals to believe in such gods, and what sorts of behaviors might believers display toward such gods? Although philosophers and religious writers have begun to deal with these questions (e.g., Hartshorne, 1984; Kushner, 1981), psychologists of religion and cognitive scientists of religion have yet to provide any answers.

Methodological integration. One criticism of the psychology of religion's research in god representations is that it relies heavily on self-report measures, which may be capable of assessing only the explicit and normative dimensions of a person's god representations (Gibson, 2007). Several researchers have attempted to make use of methodologies from social cognition and experimental psychology, such as implicit measures (Gibson, 2006), subliminal priming (Birgegard & Granqvist, 2004), and narrative comprehension (Barrett & Keil, 1996) to more directly assess the underlying cognitive representations and processes involved in religious cognition. CSR can benefit from employing validated and empirically sound methods from psychology, particularly when investigating psychological claims and constructs. Likewise, psychologists frequently draw conclusions from data collected from experimental designs that may lack ecological validity. In contrast, much of CSR research is based on cultural- and context-specific ethnographic and anthropological data that are rich in detail. Psychologists of religion should be encouraged to use multiple methods in their studies and to consider the degree of ecological validity and generalizability of their conclusions. CSR's interest in the universal aspects of religion means that a considerable proportion of its research is from non-Western cultures. Psychologists of religion should be reminded of the fact that there are more religious traditions in the world than the "great monotheisms" and that the psychology of religion in the industrial Western world may be importantly anomalous.

To sum, we see a more productive future for both psychology of religion and CSR if these two approaches, with their distinctive emphases and strengths, were more closely integrated. CSR lays a foundation for understanding cross-culturally recurrent patterns of thought we commonly regard as religious. These accounts fill in the conceptual lacunae that evolutionary and sociofunctional accounts leave. But the psychology of religion provides details on the relational, emotional, and interpersonal diversity we see built upon these cognitive foundations.

References

Astuti, R., & Harris, P. L. (2008). Understanding mortality and the life of the ancestors in rural Madagascar. *Cognitive Science, 32*, 713–740. doi:10.1080/03640210802066907

Atran, S. (2002). *In gods we trust: The evolutionary landscape of religion.* Oxford, England: Oxford University Press.

Barrett, J. L. (1998). Cognitive constraints on Hindu concepts of the divine. *Journal for the Scientific Study of Religion, 37*, 608–619. doi:10.2307/1388144

Barrett, J. L. (1999). Theological correctness: Cognitive constraint and the study of religion. *Method and Theory in the Study of Religion, 11*, 325–339. doi:10.1163/157006899X00078

Barrett, J. L. (2001). How ordinary cognition informs petitionary prayer. *Journal of Cognition and Culture, 1*, 259–269. doi:10.1163/156853701753254404

Barrett, J. L. (2002). Dumb gods, petitionary prayer, and the cognitive science of religion. In I. Pyysiainen & V. Anttonen (Eds.), *Current approaches in the cognitive study of religion* (pp. 93–109). London, England: Continuum.

Barrett, J. L. (2004). *Why would anyone believe in God?* Walnut Creek, CA: AltaMira Press.

Barrett, J. L. (2007). Is the spell really broken? Biopsychological explanations of religion and theistic belief. *Theology and Science, 5*, 57–72. doi:10.1080/14746700601159564

Barrett, J. L. (2008). Coding and quantifying counterintuitiveness in religious concepts: Theoretical and methodological reflections. *Method and Theory in the Study of Religion, 20*, 308–338. doi:10.1163/157006808X371806

Barrett, J. L., Burdett, E. R., & Porter, T. J. (2009). Counterintuitiveness in folktales: Finding the cognitive optimum. *Journal of Cognition and Culture, 9*, 271–287. doi:10.1163/156770909X12489459066345

Barrett, J. L., & Keil, F. C. (1996). Anthropomorphism and God concepts: Conceptualizing a non-natural entity. *Cognitive Psychology, 31*, 219–247. doi:10.1006/cogp.1996.0017

Barrett, J. L., Newman, R. M., & Richert, R. A. (2003). When seeing does not lead to believing: Children's understanding of the importance of background knowledge for interpreting visual displays. *Journal of Cognition and Culture, 3*, 91–108. doi:10.1163/156853703321598590

Barrett, J. L., & Nyhof, M. (2001). Spreading non-natural concepts: The role of intuitive conceptual structures in memory and transmission of cultural materials. *Journal of Cognition and Culture, 1*, 69–100. doi:10.1163/156853701300063589

Barrett, J. L., & Richert, R. A. (2003). Anthropomorphism or preparedness? Exploring children's God concepts. *Review of Religious Research, 44*, 300–312. doi:10.2307/3512389

Barrett, J. L., Richert, R. A., & Driesenga, A. (2001). God's beliefs versus Mom's: The development of natural and non-natural agent concepts. *Child Development, 72*, 50–65. doi:10.1111/1467-8624.00265

Barrett, J. L., & VanOrman, B. (1996). The effects of image use in worship on God concepts. *Journal of Psychology and Christianity, 15*, 38–45.

Beit-Hallahmi, B. (2007). Atheists: A psychological profile. In M. Martin (Ed.), *The Cambridge companion to atheism* (pp. 300–318). Cambridge, England: Cambridge University Press. doi:10.1017/CCOL0521842700.019

Benson, P., & Spilka, B. (1973). God image as a function of self-esteem and locus of control. *Journal for the Scientific Study of Religion, 12*, 297–310. doi:10.2307/1384430

Bering, J. M. (2002). Intuitive conceptions of dead agents' minds: The natural foundations of afterlife beliefs as phenomenological boundary. *Journal of Cognition and Culture, 2*, 263–308. doi:10.1163/15685370260441008

Bering, J. M. (2006). The folk psychology of souls. *Behavioral and Brain Sciences, 29*, 453–462. doi:10.1017/S0140525X06009101

Bering, J. M., & Bjorkland, D. F. (2004). The natural emergence of reasoning about the afterlife as a developmental regularity. *Developmental Psychology, 40*, 217–233. doi:10.1037/0012-1649.40.2.217

Bering, J. M., Hernández-Blasi, C., & Bjorkland, D. F. (2005). The development of "afterlife" beliefs in secularly and religiously schooled children. *British Journal of Developmental Psychology, 23*, 587–607. doi:10.1348/026151005X36498

Bering, J. M., & Johnson, D. D. P. (2005). "O Lord . . . You perceive my thoughts from afar": Recursiveness and the evolution of supernatural agency. *Journal of Cognition and Culture, 5*, 118–142. doi:10.1163/1568537054068679

Bering, J. M., McLeod, K., & Shackelford, T. K. (2005). Reasoning about dead agents reveals possible adaptive trends. *Human Nature, 16*, 360–381. doi:10.1007/s12110-005-1015-2

Birgegard, A., & Granqvist, P. (2004). The correspondence between attachment to parents and God: Three experiments using subliminal separation cues. *Personality and Social Psychology Bulletin, 30*, 1122–1135. doi:10.1177/0146167204264266

Bloom, P. (2004). *Descartes' baby: How child development explains what makes us human.* London, England: Heinemann.

Bloom, P. (2007). Religion is natural. *Developmental Science, 10*, 147–151. doi:10.1111/j.1467-7687.2007.00577.x

Bloom, P. (Ed.). (2009). *Religious belief as an evolutionary accident.* New York, NY: Oxford University Press.

Bowlby, J. (1997). *Attachment and loss: Vol. 1. Attachment.* London, England: Pimlico-Random House. (Original work published 1969)

Bowlby, J. (2004). *Attachment and loss: Vol. 2. Separation: Anxiety and anger.* London, England: Pimlico-Random House. (Original work published 1973)

Bowlby, J. (2005). *Making and breaking of affectional bonds.* New York, NY: Routledge. (Original work published 1979)

Boyer, P. (1993). Cognitive aspects of religious symbolism. In P. Boyer (Ed.), *Cognitive aspects of religious symbolism* (pp. 4–47). Cambridge, England: Cambridge University Press. doi:10.1017/CBO9780511896866.002

Boyer, P. (1994). *The naturalness of religious ideas: A cognitive theory of religion.* Berkeley: University of California Press.

Boyer, P. (1996). What makes anthropomorphism natural: Intuitive ontology and cultural representations. *Journal of the Royal Anthropological Institute, 2*, 83–97. doi:10.2307/3034634

Boyer, P. (2001). *Religion explained: The evolutionary origins of religious thought.* New York, NY: Basic Books.

Boyer, P. (2003). Religious thought and behavior as by-products of brain function. *Trends in Cognitive Sciences, 7*, 119–124. doi:10.1016/S1364-6613(03)00031-7

Boyer, P., & Ramble, C. (2001). Cognitive templates for religious concepts: Cross-cultural evidence for recall of counter-intuitive representations. *Cognitive Science, 25*, 535–564. doi:10.1207/s15516709cog2504_2

Bransford, J. D., & McCarrell, N. S. (1974). A sketch of a cognitive approach to comprehension: Some thoughts about understanding what it means to comprehend. In W. B. Weimer & D. S. Palermo (Eds.), *Cognition and the symbolic processes* (pp. 189–229). Hillsdale, NJ: Erlbaum.

Clark, K. J., & Barrett, J. L. (2010). Reformed epistemology and the cognitive science of religion. *Faith and Philosophy, 27*, 174–189.

Cohen, E. (2007). *The mind possessed: The cognition of spirit possession in an Afro-Brazilian religious tradition.* New York, NY: Oxford University Press.

Cohen, E., & Barrett, J. L. (2008a). Conceptualising possession trance: Ethnographic and experimental evidence. *Ethos, 36*, 246–267. doi:10.1111/j.1548-1352.2008.00013.x

Cohen, E., & Barrett, J. L. (2008b). When minds migrate: Conceptualising spirit possession. *Journal of Cognition and Culture, 8*, 23–48. doi:10.1163/156770908X289198

Cohen, E., & Barrett, J. L. (2011). In search of "folk anthropology": The cognitive anthropology of the person. In W. van Huyssteen & E. Wiebe (Eds.), *In search of self: Interdisciplinary perspectives on personhood* (pp. 104–122). Grand Rapids, MI: Eerdmans.

DiYanni, C., & Kelemen, D. (2005). Time to get a new mountain? The role of function in children's conceptions of natural kinds. *Cognition, 97*, 327–335. doi:10.1016/j.cognition.2004.10.002

Elkind, D. (1970). The origins of religion in the child. *Review of Religious Research, 12*, 35–42. doi:10.2307/3510932

Erikson, E. (1959). *Identity and the life cycle.* New York, NY: International Universities Press.

Evans, E. M. (2001). Cognitive and contextual factors in the emergence of diverse belief systems: Creation versus evolution. *Cognitive Psychology, 42*, 217–266. doi:10.1006/cogp.2001.0749

Exline, J. J., Fisher, M. L., Rose, E., & Kampani, S. (2006). *Emotional atheism: Can anger toward God predict decreased belief?* Unpublished manuscript, Case Western Reserve University, Cleveland, OH.

Exline, J. J., & Martin, A. (2005). Anger toward God: A new frontier in forgiveness research. In E. L. Worthington Jr., (Ed.), *Handbook of forgiveness* (pp. 73–88). New York, NY: Routledge.

Exline, J. J., Park, C. L., Smyth, J. M., & Carey, M. P. (2011). Anger toward God: Social-cognitive predictors, prevalence, and links with adjustment to bereavement and cancer. *Journal of Personality and Social Psychology, 100*, 129–148. doi:10.1037/a0021716

Forgas, J. P. (Ed.). (2001). *Handbook of affect and cognition*. Hillsdale, NJ: Erlbaum.

Freud, S. (1962). *Totem and taboo* (J. Strachey, Trans.). New York, NY: Norton. (Original work published 1913)

Geertz, A. C., & Markússon, G. (2010). Religion is natural, atheism is not: On why everybody is both right and wrong. *Religion, 40*, 152–165. doi:10.1016/j.religion.2009.11.003

Gelman, S. A., & Kremer, K. E. (1991). Understanding natural cause: Children's explanations of how objects and their properties originate. *Child Development, 62*, 396–414. doi:10.2307/1131012

Gibson, N. J. S. (2006). *The experimental investigation of religious cognition*. Unpublished doctoral dissertation, University of Cambridge, Cambridge, England.

Gibson, N. J. S. (2007). Measurement issues in God image research and practice. In G. L. Moriarty & L. D. Hoffman (Eds.), *God image handbook for spiritual counseling and psychotherapy: Research, theory, and practice* (pp. 227–246). Binghamton, NY: Haworth Press.

Gibson, N. J. S. (2008). Once more with feelings: The importance of emotion for cognitive science of religion. In J. Bulbulia, R. Sosis, E. Harris, R. Genet, C. Genet, & K. Wyman (Eds.), *The evolution of religion: Studies, theories, and critiques* (pp. 271–277). Santa Margarita, CA: Collins Foundation Press.

Goldman, R. G. (1965). *Readiness for religion*. London, England: Routledge & Kegan Paul.

Gonce, L. O., Upal, M. A., Slone, D. J., & Tweney, R. D. (2006). Role of context in the recall of counterintuitive concepts. *Journal of Cognition and Culture, 6*, 521–547. doi:10.1163/156853706778554959

Gorsuch, R. L. (1968). The conceptualization of God as seen in adjective ratings. *Journal for the Scientific Study of Religion, 7*, 56–64. doi:10.2307/1385110

Granqvist, P. (2006). On the relation between secular and divine relationships: An emerging attachment perspective and a critique of the "depth" approaches. *The International Journal for the Psychology of Religion, 16*, 1–18. doi:10.1207/s15327582ijpr1601_1

Gray, K., & Wegner, D. M. (2010). Blaming God for our pain: Human suffering and the divine mind. *Personality and Social Psychology Review, 14*, 7–16. doi:10.1177/1088868309350299

Gregory, J., & Barrett, J. L. (2009). Epistemology and counterintuitiveness: Role and relationship in epidemiology of cultural representation. *Journal of Cognition and Culture, 9*, 289–314. doi:10.1163/156770909X12489459066381

Guthrie, S. E. (1980). A cognitive theory of religion. *Current Anthropology, 21*, 181–194. doi:10.1086/202429

Guthrie, S. E. (1993). *Faces in the clouds: A new theory of religion*. New York, NY: Oxford University Press.

Hall, T. W. (2003). Relational spirituality: Implications of the convergence of attachment theory, interpersonal neurobiology, and emotional information processing. *Psychology of Religion Newsletter: American Psychological Association Division 36, 28*, 1–12.

Hall, T. W., Fujikawa, A., Halcrow, S. R., & Hill, P. C. (2009). Attachment to God and implicit spirituality: Clarifying correspondence and compensation models. *Journal of Psychology and Theology, 37*, 227–242.

Hartshorne, C. (1984). *Omnipotence and other theological mistakes*. Albany: State University New York Press.

Hill, P. C., & Gibson, N. J. S. (2008). Whither the roots? Achieving conceptual depth in psychology of religion. *Archive for the Psychology of Religions, 30*, 19–35.

Hill, P. C., & Hood, R. W. (1999). Affect, religion, and unconscious processes. *Journal of Personality, 67*, 1015–1046. doi:10.1111/1467-6494.00081

James, W. (1902). *The varieties of religious experience*. Cambridge, MA: Harvard University Press. doi:10.1037/10004-000

Jonker, H. S., Eurelings-Bontekoe, E. H. M., Zock, H., & Jonker, E. (2008). Development and validation of the Dutch Questionnaire God Image: Effects of mental health and religious culture. *Mental Health, Religion, and Culture, 11*, 501–515. doi:10.1080/13674670701581967

Kelemen, D. (1999a). The scope of teleological thinking in preschool children. *Cognition, 70*, 241–272. doi:10.1016/S0010-0277(99)00010-4

Kelemen, D. (1999b). Why are rocks pointy? Children's preference for teleological explanations of the natural world. *Developmental Psychology, 35*, 1440–1452. doi:10.1037/0012-1649.35.6.1440

Kelemen, D. (2004). Are children "intuitive theists"? Reasoning about purpose and design in nature. *Psychological Science, 15*, 295–301. doi:10.1111/j.0956-7976.2004.00672.x

Kelemen, D., & DiYanni, C. (2005). Intuitions about origins: Purpose and intelligent design in children's reasoning about nature. *Journal of Cognition and Development, 6*, 3–31. doi:10.1207/s15327647jcd0601_2

Kelemen, D., & Rosset, E. (2009). The human function compunction: Teleological explanation in adults. *Cognition, 111*, 138–143. doi:10.1016/j.cognition.2009.01.001

Kirkpatrick, L. A. (1992). An attachment-theory approach to the psychology of religion. *The International Journal for the Psychology of Religion, 2*, 3–28. doi:10.1207/s15327582ijpr0201_2

Kirkpatrick, L. A. (1994). The role of attachment in religious belief and behavior. In D. Perlman &

K. Bartholomew (Eds.), *Advances in personal relationships* (Vol. 5, pp. 239–265). London, England: Kingsley.

Knight, N. (2008). Yukatek Maya children's attributions of beliefs to natural and non-natural entitites. *Journal of Cognition and Culture, 8*, 235–243. doi:10.1163/156853708X358164

Knight, N., Sousa, P., Barrett, J. L., Atran, S. (2004). Children's attributions of beliefs to humans and God: Cross-cultural evidence. *Cognitive Science, 28*, 117–126. doi:10.1016/j.cogsci.2003.09.002

Kushner, H. (1981). *When bad things happen to good people.* New York, NY: Avon Books.

Lechner, P. L. (1989). *Application of theory and research on cognitive schemata to the concept of God.* Unpublished doctoral dissertation, Saint Louis University, Saint Louis, MO.

Lisdorf, A. (2004). The spread of non-natural concepts: Evidence from Roman prodigy lists. *Journal of Cognition and Culture, 4*, 151–173. doi:10.1163/1568537043230747 96

Lupfer, M. B., Brock, K. F., & DePaola, S. J. (1992). The use of secular and religious attributions to explain everyday behavior. *Journal for the Scientific Study of Religion, 31*, 486–503. doi:10.2307/1386858

Lupfer, M. B., & Layman, E. (1996). Invoking naturalistic and religious attributions: A case of applying the availability heuristic? The representativeness heuristic? *Social Cognition, 14*, 55–76. doi:10.1521/soco.1996.14.1.55

Lupfer, M. B., Tolliver, D., & Jackson, M. (1996). Explaining life-altering occurrences: A test of the "God-of-the-gaps" hypothesis. *Journal for the Scientific Study of Religion, 35*, 379–391. doi:10.2307/1386413

McIntosh, D. N., Silver, R. C., & Wortman, C. B. (1993). Religion's role in adjustment to a negative life event: Coping with the loss of a child. *Journal of Personality and Social Psychology, 65*, 812–821. doi:10.1037/0022-3514.65.4.812

Murken, S., Möschl, K., Müller, C., & Appel, C. (2011). Entwicklung und Validierung der Skalen zur Gottesbeziehung und zum religiösen Coping (SGrC) [Development and validation of the scales Relationship With God and Religious Coping (SGRC)]. In A. Büssung & N. Kohls (Eds.), *Spiritualität jenseits des Glaubens: Transdisziplinäre wissenschaftliche Grundlagen im Zusammenhang mit Gesundheit und Krankheit* (pp. 75–91). Heidelberg, Germany: Springer Medizin.

Murray, M. J. (2008). Four arguments that the cognitive psychology of religion undermines the justification of religious beliefs. In J. Bulbulia, R. Sosis, R. Genet, E. Harris, K. Wyman, & C. Genet (Eds.), *The evolution of religion: Studies, theories, and critiques* (pp. 365–370). Santa Margarita, CA: Collins Foundation Press.

Murray, M. J. (2009). Scientific explanations of religion and the justification of religious belief. In M. Murray & J. Schloss (Eds.), *The believing primate: Scientific, philosophical, and theological reflections on the origin of religion* (pp. 168–178). Oxford, England: Oxford University Press.

Murray, M. J., & Goldberg, A. (2009). *Evolutionary accounts of religion: Explaining and explaining away.* New York, NY: Oxford University Press.

Norenzayan, A., Atran, S., Faulkner, J., & Schaller, M. (2006). Memory and mystery: The cultural selection of minimally counterintuitive narratives. *Cognitive Science, 30*, 531–553. doi:10.1207/s15516709cog0000_68

Novotni, M., & Petersen, R. (2001). *Angry with God.* Colorado Springs, CO: Pinon Press.

Pargament, K. I. (1997). *The psychology of religion and coping: Theory, research, practice.* New York, NY: Guilford Press.

Petrovich, O. (1997). Understanding of non-natural causality in children and adults: A case against artificialism. *Psyche en Geloof, 8*, 151–165.

Petrovich, O. (1999). Preschool children's understanding of the dichotomy between the natural and the artificial. *Psychological Reports, 84*, 3–27. doi:10.2466/pr0.1999.84.1.3

Piaget, J. (1929). *The child's conception of the world.* New York, NY: Harcourt Brace.

Proudfoot, W., & Shaver, P. (1975). Attribution theory and the psychology of religion. *Journal for the Scientific Study of Religion, 14*, 317–330. doi:10.2307/1384404

Richert, R. A., & Barrett, J. L. (2005). Do you see what I see? Young children's assumptions about God's perceptual abilities. *The International Journal for the Psychology of Religion, 15*, 283–295. doi:10.1207/s15327582ijpr1504_2

Rizzuto, A. M. (1979). *The birth of the living God: A psychoanalytic study.* Chicago, IL: University of Chicago Press.

Scherer, K. R., Schorr, A., & Johnstone, T. (Eds.). (2001). *Appraisal processes in emotion: Theories, methods, research.* Oxford, England: Oxford University Press.

Slone, D. J. (2004). *Theological incorrectness: Why religious people believe what they shouldn't.* New York, NY: Oxford University Press.

Spelke, E. S., & Kinzler, K. D. (2007). Core knowledge. *Developmental Science, 10*, 89–96. doi:10.1111/j.1467-7687.2007.00569.x

Sperber, D. (1996). *Explaining culture: A naturalistic approach.* Oxford, England: Blackwell.

Spilka, B., & Schmidt, G. (1983). A general attribution theory for the psychology of religion: The influence of event-character on attributions to God. *Journal for the Scientific Study of Religion, 22,* 326–339. doi:10.2307/1385771

Spilka, B., Shaver, P. R., & Kirkpatrick, L. A. (1985). A general attribution theory for the psychology of religion. *Journal for the Scientific Study of Religion, 24,* 1–20. doi:10.2307/1386272

Stanovich, K. E., & West, R. F. (2000). Individual differences in reasoning: Implications for the rationality debate. *Behavioral and Brain Sciences, 23,* 645–665. doi:10.1017/S0140525X00003435

Streib, H., Hood, R. W., Jr., Keller, B., Csöff, R-M., & Silver, C. F. (2009). *Deconversion: Qualitative and quantitative results from cross-cultural research in the United States and Germany.* Göttingen, Germany: Vandenhoeck & Ruprecht.

Tremlin, T. (2006). *Minds and gods: The cognitive foundations of religion.* New York, NY: Oxford University Press.

Tweney, R. D., Upal, M. A., Gonce, L. O., Slone, D. J., & Edwards, K. (2006). The creative structuring of counterintuitive worlds. *Journal of Cognition and Culture, 6,* 483–498. doi:10.1163/156853706778554904

Upal, M. A., Owsianiecki, L., Slone, D. J., & Tweney, R. D. (2007). Contextualizing counterintuitiveness: How context affects comprehension and memorability of counterintuitive concepts. *Cognitive Science, 31,* 415–439.

Van Inwagen, P. (2009). Explaining belief in the supernatural—some thoughts on Paul Bloom's "religious belief as an evolutionary accident." In J. Schloss & M. Murray (Eds.), *The believing primate: Scientific, philosophical, and theological reflections on the origin of religion* (pp. 128–138). New York, NY: Oxford University Press.

Watson, P. J., Morris, R. J., Hood, R. W., Jr., Miller, L., & Waddell, M. G. (1999). Religion and the experiential system: Relationships of constructive thinking with religious. *The International Journal for the Psychology of Religion, 9,* 195–207. doi:10.1207/s15327582ijpr0903_3

Watts, F. N. (1996). Psychological and religious perspectives on emotion. *The International Journal for the Psychology of Religion, 6,* 71–87. doi:10.1207/s15327582ijpr0602_1

Watts, F. N. (2006). *Implicational and propositional religious meanings.* Unpublished manuscript, University of Cambridge, Cambridge, England.

Watts, F. N., & Williams, M. (1988). *The psychology of religious knowing.* Cambridge, Cambridge, England: Cambridge University Press.

Weeks, M., & Lupfer, M. B. (2000). Religious attributions and proximity of influence: An investigation of direct interventions and distal explanations. *Journal for the Scientific Study of Religion, 39,* 348–362. doi:10.1111/0021-8294.00029

Zahl, B. P., & Gibson, N. J. S. (2008, April). *God concepts? Depends on how you ask! Exploring measurement differences in God concept research.* Paper presented at the Christian Association of Psychological Science, Phoenix, AZ.

Zahl, B. P., & Gibson, N. J. S. (2009, August). *Improving paper and pencil measures of God representations.* Paper presented at the International Association for Psychology of Religion Congress, Vienna, Austria.

Chapter 13

RELIGION, SPIRITUALITY, AND CULTURE: CLARIFYING THE DIRECTION OF EFFECTS

Kate Miriam Loewenthal

Many years ago, in the early 1970s, I was preparing a course in the psychology of religion. There was not nearly as much to talk about then as there is now. I noticed that most of the empirical work was conducted in Western Hemisphere countries, among people of Christian background. I wondered whether the findings would change when people from other backgrounds were studied.

Tarakeshwar, Stanton, and Pargament (2003) have noted that religion has usually been overlooked in the study of cross-cultural differences. It is vital, however, to consider the interplay between religion and culture in any attempt to understand human behavior. For example, we now have evidence that risk factors for anxiety and depression vary across religious–cultural groups (e.g., Abdel-Khalek & Lester, 2007; Loewenthal et al., 1995). Other studies are revealing fascinating connections between religion, spirituality, and culture. Saroglou (2003), however, has cautioned that differences in psychological factors—personality, social attitudes, values—between cultures and religious groups may be outweighed by the similarities (p. 71). Clearly, it is too soon to draw definitive conclusions regarding the effects of religion and culture. Nevertheless, the study of religion, spirituality, and culture represents an important direction for the field.

This chapter will explore work on the relations between religion, spirituality, and culture, and in the process, it will consider theoretical, methodological, and interpretive issues. Traditionally, both cross-cultural psychologists and psychologists of religion have compared members of different groups—cultural or religious—with respect to one or more psychological factors. Examples include the study of psychological correlates of individualism versus collectivism by cross-cultural psychologists and the study of religious orientation in relation to measures of prejudice by psychologists of religion. How might these traditions—cross-cultural psychology and the psychology of religion—merge? More specifically, this chapter will focus on some ways in which culture and religion may influence each other. Theoretical and methodological developments and potential applications will be considered, adopting an integrative paradigm linking theory, research, and practice (as described in Chapter 1 of this volume).

DEFINITIONS

As elsewhere in this volume, the term *religion* refers to beliefs, practices, relationships, or experiences having to do with the sacred that are explicitly and historically rooted in established institutionalized systems. There will also be reference to work on *spirituality*, rather than religion, where spirituality refers to beliefs, practices, relationships, or experiences having to do with the sacred that are not necessarily linked to established institutionalized systems. *Culture* has been defined as "the beliefs, customs, habits and language shared by the people living in a particular time and place" (Kenrick, Neuberg, & Cialdini, 1999, p. 7). It is accepted practice to identify cultures by their geographic and ethnic

Many thanks to the editors for their constructive comments and suggestions, all of which have made this work worthwhile.

DOI: 10.1037/14045-013
APA Handbook of Psychology, Religion, and Spirituality: Vol. 1. Context, Theory, and Research, K. I. Pargament (Editor-in-Chief)
Copyright © 2013 by the American Psychological Association. All rights reserved.

labels, and where relevant, historical periods, as in "Cambodian," "African American," or "Medieval."

SOME CONCEPTUAL AND METHODOLOGICAL CHALLENGES

The psychological study of religion and culture raises some challenging issues. First, methodological issues: Many studies in the psychology of religion involve psychometric measurement of psychological and religious factors, and often the designs are cross-sectional. There have been growing calls for greater use of experimental and quasi-experimental designs, and longitudinal studies, all of which allow for stronger causal inferences (see Chapter 4 in this volume). There have also been recommendations for increased use of qualitative methodologies, allowing for the emergence of new research questions, and an enhanced understanding of the experiential aspects of the phenomena under investigation. Calls have been issued to ensure that psychometric measures are religiously and culturally appropriate, reliable, and valid; that religious sensitivities are not trampled on; and that translation and backtranslation are appropriately done (Loewenthal, 2009).

A second issue involves clarifying the direction of effects. When researchers find interactions between religion and culture, it is sometimes hard to discern when religion is affecting culture, or culture affecting religion. Even if we can make reasonable assumptions about the direction of effects, it can be hard to explain these connections and determine whether culture is mediating or moderating the relationships between religiousness and human functioning. In this chapter, we consider how religion and culture might affect each other. We also focus on some ways in which culture may mediate or moderate the ties between religion, spirituality and human behavior.

Culture is a rich and complex construct. This chapter focuses on three aspects most salient for religion. First, leading the field in popularity and influence, is individualism–collectivism, a way of depicting characteristics of cultures developed by Hofstede (1980) and by Triandis, Bontempo, Villareal, Asai, and Lucca (1988). Individualism is a dimension of social organization reflected in self-reliance, competitiveness, and low concern for one's in-group(s). Collectivism involves cooperativeness and concern for one's in-group(s). In this context, we can note parallels in current efforts to distinguish individual spirituality from collective religiousness (Heelas & Woodhead, 2005). A second dimension of culture relevant to religiousness involves concepts of modernization, secularization and improved material prosperity. Secularization theorists, led by Luckmann (1963), have argued that religion becomes less relevant in the process of modernization, including the growth of prosperity, education, individualization, and pluralism. A third religiously relevant cultural dimension has to do with the processes of acculturation, occurring when people live with and respond to a culture that differs from that of their upbringing (Berry, 1997). Acculturation can involve the importation of beliefs and practices from surrounding cultures as well as the development of distinct religious minority groups segregated from surrounding cultures. Here, we attend to social identity theory (Tajfel & Turner, 1986), which attributes crucial importance to social identity as the lens through which individuals view themselves, their world, and their relations with that world. We also draw on the concept of religion-as-culture (Cohen & Hill, 2007). Finally, we consider the effects of the political climate, including the relations between the state and religions and relations between religions themselves, including intergroup religious warfare (Roccas & Schwartz, 1997).

These cultural dimensions are not independent of each other. They are not watertight compartments, but rather they are simply conceptual spectacles for viewing societies, cultures, and their relationships to religion. Turning now to our central focus, we start to examine how religion and culture shape each other.

HOW DOES CULTURE SHAPE RELIGION?

Religion is embedded in culture. Greeley (1972) captured this point in his study of U.S. American religion (*The Denominational Society*): "For all the diversities among the three denominations (Protestant, Catholic and Jewish) . . . they are still fully American . . . with great similarities in their organizational structure, and in the behavior of their religious functionaries" (p. 203).

Religious beliefs and behavior can be affected by culture in many ways. We start with a specific illustration of mourning practices. We then examine how religion is affected by individualism–collectivism, materialism and prosperity, and political climate, values, and structure. We conclude with some specific examples of the adoption of cultural values and practices as religious.

A vivid illustration of the effects of culture on religious practices is Wikan's (1988) comparison of Muslim responses to bereavement in Egypt and in Bali. Although Islam is an all-embracing religion, local interpretations differ. Social support in Egypt and Bali is expressed in distinctive ways, "accommodating to different culturally constructed notions of self, body and interpersonal obligation" (Wikan, 1988, p. 451). In Cairo, relatives and friends of the bereaved flock in with gifts of food or money, uttering mournful shrieks, hugging and kissing the bereaved, urging them to have trust and faith that everything is from G-d. In Bali, by contrast, relatives and friends laugh and joke with the bereaved, attempting to make them forget their sorrow and to be happy. In Bali, Wikan spoke to a smiling, apparently happy girl, who said she wanted to travel to the family of a "friend" who had died suddenly. The girl mentioned that she herself was engaged, but she did not indicate any connection between her engagement and the friend who had died. Eventually it transpired that the dead friend was her fiancé. Initially, friends and relatives joked and laughed in an attempt to cheer her up. Only after a year did they begin to express sympathy; at this point, friends and relatives supposedly believed that the tragedy was safely past and that the danger of suicide had subsided. Wikan has argued that sorrow is expressed in ways that are linked to popular conceptions of health and sanity. More generally, the study highlights the influence of culture on religious practice and belief.

Individualism–Collectivism

A major influence of culture on religion is explored in studies of the relations between individualism–collectivism and religious orientation. In the 1960s, Allport (e.g., Allport & Ross, 1967) proposed a distinction between extrinsic and intrinsic religious orientations in an ingenious and influential attempt to explain the association between religion and racial prejudice. He suggested that the positive association between religion and racism is misleading. In fact, the relationship between religion and prejudice varies according to the type of religion: Extrinsic ("self-centered") religiosity would be related to intolerance, whereas the intrinsically religious (the more sincere and religiously active) would be more tolerant. In their review of empirical studies on religiousness and prejudice, Batson, Schoenrade, and Ventis (1993) concluded that intrinsic religiosity was associated with relatively low intolerance and prejudice, with the reverse being true for extrinsic religiosity (see also Chapter 24 in this volume). They also concluded that mental health was generally higher among the intrinsically religious compared with the extrinsically religious. Both conclusions may be culturally limited, with effects contingent on individualism–collectivism.

With regard to religious orientation and prejudice, we know as yet little about these relations in collectivist cultures. It does appear that extrinsic religiosity flourishes in collectivist cultures. Khan, Watson, and Habib (2005) assessed Muslims in Pakistan on the Muslim Attitudes Towards Religion Scale (MARS); Intrinsic, Extrinsic–Social, Extrinsic–Personal, and Quest religious orientation scales; and emotional empathy. Extrinsic–personal religious orientation was higher than intrinsic religious orientation among Pakistani Muslims, with the reverse pattern manifesting itself among Iranian Muslims (Watson et al., 2002). Pakistan has had a turbulent history, but its raison d'être is religion: Islam is central to its existence. Iranian culture, in contrast, carries a legacy of Westernization. Earlier Westernization in Iran may persist in the form of higher levels of individualism in Iran compared with Pakistan, and in the differences in the relative balance of extrinsic and intrinsic religiosity.

The suggestion that extrinsic religiosity flourishes in collectivist cultures is borne out by Cohen and Hill (2007; see also Chapter 37 in this volume). They compared Protestants, Catholics, and Jews on intrinsic and extrinsic religious orientation. Intrinsic orientation, they suggested, reflects the individualism of Protestant culture, which values personal religion. Extrinsic orientation, in contrast, reflects the collectivism of Jewish and Catholic cultures, which value community and ritual. Cohen and Hill (2007) found that Protestants endorsed intrinsic items relatively strongly, and Catholics endorsed extrinsic items strongly. Furthermore, the significant life-changing experiences of Protestants were more likely to involve personal encounters with G-d, whereas those of Jews and Catholics were more likely to involve ritual and social relationships (e.g., joining a congregation to say prayers for a deceased parent).

Duriez and Hutsebaut (2000) examined the relations between styles of religious belief and racism in Western European countries (Holland and Belgium) that are generally individualistic. Their work is an important development in studies of prejudice and styles of religiosity, and it echoes the suggestions made by Adorno, Frenkel-Brunswik, Levinson, and Sanford (1950) and Allport and Ross (1967) that a more tempered and flexible style of belief may help undo prejudice, at least within individualistic cultures.

Turning to the relations between religious orientation and well-being, Khan, Watson, and Habib (2005) worked with a Pakistani sample and found that extrinsic religious motivations appeared to have some beneficial mental health implications, in contrast to findings from U.S. and British Christian samples. This suggests that the conclusions reached by Batson et al. (1993) may be culturally bound rather than universal; for example, they might apply mainly to Western/Christian samples (i.e., individualistic cultures).

This conclusion is generally borne out by the work of Okulicz-Kozaryn (2010) who examined World Value Survey data from 79 countries. He looked at differences between social and individual religiosity, which broadly correspond to extrinsic and intrinsic religiosity. Okulicz-Kozaryn asserted that religion's relationship to life satisfaction is context dependent, varying across countries and cultures: Social (extrinsic) religiosity promotes social capital and satisfies the need to belong, whereas individual (intrinsic) religiosity facilitates individual experience. The empirical findings showed a bimodal relationship between religion and life satisfaction: Religion was linked with greater life satisfaction when forms of religiosity promoted social capital. Religious people were also happier in religious nations. Forms of religiosity that did not enhance social capital were not associated with greater life satisfaction; in fact, individual religiosity was tied to personal unhappiness, especially in low-religious nations. As Okulicz-Kozaryn concluded, "most of the happiness that religiosity brings about seems to come from the social setting it offers, satisfying the . . . need to belong, one of the fundamental conditions for human happiness" (p. 166). These correlational findings need to be interpreted with caution, as they do not allow causal inferences. Nonetheless, the possible link between social capital and benefits of religion may explain some of the connections between extrinsic religiosity and collectivism.

In sum, the work on religious orientation and belief style in individualist and collectivist cultures suggests that intrinsic religiosity is promoted in individualist cultures and extrinsic religiosity in collectivist culture. The implications of intrinsic and extrinsic religiousness for health and religion may vary as a function of culture.

Individualism, Materialism, and Prosperity

Individualism relates to the rise of spirituality: The growth of secularism in Western societies has been accompanied by the development of a broader view of spirituality (Hogan, 2010), often involving an emphasis on experience rather than practice. It has been suggested that spirituality involves beliefs, practices, relationships, or experiences having to do with the sacred that are, unlike religiousness, not necessarily linked to established institutionalized systems (see Chapter 1 in this volume). Zinnbauer et al. (1997) reported that a number of people in the United States defined themselves as spiritual but not religious. In their sample, 19% reported themselves as spiritual but not religious, 4% were religious but not spiritual, 74% were both religious and spiritual, and 3% were neither. Spiritual but not religious people reported that that they were likely to engage in New Age religious beliefs and practices, and they were unlikely to engage in the beliefs and practices of traditional religions.

Heelas and Woodhead (2005) studied people in the United Kingdom who regarded themselves as spiritual rather than religious. In *The Spiritual Revolution: Why Religion Is Giving Way to Spirituality*, they suggested that the emergence of spirituality is associated with postmodernity. Noting that increasing numbers of people now prefer to call themselves spiritual rather than religious, they asked whether this could be "the last gasp of religion or a radical change in the contemporary sacred scene" (p. 2). They offered the subjectivization thesis to explain changes in the forms of the sacred, particularly away from practice and ritual toward the experiential, relating these to the "massive subjective turn of modern culture" (Taylor, 1991, p.26)—a shift from objective roles and obligations to living in relation to subjective experiences, relational as much as individualistic. The key distinction is between "life-as" religion, involving obligations, and subjective-life spirituality, involving experience (Heelas & Woodhead, 2005, p. 3). We do not know whether the proportions of spiritual-but-not-religious people will continue to rise, but the phenomenon may well be linked to individualism, secularism, and issues associated with acculturation.

Individualism is not the only by-product of complex industrial societies that has import for religion. Improved material prosperity, education, pluralism, and other aspects of modernity may make religion less relevant to everyday needs and concerns. This was the argument put forward by secularization theorists, headed by Luckmann (1963). This traditional secularization hypothesis needs some reformulation, given the links between religiousness, the growth of prosperity, and other aspects of modernity and postmodernity, as seen in the former Soviet-dominated Eastern bloc countries (Pollack, 2008). How then do prosperity, materialism, and religiosity relate to one another?

Materialism may be defined as the extent to which the acquisition of material property is valued. Levels of materialism tend to be higher in less prosperous countries and so are levels of religiosity. But paradoxically, there are conflicts between materialism and many religious values. Burroughs and Rindfleisch (2002) concluded that on the individual level, materialist values are inversely related to religiosity. This conclusion appears to be limited to relatively prosperous countries, however. In less prosperous countries, the wealthier and more highly educated are as likely to place importance on religion as poorer people (Inglehart, Basanez, Dies-Medrano, Halman, & Luijkx, 2004). An important proposal (Inglehart, 1981) is that as prosperity and economic security increase, postmaterialist values develop and materialistic values decline. Postmaterialist values replace materialist concern with physical sustenance with an emphasis on belonging, self-expression, and quality of life. Postmaterialist values vary inversely with religious values (Inglehart et al., 2004). The material prosperity of cultures could affect religiosity in two ways: In conditions of low prosperity, both religion and materialist values can flourish; indeed, on the world level of analysis, materialists place greater emphasis on religion than do postmaterialists (Inglehart et al., 2004). But as prosperity increases, both materialism and religiosity decline; materialism is replaced by postmaterialism, which tends to be associated with a decline in religiosity. Because postmaterialists may feel economically secure, they may need less reassurance from religion (Inglehart et al., 2004). Thus, although there is some truth in Luckmann's (1963) secularization hypothesis, there are several complex effects. Although materialism and religiosity are inversely related in wealthy countries, they are positively related in poorer countries. Inglehart's proposals about the rise of postmaterialist values have been helpful in resolving some of the paradoxes.

Political Climate

What about the effects of the political climate, particularly the relations between the state and religion and the relations among religious groups? Explicit legal enactments and political directives can have enormous religious impact, as dramatically illustrated by attempts to suppress the practice of some or all religions or to remove the adherents of selected religions from the country.

Roccas and Schwartz (1997) examined how religion relates to individual values in different political climates. They noted that in early research, religiosity was associated with valuing conformity, security, tradition, and benevolence toward close others. Conversely, religiosity related negatively to valuing stimulation, self-direction, power, universalism, and achievement. Roccas and Schwartz proposed that opposition between church and state influences the social and psychological functions of religion in society and can affect relations between religiosity and values. They compared associations between religiosity and social values among Catholics from former Eastern bloc (European) countries with those from countries in which Catholicism is the dominant, politically favored religion. Consistent with their perspective, they found that in countries with a history of church–state opposition (Poland, Czech Republic, Hungary), religiosity correlated less positively with valuing conformity and security, less negatively with valuing power and achievement, and more positively with valuing universalism than in countries with good church–state relations (Italy, Spain, Portugal). This study controlled for religious denomination (Catholicism) while examining the moderating influence of church–state relationships. The effects observed point to the important role religious countercultures serve in the face of political opposition to religion.

Pargament, Tyler, and Steele (1979) also looked at the interplay between social organization and individual values within religious communities. They tested the hypothesis that members of churches and synagogues that were hierarchical and nonparticipatory, involving restrictive social control, would display different patterns of religiousness and mental health competence than members of horizontal, participatory churches and synagogues that enhanced individual social control. Measures of social control, authoritarian religious belief and individual psychosocial competence were used to categorize congregations into hierarchical and horizontal groups. Compared with their horizontal counterparts, members of hierarchical congregations were relatively less self-critical, were less trustful of others, and reported a greater sense of control by a powerful G-d. This study identified significant links between social organizational variables and religious and personality variables. The direction of effects is not certain; some types of individuals may be drawn toward compatible congregations, but congregational structure can also affect individual religious values. Although we cannot be sure that studies of congregations can generalize to larger levels of social–cultural analysis (i.e., countries), this work suggests the potential importance of examining the relations between political structures within countries (e.g., democracy vs. totalitarianism), the structures of their religious organizations, and the religious values and behaviors of individuals within those organizations.

Closely tied to the cultural dimension of political climate is intergroup religious conflict. Such conflicts do not bode well for psychological well-being. Francis, Robbins, Lewis, and Barnes (2008) examined the relationship between prayer, neuroticism, and psychoticism in 2,306 Northern Ireland 16- to 18-year-olds from seven Protestant and nine Catholic schools. Northern Ireland has two distinct religious communities, Protestant and Roman Catholic. Their relations are currently said to be peaceful, although they have been poor in the past. Participants who prayed more frequently had lower psychoticism scores on the Eysenck Personality Questionnaire, an often-replicated finding for which there are postulated theoretical mechanisms. The unexpected finding in this study was that although prayer was not associated with neuroticism among the Protestant sample, it was associated with neuroticism among the Catholics. The direction of causality may be related to the history of Catholic–Protestant conflict in Northern Ireland and to the position of Catholics as a relatively beleaguered and less prosperous minority: Under stress, the Catholic minority may have elevated scores on both neuroticism and praying more frequently as a means of coping. The difference between the two religious–cultural communities remains to be confirmed in further work, but the study exemplifies possible ways in which religious indicators and culture may influence each other.

In another study illustrating a similar impact of political–religious unrest, Williams, Francis, and Village (2010) analyzed multiwave data from five European countries: Great Britain, the Netherlands, Northern Ireland, Spain, and Sweden. Overall, the findings supported Durkheim's (1897/2002) analysis of the importance of the two institutions of marriage and religion for human flourishing. Closer examination of their data indicated some variations by country and time period in the associations among indexes of religiosity, happiness, and life satisfaction. Notably, in the earlier waves of the study, religious affiliation and attendance were negatively or only weakly associated with happiness and satisfaction in Northern Ireland compared with the other Western European countries studied. In the latest wave of the study, however, when Northern Ireland's troubles were much reduced, there were consistently positive and significant associations between religion and well-being in Northern Ireland. This suggests that during the Northern Ireland troubles involving severe conflict between Protestant and Roman Catholics, religious affiliation and activity were mixed blessings compared with the period following the reasonably successful peace process begun in the late 1990s. When religious affiliation was likely to be associated with victimization, the association between religion and well-being was weakened. The work of Williams et al. (2010) is valuable in detailing the effects of religious conflict and highlighting the role of historical change in relations between religious and psychological variables.

Cultural Values and Practices

Before finishing this look at the impact of culture on religious values, it is useful to consider the adoption of specific cultural values and practices. Some cultural values and practices may assume the sanctity of religious values. One example is the practice of female "circumcision" (female genital mutilation), which is widespread in Africa (Dirie & Miller, 1998; Skaine, 2005). Another example is that wives often "belong" to their husband's families throughout South Asia, and the practice may be seen as religious by Muslims, Hindus, Sikhs, and Christians from South Asia, even though it is disowned by these religious groups elsewhere. Yet another example is "binding," a form of male sexual impotence, involving the perception by a man that his male organ has been bound, and, as a result, the loss of sexual functioning. This maligned spiritual practice affecting male fertility is common in Iran and transcends religious boundaries (Muslim, Jewish, Christian; Margolin & Witztum, 1989). Such practices and beliefs are popularly perceived to have religious–spiritual bases and can have important effects on psychological functioning and well-being; yet they are not known in the same religions in other cultural contexts. Even though scholars maintain that there are no religious sources for these and other culturally carried beliefs and practices (Werbner, 2002), once they have been sanctified as religious by implicit popular consent, they become more difficult to question and change (see Chapter 14 in this volume).

In this section, we have reviewed some ways in which aspects of culture might affect religiousness. For example, the study of collectivist cultures brings into question existing conclusions about the relations between intrinsic religiosity and well-being, which may apply only in individualist cultures. Material prosperity and materialist values have shown mixed associations with religiosity, calling for further study. Political oppression, intergroup religious conflict, and warfare might also shape religiosity, highlighting the need for further study and theory.

HOW DOES RELIGION SHAPE CULTURE?

Here we reverse the directional focus and examine the impact of religion on culture. More specifically, we will consider examples of specific religious practices that pervade the surrounding society. We will also consider the enforced imposition of a religious system on an entire country.

An example of the first kind of impact relates to practices associated with feminine modesty. In many cultures and religions, it is considered modest for a woman to cover her hair. In Judaism, married orthodox women cover their hair with a scarf, hat, or wig. It was recently reported in Israel that some orthodox Jewish women had adopted the Muslim custom of the more enveloping Hijab, which covers part of the face and the shoulders (Olam, 2008). Another example, from the United Kingdom, is the report that mixed-sex hospital wards are to be abandoned. A major contributing factor to this undertaking has been campaigning by religious groups (Fleming, 2008).

Past and recent history offer examples of the imposition of entire religious systems upon countries. Islam spread rapidly in the Middle East with the introduction of the Qur'an in the 6th century by Mohamed and his followers. As a result, the earlier polytheistic religions were overtaken by monotheism. Other examples include the introduction of Buddhism in the early centuries of the first millennium to Tibet and Mongolia and the reformation of the Christian church in England, which involved suppressing Roman Catholic forms of worship and instituting the Church of England. This institution still has considerable direct political influence, as evidenced by the presence of its 21 most senior bishops in the U.K. House of Lords.

Normatively, fear of the horrendous consequences of defying the law resulted in the mass adoption of the politically favored style of religiousness. Underground countermovements aimed at preserving the suppressed religions have been widely noted. Surviving vestiges of earlier religious practices are sometimes absorbed into the dominant religion and culture. For example, pre-Christian customs involving mistletoe are common in Western Christian countries. Conversely, historians and other social scientists have noted that where religious groups continue in the teeth of suppression, they may absorb some characteristics of the dominant religion. For example, Bon, the pre-Buddhist religion of Tibet, is now said to resemble schools of Buddhism, with relatively minor variations in belief and practice (Kværne, 1995).

The imposition and development of Protestantism during the Reformation in 16th-century Northwest Europe, involved the decline of Roman Catholic Christianity. This was associated with the rise of individualism and related values (Lukes, 1971; Weber, 1904–1905/1958). Here it is important to remember Weber's thesis that the spirit of capitalism was generated by the rise of Protestantism. Building on this thesis, social psychologists identified the need to achieve as a pivotal psychological variable (e.g., McClelland, 1961). The need to achieve has been assessed using quantitative scales and measures on the basis of stories, designs, fabric coloring, and other sources. This work tested the idea that the need to achieve was higher in Protestant than in Catholic countries and that rising levels of the need for achievement predict subsequent periods of economic growth. More recently, Furnham and his colleagues (e.g., Furnham, 1990) have pursued Weberian suggestions by assessing the Protestant Work Ethic (PWE) in different cultures and subgroups, showing that PWE relates to a whole range of cultural attitudes and beliefs, such as cleanliness, obedience, and politeness.

The impact of Protestant Christianity on cultural values and psychological traits has been investigated more extensively (e.g., Furnham, 1990; McClelland, 1961) than have the effects of other religions upon cultures. There is a need for further conceptual clarification in the definitions of the culturally carried values said to be promoted by Protestantism, such as individualism and the work ethic. The interrelations of these factors can be studied further as well as the question of the degree to which these terms are culturally value-loaded. Additionally, it is important to study cultural values promoted by other religions.

RELIGION-AS-CULTURE

Sometimes religion and culture are indistinguishable. Cohen and Hill (2007) promoted the useful concept of religion-as-culture, suggesting that religious values can persist through the process of modernization in different cultures (Inglehart & Baker, 2000). Religion's effects may be more resistant to cultural change than other aspects of culture. Cohen and Hill (2007) agreed that religions may promote cultural differences and vice versa, but they are concerned with the persistence of religious values as cultural values: religion-as-culture. Their analysis leads to the question of how religion-as-culture arises. To answer this question, we turn our attention to theory and research on immigration and acculturation.

Immigration and Acculturation

All societies contain subgroups that are formed on the basis of occupation, status, age, religion, or other factors. The complexity of society is often exacerbated by immigration. Migration has been reported throughout history, often because of adversity. For example, there are the biblical accounts of the Israelites moving to Egypt to escape famine conditions, only to leave Egypt later to escape slavery. The pilgrims left England for recently discovered North

America to escape religious persecution. Sometimes, as in the shameful histories of slavery, deportation, and ethnic and religious cleansing, migration has been forced. As transport has improved in the past century, migration has become more feasible, not only to escape adversity but sometimes to improve social or economic welfare or to increase religious freedom. Subgroups in contemporary society often are formed on ethnic lines and often with religion covarying. Thus, the Israelites leaving Egypt were monotheists, the pilgrims leaving England were Puritans (Calvinists), and migrants from Bangladesh to the modern United Kingdom are Muslims. Contemporary societies are increasingly religiously and ethnically pluralist. Religious subgroups vary in their responses to the culture(s) around them, and states vary in their responses to religious and ethnic subgroups.

Religious groups respond to the societies with which they have contact in a number of possible ways. Central to this response is the process of acculturation, defined by Clanet (1990) as "the set of processes by which individuals and groups interact when they identify themselves as culturally distinct" (quoted and translated in Berry, 1997, p. 8). Berry (1997) described four varieties of acculturation strategy. These strategies reflect differences in the perceived importance of maintaining (good) relationships with wider society and the perceived importance of own-group identity, values, and customs. Table 13.1 presents the four strategies: integration (maintaining some cultural integrity but participating in the larger social network), assimilation (not holding to one's original culture and seeking daily interaction with other cultures), separation or segregation (holding one's original culture and avoiding interaction with other groups), and marginalization (little interest in one's own culture, often enforced, and little interest in relations with others, again often enforced by exclusion and discrimination). These acculturation strategies have been assessed and studied by Berry, Kim, Power, Young, and Bujaki (1989), who showed that there is usually an overall preference by individuals for one strategy over others, although preferences can vary according to context (e.g., in one's family vs. the workplace).

TABLE 13.1

Acculturation Strategies

		Importance of own-group identity and values	
		High	Low
Importance of relationships with wider society	High	Integration	Assimilation
	Low	Separation/ segregation	Marginalization

Note. From "Immigration, Acculturation, and Adaptation," by J. W. Berry, 1997, *Applied Psychology: An International Review, 46,* p. 10. Copyright 1997 by John Wiley & Sons Ltd. Adapted with permission.

Factors That Foster Religion-as-Culture

Among acculturation strategies, considerable attention has been given to separation and segregation (Douglas, 1966; Martin, 1981; Turner, 1969) and its causes and consequences. Distinctive segregated religious groups may foster religion-as-culture. Important factors include boundary maintenance, social identity, and the strength of religious beliefs.

Douglas (1966) has described the boundaries put in place by religious and other groups consisting of activities that maintain the distinction between the pure and the polluted. Boundary formation and maintenance are important processes that can affect the functioning of religious groups and thus mediate the impact of culture on religion. Turner (1969) has pointed out that religious groups in complex societies often attempt to achieve *communitas*, a community of more or less equal individuals who accept the authority of ritual elders. Martin (1981) emphasized that the process of maintaining boundaries is not static, but rather it involves dynamic tension. Loewenthal et al. (1997) offered examples of boundary maintenance in Jewish and Christian groups, examining the activities (such as Sabbath observance) involved in preserving the distinction between the "pure and the polluted." The establishment of segregated religious groups with clear boundaries can be a reaction to the complexities and perceived spiritual laxity of modern complex societies. Important effects of separation and segregation are empowerment and the establishment of a salient feature of identity: Members of small segregated religious groups may feel valued in a world that is otherwise vast, unintelligible, and alienating. These processes exemplify ways in which religion-as-culture is fostered.

In examining acculturation, the issue of social identity is growing in importance. Ysseldyk, Matheson, and Anisman (2010) argued that religious identity offers a distinctive "sacred" worldview and "eternal" group membership unmatched by other group identities. They suggest that religious identity may be a driving force for fundamentalism. Particularly when under threat, group boundaries are sharpened, and group identity and moral esteem are heightened.

In a study of identity among British Muslims in the wake of the 2001 attacks in the United States, Cinnirella et al. (in press) examined the association between ethnic, religious, and national identities and the degree to which these identities were linked with attitudes toward martyrdom and terrorism. Perpetrators of intergroup attacks normally are regarded as heroes or martyrs by those who share their group identity and aspirations—often for political and religious freedom. Attackers are often regarded as villains or terrorists, particularly by those toward whom the attacks are directed. Fifty-three percent of Cinnirella et al.'s (in press) sample were born in the United Kingdom, and 64% listed their ethnicity as Pakistani. Participants attached greatest importance and pride to their Muslim identity, less importance to ethnic identity, and least importance to British identity. High importance ratings and pride related to Muslim identity and religiosity were all linked with favorable attitudes toward religious martyrdom (suicide bombing) and terrorism (jihad, acts of violence against non-Muslims). Conversely, importance ratings and pride associated with British identity were linked with less favorable attitudes toward jihad and related acts. Using Berry's depiction of acculturation strategies, it appeared that the sample tended toward segregation or separation: The own-group identity was seen as important, whereas the host (British) identity was seen as less important. These findings suggest the relevance of the concept of identity to understanding reactions to terrorism. They also offer some evidence that a sense of host (British) national identity may mitigate support for religiously motivated acts of violence (see Chapter 26 in this volume; Volume 2, Chapter 18, this handbook).

This makes depressing reading for supporters of multiculturalism and religious tolerance, but two points are worth noting. One is that the separation response to multiculturalism is not the only one. Other strategies may also be followed, and their consequences for individual beliefs, values, and well-being may be less unpleasant. In his overview of his own and others' acculturation studies, Berry (2001) concluded that adaptation and self-esteem were optimal among those who followed the integration route. Marginalization results in poor adaptation, with separation and assimilation intermediate. One interpretation is that integration involves positive attitudes toward both one's own and the host culture, marginalization involves negative attitudes toward both, whereas separation and assimilation involve negative attitudes toward only either the host culture or one's own. Integration involves an openness to mutual accommodation and an absence of prejudice while maintaining pride in identity. Acculturation strategies and their consequences within religious groups deserve more attention from psychologists of religion, because the development of acculturation strategies is almost certainly a key mediator of the relationship between culture and religion. This work also points to the importance of religious identity in the study of beliefs, values, and behavior and the impact of culture.

The sheer strength of religious beliefs may also play a role in—or reflect—the process of acculturation and the formation of religion-as-culture. Maiello (2005) studied the religious beliefs of immigrant subgroups in Switzerland as well as members of the "resident," dominant culture. Western Europeans, Protestants, and atheists had lower levels of belief in G-d than did Eastern and Southern Europeans, Roman and Orthodox Catholics, and Muslims. Members of the majority religious and cultural groups—Western Europeans and Protestants—reported lower levels of religiosity than members of minority groups. Minority groups may show higher levels of religiosity to demonstrate the value of their minority-group identity and achieving a level of empowerment, with religion-as-culture playing an important role. Another complementary possibility is that those with stronger religious beliefs came from less prosperous countries where more importance is attached to spiritual values (Inglehart, 1981). This overview of acculturation strategies and development of religion-as-culture signals the importance of religious identity in acculturation and intergroup relations.

Religion-as-Culture and Implications for Health and Well-Being

Having examined acculturation strategies, we turn to specific examples of group norms in pluralist societies in which religion functions as culture. We will focus on religiously based norms of behavior and belief that affect health and well-being. For example, Loewenthal et al. (2003a, 2003b) examined the beliefs held by Jews and Protestants in the United Kingdom regarding alcohol use. Jews reported consuming less alcohol than did Protestants and also reported less favorable attitudes regarding drinking, being drunk, and social and recreational drinking. Jewish law and culture convey unfavorable attitudes about drunkenness, although alcohol use is prescribed in religious ritual. Although Protestants saw social drinking as relaxing and helpful in forgetting worries, Jews saw drinking as leading to loss of control, and they saw pubs as places of dangerous, wild behavior.

Albertsen, O'Connor, and Berry (2006) looked at specific religious–cultural groups in the United States and tested the hypothesis that interpersonal guilt is higher in collectivist (religious) cultures than in individualist cultures. Collectivist religious groups were Buddhist and Catholic, and individualist groups were Protestants and those who listed "none" for religion. Collectivist cultures in the study were Asian American and Latin American, whereas individualist cultures were European American. The religiously affiliated, particularly Catholics, showed higher interpersonal guilt than the religious "nones." Asian Americans generally reported higher levels of interpersonal guilt than Europeans and Latin Americans.

Examples of the varying relationships between religion and well-being can be seen when religion functions as culture. Religiously inspired caring obligations, promoted in collectivist religious–cultural groups, may have protective effects in some cases and harmful effects in others. Empirical studies have shown that caring and being cared for can promote well-being and protect against psychological disorders, particularly depression (Brown & Harris, 1978; Seligman, 2002). In collectivist groups, religion-as-culture often fosters social support, often resulting in stress moderation and greater well-being. In this vein, Shams and Jackson (1993) noted that unemployed Muslim men in a British city were less depressed if they were religiously active, praying in a cohesive mosque-based social network, a finding that may reflect the social support they received through their mosque friendships.

Caring responsibilities can become problematic, however, especially if they become too heavy. Gillard and Patton's (1999) studied different religious–cultural groups in Fiji following the disastrous hurricane Nigel. All groups interviewed reported supportive effects of their religious beliefs in coping, but there were differences between the groups with respect to the amount of practical help—financial, housing, food—demanded and received after the hurricane. Both Indian Hindus and Muslims were required by their temples and mosques to give more assistance than were the Christian Fijians. The Indian Hindus and Muslims, however, received less assistance than the Christian Fijians. Differences in these levels of support may have affected the stress levels of the Fijians, as assessed by a general measure of stress and a trauma-specific measure. The Christian Fijians indicated less stress than the other groups. Here, we see that the burden of care, obligatory in most or all religious cultures, may lower well-being, as was the case with the Fijian Hindus and Muslims. This finding may reflect the fact that Islam and Hinduism have a more collectivist ethos than Christianity.

The burdens and benefits of caring are illustrated by Loewenthal et al. (1997), who noted that the caring responsibilities of religious Jewish and Christian women were associated with a higher numbers of life events, which were themselves a product of family size. Greater numbers of life events, in turn, were associated with higher levels of anxiety. The benefits of cohesive families also were noted among both Protestants and Jews, however. Levels of depression were lowered in tandem with a characteristic of the religious lifestyle—namely, the lower number of severely disruptive life events such as marital violence.

Loewenthal and Brooke Rogers (2004) reported that strictly orthodox Jewish women were reluctant to use local religiously and culturally sensitive support services because they feared that it would be known in the community that they were having difficulty coping. Similarly, Cinnirella and Loewenthal (1999) noted reluctance in religious–cultural groups in the United Kingdom (Black Christian, Jewish, Muslim) to use psychological support and therapy for fear of stigmatization. Once it is known in these communities that there is mental illness in the family, the reputation of the family is spoiled and marriage prospects for the whole family are damaged. These studies illustrate some of the benefits and risks of the collectivist ethos, which appears to be marked in segregated groups in which religion functions as culture.

A number of studies have shown empowering effects of religion and religious identity among otherwise disempowered and marginalized minority groups. *Zar* is a form of spirit possession experienced in several middle-Eastern countries, including Ethiopians immigrating to Israel. *Zar* is generally regarded as less serious than depression (Grisaru, Budowski, & Witztum, 1997). Al-Adawi, Martin, Al-Salmi, and Ghassani (2001) have suggested that three functions are fulfilled by *Zar* and its exorcism ceremonies: Cosmology is reinforced; oppressed individuals, particularly women, may be psychologically manipulated; and exorcism may be a form of culturally defined group therapy.

The relatively greater religiosity of women in most cultures may be a general demonstration of the empowering effects of religious belief and activity among the disempowered gender (e.g., Beit-Hallahmi & Argyle, 1997). Somewhat paradoxically, Loewenthal, MacLeod, and Cinnirella (2002) reported that among non-Christian minority groups in the United Kingdom (Hindus, Jews and Muslims), men emerged as more religiously active than women. This may also reflect the empowering effects of religion for the otherwise disempowered men. In these religious traditions, men normally pray separated from women, and public religious worship is regarded as a man's obligation; women, in contrast, are free to pray privately. In their places of worship, men are able to accord respect and honor to each other and to enjoy their devotional practices together. Although women in these religious groups may indeed be disempowered, religious worship is not an arena for their empowerment.

Religious influences on beliefs about the causes and cures of mental illnesses can also affect the well-being of segregated groups in multicultural societies. These effects are likely to reflect the influence of religion-as-culture rather than the effects of religion or culture in isolation. For example, Yurkovich and Lattergrass (2008) explored Native American Indian concepts of healthiness and unhealthiness: Healthiness involves balance, harmony, and being in control of the spiritual, cognitive, emotional, and physical domains. These domains are perceived as one, and the mind–body split of Western thought is not present in Native American Indian thought (see Chapter 31 in this volume). Hence, the distinction between psychological and physical illness is an alien one within these groups. Mallinckrod, Shigeoka, and Suzuki (2005, cited in Chen & Mak, 2008, p. 443) found that people in collectivist cultures, such as Asian Americans, tended to attribute mental health problems to internal, personal causes. In contrast, those influenced by Western psychotherapeutic approaches perceived mental illness as arising from interactions between the person and the environment. Cultural–religious variations in conceptions of ill health will often influence help-seeking and the types of help that may be seen as effective.

Beliefs about spiritual factors in mental health and about spirit possession are important topics for those interested in culture, religion, and religion-as-culture, and their mental health implications. Close study has been made of beliefs in spirit possession by Dein (e.g., Dein, Alexander, & Napier, 2008). In East London, belief in *Jinn* among Bangladeshi Muslim immigrants and their children is seen as traditional. Psychological disturbances and other unexplained misfortunes and physical symptoms are often regarded as caused by a *Jinn*, or sometimes by an evil eye. Exorcism is often seen as an effective cure. Imams and lay exorcists will advise the distressed on the necessity of seeking spiritual or biomedical interventions. A *Jinn* specialist will claim to recognize the presence of a *Jinn* by signs, such as foaming at the mouth and shaking in certain parts of the body. The tendencies of East London Bangladeshis to seek spiritual rather than psychiatric help may be compounded by language barriers, inadequate service provision, and the possibility of stigma. Fear of stigmatization is particularly common among religiously cohesive minority groups. This may be exacerbated when psychological problems such as depression are seen as a result of spiritual failings (Cinnirella & Loewenthal, 1999). A further deterrent to professional help-seeking is the fear of misjudgment by professionals. Religiously normative behavior, it is feared, may be misjudged as a sign of psychiatric disturbance. In this vein, Dein and Littlewood (2007) observed that hearing the voice of G-d is commonly reported by Pentecostal Christians and is perceived as helpful in coping with difficulties and doubts. Dein and Littlewood asserted that hearing the voice of G-d cannot be *ipso facto* pathological. This point is confirmed by others who have noted that reports of "visions" and "voices" are frequent among members of some religious groups (Davies, Griffiths, & Vice, 2001; Peters, Day, McKenna, & Orbach, 1999). These experiences are also reported to be less unpleasant and more controllable than the visions and voices experienced by individuals suffering from psychosis. Many people are reluctant to share their religious experiences for fear of misjudgment. For example, Grady and Loewenthal (1997) noted that charismatic Christians who practiced glossolalia (speaking in tongues) found the practice calming and helpful; however, they were cautious about engaging in this practice in public, lest their behavior seem bizarre or pathological.

These studies illustrate some of the ways in which religion-as-culture can influence beliefs and behavior, including prejudice, beliefs about terrorism, alcohol use, caring, beliefs about the causes of mental illness, and help-seeking for mental illness. Religious identity and collectivism are important factors. A question that lurks behind many of these findings is whether religious–cultural minority groups are inherently collectivist in ethos. There are strong arguments and some evidence that Protestantism is associated with individualism. Thus, the question arises whether collectivism might be enhanced when Protestants are a nondominant minority.

APPLICATIONS AND CONCLUSIONS

We are left with a number of conclusions, questions, and potential applications. Many of the studies of religion and culture raise questions about the direction of influence between religion and culture and the distinctions between moderating and mediating effects of religion. Although cross-sectional, correlational designs are practical and popular, conclusions about causal effects are more safely made from longitudinal and (where appropriate) experimental and quasi-experimental research designs. More work using these latter designs is needed.

There is also a need for more qualitative research. Belzen (2010) has argued for a cultural psychology of religion in which a hermeneutic, generally qualitative methodological approach is taken, enabling a different level of interpretation than allowed by the individual-differences approach of cross-cultural psychology. Cultural psychology focuses on the products of culture, such as customs, religion, and language, which are the results of the coordinated action of many individuals. As a result, contextualized understandings of behaviors, thoughts and feeling are needed in different cultures and times. Belzen has suggested drawing on a wide range of disciplines for methods and sources, such as works of art, architecture, and other media.

We have seen that cultural values, including political values, and cultural change can impact religious values. Religious values, in turn, can affect cultural values. The development of the concept of religion-as-culture has pointed to the importance of studying small religious–cultural groups in pluralistic societies. We have seen that studies of individualism–collectivism and the rise of spirituality have received the lion's share of research attention in studies of the impact of cultural values and change on religious values.

On the practical level, recognition should be granted to the salience of collectivist values, reflected in the religious esteem accorded to supportive and helping behavior. Both beneficial and distressing effects need to be monitored with a view toward appropriate interventions. For example, role-related overload has been identified as a source of distress and psychiatric illness in women, particularly in religious communities in which there are heavy collectivist-type helping obligations. Efforts to foster support for carergivers may relieve distress and help to prevent or reduce potential psychiatric problems (Loewenthal & Brooke Rogers, 2004).

Prosperity and other aspects of modernity, such as materialism, have not always had an impact on religiosity in the ways suggested by secularization theory, and this area awaits further investigation. For instance, it would be worthwhile to test Inglehart's (1981) proposals that postmaterialistic values (e.g., self-expression), which are believed to replace materialistic values as prosperity increases, are negatively associated with religious values. Exploration of these proposals within postcommunist countries could be of great interest. Explorations of possible links between the rise of spirituality and postmaterialism would also be fruitful.

Segregation–separatism is a frequent consequence of migration and the formation of minority collectivist cultures. Here, religion functions as culture. There are important effects of religion-as-culture on values and well-being, with small group processes, belonging, and identity factors playing important roles. These topics await further investigation.

Although intergroup relations have been an important area of study in social psychology for many years, the roles played by religion are still poorly understood. Some headway can be made by treating religious identity as a variable. Religious identity has some special features, however, which distinguish it from other forms of identity, notably the sacred character of religious beliefs and values. Many religious believers are encouraged to be willing to sacrifice their lives for religious principles, and some are encouraged to sacrifice the lives of others. There is more to be discovered about the varieties of resistance and conformity to political oppression of religion, how these come about, and their psychological consequences. We need to know more about the conditions under which such decisions are encouraged, made, and acted upon. Another phenomenon that needs to be more fully understood is the way in which cultural values and practices can achieve the status and sanctity of spiritual values. These may make the values more resistant to change. This is of particular concern in cases in which the values are damaging, as in cases of genital mutilation or when brides are seen as the property of the husband's family.

Our overall conclusion, then, is not a simple one. There appears to be a reciprocal relationship between culture and religion. Political and social change processes interact dynamically with the adaptation and development of religious groups and their behavior and values. To gain a deeper understanding of these issues, we need to broaden our methodologies and to import understandings and concepts from other disciplines, particularly sociology, anthropology and history.

References

Abdel-Khalek, A. M., & Lester, D. (2007). Religion, health and psychopathology in two cultures: Kuwait and the USA. *Mental Health, Religion, and Culture, 10*, 537–550. doi:10.1080/13674670601166505

Adorno, T. W., Frenkel-Brunswik, E., Levinson, D. J., & Sanford, R. N. (1950). *The authoritarian personality*. New York, NY: Harper.

Al-Adawi, S., Martin, R. G., Al-Salmi, A., & Ghassani, H. (2001). Zar: Group distress and healing. *Mental Health, Religion, and Culture, 4*, 46–61.

Albertsen, E. J., O'Connor, L. E., & Berry, J. W. (2006). Religion and interpersonal guilt: Variations across ethnicity and spirituality. *Mental Health, Religion, and Culture, 9*, 67–84. doi:10.1080/13694670500040484

Allport, G. W., & Ross, J. M. (1967). Personal religious orientation and prejudice. *Journal of Personality and Social Psychology, 5*, 432–443. doi:10.1037/h0021212

Batson, C. D., Schoenrade, P. A., & Ventis, W. L. (1993). *Religion and the individual: A social-psychological perspective*. Oxford, England: Oxford University Press.

Beit-Hallahmi, B., & Argyle, M. (1997). *The psychology of religious belief, behaviour and experience*. London, England: Routledge.

Belzen, J. A. (2010). *Towards a cultural psychology of religion*. New York, NY: Springer. doi:10.1007/978-90-481-3491-5

Berry, J. W. (1997). Immigration, acculturation, and adaptation. *Applied Psychology: An International Review, 46*, 5–34.

Berry, J. W. (2001) A psychology of immigration. *Journal of Social Issues, 57*, 615–631. doi:10.1111/0022-4537.00231

Berry, J. W., Kim, U., Power, S., Young, M., & Bujaki, M. (1989). Acculturation strategies in plural societies. *Applied Psychology: An International Review, 38*, 185–206. doi:10.1111/j.1464-0597.1989.tb01208.x

Brown, G. W., & Harris, T. O. (1978). *The social origins of depression.* London, England: Tavistock.

Burroughs, J. E., & Rindfleisch, A. (2002). Materialism and well-being: A conflicting values perspective. *Journal of Consumer Research, 29*, 348–370. doi:10.1086/344429

Chen, S. X., & Mak, W. W. S. (2008). Seeking professional help: Etiology beliefs about mental illness across cultures. *Journal of Counseling Psychology, 55*, 442–450. doi:10.1037/a0012898

Cinnirella, M., & Loewenthal, K. M. (1999). Religious influences on beliefs about mental illness in minority groups: A qualitative interview study. *British Journal of Medical Psychology, 72*, 505–524. doi:10.1348/000711299160202

Cinnirella, M., Loewenthal, K. M., Lewis, C. A., Ansari, H., Rogers, M. B., & Amlot, R. (in press). Social identity and beliefs about martyrdom and terrorism amongst British Muslims. In C. A. Lewis, M. B. Rogers, R. Amlot, K. M. Loewenthal, M. Cinnirella, & H. Ansari (Eds.), *Aspects of terrorism and martyrdom: Dying for good, dying for God.* Abingdon, England: Taylor & Francis.

Clanet, C. (1990). *L'interculturel: Introduction aux approaches interculturelles en education et en sciences humaines* [The intercultural: Introduction to intercultural approaches in education and humanities]. Toulouse, France: Presses Universitaires du Mirail.

Cohen, A. B., & Hill, P. C. (2007). Religion as culture: Religious individualism and collectivism among American Catholics, Jews and Protestants. *Journal of Personality, 75*, 709–742. doi:10.1111/j.1467-6494.2007.00454.x

Davies, M. F., Griffiths, M., & Vice, S. (2001). Affective reactions to auditory hallucinations in psychotic, evangelical and control groups. *British Journal of Clinical Psychology, 40*, 361–370. doi:10.1348/014466501163850

Dein, S., Alexander, M., & Napier, D. A. (2008). Jinn, psychiatry and contested notions of misfortune among East London Bangladeshis. *Transcultural Psychiatry, 45*, 31–55. doi:10.1177/1363461507087997

Dein, S., & Littlewood, R. (2007). The voice of God. *Anthropology and Medicine, 14*, 213–228. doi:10.1080/13648470701381515

Dirie, W., & Miller, C. (1998). *Desert flower: The extraordinary journey of a desert nomad.* New York, NY: William Morrow.

Douglas, M. (1966). *Purity and danger.* London, England: Routledge Kegan Paul. doi:10.4324/9780203361832

Duriez, B., & Hutsebaut, D. (2000). The relation between religion and racism: The role of post-critical beliefs. *Mental Health, Religion, and Culture, 3*, 85–102. doi:10.1080/13674670050002135

Durkheim, E. (2002). *Suicide: A study in sociology.* Abingdon, England: Routledge. (Original work published 1897)

Fleming, N. (2008, January 28). Labour "gives up" on mixed-sex hospital wards. *Daily Telegraph.* Retrieved from http://www.telegraph.co.uk/news/uknews/1576822/Labour-gives-up-on-mixed-sex-hospital-wards.html

Francis, L. J., Robbins, M., Lewis, C. A., & Barnes, L. P. (2008). Prayer and psychological health: A study among sixth-form pupils attending Catholic and Protestant schools in Northern Ireland. *Mental Health, Religion, and Culture, 11*, 85–92. doi:10.1080/13674670701709055

Furnham, A. (1990). *The Protestant work ethic: The psychology of work-related beliefs and behaviours.* London, England: Routledge.

Gillard, M., & Patton, D. (1999). Disaster stress following a hurricane: The role of religious differences in the Fijian Islands. *Australasian Journal of Disaster and Trauma Studies, 2.* Retrieved from http://www.massey.ac.nz/~trauma/issues/1999–2/gillard.htm

Grady, B., & Loewenthal, K. M. (1997). Features associated with speaking in tongues (glossolalia). *British Journal of Medical Psychology, 70*, 185–191. doi:10.1111/j.2044-8341.1997.tb01898.x

Greeley, A. M. (1972). *The denominational society: A sociological approach to religion in America.* Glenville, IL: Scott Foresman.

Grisaru, N., Budowski, D., & Witztum, E. (1997). Possession by the "Zar" among Ethiopian immigrants to Israel: Psychopathology or culture-bound syndrome? *Psychopathology, 30*, 223–233. doi:10.1159/000285051

Heelas, P., & Woodhead, L. (2005). *The spiritual revolution: Why religion is giving way to spirituality.* Oxford, England: Blackwell.

Hofstede, G. (1980). *Culture's consequences: Individual differences in work-related values.* Beverley Hills, CA: Sage.

Hogan, M. (2010). *The culture of our thinking in relation to spirituality.* New York, NY: Nova.

Inglehart, R. (1981). Post-materialism in an environment of insecurity. *American Political Science Review, 75*, 880–900. doi:10.2307/1962290

Inglehart, R., & Baker, W. E. (2000). Modernization, cultural change, and the persistence of traditional values. *American Sociological Review, 65*, 19–51. doi:10.2307/2657288

Inglehart, R., Basanez, M., Dies-Medrano, J., Halman, L., & Luijkx, R. (2004). *Human beliefs and values: A cross-cultural sourcebook based on the 1999–2002 values surveys*. Coyacan, Mexico: Siglo XXI Editores.

Kenrick, D. T., Neuberg, S. L., & Cialdini, R. B. (1999). *Social psychology: Unravelling the mysteries*. Boston, MA: Allyn & Bacon.

Khan, Z. H., Watson, P. J., & Habib, F. (2005). Muslim attitudes toward religion, religious orientation and empathy among Pakistanis. *Mental Health, Religion, and Culture, 8*, 49–61. doi:10.1080/13674670410001666606

Kværne, P. (1995). *The Bon religion of Tibet: The iconography of a living tradition*. London, England: Serindia.

Loewenthal, K. M. (2009). The psychology of religion. In P. Clarke & P. Beyer, P. (Eds.), *Encyclopedia of world religions* (pp. 867–889). London, England: Routledge

Loewenthal, K. M., & Brooke Rogers, M. (2004). Culture sensitive support groups: How are they perceived and how do they work? *International Journal of Social Psychiatry, 50*, 227–240. doi:10.1177/0020764004043137

Loewenthal, K. M., Goldblatt, V., Gorton, T., Lubitsh, G., Bicknell, H., Fellowes, D., & Sowden, A. (1995). Gender and depression in Anglo-Jewry. *Psychological Medicine, 25*, 1051–1063. doi:10.1017/S0033291700037545

Loewenthal, K. M., Goldblatt, V., Gorton, T., Lubitsh, G., Bicknell, H., Fellowes, D., & Sowden, A. (1997). The costs and benefits of boundary maintenance: Stress, religion, and culture among Jews in Britain. *Social Psychiatry and Psychiatric Epidemiology*, 32, 200–207. doi:10.1007/BF00788239

Loewenthal, K. M., MacLeod, A. K., & Cinnirella, M. (2002). Are women more religious than men? Gender differences in religious activity among different religious groups in the UK. *Personality and Individual Differences, 32*, 133–139. doi:10.1016/S0191-8869(01)00011-3

Loewenthal, K. M., MacLeod, A. K., Cook, S., Lee, M. J., & Goldblatt, V. (2003a). Beliefs about alcohol among UK Jews and Protestants: Do they fit the alcohol-depression hypothesis? *Social Psychiatry and Psychiatric Epidemiology, 38*, 122–127. doi:10.1007/s00127-003-0609-4

Loewenthal, K. M., MacLeod, A. K., Cook, S., Lee, M. J., & Goldblatt, V. (2003b). Drowning your sorrows? Attitudes towards alcohol in UK Jews and Protestants: A thematic analysis. *International Journal of Social Psychiatry, 49*, 204–215. doi:10.1177/00207640030493006

Luckmann, T. (1963). *The invisible religion: The problems of religion in modern society*. New York, NY: Macmillan.

Lukes, S. (1971). The meaning of individualism. *Journal of the History of Ideas, 32*, 45–66. doi:10.2307/2708324

Maiello, C. (2005). Degrees of belief in God: A measure of belief for use in cross culture. *Mental Health, Religion, and Culture, 8*, 87–95. doi:10.1080/13674670410001702371

Margolin, J., & Witztum, E. (1989). Supernatural impotence: Historical review with anthropological and clinical implications. *British Journal of Medical Psychology, 62*, 333–342. doi:10.1111/j.2044-8341.1989.tb02843.x

Martin, B. (1981). *A sociology of contemporary cultural change*. Oxford, England: Blackwell.

McClelland, D. C. (1961). *The achieving society*. Princeton, NJ: Van Nostrand.

Okulicz-Kozaryn, A. (2010). Religiosity and life satisfaction across nations. *Mental Health, Religion, and Culture, 13*, 155–169. doi:10.1080/13674670903273801

Olam, T. (2008, January). *Hijab for Jewish women?* Retrieved from http://lady-date.blogspot.com/2008/01/hijab-for-jewish.women.html

Pargament, K. I., Tyler, F. B., & Steele, R. E. (1979). The Church/synagogue and the psychosocial competence of the member: In initial enquiry into a neglected dimension. *American Journal of Community Psychology, 7*, 649–664. doi:10.1007/BF00891968

Peters, E., Day, S., McKenna, J., & Orbach, G. (1999). Delusional ideas in religious and psychiatric populations. *British Journal of Clinical Psychology, 38*, 83–96. doi:10.1348/014466599162683

Pollack, D. (2008). Religious change in Europe: Theoretical considerations and empirical findings. *Social Compass, 55*, 168–186. doi:10.1177/0037768607089737

Roccas, S., & Schwartz, S. H. (1997). Church-state relations and the association of religion with values: A study of Catholics in six countries. *Cross-Cultural Research, 31*, 356–375. doi:10.1177/106939719703100404

Saroglou, V. (2003). Trans-cultural/religious constants vs. cross-cultural/ religious differences in psychological aspects of religion. *Archive for the Psychology of Religions, 25*, 71–87.

Seligman, M. (2002). *Authentic happiness*. New York, NY: Free Press.

Shams, M., & Jackson, P. R. (1993). Religiosity as a predictor of well-being and moderator of the psychological impact of unemployment. *British Journal of Medical Psychology, 66*, 341–352. doi:10.1111/j.2044-8341.1993.tb01760.x

Skaine, R. (2005). *Female genital mutilation: Legal, cultural and medical issues*. Jefferson, NC: McFarland.

Tajfel, H., & Turner, J. (1986). The social identity theory of intergroup behaviour. In S. Worchel & W. G. Austin (Eds.), *Psychology of intergroup relations* (pp. 7–24). Chicago, IL: Nelson.

Tarakeshwar, N., Stanton, J., & Pargament, K. I. (2003). Religion: An overlooked dimension in cross-cultural psychology. *Journal of Cross-Cultural Psychology, 34*, 377–394. doi:10.1177/0022022103034004001

Taylor, C. (1991). *The ethics of authenticity*. Cambridge, MA: Harvard University Press.

Triandis, H. C., Bontempo, R., Villareal, M. J., Asai, M., & Lucca, N. (1988). Individualism and collectivism: Cross-cultural perspectives on self–ingroup relationships. *Journal of Personality and Social Psychology, 54*, 323–338. doi:10.1037/0022-3514.54.2.323

Turner, V. (1969). *The ritual process: Structure and anti-structure*. London, England: Routledge & Kegan Paul.

Watson, P. J., Ghorbani, N., Davison, H. K., Bing, M. N., Hood, R. W., & Ghramaleki, A. F. (2002). Negatively reinforcing personal extrinsic motivations: Religious orientation, inner awareness, and mental health in Iran and the United States. *The International Journal for the Psychology of Religion, 12*, 255–276. doi:10.1207/S15327582IJPR1204_04

Weber, M. (1958). *The protestant ethic and the spirit of capitalism* (T. Parsons, Trans.). New York, NY: Charles Scribner's Sons. (Original work published 1904–1905)

Werbner, P. (2002). *Imagined diasporas amongst Manchester Muslims*. Oxford, England: James Curry.

Wikan, U. (1988). Bereavement and loss in two Muslim communities: Egypt and Bali compared. *Social Science and Medicine, 27*, 451–460. doi:10.1016/0277-9536(88)90368-1

Williams, E., Francis, L. J., & Village, A. (2010). Marriage, religion and human flourishing: How sustainable is the classic Durkheim thesis in contemporary Europe? *Mental Health, Religion, and Culture, 13*, 93–104.

Ysseldyk, R., Matheson, K., & Anisman, H. (2010). Religiosity as identity: Toward an understanding of religion from a social identity perspective. *Personality and Social Psychology Review, 14*, 60–71.

Yurkovich, E. E., & Lattergrass, I. (2008). Defining health and unhealthiness: Perceptions held by Native American Indians with persistent mental illness. *Mental Health, Religion, and Culture, 11*, 437–459. doi:10.1080/13674670701473751

Zinnbauer, B. J., Pargament, K. I., Cole, B., Rye, M. S., Butter, E. M., Belavich, T. G., . . . Kadar, J. L. (1997). Religion and spirituality: Unfuzzying the fuzzy. *Journal for the Scientific Study of Religion, 36*, 549–564. doi:10.2307/1387689

CHAPTER 14

SEARCHING FOR THE SACRED: TOWARD A NONREDUCTIONISTIC THEORY OF SPIRITUALITY

Kenneth I. Pargament

Traditionally, theorists in the social sciences have assumed that religious beliefs and practices are expressions of something presumably more basic, be it the need for emotional comfort, relief from the terror of dying, control of human impulses, social connectedness, evolutionary advantage, or meaning and purpose (see Part II of this volume). Although these explanations clarify the workings of religion and spirituality, they overlook a simpler possibility—that spirituality reflects a distinctive, in some ways irreducible, human motivation, a yearning for the sacred. This chapter presents a growing body of evidence that suggests that spirituality may be a distinctive human motivation and process, one that contributes in unique ways to health and well-being. Building on this perspective, the recent theoretical and empirical work of Pargament and colleagues (e.g., Hill & Pargament, 2003; Mahoney, Pargament, & Hernandez, in press; Pargament, 2002a, 2007; Pargament, Magyar-Russell, & Murray-Swank, 2005; Pargament & Mahoney, 2005), and the seminal work of other theorists and researchers (e.g., Allport, 1950; Emmons, 1999; Haidt, 2003; Piedmont, Ciarrocchi, Dy-Liacco, & Williams, 2009; see also Chapter 9 in this volume), this chapter offers a theoretical framework for understanding spirituality as a "search for the sacred," the cornerstone of religion, and a natural and normal part of life.

RELIGION AS A MULTIPURPOSE PHENOMENON

How do we explain religion? Since the founding of the social sciences, psychologists and other scientists have posited a variety of answers to this question in the effort to account for the persistence and power of the human concern with the spiritual realm. Freud (1927/1961) explained religion in two ways. First, he described religion as a bromide, a soothing response to the child's sense of fundamental anxiety when confronted with the powerful and uncontrollable forces of nature. Second, he asserted that religion arises out of the need for protection from human impulse itself, those destructive instincts that pose a threat to oneself, others, and civilization as a whole. More recently, theorists and researchers have elaborated on Freud's twofold explanation of religion. Speaking to the first of Freud's explanations of religion, terror management theorists have maintained that religion offers a way to mitigate the anxiety associated with the awareness of human finitude (Vail et al., 2010; see also Chapter 5 in this volume). Addressing Freud's second explanation, McCullough and colleagues (McCullough & Willoughby, 2009; see also Chapter 6 in this volume) have underscored the role of religion in self-regulation, including the management of undesirable thoughts, feelings, and behaviors.

Others understand religion differently. Durkheim (1915) maintained that religion is rooted primarily in social rather than psychological needs. Religious beliefs and rituals, he argued, function to unite individuals into a common faith. "If religion has given birth to all that is essential in society," he wrote, "it is because the idea of society is the soul of religion" (pp. 432–433). More recently, theorists and researchers have extended Durkheim's argument by

DOI: 10.1037/14045-014
APA Handbook of Psychology, Religion, and Spirituality: Vol. 1. Context, Theory, and Research, K. I. Pargament (Editor-in-Chief)
Copyright © 2013 by the American Psychological Association. All rights reserved.

emphasizing the role of religion in facilitating social attachment (Chapter 7 in this volume), binding people into moral communities (Graham & Haidt, 2010), and fostering social identity (Ysseldyk, Matheson, & Anisman, 2010).

Still other explanations for why people are religious have been proposed. Working from the perspective of evolutionary psychology, Kirkpatrick (2005) rejected the idea of a specific "religious instinct" but instead asserted that religion is a by-product of systems that evolved to help people understand and deal with the world. For instance, beliefs in supernatural beings can be understood as one by-product of an "agency-detection" mechanism that evolved to help people distinguish animate from inanimate objects in the environment (see Chapter 12 in this volume). Another group of theorists have emphasized the meaning-making function of religion (Geertz, 1966; Park & Folkman, 1997; see also Chapter 8 in this volume). Geertz (1966), for example, insisted that a minimal definition of religion would entail not only a belief in God but also a belief that God is not mad. Religion, he said, ensures that life's greatest problems—bafflement, suffering, injustice—are not ultimately incomprehensible.

How do we sort out these competing explanations? Perhaps there is no need to do so. Although theorists have engaged in debates about which is the most compelling explanation of religion, an alternate possibility is that each explanation is true, at least in part. There is, after all, empirical evidence to support each of these explanations of religion. According to Pargament, Mahoney, Exline, Jones, and Shafranske (see Chapter 1 in this volume), religion is a search for significance that occurs within the context of established institutions that are designed to facilitate spirituality. The concept of significance refers to a virtually limitless set of valued objects—material, physical, psychological, social, or spiritual. These classes of significant objects are not necessarily exclusive of each other. For example, as we will see shortly, spiritual significance can be attached to a wide range of tangible and intangible objects.

It is important to note that the term *significance* overlaps with the concept of *meaning* (e.g., Park & Folkman, 1997; see also Chapter 8 in this volume). The concept of meaning is often used in a narrower sense than significance to refer to a particular kind of cognition or understanding. Baumeister (1991), for example, defined *meaning* as "shared mental representations of possible relationships among things, events, and relationships" (p. 15). In contrast, *significance* is defined more broadly here to refer to valued objects that may take a variety of forms. Although the valued objects may be cognitive (e.g., meaning), they may also be social, emotional, biological, or spiritual in nature.

Religion, Pargament (1997) maintained, can be directed to the attainment of any of these values and goals. In fact, part of the power of religion lies in the fact that it can respond to the diverse needs of its adherents by offering them sacred pathways to reach a myriad of destinations—from peace of mind, identity, and self-control to intimacy with others, social justice, and a higher sense of purpose. In this sense, religion is a multipurpose phenomenon. Thus, each of the major explanatory frameworks of religion may speak to an important religious function.

As a group, however, these social scientific explanations are vulnerable to the problem of radical reductionism or the "nothing but" fallacy—that religion is nothing but an effort to find emotional comfort, nothing but a way of controlling wayward impulses, nothing but an attempt to allay the fear of dying, nothing but a way to form identity and community, nothing but an evolutionary by-product, or nothing but a source of meaning in life (Pargament, 2002b). The "nothing but" fallacy is not justified by the data. Even though empirical studies indicate that religion serves a variety of psychological and social functions, the magnitude of these effects is not large enough to indicate that these psychological and social factors fully account for religious involvement.

Consider a few examples. In one study of a well-constructed measure of meaning in life in a sample of undergraduate students, intrinsic religiousness was significantly associated with the reported presence of meaning in life, but the effect size was modest ($R^2 = .09$) (Steger, Frazier, Oishi, & Kaler, 2006). Extrinsic religiousness was unrelated to the presence of meaning in life, and neither intrinsic nor extrinsic religiousness were associated with higher levels of reported searching for meaning in life. Harding, Flannelly, Weaver, and Costa (2005) found that belief in God's existence ($R^2 = .07$) and belief in the afterlife ($R^2 = .06$) were both significantly associated with lower death anxiety, but again the effect sizes were small. In a meta-analysis of 75 samples, Sedikides and Gebauer (2010) reported significant relationships between measures of self-enhancement and two measures of religiousness: intrinsic religiousness ($R^2 = .079$) and global religiousness ($R^2 = .012$). Extrinsic religiousness was unrelated to self-enhancement. The small size of these effects suggests that no single motivational factor is sufficient to account for religiousness. Of course, it could be argued that the sum total of various psychological and social explanatory variables may eventually provide a comprehensive accounting of religiousness, but it is also possible that something else is going on with religion, motivationally speaking. We should not be too quick to explain religion away (Pargament, 2002b).

In spite of the energy that has gone into understanding why people are religious, one potential explanation has been largely overlooked by social scientists—that people are seeking something spiritual, a source of sacredness in their lives. Psychologist P. E. Johnson (1959) captured this basic yearning by stating, "It is the ultimate thou the religious person seeks most of all" (p. 70). Rather than treat the search for the "ultimate thou" as a surface expression of more basic psychological and social phenomena, this chapter considers the possibility that spirituality is an important, irreducible motive and process in and of itself. As a prelude to this presentation, it is necessary to consider the meaning of the term *spirituality*.

SPIRITUALITY AS A SEARCH FOR THE SACRED

Elsewhere, I have defined spirituality as a search for the sacred (Pargament, 1999; see Chapter 1 in this volume). There are two key terms in this definition: *sacred* and *search*.

Sacred

The term *sacred* refers not only to concepts of higher powers and God but also to other significant objects that take on spiritual character and meaning by virtue of their association with the divine (Pargament & Mahoney, 2005). In visual form, we can imagine the sacred as consisting of a core composed of traditional notions of divinity (e.g., God, Jesus, Allah, Vishnu, Lord, higher power), and a surrounding ring of significant objects that become sanctified—that is, imbued with spiritual character and meaning (Pargament, 2007). Sanctification can occur in one of two ways (Mahoney et al., in press; Pargament & Mahoney, 2005). In theistic sanctification, a significant object is linked directly with God or a higher power. For instance, some individuals perceive that God has blessed or is an intimate part of their marriage. In nontheistic sanctification, a significant object is assigned divinelike qualities, such as transcendence, boundlessness, or ultimacy. Writings about love, for instance, are often replete with references to divinelike qualities (e.g., eternal, truthful, mysterious, extraordinary).

Any object can become imbued with spiritual character. As Durkheim (1915) pointed out, "by sacred things one must not understand simply those personal beings which are called gods or spirits; a rock, a tree, a pebble, a piece of wood, a house, in a word anything can be sacred" (p. 52). Although the notion of perceiving sacredness in seemingly everyday aspects of life may seem farfetched, survey research indicates that a majority of people in the United States attribute sacred qualities to their marriages (Mahoney et al., 1999; Mahoney et al., in press), the environment (Tarakeshwar, Swank, Pargament, & Mahoney, 2001), and life in general (Doehring et al., 2009). Moreover, these studies show that people appear to sanctify both theistically and nontheistically.

Because any part of life can be assigned spiritual character, this definition of the sacred broadens the domain of scientific inquiry in the psychology of religion and spirituality beyond traditional conceptions of divinity and religious practice. The sacred as defined here encompasses not only a sacred core of divine entities but also a wider ring of seemingly secular aspects of life that have been sanctified—from loving relationships, work, and the virtues (e.g., humility, hope, and gratitude) to parenting, self-development, and social justice.

Nontheists as well as theists can perceive spiritual qualities in various aspects of life. Consider, for example, how an atheist from Sweden described the sense of boundlessness (with hints of transcendence and ultimate reality) she perceived in nature:

> Whatever happens in the world for me or others, nature is still there, it keeps going . . . the leaves fall off, new ones appear, somewhere there is a pulse that keeps going. . . . It is a spiritual feeling if we can use this word without connecting it to God. (Ahmadi, 2006, p. 73)

Thus, placing the sacred at the center of the definition of spirituality opens the door of social scientific investigation to people with diverse orientations toward religion and spirituality. Before continuing, it must be stressed that I am referring to an empirical approach here. Psychologists have nothing to offer the debate about the ontological validity of the sacred. We can, however, examine perceptions of the sacred and emotions, cognitions, and behaviors that precede, accompany, and follow these perceptions.

The Search for the Sacred

According to my definition (Pargament, 1999), spirituality does not refer to static beliefs, feelings or behaviors centered on the sacred. Instead, spirituality is best understood as a process, a *search* for the sacred that evolves and changes over the course of life (see Figure 14.1). This definition of spirituality rests on the assumption that people are motivated to discover something sacred in their lives, hold on to or conserve a relationship with the sacred, and when necessary, transform their understanding of the sacred. We turn our attention now to these three processes—discovery, conservation, and transformation—and a general theoretical framework for understanding spirituality (for an extended review, see Pargament, 2007).

Discovery. Although childhood is often thought of as a period of spiritual dormancy, there is evidence from cognitive–developmental studies that children come into this world with spiritual abilities, including the capacity to think about God as unique rather than humanlike and the ability to conceive

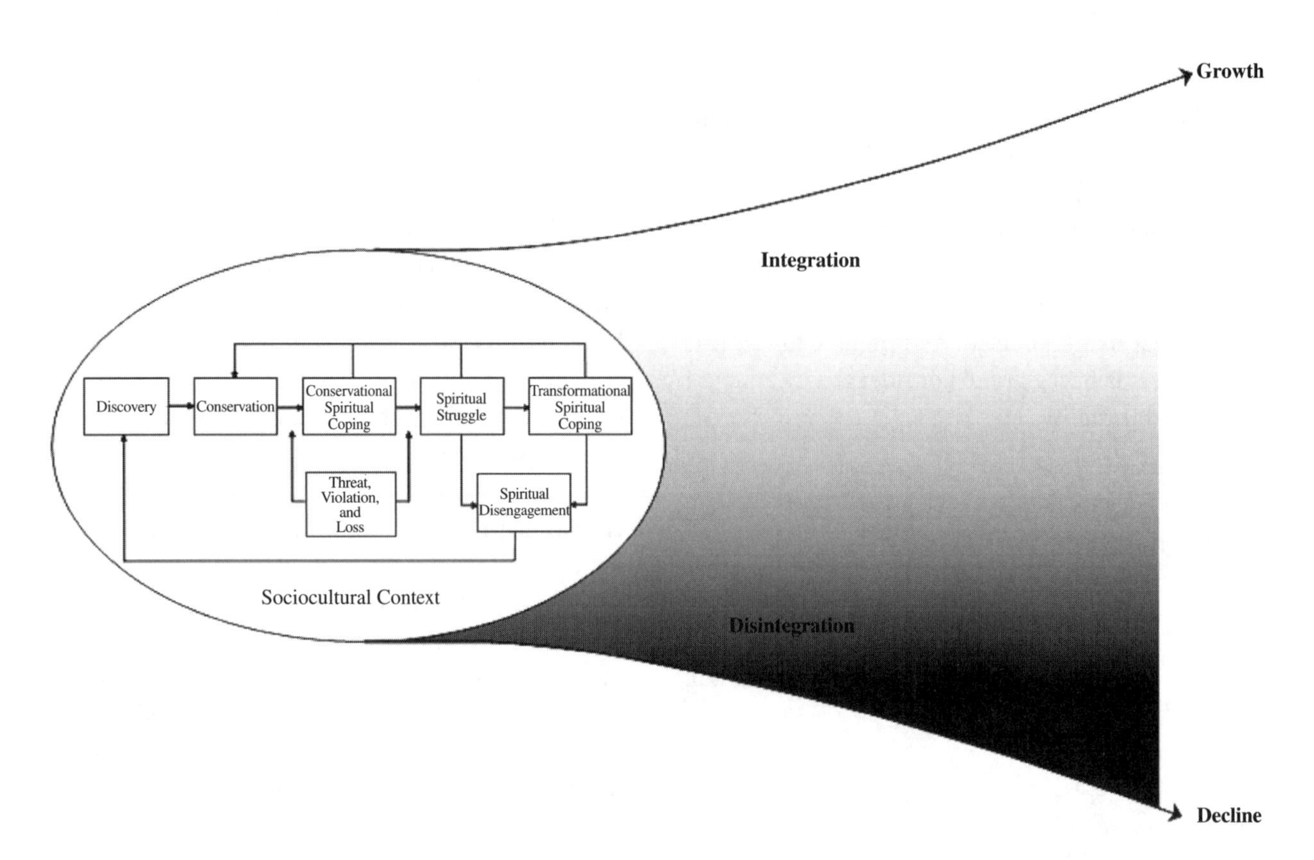

FIGURE 14.1. Search for the sacred.

of immaterial spirit and an afterlife (C. N. Johnson & Boyatzis, 2006; see also Chapters 12 and 27 in this volume). Anecdotal accounts also point to an intense interest in spiritual matters among many children, as we hear in the words of one 9-year-old interviewee:

> I'd like to find God! But He wouldn't just be there, waiting for some spaceship to land! He's not a person, you know! He's a spirit. He's like the fog and the mist. Maybe He's like something—something we've never seen here. So how can we know? You can't imagine Him, because He's so different—you've never seen anything like him . . . I should remember that God is God, and we're us. I guess I'm trying to get from me . . . to Him with my ideas when I'm looking up at the sky! (Coles, 1990, pp. 141–142)

Reports of spiritual interest of this kind often have been viewed as derivative—that is, as reflections of more basic motivations, such as a desire for comfort, predictability, or attachment. Other theorists from diverse backgrounds, however, have asserted that there may be something more fundamental to spiritual motivation. For example, Allport (1950) acknowledged that higher order motives such as spirituality may develop much of their initial power through associations with more basic motives. But he also insisted that with maturity, spirituality can become "functionally autonomous" of initial motivating fears, hungers, and desires. This mature faith "behaves no longer like an iron filing, twisting to follow the magnet of self-centered motives; it behaves rather as a master motive, a magnet in its own right, by which other cravings are bidden to order their course" (Allport, 1950, p. 64). Working from a psychodynamic perspective, Loewald (1978) asserted that the spiritual propensity is an intrinsic part of human character, not simply a defense mechanism. In the primary process of even the youngest child, he believed, we find spiritual experiences that are marked by a sense of unity and timelessness, and the capacity to enrich everyday life. Similarly, Jung (1938; see also Volume 2, Chapter 7, this handbook) maintained that the most basic of all drives is not sexuality but rather the desire to recover and integrate the various levels of the self, including the spiritual dimension. More recently, Jones (2002) has argued that psychologists do not need to limit their analyses to the psychological and social functions of the sacred; they can broaden their focus to include the sacred as a primary desire that "lures us forward," grounding our efforts to know the world (p. 111). Neuroscientists have also suggested that people may be, in some respects, "hard-wired" for spirituality. Newberg and Waldman (2006) maintained that "we are biologically inclined to ponder the deepest nature of our being and the deepest secrets of the universe . . . born to believe" (pp. xvii–xviii). Along similar lines, cognitive psychologists have found that young children may be predisposed to perceive powerful and caring figures in their lives, including gods. Chapter 12 in this volume reviews several studies that indicate that it may take longer for children to learn about the limitations in the minds of people in their worlds. The chapter authors suggest that beliefs in omniscient gods may be the cognitive default option in the developing mind.

The literature contains numerous examples of individuals who reportedly discover something sacred, even at an early age (e.g., Hardy, 1979), either through revelation, socialization, or a more active searching process. Perceptions of the sacred can be elicited through experiences later in life. Religious wedding rituals, for instance, are designed to imbue the marriage with a sense of sacredness through several ingredients, including verbal behaviors (e.g., vows, prayer), nonverbal behaviors (e.g., exchanging blessed rings), and religious legitimation (e.g., presence of clergy; Mahoney et al., in press). In this vein, Lambert and Dollahite (2008) conducted a qualitative study of religious couples who described how the wedding ceremony fostered the sense that God was an active party in their marriage.

Whenever it occurs, the discovery of the sacred has several noteworthy implications, according to empirical studies. First, people invest more of themselves in the pursuit of those things they hold sacred. For instance, individuals who view the environment as sacred are more likely to invest personal funds in environmental causes (Tarakeshwar,

Swank, Pargament, & Mahoney, 2001). Similarly, workers of various occupations who define their work as a "calling" have fewer absences than those who define their work as a job (Wrzesniewski, McCauley, Rozin, & Schwartz, 1997; see also Volume 2, Chapter 31, this handbook).

Second, perceptions of the sacred appear to act like an emotional generator. Consistent with the writings of Rudolf Otto (1928) who described the *mysterium*, the fascinating and overpowering feelings that accompany consciousness of the divine, empirical studies have tied perceptions of the sacred to a variety of spiritually related emotions, including elevation and awe (Haidt, 2003) and gratitude (Emmons & Crumpler, 2000).

Third, people derive more support, strength, and satisfaction from those parts of their lives that they hold sacred. For example, in a study of adults in steady dating or cohabitating relationships, greater belief that God was at the center of the relationship was associated with higher levels of satisfaction with the relationship, even after accounting for the effects of kindness, consideration, and criticism between partners (Henderson et al., 2010). In a longitudinal study of recently married couples, greater sanctification of sexuality was predictive of greater sexual and marital satisfaction as well as more frequent sexual intercourse 1 year later, after controlling for initial levels of marital satisfaction (Hernandez & Mahoney, 2009). A sample of working mothers who sanctified their jobs reported more positive affect, less interrole conflict, and greater satisfaction with their work (Hall, Oates, Anderson, & Willingham, 2012).

Fourth, sacred objects are likely to become organizing forces that lend coherence to other lower level goals and motivations. This point is illustrated by the work of Emmons (1999), who examined spiritual motivation within the larger context of research on personal goals and strivings. Emmons had participants generate lists of their goals and, in the process, found that spiritual strivings regularly appeared. Spiritual strivings pertained to "ultimate concerns" or a transcendent level of experience (e.g., "discern and follow God's will for my life"; "be aware of the spiritual meaningfulness of my life"; Emmons, 1999, pp. 89–91). Emmons maintained that these spiritual motives are unique not only in their content, for they alone refer to a transcendent realm, but also in their "primacy within a person's overall goal hierarchy" (p. 90). Consistent with his assertion, Emmons found that in comparison with other goals, spiritual strivings correlated more strongly with measures of well-being. Moreover, these strivings were uniquely linked to less conflict and greater coherence within the individual's goal system.

Conservation. The search for the sacred does not end with discovery. Once people discover something they perceive as sacred, they engage in efforts to hold on to or conserve it. Toward this end, individuals can take a variety of conservational spiritual pathways, traditional or nontraditional. These include the pathways of spiritual practice (e.g., ritual, music), spiritual knowledge (e.g., study of sacred texts, scientific inquiry), spiritual experience (e.g., meditation, walks outdoors), and spiritual relationships (e.g., church involvement, social action). What religious scholar Martin Marty wrote in the 1960s still applies in the 21st century:

> In search of spiritual expression, people speak in tongues, enter Trappist monasteries, build on Jungian archetypes, go to southern California and join a cult, become involved "where the action is" in East Harlem, perceive "God at work in the world," see Jesus Christ as the man for others, hope for liberation by the new morality, study phenomenology, share the Peace Corps experience, borrow from cosmic synthesis, and go to church. (cited in Roof, 1993, p. 242)

Clearly, people can follow any number of spiritual pathways in search of the sacred. One way to think about these pathways is as an orienting system, a relatively stable set of beliefs, practices, relationships, and emotions, that help guide the individual's attempt to develop a relationship with the sacred (Pargament, 1997). Piedmont has made a similar point. Drawing on a significant body of theory and research, he has suggested that religiousness and spirituality can be understood as dimensions of personality and motivation that are distinctive from established personological frameworks, such as the Five-Factor Model of personality (see Piedmont, Mapa, & Williams, 2006; see also Chapter 9 in this volume).

Spiritual pathways can serve a number of psychological, social, and physical purposes as well as spiritual purposes. In this vein, reviews of the now voluminous empirical literature on the links between spirituality and health indicate that various spiritual beliefs and practices are generally associated with better health and well-being (e.g., see Koenig, King, & Carson, 2012; T. B. Smith, McCullough, & Poll, 2003; see also Volume 2, Chapter 14, this handbook). Even though theorists have posited a variety of psychological and social mechanism to explain these effects, empirical attempts to test these potential mediating variables have not been particularly successful, with some exceptions (e.g., Carrico et al., 2006). For example, Ironson, Stuetzle, and Fletcher (2006) studied HIV-positive individuals over a 4-year period. They found that those who reported increases in religiousness or spirituality after diagnosis had significantly greater preservation of CD4 cells. They were unable to explain these effects statistically through the mediating pathways of hopelessness, optimism, secular coping, or social support. Working with a longitudinal data set from a community sample from the San Francisco Bay area born in the 1920s, Wink, Dillon, and Larsen (2005) found that greater involvement in religious institutional life buffered the effects of depression associated with poor physical health. These effects could not be explained by differences in levels of general social support in the sample. C. G. Ellison and his colleagues studied the relationships between religious involvement, psychological distress, and well-being in a large-scale study of adults in Detroit (C. G. Ellison, Boardman, Williams, & Jackson, 2001). The connections between the religious variables and the measures of distress and well-being were not mediated by psychosocial resources, including self-esteem, mastery, and social support. C. G. Ellison et al. (2001) concluded:

> The salutary effects of religious involvement cannot be explained away in terms of social or psychological resources, at least insofar as these constructs are conventionally conceptualized and measured. . . . Religious groups and traditions may foster distinctive sets of spiritual or psychosocial resources. (p. 243)

The conclusion of C. G. Ellison et al. (2001) raises the simpler possibility that religion and spirituality have direct effects on various indicators of well-being. After all, spiritual pathways are designed first and foremost to sustain an individual's relationship with the sacred. For example, to the spiritually minded, rituals are not meaningless repetitive actions or devices primarily designed to achieve nonspiritual ends. Rather they recreate a world that the individual can reenter and then replay and reexperience ultimate life dramas. In this sense, rituals are ways of "reactualizing sacred history" that keep people "close to the gods" (Eliade, 1957, p. 202; see also Chapter 18 in this volume).

Empirical studies suggest that people who follow spiritual pathways are, in fact, more likely to conserve their relationship with the sacred. For instance, according to one national survey, 95% of those who pray feel that their prayers have been answered (Gallup & Lindsay, 1999). Similarly, other studies show that those who attend religious services more often, pray more regularly, and engage in more spiritual study score higher on measures of closeness to God, spiritual growth, and spiritual well-being (e.g., C. W. Ellison & Smith, 1991; Pargament et al., 1990). Furthermore, people are more likely to preserve and protect those aspects of their lives they perceive as sacred (Mahoney et al., in press; Pargament & Mahoney, 2005). Among college students, stronger perceptions of one's body as sacred were associated with more health-protective behaviors, such as getting enough sleep, eating better, wearing a seat belt, and avoiding illicit drug use (Mahoney et al., 2005). In a study of married couples, higher levels of sanctification of their marriage were tied to reports of less marital conflict and dysfunctional communication (Mahoney et al., 1999). As a group, these studies suggest that the effects of spiritual pathways on health and well-being may be irreducibly tied, at least in part, to their spiritual design and function.

The effort to conserve the sacred is not invariably smooth and easy. Major life crises and transitions arise that can challenge, threaten, or damage the individual's significant objects, including sacred objects. Events that cut to the core of the individual's spiritual values, beliefs, and practices may be especially problematic. For example, in a study of community members who had experienced a major stressor (e.g., illness, accident, natural disaster, divorce) in the past 2 years, 38% perceived their stressor as a loss of something they perceived as sacred and 24% perceived their stressor as a sacred violation (Pargament, Magyar, Benore, & Mahoney, 2005). Furthermore, perceptions of sacred loss and violation were associated with significantly higher levels of emotional distress. In the interpersonal realm, perceptions that others are intentionally violating one's sacred values may have potentially powerful consequences. In this vein, Christians who saw Jews and Muslims as desecrating Christianity were more likely to hold anti-Jewish and anti-Muslim attitudes respectively (Pargament, McConnell, Mahoney, & Silberman, 2007; Raiya, Pargament, Mahoney, & Trevino, 2008).

In times of stress, however, people can draw on a variety of distinctive spiritual coping methods to sustain themselves not only psychologically, socially, and physically but spiritually as well. These include spiritual support, benevolent spiritual reframing, church-based support, and purification rituals (for a review, see Pargament, 1997). Coping methods such as these have been linked to greater health and well-being (e.g., Ano & Vasconcelles, 2005; Pargament, 2011; see Chapter 19 in this volume). Again, with some exceptions (e.g., Ai, Park, Huang, Rodgers, & Tice, 2007; McIntosh, Silver, & Wortman, 1993), attempts to account for these effects through a variety of explanatory psychosocial mechanisms have not been largely successful. For instance, Tix and Frazier (1998) studied patients undergoing kidney dialysis and their loved ones. Higher levels of religious coping, they found, predicted greater life satisfaction 12 months and 30 months posttransplantation after controlling for cognitive restructuring, internal control, and social support. They concluded that "religious coping adds a unique component to the prediction of adjustment to stressful life events that cannot be accounted for by other established predictors" (Tix & Frazier, 1998, p. 42). Similarly, Krause (2006) studied a national sample of elders and compared the role of emotional support received from church versus support received outside of the church as buffers of the effects of financial strain on self-rated health. Church-based emotional support emerged as a buffer, but secular support did not. In a study of a community sample of divorced individuals, Krumrei, Mahoney, and Pargament (2009) found that positive religious coping methods were predictive of greater posttraumatic growth following divorce, even after controlling for the effects of secular coping methods.

How do we make sense of these findings? Once again, the key may lie in the spiritual design and function of these coping methods. Perhaps more so than other methods of coping, spiritual coping methods are tailored to provide solutions to problems of human finitude and insufficiency (Pargament, 1997). In spiritual coping, people can find support when other forms of social support are hard to come by, ultimate explanations when the events of the world seem incomprehensible, and a sense of control when life seems out of control. Like other spiritual pathways, spiritual coping methods are designed to conserve and sustain the individual's relationship with the sacred. Empirical studies indicate that spiritual coping activities are successful in this regard. In times of major crises, many people turn to their faith for help in coping, and, as telling, faith for most people remains resilient. For instance, in one survey study of Jewish Holocaust survivors, 61% reported no change in their religious behavior from before the Holocaust to the present time (Brenner, 1980). In another study of people who had experienced multiple traumas, only 8% reported a decline in their religiousness (Falsetti, Resick, & Davis, 2003).

Transformation. At times, however, life events and transitions can push people beyond their resources. During these periods, many people experience spiritual struggles. Spiritual struggles refer to tensions, questions, and conflicts centering on sacred matters (see Pargament, Murray-Swank, Magyar, &

Ano, 2005; see also Chapter 25 in this volume). We can distinguish among at least three types of spiritual struggles: (a) interpersonal struggles involving conflicts and tensions with family, friends, clergy, or church around spiritual issues; (b) intrapersonal struggles that focus on internal questions and doubts about matters of faith as well as intrapsychic conflicts between higher and lower aspects of oneself; and (c) divine struggles that involve negative emotions toward God, such as anger, anxiety, fear, and feelings of abandonment. Listen to how one 14-year-old Nicaraguan girl voiced her own struggles with God:

> Many times I wonder how there can be a God—a loving God and where He is . . . I don't understand why He lets little children in Third World countries die of starvation . . . I believe in God and I love Him, but sometimes I just don't see the connection between a loving God and a suffering hurting world. Why doesn't He help us—if He truly loves us? It seems like He just doesn't care? Does He? (Kooistra, 1990, pp. 91–92)

Survey studies indicate that these kinds of struggle are not uncommon. For instance, only 35% of a national sample of Presbyterians reported that they never had any religious doubts (Krause, Ingersoll-Dayton, Ellison, & Wulff, 1999). Empirical studies have also demonstrated robust relationships between spiritual struggles and distress, including poorer psychological functioning and poorer physical health (for a review, see Exline & Rose, 2005; see also Chapter 25 in this volume). Spiritual struggles have even been tied to a greater risk of dying. In a longitudinal study, Pargament, Koenig, Tarakeshwar, and Hahn (2001) followed a group of medically ill elder patients and found that spiritual struggles at baseline were predictive of higher levels of mortality 2 years later, even after controlling for selective attrition, demographic variables, and baseline physical and mental health. Divine struggles in particular were associated with a 22% to 33% greater risk of dying.

The effects of spiritual struggles have not been fully reduced to other explanatory variables. Pearce, Singer, and Prigerson (2006) studied 162 informal caregivers of terminally ill cancer patients and found that struggles were tied to more burden, poorer quality of life, less satisfaction, and greater likelihood of major depressive and anxiety disorders. The effects were partially but not fully mediated through social support, optimism, and self-efficacy. Similarly, working with a sample of women dealing with panic disorder, Trenholm, Trent, and Compton (1998) found that intrapsychic spiritual conflicts predicted psychological distress after controlling for conventional explanations (e.g., state anxiety, irrational thinking, hypochondriasis). Higher levels of spiritual struggle have been predictive of increases in depression among divorced individuals, after accounting for the effects of secular struggles (Krumrei, Mahoney, & Pargament, 2009).

Those unable to find compelling ways to resolve their spiritual struggles may disengage from the search for the sacred, temporarily or permanently. In this vein, Exline and Martin (2005) found that although most college students who experienced negative feelings toward God reported that their feelings decreased over time, 9% decided not to believe in God. These students might have taken up the spiritual quest once again at a later point in their lives. In other instances, spiritual struggles lead to a third spiritual process, transformation—that is, profound changes in the individual's understanding of or approach to the sacred. To facilitate this process, people can draw on several transformational methods of spiritual coping, such as rites of passage, forgiveness, and conversion. A small but growing body of research suggests that spiritual transformations are not at all rare and often have a long-lasting impact on the individual's health and well-being (e.g., Freedman & Enright, 1996; Miller & C'de Baca, 2001; Paloutzian, Richardson, & Rambo, 1999; see also Chapters 22 and 23 in this volume).

As with other elements of the search for the sacred, the process of spiritual transformation may be distinctive in some respects. In one of the few studies in this area, Cohen, Gruber, and Keltner (2010) used survey and narrative methods to compare experiences of spiritual transformation with those involving a profound sense of beauty. Both types of experience were associated with high levels of awe and were quite positive in nature. However, spiritual transformational experience differed from experiences of profound beauty in several ways. Consistent with the notion that spiritual transformation grows out of spiritual struggle, experiences of spiritual transformation were tied to reports of greater uncertainty, problems, turmoil, and obstacles as well as negative emotions, including sadness, worry, guilt, and pain. In comparison with experiences of profound beauty, spiritual transformation was also associated with signs of more deep-seated changes in the ways participants understood themselves and the world and in a greater sense of purpose in life.

Once a spiritual transformation takes place, the individual typically returns to the process of conservation and the effort to sustain a relationship with the newly transformed understanding of the sacred. Thus, viewed from this perspective, spirituality is a dynamic process that evolves in diverse ways over the life span.

IMPLICATIONS

In spite of their differences, psychologists and spiritually minded individuals share an assumption: There is more to life than meets the eye. Beneath the surface of human behavior, psychologists see deeper forces of personality, environment, genetics, physiology, the unconscious, and evolution at play. Spiritual individuals also see a deeper dimension in life, but this is a dimension of a different kind, one marked by such terms as karma, divine will, devils, angels, miracles, and transcendence. Perhaps because psychologists tend to be skeptical about the reality of divine forces (see Volume 2, Chapter 2, this handbook) and because these forces cannot be measured directly, they have largely ignored the interpretive phenomenology of spiritual people themselves and, instead, presumed a deeper psychological or social basis to religious and spiritual expression. Certainly, there is merit to the effort to understand religion and spirituality at other levels of analysis, psychological, social, or physical, but a purely reductionistic analysis is necessarily limited. In its most radical form, a reductionistic approach can lead researchers and practitioners to minimize or even ignore the religious dimension. After all, why focus on religion when it can be fully explained by secular mediators? One psychologist articulated this perspective:

> The psychological processes by which religion affects subjective well-being and psychological and physical health are interesting and important, and research on them is easily justified; however, they have very little to do with religion per se, and there is nothing that necessarily leads from an interest in these processes to a focus on religion. (Funder, 2002, p. 214)

This chapter offers a caution against efforts to "explain religion away" (Pargament, 2002a). I have asserted that there are some good reasons to treat spirituality as a significant motivation and process in and of itself. True, psychologists have no tools to measure God or to confirm or disconfirm the existence of a higher power. We can, however, examine perceptions of sacredness, reports of spiritual motivation, and the process of spiritual evolution over the life span as they affect human functioning. By doing so, we place these distinctive spiritual phenomena where they belong—at the center of the psychology of religion and spirituality. This chapter concludes with a discussion of some of the theoretical, practical, and empirical advantages of treating spirituality as a distinctive motive and process.

Theoretical Implications

Theoretically, this nonreductive perspective on spirituality offers one way to resolve the tensions that have arisen in conceptualizations of the terms *spiritual* and *religious*. Over past decades, the notions of spirituality and religion have become polarized (see Chapter 1 in this volume). The phrase "you can be spiritual without being religious" has become almost a mantra in the 21st century, at least in academic circles. Spirituality is increasingly viewed as a highly personal, subjective, positive process, whereas religion in contrast, is increasingly seen as an institutional, restrictive, and negative phenomenon (Zinnbauer & Pargament, 1999). From the perspective of this chapter, spirituality represents the core function of religious life. Certainly, religion serves other purposes as well, but to reduce religious motivation purely to psychological, social, and physical functions overlooks the raison d'être of religion—the yearning for a connection with the sacred. This is not to say that spiritually oriented individuals cannot and do not pursue the sacred outside of traditional religious pathways. Any attempt to understand spirituality as a purely individual, context-free process, however, is bound to be limited, for spirituality always unfolds within a larger field of religious, institutional, and cultural forces, including those in the United States that encourage individualism and privatization. The individual who defines his or her spirituality in reaction to traditional religious pathways is nonetheless affected by that larger context. Thus, the perspective in this paper locates spirituality squarely within the province of the psychology of religion.

It does not follow, however, that spirituality has a narrow and limited set of implications. Defined as a distinctive motivation and process, the construct of spirituality may contribute to a broader and deeper understanding of many other aspects of human functioning. Many of the chapters in this volume have highlighted ways that religion and spirituality can be understood through the perspective of mainstream psychological theories. Consistent with the integrative paradigm of this handbook (see Chapter 1 in this volume), however, these same chapters have demonstrated ways in which theory and research on religion and spirituality enrich mainstream thought in psychology, including theories of attachment (see Chapter 7 in this volume), cognitive development (see Chapter 12 in this volume), coping (see Chapter 19 in this volume), personality (see Chapter 9 in this volume), modeling (see Chapter 10 in this volume), marital and family functioning (see Chapter 20 in this volume), and culture (see Chapter 13 in this volume)

Practical Implications

The present approach also has implications for the ways psychologist evaluate and approach spirituality in their applied work.

Evaluating spirituality. As defined here, spirituality is a natural and normal part of life. But no theory of spirituality would be complete without attending to its capacity to elicit both the highest and lowest of human expressions (see Volume 2, Chapter 4, this handbook). Elsewhere, I have proposed the concept of "spiritual integration" to help guide evaluations of spirituality in ways that are grounded in the character of spirituality itself (Pargament, 2007). A well-integrated spirituality is not defined by a specific belief, practice, emotion, or relationship, but rather by the degree to which the various spiritual ingredients work together in synchrony. Thus, we can imagine a variety of effective spiritualities. What they share is a high degree of integration, marked by breadth and depth, responsivity to life situations, flexibility and continuity, and a concept of the sacred that is large enough to encompass the full range of human potential and luminous enough to provide the individual with a powerful guiding vision. At lower levels of integration, spirituality is characterized by a lack of breadth and depth, an insensitivity to life demands, rigidity or instability, and concepts of the sacred that misdirect the individual in the pursuit of spiritual value (see Figure 14.1).

Consider an example. Empirical studies have shown that people who passively defer the responsibility for problem solving to God generally manifest poorer mental health than those who view God as more of a partner or collaborator in problem solving (e.g., Yangarber-Hicks, 2004). And yet, this seemingly straightforward finding obscures a more complex yet vital point: The value of passive deferral to a higher power varies from situation to situation. Passive deferral in response to situations that call for action and initiative on the part of the individual, such as the discovery of a lump in the breast, may have deadly consequences (see Baider & De-Nour, 1986). Equally problematic, however, is the stubborn insistence on personal initiative in situations that are beyond human control, as in exhaustive and futile self-directed efforts to cure a terminal illness (see Bickel et al., 1988). The most effective spirituality—a well-integrated spirituality—may rest on spiritual discernment, the kind of wisdom embodied in Reinhold Niebuhr's Serenity Prayer: "God grant me the serenity to accept the things I cannot change; courage to change the things I can; and wisdom to know the difference."

Drawing on spiritual resources. A nonreductive approach to spirituality can also alert practitioners to the possibility of distinctive spiritual resources that can be drawn on to facilitate health and well-being. For example, Goldstein (2007) developed an intervention in which participants were taught to "cultivate sacred moments" in their lives by focusing on a sacred, precious, or special object (e.g., heirloom, childhood memorabilia, something from nature) for a minimum of 5 min a day, 5 days a week, over 3 weeks. Participants in the intervention experienced significant improvements in subjective well-being, personal well-being, and daily spiritual experiences over the course of the intervention and again 6 weeks later. Participants also commonly reported experiencing qualities and emotions related to the sacred, such as interconnectedness, sweet-sadness, gratitude, and humility. Moreover, the intervention was equally effective as a daily writing task. Avants, Beitel, and Margolin (2005) developed and tested an 8-week therapy for cocaine- and opioid-dependent clients that was designed to help them replace an "addict self-schema" with a "spiritual self-schema" through the use of spiritual resources, such as prayers and affirmation, spiritual reframing, meditation, and training in spiritual virtues. Participants manifested significant reductions in drug use and HIV-risk behaviors. They also experienced significant shifts toward a spiritual self-schema, and these shifts, in turn, were associated with declines in drug use and HIV-risk behavior.

If spirituality represents a distinctive resource, then we might expect spiritually integrated forms of treatment to be equally, or even more, effective than their secular counterparts. An emerging empirical literature provides some initial support for this conclusion (e.g., Pargament, 2007; T. B. Smith, Bartz, & Richards, 2007; Wachholtz & Pargament, 2008; see also Volume 2, Chapter 34, this handbook). For example, Richards, Berrett, Hardman, and Eggett (2006) compared the effectiveness of three treatments for women with eating disorders in an inpatient setting: a spirituality group that read and discussed a spiritual workbook; a cognitive group that read and discussed a cognitive–behavioral workbook; and an emotional support group that discussed nonspiritually related topics (e.g., nutrition, self-esteem). Although participants in all three groups reported positive changes, the members of the spirituality group manifested greater declines in symptom distress, relationship distress, and social role conflict, and more improvement in eating attitudes and spiritual well-being. Similarly, Wachholtz and Pargament (2008) randomly assigned chronic headache sufferers to groups that were taught to meditate to a spiritual mantra, meditate to nonspiritual mantras, and progressive muscle relaxation. In comparison with the other groups, those who were taught to meditate to a spiritual mantra showed significantly greater improvements in pain tolerance, headache frequency, headache self-efficacy, and mood.

Empirical Implications

Finally, the present approach to spirituality points to new directions and questions for empirical study. As noted, in the effort to uncover explanations for the links between indices of religiousness and health and well-being, researchers have proposed and tested a variety of psychological, social, and physical mediating variables, with limited success. In addition to these explanatory candidates, it might be worth considering more fine-grained spiritual variables as potential mediators in future research (e.g., Fincham, Lambert, & Beach, 2010). Studies of church attendance–mortality connection offer a case in point. Frequent church attendance has been consistently linked with a significantly lower risk of mortality (e.g., McCullough, Hoyt, Larson, Koenig, & Thoresen, 2000). Attempts to account for these effects through psychological and social mechanisms (e.g., better health practices, social support, coherence) have not proven very successful. An alternate possibility is that the effects of church attendance on mortality are mediated through more proximal spiritual variables. For instance, people who attend church frequently may be exposed to a more regular "dose" of spiritual emotions, such as uplift, awe, and gratitude, through the mechanisms of religious music, sermons, testimonies, rituals, and so on (see Chapter 18 in this volume). Or they may be more likely to view their bodies in spiritual terms (e.g., sacred vessel, carrier of a divine spark). These explanations may also account for the greater church attendance–longevity benefit of African Americans in comparison with White Americans (McCullough et al., 2000). African American churches may be particularly effective in promoting spiritually uplifting experiences in their members and encouraging their members to see themselves and the world through a sacred lens.

To extend this line of questioning, is it possible that some effects of secular treatments are in fact mediated through spiritual variables? This turns the reductionistic question (i.e., whether spirituality can be explained in terms of presumably more basic phenomena) neatly around on its head; here we consider whether the critical ingredients of effective treatments may be spiritual in nature. The idea may not be far-fetched. Indeed, there is evidence that secular treatments affect people spiritually as well as psychologically, socially, and physically. For instance, Tisdale et al. (1997) evaluated the effects of a psychiatric inpatient program. The program was secular, consisting of individual, group, milieu, and psychotropic interventions. It was not surprising to find that the program was effective in improving the personal adjustment of the patients. What was surprising was the finding that patients also reported significant changes toward more positive images of God. Furthermore, shifts in image of God were linked with other personal improvements in the lives of the patients. Similarly, one study of women in treatment for eating disorders found that improvements in spiritual well-being were associated with positive changes in body image, healthier attitudes toward eating, reduced conflict in relationships, and reductions in psychological symptoms (F. T. Smith, Hardman, Richards, & Fischer, 2003). These findings are quite preliminary in nature, but they raise the intriguing possibility that spiritual variables may be important ingredients of change that occurs through even ostensibly secular psychological interventions.

Other important questions that grow out of a nonreductive approach to spirituality center on perceptions of the sacred as a phenomenon of interest. For example, how do perceptions of the sacred differ from other aspects of life that may be seen as important but not sacred? How do people develop their understandings of sacredness in their lives? What leads to the growth of broad and deep conceptualizations of the sacred as opposed to narrow and shallow conceptualizations? What factors foster the development of tolerance or intolerance to representations of the sacred that are different from one's own? What determines whether struggles in the search for the sacred lead to spiritual transformation, disengagement, growth or decline? More generally, what promotes high rather than low levels of spiritual integration?

CONCLUSION

In this chapter, I have cautioned against efforts to fully reduce religion and spirituality to purely psychological, social, and physical processes. I have marshaled some evidence in support of a simpler possibility, that spirituality is a distinctive human motivation and process in and of itself. This perspective has significant theoretical, practical, and empirical implications. More generally, I believe it contributes greater depth, breadth, and balance to the study of religion and spirituality—dimensions of life that may be at least partially irreducible and at least partially responsible for our distinctiveness as human beings. The "jury is still out" on this parsimonious yet provocative perspective, but even if additional studies succeed in identifying a set of explanatory factors that fully account for the effects of religion and spirituality, a reductionistic approach to these phenomena would remain problematic. Why? Because a substantial portion of the world's population looks at life through a sacred lens, a lens that colors, filters, and clarifies their view of reality. Psychologists who encourage people to replace their glasses with psychological prescriptions are unlikely to meet with a great deal of success. Instead, they are likely to encounter active resistance or, even more often, dismissive shrugs that convey the message "You just don't understand." A nonreductive psychology of religion and spirituality lends itself to a more collaborative, respectful, and productive relationship with diverse individuals and communities because it takes seriously their own visions of the world.

References

Ahmadi, F. (2006). *Culture, religion, and spirituality in coping: The example of cancer patients in Sweden.* Uppsala, Sweden: Acta Universitatis Upsaliensis.

Ai, A. L., Park, C. L., Huang, B., Rodgers, W., & Tice, T. N. (2007). Psychosocial mediation of religious coping styles: A study of short-term psychological distress following cardiac surgery. *Personality and Social Psychology Bulletin, 33,* 867–882. doi:10.1177/0146167207301008

Allport, G. (1950). *The individual and his religion.* New York, NY: Macmillan.

Ano, G. G., & Vasconcelles, E. B. (2005). Religious coping and psychological adjustment to stress: A meta-analysis. *Journal of Clinical Psychology, 61,* 461–480. doi:10.1002/jclp.20049

Avants, S. K., Beitel, M., & Margolin, A. (2005). Making the shift from "addict self" to "spiritual self": Results from a Stage I study of spiritual self-schema (3-S) therapy for the treatment of addiction and HIV risk behavior. *Mental Health, Religion, and Culture, 8,* 167–177. doi:10.1080/13694670500138924

Baider, L., & De-Nour, A. K. (1986). The meaning of a disease: An exploratory study of Moslem Arab women after a mastectomy. *Journal of Psychosocial Oncology, 4,* 1–13. doi:10.1300/J077v04n04_01

Baumeister, R. F. (1991). *Meanings of life.* New York, NY: Guilford Press.

Bickel, C. O., Ciarrocchi, J. W., Sheers, N. J., Estadt, B. K., Powell, D. A., & Pargament, K. I. (1998). Perceived stress, religious coping styles, and depressive affect. *Journal of Psychology and Christianity, 17,* 33–42.

Brenner, R. R. (1980). *The faith and doubt of Holocaust survivors.* New York, NY: Free Press.

Carrico, A. W., Ironson, G., Antoni, M. H., Lechner, S. C., Duran, R. E., Kumar, M., & Schneiderman, N. (2006). A path model of the effects of spirituality on depressive symptoms and 24-h urinary-free cortisol in HIV-positive persons. *Journal of Psychosomatic Research, 61,* 51–58. doi:10.1016/j.jpsychores.2006.04.005

Cohen, A. B., Gruber, J., & Keltner, D. (2010). Comparing spiritual transformations and experiences of profound beauty. *Psychology of Religion and Spirituality, 2,* 127–135. doi:10.1037/a0019126

Coles, R. (1990). *The spiritual lives of children.* Boston, MA: Houghton Mifflin.

Doehring, C., Clarke, A., Pargament, K. I., Hayes, A., Hammer, D., Nikolas, M., & Hughes, P. (2009). Perceiving sacredness in life: Correlates and predictors. *Archive for the Psychology of Religion, 31,* 55–73. doi:10.1163/157361209X371492

Durkheim, E. (1915). *The elementary forms of religious life.* New York, NY: Free Press.

Eliade, M. (1957). *The sacred and the profane: The nature of religion.* New York, NY: Harvest Books.

Ellison, C. G., Boardman, J. D., Williams, D. R., & Jackson, J. S. (2001). Religious involvement, stress, and mental health: Findings from the 1995 Detroit area study. *Social Forces, 80,* 215–249. doi:10.1353/sof.2001.0063

Ellison, C. W., & Smith, J. (1991). Toward an integrative measure of health and well-being. *Journal of Psychology and Theology, 19,* 35–48.

Emmons, R. A. (1999). *The psychology of ultimate concerns.* New York, NY: Guilford Press.

Emmons, R. A., & Crumpler, C. A. (2000). Gratitude as human strength: Appraising the evidence. *Journal of Social and Clinical Psychology, 19,* 56–69. doi:10.1521/jscp.2000.19.1.56

Exline, J. J., & Martin, A. (2005). Anger toward God: A new frontier in forgiveness research. In E. L. Worthington (Ed.), *Handbook of forgiveness* (pp. 73–88). New York, NY: Routledge.

Exline, J. J., & Rose, E. (2005). Religious and spiritual struggles. In R. F. Paloutzian & C. L. Park (Eds.), *Handbook of the psychology of religion and spirituality* (pp. 315–330). New York, NY: Guilford Press.

Falsetti, S. A., Resick, P. A., & Davis, J. L. (2003, August). Changes in religious beliefs following trauma. *Journal of Traumatic Stress, 16,* 391–398. doi:10.1023/A:1024422220163

Fincham, F. D., Lambert, N. M., & Beach, R. H. (2010). Faith and unfaithfulness: Can praying for your partner reduce infidelity. *Journal of Personality and Social Psychology, 99,* 649–659. doi:10.1037/a0019628

Freedman, S. R., & Enright, R. D. (1996). Forgiveness as an intervention goal with incest survivors. *Journal of Consulting and Clinical Psychology, 64,* 983–992. doi:10.1037/0022-006X.64.5.983

Freud, S. (1927/1961). *The future of an illusion.* New York, NY: Norton.

Funder, D. C. (2002). Why study religion? *Psychological Inquiry, 13,* 213–214.

Gallup, G., Jr., & Lindsay, D. M. (1999). *Surveying the religious landscape: Trends in U.S. beliefs.* Harrisburg, PA: Morehouse.

Geertz, C. (1966). Religion as a cultural system. In M. Banton (Ed.), *Anthropological approaches to the study of religion* (pp. 1–46). London, England: Tavistock.

Goldstein, E. D. (2007). Sacred moments: Implications on well-being and stress. *Journal of Clinical Psychology, 63,* 1001–1019. doi:10.1002/jclp.20402

Graham, J., & Haidt, J. (2010). Beyond beliefs: Religions bind individuals into moral communities. *Personality and Social Psychology Review, 14,* 140–150. doi:10.1177/1088868309353415

Haidt, J. (2003). Elevation and the positive psychology of morality. In C. L. M. Keyes & J. Haidt (Eds.), *Flourishing: Positive psychology and the life well-lived* (pp. 275–289). Washington, DC: American Psychological Association. doi:10.1037/10594-012

Hall, M. E. L., Oates, K. L. M., Anderson, T. L., & Willingham, M. M. (2012). Calling and conflict: The sanctification of work in working mothers. *Psychology of Religion and Spirituality, 4*, 71–83. doi:10.1037/a0023191

Harding, S. R., Flannelly, K. J., Weaver, A. J., & Costa, K. G. (2005). The influence of religion on death anxiety and death acceptance. *Mental Health, Religion, and Culture, 8*, 253–261. doi:10.1080/13674670412331304311

Hardy, A. (1979). *The spiritual nature of man: A study of contemporary religious experience.* Oxford, England: Clarendon Press.

Henderson, A. K., Ellison, C. G., & Glenn, N. D. (2010). *Religion and relationship quality among cohabitating and dating couples.* Manuscript submitted for publication.

Hernandez, K. M., & Mahoney, A. (2009). *Sex through a sacred lens: The longitudinal effects of sanctifying marital sexuality* (Working paper, National Marriage and Family Research Center, Bowling Green, OH). Retrieved from http://ncmr.bgsu.edu/data/working-papers.html

Hill, P. C., & Pargament, K. I. (2003). Advances in the conceptualization and measurement of religion and spirituality: Implications for physical and mental health research. *American Psychologist, 58*, 64–74. doi:10.1037/0003-066X.58.1.64

Ironson, G., Stuetzle, R., & Fletcher, M. A. (2006). An increase in religiousness/spirituality occurs after HIV diagnosis and predicts slower disease progression over 4 years in people with HIV. *Journal of General Internal Medicine, 21*, S62–S68. doi:10.1111/j.1525-1497.2006.00648.x

Johnson, C. N., & Boyatzis, C. J. (2006). Cognitive-cultural foundations of spiritual development. In E. C. Roehlkepartain, P. E. King, L. Wagener, & P. L. Benson (Eds.), *The handbook of spiritual development in childhood and adolescence* (pp. 211–223). Thousand Oaks, CA: Sage.

Johnson, P. E. (1959). *Psychology of religion.* Nashville, TN: Abingdon Press.

Jones, J. W. (2002). *Terror and transformation: The ambiguity of religion in psychoanalytic perspective.* New York, NY: Brunner-Routledge.

Jung, C. G. (1938). *Psychology and religion.* New Haven, CT: Yale University Press.

Kirkpatrick, L. A. (2005). *Attachment, evolution, and the psychology of religion.* New York, NY: Guilford Press.

Koenig, H. G., King, D., & Carson, V. B. (2012). *Handbook of religion and health* (2nd ed.). Oxford, England: Oxford University Press.

Kooistra, W. P. (1990). *The process of religious doubting in adolescents raised in religious environments.* Unpublished doctoral dissertation, Bowling Green State University, Bowling Green, OH.

Krause, N. (2006). Exploring the stress-buffering effects of church-based and secular social support on self-rated health in late life. *The Journals of Gerontology, Series B: Psychological Sciences and Social Sciences, 61*, S35–S43. doi:10.1093/geronb/61.1.S35

Krause, N., Ingersoll-Dayton, B., Ellison, C. G., & Wulff, K. M. (1999). Aging, religious doubt, and psychological well-being. *The Gerontologist, 39*, 525–533. doi:10.1093/geront/39.5.525

Krumrei, E. J., Mahoney, A., & Pargament, K. I. (2009). Divorce and the divine: The role of spiritual appraisals, coping, and struggles for adults' post-divorce adjustment. *Journal of Marriage and Family, 71*, 373–383. doi:10.1111/j.1741-3737.2009.00605.x

Lambert, N. M., & Dollahite, D. C. (2008). The threefold cord—Marital commitment in religious couples. *Journal of Family Issues, 29*, 592–614. doi:10.1177/0192513X07308395

Loewald, H. (1978). *Psychoanalysis and the history of the individual.* New Haven, CT: Yale University Press.

Mahoney, A., Carels, R. A., Pargament, K. I., Wachholtz, A., Leeper, L. E., Kaplar, M., & Frutchey, R. (2005). The sanctification of the body and behavioral health patterns of college students. *The International Journal for the Psychology of Religion, 15*, 221–238. doi:10.1207/s15327582ijpr1503_3

Mahoney, A., Pargament, K. I., & Hernandez, K. M. (in press). Heaven on earth: Beneficial effects of sanctification for individual and interpersonal well-being. In J. Henry (Ed.), *Oxford handbook of happiness.* New York, NY: Oxford University Press.

Mahoney, A., Pargament, K. I., Jewell, T., Swank, B., Scott, E., Emery, E., . . . Rye, M. (1999). Marriage and the spiritual realm: The role of proximal and distal religious constructs in marital functioning. *Journal of Family Psychology, 13*, 321–338. doi:10.1037/0893-3200.13.3.321

McCullough, M. E., Hoyt, W. T., Larson, D. B., Koenig, H. G., & Thoresen, C. (2000). Religious involvement and mortality: A meta-analytic review. *Health Psychology, 19*, 211–222. doi:10.1037/0278-6133.19.3.211

McCullough, M. E., & Willoughby, B. (2009). Religion, self-regulation, and self-control: Associations, explanations, and implications. *Psychological Bulletin, 135*, 69–93. doi:10.1037/a0014213

McIntosh, D. N., Silver, R. C., & Wortman, C. B. (1993). Religion's role in adjustment to a negative life event: Coping with the loss of a child. *Journal of Personality and Social Psychology, 65*, 812–821. doi:10.1037/0022-3514.65.4.812

Miller, W. R., & C'de Baca, J. (2001). *Quantum change; When epiphanies and sudden insights transform ordinary lives*. New York, NY: Guilford Press.

Newberg, A., & Waldman, M. R. (2006). *Born to believe: God, science, and the origin of ordinary and extraordinary beliefs*. New York, NY: Free Press.

Otto, R. (1928). *The idea of the holy: An inquiry into the non-rational factor in the idea of the divine and its relation to the rational*. London, England: Oxford University Press.

Paloutzian, R. F., Richardson, J. T., & Rambo, L. R. (1999). Religious conversion and personality change. *Journal of Personality, 67*, 1047–1079. doi:10.1111/1467-6494.00082

Pargament, K. I. (1997). *The psychology of religion and coping: Theory, research, practice*. New York, NY: Guilford Press.

Pargament, K. I. (1999). The psychology of religion and spirituality? Yes and no. *The International Journal for the Psychology of Religion, 9*, 3–16. doi:10.1207/s15327582ijpr0901_2

Pargament, K. I. (2002a). The bitter and the sweet: An evaluation of the costs and benefits of religiousness. *Psychological Inquiry, 13*, 168–181. doi:10.1207/S15327965PLI1303_02

Pargament, K. I. (2002b). Is religion nothing but . . . ? Explaining religion versus explaining religion away. *Psychological Inquiry, 13*, 239–244. doi:10.1207/S15327965PLI1303_06

Pargament, K. I. (2007). *Spiritually integrated psychotherapy: Understanding and addressing the sacred*. New York, NY: Guilford Press.

Pargament, K. I. (2011). Religion and coping: The current state of knowledge. In S. Folkman (Ed.), *Oxford handbook of stress, health, and coping* (pp. 269–288). New York, NY: Oxford University Press.

Pargament, K. I., Ensing, D. S., Falgout, K., Olsen, H., Reilly, B., Van Haitsma, K., . . . Warren, R. (1990). God help me (I): Religious coping efforts as predictors of the outcomes to significant negative life events. *American Journal of Community Psychology, 18*, 793–824. doi:10.1007/BF00938065

Pargament, K. I., Koenig, H. G., Tarakeshwar, N., & Hahn, J. (2001). Religious struggle as a predictor of mortality among medically ill elderly patients: A two-year longitudinal study. *Archives of Internal Medicine, 161*, 1881–1885. doi:10.1001/archinte.161.15.1881

Pargament, K. I., Magyar, G. M., Benore, E., & Mahoney, A. (2005). Sacrilege: A study of sacred loss and desecration and their implications for health and well-being in a community sample. *Journal for the Scientific Study of Religion, 44*, 59–78. doi:10.1111/j.1468-5906.2005.00265.x

Pargament, K. I., Magyar-Russell, G. M., & Murray-Swank, N. A. (2005). The sacred and the search for significance: Religion as a unique process. *Journal of Social Issues, 61*, 665–687. doi:10.1111/j.1540-4560.2005.00426.x

Pargament, K. I., & Mahoney, A. (2005). Sacred matters: Sanctification as a vital topic for the psychology of religion. *The International Journal for the Psychology of Religion, 15*, 179–198. doi:10.1207/s15327582ijpr1503_1

Pargament, K. I., McConnell, K., Mahoney, A., & Silberman, I. (2007). They killed our Lord: The perception of Jews as desecrators of Christianity as a predictor of anti-Semitism. *Journal for the Scientific Study of Religion, 46*, 143–158. doi:10.1111/j.1468-5906.2007.00347.x

Pargament, K. I., Murray-Swank, N., Magyar, G., & Ano, G. (2005). Spiritual struggle: A phenomenon of interest to psychology and religion. In W. R. Miller & H. Delaney (Eds.), *Judeo-Christian perspectives on psychology: Human nature, motivation, and change* (pp. 245–268). Washington, DC: American Psychological Association. doi:10.1037/10859-013

Park, C. L., & Folkman, S. (1997). Meaning in the context of stress and coping. *Review of General Psychology, 1*, 115–144. doi:10.1037/1089-2680.1.2.115

Pearce, M. J., Singer, J. L., & Prigerson, H. G. (2006). Religious coping among caregivers of terminally ill cancer patients: Main effects and psychosocial mediators. *Journal of Health Psychology, 11*, 743–759. doi:10.1177/1359105306066629

Piedmont, R. L., Ciarrocchi, J. W., Dy-Liacco, G. S., & Williams, J. E. G. (2009). The empirical and conceptual value of the Spiritual Transcendence and Religious Involvement scales for personality research. *Psychology of Religion and Spirituality, 1*, 162–179. doi:10.1037/a0015883

Piedmont, R. L., Mapa, A. T., & Williams, J. E. G. (2006). A factor analysis of the Fetzer/NIA Brief Multidimensional Measure of Religiousness/Spirituality (MMRS). *Research in the Social Scientific Study of Religion, 17*, 177–196.

Raiya, H. A., Pargament, K. I., Mahoney, A., & Trevino, K. (2008). When Muslims are perceived as a religious threat: Examining the connection between desecration, religious coping, and anti-Muslim attitudes. *Basic and Applied Social Psychology, 30*, 311–325. doi:10.1080/01973530802502234

Richards, P. S., Berrett, M. E., Hardman, R. K., & Eggett, D. L. (2006). Comparative efficacy of spirituality, cognitive, and emotional support groups for treating eating disorder inpatients. *Eating Disorders, 14*, 401–415. doi:10.1080/10640260600952548

Roof, W. C. (1993). *A generation of seekers: The spiritual journeys of the baby boom generation*. San Francisco, CA: Harper & Row.

Sedikides, C., & Gebauer, J. E. (2010). Religiosity as self-enhancement: A meta-analysis of the relation between socially desirable responding and religiosity. *Personality and Social Psychology Review, 14*, 17–36. doi:10.1177/1088868309351002

Smith, F. T., Hardman, R. K., Richards, P. S., & Fischer, L. (2003). Intrinsic religiosity and spiritual well-being as predictors of treatment outcome among women with eating disorders. *Eating Disorders, 11*, 15–26. doi:10.1080/10640260390167456-2199

Smith, T. B., Bartz, J. D., & Richards, P. S. (2007). Outcomes of religious and spiritual adaptations to psychotherapy: A meta-analytic review. *Psychotherapy Research, 17*, 643–655. doi:10.1080/10503300701250347

Smith, T. B., McCullough, M. E., & Poll, J. (2003). Religiousness and depression: Evidence for a main effect and the moderating influence of stressful life events. *Psychological Bulletin, 129*, 614–636. doi:10.1037/0033-2909.129.4.614

Steger, M. F., Frazier, P., Oishi, S., & Kaler, M. (2006). The Meaning in Life Questionnaire: Assessing the presence of and search for meaning in life. *Journal of Counseling Psychology, 53*, 80–93. doi:10.1037/0022-0167.53.1.80

Tarakeshwar, N., Swank, A. B., Pargament, K. I., & Mahoney, A. (2001). The sanctification of nature and theological conservatism: A study of opposing religious correlates of environmentalism. *Review of Religious Research, 42*, 387–404. doi:10.2307/3512131

Tisdale, T. C., Keys, T. L., Edwards, K. J., Brokaw, B. F., Kemperman, S. R., Cloud, H., . . . Okamoto, T. (1997). Impact of treatment on God image and personal adjustment, and correlations of God image to personal adjustment and object relations adjustment. *Journal of Psychology and Theology, 25*, 227–239.

Tix, A. P., & Frazier, P. A. (1998). The use of religious coping during stressful life events: Main effects, moderation, and mediation. *Journal of Consulting and Clinical Psychology, 66*, 411–422. doi:10.1037/0022-006X.66.2.411

Trenholm, P., Trent, J., & Compton, W. C. (1998). Negative religious conflict as a predictor of panic disorder. *Journal of Clinical Psychology, 54*, 59–65. doi:10.1002/(SICI)1097-4679(199801)54:1<59::AID-JCLP7>3.0.CO;2-P

Vail, K. E., Rothschild, Z. K., Weise, D. R., Solomon, S., Pyszczynski, T., & Greenberg, J. (2010). A terror management analysis of the psychological functions of religion. *Personality and Social Psychology Review, 14*, 84–94. doi:10.1177/1088868309351165

Wachholtz, A. B., & Pargament, K. I. (2008). Migraines and meditation; Does spirituality matter? *Journal of Behavioral Medicine, 31*, 351–366. doi:10.1007/s10865-008-9159-2

Wink, P., Dillon, M., & Larsen, B. (2005). Religion as moderator of the depression-health connection: Findings from a longitudinal study. *Research on Aging, 27*, 197–220. doi:10.1177/0164027504270483

Wrzesniewski, A., McCauley, C., Rozin, P., & Schwartz, B. (1997). Jobs, careers, and callings: People's relations to their work. *Journal of Research in Personality, 31*, 21–33. doi:10.1006/jrpe.1997.2162

Yangarber-Hicks, N. (2004). Religious coping styles and recovery from serious mental illnesses. *Journal of Psychology and Theology, 32*, 305–317.

Ysseldyk, R., Matheson, K., & Anisman, H. (2010). Religiosity as identity: Toward an understanding of religion from a social identity perspective. *Personality and Social Psychology Review, 14*, 60–71.

Zinnbauer, B., & Pargament, K. I. (1999). The emerging meanings of religiousness and spirituality: Problems and prospects. *Journal of Personality, 67*, 889–919. doi:10.1111/1467-6494.00077

Part III

HOW PEOPLE ARE RELIGIOUS AND SPIRITUAL: EXPRESSIONS AND EXPERIENCES

Chapter 15

GOD IMAGE AND THE SACRED

Todd W. Hall and Annie M. Fujikawa

The notion of the God image as a psychological construct dates back to the 19th century, with much of the theoretical discussion being initiated by Freud (1913/1950, 1927/1961). Although the God image generally refers to one's personal view of God, numerous theoretical lines are converging in suggesting two broad layers to the God image that are based on two distinct types of knowledge: explicit, or propositional knowledge of God, and implicit, or experiential knowledge of God (e.g., Rizzuto, 1979; see also Volume 2, Chapter 6, this handbook). Although these layers are distinct, they are all part of an individual's personal view of God, and can certainly influence each other, although they may also operate somewhat independently.

A person's God image not only has multiple layers in terms of how the information is processed, but it also has multiple dimensions such as the biological, cognitive, emotional, motivational, behavioral, and relational dimensions. In addition, we can think of the God image interacting in reciprocal ways with multiple levels, such as the individual, familial, organizational, and community levels. These layers, dimensions, and levels of the God image have a multidirectional impact, meaning they cause certain outcomes, but they are also influenced by contextual factors, both of which are the result of complex processes. Finally, it is important to point out that the God image has multiple valences—that is, a person's God image exists on a continuum ranging from positive and health inducing to negative and health diminishing.

As part of the integrative paradigm of this handbook, our goal in this chapter is to integrate as much as possible the various layers, dimensions, levels, directionalities, and valences within several foundational conceptual headings related to the God image: terminology and the layers of the God image, the nature and formation of the God image, the God image and psychological functioning, contextual influences on the God image, the transformation of the God image, and measurement issues. Although theory and research will lay the foundation for this chapter, we will discuss implications for practice throughout the various sections.

TERMINOLOGY AND LAYERS OF THE GOD IMAGE

In reviewing the literature on the God image, one is quickly confronted with the fact that various terms are used to refer to an individual's personal view of God. The three main terms found in the literature—God image, God concept, and God representation—are often used interchangeably and inconsistently, which promotes conceptual confusion. Generally, the term *God concept* has been used to refer to more conscious, propositional beliefs about God. In contrast, the terms *God image* and *God representation* generally have been used to refer to a more experiential view of God. Jones (2007) highlighted these two layers in his discussion of two approaches to people's beliefs about God: (a) the correlational approach that uses empirical methods and focuses

DOI: 10.1037/14045-015
APA Handbook of Psychology, Religion, and Spirituality: Vol. 1. Context, Theory, and Research, K. I. Pargament (Editor-in-Chief)
Copyright © 2013 by the American Psychological Association. All rights reserved.

on associations between beliefs about God and personality traits and behaviors and (b) the clinical psychodynamic approach that "suggests ways in which these beliefs are rooted in and linked to the person's developmental history, their character, and personality style" (p. 34). These two approaches as described by Jones generally parallel the distinction between the explicit, conscious God concept, and the implicit, nonconscious God image.

These two layers of the God image correspond to two types of knowledge that have emerged in recent decades in cross-disciplinary research on emotion, ways of knowing, and memory (e.g., Bucci, 1997; Siegel, 2012; Solms & Turnbull, 2002): explicit knowledge and implicit relational knowledge (The Process of Change Study Group, 1998). In light of this, and in the hopes of providing some consistency and clarity in this chapter and the broader literature, we propose the term *explicit God image* for the more conscious, propositional view of God. For the less conscious, experiential view of God, we propose the term *implicit God image*. Both layers of the God image and types of knowledge of God are important and related, albeit in complex ways. Thus, in this conceptualization, one's overall God image includes both explicit and implicit layers, and people vary in meaningful ways in terms of the degree of integration of these two layers.

THE FORMATION OF GOD IMAGE AND PSYCHOLOGICAL FUNCTIONING

Because theories of the God image historically derive so heavily from Freud, many of the theoretical developments about the nature and formation of the God image come from psychoanalytic theory. Attachment theory, which developed out of Bowlby's critique of Freudian and Kleinian psychoanalytic theories (Bowlby, 1969, 1973, 1980) and has much conceptual overlap with more contemporary psychoanalytic theories such as object relations theory (Hall, 2007a, 2007b), has perhaps become the dominant framework for theory and research in recent years. Thus, in presenting a broad overview of the nature and formation of the God image in this section, it is necessary to review developments within psychoanalytic theory and attachment theory for the sake of historical context as well as for substantive contributions that come from these fields.

Freud and the God Image

There appear to be two aspects to Freud's explanation of religion in general, and the God image in particular, which draw from both sides of the ambivalence associated with children's images of their father. The first aspect of Freud's notion of the God image builds on his theory of infantile sexuality and instinctual drives (Freud, 1905/1953). As part of Freud's instinct theory, he postulated that children (he focused on male children in this discussion) internalize a representation of their father as a way to resolve the Oedipus complex. In this resolution, the son must abandon the Oedipal desires and internalize a representation of the father referred to as the "ego-ideal," which then regulates his guilt and instinctual impulses. The ego ideal is a key component of the superego, which Freud later developed as part of the structural model of the mind. The image of the father, then, is associated with the superego functions of constraint and guilt. Freud stated, "The god of each of them is formed in the likeness of the father, his personal relation to God depends on his relation to his father . . . at bottom God is nothing other than an exalted father" (Freud, 1913/1950, p. 147). On the basis of the Oedipal resolution, we can see why this version of the God image is, as Jones (2007) put it, a "patriarchal deity of law, guilt, and subjugation" (p. 35).

The other side of the father image that contributes to Freud's theory of the God image is the idealized identification with father. Freud (1927/1961, 1907/1959) viewed the God image as the result of a neurotic organization created by the human mind to defend one's self against a sense of helplessness in the face of the uncertainties of life and one's mortality. This version of Freud's God image is still made up of projections of the images of parents, primarily the father, but now elevated to an exalted, all-powerful figure who can help the believer escape the perils of life and death. The believer is portrayed by Freud as childlike, dependent, and immature, whereas the God image is portrayed as powerful, majestic, and transcendent (Meissner, 2009). Religious beliefs and the God image for Freud are, as he put it, "illusions, fulfillments of the oldest, strongest and most urgent wishes of mankind" (Freud, 1927/1961, p. 30).

The God image and concomitant belief in God function as a defense and are therefore pathological according to Freud. Maturing involves giving up the defensive illusion that there is a grand father figure in the sky who will protect one from the harsh realities of life. Although the God image in Freud's theory does contribute to psychological functioning by helping people cope with anxiety, it does not contribute to mature psychological functioning or development. This view has been critiqued by more relational psychoanalytic authors (e.g., Meissner, 2009; Rizzuto, 1979, 1998) who have suggested that the God image can have a positive or negative impact on psychological functioning. Constructs of the God image were broadened by later psychoanalytic theorists in a turn toward a relational view of the God image sparked by Rizzuto (1979, 1998).

Object Relations Theory and the God Image

Rizzuto (1979) catalyzed a shift in our understanding of the God image with her book *The Birth of the Living God,* in which she investigated "the possible origins of the individual's private representation of God" (p. 3). This work opened up new territory for a more nuanced understanding of the God image as having a potentially positive or negative impact on psychological functioning, rather than being primarily pathological as was the case with Freud's theory. She proposed that object representations are a special case of several broader psychological processes: "representing, remembering, fantasizing, interpreting, and integrating experiences with others through defensive and adaptive maneuvers" (p. 75). These complex processes, which are all intricately intertwined, form representations of the other ("object") at the time when two people interact. These representations are a combination of somatic sensations (e.g., of being held by mother), emotion communicated through nonverbal channels (e.g., tone of voice, facial expressions), and the subjective meaning associated with these experiences. Moreover, specific memories are consolidated into increasingly complex object representations over time in an effort to create a coherent internal world (Jones, 2007).

Building on this general theory of object representations, and her own case study research, Rizzuto (1979) proposed that the (implicit) God image is essentially a mental representation (or "object representation") initially formed from the parent–child relationship in the earliest period of life. More specifically, the God image is first formed in the context of eye contact or gazing with mother, early nursing, and being mirrored by the mother. These experiences then interact with sociocultural phenomena related to God for most children, and with religious experiences for some. For example, most children hear God described and observe people behave toward this "God" in ways that cause them to sense that God is "powerful, respectable, rules everything, and is everywhere" (Rizzuto, 1979, p. 194). The people closest to the child who possess these characteristics are her mother and father. Because of this, the God image is naturally built out of the content of the parental images. Early relational experiences represent only half of Rizzuto's God image, however. The other half stems from a child's capacity to "create" a God according to her needs. The God image, then, is a special type of object representation: a "transitional object."

The classic example of a transitional object is the proverbial teddy bear that carries the mother's presence in her absence. The God image is similar to a transitional object in that it also carries a sense of the attachment figure's presence (in this case, God as a perceived attachment figure)—or lack thereof—when no one is physically present, because it is formed out of early object representations. Children eventually grow out of their need for transitional objects like a teddy bear and cast them aside. This, however, does not typically happen with the God image according to Rizzuto (1979). In contrast, people increasingly invest emotional energy in the God image throughout development, rather than investing less energy over time as with typical transitional objects. On the basis of this observation, Rizzuto proposed that the God image is a special kind of transitional object—that is, one that continues to develop throughout each consecutive psychological stage as part of the process of maintaining one's sense of self. Thus, a key psychological function of the God image according to Rizzuto is to help maintain a sense of self and relatedness to emotionally significant people in one's life.

Jones (2007) has critiqued Rizzuto's (1979) theory of the God image as a special kind of transitional object. He clarified that the God image is not a special kind of transitional object, but rather, because it is a mental representation (i.e., an internal object), it is a special kind of mental representation. Jones proposed that the God image is linked to the capacity for a certain kind of transitional experience that holds together subjective experience and objective reality. The implication of this is that people continue to invest emotional energy in their God image not because it is a special type of transitional *object* but rather because it is a mental representation that facilitates the capacity for transitional experience. Because of this quality, the God image may foster the capacity for imaginative play and creativity that become the basis for the arts, sciences, and culture making.

Research on Object Relations Theory and the God Image

Rizzuto's work led to numerous empirical studies linking God image to a level of object relations development. The theoretical hypothesis from an object relations perspective is that the (implicit) God image generally corresponds to parental images. Numerous studies have supported the idea that object relations maturity is associated with images of God as loving and nurturing (Bauman, 1995; Brokaw & Edwards, 1994; Spear, 1994; Wootton, 1991). These results have been demonstrated with paternal parenting style (Dean, 1988); with a composite of experiences with both parents (Birky & Ball, 1988); with those who lost a parent as a child (Shackel, 2000); with Jewish, Muslim, and Protestant subjects (Tisdale, 1997); and within an inpatient treatment population (Key, 1994). Although both father and mother images contribute to the God image, when one parent is preferred or idealized, that parental image tends to be more reflective of the God image (Birky & Ball, 1988). Research has also found that higher levels of childhood physical and sexual abuse and neglect are associated with viewing God as less loving and more distant (Reinert & Edwards, 2009). In sum, the empirical research on object relations and God image consistently indicates that those who have loving and nurturing parental images generally develop loving and nurturing images of God.

Attachment Theory and the God Image

The application of attachment theory (Bowlby, 1969, 1973, 1980) to the God image parallels more general theoretical developments in psychoanalysis (Hall, 2007a, 2007b) and psychology in general (Siegel, 2012). These developments represent a turn toward relationality and the notion that there are multiple levels of emotional information processing. In the early 1990s, Kirkpatrick and colleagues (Kirkpatrick, 1992; Kirkpatrick & Shaver, 1990) applied attachment theory to people's experiences of God giving rise to an attachment theory perspective of the God image and the subfield of "attachment to God."

Current conceptualizations within attachment theory assert that as a result of repeated patterns of emotional communication, infants develop internal organizations of the emotions, sensations, behaviors, and cognitions involved in their efforts to maintain felt security with a particular attachment figure (Bowlby, 1969). Bowlby (1969) conceptualized these internal organizations as "internal working models" of self and others, which are a form of implicit memory. Once developed, these internal working models serve as templates for interpreting and responding to future attachment figures, thereby influencing peoples' images of others and God. Research has shown that these attachment templates take the form of four major categories: one form of secure attachment and three forms of insecure attachment—preoccupied, dismissing, and disorganized (Ainsworth et al., 1978).

Within attachment theory, God is conceptualized as an attachment figure (Proctor, Miner, McLean, Devenish, & Bonab, 2009), and the God image is understood as an internal working model, which is similar to an object representation in object relations theory. Attachment theory contends, like object relations theory, that the God image is based on the internalization of early experiences with attachment figures and thus will tend to fit into one (or more) of the four attachment categories. Attachment theorists have studied how internal working models of God (what we might think of as an "attachment-based God image") relate to internal working models of human attachment figures. In the next section, we review this attachment research in the context of our broader review of theory and research on the psychological functioning of the God image.

Research on Attachment Theory and the God Image

Paralleling the application of object relations theory to understanding the God image, in the early 1990s, social and personality psychologists began applying attachment theory to religious experience, which has led to a growing body of research on the psychological functioning of the God image from an attachment perspective. Attachment researchers suggest that God clearly fits the definition of an attachment figure (Kirkpatrick & Shaver, 1990; Proctor et al., 2009). Just as with parents or other attachment figures, people tend to turn to God for comfort and safety when they are distressed. Attachment research has also investigated the association between human and divine attachment, which parallels earlier object relations research on the relationship between parental images and the God image (for an in-depth discussion on attachment theory, see Chapter 7 in this volume).

Kirkpatrick and Shaver (1990) suggested two alternative, and seemingly competing, hypotheses with respect to the association between human and divine attachment, which they termed *compensation* and *correspondence*. The conceptual question at issue is whether the God image *corresponds* to internal working models of human attachment figures, or, in contrast, whether the God image *compensates*, or substitutes, for the lack of secure attachment relationships with primary caregivers. Research in this conceptual framework has yielded mixed findings that present a seemingly confusing picture. In light of numerous studies providing partial support for both hypotheses, revisions have been made to account for these seemingly discrepant findings.

In the most recent revision, Granqvist (2002) proposed a "two-level correspondence" model. The first level is "socialized correspondence" in which one's religious beliefs and values are similar to parents, but only for secure individuals. The second level or component, referred to as a "secondary effect," is internal working model (IWM) correspondence, in which IWMs of self and others correspond to IWMs of God. Granqvist also concluded that individuals with insecure attachment histories engage in emotional compensation more than those with secure histories.

We have suggested elsewhere (Hall, Fujikawa, Halcrow, Hill, & Delaney, 2009) that these mixed findings result from two different, broad theoretical schools of thought: the implicit–developmental perspective and the social–cognitive perspective. Although both schools argue that their work is grounded in Bowlby's original formulations of attachment models, George and West (1999) have cogently argued that this is not the case. The underlying theoretical differences between these two schools of thought account for the different methodologies and mixed research findings.

Social–cognitive theorists define mental representations "in terms of cognitive attribution[s]" (George & West, 1999, p. 291) of self and other, either positive or negative. In this formulation, different constellations of positive or negative self and other models represent four different attachment classifications. Such cognitive attributions are assumed to be conscious enough that individuals are able to articulate their views via self-report. The social–cognitive perspective implies a notion of compensation in which a secure God image develops immediately despite insecure internal working models of human attachment and thereby compensates for insecure human attachment models (Hall et al., 2009; Miner, 2009). In addition, in its focus on cognitive attributions, research from this perspective emphasizes the explicit God image and generally does not distinguish between the explicit and implicit layers of the God image.

The implicit–developmental perspective focuses on IWMs as implicit templates for how one expects relationships to feel and how one views him- or herself throughout childhood and into adulthood (Sroufe, Egeland, Carlson, & Collins, 2005). Since Bowlby (1969) stated that the activation of IWMs and attachment behaviors are specific to the context of attachment relationships that have been activated under such conditions as fear or safety, theorists from this perspective seek to measure attachment by activating this system. Researchers have developed creative ways to activate the attachment system to assess infant attachment in Ainsworth's strange situation protocol (Ainsworth et al., 1978) and adult attachment in the Adult Attachment Interview (AAI; George, Kaplan, & Main, 1996). The implicit–developmental perspective, in contrast to the social–cognitive perspective, argues for the importance of distinguishing between the explicit and implicit layers of the God image, because the relationship between IWMs (or images) for humans and God is different for these two layers.

This contemporary framework on the nature of implicit mental representations found in the implicit–developmental perspective contraindicates the social–cognitive model of parallel compensation, and research supports this. For example, individuals categorized as the compensation group (those who reported insecure attachment with parents in their childhood but secure attachment to God currently) have been shown to be no better psychologically adjusted than those who report insecure attachment with parents in childhood and with God currently (Miner, 2009). This directly contradicts what would be expected if the implicit God image were in fact positive and compensating for a negative self-image by coexisting with it.

Returning to the distinction between the two layers of the God image, we have suggested that the implicit–developmental perspective makes sense of the mixed findings in that correspondence holds for the implicit God image, whereas human attachment IWMs are largely independent of the explicit God image. In an initial self-report study, we found support for correspondence in terms of how people experience God, and as predicted, no evidence for compensation in terms of cognitive and behavioral aspects of spiritual functioning (Hall et al., 2009).

In addition, implicit methodologies have tested this theory more directly and provide support for correspondence for the implicit God image. Birgegard and Granqvist (2004) used subliminal separation cues to assess implicit (or unconscious) attachment dynamics with God. They found that when subjects' attachment systems were activated using subliminal priming, those who were classified as secure (via a self-report measure of human attachment) were more likely to turn toward God, whereas those with insecure attachments were more likely to turn away from God. Whereas Birgegard and Granqvist (2004) used a self-report measure of attachment, Fujikawa (2010) conducted the first study we know of using an implicit interview-based measure of both adult and God attachment. The interview measuring God attachment was modeled after the AAI and was coded using the AAI's system, which allowed for statistical analyses to measure the association between continuous attachment security and categorical attachment classification. She found a significant correlation between adult and God attachment and security. In addition, she found 65% continuity between Secure, Dismissing, and Preoccupied attachment classifications across human and God attachment interviews, and a correlation (Cramér's *V*) of .50. Thus, when using measures designed to access implicit processes, we see correspondence for the implicit God image.

In summary, the balance of theory and research suggests that the implicit God image is not substantially discrepant from mental representations of human attachment figures, but rather generally parallels them. Furthermore, the scope of theory and research suggests that the God image and IWMs of human attachment figures can transform each other through a developmental, relational process. Attachment theory, within the broader context of cognitive and affective neuroscience, also suggests some insights into the relationship between implicit and explicit layers of the God image.

THE RELATIONSHIP BETWEEN IMPLICIT AND EXPLICIT GOD IMAGES

As mentioned at the outset of this chapter, there are two broad layers of the God image, implicit and explicit. Research on emotional information processing (Bucci, 1997) and affective neuroscience (Solms & Turnbull, 2002) suggests that these layers of the God image represent distinct forms of information processing. The explicit God image is a more conscious, verbal view of God, although it is still a *personal* view of God. It is not the same thing as abstract theological knowledge. The explicit God image is based on autobiographical memory (Cozolino, 2002; Siegel, 2012; Solms & Turnbull, 2002), which is an explicit form of memory that is a narrative of one's life events. These conscious beliefs about God, however, "rest on unconscious processes, and come with a long and complicated developmental history" (Jones, 2007, p. 41). These unconscious processes are part of the implicit God image, which is based on implicit memory that is stored in emotions and gut-level sensations.

Two dimensions help us understand the relationship between the implicit and explicit God images: valence and degree of integration. Both the explicit and implicit God images vary on a continuum from positive to negative. In addition, the degree to which the explicit "rests" on the implicit is a function of the degree of integration between the implicit and explicit God images. Research on attachment styles and on illusory mental health provides some interesting clues as to how the valence and degree of integration may form subtypes in terms of the relationship between implicit and explicit God images, and furthermore, a possible developmental progression of these subtypes.

Attachment styles may predict the degree and nature of the discrepancy–integration between the explicit and implicit God images. Research by Shedler, Mayman, and Manis (1993) on illusory mental health provided a model suggesting this may be the case. Shedler et al. (1993) developed the concept of the "illusion of mental health." They hypothesized that there are two subgroups among people who look healthy on self-report mental health scales. One subgroup is genuinely psychologically healthy, and the other is distressed and maintains the illusion of mental health by defensive processes that deny psychological distress. They distinguished genuine mental health from illusory mental health by using both self-report measures (explicit) and clinical (implicit) judgment. Those who looked healthy on self-report measures and were judged healthy by a clinician were classified as genuinely mentally healthy. Those who looked distressed on self-report scales and were judged distressed by a clinician were classified as manifestly distressed. In contrast, those who looked healthy on self-report scales but were judged distressed by a clinician were classified as maintaining illusory mental health. On the basis of the notion that psychological defense has a physiological cost, Shedler et al. hypothesized that the illusory mental health group would demonstrate more physiological reactivity than the genuine mental health group and the manifestly distressed group when exposed to psychological stressors. Using heart rate and blood pressure as measures of reactivity, the illusory mental health group was indeed significantly more reactive than the other two groups when conducting mental arithmetic, Thematic Apperception Test stories, and phrase association tasks.

On the basis of the theoretical conceptualizations of the three main attachment groups, we would suggest that they parallel the three groups in the Shedler et al. (1993) study. The genuinely healthy group likely represents a secure attachment group, the manifestly distressed group likely represents preoccupied attachment, and the illusory group likely represents dismissing attachment. The pattern of responses to both implicit and explicit measures for each group gives us insight into the relationship between the implicit and explicit God images for each group.

The secure attachment group, or genuinely healthy group, will likely have more positive implicit and explicit God images that will be consistent with each other. They tend to have positive implicit images of self and others and this will likely translate into a more positive implicit God image. Because there is no reason to defend against pain involved in a positive implicit God image, this will facilitate conscious awareness of a more positive view of God.

The preoccupied attachment, or manifestly distressed group, tends to be highly anxious and is easily flooded by negative emotions about themselves (Siegel, 2012). They experience more negative self-related emotions than securely attached people and are more consciously aware of negative self-related emotions than people who tend toward a dismissing state of mind. Thus, they will likely have a more negative implicit God image than securely attached people. Whereas dismissing people also have negative implicit self-related emotions and God images, preoccupied people are more likely to be aware of their negative implicit God image. This would suggest that their explicit God image will tend to be more negative and fairly consistent with their implicit God image.

The dismissing attachment, or illusory healthy, group likely maintains the largest disconnect between their implicit and explicit God images. People with a dismissing state of mind have less access to their implicit, internal world, which is often filled with pain and neglect. This is partly a function of their attachment system being deactivated. As a result, they report that they are doing fine, as seen in the Shedler et al. (1993) study, but the implicit level (the physiological reactivity in Shedler et al.'s, 1993, study) tells a different story. With the dismissing group, we predict the least degree of integration of the two layers of the God image.

Object relations and attachment theories have contributed significantly to our understanding of the God image. In addition, research going back several decades has explored the God image in relation to self-esteem and general personality characteristics, to which we now turn.

Self-Esteem and the God Image

The seminal work of Benson and Spilka (1973) established the positive relationship between a person's God image and self-esteem. That is, self-esteem was positively correlated with loving and accepting God images and negatively correlated with rejecting images. A study conducted in a sample of 12- to 15-year-olds in Scotland confirmed these findings (Francis, Gibson, & Robbins, 2001), suggesting that the relationship between God image and self-esteem remains fairly stable across the life span. From this starting point, additional research brought about a more nuanced understanding of the link between God image and self-concept. Using attachment theory as their theoretical framework, Dickie, Ajega, Kobylak, and Nixon (2006) found that the relationship between attachment to parents and God image was moderated by the way the person views him- or herself, although differently for males and females, and for different concepts of God:

> The concept of God as nurturing related differently to parent concepts than did concepts of God as powerful or punishing/judging. Seeing God as nurturing is more related to self-concept (for daughters) and self-esteem (for sons) than to perceptions of parents. (p. 66)

Although Dickie et al. employed self-report measures, the implications of these results can be better understood in light of the discussion about the relationship between self-report measures and implicit processes, whereby we can conclude that explicit and implicit aspects of self-concept and self-esteem differentially moderate the association between God image and human attachment.

Personality and the God Image

Another line of inquiry has been the link between personality and God image. Braam, Mooi, Schaap Jonker, van Tilburg, and Deeg (2008) explored the associations between personality, as conceptualized by the five-factor model, and God image in older adults in the Netherlands. After controlling for the possible confounding factors of depression, functional limitations, and age, they found a significant relationship between Agreeableness and perceiving God as supportive, as well as Neuroticism and anxious feelings toward God. Previously significant associations dropped to insignificance when controlling for the confounding factors, suggesting that the connection between personality and God image are influenced by current mood, age, and education. Another study found similar mediational effects for psychological distress (Eurelings-Bontekoe, Hekman-Van Steeg, & Verschuur, 2005). In addition, positive personality characteristics have been found to be associated with feeling that God is caring, and feelings of incompetence and depression have been shown to be associated with a negative image of God (Greenway, Milne, & Clarke, 2003). Exline, Yali, and Sanderson (2000) investigated religious strain, depression, and suicidality in clinical and nonclinical samples and discovered that depression was associated with feeling alienated from God. Robbins, Francis, and Kerr (2006) added to our understanding of the relationship between God image and personality by including a separate measure for empathy. They found that a positive God image was a significant predictor of greater empathic capacity, even after controlling for personality variables.

Personality pathology has also been linked to more negative feelings about God. Schaap-Jonker, Eurelings-Bontekoe, Verhagen, and Zock (2002) found that those higher in cluster-A personality disorder symptoms, particularly borderline personality disorder, tended to experience God as more passive and had more negative feelings toward God. Furthermore, they found that higher levels of anxiety and depression were associated with negative feelings toward God. Eurelings-Bontekoe et al. (2005) conducted a follow-up study to the Schaap-Jonker et al. (2002) study with a nonclinical sample. Their results suggested a link between positive personality traits, such as being self-directed and cooperative, and having positive feelings toward God, although this relationship was mediated by psychological distress.

Without the ability to determine causation, we are left to speculate as to the direction of the relationship between the God image and aspects of personality and psychological functioning. Does a negative image of God color the perception of self, other, and the world in a pessimistic light, leading to depression? Or conversely, do experiences of depression affect how one views God? It would seem overly simplistic to assume that the relationship is not bidirectional. Although future research is needed to answer these questions directly, on the basis of our knowledge of implicit processes and attachment dynamics we suggest that the implicit God image and its corresponding aspects of self both influence our appraisal of events and are reciprocally influenced by them. Therefore, it is not surprising that in general, those with a positive God image tend to be more empathic, have more positive views of self, and less personality pathology.

CONTEXTUAL INFLUENCES ON THE GOD IMAGE

Although traditional models of God image development and formation have focused mainly on intrapsychic processes, increasingly researchers are looking to understand the contextual factors that influence the God image. Such contextual factors include denominational differences (Noffke & McFadden, 2001), race (Hoffman et al., 2008), gender (Foster & Babcock, 2001), and sexual orientation (Hoffman, Knight, Boscoe-Huffman, and Stewart, 2007).

Noffke and McFadden (2001) found differences between Evangelicals, Methodists, and Catholics in God images, in that Evangelicals rated God as significantly more vindictive and had higher ratings of God as stern father and supreme ruler, than both Methodists and Catholics. Although denominational difference was not the main focus of the study by Schaap-Jonker, Eurelings-Bontekoe, Zock, and Jonker (2008), they nonetheless found that orthodox church members experienced God more as a judge than nonorthodox church members. We may therefore speculate that perhaps religious teachings and the differential emphasis on certain theological doctrines within denominations influence an individual's explicit God image.

There is very little research on how specific aspects of diversity affect the God image. Preliminary work has theorized about the potential impact of specific individual differences. Hoffman (2007), for example, suggested that individuals who identify themselves as lesbian, gay, bisexual, transgender are particularly affected by experiences of judgment within faith communities and that these experiences more directly affect their God image than attachment relationships. Research is needed to directly investigate this hypothesis.

With regard to gender, Hoffman et al. (2007) suggested that women's God images are negatively affected by the prominence of masculine language within the Bible, Jesus's gender, and the portrayal of women as temptresses that lead men astray. These aspects may act to distance women from feeling as though the object of their faith is similar to them and can understand their experiences. Previous research has found that compared with men, women tended to have a more positive image of God (Krejci, 1998) and placed greater emphasis on the healing aspect of God's character (Nelsen, Cheek, & Au, 1985). Krejci (1998) employed multidimensional scaling analysis to uncover the cognitive schemas individuals possess for their God images. Analysis revealed that both men and women tend to organize their God images schema on three dimensions, each existing on continuums: judging–nurturing, controlling–saving, and concrete–abstract. What differed between men and women was the salience of specific dimensions, in that women place greater emphasis on the controlling–saving image than men.

Similarly, Hoffman et al. (2007) proposed that racial minorities feel unable to relate to Jesus as he has been socially constructed and portrayed as a Caucasian male. These areas of diversity are understudied and are critical to understanding the complexity of an individual's God image. Building on these theoretical foundations, Hoffman et al. (2008) investigated the relationship between White and non-White ethnic identification and God image. Although the sample was small, preliminary results suggested that an individual's identification as Caucasian was negatively correlated with the egocentric and benevolence factors. In other words, those who more strongly identified as Caucasian were less likely to view God as unconditionally loving or as always being there for them. It would seem that racial identification affects God image and further research is needed to flesh out this impact.

The God image also can be understood from a developmental perspective. That is, the God image may be viewed cross-sectionally at varying developmental stages (de Roos, Miedema, & Iedema, 2001; Dickie et al., 2006; Francis, Gibson, & Robbins, 2001; Reinert & Edwards, 2009). Because cross-sectional research focuses on correlates at a single point in time, it does not address how God images change as a function of development. To our knowledge, such longitudinal research has not been conducted. Some research, however, does speak to the nature of the God image among children.

Early research on the explicit God image suggests that its development corresponds to Piaget's cognitive developmental stages. Several studies have found that as children move from concrete operational thinking to formal operational thinking, their explicit God image tends to shift from a more concrete, objective, and anthropomorphic one to a more abstract, subjective concept of God as Spirit (Baker & Koppe, 1959). Rizzuto's (1979) research also has supported this developmental trajectory along Piagetian lines for the implicit God image.

Childhood is distinct from other times in life in terms of the possible impact of secondary attachment relationships, such as teachers and coaches. Similar to Dickie et al. (2006), de Roos et al. (2001) found that working models of self and others mediate the association between the child–teacher relationship and loving explicit God images. Interestingly, de Roos et al. uncovered that in their sample of children from nonreligious homes receiving religious education at school, the child–teacher relationship was related to loving explicit God images, whereas the mother–child relationship was not related. It would seem that attachment dynamics interact with how attachment figures present God to children, thus shaping their God image. Perhaps, as de Roos et al. proposed, socialization processes are at work with young children.

THE TRANSFORMATION OF THE GOD IMAGE

The God image typically changes over time as part of the course of normal development. In addition, it can change as the result of psychological interventions aimed at healing and transforming the God image. Given the research on how a person's God image uniquely affects many aspects of psychological functioning, intervening to transform an individual's God image to be more positive can directly affect many aspects of his or her life. Although the research in this area is limited, a few studies have directly investigated such interventions as psychotherapy on a person's God image. Tisdale et al. (1997) found that psychotherapy for individuals who began inpatient treatment and continued on an outpatient basis had a positive impact on his or her God image. Cheston, Piedmont, Eanes, and Lavin (2003) added to our understanding of the impact of psychotherapy on God image in terms of the amount of emotional and spiritual change the participants experienced. They found that the amount of growth was associated with changes in God image. That is, more emotional and spiritual growth, as measured by therapist's ratings, were related to perceiving God "as becoming more emotionally stable, less assertive, and more compassionate and loving" (Cheston et al., 2003, p. 103).

Recently researchers have designed treatment protocols to address spirituality in psychotherapy. Murray-Swank and Pargament (2005) investigated the impact of spiritually integrated psychotherapy on spiritual well-being, religious coping, and God image for two women with a history of sexual abuse. Results showed that after the eight-session intervention, the women had an increase in positive God images. Similarly Thomas, Moriarty, and Anderson (2011) found a significant decrease in negative God images (e.g., distant, harsh, and disapproving) and a significant increase in positive God images (e.g., intimate, supportive, and accepting) after a group therapy intervention with 26 subjects. Furthermore, numerous case studies detailed in the *God Image Handbook for Spiritual Counseling and Psychotherapy* (Moriarty & Hoffman, 2007) provide examples of the impact of specific therapeutic modalities on an individual's image of God, including attachment-based psychoanalytic therapy (Noffke & Hall, 2007), time-limited dynamic therapy (Moriarty, 2007), existential–integrative psychotherapy (Hoffman, 2007), rational emotive behavior therapy (Johnson, 2007), theistic psychotherapy (O'Grady & Richards, 2007), and liberal Protestant pastoral psychotherapy (Doehring, 2007).

DIRECTIONS FOR FUTURE RESEARCH

The field of God image theory and research has come a long way since its inception. There remains, however, a need for theoretically driven research aimed at answering specific questions. For example, as research on correspondence versus compensation in attachment theory has developed in the past decade, research and theory are increasingly mutually informing one another (e.g., Birgegard & Granqvist, 2004; Hall et al., 2009). At a broad level, we believe this positive direction needs to characterize the next phase of investigation of the God image. Research needs to utilize broad psychological theories of the God image to develop conceptual hypotheses about (a) the relationship between the implicit and explicit God images; (b) how various contextual variables influence or correlate with the God image, and how each of these relate to the various layers of the God image; and (c) how various interventions affect the God image. Advancement in all of these major areas requires progress in measuring the God image. In the following sections, we address measurement issues first, and then briefly highlight some suggestions for future research in these three major areas.

Measurement Issues

Measurement issues go hand in hand with the distinction between the layers of the God image and the future of research in the field. The clear challenge for the field is measuring the implicit God image. There is controversy between self-report and implicit measurement methods in attachment research, and this applies to the measurement of the God image as well. Although self-reports of the God image clearly have limitations in accessing people's implicit God image, there is some evidence that self-reports of attachment predict meaningful outcomes on implicit measures. Shaver and Mikulincer (2002), for example, have argued that

> social psychologists and others who use self-report measures view them as convenient surface indicators of differences in attachment-related cognitions, emotions, and behavioral tendencies which are partly unconscious, indicators that can be examined *in relation to more direct measures of unconscious processes* to see whether those processes work the way attachment theory leads us to expect. (p. 137)

Therefore, self-report measures can be seen as valid indicators of implicit processes if their relationship to implicit measures can be empirically supported. There is some support from a study by Berant, Mikulincer, Shaver, and Segal (2005) investigating the convergence of a self-report measure of attachment and the Rorschach, considered to be a valid measure of unconscious–implicit processes. Their findings "support the contention that self-reports of attachment anxiety and avoidance are associated with theoretically predictable implicit aspects of attachment psychodynamics" (Berant et al., 2005, p. 77). This provides initial justification for the use of self-report measures as a means to assess implicit processes.

Thus, it appears that self-report measures can to some extent access implicit processes related to the God image. This notwithstanding, measurement of the implicit God image needs to advance if the field is going to progress. Gibson (2007) reviewed the research on correspondence versus compensation in attachment to God and provided a number of helpful procedures with regard to self-report measures that can improve access to multiple layers of the God image. For example, he suggested that researchers provide different sets of instructions for answering the same items multiple times to highlight disparity between different layers of the God image. Another recommended method is to use inventories that measure each item on more than one dimension. Gibson also suggested that researchers can manipulate the schemas that are activated at the time a measure is administered. The AAI similarly attempts to activate the attachment system by going quickly into questions about the person's primary attachment relationships. We have used this methodology to conduct a spiritual attachment interview focused on attachment to God (Fujikawa, 2010); however, in line with Gibson's suggestion, surveys could be completed after doing a spiritual attachment interview.

There is also a need to conduct more qualitative research, using methodologies such as grounded theory, and combining this with quantitative measures. As an example, we are currently conducting an interview study using grounded theory and linking these results to quantitative measures. It is our hope that researchers will more frequently employ implicit measures and mixed methods studies to advance the field of God image.

Implicit Versus Explicit God Images

If the field of God image research is going to advance, investigators should explore the nature of the relationship between implicit and explicit God images. We suggested one hypothesis for how implicit and explicit God images may relate to one another. More specifically, we proposed that attachment styles may predict the degree and nature of the discrepancy and integration between the explicit and implicit God images. Very little research addresses this question, however. Most of the research to date has focused on basic correlates of the God image, and more recently, on the nature of the relationship between parental images and God image. Research is needed to investigate, for example, whether attachment styles do indeed indicate specific pathways for the development and integration of the implicit and explicit God images.

Contextual Factors

The God image is clearly a multidimensional construct that is associated with and affected by many factors. Among the many factors that may affect the God image, we need more research on contextual factors and the God image, such as sexual orientation, gender, diversity, identity development, and the impact of religious–spiritual teaching and authority figures on the God image. In addition, we have a high level of understanding of the impact of cognitive development (e.g., Rizzuto, 1979), but we know relatively less about the impact of stages of life and identity development. Recent developments such as the notion of "emerging adulthood" (roughly 18 to 29) (Arnett, 2004) as a life stage presents an opportunity to better understand how the God image is affected and formed by this critical developmental stage.

Treatment Interventions

A number of treatment interventions have been developed and applied to the God image. The *God Image Handbook for Spiritual Counseling and Psychotherapy* (Moriarty & Hoffman, 2007) presented case studies from six different therapeutic modalities. These case studies represent a significant contribution by providing clinicians a window into what it looks like to address the God image in therapy. Beyond case studies, however, there is very little research examining the efficacy of therapeutic interventions on the God image. Generally, the research in this area has examined the impact of traditional psychotherapy modalities on the God image, rather than interventions targeted at the God image. Studies investigating the impact of targeted interventions on the God image are beginning to appear (Murray-Swank & Pargament, 2005; Thomas et al., 2011). The results are encouraging but need to be replicated with larger numbers of participants and control groups.

CONCLUSION

The God image generally refers to one's personal view of God. It is theorized to be a special kind of mental representation that facilitates "transitional experience"; that is, "an intermediate area of experiencing to which inner reality and external reality both contribute" (Winnicott, 1971, p. 2). The predominant theories have suggested that the God image is formed from one's experiences with early attachment figures and from one's psychological needs. The God image has several layers, including a more conscious, propositional layer (the explicit God image) and a nonconscious, experiential layer (the implicit God image). Research suggests that the implicit God image accounts more for how people experience God. People vary in meaningful ways in terms of the degree of integration of these two layers. We suggested that the degree of integration interacts with attachment security in influencing developmental pathways for the God image. Research has found the God image to be associated in meaningful ways with psychological functioning, personality variables, and contextual factors. The theoretical framework for the God image has moved from early Freudian drive theory to more relational theories, such as object relations theory, and most recently, to a broader relational paradigm based on attachment theory and neuroscience. Interventions on the God image have shown promising results but need further research to corroborate them. To advance the field, the next phase needs to build on more sophisticated measurement methodologies and theoretically derived hypotheses that inform, and are informed by, empirical research.

References

Ainsworth, M. D. S., Blehar, M. C., Waters, E., & Wall, S. (1978). *Patterns of attachment: A psychological study of the strange situation*. Hillsdale, NJ: Erlbaum.

Arnett, J. J. (2004). *Emerging adulthood: The winding road from the late teens through the twenties*. Oxford, England: Oxford University Press.

Baker, W. G., & Koppe, W. A. (1959). *Children's religious concepts* (Character Research Report). Schenectady, NY: Union College.

Bauman, P. J. (1995). Correlations among marital intimacy, object relations, mental representations of God and spiritual well-being. *Dissertation Abstracts International: Section B. Sciences and Engineering, 55*(11).

Benson, P., & Spilka, B. (1973). God image as a function of self-esteem and locus of control. *Journal for the Scientific Study of Religion, 12*, 297–310. doi:10.2307/1384430

Berant, E., Mikulincer, M., Shaver, P., & Segal, Y. (2005). Rorschach correlates of self-reported attachment dimensions: Dynamic manifestations of hyperactivating and deactivating strategies. *Journal of Personality Assessment, 84*, 70–81. doi:10.1207/s15327752jpa8401_13

Birgegard, A., & Granqvist, P. (2004). The correspondence between attachment to parents and God: Three experiments using subliminal separation cues. *Personality and Social Psychology Bulletin, 30*, 1122–1135. doi:10.1177/0146167204264266

Birky, I. T., & Ball, S. (1988). Parental trait influence on God as an object representation. *Journal of Psychology: Interdisciplinary and Applied, 122*, 133–137. doi:10.1080/00223980.1988.9712698

Bowlby, J. (1969). *Attachment and loss: Vol. 1. Attachment*. New York, NY: Basic Books.

Bowlby, J. (1973). *Attachment and loss: Vol. 2. Separation: Anxiety and anger*. New York, NY: Basic Books.

Bowlby, J. (1980). *Attachment and loss: Vol. 3. Loss, sadness and depression*. New York, NY: Basic Books.

Braam, A., Mooi, B., Schaap Jonker, J., van Tilburg, W., & Deeg, D. (2008). God image and five-factor model personality characteristics in later life: A study among inhabitants of Sassenheim in the Netherlands. *Mental Health, Religion, and Culture, 11*, 547–559. doi:10.1080/13674670701641886

Brokaw, B. F., & Edwards, K. J. (1994). The relationship of God image to level of object relations development. *Journal of Psychology and Theology, 22*, 352–371.

Bucci, W. (1997). *Psychoanalysis and cognitive science*. New York, NY: Guilford Press.

Cheston, S. E., Piedmont, R. L., Eanes, B., & Lavin, P. (2003). Changes in client's images of God over the course of outpatient therapy. *Counseling and Values, 47*, 96–108. doi:10.1002/j.2161-007X.2003.tb00227.x

Cozolino, L. (2002). *The neuroscience of psychotherapy: Building and rebuilding the human brain*. New York, NY: Norton.

Dean, T. L. (1988). The relationship between father's parenting style, concept of God, and spiritual well being in Christian college-age women. *Dissertation Abstracts International: Section B. Sciences and Engineering, 49*, 2374.

de Roos, S. A., Miedema, S., & Iedema, J. (2001). Attachment, working models of self and others, and God concept in kindergarten. *Journal for the Scientific Study of Religion, 40*, 607–618. doi:10.1111/0021-8294.00080

Dickie, J., Ajega, L., Kobylak, J., & Nixon, K. (2006). Mother, father, and self: Sources of young adult's God concepts. *Journal for the Scientific Study of Religion, 45*, 57–71. doi:10.1111/j.1468-5906.2006.00005.x

Doehring, C. (2007). A liberal protestant theological approach and the God image: The role of god images in recovery from sexual and physical abuse. In G. Moriarty & L. Hoffman (Eds.), *God image handbook for spiritual counseling and psychotherapy: Research, theory, and practice* (pp. 211–226). Philadelphia, PA: Haworth Press.

Eurelings-Bontekoe, E., Hekman-Van Steeg, J., & Verschuur, M. (2005). The association between personality, attachment, psychological distress, church denomination and the God concept among a non-clinical sample. *Mental Health, Religion, and Culture, 8*, 141–154. doi:10.1080/13674670412331304320

Exline, J. J., Yali, A. M., & Sanderson, W. C. (2000). Guilt, discord, and alienation: The role of religious strain in depression and suicidality. *Journal of Clinical Psychology, 56*, 1481–1496. doi:10.1002/1097-4679(200012)56:12<1481::AID-1>3.0.CO;2-A

Foster, R., & Babcock, R. (2001). God as a man versus God as a woman: Perceiving God as a function of the gender of God and the gender of the participant. *The International Journal for the Psychology of Religion, 11*, 93–104. doi:10.1207/S15327582IJPR1102_02

Francis, L., Gibson, H., & Robbins, M. (2001). God images and self-worth among adolescents in Scotland. *Mental Health, Religion, and Culture, 4*, 103–108.

Freud, S. (1950). *Totem and taboo* (J. Strachey, Trans.). New York, NY: Norton. (Original work published 1913)

Freud, S. (1953). Three essays on the theory of sexuality. In J. Strachey (Ed.), *The standard edition of the complete psychological works of Sigmund Freud* (Vol. 7, pp. 125–245). London, England: Hogarth Press. (Original work published 1905)

Freud, S. (1959). Obsessive actions and religious practices. In J. Strachey (Ed.), *The standard edition of the complete psychological works of Sigmund Freud* (Vol. 9, pp. 115–127). London, England: Hogarth Press. (Original work published 1907)

Freud, S. (1961). The future of an illusion. In J. Strachey (Ed.), *The standard edition of the complete psychological works of Sigmund Freud* (Vol. 21, pp. 1–56). London, England: Hogarth Press. (Original work published 1927)

Fujikawa, A. (2010). *The relationship between adult and God attachment: A coherence analysis.* Unpublished doctoral dissertation, Biola University, La Mirada, CA.

George, C., Kaplan, N., & Main, M. (1996). *Adult attachment interview protocol* (3rd ed.). Unpublished manuscript, University of California at Berkeley.

George, C., & West, M. (1999). Developmental vs. social personality model of adult attachment and mental ill health. *British Journal of Medical Psychology, 72*, 285–303. doi:10.1348/000711299159998

Gibson, N. J. S. (2007). Measurement issues in God image research and practice. In G. Moriarty & L. Hoffman (Eds.), *God image handbook for spiritual counseling and psychotherapy: Research, theory, and practice* (pp. 227–246). Philadelphia, PA: Haworth Press.

Granqvist, P. (2002). Attachment and religiosity in adolescence: Cross-sectional and longitudinal evaluations. *Personality and Social Psychology Bulletin, 28*, 260–270. doi:10.1177/0146167202282011

Greenway, A., Milne, L., & Clarke, V. (2003). Personality variables, self-esteem, and depression in an individual's perception of God. *Mental Health, Religion, and Culture, 6*, 45–58. doi:10.1080/1867467021000029381

Hall, T. W. (2007a). Psychoanalysis, attachment, and spirituality: Part I. The emergence of two relational traditions. *Journal of Psychology and Theology, 35*, 14–28.

Hall, T. W. (2007b). Psychoanalysis, attachment, and spirituality: Part II. The spiritual stories we live by. *Journal of Psychology and Theology, 35*, 29–42.

Hall, T. W., Fujikawa, A., Halcrow, S., Hill, P. C., & Delaney, H. (2009). Attachment to God and implicit spirituality: Clarifying correspondence and compensation models. *Journal of Psychology and Theology, 37*, 227–242.

Hoffman, L. (2007). Existential-integrative psychotherapy and God image. In G. Moriarty & L. Hoffman (Eds.), *God image handbook for spiritual counseling and psychotherapy: Research, theory, and practice* (pp. 105–137). Philadelphia, PA: Haworth Press.

Hoffman, L., Hoffman, J., Dillard, K., Clark, J., Acoba, R., Williams, F., & Jones, T. T. (2008). Diversity and the God image: Examining ethnic differences in the experience of God for a college age population. *Journal of Psychology and Theology, 36*, 26–41.

Hoffman, L., Knight, S., Boscoe-Huffman, S., & Stewart, S. (2007). Diversity issues and the God image. In G. Moriarty & L. Hoffman (Eds.), *God image handbook for spiritual counseling and psychotherapy: Research, theory, and practice* (pp. 257–279). Philadelphia, PA: Haworth Press.

Johnson, B. (2007). Rational emotive behavior therapy and the God image. In G. Moriarty & L. Hoffman

(Eds.), *God image handbook for spiritual counseling and psychotherapy: Research, theory, and practice* (pp. 157–181). Philadelphia, PA: Haworth Press.

Jones, J. (2007). Psychodynamic theories of the evolution of the God image. In G. Moriarty & L. Hoffman (Eds.), *God image handbook for spiritual counseling and psychotherapy: Research, theory, and practice* (pp. 33–55). Philadelphia, PA: Haworth Press.

Key, T. L. (1994). *Impact of inpatient psychiatric treatment on object relations maturity, self-esteem, and God image.* Unpublished doctoral dissertation, Biola University, La Mirada, CA.

Kirkpatrick, L. A. (1992). An attachment theory approach to the psychology of religion. *The International Journal for the Psychology of Religion, 2*, 3–28. doi:10.1207/s15327582ijpr0201_2

Kirkpatrick, L. A., & Shaver, P. R. (1990). Attachment theory and religion: Childhood attachments, religious beliefs, and conversion. *Journal for the Scientific Study of Religion, 29*, 315–334. doi:10.2307/1386461

Krejci, M. (1998). Gender comparison of God schemas: A multidimensional scaling analysis. *The International Journal for the Psychology of Religion, 8*, 57–66. doi:10.1207/s15327582ijpr0801_7

Meissner, W. W. (2009). The God question in psychoanalysis. *Psychoanalytic Psychology, 26*, 210–233. doi:10.1037/0736-9735.26.2.210

Miner, M. (2009). The impact of child–parent attachment, attachment to God and religious orientation on psychological adjustment. *Journal of Psychology and Theology, 37*, 114–124.

Moriarty, G. (2007). Time limited dynamic psychotherapy and God image. In G. Moriarty & L. Hoffman (Eds.). *God image handbook for spiritual counseling and psychotherapy: Research, theory, and practice* (pp. 79–104). Philadelphia, PA: Haworth Press.

Moriarty, G., & Hoffman, L. (Eds.). (2007). *God image handbook for spiritual counseling and psychotherapy: Research, theory, and practice.* Philadelphia, PA: Haworth Press.

Murray-Swank, N., & Pargament, K. (2005). God, where are you? Evaluating a spiritually-integrated intervention for sexual abuse. *Mental Health, Religion, and Culture, 8*, 191–203. doi:10.1080/13694670500138866

Nelson, H. M., Cheek, N. H., & Au, P. (1985). Gender differences in images of God. *Journal for the Scientific Study of Religion, 24*, 396–402. doi:10.2307/1385990

Noffke, J., & Hall, T. W. (2007). Attachment psychotherapy and God image. In G. Moriarty & L. Hoffman (Eds.), *God image handbook for spiritual counseling and psychotherapy: Research, theory, and practice* (pp. 57–78). Philadelphia, PA: Haworth Press.

Noffke, J., & McFadden, S. (2001). Denominational and age comparisons of God concepts. *Journal for the Scientific Study of Religion, 40*, 747–756. doi:10.1111/0021-8294.00089

O'Grady, K., & Richards, P. S. (2007). Theistic psychotherapy and the God image. In G. Moriarty & L. Hoffman (Eds.), *God image handbook for spiritual counseling and psychotherapy: Research, theory, and practice* (pp. 183–209). Philadelphia, PA: Haworth Press.

The Process of Change Study Group. (1998). Noninterpretive mechanisms in psychoanalytic therapy: The "something more" than interpretation. *International Journal of Psychoanalysis, 79*, 903–921.

Proctor, M., Miner, M., McLean, L., Devenish, S., & Bonab, B. (2009). Exploring Christians' explicit attachment to God representations: The development of a template for assessing attachment to God experiences. *Journal of Psychology and Theology, 37*, 245–264.

Reinert, D., & Edwards, C. (2009). Attachment theory, childhood mistreatment, and religiosity. *Psychology of Religion and Spirituality, 1*, 25–34. doi:10.1037/a0014894

Rizzuto, A-M. (1979). *The birth of the living God.* Chicago, IL: University of Chicago Press.

Rizzuto, A-M. (1998). *Why did Freud reject God? A psychodynamic interpretation.* New Haven, CT: Yale University Press.

Robbins, M., Francis, L., & Kerr, S. (2006). God images and empathy among a group of secondary school pupils in South Africa. *Religion and Theology, 13*, 173–194.

Schaap-Jonker, H., Eurelings-Bontekoe, E., Verhagen, P., & Zock, H. (2002). Image of God and personality pathology: An exploratory study among psychiatric patients. *Mental Health, Religion, and Culture, 5*, 55–71. doi:10.1080/13674670110112712

Schaap-Jonker, H., Eurelings-Bontekoe, E., Zock, H., & Jonker, E. (2008). Development and validation of the Dutch Questionnaire God Image: Effects of mental health and religious culture. *Mental Health, Religion, and Culture, 11*, 501–515. doi:10.1080/13674670701581967

Shackel, S. K. (2000). The effects of parental death during childhood on adult experience of God. *Dissertation Abstracts International: Section B. Sciences and Engineering, 61*(11) (UMI No. 9994818).

Shaver, P. R., & Mikulincer, M. (2002). Attachment-related psychodynamics. *Attachment and Human Development, 4*, 133–161. doi:10.1080/146167 30210154171

Shedler, J., Mayman, M., & Manis, M. (1993). The illusion of mental health. *American Psychologist, 48*, 1117–1131. doi:10.1037/0003-066X.48.11.1117

Siegel, D. J. (2012). *The developing mind* (2nd ed.). New York, NY: Guilford Press.

Solms, M., & Turnbull, O. (2002). *The brain and the inner world.* New York, NY: Other Press.

Spear, K. (1994). *Conscious and pre-conscious God representations: An object relations perspective.* Unpublished doctoral dissertation, Fuller Theological Seminary, Pasadena, CA.

Sroufe, L., Egeland, B., Carlson, E., & Collins, W. (2005). *The development of the person: The Minnesota study of risk and adaptations from birth to adulthood.* New York, NY: Guilford Press.

Thomas, M. J., Moriarty, G. L., & Anderson, E. L. (2011). The effect of a manualized group treatment protocol on God image and attachment to God. *Journal of Psychology and Theology, 39,* 44–58.

Tisdale, T. C. (1997). A comparison of Jewish, Muslim, and Protestant faith groups on the relationship between level of object relations development and experience of God and self. *Dissertation Abstracts International: Section B. Sciences and Engineering, 58*(9) (UMI No. 9810887).

Tisdale, T. C., Key, T. L., Edwards, K., Brokaw, B. F., Kemperman, S. R., & Cloud, H. (1997). Impact of treatment on God image and personal adjustment, and correlations of the God image to personal adjustment and object relations development. *Journal of Psychology and Theology, 25,* 227–239.

Winnicott, D. W. (1971). *Playing and reality.* London, England: Tavistock.

Wootton, R. J. (1991). God-representation and its relation to object relations and defensive functioning. *Dissertation Abstracts International: Section B. Sciences and Engineering, 51,* 5600.

CHAPTER 16

PRAYER: A REVIEW OF THE EMPIRICAL LITERATURE

Kevin L. Ladd and Bernard Spilka

It would be easy to fill this entire chapter with definitions of prayer. Instead, we selectively follow the lead of Watts (2001b), who simply argued that prayer is theistically oriented behavior. This presupposes nothing about the content or function of prayer; it merely observes that the behavior has an intended "target" or recipient. It further provides us with a way to separate prayer and meditation. Although prayer may include components of rest, quietude, and waiting or listening (Baesler, 2003; Dein & Littlewood, 2008), meditation is often unrelated to any theistic understanding (Brown, 1994). If the research focus is clearly on theistic meditation, we consider it prayer, otherwise we exclude it from this review; meditation per se is treated elsewhere in this handbook (see Chapter 17, this volume and Volume 2, Chapter 10, this handbook). Likewise, we distinguish prayer from healing touch, energy therapy, healing energy, spiritual healing, or therapeutic touch (Jonas & Crawford, 2003; Wardell & Weymouth, 2004), as most such practices are nontheistic. Ours is a tight definition of prayer, but it reflects a substantial portion of the empirical literature and helps to focus this contribution. In the course of this chapter, we first discuss possible models of prayer, then critically review the existing empirical literature. Although it is not feasible for the review to be exhaustive in scope, we cover areas that have received sustained attention: history, health, coping, development, neuroscience, personality, and interpersonal relationships. We close each of the sections, and the chapter, with practical suggestions for further developing the area of study.

PRELIMINARY NOTES

Is prayer a religious or a spiritual practice? In keeping with the parameters of this handbook, prayer is a religious phenomenon because it is deeply rooted in formal institutions of faith. It is also a spiritual discipline because its theistic orientation, by definition, indicates that practitioners are brought into relationship with what they consider sacred. For these reasons, we use the language of "religious and spiritual" in this chapter as necessary.

Perhaps most important is that prayer is multidimensional in expression, motivation, and cognition. Many studies default to simple indexes of prayer frequency, a practice akin to a physician evaluating health by inquiring if a patient is dead or alive; it provides basic data, but the analysis can be deepened to the benefit of all involved. Prayer is, however, "thick" and has various predictable forms of content (Janssen, de Hart, & den Draak, 1990; Ladd & Spilka, 2002, 2006; Poloma & Gallup, 1991), expressive mediums (Begbie, 2001; Inge, 2001), uses of the body (Savage, 2001; Tilby, 2001), social contexts (Elliott, 2001), and modes and times of engagement (Baesler, 2003). It is imperative that researchers clearly articulate what aspects of prayer they are exploring and under what conditions their exploration is taking place; this often is not the case in the existing literature.

POTENTIAL MODELS OF PRAYER

Many, though not all, of the ideas sketching the basic elements of prayer and how they function

DOI: 10.1037/14045-016
APA Handbook of Psychology, Religion, and Spirituality: Vol. 1. Context, Theory, and Research, K. I. Pargament (Editor-in-Chief)
Copyright © 2013 by the American Psychological Association. All rights reserved.

concern themselves with the specific way of praying known as "intercessory" prayer. This emphasis on praying for the well-being of someone or something other than the self is a reflection of two factors. First, much of the empirical research funding has appeared in medical contexts (e.g., Benson et al., 2006). Second, this kind of prayer has great potential for application. If prayer could somehow be employed explicitly and in a controlled fashion as a health care strategy, the implications could revolutionize the medical field. Where possible in the following material, we move beyond notions of intercessory prayer in search of a more encompassing model.

Levin reported in 1996 that there were "more than 150 published empirical studies" (p. 66) potentially in support of the healing effect of prayer or related phenomena (e.g., yoga, touch therapy). Although Levin's definition of prayer is much wider than that employed in this chapter, we embrace his framework of how to approach the study of prayer and similar phenomena. He proposed that two dimensions must be considered. The first dimension (naturalistic–supernatural) addresses the extent to which the proffered explanation implies or requires a referent (e.g., God or other supernatural agents) acting outside of the principles of nature to effect healing. The second dimension (local–nonlocal) identifies whether the activity adheres to normal space–time laws or if it occurs outside those parameters. The resulting four quadrants help investigators articulate the character of their work. For instance, a researcher's interest might be focused on the potential effects of prayer described in the naturalistic–local quadrant (e.g., social support). Others may wish to explore features of prayer that are naturalistic–nonlocal (e.g., "extended mind" or Qigong), many of which draw on conceptualizations from Eastern traditions. Might prayer's influence be local–supernatural (e.g., direct intervention of a deity)? If so, the questions asked will probably revolve around the interaction between faith and healing. Or is prayer best considered a nonlocal–supernatural (e.g., nonempirical) event most effectively described in theological terms? A recent overview of the theoretical literature by Breslin and Lewis (2008) aligned nicely with Levin's (1996) system.

In related work, Levin (2009) broadened his model to consider not just the specific practice of prayer per se but the wider concept of faith in which prayer occurs. He noted that faith is thought to effect healing in many of the same ways that prayer has been argued to "work" over the past century—namely, by motivating healthy behavior, enhancing social support, creating positive cognitive schema, modulating affect, and stimulating psychophysiological responses. In this formulation, prayer becomes one way in which faith is expressed in behavior. This is a particularly important shift because it aligns with the actual theology underlying prayer (e.g., perceived relationship building with both God and humans) rather than forcing prayer into a physically causal role in which prayer is viewed as a tool to manipulate and control one's immediate environment. Faith (and by extension prayer) thus is viewed not as a component that can be simply grafted on to a person's life but rather as a way of living that is cultivated over time.

Although Levin (1996, 2009) has offered a comprehensive way to think about prayer, and more broadly faith, most models arise within specific theoretical domains. For instance, Baesler (2003) worked within the context of prayer as communication, both active and receptive; Dein and Littlewood (2008) stressed the need to explore the latter. Francis and Robbins (2008) advocated a Jungian approach, whereas Maltby, Lewis, and Day (2008) employed a cognitive–behavioral framework in line with the clinical applications highlighted by J. Harris et al. (2010) as well as others (Bade & Cook, 2008; Laird, Snyder, Rapoff, & Green, 2004). Janssen, de Hart, and den Draak (1990) oriented their efforts toward symbolic interactionism. Ladd and Spilka (2002, 2006; Ladd, 2010) looked to theories that highlight how people create meaningful networks or connections using social information (Modée, 2005); physical, emotional, and other forms of mimicry (Girard, Antonello, Rocha, & Kirwan, 2007; Lakin & Chartrand, 2003; Lakin, Jefferis, Cheng, & Chartrand, 2003); and cognitive processes (Tremlin, 2006). Poloma and Gallup (1991) organized forms of prayer on the basis of a nationally (United States) representative sample. These approaches, developed to answer different sorts of questions within distinct academic traditions from psychology to communications and sociology, offer slightly different constellations to describe the ways in which people pray (e.g., intercession, petition, etc.). Can the independently constructed frameworks be consolidated?

Although each of these viewpoints adds discrete information to our knowledge of the topic, the process of sifting through the findings to arrive at some consensus model is made especially challenging by two conditions. First, nearly all of the models utilize different multidimensional instruments of prayer with some clear conceptual overlap (Breslin, Lewis, & Shevlin, 2010). Second, many of these initial efforts have not yet received extensive empirical or theoretical follow-up, so the reliability and validity of many formulations is unknown.

THE STATE OF THE PRAYER LITERATURE

To better understand what is available for examination, we searched the CINAHL (nursing and allied health), PsycINFO, socINDEX, and MEDLINE databases. Initially we sought any article containing the sole term *prayer* in either the title or subject position. With this loose strategy, a total of 3,226 documents were returned. There were, however, a number of duplicates and materials that were quite peripheral and not relevant. For instance, colloquial phrases, such as "on a wing and a prayer," rarely proved to represent investigations of prayer per se. Tightening our criteria, we specified peer-reviewed articles, eliminated CINAHL/MEDLINE overlap, accepted only research articles in CINAHL, and included dissertations. With this conservative search strategy, we located a total of 1,362 works. The results appear in Figure 16.1.

After searching each year separately, it became apparent that analyses of the literature by 5-year groupings portrayed the development of the field rather well. Before 1960, each year had few publications, hence they were combined. As the figure demonstrates, the period from 2000 to 2009 contains 885 documents, or 65% of all the works identified. Looking across the entire figure, it is also interesting to note that MEDLINE references outpace psychology references until 2005–2009 when explicitly psychologically oriented materials take the lead.

These data are limited by the fact that they include only peer-reviewed documents in English. There were, however, significant developments in the field of prayer outside these parameters. For instance, Heiler's (1918) well-known volume outlined a variety of kinds of prayer; German texts by Bolley (1930) and Eller (1937) were also explicitly cast in the mold of psychology of religion. More recently, Hauenstein (2002) added another

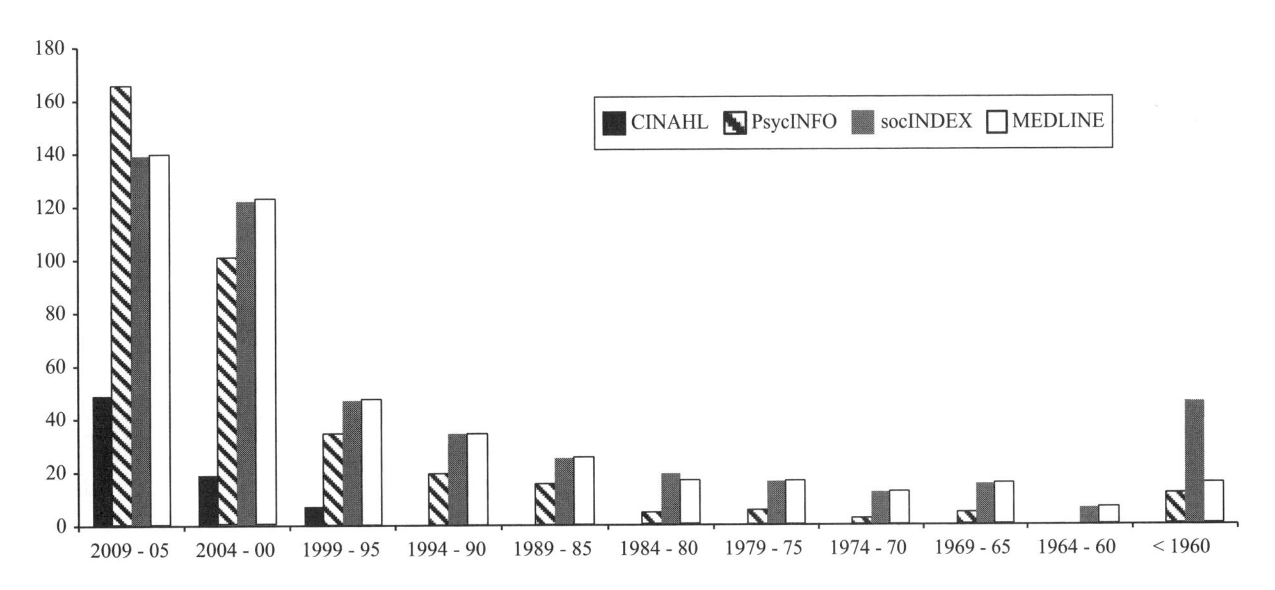

FIGURE 16.1. Frequency count of documents in four databases containing *prayer* in either their title or subject listing.

important book featuring both a literature review and empirical investigation. In French, Segond (1911) produced an early work and Puglisi (1928) offered an Italian perspective. Also, although on the periphery of the psychology of religion proper, Cabrol's (1900) text offered insight concerning the practical aspects of how prayers in the Catholic tradition were understood. Within the English language, as older texts, those of Hodge (1931), Jellett (1878), and Romanes (1874) represented early forays into the scientific psychology of prayer. Poloma and Gallup's (1991) survey, Brown's (1994) extensive treatment of the subject, and the volume of new material edited by Watts (2001a) provide contemporary orientations.

A further limitation is that the bulk of the material on prayer found in these databases relates to Christian practices. Brown (1994) and Levin (1996, 2009) are notable exceptions. Books about prayer in various traditions abound; however, the vast majority are devotional in nature. Although we do not consider many texts of that nature in this chapter, familiarity with this literature is critical. Without an understanding of the belief context in which the prayers are practiced, researchers run the risk of asking the wrong questions and misinterpreting data.

Many of these cited works emphasize theory or theology over empirical data. They speculate on the roles of prayer in the lives of practitioners and how prayer relates to psychological principles. Still, even well-reasoned arguments need verification from objective data.

EXISTING REVIEWS OF EMPIRICAL PRAYER LITERATURE

Books, scrolls, and oral traditions articulating the nature and role of prayer have clearly existed for a very long time (Zaleski & Zaleski, 2005). Although those resources add much to our understanding of the broad history of praying, our attention here is necessarily limited to the more narrow category of work that constitutes a scientific approach to this spiritual discipline.

Early Perspectives

Among the first to write in a sustained fashion on the topic of prayer psychology was Strong (1909). Although there was little empirical material for her to review, much of what she penned remains valid and insightful. For Strong, prayer is a social practice, primarily undertaken in social settings. This process establishes an enriched sense of self. Such an outlook is not hers alone, but accords well with the earlier, less extensive evaluation of prayer made by James (1902). As part of this emergent self-understanding, Strong has noted that people discriminate among prayers using two criteria. First, they intuitively monitor which prayers are efficacious in which situations. If a particular mode of prayer routinely fails to have a demonstrable effect according to the pray-er's definition, the individual gradually ceases to pray in that fashion. Strong provided the example of a young woman who stopped praying for higher exam marks after repeated lack of success, noting that this resulted in significant embarrassment for having attempted to use prayer for such purposes.

A second way that people censor their prayers, according to Strong (1909), is based on social norms. Situations that call for prayer are circumscribed by what the surrounding group deems appropriate. Individuals are unlikely to pray in opposition to group standards, with the notable exception of "prophets" whose stated role is to offer an alternative to the status quo.

More Modern Perspectives

Leaping forward nearly a century brings us to a point at which Finney and Maloney (1985) had more empirical material with which to work. They moved beyond studies focused on the frequency of prayer and explored the literature on development, motivation, and outcomes of both verbal and silent praying. With regard to developmental issues, they noted that prayer is generally analyzed according to Piagetian stages of understanding. Moreover, in the process of development, individuals' prayers reflect declining expectations of materialistic outcomes, a progression from vague to intimate "conversation," and a transition from egocentric to altruistic content. The single empirical study that concerned motivation led the authors to tentatively note that petitionary prayer helped reduce frustration and increased positive adaptation to novel contexts. The authors summarized six studies relevant to verbal prayer. They concluded that positive petitionary prayer might be useful in the context of therapy. They further noted that intercessory–reflective prayers were less effective than simple muscle relaxation exercises for reducing stress. After critiquing two articles dealing with contemplative prayer, Finney and Maloney basically set them aside because of methodological and analytic problems. They did allow, however, that contemplative prayer might help practitioners develop a sense of self, in part because of its reflective quality.

Brown's (1994) full-length text covers empirical work that is both qualitative and quantitative. He reviewed a wide variety of surveys that were not considered by Finney and Maloney (1985), including some from the early 1900s, concerning the practice and content of prayer. At the risk of vastly oversimplifying this important volume, one recurrent theme is that empirical research, in Brown's reading, had shifted toward conceptualizing prayer as a form of coping. From that perspective, he presented literature to support the notion that engaging in prayer can be both a help and a hindrance depending on many factors. It is noteworthy that Brown included an entire section on antiprayer or cursing as one of these factors. Although empirical studies in that arena were few in number, they represent a viewpoint critical to a well-developed understanding of that practice.

One year later, Francis and Evans (1995) published a more circumscribed review of empirical work. They stressed prayer practice (as derived from surveys), developmental–social issues, and subjective and objective effectiveness. With regard to practice, the authors concluded that private prayer behavior is more common than public behavior (e.g., in formal worship settings); people are more likely to pray when removed from public forums. Although Francis and Evans (1995) used more liberal criteria for the inclusion of studies in their review than did Finney and Maloney (1985), their conclusions about developmental issues are consistent with earlier reviews. Expanding slightly on the topic, this article also noted that developmental facets of prayer are heavily influenced by social factors, such as the presence or absence of siblings, school conditions, and so forth.

Concerning possible subjective effects of prayer, the results presented suggest a positive relation between good health conditions and the frequency of prayer among individuals less than roughly 60 years of age. This correlation apparently becomes negative in older samples. The missing component here is a study controlling for the amount and degree of illness. Such an effort would address the question of whether this is a true curvilinear relation or if overall health conditions are confounding the findings. Another, more compelling, alternative would be a longitudinal investigation that could demonstrate the extent to which specific individuals did or did not change their approach to prayer across the life span.

The objective effects of prayer are reviewed as being at least suggestive that prayer could have an influence on physical health. The review, however, does not critique the materials presented but instead takes the findings at face value. Most of these are offered by the original authors as percentage differences between prayer and no-prayer conditions without benefit of statistical tests. In one prominent instance, the well-known Byrd (1988) study is offered as confirmatory evidence of prayer's influence on physical well-being via intercessory prayer, yet that work has since been thoroughly discredited (Benson et al., 2006; Hood, Hill, & Spilka, 2009; Sloan, 2006). For these reasons, we disagree with the conclusion of Francis and Evans (1995) and believe that at that point in time the evidence did not support any objective efficacy for intercessory prayer.

In a work appearing in the same year, McCullough (1995) took a narrower empirical approach in his review of the literature. He explored the relation between prayer and health. In particular, the article addressed subjective well-being, coping, psychiatric symptoms, and intercessory efficacy. As with the previous reviews, the author concluded that although single-item measures of the frequency of prayer had reliability problems, the intensity of the prayer experience positively related to increased subjective well-being. The report on the status of coping strategies and psychiatric symptoms is that their relations to the practice of prayer are mixed, partially because of compromised methodologies, including reliance on the measurement of prayer purely on the basis of frequency. As with the Francis and Evans (1995) review, McCullough's verdict on objective efficacy is based largely on his acceptance of the Byrd (1988) article. Our position remains the same—that is, the Byrd study is critically flawed and does not provide support for intercessory prayer's objective efficacy (Hood, Hill, & Spilka, 2009; Sloan, 2006). We next offer a brief review of the Byrd study and its critiques.

Byrd (1988) split 393 coronary patients into two ostensibly equal groups: an experimental treatment group, the members of which were regularly prayed for, and a control group that received only the standard therapy. A randomized double-blind procedure was used to construct the groups. Initially, on all variables, the two groups were comparable. Despite the substantial size of the initial two groups, the majority of the variables had fewer than 10 subjects each, some with none or a single patient. Following a period of prayer, the groups were again compared on 29 variables. Utilizing the .05 probability level, six of the measures achieved significance. These differences favored the treatment group. When taking into account the large number of comparisons (a Bonferroni adjustment), the stated .05 level drops to an actual .0017. By this corrected index, only one difference reached significance with a value of .002. On the basis of chance alone, one to two indications of significance might result, so the interpretation is highly ambiguous at best. Byrd further combined variables to create a "severity score," which also favored the prayed-for patients. He, however, did not indicate that he was "unblinded" when making this comparison (Tessman, personal communication, May 25, 2008). Later work failed to support this finding (W. S. Harris et al., 1999). There was also reason to doubt the equivalence of the two groups in health, as a later assessment suggested that the control group participants may have been sicker from the beginning than their prayed-for counterparts. For additional questions and critiques, readers are referred to Sloan (2006), Sloan and Ramakrishnan (2006), Tessman and Tessman (2000), and the W. A. Harris and Tessman (2001) debate.

Although not a part of the empirical review component of his article, McCullough (1995) does reiterate Finney and Maloney's (1985) observation of a critical point concerning prayer's objective efficacy. The theology that supports prayer commends the practice as a way for individuals to develop a relationship with God (cf. Baesler, 2003); any other effect is secondary. By virtue of this understanding of prayer, tangible effects, from the praying person's viewpoint, are not guaranteed to result. Physical effects, therefore (e.g., changes in health status), should be statistically neutral. In a wider sense, research on *prayer* may be tantamount to investigating "perceived quality of relationship with God." This is why a single-item measure of frequency is problematic. Knowing how *often* a person speaks to his relatives does not provide information about the psychological quality of the relationship. More specific indexes of how people pray can be useful precisely because they detail more closely the nature of the perceived relationship with God (Janssen, de Hart, & den Draak, 1990; Ladd & Spilka, 2002; 2006; Poloma & Gallup, 1991). Such ideas are already present in Strong's (1909) work, but they have been largely obscured in the intervening years.

Intercessory Prayer Considerations and Health

Astin, Harkness, and Ernst (2000) explored work on distant healing, including intercessory prayer studies. They argued that because positive effects were demonstrated approximately 57% of the time, intercessory prayer studies were worth refining and continuing. This reading was almost immediately challenged by Sampson (2000), who pointed out numerous flaws in both the study evaluation and the overall logic guiding the conclusion. Sampson suggested that because of a host of biases, the literature does not support the objective efficacy of intercessory prayer.

Oman and Thoresen (2002) covered several intercessory prayer studies as they sought to answer the question, "Does religion or spirituality cause health?" They concluded that the extant investigations tend to be more carefully detailed with regard to medical issues (e.g., definitions of illness) than psychological issues (e.g., definitions of prayer that align to real-world practices). In particular, they raised concerns about "distance" prayer and the fact that myriad confounding variables are frequently not controlled. For instance, how can an experimenter be certain that some group receives absolutely no prayer from any source? They further assert that well-controlled studies could be of benefit; however, they do not offer specific examples of how this might be accomplished.

An additional four reviews of prayer and health (Hodge, 2007; Masters & Spielmans, 2007; Masters, Spielmans, & Goodson, 2006; Roberts, Ahmed, Hall, & Davison, 2009) affirm what is becoming a consensus: There is little, if any, empirical evidence that intercessory prayer has a demonstrable effect on the health of those for whom prayers are offered (see especially Benson et al., 2006).

Prayer's role in primary care was reviewed by Hollywell and Walker (2009). Although they reported an overall positive relation between prayer frequency and good health, we have discussed the problems associated with using a single-item measure of prayer frequency, so we do not consider this strong evidence. The authors, however, have suggested that different ways of praying can mediate between faith and health. For instance, among those who perceived a caring God, prayers were associated with improved health; for those who did not share this perception and its assumed relationship, prayers were linked to greater distress levels.

From the practical vantage point of counseling, Curtis and Robertson (2009) reviewed the recent literature on prayer and meditation. They reported that the expectancy of receiving intercessory prayer (as compared with actually receiving intercessory prayer) was a better predictor of positive health effects. In addition, they found that evidence was lacking for any robust support for the notion that personal prayer (praying for oneself) resulted in better health conditions.

As is obvious from these reviews, the bulk of attention has focused on investigations of prayer and health. Studies frequently strive to evaluate the extent to which prayers can influence the physical world. Beyond the obvious similarity of exploring the outcomes and efficacy of prayer, such studies share the critical flaw of confusing psychological and theological levels of measurement. From the perspective of the practitioner, prayer is a spiritual discipline with a spiritual goal. Although this certainly does not preclude demonstrable physical effects, it emphasizes supraphysical (sacred) effects as the primary outcomes. The fact that null or ambiguous findings dominate the literature—and undoubtedly the "file drawer" as well—is not solid evidence of prayer's efficacy (or inefficacy). The physical dependent variables simply fail to adequately represent the full range of prayer content and meaning. Thinking about prayer solely as a human act has yielded studies that have missed the point elucidated across faith traditions: Prayers express human conditions, but practitioners believe that the outcomes are determined in a nonphysical realm.

Prayer and Coping Strategies

What then of a possible relation between prayer and psychological processes, such as coping or finding meaning? Brown (1994) correctly inferred that research seeking links between prayer and coping was on the increase. The expansion, however, has primarily been with a more generalized focus on religious or spiritual coping that includes prayer as one among many options. For instance, Pargament, Koenig, and Perez's (2000) formulation of the Religious Coping Inventory (RCOPE) spurred considerable research; yet, because prayer's inclusion is not structured as a central factor, its influence is hard to partial out.

Along the same lines, two empirical literature reviews (Johnson, Elbert-Avila, & Tulsky, 2005; Thuné-Boyle, Stygall, Keshtgar, & Newman, 2006) focused on religious and spiritual beliefs and practices included brief mentions of prayer as important within the various samples explored (African Americans and cancer patients, respectively). Yet they could not provide detailed conclusions because prayer was measured in rather cursory fashion, primarily by frequency, and the contexts in which the prayer was practiced (e.g., alone or in groups) were not consistently delineated. The main feature that can be garnered from these efforts is that people consider prayer important in the coping process, but it is not always clear what that means outside of specific samples that employ measures developed for use in single studies.

Similarly, in a review of literature relevant to prayer and coping with pain (Wachholtz, Pearce, &

Koenig, 2007), the authors identified several ways that practices such as prayer might influence experiences of pain: by providing a sense of meaning, purpose, increased control, or self-efficacy; by serving as a distraction; by serving as a means of giving and receiving social support; and by facilitating relaxation. These findings are tempered with the caveat that many of the studies used an index of prayer that equated prayer and hoping, thus characterizing prayer as a passive form of coping. Jones et al. (2008) likewise found that some groups used "hoping and praying" as one of several strategies for coping with chronic osteoarthritis pain. Neither article argues that hope and praying constitute identical constructs. Furthermore, the authors were careful to state that the decision to employ a strategy and its actual effectiveness are questions requiring different levels of analysis. It is possible to draw the same sort of conclusion about two recent investigations (Hodge, 2010; Nakonz & Shik, 2009) of women in Sub-Saharan Africa with regard to how they cope while living with HIV/AIDS: Prayer is a prevalent strategy, but the nature of those prayers or actual outcomes remains unknown.

J. Harris et al. (2010) explored the relation between prayer and post-traumatic growth, suggesting that prayer might serve to foster acceptance, assistance, a calming focus, or a way to defer or avoid the situation. Among these, only the calming feature emerged as predictive of growth. This relation was probably a result of a conceptual overlap involving the use of the total score for an interpersonal trauma index that included a spiritual change subscale.

Among these studies relating prayer and coping, a few efforts (Bänziger, Van Uden, & Janssen, 2008; Ladd & Spilka, 2006; Laird, Snyder, Rapoff, & Green, 2004) stand apart for using thoroughly multidimensional approaches. The benefit of employing these more detailed measures is that they help to assess specific ways in which people engage in prayer and how those various prayers are associated with coping. For instance, Bänziger et al. (2008) as well as Ladd and Spilka (2006) used Pargament's (1997) indexes of religious coping, but the two studies employed different prayer measures. Nonetheless, from these investigations it is possible to see that individuals who perceive a distinct role for God in the coping process are likely to practice a variety of prayers, with the exception of those invoking personal petitions or pursuing contemplative purposes. People who do not readily include God when addressing stressful situations are either ambivalent or negative toward most forms of prayer. Laird et al. (2004) addressed how prayers were used among two samples of individuals dealing with arthritis. Using a variety of health criteria and many possible predictors, only prayers of thanksgiving and reception (contemplation) negatively predicted the subjective impact of osteoarthritis.

Empirical studies of prayer and coping are greatly limited by the use of prayer measures that are efficient but simplistic. What emerges thus far from this literature is the observation that many people pray with regularity when faced with stressors. A review by the American Psychological Association (2008) indicated that 37% of their respondents utilized prayer to manage stress. Although among all stress-reducing techniques prayer was in eighth place, it was in first place regarding its helpfulness, with 77% of the sample considering it their most successful stress management procedure. Various efforts suggest that the objective effects of the practice are less apparent than are the limited subjective effects.

DEVELOPMENT AND PRAYER

The majority of investigations of prayer are cross-sectional as opposed to longitudinal in nature. When juxtaposing the various efforts, however, it is still possible to piece together a sketch of prayer across the life span.

Children

Since Francis and Evans's (1995) earlier review, 16 studies have explored developmental issues in relation to prayer. Of these, the majority note that like adults, children practice prayer frequently (Humphrey, Hughes, & Holmes, 2008; see also Chapter 27 in this volume). Prayer is more common among youngsters who have a positive attitude toward Christianity and attend services (Robbins, Babington, & Francis, 2004). Krause and Ellison (2007) added that individuals religiously socialized early in life highly value practices such as prayer and are more likely to continue them into adulthood.

Broaching the topic of intercessory prayer in a childhood context, Mathai and Bourne (2004) set aside previous reviews and claim that there is sufficient merit to further investigation. Their findings suggested, however, that on a variety of indexes of well-being, children with psychiatric disorders fared no better when they received intercessory prayers than when they did not receive them as part of the experimental condition. This study, as well as other experimental studies of similar design, has some specific challenges. It is hard to justify the assumption that the "no-prayer" group received absolutely no prayer from any source. It is feasible to argue that the effects of extra-study prayers will be randomly distributed across the conditions and therefore statistically balance each other. This is not compelling, however, because we know of no study that has empirically demonstrated anything about the dosage effects of prayer. Theologians can easily say that it is an issue of quality, not quantity, contending that a single prayer can be as effective as many prayers.

Seeking to understand how emotions and prayer relate in the minds of children, Bamford and Lagattuta (2010) helped open a new line of thinking. They demonstrated via an experiment that younger children (between 4 and 6 years of age) thought that positive emotions would motivate prayer. In contrast, older (8-year-old) children and adults thought that negative emotions prompted prayers. These older participants (including adults) also thought more widely about prayer as a means of finding help, a time of relating to God with regard to giving thanks or more simply communicating. This study dovetails nicely with earlier work by Barrett (2001) that outlined how Christians, Muslims, and Jews tend to restrict their prayers (especially those of petition) to psychological domains, such as emotional regulation. This agrees with the findings of Wooley and Phelps (2000) that showed how children's use of prayer shifted in accord with their changing theories of mind but in ways that sometimes violated the norms. For instance, young children knew that human–human communication needed speech, but they believed that human–God interaction could occur silently. On the other hand, wishing and praying were not always well-differentiated concepts until later childhood. Developmental features that facilitate the shift from earlier to later ways of understanding and engaging prayer remain to be discovered. It seems that one helpful way forward is to expand studies of this nature, linking cognitive development and the practice of prayer.

Older Adults

As with the literature concerning children, research on prayer among older adults is somewhat limited (for a review, see Chapter 29 in this volume). Using the same cutoff for Francis and Evans's (1995) review, roughly 20 peer-reviewed articles are available. Many of them are similar to the presentation by Arcury, Quandt, McDonald, and Bell (2000) that reported on a sample of African Americans, European Americans, and Native Americans in North Carolina. Arcury et al. concluded that many of these older people view prayer as an important part of their health self-management. No outcomes were reported, so we do not know the degree to which this inference is accurate.

In a more nuanced approach, Krause (2003) stated that prayer alters the extent to which financial stressors contribute to poor health. He also observed that praying for others may offer health benefits to those over 60 years of age. Furthermore, African Americans in his sample engaged in prayer for others more often than did the White Americans. Using measures of both trust associated with praying and frequency of private prayer, Krause (2008) further found a weak relation between prayer and depression later in life, particularly when considering trauma experienced across the life span. The results are more complex for childhood trauma, showing that early traumatic experience corresponds to greater depression among those with low trust and to less depression among those with high trust in prayer. Frequency of prayer failed to offset effects of either lifetime or childhood trauma.

Others have reported that frequency of prayer is linked negatively to self-perceptions of health, physical health, functional abilities, and mental health (Hank & Schaan, 2008). One study suggested that frequency of prayer was unrelated to depressive symptoms except for a negative relation among those who had no ties to any specific faith tradition (Braam, Deeg, Poppelaars, Beekman, & van Tilburg, 2007). In other words, for many older people, prayer and poor health go together.

This position was mildly countered by Ai, Tice, Huang, Rodgers, and Bolling (2008), who used the four ways of praying identified by Poloma and Gallup (1991). From among the four approaches to prayer, only petitionary prayer (mediated by optimism) related significantly to postoperative well-being. On the other hand, prayers resembling conversations with God tied into acute stress. In a related study, Ai et al. (2010) reported that the preoperative intention to employ prayer as a part of a coping strategy was related to greater optimism and hope 30 months postsurgery.

Among older adults, prayer appears to be readily employed for various purposes. In many cases, praying has been associated with poorer functioning, although it is not possible to discern the causal direction. There is a little evidence that a strong trust in prayer in later life relates to better psychological health, but that may be confounded by the experience of extreme health challenges.

Research on developmental issues has begun to move beyond reliance on unidimensional measurements of prayer behavior. Among children in particular, an emphasis on the cognitive complexity of prayer in relation to emerging theories of mind shows considerable promise. The study of older adults, however, remains largely dominated by interest in outcomes, especially in the realm of health. There is a clear need to continue to move beyond correlational designs to parse questions of causality at all ages. Given the sweep of literature reviewed up to this point, it seems unlikely that a clear, causal influence would be observed, even with true experimental approaches. Although the language of prayer sounds causal, its theistic nature means that it is understood by practitioners as being filtered through a divine will. Content must be evaluated in relation to that caveat. That being the case, we think that developmentally oriented projects can fruitfully continue along at least two dimensions. One will follow the lead of Krause (2003, 2008) and think about health outcomes not as simply caused by prayers of various kinds, but as complexly related to a constellation of prayer behaviors. The influence of intentions, actual praying, and the physiology of prayer across the life span may be of particular merit. A second possible developmental line of inquiry may include shifting from outcome measures to process evaluations. Exploring the ways in which younger and older people think about their praying and how those thoughts correspond to other cognitive processes (Wooley & Phelps, 2000) will continue to provide important information, especially when longitudinal designs are developed.

PRAYER AND NEUROSCIENCE

A newer area of prayer investigations revolves around ever-improving technology for isolating brain activation. For example, Newberg and colleagues (Newberg et al., 2001; Newberg, Pourdehnad, Alavi, & d'Aquili, 2003; Newberg, Wintering, Morgan, & Waldman, 2006) used single-photon emission computed tomography (SPECT) to investigate brain activity during centering prayer (focusing on a sacred word or phrase as a means of entering the presence of the divine) as practiced by Franciscan nuns. They reported increased activation in the prefrontal cortex and the inferior parietal area. These areas deal with attention and language, respectively.

Schjødt, Stødkilde-Jørgensen, Geertz, and Roepstorff (2008) looked at functional magnetic resonance imaging (fMRI) scans of participants improvising prayer, reciting the Lord's Prayer or reciting a well-known rhyme, making wishes to Santa, and counting backward from 100. They observed increases in caudate nucleus activity during recitation of the Lord's Prayer and slightly less so during improvised prayer. Their interpretation was that prayer stimulates the dopaminergic system of the dorsal striatum, a part of the reward system. In another study, Schjødt, Stødkilde-Jørgensen, Geertz, and Roepstorff (2009) again looked at improvised prayer, the Lord's Prayer, recitation of a nursery rhyme, and wishing to Santa, but this time they utilized a sample of highly religious individuals. During improvised prayer, more so than Lord's Prayer recitation, areas of the brain associated with theory of mind—the temporoparietal junction, temporopolar region, and left medial prefrontal cortex—displayed increased activity. The authors attributed this to the less personal nature of the Lord's Prayer. Schjødt et al. (2009) also found that the area of the brain associated with autobiographical memory, the temporopolar area, was active during improvised prayer. They believed that this was due to the necessity of recall inherent in the praying process. The precuneus (self-reflection) was active during improvised prayer and wishing to Santa. The authors associated this with the expression of one's own desires when openly praying to God and stating wishes to Santa. The activation of the prefrontal cortex is consistent in these investigations of prayer, but other areas of the brain found to be active are unique to the individual study (Azari et al., 2001; Schjødt et al., 2008, 2009).

Although such sophisticated technologies are providing unique information, if ever there was an area demanding replication, this is it. Simultaneously, caution must be exercised concerning the extent to which these methods can inadvertently dictate the nature of questions asked. Researchers must keep in mind that technology is most useful as a tool to answer theoretically derived inquiries. In other words, psychological prayer components must be at least as painstakingly detailed as their physiological–brain components and correlates. Elsewhere (Ladd, Cook, Foreman, & Ritter, 2012), we have demonstrated experimentally that the prayers evoked during these highly noisy, disruptive procedures are substantially different than typical prayers. This means that not only are operationalizations of prayer difficult to assess but also the nature of the experience itself may radically alter the ability to pray in a typical fashion, rendering the data highly questionable.

PRAYER AND PERSONALITY

Roughly two dozen articles have appeared in this area since Francis and Evans (1995) reviewed the literature. Some efforts by Francis and his colleagues have aimed to show how the personality system of Eysenck and Eysenck (1991), which emphasizes extraversion, neuroticism, and psychoticism, relates to the frequency of prayer among a variety of samples. Representative of this work, Francis, Robbins, Lewis, and Barnes (2008) indicated that Catholic and Protestant 16- to 18-year-olds who pray frequently score lower on the psychoticism scale than do those who pray less frequently. Catholic students evidence a statistically significant but very small .09 correlation between prayer frequency and neuroticism; the large sample size (Catholic $n = 1{,}246$) makes this a significant relation. This is an instance in which an effect-size analysis would be appropriate. This critique, however, is pertinent to many studies in the psychology of prayer. Relative to this work, these findings are tempered by the fact that the psychoticism and neuroticism scales have alpha coefficients of .40 and .66, respectively; the psychoticism scale is consistently plagued by similarly low reliabilities (cf. Robbins, Francis, & Edwards, 2008).

Using a list of adjectives in Polish that loosely approximated the widely used NEO Five-Factor Inventory (NEO FFI), Kosek (2000) asked Polish seminarians about the extent to which they prayed because they liked God. Neuroticism (positively) and extraversion (negatively) were significant predictors of the propensity to pray to a God who was perceived as likeable. These studies share a common reliance on single-item measures of prayer along with the difficulties associated with such a simple but vague index.

Francis and Robbins (2008) provided an intriguing investigation of the relation of prayer to Jungian ideas. Relying on four experts to generate prayer-related questions keyed to the eight Jungian types (introverted, extraverted, sensing, intuitive, thinking, feeling, judging, and perceiving), an unspecified factor analytic procedure reduced the pool to seven items per type (56 total). Five of the eight prayer scales showed reliability greater than.65. These prayer scales were correlated with participant's Keirsey Temperament Sorter results to demonstrate the extent to which they tapped similar constructs. With an N of just over 1,500, the majority of the correlations with $p < .05$ had an absolute value of less than .20. This means that most of the relations had more mathematical than practical significance; this is always a challenge in such large studies. The extraverted prayer scale correlated as predicted with a measure of extraverted personality. Of the remaining seven scales, sensing correlated significantly with two different types, introverted and thinking correlated with three different types, and the other four scales displayed significant associations to all of the types. In other words, the Jungian-based scales of prayer and personality associated significantly, though somewhat indiscriminately, with each other. Although this use of personality theory ultimately may prove fruitful, the difficulty in specifying the relation between prayer scales and personality types signals the need for further refinement.

Two other articles used multidimensional prayer indexes to capture various ways of praying. Ladd, Ladd, Harner, et al. (2007) worked with the Ladd and Spilka (2002, 2006) prayer scales in conjunction with the Abridged Big-Five Circumplex of DeRaad (2000). Participants self-rated themselves on prayer and personality dimensions. A close peer then independently rated them. Across participants and raters, 11 of the 16 reliabilities were greater than .65 (with two at .62 and one at .64). Participant and peer scores were similar, although peers seemed more confident about the participant's personality characteristics as opposed to prayer preferences. Correlations were of the same magnitude as in the Francis and Robbins (2008) study; however, the smaller sample size ($N = 70$ participants; 70 raters) did not result in statistical significance.

Looking at the magnitude of the correlations, a pattern similar to the Francis and Robbins (2008) findings emerges in which multiple ways of praying are associated with multiple facets of personality. Taken as a pair, these two studies may indicate that regardless of personality characteristics, people enjoy a wide variety of praying options. Still, the observations need replication plus a better understanding of what they mean.

An additional relevant article links the Ladd and Spilka (2002, 2006) scales to indexes of personal character (Peterson & Seligman, 2004). Using canonical correlation, Ladd, Ladd, Ashbaugh, et al. (2007) presented data showing that the personal trait of transcendence (e.g., awe, gratitude) was associated with prayer frequency, duration, experience, and attendance at services in addition to the internal prayer experience of the self and others. The data also indicated that the character trait of humanity (e.g., kindness, intimacy) was tied to being female and to prayers of intercession for others, intense personal evaluation, and asking for material things (petition). In a third finding, wisdom, courage, justice, and transcendence characteristics related to prayers of suffering with others, self-reflection, rest, upholding traditions, and being willing to question God. The final canonical variate reflected a link between zestful living, modesty, humor traits, and traditional forms of praying, frequent attendance, and younger age. Complex meanings are evident, but there is a need to clarify such possibilities in greater detail.

The empirical literature on prayer and personality shows some movement toward developing and using robust indexes of prayer's multiple dimensions. Although there are clearly psychometric and interpretive challenges to be met, such should be expected when beginning to grapple seriously with these involved constructs.

PRAYER IN RELATIONSHIPS

Baesler (2003) systematically advanced the idea that prayer is a form of interpersonal communication. In the broad context of social relations, Loveland, Sikkink, Myers, and Radcliff (2005) used the concept of intercessory prayer to examine the underpinnings of civic involvement. They indicated that praying is positively associated with increased participation in social activities, particularly those in which the person has the chance to offer direct care for individuals.

More tightly circumscribed explorations of this possibility suggest that couples whose faith tradition includes prayer may find that it helps to improve the quality of their familial interactions (Beach, Fincham, Hurt, McNair, & Stanley, 2008; Butler, Stout, & Gardner, 2002; see Volume 2, Chapter 24, this handbook). It also has been demonstrated experimentally that those who engage in prayer for their partner on a regular basis increase in relationship satisfaction and participate in fewer romantic behaviors outside the relationship. They are seen by others to be more committed to their partner than are people in the control condition (Fincham, Lambert, & Beach, 2010). Likewise, higher relationship satisfaction was observed among those engaging in petitionary prayer (Fincham, Beach, Lambert, Stillman, & Braithwaite, 2008). These studies by Fincham and colleagues employ measures of prayer that are unidimensional in accord with their research goals. They thereby maintain a high level of efficiency without needing to resort to more ambiguous single items measuring global frequency of prayer. This is a relatively simple departure from the bulk of the empirical literature, but it provides a wealth of information because it is guided by well-developed hypotheses derived from theory.

One additional stream of research in this area concerns the process of prayer as a means of self-disclosure. Among the first studies to address this topic, VandeCreek, Janus, Pennebaker, and Binau (2002) randomly assigned participants (seminary students) to write about a highly challenging experience either as a simple disclosure, a letter to God, or a prayer. Using a computer program to count word frequency, they reported no linguistic differences across the groups with regard to causal expressions or negative emotions. Differences did emerge, however, with lower levels of insight and positive emotions in the simple disclosure condition. The main difficulty with this sort of approach is that the computer programs do not consider context. Both "I love praying" and "I do not love praying" add weight to the "love" outcome; however, the meaning is clearly not the same.

A recent effort by Grossoehme et al. (2010) reviewed similar studies, noting a theme in written prayers from various contexts of a God perceived as available and caring. This work used a computer program to generate word counts of prayers written in a hospital chapel's designated book. Not surprisingly, the content of these spontaneous prayers is different from the content in disclosure writing samples in which the participants were given instructions (VandeCreek, Janus, Pennebaker, & Binau, 2002). The conclusion by Grossoehme et al. that written prayers and emotional disclosures are different supports the report of VandeCreek et al. (2002). This, however, is virtually a foregone conclusion because the comparison groups are so thoroughly distinct at the onset. A more tightly structured analysis is apparent in the work of Cadge and Daglian (2008), who concurred that spontaneous written prayers include concepts of an available, caring God toward which people direct their thanks and petitions.

Future work in this area should attend to the view that human–human and human–divine interactions may look alike on the surface and even act similarly on a neural level (Schjødt et al., 2009). Still, the phenomenological experience of the two event patterns can be very different. This is reflected in the fact that individuals use different content and explore different emotions depending on whether they are praying or in a conversation with a close friend (Ladd, Vreugdenhil, Ladd, & Cook, in press).

With regard to relationships, we see two clear ways forward. One maps out how prayer functions within intimate contexts. This approach will become even more helpful as it expands to include family or other kinds of social arrangements. The second path explores how prayer, as a form of personal linguistic disclosure, is both similar to and different from other forms of disclosure. This strategy will become stronger as computer programming (or hand coding!) explicitly takes into account contexts both within the language itself and the settings in which these expressions are created.

PRACTICAL IMPLICATIONS AND CONCLUSIONS

Being able to coherently describe the practice of prayer is the first step toward systematically evaluating its role in various aspects of life. Chief among these roles is the relation of prayer to the topic of coping. In general, we regard prayer as a process of "connecting" to self, others, and the sacred. To a certain degree, these are sufficiently significant psychological sources of motivation in and of themselves. Unintentional effects of the perceived success or failure of desired contacts may be relevant to understanding coping processes. For instance, it may be the case that the physical features of praying (e.g., head bowing, closing eyes) might more or less automatically result in the activation and expression of emotions (Ladd & McIntosh, 2008).

Individuals who pray may find a particular mode of praying that is exceptionally comfortable. The dilemma is that at some point, perhaps in a crisis or maybe in the midst of more general malaise, one can experience an inability to pray in that formerly comfortable manner. This might result in a compounding of the initial source of discomfort because the familiar mechanism for coping is no longer readily available.

These circumstances require sensitivity on the part of clinicians or spiritual advisors who want to help people discover other meaningful ways of praying. For instance, those who previously relied heavily on spontaneous prayers may discover that traditional, codified prayers help them regain or broaden one's sense of the prayerful. Alternatively, it can be useful for an individual to explore fresh postures during prayer (Ladd, Cook, Foreman, Ritter, & Cora, 2010). If kneeling was common, perhaps standing would aid the person's sense of being able to focus. If being physically still was the norm, then walking or other bodily movement might enable the person to reconnect with their valued practice. One must not lose sight of the fact that prayer probably has been with humanity since, at least, the Paleolithic Era (Wallace, 1966). For many centuries, the literate have offered their insights and practices to a spiritually hungry audience. There is a plethora of research possibilities in this literature.

As with other situations, it is probably most useful to know about these alternatives well in advance of actually needing them. "Spiritual triage" may be able to staunch an existential crisis, but it is not likely to be a stable ongoing resource. Those interested in preventative measures in this realm could consider events allowing people the opportunity to explore multiple avenues toward prayer.

Our position is categorically *not* that prayer is simply an effective tool to promote positive coping. The situation is far more complex than that because, as with any sort of relationship, the quality and conditions of the connection matter greatly. Clearly, prayer may have both positive and negative aspects, although the negatives have thus far received little formal research attention. This may be because people are susceptible to social desirability pressures and are therefore reticent to discuss negative experiences with prayer. Regardless, researchers are only just scratching the surface of the complexity of this quintessential religious and spiritual practice (Spilka & Ladd, in press).

References

Ai, A. L., Ladd, K. L., Peterson, C. C., Cook, C. A., Shearer, M. M., & Koenig, H. G. (2010). Long-term adjustment after surviving open heart surgery: The effect of using prayer for coping replicated in a prospective design. *The Gerontologist, 50,* 798–809. doi:10.1093/geront/gnq046

Ai, A. L., Tice, T. N., Huang, B., Rodgers, W., & Bolling, S. F. (2008). Types of prayer, optimism, and well-being of middle-aged and older patients undergoing open-heart surgery. *Mental Health, Religion, and Culture, 11,* 131–150. doi:10.1080/13674670701324798

American Psychological Association. (2008). *Stress in America.* Retrieved from http://www.apa.org/news/press/releases/stress/index.aspx

Arcury, T. A., Quandt, S. A., McDonald, J., & Bell, R. A. (2000). Faith and health self-management of rural older adults. *Journal of Cross-Cultural Gerontology, 15,* 55–74. doi:10.1023/A:1006741625617

Astin, J. A., Harkness, E., & Ernst, E. (2000). The efficacy of "distant healing": A systematic review. *Annals of Internal Medicine, 132,* 903–910.

Azari, N. P., Nickel, J., Wunderlich, G., Niedeggen, M., Hefter, H., Tellmann, L., Herzog, H., Stoerig, P., Birnbacher, D., & Seitz, R. J. (2001). Short communication: Neural correlates of religious experience. *European Journal of Neuroscience, 13,* 1649–1652.

Bade, M. K., & Cook, S. W. (2008). Functions of Christian prayer in the coping process. *Journal for the Scientific Study of Religion, 47,* 123–133. doi:10.1111/j.1468-5906.2008.00396.x

Baesler, E. J. (2003). *Theoretical explorations and empirical investigations of communication and prayer.* Lewistown, NY: Edwin Mellen Press.

Bamford, C., & Lagattuta, K. H. (2010). A new look at children's understanding of mind and emotion: The case of prayer. *Developmental Psychology, 46,* 78–92. doi:10.1037/a0016694

Bänziger, S., Van Uden, M., & Janssen, J. (2008). Praying and coping: The relation between varieties of praying and religious coping styles. *Mental Health, Religion, and Culture, 11,* 101–118. doi:10.1080/13674670600748386

Barrett, J. L. (2001). How ordinary cognition informs petitionary prayer. *Journal of Cognition and Culture, 1,* 259–269. doi:10.1163/156853701753254404

Beach, S. R. H., Fincham, F. D., Hurt, T. R., McNair, L. M., & Stanley, S. M. (2008). Prayer and marital intervention: A conceptual framework. *Journal of Social and Clinical Psychology, 27,* 641–669. doi:10.1521/jscp.2008.27.7.641

Begbie, J. (2001). Prayer and music. In F. Watts (Ed.), *Perspectives on prayer* (pp. 67–80). London, England: SPCK.

Benson, H., Dusek, J. A., Sherwood, J. B., Lam, P., Bethea, C. F., Carpenter, W., . . . Hibberd, P. L. (2006).

Study of the therapeutic effects of intercessory prayer (STEP) in cardiac bypass patients: A multicenter randomized trial of uncertainty and certainty of receiving intercessory prayer. *American Heart Journal, 151*, 934–942. doi:10.1016/j.ahj.2005.05.028

Bolley, A. (1930). *Gebetsstimmung und Gebet. Empirische Untersuchungen zur Psychologie des Gebetes* [Prayer and its moods: An empirical investigation of the psychology of prayer]. Düsseldorf, Germany: Pädagogischer.

Braam, A. W., Deeg, D. J. H., Poppelaars, J. L., Beekman, A. T. F., & van Tilburg, W. (2007). Prayer and depressive symptoms in a period of secularization: Patterns among older adults in the Netherlands. *American Journal of Geriatric Psychiatry, 15*, 273–281. doi:10.1097/JGP.0b013e31802d0ae8

Breslin, M. J., & Lewis, C. (2008). Theoretical models of the nature of prayer and health: A review. *Mental Health, Religion, and Culture, 11*, 9–21. doi:10.1080/13674670701491449

Breslin, M. J., Lewis, C. A., & Shevlin, M. (2010). A psychometric evaluation of Poloma and Pendleton's (1991) and Ladd and Spilka's (2002, 2006) measures of prayer. *Journal for the Scientific Study of Religion, 49*, 710–723. doi:10.1111/j.1468-5906.2010.01541.x

Brown, L. B. (1994). *The human side of prayer.* Birmingham, AL: Religious Education Press.

Butler, M. H., Stout, J. A., & Gardner, B. C. (2002). Prayer as a conflict resolution ritual: Clinical implications of religious couples' report of relationship softening, healing perspective, and change responsibility. *American Journal of Family Therapy, 30*, 19–37. doi:10.1080/019261802753455624

Byrd, R. C. (1988). Positive therapeutic effects of intercessory prayer in a coronary care unit population. *Southern Medical Journal, 81*, 826–829. doi:10.1097/00007611-198807000-00005

Cabrol, F. (1900). *Le livre de la prière antique* [The ancient book of prayer]. Poitiers, France: H. Oudin.

Cadge, W., & Daglian, M. (2008). Blessings, strength, guidance: Prayer frames in a hospital prayer book. *Poetics, 36*, 358–373. doi:10.1016/j.poetic.2008.06.011

Curtis, R., & Robertson, P. (2009). Prayer and meditation: A review of research. *Counselling and Spirituality, 28*(2), 11–32.

Dein, S., & Littlewood, R. (2008). The psychology of prayer and the development of the Prayer Experience Questionnaire. *Mental Health, Religion, and Culture, 11*, 39–52. doi:10.1080/13674670701384396

De Raad, B. (2000). *The Big Five personality factors: The psycholexical approach to personality*. Seattle, WA: Hogrefe & Huber.

Eller, E. (1937). *Das Gebet: Religionspsychologische Studien* [Prayer: Studies in the psychology of religion] Paderborn, Germany: Ferdinand Schöingh.

Elliott, C. (2001). Prayer and society. In F. Watts (Ed.), *Perspectives on prayer* (pp. 15–26). London, England: SPCK.

Eysenck, H. J., & Eysenck, S. B. G. (1991). *Manual of the Eysenck Personality Scales.* London, England: Hodder & Stoughton.

Fincham, F. D., Beach, S. R. H., Lambert, N., Stillman, T., & Braithwaite, S. R. (2008). Spiritual behaviors and relationship satisfaction: A critical analysis of the role of prayer. *Journal of Social and Clinical Psychology, 27*, 362–388. doi:10.1521/jscp.2008.27.4.362

Fincham, F. D., Lambert, N. M., & Beach, S. R. H. (2010). Faith and unfaithfulness: Can praying for your partner reduce infidelity? *Journal of Personality and Social Psychology, 99*, 649–659. doi:10.1037/a0019628

Finney, J. R., & Maloney, H. (1985). Empirical studies of Christian prayer: A review of the literature. *Journal of Psychology and Theology, 13*(2), 104–115.

Francis, L. J., & Evans, T. E. (1995). The psychology of Christian prayer: A review of empirical research. *Religion, 25*, 371–388. doi:10.1016/S0048-721X(05)80021-1

Francis, L. J., & Robbins, M. (2008). Psychological type and prayer preferences: A study among Anglican clergy in the United Kingdom. *Mental Health, Religion, and Culture, 11*, 67–84. doi:10.1080/13674670701619445

Francis, L. J., Robbins, M., Lewis, C. A., & Barnes, L .P. (2008). Prayer and psychological health: A study among sixth-form pupils attending Catholic and Protestant schools in Northern Ireland. *Mental Health, Religion, and Culture, 11*, 85–92. doi:10.1080/13674670701709055

Girard, R., Antonello, P., Rocha, J. C. C., & Kirwan, M. (2007). *Evolution and conversion: Dialogues on the origins of culture.* New York, NY: Continuum.

Grossoehme, D. H., VanDyke, R., Jacobson, C. J., Cotton, S., Ragsdale, J. R., & Seid, M. (2010). Written prayers in a pediatric hospital: Linguistic analysis. *Psychology of Religion and Spirituality, 2*, 227–233. doi:10.1037/a0020035

Hank, K., & Schaan, B. (2008). Cross-national variations in the correlation between frequency of prayer and health among older Europeans. *Research on Aging, 30*, 36–54. doi:10.1177/0164027507307923

Harris, J., Erbes, C., Engdahl, B., Tedeschi, R., Olson, R., Winskowski, A. M. M., & McMahill, J. (2010). Coping functions of prayer and posttraumatic growth. *The*

International Journal for the Psychology of Religion, 20, 26–38. doi:10.1080/10508610903418103

Harris, W. A., & Tessman, I. (2001, March 13). *Is there scientific evidence that intercessory prayer speeds medical recovery? A debate.* Retrieved from http://www.csicop/org/articles/20010810-prayer/index.html

Harris, W. S., Gowda, M., Kolb, J. W., Strychacz, C. P., Vacek, J. L., Jones, P. G., . . . McCallister, B. D. (1999). A randomized, controlled trial of the effects of remote, intercessory prayer on outcomes in patients admitted to the coronary care unit. *Archives of Internal Medicine, 159*, 2273–2278. doi:10.1001/archinte.159.19.2273

Hauenstein, H. U. (2002). *Auf den Spuren des Gebets: Methoden und Ergebnisse der empirischen Gebetsforschung* [On the trail of prayer: Methods and results of empirical prayer research]. Heidelberg, Germany: Asanger.

Heiler, F. (1918). *Das Gebet: Eine Religionsgeschichtliche und Religionspsychologische Untersuchung* [A study in the history and psychology of prayer]. Munich, Germany: Reinhardt.

Hodge, A. J. (1931). *Prayer and its psychology*. London, England: SPCK.

Hodge, D. R. (2007). A systematic review of the empirical literature on intercessory prayer. *Research on Social Work Practice, 17*, 174–187. doi:10.1177/1049731506296170

Hodge, D. R. (2010). Sub-Saharan African women living with HIV/AIDS: An exploration of general and spiritual coping strategies. *Social Work, 55*, 27–37. doi:10.1093/sw/55.1.27

Hollywell, C., & Walker, J. (2009). Private prayer as a suitable intervention for hospitalised patients: A critical review of the literature. *Journal of Clinical Nursing, 18*, 637–651.

Hood, R. W., Jr., Hill, P., & Spilka, B. (2009). *The psychology of religion: An empirical approach* (4th ed.). New York, NY: Guilford Press.

Humphrey, N., Hughes, H. M., & Holmes, D. (2008). Understanding prayer among African American children: Preliminary themes. *Journal of Black Psychology, 34*, 309–330. doi:10.1177/0095798408319885

Inge, D. (2001). Prayer and poetry. In F. Watts (Ed.), *Perspectives on prayer* (pp. 53–66). London, England: SPCK.

James, W. (1902). *Varieties of religious experience*. New York, NY: Longmans, Green.

Janssen, J., de Hart, J., & den Draak, C. (1990). A content analysis of the praying practices of Dutch youth. *Journal for the Scientific Study of Religion, 29*, 99–107. doi:10.2307/1387033

Jellett, J. H. (1878). *The efficacy of prayer: Being the Donnellan Lectures for the year 1877*. Dublin, Ireland: Hodges, Foster, & Figgis.

Johnson, K. S., Elbert-Avila, K., & Tulsky, J. (2005). The influence of spiritual beliefs and practices on the treatment preferences of African Americans: A review of the literature. *Journal of the American Geriatrics Society, 53*, 711–719. doi:10.1111/j.1532-5415.2005.53224.x

Jonas, W. B., & Crawford, C. C. (2003). Science and spiritual healing: A critical review of spiritual healing, "energy" medicine, and intentionality. *Alternative Therapies in Health and Medicine, 9*(2), 56–61.

Jones, A. C., Kwoh, C., Groeneveld, P., Mor, M., Geng, M., & Ibrahim, S. (2008). Investigating racial differences in coping with chronic osteoarthritis pain. *Journal of Cross-Cultural Gerontology, 23*, 339–347. doi:10.1007/s10823-008-9071-9

Kosek, R. B. (2000). The desire for God: An assessment of seminarians' spirituality through the lens of the "Big Five." *Pastoral Psychology, 49*, 43–50. doi:10.1023/A:1004621531794

Krause, N. (2003). Praying for others, financial strain, and physical health status in late life. *Journal for the Scientific Study of Religion, 42*, 377–391. doi:10.1111/1468-5906.00189

Krause, N. (2008). Lifetime trauma, prayer, and psychological distress in later life. *The International Journal for the Psychology of Religion, 19*, 55–72. doi:10.1080/10508610802471112

Krause, N., & Ellison, C. G. (2007). Parental religious socialization practices and self-esteem in late life. *Review of Religious Research, 49*(2), 109–127.

Ladd, K. L. (2010, May). *Prayer and health: A strategy to move beyond ambiguous results.* Paper presented at the Second European Conference on Religion, Spirituality, and Health. University of Bern, University Hospital, Bern, Switzerland.

Ladd, K. L., Cook, C. A., Foreman, K. M., & Ritter, E. A. (2012). *Prayer and neuroimaging: An experimental investigation of questions of validity*. Manuscript submitted for publication.

Ladd, K. L., Cook, C. A., Foreman, K. M., Ritter, E. A., & Cora, J. (2010, March). *The influence of posture on prayer experience: Preliminary findings.* Paper presented at the American Psychological Association Division 36 Mid-Winter Conference on Religion and Spirituality, Columbia, MD.

Ladd, K. L., Ladd, M. L., Ashbaugh, P., Trnka, D., Harner, J., Pierre, K. T., & Swanson, T. (2007). Inward, outward, upward prayers and personal character. *Research in the Social Scientific Study of Religion, 18*, 209–231. doi:10.1163/ej.9789004158511.i-301.80

Ladd, K. L., Ladd, M. L., Harner, J., Swanson, T., Metz, T., Pierre, K. T., & Trnka, D. (2007). Inward, outward, upward prayer and Big Five personality traits. *Archive for the Psychology of Religion, 29*, 151–175. doi:10.1163/008467207X188711

Ladd, K. L., & McIntosh, D. N. (2008). Meaning, God, and prayer: Physical and metaphysical aspects of social support. *Mental Health, Religion, and Culture, 11*, 23–38. doi:10.1080/13674670701475053

Ladd, K. L., & Spilka, B. (2002). Inward, outward, upward: Cognitive aspects of prayer. *Journal for the Scientific Study of Religion, 41*, 475–484. doi:10.1111/1468-5906.00131

Ladd, K. L., & Spilka, B. (2006). Inward, outward, upward prayer: Scale reliability and validation. *Journal for the Scientific Study of Religion, 45*, 233–251. doi:10.1111/j.1468-5906.2006.00303.x

Ladd, K. L., Vreugdenhil, S., Ladd, M.L., & Cook, C (in press). Interpersonal conversations and prayers: Differences of content and attachment functions. *Journal of Communication and Religion.*

Laird, S., Snyder, C., Rapoff, M., & Green, S. (2004). Measuring private prayer: Development, validation, and clinical application of the multi-dimensional prayer inventory. *The International Journal for the Psychology of Religion, 14*, 251–272. doi:10.1207/s15327582ijpr1404_2

Lakin, J. L., & Chartrand, T. L. (2003). Using nonconscious behavioral mimicry to create affiliation and rapport. *Psychological Science, 14*, 334–339. doi:10.1111/1467-9280.14481

Lakin, J. L., Jefferis, V. E., Cheng, C. M., & Chartrand, T. L. (2003). The Chameleon Effect as social glue: Evidence for the evolutionary significance of nonconscious mimicry. *Journal of Nonverbal Behavior, 27*, 145–162. doi:10.1023/A:1025389814290

Levin, J. S. (1996). How prayer heals: A theoretical model. *Alternative Therapies in Health and Medicine*, 2(1), 66–73.

Levin, J. S. (2009). How faith heals: A theoretical model. *EXPLORE: The Journal of Science and Healing, 5*, 77–96. doi:10.1016/j.explore.2008.12.003

Loveland, M. T., Sikkink, D., Myers, D. J., & Radcliff, B. (2005). Private prayer and civic involvement. *Journal for the Scientific Study of Religion, 44*, 1–14. doi:10.1111/j.1468-5906.2005.00261.x

Maltby, J., Lewis, C. A., & Day, L. (2008). Prayer and subjective well-being: The application of a cognitive-behavioural framework. *Mental Health, Religion, and Culture, 11*, 119–129. doi:10.1080/13674670701485722

Masters, K. S., & Spielmans, G. I. (2007). Prayer and health: Review, meta-analysis, and research agenda. *Journal of Behavioral Medicine, 30*, 329–338. doi:10.1007/s10865-007-9106-7

Masters, K. S., Spielmans, G. I., & Goodson, J. T. (2006). Are there demonstrable effects of distant intercessory prayer? A meta-analytic review. *Annals of Behavioral Medicine, 32*, 21–26. doi:10.1207/s15324796abm3201_3

Mathai, J., & Bourne, A. (2004). Pilot study investigating the effect of intercessory prayer in the treatment of child psychiatric disorders. *Australasian Psychiatry, 12*, 386–389.

McCullough, M. E. (1995). Prayer and health: Conceptual issues, research review, and research agenda. *Journal of Psychology and Theology, 23*(1), 15–29.

Modée, J. (2005). *Artifacts and supraphysical worlds.* Lund, Sweden: Lund University.

Nakonz, J., & Shik, A. (2009). And all your problems are gone: Religious coping strategies among Philippine migrant workers in Hong Kong. *Mental Health, Religion, and Culture, 12*, 25–38. doi:10.1080/13674670802105252

Newberg, A., Alavi, A., Baime, M., Pourdehnad, M., Santanna, J., & d'Aquili, E. (2001). The measurement of regional cerebral blood flow during the complex cognitive task of meditation: A preliminary SPECT study. *Psychiatry Research: Neuroimaging, 106*, 113–122. doi:10.1016/S0925-4927(01)00074-9

Newberg, A., Pourdehnad, M., Alavi, A., & d'Aquili, E. G. (2003). Cerebral blood flow during meditative prayer: Preliminary findings and methodological issues. *Perceptual and Motor Skills, 97*, 625–630.

Newberg, A. B., Wintering, N. A., Morgan, D., & Waldman, M. R. (2006). The measurement of regional cerebral blood flow during glossolalia: A preliminary SPECT study. *Psychiatry Research: Neuroimaging.* doi:10.1016/j.pscychresns.2006.07.001

Oman, D., & Thoresen, C. E. (2002). "Does religion cause health?": Differing interpretations and diverse meanings. *Journal of Health Psychology, 7*, 365–380. doi:10.1177/1359105302007004326

Pargament, K. I. (1997). *The psychology of religion and coping.* New York, NY: Guilford Press.

Pargament, K. I., Koenig, H. G., & Perez, L. M. (2000). The many methods of religious coping: Development and initial validation of the RCOPE. *Journal of Clinical Psychology, 56*, 519–543. doi:10.1002/(SICI)1097-4679(200004)56:4<519::AID-JCLP6>3.0.CO;2-1

Peterson, C., & Seligman, M. E. P. (2004). *Character strengths and virtues: A handbook and classification.* Washington, DC: American Psychological Association and Oxford University Press.

Poloma, M. M., & Gallup, G. H., Jr. (1991). *Varieties of prayer: A survey report.* Philadelphia, PA: Trinity Press.

Puglisi, M. (1928). *La Preghiera* [Prayer]. Torino, Italy: Fratelli Bocca.

Robbins, M., Babington, P., & Francis, L. J. (2004). Correlations between attitude toward Christianity, prayer, and church attendance among 9–11 year olds. *Psychological Reports, 94*, 305–306. doi:10.2466/pr0.94.1.305-306

Robbins, M., Francis, L. J., & Edwards, E. (2008). Prayer, personality, and happiness: A study among undergraduate students in Wales. *Mental Health, Religion, and Culture, 11*, 93–99. doi:10.1080/13674670701702548

Roberts, L., Ahmed, I., Hall, S., & Davison, A. (2009, April 15). Intercessory prayer for the alleviation of ill health. *Cochrane Database of Systematic Reviews, 2*, CD000368.

Romanes, G. J. (1874). *Christian prayer and general laws: Being the Burney prize essay for the year 1873.* London, England: Macmillan.

Sampson, W. I. (2000). Are systematic reviews and meta-analyses sufficient as well as necessary for assessing the medical effectiveness of prayer? *Scientific Review of Alternative Medicine, 4*(2), 12–16.

Savage, S. (2001). Prayer and the body. In F. Watts (Ed.), *Perspectives on prayer* (pp. 97–110). London, England: SPCK.

Schjødt, U., Stødkilde-Jørgensen, H., Geertz, A. W., & Roepstorff, A. (2008). Reward prayers. *Neuroscience Letters, 443*, 165–168. doi:10.1016/j.neulet.2008.07.068

Schjødt, U., Stødkilde-Jørgensen, H., Geertz, A. W., & Roepstorff, A. (2009). Highly religious participants recruit areas of social cognition in personal prayer. *Social Cognitive and Affective Neuroscience, 4*, 199–207. doi:10.1093/scan/nsn050

Segond, J. (1911). *La prière: Essai de psychologie religieuse* [Prayer: A study in the psychology of religion]. Paris, France: Félix Alcan.

Sloan, R. P. (2006). *Blind faith.* New York, NY: St. Martin's Press.

Sloan, R. P., & Ramakrishnan, R. (2006). Science, medicine, and intercessory prayer. *Perspectives in Biology and Medicine, 49*, 504–514. doi:10.1353/pbm.2006.0064

Spilka, B., & Ladd, K. L. (in press). *The psychology of prayer: A scientific approach.* New York, NY: Guilford Press.

Strong, A. L. (1909). *The psychology of prayer.* Chicago, IL: University of Chicago Press.

Tessman, I., & Tessman, J. (2000). Efficacy of prayer: A critical evaluation of claims. *Skeptical Inquirer, 24*(2), 31–33.

Thuné-Boyle, I. C., Stygall, J. A., Keshtgar, M. R., & Newman, S. P. (2006). Do religious/spiritual coping strategies affect illness adjustment in patients with cancer? A systematic review of the literature. *Social Science and Medicine, 63*, 151–164. doi:10.1016/j.socscimed.2005.11.055

Tilby, A. (2001). Prayer and sexuality. In F. Watts (Ed.), *Perspectives on prayer* (pp. 81–96). London, England: SPCK.

Tremlin, T. (2006). *Minds and gods: The cognitive foundations of religion.* New York, NY: Oxford University Press.

VandeCreek, L., Janus, M., Pennebaker, J. W., & Binau, B. (2002). Praying about difficult experiences as self-disclosure to God. *The International Journal for the Psychology of Religion, 12*, 29–39. doi:10.1207/S15327582IJPR1201_04

Wachholtz, A. B., Pearce, M. J., & Koenig, H. (2007). Exploring the relationship between spirituality, coping, and pain. *Journal of Behavioral Medicine, 30*, 311–318. doi:10.1007/s10865-007-9114-7

Wallace, A. F. C. (1966). *Religion: An anthropological view.* New York, NY: Random House.

Wardell, D. W., & Weymouth, K. (2004). Review of studies of healing touch. *Journal of Nursing Scholarship, 36*, 147–154. doi:10.1111/j.1547-5069.2004.04012.x

Watts, F. (2001a). *Perspectives on prayer.* London, England: SPCK.

Watts, F. (2001b). Prayer and psychology. In F. Watts (Ed.), *Perspectives on prayer* (pp. 39–52). London, England: SPCK.

Wooley, J. D., & Phelps, K. E. (2000). The development of children's beliefs about prayer. *Journal of Cognition and Culture, 70*, 571–587.

Zaleski, P., & Zaleski, C. (2005). *Prayer: A history.* New York, NY: Houghton Mifflin.

Chapter 17

CONTEMPORARY SPIRITUAL MEDITATION: PRACTICES AND OUTCOMES

Amy B. Wachholtz and Elizabeth T. Austin

A student went to his meditation teacher and said, "My meditation is horrible! I feel so distracted, my legs ache, and I'm constantly falling asleep!"

"It will pass," said the teacher.

A week later, the student came back to his teacher. "My meditation is wonderful! I feel so aware, so peaceful, so alive!"

"It will pass," said the teacher.

—Unattributed

Historically, meditation has rarely been a source of controversy. Recently, however, there have been some heated discussions about the role of meditation and its impact on physical, mental, and spiritual health, particularly in relationship to specific religious groups. Questions have also been raised as to what makes meditation, meditation? What are the unique factors? Is there such a thing as a nonspiritual form of meditation? How does spiritual meditation affect mental, physical, and spiritual health? These questions will be explored in this chapter.

DEFINITION OF MEDITATION

The term *meditation* describes a practice that encompasses thousands of different forms that have a part of thousands of religious cultures over thousands of years. Each of these traditions has its unique view of what defines meditation. There may be movement or stillness. The mind may be highly focused or blank. Despite these differences, it is generally agreed that meditation involves some type of intentional control of the mind and body to enhance the biological, psychological, social, or spiritual functioning of the individual.

Meditation in the Major Religious Traditions

In the Buddhist traditions, learning to meditate is considered a great gift, with the primary goals of transforming the mind and exploring the self and the world. Toward these ends, a host of specific meditation strategies are used across the various Buddhist schools. *Anapanasati*, breath meditation, is frequently incorporated. Others emphasize *shamatha*, or calm abiding, and *vipassana*, referring to insight. Compassion meditation derives from Zen Buddhism. Theravada Buddhism emphasizes the development of mindfulness (*sati*) and concentration (*samadhi*).

Hindu practices refer to meditation as a process of becoming calm and focused in which one perceives the self or soul (*ātman*) within oneself. Yoga is incorporated into the Hindu meditative traditions, which combines ethics (*yamas*); postures (*asanas*); breath control (*pranayama*); withdrawal from the senses (*pratyahara*); focused mind (*dharana*); meditation (*dhyana*); and *samadhi*, which is the union of the *ātman* with the omnipresent. This is the ultimate goal for Hindu Yogis.

In the Muslim tradition, meditative prayer is an obligation of the individual at least five times a day. The practice of peaceful prayer is intended to serve as a template for conduct during the day, transforming it ideally into one single and sustained meditation. Sufi Muslim traditions place an emphasis on a

DOI: 10.1037/14045-017
APA Handbook of Psychology, Religion, and Spirituality: Vol. 1. Context, Theory, and Research, K. I. Pargament (Editor-in-Chief)
Copyright © 2013 by the American Psychological Association. All rights reserved.

concentration meditation technique, involving high-intensity and sharply focused introspection

Christian traditions have various meditative practices, including *Lectio Divina*, a slow contemplative praying of scripture, rosary meditations, and Eucharistic Adoration specific to Catholicism. In Eastern Orthodoxy, the Jesus Prayer is repeated silently to the self in the practice of *Hesychast*. Similarly, other Western Christian meditative practices rely on the repetition of a single word or short phrase, similar to a mantram.

Judaism incorporates meditative practices as evidenced by references in the Torah and Hebrew Bible to contemplative meditation. This concept is best embodied in the mystical tradition of Kabbalah. Meditative methods in the Kabbalist practices include the mental visualization of the supernatural realms the soul navigates through to achieve certain ends.

TYPES OF MEDITATION

Although meditation may come in many forms, almost all types of meditation fall into the four-square format. This format differentiates between what is occurring physically during the meditation (movement vs. still) and the cognitive focus during the meditation (singularly focused vs. clearing the mind). It would be impossible to describe every type of meditation practice, but some of the major variations are described in Exhibit 17.1.

Empirical studies have not examined whether the various types of meditation result in different

Exhibit 17.1
Examples of Major Forms of Meditation

Moving–Singular Focus

- *Buddhist Walking*: flood the senses to heighten a reverent awareness of small details in the environment; then take a step forward and repeat the process (Coleman, 1999).
- *Sema Dance*: From Sufi Islam, the dance symbolizes planetary rotation, movement of blood from the heart, with a focus on drawing closer to God (Wachholtz & Pearce, 2010).
- *In Vivo Mantra*: brief statements practiced during daily life to increase salience of spiritual qualities or to increase feelings of closeness to a higher power (Bormann et al., 2005).

Stationary–Singular Focus

- *Sacred Object*: focus on a holy object, image, or idea to identify or absorb the spiritual characteristics that can be learned from that object/image (Kozhevnikov et al., 2009).
- *Passage*: similar to above, but focused on a short text (e.g., 23rd Psalm; Oman et al., 2006).
- *Breath:* focus on the sensation of individual breaths to increase reverence for the human body and to focus the mind (Rappaport & Cammer, 1977).
- *Loving Kindness*: from the Buddhist tradition and asks the practitioner to project love to a progressively expansive group of people from self to the entire world (Carson et al., 2005).
- *Relaxation Response*: initially designed as a nonspiritual mantra technique that was practiced in away from other activities (Benson, 1975). Over time, the "Faith Factor" was identified as participants often reported spiritual benefits from this technique (Benson & Proctor, 1984).

Clearing the Mind–Moving Meditation

- *Laughing Yoga*: a group practice of laughing to clear the mind of stressors so that the natural state of spiritual joy can take over (Wachholtz & Pearce, 2010).
- *Tai Chi/Yoga:* requires stylized physical movements (known as "forms") that reflect the balance of the universe and bring balance to the mind and spirit (Butler et al., 2008).
- *Sacred Dance*: expression of spiritual ideas via the body (Wachholtz & Pearce, 2010).

Clear Clearing the Mind–Stationary Meditation

- *Formless/Zen*: a Buddhist practice that encourages being present and open with an unbiased observation of internal cognitive–spiritual experiences (Kozhevnikov et al., 2009). This Buddhist practice has been absorbed by the modern mindfulness movement and is often referred to as mindfulness or Mindfulness-Based Stress Reduction (MBSR).
- *Contemplative Prayer:* a form of prayerful meditation; it might begin with a question or topic, and then it moves to being open to communicating with a higher power (Johnson et al., 2009).

outcomes among meditators. Some early functional magnetic resonance imaging (fMRI) research identified distinctive forms of brain activation during focused versus nonfocused forms of meditation (Liou et al., 2006; Chapter 11 in this volume). But only a small number of studies have explored whether these distinctive brain activation patterns associated with different types of meditation lead to observable outcome differences.

In one of the few studies exploring differences in meditation types, Passage Meditation (PM; focused meditation type) was compared with mindfulness-based stress reduction (MBSR; mind-clearing meditation type) and a wait-list control group among college students (Shapiro, Schwartz, & Bonner, 1998). Participants were given 8 weeks of training in 90-min weekly sessions. At the 8-week follow-up, participants in the PM and MBSR group showed few outcome differences; both treatment groups had significantly lower self-reported stress levels and higher levels of forgiveness than the control group (Shapiro et al., 1998).

Early evidence suggests that there may be few phenotypic outcome differences among the four-square meditation types (Shapiro et al., 1998). Although there are many opinion papers in the literature, there is not enough empirical evidence to generate firm conclusions about differential effects of the various meditation styles. Furthermore, the relationship between individual variables and the type of meditation intervention may affect outcomes. For example, certain forms of meditation may have a differential impact on the basis of the condition that is treated or personality styles. Additionally, religious or cultural variables could influence the adherence or outcomes to different forms of meditation. Although these are intriguing ideas to speculate about, to date, these issues are inadequately articulated in the empirical literature.

MODELS OF CHANGE AND EFFICACY

Since the late 1990s, progress has been made linking the changes engendered by spiritual meditation with changes in physiological and psychological outcomes. Researchers have speculated about the physiological pathways mediating these connections. Models focusing on psychoneuroimmunology or psychoneuroendocrinology have yielded putative physiological mechanisms linking spirituality or religion and health (Seeman, Dubin, & Seeman, 2003; Seybold, 2007). Other models focus on the bio-psycho-social-spiritual pathways that lead to change (Uchino, Cacioppo, & Kiecolt-Glaser, 1996; Wachholtz, Pearce, & Koenig, 2007).

IS SPIRITUALITY A CRITICAL COMPONENT OF MEDITATION?

The study of secular meditation raises the intriguing question as to whether the beneficial effects of meditation that have been reported in the literature are at least partly due to the implicitly spiritual nature of meditation. The concept of secular meditation is a relatively new idea in the historical context of meditation practice. Early researchers such as Herbert Benson and the Relaxation Response (Benson, 1975), and Jon Kabat-Zinn's MBSR (Kabat-Zinn, 2003; Kabat-Zinn & Borysenko, 1990) have been ambivalent toward the concept of spirituality in meditation. Even contemporary reviews of meditation research acknowledge the historical–religious background of meditation, but they often neglect the potential role of spirituality as a mechanism of change (Shapiro et al., 2006) or as a potential outcome of meditation practice (Walsh & Shapiro, 2006).

Early meditation researchers may have distanced themselves from spiritual meditation research, which at the time was primarily focused on transcendental meditation (TM; Raskin, Bali, & Peeke, 1980), in an effort to foster greater acceptance by the biomedical community. Despite this attempt to separate spiritual and secular practices, follow-up studies have suggested that what was thought to be a "secular" practice appears to be too closely intertwined with spirituality to be considered completely independent of spiritual constructs (Benson & Proctor, 1984; Carmody, Reed, Kristeller, & Merriam, 2008; Shapiro et al., 1998). By the mid- to late 1990s, researchers were becoming increasingly aware that these secular practices likely had spiritual influences. In 1997, Astin published a study on the 8-week MBSR program that assessed the influence of mindfulness on chronic pain and spirituality. The participants in the secular MBSR program reported significantly more spiritual experiences than the control group as well as a significant decrease in chronic pain. A number of later studies have supported the concept that secular meditation techniques taught in a secular context can create positive spiritual effects for practitioners, such as increased spiritual well-being and spiritual meaning making (Carmody et al., 2008).

Because secular meditation techniques grew out of spiritual traditions, it is possible that some of the beneficial effects of secular meditation may be rooted in spirituality. The experience of external silence (a rarity in the modern world), decreases the focus on the minutiae of everyday life, and during this time, the person naturally seems to gravitate toward spirituality (Wachholtz & Pargament, 2005). Thus, a presumably secular technique may have indivisible aspects of spirituality embedded within it (Astin, 1997). Therefore, ostensibly secular meditation tasks may represent *less* spiritually oriented, rather than *non*spiritually oriented, meditation types. The lack of information on the spiritual impact of meditation in many research populations for which there are "secular" meditation studies may arise from a paucity of spiritual assessments in these studies (Greeson, 2009), as opposed to an actual absence of spiritual impact.

Part of the argument about secular versus sacred includes the question about the role of "meaningless" phrases versus spiritually meaningful phrases. The original Relaxation Response involved chanting any syllable or phrase (Benson, 1975). Even within spiritual meditation research, a TM novice will be prescribed a mantra but not necessarily told what it means (Yogi, 2001). This, however, has become a point of contention with non-TM meditation researchers whose research supports the use of a spiritually meaningful phrase (e.g., Bormann & Oman, 2007; Wachholtz & Pargament, 2005, 2008; Wolf & Abell, 2003). Wolf and Abell (2003) explored this question to see whether a meaningful phrase affects meditators differently than a meaningless phrase over 28 days. The three groups were exposed to (a) a spiritually meaningful phrase, (b) meaningless combination of Sanskrit syllables, and (c) nonphrase control. They found that the spiritually meaningful phrases were more effective for reducing stress and depression. They were not able to identify, however, whether it was the specific meaning of the words that created significant change in the participants. Oman and Driskill (2003) posited that the frequent repetition of a holy name was likely "to make a person's associated spiritual feelings, attitudes, and beliefs more salient and accessible to consciousness, and thus more easily translated into spiritual choices for daily living" (p. 11). Therefore, meditating on spiritually meaningful words may be more powerful because it increases the salience for other spiritual ideas.

To identify whether the spiritual focus of the meditation is a critical variable in producing change in meditation practice, Wachholtz and Pargament (2005, 2008) completed a series of studies comparing secular and spiritual forms of meditation. All of the meditation types included a cognitive focus, one of the meditation types (progressive muscle relaxation) incorporated movement, and the remainder were nonmovement meditations. Outcomes included mood, cardiac variables, and pain levels. In the first study, there were no observed differences in cardiac responses to stress across the different meditation groups. Across the study series, however, spiritual meditation had a greater impact than the secular forms of meditation on psychological, pain tolerance, and spiritual variables. As a result, for individuals who have a spiritual belief system, explicitly spiritual forms of meditation may have a value-added benefit.

It could be argued that meditation is, by definition, a spiritual practice (Kristeller, 2010). Alternatively, it may be that for practitioners the term *meditation* connotes a spiritual practice that is integral to the act, thereby increasing the salience of spirituality during the practice. At the same time, deeming a practice "secular" may increase its accessibility to individuals not usually amenable to spiritual practice and may permit broader dissemination. We have a rich scientific tradition of mindfulness and the relaxation response (see Volume 2, Chapter 10, this handbook), but these interventions are generally conceived of as "secular" meditation by their authors. As empiricists, we cannot assume that there is a factor influencing the outcomes of a study if that factor is not named or measured. Therefore, in this chapter, we elected to cast a wide net in terms of inclusion of literature that includes explicitly spiritual meditation, spiritual assessment of meditation, or spiritual aspects of meditation. The studies are of varying quality, with unfortunately only a select few meeting the Consolidated Standards for Reporting Trials criteria for design and quality of intervention research reporting. A host of exploratory and effectiveness studies illustrate the applicability of spiritual meditation. We expect that the quality of research in spiritual meditation will improve in the coming decade, analogous to the developmental trajectory of the literature explicating the efficacy, applicability, and effective components of mindfulness and relaxation response interventions. There is also the hope that we will reach greater clarity on the discrimination between "secular" and "spiritual" forms of meditation.

MEDITATION AND MENTAL HEALTH

There is an emerging consensus that meditation practices facilitate improvement and recovery from a host of mental health problems (Shapiro & Walsh, 2003), including depression, anxiety, posttraumatic stress disorder (PTSD), attention-deficit/hyperactivity disorder (ADHD), substance abuse, personality disorders, and antisocial behavior. Mindfulness meditation techniques are heavily represented in the compendium of studies supporting the use of meditation strategies in therapeutic practice. There are only a handful of well-constructed studies examining spiritually integrated meditation as a treatment for psychiatric conditions. This body of work represents a promising first look at incorporating a spiritual component into intervention trials, but it lacks effective components analyses to determine what spirituality contributes specifically to the effectiveness of the interventions.

Depression

Depression occurs at a high rate in our population. Effective treatment has been challenging despite the proliferation of pharmaceutical options, especially in light of recent data indicating that pharmacotherapy is relatively ineffective for mild to moderate depression (Fournier et al., 2010). The development of treatment strategies that are effective, safe, and efficient is essential to add to the range of options for patients. There is growing evidence that spiritual meditation and meditative styles of yoga are effective interventions in managing mild and moderate depression.

Butler et al. (2008) compared three group interventions (meditation–hatha yoga, hypnosis, and psychoeducation) in patients with depression over a 12-week intervention. They employed a meditation–hatha yoga protocol emphasizing the meditative spiritual practices of surrender. They found a remission rate of 77% in the meditation–yoga group, which is comparable to that reported in combination antidepressant and psychotherapy studies.

Researchers found similar effects with Siddha Samadhi Yoga (Kozasa et al., 2008). Study participants reported symptoms of anxiety or depression, were naive to meditation and yoga, and were not in active mental health treatment. The 2-week intervention incorporated focused breathing exercises and Samadhi meditation, which uses spiritual meditation with mindful self-observation and a spiritual mantra. Participants meditated 20 min twice daily. After 2 weeks of meditation, anxiety and depression scores were significantly reduced, and there were significant increases in well-being and reduction of tension.

Similarly, Chan et al. (2009) employed a 4-week mind–body intervention incorporating Chan (or *Zen* in non-Chinese literature) practices as a component of the intervention called *Dejian*. Chan principles include the idea that problems are associated with greed, anger, and blaming; healing requires observing and fixing the relationship between the self and nature. This philosophy was integrated with *Dan Tien* breathing exercises during the training sessions. Ninety-six percent of the *Dejian* group reported the intervention was helpful in enhancing health, feeling more alert, and increasing concentration.

Despite limitations related to small sample sizes and a frequent lack of control groups, these studies offer evidence that meditation has positive effects on the overall well-being of individuals who are depressed or dysthymic. These interventions are relatively brief, yet yield clinically relevant changes in mood and overall well-being. It is not clear, however, what component of the intervention accounts for the improvement because the majority of these protocols incorporated both physical relaxation strategies and a spiritual meditative component.

Stress and Anxiety

Stress and anxiety are the most commonly studied outcomes in meditation research. MBSR (Kabat-Zinn, 2003), among other techniques, have made significant contributions to the field of stress management in an effort to reduce its impact on physical and emotional conditions (Baer, 2003). Many MBSR researchers do not conceptualize mindfulness meditation as a spiritual practice and do not explore potential spiritual effects of this form of meditation. Therefore, we have limited our review of this literature to only those studies measuring spiritual–religious outcomes. Outside of the realms of MBSR and TM, there is a relative paucity of high-quality studies examining the effect of spiritual meditation practices on stress and anxiety utilizing rigorous methodology or active control groups.

Stress. One of the few randomized controlled trials of meditation was conducted by Oman, Hedberg, and Thoresen (2006), comparing passage meditation plus an in vivo mantram (see Exhibit 17.1) to a wait list control group in health care professionals. The study examined the effects of meditation training in stress, mental health, and well-being in 27 health care professionals. Participants were instructed in the meditation techniques in weekly 2-hr sessions over an 8-week period. Rapid and robust effects on perceived stress, and improvements in mental heath and vitality were reported. The authors identified that the beneficial effects may be due to the ease of integrating the intervention into the participants' daily lives and the ability of the Eight Point Program meditation to be used with multiple culturally appropriate adaptations.

Similar findings were reported in a later study conducted with undergraduates (Shapiro, Oman, Thoresen, Plante, & Flinders, 2008). In this study, MBSR was compared with a spiritual meditation program in 29 undergraduates. Increases in mindfulness as assessed by the Mindfulness Attention Awareness Scale were achieved with both active interventions and this was associated with reduction in perceived stress and rumination. Differences between the interventions were observed on constructs of forgiveness and rumination. The meditation program was associated with increased forgiveness, whereas the MBSR group had greater reductions in rumination.

Anxiety. A Cochrane review of randomized controlled trials for the use of meditation in management of anxiety (Krisanaprakornkit, Sriraj, Piyavhatkul, & Laopaiboon, 2009) found two studies meeting their rigorous criteria for inclusion. Both studies compared treatments incorporating meditation practices to more traditional treatments for anxiety. Raskin et al. (1980) compared TM, electromyography-biofeedback, and relaxation therapy in an 18-week study of the treatment of anxiety neurosis. Participants in all three groups reported reductions in situational anxiety and symptomatic distress, but there were no differences between the three interventions. Shannahoff-Khalsa et al. (1999) compared Kundalini yoga, with a focus on a spiritually focused breathing meditation, to mindfulness meditation in the treatment of obsessive–compulsive disorder. No differences were identified for obsessive–compulsive disorder; however, the group using the spiritual practice of Kundalini yoga had significant improvements on stress and life purpose.

In treating combat veterans, Bormann and colleagues (2005) reported the successful use of spiritual mantram meditation in managing PTSD symptoms and improving quality of life. Male veterans ($N = 29$) were recruited from a PTSD treatment program. They were randomly assigned to a treatment or delayed control condition. Participants in the active group attended a 6-week spiritual mantram intervention program. Participants were assigned a mantram from a representative list of major spiritual traditions to minimize the likelihood of confound by affirmation or other types of cognitions. They were asked to repeat the mantram as often as possible to train their attention. In addition, they were taught the concepts of slowing down and using the mantram as a means to shift attentional focus away from reactive or triggering thoughts. Results indicated that participants in the active intervention reported a large effect size ($d = -.72$) on self-reported PTSD, with spiritual well-being evidencing a medium to large effect ($d = .67$).

Similarly, active intervention yielded improvements on measures of quality of life and psychological distress. Retention was high in this group, and the participants reported that they were satisfied with the intervention.

In a study assessing the use of spiritual meditation to manage a specific fear, the mantram intervention was successfully implemented in a very small sample of women and men reporting childbirth-related fears. Hunter et al. (2011) reported preliminary results from a study integrating the mantram intervention into childbirth education classes. Unlike the PTSD sample in the previous mantram study, attrition in this sample was very high, with only five active intervention subjects completing follow-up interviews. Nonetheless, the intervention was perceived to be helpful by the participants in managing fear in the hospital setting and facilitated interaction with the hospital staff during delivery. Most continued using the spiritual mantram techniques long after delivery to cope with the feelings of being overwhelmed as new parents.

These studies were all limited in terms of small sample sizes, which affected treatment effect sizes and generalizability. Nonetheless, there is promise in the use of these interventions that incorporate focused attention and relaxation in the amelioration of symptoms.

Attention-Deficit/Hyperactivity Disorder

The management of ADHD has provoked much debate as this prevalent, chronic condition has significant impact on functional capacity and mood. Two small feasibility studies incorporated spiritual meditation as a mental training strategy to regulate attention and manage stress and anxiety associated with behavioral dysregulation.

A TM technique was employed (Grosswald, Stixrud, Travis, & Bateh, 2008) in 10 children diagnosed with ADHD in a school setting. Over a 3-month period, students were given instruction in TM and asked to meditate for 10 min daily. Improvements were seen in measures of stress, anxiety, and ADHD symptoms. Similarly, a feasibility study implementing a modified mindfulness meditation was conducted by Zylowska et al. (2007) in 24 adults and 8 adolescents. The Mindfulness Awareness Practices for ADHD program was implemented for 8 weeks. This program includes ADHD psychoeducation, shorter sitting meditation periods, and the addition of the spiritually based loving kindness meditation to enhance low self-esteem. The intervention was well received. Self reported measures of ADHD symptoms improved, and there was evidence of improved performance on tests of neurocognitive impairment.

Personality Disorders

Linehan's (1993) dialectal behavior therapy (DBT) was one of the first treatments to incorporate meditation into a behavioral treatment protocol for severe mental illness. The meditative–mindfulness component is derived from Zen Buddhist spiritual practices and is designed to reduce interpersonal sensitivity and encourage responsiveness to interpersonal situations. Although not an explicitly spiritual practice, secular mindfulness strategies that are derived from spiritual practices have been demonstrated to enhance the practitioner's sense of spirituality (Carmody, Reed, Kristeller, & Merriam, 2008). A controlled trial (Linehan et al., 2006) comparing DBT with nonbehavioral treatment by experts yielded greater improvement in parasuicidal behaviors and treatment retention in the DBT cohort. Essential components research is under way to clarify the most effective aspects of the intervention, and it will be interesting to explore how directly and how much a spiritual dimension contributes to efficacy in these interventions.

Antisocial–Criminal Behavior

A number of studies reporting on the implementation of TM in correctional settings have demonstrated both proximal and longitudinal changes in stress, aggression and psychological well-being as well as recidivism rates (e.g., Alexander & Orme-Johnson, 2003; Rainforth, Alexander, & Cavanaugh 2003). In addition, TM participants had more constructive cognitive processes, which the authors posited may be attributable to redressing the impact of chronic stress (Alexander & Orme-Johnson, 2003).

Conclusion

The emerging evidence indicates that spiritual meditation techniques, such as TM and mantram meditation, represent effective, well-accepted, and often brief intervention strategies for symptom management across a range of mental health conditions. The studies thus far represent a good beginning. There are several challenging issues to be addressed in future research. The sample sizes, retention, and lack of an active control group make generalization of the results, however compelling, problematic. Oman, Hedberg, and Thoresen (2006) and Linehan et al. (2006) addressed some of these concerns in their study designs. But the authors noted that the inclusion of active controls in meditation research generally has posed a difficult challenge to the field, and creative solutions to this dilemma allowing for comparative efficacy studies will enhance the clinical acceptance of these treatment paradigms.

It will be interesting to explore the active components of these treatments. Most of the interventions reviewed incorporate a relaxation component and a shift in attentional focus away from triggering thoughts and emotions. What does spirituality per se contribute in terms of incremental efficacy? As noted previously, secular forms of meditation may unintentionally enhance spirituality as part of the phenomenological experience for participants. In future research, it will be important to assess changes in spiritual experiences as well as changes in symptom severity to parse out the effective components of these interventions.

Finally, there is the question of treatment matching. Each of the interventions was applied uniformly across the samples. Future studies should assess an individual's spirituality and faith before intervention and test whether matching on those dimensions enhances effectiveness and retention.

MEDITATION AND PHYSICAL HEALTH

Recent theoretical and empirical articles have suggested that spirituality has a positive impact on physical health (e.g., Oman & Beddoe, 2005; Sulmasy, 2002). Other studies point to the beneficial physical effects of meditation, including recent research that suggests that meditation can positively affect humans on a subcellular level (Epel, Daubenmier, Moskowitz, Folkman, & Blackburnc, 2009). Considering the potentially positive physical health outcomes identified in the individual fields of spirituality and meditation, the combined team of spirituality plus meditation has the potential to create a meaningful impact. Questions such as treatment matching, dosing effects, and appropriate treatment populations continue to intrigue researchers.

Neurological Imaging Studies

fMRI studies on mindfulness meditation practitioners show increased activity in the dorso-lateral prefrontal cortex (Ritskes, Ritskes-Hoitinga, Stodkilde-Jorgensen, Baerentsen, & Hartman, 2003) and decreased activity in the anterior cingulated cortex and left frontal cortex (Baerentsen, 2001). Research suggests that these changes increase emotion regulation and ability to suppress negative emotions (Lévesque et al., 2003; see also Chapter 11 in this volume).

fMRI studies using spiritual meditation and spiritual imagery in the context of laboratory-induced pain indicate that the right ventral-lateral prefrontal cortex is uniquely activated when spiritual individuals use spiritual imagery or meditation as a pain coping resource compared with nonspiritual individuals and secular imagery (Wiech et al., 2008). When this area is activated, there is a decrease in reported pain severity (Wiech et al., 2008). There may be a value-added benefit to spirituality in the context of meditation for analgesia.

There are shared areas of neurological activation among meditation practitioners, but there are unique areas of neural activity as well. In a study of focused meditation attention, Christian nuns engaged in prayerful meditation (Newberg, Pourdehnad, Alavi, & d'Aquili, 2003). They showed elevated activation in the prefrontal cortex, inferior parietal lobes, and inferior frontal lobes. This is in contrast to Tibetan Buddhist meditators using mind-clearing meditation, who showed increased blood flow to the right thalamus, bilateral prefrontal cortex, inferior frontal lobes, and right medial temporal lobe (Newberg et al., 2001). Although this work is still in the early stages, it does show that the differences in mental focus may affect the brain differently, although we do not know yet what these changes mean from a functional standpoint.

Researchers have begun asking whether meditating on spiritual ideals, such as compassion, changes brain activity? When Tibetan Buddhist monks engaged in compassion meditation, researchers found high levels of gamma waves (attention, working memory, learning) during both baseline and meditation phases (Lutz et al., 2004). The gamma waves were higher in the meditators than meditation-naive controls, suggesting this is a unique outcome of long-term meditation practice, consistent with the concept of brain plasticity (Davidson & Lutz, 2008).

Neurology

A small study of 32 stroke patients suggested that private religious practices (including spiritual meditation and prayer) may reduce emotional distress after a stroke but do not necessarily influence physical health outcomes (Johnstone, Franklin, Yoon, Burris, & Shigaki, 2008). Similarly, other researchers have reported that spiritual coping influences mental, but not physical, health after a stroke (Giaquinto, Spiridigliozzi, & Caracciolo, 2007). Studies, however, are needed to identify whether spiritual meditation's influence on mental health affects physical rehabilitation due to mediational factors (e.g., adherence to physical therapy).

General cognitive and physical health in an older population appears to be positively affected by spiritual meditation specifically in the areas of longevity, physical health, mental health, and cognitive aging (Lindberg, 2005). A study compared TM, mindfulness meditation, relaxation, and no-treatment control groups in a sample of 73 nursing home residents (Alexander, Langer, Newman, Chandler, & Davies, 1989). After 12 weeks of 20-min daily practice, the mindfulness group, followed closely by the TM group showed greater internal locus of control compared with the other two groups. At the 3-year follow-up, the TM group, followed by the mindfulness group, showed significant improvement on learning ability, cognitive flexibility, verbal fluency, behavioral flexibility, mental health variables, blood pressure, and longevity. A number of neurological disorders, such as amyotrophic lateral sclerosis, have not been empirically studied using spiritual meditation techniques.

Cardiology

Studies of spiritual meditation focusing on cardiovascular issues include interventions to manage distress associated with the occurrence of disease (Ai et al., 2007; Ditto, Eclache, & Goldman, 2006) and to target prevention by addressing risk factors associated with the development of heart disease.

Ai and colleagues completed a series of studies exploring prayer and meditation on cardiac patients. Prayer coping following surgery was associated with optimism and fewer symptoms of anxiety and depression (Ai et al., 2007). A more recent study examined the effects of four prayer types (petitionary, conversational, ritual, and meditative) on psychosocial well-being and postoperative health among patients undergoing open-heart surgery (Ai, Tice, Huang, Rodgers, & Bolling, 2008). Their sample of 335 patients completed a series of in-person and telephone interviews and standard questionnaire assessment of depression and anxiety. They found that petitionary prayer was associated with optimism and less psychological distress than conversational prayer, meditative prayer, or ritual prayer. Interestingly, conversational prayer, the most common type endorsed by participants and in national surveys, was associated with acute stress and counteracted the beneficial contribution of optimism on psychosocial measures of well-being. This study highlights the complex nature of meditation and prayer, and supports the idea that a unitary approach to spiritual practices does not capture all aspects of the effects (see Chapter 16 in this volume).

Relaxation strategies have long been employed in interdisciplinary secondary prevention programs to reduce the impact of stress on future cardiac morbidity, yielding a reduction in cardiac arrhythmias and reduction in myocardial infarction (e.g., Benson, Alexander, & Feldman, 1975; Dusseldorp, van Elderen, Maes, Meulman, & Kraaij, 1999). In recent years, spiritual meditation practices have been incorporated into primary prevention strategies in an effort to manage modifiable cardiac risk factors, such as hypertension and metabolic syndrome.

Similar to Benson's (1975) work on the relaxation response, some studies suggest that the cardiovascular benefits seen from spiritual meditation may be related to the rhythmic nature of the mediation. Bernardi et al. (2001) used 23 healthy adults to compare recitation of the rosary to the mantra, "om-mani-padme-om," repeated on 10-s cycles. They found that a rhythm of six beats per minute induced positive psychological and physiological effects. They suggested that mantras may have evolved because of their ability to synchronize the cardiovascular rhythm, giving rise to feelings of well-being and increased responsiveness to the religious message.

A meta-analysis of nine studies on blood pressure response to TM was published by Anderson, Liu, and Kryscio (2008). TM was associated with reductions in systolic and diastolic blood pressure in both hypertensive and normotensive individuals. Such large decreases in blood pressure could yield a significant risk reduction for cardiovascular disease.

Metabolic syndrome is a constellation of risk factors (hypertension, elevated blood lipids, central adiposity, and insulin resistance) that has received increasing attention in the development of cardiovascular disease. In a 16-week trial of TM versus health education in a sample 103 patients with stable cardiac disease, Paul-Labrador et al. (2006) found TM was more effective in reducing systolic blood pressure, mean arterial blood pressure, and insulin resistance. In addition, fasting blood glucose and insulin levels were improved in the TM participants compared with health education, reflecting improved glycemic control.

Gastrointestinal Issues

There is a more robust literature emerging in the use of mindfulness-based interventions for eating disorders, such as anorexia nervosa, bulimia nervosa, and binge eating disorders (Kristeller, Baer, & Quillian-Wolever, 2006). Spirituality in the meditative component of an intervention may also be a useful tool in helping patients overcome eating disorders (Jacobs-Pilipski, Winzelberg, Wilfley, Bryson, & Taylor, 2005). In research involving the group Overeaters Anonymous, successful participants with both binge eating and bulimic disorders report that spirituality and meditation were a significant part of their success (Westphal & Smith, 1996). Approximately 92% of regular Overeaters Anonymous attendees have reported at least weekly prayer and meditation (Kriz, 2002) to help them maintain healthy eating behaviors.

Pain

Chronic pain is often accompanied by multiple psychosocial stressors and comorbidities. Spiritual meditation is beginning to be recognized as a potential tool to treat both acute and chronic pain (e.g., Carson et al., 2005; Wachholtz & Pargament, 2005, 2008).

Treating chronic pain with some form of meditation or relaxation has become common practice in psychosocial pain management (Keefe, Abernethy, & Campbell, 2005). The inclusion of spiritual meditation, however, is a less frequent addition to psychosocial pain management. Early empirical research suggests there are a number of chronic pain disorders that do respond well to the use of spiritual meditation techniques. In a study of Loving-Kindness meditation (see Exhibit 17.1) versus usual care, Carson et al. (2005), tested 43 patients with chronic back pain in an 8-week, 90-min group intervention with daily meditation practice. At the 3-month follow-up, the Loving-Kindness group showed improvements on usual pain levels, worst pain levels, emotional distress, anxiety, hostility, and phobias. Although these results are interesting, the most unique contribution is the authors' exploration of dosing, or the effect of time spent in meditation; the more time spent performing the meditation practice, the greater the pain reduction (Carson et al., 2005). The research is not yet at a point where clinicians can prescribe different "dosages" for specific conditions, but it does encourage clinicians to consider the appropriate "dose" of meditation to avoid undertreating (causing doubts about meditation efficacy) or overtreating (risking low adherence due to time burden).

For intermittent severe pain, such as migraine headaches, spiritual meditation appears to be a viable coping resource (Wachholtz & Pargament, 2008). A recent study randomly assigned 83 mediation-naive frequent migraineurs to one of four conditions: Spiritual Meditation, Internally Focused Secular Meditation, Externally Focused Secular Meditation, or Muscle Relaxation. Each of the meditation groups was asked to choose from four target phrases that would provide focus for their meditation time. The internal meditation group chose from four self-affirmation statements. The spiritual meditation group chose from four positive statements about their higher power. The external meditation group had four neutral statements. Participants practiced for 20 min a day for 4 weeks. At the post-test, the spiritual meditation group had greater decreases compared with the other groups on measures of (a) migraine frequency, (b) anxiety, and (c) negative affect. The spiritual meditation group also showed greater increases in pain tolerance, headache-related self-efficacy, spiritual experiences, and existential well-being.

It is conceivable that spiritual meditation would also be useful for other intermittent pain conditions. For example, there is evidence that spirituality may be a protective factor in sickle cell pain (e.g., Harrison et al., 2005; O'Connell-Edwards et al., 2009), and therefore spiritual coping resources may be useful. Although multiple papers suggest the use of spiritual meditation in sickle cell patients, however, there is limited empirical testing, and some evidence suggests that private religious or spiritual techniques are not associated with pain levels during a pain crisis (Harrison et al., 2005). But lack of empirical evidence prevents a definitive statement.

In the context of acute pain episodes, spiritual meditation may be an adaptive coping mechanism. Wachholtz and Pargament (2005) conducted a brief 2-week study in which meditation-naive participants were taught a spiritual meditation, a secular meditation, or a progressive muscle relaxation, and then completed a cold-pressor pain task both before and after the 2-week intervention. The spiritual meditation group reported no differences in pain severity; however, they did display greater pain tolerance, almost twice as long, compared with the other groups. The spiritual group also had improvements in anxiety, positive mood, and spiritual health (Wachholtz & Pargament, 2005). Particularly notable in this study was its focus on acute pain and brief meditation training. The results of this study suggest that meditation-naive individuals initiating spiritual meditation practice can quickly gain the ability to increase pain tolerance.

Cancer

In general, spiritual interventions have somewhat mixed empirical results in a cancer population. A meta-analysis on biological, psychological, and spiritual outcomes from spiritually based interventions for cancer patients indicated generally small to moderate effect sizes across all three outcome domains (Kaplar, Wachholtz, & O'Brien, 2004). Although spiritual meditation does not appear to have been widely tested individually, spiritual meditation has been an important component in a number of interventions. Targ and Levine (2002) randomized 181 women to a 12-week support or mind-body-spirit treatment group. Both groups showed improvements on anxiety, quality of life, and spiritual well-being. The mind-body-spirit group had greater treatment satisfaction and adherence than the support group (Targ & Levine, 2002). Although specific outcomes may not differ, for individuals who are seeking mind-body-spirit treatment, a spiritually based meditation may offer a better treatment match, therefore increasing adherence and allowing for a greater dose-response effect.

In one of the few tests explicitly exploring spiritual meditation, a centering prayer group meditation intervention was pilot tested with 10 women experiencing recurring ovarian cancer. The women received three 1-hr sessions over a period of 9 weeks while they were in the oncology clinic receiving chemotherapy. At the post-test, and 3- and 6-month follow-up periods, participants showed improvement in depression, anxiety, emotional well-being, and spiritual well-being (Johnson et al., 2009). The unique aspect of this study is that it offered a healthy alternative to the frequently reported experiences during chemotherapy of anxiety, rumination, and boredom. Furthermore, the intervention was offered during a time that was already set aside for chemotherapy, so participants were not asked to make an additional time commitment.

HIV/AIDS

The data on spirituality in an HIV-positive population are fairly encouraging (Ironson & Hayward, 2008). There are a number of validated spiritually integrated treatment manuals incorporating spiritual meditation (Pargament et al., 2004; Tarakeshwar, Pearce, & Sikkema, 2005).

Multiple studies have identified the positive psychological effects (e.g., Bormann & Carrico, 2009) and physiological effects (Bormann, Aschbacher, Wetherell, Roesch, & Redwine, 2009) of spiritual meditation among HIV-positive patients. In Bormann et al. (2009), 71 HIV-positive adults were randomly assigned to spiritual meditation or to HIV education. Both groups experienced five 90-min long weekly group classes, four follow-up individual phone calls, and another group meeting at Week 10. Individuals in the spiritual meditation condition were asked to practice a mantra-based spiritual meditation as often as possible during their daily lives. This study found a time-lagged effect of faith on cortisol. Faith levels in the previous time point influenced cortisol levels at subsequent time points suggesting that faith and meditation techniques may not have an instantaneous effect, yet over time, they can reduce the impact of stress in the context of HIV.

Conclusion

Individuals with different physical health conditions appear to respond differently to spiritual meditation. Although some conditions have more positive health outcomes (e.g., HIV, pain), other conditions have more mixed physical health results (e.g., cancer). And because spiritual meditation is so understudied in some medical conditions, no empirically based conclusions can be made at this juncture (e.g., multiple sclerosis, amyotrophic lateral sclerosis, Parkinson's disease). Furthermore, spiritual meditation appears to have different efficacy timelines depending on the condition being treated. For some conditions, the effects of spiritual meditation appear almost immediate, whereas for others, there is more of a delay before beneficial outcomes are evident. These differences in time-to-effect may be related to differences in the speed of activation for physiological mediators across various conditions. Increased diversification of research and use of biomarkers will inform this area of research and its potential usefulness in treating medical illness.

MEDITATION AND SPIRITUAL HEALTH

Spiritual forms of meditation are generally conducive to improving spiritual health. Medical students taught a combined mindfulness–loving-kindness meditation showed significant improvements on not only anxiety, depression, psychological distress, and empathy but also spiritual experiences (Shapiro et al., 1998).

Passage meditation may enhance compassionate love among hospital-based health workers (Oman, Thoresen, & Hedberg, 2010). In a study including a disparate group of health care workers (nurses, physicians, chaplains, psychologists, social workers, etc.), participants were provided an 8-week, 2-hr weekly group education session focusing on passage meditation. At the 19-week follow-up, compared with wait-list controls, passage meditators showed significant improvements in compassionate love, altruism, perspective taking, and forgiveness; treatment adherence and stress reduction mediating these findings (Oman et al., 2010).

Holy Name meditation (Oman & Driskill, 2003) or mantram meditation involves frequent brief periods of meditation during the day that focus on repeating a sacred or holy word. This technique is an effective meditation style that allows individuals to use spiritual meditation "on the fly" to achieve spiritual well-being. Forty-two hospital clinicians were taught mantram repetition (Bormann et al., 2006). After a series of 90-min classes over 5 weeks, participants had improvements in their stress, anger, and anxiety levels, quality of life, and spiritual well-being. Identifying a dosage effect by comparing frequent to infrequent meditators the team found more practice leads to greater improvements in anxiety, religious well-being, and spiritual well-being (Bormann et al., 2006). This suggests that whereas traditional forms of sitting meditation may be beneficial to patients, there is also a benefit to using in vivo forms of meditation. In vivo meditation may be particularly useful for clients initiating a meditation practice. It provides additional evidence for the "dose effect" of meditation—more practice equals better results.

Spiritual forms of meditation have been used to treat a number of mental and physical disorders. They are also receiving attention as a way to maintain wellness (Myers & Williard, 2003). With empirical evidence emerging from studies of both children (Cotton, Zebracki, Rosenthal, Tsevat, &

Drotar, 2006) and aging adults (Ai, 2000), it appears that spiritual meditation can be used to improve spiritual health across the life span. The empirical research in this field is providing greater evidence that spiritual meditation may be a positive tool for individuals. However, asking patients to engage in a practice during their already busy days may be burdensome and (initially) create more stress. The recent research into in vivo forms of meditation may provide an alternative approach to help patients successfully integrate a spiritual meditation practice into their lives.

FUTURE RESEARCH DIRECTIONS

Despite what we know about spiritual meditation, there are a number of unexplored areas. One area focuses on the identification of biomarkers and biological pathways through which spiritual meditation affects the body. The other area still largely unexplored involves tailoring spiritual meditation to the individual. To date, the research has used a "one-size-fits-all" model. The unique nature of spirituality suggests that tailoring a spiritual intervention to the patient's needs may provide better adherence and outcomes. Therefore, identifying factors predicting successful biopsychosocial–spiritual health outcomes in the context of individual differences, and specific diseases will be crucial to understanding the impact of spiritual meditation.

References

Ai, A. L. (2000). Spiritual well-being, spiritual growth, and spiritual care for the aged: A cross-faith and interdisciplinary effort. *Journal of Religious Gerontology, 11*, 3–28. doi:10.1300/J078v11n02_02

Ai, A. L., Peterson, C., Tice, T. N., Huang, B., Rodgers, W., & Bolling, S. F. (2007). The influence of prayer coping on mental health among cardiac surgery patients: The role of optimism and acute distress. *Journal of Health Psychology, 12*, 580–596. doi:10.1177/1359105307078164

Ai, A. L., Tice, T. N., Huang, B., Rodgers, W., & Bolling, S. F. (2008). Types of prayer, optimism, and well-being of middle-aged and older patients undergoing open-heart surgery. *Mental Health, Religion, and Culture, 11*, 131–150.

Alexander, C., Langer, E., Newman, R., Chandler, H., & Davies, J. (1989). Transcendental meditation, mindfulness, and longevity: An experimental study with the elderly. *Journal of Personality and Social Psychology, 57*, 950–964. doi:10.1037/0022-3514.57.6.950

Alexander, C., & Orme-Johnson, D. (2003). Walpole study of the transcendental meditation program in maximum security prisoners II. *Journal of Offender Rehabilitation, 36*, 127–160. doi:10.1300/J076v36n01_07

Anderson, J. W., Liu, C., & Kryscio, R. J. (2008). Blood pressure response to transcendental meditation: A meta-analysis. *American Journal of Hypertension, 21*, 310–316. doi:10.1038/ajh.2007.65

Astin, J. (1997). Stress reduction through mindfulness meditation: Effects on psychological symptomatology, sense of control, and spiritual experiences. *Psychotherapy and Psychosomatics, 66*, 97–106. doi:10.1159/000289116

Baer, R. (2003). Mindfulness training as a clinical intervention: A conceptual and empirical review. *Clinical Psychology: Science and Practice, 10*, 125–143. doi:10.1093/clipsy.bpg015

Baerentsen, K. (2001). Onset of meditation explored with fMRI. *NeuroImage, 13*, 297. doi:10.1016/S1053-8119(01)91640-4

Benson, H. (1975). *The relaxation response.* New York, NY: Morrow.

Benson, H., Alexander, S., & Feldman, C. L. (1975). Decreased premature ventricular contractions through use of the relaxation response in patients with stable ischemic heart disease. *Lancet, 306*, 380–382. doi:10.1016/S0140-6736(75)92895-0

Benson, H., & Proctor, W. (1984). *Beyond the relaxation response.* New York, NY: Times Books.

Bernardi, L., Steight, P., Bandinelli, G., Cencetti, S., Fattorini, L., Wdowczyc-Szulc, J., & Lagi, A. (2001). Effect of rosary prayer and yoga mantras on autonomic cardiovascular rhythms: A comparative study. *BMJ, 323*, 1446–1449. doi:10.1136/bmj.323.7327.1446

Bormann, J. E., Aschbacher, K., Wetherell, J. L., Roesch, S., & Redwine, L. (2009). Effects of faith/assurance on cortisol levels are enhanced by a spiritual mantram intervention in adults with HIV: A randomized trial. *Journal of Psychosomatic Research, 66*, 161–171. doi:10.1016/j.jpsychores.2008.09.017

Bormann, J. E., Becker, S., Gershwin, M., Kelly, A., Pada, L., Smith, T. L., & Gifford, A. L. (2006). Relationship of frequent mantram repetition to emotional and spiritual well-being in healthcare workers. *Journal of Continuing Education in Nursing, 37*, 218–224.

Bormann, J. E., & Carrico, A. (2009). Increases in positive reappraisal coping during a group-based mantram intervention mediate sustained reductions in anger in HIV-positive persons. *International*

Journal of Behavioral Medicine, 16, 74–80. doi:10.1007/s12529-008-9007-3

Bormann, J., & Oman, D. (2007). Mantram or holy name repetition: Health benefits from a portable spiritual practice. In T. G. Plante & C. E. Thoresen (Eds.), *Spirit, science, and health: How the spiritual mind fuels physical wellness* (pp. 94–112). Westport, CT: Praeger.

Bormann, J. E., Smith, T. L., Becker, S., Gershwin, M., Pada, L., Grudzinski, A. H., & Nurmi, E. A. (2005). Efficacy of frequent mantram repetition on stress, quality of life, and spiritual well-being in veterans: A pilot study. *Journal of Holistic Nursing, 23*, 395–414. doi:10.1177/0898010105278929

Butler, L. D., Waelde, L., Hastings, T. A., Chen, X., Symons, B., Marshall, J., . . . Spiegel, D. (2008). Meditation with yoga, group therapy with hypnosis, and psychoeducation for long-term depressed mood: A randomized pilot trial. *Journal of Clinical Psychology, 64*, 806–820. doi:10.1002/jclp.20496

Carmody, J., Reed, G., Kristeller, J., & Merriam, P. (2008). Mindfulness, spirituality, and health-related symptoms. *Journal of Psychosomatic Research, 64*, 393–403. doi:10.1016/j.jpsychores.2007.06.015

Carson, J. W., Keefe, F. J., Lynch, T. R., Carson, K. M., Goli, V., Fras, A. M., & Thorp, S. R. (2005). Loving-Kindness Meditation for chronic low back pain: Results from a pilot trial. *Journal of Holistic Nursing, 23*, 287–304. doi:10.1177/0898010105277651

Chan, A., Cheung, M., Tsui, W., Sze, S., & Shi, D. (2009). *Dejian* mind-body intervention of depressive mood of community-dwelling adults: A randomized controlled trial. *eCam, 09*, 1–8.

Coleman, J. W. (1999). The new Buddhism: Some empirical findings. In D. R. Williams & C. S. Queen (Eds.), *American Buddhism: Methods and findings in recent scholarship* (pp. 91–116). Abington, England: Curzon Press.

Cotton, S., Zebracki, K., Rosenthal, S. L., Tsevat, J., & Drotar, D. (2006). Religion/spirituality and adolescent health outcomes: A review. *Journal of Adolescent Health, 38*, 472–480. doi:10.1016/j.jadohealth.2005.10.005

Davidson, R. J., & Lutz, A. (2008). Buddha's brain: Neuroplasticity and meditation. *IEEE Signal Processing, 25*, 176, 172–174. doi:10.1109/MSP.2008.4431873

Ditto, B., Eclache, M., & Goldman, N. (2006). Short-term autonomic and cardiovascular effects of mindfulness body scan meditation. *Annals of Behavioral Medicine, 32*, 227–234. doi:10.1207/s15324796abm3203_9

Dusseldorp, E., van Elderen, T., Maes, S., Meulman, J., & Kraaij, V. (1999). A meta-analysis of psychoeducational programs for coronary heart disease patients. *Health Psychology, 18*, 506–519. doi:10.1037/0278-6133.18.5.506

Epel, E., Daubenmier, J., Moskowitz, J., Folkman, S., & Blackburnc, E. (2009). Can meditation slow rate of cellular aging? Cognitive stress, mindfulness, and telomeres. *Annals of the New York Academy of Sciences, 1172*, 34–53.

Fournier, J. C., DeRubeis, R. J., Hollon, S. D., Dimidjian, S., Amsterdam, J. D., Shelton, R. C., & Fawcett, J. (2010). Antidepressant drug effects and depression severity. *JAMA, 303*, 47–53. doi:10.1001/jama.2009.1943

Giaquinto, S., Spiridigliozzi, C., & Caracciolo, B. (2007). Can faith protect from emotional distress after stroke? *Stroke, 38*, 993. doi:10.1161/01.STR.0000257996.26950.59

Greeson, J. M. (2009). Mindfulness research update: 2008. *Complementary Health Practice Review, 14*, 10–18. doi:10.1177/1533210108329862

Grosswald, D. J., Stixrud, W. R., Travis, F., & Bateh, M. A. (2008). Use of the TM technique to reduce symptoms of ADHD by reducing stress and anxiety: An exploratory study. *Current Issues in Education, 10*(2). Retrieved from http://cie.ed.asu.edu/volume10/number2

Harrison, M. O., Edwards, C. L., Koenig, H. G., Bosworth, H. B., Decastro, L., & Wood, M. (2005). Religiosity/Spirituality and pain in patients with sickle cell disease. *Journal of Nervous and Mental Disease, 193*, 250–257. doi:10.1097/01.nmd.0000158375.73779.50

Hunter, L., Bormann, J., Belding, W., Sobo, E. J., Axman, L., Reseter, B. K., . . . Anderson, V. M. (2011). Satisfaction and use of a spiritually based mantram intervention for childbirth-related fears in couples. *Applied Nursing Research, 24*, 138–146. doi:10.1016/j.apnr.2009.06.002

Ironson, G., & Hayward, H. S. (2008). Do positive psychosocial factors predict disease progression in HIV-1? A review of the evidence. *Psychosomatic Medicine, 70*, 546–554. doi:10.1097/PSY.0b013e318177216c

Jacobs-Pilipski, M. J., Winzelberg, A., Wilfley, D. E., Bryson, S. W., & Taylor, C. B. (2005). Spirituality among young women at risk for eating disorders. *Eating Behaviors, 6*, 293–300. doi:10.1016/j.eatbeh.2005.03.003

Johnson, M. E., Dose, A. M., Pipe, T. B., Petersen, W. O., Huschka, M., Gallenberg, M. M., . . . Frost, M. H. (2009). Centering prayer for women receiving chemotherapy for recurrent ovarian cancer: A pilot study. *Oncology Nursing Forum, 36*, 421–428. doi:10.1188/09.ONF.421-428

Johnstone, B., Franklin, K., Yoon, D., Burris, J., & Shigaki, C. (2008). Relationships among religiousness, spirituality, and health for individuals with stroke. *Journal of Clinical Psychology in Medical Settings, 15*, 308–313. doi:10.1007/s10880-008-9128-5

Kabat-Zinn, J. (2003). Mindfulness-based interventions in context: Past, present, and future. *Clinical Psychology: Science and Practice, 10*, 144–156. doi:10.1093/clipsy.bpg016

Kabat-Zinn, J., & Borysenko, J. (1990). *Full catastrophe living: How to cope with stress, pain and illness using mindfulness meditation.* New York, NY Random House.

Kaplar, M. E., Wachholtz, A. B., & O'Brien, W. H. (2004). The effect of religious and spiritual interventions on the biological, psychological, and spiritual outcomes of oncology patients. *Journal of Psychosocial Oncology, 22*, 39–49. doi:10.1300/J077v22n01_03

Keefe, F. J., Abernethy, A. P., & Campbell, L. C. (2005). Psychological approaches to understanding and treating disease-related pain. *Annual Review of Psychology, 56*, 601–630. doi:10.1146/annurev.psych.56.091103.070302

Kozasa, E. H., Santos, R., Rueda, A., Benedito-Silva, A., Ornellas, E., Leite, F., & Leite, J. (2008). Evaluation of Siddha Samadhi Yoga for anxiety and depression symptoms: A preliminary study. *Psychological Reports, 103*, 271–274.

Kozhevnikov, M., Louchakova, O., Josipovic, Z., & Motes, M. A. (2009). Enhancement of visuospatial processing efficiency through Buddhist deity meditation. *Psychological Science, 20*, 645–653. doi:10.1111/j.1467-9280.2009.02345.x

Krisanaprakornkit, T., Sriraj, W., Piyavhatkul, N., & Laopaiboon, M. (2009). Meditation therapy for anxiety disorders. *Cochrane Database of Systematic Reviews*, 25(1), CD004998. doi:10.1002/14651858.CD004998.pub2

Kristeller, J. (2010). Spiritual engagement as a mechanism of change in mindfulness and acceptance based therapies. In R. Baer (Ed.), *Assessing mindfulness and acceptance processes in clients: Illuminating the theory and practice of change* (pp. 155–184). Oakland, CA: Context Press.

Kristeller, J., Baer, R., & Quillian-Wolever, R. (2006). Mindfulness-based approaches to eating disorders. In R. Baer (Ed.), *Mindfulness-based treatment approaches: Clinician's guide to evidence base and applications* (pp. 75–92). New York, NY: Academic Press.

Kriz, K. L. M. (2002). *The efficacy of overeaters anonymous in fostering abstinence in binge-eating disorder and bulimia nervosa.* Unpublished dissertation, Virginia Polytechnic Institute and State University, Falls Church, VA.

Lévesque, J., Fanny, E., Joanette, Y., Paquette, V., Mensour, B., Beaudoin, G., . . . Beauregard, M. (2003). Neural circuitry underlying voluntary suppression of sadness. *Biological Psychiatry*, *53*, 502–510. doi:10.1016/S0006-3223(02)01817-6

Lindberg, D. A. (2005). Integrative review of research related to meditation, spirituality, and the elderly. *Geriatric Nursing, 26*, 372–377. doi:10.1016/j.gerinurse.2005.09.013

Linehan, M. M., Comtois, K. A., Murray, A. M., Brown, M. Z., Gallop, R. J., Heard, H. L., . . . Lindenboim, M. (2006). Two-year randomized controlled trial and follow-up of dialectical behavior therapy vs therapy by experts for suicidal behaviors and borderline personality disorder. *Archives of General Psychiatry*, *63*, 757–766. doi:10.1001/archpsyc.63.7.757

Linehan, M. M. (1993). *Cognitive-behavioral treatment of borderline personality disorder.* New York, NY: Guilford Press.

Liou, C. H., Hsieh, C. W., Hsieh, C. W., Wang, C. H., Lee, S. C., & Chen, J. H. (2006). Forced and non-forced Chinese meditation studies. *World Congress on Medical Physics and Biomedical Engineering, 14*, 3602–3604.

Lutz, A., Greischar, L. L., Rawlings, N. B., Ricard, M., & Davidson, R. J. (2004). Long-term meditators self-induce high-amplitude gamma synchrony during mental practice. *Proceedings of the National Academy of Sciences of the United States of America, 101*, 16369–16373. doi:10.1073/pnas.0407401101

Myers, J. E., & Williard, K. (2003). Integrating spirituality into counselor preparation: A developmental wellness approach. *Counseling and Values, 47*, 142–155. doi:10.1002/j.2161-007X.2003.tb00231.x

Newberg, A., Alavi, A., Baime, M., Pourdehnad, M., Santanna, J., & d'Aquili, E. G. (2001). The measurement of regional cerebral blood flow during the complex cognitive task of meditation: A preliminary SPECT study. *Psychiatry Research: Neuroimaging, 106*, 113–122. doi:10.1016/S0925-4927(01)00074-9

Newberg, A., Pourdehnad, M., Alavi, A., & d'Aquili, E. G. (2003). Cerebral blood flow during meditative prayer: Preliminary findings and methodological issues. *Perceptual and Motor Skills, 97*, 625–630.

O'Connell-Edwards, C., Edwards, C., Pearce, M., Wachholtz, A., Wood, M., Muhammad, M., . . . Robinson, E. (2009). Religious coping and pain associated with sickle cell disease: Exploration of a non-linear model. *Journal of African American Studies, 13*, 1–13. doi:10.1007/s12111-008-9063-4

Oman, D., & Beddoe, A. (2005). Health interventions combining meditation with learning from spiritual exemplars: Conceptualization and review. *Annals of Behavioral Medicine, 29*, S126.

Oman, D., & Driskill, J. D. (2003). Holy name repetition as a spiritual exercise and therapeutic technique. *Journal of Psychology and Christianity, 22*, 5–19.

Oman, D., Hedberg, J., & Thoresen, C. E. (2006). Passage meditation reduced perceived stress in health professionals: A randomized controlled trial.

Journal of Consulting and Clinical Psychology, 74, 714–719. doi:10.1037/0022-006X.74.4.714

Oman, D., Thoresen, C. E., & Hedberg, J. (2010). Does passage meditation foster compassionate love among health professionals? A randomized trial. *Mental Health, Religion, and Culture, 13*, 129–154. doi:10.1080/13674670903261954

Pargament, K. I., McCarthy, S., Shah, P., Ano, G., Tarakeshwar, N., Wachholtz, A. B., . . . Duggan, J. (2004). Religion and HIV: A review of the literature and clinical implications. *Southern Medical Journal, 97*, 1201–1209. doi:10.1097/01.SMJ.0000146508.14898.E2

Paul-Labrador, M., Polk, D., Swyer, J. H., Velasquez, I., Nidich, S., Rainforth, M., . . . Merz, C. N. (2006). Effects of a randomized controlled trial of transcendental meditation on components of the metabolic syndrome in subjects with coronary heart disease. *Archives of Internal Medicine, 166*, 1218–1224. doi:10.1001/archinte.166.11.1218

Poloma, M. M., & Gallup, G. H., Jr. (1991). *Varieties of prayer: A survey report*. Philadelphia, PA: Trinity Press.

Rainforth, M., Alexander, C. N., & Cavanaugh, K. (2003). Effects of the TM program on recidivism among former inmates of Folsom Prison: Survival analysis of 15-year follow-up data. *Journal of Offender Rehabilitation, 36*, 181–203.

Rappaport, A. F., & Cammer, L. (1977). Breath meditation in the treatment of essential hypertension. *Behavior Therapy, 8*, 269–270.

Raskin, M., Bali, L. R., & Peeke, H. V. (1980). Muscle biofeedback and transcendental meditation: A controlled evaluation of efficacy in the treatment of chronic anxiety. *Archives of General Psychiatry, 37*, 93–97. doi:10.1001/archpsyc.1980.01780140095011

Ritskes, R., Ritskes-Hoitinga, M., Stodkilde-Jorgensen, H., Baerentsen, K., & Hartman, T. (2003). MRI scanning during Zen meditation: The picture of enlightenment? *Constructivism in the Human Sciences, 8*, 85–90.

Seeman, T. E., Dubin, L. F., & Seeman, M. (2003). Religiosity/spirituality and health. A critical review of the evidence for biological pathways. *American Psychologist, 58*, 53–63. doi:10.1037/0003-066X.58.1.53

Seybold, K. S. (2007). Physiological mechanisms involved in religiosity/spirituality and health. *Journal of Behavioral Medicine, 30*, 303–309. doi:10.1007/s10865-007-9115-6

Shannahoff-Khalsa, D., Ray, L., Levine, S., Gallen, C., Schwartz, B., & Sidorowich, J. (1999). Randomized controlled trial of yogic meditation techniques for patients with obsessive compulsive disorder. *CNS Spectrums, 4*, 34–47.

Shapiro, S. L., Carlson, L. E., Astin, J. A., & Freedman, B. (2006). Mechanisms of mindfulness. *Journal of Clinical Psychology, 62*, 373–386. doi:10.1002/jclp.20237

Shapiro, S. L., Oman, D., Thoresen, C. E., Plante, T. G., & Flinders, T. (2008). Cultivating mindfulness: Effects on well-being. *Journal of Clinical Psychology, 64*, 840–862. doi:10.1002/jclp.20491

Shapiro, S. L., Schwartz, G. E., & Bonner, G. (1998). Effects of mindfulness-based stress reduction on medical and premedical students. *Journal of Behavioral Medicine, 21*, 581. doi:10.1023/A:1018700829825

Shapiro, S. L., & Walsh, R. (2003). An analysis of recent meditation research and suggestions for future directions. *Humanistic Psychologist, 31*, 86–114. doi:10.1080/08873267.2003.9986927

Sulmasy, D. P. (2002). A biopsychosocial-spiritual model for the care of patients at the end of life. *The Gerontologist, 42*, 24–33. doi:10.1093/geront/42.suppl_3.24

Tarakeshwar, N., Pearce, M. J., & Sikkema, K. J. (2005). Development and implementation of a spiritual coping group intervention for adults living with HIV/AIDS: A pilot study. *Mental Health, Religion, and Culture, 8*, 179–190. doi:10.1080/13694670500138908

Targ, E. F., & Levine, E. G. (2002). The efficacy of a mind-body-spirit group for women with breast cancer: A randomized controlled trial. *General Hospital Psychiatry, 24*, 238–248. doi:10.1016/S0163-8343(02)00191-3

Uchino, B. N., Cacioppo, J. T., & Kiecolt-Glaser, J. K. (1996). The relationship between social support and physiological processes: A review with emphasis on underlying mechanisms and implications for health. *Psychological Bulletin, 119*, 488–531. doi:10.1037/0033-2909.119.3.488

Wachholtz, A. B., & Pargament, K. (2005). Is spirituality a critical ingredient of meditation? Comparing the effects of spiritual meditation, secular meditation, and relaxation on spiritual, psychological, cardiac, and pain outcomes. *Journal of Behavioral Medicine, 28*, 369–384. doi:10.1007/s10865-005-9008-5

Wachholtz, A. B., & Pargament, K. (2008). Migraines and meditation: Does spirituality matter? *Journal of Behavioral Medicine, 31*, 351–366. doi:10.1007/s10865-008-9159-2

Wachholtz, A. B., & Pearce, M. J. (2010). "Shaking the blues away": Energizing spiritual practices for the treatment of chronic pain. In T. Plante (Ed.), *Contemplative practices in action: Spirituality, meditation, and health* (pp. 205–224). Santa Barbara, CA: Praeger.

Wachholtz, A. B., Pearce, M. J., & Koenig, H. G. (2007). Exploring the relationship between spirituality, coping, and pain. *Journal of Behavioral Medicine, 30*, 311–318. doi:10.1007/s10865-007-9114-7

Walsh, R., & Shapiro, S. (2006). The meeting of meditative disciplines and western psychology: A mutually enriching dialogue. *American Psychologist, 61*, 227–239. doi:10.1037/0003-066X.61.3.227

Westphal, V. K., & Smith, J. E. (1996). Overeaters Anonymous: Who goes and who succeeds? *Eating Disorders, 4*, 160–170. doi:10.1080/10640269608249183

Wiech, K., Farias, M., Kahane, G., Shackel, N., Tiede, W., & Tracey, I. (2008). An fMRI study measuring analgesia enhanced by religion as a belief system. *Pain, 139*, 467–476. doi:10.1016/j.pain.2008.07.030

Wolf, D., & Abell, N. (2003). Examining the effects of meditation techniques on psychosocial functioning. *Research on Social Work Practice, 13*, 27–42. doi:10.1177/104973102237471

Yogi, M. M. (2001). *Science of being and art of living: Transcendental meditation.* New York, NY: Penguin.

Zylowska, L., Ackerman, D. L., Yang, M., Futrell, J. L., Horton, N. L., Hale, T. S., . . . Smalley, S. L. (2007). Mindfulness meditation training in adults and adolescents with ADHD: A feasibility study. *Journal of Attention Disorders, 11*, 737–746. doi:10.1177/1087054707308502

CHAPTER 18

RITUALS AND PRACTICES

Ellen L. Idler

In the psychological and social scientific study of religion in the 20th century, religious rites are notable for being absolutely central to the work of some leading thinkers and virtually absent from the work of others. Durkheim's *The Elementary Forms of the Religious Life* (1915/1965), van Gennep's *The Rites of Passage* (1908/1960), Turner's *The Ritual Process* (1969/1977), Wallace's *Religion: An Anthropological View* (1966), and Douglas's *Purity and Danger* (1966) are classic sociological and social anthropological texts that place ritual at the center of the understanding of what religion is and does. By contrast, major treatments of religion by psychologists William James (*The Varieties of Religious Experience*, 1901–1902/1978) and Gordon Allport (*The Individual and His Religion*, 1956), or sociologists Rodney Stark and William Sims Bainbridge (*A Theory of Religion*, 1987/1996) ignore the topic almost completely. Within the psychoanalytic canon, writing on ritual is not absent but was often used as the backdrop against which new concepts were developed: Freud (1906–1908/1959) explicated the obsessive acts of neurotics by comparing them with religious rituals. Jung (1960), in his 1937 Terry Lectures, drew attention to "original religious experience" and away from "ritualistic performances" and "codified and dogmatized creeds" (1960, pp. 4, 6) although in his later work he suggested that ritual forms and symbols express transformative, universal images and themes. Erikson's (1966) examples of ritualization at various stages of psychosocial development were explicitly nonreligious, but in his 1968 book *Identity: Youth and Crisis*, he stressed religion's importance in supporting "the ritual restoration of a sense of trust," which is the foundation of all later development (p. 106; see also Chapter 29, this volume), and in his later writings he increasingly spoke about the important role of religion. As these examples show, the differential attention to religious ritual was not a function of discipline ("psychological" vs. "social" sciences) and it was not a function of the academic fashion of one period of the 20th century versus another.

It is also the case that until the middle of the 20th century, the subject of ritual could be discussed straightforwardly as a central aspect of religion without acknowledgment of the criticism of the concept that had become the lens through which, by at least the 1980s, most Western thinkers had come to see it. In 1966, Mary Douglas's *Purity and Danger* treated religious ritual matter-of-factly as the practice of distinguishing the clean from the unclean and the inside from the outside, which could "bind believers to the higher purposes of their religion" (p. 175). By 1973, however, distinct cultural changes had taken place, leading her to write in *Natural Symbols* about the "wide-spread, explicit rejection of rituals as such. Ritual is become a bad word signifying empty conformity" (Douglas, 1973, p. 19). Douglas linked this profound shift in perception to ongoing processes of secularization and the privatization of religious experience. Whatever the causes, however, major works on ritual written since mid-century have had to address the meaning of ritual by first addressing its (assumed) meaninglessness in the modern world.

DOI: 10.1037/14045-018
APA Handbook of Psychology, Religion, and Spirituality: Vol. 1. Context, Theory, and Research, K. I. Pargament (Editor-in-Chief)
Copyright © 2013 by the American Psychological Association. All rights reserved.

Given this movement of the field, then, one might have thought that 21st-century social scientific research on ritual, if it existed at all, would be fundamentally akin to the study of a species nearing extinction—interesting for what it tells us about the past and useful for knowing the conditions of the present causing its demise. But, surprisingly, in the past decade or so there has been a real upwelling of research interest in the subject of ritual—as a living, not as a dead or dying thing—coming from the newly developing interdisciplinary fields of the evolutionary and cognitive science of religion. Ritual has again become central to the understanding of religion, as religion has again become central to our understanding of the 21st-century world in which we live. This chapter on ritual draws on the classic texts and on the newer works as well, including especially those of Bell (1992/2009); Rappaport (1999); Boyer (2001); McCauley and Lawson (2002); Seligman, Weller, Puett, and Simon (2008); and Wade (2009). Wallace wrote in 1966 that "ritual is religion in action; it is the cutting edge of the tool" (p. 102), and ritual does indeed seem to be the cutting-edge point of entry for the new wave of scholarship on this most ancient of human activities, religious observance.

One of the most notable aspects of ritual practices is their cyclical nature, a dimension we overlay on the work mentioned thus far. Sometimes the cycles are very short, with frequent repetitions in a single day. Other rituals are observed once only in a lifetime. Many accounts of ritual focus on a single type, such as puberty rituals, and consequently generalize about the entire phenomenon from a narrow perspective. In this chapter, for conceptual and theoretical clarity, we focus specifically on ritual practices that represent and are associated with religious traditions. We use the lens of a life course approach to religious ritual practice and ask (a) what religious rituals are; (b) who participates in them; (c) where they are performed; (d) when and how often they are performed; (e) why they are important; and (f) throughout the chapter, where the new research seems to be taking us. This focus on ritual swings the field of research on religion back to a more balanced approach to the study of religion as both belief *and* practice and to a more embodied, performative conception of that practice.

WHAT ARE RELIGIOUS RITUALS?

It might seem that the obvious place to start in defining what religious rituals are would be with participants' own accounts of what they are doing and what it means. We might ask, what are individuals intending by their actions? What do the actors say they are doing? What do they think have they accomplished when they are finished? As Boyer (2001) pointed out, however, acting in rituals is not quite the same as acting in other contexts: The connection between what one is actually doing in a ritual (e.g., eating a wafer dipped in wine) and what is supposed to happen afterward as a result of the act may be hard for observers and even participants to see. The essence of ritual, in fact, is that it is performed according to rules set down by others in the past and that these actions are not at all open to the motivated intentions or the self-directed agency of the individuals performing them. So it may be less useful, from a research perspective, to seek an actor's account of the meaning of his or her ritual actions than it is for just about any other type of action he or she performs. Seligman et al. (2008) thus argued that although the subjective meaning of ritual has been the entry point for most social scientific research, we may find out more by focusing on the *doing* of ritual than we can by focusing on the participants' subjective *understanding* of it.

Even the briefest reading of the anthropological literature on religious ritual reveals a bewildering array of ritual practices, present in the earliest human settlements, and in all of the world's faith traditions. At a minimum, religious rituals consist of words and acts—things that must be said (*legoumena*) and things that must be done (*dromena*; Berger, 1967). Rappaport (1999) offered a formal definition of ritual: "The performance of more or less invariant sequences of formal acts and utterances not entirely encoded by the performers" (p. 24). This definition is useful as a starting place because it says nothing about either the substance (content) of rituals or their functions (consequences). With this minimal definition, it is clear that not all ritual behaviors are religious in nature, and also that not all religious acts are rituals, but Rappaport's basic argument is that "ritual as defined here is the ground from which religion grows" (Rappaport, 1999, p. 26). *Religious* rituals, or "liturgical orders" are formal, invariant, elaborated, linked words and acts that refer to and enact the performer's relationship to the sacred. Rappaport argued that a formal definition in fact logically implies the social and material consequences that one finds in the more traditional functional approaches to defining religious ritual, including the establishment of social order, the development of morality, the generation of the concept and the experience of the sacred, and the awareness of the divine. So we take this definition as our starting point for examining the substance and functions of religious ritual.

Following Rappaport (1999), "performance" is meant to convey the condition that a ritual cannot exist without being enacted; liturgical orders may exist in books, but they are not rituals unless they are performed. Moreover, the performance of religious ritual involves everyone present, including congregants, as an "actor" with a role in the ritual, in a way that theater performances or sporting events do not encompass their audiences who are there simply as spectators. The acts and utterances of the ritual are "formal" in the sense that they take place in specific places, at specific times, they are stylized and ceremonial, and they are undertaken with great seriousness. Rappaport's definition emphasized that the performers of rituals are following prescribed patterns of behavior that were encoded by others; they are "acting out" the complex behavioral form of the ritual according to conventions established in the past. Rituals are performed "invariantly" because their historical continuity over generations and millennia can only have been preserved by "faithful" repetition; individuals may in fact recapitulate the ritual imperfectly, but the goal is to achieve similarity of performance, not to improvise or be spontaneous.

Religious rituals are composed of both utterances and deeds that form a single whole. The words said during a ritual performance are themselves "performative" (Bell, 1992/2009); they are not discursive and they do not necessarily narrate the actions that accompany them. The string of words and the sequence of acts are "fused" in a sense, from one word to the next, and one action to the next—and they are also fused across these sequences to each other, in a kind of ladder structure. Because they are fused, there is a "binariness" to ritual: Either it is being performed or not being performed (there is no halfway state); a person is within a ritual time or place or not (one does not multitask during rituals). The rungs on the ladder are the connections between the words and the deeds that reinforce the strength of the whole apparatus. The Roman Catholic Rosary is said with beads in hand, each bead marking the progress through the complete ritual (Dominican Fathers, 2012). Muslim prayer, *Salat* (or *Namaz*), is said five times a day, accompanied by a set of postures that begin from standing, move to bowing, and end with kneeling, with specific recitations at each movement (Islamic Voice, 2003). The act signals the next word, the word signals the next act.

The combination of words with acts fuses the physical, sensory experience of the ritual into a single whole with its cognitive dimensions. McCauley and Lawson (2002) proposed that "sensory pageantry" is required so that rituals, particularly the most complex and least often performed, can be remembered over time, because the body memory assists the cognitive memory. The "tuning" or coordination of individual bodies and individual memories also permits the intercalation of the physical experience and cognition of the entire group of ritual participants. Music, drumming, chanting, dance—the near-universal features of ritual practices of the world's religions—are especially powerful synchronizers. Wallace (1966) noted that there are "few, if any, religious systems in which *dancing, singing, chanting, poesy, and the playing of musical instruments* do not play an important part in ceremony" (p. 54). The 1998 National Congregations Study found that 96% of U.S. congregations of all faith traditions reported singing by congregation members, making it the single most common element found in worship services (Chaves, 2004). Fasting, as in the Muslim observance of Ramadan, is another example of the fusing of word (praise to Allah for the gift of the Qur'an) with the deed of abstaining from food from dawn until sundown

(Islam 101, 2012). As suggested by these examples, it is obvious but important to point out that the somatic experiences of rituals may be pleasurable, to the point of being wildly ecstatic and exhilarating, or slightly to extremely unpleasant, in the case of ascetic fasting, mortification, or circumcision. In fact, rituals of scarification or mutilation, that forever mark the participant, are likely among the most intensely remembered, leaving the individual with a permanently changed physical body as a felt and visible daily reminder and perhaps also an emotional sense of pride or accomplishment at having withstood the experience.

We have noted that rituals impose a binary structure on time and experience—they have an on-off quality. In addition, many rituals have internal structures first identified by van Gennep (1908/1960): The "life crisis" rituals he called *les rites de passage* move individuals (at the times of puberty, marriage, parenthood, or death) from one well-defined state to another through three stages of separation, transition, and incorporation. Turner (1969/1977) further elaborated the structure of the middle phase of the ritual, during which the participants leave their familiar world and pass through a state of what Turner called "liminality." In this transitional or limbo state, the ritual subjects are neither the people they once were, nor the people they are soon to become; they are special, vulnerable, and also dangerous because they exist outside the social order. The most important quality of this period for Turner was its capacity for creating "communitas" for those who participate, a short-lived period when the rationality of everyday life, social conventions, and structures are cast aside and participants experience altered states of consciousness and a sense of transcendence.

Not all rituals carry the drama of rites of passage, which are performed once in a lifetime. But all rituals have an internal structure with a beginning, middle, and end that carry individuals through time, from one moment of taken-for-granted everyday life, to another time or place, and then back again to daily life. That opening out of daily life carries the potential of taking the individual to the realm of the sacred, where the presence of the divine may be sensed. To summarize this discussion of the formal, structural (as opposed to the functional or substantive) aspects of ritual: A ritual must be performed to exist; its performance does not vary over time; it entails both words and physical actions; it frequently involves music or rhythm; the words and actions of the ritual are coordinated within and between performers; it creates a time unto itself, set distinctly apart from the experience of everyday life; and that time offers the opening for communicating with ancestors, spirits, gods, or God.

WHO PERFORMS RITUALS?

If ritual is the cutting edge of the tool of religion, then all people practicing religion are at least occasionally practicing ritual as well. Evidence of ritual practice, particularly in burial, goes back to the most ancient of human settlements (Wade, 2009); signs of preparation of the body and the presence of goods in the grave—ritual practices—unquestionably mark these sites as those of our human ancestors. In preparing the deceased for their journey into the next world and sending them there with messages of respect, ancient human peoples have communicated across the millennia to us as well, about the ways in which they conducted their most significant activities (Kellehear, 2007). Thus, with the important exception of the growing number of secular people in many industrial societies, religious ritual is practiced to some extent, by most human beings, around the world, and it has been a feature of human activity since the earliest human societies formed.

A second question related to who performs rituals concerns who does what within the structure of the ritual itself. As we have noted, rituals are formalized activities performed according to rules set down by someone other than the present actors. An important element of those rules governs who can do what, meaning that all participants have a specific role to play. For one thing, only insiders may participate. Membership in the group may be a matter of birth or lineage, or a result of having participated in a necessary prior ritual. Most Christian churches practice "closed communion," restricting participation in the celebration of Holy Communion to those who have been (at least) baptized a Christian, but usually there are additional requirements, including completing catechism instruction, making confession, or even being a member of the specific parish.

Among the insiders, there are well-defined roles of ritual specialists, such as priests or shamans as well as novices or initiates, elders or wise men, acolytes or assistants, and congregants. As we have said, even at the least specialized level, some prior ritual performance is usually necessary for full membership in the laity. And as we have also said, rituals involve the entire group—there are no disengaged spectators. Lay congregants kneel, sing, dance, and speak responsively; they may lay on hands to bless others, cross themselves, or pray in unison. Knowledge of how to correctly perform these activities comes through imitation, informal socialization, and formal instruction, often from earliest childhood (Wuthnow, 2000). But only those who have received additional training and consecration can assume the responsibilities of leading the ritual—in other words, prior rituals legitimize the practice of subsequent rituals. Moreover, the validity of a ritual's performance, such as a wedding, depends on the legitimacy of the one leading it, the official ordination of the priest or clergy (McCauley & Lawson, 2002).

Because of its socially structured roles, every performance of a ritual is informative. The performance tells everyone present who *is* and who *is not* a member of the group. The enactment tells them their position in the structure of the group by making their relationships with others visible, and by providing them with examples of their former, and perhaps, their future social roles. And in doing so, it provides each individual with a role that constitutes a portion, perhaps a quite central portion, of his or her social identity. As Rappaport (1999) expressed it, "in *all* [emphasis in original] rituals private psychophysical processes and public orders are at once articulated to each other and buffered against each other" (p. 105). By enacting the ritual, the performer displays his or her role to the public and at the same time internalizes it as "Who I Am."

Since earliest human history almost all people have practiced religious rituals. Ritual religious practice takes place in social groups in which individuals have membership by virtue of prior initiation rituals, so the performance of religious ritual is an expression of who and what the social group is. Moreover, the internal structure of the social group is enacted by ritual performances in which actors take on specific, highly codified roles for which they may have studied and trained for years. Religious rituals are, in a sense, stories that tell individuals and the groups of which they are members who they are and where they came from.

WHERE ARE RELIGIOUS RITUALS PERFORMED?

Religious rituals take place often, although not always, in special, sacred places. Eliade wrote that "every sacred space implies a hierophany, an irruption of the sacred that results in detaching a territory from the surrounding cosmic milieu and making it qualitatively different" (Beane & Doty, 1975, p. 144). Eliade's first example of a hierophany, or a breakthrough of the sacred into the world, draws on the dream of Jacob in the Hebrew Bible: In his dream, a ladder reached up to "the house of God, the gate of heaven" (Beane & Doty, 1975, p. 144). Other Eliade examples also draw on architectural metaphors as the locations for their hierophanies, such as "the doors of the gods" or "the sanctuary." Brandon (1975), in fact, argued that architecture itself—from Stonehenge to the Minoan sanctuaries of Crete, to the Egyptian temples—was created in the first place to serve religion; ancient cultures invested heavily in these palaces for the gods, also the settings for worship and ritual. A 1,000-year-old cathedral that took 400 years to build does not just provide a space, however beautiful, for ritual observances to take place—it is a soaring demonstration of the continuity and significance of those observances. In these places, the stories of the faith are told in the symbols and iconography present in these spaces; frescos or friezes on the walls of these buildings may depict stories from sacred texts that present-day rituals reenact, millennia later, while participants experience the awe inspired by their sacred surroundings.

More modern settings for religious worship, particularly in the United States, are diverse in size, resources, and architectural style. All have some space marked off as "sacred space," where the symbols of the faith are kept and worship services are held. A 1997 study of a sample of U.S. congregations found great variation in these physical spaces, from beautiful but expensive old buildings in need of repair and heat, to storefronts or tents set up in parking lots, but all served effectively as sacred settings for worship (Ammerman, 1997). Sometimes, as in Jacob's dream at Haran, or the appearance of the Virgin Mary at Lourdes, an ordinary place was revealed as sacred first, and the building of the altar or shrine as the location for ritual practices came second. More often in modern times, a mosque or synagogue or temple is built and subsequently sanctified by the religious rituals that come to be practiced there. In either case, the space and the ritual activities that take place there support each other in making the stories of the faith manifest.

WHEN AND HOW OFTEN ARE RITUALS PERFORMED?

One feature of ritual religious practice fundamental to its meaning is its cyclical character, and by corollary, the connection of these cycles to the lived course of life. Ritual cycles might be thought of as concentric rings, with some spinning at very high frequencies nested inside others spinning at medium frequencies, nested inside others that make their circle only once in a person's life. To consider ritual practice as a whole, one must employ definitions and formal features that apply to all of the frequencies and that optimally illuminate the connections between them. This has not often been the case with work in this area, however, and major scholarly treatments of ritual often focus rather narrowly on one cycle or another in their theorizing, generalizing about ritual practice as a whole, but providing examples only from, for example, life course transition rituals such as marriage or puberty initiation rites. For example, Wallace (1966) observed that there are calendrical rituals based on the seasons or the time of year, and noncalendrical rituals like rites of passage that occur when there are candidates or the need arises. He further argued that all societies observe both types, and additionally that the calendrical rituals are communal and concerned with the needs of the social group as a whole, whereas noncalendrical rituals may or may not be communal as they serve the purposes of individuals. A wider view of ritual cycles, however, would extend to units of time both smaller (days, parts of days) and greater than (once only) those that are captured by the concept of the annual calendar.

Figure 18.1 represents the maximum potential for religious ritual performance over the life course for an individual born into an environment in which such practice was encouraged from an early age, and

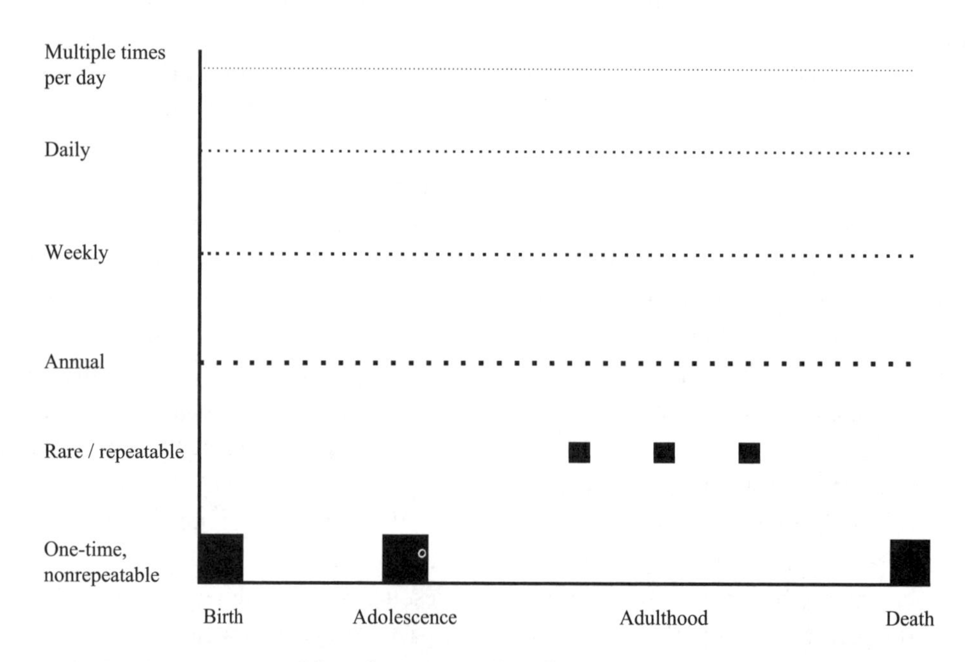

FIGURE 18.1. Potential for religious ritual performance over the life course.

who continued those practices throughout his or her lifetime. Along the *y*-axis is the frequency with which rituals are performed, which could be as often as multiple times per day, or daily, weekly, annually, rarely, or once only per lifetime. With the life course presented along the *x*-axis, Figure 18.1 presents the overlay and accumulation of ritual experience that could occur throughout the lifetime of a person with the maximum level of religious practice. An 80-year-old woman could have celebrated 80 Passovers or Easters but no more. A 30-year-old man could have said evening prayers $30 \times 365 = 10{,}950$ times. Rituals repeated multiple times per day, such as grace said before three meals per day or Muslim prayers said five times per day, could reach numbers many times that. The lowest frequency is for rituals observed only once. Many one-time-only religious rituals are tied to moments in the life course and would be appropriately performed only at that time. And there are some rituals, such as marriage or ordination in a religious institution that may not occur at all for some persons or that could potentially be performed more than once. One additional feature of Figure 18.1 to be noted is that it takes the perspective of the individual subject or participant in the ritual. One can be baptized only once, but one could participate in a baptism as a parent as many times as one has children, or even more often as a godparent, or even more often as a member of the clergy or congregation.

Figure 18.1 represents the *maximum* potential for religious ritual performance over the lifetime. The actual frequency of performance for any individual, however, in most cases would be less completely filled-in, perhaps with gaps in the lines for periods of the life course when religious observance often declines, as in young adulthood, or in old age when physical infirmity prevents attendance at worship services. One might also imagine the profile of an individual with a secular upbringing who experiences conversion in middle age, and begins a pattern of frequent observance where none had existed before. Or another profile might be seen for individuals who participate in annual or ceremonial rituals but none of those in the upper part of the figure that occur more frequently. Ritual observance profiles might also be expected to differ by faith tradition, as the requirements for ritual practice do. Our recent research in a religiously diverse regional sample found, in fact, that conservative Protestants were significantly more likely to participate in daily devotional activities than any other religious group in the sample (Orthodox Christians, mainline Protestants, Roman Catholics, Hindus, Jews, and other religions) with the single exception of Muslims, who also scored very high on this measure (Idler et al., 2009). Thus, Figure 18.1 is intended as a hypothetical maximum for potential performance, not as a norm.

Rituals Performed Only Once in the Life Course

Much of the scholarship on ritual practice, beginning especially with van Gennep (1908/1960), is focused on those rites that are performed only once with any particular individual as the subject of the ritual. Because such rituals move individuals from one state to another, because they are associated with a small number of key moments in the life course, and because they are performed relatively rarely, they are invested with great significance. McCauley and Lawson (2002) have argued that in these nonrepeatable rituals, the effects are "super-permanent" and do not need to be repeated because gods (their term is "culturally postulated super-human agents" [CPS agents]) are believed to take an intimate role, and the act is done "once and for all" (p. 122). Some such rituals are triggered by events—a Jewish *bris* must take place on the eighth day after birth, regardless of whether the day is a Sabbath or other holiday. A Jewish burial must take place within 24 hours of the death. Puberty or initiation rituals are less precisely timed; social puberty and physiological puberty are not identical, and young adolescents frequently undergo these ceremonies as a group, at a single time, or when there is an approximate correlation with their own states of physiological development. The other relevant aspect of ritual timing is length. Scholars connect the rarity and profundity of these one-time-only rituals with their longer length and greater elaboration (Rappaport, 1999). McCauley and Lawson (2002) further argued that the "sensory pageantry," or elaborateness and complexity of the ritual performance, will be greatest for these one-time rituals precisely because they are so rarely performed, making them most difficult for ritual specialists to remember; the cues elicited by the involvement of a wide range of sensory modalities increases the competence of the performers in retaining the essential invariability of the ritual. Moreover, McManus (1979) argued that the longer a ritual continues, the more profound the effect on consciousness, because the person is so radically removed from the cognitions, emotions, and social interactions of daily life that new forms of understanding and relationships can form.

Among these one-time-only rituals, those of birth and death are focused on the isolated individual subject: We enter life, and leave it, alone. Infant baptism, for Christians who practice it, is a ritual cleansing or purification by which the child is named and becomes one with the mystical body of the Church and the spiritual body of Jesus Christ. The Hindu funeral ends with the ashes of the deceased being taken to the holy Ganges River 12 days after the death and returned to the waters. In both cases, the single individual who is the subject of the ritual is surrounded by family, ritual specialists, and the religious community—the immediate society—that he or she is entering at the beginning of life or departing at the end (Parkes, Laungani, & Young, 1997). Puberty rituals, on the other hand, are quite often performed with groups of subjects—all of them fully immersed in their lives and communities, and ready to take on more adult roles in their families, societies, and religious faith. Cohort-based practices such as these—tribal "bush schools," *bar* or *bat mitzvahs*, confirmation—are especially significant to social groups. They underscore the meaning of an entire cohort's ascension to the social ranks of adulthood, presenting—to themselves and to their elders—the visible set of future leaders of the society.

Thus the one-time-only rituals are profoundly connected with the life course, marking its beginning, middle, and end. These rites are dramatic and highly sensory; they may go on for days at a time, they sometimes entail permanent physical alterations in the body, and to the extent that this new identity is a central one for the individual, he or she emerges changed forever in his or her own eyes, and in the eyes of others.

Rare but Repeatable Rituals

A second category of ritual frequency is composed of observances that may or may not take place during an otherwise-observant believer's life, and for which there is also the possibility of repeating the event. We include here marriages, pilgrimages, ordinations, and healing rituals. Such rituals are marked in Figure 18.1 as taking place in adulthood because they generally are undertaken by choice and may require the consent of a person of legal age. Thus, there is an approximate kind of life course timing connected with these rituals, but the triggers are not related to biological growth or maturation in the same way as they are in the previous group. As in the one-time-only category, these rituals are elaborate, involve sensory pageantry, and may take place as a days-long unfolding of events.

Some of these rituals (marriage, ordination) do create a significant change in social status in the same way as do the once-only rituals. But unlike those of the previous category, the social status changes here can be undone—a married person can get divorced, a priest can be defrocked. Marriage and ordination (in celibate orders) also have an interesting alternative quality—one can be the subject of one ritual or the other, but not both—or at least not until the first one has been undone. Both marriage and ordination have effects on the social group of the subjects: Marriages portend the survival of society in general and the religious group of the celebrants in particular through procreation, whereas ordination promises the persistence of the religious group's leadership and its institutional permanence.

Pilgrimages and healing rituals also have interesting relationships to each other. Unlike marriage and training for the priesthood or clergy, for which all faith traditions make provisions, the centrality of pilgrimages and healing rituals are more theologically specific. One might be a lifelong observant member of a religious faith without ever participating in either a pilgrimage or a healing ritual. Or one might make regular pilgrimages to sacred places, for purposes that may include healing. The two most-visited Christian shrines are Fatima in Portugal and Lourdes in France, both sites of visions of Mary, the mother of Jesus, and reputed to be places of miraculous healing. The *Hajj*, the pilgrimage to Mecca, one of the five pillars of Islam, is to be completed during the lifetime of faithful Muslims, if they are able, and if they can afford it, and there are no prohibitions on performing the *Hajj* more than once. Once the believer has decided to make this pilgrimage, however, specific timing is in place in accordance with the Islamic calendar. Healing rituals, on the other hand, are prompted by need and may take place in response to requests. Even if liturgical healing services are offered on a regular, calendrical basis by religious groups, they are likely to be participated in by congregants only in times of need, making them noncalendrical from the perspective of the individual.

This category of rituals, then, shares some of the characteristics of the once-only rituals: They may mark important transitions from one stage of the life course to another, they have an impact on the social structure in which they take place, and they are frequently highly elaborated. What they do not share with once-only rituals, and what is quite distinct about them, is the characteristic of individual agency that initiates them and without which they cannot take place.

Annual Rituals

Calendrical rituals occur regularly according to some cycle in nature. The annual movement of the Earth around the Sun, made observable to ancient peoples by the lengthening and shortening of daylight, provided the basis for the earliest calendrical rituals. Agricultural cycles, not unrelated to astronomical cycles, provided the basis for annual observances related to planting and harvesting. Planting and harvest rituals of the ancient world, for example, were adapted by Jews and Christians who suited them to their own purposes: Passover, the commemoration of the exodus of the enslaved Hebrews from Egypt, was timed to coincide with the barley festival of the ancient Near East; Easter followed naturally as Jesus's death and resurrection took place after he celebrated Passover with his disciples (Zerubavel, 1985). Rappaport (1999) noted that it is not coincidental that annual religious holidays tend to cluster in the fall, winter, and spring seasons, because the summer was occupied with subsistence needs, and people were too busy. All of the world's major religions observe multiple annual holidays, in which believers participate in the most fundamental rituals of the faith: The most important holidays of the major world religions would include Ramadan (Islam), Yom Kippur (Judaism), Easter (Christianity), Diwali (Hinduism), and Wesak (Buddhism) (Salamone, 2010).

The celebration of annual religious festivals, including the preparation for them, time off from work, attendance at religious services, and participation in related family observances, may be the most prominent markers of religious identity in modern societies. Less observant members of religious groups, who do not attend religious services or otherwise practice the faith of their parents may still participate in annual holiday rituals, under pressure from family or other religious group members. Unlike weekly religious observances, which are accommodated to the work week, annual holidays frequently interrupt the regular calendar of responsibilities, providing occasions for travel and extended family gatherings that may include, in addition to the religious ritual, the preparation of special foods, decoration of the home and place of worship, the wearing of special clothes, and the giving of gifts.

As annual celebrations, these occasions "mark time" in the aging of individuals and families. The level of sensory pageantry is still high, making them memorable occasions. Unlike the one-time life course rituals or the self-initiated adulthood rituals that we have discussed to this point, annual rituals provide even young children with the experience of encoded, invariant ritual that they can both remember from their past and anticipate in their future. Indeed, the role of children in certain holidays, for example, the Jewish Seder, or Muslim Eid al-Fitr, is given special status. But all annual holidays represent an opportunity to tell and retell the central stories of the faith and to enact them in ritual. Across the life course, the experience of annual holidays accumulates. By middle age, an individual with regular observances will be able to remember his or her own childhood celebrations with grandparents who are no longer alive. By the time of old age, an individual may remember similar observances going back 80 years or more, celebrated with two generations of family members now dead, and two, or even three, who come after.

The annual rituals, then, exist in the middle range of frequency. They are frequent enough to be remembered, compared, and anticipated with accuracy. And yet they are infrequent enough to be special, remembered distinctly as "the last Yom Kippur Papa was with us" or "our first Ramadan after we were married." As calendrical rituals, individual agency plays less of a role than it does for other types of rituals, particularly because there is pressure on the less observant to participate. But because they are calendrical rituals and because they originated in seasonal festivals, they mark the passage of time from one season to the next, as from Lent to Pentecost, or even from one year to the next, as in Rosh Hashanah or other religious new year observances, when the religious calendar does not coincide with the secular calendar.

Weekly Rituals

The weekly ritual of a day of rest and religious observance is a more central feature of the monotheistic religions of Judaism, Christianity, and Islam than it is of Hinduism and Buddhism. All three monotheistic faiths observe a "seven day circle" (Zerubavel, 1989), although the day chosen for the holy day, or Sabbath, is different for each. Jews began by keeping the 7th day as the day on which God rested in the Genesis account of creation. The emphasis in Jewish law on activities permitted and not permitted on the Sabbath was (and remains) essential to the meaning of the faith; Jesus's contention with these laws is a frequent theme of the New Testament. Early Christians distinguished themselves from Jews by their similar-yet-different observance of the Sabbath on the first, rather than the last day of the week. "Sunday" was the day in the Genesis account on which God created the light and the darkness; it was also the day of Christ's resurrection, the third day following the crucifixion. Islam, the third of the three monotheistic faiths, observes Friday as its holy day, distinct from both Christians and Jews. This is the day, again drawing back to Genesis, in which Adam was created (Rappaport, 1999).

Chaves (2004) studied the content of weekly religious services in a probability sample of U.S. congregations of all faiths. The performance of these weekly rituals is the single most important purpose of congregations in the United States; it is the way in which they produce religion. As we noted, music—specifically singing by the congregation—was the single most frequently occurring feature of these services. A sermon, drasha, or homily was second, and the performance of instrumental music was third; these three features occurred in more than 90% of services of all faiths. At the level of the individual, data from the 2008 General Social Survey shows that 32.4% of U.S. residents sampled said that they attended religious services nearly every week or more often. This differed by faith: For Protestants, it was 43.6%, for Roman Catholics 33.3%, and for Jews 12.2%. If we also included those who attended one to three times per month, the figures would jump to more than 50% for Protestants and Roman Catholics, and up to 25% for Jews (Association of Religion Data Archives, 2008). Thus, weekly (or almost weekly) religious ritual observances are a common feature of Americans' lives, and those observances include both speech and acts, and music, which is often a combination of the two.

We have noted that congregants are not idle onlookers at religious services, but rather they are active participants. Besides singing, they may read responsively, recite in unison and from memory, kneel or genuflect, cross themselves, or receive communion from the priest, elders, or deacons. Murphy (1979) provided an account of the Roman Catholic Mass that shows the intimate involvement of the congregation as active participants, both as single individuals and as a whole body. Beginning with the entrance of the priest at the rear of the church accompanied by singing and the rhythmic movement of incense in the air, to the priest's ascending of the altar, the leading of communal confession of sins, the reading of the Gospels, the celebration of the Eucharist, and the final passing of the Peace of Christ, the congregation as a whole is entrained and synchronized in their focus of attention, experiencing the same physical sensations, hearing the same words, feeling the same vibrations of the music, and assuming the same postures.

Over the life course, the repeated experience of the mass or another frequently celebrated rite builds up a reservoir of memories of the ritual from which the distinctive memory of a single observance would be hard to single out. Initially, however, children have to be instructed in the rituals of their faith. Orsi (2005) provided a fascinating account of the education and training of Catholic children in the United States in the 20th century, in which imitative behavior included costumed role-playing and candy wafers as substitutes for communion wafers. The invariant nature of religious rituals makes them a unique source of continuity and stability through the entire life course. In old age, lifelong weekly religious observance may become hard to sustain as functional decline sets in; however, religious congregations are frequently proactive in providing transportation to services and hearing and visual aids for those with sensory impairments. In our study of a sample of community residents in their last 12 months of life, we found no decline in average levels of attendance at religious services until the last 6 months of life, and even then the sampled respondents were attending services an average of once per month or more often (Idler, Kasl, & Hays, 2001).

Weekly ritual observance alternates with the week of school or work in the world for younger people, and perhaps with a week of social isolation and inactivity for older persons. Thus, it is a calendrical ritual, but one that is entirely socially constructed; no model exists in nature for cycles of 7 days. The sensory pageantry of the service is less elaborate than for other, less frequently performed rituals that we have discussed. But faiths differ in their levels of sensory pageantry, and if found at a lower level overall, it is certainly present to a greater or lesser degree. Finally, if there is historical individual agency evident in the very construction of a 7-day religious ritual cycle, there is also a great deal of agency evident in the participation levels of individuals, certainly more than for those rituals that occur less frequently.

Daily or Multiple Daily Rituals

The final category is for rituals that are performed once a day or more than once a day. This set of activities is engaged in throughout the entire 7-day cycle and thus takes place in homes, workplaces, and other settings of daily life. The most common specific activities falling in this category would be prayer, meditation, contemplation, yoga, and other spiritual disciplines. The 2008 General Social Survey found that 30% of U.S. respondents said they prayed once per day, and an additional 28% prayed more than once per day (Association of Religion Data Archives, 2008). As might be expected, these figures differ by faith tradition: 70% of Protestants, 60% of Roman Catholics, and 37% of Jews prayed once or more per day. As Seligman et al. (2008) pointed out, however, not all prayers are ritual prayers; supplicatory, intercessory, event-responsive prayers are not ritual prayers. Ritual prayers are "performative, repetitive, subjunctive, anti-discursive, and social (even when done alone)" (Seligman et al., 2008, p. 117). Ritual prayers are distinguished by their rigid scheduling (as in the public calls of the muezzin for prayer in Muslim countries), or by their accompanying gestures (as in the Christian sign of the cross), or by their use of ritual objects (as in the Hindu daily *puja*).

The daily or multiple-daily performance of these rituals raises a number of interesting issues. At this high level of frequency, and especially if the ritual practice is lengthy, the total amount of time during the day (every day) that the individual is spending in ritual performance may be quite great. As Rappaport (1999) noted, the balance between mundane time and sacred time may be shifted radically in the direction of sacred time, particularly in religious orders or orthodox sects in which these conditions of long temporality and high frequency are met.

McCauley and Lawson (2002) predict this dimension of sensory pageantry to be at its lowest, in that these rituals are performed in private or within the small group of the family, and the risk of forgetting something repeated so often is minimal. In the group of rituals performed in the context of daily life, however, the involvement of the physical body is a prominent feature. For many Orthodox Jews, morning prayers are accompanied by the binding of phylacteries to the forehead and arms. For the faithful Muslim, the daily prayers (*Salat*) are enacted through 11 ritual postures, which themselves are preceded by ritual ablutions of the face, hands, neck, and feet. For the Christian, making the sign of the cross by touching the forehead and chest in four places invokes in an instant the story of the crucifixion, Christ's suffering, and the complex symbol of the Trinity—Father, Son, and Holy Ghost. A continual daily immersion in such physically enacted rituals can create, as Orsi (2005) described it, a level of "body awareness that can operate below the level of consciousness" (p. 108). Orsi recounted an interview with an "activist nun" who found herself in a dangerous riot and, afraid for her life, found a memorized prayer from her childhood welling up inside her:

> She was not "saying this prayer," Margaret explained to me. The prayer was "echoing in my body." Her childhood prayer was saying her. The disciplined instruction in praying she had received as a child and adolescent, the determination of adults to embody praying in her, had done its work. (p. 108)

The extent of the individual's choice in participating in these rituals, or what we have been calling individual agency, might be expected to be at a maximum, given the privacy of daily life. Moreover, some of these rituals may be performed in private, which is completely unlike the other rituals we have discussed. Whether a private ritual has been performed or not performed would be known only to the individual. In these cases, agency is at a maximum. Other daily rituals, the Hindu *puja* or the Muslim *salat*, are done in the presence of others in the home or the workplace, and the failure to perform them would be noted and perhaps sanctioned.

To summarize this section on the frequency of ritual repetition and its association with the life course, we return to the binary nature of ritual. As we have said, there is an on–off quality, a wholly-there or wholly-not-there quality to the time and place of ritual observance. We might think of a figure–ground relationship, in which the figure is clearest where its edges meet the ground. Or we might also think of a light switch, turning on banks of giant floodlights for rituals that happen only once in a person's lifetime, or ordinary spotlights for those that happen only rarely. The space between these ritual observances could be completely dark, for quite long periods of time. Our light switch for daily rituals, however, might be likened to a small candle-bulb that does not light up a very big space. But the fact that it is turned on and off frequently could leave the individual in a nearly perpetual kind of afterglow, with only few and short periods of darkness in between.

WHY ARE RITUALS IMPORTANT? WHAT DO THEY DO TO AND FOR US?

By taking a formal or structural approach, this chapter has thus far avoided the subject of the functions of ritual. Functional explanations of social phenomena have had a long history in the social sciences, going back in fact to some of the same works in the anthropology and sociology of religion that also began the study of ritual—those of Durkheim, Mauss, and Malinowski. They conceived of societies as organic wholes, in which social actions (such as ritual) "functioned" in some way to perpetuate the society; otherwise, the society would not continue to exist. Functional explanations fell out of favor in the second half of the 20th century; they were critiqued as being ad hoc, incomplete, politically conservative, not allowing a role for individual agency, and failing to explain social change or the existence of free riders (individuals who fail to follow social norms and "ride for free" because everyone else maintains the social order for them). But, as Boyer (2001) pointed out, if you have something new and you want to know about it, it is undeniably useful to know what it does. Even if the function of a thing is not the whole story, it is certainly an important part—Boyer called understanding the function of a thing necessary, if not always sufficient. In this section, we consider not only the social functions of ritual but also the more recent and quite interesting research on its biological and psychological functions.

The Physiological Level

As we have noted, rituals consist of both words and acts—that is, they involve the complex physiological processes of the body, including its neurological, sensory, respiratory, digestive, sexual, reproductive, cardiac, and musculoskeletal systems. These physiological processes have their own cyclical patterns that interplay with the cyclical patterns of religious ritual practice that we have been delineating. Some of the most interesting new research has come from studies of the physical effects of the most frequently repeated rituals: daily prayer and meditation (see Chapters 11, 16, and 17 in this volume). Ellis (2009) studied religion's ocular behaviors, noting the universality of closing or covering the eyes in prayer. Feierman (2009) identified what he called "lower-*or*-smaller-*or*-more-vulnerable behavior (LSV behavior)," a physically portrayed submissiveness to higher authority also found in all the world's religions (p. 76). Bernardi et al. (2001) have shown that recitation of either the Ave Maria prayer or a yogic mantra recited six times per minute stabilized respiratory rates at favorable lower levels and increased the subjects' cardiovascular rhythms, also a positive outcome. Lex (1979) reported on the effect of ritual on the brain and its ability to permit right hemisphere dominance and synchronization of cortical rhythms in both right and left hemispheres. These physiological effects may be short lived, even as brief as the experience of a shiver down the spine, but if they are repeated daily or even more often, they could have long-lasting effects by altering the baseline for those functions in daily life.

The physiological effects of less frequently performed ritual performances might include these effects as well as others related to the different activities of weekly observances that take place in the social context of a congregation. Drumming, dancing, singing, gesturing, and speaking in unison may amplify effects at the individual level with reverberations and group-driven tempos that are felt physically. The rhythm of a drum may approximate the pace of heartbeats, and the singing of chants or hymns with a regular cadence will entrain the respiration of all members of the group, timing their inhaling and exhaling so that they are breathing as a single organism.

In contrast to the "activity" of weekly worship, there is the equally important withdrawal from ordinary work during the observance of the Friday, Saturday, or Sunday Sabbath (Shulevitz, 2010). On this once-a-week day of rest, Sabbath observers refrain from work completely, and substitute family-centered or contemplative activities, providing physical relaxation and relief from stress (A. D. Goldberg, 1986).

Ritual practice may and often does intersect with sexuality and fertility. Some of the intersection may be driven by the religious ritual cycle (forbidding or encouraging sexual intercourse on the Sabbath) or by the longer biological cycles of women's menstrual cycles, or childbirth, or nursing. All religions regulate marriage, either by outlawing it, as in celibate sects, or by sanctifying monogamy or even polygamy, through religious ritual. The regulation and the promotion of fertility bears a natural relationship to the rate at which religious groups reproduce themselves; Wade (2009) argued that it makes perfect evolutionary sense that religions with ritual practices that maximize fertility would more successfully perpetuate themselves.

Similarly, religious rituals concerning food are central to all faiths and can be found at cycles of varying frequency. The 2005 Baylor Religion Survey found that 19% of U.S. respondents said "table prayers" or grace before *all* meals, with only 11% saying they never prayed before meals (Association of Religion Data Archives, 2005). The Jewish Sabbath begins after sundown on Fridays with a specially prepared family meal accompanied by candle-lighting and ritual blessings. Shulevitz (2010) noted that God's introduction of the concept of the Sabbath to the children of Israel in the wilderness, after the exodus from Egypt, comes by way of an order to gather twice as much manna on Friday (the 6th day) because there would be no new manna from heaven on the 7th day. The periodic Christian celebration of the Eucharist commemorates a Passover meal, the Last Supper taken by Jesus Christ with his disciples.

The ritual alternative to eating is fasting or the deliberate abstention from eating for extended periods of time, which is sometimes, although not always, concluded with feasting, even overindulgence. R. Goldberg (2009) noted the practice of fasting in all of the world's religions, particularly the "community-centered" religions of Catholicism, Hinduism, Islam, Judaism, and Mormonism, and less so in the "noncommunalist" faiths of Buddhism and Protestantism. Physiologically, fasting may purify, detoxify, and heal the body, promote visionary or transcendental experiences, or regulate fertility. A study of cholesterol levels among Bedouin

Muslims in Israel found that the day-long fasts followed by evening feasts during the month of Ramadan resulted in significantly higher high-density lipoprotein (HDL; "good") cholesterol levels among participants compared with nonobservant Muslims; there were no differences in low-density lipoprotein or triglyceride levels or body mass index, and the participants' HDL levels returned to baseline after 4 weeks (Maislos et al., 1998).

In the field of research on religion as a factor in health outcomes, studies find a generally consistent positive effect of religious participation on survival. Some studies focus specifically on the health effects of ritual practice. The pattern of deaths around the Sabbath was studied by Anson and Anson (2001), using Israeli mortality records from 1983 to 1992. They found that for all men and for younger women, there was a significant trend of fewer deaths from all causes in the days before each Sabbath and more deaths in the days immediately following. Idler and Kasl (1992), in a study of elderly Jewish and Christian persons in the United States, found significantly fewer deaths of Christians in the 30 days before the annual Christian holidays of Christmas and Easter compared with the 30 days after those holidays. The pattern was the same for observant Jews around the Jewish holidays of Passover, Rosh Hashanah, and Yom Kippur, and as expected, there were no such patterns for either group around the other's holidays. Studies of the health effects of religiousness in general are done both at the level of the individual (e.g., Hummer, Rogers, Nam, & Ellison, 1999) and at the level of the group, that is, a comparison of one (highly observant) religious group such as the Mormons or Seventh Day Adventists with a standard population (e.g., Enstrom & Breslow, 2008). Overall the findings show a consistent pattern of lower mortality risk for the more religiously observant groups or individuals (Idler, 2011). Even though these are studies of religious participation or membership in general, it is the ritual-relevant measure of an individual's attendance at religious services or his or her membership in a ritual-laden religious group that proves to be related to longer life expectancy, and not more internal, subjective dimensions such as spirituality or the importance to the individual of their religion (Powell, Shahabi, & Thoresen, 2003). Such studies usually focus on mechanisms like lower cigarette smoking, alcohol use, or better diet and exercise, or more social support among the religiously observant. An additional pathway, suggested by the specific association of lower mortality with the public, performative dimension of religious attendance, is that religious practice may act to promote health in a direct way, by regulating one or more of the body's physiological systems that, as we have seen, are the site of ritual performance.

The Psychological Level

The psychology of ritual might be thought of most immediately as its effect on affective states, and indeed there is a long tradition of research in that area. But some of the most interesting new research concerns not the emotional but rather the cognitive dimensions of ritual. McGuire and Tiger (2009) stated it simply: "Rituals focus attention" (p. 131). Imaging studies show an enhanced flow of blood to the brain, particularly to the amygdala and the prefrontal cortex, during ritual observance (Feierman, 2009). Physiological changes in the brain's normal hemispheric function may enable ritual participants to perceive logical paradoxes or polar opposites as unified wholes, creating cognitive resolution in cases in which there was division (d'Aquili & Laughlin, 1979). At the same time, Barrett (2002) has employed theory of mind and other "ordinary" social cognitions in the study of the perception of ritual; he found that predictions about ritual effectiveness are driven by some of the same cognitive processes we use in everyday life. Boyer (2001) has called rituals "cognitive gadgets" or "*snares for thought* that produce highly salient effects by activating special systems in the mental basement" (pp. 240, 263); his work stressed the evolutionary aspects of religion, arguing that we are "wired" to practice rituals. Rituals persist because they serve functions; they somewhat miraculously collapse an elaborate and complex set of meanings and relationships into a familiar form that can be known and practiced by persons with a wide range of cognitive abilities. There is much more to learn about our human capacity for participating in and transmitting rituals. In sum, at the same time as the recent scholarship has emphasized the *practice* of ritual as opposed to its subjective *meaning*, this scholarship has concerned itself with the cognitive processes associated with these practices, particularly as they are revealed by new research on the brain.

Boyer (2001) and Fiske and Haslam (1997) have noted the analogy of the repetitiveness and contagion concerns of ritual practice with the mental illness of obsessive compulsive disorder, as did Freud (1906–1908/1959). But most research depicts the overall mental health effects of ritual practice as positive. The copresence of ritual participants and their synchronized behaviors leads the individual to feelings of deindividuation, or the loss of a sense of a separate self, and a concomitant sense of unity and positive feelings toward the group (Marshall, 2002). McGuire and Tiger (2009), in summing up the complex set of physiologically driven (through the production of endorphins, oxytocin, and dopamine) psychological effects that rituals have on human consciousness, called these effects "brainsoothing" (p. 125). Ovieda (2009), drawing on the neuroscientific theories of Antonio Damasio, argued that the practice of religious rituals engenders emotional somatic markers that may have either negative or positive content. Idler et al.'s study (2009) of religious experiences found "positive worship emotions" (feelings of energy, calm, joy, and being healed during worship services) to be more highly correlated with the importance of worship practices for the individual (music, prayer, reading sacred texts, sermons, participating in rituals, and awareness of the setting) than they were with any other dimension of religious experience. "Sad worship emotions" (crying, feeling sad, feeling goose bumps, and feeling choked up) were most highly correlated with positive worship emotions, but the overall level of sad emotions was much lower than the level of positive emotions (Idler et al., 2009). The combination of LSV (lower, smaller, vulnerable) behaviors indicative of submission to a higher authority, with the deindividuation of the self in the midst of a group exhibiting synchronized, sensorily stimulating, and well-being-enhancing behaviors may lead to emotionally satisfying feelings of being surrounded, protected, and comforted. Indeed, it is hard to see why individuals under conditions of choice would make the substantial sacrifice of time and resources required for the frequent practice of religious ritual if they did not derive, on balance, at least some positive benefit from their practice.

The Social Level

Following the insights of Durkheim and the early 20th-century social anthropologists, the primary outcome or function of religious ritual has been seen as its power to create, enhance, and maintain social structure and its solidarity. The simple functional argument is that if individuals devote significant amounts of time, energy, and resources to the performance of group-based religious rituals, the practices must be serving some purpose of benefiting and maintaining the social group, by reducing or resolving conflict, enforcing social control, reinforcing the social order and its relations of power, and promoting social harmony and cohesion. At a more complex level, in performing religious rituals, Durkheim (1915/1965) argued, societies collectively represent themselves—they reveal to themselves the whole of what and who they are. In a ritual observance, dispersed people come together to a special, sacred place. There they sing or dance or speak with others, moving and breathing in unison, performing the most important stories of their faith; the activity draws the participants into the state of *communitas* and vividly reminds them—enacts for them—that there is a whole that they are always a part of, even if the collective representations of it are only periodic. Religious rituals are simultaneously models *of* our social world and models *for* that world.

Mary Douglas (1966, 1973) has argued that the familiar form of the human body is an at-hand representation of any bounded social system, better able to represent complex social forms than other natural or man-made structures like trees or architecture. Bodies and societies have both structures and functions; they have insides and outsides, boundaries that must be protected, openings that can emit and admit, and they have a consciousness of the whole—particularly when engaged in collective representation through religious ritual. In Douglas's terms, bodies are "natural symbols" for the set of grid (social classifications) and group (social control) dimensions of a society. Douglas, however, did not develop the analogy of body and society that we have been developing here with the additional critical dimension of time. Ritual performances do capture the tie between the physical and the social body as they are performed, in the moment. But even more important, the essential dimension of ritual is that it is repeated over and over during the course of any individual's lifetime, as he or she ages and accumulates the continuous thread of ritual performance over time.

We have noted the connections between society, the body, rituals, and the passage of time. The rarely performed and one-time-only rituals move individuals from one stage of the life course to the next. Rites of passage mark the moment when boys become men and girls become women. All of an individual's life before the ritual was childhood; all of it from then on is adulthood. These turning points in individual lives also mark the flow of groups of same-age people through the social structure, a continuous progression of cohorts through the age structure of the society that infuses it with youthful energy and ideas and promise for the future. But it is at the end of life when the collective representation of the social group is perhaps most critical. Death is a threat—to the individual certainly, and to his or her family and the social structure he or she is a part of. The power of ritual, to bring people together, to have them collectively represent themselves as ongoing, persisting, living, continuous things is simultaneously a cognitive and emotional source of solace. To those at the end of life, whose own death is near, the sights and sounds of multiple younger generations are evidence of what one has done over one's life and what will carry on in one's name. For the young, experiencing the unknown of death for the first time, ritual provides a cognitive map of what to do, and the comfort of the group in doing it together. The individual may not survive—in fact, none of us will—but religious ritual, recapitulated since ancient times, is prima facie evidence that each individual self is part of something much larger, both permanent and transcendent.

FINAL THOUGHTS

We began this chapter by noting the move from the straightforward consideration of religious ritual in the first half of the 20th century, to its negation as "ritualism" in the second half, to its resurrection as a respectable topic for investigation in the 21st century. Some of the most interesting new work takes this third stage not as a romantic or in-denial return to the first, but it instead uses the skepticism of the culture to underscore the continuing power of ritual. Rappaport (1999), for example, argued that liturgical orders are public orders, and the performance of them, regardless of an individual's perceived state of grace or faith, implies the acceptance of them; the social efficacy of ritual, in fact, lies in the possible disparity between individual states and the public order. Seligman et al. (2008) tied what they see as the modern overemphasis on "sincerity" to the influence of Protestantism; they argued that we should shift our attention away from the search for inner certainty and authenticity and focus instead on practice. They see danger in perfectionistic truth standards in all of the world's religions that look only inward; ritual practice, by contrast, accepts human flaws and the consequent need for purification, over and over again, like brushing one's teeth. This new work, in fact, turns the "meaningless ritualism" critique of ritual that was so widely accepted in the 1980s and 1990s on its head: Religious ritual can succeed at all of the things we have been saying it succeeds at, whether the performer actually believes in it or not. That makes it a very powerful thing.

Religious ritual is practice that has an impact on physical, emotional, cognitive, and spiritual–religious states. There are structural similarities in the rituals of the world religions, including, importantly, ritual cycles embedded in the life course that we experience as we age. Rituals link the physical body with the social body, and many are relevant to the human cycles of eating, sleeping, having sex and babies, and eventually dying. Ritual materializes religion; it makes it available to the senses; it takes place in specific contexts, at specific times, among specific people with ongoing relationships with each other. Its effects are to reliably bring individuals into collective states with access to the transcendent, to manifest simultaneously the social hierarchy and the underlying equality of members of the social group, and to facilitate the entrainment of a complex set of cognitive, emotional, and physical states into one collective consciousness.

As an area of research, religious ritual has been entraining scholars in many fields for more than 100 years. Research in the field of religion, spirituality, and psychological and physical well-being has tended to privilege the internal, subjective beliefs and experiences of religiousness and spirituality, but that appears to be changing as exciting new theories and research techniques emerge. With these theoretical and methodological doors to religious ritual opened up, many fundamental research questions can be raised. What do the patterns of religious ritual involvement over the life course typically look like for members of different faith traditions? What do they look like for different birth cohorts within those traditions? What are the consequences of ritual practice for the body, mind, and spirit during the practice itself, and during the hours, days, and years afterward? What is the role of daily, weekly, annual, and once-only rituals during life crises or transitions? What are the consequences of ritual practice for those communities in which they are a prominent or nearly universal feature of community life, and those in which there is more diversity or in which they are mostly absent or quite unusual? Under what conditions can new rituals arise? How might individuals personalize rituals? Does belief in ritual in fact make a difference? Bringing the rich specificity and diversity of the experience of religious ritual practice into research will deepen this research and ground it in reality while drawing us out of our sometimes-superficial or simplistic approaches to the subject. Religion is not one thing, it is many things, and the best way to see that is to observe its practices. With the development of new technology for brain imaging, methods for more sophisticated epidemiologic and health research, attention to measurement and examination of the role of ritual across the life course and in aging populations, and new thinking in cognitive science and the behavioral and social sciences, much more is promised.

References

Allport, G. W. (1956). *The individual and his religion: A psychological interpretation.* New York, NY: Macmillan.

Ammerman, N. T. (1997). *Congregation and community.* New Brunswick, NJ: Rutgers University Press.

Anson, J., & Anson, O. (2001). Death rests a while: Holy day and Sabbath effects of Jewish mortality in Israel. *Social Science and Medicine, 52*, 83–97. doi:10.1016/S0277-9536(00)00125-8

Association of Religion Data Archives. (2005). *Table prayers.* Retrieved from http://www.thearda.com/quickstats/qs_69.asp

Association of Religion Data Archives. (2008). *Frequency of prayer.* Retrieved from http://www.thearda.com/quickstats/qs_104.asp

Barrett, J. L. (2002). Smart gods, dumb gods, and the role of social cognition in structuring ritual intuitions. *Journal of Cognition and Culture, 2*, 183–193. doi:10.1163/15685370260225080

Beane, W. C., & Doty, W. G. (Eds.). (1975). *Myths, rites, symbols: A Mircea Eliade reader.* New York, NY: Harper Colophon.

Bell, C. (1992/2009). *Ritual theory, ritual practice.* New York, NY: Oxford University Press.

Berger, P. (1967). *The sacred canopy: Elements of a sociological theory of religion.* New York, NY: Doubleday.

Bernardi, L., Sleight, P., Bandinelli, G., Cencetti, S., Fattorini, L., Wdowczyc-Szulc, J., & Lagi, A. (2001). Effect of rosary prayer and yoga mantras on autonomic cardiovascular rhythms: Comparative study. *BMJ, 323*, 1446–1449. doi:10.1136/bmj.323.7327.1446

Boyer, P. (2001). *Religion explained: The evolutionary origins of religious thought.* New York, NY: Basic Books.

Brandon, S. G. F. (1975). *Man and god in art and ritual.* New York, NY: Charles Scribner's.

Chaves, M. (2004). *Congregations in America.* Cambridge, MA: Harvard University Press.

d'Aquili, E. G., & Laughlin, C. D. (1979). The neurobiology of ritual trance. In E. G. d'Aquili, C. D. Laughlin, & J. McManus (Eds.), *The spectrum of ritual: A biogenetic structural analysis* (pp. 152–182). New York, NY: Columbia University Press.

Dominican Fathers. (2012). *Rosary center.* Retrieved from http://www.rosary-center.org/index.htm

Douglas, M. (1966). *Purity and danger: An analysis of the concepts of pollution and taboo.* London, England: Routledge & Kegan Paul. doi:10.4324/9780203361832

Douglas, M. (1973). *Natural symbols: Explorations in cosmology.* New York, NY: Random House.

Durkheim, E. (1965). *The elementary forms of the religious life.* New York, NY: Free Press. (Original work published 1915)

Enstrom, J. E., & Breslow, L. (2008). Lifestyle and reduced mortality among active California Mormons, 1980–2004. *Preventive Medicine, 46*, 133–136. doi:10.1016/j.ypmed.2007.07.030

Erikson, E. H. (1966). Ontogeny of ritualization in man. *Philosophical Transactions of the Royal Society of London Series B, Biological Sciences, 251*, 337–349. doi:10.1098/rstb.1966.0019

Feierman, J. R. (2009). The evolutionary history of religious behavior. In J. R. Feierman (Ed.), *The biology of religious behavior: The evolutionary origins of faith and religion* (pp. 71–86). Santa Barbara, CA: Praeger.

Fiske, A. P., & Haslam, N. (1997). Is obsessive-compulsive disorder a pathology of the human disposition to perform socially meaningful rituals? Evidence of similar content. *Journal of Nervous and Mental Disease, 185*, 211–222. doi:10.1097/00005053-199704000-00001

Freud, S. (1959). *The complete psychological works of Sigmund Freud* (the standard edition; Vol. IX, pp. 117–127, J. Strachey, Ed.). New York, NY: Norton. (Original work published 1906–1908)

Goldberg, A. D. (1986). The Sabbath as dialectic: Implications for mental health. *Journal of Religion and Health, 25*, 237–244. doi:10.1007/BF01534020

Goldberg, R. (2009). The adaptiveness of fasting and feasting rituals: Costly adaptive signals? In J. R. Feierman (Ed.), *The biology of religious behavior: The evolutionary origins of faith and religion* (pp. 190–203). Santa Barbara, CA: Praeger.

Hummer, R. A., Rogers, R. G., Nam, C. B., & Ellison, C. G. (1999). Religious involvement and U.S. adult mortality. *Demography, 36*, 273–285. doi:10.2307/2648114

Idler, E. L. (2011). Religion and adult mortality. In R. G. Rogers & E. Crimmins (Eds.), *International handbook of adult mortality* (pp. 345–377). New York, NY: Springer-Verlag.

Idler, E. L., Boulifard, D. A., Labouvie, E., Chen, Y. Y., Krause, T. J., & Contrada, R. J. (2009). Looking inside the black box of "attendance at services": New measures for exploring an old dimension in religion and health research. *The International Journal for the Psychology of Religion, 19*, 1–20. doi:10.1080/10508610802471096

Idler, E. L., & Kasl, S. V. (1992). Religion, disability, depression, and the timing of death. *American Journal of Sociology, 97*, 1052–1079. doi:10.1086/229861

Idler, E. L., Kasl, S. V., & Hays, J. C. (2001). Patterns of religious practice and belief in the last year of life. *The Journals of Gerontology, Series B: Psychological Sciences and Social Sciences, 56*, S326–S334. doi:10.1093/geronb/56.6.S326

Islamic Voice. (2003). *Health benefits of prayer postures*. Retrieved from http://www.islamicvoice.com/march.2003/living.htm

Islam 101. (2012). *How to's of fasting*. Retrieved from http://www.islam101.com/ramadan/ramadan.htm

James, W. (1978). *The varieties of religious experience*. Garden City, NY: Doubleday. (Original work published (1901–1902).

Jung, C. G. (1960). *Psychology and religion*. New Haven, CT: Yale University Press.

Kellehear, A. (2007). *A social history of dying*. London, England: Oxford University Press. doi:10.1017/CBO9780511481352

Lex, B. W. (1979). The neurobiology of ritual trance. In E. G. d'Aquili, C. D. Laughlin, & J. McManus (Eds.), *The spectrum of ritual: A biogenetic structural analysis* (pp. 117–151). New York, NY: Columbia University Press.

Maislos, M., Abou-Rabian, Y., Zuili, I., Iordash, S., & Shany, S. (1998). Gorging and plasma HDL cholesterol—the Ramadan model. *European Journal of Clinical Nutrition, 52*, 127–130. doi:10.1038/sj.ejcn.1600526

Marshall, D. (2002). Behavior, belonging, and belief: A theory of ritual practice. *Sociological Theory, 20*, 360–380. doi:10.1111/1467-9558.00168

McCauley, R. N., & Lawson, E. T. (2002). *Bringing ritual to mind: Psychological foundations of cultural forms*. Cambridge, England: Cambridge University Press. doi:10.1017/CBO9780511606410

McGuire, M. T., & Tiger, L. (2009). The brain and religious adaptations. In J. R. Feierman (Ed.), *The biology of religious behavior: The evolutionary origins of faith and religion* (pp. 125–140). Santa Barbara, CA: Praeger.

McManus, J. (1979). Ritual and human social cognition. In E. G. d'Aquili, C. D. Laughlin, & J. McManus (Eds.), *The spectrum of ritual: A biogenetic structural analysis* (pp. 216–248). New York, NY: Columbia University Press.

Murphy, G. R. (1979). A ceremonial ritual: The Mass. In E. G. d'Aquili, C. D. Laughlin, & J. McManus (Eds.), *The spectrum of ritual: A biogenetic structural analysis* (pp. 318–341). New York, NY: Columbia University Press.

Orsi, R. A. (2005). *Between heaven and earth: The religious worlds people make and the scholars who study them*. Princeton, NJ: Princeton University Press.

Ovieda, L. (2009). Is religious behavior "internally guided" by religious feelings and needs? In J. R. Feierman (Ed.), *The biology of religious behavior: The evolutionary origins of faith and religion* (pp. 141–156). Santa Barbara, CA: Praeger.

Parkes, D. M., Laungani, P., & Young, B. (1997). *Death and bereavement across cultures*. New York, NY: Routledge.

Powell, L. H., Shahabi, L., & Thoresen, C. E. (2003). Religion and spirituality: Linkages to physical health. *American Psychologist, 58*, 36–52. doi:10.1037/0003-066X.58.1.36

Rappaport, R. (1999). *Ritual and religion in the making of humanity*. New York, NY: Cambridge University Press.

Salamone, F. (2010). *Routledge encyclopedia of religious rites, rituals and festivals*. New York, NY: Routledge.

Seligman, A. B., Weller, R. P., Puett, M. J., & Simon, B. (2008). *Ritual and its consequences: An essay on the limits of sincerity*. New York, NY: Oxford University Press. doi:10.1093/acprof:oso/9780195336009.001.0001

Shulevitz, J. (2010). *The Sabbath world: Glimpses of a different order of time*. New York, NY: Random House.

Stark, R., & Bainbridge, W. S. (1996). *A theory of religion*. New Brunswick, NY: Rutgers University Press. (Original work published 1987)

Turner, V. W. (1977). *The ritual process: Structure and anti-structure*. Ithaca, NY: Cornell University Press. (Original work published 1969)

van Gennep, A. (1960). *The rites of passage*. Chicago, IL: University of Chicago Press. (Original work published 1908)

Wade, N. (2009). *The faith instinct: How religion evolved and why it endures*. New York, NY: Penguin Press.

Wallace, A. F. C. (1966). *Religion: An anthropological view*. New York, NY: Random House.

Weber, M. (1922/1963). *The sociology of religion*. Boston, MA: Beacon Press.

Wuthnow, R. (2000). *Growing up religious: Christians and Jews and their journeys of faith*. Boston, MA: Beacon Press.

Zerubavel, E. (1985). *Hidden rhythms: Schedules and calendars in social life*. Berkeley: University of California Press.

Zerubavel, E. (1989). *The seven day circle: The history and meaning of the week*. Chicago, IL: University of Chicago Press.

CHAPTER 19

RELIGIOUS AND SPIRITUAL COPING: CURRENT THEORY AND RESEARCH

Terry Lynn Gall and Manal Guirguis-Younger

For decades, religion was marginalized within the context of mainstream psychological theory and research. Yet, studies began to emerge in the mid- to late 1980s revealing religion's relevance to physical health and emotional well-being. With the advent of Pargament's (1997) seminal work *The Psychology of Religion and Coping,* this field of research ignited. Today hundreds of articles exist on religious and spiritual coping, covering an array of populations and life stressors, including physical illness (Pargament, Koenig, Tarakeshwar, & Hahn, 2004), childhood trauma (Gall, Basque, Damasceno-Scott, & Vardy, 2007), bereavement (McIntosh, Silver, & Wortman, 1993), divorce (Shortz & Worthington, 1994), and natural or man-made disasters (Maton, 1989). The purpose of this chapter is to present the major theoretical frameworks and review the measurements used in the field of religious and spiritual coping. This chapter also highlights the main empirical findings regarding religious and spiritual coping, including its prevalence, relationship to aspects of well-being, functions in the process of coping, and implications for adjustment and intervention. Finally, we consider the limitations of this research domain and suggest some future research directions. Consistent with the integrative paradigm of the psychology of religion and spirituality (see Chapter 1 in this volume), we recognize that religion and spirituality function in complex, multifaceted ways in coping with life stress. Religious and spiritual coping is a rich field of research with broad implications for the psychological, physical, social, and spiritual well-being of individuals, families, and communities.

THEORETICAL FRAMEWORKS OF RELIGIOUS AND SPIRITUAL COPING

The study of religious and spiritual coping has been approached from the viewpoint of psychosocial theories, including social–cognitive (Carone & Barone, 2001), cognitive schema (Dull & Skokan, 1995; McIntosh, 1995), attribution (Roesch & Ano, 2003), biopsychosocial (Sulmasy, 2002; Wachholtz, Pearce, & Koenig, 2007), and personality (Schottenbauer, Rodriguez, Glass, & Arnkoff, 2006). Religious and spiritual coping have also been integrated within theories pertaining to specific populations or life circumstances, such as the gate control theory of chronic pain (Rippentrop, 2005), the stress–adjustment model of acculturation (Navara & James, 2005), and terror management theory (Edmondson, Park, Chaudoir, & Wortmann, 2008). By far, the most commonly adopted theoretical approach is the transactional model of stress and coping (Lazarus & Folkman, 1984), which encompasses cognitive and behavioral processes (Bjorck & Thurman, 2007; Pearce, Singer, & Prigerson, 2006; Prado et al., 2004).

Cognitive Models

Most theories highlight the cognitive role of religion and spirituality in coping. It has been argued that religion and spirituality operate as part of a general orienting framework (Pargament, 1997) or as a superordinate schema (Dull & Skokan, 1995) that determines how a situation will be appraised, which resources will be activated, and which coping methods will be implemented in response to a stressor.

DOI: 10.1037/14045-019
APA Handbook of Psychology, Religion, and Spirituality: Vol. 1. Context, Theory, and Research, K. I. Pargament (Editor-in-Chief)
Copyright © 2013 by the American Psychological Association. All rights reserved.

Dull and Skokan (1995) proposed that as a cognitive schema, religious and spiritual factors can have an impact on a person's "illusions" about an event. For example, belief in a higher power might engender a sense of optimism, control, or meaning that would affect stress levels and perhaps health. Daaleman, Cobb, and Frey (2001) proposed that core beliefs such as spirituality can affect agency and well-being through the mediating pathways of life schema and positive intentionality. Although these models are insightful, they emphasize the cognitive role of religion in the coping process.

Transactional Model

Some researchers have adopted the transactional model of stress and coping as a framework for understanding religious and spiritual coping (Gall et al., 2005; Pargament, 1997). In the transactional model, the impact of life event stress is seen to be mediated by a person's cognitive appraisal of a situation and the selection of coping behaviors (Lazarus & Folkman, 1984). A strength of the transactional model is that it provides a conceptual scaffold or framework to illuminate the multidimensional aspects of religion and spirituality and their roles within the coping process (Park & Folkman, 1997). As Gall et al. (2005) posited, religious and spiritual resources can function at the level of person or dispositional factors (e.g., belief in God), primary and secondary appraisals (e.g., God attributions), coping behavior (e.g., prayer), coping resources (e.g., religious support), and meaning making (e.g., spiritual reappraisal).

A person's *spiritual disposition,* which includes elements such as denomination, doctrinal beliefs, religious orientation (intrinsic/extrinsic), religious–spiritual coping styles, and spiritual attachment, may drive other processes of appraisal, coping, and meaning making. Research has supported the importance of spiritual disposition in relation to the coping process. In particular, belief in a just and benevolent God seems to provide a framework of control that is experienced as more benign than that of fate (Pargament, Sullivan, Tyler, & Steele, 1982).

Religion and spirituality can also emerge at the points of cognitive appraisal and coping. For example, individuals who engage in positive spiritual appraisals report more religious coping (Shortz & Worthington, 1994), more positive reframing (Gall, 2003; Miner & McKnight, 1999), and better adjustment to negative events (Pargament et al., 1990). Individuals can also mobilize a variety of religious and spiritual coping strategies that can be public (e.g., religious service attendance), private (e.g., prayer), or nontraditional (e.g., meditation) in nature (Harrison, Koenig, Hays, Eme-Akwari, & Pargament, 2001; Pargament, 1997). For example, prayer functions in multiple ways (Bade & Cook, 2008; see also Chapter 16 in this volume) and can be effective at many levels in dealing with crises (e.g., McCullough & Larson, 1999).

People also call on various forms of religious and spiritual support when faced with stressful events (Koenig, McCullough, & Larson, 2001). For example, they may cultivate an attachment bond with a higher power, or they may pursue spiritual connections with nature (Burkhardt, 1994) and other people such as clergy (Koenig, 1997). In general, religious or spiritual support seems to predict positive health factors, such as lower morbidity for hypertension (Ferraro & Koch, 1994). In contrast, a lack of religious involvement predicts problems such as higher mortality rates (Oman & Reed, 1998; Strawbridge, Shema, Cohen, & Kaplan, 1997).

Finally, spirituality and religion can function at the level of situational meaning or reappraisal (Park & Folkman, 1997). Studies have shown that religion and spirituality often help people find meaning in stressful events (Borras et al., 2007; Cohen, 2002; Gordon et al., 2002; Murphy, Johnson, & Lohan, 2003; Vickberg et al., 2001). Stressful events can be reframed as spiritual opportunities that offer benefits (Pargament, 1997) or a chance to rearrange priorities (Angen, 2000; Emmons, 1999), gain insights (Pryds, Back-Pettersson, & Segesten, 2000), or learn lessons (Ersek & Ferrell, 1994). Spirituality can help people to see an event as part of a bigger picture or overall purpose—meanings that can support the integration of an event within one's life story (Gall & Cornblat, 2002).

Spiritual Process Model

Although the models by Dull and Skokan (1995) and Gall et al. (2005) illuminate the functional links between religious and spiritual coping and adjustment, Pargament and colleagues have argued that they may fall short in not sufficiently addressing spiritual well-being as a unique outcome of the coping process (see Chapter 1 in this volume). To address this gap, Pargament (2007) proposed a model that emphasizes the development of a relationship with one particular form of significance: the sacred. In the discovery phase of this process, an individual may draw on religious beliefs and teachings as a means to identify the sacred. As a sense of the sacred emerges and consolidates into identity, individuals enter a phase of conservation wherein they engage in religious and spiritual beliefs and practices, including coping methods, to protect that which they hold to be sacred. The sense of the sacred can be disrupted by negative events, such as bereavement (Tedeschi & Calhoun, 2006), or challenged by exposure to different beliefs or teachings. These events may trigger a spiritual struggle, followed by a phase of spiritual transformation, which can involve growth or disengagement. Those who transform their sense of the sacred and redefine their spiritual identity reenter the process of conservation, whereas those who disengage may abandon their spiritual quest permanently or until a time of new discovery.

Research has provided some support for parts of this model of spiritual development. For example, studies suggest that crisis events can have a significant impact on an individual's spiritual disposition (Brotherson & Soderquist, 2002), even for those who are considered to be more religious (Bell-Meisenhelder & Marcum, 2004; Fater & Mullaney, 2000). It is clear that the impact of events on spiritual disposition can be positive or negative (Falsetti, Resick, & Davis, 2003; Ironson, Stuetzle, & Fletcher, 2006; McMinn, Kerrick, Duma, Campbell, & Jung, 2008; Tarakeshwar, Khan, & Sikkema, 2006); however, more research is needed to identify specific factors that predict a negative versus positive impact of events on religious and spiritual beliefs. Furthermore, the impact of events on beliefs may evolve differently for religious versus nonreligious individuals (Cole, Hopkins, Tisak, Steel, & Carr, 2008). Those who are initially less religious may find it difficult to access religious coping in a positive way in response to major life events. Finally, a few studies have shown that a disruption in spiritual disposition can set the stage for spiritual growth and transformation (Ridge, Williams, Anderson, & Elford, 2008; Sorajjakool, Aja, Chilson, Ramírez-Johnson, & Earll, 2008; Thomas & Retsas, 1999).

MEASUREMENT OF RELIGIOUS AND SPIRITUAL COPING

One limitation of many religious coping studies is a reliance on single-item measures of the frequency of religious activities (e.g., service attendance, prayer) or global measures that broadly assess religion's role in coping (e.g., Religion subscale of the Brief COPE; Carver, 1997).

To address these limitations, Pargament, Koenig, and Perez (2000) developed the RCOPE, which was designed to focus specifically on religious and spiritual coping. On the basis of a literature review, the authors identified five fundamental functions of religion in coping: meaning (positive and negative religious reappraisal), control (active and passive ways of gaining mastery), comfort (spiritual connection, support, spiritual discontent), intimacy (seeking religious support from others, interpersonal spiritual discontent), and life transformation (religious direction, conversion). These fundamental functions served as a theoretical basis for the RCOPE, and coping items were developed for each area. The resulting measure included 21 religious coping methods, providing a comprehensive way to assess religion and spirituality in coping. Although the RCOPE has not been used widely in its full form because of its length, researchers have used a selection of subscales based on theoretical considerations and stressor-specific contextual factors (e.g., Gall, Guirguis-Younger, Charbonneau, & Florack, 2009).

The RCOPE was also developed in a brief format that includes positive and negative coping subscales. Positive religious coping refers to a connection with the transcendent, with others, and a vision of the world as good, whereas negative religious coping involves spiritual struggle with oneself, others, and the transcendent. The Brief RCOPE has been used widely in research examining the role of spirituality in coping with crises (Pargament, Feuille, & Burdzy,

2011). It has demonstrated reliability in a variety of samples in North America facing a variety of stressors. Moreover, the Brief RCOPE was shown to have validity within a sample of Pakistani Muslims (Khan & Watson, 2006) and was used along with qualitative interviews to develop a measure appropriate for Hindus (Tarakeshwar, Pargament, & Mahoney, 2003). Rosmarin, Pargament, and Flannelly (2009) also developed and validated a religious coping measure for use with Jewish populations, the JCOPE. Although these extensions of the RCOPE are promising, much remains to be done in terms of developing culturally sensitive measures. For example, cultural groups may differ in their levels of reliance on spiritual or religious coping and their choices of specific religious coping methods (e.g., Abraído-Lanza, Vasquez, & Echeverria, 2004; Chatters, Taylor, Jackson, & Lincoln, 2008; see also Chapters 30 and 32 in this volume).

MAJOR FINDINGS ON RELIGIOUS AND SPIRITUAL COPING

In the sections that follow, we address the use of religious and spiritual coping and its relationship to physical and psychological well-being.

Turning to Religion and Spirituality

Not surprisingly, highly religious individuals often rely on religious and spiritual strategies to cope with stress. Bell-Meisenhelder and Marcum (2004) reported that 92% of their sample of Presbyterian clergy turned to God for support after the terrorist attacks of September 11, and 74% prayed and 28% went to church more than usual. McMinn et al. (2008) also found that 88% of a sample of women married to clergy used spiritual practices (e.g., prayer) to cope with stress. Yet religious and spiritual coping are by no means limited to the highly religious. For example, family members of homicide victims (Thompson & Vardaman, 1997) and bereaved parents (Brotherson & Soderquist, 2002) rely heavily on religious coping. Also, 97% of a sample of 151 female survivors of domestic abuse reported that they relied on God as a source of comfort and strength to some degree, with 76% of these individuals stating that they relied on God a great deal in this regard (Gillum, Sullivan, & Bybee, 2006). In addition, a vast majority of individuals (90%) turned to religion as a means of coping after the September 11 terrorist attacks (Schuster et al., 2001).

Religious and spiritual coping have consistently emerged as resources to help people cope with physical illness and disability. About 63% of individuals with chronic illness stated that religious beliefs were important in their lives and that their belief in God, church, and the use of prayer helped them cope (Gordon et al., 2002). Religiosity may be particularly important for coping with life-threatening illness, such as end-stage pulmonary disease (Burker, Evon, Sedway, & Egan, 2004) and HIV/AIDS (Baesler, Derlega, Winstead, & Barbee, 2003; Siegel & Schrimshaw, 2002). For example, 78.8% of advanced cancer patients reported that religion helped them cope, and 31.6% underscored that religion played a critical role in their continued investment in life (Phelps et al., 2009). Furthermore, 55.9% prayed, meditated, or engaged in religious study daily. In another study, 51% of women who had a myocardial infarction reported being deeply religious, 66% were involved in a church group, and 78% said that religion brought them personal strength and comfort (Kamm-Steigelman, Kimble, Dunbar, Sowell, & Bairan, 2006). Religious and spiritual coping is also a common strategy for those facing mental health issues (Bhui, King, Dein, & O'Connor, 2008), including disorders such as schizophrenia (Awara & Fasey, 2008; Mohr, Gilliéron, Borras, Brandt, & Huguelet, 2007).

It is the rare study that finds religion or spirituality to be an uncommon coping strategy. Wasteson, Nordin, Hoffman, Glimelius, and Sjöden (2002) reported that religious coping was the least-used strategy compared with forms of nonreligious coping (e.g., acceptance) among patients with gastrointestinal cancer at a Swedish hospital. Religion and spirituality may not be central to coping for those who are less traditionally religious, such as those from European culture as compared with North American culture (Stifoss-Hanssen, 1999). Indeed, research has shown that certain groups rely on religious coping more than others, including older adults (Bergan & McConatha, 2000)—in particular, the rural elderly (Zorn & Johnson, 1997), African Americans and women (Levin, Taylor, & Chatters, 1994), the physically disabled (Johnstone, Glass, & Oliver, 2007), those with lower mobility (Fitchett, Rybarczyk, DeMarco, & Nicholas, 1999), and widowed individuals (Roff et al., 2007). Groups that are more religious (e.g., African Americans) may find that religious coping resources are more readily available or especially compelling choices under stressful conditions (Pargament, 1997). Also, those with fewer resources (e.g., social support, financial stability, health) may turn to religion as an additional avenue of support.

Relationship to Well-Being

Psychological health. Positive aspects of religious and spiritual coping have been linked with lower levels of distress (Tix & Frazier, 1998), less depression and anxiety (Baider et al., 1999; Braxton, Lang, Sales, Wingood, & DiClemente, 2007; Lee, 2007), less hopelessness (Arnette, Mascaro, Santana, Davis, & Kaslow, 2007), less perceived stress (Arévalo, Prado, & Amaro, 2008), and less severe posttraumatic or stress-related symptoms, such as numbness and evasion (Bell-Meisenhelder & Marcum, 2004). Religious and spiritual coping are also linked with indicators of good mental health, including greater happiness, quality of life, and psychological well-being (Abraído-Lanza et al., 2004; Ayele, Mulligan, Gheorghiu, & Reyes-Ortiz, 1999; Gillum et al., 2006; Lee, 2007) as well as greater posttraumatic or stress-related growth and positive life changes (Frazier, Tashiro, Berman, Steger, & Long, 2004; Pargament et al., 2004; Proffitt, Cann, Calhoun, & Tedeschi, 2007) within the context of significant life stress.

Physical health. Religious and spiritual factors have been related to better self-rated physical health (Boswell, Kahana, & Dilworth-Anderson, 2006), slower disease progression for HIV-1 (Ironson & Hayward, 2008), fewer complications following coronary artery bypass surgery (Ai, Wink, Tice, Bolling, & Shearer, 2009), and higher T-helper-inducer cell counts in HIV patients (Woods, Antoni, Ironson, & Kling, 1999). Most strikingly, religious and spiritual coping have been related to lower mortality rates (Fitzpatrick et al., 2007). Yet results on the religion–health link are not always consistent. Ai, Peterson, Bolling, and Rodgers (2006) found that positive religious coping (e.g., seeking spiritual support) before cardiac surgery predicted better short-term global functioning postsurgery, whereas prayer postsurgery was related to poorer functioning in cross-sectional analyses. According to the authors, the longitudinal analysis suggests that strong faith plays a protective role in recovery from postcardiac surgery, whereas the cross-sectional results suggest that the use of prayer may be mobilized to deal with a crisis situation, such as poor functioning postsurgery.

Making Sense of Contradictory Findings

Although most studies suggest a positive association between religious and spiritual coping and well-being, some have found no association with such outcomes as emotional distress (Holland et al., 1999; Kamm-Steigelman et al., 2006) or suggest a negative effect of religious coping on well-being (Roff, Durkin, Sun, & Klemmack, 2007). For example, Pargament et al. (1999) reported that collaborative, self-directing, and pleading (but not deferral) coping styles were related to greater anxiety and depression for those awaiting a loved one undergoing surgery. Richards and Folkman (1997) found that bereaved individuals who spoke of religion and spirituality in coping with the death of a loved one from AIDS reported more depression and anxiety and less positive states of mind compared with those who did not reference religion and spirituality. Similarly, spiritual coping was linked with more grief among bereaved HIV-positive individuals, particularly Whites (Tarakeshwar, Hansen, Kochman, & Sikkema, 2005). Finally, Loewenthal, MacLeod, Goldblatt, Lubitsh, and Valentine (2000) found that religious cognitions (e.g., God in control) were related to higher levels of intrusive thoughts for those coping with major life events.

Such contradictory findings may reflect methodological limitations in the measurement of religious and spiritual coping. Many studies continue to rely on global measures of religion and spirituality, which may not be sensitive indicators of adjustment in some circumstances. Links between religious coping and negative outcomes may also reflect the limitations of cross-sectional designs that cannot parse out the effects of religious coping on adjustment from the mobilizing effects of severe stress and limited resources on religious coping (Pargament, 1997). In addition, the complexity of religious coping (e.g., multifunctions) may account for some contradictory results. For example, Phelps et al. (2009) revealed that an individual's engagement in religious coping may reflect a positive process (e.g., support of a fighting spirit) in response to advanced cancer or a negative process (e.g., denial) that has implications for the well-being of the patient as well as others in the patient's life.

Are Religion and Spirituality Only a Proxy for Other Psychosocial Variables?

Despite evidence that religious and spiritual factors are related to indicators of physical and mental well-being, critics (e.g., Sloan, Bagiella, & Powell, 2001) have argued that such effects are modest at best. At worst, they may be confounded by conceptual overlap with other constructs such as social support. Such critiques raise questions about whether religious and spiritual coping add anything unique to the study of stress and adjustment. Yet, research has shown that religious and spiritual coping often contribute to well-being after controlling the effects of demographic, medical, and psychosocial variables, including global indicators of religiosity and spirituality. For example, in young adults with serious mental illness, religious strategies tied to difficulty in meaning making (e.g., feeling punished by God, questioning God's powers) were related to increases in psychological distress and perceptions of personal loss over 1 year, beyond the roles of demographic and global religious indicators (Phillips & Stein, 2007). In a longitudinal study of geriatric patients, positive religious coping predicted lower levels of depression at a 6-month follow-up beyond the contributions of age, gender, education, previous history of depression, use of electroconvulsive therapy, and social support (Bosworth, Park, McQuoid, Hays, & Steffens, 2003). In addition, Ai et al. (2009) found that the relationship between spiritual struggle, behavior coping, and excess plasma interleukin-6 among cardiac patients remained significant after controlling for medical variables.

Religious and Spiritual Coping: What Roles Do They Play?

It is not enough to establish a link between religious–spiritual factors and well-being; it is important to clarify how these factors shape the coping process. Siegel, Anderman, and Schrimshaw (2001, p. 631) outlined three pathways through which religious and spiritual factors might affect health and well-being: (a) offering a cognitive framework to interpret events, (b) enhancing coping efforts, and (c) increasing access to social support and facilitating social integration.

Studies have shown that religious and spiritual factors can provide a framework to help people interpret stressors. Gall et al. (2007) found that adult survivors of childhood sexual abuse who had a sense of a benevolent God reported greater hope and self-acceptance, two factors that predicted less depressive mood and greater resolution of the abuse. Religious and spiritual coping can also affect general coping efforts and the use of social support. Canada et al. (2006) found that religious and spiritual beliefs were linked to higher functional well-being and higher quality of life among women with ovarian cancer through the mediating pathway of active coping. In a sample of African American mothers with HIV, Prado et al. (2004) found that religious involvement predicted more active coping and accessibility of social support and less reliance on avoidance coping, factors that in turn predicted less emotional distress. Among caregivers of disabled older adults, those who used religious and spiritual coping had better relationships with those receiving their care, which in turn predicted less depression for caregivers (Chang, Noonan, & Tennstedt, 1998).

Although such findings are promising, many studies that investigate religious and spiritual coping and adjustment are limited by reliance on cross-sectional data and potential overlap in the measurement of predictor, mediator, and outcome variables. In one study, the finding that nonreligious coping accounted fully for the link between religious coping and depression was compromised by the degree of conceptual overlap between the measure of "depressive coping" and the outcome measure of depression (Zwingmann, Wirtz, Müller, Körber, & Murken, 2006). In contrast, a longitudinal study of breast cancer patients (Gall, Kristjansson, Charbonneau, & Florack, 2009) showed only weak support for the idea that a link between negative God image and emotional distress was mediated by attitudes or social well-being. Mediation models are further complicated by the possibility that associations between religious coping and outcomes may be nonlinear. In a study of spouses of lung cancer patients, Abernethy, Chang, Seidlitz, Evinger, and Duberstein (2002) found that the moderate use of religious coping was related to less spousal depression, whereas low and high reliance on religious coping were linked with more depression. Perhaps there is a level of healthy reliance on religious coping that does not preclude the use of other adaptive strategies.

The Specific Nature of Religious and Spiritual Coping

As mentioned earlier, some of the inconsistencies in this research area may reflect the use of global or nonspecific measures of religious and spiritual coping (Pargament, 1997). In a study of HIV-infected gay men (Woods et al., 1999), a global measure of religious coping was related to lower depression but not to immune markers. In contrast, specific religious activities (e.g., prayer) were related to greater presence of immune markers (CD41) but not depression. Johnstone, Franklin, Yoon, Burris, and Shigaki (2008) also found that specific religious coping, but not general religiosity, was related to better mental health for stroke patients. Such findings underscore the importance of specificity in the measurement of religious and spiritual coping.

At the very least, a distinction must be made between positive and negative religious coping, as it may have differential implications for physical and mental well-being (Pargament & Brant, 1998; Pargament et al., 2004). In a study on medical compliance in the context of congestive heart failure, Park, Moehl, Fenster, Suresh, and Bliss (2008) found that religious support and positive religious coping were associated with adherence to dietary recommendations, whereas negative religious coping was not related to any measures of adherence (cross-sectionally). Furthermore, positive religious coping and receipt of religious social support predicted better adherence, whereas negative religious coping predicted poorer adherence to recommendations regarding substance use. Pearce et al. (2006) found that negative religious coping (as compared with positive coping) was more consistently related to poorer adjustment (e.g., poor quality of life, depression) in a sample of caregivers of terminally ill patients. In another study of advanced cancer patients, positive religious coping was related to higher quality of life, and negative religious coping was related to poorer quality of life, beyond the roles of sociodemographic variables, depression history, and self-efficacy (Tarakeshwar, Vanderwerker, et al., 2006). Ai, Peterson, and Huang (2003), in studying the effects of trauma on positive expectations for Muslim refugees from Kosovo and Bosnia, found that positive religious coping was related to optimism but not hope, whereas negative religious coping was related to hope but not optimism. Finally, in a meta-analysis of 49 studies, Ano and Vasconelles (2005) reported a moderate association between positive religious coping and psychological well-being and a slight inverse relationship between positive strategies and psychological distress. They also reported a modest but consistent link between negative religious coping and poor psychological well-being.

The role of negative religious and spiritual coping should not be underestimated. Although less frequent than positive religious coping, negative religious coping can have a significant impact on adjustment (Pargament, 1997). Negative spiritual coping that manifests as anger, complaint, or pleading for a miracle in relationship to God can have negative implications for adaptation in the context of breast cancer survivorship (Gall & Cornblat, 2002). Negative religious coping was also related to greater levels of anxiety and depression in a national sample of adults; these links were heightened in the context of recent illness (McConnell, Pargament, Ellison, & Flannelly, 2006). Seeing one's mental illness as a punishment from God has been shown to predict more distress and a sense of personal loss both cross-sectionally and longitudinally (Phillips & Stein, 2007). In another study, individuals who viewed their illness and need for a lung transplant as a punishment from God experienced greater depression, anxiety, and disability from their condition

(Burker, Evon, Sedway, & Egan, 2005). Among myeloma patients during the time of stem cell collection, negative religious coping was associated with greater anxiety, depression, and transplant concerns and poorer emotional well-being immediately following stem cell transplantation (Sherman, Plante, Simonton, Latif, & Anaissie, 2009). In a longitudinal study with patients receiving medical rehabilitation, Fitchett et al. (1999) found that negative religious coping predicted lower recovery of somatic autonomy beyond the contribution of baseline measures. In another longitudinal study of medically ill elders, Pargament et al. (2001) found that negative religious coping was predictive of greater risk of mortality, after controlling for other variables.

Pargament et al. (2004) found that it is the chronic engagement of negative religious coping that has important implications for physical and mental well-being over time. The use of negative religious coping may signal that a person is engaging in a process of spiritual struggle (Pargament, 2003). If prolonged, spiritual struggle may undermine an individual's physical health. For example, Ai et al. (2010) showed that spiritual struggle was associated with increased levels of inflammatory cytokines for individuals facing cardiac surgery, thus having direct implications for the physical health and recovery of the patient (for a more in-depth presentation on the phenomenon of spiritual struggle, see Chapter 25 in this volume).

Finally, research has shown that finer distinctions may be required to further tease out the roles of negative and positive aspects of religious and spiritual coping. Burker et al. (2005) showed that measures of specific forms of religious coping (as assessed by the RCOPE) were related to emotional distress for lung transplant patients, whereas a global measure of coping (Religion subscale of the COPE) was not. Punishing reappraisal was the strategy most strongly associated with depression. In a study of adults bereaved from the homicide of a family member, Thompson and Vardaman (1997) found religious support to be related to less distress, whereas pleading, good deeds, and religious discontent were associated with greater distress. In another study, religious discontent and pleading coping were related to greater distress and lower life satisfaction for long-term breast cancer survivors, whereas religious avoidance, good deeds, and spiritually based coping were related to optimism (Gall, 2000). Researchers also need to be aware of subtle distinctions within the categories of positive and negative religious coping. In a longitudinal study on breast cancer, Gall, Charbonneau, and Florack (2011) found that women who engaged in more passive negative religious strategies (e.g., passive deferral to God) compared with more active negative strategies (e.g., spiritual discontent) reported less posttraumatic growth over the long term. Finally, in a longitudinal study following women newly diagnosed with breast cancer, Gall, Guirguis-Younger, et al. (2009) revealed that the issue of specificity in assessment was critical to understanding the trajectory of religious and spiritual coping across time. Although many negative and positive religious strategies peaked around surgery, spiritual meaning-making strategies remained elevated or gradually increased up to 2 years postdiagnosis.

INTEGRATING SPIRITUALITY IN INTERVENTION

A compelling body of evidence indicates that spirituality is implicit in many aspects of coping and can affect treatment outcome. This is one reason why researchers are beginning to examine the impact of incorporating spirituality into treatment. The evidence seems to suggest that integrating spirituality as a component of treatment can improve outcomes for both physical and mental health interventions (see Volume 2, Chapter 34, this handbook). For example, migraine sufferers exposed to meditations with spiritual content had better outcomes than those exposed to secular content (Wachholtz & Pargament, 2008). Similar results were reported by Tarakeshwar, Pearce, and Sikkema (2005), who demonstrated that an 8-week spiritually focused support group with HIV participants resulted in significant reduction in depression and improved coping. Although research in this area needs to develop further, early findings suggest that integrating spirituality can enhance clinical outcomes (e.g., Murray-Swank & Pargament, 2005). Many questions remain regarding how and when it is best to draw on spiritual resources and use them to catalyze or boost the goals of treatment.

FUTURE RESEARCH: CONSIDERING CONTEXT

There are many influences on the role of religion and spirituality in coping, and some of these influences are unique in groups defined by age and development, culture, and social role. A natural next step would be to extend the religious–spiritual coping concept to the realm of couples, families, and greater communities.

For example, some aspects of religion and spirituality and their roles in coping may be dictated by developmental factors; it is important to consider how spirituality evolves throughout the life span. There is recent evidence that children and adolescents use a variety of methods of spiritual and religious coping when faced with health issues (e.g., Benore, Pargament, & Pendleton, 2008; Pendleton, Cavalli, Pargament, & Nasr, 2002) in a way that is different from adults and generally supportive of positive coping. Park, Edmondson, Hale-Smith, and Blank (2009) found that young adult cancer survivors who had daily spiritual experiences were more likely to exhibit positive health behaviors. These authors suggested that spirituality and religion play an important role in the life choices of these young adults and may have an impact on long-term health outcomes. There is much to learn about how spirituality and religion evolve throughout the life span and the significance they have for coping with various life transitions during different developmental phases.

Spirituality and religion also play a role in various family dynamics and are invoked in crises related to couple and familial relationships (see Chapter 20 in this volume). For example, Krumrei, Mahoney, and Pargament (2009) reported that those who experience divorce often use spiritual coping, which is linked to higher levels of growth. Other important issues include the role of religious coping as compensating for a lack of support from a partner and its role in the process of forgiveness of transgressions in intimate relationships. The quality and nature of relationships within families may be influenced by the role of spirituality within the family dynamic. Although research is sparse in this area, some promising work shows that mutual disclosure about religious and spiritual beliefs enhances the quality of relationship between mothers and adolescent children dealing with disagreements, even if spirituality was considered important by only one member of the dyad (Brelsford & Mahoney, 2008). The same study reported that greater sharing of spiritual values was associated with relationship satisfaction and more collaborative resolution of disagreements. These new studies represent the beginnings of a deeper look into the role of spirituality and religion in family coping.

More broadly, cultural context must play a role in the use of religious coping. For example, how do communities use religious and spiritual resources to cope with issues such as cultural oppression (a daily stressor) or genocide (an extreme crisis)? Many communities reacted to the September 11 terrorist attacks by turning to shared prayers and vigils (e.g., Schuster et al., 2001). This is not a unique reaction, and many communities look to spirituality and religion in times of crisis that touch the whole community. Lawson and Thomas (2007) reported that survivors of Hurricane Katrina named many forms of spiritual and religious coping, both on an individual level (e.g., religious reading, prayer) and on a community level (e.g., assisting others). Respondents in this study saw coming together as a community and helping those in need as an extension of their religious and spiritual philosophy and a way of coping as a community. Similar findings emerged when looking at specific cultural groups. For example, Hazel and Mohatt (2001) reported a study on the role of spirituality in an Alaskan Native community's dealing with issues of alcohol consumption. Native spirituality, rooted in community practices and shared values, emerged as an important tool for coping and maintaining sobriety (e.g., native traditions, ceremonies, hunting). As mentioned, religious coping is also highly salient for African Americans (see Chapter 30 in this volume). For example, Bacchus (2008) reported that 97% of Black women used spirituality as a coping resource, and 69% stated that prayer was used a great deal to cope with job stress. In a qualitative study, many African American women spontaneously introduced spirituality as an important component of how they coped with being HIV-positive mothers (Polzer Casarez & Miles, 2008).

Even though some attention has been paid to the cultural dimension of religious and spiritual coping, much work remains. Understanding how other cultural and religious communities cope is crucial in a time when many serious, prolonged political conflicts are partly rooted in religious and cultural differences. The interaction of religion, spirituality, and culture is significant in forming shared values and beliefs that may affect meaning making, coping dispositions, and coping strategies. Although work has begun, more research is needed to develop measures of religious coping that will be suitable for diverse groups, such as Muslims, Hindus, and Jews, as well as substitutive mechanisms in communities adhering to secular values. For example, Van Uden, Pieper, and Alma (2004) reported that the concept of a personal God may not be salient in less theistic or religiously based cultures, such as among the Dutch. A culturally driven conceptualization of the nature of God may have a strong impact on coping during crisis and the role of spirituality. Measures also need to include strategies that reflect the perspectives of those who are nontraditionally religious or identify as spiritual but not religious.

It is clear that understanding the individual and cultural contexts of religious and spiritual coping is essential to grasping its meaning and function across religious traditions, ages, gender, social role, and ethnicity. Perhaps the most important application of these findings will be to develop spiritually integrated treatments that can support coping by mobilizing spiritual resources to achieve better management of stress and enhance clinical outcomes.

References

Abernethy, A. D., Chang, T., Seidlitz, L., Evinger, J. S., & Duberstein, P. R. (2002). Religious coping and depression among spouses of people with lung cancer. *Psychosomatics, 43*, 456–463. doi:10.1176/appi.psy.43.6.456

Abraído-Lanza, A. F., Vasquez, E., & Echeverria, S. E. (2004). En las manos de Dios (In God's hands): Religious and other forms of coping among Latinos with arthritis. *Journal of Consulting and Clinical Psychology, 72*, 91–102. doi:10.1037/0022-006X.72.1.91

Ai, A. L., Pargament, K., Kronfol, Z., Tice, T. N., & Appel, H. (2010). Pathways to postoperative hostility in cardiac patients: Mediation of coping, spiritual struggle, and interleukin-6. *Journal of Health Psychology, 15*, 186–195. doi:10.1177/1359105309345556

Ai, A. L., Peterson, C., Bolling, S. F., & Rodgers, W. (2006). Depression, faith-based coping, and short-term postoperative global functioning in adult and older patients undergoing cardiac surgery. *Journal of Psychosomatic Research, 60*, 21–28. doi:10.1016/j.jpsychores.2005.06.082

Ai, A. L., Peterson, C., & Huang, B. (2003). The effect of religious-spiritual coping on positive attitudes of adult Muslim refugees from Kosovo and Bosnia. *The International Journal for the Psychology of Religion, 13*, 29–47. doi:10.1207/S15327582IJPR1301_04

Ai, A. L., Wink, P., Tice, T. N., Bolling, S. F., & Shearer, M. (2009). Prayer and reverence in naturalistic, aesthetic, and socio-moral contexts predicted fewer complications following coronary artery bypass. *Journal of Behavioral Medicine, 32*, 570–581. doi:10.1007/s10865-009-9228-1

Angen, M. (2000, June). *Meaning making in illness: A potent human magic.* Presented at the 2000 Conference on Meaning, Vancouver, British Columbia, Canada. Retrieved from http://www.meaning.ca/pdf/2000proceedings/maureen_angen.pdf

Ano, G. G., & Vasconelles, E. B. (2005). Religious coping and psychological adjustment to stress: A meta-analysis. *Journal of Clinical Psychology, 61*, 461–480. doi:10.1002/jclp.20049

Arévalo, S., Prado, G., & Amaro, H. (2008). Spirituality, sense of coherence, and coping responses in women receiving treatment for alcohol and drug addiction. *Evaluation and Program Planning, 31*, 113–123. doi:10.1016/j.evalprogplan.2007.05.009

Arnette, N. C., Mascaro, N., Santana, M. C., Davis, S., & Kaslow, N. J. (2007). Enhancing spiritual well-being among suicidal African American female survivors of intimate partner violence. *Journal of Clinical Psychology, 63*, 909–924. doi:10.1002/jclp.20403

Awara, M., & Fasey, C. (2008). Is spirituality worth exploring in psychiatric out-patient clinics? *Journal of Mental Health, 17*, 183–191. doi:10.1080/09638230701498390

Ayele, H., Mulligan, T., Gheorghiu, S., & Reyes-Ortiz, C. (1999). Religious activity improves life satisfaction for some physicians and older patients. *Journal of the American Geriatrics Society, 47*, 453–455.

Bacchus, D. (2008). Coping with work-related stress: A study of the use of coping resources among professional black women. *Journal of Ethnic and Cultural Diversity in Social Work, 17*, 60–81. doi:10.1080/15313200801906443

Bade, M. K., & Cook, S. W. (2008). Functions of Christian prayer in the coping process. *Journal for the*

Scientific Study of Religion, 47, 123–133. doi:10.1111/j.1468-5906.2008.00396.x

Baesler, E. J., Derlega, V. J., Winstead, B. A., & Barbee, A. (2003). Prayer as interpersonal coping in the lives of mothers with HIV. *Women and Therapy, 26*, 283–295. doi:10.1300/J015v26n03_07

Baider, L., Russak, S. M., Perry, S., Kash, K., Gronert, M., Fox, B., . . . Kaplan-Denour, A. (1999). The role of religious and spiritual beliefs in coping with malignant melanoma: An Israeli sample. *Psycho-Oncology, 8*, 27–35. doi:10.1002/(SICI)1099-1611(199901/02)8:1<27::AID-PON334>3.0.CO;2-V

Bell-Meisenhelder, J., & Marcum, J. P. (2004). Responses of clergy to 9/11: Posttraumatic stress, coping, and religious outcomes. *Journal for the Scientific Study of Religion, 43*, 547–554. doi:10.1111/j.1468-5906.2004.00255.x

Benore, E., Pargament, K. I., & Pendleton, S. (2008). An initial examination of religious coping in children with asthma. *The International Journal for the Psychology of Religion, 18*, 267–290. doi:10.1080/10508610802229197

Bergan, A., & McConatha, J. T. (2000). Religiosity and life satisfaction. *Activities, Adaptation, and Aging, 24*, 23–34. doi:10.1300/J016v24n03_02

Bhui, K., King, M., Dein, S., & O'Connor, W. (2008). Ethnicity and religious coping with mental distress. *Journal of Mental Health, 17*, 141–151. doi:10.1080/09638230701498408

Bjorck, J. P., & Thurman, J. W. (2007). Negative life events, patterns of positive and negative religious coping, and psychological functioning. *Journal for the Scientific Study of Religion, 46*, 159–167. doi:10.1111/j.1468-5906.2007.00348.x

Borras, L., Mohr, S., Brandt, P.-Y., Gilliéron, C., Eytan, A., & Huguelet, P. (2007). Religious beliefs in schizophrenia: Their relevance for adherence to treatment. *Schizophrenia Bulletin, 33*, 1238–1246. doi:10.1093/schbul/sbl070

Boswell, G. H., Kahana, E., & Dilworth-Anderson, P. (2006). Spirituality and healthy lifestyle behaviors: Stress counter-balancing effects on the well-being of older adults. *Journal of Religion and Health, 45*, 587–602. doi:10.1007/s10943-006-9060-7

Bosworth, H. B., Park, K.-S., McQuoid, D. R., Hays, J. C., & Steffens, D. C. (2003). The impact of religious practice and religious coping on geriatric depression. *International Journal of Geriatric Psychiatry, 18*, 905–914. doi:10.1002/gps.945

Braxton, N. D., Lang, D. L., Sales, J. M., Wingood, G. M., & DiClemente, R. J. (2007). The role of spirituality in sustaining the psychological well-being of HIV-positive black women. *Women and Health, 46*, 113–129. doi:10.1300/J013v46n02_08

Brelsford, G. M., & Mahoney, A. (2008). Spiritual disclosure between older adolescents and their mothers. *Journal of Family Psychology, 22*, 62–70. doi:10.1037/0893-3200.22.1.62

Brotherson, S. E., & Soderquist, J. (2002). Coping with a child's death: Spiritual issues and therapeutic implications. *Journal of Family Psychotherapy, 13*, 53–86. doi:10.1300/J085v13n01_04

Burker, E. J., Evon, D. M., Sedway, J. A., & Egan, T. (2004). Religious coping, psychological distress and disability among patients with end-stage pulmonary disease. *Journal of Clinical Psychology in Medical Settings, 11*, 179–193. doi:10.1023/B:JOCS.0000037612.31730.56

Burker, E. J., Evon, D. M., Sedway, J. A., & Egan, T. (2005). Religious and non-religious coping in lung transplant candidates: Does adding God to the picture tell us more? *Journal of Behavioral Medicine, 28*, 513–526. doi:10.1007/s10865-005-9025-4

Burkhardt, M. A. (1994). Becoming and connecting: Elements of spirituality for women. *Holistic Nursing Practice, 8*(4), 12–21.

Canada, A. L., Parker, P. A., de Moor, J. S., Basen-Engquist, K., Ramondetta, L. M., & Cohen, L. (2006). Active coping mediates the association between religion/spirituality and quality of life in ovarian cancer. *Gynecologic Oncology, 101*, 102–107. doi:10.1016/j.ygyno.2005.09.045

Carone, D. A., & Barone, D. F. (2001). A social cognitive perspective on religious beliefs: Their functions and impact on coping and psychotherapy. *Clinical Psychology Review, 21*, 989–1003. doi:10.1016/S0272-7358(00)00078-7

Carver, C. S. (1997). You want to measure coping but your protocol's too long: Consider the Brief COPE. *International Journal of Behavioral Medicine, 4*, 92–100. doi:10.1207/s15327558ijbm0401_6

Chang, B-H., Noonan, A. E., & Tennstedt, S. L. (1998). The role of religion/spirituality in coping with caregiving for disabled elders. *The Gerontologist, 38*, 463–470. doi:10.1093/geront/38.4.463

Chatters, L. M., Taylor, R. J., Jackson, J. S., & Lincoln, K. D. (2008). Religious coping among African American, Caribbean blacks, and non-Hispanic whites. *Journal of Community Psychology, 36*, 371–386. doi:10.1002/jcop.20202

Cohen, S. R. (2002). What determines the quality of life of terminally ill cancer patients from their own perspective? *Journal of Palliative Care, 18*, 48–58.

Cole, B. S., Hopkins, C. M., Tisak, J., Steel, L., & Carr, B. I. (2008). Assessing spiritual growth and spiritual decline following a diagnosis of cancer: Reliability and validity of the Spiritual Transformation Scale. *Psycho-Oncology, 17*, 112–121. doi:10.1002/pon.1207

Daaleman, T. P., Cobb, A. K., & Frey, B. B. (2001). Spirituality and well-being: An exploratory study of the patient perspective. *Social Science and Medicine, 53*, 1503–1511. doi:10.1016/S0277-9536(00)00439-1

Dull, V. T., & Skokan, L. A. (1995). A cognitive model of religion's influence on health. *Journal of Social Issues, 51*, 49–64. doi:10.1111/j.1540-4560.1995.tb01323.x

Edmondson, D., Park, C. L., Chaudoir, S. R., & Wortmann, J. H. (2008). Death without God: Religious struggle, death concerns, and depression in the terminally ill. *Psychological Science, 19*, 754–758. doi:10.1111/j.1467-9280.2008.02152.x

Emmons, R. A. (1999). *The psychology of ultimate concerns: Motivation and spirituality in personality.* New York, NY: Guilford Press.

Ersek, M., & Ferrell, B. R. (1994). Providing relief from cancer pain by assisting in the search for meaning. *Journal of Palliative Care, 10*(4), 15–22.

Falsetti, S. A., Resick, P. A., & Davis, J. L. (2003). Changes in religious beliefs following trauma. *Journal of Traumatic Stress, 16*, 391–398. doi:10.1023/A:1024422220163

Fater, K., & Mullaney, J. A. (2000). The lived experience of adult male survivors who allege childhood sexual abuse by clergy. *Issues in Mental Health Nursing, 21*, 281–295. doi:10.1080/016128400248095

Ferraro, K. F., & Koch, J. R. (1994). Religion and health among Black and White adults: Examining social support and consolation. *Journal for the Scientific Study of Religion, 33*, 362–375. doi:10.2307/1386495

Fitchett, G., Rybarczyk, B. D., DeMarco, G. A., & Nicholas, J. J. (1999). The role of religion in medical rehabilitation outcomes: A longitudinal study. *Rehabilitation Psychology, 44*, 333–353. doi:10.1037/0090-5550.44.4.333

Fitzpatrick, A. L., Standish, L. J., Berger, J., Kim, J., Calabrese, C., & Polissar, N. (2007). Survival in HIV-1 positive adults practicing psychological or spiritual activities for one year. *Alternative Therapies in Health and Medicine, 13*, 18–24.

Frazier, P., Tashiro, T., Berman, M., Steger, M., & Long, J. (2004). Correlates of levels and patterns of positive life changes following sexual assault. *Journal of Consulting and Clinical Psychology, 72*, 19–30. doi:10.1037/0022-006X.72.1.19

Gall, T. L. (2000). Integrating religious resources within a general model of stress and coping: Long-term adjustment to breast cancer. *Journal of Religion and Health, 39*, 167–182. doi:10.1023/A:1004670717144

Gall, T. L. (2003). The role of religious resources for older adults coping with illness. *Journal of Pastoral Care and Counseling, 57*, 211–224.

Gall, T. L., Basque, V., Damasceno-Scott, M., & Vardy, G. (2007). Spirituality and the current adjustment of adult survivors of childhood sexual abuse. *Journal for the Scientific Study of Religion, 46*, 101–117. doi:10.1111/j.1468-5906.2007.00343.x

Gall, T. L., Charbonneau, C., Clarke, N. H., Grant, K., Joseph, A., & Shouldice, L. (2005). Understanding the nature and role of spirituality in relation to coping and health: A conceptual framework. *Canadian Psychology, 46*(2), 88–104.

Gall, T. L., Charbonneau, C., & Florack, P. (2011). The relationship between religious/spiritual factors and perceived growth following a diagnosis of breast cancer. *Psychology and Health, 26*, 287–305. doi:10.1080/08870440903411013

Gall, T. L., & Cornblat, M. W. (2002). Breast cancer survivors give voice: A qualitative analysis of spiritual factors in long-term adjustment. *Psycho-Oncology, 11*, 524–535. doi:10.1002/pon.613

Gall, T. L., Guirguis-Younger, M. J., Charbonneau, C., & Florack, P. (2009). The trajectory of religious coping across time in response to the diagnosis of breast cancer. *Psycho-Oncology, 18*, 1165–1178. doi:10.1002/pon.1495

Gall, T. L., Kristjansson, E., Charbonneau, C., & Florack, P. (2009). A longitudinal study on the role of spirituality in response to the diagnosis and treatment of breast cancer. *Journal of Behavioral Medicine, 32*, 174–186. doi:10.1007/s10865-008-9182-3

Gillum, T. L., Sullivan, C. M., & Bybee, D. I. (2006). The importance of spirituality in the lives of domestic violence survivors. *Violence Against Women, 12*, 240–250. doi:10.1177/1077801206286224

Gordon, P. A., Feldman, D., Crose, R., Schoen, E., Griffing, G., & Shankar, J. (2002). The role of religious beliefs in coping with chronic illness. *Counseling and Values, 46*, 162–174. doi:10.1002/j.2161-007X.2002.tb00210.x

Harrison, M. O., Koenig, H. G., Hays, J. C., Eme-Akwari, A. G., & Pargament, K. I. (2001). The epidemiology of religious coping: A review of recent literature. *International Review of Psychiatry, 13*, 86–93. doi:10.1080/09540260120037317

Hazel, K. L., & Mohatt, G. V. (2001). Cultural and spiritual coping in sobriety: Informing substance abuse prevention for Alaska Native communities. *Journal of Community Psychology, 29*, 541–562. doi:10.1002/jcop.1035

Holland, J. C., Passik, S., Kash, K. M., Russak, S. M., Gronert, M. K., Sison, A., . . . Baider, L. (1999). The role of religious and spiritual beliefs in coping with malignant melanoma. *Psycho-Oncology, 8*, 14–26. doi:10.1002/(SICI)1099-1611(199901/02)8:1<14::AID-PON321>3.0.CO;2-E

Ironson, G., & Hayward, H. (2008). Do positive psychosocial factors predict disease progression in HIV-1?

A review of the evidence. *Psychosomatic Medicine, 70,* 546–554. doi:10.1097/PSY.0b013e318177216c

Ironson, G., Stuetzle, R., & Fletcher, M. A. (2006). An increase in religiousness/spirituality occurs after HIV diagnosis and predicts slower disease progression over 4 years in people with HIV. *Journal of General Internal Medicine, 21,* S62–S68. doi:10.1111/j.1525-1497.2006.00648.x

Johnstone, B., Franklin, K. L., Yoon, D. P., Burris, J., & Shigaki, C. (2008). Relationships among religiousness, spirituality, and health for individuals with stroke. *Journal of Clinical Psychology in Medical Settings, 15,* 308–313. doi:10.1007/s10880-008-9128-5

Johnstone, B., Glass, B. A., & Oliver, R. E. (2007). Religion and disability: Clinical, research, and training considerations for rehabilitation professionals. *Disability and Rehabilitation, 29,* 1153–1163. doi:10.1080/09638280600955693

Kamm-Steigelman, L., Kimble, L. P., Dunbar, S., Sowell, R. L., & Bairan, A. (2006). Religion, relationships and mental health in midlife women following acute myocardial infarction. *Issues in Mental Health Nursing, 27,* 141–159. doi:10.1080/01612840500436925

Khan, Z. H., & Watson, P. J. (2006). Construction of the Pakistani religious coping practices scale: Correlation with religious coping, religious orientation, and reactions to stress among Muslim university students. *The International Journal for the Psychology of Religion, 16,* 101–112. doi:10.1207/s15327582ijpr1602_2

Koenig, H. G. (1997). Use of religion by patients with severe medical illness. *Mind/Body Medicine, 2,* 31–36.

Koenig, H. G., McCullough, M. E., & Larson, D. B. (2001). *Handbook of religion and health.* Oxford, England: Oxford University Press. doi:10.1093/acprof:oso/9780195118667.001.0001

Krumrei, E. J., Mahoney, A., & Pargament, K. (2009). Divorce and the divine: The role of spirituality in adjustment to divorce. *Journal of Marriage and Family, 71,* 373–383. doi:10.1111/j.1741-3737.2009.00605.x

Lawson, E. J., & Thomas, C. (2007). Wading in the waters: Spirituality and older Black survivors. *Journal of Health Care for the Poor and Underserved, 18,* 341–354. doi:10.1353/hpu.2007.0039

Lazarus, R. S., & Folkman, S. (1984). *Stress, appraisal, and coping.* New York, NY: Springer.

Lee, E.-K. O. (2007). Religion and spirituality as predictors of well-being among Chinese American and Korean American older adults. *Journal of Religion, Spirituality, and Aging, 19,* 77–100. doi:10.1300/J496v19n03_06

Levin, J. S., Taylor, R. J., & Chatters, L. M. (1994). Race and gender differences in religiosity among older adults. Findings from four national surveys. *The Journals of Gerontology, Series B: Psychological Sciences and Social Sciences, 49,* S137–S145.

Loewenthal, K. M., MacLeod, A. K., Goldblatt, V., Lubitsh, G., & Valentine, J. D. (2000). Comfort and joy? Religion, cognition, and mood in Protestants and Jews under stress. *Cognition and Emotion, 14,* 355–374. doi:10.1080/026999300378879

Maton, K. I. (1989). The stress-buffering role of spiritual support: Cross-sectional and prospective investigations. *Journal for the Scientific Study of Religion, 28,* 310–323. doi:10.2307/1386742

McConnell, K. M., Pargament, K. I., Ellison, C. G., & Flannelly, K. J. (2006). Examining the links between spiritual struggles and symptoms of psychopathology in a national sample. *Journal of Clinical Psychology, 62,* 1469–1484. doi:10.1002/jclp.20325

McCullough, M., & Larson, D. (1999). Prayer. In W. Miller (Ed.), *Integrating spirituality into treatment* (pp. 85–110). Washington, DC: American Psychological Association. doi:10.1037/10327-005

McIntosh, D. N. (1995). Religion-as-schema, with implications for the relation between religion and coping. *The International Journal for the Psychology of Religion, 5,* 1–16. doi:10.1207/s15327582ijpr0501_1

McIntosh, D. N., Silver, R. C., & Wortman, C. B. (1993). Religion's role in adjustment to a negative life event: Coping with the loss of a child. *Journal of Personality and Social Psychology, 65,* 812–821. doi:10.1037/0022-3514.65.4.812

McMinn, M. R., Kerrick, S. P., Duma, S. J., Campbell, E. R., & Jung, J. B. (2008). Positive coping among wives of male Christian clergy. *Pastoral Psychology, 56,* 445–457. doi:10.1007/s11089-008-0122-5

Miner, M., & McKnight, J. (1999). Religious attributions: Situational factors and effects on coping. *Journal for the Scientific Study of Religion, 38,* 274–286. doi:10.2307/1387794

Mohr, S., Gilliéron, C., Borras, L., Brandt, P.-Y., & Huguelet, P. (2007). The assessment of spirituality and religiousness in schizophrenia. *Journal of Nervous and Mental Disease, 195,* 247–253. doi:10.1097/01.nmd.0000258230.94304.6b

Murphy, S. A., Johnson, C., & Lohan, J. (2003). Finding meaning in a child's violent death: A five-year prospective analysis of parents' personal narratives and empirical data. *Death Studies, 27,* 381–404. doi:10.1080/07481180302879

Murray-Swank, N. A., & Pargament, K. I. (2005). God, where are you? Evaluating a spiritually-integrated intervention for sexual abuse. *Mental Health, Religion, and Culture, 8,* 191–203. doi:10.1080/13694670500138866

Navara, G. S., & James, S. (2005). Acculturative stress of missionaries: Does religious orientation affect religious coping and adjustment? *International Journal of Intercultural Relations, 29*, 39–58. doi:10.1016/j.ijintrel.2005.04.004

Oman, D., & Reed, D. (1998). Religion and mortality among the community-dwelling elderly. *American Journal of Public Health, 88*, 1469–1475. doi:10.2105/AJPH.88.10.1469

Pargament, K. I. (1997). *The psychology of religion and coping*. New York, NY: Guilford Press.

Pargament, K. I. (2003, August). *Recognizing and addressing spiritual struggles*. Paper presented at the 111th Annual Convention of the American Psychological Association, Toronto, Ontario, Canada.

Pargament, K. I. (2007). *Spiritually integrated psychotherapy: Understanding and addressing the sacred*. New York, NY: Guilford Press.

Pargament, K. I., & Brant, C. R. (1998). Religion and coping. In H. G. Koenig (Ed.), *Handbook of religion and mental health* (pp. 111–128). San Diego, CA: Academic Press. doi:10.1016/B978-012417645-4/50075-4

Pargament, K. I., Cole, B., VandeCreek, L., Belavich, T., Brant, C., & Perez, L. (1999). The vigil: Religion and the search for control in the hospital waiting room. *Journal of Health Psychology, 4*, 327–341. doi:10.1177/135910539900400303

Pargament, K. I., Ensing, D. S., Falgout, K., Olsen, H., Reilly, B., Van Haitsma, K., & Warren, R. (1990). God help me: I. Religious coping efforts as predictors of the outcomes to significant negative life events. *American Journal of Community Psychology, 18*, 793–824. doi:10.1007/BF00938065

Pargament, K. I., Feuille, M., & Burdzy, D. (2011). The Brief RCOPE: Current psychometric status of a short measure of religious coping. *Religions, 2*, 51–76. doi:10.3390/rel2010051

Pargament, K. I., Koenig, H. G., Tarakeshwar, N., & Hahn, J. (2001). Religious struggles as a predictor of mortality among medically ill elderly patients: A 2-year longitudinal study. *Archives of Internal Medicine, 161*, 1881–1885. doi:10.1001/archinte.161.15.1881

Pargament, K. I., Koenig, H. G., Tarakeshwar, N., & Hahn, J. (2004). Religious coping methods as predictors of psychological, physical, and social outcomes among medically ill elderly patients: A two-year longitudinal study. *Journal of Health Psychology, 9*, 713–730. doi:10.1177/1359105304045366

Pargament, K. I., Sullivan, M. S., Tyler, F. B., & Steele, R. E. (1982). Patterns of attribution of control and individual psychosocial competence. *Psychological Reports, 51*, 1243–1252. doi:10.2466/pr0.1982.51.3f.1243

Park, C. L., Edmondson, D., Hale-Smith, A., & Blank, T. (2009). Religiousness/spirituality and health behaviors in younger adult cancer survivors: Does faith promote a healthier lifestyle? *Journal of Behavioral Medicine, 32*, 582–591. doi:10.1007/s10865-009-9223-6

Park, C. L., & Folkman, S. (1997). Meaning in the context of stress and coping. *Review of General Psychology, 1*, 115–144. doi:10.1037/1089-2680.1.2.115

Park, C. L., Moehl, B., Fenster, J. R., Suresh, D. P., & Bliss, D. (2008). Religiousness and treatment adherence in congestive heart failure patients. *Journal of Religion, Spirituality, and Aging, 20*, 249–266. doi:10.1080/15528030802232270

Pearce, M. J., Singer, J. L., & Prigerson, H. G. (2006). Religious coping among caregivers of terminally ill cancer patients. Main effects and psychosocial mediators. *Journal of Health Psychology, 11*, 743–759. doi:10.1177/1359105306066629

Pendleton, S. M., Cavalli, K. S., Pargament, K. I., & Nasr, S. Z. (2002). Religious/spiritual coping in childhood cystic fibrosis: A qualitative study. *Pediatrics, 109*, e8. doi:10.1542/peds.109.1.e8

Phelps, A. C., Maciejewski, P. K., Nilsson, M., Balboni, T. A., Wright, A. A., Paulk, E., . . . Prigerson, H. G. (2009). Religous coping and use of intensive life-prolonging care near death in patients with advanced cancer. *JAMA, 301*, 1140–1147. doi:10.1001/jama.2009.341

Phillips, R. E., III, & Stein, C. H. (2007). God's will, god's punishment, or god's limitations: Religious coping strategies reported by young adults living with serious mental illness. *Journal of Clinical Psychology, 63*, 529–540. doi:10.1002/jclp.20364

Polzer Casarez, R. L., & Miles, M. S. (2008). Spirituality: A cultural strength for African American mothers with HIV. *Clinical Nursing Research, 17*, 118–132. doi:10.1177/1054773808316735

Prado, G., Feaster, D. J., Schwartz, S. J., Pratt, I. A., Smith, L., & Szapocznik, J. (2004). Religious involvement, coping, social support, and psychological distress in HIV-seropositive African American mothers. *AIDS and Behavior, 8*, 221–235. doi:10.1023/B:AIBE.0000044071.27130.46

Proffitt, D., Cann, A., Calhoun, L. G., & Tedeschi, R. G. (2007). Judeo-Christian clergy and personal crisis: Religion, posttraumatic growth and well being. *Journal of Religion and Health, 46*, 219–231. doi:10.1007/s10943-006-9074-1

Pryds, J. K., Back-Pettersson, S., & Segesten, K. (2000). The meaning of "not giving in". *Cancer Nursing, 23*, 6–11.

Richards, T. A., & Folkman, S. (1997). Spiritual aspects of loss at the time of a partner's death from AIDS. *Death Studies, 21*, 527–552. doi:10.1080/074811897201769

Ridge, D., Williams, I., Anderson, J., & Elford, J. (2008). Like a prayer: The role of spirituality and religion for people living with HIV in the UK. *Sociology of Health and Illness, 30*, 413–428. doi:10.1111/j.1467-9566.2007.01062.x

Rippentrop, A. E. (2005). A review of the role of religion and spirituality in chronic pain populations. *Rehabilitation Psychology, 50*, 278–284. doi:10.1037/0090-5550.50.3.278

Roesch, S. C., & Ano, G. (2003). Testing an attribution and coping model of stress: Religion as an orienting system. *Journal of Psychology and Christianity, 22*, 197–209.

Roff, L. L., Durkin, D., Sun, F., & Klemmack, D. L. (2007). Widowhood, religiousness, and self-assessed well-being among older adults. *Journal of Religion, Spirituality, and Aging, 19*, 43–59. doi:10.1300/J496v19n04_04

Rosmarin, D. H., Pargament, K. I., & Flannelly, K. J. (2009). Religious coping among Jews: Development and initial validation of the JCOPE. *Journal of Clinical Psychology, 65*, 670–683. doi:10.1002/jclp.20574

Schottenbauer, M. A., Rodriguez, B. F., Glass, C. R., & Arnkoff, D. B. (2006). Religious coping research and contemporary personality theory: An exploration of Endler's (1997). integrative personality theory. *British Journal of Psychology, 97*, 499–519. doi:10.1348/000712606X97840

Schuster, M. A., Stein, B. D., Jaycox, L. H., Collins, R. I., Marshall, G. N., Elliott, M. N., . . . Berry, S. H. (2001). A national survey of stress reactions after the September 11, 2001, terrorist attacks. *New England Journal of Medicine, 345*, 1507–1512. doi:10.1056/NEJM200111153452024

Sherman, A. C., Plante, T. G., Simonton, S., Latif, U., & Anaissie, E. J. (2009). Prospective study of religious coping among patients undergoing autologous stem cell transplantation. *Journal of Behavioral Medicine, 32*, 118–128. doi:10.1007/s10865-008-9179-y

Shortz, J. L., & Worthington, E. L. (1994). Young adults' recall of religiosity, attributions, and coping in parental divorce. *Journal for the Scientific Study of Religion, 33*, 172–179. doi:10.2307/1386603

Siegel, K., Anderman, S. J., & Schrimshaw, E. W. (2001). Religion and coping with health-related stress. *Psychology and Health, 16*, 631–653. doi:10.1080/08870440108405864

Siegel, K., & Schrimshaw, E. W. (2002). The perceived benefits of religious and spiritual coping among older adults living with HIV/AIDS. *Journal for the Scientific Study of Religion, 41*, 91–102. doi:10.1111/1468-5906.00103

Sloan, R. P., Bagiella, E., & Powell, T. (2001). Without a prayer: Methodological problems, ethical challenges, and misrepresentations in the study of religion, spirituality, and medicine. In T. G. Plante & A. C. Sherman (Eds.), *Faith and health: Psychological perspectives* (pp. 339–354). New York, NY: Guilford Press.

Sorajjakool, S., Aja, V., Chilson, B., Ramírez-Johnson, J., & Earll, A. (2008). Disconnection, depression, and spirituality: A study of the role of spirituality and meaning in the lives of individuals with severe depression. *Pastoral Psychology, 56*, 521–532. doi:10.1007/s11089-008-0125-2

Stifoss-Hanssen, H. (1999). Religion and spirituality: What a European ear hears. *The International Journal for the Psychology of Religion, 9*, 25–33. doi:10.1207/s15327582ijpr0901_4

Strawbridge, W. J., Shema, S. J., Cohen, R. D., & Kaplan, G. A. (1997). Religious attendance increases survival by improving and maintaining good health behaviors, mental health, and social relationships. *Annals of Behavioral Medicine, 23*, 68–74. doi:10.1207/S15324796ABM2301_10

Sulmasy, D. P. (2002). A biopsychosocial-spiritual model for the care of patients at the end of life. *The Gerontologist, 42*, 24–33. doi:10.1093/geront/42.suppl_3.24

Tarakeshwar, N., Hansen, N., Kochman, A., & Sikkema, K. J. (2005). Gender, ethnicity, and spiritual coping among bereaved HIV-positive individuals. *Mental Health, Religion, and Culture, 8*, 109–125. doi:10.1080/13674670412000240383

Tarakeshwar, N., Khan, N., & Sikkema, K. J. (2006). A relationship-based framework of spirituality for individuals with HIV. *AIDS and Behavior, 10*, 59–70. doi:10.1007/s10461-005-9052-8

Tarakeshwar, N., Pargament, K. I., & Mahoney, A. (2003). Initial development of a measure of coping among Hindus. *Journal of Community Psychology, 31*, 607–628. doi:10.1002/jcop.10071

Tarakeshwar, N., Pearce, M. J., & Sikkema, K. J. (2005). Development and implementation of a spiritual coping group intervention for adults living with HIV/AIDS: A pilot study. *Mental Health, Religion, and Culture, 8*, 179–190. doi:10.1080/13694670500138908

Tarakeshwar, N., Vanderwerker, L. C., Paulk, E., Pearce, M. J., Kasl, S. V., & Prigerson, H. G. (2006). Religious coping is associated with the quality of life of patients with advanced cancer. *Journal of Palliative Medicine, 9*, 646–657. doi:10.1089/jpm.2006.9.646

Tedeschi, R. G., & Calhoun, L. G. (2006). Time or change? The spiritual challenges of bereavement and loss. *Omega: Journal of Death and Dying, 53*(1–2), 105–116.

Thomas, J., & Retsas, A. (1999). Transacting self-preservation: A grounded theory of the spiritual dimensions of people with terminal cancer. *International Journal of Nursing Studies, 36*, 191–201. doi:10.1016/S0020-7489(99)00012-7

Thompson, M. P., & Vardaman, P. J. (1997). The role of religion in coping with the loss of a family member to homicide. *Journal for the Scientific Study of Religion, 36*, 44–51. doi:10.2307/1387881

Tix, A. P., & Frazier, P. A. (1998). The use of religious coping during stressful life events: Main effects, moderation, and mediation. *Journal of Consulting and Clinical Psychology, 66*, 411–422. doi:10.1037/0022-006X.66.2.411

Van Uden, M., Pieper, J., & Alma, H. (2004). Bridge over troubled water: Further results regarding the Receptive Coping Scale. *Journal of Empirical Theology, 17*, 101–114. doi:10.1163/1570925041208916

Vickberg, S. M., Duhamel, K. M., Smith, M. Y., Manne, S. L., Winkel, G., Papadopoulos, E. B., & Redd, W. H. (2001). Global meaning and psychological adjustment among survivors of bone marrow transplant. *Psycho-Oncology, 10*, 29–39. doi:10.1002/1099-1611(200101/02)10:1<29::AID-PON482>3.0.CO;2-Y

Wachholtz, A. B., & Pargament, K. I. (2008). Migraines and meditation: Does spirituality matter. *Journal of Behavioral Medicine, 31*, 351–366. doi:10.1007/s10865-008-9159-2

Wachholtz, A. B., Pearce, M. J., & Koenig, H. (2007). Exploring the relationship between spirituality, coping and pain. *Journal of Behavioral Medicine, 30*, 311–318. doi:10.1007/s10865-007-9114-7

Wasteson, E., Nordin, K., Hoffman, K., Glimelius, B., & Sjöden, P.-O. (2002). Daily assessment of coping in patients with gastrointestinal cancer. *Psycho-Oncology, 11*, 1–11. doi:10.1002/pon.542

Woods, T. E., Antoni, M. H., Ironson, G. H., & Kling, D. W. (1999). Religiosity is associated with affective and immune status in symptomatic HIV-infected gay men. *Journal of Psychosomatic Research, 46*, 165–176. doi:10.1016/S0022-3999(98)00078-6

Zorn, C. R., & Johnson, M. T. (1997). Religious well-being in noninstitutionalized elderly women. *Health Care for Women International, 18*, 209–219. doi:10.1080/07399339709516276

Zwingmann, C., Wirtz, M., Müller, C., Körber, J., & Murken, S. (2006). Positive and negative religious coping in German breast cancer patients. *Journal of Behavioral Medicine, 29*, 533–547. doi:10.1007/s10865-006-9074-3

CHAPTER 20

THE SPIRITUALITY OF US: RELATIONAL SPIRITUALITY IN THE CONTEXT OF FAMILY RELATIONSHIPS

Annette Mahoney

"Soul mate." "Kindred spirits." "A match made in heaven." "Sacred vows." "The miracle of birth." "A family that prays together stays together." These commonplace phrases speak to entrenched historical ties between faith and family life. Hundreds of self-help books and diverse religious communities offer advice on how to draw on the sacred to build a healthy family. Social scientists, however, have primarily been curious about the "spirituality of me" rather than the "spirituality of us." For instance, the field of the psychology of religion and spirituality has devoted itself to uncovering positive and negative roles that faith plays for the health and well-being for individuals, rather than for relationships (Hood, Hill, & Spilka, 2009; Koenig, McCullough, & Larson, 2001; Paloutzian & Park, 2005). Furthermore, the comparatively small number of peer-reviewed, scientific studies devoted to faith and family life depend heavily on global indicators of a given family member's own religiousness. For example, about 75% to 80% of quantitative studies published in the past 3 decades on the intersection of faith and family have relied on one- or two-item measures of a spouse's or a parent's religious affiliation (e.g., Catholic, Protestant, Jewish, none, other), frequency of worship attendance, self-reported salience of religion in daily life, or biblical literalism (Mahoney, 2010; Mahoney, Pargament, Swank, & Tarakeshwar, 2001). But although people who more often attend services and say religion is important tend to report better family functioning, the magnitude of such associations is small (Mahoney, 2010; Mahoney et al., 2001). More problematic, global items offer little insight into unique ways that religion and spirituality can help or harm family relationships. For instance, a therapist who learns that a client attends a Methodist church twice a month would have few clues about specific spiritual beliefs the client holds about family life that could be part of the problem or the solution in the client's marital and parental difficulties. Similarly, policy makers who know that higher attendance at any place of worship in the United States is statistically, but weakly, linked to lower rates of divorce or child physical abuse would presumably hesitate to make the blank injunction that all parents go to religious services more often to protect U.S. children from marital dissolution or child maltreatment. Rather, societies and therapists around the globe would benefit from a deeper appreciation of the specific ways that spirituality, pursued within and outside of different religious institutions, can help bind families together or tear them apart.

My goal in this chapter is to provide scientists and practitioners with a map to guide in-depth explorations into various ways that spiritual beliefs or practices can be integrated into family relationships. My assumption is that both scholars who want to understand all types of families as well as practitioners who want to help unhappy families would benefit from richer conceptual models to guide research and practice on faith and family life. Thus, I focus on three tiers of spiritual mechanisms that could operate as either helpful resources or painful struggles in the co-occurring searches for the sacred and for family relationships. These three tiers

DOI: 10.1037/14045-020
APA Handbook of Psychology, Religion, and Spirituality: Vol. 1. Context, Theory, and Research, K. I. Pargament (Editor-in-Chief)
Copyright © 2013 by the American Psychological Association. All rights reserved.

of mechanisms are embedded in a conceptual framework I have previously introduced (Mahoney, 2010), labeled "relational spirituality," which is summarized in Table 20.1. I start with an overview of key elements of the framework. I then spend the bulk of the chapter elaborating the three tiers of mechanisms (relationship with God, family relationship, relationship with religious community). For each tier, I start with an overview, which is followed by a discussion of possible mechanisms in that tier that could function as spiritual resources and then mechanisms that reflect spiritual struggles. Both resources and struggles in each tier are divided according to three stages of family life (discovery, maintenance, and transformation). Throughout I illustrate various mechanisms, highlighting available studies and pointing out gaps in direct evidence. Although I mention some findings based on global markers of religiousness (also see top row of Table 20.1), because of space constraints, I refer researchers elsewhere for lengthier, more technical reviews and critiques of these findings written for researchers (e.g., Dollahite & Marks, 2009; Mahoney, 2010; Mahoney et al., 2001), and a related summary written for general audiences (Mahoney, 2009). Readers can also access citation lists of all the peer-reviewed studies that I located from 1980 to 1999 in Mahoney et al. (2001) and from 1999–2009 at http://www.bgsu.edu/departments/psych/spirituality, which also has measures posted to assess some of the spiritual mechanisms discussed in this chapter (e.g., sanctification of marriage or parenting; benevolent prayer for a partner).

RELATIONAL SPIRITUALITY FRAMEWORK: OVERVIEW OF KEY ELEMENTS

Overview of Spirituality and Religion

For the purpose of this chapter, *spirituality* refers to "the search for the sacred" (see Chapter 1 in this volume) and the two elements of this definition merit review. In brief, at its core, *the sacred* refers to human perceptions of the divine, God, or transcendent reality, but any aspect of life can be perceived as possessing divine character and significance (Mahoney, Pargament, & Hernandez, in press; Pargament & Mahoney, 2005). Thus, the heart of the sacred can extend to family relationships as well as other domains of life (e.g., career, community work, nature), with individuals differing in the constellation of elements that encompass the entire sphere of the sacred (Mahoney et al., in press). *The search* includes three dynamic and recursive stages of the discovery, maintenance, and transformation of the sacred across the life span (Pargament, 2007). Discovery refers to developing an orientation to the sacred via proactive or passive journeys down solitary or communal roads of learning. Maintenance involves efforts to conserve one's orientation to the sacred during ordinary daily life and in times of trouble. Transformation refers to seeking out a fundamentally different orientation to the sacred, whether gradually or rapidly prompted by life transitions or crises.

For the purpose of this chapter, *religion* refers to "the search for significance that occurs within the context of established institutions that are designed to facilitate spirituality" (see Chapter 1 in this volume). As Pargament (1997, 2007) has discussed, the search for significance involves identifying the most important destinations to pursue in life, and the pathways to take to arrive at one's most cherished goals. Historically and across cultures, religious institutions have influenced this identification process, helping to define and reinforce cultural norms about what ends in life should be of ultimate value and what means should be used to reach desired ends (see Chapter 1 in this volume). Religious institutions have particularly set forth and defended norms about the destinations and pathways that people should pursue to fulfill sacred ideals about family life. For example, in conservative and many mainline Christian groups, the "good family" that people should intentionally aim to create includes a married heterosexual couple with biological children (Edgell, 2003, 2005; Onedera, 2008), whereas some liberal Christian groups affirm that the intentional creation of same-sex or single-parent families can be equally good in the eyes of God (Onedera, 2008; Ruether, 2000). In either case, Christians who adhere to the norms advocated by their religious subgroup may more easily draw on spirituality as a resource to form and sustain their families. Conversely, Christians who deviate from familial norms endorsed by their religious

TABLE 20.1

Relational Spirituality Framework

Relational spirituality framework		Stages of family relationships: Discovery — Goal: Create and structure bond	Maintenance — Goal: Conserve and protect bond	Transformation — Goal: Reform or exit distressed bond
Markers of spiritual mechanisms Importance of religion and/or attendance is related to . . .		Better odds of marriage not cohabitation; women wanting and having children when married; and married men spending time with offspring.	Better odds of marital satisfaction and positive parenting, and lower odds of divorce, infidelity, domestic violence, and child physical abuse.	Almost no research focuses on subsamples of distressed families coping with domestic violence, infertility, infidelity, child abuse, and other serious issues.
Three tiers of spiritual mechanisms (Illustrative mechanisms in italics)				
Tier 1: Relationship with God	**Resources**	*Support from God* * May motivate creation of committed adult union and parent–child relationship. * May guide formation and strengthen commitment to traditional or nontraditional family structures.	*Prayer for a partner's well-being* √ Improves relationship quality. *Serenity prayer about relationship* * May aid good decisions and skills to mindfully accept or proactively address relationship imperfections.	*Support from God to cope effectively* √ Predicts less depression and more personal growth over time for postdivorce adjustment. * May enhance coping with many family crises or dysfunction.
	Struggles	*Struggles with God* * Over the creation or structure of adult union or family unit may weaken relationship commitment and stability.	*Displace dyadic struggles onto God* * May undermine effective resolution of dyadic conflict.	*Turn to God to forgive* (TGF) *struggles* √ TGF struggles over divorce predict less forgiveness of ex-spouse and more dyadic verbal hostility over time.
Tier 2: Relationship with family member(s) invested with spiritual properties	**Resources**	*Sanctification of marriage* √ Wedding vows tied to viewing marriage as sacred by heterosexuals and, in turn, self-reported commitment. *Sanctification of parenthood* * May motivate planned pregnancy and commitment to parent–child bond.	*Sanctification of adult union* √ Enhances relationship quality for married, same-sex, and cohabiting couples. *Spiritual disclosure and intimacy* √ Relates to relational quality for college students and mothers.	*Sanctification of marriage* * Sanctification may motivate efforts to repair a distressed marriage.
	Struggles	*Struggles over sanctification of family unit* * Infertility may trigger spiritual struggles over acceptable means to form a sacred parent–child relationship.	*Spiritual one-upmanship* √ Tied to greater verbal hostility and relational distress in college student–parent relationship.	*Desecration or sacred loss* √ Viewing divorce or parental divorce as a sacred injury relates to greater postdivorce personal distress.

(*Continued*)

TABLE 20.1 (*Continued*)

Relational Spirituality Framework

Tier 3: Relationship with religious community	**Resources**	*Support from religious group* * May motivate public formation of committed bond and viewing it as sacred.	*Support from religious group* * May encourage helpful Tier 1 and Tier 2 spiritual mechanisms.	*Support from religious group* √ Is tied to leaving and reconciling with abusive partners.
	Struggles	*Struggles with religious group* * Over the creation or structure of family bond may decrease public formation and commitment to family relationships.	*Triangulation of religious group* * May reinforce harmful Tier 1 and Tier 2 spiritual mechanisms.	*Struggles with religious group* * May escalate blame, hostility, and physical aggression by abusive parents or between spouses.

Note. √ findings exist; * studies needed.

subgroup may more often experience spiritual struggles that intensify family-related distress and jeopardize their access to spiritual resources to strengthen their families. The dual-edged potential of religion to help or hinder peoples' efforts to integrate spirituality and family life echoes throughout this chapter.

Overview of Stages of Family Relationships

For the purpose of this chapter, *relational spirituality* refers to situations in which the search for the sacred is united, for better or worse, with the search for human relationships. Given that this chapter focuses on family life, the relational spirituality framework in Table 20.1 is designed to capture the multidimensional intersections of these co-occurring searches within a family context. Paralleling an individual's search for the sacred (i.e., spirituality), the relational spirituality framework discriminates three recursive stages over time in an individual's search for relationships: (a) discovery—creating and structuring the relationships, (b) maintenance—conserving and protecting the relationships, and (c) transformation—reforming or exiting distressed relationships that call for fundamental change. As seen in Table 20.1, the diverse family topics that have been empirically linked to global markers of religiousness can be sorted into these three stages, including issues pertaining to the formation of family relationships (e.g., union formation, maternal fertility), their maintenance (e.g., marital satisfaction or sexual fidelity; parental warmth or use of spanking), and their transformation when family crises or dysfunction occurs (e.g., coping with divorce and domestic violence). As is discussed in more detail in Mahoney et al. (2001) and Mahoney (2010), greater religious attendance and overall salience of religion tends to be tied to the formation of traditional family bonds (i.e., married heterosexuals, birth of children within marriage) and the maintenance of traditional or nontraditional family ties. Yet, such broad generalizations can frustrate both researchers and clinicians who want deeper insights into more malleable, specific, and unique spiritual cognitions or behaviors that contribute to harmony or strife across diverse family relationships. For example, although higher religious attendance could signal many distinctive spiritual constructs that influence family functioning, greater involvement in a religious group may reflect psychosocial processes that are not unique to religious institutions, such as social support or coercion to adhere to socially conservative norms about family life.

Overview of Three Tiers of Spiritual Mechanisms

To advance theory and research on unique spiritual constructs that may shape family relationships, the relational spirituality framework discriminates three tiers of mechanisms that could operate in the discovery, maintenance, and transformation of family relationships. Namely, Mahoney (2010) has suggested that the search for family relationships could be influenced by (a) one or more family member's relationship with the divine/God, (b) one or more family relationships invested with spiritual properties, and (c) one or more family member's relationship with religious communities. The rest of this chapter illustrates these three sets of processes across the three major stages of family relationships. The substantive content of the spiritual cognitions and practices manifested within a particular spiritual mechanism determines whether the process is likely to help or harm relational (and individual) functioning in a particular relationship context.

TIER 1: RELATIONSHIP WITH GOD IN THE SEARCH FOR FAMILY RELATIONSHIPS

Tier 1: Overview

Consistent with scholarship on spiritual development (see Chapter 28 in this volume), an individual's search for the sacred involves developing an understanding of the divine, God, or transcendent reality, and taking a position in relation to this central element of the sacred. For many, such a connection represents a psychologically powerful bond. For example, people speak of having formed a personal relationship with an external deity who has well-delineated characteristics (see Chapter 15 in this volume); however, people also speak of experiencing profound connections to a spark of the divine within the self or to supernatural forces that permeate all of existence (Pargament, 2007; see Volume 2, Chapter 7, this handbook). People travel along diverse cognitive and behavioral pathways to foster their felt connections to supernatural forces, within and outside the self. These pathways range from solitary exploration to engagement in religious networks. From a family system's perspective, these endeavors may yield a perceived connection with the divine that operates alongside other family relationships, with or without the awareness of other family members. Given that empirical studies of faith and family life rely virtually exclusively on samples drawn from monotheistic societies that are predominantly composed of Christians with minorities of nonaffiliated individuals, Jews, Latter Day Saints, or Muslims, I hereafter use the term *God* in this chapter to refer to individuals' felt connection with the core of the sacred, recognizing that peoples' images of God—theistic or nontheistic, tangible or abstract, immanent or transcendent, personal or transpersonal—vary widely across individuals, communities, and cultures (see Part III in this volume).

Tier 1 Resources: Family Member's Relationship With God as a Resource

Discovery stage. Conceptually, people can come to know God as a trusted figure who affirms their goals for family relationships and helps them to reach these ends (Mahoney, 2005). Indeed, religions offer abundant and diverse messages about God's intentions for family life that people use to reinforce their choices in forming family ties (Onedera, 2008). Empirical findings hint that people may often seek God's affirmation for their approach to creating a stable intimate union. For example, higher religious attendance and importance of religion increases the likelihood that heterosexual couples marry instead of cohabit and that same-sex couples cement their bond via commitment ceremonies and legal procedures (e.g., wills, mortgages; Mahoney, 2010). Furthermore, significant parallelism exists between the style of one's attachment to God and to romantic partners, implying that a secure attachment to God provides people with a secure sense of self that helps them select well-matched partners (see Chapter 7 in this volume). Conversely, people who report insecure attachments to God tend to form unions marked by ambivalence or anxiety that bode poorly for relational and individual adjustment. Yet studies are needed that directly identify specific ways that individuals turn to God to help them define and prioritize the qualities they seek in a romantic partner and to decide when an intimate relationship merits matrimony or long-term commitment. One important question is whether people of all ages turn to God to cope with frustration when dating, rather than become involved with an unsuitable partner or give up the quest entirely. Another key question is whether people rely on God after a romance has begun to make adaptive decisions about the pace and order that the pair journeys through the stages of causal dating, monogamous dating, sexual intercourse, cohabitation, marriage, and becoming coparents.

When it comes to forming family units, religious attendance and importance increases the odds that women intend to become mothers, bear children within marriage, and get married after a nonmarital birth (Mahoney, 2010). Married men who attend services more often also tend to spend more leisure time with children rather than being absent or disengaged fathers (Mahoney, 2010). Only one study, which focused on adoption, could be located that has examined associations between religious factors and intentionally creating a nontraditional family unit (Hollingsworth, 2000). Specifically, greater importance of religion emerged as a strong factor tied to adoption by White U.S. women out of a host of other motivations and fertility issues. No studies were found on religious factors in becoming a step- or foster parent or on the use of assisted reproductive technology. To the degree that religious attendance or importance are proxy variables for a supportive relationship with God, the above findings hint that a sense of being called to parenthood by God could motivate men and women's decisions to create a parent–child relationship. But, once again, studies are needed that directly examine specific ways that men or women may turn to God to facilitate their decisions about the timing and family context to form a parent-child bond. Hypothetically, partnered and single individuals from different sexual orientations may invest more effort in pursuing planned parenthood, whether via conventional or unconventional routes, if they believe God validates their chosen ends and means (Mahoney & Krumrei, in press).

Maintenance stage. God is often portrayed by religious traditions as a source of strength that people can rely on to enact virtues to sustain family bonds after they are formed (Onedera, 2008; see Volume 2, Chapter 9, this handbook). Because greater general religiousness marginally, but persistently, predicts lower risk of divorce and greater martial satisfaction, especially if spouses are religiously similar (Mahoney, 2010), researchers have begun to try to uncover specific and robust ways that adults may partner with God to help them maintain their unions. One compelling program of research by Fincham, Beach, Lambert, Stillman, and Braithwaite (2008) found that benevolent prayer for a romantic partner facilitates relational quality. In their exemplary series of studies with college students, these researchers found that privately praying for a romantic partner's well-being increased relationship satisfaction longitudinally (Fincham et al., 2008); furthermore, these effects persisted beyond the impact of other key positive and negative relationship processes and how often either the individual or the pair prayed. Their experimental studies also found that praying for a person with whom one has a close relationship increased the prayer's selfless concern, gratitude, and forgiveness of the other person (see Volume 2, Chapter 24, this handbook). In addition, Beach et al. (2011) conducted a randomized experiment with African American couples recruited from the community to test the effects of benevolent prayer for a spouse. Specifically, couples were randomly assigned to one of three conditions: (a) a marital education program that previously has been found to improve marital quality (i.e., the Prevention and Relationship Enhancement Program [PREP]), (b) the same program supplemented with a module focused on private prayer for partner, and (c) self-help reading materials only. Over time, prayer for partner enhanced marital outcomes for wives beyond the beneficial effects of participating in PREP or self-help efforts. Prayer, however, did not function as an added resource beyond PREP for husbands' marital satisfaction.

In theorizing why benevolent prayer for another's well-being predicts desirable relational outcomes, Fincham and Beach (see Volume 2, Chapter 24, this handbook) reason that this kind of prayer may help humans cope effectively with interpersonal conflict by shifting the praying person's motivational attention away from winning an immediate battle and toward the long-term goal of protecting the union. Prayer may help prime spouses to inhibit their use of tactics during conflicts that are counterproductive for the relationship, such as verbal hostility or withdrawal, and instead proactively engage in collaboration, compromise, or acceptance. Prayer may facilitate this motivational shift by reminding individuals of God's loving views of each partner, God's desire for marital permanence, and God's directives to be selfless, patient, honest, accountable, compassionate, and forgiving. Further prayer has been shown to heighten the perception that a relationship itself is a sacred gift from God that, as elaborated in a later section, may intensify people's motivation to act in productive ways that preserve their bond.

These speculations that prayer for a partner can help couples manage conflict effectively dovetail with findings from qualitative research on marriage that resonate with theologian Reinhold Niebuhr's well-known "serenity prayer." Namely, in one qualitative study of 20 Catholics in long-term marriages, many spouses reported that their relationship with God, prayer, and meditation helped them both to accept their spouse's shortcomings (i.e., serenity to accept what cannot be changed) and to nondefensively initiate discussions to resolve marital disputes (i.e., courage to change what can be changed; Marsh & Dallos, 2000), thereby inhibiting harmful expressions of anger toward the spouse. Similar findings emerged in qualitative interviews with 57 highly religious couples in long-term marriages (average 21 years) from diverse religious traditions (Catholic; Jewish; Muslim; Fundamentalist, Evangelical and Mainline Protestant; Greek Orthodox). These couples said that religion motivated them (a) to focus on a sacred vision and purpose of the marriage and (b) to enact relational virtues to fulfill the goals of marriage (Lambert & Dollahite, 2006). They also claimed that their relationship with God provided perspective on their partner's limitations and reminded them of the overarching goal of marital permanence, which helped them proactively address marital conflicts (Lambert & Dollahite, 2006), avoid sexual infidelity (Dollahite & Lambert, 2007), and strengthen their commitment (Lambert & Dollahite, 2007). As one spouse put it:

> We've been married over 19 years and sometimes your spouse drives you crazy, but you love him. And sometimes you just have to see him as God sees him. Not sometimes, all the time, actually. . . . The set of wonderful qualities that you married him for are always, and that they can never lose that, then it just helps you get over the tough spots. (Lambert & Dollahite, 2007, p. 605)

The ubiquity of prayer for a loved one extends to the parenting context. In a 2002 national survey, for example, 60% of parents of adolescents said they prayed for their teen daily, with another 20% saying they did this a few times per week (National Center for Family & Marriage Research, 2011). In addition, greater religious attendance or salience has been repeatedly tied to more positive parenting in traditional and nontraditional families (Mahoney, 2010; Mahoney et al., 2001). Collectively, these findings imply that some parents experience God as an authority or coparental figure who wants them to make sacrifices to satisfy their children's spiritual, nutritional, educational, and medical needs, and to help them be more engaged and efficacious in their parenting. Such salutary links, however, did not emerge in two quantitative studies in which parents were specifically asked about turning to God to cope with parenting at-risk preschoolers (Dumas & Nissley-Tsiopinis, 2006) or children with autism (Tarakeshwar & Pargament, 2001). The null findings in these two cross-sectional studies may reflect stress-mobilization processes in which more stressed parents may call on God more often when they are taxed or overwhelmed, but the potential benefits of seeking divine support become evident only later.

More research is needed that pinpoints family members' felt relationships with God as a resource for different levels of family systems, including dyadic relationships (e.g., marital, parent–child), triadic units (e.g., coparents and one child, one parent and two siblings), and whole family dynamics. Important leads for further work include qualitative research suggesting that agreement between evangelical Christian parents about God's intentions for their parenting goals and practices strengthens their coparenting alliance and mutual investment in parenting (Edgell, 2005). Other qualitative studies suggest that single parents often experience God as an ever-present, unique ally who helps them parent responsibly without a partner (Sparks, Peterson, &

Tangenberg, 2005). Finally, parents and offspring who have a similar type of relationship with God may enjoy a high degree of relational cohesiveness (e.g., Abbott, Berry, & Meredith, 1990).

Transformation stage. Surveys of national or community samples of families find that higher religious attendance by Americans lowers the risk of divorce, infidelity, domestic violence, and child physical abuse (Mahoney, 2001; Mahoney et al., 2001). Assuming religious attendance reflects a positive relationship with God for some people, these findings imply that seeking support from God may help in *preventing* relational problems from occurring in families. A very different question is whether a supportive relationship with God could help in *intervening* after family dysfunction or crises occur. Ample research on religious coping with nonfamilial stressors (e.g., natural disasters, illness; Pargament, 1997, 2007; see also Chapter 19 in this volume) suggests that people may often turn to God to help them respond adaptively to major familial stressors.

Yet available research offers families, clergy, and practitioners little guidance on ways on that faith could be part of the solution for highly distressed couples or families because studies thus far have focused on community samples, with two notable exceptions. First, qualitative interviews of female survivors of domestic violence suggest that some women rely on their relationship with God for courage to confront mistreatment by partners and to require change as a condition of reconciliation (Nason-Clark, 1997; Yick, 2008). But to initiate change, women with conservative religious identities must often alter their understanding of God's views about women's rights within marital relationships and adopt the view that God condones divorce if partners will not change. Second, a quantitative study found that divorcees who more often turned to God as a source of support during the year after their divorce reported greater personal growth longitudinally but, unexpectedly, not less depression or conflict with an ex-spouse (Krumrei, Mahoney, & Pargament, 2011b). Also contrary to expectations, a study of parental divorce found that college students who recalled seeking more support from God when their parents divorced within the prior 5 years were more likely to report psychological distress currently (Warner, Mahoney, & Krumrei, 2009). These studies highlight the need for more research with distressed familial subgroups on the ways that people can rely on a relationship with God to reform or exit problematic family structures or processes and adaptively recover from broken family ties.

Tier 1 Struggles: Family Member's Relationship With God as a Struggle

Discovery stage. As people search for family relationships, they may encounter conflicts with God. Just as interpersonal conflict can be defined as an incompatibility between individuals or groups in their selection and pursuit of goals (Fincham & Bradbury, 1991), people may encounter serious incompatibilities in their own desires versus what they view as God's "will" about family life. Such conflicts with God represent one type of spiritual struggle (see Chapter 25 in this volume). Broadly speaking, situations that threaten or harm people's spirituality often trigger spiritual struggles to conserve or transform their approach to the sacred, including their connection to the divine (Pargament, 1997, 2007). Indeed, people may wrestle with God over the ideal ends and means in their search for family relationships. An inability to reconcile their own and God's wishes about family matters may mire people down in spiritual, relational, and psychological turmoil as people face the choice to leave either God or loved ones behind.

To illustrate the potential conflict that people could experience with God about the formation of family ties, consider the situation faced by nonheterosexuals raised to believe that God only approves of heterosexual relationships (see Chapter 34 in this volume). Many individuals appear to reject this notion and instead sustain a connection to God as they pursue same-sex unions. Specifically, a national U.S. survey found no differences in how often bisexual, gay, and lesbian individuals pray compared with heterosexuals, with all groups praying, on average, between once a day to several times per week (Sherkat, 2002; personal communication, August 19, 2011). Yet studies are needed that directly examine struggles with God that people from any sexual orientation face when their goal to be married seems unattainable. For example, those who view God as an all-loving, omnipotent being who desires marriage for faithful followers may become angry or confused with God if they have prayed for a spouse and patiently followed what they perceive are God's mandates for dating, but years go by without a suitable partner materializing. This may be taken as a sign that God has failed to intervene. Another line of needed research involves struggles with God over the best pathways to establish a union. For example, people who violate what they believe God desires, perhaps cohabiting before engagement or having a child out of wedlock, may persist in a dysfunctional relationship with an uncommitted partner, hoping that eventually marriage will make things right in God's eyes.

Painful struggles with God might also emerge when people form family units, although studies are needed. One relevant finding is that unmarried U.S. fathers who live in impoverished, urban cities are less likely to live with or spend time with their offspring if they have a conservative Christian background (Wildeman, 2008). Perhaps unmarried parents who view the circumstances of the birth of a child as contrary to God's precepts more often experience a sense of shame or unworthiness that compromises their attachment to their child. Married spouses might also struggle with God over their ambivalence about an unintended pregnancy that interferes with forming a strong parent–child or coparental alliance.

Maintenance stage. People in distressed relationships might also seek support from God to maintain family ties in ways that backfire. For example, Butler and Harper (1994) described ways that couples in marital therapy may privately seek solace from God and displace their marital woes onto God rather than effectively communicate with their spouse. More controlled research needs to examine the seemingly rare, but potentially toxic, ways that individuals may turn to God to cope with marital difficulties. For example, some may pray for God to change the spouse rather than directly confront marital issues. People may also struggle with God over a secret desire to exit a dissatisfying marriage, especially in absence of clear-cut violations of marital vows that might justify a divorce in God's eyes. Such undisclosed struggles could take a toll on individuals, exacerbating private misgivings that further strain the marriage.

Given that children and adolescents from more religiously engaged families tend to exhibit fewer behavioral problems than other families (e.g., Smith, 2005), some parents may feel a strong sense of responsibility to God to socialize their offspring effectively. Such parents may, in turn, experience struggles with God if they have difficulties eliciting and maintaining positive child behavior. Such struggles could range from feelings of shame, guilt, or punishment about parental ineffectiveness to confusion and anger with God about their children's problems to doubts and despair about God's failure to intervene. Two studies have examined spiritual struggles with parenting, both of which used negative religious coping with items that predominantly assessed strain in a parent's relationship with God. For both parents of at-risk preschoolers (Dumas & Nissley-Tsiopinis, 2006) and children with autism (Tarakeshwar & Pargament, 2001), greater spiritual struggles were correlated with greater parental distress and depression. Clearly, more research is needed on ways that parents' relationships God could exacerbate poor parental and coparental adjustment, particularly when youth exhibit maladjustment.

Transformation stage. As noted, studies on faith and family life have overwhelmingly relied on national or community samples rather than subgroups of distressed couples or families. As a result, much remains to be learned about ways that people may become mired in struggles with God that thwart radical change in the face of family crises or dysfunction. Two lines of research highlight the possibility that faith could be part of the problem in some distressed families. First, qualitative studies of female survivors of domestic violence indicate that some women struggle with God about whether forgiveness requires them to reconcile with an abusive partner. Others wrestle with the risk of losing their relationship with God by failing to make the marriage work, particularly if children are involved, versus their risks of reconciling repeatedly with an abusive partner who verbally repents but fails to change behaviorally (Nason-Clark, 1997; Yick, 2008). Second, quantitative research on postdivorce adjustment indicates that the more that divorcees engaged in negative spiritual coping strategies in the year following the marital dissolution, the more depression and conflict with the ex-spouse they longitudinally reported. These adverse effects remained after controlling for initial postdivorce adjustment, overall religious involvement, and nonreligious methods of coping with divorce during the subsequent year (Krumrei et al., 2011b). Furthermore, the more divorcees specifically turned to God to try to forgive themselves, their ex-spouse, and God for their divorce over time, the more they viewed their ex-spouse as controlled by demonic forces and the more both ex-spouses engaged in verbal aggression with each other (Krumrei, Mahoney, & Pargament, 2008). College students who reported having had spiritual struggles with parental divorce when it occurred also reported greater current psychosocial maladjustment (Warner et al., 2009). These initial findings highlight the need for more research with distressed samples to better understand maladaptive ways of turning to God to cope with family problems, such as triangulating God into dysfunctional family dynamics, which then escalates individual and family maladjustment.

TIER 2: A FAMILY RELATIONSHIP AS SPIRITUAL IN THE SEARCH FOR FAMILY RELATIONSHIPS

Tier 2: Overview

The search for the sacred can be woven into the search for family relationships when a family relationship itself is invested with spiritual properties. Religions offer people a myriad of spiritual beliefs and rituals that transport family relationships to the sacred realm (Onedera, 2008). Religious weddings and baby-naming ceremonies vividly exemplify occasions in which family bonds are enveloped in a rich web of spiritual cognitions, behaviors, and emotions. In turn, viewing family bonds through a sacred lens and engaging in spiritual activities with family members may help motivate people to create and maintain family ties. Yet when family relationships go awry, people may encounter painful struggles as they attempt to conserve or transform their understanding of a given family bond as a spiritual end and means. This section focuses on ways that family relationships themselves can function as a spiritual resource or struggle. Emerging research shows that even those who do not report having a personal or close relationship with a deity nevertheless often experience family life as having a spiritual dimension. For example, all of the heterosexual couples from diverse religious traditions who Dollahite and colleagues recruited for qualitative interviews because they were highly religious imbued their marriage with divine qualities, but not all of them construed God as an interactive third "person" in the union (Goodman & Dollahite, 2006).

Tier 2 Resources: Spiritual Family Relationship as a Resource

Discovery stage. Studies on the sanctification of intimate adult relationships indicate that many U.S. heterosexual and same-sex couples perceive their marital or cohabiting union as having a spiritual dimension (for a review, see Mahoney et al., in press). "Sanctification" is a construct broadly conceptualized for psychological research as "perceiving an aspect of life as having divine significance and meaning" (Mahoney et al., in press; Pargament & Mahoney, 2005). Thus far, sanctification has been operationalized in two ways. Nontheistic sanctification involves perceiving a relationship as having sacred qualities. For example, in a study of married couples pregnant with their first child, most spouses agreed to some degree (i.e., ratings above anchor of "neutral" to "strongly agree") that my marriage "is sacred to me" (93% of wives; 90% of husbands), "seems like a miracle to me" (88%, 73%), and "connects my spouse and me to something greater than ourselves" (84%, 78%; Mahoney, Pargament, & DeMaris, 2009). Likewise, most of these couples endorsed items tapping into theistic sanctification, which refers to perceiving a bond to be a manifestation of God. Examples include "God played a role in how I ended up being married to my spouse" (86% of wives; 79% of husbands),

"I see God's handiwork in my marriage" (84%, 74%), and "In mysterious ways, God touches my marriage" (79%; 74%). Notably these married couples from the U.S. Midwest attended religious services at rates similar to other married U.S. couples with children, implying that many married Americans may view their marriages as having divine significance. Furthermore, in a national sample of dating and cohabiting couples, 55% of respondents endorsed "strongly agree" to the statement "God is at the center of my relationship" (Henderson, Ellison, & Glenn, 2010). Similarly, many parents also report that they view parenting as a sacred calling (Mahoney et al., in press).

Consistent with the benefits of sanctification for other aspects of life, greater sanctification of an adult union is tied to greater relational satisfaction, net of other factors (Mahoney et al., in press). Thus, although studies are needed to verify whether sanctification beliefs facilitate the formation of couples' relationships, hypothetically people may often strive to find a "soul mate" who elicits the perception that their union possesses sacred qualities or involves God's intentions or actions. The sanctification of parenthood may likewise intensify adults' efforts to do whatever is necessary to form a divine parent–child relationship. When a sacred family relationship appears possible, people may more often form a commitment to a partner or child and invest resources to firmly establish their bond.

Maintenance stage. Growing evidence supports the finding that viewing a family relationship as sanctified helps to maintain the quality of the formed bond. For example, in surveys of national and community samples of generally happily married couples, greater sanctification of marriage predicts less marital conflict and greater marital satisfaction and commitment after controlling for demographics, spouses' general religiousness, and unmeasured characteristics (i.e., fixed-effects modeling) of couples' relationships (DeMaris, Mahoney, & Pargament, 2010; Ellison, Henderson, Glenn, & Harkrider, 2011; Lichter & Carmalt, 2009; Mahoney et al., 1999). Perceiving sexual relations with a partner as sanctified also covaries strongly with greater sexual satisfaction among newlyweds (Hernandez, Mahoney, & Pargament, 2011) and unmarried college students involved in "loving relationships" (N. A. Murray-Swank, Pargament, & Mahoney, 2005). Furthermore, although newlyweds are less prone to appraise their sex lives as connected to God or marked by sacred qualities than the marriage as a whole, viewing marital sexuality as sacred robustly predicts sexual and marital quality longitudinally (Hernandez & Mahoney, 2012). Finally, greater similarity between spouses on sanctity of marriage predicts marital quality beyond the impact of the degree that each spouse personally views their marriage in a sacred light (Lichter & Carmalt, 2009).

When it comes to parent–child relationships, wide variation exists within and across religious subcultures about the goal of fostering children's obedience versus autonomy and the disciplinary method of spanking (Ellison & Bradshaw, 2008), but a broad agreement exists that parents should be affectionate and devoted to their children (Onedera, 2008). Thus, greater sanctity of parenting may translate into differing patterns of parenting depending on how people construe spiritually responsible parental goals and methods. For example, an initial study found that greater sanctification of parenting was tied to more spanking and positive interactions with their children when mothers interpreted the Bible literally (A. Murray-Swank, Mahoney, & Pargament, 2006). In contrast, greater sanctification was tied to less spanking and did not alter relatively high levels of positive mother–child interactions for mothers with more liberal views of the Bible. For all mothers, sanctification related to less verbal hostility and more consistency in parenting.

In another initial, small-scale study, greater sanctification of parenting related to greater use of positive strategies by mothers and fathers (e.g., praise, induction) to elicit young children's moral conduct (Volling, Mahoney, & Rauer, 2009). Finally, parents from a low-income, urban setting who reported greater sanctification of parenting also reported greater investment of effort to care for their children but not parental satisfaction or efficacy (Dumas & Nissley-Tsiopinis, 2006). Overall, viewing parenting as a sacred mission seems to strengthen parents' pursuit of their parenting goals and their reliance on their preferred childrearing methods, but more studies are needed to confirm this conclusion.

In addition to having spiritual cognitions about a given family bond, family members can behaviorally integrate spirituality into their relationships by participating in spiritually focused activities together. Numerous studies have found that similarity in spouses' attendance at religious services predicts marital quality better than either spouse's own attendance (Mahoney, 2010; Mahoney et al., 2001). Furthermore, the more couples say they engage in spiritual activities together, the better marital interaction patterns they report (Fiese & Tomcho, 2001; Lichter & Carmalt, 2008; Mahoney et al., 1999). Yet one could argue that any ritualistic or recreational activity that family members share in common could facilitate relational quality. Thus, studies are needed that target ways people overtly engage in unique spiritual activities together that may enhance their relationships. Two such examples of constructs that tap into behavioral manifestations of dyadic spirituality that could be witnessed by others (e.g., children, researchers) are highlighted next.

First, Brelsford and Mahoney (2008) examined the extent to which mothers and college students attending a Midwestern state university reported they candidly discussed their spiritual journeys, questions, and doubts with one another, a construct labeled "spiritual disclosure." Greater dialogue about spiritual matters was associated with greater use of collaborative methods to resolve conflict, even controlling for the degree to which the pair discussed other sensitive topics and each party reported religion or spirituality to be personally important. Second, Brelsford and Mahoney (2009) examined the extent to which mothers and college students suggested to one another that they rely on God and spirituality as a mediator during conflictual interactions, a construct labeled here as "spiritual mediation" (this construct was previously labeled "theistic mediation" but was assessed with both theistic and nontheistic items). More specifically, both family members reported the degree that each party openly suggested the pair call on God and spirituality to help them listen to one another, remain calm and nondefensive, and use compromise or collaboration when discussing conflicts. Greater levels of theistic meditation were related to fewer conflicts, higher levels of relationship satisfaction, and more adaptive communication strategies.

This section has showcased initial findings on a few possible mechanisms for which researchers assessed cognitions or behaviors that infused family relationships with spiritual properties. In moving forward to replicate and expand this body of research, investigators need to identify spiritual mechanisms likely to apply to traditional and nontraditional families. For example, two initial qualitative studies revealed that same-sex couples, like heterosexual couples, often believe that their union possesses divine, transcendent qualities (Rostosky, Riggle, Brodnicki, & Olson, 2008) and are similar in intrinsic religiosity (i.e., depth and salience of internal religiousness), with both factors predicting greater relationship satisfaction (Rostosky, Otis, Riggle, Kelly, & Brodnicki, 2008); however, unlike heterosexual couples, same-sex couples rarely talk about calling on God as a third party to help them sustain their union, and similarity in religious attendance or activities was not related to relationship happiness. This pattern of findings suggests that some spiritual mechanisms, such as sanctification and spiritual disclosure, may apply to diverse types of couples and families. Other spiritual mechanisms, however, may play a prevalent role in subsamples in which family members mutually experience God as an invisible but active "person" in their family system. Theistic meditation represents this type of construct. Overall, more empirical work needs to uncover specific spiritual processes that help people maintain their chosen family bonds.

Transformation stage. When families face serious family crises or dysfunction, they may tap into unrealized or new perspectives about the spiritual nature of their bonds to help them adaptively rework family structure and processes. Again, systematic empirical research on such change processes needs to be conducted. Hypothetically, people could draw on spiritual beliefs or behaviors centered on family life to help them transform their family when a member ceases to fulfill an established family function. Consider, for example, a heterosexual couple who marry, agreeing that their family structure will embody their respective spiritual callings in life by him earning money in the labor market to support the family and her working as a stay-at-home mother. What happens, however, if he becomes unemployable and disabled because of a medical or mental illness? Faced with the challenge of altering their martial roles, the couple might unite around the superordinate goal of family stability. By sanctifying this goal, they may better adjust to the wife becoming the primary wage earner. Alternatively, when a family member violates normative expectations about how to treat another family member, such as acting out sexually or aggressively, family members may reflect more deeply on family dynamics that match their spiritual values; such deliberations may facilitate confrontation and confession, and forgiveness and repentance as people strive to keep their family intact, but they may radically change their relational processes to maintain their relationships.

Tier 2 Struggles: Spiritual Family Relationship as a Struggle

Discovery stage. Social science studies on faith and family life have been dominated by the conceptual lens of "religious familism," a term that refers to the ideology that the family is the central unit of social order and should be governed by certain religious imperatives (Edgell, 2005; Wilcox, 2006). Sociological work on religious familism in the United States has highlighted ways that mainline religions, particularly conservative branches of U.S. Protestantism, have promoted certain norms about family structure. Namely, traditional religious doctrines idealize and reinforce American, middle-class, and mid-20th-century views of "the good family" as being composed of married heterosexuals who bear and raise biological children (Browning & Clairmont, 2006; Edgell, 2005). In response, researchers have sought to determine whether public involvement in organized religion is related to the higher likelihood of men and women getting married, women giving birth, and heterosexuals fulfilling traditional roles as husbands and wives in a family. Yet researchers have left largely untouched the spiritual dilemmas that people face if they are unable to create traditional or untraditional family relationships. Because I was unable to locate empirical studies focused on spiritual struggles triggered by difficulties in forming family relationships, I illustrate the need for such work by discussing infertility.

For centuries, traditional doctrines across major world religions have held that procreation and thus sexual intercourse should occur only between a married man and woman (Browning & Clairmont, 2006; Ruether, 2000). In turn, the conception and birth of a biological child has been portrayed as a living, spiritual symbol of marital love. Thus, many people may implicitly or explicitly assume that conceiving children via sexual intercourse is inherent to creating a spiritual family unit. Indeed, 78% of husbands and 84% of wives from a region in the U.S. Midwest perceived their first pregnancy to be a manifestation of God and marked by sacred qualities to some degree (Mahoney, Pargament, & DeMaris, 2009). Notably, these married couples attended religious services at rates similar to other married U.S. couples with children, implying that many people may feel spiritually called to have biological children with a spouse. The experience of infertility obviously blocks this goal, raising complex questions. Infertile couples may struggle with the traditional concepts that (a) biological relatedness is necessary or sufficient to define a parent–child bond as sacred, or (b) "natural" methods are spiritually superior to "non-natural" routes to establish parenthood, such as assisted reproductive technology and surrogate birth mothers, or the adoption of donor eggs, sperm, embryos, or children. Same-sex couples or unmarried individuals who desire parent–child relationships may wrestle with choices brought about by technology that conflict with their assumptions on the spiritually ideal way to form family bonds. Prior research on negative spiritual coping with nonfamilial issues would predict that spiritual struggles with infertility as well as other roadblocks to forming family relationships could intensify individual and relational distress, but studies are needed to confirm such predictions. Hopefully, the next decade will usher in such work.

Maintenance stage. Whereas open-minded spiritual dialogues and shared spiritual activities seem to sustain harmonious family processes, spiritual struggles between family members appear to produce the opposite effect. Before reviewing such evidence, it must be emphasized that serious intrafamilial disputes focused on faith are the exception, not the rule. For example, religion falls near the bottom of topics that newlyweds report cause marital arguments (Oggins, 2003). Nevertheless, because spirituality can deeply anchor one's priorities in life, including family goals, and shape the pursuit of these ends (Mahoney, 2005), spiritually grounded clashes may be especially destructive, even if infrequent. This paradox is evident in sociological research on domestic violence and marital conflict. On one hand, higher religious attendance substantially decreases the risk of being the victim or perpetrator of domestic violence in dating, cohabiting, and marital unions (Mahoney, 2010), and spouses' personal involvement in religion neither increases nor decreases the frequency of marital conflicts (Mahoney et al., 2001). On the other hand, the small fraction of married couples (around 8%) who display major discrepancies in their interpretation of the Bible are far more likely to argue with each other (Curtis & Ellison, 2002) and to report that husbands are physically aggressive toward their wives (Ellison, Bartkowski, & Anderson, 1999) than couples who have similar Biblical attitudes. Although it also rarely occurs, conflict between parents over religion predicts greater child maladjustment (Bartkowski, Xu, & Levin, 2008), implying that spiritual struggles between spouses can escalate coparenting conflict and ineffective parenting.

Marked dissimilarity between parents and adolescents on global religious variables, such as religious attendance or importance of religion, are also atypical, but this dissimilarity decreases satisfaction with the relationship (Mahoney, 2010). Qualitative observations also reveal that highly religiously parents who dispense heavy-handed lectures, rather than taking an open-minded approach during spiritual discussions with teens, unwittingly alienate their adolescents (Dollahite & Thatcher, 2008). Finally, in an initial quantitative study on dyadic spiritual struggles in a family context, Brelsford and Mahoney (2009) examined the extent to which mothers and college students openly aligned with God and spirituality against the other party during conflicts, a construct labeled here as "spiritual one-upmanship" (the construct was previously labeled "theistic triangulation" but was assessed with both theistic and nontheistic items). Specifically, both family members reported the degree to which each overtly suggested their position was spirituality superior and backed up by God's support. As expected, greater spiritual one-upmanship was related to less satisfaction with the relationship and more use of verbal hostility and stonewalling during disputes. Although more studies are needed, these findings highlight maladaptive ways family members can pull spirituality into marital and parent–adolescent interactions.

Another key direction for future research is to identify unique spiritual mechanisms that sustain excessively rigid or harsh parenting of children. Critics of corporal punishment have argued that parents may lean on certain Bible passages to defend physically abusive parenting (Rodriguez & Henderson, 2010). Parenthetically, the more that parents from a broad array of Christian denominations endorse orthodox attitudes about the Bible, God's role in their lives, and the authority of their religious community, the more they value child obedience and conformity (Mahoney et al., 2001). Yet the hypothesis that highly devout Christian parents are more likely than other parents to justify physically abusive acts on spiritual grounds has not been verified. The closest study to date examined links between religious orientation and the risk of physical child abuse on the basis of responses to the Child Abuse Potential Inventory (CAPI) by 207 regularly attending Christians across the spectrum of liberal to conservative denominations (Rodriguez & Henderson, 2010). The more respondents indicated that they used religion for self-serving and instrumental purposes (i.e., extrinsic orientation), the higher their CAPI scores, a link exacerbated by greater social conformity. But the degree to which religion was well integrated into participants' identities and pursued for its own sake (i.e., intrinsic orientation) was unrelated to their CAPI scores. Dyslin and Thomsen (2005) found the same results for college students' risk of abusing hypothetical offspring. Furthermore, a longitudinal study found that frequent religious attendance by U.S. parents markedly decreased, not increased, the incidence of physical abuse substantiated by the child protective system (Brown, Cohen, Johnson, & Salzinger, 1998). Also, in low-income and minority families, greater religious attendance and importance of spirituality to single mothers correlates with less risk of child maltreatment (e.g., Carothers, Borkowski, Lefever, & Whitman, 2005). Thus, despite the finding that U.S. parents who belong to conservative Christian groups or interpret the Bible literally are more likely to spank children than other parents (Mahoney, 2010; Mahoney et al., 2001), adults who take their chosen faith seriously appear to be less likely to be physically abusive toward children than other adults. Yet a minority of parents may exploit certain spiritual beliefs about parenting to justify child maltreatment, a possibility underscored by 21% of U.S. Midwestern college students who had a history of physical maltreatment, recalling the perpetrator had used spiritual rationales to justify their conduct (Bottoms, Nielsen, Murray, & Filipas, 2004). Clearly, more research is needed to identify specific spiritual beliefs about parenting that perpetuate and discourage physical maltreatment of youth.

Transformation stage. In this section, I discuss emerging evidence that family crises or dysfunction can be interpreted in a negative spiritual light that exacerbates peoples' suffering over family difficulties. I highlight three constructs that reflect the danger of investing family structures or processes with either divine or demonic significance: sacred loss, desecration, and demonization. Recent studies on postdivorce adjustment illustrates that all three spiritual mechanisms appear to intensify personal and relational distress when relationships break down.

Sacred loss and desecration involve spiritual cognitions that an event has injured an aspect of life thought to embody sacred qualities or God's presence (Pargament, Magyar, Benore, & Mahoney, 2005). A divorce, for example, could be appraised as an event that causes a marriage to fall from the sacred realm. Sacred loss appraisals focus on a sense of sacred loss, such as "Something I held as sacred is no longer present in my life," or "I lost something I thought God wanted for me." Desecration appraisals focus on a sense of intentional violation or harm of a sacred object, such as "Something that was sacred to me was destroyed" or "A part of my life that God made sacred was attacked." In an initial study on spiritual coping with divorce with adults from the Midwest, three quarters of respondents endorsed such negative spiritual appraisals about their recent divorce even though they, like other divorcees, were less religiously or spiritually engaged than the general U.S. population (Krumrei et al., 2009, 2011b). About one third of college students at a Midwestern state university also endorsed these negative spiritual beliefs about their parents' divorce (Warner et al., 2009). Furthermore, the two appraisals were essentially fused together for divorcees and children of divorce (correlated around .90). Thus, the more family members viewed a divorce as a sacred loss, the more they also viewed the divorce as a violation of sacred vows. In contrast, in a study of a wide range of negative life events, sacred loss and desecration cognitions were uncorrelated (Pargament et al., 2005). Thus, life stressors that tend to be viewed as beyond human control (e.g., natural disasters, accidents, illness) often may be perceived as a sacred loss without attributions of spiritual culpability, whereas divorce typically may be seen as a spiritual loss due to human culpability. Furthermore, these two negative spiritual appraisals were not found to have a psychosocial "upside" for postdivorce adjustment, whereas sacred loss triggered by diverse stressors was tied to greater personal growth. For example, the more divorcees viewed their divorce as a sacred loss and desecration, the more depression and dysfunctional conflict tactics with the ex-spouse they reported longitudinally, even after accounting for typically helpful nonspiritual and spiritual coping strategies (Krumrei et al., 2011b). Likewise, college students who retrospectively recalled experiencing their parental divorce as a spiritual loss and desecration reported greater current personal and family-related distress (Warner et al., 2009).

Demonization refers to interpreting someone or something as being controlled by destructive powers of a transcendental nature (Krumrei, Mahoney, & Pargament, 2011b; Pargament, 1997). More specifically, a demonic appraisal is the belief that the devil or demonic forces directly or indirectly caused an event. Such beliefs offer a means to understand suffering while conserving the belief in a just world or benevolent God. In the case of Krumrie et al.'s (2011a) study of 100 divorcees, 48% viewed their divorce as demonic in one or more of the following three ways: demonized the divorce itself (36%), believed their ex-spouse was operating under demonic influences (43%), and viewed themselves as under the control of demonic forces (31%). Greater anger and posttraumatic anxiety symptoms, such as intrusive negative thoughts and avoidance, covaried with all three forms of demonization. Greater depression was also associated with greater demonization of the divorce or oneself.

Taken together, these initial findings indicate that family difficulties can deeply threaten peoples' assumptions about the sanctity of family relationships. Thus, paradoxically, to the degree that people invest family relationships with spiritual properties, they may incur added costs when these relationships go awry. Far more research is needed to understand the spiritual struggles that people face if they are challenged to reform family dynamics that transgress their spiritual values or to let go entirely of bonds they once held sacred. One important line of future research revolves around distressed couples' perceptions that a partner has desecrated their relationship by engaging in serious wrongdoing, such as infidelity, domestic violence, compulsive gambling or spending, or pornography addiction. Another critical line of research involves how parents and children manage their relationships when any family member engages in behavior that deeply contradicts the stated spiritual virtues that their relationships should embody, such as parents neglecting or maltreating their children, or children treating parents in ways the parents view as reprehensible.

TIER 3: RELATIONSHIP WITH A RELIGIOUS COMMUNITY IN THE SEARCH FOR FAMILY RELATIONSHIPS

Tier 3: Overview

The third tier in the relational spirituality framework addresses family member(s) relationships with religious communities. Religious communities may support or reject the spiritual cognitions or behaviors that people use to discover, maintain, and transform their family relationships. In turn, individuals may be attracted or repelled by various religious subgroups' views of their family, and thus may experience a religious community as an added source of support or strain on the basis of the goodness of fit between the respective parties' approach to family life. In addition, people who deviate from familial norms advocated by their religious group may more often experience spiritual struggles that intensify family-related distress and jeopardize access to spiritual resources to strengthen their families. People embedded in a religious network that affirms their family choices, however, may more readily draw on spirituality as a resource to form and sustain their families. Thus, although people may rely strictly on private efforts to build a relationship with God or invest their family relationships with spiritual properties, religious communities constitute public social groups that are uniquely positioned to reinforce the spiritual mechanisms already discussed in this chapter. Religious groups can also offer families socially based spiritual resources and struggles that have no direct parallels in secular organizations. Before elaborating, three broad cultural issues pertinent to Tier 3 need recognition not addressed in the discussions of Tier 1 or Tier 2.

Three Cultural Considerations

Although religious groups may endorse norms for family life that fall anywhere along the continuum of progressive to conservative social values for family life also advocated by civic or political organizations (e.g., pro- or antigay marriage), a unique value that diverse religious groups share is to help people integrate spirituality into daily life. In short, religious communities represent a distinctive public context in which family members are likely to be exposed to and encouraged to adopt various spiritual cognitions and behaviors about family life. These include the spiritual processes covered in this chapter, such as benevolent prayer, sanctification, or sacred loss–desecration. As sociologists have emphasized, however, religious groups can serve nonspiritual, social functions that other well-organized and well-funded community organizations could provide to families. These generic social functions include heightening the family's integration into their broader culture; providing structured opportunities to invest time in family activities, alongside families with similar values; and aiding in the socialization of children (Edgell, 2005, Wilcox, 2006). Of course, people may often interpret seemingly secular functions served by religious communities as spiritual. For example, a "secular" marital education program or parent support group delivered in a religious setting may be perceived by participants as a "blessing." Furthermore, qualitative studies of couples and single parents often indicate that religious groups simultaneously fulfill spiritual and nonspiritual functions (e.g., Goodman & Dollahite, 2006; Sparks et al., 2005). Thus, attending religious services may reinforce adaptive spiritual beliefs or behaviors (e.g., prayer for partner) as well as humanistic virtues widely promoted by religious and secular groups as being helpful to family relationships (e.g., compassionate love, forgiveness). To date, however, quantitative studies that have attempted to assess the role of religious communities for family life have relied heavily on global markers, such as religious affiliation or attendance rates. Such single-item measures confound the spiritual and nonspiritual functions that religious groups may serve, making it difficult to untangle and appreciate these distinctive, but co-occurring, roles that religious communities can serve for family life.

Second, the extent to which religious communities help or hinder family life rests in the eye of the beholder and the particular aspect of family life under consideration. The differentiation of the three stages of family relationships in the relational spirituality framework illuminates points of division and consensus across religious communities. In broad strokes, issues related to the discovery and transformation of family relationships tend to generate religiously based conflict, whereas diverse religious subgroups tend to agree about the ideal ways to maintain family bonds. Regarding the discovery stage, as noted, debates exist in religious circles about bestowing equal spiritual status to the intentional formation of traditional and nontraditional families. For the stage of maintenance, however, religious (and secular) subgroups tend to speak in one voice about the desirability of sustaining healthy family relationships and the optimal pathways to reach this goal, such as being loving, selfless, forgiving, faithful, and honest in kinship circles. In short, broad cultural consensus tends to exist about the virtues that ideally should permeate family bonds so they endure. Yet opinion again differs widely within and across religious subgroups about the transformation stage and defensible grounds to reform or exit distressed relationships. For instance, some theologians argue that believers who ground their ultimate sense of significance in a secure relationship with God should demand change or sever family relationships that are dysfunctional, rather than enable their own mistreatment (Ruether, 2001). Others point out the need for greater effort and self-sacrifice to sustain family bonds (Browning & Clairmont, 2006), as evidenced by nontrivial rates of divorce by Catholics (28%), Protestants (34%), and "born again" Christians (33%; Barna Group, 2009). The dilemma that religious groups face is determining when justice is best served by insisting a marriage can be saved or by supporting all family members when an irreparably damaged marriage ends.

Third, religious institutions face obvious challenges in responding to the growing pluralism of family structures in modern societies. Some social scientists postulate that religious institutions will survive in the 21st century to the degree they defend and support nuclear families who most often engage in communal worship (Wilcox, 2006). For example, 56% of married parents with children attend religious services two to three times per month compared with 39% of single mothers or 39% of cohabiting couples with children (Centers for Disease Control and Prevention, 2012). Other scholars predict that religious institutions will thrive to the degree they increase their affirmation and outreach to the rising number of nontraditional families (Edgell, 2005). In the United States, for example, in the 1960s, 91% of U.S. minors lived with married, biological parents; this rate dropped to 69% by 2009, with 27% of minors living with single parents, 10% with married stepparents, and 9% with cohabiting couples or nonparental caregivers (Kreider & Ellis, 2011, Figure 6, p. 9). Yet 77% of single mothers and 78% of cohabiting couples report that religion is "somewhat" or "very important" to their daily life, compared with 89% of married parents (U.S. National Survey of Family Growth, 2006–2008). Thus many people in traditional and nontraditional families appear to value something that religion offers. The unanswered question is "what is it?"

Tier 3 Resources: Relationship With a Religious Community as a Resource

Discovery stage. Scarce research has addressed specific ways that people may draw support from religious communities to form family relationships. The need for such research is illustrated by inconclusive evidence that heterosexuals rely on their religious community to help structure their roles in marriage (Edgell, 2005; Hernandez & Mahoney, 2012). Conceptually, researchers have highlighted alternative Christian models that may influence marital roles. A complementary model holds that God intends for men and women to hold distinct, traditional roles in the family. In its most extreme form, men are assigned the role of sole breadwinner who holds authority over family decisions. In turn, women are ascribed the role of full-time homemaker, particularly after children are born. A contrasting model of egalitarianism in Christian circles argues that husbands and wives should hold equal authority in family life, divide domestic labor evenly, and mutually pursue paid labor. Hypothetically, people would be more likely to create family systems consistent with their religious group's stance on this complementary–egalitarian continuum.

Yet empirical evidence, on the basis of national surveys of religious denomination and attendance as well as qualitative interviews of religious subgroups, reveals a far more complex picture of religion and *attitudes* about gender relations in families than implied by these two polarized models (Edgell, 2005). Muslims and conservative Christian Protestants living in the United States hold far more diverse and flexible attitudes about feminism, women's labor market participation, and familial hierarchy than implied by conservative religious teachings (Edgell, 2005; Hernandez & Mahoney, 2012). Even more telling are studies focused on *behavioral* indexes of gender roles that find virtually no differences in how married Christians who belong to liberal versus conservative denominations manage decision making or divide household labor (Mahoney, 2010). Greater religious attendance, Biblical conservatism, and sanctification of parent–infant relationships, however, are associated with married couples adopting a traditional division of labor in daily infant care tasks after the transition to parenthood (DeMaris, Mahoney, & Pargament, 2011). Yet, recent qualitative research has found that working Christian mothers who view their career as a sacred endeavor blessed by God feel less strain in juggling conflicting work–domestic roles (e.g., Oates, Hall, & Anderson, 2005).

More research is needed to clarify the extent to which diverse religious communities shape the formation and structure of diverse family units and reinforce related spiritual beliefs or practices. One initial study found that same-sex couples who were more involved in their religious community were more likely to hold a public commitment ceremony and take legal steps to form a committed union (Oswald, Goldberg, Kuvalanka, & Clausell, 2008). Thus, involvement in religious communities may facilitate peoples' pursuit of conventional or unconventional family relationships by offering people unique public rituals to solidify their family bonds and infuse them with spiritual significance (e.g., religious wedding and baby-naming ceremonies). Religious groups may help people locate partners who hold a similar spiritual vision of adult unions as well as facilitate shared spirituality between parents and children, which, in turn, may increase their mutual commitment to their family relationships.

Maintenance stage. In qualitative studies of highly religious and married heterosexuals with children, couples from diverse religious traditions report that involvement in their religious communities increases their belief that their marriage has spiritual purposes and their level of engagement in family spiritual activities at home (Dollahite & Marks, 2009; Goodman & Dollahite, 2006). Consistent with these findings, greater general religiousness modestly correlates with the helpful specific spiritual mechanisms reviewed in Tier 1 and Tier 2, including benevolent prayer for partner (Fincham et al., 2008); the sanctification of marriage (e.g., Mahoney et al., 1999), cohabiting unions (Henderson et al., 2010), marital sexuality (Hernandez et al., 2011), and parenting (A. Murray-Swank et al., 2006); and theistic meditation (Brelsford & Mahoney, 2009). Thus, not surprisingly, greater involvement in religious groups appears to facilitate specific spiritual cognitions or behaviors about family life that are associated with better family functioning. Yet studies are needed that spell out direct and mediated pathways of influence between involvement in religious communities and specific spiritual mechanisms for family outcomes. More research is also needed to pinpoint ways that religious groups may motivate family members to adopt virtues that could help them sustain their bonds, such as compassionate love, sacrifice, gratitude, forgiveness, acceptance, and sexual fidelity.

Furthermore, research is needed to identify spiritual mechanisms that, by definition, involve social processes via religious groups that people are unlikely to experience in other social contexts. Possible examples include family members looking up to members of a religious community for inspiration or aid to form or maintain family ties (e.g., spiritual role models; see Chapter 10 in this volume), having spiritually intimate dialogues with fellow believers about family issues, and engaging in joint prayer with or soliciting benevolent prayers from others. In addition, research is needed that clarifies ways that religious organizations may enhance the impact of family-oriented prevention or intervention programs that religious groups offer to their members and other families in their communities. For example, although religious organizations routinely offer premarital, marital, and parenting education programs, little controlled research appears to have evaluated the penetration rates, efficacy, or effectiveness of "church-based" programs, and whether these programs capitalize on participants' spirituality to enhance outcomes. Initial work on integrating prayer for partner into standard marital educational programs illustrates the potential value of augmenting a "secular" marital program with spiritual activities (see Volume 2, Chapter 24, this handbook). Tremendous potential remains for similar collaborative efforts between religious communities and family experts that productively taps into spiritual resources in a respectful and scientifically rigorous manner to strengthen diverse families.

Transformation stage. Ideally, religious leaders and communities could help families confront and recover effectively from serious family problems. Some surveys suggest that people more often turn to clergy for help with marital or family issues than to mental health professionals (Chalfant et al., 1990). Yet clergy often report that couples wait too long before they seek help and they feel unequipped to handle the severity of many problems presented to them (see Volume 2, Chapter 9, this handbook). Qualitative research on victims of domestic violence suggests that women can gain support from their community either to leave or to reconcile with an abusive spouse (Nason-Clark, 1997; Yick, 2008). Yet systematic or controlled studies could not be located that have examined the success of interventions carried out by or in collaboration with religious groups for distressed or clinic-referred couples or families. Hopefully, more in-depth collaborative efforts will develop between religious groups and family intervention specialists to intervene with and generate positive outcomes for distressed families.

Tier 3 Struggles: Relationship With a Religious Community as a Struggle

Discovery stage. Hypothetically, individuals who violate the norms of their religious community to establish an adult union or parent–child bond may be at greater risk to experience spiritually based conflicts with their religious community. Yet systematic research is needed to uncover the struggles that people encounter with religious communities over their choices to form family ties and how such conflicts may undermine peoples' efforts to establish stable relationships with partners or offspring. For example, although a growing body of research shows that homosexuals who feel rejected by their religious communities report greater psychological distress (see Chapter 34 in this volume), it is unclear whether such struggles undermine their desire or ability to establish a committed relationship with a partner. Similarly, scarce research exists on the prevalence or implications of struggles that people encounter with religious networks when they do not form a traditional family because of infertility or nonmarital births. Little also appears to be known empirically about the impact of feeling judged by or upset with religious leaders or fellow believers who may view a prospective union as spiritually subpar because the fiancé is from a different faith tradition (i.e., interfaith marriages) or because of either partner's history of premarital sexuality, cohabitation, nonmarital birth, or divorce. In all of these instances, people may turn away or be turned away from engaging in public religious rituals to solidify their family bonds (see Volume 2, Chapter 9, this handbook). In turn, they may be more likely to view family ties as strictly private matters; dismiss any potential "added value" of solidifying a family unit by getting married before cohabiting or conceiving a child; and reject organized religion as a resource that could facilitate the helpful spiritual mechanisms highlighted previously in Tier 1, Tier 2, or Tier 3.

Maintenance stage. Although spiritual communities ideally could help families access helpful spiritual and nonspiritual resources to sustain healthy family dynamics, these communities could function in the reverse manner by reinforcing harmful spiritual mechanisms highlighted in Tier 1 and Tier 2. Again, however, scarce systematic research has examined the prevalence or implications of family members' turning to members of their religious communities in ways that maintain negative spiritual processes or family dynamics. Although it is well established that family dyads who report dissimilar rates of religious attendance tend to report poorer relational quality (Mahoney, 2010; Mahoney et al., 2001), more research needs to clarify why this may be the case. For example, a married individual may turn to a clergy member or fellow believer for support to tolerate an excessively domineering spouse, which, in turn, might fuel unhealthy power imbalances in the union. Alternatively, a spouse may align with members of a religious community in a judgmental manner against a spouse who holds more liberal or conservative views of family life, which could escalate conflict between the spouses. Similarly, parents may counterproductively triangulate religious groups into conflict with adolescents who explore or develop an identity that triggers parental anxiety. Parents from religious groups with highly conservative social values, for example, may worry their teens will adopt excessively permissive attitudes or actions about media, sexuality, or alcohol use because of their exposure to more liberal peer groups. Conversely, parents committed to religious groups with liberal social values (as well as parents who eschew organized religion entirely) may fear that their teens will become excessively intolerant or exclusionary as a result of closer involvement with conservative peers. Parents who try to draw on religious communities with conservative or liberal ideology to back up their own position may escalate conflict between themselves and their teens and inadvertently push their teens to differentiate their identities in ways that are even more out of line with the parents' (and teen's) faith. Hopefully, more fine-grained empirical work will be conducted to identify specific ways that religious communities may escalate distance or hostility within families.

Transformation stage. People may encounter a variety of spiritual struggles with religious communities when their family relationships seriously go awry. These struggles, in turn, could compromise family members' effective coping. For example, one or more family members may feel spiritual shame about family dysfunction in the eyes of their religious community and harbor fears of being stigmatized, rejected, or judged by their spiritual group. To be protected from such social criticism, a family member may disclose problems to trusted members of their religious group to form alliances with them against other family members. Such triangulation processes may escalate counterproductive cycles of blame and hostility between family members, particularly if religious leaders or fellow believers take sides. Alternatively, family members and religious communities may mutually engage in a "don't ask, don't tell" pattern when dysfunction occurs within family systems, which cuts off families from spiritual and nonspiritual resources that religious communities could offer to help them confront and cope adaptively with serious family issues. Limited in-depth research has investigated these possibilities in distressed subsamples of families. Studies on divorce, however, highlight a tendency toward silence and distance between family members and religious communities when family systems break down. For example, in a national survey of young adults whose parents had divorced, only 25% reported that anyone from their religious community had ever talked to them about the divorce (Marquardt, 2005). Interestingly, older adolescents whose parents divorce are more likely to transition from being "religious and spiritual" to "spiritual but not religious" (Zhai, Ellison, Stokes, & Glenn, 2008). They also decrease their religious attendance but say they feel equally close to God compared with peers from maritally intact families (Zhai, Ellison, Glenn, & Marquardt, 2007). These findings highlight that family difficulties may create a wedge between families and religious community, even as people privately seek support from God to cope.

SUMMARY: INTEGRATION AND RECIPROCITY

In this chapter, I have illustrated three tiers of spiritual beliefs and practices that may help or harm family relationships. Hopefully, researchers and clinicians will be inspired to delve into these mechanisms. These three tiers of mechanisms often may be tightly interwoven, with people experiencing little dissonance in their connections to God, family members, and their religious community. For example, individuals who hold traditional theistic views of God and favor family units headed by married heterosexuals with children may readily find support in socially conservative religious groups that promote marriage and parenthood relatively early in life. Such people may pray alone, with their spouse, and with their religious community to facilitate their efforts to form and maintain a traditional family. A parallel case of integration could be made for individuals who pursue nontraditional searches for both spirituality and family life. The differentiation of the three tiers, however, shines light on debilitating spiritual struggles that people could face in their search for family bonds. For example, those raised in socially conservative religious groups may experience painful spiritual conflicts internally, with God, or with others if they pursue unconventional family bonds. Likewise, those raised with no or loose ties to a religious group may struggle to establish or maintain belief in the sanctity of any type of family unit and may have less access to spiritual practices to strengthen their family. Thus, the stages of discovery and maintenance most likely shape each other across the unfolding of the family life cycle, as people adjust their family structure and processes to accommodate the developmental needs of all family members. Presumably, spirituality could help people cope with the continual challenges to balance firmness versus flexibility in their family structure, and warmth versus control within and across family subsystems over time. Yet spirituality could also trigger or intensify family crises or dysfunction that emerge. Hopefully this chapter will spur further investigation of people's efforts, for better or worse, to integrate all three tiers of spiritual resources across all three stages of family life.

References

Abbott, D. A., Berry, M., & Meredith, W. H. (1990). Religious belief and practice: A potential asset for helping families. *Family Relations, 39*, 443–448. doi:10.2307/585226

Barna Group. (2009, May 8). *Family/kids*. Retrieved from http://www.barna.org/barna update/article/15 familykids/42 new marriage and divorce statistics

Bartkowski, J. P., Xu, X. H., & Levin, M. L. (2008). Religion and child development: Evidence from the early childhood longitudinal study. *Social Science Research, 37*, 18–36. doi:10.1016/j.ssresearch.2007. 02.001

Beach, S. R. H., Hurt, T. R., Fincham, F. D., Kameron, J., Franklin, K. J., McNair, L. M., & Stanley, S. M. (2011). Enhancing marital enrichment through spirituality: Efficacy data for prayer focused relationship enhancement. *Psychology of Religion and Spirituality, 3*, 201–216. doi:10.1037/a0022207

Bottoms, B. L., Nielsen, M., Murray, R., & Filipas, H. (2004). Religion-related child physical abuse: Characteristics and psychological outcomes. *Journal of Aggression, Maltreatment, and Trauma, 8*, 87–114. doi:10.1300/J146v08n01_04

Brelsford, G. M., & Mahoney, A. (2008). Spiritual disclosure between older adolescents and their mothers. *Journal of Family Psychology, 22*, 62–70. doi:10.1037/0893-3200.22.1.62

Brelsford, G. M., & Mahoney, A. (2009). Relying on God to resolve conflict: Theistic mediation and triangulation in relationships between college students and mothers. *Journal of Psychology and Christianity, 28*, 291–301.

Brown, J., Cohen, P., Johnson, J. G., & Salzinger, S. (1998). A longitudinal analysis of risk factors for child maltreatment: Findings of a 17-year prospective study of officially recorded and self-reported child abuse and neglect. *Child Abuse and Neglect, 22*, 1065–1078. doi:10.1016/S0145-2134(98)00087-8

Browning, D. S., & Clairmont, D. A. (Eds.). (2006). *American religions and the family: How faith traditions cope with modernization and democracy*. New York, NY: Columbia University Press.

Butler, M. H., & Harper, J. M. (1994). The divine triangle: God in the marital system of religious couples. *Family Process, 33*, 277–286. doi:10.1111/j.1545-5300.1994.00277.x

Carothers, S. S., Borkowski, J. G., Lefever, J. B., & Whitman, T. L. (2005). Religiosity and the socio-emotional adjustment of adolescent mothers and their children. *Journal of Family Psychology, 19*, 263–275. doi:10.1037/0893-3200.19.2.263

Centers for Disease Control and Prevention. (2012). *National Survey of Family Growth*. Retrieved from http://www.cdc.gov/nchs/nsfg.htm

Chalfant, H. P., Heller, P. L., Roberts, A., Briones, D., Aguirrehochbaum, S., & Farr, W. (1990). The clergy as a resource for those encountering psychological distress. *Review of Religious Research, 31*, 305–313. doi:10.2307/3511620

Curtis, K. T., & Ellison, C. G. (2002). Religious heterogamy and marital conflict—Findings from the national survey of families and households. *Journal of Family Issues, 23*, 551–576.

DeMaris, A., Mahoney, A., & Pargament, K. I. (2010). Sanctification of marriage and general religiousness as buffers of the effects of marital inequity. *Journal of Family Issues, 31*, 1255–1278. doi:10.1177/0192513X10363888

DeMaris, A., Mahoney, A., & Pargament, K. I. (2011). Doing the scut work of childcare: Does religiousness encourage greater father involvement? *Journal of Marriage and Family, 73*, 354–368. doi:10.1111/j.1741-3737.2010.00811.x

Dollahite, D. C., & Lambert, N. M. (2007). Forsaking all others: How religious involvement promotes marital fidelity in Christian, Jewish, and Muslim couples. *Review of Religious Research, 48*, 290–307.

Dollahite, D. C., & Marks, L. D. (2009). A conceptual model of family and religious processes in a diverse, national sample of highly religious families. *Review of Religious Research, 50*, 373–391.

Dollahite, D. C., & Thatcher, J. Y. (2008). Talking about religion: How religious youth and parents discuss their faith. *Journal of Adolescent Research, 23*, 611–641. doi:10.1177/0743558408322141

Dumas, J. E., & Nissley-Tsiopinis, J. (2006). Parental global religiousness, sanctification of parenting, and positive and negative religious coping as predictors of parental and child functioning. *The International Journal for the Psychology of Religion, 16*, 289–310. doi:10.1207/s15327582ijpr1604_4

Dyslin, C. W., & Thomsen, C. J. (2005). Religiosity and risk of perpetrating child physical abuse: An empirical investigation. *Journal of Psychology and Theology, 33*, 291–298.

Edgell, P. (2003). In rhetoric and practice: Defining "the good family" in local congregations. In M. Dillon (Ed.), *Handbook of the sociology of religion* (pp. 164–179). New York, NY: Cambridge University Press.

Edgell, P. (2005). *Religion and family in a changing society*. Princeton, NJ: Princeton University Press.

Ellison, C. G., Bartkowski, J. P., & Anderson, K. L. (1999). Are there religious variations in domestic violence? *Journal of Family Issues, 20*, 87–113. doi:10.1177/019251399020001005

Ellison, C. G., & Bradshaw, M. (2008). Religious beliefs, sociopolitical ideology, and attitudes toward corporal punishment. *Journal of Family Issues, 30*, 320–340. doi:10.1177/0192513X08326331

Ellison, C. G., Henderson, A. K., Glenn, N. D., & Harkrider, K. E. (2011). Sanctification, stress, and marital quality. *Family Relations, 60*, 404–420. doi:10.1111/j.1741-3729.2011.00658.x

Fiese, B. H., & Tomcho, T. J. (2001). Finding meaning in religious practices: The relation between religious holiday rituals and marital satisfaction. *Journal of Family Psychology, 15*, 597–609. doi:10.1037/0893-3200.15.4.597

Fincham, F. D., Beach, S. R. H., Lambert, N. M., Stillman, T., & Braithwaite, S. (2008). Spiritual behaviors and relationship satisfaction: A critical analysis of the role of prayer. *Journal of Social and Clinical Psychology, 27*, 362–388. doi:10.1521/jscp.2008.27.4.362

Fincham, F. D., & Bradbury, T. M. (1991). Marital conflict: Towards a more complete integration of research and treatment. In J. Vincent (Ed.), *Advances in family intervention, assessment, and theory* (Vol. 5, pp. 1–24). London, England: Kingsley.

Goodman, M. A., & Dollahite, D. C. (2006). How religious couples perceive the influence of God in their marriage. *Review of Religious Research, 48*, 141–155.

Henderson, A. K., Ellison, C. G., & Glenn, N. D. (2010). *Religion and relationship quality among cohabiting and dating couples*. Manuscript submitted for publication.

Hernandez, K. M., & Mahoney, A. (2012). Balancing sacred callings in career and family life. P. Hill & B. Dik (Eds.), *Advances in workplace spirituality: Theory, research, and application* (pp. 135–156). Charlotte, NC: Information Age.

Hernandez, K. M., Mahoney, A., & Pargament, K. I. (2011). Sanctification of sexuality: Implications for newlyweds' marital and sexual quality. *Journal of Family Psychology, 25*, 775–780. doi:10.1037/a0025103

Hollingsworth, L. D. (2000). Who seeks to adopt a child? Findings from the national survey of family growth. *Adoption Quarterly, 3*, 1–23. doi:10.1300/J145v03n03_01

Hood, R. W., Hill, P. C., & Spilka, B. (2009). *The psychology of religion: An empirical approach* (4th ed.) New York, NY: Guilford Press.

Koenig, H. G., McCullough, M. E., & Larson, D. B. (2001). *Handbook of religion and health.* New York, NY: Oxford University Press. doi:10.1093/acprof:oso/9780195118667.001.0001

Kreider, R. M., & Ellis, R. (2011, June). Living arrangements of children: 2009. *Current Population Reports*, P70-126, U.S. Census Bureau. Washington, DC. Retrieved from http://www.census.gov/prod/2011pubs/p70-126.pdf

Krumrei, E. J., Mahoney, A., & Pargament, K. I. (2009). Divorce and the Divine: The role of spirituality in adjustment to divorce. *Journal of Marriage and Family, 71*, 373–383. doi:10.1111/j.1741-3737.2009.00605.x

Krumrei, E. J., Mahoney, A., & Pargament, K. I. (2011a). Demonic dimensions of divorce: The prevalence of demonization of divorce and links to adult post-divorce adjustment. *Family Relations, 60*, 90–103. doi:10.1111/j.1741-3729.2010.00635.x

Krumrei, E. J., Mahoney, A., & Pargament, K. I. (2011b). Spiritual stress and coping model of divorce: A longitudinal study of a community sample. *Journal of Family Psychology, 25*, 973–985. doi:10.1037/a0025879

Krumrei, E. J., Mahoney, A., & Pargament, K. P. (2008). Turning to God to forgive: More than meets the eye. *Journal of Psychology and Christianity, 27*, 302–310.

Lambert, N. M., & Dollahite, D. C. (2006). How religiosity helps couples prevent, resolve, and overcome marital conflict. *Family Relations, 55*, 439–449. doi:10.1111/j.1741-3729.2006.00413.x

Lambert, N. M., & Dollahite, D. C. (2007). The threefold cord: Marital commitment in religious couples. *Journal of Family Issues, 29*, 592–614. doi:10.1177/0192513X07308395

Lichter, D. T., & Carmalt, J. H. (2009). Religion and marital quality in low-income couples. *Social Science Research, 38*, 168–187. doi:10.1016/j.ssresearch.2008.07.003

Mahoney, A. (2005). Religion and conflict in family relationships. *Journal of Social Issues, 61*, 689–706. doi:10.1111/j.1540-4560.2005.00427.x

Mahoney, A. (2009). *Marriage and family, faith, and spirituality among emerging adults.* Catholic University of America, Institute for Policy Research and Catholic Studies, The Changing Sea. Retrieved from http://www.changingsea.net/essays/Mahoney.pdf

Mahoney, A. (2010). Religion in families 1999–2009: A relational spirituality framework. *Journal of Marriage and Family, 72*, 805–827. doi:10.1111/j.1741-3737.2010.00732.x

Mahoney, A., & Krumrei, E. J. (in press). Questions left unaddressed by religious familism: Is spirituality relevant to nontraditional families? In L. Miller (Ed.), *The Oxford handbook of the psychology of spirituality.* Oxford, England: Oxford University Press.

Mahoney, A., Pargament, K. I., & DeMaris, A. (2009). Couples viewing marriage and pregnancy through the lens of the Sacred: A descriptive study. *Research in the Social Scientific Study of Religion, 20*, 1–46. doi:10.1163/ej.9789004175624.i-334.7

Mahoney, A., Pargament, K. I., & Hernandez, K. M. (in press). Heaven on earth: Beneficial effects of sanctification for individual and interpersonal well-being. In J. Henry (Ed.), *Oxford book of happiness.* Oxford, England: Oxford University Press.

Mahoney, A., Pargament, K. I., Jewell, T., Swank, A. B., Scott, E., Emery, E., & Rye, M. (1999). Marriage and the spiritual realm: The role of proximal and distal religious constructs in marital functioning. *Journal of Family Psychology, 13*, 321–338. doi:10.1037/0893-3200.13.3.321

Mahoney, A., Pargament, K. I., Swank, A., & Tarakeshwar, N. (2001). Religion in the home in the 1980s and 90s: A meta-analytic review and conceptual analysis of religion, marriage, and parenting. *Journal of Family Psychology, 15*, 559–596. doi:10.1037/0893-3200.15.4.559

Marquardt, E. (2005). *Between two worlds: The inner lives of children of divorce.* New York, NY: Crown.

Marsh, R., & Dallos, R. (2000). Religious beliefs and practices and Catholic couples' management of anger and conflict. *Clinical Psychology and Psychotherapy, 7*, 22–36. doi:10.1002/(SICI)1099-0879(200002)7:1<22::AID-CPP217>3.0.CO;2-R

Murray-Swank, A., Mahoney, A., & Pargament, K. I. (2006). Sanctification of parenting: Links to corporal punishment and parental warmth among biblically conservative and liberal mothers. *The International Journal for the Psychology of Religion, 16*, 271–287. doi:10.1207/s15327582ijpr1604_3

Murray-Swank, N. A., Pargament, K. I., & Mahoney, A. (2005). At the crossroads of sexuality and spirituality: The sanctification of sex by college students. *The International Journal for the Psychology of Religion, 15*, 199–219. doi:10.1207/s15327582ijpr1503_2

Nason-Clark, N. (1997). *The battered wife: How Christians confront family violence.* Louisville, KY: Westminster John Knox Press.

National Center for Family & Marriage Research. (2011). *Measures snapshot: National longitudinal study of adolescent health, parent questionnaire.* Retrieved from http://ncfmr.bgsu.edu/pdf/measuressnapshot/religion/file91847.pdf

Oates, K. L., Hall, M. E., & Anderson, T. L. (2005). Calling and conflict: A qualitative exploration of interrole conflict and the sanctification of work in Christian mothers in academia. *Journal of Psychology and Theology, 33*, 210–223.

Oggins, J. (2003). Topics of marital disagreements among African-American and Euro-American newlyweds. *Psychological Reports, 92*, 419–425. doi:10.2466/pr0.2003.92.2.419

Onedera, J. D. (2008). *The role of religion in marriage and family counseling.* New York, NY: Routledge.

Oswald, R. F., Goldberg, A., Kuvalanka, K., & Clausell, E. (2008). Structural and moral commitment among same-sex couples: Relationship duration, religiosity, and parental status. *Journal of Family Psychology, 22*, 411–419. doi:10.1037/0893-3200.22.3.411

Paloutzian, R. F., & Park, C. L. (2005). *Handbook of the psychology of religion and spirituality.* New York, NY: Guilford Press.

Pargament, K. I. (1997). *The psychology of religion and coping: Theory, research, practice.* New York, NY: Guilford Press.

Pargament, K. I. (2007). *Spiritually integrated psychotherapy: Understanding and addressing the sacred.* New York, NY: Guilford Press.

Pargament, K. I., Magyar, G. M., Benore, E., & Mahoney, A. (2005). Sacrilege: A study of sacred loss and desecration and their implications for health and well-being in a community sample. *Journal for the Scientific Study of Religion, 44*, 59–78.

Pargament, K. I., & Mahoney, A. (2005). Sacred matters: Sanctification as a vital topic for the psychology of religion. *The International Journal of the Psychology of Religion, 15*, 179–198. doi:10.1207/s15327582ijpr1503_1

Rodriguez, C. M., & Henderson, R. C. (2010). Who spares the rod? Religious orientation, social conformity, and child abuse potential. *Child Abuse and Neglect, 34*, 84–94. doi:10.1016/j.chiabu.2009.07.002

Rostosky, S. S., Otis, M. D., Riggle, E. D. B., Kelly, S., & Brodnicki, C. (2008). An exploratory study of religiosity and same-sex couple relationships. *Journal of GLBT Family Studies, 4*, 17–36. doi:10.1080/15504280802084407

Rostosky, S. S., Riggle, E. B., Brodnicki, C., & Olson, A. (2008). An exploration of lived religion in same-sex couples from Judeo-Christian traditions. *Family Process, 47*, 389–403. doi:10.1111/j.1545-5300.2008.00260.x

Ruether, R. R. (2001). *Christianity and the making of the modern family.* Boston, MA: Beacon Press.

Sherkat, D. E. (2002). Sexuality and religious commitment in the United States: An empirical examination. *Journal for the Scientific Study of Religion, 41*, 313–323. doi:10.1111/1468-5906.00119

Smith, C. (with Denton, M. L.). (2005). *Soul searching: The religious and spiritual lives of American teenagers.* New York, NY: Oxford University Press.

Sparks, A., Peterson, N. A., & Tangenberg, K. (2005). Belief in personal control among low-income African American, Puerto Rican, and European American single mothers. *Affilia, 20*, 401–415. doi:10.1177/0886109905279872

Tarakeshwar, N., & Pargament, K. (2001). Religious coping in families of children with autism. *Focus on Autism and Other Developmental Disabilities, 16*, 247–260. doi:10.1177/108835760101600408

Volling, B. L., Mahoney, A., & Rauer, A. J. (2009). Sanctification of parenting, moral socialization, and young children's conscience development. *Psychology of Religion and Spirituality, 1*, 53–68. doi:10.1037/a0014958

Warner, H. L., Mahoney, A., & Krumrei, E. J. (2009). When parents break sacred vows: The role of spiritual appraisals, coping and struggles for young adults' adjustment to parental divorce. *Psychology of Religion and Spirituality, 1*, 233–248. doi:10.1037/a0016787

Wilcox, W. B. (2006). Family. In H. R. Ebaugh (Ed.), *Handbook of religion and social institutions* (pp. 97–116). New York, NY: Springer.

Wildeman, C. (2008). Conservative Protestantism and paternal engagement in fragile families. *Sociological Forum, 23*, 556–574. doi:10.1111/j.1573-7861.2008.00076.x

Yick, A. G. (2008). A metasynthesis of qualitative findings on the role of spirituality and religiosity among culturally diverse domestic violence survivors. *Qualitative Health Research, 18*, 1289–1306. doi:10.1177/1049732308321772

Zhai, J. E., Ellison, C. G., Glenn, N. D., & Marquardt, E. (2007). Parental divorce and religious involvement among young Adults. *Sociology of Religion, 68*, 125–144. doi:10.1093/socrel/68.2.125

Zhai, J. E., Ellison, C. G., Stokes, C. E., & Glenn, N. D. (2008). "Spiritual, but not religious": The impact of parental divorce on the religious and spiritual identities of young adults in the United States. *Review of Religious Research, 49*, 379–394.

CHAPTER 21

MYSTICAL EXPERIENCE: CONCEPTUALIZATIONS, MEASUREMENT, AND CORRELATES

Ralph W. Hood Jr. and Leslie J. Francis

Mysticism has been a topic of central interest to the psychology of religion from the early days of the discipline. In his foundational study, James (1902/1985) referred to mysticism as "the root and center" of religion (p. 301). Within the broader field of religious studies, Hick (1989) has maintained that mysticism is integral to all faith traditions and can be expressed in both personal and impersonal terms. The discussion of mysticism is vast. McGinn (1991) identified three distinct literatures in the field that he references as theological, philosophical, and comparative–psychological. To these should be added a fourth literature grounded in measurement-based psychology. Much of this measurement-based literature centers on two scales, the Mysticism Scale (the M Scale) developed by Hood (1975) and the Mystical Orientation Scale (MOS) developed by Francis and Louden (2000a). To provide an overview of this field, this chapter (a) discusses the definition of mysticism, (b) reviews how mysticism has been accessed in survey studies, (c) introduces Hood's M Scale and Francis and Louden's MOS, (d) considers the dimensionality of mysticism, (e) examines the association between mysticism and personality, and (f) explores whether mysticism is linked to psychopathology.

DEFINING MYSTICISM

For definitions to be useful within measurement-based approaches to psychology, they need to be clear, structured, and amenable to operationalization (Francis, 2009). The definition of mysticism offered by Happold (1963) meets these criteria. It embraces seven key components.

The first four characteristics were originally proposed at the beginning of the 20th century by James (1902/1985). The first of James's defining characteristics of mysticism is *ineffability*, which is a negative description emphasizing the private or incommunicable quality of the experience. The subject of this state of mind says that "it defies expression that no adequate report of its contents can be given in words" (James, 1902/1985, p. 302). It appears to follow that this characteristic or quality of mysticism must be directly experienced with the consequence that mystical states are more like states of feeling than like states of intellect. The second of James's defining characteristics of mysticism is *noesis*. This noetic quality pertains to states of insight into levels of truth inaccessible to the discursive intellect. According to James, "they are illuminations, revelations, full of significance and importance, all inarticulate though they remain; and as a rule they carry with them a curious sense of authority after-time" (1902/1985, p. 302). The third of James's defining characteristics of mysticism is *transiency*. Transiency describes the brief, inconstant, and intermittent nature of the experience. Mystical states do not endure for long, although they may recur, "and from one recurrence to another it is susceptible of continuous development in what is felt as inner richness and importance" (James, 1902/1985, p. 302). The fourth of James's defining characteristics of mysticism is *passivity*. Passivity emphasizes both the experience of being controlled by a superior power

DOI: 10.1037/14045-021
APA Handbook of Psychology, Religion, and Spirituality: Vol. 1. Context, Theory, and Research, K. I. Pargament (Editor-in-Chief)
Copyright © 2013 by the American Psychological Association. All rights reserved.

and the undeserved, gratuitous nature of the mystical experience. James differentiated mystical states, strictly so called, from allied occurrences of what he referred to as prophetic speech, automatic writing, and mediumistic trance. Whereas these allied occurrences may be looked on as an interruption, an invasion of the subject's inner life with no residual recollection or significance, mystical states are never merely interruptive. Both memories of the content of mystical experiences and a profound sense of their importance remain with the subject (James, 1902/1985, pp. 302–303).

Moving to Happold's (1963) defining characteristics of mysticism, the fifth characteristic is *consciousness of the oneness of everything*. In this sense, existence is perceived as a unity. Although it may be expressed in different ways by Hindu, Sufi, and Christian contemplatives, the resolution of the dilemma of duality through this sense of the oneness of everything "is at the heart of the most highly developed mystical consciousness" (Happold, 1963, p. 47). Happold's sixth defining characteristic of mysticism is a *sense of timelessness*. According to the mystics, experiences appear to have a timeless quality, which are in an entirely different dimension from that of any known sense of time.

Finally, Happold's seventh aspect of mysticism is called *true ego*. True ego is described as "the conviction that the familiar phenomenal *ego* is not the real *I*" (Happold, 1963, p. 48). According to Happold (1963), "by the *self* Jung does not mean what we normally mean by the word. Rather, it has affinities with the self of Hindu psychology" (p. 50). In Hinduism, the *true self* is called *Atman*, which is immortal, constant, unchanging, and not bound by space or time. In Christian mysticism, the notion of true ego has several names, the *spark*, the *soul spark*, the *center*, the *apex of the soul*, or the *ground of the spirit*. Whatever the nature of this entity, it has been described as closely akin to the divine and sharing in the life of God.

SURVEY STUDIES OF MYSTICAL EXPERIENCE

Hood, Hill, and Spilka (2009, p. 338) distinguished between two ways in which mysticism has been operationalized in survey studies: open-ended responses to specific questions intuitively assumed to tap mystical experience, and an established set of well-tested survey questions. Hood et al. reviewed studies using open-ended responses (pp. 338–342). The value of open-ended responses is that people readily respond to inquiries indicating that mystical experience is not rare. Survey studies have documented this more precisely and confirm the commonality of the report of mystical experience. As we will see, however, these studies have run into the same problem open-ended inquires have: Exactly what are people affirming when they respond positively to inquiries of survey questions assumed to tap into mystical experiences?

There are four survey questions that have been fairly consistently used so that comparisons over time can be made. Hood et al. (2009, pp. 344–347) identified each question by the name of the researcher most associated with it. The specific questions are as follows:

1. The Stark question: "Have you ever as an adult had the feeling that you were somehow in the presence of God?" (Glock & Stark, 1965).
2. The Bourque question: "Would you say that you have ever had a 'religious or mystical experience'—that is, a moment of sudden religious awakening or insight?" (Back & Bourque, 1970).
3. The Greeley question: "Have your ever felt as though you were close to a powerful spiritual force that seemed to lift you out of yourself?" (Greeley, 1974).
4. The Hardy question: "Have you ever been aware of or influenced by a presence or power, whether you call it God or not, which is different from your everyday self?" (Hay & Morisy, 1978). This is slightly modified from a question originally used in a widely circulated pamphlet designed to elicit mail in responses from residents of the United Kingdom (Hardy, 1979).

It is readily apparent that these four questions share some conceptual overlap, but we are left with several serious problems. First, to the best of our knowledge, these four questions have not been used simultaneously in a single survey, so we do not know how they are correlated. Second, in two separate studies, Thomas and Cooper (1978, 1980) asked people who answered the Greeley question affirmatively to describe in detail the nature of their experiences. Often the responses were uncodeable. Using their own definition of *mystical* as an ineffable sense of unity with God or nature, less than 2% in the first study and 1% in the second study were mystical experiences. Third, the questions elicit different response rates depending on their specific phrasing. For instance, the highest rate was for the Stark question, which they assumed measured *feeling* rather than belief (Glock & Stark, 1965, p. 157). However, 72% of their sample (*N* = 2,871) of predominantly Protestant church members answered "yes." Using the Greeley question in a General Social Survey (GSS; *N* = 1468) only 35% answered "yes" (Davis & Smith, 1994).

Some indication of changes in the report of mystical experience can be gleaned from studies that have employed the same question over several years. Using the Bourque question, Back and Bourque (1970, p. 489) cited results from three Associated Press surveys conducted in the United States in 1962, 1966, and 1967. Over time, the percentage of persons answering "yes" increased from 21% in 1962 (*N* = 3,232) to 32% in 1966 (*N* = 3,518) to 41% in 1967 (*N* = 3,168). Gallup (1978) used this item in a national survey in the United States (*N* = 1,500) in 1976 and found that 31% answered affirmatively.

The Greeley question has been most used in the GSS. Yamane and Polzer (1994) analyzed ordinal ranked responses from the GSS to this question in 1983, 1984, 1988, and 1989 (*N* = 5,420). Respondents who answered affirmatively could select from three options: "once or twice," "several times," or "often." Converting these to a percentage of "yes" as a nominal category, regardless of frequency, yielded 2,183 affirmative responses, or an overall affirmative response rate of 40% of the total sample that reported ever having had the experience. Independent assessment of affirmative responses for each year suggested a slight but steady decline from 39% for 1983–1984 to 31% for 1989.

The Hardy question has been most typically used in the United Kingdom. Data suggest that face-to-face interviews produced higher rates of affirmation than anonymous survey conditions. In one study (Hay & Morisy, 1978), names in England were randomly drawn from the electoral register, supplemented with names drawn at random of nonelectors from the households of the selected electors. In this study, 36% (*N* = 1,865) answered the Hardy question affirmatively, indicating comparable data to the GSS in the United States using the Greeley question. Asking the Hardy question in a face-to-face interview in an industrial area of England, however, Hay and Morisy (1985) found the high affirmative response rate of 72% (*N* = 172). Hay (1994) also found a 65% affirmative response in a random sample of postgraduate students at Nottingham University, England, who knew they would be interviewed about their affirmative response after they responded to the survey. Hay (1994, p. 8, Table 3) also cited a study by Lewis in which a high affirmative response rate to the Hardy question was obtained in a British sample of 108 nurses from two different hospitals in Leeds.

The Hardy question has been used in the United States, Britain, and Australia allowing for some cross-cultural comparisons with the same question. This compares with an affirmative rate of 44% obtained in previously unpublished data based on an Australian sample (*N* = 1,228) by the Australian affiliate of the Gallup Poll organization cited by Hay (1994, p. 7). A survey in the United States of 3,000 people produced a 31% affirmative response rate, closely matching the 35% response rate produced in a sample of 3,062 from the Princeton Research Center (1978, cited by Hay, 1994) a few years earlier. Hay (1994, p. 7, Table 1) also cited two unpublished Gallup Polls commissioned by the Hardy Centre in 1985, indicating a 33% affirmative response to the Hardy question in a sample of 1,030 in Britain, and a 10% higher rate (43%) for a similar sample of 1,525 in the United States.

Three main conclusions can be drawn from such survey studies. First, somewhere in the range of one third of Americans, Britons, and Australians affirm experiences of some spiritual nature, often more frequently by females than males. Second, the reports increase if individuals are in face-to-face interviews or know they will talk about their experiences later. Finally, the assumption that mystical experiences (if these questions tap them) are rare is unfounded (see Zaehner, 1957). Indeed, it may be that only with anonymity or sensitive interviewers interested in these experiences will individuals who have them talk about them (Tamminen, 1991). One should be able to construct measures of mysticism and not only confirm the existence of the report of these experiences but also seek meaningful patterns of correlations and determine conditions under which these experiences occur.

THE MEASUREMENT OF MYSTICISM

Hood (1975) developed the M Scale to operationalize the phenomenologically derived common core of mysticism initially advanced by Stace (1960). In terms of the integrative paradigm for the psychology of religion (see Chapter 1 in this volume), having an empirical measure of phenomenologically derived criteria of mysticism has several advantages. First, it links with the considerable philosophical and theological literature surrounding the debate over whether mysticism is always a socially constructed and hence linguistically and culturally determined experience (Katz, 1977) or whether mysticism is an exception and is in fact a largely unmediated and hence universal experience that is less a volitional attainment of the sacred than a response to a perceived encounter with the sacred (Hood, in press). Hood and his colleagues believed this largely conceptually based literature could also be approached empirically if Stace's common core criteria could be measured and addressed empirically. Stace had determined that mysticism could be understood in terms of an introvertive experience of unity (in which one experiences a unity that involves the dissolution of the empirical self), an extrovertive experience of unity (in which one perceives a unity of all things), and associated family resemblances of additional criteria common to both types of experiences (Stace, 1960).

The M Scale consists of 32 items (16 positively worded and 16 negatively worded items), covering all but one (paradoxicality) of the original common core criteria of mysticism proposed by Stace (1960). Independent investigators (Caird, 1988; Hood, 1975; Reinert & Stifler, 1993) identified two factors to the M Scale. For our purposes, Factor I consists of items assessing an experience of unity (introvertive or extrovertive), whereas Factor II consists of items referring to interpretation of these experiences. This is compatible with Stace's claim that a common experience (mystical experience of unity) may be variously interpreted.

Francis and Louden (2000a) developed the MOS to operationlize Happold's (1963) definition of mysticism. They proposed three items to access each of the seven components. Respondents were asked, "How important are the following experiences to your faith?" They were requested to rate each of the 21 items by circling a number on a 5-point scale from 1 (*not at all*) to 5 (*a great deal*). Tested on a sample of 1,468 Roman Catholic priests in England and Wales, these 21 items all loaded highly (between .46 and .79) on the first factor of the unrotated solution proposed by principal component analysis, and generated an alpha coefficient of internal consistency reliability of .94 (Cronbach, 1951). In a second study, Bourke, Francis, and Robbins (2004) checked the internal consistency reliability of the MOS among a sample of 168 church musicians (130 men and 38 women). In this new study, the 21 items also generated an alpha coefficient of .94, with the rest-of-scale correlations ranging between .45 and .78.

Alongside the MOS, Francis and Louden (2004) developed the Short Index of Mystical Orientation (SIMO), a nine-item instrument intended for use when time and space were restricted. Among the original sample of 1,468 Roman Catholic priests, the SIMO recorded an alpha coefficient of .86 and a correlation of .97 with the MOS. Although the range of information gathered by the SIMO is restricted, it can be said to serve as a functional equivalent to the longer measure.

Two other promising measures of mysticism can also be noted, although as yet (unlike the M Scale and the MOS) they have not generated a significant body of empirical findings. First, the measure of transliminality developed by Thalbourne (1998) maps well onto James's (1902/1985) understanding of mysticism. It is a single-factor scale measuring essentially subliminal states of consciousness. James placed mysticism in a context of numerous experiences (his "mystical ladder"), including those that are at best tangential to mysticism. Barnard (1997, p. 63) has noted that ultimately James equated mystical experience with any submarginal or subliminal state, including diabolical states that James (1902/1985) identified as a "sort of religious mysticism turned upside down" (p. 337). Thalbourne and Delin (1994, p. 25) coined the term *transliminal* to refer to a common underlying factor that is largely an involuntary susceptibility to inwardly generated psychological phenomena of an ideational and affective kind. Transliminality, however, is also related to a hypersensitivity to external stimulation (Thalbourne, 1998, p. 403), such that transliminality becomes a Jamesian measure of the submarginal region in which "'seraph and snake' abide there side by side" (James, 1902/1985, p. 338). This submarginal region includes phenomena of such a wide variety that it is hard to give them a single name.

Second, Edwards and Lowis (2008b) developed a measure of attitudes toward mysticism as distinguished from reported mystical experience. This promising measure has been used in one study suggesting that attitudes toward mysticism and mystical experience, as measured by the MOS (Francis & Louden, 2000a), may relate differently to personality dimensions, such as psychoticism (Edwards & Lowis, 2008a).

THE DIMENSIONALITY OF MYSTICISM

One of the major questions examined by Hood's M Scale concerned the dimensionality of mysticism. The original analyses conducted by Hood (1975) generated a two-factor solution, with Factor I assessing an experience of unity and Factor II referring to interpretation of these experiences. Other analyses also supported two-factor solutions (Caird, 1988; Holm, 1982; Reinert & Stifler, 1993). Early factor-analytic studies were far from definitive; notably, they suffered from inadequate subject-to-items ratios. Hood and his colleagues first proposed a three-factor solution to the M Scale on the basis of a more adequate item-to-subject ratio (Hood, Morris, & Watson, 1993). This three-factor solution fitted Stace's (1960) phenomenology of mysticism quite nicely in that both introvertive and extrovertive mysticism emerged as separate factors, along with a third interpretative factor.

Hood and Williamson (2000) created two additional versions of the M Scale. Each paralleled the original M Scale, but, where appropriate, they made reference to God or to Christ rather than to reality. Both the original M Scale and either the God-language version or the Christ-language version were given to relevant Christian-committed samples. The factor structures for all three versions matched Stace's (1960) phenomenologically derived model quite well. For all versions of the scale, clear introvertive, extrovertive, and interpretative factors emerged. The exception was that, as Hood and Williamson (2000) anticipated, ineffability emerged as part of the introvertive factor in all samples and not as part of the interpretative factor (as suggested by Stace). As Hood and Williamson noted, however, an experience devoid of content is inherently "ineffable," as there is no content to describe. Forman (1990) has made the same argument in identifying what he called a pure consciousness experience, which, having no content, cannot be described. Finally, Hood and his colleagues translated the M Scale into Persian and administered this scale to a sample of Iranian Muslims (Hood et al., 2001). The scale in its original English version was also administered to a U.S. sample. Confirmatory factor analysis was then used to compare Hood's model of mysticism in both samples (with ineffability as part of introvertive mysticism) directly with other possible models, including Stace's (where ineffability is part of the interpretative factor). The overall results showed that although both Stace's model and Hood's model fit the data, Hood's model fit the data better than Stace's model. Empirically, there is strong support to claim that as operationalized from Stace's criteria, mystical experience is identical as measured across diverse samples, whether expressed in language referring to "reality" or with either "God" or "Christ" references. Thus, in terms of the new integrative paradigm, Hood's measure of mysticism conforms to the phenomenologically derived common core of Stace and links directly to conceptual literatures on the commonality of mystical experience that can at least be partly addressed empirically. Belzen (2009) criticized the common core conceptually by stating that "he [Hood] designed an instrument to answer the question tested it out, and lo and behold, a common core shows up—*but* [emphasis in original] the instrument was based on a conceptualization of mysticism, by Stace (1960), that *presupposes* [emphasis in original] a common core" (pp. 217–218). Rather than a telling critique, however, Belzen's claim is precisely where theory-driven measurement empiricism advances a specific claim. Neither Stace nor Hood presupposed a common core. Stace claimed to identify it empirically from a catholicity of cross-culturally derived phenomenological descriptions of mystical experiences. Hood created the scale to measure and test the commonality of these experiences and demonstrated empirically that the pattern or clustering of these items is consistent across cultures—revealing introvertive, extrovertive, and interpretive factors. This provides a purely empirical base of support for the common core thesis.

Given that the M Scale was developed as a specific operationalization of Stace's (1960) phenomenological work, it is a theory-driven scale in which empiricism is balanced with conceptual concerns central to the other literatures on mysticism (Hood, 2006). It is commonly employed as the most widely used empirical measure of mysticism (Lukoff & Lu, 1988). Much of the empirical research, however, has used the original two-factor solution proposed by Hood (1975). This is not a major conceptual issue for Stace's common core theory because the criteria are seen as sharing a family resemblance and because introvertive and extrovertive mysticism are seen to be variations of a single experience of unity (Hood, 1989; Stace, 1960). The two-factor solution allows for identification of the minimal phenomenological properties of experiences of union (Factor I) and interpretative factors (Factor II) that empirically have different predicted consequences.

The initial publication of the M Scale related it to several other measures using independent samples of students (Hood, 1975). In a sample of 52 students at a Protestant college, Factor II correlated more strongly with a measure of religious experience expressed in explicit religious language than did Factor I. In the same study with another sample of 83 college students, Factor I correlated (−.75) more strongly with a measure of ego permissiveness (Taft, 1970) than did Factor II (−.43; Hood, 1975). Insofar as Taft's ego permissiveness measure is related to openness to a wide range of anomalous experiences, including ecstatic emotions, intrinsic arousal, and peak experiences, it is not surprising that Factor I correlated more strongly with this measure than Factor II. In Hood's (1975) original report, the M Scale factors correlated with a measure of intrinsic religion in roughly the same magnitude in a sample of 65 fundamentalist college students enrolled in a religious college in the South (Factor I = .68, Factor II = .58). In a separate study, Hood (1976) found both frequent attendees and nonattendees had similar high scores on Factor I of the M Scale, but only frequent church attendees had high Factor II scores. These simple correlational studies suggest that we can distinguish between those who self-identify as religious and those who do not (many of whom are likely to self-identify as spiritual). Frequent church attendees both report the minimal phenomenological properties of mystical experience and interpret them in religious language. Infrequent or nonattendees report similar experiences in terms of Factor I but do not use religious language to describe them. Factor I contains the preponderance of unity items and these are more likely to be endorsed by those who are not self-identified as religious but who still are open to mystical experiences of unity.

In another correlational study, Zinnbauer et al. (1997, p. 553) used a modified form of Hood's M Scale (unity items only) and found that in their overall sample, self-rated religiousness did not correlate with mystical experience ($r = -.04$), but self-rated spirituality did ($r = .27, p < .001$). Furthermore, there was a significant difference between the mean mysticism scores for the "equally spiritual and religious" group and the "spiritual but not religious" group, with the latter scoring significantly higher. The differential correlation of Factors I and II in the two samples is congruent with Stace's (1960) theory that experience can be separated from interpretation in varying degrees. Factor I correlates more strongly with measures of experience minimally interpreted, and Factor II correlates with measures of experience more extensively interpreted in religious language.

Holm (1982) translated the M Scale into Swedish and found a similar two-factor solution with only minor variations. He identified a general mysticism factor (Factor I) and an interpretation factor (Factor II) that paralleled Hood's with only minor variation. Holm identified Factor I as a "general mysticism factor" and Factor II as an interpretation factor that "covered experiences with an expressly Christian profile" (1982, p. 273). Only the latter factor correlated strongly with a measure of intrinsic religion and with other religious variables, such as prayer, and frequency of Church attendance. He concluded that the M Scale functioned in Finnish and Swedish culture as it does in U.S. culture. He also supported our distinction between experience and interpretation in that mysticism can occur both within and outside faith traditions and hence may or may not be religiously interpreted (Holm, 1982, pp. 276–2176; Hood et al., 2009, pp. 372–379).

Overall, the findings from research employing either of the earlier two-factor solutions or the more recent three-factor solution are compatible with Stace's (1960) basic phenomenologically derived common core thesis. First, the two-factor solutions confirm a distinction between what have been identified as experiences of unity that lie at the core of mystical experience and an interpretative dimension that meaningfully frames these experiences. Second, the three-factor solution separates the experiences of unity into introvertive and extrovertive while maintaining the distinction between these experiences and how they are interpreted.

Mysticism and Personality

One of the major questions examined by Francis and Louden's measures (MOS and SIMO) concerns the connection between mysticism and personality. Studies in this field have employed two different models of personality.

Working within a British context, Francis and his colleagues began by examining the association between mystical orientation and Eysenck's three-dimensional model of personality. Eysenck's model argues that individual differences can be best summarized in terms of the three higher order factors of Extraversion, Neuroticism, and Psychoticism. The high scorer on the Extraversion scale could be described as sociable, carefree, and optimistic. The high scorer on the Neuroticism scale could be characterized in one word as a worrier. The high scorer on the Psychoticism scale could be described as cold, impersonal, and insensitive. The low scorers on each of these dimensions are characterized by the opposite traits. A major strength of Eysenck's theory concerns the way in which he conceptualized and located neurotic disorders on a continuum with one dimension of normal personality and psychotic disorders on a continuum with a second (orthogonal) dimension of normal personality. These three higher order factors, together with a lie scale, have been operationalized in a series of measures, including the Eysenck Personality Questionnaire (Eysenck, & Eysenck, 1975) and the Revised Eysenck Personality Questionnaire (Eysenck, Eysenck, & Barrett, 1985).

In the first study designed to locate the SIMO within Eysenck's dimensional model of personality, Francis and Thomas (1996) built on Caird (1987) who drew attention to two conflicting views regarding the theoretical relationship between mysticism and Eysenck's dimensional model of personality (Eysenck, & Eysenck, 1975). Caird cited the Group for the Advancement of Psychiatry (1976), which has regarded mystical experiences as essentially introvertive, with neurotic and psychotic sufferers especially tempted to seek relief in these ways. Caird noted, in contrast, that Maslow (1964) identified mystical experiences with peak experiences, more characteristic of health than of neurosis or psychosis. Testing these conflicting theories among a sample of 222 Anglican clergymen who completed the SIMO alongside the short-form Revised Eysenck Personality Questionnaire (Eysenck et al., 1985), Francis and Thomas (1996) found empirical support for neither view. The data demonstrated a positive correlation between mystical orientation and extraversion, but no relationship between mystical orientation and either neuroticism or psychoticism.

In the second study designed to locate the MOS within Eysenck's dimensional model of personality, Francis and Louden (2000a) tested the same theories among the sample of 1,468 Roman Catholic priests who completed the MOS alongside the Eysenck Personality Questionnaire (Eysenck &

Eysenck, 1975). The data also demonstrated a positive correlation between mystical orientation and extraversion but no relationship between mystical orientation and either neuroticism or psychoticism.

The second model of personality within which individual differences in mystical orientation have been located is the model of psychological type originally proposed by Jung (1971) and developed and operationalized by instruments like the Myers–Briggs Type Indicator (Myers & McCaulley, 1985), the Keirsey Temperament Sorter (Keirsey, 1998), and the Francis Psychological Type Scales (Francis, 2005). These instruments are designed to distinguish between two perceiving functions (sensing and intuition), two judging functions (thinking and feeling), two orientations (introversion and extraversion), and two attitudes toward the outer world (judging and perceiving). These instruments are designed primarily to categorize individuals within dichotomous psychological types not to locate individuals along dimensions of personality. The Eysenckian and the Jungian understandings of introversion and extraversion are far from synonymous. Eysenck is concerned with identifying social behavior, whereas Jung is concerned with identifying sources of energy (see Volume 2, Chapter 7, this handbook).

Since the early 1990s there has been considerable expansion in the number of empirical studies within the psychology of religion concerned with the relationship between psychological type and a variety of indexes assessing aspects of religiosity, and leading to the creative dialogue between empirical data and the development of theory. In particular, Ross's work began to point to the central role of the perceiving process (sensing or intuition) in predicting preferred ways of being religious or expressing religiosity. For example, Ross, Weiss, and Jackson (1996) found intuitives contrasted to sensers in terms of greater comfort with regard to complexity of religious belief, whereas sensers tended to be more definite in regard to what counted as religious to them. Sensers evidenced firmer boundaries between what was secular and what was sacred. Intuitives showed a more welcoming attitude toward religious change, viewing new insights as essential for a healthy religious life and "narrow-minded religion" as a significant problem. Sensing types by contrast saw religious change as a problem and change in personal faith as an indication of weakness. Ross and Jackson (1993) concluded in their study of Catholics that the pattern of responses to individual items suggested that religion functioned in different ways for sensing and for intuitive types. According to this study, religion tended to function as a guide to right living for sensers and as a source of insight for intuitives.

In a subsequent article, Francis and Ross (1997, p. 95) set out to examine differences between sensing types and intuitive types with regard to preferences in Christian spirituality and to test the following specific hypothesis: that sensers would display a greater preference for traditional expressions of Christian spirituality (like church attendance and personal prayer), whereas intuitives would display a greater openness to the experiential aspects of spirituality (like witnessing a fine sunset or being inspired by a star-filled sky).

Ross's general theory that the perceiving process (sensing or intuition) plays a central role in predicting preferred ways of being religious or expressing religiosity, together with the findings presented by Francis and Ross (1997) that intuitives show a higher appreciation than sensers of experiential spirituality, leads to the clear hypothesis that intuitives will record higher scores than sensers on the indexes of mystical orientation. There are no similar theoretical grounds for predicting a significant relationship between mystical orientation and the judging process (thinking or feeling), the psychological orientations (introversion or extraversion), or the attitudes toward the outer world (judging or perceiving).

In a first study designed to test the relationship between psychological type and mystical orientation, Francis and Louden (2000b) administered the Keirsey Temperament Sorter (Keirsey, 1998) and the SIMO to a sample of 100 student and adult church attenders. Their data provided only partial support for the hypotheses advanced on the basis of Ross's work. Consistent with these hypotheses, they found a significant relationship between mystical orientation and the perceiving function: Intuitives recorded a significantly higher mean score than sensers. Also consistent with these hypotheses, they found no significant relationship between mystical orientation and either the distinction between introversion and extraversion or the distinction between judging and perceiving. On the other hand, contrary to prediction, they also found a significant relationship between mystical orientation and the judging function: Feelers recorded a significantly higher mean score than thinkers.

In a second study, Francis (2002) administered the Myers–Briggs Type Indicator (Myers & McCaulley, 1985) and the SIMO to a sample of 543 participants who attended workshops concerned with personality and spirituality. Their data provided only partial confirmation for the findings reported by Francis and Louden (2000b). Like the earlier study, this second study found no significant relationship between mystical orientation and either psychological orientation (introversion or extraversion) or attitude toward the outer world (judging or perceiving). Like the earlier study, this second study found a significant relationship between mystical orientation and the judging process: Feelers recorded significantly higher mean scores than thinkers. Unlike the earlier study, this second study found no significant relationship between mystical orientation and the perceiving process (sensing or intuition).

Taken together, these two studies begin to call into question Ross's contention that the perceiving process is central to individual differences in religious expression, at least as far as mystical orientation is concerned. There are, however, two crucial ways in which both studies reported by Francis and Louden (2000b) and Francis (2002) may be criticized as being perhaps preliminary enquiries. First, both studies employ the short form of the mystical orientation measure, which samples the domain of mystical orientation less comprehensively and less adequately than the longer form. Second, both studies are based on somewhat odd samples: A small group of only 100 churchgoers and a larger group of workshop participants.

In a third study designed to rectify these shortcomings, Francis, Village, Robbins, and Ineson (2007) administered the Francis Psychological Type Scales (Francis, 2005) and the MOS to a sample of 318 individuals who have stayed at the Benedictine retreat house associated with Ampleforth Abbey. These data found closer support for Ross's hypothesis: They demonstrated a significant relationship between mystical orientation and the perceiving process (sensing and intuition) but no relationship between mystical orientation and psychological orientation (introversion and extraversion), the judging process (feeling and thinking), and attitudes toward the outer world (judging and perceiving).

Taken together, the two sets of studies (employing Eysenck's dimensional model of personality and Jung's model of psychological type) have demonstrated that the notion of mysticism proposed by Happold (1963) and operationalized by the MOS (Francis & Louden, 2000a) is not associated with indicators of psychological pathology (neuroticism and psychoticism) but is associated with individual differences in normal personality as conceptualized and operationalized by the Eysenckian notion of extraversion and by the Jungian distinction between sensing and intuition.

Mysticism and Psychopathology

The Hood (1975) M Scale has been employed in a number of studies to deepen examination of the claim that mysticism itself is a form of pathology or that some forms of mysticism are pathological. Part of the issue is purely conceptual (Hood & Byrom, 2010), but the issue can also be addressed empirically. For instance, Factor II (but not Factor I) significantly correlated with the Lie (L) scale of the Minnesota Multaphasic Personality Inventory (MMPI). This scale presumably measures the tendency to lie or present oneself in a favorable social light. Insofar as Factor II represents a traditional religious stance, however, Hood suggested that high L scores for Factor II may represent the fact that traditionally religious individuals are less likely to engage in deviant social behaviors as measured by the L scale. Factor I did significantly correlate with two scales on the MMPI concerned with bodily processes (hypochondriasis) and intense experiential states (hysteria), which in nonpathological terms are likely to be compatible with mystical experience.

Spanos and Moretti (1988) provided further recognition that mysticism need not be associated with pathology. They directly correlated the M Scale with the Tellegen and Atkinson (1974) Absorption Scale and with three measures of hypnosis. Overall, the M Scale correlated positively with all of these measures. When mysticism was used as the criterion variable, regression analyses using the four hypnosis measures, absorption, and two other variables (neuroticism and psychosomatic symptoms) indicated that absorption was the best predictor of M Scale scores with only one of the hypnosis measures adding any additional predictive power. Neither neuroticism nor psychosomatic symptom scales were predictive of the M Scale.

Byrom (2009) found that a measure of magical ideation, assumed to be a measure of psychosis proneness appropriate for use with nonclinical populations, positively correlated with total M Scale scores. Using the three-factor solution, with a relatively large *N* (211), Byrom found that magical ideation significantly correlated with all subscales but that it shared only 2% of the common variance with the interpretation scale ($r = .16$). Proneness to psychosis is more associated with the phenomenology of experiences of unity than with their interpretation if one assumes that interpretation accounts for more religiously committed individuals. Furthermore, this measure of magical ideation was specifically designed to tap the belief that there is a causal connection between events that cannot be connected by the concepts of a particular culture (Eckblad & Chapman, 1983, p. 215). This is consistent with the fact that the same conditions that facilitate mystical *experiences* trigger paranormal ones as well (Hood, 1989, 2006). Thus, magical ideation correlated much more strongly with the introvertive ($r = .53$) and extrovertive ($r = .44$) factors, with shared variance with the magical ideation measure of 28% and 19%, respectively (Byrom, 2009).

Stifler, Greer, Sneck, and Dovenmuehle (1993) used the M Scale alongside other measures to compare samples ($n = 30$ each): psychiatric inpatients to advanced members of various contemplative groups. The psychiatric inpatients met the diagnostic criteria of the third edition of the *Diagnostic and Statistical Manual of Mental Disorders* (American Psychiatric Association, 1987) and also displayed "notable religiously oriented symptoms" (Stifler et al., 1993, p. 368). Stifler et al. found that the psychotic and contemplative groups could not be distinguished from one another on their mysticism scores but that both differed from a group of staff used as controls. Individuals with psychosis were not distinguished from those without it by mystical experience but rather by dimensions of personality structure. The psychotic mystics exhibited resistance and rigidity as opposed to nonpsychotic mystics, who exhibited openness and fluidity. This study is consistent with the study by Campbell, Lee, and Cothran (2010), who used the M Scale alongside several other measures to assess a large sample ($N = 777$) of university students relevant to predicting religion and spirituality. They found that a measure of openness correlated more strongly with mysticism and with a measure of spirituality than it did with intrinsic religiosity. Furthermore, using the two-factor solution of a measure of the five-factor model of personality adopted by Streib, Hood, Keller, Csöff, and Silver (2009), they found that traditionalism (combined agreeableness, conscientiousness, and positive affect) predicted both intrinsic religiosity and the interpretive factor of the M Scale. On the other hand, transformation (openness combined with extraversion) correlated more strongly with introvertive and extrovertive factors of the M Scale. Thus, there may be a critical balance between openness or transformation and mystical experience that can produce distress for some who do not have a frame within which to interpret mystical experiences. People within faith traditions need not have mystical experiences, but, if they do have mystical experiences, they are likely to have a meaningful frame within which to interpret them. For instance, among forms of prayer, contemplative prayer has been shown to be most strongly correlated with Factor I of the M Scale and with Factor II as well in studies of religiously committed people (Hood, Morris, & Watson, 1989).

Religiously committed people may have a ready frame within which to interpret and shape mystical experiences. Other frames may be available that are not linked to religion, however. For instance, Mercer and Durham (1999) found scores on the M Scale to be significantly correlated with scores on a measure of gender orientation; people with female and androgynous orientations had higher M Scale scores than people with masculine orientations. Mercer and Durham suggested that people who report mystical experiences may have a schema through which they process data in a way that facilitates the unity of reality inherent in mystical experiences. Neither mystical experience itself, nor the framing of it in faith traditions, can be meaningfully identified with psychopathology, but rather mystical experience is possible across those with and without psychological distress (Lukoff, 1985).

The M Scale is unique in that it has been used in two experimental studies to elicit mystical experience. In one study, a private all-male high school cooperated in an assessment of the possibility that various planned nature activities as part of week-long program might elicit mystical experiences (Hood, 1977). Just before participating in each activity, participants were administered a measure of subjective, anticipatory stress for that activity. Immediately after each activity, the participants completed the M Scale, to assess mystical experience. Participants varied in their anticipation of stress for all activities, except for canoeing a peaceful stream, which none anticipated as stressful. On four other activities (such as staying alone with only a tarp at night), however, participants varied in their anticipation of stress. Because anticipatory stress varied across situations, whether or not a particular person anticipated a given situation as stressful was not simply a function of its independently assessed setting stress. Second, in stressful situations, those anticipating low stress scored higher on mysticism than those anticipating high stress. The hypothesis was that neither setting stress per se nor anticipatory stress alone would elicit mystical experiences. The comparisons between M Scale scores for each high-stress activity anticipated as nonstressful supported the hypothesis that the interaction between these two types of stress elicits reports of mystical experience. Thus, stress incongruity elicited reports of mystical experience, not simply stress per se, either anticipatory or situational. Given the congruity between anticipated stress and setting stress (both low), low M Scale scores resulted, as predicted. However, in high-stress activities anticipated as high in stress, low M Scale scores were also hypothesized and obtained. Only the incongruity between setting and anticipatory stress produced high M Scale scores.

A second experimental study used an entheogen under favorable set and setting conditions to elicit mystical experiences (Griffiths, Richards, Johnson, McCann, & Jesse, 2008). Thirty entheogenic naive volunteers with stated religious or spiritual interests received psilocybin and menthylphenidate (Ritalin) in counterbalanced order over two sessions. An additional six randomly assigned volunteers received methylphenidate on the first two sessions and unblinded psilocybin on the third session. The purpose of this condition was to obscure the study design to both participants and guides.

All participants were administered the M Scale (along with other measures). We will discuss only the results concerning the M Scale here. Before the study, 2 months after the study, and again for a third time in a follow-up, participants took the M Scale. Two months after the experiment, psilocybin participants had higher scores of the M Scale than the methylphenidate controls. Scores on the M Scale after psilocybin predicted the spiritual significance of the experience ($r = .77$) in a 12- to 14-month follow-up (Griffiths et al., 2008). All three factors of the M Scale were significantly greater than the initial screening scores at both the 2-month and 14-month follow-ups for those receiving psilocybin.

A third experimental study used an isolation tank to elicit mystical experiences (Hood, Morris, & Watson, 1990). Hood and his colleagues placed individuals in a sensory isolation tank to maximize solitude. The tank was equipped with an intercom system so that a participant could communicate with an experimenter in another room. Participant religious orientation was assessed before participating in the study. Neither the participants nor the investigators knew their scores until after the experiment. Just before entering the isolation tank, participants were given a specific religious set or nonreligious control set that they should be as silent as possible and open to whatever religious revelation or insight (nonreligious set).

A modified version of the M Scale was used that allowed a simple "yes" or "no" response to each item, so that the participants could respond over the intercom while still in the isolation tank. When participants were not presented with a religious set, none of the groups differed in the minimal phenomenological properties of mysticism (Factor I). As anticipated, the isolation tank was able to facilitate mystical experience in persons regardless of religious type. Interestingly, intrinsic participants scored as high on religious interpretation (Factor II) of the experience in the control condition as in the experimental condition. Extrinsics did not describe or interpret their experiences in religious language in the control condition as indicated by a significant difference between Factor II scores between the experimental and control conditions. Thus the isolation tank elicited similar experiences in participants regardless of their religious orientation. The difference in Factor II under set conditions for the religious types, however, suggests that only intrinsic persons consistently interpreted their tank experiences as religious regardless of set conditions.

CONCLUSION AND SUGGESTIONS FOR FUTURE RESEARCH

We can draw three major conclusions from the research reviewed. First, from survey studies, we can note that single questions that apparently make some reference to mystical experiences reveal that they are common in the United States, Australia, and Britain. The commonality of the report of such experiences can be taken as prima facie evidence that they are unlikely to be pathological and clearly are not, as some have suggested, rare events.

Second, both the MOS and the M Scale have been developed from conceptual models, linking the empirical research using these scales to a rich conceptual literature often ignored by psychologists. Both research traditions using these scales allow for integrating psychology with theology (more likely with the MOS) and phenomenology (more likely with the M Scale).

Finally, one can study empirically the report of mystical experience. Although much of the research using both of these scales is correlational, the findings with both measures are consistent in rejecting the claim that mystical experience is either an instance of pathology itself or more common among person who are pathological. Furthermore, it is possible to facilitate the occurrence of these experiences, as noted in particular with research using the M Scale. That the same experience can be facilitated by such diverse triggers as set or setting stress incongruity, intense solitude in an isolation tank, or ethnogeny suggests that mystical experience is not only part of the search for the sacred, but likely as well a response to it.

The foregoing review of empirical research on mystical experience offers pointers for future research in this field. In particular, the research traditions employing the MOS and the M Scale could be extended in three ways. First, existing research employing correlational studies has demonstrated the value of this basic approach for establishing the correlates of individual differences in mystical orientation and mystical experience. This form of study could be extended to include a wide range of covariates. Second, as yet, few experimental studies have employed the MOS or M Scale to monitor specific impacts on mysticism scores. New research could examine the effects of specific environmental or situational stimuli, such as music, meditation, natural beauty, or holy sites. Third, there would be value in including the MOS or the M Scale in some longitudinal studies to understand the long-term implications of mystical experience

References

American Psychiatric Association. (1987). *Diagnostic and statistical manual of mental disorders* (3rd ed., rev.). Washington, DC: Author.

Back, K. W., & Bourque, L. (1970). Can feelings be enumerated? *Behavioral Science, 15*, 487–496. doi:10.1002/bs.3830150603

Barnard, G. W. (1997). *Exploring unseen worlds: William James and the philosophy of mysticism.* Albany: State University of New York Press.

Belzen, J. A. (2009). Studying the specificity of spirituality: Lessons from the psychology of religion. *Mental Health, Religion, and Culture, 12*, 205–222. doi:10.1080/13674670802456606

Bourke, R., Francis, L. J., & Robbins, M. (2004). Mystical orientation among church musicians. *Transpersonal Psychology Review*, *8*(2), 14–19.

Byrom, G. N. (2009). Differential relationships between experiential and interpretive dimensions of mysticism and schizotypal magical ideation in a university sample. *Archive for the Psychology of Religion, 31*, 127–150.

Caird, D. (1987). Religiosity and personality: Are mystics introverted, neurotic, or psychotic? *British Journal of Social Psychology, 26*, 345–346. doi:10.1111/j.2044-8309.1987.tb00798.x

Caird, D. (1988). The structure of Hood's Mysticism Scale: A factor analytic study. *Journal for the Scientific Study of Religion, 27*, 122–127. doi:10.2307/1387407

Campbell, M. L., Lee, S. A., & Cothran, L. D. (2010). Mysticism matters: Distinguishing between intrinsic, extrinsic religiosity, and spirituality using higher-order factors of personality and mysticism. *Archive for the Psychology of Religion, 32*, 1–22.

Cronbach, L. J. (1951). Coefficient alpha and the internal structure of tests. *Psychometrika, 16*, 297–334. doi:10.1007/BF02310555

Davis, J. A., & Smith, T. W. (1994). *General Social Surveys, 1972–1994* [Machine-readable data file]. Chicago, IL: National Opinion Research Center [Producer]; Storrs: Roper Center for Public Opinion Research, University of Connecticut [Distributor].

Eckblad, M., & Chapman, L. J. (1983). Magical ideation as a measure of schizotypy. *Journal of Consulting and Clinical Psychology, 51*, 215–225.

Edwards, A. C., & Lowis, M. J. (2008a). Attitudes to mysticism: Relationship with personality in Western and Eastern traditions. *Spirituality and Health International, 9*, 145–160. doi:10.1002/shi.342

Edwards, A. C., & Lowis, M. J. (2008b). Construction and validation of a scale to assess attitudes to mysticism: The need for a new scale for research in the psychology of religion. *Spirituality and Health International, 9*, 16–31. doi:10.1002/shi.330

Eysenck, H. J., & Eysenck, S. B. G. (1975). *Manual of the Eysenck Personality Questionnaire (adult and junior)*. London, England: Hodder & Stoughton.

Eysenck, H. J., Eysenck, S. B. G., & Barrett, P. (1985). A revised version of the psychoticism scale. *Personality and Individual Differences, 6*, 21–29. doi:10.1016/0191-8869(85)90026-1

Forman, R. K. C. (Ed.). (1990). *The problem of pure consciousness: Mysticism and philosophy*. New York, NY: Oxford University Press.

Francis, L. J. (2002). Psychological type and mystical orientation: Anticipating individual differences within congregational life. *Pastoral Sciences, 21*, 77–99.

Francis, L. J. (2005). *Faith and psychology: Personality, religion and the individual*. London, England: Darton, Longman & Todd.

Francis, L. J. (2009). Comparative empirical research in religion: Conceptual and operational challenges within empirical theology. In L. J. Francis, M. Robbins, & J. Astley (Eds.), *Empirical theology in texts and tables: Qualitative, quantitative and comparative perspectives* (pp. 127–152). Leiden, the Netherlands: Brill. doi:10.1163/ej.9789004168886.i-408.48

Francis, L. J., & Louden, S. H. (2000a). The Francis–Louden Mystical Orientation Scale (MOS): A study among Roman Catholic priests. *Research in the Social Scientific Study of Religion, 11*, 99–116.

Francis, L. J., & Louden, S. H. (2000b). Mystical orientation and psychological type: A study among student and adult churchgoers. *Transpersonal Psychology Review, 4*(1), 36–42.

Francis, L. J., & Louden, S. H. (2004). A short index of mystical orientation (SIMO): a study among Roman Catholic priests. *Pastoral Psychology, 53*, 49–51. doi:10.1023/B:PASP.0000039325.40451.65

Francis, L. J., & Ross, C. F. J. (1997). The perceiving function and Christian spirituality: Distinguishing between sensing and intuition. *Pastoral Sciences, 16*, 93–103.

Francis, L. J., & Thomas, T. H. (1996). Mystical orientation and personality among Anglican clergy. *Pastoral Psychology, 45*, 99–105. doi:10.1007/BF02260016

Francis, L. J., Village, A., Robbins, M., & Ineson, K. (2007). Mystical orientation and psychological type: An empirical study among guests staying at a Benedictine Abbey. *Studies in Spirituality, 17*, 207–223. doi:10.2143/SIS.17.0.2024649

Gallup, C., Jr. (1978). *The Gallup Poll: 1972–1977*. Washington, DC: Scholarly Resources.

Glock, C. Y., & Stark, R. (1965). *Religion and society in tension*. Chicago, IL: Rand McNally.

Greeley, A. M. (1974). *Ecstasy: A way of knowing*. Englewood Cliffs, NJ: Prentice-Hall.

Griffiths, R. R., Richards, W. A., Johnson, M. W., McCann, U. D., & Jesse, R. (2008). Mystical-type experiences occasioned by psilocybin mediate the attribution of personal meaning and spiritual significance 14 months later. *Journal of Psychopharmacology, 22*, 621–632. doi:10.1177/0269881108094300

Griffiths, R. R., Richards, W. A., McCann, U., & Jesse, R. (2006). Psilocybin can occasion mystical-type experience having substantial and sustained personal meaning and significance. *Psychopharmacology, 187*, 268–283. doi:10.1007/s00213-006-0457-5

Group for the Advancement of Psychiatry. (1976). *Mysticism: Spiritual quest or psychological disorder?* New York, NY: Author.

Happold, F. C. (1963). *Mysticism: A study and an anthology*. Harmondsworth, England: Penguin.

Hardy, A. (1979). *The spiritual nature of man: A study of contemporary religious experience*. Oxford, England: Clarendon Press.

Hay, D. (1994). "The biology of God": What is the current status of Hardy's hypothesis? *The International Journal for the Psychology of Religion, 4*, 1–23. doi:10.1207/s15327582ijpr0401_1

Hay, D., & Morisy, A. (1978). Reports of ecstatic, paranormal, or religious experience in Great Britain and the United States: A comparison of trends. *Journal for the Scientific Study of Religion, 17*, 255–268. doi:10.2307/1386320

Hay, D., & Morisy, A. (1985). Secular society, religious meanings: A contemporary paradox. *Review of Religious Research, 26*, 213–227.

Hick, J. (1989). *An interpretation of religion*. New Haven, CT: Yale University Press. doi:10.1057/9780230371286

Holm, N. G. (1982). Mysticism and intense experiences. *Journal for the Scientific Study of Religion, 21*, 268–276. doi:10.2307/1385891

Hood, R. W., Jr. (1975). The construction and preliminary validation of a measure of reported mystical experience. *Journal for the Scientific Study of Religion, 14*, 29–41. doi:10.2307/1384454

Hood, R. W., Jr. (1976). Mystical experience as related to present and anticipated future church participation. *Psychological Reports, 39*, 1127–1136. doi:10.2466/pr0.1976.39.3f.1127

Hood, R. W., Jr. (1977). Eliciting mystical states of consciousness with semi-structured nature experiences. *Journal for the Scientific Study of Religion, 16*, 155–163. doi:10.2307/1385746

Hood, R. W., Jr. (1989). Mysticism, the unity thesis, and the paranormal. In G. K. Zollschan, J. F. Schumaker, & G. F. Walsh (Eds)., *Exploring the paranormal: Perspectives on belief and experience* (pp. 117–130). New York, NY: Avery.

Hood, R. W., Jr. (2006). The common core thesis in the study of mysticism. In P. McNamara (Ed.), *Where God and science meet* (Vol. 3, pp. 119–138). Westport, CT: Praeger.

Hood, R. W., Jr. (in press). Another epistemic evaluation of Freud's oedipal theory of religion. In Benjamin Beit-Hallahmi (Ed.), *Psychoanalysis and theism: Critical reflections on the Grünbaum thesis*. Lanham, MD: Jason Aronson.

Hood, R. W., Jr., & Byrom, G. (2010). Mysticism, madness, and mental health. In J. H. Ellens (Ed.), *The healing power of spirituality: Vol. 3. Psychodynamics* (pp. 171–191). Westport, CT: Praeger.

Hood, R. W., Jr., Ghorbani, N., Watson, P. J., Ghramaleki, A. F., Bing, M. B., Davison, H. R., . . . Williamson, P. J. (2001). Dimensions of the Mysticism Scale: Confirming the three factor structure in the United States and Iran. *Journal for the Scientific Study of Religion, 40*, 691–705. doi:10.1111/0021-8294.00085

Hood, R. W., Jr., Hill, P. C., & Spilka, B. (2009). *The psychology of religion: An empirical approach* (4th ed.). New York, NY: Guilford Press.

Hood, R. W., Jr., Morris, R. J., & Watson, P. J. (1989). Prayer experience and religious orientation. *Review of Religious Research, 31*, 39–45. doi:10.2307/3511022

Hood, R. W., Jr., Morris, R. J., & Watson, P. J. (1990). Quasi-experimental elicitation of the differential report of religious experience among intrinsic and indiscriminately pro-religious types. *Journal for the Scientific Study of Religion, 29*, 164–172. doi:10.2307/1387425

Hood, R. W., Jr., Morris, R. J., & Watson, P. J. (1993). Further factor analysis of Hood's Mysticism Scale. *Psychological Reports, 73*, 1176–1178. doi:10.2466/pr0.1993.73.3f.1176

Hood, R. W., Jr., & Williamson, W. P. (2000). An empirical test of the unity thesis: The structure of mystical descriptors in various faith samples. *Journal of Christianity and Psychology, 19*, 222–244.

James, W. (1985). *The varieties of religious experience: A study in human nature*. Cambridge, MA: Harvard University Press. (Original work published 1902)

Jung, C. G. (1971). *Psychological types: The collected works* (Vol. 6). London, England: Routledge & Kegan Paul.

Katz, S. T. (1977). *Mysticism and philosophical analysis*. New York, NY: Oxford University Press.

Keirsey, D. (1998). *Please understand me: 2*. Del Mar, CA: Prometheus Nemesis.

Lukoff, D. (1985). The diagnosis of mystical experience with psychotic features. *Journal of Transpersonal Psychology, 17*, 155–181.

Lukoff, D., & Lu, F. G. (1988). Transpersonal psychology research review topic: Mystical experience. *Journal of Transpersonal Psychology, 20*, 161–184.

Maslow, A. H. (1964). *Religions, values, and peak-experiences*. Columbus: Ohio State University.

McGinn, B. (1991). Appendix: Theoretical foundations: The modern study of mysticism. In B. McGinn (Ed.), *The foundations of mysticism* (pp. 265–343). New York, NY: Crossroads.

Mercer, C., & Durham, T. W. (1999). Religious mysticism and gender orientation. *Journal for the Scientific Study of Religion, 38*, 175–182. doi:10.2307/1387592

Myers, I. B., & McCaulley, M. H. (1985). *Manual: A guide to the development and use of the Myers–Briggs Type Indicator*. Palo Alto, CA: Consulting Psychologists Press.

Reinert, D. F., & Stifler, K. R. (1993). Hood's Mysticism Scale revisited: A factor-analytic replication. *Journal for the Scientific Study of Religion, 32*, 383–388. doi:10.2307/1387178

Ross, C., & Jackson, L. M. (1993). *Orientation to religion and Jungian type preference among Canadian Catholics.* Paper presented at the 101st Annual Convention of the American Psychological Association, Toronto, Ontario, Canada.

Ross, C. F. J., Weiss, D., & Jackson, L. M. (1996). The relation of Jungian psychological type to religious attitudes and practices. *The International Journal for the Psychology of Religion, 6,* 263–279. doi:10.1207/s15327582ijpr0604_3

Spanos, N. P., & Moretti, P. (1988). Correlates of mystical and diabolical experiences in a sample of female university students. *Journal for the Scientific Study of Religion, 27,* 105–116. doi:10.2307/1387405

Stace, W. T. (1960). *Mysticism and philosophy.* Philadelphia, PA: Lippincott.

Stifler, K., Greer, J., Sneck, W., & Dovenmuehle, R. (1993). An empirical investigation of the discriminability of reported mystical experiences among religious contemplatives, psychotic inpatients, and normal adults. *Journal for the Scientific Study of Religion, 32,* 366–372. doi:10.2307/1387176

Streib, H., Hood, R. W., Jr., Keller, B., Csöff, R.-M., & Silver, C. (2009). *Research in contemporary religion: Vol. 4. Deconversion: Qualitative and quantitative results from cross-cultural research in Germany and the United States.* Göttingen, Germany: Vandenhoeck & Rupprecht.

Taft, R. (1970). The measurement of the dimensions of ego permissiveness. *Personality, 1,* 163–184.

Tamminen, K. (1991). *Religious development in childhood and youth: An empirical study.* Helsinki, Finland: Suomalainen Tiedeakatemia.

Tellegen, A., & Atkinson, G. (1974). Openness to absorbing and self-altering experiences ("absorption"), a trait related to hypnotic susceptibility. *Journal of Abnormal Psychology, 83,* 268–277. doi:10.1037/h0036681

Thalbourne, M. A. (1998). Transliminality: Further correlates and a short measure. *Journal of the American Society for Psychical Research, 92,* 402–419.

Thalbourne, M. A., & Delin, P. S. (1999). Transliminality: Its relation to dream life, religiosity, and mystical experience. *The International Journal for the Psychology of Religion, 9,* 45–61.

Thomas, L. E., & Cooper, P. E. (1978). Measurement and incidence of mystical experiences: An exploratory study. *Journal for the Scientific Study of Religion, 17,* 433–437. doi:10.2307/1385407

Thomas, L. E., & Cooper, P. E. (1980). Incidence and psychological correlates of intense spiritual experiences. *Journal of Transpersonal Psychology, 12,* 75–85.

Yamane, D., & Polzer, M. (1994). Ways of seeing ecstasy in modern society: Experimental-expressive and cultural-linguistic views. *Sociology of Religion, 55,* 1–25. doi:10.2307/3712173

Zaehner, R. C. (1957). *Mysticism, sacred and profane: An inquiry into some varieties of praenatural experience.* London, England: Oxford University Press.

Zinnbauer, B. J., Pargament, K. I., Cole, B., Rye, M. S., Butter, E. M., Belavich, T. G., . . . Kadar, J. L. (1997). Religion and spirituality: Unfuzzying the fuzzy. *Journal for the Scientific Study of Religion, 36,* 549–564. doi:10.2307/1387689

CHAPTER 22

SPIRITUAL EXPERIENCE: CONVERSION AND TRANSFORMATION

Steven J. Sandage and Shane P. Moe

Everything became new. My horses and hogs and even everybody seemed changed.

—Converted farmer interviewed by E. D. Starbuck (1899, p. 120)

Conversion and transformation constitute two perennial topics of interest for psychologists of religion. By the early 1900s, significant psychological contributions to the study of religious conversion had already emerged in the work of G. Stanley Hall and Edwin Starbuck and in the classic work of William James. Each of these researchers was drawn to investigate dramatic changes in religious experience and the potential consequences of such changes. Throughout the 20th and 21st centuries, psychologists and sociologists of religion have studied various aspects of religious conversion. In the past decade, we have seen a broadening of the contemporary field and a growing literature on spiritual transformation arising from recognition that (a) people experience a variety of types of spiritual changes beyond an initial "conversion" and (b) spiritual changes occur outside explicitly religious contexts. This chapter offers an overview of theoretical models and empirical research on conversion and spiritual transformation and concludes with integrative directions for future research and practice.

CLASSIC AND CONTEMPORARY PARADIGMS

Hood, Hill, and Spilka (2009) have contrasted the classic and contemporary research paradigms on conversion and transformation. In the classic paradigm, the focus was on dramatic religious conversions of a passive subject transformed through an emotional process, most typically during adolescence. The Apostle Paul's conversion on the road to Damascus was viewed as a prototypical conversion in its perceived suddenness and focus on the resolution of an internal crisis of individual sin and guilt, resting on an interpretation of the New Testament that some contemporary theologians would broaden in more relational and developmental directions (Shults & Sandage, 2006). Hood et al. noted that this early classic paradigm of conversion research was dominated by psychologists, but sociologists came to shape much of the "contemporary" research in the second half of the 20th century. The contemporary research paradigm shifted toward a stronger recognition that conversion and transformation can be gradual as well as sudden, an insight that emerged as early as the second generation of conversion researchers (e.g., Pratt, 1920). Contemporary researchers increasingly viewed the human subject as a less passive and more active agent seeking meaning and striving toward goals. The classic emphasis on an intra-individual and emotional process gave way to more cognitive and contextual models of conversion that attended to sociocultural dynamics that precipitate spiritual change. Finally, a growing awareness of spiritual and religious diversity has led to the questioning of universal models of conversion and to efforts to investigate differing conversion "motifs" (Lofland & Skonovd, 1981) and differing populations and contexts.

This project was supported by Grant No. 2266 from the Fetzer Institute.

DOI: 10.1037/14045-022
APA Handbook of Psychology, Religion, and Spirituality: Vol. 1. Context, Theory, and Research, K. I. Pargament (Editor-in-Chief)
Copyright © 2013 by the American Psychological Association. All rights reserved.

Definitions

The earlier focus on conversion has shifted toward a recent emphasis on spiritual transformation in the psychology of religion. Psychologists have typically defined "conversion" as a "radical transformation of the self" (Hood et al., 2009, p. 209) through a process (sudden or gradual) that is more discrete than maturation. This focus on conversion as a radical change in the self goes back to the work of William James (1902/1958) who suggested "a self, hitherto divided and consciously wrong inferior and unhappy, becomes unified and consciously right superior and happy" (p. 157). Conversions are also understood as involving radical consequences in terms of concerns, values, identity, or actions. Most of the psychological research on conversion has traditionally focused on *religious* conversions. Transformations, however, occur beyond the bounds of religious contexts, and those reporting powerful transformations of the self, or "quantum changes," do not always understand such changes in relation to the sacred (Miller & C'de Baca, 2001). So, Hood et al. (2009) have suggested using the term *conversion* to refer to radical transformations of the self in association with religious institutions, whereas *spiritual transformations* are similar changes outside of religious institutions (p. 208). One problem with this view is that many religious traditions view conversion as a one-time event, which would make it confusing to use the term for subsequent changes. Paloutzian (2005) offered a slightly different solution by viewing religious conversion as a subset of the broader category of spiritual transformation, with the latter referring to a change in the "meaning system a person holds as a basis for self-definition, the interpretation of life, and overarching purposes and ultimate concerns" (p. 334). In Paloutzian's model, religious conversion is essentially a religious version of a spiritual transformation. We prefer the approach of Paloutzian (2005) in viewing spiritual transformation as the broader category with religious conversions as a subset.

Pargament (2007) has suggested defining spirituality as a "search for the sacred" and "spiritual transformation" as a change in the place or character of, or pathways toward, the sacred in a person's life. Shults and Sandage (2006) adapted these definitions to fit an interdisciplinary relational framework, defining spirituality as "ways of relating to the sacred" (p. 161). Theorists in the area of spiritual transformation agree the term "transformation" should refer to a profound, qualitative change or what family systems researchers have called *second-order change*. From a relational perspective, a spiritual transformation involves a profound integrative change in how a person relates to the sacred (Shults & Sandage, 2006). This might involve a shift from spiritual disinterest or obedience to deep intimacy with the sacred. Not all spiritual transformations have positive consequences, however (Pargament, 2007). A negative spiritual transformation might move a person from hopeful trust toward bitter disappointment or anger at God or the sacred. Spiritual transformation can also involve a shift in the contexts in which a person relates to the sacred, something occasionally called religious or spiritual "switching." For example, a person might switch within a religious tradition from Orthodox to Reformed Judaism. Or a person might move across traditions, such as from Catholicism to Native American spirituality. A national survey in the United States suggests religious switching is extremely common (Pew Forum on Religion & Public Life, 2008). A change in external affiliation is not a spiritual transformation, however, unless it represents an internalized psychological shift in the way the person actually relates to the sacred.

THEORETICAL MODELS

In this section we offer an overview of contemporary theoretical models of conversion and spiritual transformation that have emerged in psychological literature. To organize our overview of models, we will draw on the work of sociologist of religion Wuthnow (1998). Wuthnow has argued that the United States has undergone a spiritual transformation in the past 60 years, moving from a nation of primarily spiritual dwellers to an increasing number of spiritual seekers. Traditionally, spiritual dwelling has involved relating to the sacred through a secure sense of rootedness and stability by participating in a religious tradition and local community. Beginning in the 1950s, many people became spiritual seekers who started relating to the sacred by questing beyond traditional religious institutions and by searching for new spiritual meanings and practices. This shift from dwelling to seeking intensified in the 1960s and was prompted by numerous sociological factors in the Western Hemisphere, including (a) sociopolitical questioning of institutions, (b) an existential emphasis on the search for personal meaning, (c) the popularization of religion and spirituality through various forms of media that provide "access" to the sacred beyond the local congregation, and (d) the rising exposure to spiritual and religious diversity in practices to promote well-being. At one level, Wuthnow was describing a socially transformative shift away from religious institutions toward noninstitutional forms of spirituality. Yet, Wuthnow's model of spiritual dwelling and seeking has been interpreted as pointing to an underlying dialectical dynamic of spiritual stability (dwelling) and spiritual process (seeking) within spiritual development (Shults & Sandage, 2006). Wuthnow has suggested that some approaches to spirituality combine aspects of dwelling and seeking, an idea that has received some empirical support (Williamson & Sandage, 2009).

Wuthnow's (1998) model not only provides valuable insights into changes in the broader social context of spirituality in the United States, but his categories of spiritual dwelling and seeking provide a useful heuristic for understanding differing themes in theoretical models of conversion and spiritual transformation. Some contemporary models emphasize spiritual dwelling and emotional security, and such models resonate with the classic model of conversion or transformation as pursuit of a compensatory source of psychological and spiritual stability. Several other models of conversion and transformation have emphasized spiritual seeking of new meaning and greater agency or complexity, which fit trends within the contemporary paradigm. Finally, a few models can be characterized as integrating the dialectic of spiritual dwelling and seeking.

Models of Spiritual Dwelling

Ullman's (1989) study comparing 40 religious converts (to Roman Catholicism, Orthodox Judaism, Hare Krishna, or Baha'i) and 30 nonconverts drew on psychoanalytic theory in interpreting her participants as attempting to find a relational experience for dwelling in emotional security to compensate for family-of-origin deficits. She suggested "conversion pivots around a sudden attachment, an infatuation with a real or imagined figure which occurs on a background of great emotional turmoil" (Ullman, 1989, p. xvi). Like James (1902/1958) and Pratt (1920) before her, Ullman likened religious conversion to falling in love. Consistent with the classic paradigm, her focus was on the emotional and relational dynamics of religious conversion and the pursuit of a safe haven or psychological salvation in relationship to a parental authority figure, a transcendent love object, or an accepting peer community. Her research suggested that up to 80% of converts reported a precipitating period of emotional distress before conversion. Ullman, however, did note a subgroup of her sample who seemed to convert out of a different motivation—that is, the quest for existential meaning. She viewed these questers as more internally motivated and as less driven by emotional wounds, and this group fits our category of spiritual seeking.

Similar to Ullman, Kirkpatrick's (2005; see Chapter 7 in this volume) program of research on conversion and spiritual change, grounded in attachment theory, also suggested that conversion might represent attempted compensation for emotional and relational insecurity. This model draws a parallel between the attachment system, particularly the safe haven function, and spiritual and religious experience. Once activated, the attachment system prompts the human organism to seek proximity and security in relation to attachment figures. In an analogous fashion, much spiritual and religious behavior can be interpreted as representing attempts to dwell within the safety and security of Divine love, protection, and provision, particularly in theistic traditions. God(s) and spiritual beings can be likened to sacred attachment figures who "provide" varying degrees of emotional security depending on the psychological development of the devotee and their prior experiences with human attachment figures.

Kirkpatrick and other attachment-based theorists (Granqvist, 2002; Granqvist & Kirkpatrick, 2004; Granqvist, Mikulincer, & Shaver, 2010) have developed a two-process model of spiritual and religious change. Those who develop a secure style of attachment with caregivers can be expected to develop spiritual and religious perspectives that *correspond* to those of their parents. Loving and secure family relationships set the stage for a gradual, nondramatic process of spiritual and religious socialization. There are no significant emotional and relational deficits that generate the need for dramatic transformations. Conversely, those who develop an insecure style of attachment with caregivers may approach spiritual and religious experience in a *compensatory* fashion as a way of overcoming emotional insecurity. This could lead to dramatic spiritual or religious transformations because an experience of God's love or spiritual acceptance may be profoundly different from prior attachment experiences and the person's prior internal working model of relationships. Conversely, a person with insecure attachments to highly religious parents might also find it deeply relieving to compensate by shifting away from or "losing" their parents' religious beliefs and the associated anxiety of those relational dynamics (Kirkpatrick & Shaver, 1990). Kirkpatrick has compared the correspondence and compensation processes to James's (1902/1958) classic two-fold model of religious temperaments of the healthy-minded (or once born) and sick soul (twice born), respectively. Attachment theory posits the two main attachment functions of a (a) safe haven for protection and (b) a secure base for exploration. Attachment theorists in the psychology of religion, however, have tended to focus on the safe haven function, suggesting spiritual and religious transformations are primarily motivated by a desire to dwell in emotional security and are prompted by experiences of relational loss or developmental transitions, such as adolescence. Granqvist and Kirkpatrick (2004) specifically differentiated their attachment-based model of conversion with the focus on "emotionally and relationally based needs" from models that emphasize "cognitive/existential meaning" and questing (p. 226). We consider empirical tests of attachment-based models in the following section.

Models of Spiritual Seeking

Hay (2001) has offered the critique that "emotional problem-solving" or compensatory models of conversion or transformation reflect a culturally specific Puritan or Pietistic Christian bias that does not generalize to all religious traditions or experiences. Interestingly, he even invoked Jonathan Edwards's own description of his conversion experience to suggest it moved from an initial fear of damnation (arguably a spiritual attachment issue) to what Hay (2001) interpreted as a "new way of seeing" (p. 244) or making meaning. Several contemporary models of conversion and transformation reflect an emphasis on spiritual seeking of new meaning and complexity of consciousness. For example, Batson, Schoenrade, and Ventis (1982/1993) developed a social constructivist and cognitive restructuring model in which existential crises or discrepancies of meaning lead to spiritual searching or questing and eventual creative transformation into greater differentiation and integration. The Batson et al. model suggested that emotions can offer motivational force, but the focus is on transformation into a more flexible and complex cognitive structure for meaning making than attachment security. This is similar to Loder's (1989) theologically integrative existential and developmental model in which transformation begins with a "rupture in the knowing context" (p. 37) and proceeds to an interlude for scanning and differentiating until a constructive insight is achieved.

Hill (2002) also proposed a model of spiritual transformation in which seeking new meaning is the core motivation. Rather than simply providing emotional security or resolution of anxiety, Hill suggested spiritual transformations can lead to meaning frameworks that can expand positive emotional experience. Although negative emotions (e.g., fear) might tend to motivate sudden and dramatic transformation aimed at restoring safety and security, positive emotions might tend to be associated with a more gradual opening to new meaning and understanding. Paloutzian (2005) has utilized Hill's work in offering a related social cognitive model of spiritual transformation of "meaning systems," activated by discrepancies, doubts, or discontinuities or what Loder (1989) called "the existential void." These discontinuities necessitate changes in systems of meaning, which include cognitive, emotional, motivational, and behavioral elements. Various kinds of stressors can prompt the disequilibrium that leads to transformations in spiritual meaning, such as changes in overall purpose in life, ultimate concerns, or self-definition.

These spiritual-seeking models of transformation above have tended to employ cognitive and existential psychology, yet advances in neurobiology are also contributing to seeking-oriented models. Albright (2006) has drawn on neurobiology and complexity theory to view spiritual transformation as an emergent, self-organizing process of evolution in which an embodied organism seeks greater complexity of neural patterning in the brain. Spiritual transformation in this model involves the dynamic reorganization of the brain characterized by qualities of increased convergence, emergence, synergy, and complexity. This is an evolutionary process of seeking to adapt to an ever-changing universe.

Dialectical Models

A third group of theoretical models of conversion and spiritual transformation can be characterized as dialectical, integrating the dimensions of spiritual dwelling and seeking. For example, Rambo's (1993) dialectical and process-oriented stage model of religious conversion is one of the most holistic by giving significant consideration to contextual, relational, emotional, and meaning-oriented dimensions of change. Rambo's nonlinear stages include a crisis in a given context that leads to questing (seeking) for meaning and eventually commitment (dwelling) to a group or community as aspects of the overall process of change. Rambo's model is one of the few that attempts to consider both sociocultural or contextual factors outside the person as well as intrapsychic factors in understanding the process of conversion. This model also highlights the roles of both relationships and the need for meaning as part of the "matrix of transformation" (Rambo, 1993, p. 107).

Jones's (2002) model drew on relational psychoanalysis (e.g., Winnicott, Kohut) to view spiritual transformation as a developmental and relational process. Jones suggested that transformation is generated both by relational desires and by the need for reconstructed meaning following spiritual deidealization. Relating to the sacred involves a growth-enhancing search for "a transformational object that can facilitate the integration of new experience" (Jones, 2002, p. 87). In Jones's view, spiritual transformation is shaped by prior relational experiences but is oriented toward creativity and new meaning. He sought to integrate psychological theorists and Eastern and Western spiritual traditions to suggest a view of transformation as nonlinear and inclusive of *dark nights of the soul* or periods of spiritual ambiguity and struggle.

Welwood's (2000) dialectical Buddhist model of spiritual and psychological transformation integrated an awareness of pure being (dwelling) with an actualization of development (seeking) for everyday life. In his model, realization involves liberation of the conditioned self into an awareness of ultimate truth, whereas transformation involves the integration of spiritual development with the rest of life into a more human presence. So realization involves dwelling in spiritual awareness and transformation involves actively seeking practical spiritual embodiment. A unique feature of Welwood's model is his developmental understanding of "spiritual bypassing" (Welwood, 2000, p. 11), or a defensive process among some persons who overspiritualize experience to avoid the pain or difficulty of certain psychological issues. This means someone might self-report a profound change into heightened spiritual awareness, but this could represent a defensive or dissociative process in some cases. Welwood's model would lead to assessing developmental qualities of personal and relational maturity to help validate an actual transformation. Like Jones (2002), he offered an integration of psychological theory and spiritual tradition.

Pargament's (2007) model suggested that spirituality involves both conserving and transforming forms of spiritual coping within a sociocultural context. People often attempt to hold onto or conserve sacred meaning through various coping mechanisms, such as positive reappraisals of negative events or engaging in spiritual purification. Spiritual struggles, however, can lead to new forms of coping that represent a spiritual transformation. For example, a person may move from a focus on anger over injustice to valuing forgiveness on the basis of a spiritual transformation. Pargament's model considers both the conserving and transforming functions of spirituality, thereby acknowledging the dialectical needs for stability (dwelling) and growth (seeking).

Like Jones (2002), he also acknowledged the constructive potential for spiritual struggles or even trauma to catalyze transformations without suggesting this is always the outcome.

Shults and Sandage (2006; Williamson & Sandage, 2009) utilized Wuthnow's (1998) constructs of spiritual dwelling and sought to develop a dialectical and relational model of spiritual transformation. Similar to Pargament (2007), they suggested that spiritual development involves an ongoing process of attempting to balance spiritual dwelling and seeking, with various struggles and discontinuities (e.g., "dark nights of the soul") serving as potential catalysts for transformative change. They focused on relationships as providing a key crucible or holding environment for spiritual transformation resulting in new ways of relating to the sacred. Like Welwood (2000), their model integrated psychology with a particular spiritual tradition—in this case, contemplative Christian spirituality. They also defined spiritual maturity in relation to increased differentiation, which is achieved in response to a transformative intensification of anxiety.

EMPIRICAL RESULTS

This section offers a brief overview of empirical research on conversion and spiritual transformation. Research in this area tended to focus on correlates and consequences through the 1990s, as summarized in prior reviews. The field is now advancing toward (a) empirical tests of theoretical models and (b) investigations of diverse populations and contexts.

Correlates and Consequences

Paloutzian, Richardson, and Rambo (1999) conducted a thorough review of the literature to that date to investigate the impact of conversion upon personality. Drawing on the work of McAdams (1994), they adopted a three-level conceptualization of personality characterized by increasing complexity at comprehensively higher personality levels. They found that conversions to new belief systems and faith communities had "little appreciable effect" (Paloutzian et al., 1999, p. 1073) at the lowest level of personality (Level 1)—that of one's most basic personality traits and temperaments (such as the Big Five traits of Openness to Experience, Conscientiousness, Extroversion, Agreeableness, and Neuroticism). The authors suggested that these basic aspects of one's personality, commonly taken to stabilize during young adulthood, were more likely to serve as predisposing or contributing factors, shaping the course or object of one's religious or spiritual change. This proved to be the case regardless of whether the conversion took place suddenly or gradually, and whether the conversion was to a traditional religion or a new religious movement.

Despite the limited influence on Level 1 of personality, the Paloutzian et al. (1999) review suggested that religious conversion did have significant effects at Level 2 of personality, or the level of goals and strivings, values, motivations, feelings, behaviors (including coping strategies), and relational attachment style. This mid-level dimension of personality reflects, perhaps among other things, the functional expression of one's more basic traits and personal adaptation to diverse situations. This suggests that conversions typically do not change a person's basic personality traits or character but can transform the ways they adapt to life.

Miller and C'de Baca's (1994, 2001; C'de Baca & Wilbourne, 2004; Miller, 2004) research illustrated mid-level change as a result of a transformation. They investigated the experiences of 55 people who had experienced some sort of *quantum change*—"a vivid, surprising, benevolent, and enduring personal change" (Miller & C'de Baca, 2001, p. 4), although not all explicitly interpreted their transformation in spiritual terms. They found the chief effects of these changes to consist in an increase of positive emotion and a significant shift in values or priorities, with spirituality showing the greatest gain. Similarly, they found increases in participants' valuing of compassion, cherishing of the present, practicing of virtue, and relational connectedness and depth. Men's and women's changes tended to work against stereotyped gender polarities, a finding similar to results from Zinnbauer and Pargament (1998; Mahoney & Pargament, 2004). C'de Baca and her colleagues found that these positive effects appeared to have been sustained an average of 10 and even 20 years after the experience (Miller & C'de Baca, 1994; C'de Baca & Wilbourne, 2004). Like many studies in this area, these findings are not without their limitations, as the reports came from self-selected participants, were based on significantly retrospective accounts, and lacked any third-party confirmation.

If conversions and transformations appear to produce little change at Level 1 but significant effects at Level 2 of personality, what can be said for the even more complex and comprehensive third level—that of integrative life narrative? Paloutzian et al. (1999) answered the query: "It is here that the changes due to religious conversion are most encompassing" (p. 1068). This is where religious conversions and spiritual transformations produce second-order perceptual and belief changes of the highest order, the kind that most profoundly shape—but also emerge out of—our goals and strivings, values, attitudes, feelings, behaviors (including coping strategies), and relational attachment styles. Of course, the entire history of inquiry into conversion and spiritual transformation attests to profound shifts in the ways one perceives the sacred, the world, and oneself, whether these shifts come all at once (as emphasized in the classical paradigm and dwelling-oriented models) or in a more progressive fashion (as emphasized in the contemporary paradigm and some of the seeking-oriented and dialectical models). Narrative psychology, quite naturally, is emerging as a prominent frontier for the investigation of Level 3 personality effects vis-à-vis religious conversions and spiritual transformations. As McAdams (2006) stated, "Human lives are cultural texts that can interpreted as stories" (p. 14). And these culturally influenced "narrative identities," as he called them, potentially provide our lives with meaning, unity, and purpose, some of the highest order functions served by religiousness or spirituality, in general.

In particular, McAdams's (2006) research has found that highly generative adults frequently have a strong theme of *redemption* in their narrative self-identity, with redemption meaning a transformation of negative events into something positive that eventually leads to caring for others. Redemptive identities are often, although not always, influenced by spiritual or religious traditions. But even secular versions of redemptive narratives can operate as sources of idealization similar to the sacred and may even carry vestiges of religious heritage.

This tri-part understanding of personality can serve as a heuristic for studying the psychological dynamics of religious conversions and spiritual transformations. As might be evident by this point, Level 2 personality functions surface not only among the *outcome* correlates of conversion and transformation but also among the contributing *process* correlates. Whereas the direction of influence in the relationship between Level 1 personality traits and religious conversions or transformations would appear to flow, if at all, from the former to the latter, the relationship between Level 2 personality functions and conversions or transformations is clearly more reciprocal. Thus, we commonly find emotional concerns, values, motivations, and behaviors not only changing partly as a result of conversions or transformations, but also we find them factoring into the impetus behind those conversions or transformations. This is evident in Ullman's (1989) and Granqvist and Kirkpatrick's (2004; Kirkpatrick, 2005) findings regarding the emotional and attachment-related salience of religious conversions for spiritual *dwelling*. And whereas Miller and C'de Baca's (2001) research highlighted transformation outcomes in the areas of personal values, behavior, and relational styles, the *seeking-oriented* models of spiritual transformation give prominence to such contributory Level 2 process correlates as personal strivings after meaning and the resolution of existential questions (Batson et al., 1982/1993; Hill, 2002; Paloutzian, 2005).

An emerging interest in *meaning* in the broader field of the psychology of religion directs scholars' attention toward that third, most complex and comprehensive level of personality. And perhaps it is the complex and reciprocal relationship between this cultural worldview level of personality and mid-level personality functions that holds the key to understanding spiritual transformations of the dialectical relationship between dwelling and seeking. It might also constitute the nexus—or perhaps *metanexus*—of transformations in the complexity of consciousness, differentiation, and integration in relation to the sacred.

Theoretical Model Testing

One important advance in research in this area is the growing number of empirical studies that explicitly tested theoretical models of conversion or spiritual transformation discussed in the section Correlates and Consequences. Kahn and Greene (2004) tested Rambo's (1993) process model of religious conversion by developing a new measure based on a sample of adults reporting a religious conversion (broadly defined) across numerous traditions. The sample included some participants who had left a religious affiliation for atheism or agnosticism. Items were designed to fit each of Rambo's seven dimensions of the conversion process (Context, Crisis, Quest, Encounter, Interaction, Commitment, Consequences), although Batson and Schoenrade's (1991a, 1991b) 12-item Quest Scale was used to measure Rambo's quest dimension. The context scale items did not achieve an adequate reliability and were deleted from further analyses. Factor analysis yielded six factors the researchers labeled (a) *redemptive love*, (b) *zealous dedication*, (c) *dysphoric need*, (d) *openness to uncertainty*, (e) *extrinsic crisis*, and (f) *experiential learning*. The redemptive love items appeared to closely correspond with Rambo's consequences dimension, the dysphoric need and extrinsic crisis items corresponded with Rambo's crisis dimension (internal and external crises, respectively), and the experiential learning items corresponded with Rambo's interaction dimension. Zealous dedication items were intended to correspond with Rambo's commitment dimension, although converts to conservative–evangelical Protestantism scored higher in this dimension than other participants. Younger ages at conversion were also associated with higher levels of zealous dedication, whereas older ages at conversion were associated with higher levels of extrinsic crisis. Converts to non-Christian religions scored higher than conservative–evangelical Protestant participants in openness to uncertainty items drawn from the Quest Scale, and this dimension was positively related to higher education. The researchers raised questions about the specific theoretical connections between questing and conversion, such as how seeking eventuates in conversion in some cases versus ongoing searching in others. This study supports the need for multidimensional models of conversion and transformation and the possibility that some dimensions may be more prominent within certain traditions or developmental periods.

Zinnbauer and Pargament (1998) tested a model of spiritual conversion based on Pargament's (1997) coping theory of conversion as a radical change or transformation of the self that is precipitated by stress. They defined *spiritual conversion* as "one type of religious conversion in which the self becomes identified with a spiritual force" (Zinnbauer & Pargament, 1998, p. 162). Their sample and cross-sectional design allowed a comparison of the retrospective reports of Christian undergraduate and graduate students (ages 18–26) across three groups: (a) spiritual converts (in the previous 2 years), (b) nonconverts who reported a gradual increase in religiousness, and (c) religious adherents who did not report change. The spiritual converts and gradual religious changers reported higher levels of precipitating stress 2 years earlier and greater increases in self development and spirituality over the past 2 years than did the nonchange group. The only difference between the spiritual convert and gradual religious change groups was that the former reported higher levels of life transformation as a result of their experiences. This was based on a new eight-item measure developed in this study—The Degree Life Is Transformed scale. The results also included some gender effects, with women generally increasing in spirituality more than men over time. Women who experienced religious change also (a) reported greater improvement in sense of self and self-confidence compared with women and men, in general, and (b) increased in self-reliance, whereas male religious changers tended to decrease in self-reliance, a finding similar to gender effects found by Miller and C'de Baca (2001). The results of this study generally supported theorized connections between conversion and stress, selfhood, and holistic life transformation, although the differences between sudden and gradual religious changes appeared more tenuous.

Cole, Hopkins, Tisak, Steel, and Carr (2008) used Pargament's (2007) model to frame their findings on spiritual change in response to a cancer diagnosis. They developed a 40-item Spiritual Transformation

Scale, which is unique in measuring both spiritual growth and spiritual decline. Spiritual growth was associated with more threatening illness and with posttraumatic growth. Spiritual decline was positively associated with depression and negatively associated with spiritual well-being. Spiritual decline seems to measure a set of spiritual struggles that are distinct from low levels of posttraumatic growth.

Empirical studies of conversion and spiritual transformation based on attachment theory represent the largest body of theory-driven psychological research in this area (for reviews, see Granqvist & Kirkpatrick, 2004; Kirkpatrick, 2005). For example, individuals reporting a history of avoidant attachment with parents were more likely to experience a sudden religious conversion than those with a secure style of attachment. Longitudinal studies with adult samples have also found insecure attachment to be associated with conversion and increases in religiosity over time. Granqvist (2002; see Chapter 7 in this volume) reformulated attachment hypotheses based on prior studies to suggest "socialized correspondence" for individuals with a secure style of attachment and "emotional compensation" for individuals with an insecure style of attachment. That is, those with a secure style of attachment are generally socialized into a spiritual and religious orientation that corresponds to that of their parents. They do not experience significant emotional or relational deficits that motivate compensatory experiences with the sacred. In contrast, those with an insecure style of attachment may relate to the sacred primarily out of a need for emotional compensation to help regulate affective distress, particularly during times of transition or loss.

Granqvist and Kirkpatrick (2004) conducted a meta-analysis of 11 studies ($N = 1,465$) conducted in the United States and Sweden examining links between religious conversion and perceived childhood attachment. As hypothesized, nonsudden conversions and gradual religious changes were associated with a perceived history of secure attachment, whereas sudden religious conversions tended to be associated with a perceived history of insecure attachment. The effect sizes ranged from small to medium. Gender differences were not found, which differentiates attachment theory research from some other studies of conversion and transformation. Granqvist and Kirkpatrick suggested the classic paradigm of conversion research may best fit those with an insecure attachment history who are more prone to convert suddenly and passively with antecedent emotional distress. In contrast, the contemporary paradigm of conversion (and transformation) research may better fit those with secure attachment histories because spiritual and religious change is more likely to be gradual, noncompensatory, and reflective of active seeking.

Sandage and colleagues have tested the relational model of spiritual transformation (Shults & Sandage, 2006) in two cross-sectional studies of Christian graduate-level seminary students. A dichotomous measure of spiritual transformation was adapted from Miller and C'de Baca's (2001) quantum change research to assess whether participants reported a dramatic spiritual change during the previous year. In support of the model, the researchers found empirical evidence that those reporting a recent spiritual transformation differ from those who do not with respect to the dialectical relationship between spiritual dwelling and seeking. For example, the curvilinear relationship between spiritual questing and a dwelling-oriented measure of spiritual maturity was moderated or altered by a report of a recent spiritual transformation (Sandage, Link, & Jankowski, 2010). A second study found spiritual questing was negatively related with generativity among those not reporting a recent spiritual transformation but showed a curvilinear pattern with generativity for those who did (Sandage, Hill, & Vaubel, 2011). That is, moderate levels of spiritual questing were associated with the highest levels of generativity for those reporting a recent spiritual transformation, and this effect held after controlling for impression management. Although the cross-sectional design of these two studies limited interpretations of causality, the results showed that those reporting a recent spiritual transformation tended to display a greater integration of spiritual dwelling and seeking than those who did not. Measures of spiritual dwelling and seeking are sometimes inversely related; however, these two studies show a different, nonlinear pattern for those reporting spiritual changes. These studies also suggest that future work on spiritual transformation may benefit from the investigation of nonlinear effects as well as inclusion of measures of both spiritual dwelling and seeking to test dialectical models.

DIVERSE POPULATIONS AND CONTEXTS

Like many areas in the psychology and sociology of religion, research on conversion and spiritual transformation has been limited by an overrepresentation of Christian and European American samples and contexts. Several recent studies illustrate the benefits of intentionally investigating these constructs in more diverse populations. For example, Danzig and Sands (2007) conducted a qualitative study with 48 *baalei teshuvah*—that is, Jewish women and men who undergo a spiritual transformation toward becoming Orthodox. They identified several nonlinear processes that contributed to a gradual spiritual transformation or intensification of spiritual commitment, including a strong emphasis on relational dynamics and actively seeking meaning to overcome a sense of existential vacuum. The multidimensional relational dynamics included family dissension and deficits as antecedents (similar to Ullman's findings) as well as positive relationships with spiritual models or exemplars (e.g., teachers, Rabbis, family members). They also identified a common process of idealization and deidealization that was part of immersion into spiritual community, which resonated with Jones's (2002) model. Overall, Danzig and Sands's results suggested a model of spiritual transformation among *baalei teshuvah*, which includes strong elements of spiritual dwelling and seeking.

Islam, the second largest religious group in the world, has been grossly understudied in the psychology of religion. Several studies have started to shape a body of literature on Islamic conversion and transformation. Lakhdar, Vinsonneau, Apter, and Mullet (2007) developed an inventory of conversion motives that they tested in a sample of French adolescents and adults who had converted to Islam. Overall, their results suggested the primary motives for conversion were active and personal or "telic" in the sense of seeking purpose or growth. Passive or societal motives were clearly secondary, and conversion motivated by marriage or interpersonal attachment was negatively related to regularity of prayer. The latter effect supported their hypothesis that more extrinsic reasons for conversion might be associated with lower levels of religious observance.

Maslim and Bjorck (2009) also studied motives for conversion to Islam but focused on women in the United States. Like Lakhdar et al. (2007), they found that active reasons (e.g., preferring Islamic values or seeking an increased sense of identity) were predominant over passive or social reasons (e.g., marrying a Muslim or feeling marginalized by their former faith). At the same time, they found that a majority of participants indicated multiple reasons for conversion to Islam, including relational motivations, seeking meaning, and a good fit with their views on ethnicity and gender. As with Lakhdar et al., converting because of marriage or because of friends were both negatively correlated with regularity of prayer, suggesting that those may be extrinsic motivations that are not associated with consistent religious practice. Ethnicity did show some effect on the results. Compared with women of Caucasian descent, women of African descent ascribed more importance to motives of believing in Islamic values, being dissatisfied with their former faith, and gaining an increased sense of identity and independence. Participants were recruited online through the website of a North American magazine focused on Muslim women, and women who would seek out such a publication are probably relatively committed to their cultural and religious identity.

Abu-Raiya, Pargament, Mahoney, and Stein (2008) used an international sample in developing a multidimensional measure of Islamic religiousness, which included a six-item Islamic Religious Conversion subscale with strong reliability. This subscale also showed incremental validity in regression analyses with higher scores predicting higher levels of General Islamic Well-Being and Satisfaction With Life and lower levels of depression and anger even after controlling for demographic variables, social desirability, and global religiousness. These three quantitative studies of Islamic conversion offer a set of measures and findings that can be useful for future research, although the samples were heavily weighted toward the United States and Europe.

LeBlanc's (2007) ethnographic study of the religious transformation of West African Muslim women in the Republic of Côte d'Ivoire highlighted important contextual factors that can be revealed in qualitative research. She interviewed women about the experience of *imaniya*, which is a change in Muslim religious practice that means "assuming one's faith" (LaBlanc, 2007, p. 36) or religious intensification. For women in particular, imaniya is understood to be associated with humility, modesty, and purification. LeBlanc's findings showed the tensions for Muslim women who challenge traditional gender roles by becoming educated, French-speaking, and professionally employed, which can reduce their chances of attracting marital partners among Muslim men. In fact, in the traditional Dioula language an "adult woman" is one who is married and a mother, roles that are considered central to the transmission of the revival of Islamic religious education in that region. Many of the educated women in LeBlanc's (2007) study navigated this social landscape through involvement in neighborhood Islamic associations, which allowed them social access to peers in public spaces or "matrimonial markets" (p. 44) without compromising the humility and piety that is considered appropriate for women. LeBlanc argued that imaniya facilitates marriage in this context for well-educated women who might otherwise be considered secular and suspect, and this also allowed some participants to channel their professional skills into public leadership roles in Islamic nongovernmental organizations following marriage and motherhood. LeBlanc's multifaceted sociopolitical analysis leads her to caution against simplistic interpretations of these women's religious transformations as passive acceptance of hierarchical gender roles but rather a complex process through which women redefine religious virtues (e.g., humility) and negotiate the tensions between agency and community.

Religious conversions were embedded in the renegotiation of cultural expectations of gender roles for Taiwanese immigrant women in southern California studied by Chen (2005). She interviewed 28 Taiwanese women (15 Buddhists and 13 Christians) who had converted from traditional Confucianism to Buddhism or Christianity. Chen noted that whereas some prior studies have suggested immigrant religion tends to support traditional patriarchy, the women in this study tended to use their new religion to challenge traditional gender roles in favor of a more egalitarian view of gender. She explained, "religion is a catalyst for transformation as its rejection of this world becomes a metaphor that these women use to reject certain kinship expectations that they now find constraining in the United States" (Chen, 2005, p. 354). As in the LeBlanc (2007) study, the religious involvement of these women might seem to reinforce relatively conservative gender roles unless they are viewed within a wider cultural context and with an awareness of the overall transformation process. Chen showed that the religious conversions of these women achieved a sense of liberation, although it is liberation from what they experience as excessive kinship obligations that could preclude education and employment outside the home. Her results highlighted the connections between religious conversions and processes of acculturation for immigrant populations.

African American women are another vastly underrepresented group in research on conversion and spiritual transformation. Lee (2008) sought to move the field beyond this omission by interviewing 13 African American women about their Christian conversion narratives. Interestingly, all her participants viewed their conversion as more of a gradual process than a sudden event and frequently mentioned the influence of religious roots in their upbringing. This finding raises important questions for attachment-based models of conversion. It is possible all of the participants had secure attachment histories leading to a gradual process of conversion. Or, there may be cultural influences on the interpretation of conversion that have been largely unaddressed in attachment-based models as well as the wider field of spiritual transformation. Participants in Lee's study also tended to view conversion (a) as distinct from salvation and (b) necessarily expressed through concrete actions. A few participants suggested those concrete actions might include more conservative choices in dress and jewelry, again revealing some of the unique findings that emerge through the thick description obtained via qualitative research. Distinctions between conversion and salvation also suggest theological nuances and the need for interdisciplinary collaboration between social scientists and religious scholars.

FUTURE RESEARCH DIRECTIONS

Efforts to advance research could start with measurement development. Some quantitative measures of conversion and transformation have been mentioned in this chapter (e.g., see Abu-Raiya et al., 2008; Cole et al., 2008; Kahn & Greene, 2004; Zinnbauer & Pargament, 1998), although most have not been repeatedly tested in published studies. The literature also now clearly supports a view of conversion and transformation as multidimensional, which suggests the need for further theory-driven psychometric work along with validity studies using the quality measures that are now available. Like many areas of psychology, the research to date largely is based on self-report measures and there is a great need for studies using implicit measures or observer ratings. Most of the research in this area is cross sectional, qualitative, or ethnographic, and the field could be advanced through more longitudinal, experimental, and mixed-method designs. Zinnbauer and Pargament (1998), in one of the few mixed-method studies, highlighted the limitation of using retrospective or postconversion reports of preconversion functioning because standards of evaluation may change following a conversion. Longitudinal designs may also need to account for differing patterns of change, including nonlinear changes over time. It is also striking that the hundreds of empirical studies of psychotherapy have yielded so little data on spiritual changes during the therapy process. Numerous well-studied virtues (e.g., hope, gratitude, forgiveness) in the field of positive psychology might also be integrated into spiritual transformation research (see Chapter 23 in this volume; see Volume 2, Chapter 25, this handbook).

The growing attention to diversity in this field needs continued development. Some groups and contexts continue to be understudied. The available research suggests that universal theories of conversion and transformation are highly suspect and need to be contextualized with respect to various cultural, religious, and spiritual traditions. Moderator effects for gender, culture, and other forms of diversity need to be more carefully tested. It is also important for spiritual transformation to be further studied beyond the convenience of college samples to access greater diversity. For example, emerging studies of spiritual transformation have investigated a variety of contexts, including HIV/AIDS (Ironson, Kremer, & Ironson, 2006), surviving sexual violence (Knapik, Martsolf, & Draucker, 2008), incarceration (Kerley & Copes, 2009), and bereavement (Cait, 2004). Contexts involving human loss, transition, and trauma are particularly ripe for the study of spiritual transformation. Smith's (2006) nationally representative survey of spiritual transformation in the United States suggested self-reports of spiritual and religious changes are common (50%), and personal problems such as an illness, accident, or death of someone close were frequently cited as precipitating a spiritual transformation.

The history of the psychology of religion also includes too many examples of reductionistic explanations of spiritual or religious experience that are divorced from the interpretive horizon of the participants. In that vein, the paradigm of indigenous psychology (Kim, Yang, & Hwang, 2006) could be useful for rooting empirical research within the indigenous meaning and cultural or spiritual traditions of a particular group. The integrative paradigm promoted in this handbook is also consistent with greater interdisciplinary collaboration between psychologists and sociologists or anthropologists to integrate understandings of individual and contextual dynamics of change. Integration could be further enhanced as social scientists collaborate with religious scholars or spiritual leaders to accurately interpret indigenous understandings of spiritual transformation. Koss-Chioino's (2006) work with spirit healers in Puerto Rico provided a valuable example.

PRACTICAL APPLICATIONS

Several practical implications follow from this overview of conversion and spiritual transformation. First, practitioners are wise to attend to the multiple cultural, relational, and developmental factors that might be related to conversions or spiritual transformations reported by their clients. Rather than holding a singular perspective on reasons for spiritual and religious change, clinicians might assess the multiple dimensions suggested by the research in this chapter. Are there recent developmental or life-cycle transitions operative in the client's life (e.g., young adulthood, midlife, divorce)? Are acculturation processes related to recent spiritual or religious changes? Does the client seem to be seeking a new relational experience or greater cognitive complexity following a trauma, loss, or relational injury? Is the client seeking out new spiritual or religious coping resources to deal with a particular life challenge or struggle? Higher levels of family triangulation have been associated with increased religious questing in young adults (Rootes, Jankowski, & Sandage, 2010), so the intersections between certain relational dynamics and potential changes are worth exploring. Spiritual or religious genograms can be a useful tool for mapping patterns of intergenerational change in a client's family of origin for clients who are comfortable discussing those issues.

Some clients may be hesitant to discuss dramatic spiritual experiences with clinicians out of fear of being thought "crazy," so it can be particularly important to maintain a respectful and empathic stance to gain the trust of such clients. To do so, clinicians may need to examine their own countertransference about issues of spirituality and religion, especially those forms that lie outside their own familiarity and worldviews or forms that trigger difficult associations in the clinicians' past. It has been our observation that some clinicians prefer dwelling-oriented spiritualities, whereas others prefer seeking-oriented spiritualities. Yet clients can be moving toward either category (or an integration of the two). Consultation with professionals who are well informed about particular spiritual or religious traditions can be helpful in maintaining clinical objectivity.

Couple and family conflicts can also arise as differences in spiritual dwelling and seeking emerge. A spiritual transformation is not always popular with a person's spouse or family members. For example, some adolescent or young adult clients may present mental health symptoms of anxiety or depression that could be due to conflicts over a recent conversion away from their family's religious tradition to another faith or even a deconversion away from all religion. Or, spouses, may go through spiritual transformations that result in a greater sense of agency, self-regard, and spiritual leadership, which could contribute to tensions in their relationships if their partners hold more conservative spiritual or religious orientations regarding gender (Mahoney & Pargament, 2004). Spouses or family members might feel abandoned, and the transformed individual might feel engulfed by extreme resistance. Therapists doing couples or family work in such cases can find themselves quickly triangulated and will be challenged to maintain a systemic perspective to avoid taking a side on whether the recent conversion or transformation is "a good thing." In such cases, what is needed, beyond the individual transformation, is a secondary mesosystemic transformation of the relationship between the individual and his or her other relationships to integrate the changes toward greater differentiation. Virtues like forgiveness, acceptance, compassion, or humility might be useful as integrative or bridging constructs within relational systems in which spiritual or religious differences have become problematic. The therapist needs to be sensitive to the ways such virtue language can become a source of further conflict.

There is the question of whether therapists should ever try to facilitate spiritual transformations, to which we offer a qualified "yes." On the one hand, therapists have an ethical responsibility to respect their clients and traditions and values, so it would be improper to try to persuade a client to practice a different faith (see Volume 2, Chapter 3, this handbook). Clients can be encouraged to explore the transformative possibilities for psychological and relational growth within their own traditions, and in some cases, the search may lead clients toward new traditions. Another qualification is that clients from spiritual or religious traditions that focus on sudden, dramatic transformations may have unrealistic expectation about the process of change in psychotherapy. For such clients, it could be important to help them manage spiritual disappointment if change is harder or more gradual than they expected.

There are clinical situations in which second-order change or transformation is typically a necessary goal. For example, couples therapy often requires transformative change to overcome the risk of relationship dissolution and alter dysfunctional relational patterns. Fincham, Stanley, and Beach's (2007) emphasis on nonlinear transformative processes, such as forgiveness, commitment, and sanctification, represented a key emerging trend in relationship science. Forgiveness involves a transformation in interpersonal motivations that may be necessary to sustain close relationships following conflict (McCullough, Bono, & Root, 2007). Spiritually transformative changes with couples and families in therapy often will involve first tolerating increased levels of anxiety and conflict as the system destabilizes, a truth found in many spiritual and religious traditions (Schnarch, 1997).

Clients who meet criteria for personality disorders also necessitate transformation as they evidence pervasive problems in their sense of self and relational functioning, including spiritual impairment and pathology. For personality-disordered clients who value their spiritual or religious commitments, therapeutic progress will include a transformation in the way such clients relate to both the sacred and human others. Relational dynamics between the client and therapist are likely to be a key source of transformative gain as attachment templates are changed.

There has also been a long history of recognition that individuals with substance disorders need a spiritual transformation rather than simple, first-order behavioral change. Margolin et al. (2007) have found empirical support for spiritual self-schema (3-S+) therapy in reducing impulsive behavior and increasing spiritual practice among HIV-positive drug users. Their approach combines Buddhist mindfulness practice with interventions to transform addict self-schemas toward spiritual self-schemas and teaches virtue practices of compassion, gratitude, forgiveness, wisdom, and courage. This represents the best of the psychology of religion and spirituality—integrating psychological science with the richness of sacred traditions to alleviate suffering and enhance human growth.

Finally, spiritual and religious leaders and educators are uniquely positioned to inform adolescents and adults about the processes of spiritual development that are involved in conversion and transformation. Leaders and educators could utilize an integration of sacred traditions and empirical research in helping laypeople cope with spiritual struggles and understand the possibilities of spiritual growth and change. Well-informed, authentic, and integrative approaches might serve a preventative function by limiting the risk that processes of spiritual struggle and change will become disempowering or relationally divisive within families and communities.

References

Abu-Raiya, H., Pargament, K. I., Mahoney, A., & Stein, C. (2008). A psychological measure of Islamic religiousness: Development and evidence for reliability and validity. *The International Journal for the Psychology of Religion, 18*, 291–315. doi:10.1080/10508610802229270

Albright, C. R. (2006). Spiritual growth, cognition, and complexity: Faith as a dynamic process. In J. D. Koss-Chioino & P. Hefner (Eds.), *Spiritual transformation and healing: Anthropological, theological, neuroscientific, and clinical perspectives* (pp. 168–186). Walnut Creek, CA: AltaMira Press.

Batson, C. D., & Schoenrade, P. A. (1991a). Measuring religion as quest: 1. Validity concerns. *Journal for the Scientific Study of Religion, 30*, 416–429.

Batson, C. D., & Schoenrade, P. A. (1991b). Measuring religion as quest: 2. Reliability concerns. *Journal for the Scientific Study of Religion, 30*, 430–447.

Batson, C. D., Schoenrade, P., & Ventis, W. L. (1993). *Religion and the individual: A social–psychological perspective.* New York, NY: Oxford University Press. (Original work published 1982)

Cait, C. (2004). Spiritual and religious transformation in women who were parentally bereaved as adolescents. *Omega: Journal of Death and Dying, 49*, 163–181.

C'de Baca, J., & Wilbourne, P. (2004). Quantum change: Ten years later. *Journal of Clinical Psychology, 60*, 531–541. doi:10.1002/jclp.20006

Chen, C. (2005). A self of one's own: Taiwanese immigrant women and religious conversion. *Gender and Society, 19*, 336–357. doi:10.1177/0891243204273125

Cole, B. S., Hopkins, C. M., Tisak, J., Steel, J. L., & Carr, B. I. (2008). Assessing spiritual growth and decline following a diagnosis of cancer: Reliability and validity of the spiritual transformation scale. *Psycho-Oncology, 17*, 112–121. doi:10.1002/pon.1207

Danzig, R. A., & Sands, R. G. (2007). A model of spiritual transformation of *Baalei Teshuvah*. *Journal of Religion and Spirituality in Social Work: Social Thought, 26*, 23–48. doi:10.1300/J377v26n02_02

Fincham, F. D., Stanley, S. M., & Beach, S. R. H. (2007). Transformative processes in marriage: An analysis of emerging trends. *Journal of Marriage and Family, 69*, 275–292. doi:10.1111/j.1741-3737.2007.00362.x

Granqvist, P. (2002). Attachment and religiosity in adolescence: Cross-sectional and longitudinal evaluation. *Personality and Social Psychology Bulletin, 28*, 260–270. doi:10.1177/0146167202282011

Granqvist, P., & Kirkpatrick, L. A. (2004). Religious conversion and perceived childhood attachment: A meta-analysis. *The International Journal for the Psychology of Religion, 14*, 223–250. doi:10.1207/s15327582ijpr1404_1

Granqvist, P., Mikulincer, M., & Shaver, P. R. (2010). Religion as attachment: Normative processes and individual differences. *Personality and Social Psychology Review, 14*, 49–59. doi:10.1177/1088868309348618

Hay, D. (2001). The cultural context of stage models of religious experience. *The International Journal for the Psychology of Religion, 11*, 241–246. doi:10.1207/S15327582IJPR1104_03

Hill, P. C. (2002). Spiritual transformation: Forming the habitual center of personal energy. *Research in the Social Scientific Study of Religion, 13*, 87–108.

Hood, R. W., Jr., Hill, P. C., & Spilka, B. (2009). *The psychology of religion: An empirical approach* (4th ed.). New York, NY: Guilford Press.

Ironson, G., Kremer, H., & Ironson, D. S. (2006). Spirituality, spiritual experiences, and spiritual transformations in the face of HIV. In J. D. Koss-Chioino & P. Hefner (Eds.), *Spiritual transformation and healing: Anthropological, theological, neuroscientific, and clinical perspectives* (pp. 241–262). Lanham, MD: AltaMira Press.

James, W. (1958). *Varieties of religious experience: A study in human nature.* New York, NY: Modern Library. (Original work published 1902)

Jones, J. W. (2002). *Terror and transformation: The ambiguity of religion in psychoanalytic perspective.* New York, NY: Brunner-Routledge.

Kahn, P. J., & Greene, A. L. (2004). "Seeing conversation whole": Testing a model of religious conversion. *Pastoral Psychology, 52*, 233–258. doi:10.1023/B:PASP.0000010025.25082.25

Kerley, K. R., & Copes, H. (2009). "Keepin' my mind right": Identity maintenance and religious social support in the prison context. *International Journal of Offender Therapy and Comparative Criminology, 53*, 228–244. doi:10.1177/0306624X08315019

Kim, U., Yang, K., & Hwang, K. (Eds.). (2006). *Indigenous and cultural psychology: Understanding people in context.* New York, NY: Springer.

Kirkpatrick, L. A. (2005). *Attachment, evolution, and the psychology of religion.* New York, NY: Guilford Press.

Kirkpatrick, L. A., & Shaver, P. R. (1990). Attachment theory and religion: Childhood attachments, religious beliefs, and conversion. *Journal for the Scientific Study of Religion, 29*, 315–334. doi:10.2307/1386461

Knapik, G. P., Martsolf, D. S., & Draucker, C. B. (2008). Being delivered: Spirituality in survivors of sexual violence. *Issues in Mental Health Nursing, 29*, 335–350. doi:10.1080/01612840801904274

Koss-Chioino, J. D. (2006). Spiritual transformation, relation and radical empathy: Core components of the ritual healing process. *Transcultural Psychiatry, 43*, 652–670. doi:10.1177/1363461506070789

Lakhdar, M., Vinsonneau, G., Apter, M. J., & Mullet, E. (2007). Conversion to Islam among French adolescents and adults: A systematic inventory of motives. *The International Journal for the Psychology of Religion, 17*, 1–15.

LeBlanc, M. N. (2007). *Imaniya* and young Muslim women in Cote d'Ivoire. *Anthropologica, 49*, 35–50.

Lee, P. C. (2008). Christian conversion stories of African American women: A qualitative analysis. *Journal of Psychology and Christianity, 27*, 238–252.

Loder, J. E. (1989). *The transforming moment* (2nd ed.). Colorado Springs, CO: Helmers & Howard.

Lofland, J., & Skonovd, N. (1981). Conversion motifs. *Journal for the Scientific Study of Religion, 20*, 373–385. doi:10.2307/1386185

Mahoney, A., & Pargament, K. I. (2004). Sacred changes: Spiritual conversion and transformation. *Journal of Clinical Psychology, 60*, 481–492. doi:10.1002/jclp.20007

Margolin, A., Schuman-Olivier, Z., Beitel, M., Arnold, R. M., Fulwiler, C. E., & Avants, S. K. (2007). A preliminary study of spiritual self-schema (3-S+) therapy for reducing impulsivity in HIV-positive drug users. *Journal of Clinical Psychology, 63*, 979–999. doi:10.1002/jclp.20407

Maslim, A. A., & Bjorck, J. P. (2009). Reasons for conversion to Islam among women in the United States. *Psychology of Religion and Spirituality, 1*, 97–111. doi:10.1037/a0015735

McAdams, D. P. (1994). Can personality change? Levels of stability and growth in personality across the lifespan. In T. F. Heatherton & J. L. Weinberger (Eds.), *Can personality change?* (pp. 299–313). Washington, DC: American Psychological Association. doi:10.1037/10143-027

McAdams, D. P. (2006). *The redemptive self.* New York, NY: Oxford University Press.

McCullough, M. E., Bono, G., & Root, L. M. (2007). Rumination, emotion, and forgiveness: Three longitudinal studies. *Journal of Personality and Social Psychology, 92*, 490–505. doi:10.1037/0022-3514.92.3.490

Miller, W. R. (2004). The phenomenon of quantum change. *Journal of Clinical Psychology, 60*, 453–460. doi:10.1002/jclp.20000

Miller, W. R., & C'de Baca, J. (1994). Quantum change: Toward a psychology of transformation. In T. F. Heatherton & J. L. Weinberger (Eds.), *Can personality change?* (pp. 253–280). Washington, DC: American Psychological Association. doi:10.1037/10143-011

Miller, W. R., & C'de Baca, J. (2001). *Quantum change: When epiphanies and sudden insights transform ordinary lives.* New York, NY: Guilford Press.

Paloutzian, R. F. (2005). Religious conversion and spiritual transformation: A meaning-system analysis. In R. F. Paloutzian & C. L. Park (Eds.), *Handbook of the psychology of religion and spirituality* (pp. 331–347). New York, NY: Guilford Press.

Paloutzian, R. F., Richardson, J. T., & Rambo, L. R. (1999). Religious conversion and personality change. *Journal of Personality, 67*, 1047–1079. doi:10.1111/1467-6494.00082

Pargament, K. I. (1997). *The psychology of religion and coping: Theory, research, and practice.* New York, NY: Guilford Press.

Pargament, K. I. (2007). *Spiritually integrated psychotherapy: Understanding and addressing the sacred.* New York, NY: Guilford Press.

Pew Forum on Religion & Public Life. (2008). *U.S. religious landscape survey.* Washington, DC: Pew Research Center.

Pratt, J. B. (1920). *The religious consciousness.* New York, NY: Macmillan. doi:10.1037/10884-000

Rambo, L. R. (1993). *Understanding religious conversion.* New Haven, CT: Yale University Press.

Rootes, K. M. H., Jankowski, P. J., & Sandage, S. J. (2010). Bowen family systems theory and spirituality: Exploring the relationship between triangulation and religious questing. *Contemporary Family Therapy, 32*, 89–101. doi:10.1007/s10591-009-9101-y

Sandage, S. J., Hill, P. C., & Vaubel, D. C. (2011). Relational spirituality, generativity, and mental health: Relationships and pathways. *The International Journal for the Psychology of Religion, 21*, 1–16. doi:10.1080/10508619.2011.532439

Sandage, S. J., Link, D. C., & Jankowski, P. J. (2010). Quest and spiritual development moderated by spiritual transformation. *Journal of Psychology and Theology, 38*, 15–31.

Schnarch, D. (1997). *Passionate marriage: Keeping love and intimacy alive in committed relationships* (Rev. ed.). New York, NY: Henry Holt.

Shults, F. L., & Sandage, S. J. (2006). *Transforming spirituality: Integrating theology and psychology.* Grand Rapids, MI: Baker Academic.

Smith, T. W. (2006). The national spiritual transformation study. *Journal for the Scientific Study of Religion, 45*, 283–296. doi:10.1111/j.1468-5906.2006.00306.x

Starbuck, E. D. (1899). *The psychology of religion.* New York, NY: Scribner.

Ullman, C. (1989). *The transformed self: The psychology of religious conversion.* New York, NY: Plenum.

Welwood, J. (2000). *Toward a psychology of awakening: Buddhism, psychotherapy, and the path of personal and spiritual transformation.* Boston, MA: Shambhala.

Williamson, I. T., & Sandage, S. J. (2009). Longitudinal analyses of religious and spiritual development among seminary students. *Mental Health, Religion, and Culture, 12*, 787–801. doi:10.1080/13674670902956604

Wuthnow, R. (1998). *After heaven: Spirituality in America since the 1950s.* Berkeley: University of California Press.

Zinnbauer, B. J., & Pargament, K. I. (1998). Spiritual conversion: A study of religious change among college students. *Journal for the Scientific Study of Religion, 37*, 161–180. doi:10.2307/1388035

CHAPTER 23

THE VIRTUES: GRATITUDE AND FORGIVENESS

Robert D. Carlisle and Jo-Ann Tsang

Let us rise up and be thankful; for if we didn't learn a lot today, at least we learned a little, and if we didn't learn a little, at least we didn't get sick, and if we got sick, at least we didn't die; so, let us all be thankful. (Buscaglia, 1992, p. 102)

He that cannot forgive others breaks the bridge over which he himself must pass if he would ever reach heaven, for everyone has need of forgiveness. (Herbert, 1809, p. 63)

A primary function of religion is to help individuals deal with existential questions (Batson, Schoenrade, & Ventis, 1993). Words of wisdom, such as those opening this chapter, provide answers to questions about the meaning of life, death, and our relationships with others. Gratitude (e.g., Emmons & Crumpler, 2000) and forgiveness (Rye et al., 2000) are central in much of religion's wisdom. In addition, these virtues are perceived to be so foundational to religion that a number of measures of religiousness and spirituality have incorporated items on forgiveness and gratitude (e.g., Fetzer Institute/National Institute on Aging Working Group, 1999; Koenig, 2008). Yet, psychological research on forgiveness and gratitude has taken place largely outside of the context of religiousness. We begin by briefly discussing the role of gratitude and forgiveness in several world religions. After reviewing the general literature, we outline research relating these virtues to religion and discuss whether a religious context adds something qualitatively different to gratitude and forgiveness compared with their secular counterparts.

Although this handbook encompasses both religiousness and spirituality, we more often refer to *religiousness* rather than to both terms. This is because most research has looked at religiousness in the traditional sense, and less research has examined nontraditional spiritual beliefs or personalized spiritual beliefs independent of religious tradition. We use the term *spirituality* when theory or research specifically addresses the concept.

THEOLOGICAL SIGNIFICANCE OF GRATITUDE AND FORGIVENESS

Long before psychology even noticed these concepts, religions have encouraged gratitude and forgiveness. These virtues may even be theologically linked. For instance, in Christianity it is inferred in the parable of the unforgiving servant (Matthew 18:23–35) that individuals who fail to forgive others show ingratitude toward God for divine forgiveness.

Religion and Gratitude

Numerous aspects of Judaism underscore the importance of expressing gratitude toward God. The Psalms (Emmons & Crumpler, 2000), the practice of sacrificing one's first fruits, and prayers of gratitude such as the Passover *dayenu* prayer (Schimmel, 2004) all contain strong themes of gratitude. Schimmel further noted that gratitude and love for God motivated followers of Judaism to obey God's commandments. Several Biblical stories describe the importance of expressing gratitude toward human

DOI: 10.1037/14045-023
APA Handbook of Psychology, Religion, and Spirituality: Vol. 1. Context, Theory, and Research, K. I. Pargament (Editor-in-Chief)
Copyright © 2013 by the American Psychological Association. All rights reserved.

benefactors, such as the story of Joshua and Rahab. Judaism also teaches adherents to be particularly grateful toward parents and religious teachers. Gratitude toward others is said to build gratitude as a character trait as well as to increase gratitude toward God (Schimmel, 2004). Emmons and Kneezel (2005) noted the centrality of gratitude in Judeo-Christian tradition, calling gratitude a natural response to a benevolent deity. They emphasized the link between grace and gratitude in Christianity, citing the letters of Paul. Roberts (2007) further observed that the views of life as a gift and people as interdependent both foster gratitude within Christianity. Gratitude for creation, preservation, and ultimately salvation allows Christians to be grateful to God even in negative circumstances (Roberts, 2004, 2007). Gratitude is also important in Islam (Emmons & Crumpler, 2000). The Qur'an consistently emphasizes gratitude toward Allah. Likewise, some of the pillars of Islam, such as fasting during Ramadhan and daily prayers, either facilitate or are a response to gratitude toward Allah (Emmons & Crumpler, 2000). Gratitude is likewise a key emotion in Buddhism. Several Theravada Buddhist historical narratives were written not only to model gratitude but also to induce gratitude in the religious community for sacrifices made by Buddha and other bodhisattvas (Berkwitz, 2003). Believers are thus united in their gratitude for historical religious benefactors, leading them to revere the religious figures and increase their own piety in response. On a spiritual level, Komter (2004) discussed gratitude from an ecological standpoint. She noted that the experience of gratitude helps humans comprehend their relationship to nature, a relationship in which the abundance provided by nature must be returned to sustain life.

Religion and Forgiveness

Jewish forgiveness is exemplified in the belief that as God forgives us, we must also forgive others. Forgiveness is conditional upon the repentance of the transgressor, but if forgiveness is sought and not given, the unforgiving person commits a sin. In contrast to Christians, Jews are more likely to believe that some sins are unforgivable (Cohen, Malka, Rozin, & Cherfas, 2006; Rye et al., 2000). Christianity also views forgiveness as central to its tenets. Jesus emphasized the importance of forgiveness when he admonished followers to forgive "seventy times seven" times (Mathew 18:21–22). As with Judaism, forgiving others in Christianity is a response to divine forgiveness (Marty, 1998). Adherents of Islam forgive to follow the example of Muhammad and the commandments of Allah (Rye et al., 2000). For example, in the Qur'an it is written that after many years of war in Mecca, Muhammad forgave all who fought against him. In Islam, a victim may engage in retaliation equal to the original offense but risks making too strong of a retribution, which would result in sin.

The concept of forgiveness is not limited to Western religions (Rye et al., 2000). Buddhism discusses forbearance and compassion, which are similar to forgiveness. Both facilitate the reduction of suffering, a major goal in Buddhism (Higgins, 2001). Hinduism focuses on the role of forgiveness in promoting good karma. Forgiveness and forbearance are important for Hindus who strive toward the path of righteousness (Klostermaier, 1994). One example of forgiveness in this tradition is the forgiveness that Varuna (Guardian of the Rita or cosmic order) gives to humans for their lying and drunkenness.

WHAT MAKES PEOPLE GRATEFUL? WHAT HELPS PEOPLE FORGIVE?

We next present psychological definitions of gratitude and forgiveness, and briefly review the existing research on these virtues.

Gratitude

Gratitude is a positive emotion that is experienced when people perceive that someone has intentionally given them a valued benefit (McCullough, Kilpatrick, Emmons, & Larson, 2001). Research has demonstrated gratitude's positive valence (e.g., Baron, 1984; Ellsworth & Smith, 1988; Emmons & McCullough, 2003) and social nature (Ellsworth & Smith, 1988; Weiner, Russell, & Lerman, 1978). Taking the previous literature into account, we define *gratitude* as *"a positive emotional reaction to the receipt of a benefit that is perceived to have resulted from the good intentions of another"* (Tsang, 2006, p. 139).

McCullough and colleagues theorized that gratitude serves important moral and social functions (e.g., McCullough, Kilpatrick, et al., 2001; McCullough, Kimeldorf, & Cohen, 2008). First, gratitude serves as a *benefit detector* (McCullough et al., 2008) in a manner analogous to the informational function of emotions (Epstein, 1984; Schwarz, 1990). Specifically, gratitude provides information about the value, cost, intentionality, and role-independent nature of a benefit from another person. People tend to feel more grateful for favors that are of higher value (Tsang, 2007), are more costly to the benefactor (Okamoto & Robinson, 1997), and are intentional rather than accidental (Tesser, Gatewood, & Driver, 1968). People are likewise more inclined to feel grateful for favors that are not dictated by social roles; for instance, individuals report feeling more gratitude for favors from people who are less close to them (Bar-Tal, Bar-Zohar, Greenberg, & Hermon, 1977) and from higher status benefactors (Becker & Smenner, 1986; Hegtvedt, 1990). Second, gratitude functions as a *motivator of prosocial behavior* (McCullough et al., 2008), causing beneficiaries to return the favor to the benefactor (Tsang, 2006, 2007) and to unrelated others (Bartlett & DeSteno, 2006; DeSteno, Bartlett, Baumann, Williams, & Dickens, 2010) and also reducing hostile behavior (Baron, 1984). Third, gratitude expressed by the beneficiary can be a *reinforcer of prosocial behavior* in the benefactor (McCullough et al., 2008). Expressions of thanks have been shown to increase return sales (Carey, Clicque, Leighton, & Milton, 1976) and increase the amount of tips left for wait staff (Rind & Bordia, 1995).

Positive Variables Associated With Gratitude

Both state and trait gratitude are empirically linked with various positive psychological states (Emmons & Crumpler, 2000; McCullough, Emmons, & Tsang, 2002; Seligman, Steen, Park, & Peterson, 2005; Wood, Froh, & Geraghty, 2010). Emmons and McCullough (2003) found that individuals who completed gratitude journals for several weeks reported more positive life appraisals and better expectations for the coming week, compared with individuals who wrote about daily hassles. Gratitude is also related to decreased depression (Fredrickson, Tugade, Waugh, & Larkin, 2003), increased positive affect (Froh, Kashdan, Ozimkowski, & Miller, 2009), and increased meaning in life (Kashdan, Uswatte, & Julian, 2006; Lambert, Graham, & Fincham, 2009). In some cases, gratitude has even been related to physical health, such as fewer physical symptoms of illness (Emmons & McCullough, 2003).

Gratitude can have positive interpersonal consequences (Fredrickson, 2004; Lambert, Clark, Durtschi, Fincham, & Graham, 2010). Consistent with the prosocial motivator function (McCullough et al., 2008), individuals induced to be grateful are more likely to behave prosocially (Bartlett & DeSteno, 2006; DeSteno et al., 2010; Tsang, 2006, 2007), promoting positive interpersonal relationships. Gratitude also leads to increased liking for the benefactor, and it facilitates the use of constructive conflict management skills (Baron, 1984). Emmons and McCullough (2003) found that participants in a gratitude journal intervention were more likely than controls to report recently offering emotional support and helping others solve problems.

Trait gratitude is also associated with positive variables (Wood et al., 2010). McCullough and colleagues (2002) found that a grateful disposition was positively related to self- and other-reported well-being factors, such as life satisfaction, vitality, happiness, optimism, hope, and positive affect, and negatively related to anxiety and depression. They also found links between a grateful disposition and prosocial traits, such as empathy, self-reported prosocial behaviors and traits, agreeableness, and religiousness. Watkins, Woodward, Stone, and Kolts (2003) found additional positive relationships between a grateful disposition and intrinsic religiousness and internal and divine locus of control, and negative relationships with aggression, extrinsic religiousness, and narcissism. Thus gratitude, both as a temporary state and a more permanent trait, seems related to good psychological, physical, and interpersonal functioning.

Forgiveness

Forgiveness can be viewed from several different perspectives: as a response, a disposition, or a relationship characteristic. Forgiveness as a response, or state forgiveness, can be defined as a post-transgression transformation from negative motivations, such as avoidance and revenge, to more positive motivations, such as benevolence (e.g., McCullough, 2001; McCullough & Witvliet, 2002). Forgiveness as a disposition can be defined as the propensity to forgive (e.g., Mullet, Neto, & Riviere, 2005). Forgiveness as a relationship characteristic is similar to intimacy and trust (McCullough & Witvliet, 2002). Forgiveness is considered an intrapersonal concept, in contrast to more interpersonal concepts such as reconciliation, which entail behavioral change toward the transgressor (e.g., Freedman, 1998; Tsang, McCullough, & Fincham, 2006). Forgiveness is also differentiated from pardoning, condoning, excusing, forgetting, and denying (Enright & Coyle, 1998).

A number of variables are associated with forgiveness. Empathy for the transgressor (McCullough et al., 1998; McCullough & Witvliet, 2002; McCullough, Worthington, & Rachal, 1997) predicts increased forgiveness, whereas rumination (e.g., McCullough, Bellah, Kilpatrick, & Johnson, 2001) and attributions of transgressor responsibility (e.g., McCullough et al., 2003; Weiner, Graham, Peter, & Zmuidinas, 1991) predict decreased forgiveness. The majority of research on gratitude and forgiveness has been done in Western cultures. In one exception, Fu, Watkins, and Hui (2004) found that the tendency to forgive in a Chinese sample was correlated with relationship preservation. The authors theorized that individuals in a collectivist culture are more concerned with forgiving for solidarity reasons than for the personality reasons emphasized in more individualistic cultures.

Positive Variables Associated With Forgiveness

Although forgiveness may not be appropriate in all circumstances (e.g., Lamb, 2002), many of the psychological, physical, and interpersonal variables associated with forgiveness tend to be beneficial.

Forgiveness is correlated with a host of positive psychological variables (e.g., Lawler et al., 2003; Witvliet, Phipps, Feldman, & Beckham, 2004). Toussaint, Williams, Musick, and Everson-Rose (2008) found in a nationally representative population that feeling forgiven by others, by the self, and by God all predict fewer depressive episodes in women, and forgiveness of self predicted fewer episodes in men. Forgiveness has also been linked with physiological indicators of health. Lawler et al. (2003) found that forgiveness for a betrayal was related to lower blood pressure and heart rate among college students. Witvliet and colleagues also found that compared with imagining holding a grudge, imagining forgiveness led to a lowered physiological stress response as manifested in corrugator electromyography, skin conductance, and heart-rate measures (Witvliet, Ludwig, & Vander Laan, 2001; Witvliet, Worthington, et al., 2008). In addition, forgiveness is related to positive interpersonal states. Fincham and Beach (2002) found that among women, both positive (benevolence) and negative (avoidance and revenge) dimensions of forgiveness predicted marital satisfaction, whereas with men only the negative dimension predicted satisfaction (Fincham & Beach, 2002). Several other studies show correlations between forgiveness and positive qualities in other types of relationships (Berry & Worthington, 2001; Fincham, Paleari, & Regalia, 2002; Karremans, Van Lange, Ouwerkerk, & Kluwer, 2003).

RESEARCH ON GRATITUDE AND FORGIVENESS AS RELIGIOUS VIRTUES

Religious tenets might encourage believers to be more grateful and more forgiving, but do religious people really show more of these virtues? Research on this question is still in its infancy and is therefore sparse, largely cross sectional, and often limited to Christian samples.

Gratitude

Correlational research has shown thanksgiving to be a common theme in Christian prayer (Bade & Cook, 2008; McKinney & McKinney, 1999). Laird, Snyder, Rapoff, and Green (2004) found in a sample of undergraduates that prayers of thanksgiving were related to increased weekly prayer frequency, longer prayer duration, belief that one's prayers have an effect on one's own and others' lives, and intrinsic religious orientation. Laird and colleagues also examined prayer among individuals visiting an arthritis clinic, finding that thanksgiving prayer in this sample was related to a dispositional measure of hope. Also, for patients with osteoarthritis who prayed, thanksgiving was related to increases in subjective well-being.

General gratitude as well as gratitude toward God are common themes mentioned by religious individuals (Griffith, 1998; Samuels & Lester, 1985). Krause and Ellison (2009) studied gratitude toward God in older African and European Americans in the United States. They found that self-reports of church attendance were positively related to perceptions of increased church cohesiveness, which was in turn related to perceptions of increased social support, and feeling more closely connected to others. This close connection to others was associated with increased reports of gratitude toward God, both concurrently and 3 years later. These data point to a potential interplay between social interactions and gratitude toward God. Other research has shown that gratitude toward God is related to important positive variables. For example, gratitude toward God has been shown to attenuate the relationship between stress and poorer health in a sample of older Americans, especially older women (Krause, 2006).

Research has also uncovered links between a grateful disposition and religious variables such as general religiousness (McCullough et al., 2002), religious orientation, the divine control subscale of locus of control (Watkins et al., 2003), prayer frequency (Lambert, Fincham, Braithwaite, Graham, & Beach, 2009), and spirituality (Adler & Fagley, 2005; Diessner & Lewis, 2007; McCullough et al., 2002). Emmons and Kneezel (2005) reported a positive relationship between state and trait gratitude and a host of religiousness–spirituality measures in a population of individuals with neuromuscular disorders. In addition to some of the relationships mentioned thus far, they found that striving sanctification and the degree to which strivings helped participants feel close to God were also positively related to dispositional and daily gratitude.

Longitudinal research has also been conducted on gratitude and religion. As mentioned, Krause and Ellison (2009) found that the relationship between closeness to others in one's church and gratitude toward God persisted after 3 years, although the longitudinal relationship was weaker than the relationship with immediate gratitude. Lambert, Fincham, et al. (2009) found that prayer frequency was related to dispositional gratitude 6 weeks later (see also Volume 2, Chapter 24, this handbook). This cross-lagged effect remained significant after controlling for religious participation. In a second sample they replicated the longitudinal relationship between prayer and gratitude controlling for social desirability and religiousness.

Some experiments have provided a stronger test for causal relationship between religion and gratitude. Lambert, Fincham, et al. (2009), in an additional study, instructed some participants to engage in daily prayer for 4 weeks and others to engage in daily activities not associated with prayer. Participants who were induced to pray daily reported higher levels of grateful personality after 4 weeks compared with individuals in the nonpraying conditions. This effect remained when controlling for initial prayer frequency and religiousness.

In contrast, data from our lab suggest that religious salience increases prosocial behavior in general, but not gratitude specifically (Tsang, Schulwitz, & Carlisle, 2012). Religion was primed for half of the undergraduate participants via a scrambled sentence task. Then, some participants received a generous amount of raffle tickets from a distribution partner, whereas others were told they received a generous amount of tickets by chance. When given the opportunity, participants who received the favor from the partner were more generous in return. Participants for whom religion was made salient were also marginally more generous, whether or not their partner had done them a favor previously. The interaction between religious salience and favor was not significant. Thus, religious salience slightly increased prosocial behavior, but it did not have a special effect on gratitude per se.

It seems, then, that much research links gratitude and religiousness. Stronger evidence has been found for the relationship between religious and spiritual variables with trait rather than state gratitude, and most of the supporting studies have been correlational.

Forgiveness

Forgiveness likewise correlates with several religious and spiritual variables. Rye et al. (2001) tested the psychometrics of two forgiveness measures, both of which correlated with religious and existential well-being. Leach and Lark (2004) found that spiritual transcendence was related to increased forgiveness in Christian undergraduates. Brown, Barnes, and Campbell (2007) found that the tendency to forgive increased with religious fundamentalism. In a study examining both Christian clergy and a lay population, Macaskill (2007) found that as religious involvement increased, forgiveness also increased. Schultz, Tallman, and Altmaier (2010) found forgiveness to be related to increased posttraumatic growth. This relationship was mediated by religious and spiritual importance, suggesting that the effectiveness of forgiveness was primarily through religious variables.

Another new variable that may be related to forgiveness is spiritual similarity. Davis et al. (2009) found that self-reports of forgiveness increased as spiritual similarity to the transgressor increased. In a second study, some participants recalled a transgression by a person spiritually close to them, whereas others recalled a transgression by someone spiritually dissimilar to them. They found that those recalling transgressions by spiritually closer transgressors were more likely to forgive. These studies suggest that people might be more willing to forgive members of their in-group compared with out-group members, which would point to possible relationships between stereotyping and prejudice and the tendency to forgive.

Recently, Lambert, Fincham, Stillman, Graham, and Beach (2010) found both experimentally and longitudinally that prayer increased forgiveness. In Study 1, participants who were instructed to pray for their significant other expressed more forgiveness toward them. In Study 2, participants who prayed for a friend every day for 4 weeks expressed more forgiveness toward the friend compared with participants in control groups who were not asked to pray. Although more research is needed regarding the mechanism underlying this effect, the finding does suggest that some aspects of religion may play a causal role in forgiveness.

Research has also examined differences among Christian denominations. Toussaint and Williams (2008) conducted a phone survey and showed that Protestants report valuing and seeking forgiveness more than Catholics. Research has also found individual differences in beliefs within the same denomination. Exline (2008) investigated differences in beliefs about forgiveness in a sample of Baptists. She hypothesized that among religious adherents, there are differences in how people view core beliefs on forgiveness, including such beliefs as (a) forgiveness as a divine mandate, (b) God as merciful and just, (c) God's forgiveness toward the self, (d) conditionality of God's forgiveness, and (e) unforgivable sins. Exline (2008) found slight differences in endorsement of the beliefs among Baptists in this sample.

Only a few studies have compared differences in forgiveness between religions. Cohen et al. (2006) found that Jews were more likely than Protestants to believe in unforgivable sins. Fox and Thomas (2008) found a tendency toward less self-reported forgiveness among Muslims and Jews compared with Christians. Ahmed (2009), in a comparison of Muslim and Christian youth, found that highly religious Muslim youth reported greater dispositional forgiveness compared with less religious Muslim youth, but there was no relationship between high religiousness and forgiveness within the Christian sample. More research is needed looking at forgiveness across and within different denominations and religious groups, not only to describe differences but also to explain why differences exist.

IS THERE SOMETHING SPECIAL ABOUT GRATITUDE AND FORGIVENESS IN A RELIGIOUS CONTEXT?

Because much of the research on gratitude and forgiveness has been done outside of a religious context, little is empirically known about the religious aspects of these virtues. A number of research questions are relevant to the unique effects of religion on gratitude and forgiveness. First, researchers could ask whether religious contexts and individual differences in religiousness are related to increased gratitude and forgiveness. Second, researchers could ask whether gratitude and forgiveness within religious contexts have different effects than their nonreligious counterparts, or if the effects are stronger inside rather than outside religious contexts. Currently, the former question has received more attention than the latter.

Gratitude

Little research exists on whether religion uniquely affects gratitude. Emmons and Kneezel (2005) found that Christians scored higher than nonreligious participants on grateful personality, but their nonreligious sample was very small. Ahmed (2009) found that religiousness was highly correlated with increased gratitude in both Muslim and Christian youth. As described earlier, Lambert, Fincham, et al. (2009) found a positive effect of prayer on gratitude using correlational, longitudinal, and experimental methods. In contrast, Tsang et al. (2012) found that whereas religious salience increased general prosocial behavior, it did not uniquely affect gratitude responses, measured either behaviorally or via self-report. Lambert, Graham, and Fincham (2009), in their prototype analysis of gratitude, found that laypeople did in fact characterize gratitude as religious or spiritual, but this characterization was rated 5.52 on a 1-to-8 scale of centrality. Although religiousness and spirituality are moderately central features of laypeople's conceptions of gratitude, other features, such as compassion, helpfulness, and friendship, were seen as more central to gratitude.

What are some theoretical reasons for predicting a unique relationship between gratitude and religion and spirituality? Krause and Ellison (2009) speculated on some religious variables that may facilitate gratitude. For instance, feelings that prayers have been answered, feelings of God's presence in one's life, and acknowledgment of God's many gifts may all affect feeling grateful toward God. Additionally, Krause and Ellison suggested that certain aspects of church worship service and ritual might affect gratitude toward God. These religious context variables have yet to be researched, but they would be relevant to the question of whether religious contexts have unique effects on gratitude.

Although gratitude exists both within and outside of religious contexts, individuals might find it easier to experience gratitude in situations that encourage religiousness. For example, although gratitude for positive events could occur easily in both religious and nonreligious contexts, gratitude in the midst of negative events might happen more frequently in religious contexts and for religious individuals. Schimmel (2004) described a tradition in Judaism of being thankful for misfortune. He noted that Jewish teachings state that "One blesses over misfortune just as one blesses over good, for it is said 'Love the Lord your God . . . with all your soul' (Deuteronomy 6:5), even if he takes your soul" (*Mishnah*, Berakhot 9:5, as cited in Schimmel, 2004, p. 42). Similarly, Roberts (2004) noted that Christian theology encourages believers to be thankful in all circumstances because under a benevolent God things that seem negative should still ultimately work out for good. In the midst of negative events, Christians should still be grateful to God for salvation. Some empirical research speaks to gratitude for misfortune within a religious framework. Bade and Cook (2008), in their study of concept maps of prayer and coping, asked Christian undergraduates to write about ways they used prayer in response to personal problems. The theme of "Realize that what is happening in my life is good, even if it seems awful or painful at the time" clustered with other gratitude themes, including "Give thanks" and "Praise God for what God has done in my life," along with themes related to trust in God (Bade & Cook, 2008, p. 127). Therefore, although gratitude appears in both religious and nonreligious contexts, gratitude in the face of misfortune might occur more frequently within religious contexts.

Another type of gratitude that might occur more often in religious and spiritual contexts is that of a transcendent, less benefactor-specific gratitude. Komter (2004) outlined an ecological, spiritual understanding of gratitude and contrasted it with psychological, social, and cultural understandings of gratitude. The ecological level of gratitude helps humans understand their relationship to nature and the world and guides them in maintaining equilibrium with nature. Just as individuals receive from nature, they also are obligated to give back to nature to maintain the cosmic balance. This understanding of gratitude is very different from the psychological and social levels of gratitude studied by most psychologists, which look at how individuals feel grateful to specific people for particular benefits. Steindl-Rast (2004) also distinguished between *personal* gratitude that occurs when we receive a benefit from someone, and *transpersonal* gratitude that occurs when we perceive overwhelming cosmic oneness. In contrast to personal gratitude, transpersonal gratitude is universal, spontaneous, unconditional, and unreflective. Steindl-Rast called transpersonal gratitude "the mystic dimension of gratitude" (2004, p. 288) and theorized that of the two, transpersonal gratitude may be more linked to religion.

Lambert, Graham, and Fincham (2009) empirically tested the distinction between "benefit-triggered gratitude" and a more generalized gratitude, defined as "an emotion or state resulting from an awareness and appreciation of that which is valuable and meaningful to oneself" (p. 1194). Participants in one study were presented with scenarios representing each type of gratitude and were asked to rate how well each scenario characterized gratitude. Participants endorsed the benefit-triggered gratitude scenarios as being more prototypical, but they still rated generalized gratitude scenarios above the mean. The modal response was to rate the two as equally representative of gratitude. Lambert, Graham, and Fincham's generalized gratitude is conceptualized similarly to Steindl-Rast's (2004) transpersonal gratitude. They presented data from an additional study examining the generation of gratitude narratives. They mentioned that God appeared as a subtheme in generalized gratitude narratives, in support of the religious nature of generalized gratitude.

Forgiveness

Forgiveness is also theoretically linked to religion. Because all major religions emphasize forgiveness, one might suspect that religious people are more forgiving than nonreligious people. There is mixed evidence for this hypothesis. Religious people report valuing forgiveness more and being more forgiving in general, but when specific events are measured, religious people are often no different in how much they forgive (McCullough & Worthington, 1994).

Ongoing research in our lab has been consistent with this religion–forgiveness discrepancy (Carlisle, Tsang, & Ahmad, 2010). Half of the participants in our study were offended by a distribution partner who gave two of 10 raffle tickets, whereas participants in the control condition received the same negative distribution outcome distributed by chance. Participants who later received restitution showed more behavioral forgiveness by distributing more raffle tickets back to their partner, whereas participants who later received an apology from their partner reported more forgiveness. Consistent with the religion–forgiveness discrepancy, although many religious measures were correlated with dispositional forgiveness, religiousness was related neither to behavioral nor to self-reported forgiveness for the specific study transgression.

Tsang et al. (2005) suggested two possible explanations for this discrepancy: (a) It is a measurement problem, or (b) religious people are able to use different religious meaning systems to rationalize their unforgiveness. They presented data from three studies to test the first explanation. In Study 1, highly religious participants were no more likely to forgive a past transgression than those low in religiousness, replicating the religion–forgiveness discrepancy. In Study 2, the measurement confound of recall bias was attenuated by restricting potential participants to those who had experienced an offense within the past 2 months. Participants who scored higher in intrinsic religiosity were lower in revenge motivation, indicating some forgiveness. In Study 3, religious people showed higher levels of forgiveness when aggregate measures of forgiveness were used. These studies indicate that the discrepancy between the value that religious individuals place on forgiveness and ratings of their actual forgiveness for specific transgressions may in part be a measurement issue.

Tsang et al. (2005) proposed an additional rationalization explanation for the discrepancy. They hypothesized that religions teach people to forgive, but they also give adherents multiple meaning systems from which they can draw to justify forgiving and unforgiving behavior alike. They conducted a pilot study in which participants completed measures with items that endorsed God's justice as well as God's forgiveness. Results showed that people who endorsed a just and vengeful God or had a more vengeful religious meaning system had lower forgiveness scores. This study gives some support to the rationalization hypothesis, but more research is needed with larger samples and experimental studies with behavioral measures.

Barnes and Brown (2010) proposed a third explanation for the religion–forgiveness discrepancy. They posited that individuals often show a value-congruent bias when predicting future behaviors, meaning that individuals place more weight on their values than they do on their past behaviors when forecasting future behaviors. Individuals are thus often in error because past behaviors are the better predictor. In two studies, Barnes and Brown applied this theory to the religion–forgiveness discrepancy and found that the relationship between religiousness and forgiveness forecasts was mediated by the value a person places on forgiveness. This was after they controlled for prior forgiveness experiences and past forgiveness tendencies, providing support for a value-congruent bias explanation of the discrepancy.

Another reason why it has been difficult to uncover a clear relationship between religiousness and forgiveness is that the effect might be more complex than previously thought. For instance, Witvliet, Hinze, and Worthington (2008) found that religion interacted with offense severity in predicting forgiveness, in that religious people forgave more severe transgressions than did less religious people. Powers, Nam, Rowatt, and Hill (2007) found that participants scoring high in both humility and spiritual transcendence were more likely to forgive than those low in both; but if they were high in only one of these variables, they were no more likely to forgive than someone who was low in both. If these interactions replicate, researchers might find religious people to be more forgiving than nonreligious people only if they take other important variables into account.

Schultz et al. (2010) uncovered a complex relationship between forgiveness, posttraumatic growth, and religion. They found a relationship between self-reported forgiveness for an offense and posttraumatic growth. The relationship between the benevolence dimension of forgiveness and growth was mediated by self-reports of religious and spiritual importance. Researchers went beyond the question of "Are religious people more forgiving?" to an additional question of "Do religion and spirituality have an effect on some of the outcomes of forgiveness?"

Another topic relevant to religious forgiveness is anger at God. Many people who report being angry at God simultaneously believe that God is perfect, and a perfect God does not need forgiveness. For this reason Exline and Martin (2005) referred to "resolving anger toward God" rather than "forgiving God." Space is not available here for a complete review of the anger at God research (for a review, see Exline & Martin, 2005), but many of the psychological consequences of feeling anger toward God are similar to outcomes linked to unforgiveness of human transgressors. This new area of research therefore has potential to overlap with research on religiousness, spirituality, and forgiveness.

LIMITATIONS OF CURRENT RESEARCH

Research on forgiveness, gratitude, and religiousness has been mostly limited to the examination of Christian participants in Western cultures. There is scant research examining these variables in other religions and cultures. Additionally, much of the research is cross sectional and utilizes self-report data, which may be problematic for several reasons. First, forgiveness and gratitude measures may be prone to social desirability biases (Rye et al., 2001; Tsang, 2006). Second, many self-report studies on religion and forgiveness or gratitude have participants engage in recall of actual offenses or favors. This is problematic because of recall bias: Individuals might remember past experiences differently. Third, the correlational, cross-sectional nature of most of the research on forgiveness, gratitude, and religion makes it impossible to rule out third-variable confounds or to resolve ambiguity about causal direction.

Researchers need to more systematically examine when people are forgiving and grateful, and when they are not, and investigate the role that religiousness and spirituality might play in this process. The field would especially benefit from the increased use of experimental studies to determine the causal role that religious salience and other religious variables have on both forgiveness and gratitude (e.g., McCullough, 2001; Rye et al., 2001).

Potential Theoretical Directions for Research in Religion, Gratitude, and Forgiveness

As noted, there may be aspects of gratitude or forgiveness that link these virtues in a special way to religion and spirituality. There are also some higher level issues that may be relevant to this area. Emmons (2000) discussed the possible existence of a spiritual intelligence. One characteristic of spiritually intelligent individuals is the ability to consistently exercise virtues, including gratitude and forgiveness. Empirically, then, the virtues hypothetically tied to spiritual intelligence, including gratitude and forgiveness, should cluster together. In addition, one would predict that as spiritual intelligence was cultivated, virtues linked to spiritual intelligence, such as forgiveness and gratitude, should increase on both the state and trait level.

The issue of altruistic motivation, usually discussed within the context of prosocial behavior (e.g., Batson, 1991), might also be relevant to this area. Batson and his colleagues define altruism as prosocial motivation to increase the welfare of a person in need. This is contrasted with egoism, which is the motivation to help another to receive benefit or to avoid punishment for the self. Research on religious orientation and prosocial motivation has demonstrated that individuals who score high in intrinsic religiousness tend to help more than those scoring low, but their motivation is more egoistically oriented toward looking good. In contrast, individuals scoring high in quest religiousness, who see religion as an open-ended journey, do not necessarily help more; but their patterns of help tend to be consistent with altruistic motivation (Batson et al., 1993).

It should be possible to examine whether and in what contexts expressions of gratitude and forgiveness are altruistically or egoistically motivated. Many psychologists have theorized that gratitude is altruistic—that is, they suggest that the experience of gratitude leads the person to have the ultimate goal of benefiting his or her benefactor in return (e.g., Baumgarten-Tramer, 1938; cf. Baumeister & Ilko, 1995). Yet, a number of egoistic motivations might also underlie gratitude. For instance, gratitude can be expressed for self-presentational reasons. Because of the positive value that many place on gratitude, an individual who expresses gratitude will be looked on favorably. In addition, individuals can be egoistically motivated to secure further benefits. People might intuitively know that the expression of gratitude serves as a reinforcer of prosocial behavior. If so, individuals who wanted to secure further benefits would be motivated to reinforce the benefactor by expressing gratitude (e.g., Baumgarten-Tramer, 1938; Heider, 1958).

Similarly, forgiveness may be motivated by both egoistic and altruistic reasons. An individual might forgive a transgressor egoistically, for instance because the person's community expects a forgiving response. On the other hand, people can forgive altruistically, for instance because they care about the transgressor and do not want to see him or her feel guilty. Bud Welch is one example of potentially altruistic forgiveness: He forgave Timothy McVeigh for the death of his daughter in the 1995 Oklahoma City bombing after he began to feel sympathy for McVeigh's father, Bill. Mr. Welch's forgiveness was likely altruistically motivated out of compassion for McVeigh and for his family (Carrubba, 2000).

Researchers can press the altruism issue further and ask whether religion promotes egoistic or altruistic gratitude and forgiveness. Are religious individuals egoistically motivated to express gratitude to curry God's favor? Or is gratitude a more altruistic celebration of undeserved kindness (Steindl-Rast, 2004)? Likewise, do religious individuals express forgiveness as an egoistic demonstration of righteousness, or do they forgive out of love for the transgressor and gratitude toward God? Research on altruism and religion can inform our predictions for forgiveness and gratitude. Just as intrinsic religiousness is associated with the egoistic helping motivation of upholding appearances, intrinsic religion might also relate to the expression of gratitude and forgiveness out of a need to appear pious. In contrast, quest religiousness might be related to expressions of gratitude and forgiveness that are more centered around the objects of gratitude and forgiveness, rather than on the individual him or herself. This again moves research beyond questions of "Are religious people more grateful and forgiving?" to "What types of forgiving and grateful motivations might religion facilitate?"

Practical Implications of Research

If research determines that religious or spiritual contexts encourage gratitude and forgiveness, clinicians will have another tool by which to facilitate these virtues, at least among religious populations. For example, Lambert and colleagues' research on the effects of prayer on gratitude (Lambert, Fincham, et al., 2009) and forgiveness (Lambert, Fincham, et al., 2010) could be applied to interventions with religious populations. This would be especially useful if religious and spiritual interventions were shown to be more effective at increasing these virtues than their secular counterparts. Current research suggests that people in religious interventions do not forgive any more than do those in nonreligious interventions (Rye, 2005; Rye et al., 2000, 2005). One conclusion that might be drawn from these results is that religion does not add anything to a forgiveness intervention. Yet, participants in the secular interventions report using religious skills to help them forgive that are similar to those skills reported by participants in religious interventions. Thus, religion and virtues such as forgiveness and gratitude may be strongly linked in people's minds, making it important to conduct systematic research to tease apart any unique effects of religion and spirituality.

CONCLUSION

Despite the theological relevance of gratitude and forgiveness, there has been little research on the relationship between religiousness and spirituality and these virtues. There has been even less research examining whether gratitude and forgiveness that occur in religious or spiritual contexts are uniquely different from their secular counterparts. With the renewed focus that positive psychology has brought both to the virtues and to the scientific study of religiousness and spirituality, we are hopeful that research in this area will increase and shed light on basic research questions and their practical and clinical application. In this way, perhaps psychology and religion can work together to help people rise up, be thankful, and cross the bridge to forgiveness.

References

Adler, M. G., & Fagley, N. S. (2005). Appreciation: Individual differences in finding value and meaning as a unique predictor of subjective well-being. *Journal of Personality, 73*, 79–114. doi:10.1111/j.1467-6494.2004.00305.x

Ahmed, S. (2009). Religiosity and presence of character strengths in American Muslim youth. *Journal of Muslim Mental Health, 4*, 104–123. doi:10.1080/15564900903245642

Bade, M. K., & Cook, S. W. (2008). Functions of Christian prayer in the coping process. *Journal for the Scientific Study of Religion, 47*, 123–133. doi:10.1111/j.1468-5906.2008.00396.x

Barnes, C. D., & Brown, R. P. (2010). A value-congruent bias in the forgiveness forecasts of religious people. *Psychology of Religion and Spirituality, 2*, 17–29. doi:10.1037/a0017585

Baron, R. A. (1984). Reducing organizational conflict: An incompatible response approach. *Journal of Applied Psychology, 69*, 272–279. doi:10.1037/0021-9010.69.2.272

Bar-Tal, D., Bar-Zohar, Y., Greenberg, M. S., & Hermon, M. (1977). Reciprocity behavior in the relationship between donor and recipient and between harm-doer and victim. *Social Psychology Quarterly, 40*, 293–298.

Bartlett, M. Y., & DeSteno, D. (2006). Gratitude and prosocial behavior: Helping when it costs you. *Psychological Science, 17*, 319–325. doi:10.1111/j.1467-9280.2006.01705.x

Batson, C. D. (1991). *The altruism question*. Hillsdale, NJ: Erlbaum.

Batson, C. D., Schoenrade, P. A., & Ventis, W. L. (1993). *Religion and the individual*. New York, NY: Oxford University Press.

Baumeister, R. F., & Ilko, S. A. (1995). Shallow gratitude: Public and private acknowledgement of external help in accounts of success. *Basic and Applied Social Psychology, 16*, 191–209.

Baumgarten-Tramer, F. (1938). "Gratefulness" in children and young people. *The Pedagogical Seminary and Journal of Genetic Psychology, 53*, 53–66.

Becker, J. A., & Smenner, P. C. (1986). The spontaneous use of thank you by preschoolers as a function of sex, socioeconomic status, and listener status. *Language in Society, 15*, 537–545. doi:10.1017/S0047404500012008

Berkwitz, S. C. (2003). History and gratitude in Theravada Buddhism. *Journal of the American Academy of Religion American Academy of Religion, 71*, 579–604. doi:10.1093/jaarel/lfg078

Berry, J. W., & Worthington, E. L., Jr. (2001). Forgivingness, relationship quality, stress while imagining relationship events, and physical and mental health. *Journal of Counseling Psychology, 48*, 447–455. doi:10.1037/0022-0167.48.4.447

Brown, R. P., Barnes, C. D., & Campbell, N. J. (2007). Fundamentalism and forgiveness. *Personality and Individual Differences, 43*, 1437–1447. doi:10.1016/j.paid.2007.04.025

Buscaglia, L. F. (1992). *Born for love: Reflections on loving.* New York, NY: Ballantine Books.

Carey, J. R., Clicque, S. H., Leighton, B. A., & Milton, F. (1976). A test of positive reinforcement of customers. *Journal of Marketing, 40*, 98–100. doi:10.2307/1251075

Carlisle, R. D., Tsang, J., & Ahmad, N. (2010, October). *Unforgiveness in the lab: A test of the religion-forgiveness discrepancy*. Paper presented at the annual conference of the Society for the Scientific Study of Religion, Baltimore, MD.

Carrubba, S. M. (2000, April). Oklahoma City bombing: Two fathers and forgiveness. *St. Anthony Messenger.* Retrieved from http://www.americancatholic.org/messenger/Apr2000/feature2.asp

Cohen, A. B., Malka, A., Rozin, P., & Cherfas, L. (2006). Religion and unforgivable offenses. *Journal of Personality, 74*, 85–117. doi:10.1111/j.1467-6494.2005.00370.x

Davis, D. E., Worthington, E. L., Hook, J. N., Van Tongeren, D. R., Green, J. D., & Jennings, D. J. (2009). Relational spirituality and the development of the Similarity of the Offender's Spirituality Scale. *Psychology of Religion and Spirituality, 1*, 249–262. doi:10.1037/a0017581

DeSteno, D., Bartlett, M. Y., Baumann, J., Williams, L. A., & Dickens, L. (2010). Gratitude as moral sentiment: Emotion-guided cooperation in economic exchange. *Emotion, 10*, 289–293. doi:10.1037/a0017883

Diessner, R., & Lewis, G. (2007). Further validation of the Gratitude, Resentment, and Appreciation Test (GRAT). *Journal of Social Psychology, 147*, 445–447. doi:10.3200/SOCP.147.4.445-448

Ellsworth, P. C., & Smith, C. A. (1988). Shades of joy: Patterns of appraisal differentiating pleasant emotions. *Cognition and Emotion, 2*, 301–331. doi:10.1080/02699938808412702

Emmons, R. A. (2000). Is spirituality an intelligence? Motivation, cognition, and the psychology of ultimate concern. *The International Journal for the Psychology of Religion, 10*, 3–26. doi:10.1207/S15327582IJPR1001_2

Emmons, R. A., & Crumpler, C. A. (2000). Gratitude as human strength: Appraising the evidence. *Journal of Social and Clinical Psychology, 19*, 56–69. doi:10.1521/jscp.2000.19.1.56

Emmons, R. A., & Kneezel, T. T. (2005). Giving thanks: Spiritual and religious correlates of gratitude. *Journal of Psychology and Christianity, 24*, 140–148.

Emmons, R. A., & McCullough, M. E. (2003). Counting blessings versus burdens: An experimental investigation of gratitude and subjective well-being in daily life. *Journal of Personality and Social Psychology, 84*, 377–389. doi:10.1037/0022-3514.84.2.377

Enright, R. D., & Coyle, C. T. (1998). Researching the process model of forgiveness within psychological interventions. In E. L. Worthington Jr. (Ed.), *Dimensions of forgiveness: Psychological research and theological perspectives* (pp. 139–161). Radnor, PA: Templeton Foundation Press.

Epstein, S. (1984). Controversial issues in emotion theory. In P. Shaver (Ed.), *Review of personality and social psychology* (pp. 64–88). Beverly Hills, CA: Sage.

Exline, J. J. (2008). Beliefs about God and forgiveness in a Baptist Church sample. *Journal of Psychology and Christianity, 27*, 131–139.

Exline, J. J., & Martin, A. (2005). Anger toward God: A new frontier in forgiveness research. In E. L. Worthington Jr. (Ed.), *Handbook of forgiveness* (pp. 73–88). New York, NY: Brunner-Routledge.

Fetzer Institute/National Institute on Aging Working Group. (1999). *Multidimensional measurement of religiousness/spirituality for use in health research: A report of the Fetzer Institute/National Institute on Aging Working Group.* Kalamazoo, MI: John E. Fetzer Institute.

Fincham, F. D., & Beach, S. R. H. (2002). Forgiveness in marriage: Implications for psychological aggression and constructive communication. *Personal Relationships, 9*, 239–251. doi:10.1111/1475-6811.00016

Fincham, F. D., Paleari, F. G., & Regalia, C. (2002). Forgiveness in marriage: The role of relationship quality, attributions, and empathy. *Personal Relationships, 9*, 27–37. doi:10.1111/1475-6811.00002

Fox, A., & Thomas, T. (2008). Impact of religious affiliation and religiosity on forgiveness. *Australian Psychologist, 43*, 175–185. doi:10.1080/00050060701687710

Fredrickson, B. L. (2004). Gratitude, like other positive emotions, broadens and builds. In R. A. Emmons & M. E. McCullough (Eds.), *The psychology of gratitude* (pp. 144–166). New York, NY: Oxford University Press. doi:10.1093/acprof:oso/9780195150100.003.0008

Fredrickson, B. L., Tugade, M. M., Waugh, C. E., & Larkin, G. R. (2003). What good are positive emotions in crises? A prospective study of resilience and emotions following the terrorist attacks on the United States on September 11th, 2001. *Journal of Personality and Social Psychology, 84*, 365–376. doi:10.1037/0022-3514.84.2.365

Freedman, S. (1998). Forgiveness and reconciliation: The importance of understanding how they differ. *Counseling and Values, 42*, 200–216. doi:10.1002/j.2161-007X.1998.tb00426.x

Froh, J. J., Kashdan, T. B., Ozimkowski, K. M., & Miller, N. (2009). Who benefits the most from a gratitude intervention in children and adolescents? Examining positive affect as a moderator. *Journal of Positive Psychology, 4*, 408–422. doi:10.1080/17439760902992464

Fu, H., Watkins, D., & Hui, E. K. (2004). Personality correlates of the disposition towards interpersonal forgiveness: A Chinese perspective. *International Journal of Psychology, 39*, 305–316. doi:10.1080/00207590344000402

Griffith, R. M. (1998). "Joy unspeakable and full of glory": The vocabulary of pious emotion in the narratives of American Pentecostal women, 1910–1945. In P. N. Stearns & J. Lewis (Eds.), *An emotional history of the United States* (pp. 218–240). New York, NY: New York University Press.

Hegtvedt, K. A. (1990). The effects of relationship structure on emotional responses to inequity. *Social Psychology Quarterly, 53*, 214–228. doi:10.2307/2786960

Heider, F. (1958). *The psychology of interpersonal relations*. Hillsdale, NJ: Erlbaum. doi:10.1037/10628-000

Herbert, E. H. (1809). *The life of Edward Lord Herbert, of Cherbury*. Edinburgh, Scotland: James Ballantyne. Retrieved from http://archive.org/details/lifeofedwardlord00herb

Higgins, R. (2001). Buddhists practice forgiveness: Mindful suffering. *Christian Century, 118*, 9–10.

Karremans, J. C., Van Lange, P. A. M., Ouwerkerk, J. W., & Kluwer, E. S. (2003). When forgiving enhances psychological well-being: The role of interpersonal commitment. *Journal of Personality and Social Psychology, 84*, 1011–1026. doi:10.1037/0022-3514.84.5.1011

Kashdan, T. B., Uswatte, G., & Julian, T. (2006). Gratitude and hedonic and eudaimonic well-being in Vietnam War veterans. *Behaviour Research and Therapy, 44*, 177–199. doi:10.1016/j.brat.2005.01.005

Klostermaier, K. K. (1994). *A survey of Hinduism*. Albany: State University of New York Press.

Koenig, H. G. (2008). Concerns about measuring "spirituality" in research. *Journal of Nervous and Mental Disease, 196*, 349–355. doi:10.1097/NMD.0b013e31816ff796

Komter, A. E. (2004). Gratitude and gift exchange. In R. A. Emmons & M. E. McCullough (Eds.), *The psychology of gratitude* (pp. 194–212). Oxford, England: Oxford University Press. doi:10.1093/acprof:oso/9780195150100.003.0010

Krause, N. (2006). Gratitude toward God, stress, and health in late life. *Research on Aging, 28*, 163–183. doi:10.1177/0164027505284048

Krause, N., & Ellison, C. G. (2009). Social environment of the church and feelings of gratitude toward God. *Psychology of Religion and Spirituality, 1*, 191–205. doi:10.1037/a0016729

Laird, S. P., Snyder, C. R., Rapoff, M. A., & Green, S. (2004). Measuring private prayer: Development, validation, and clinical application of the multidimensional prayer inventory. *The International Journal for the Psychology of Religion, 14*, 251–272. doi:10.1207/s15327582ijpr1404_2

Lamb, S. (2002). Women, abuse, and forgiveness: A special case. In J. G. Murphy & S. Lamb (Eds.), *Before forgiving: Cautionary views of forgiveness in psychotherapy* (pp. 155–171). London, England: Oxford University Press. doi:10.1093/acprof:oso/9780195145205.003.0009

Lambert, N. M., Clark, M. S., Durtschi, J., Fincham, F. D., & Graham, S. M. (2010). Benefits of expressing gratitude: Does expressing gratitude to a partner change one's view of the relationship? *Psychological Science, 21*, 574–580. doi: 10.1177/0956797610364003

Lambert, N. M., Fincham, F. D., Braithwaite, S. R., Graham, S. M., & Beach, S. R. H. (2009). Can prayer increase gratitude? *Psychology of Religion and Spirituality, 1*, 139–149. doi:10.1037/a0016731

Lambert, N. M., Fincham, F. D., Stillman, T. F., Graham, S. M., & Beach, S. R. H. (2010). Motivating change in relationships: Can prayer increase forgiveness? *Psychological Science, 21*, 126–132. doi:10.1177/0956797609355634

Lambert, N. M., Graham, S. M., & Fincham, F. D. (2009). A prototype analysis of gratitude: Varieties of gratitude experiences. *Personality and Social Psychology Bulletin, 35*, 1193–1207. doi:10.1177/0146167209338071

Lawler, K. A., Younger, J. W., Piferi, R. L., Billington, E., Jobe, R., Edmondson, K., & Jones, W. H. (2003). A change of heart: Cardiovascular correlates of forgiveness in response to interpersonal conflict. *Journal of Behavioral Medicine, 26*, 373–393. doi:10.1023/A:1025771716686

Leach, M. M., & Lark, R. (2004). Does spirituality add to personality in the study of trait forgiveness? *Personality and Individual Differences, 37*, 147–156. doi:10.1016/j.paid.2003.08.007

Macaskill, A. (2007). Exploring religious involvement, forgiveness, trust, and cynicism. *Mental Health, Religion, and Culture, 10*, 203–218. doi:10.1080/13694670600616092

Marty, M. E. (1998). The ethos of Christian forgiveness. In E. L. Worthington Jr. (Ed.), *Dimensions of forgiveness* (pp. 9–28). Philadelphia, PA: Templeton Foundation Press.

McCullough, M. E. (2001). Forgiveness: Who does it and how do they do it? *Current Directions in Psychological Science, 10*, 194–197. doi:10.1111/1467-8721.00147

McCullough, M. E., Bellah, C. G., Kilpatrick, S. D., & Johnson, J. L. (2001). Vengefulness: Relationships with forgiveness, rumination, well-being, and the Big Five. *Personality and Social Psychology Bulletin, 27*, 601–610. doi:10.1177/0146167201275008

McCullough, M. E., Emmons, R. A., & Tsang, J. (2002). The grateful disposition: A conceptual and empirical topography. *Journal of Personality and Social Psychology, 82*, 112–127. doi:10.1037/0022-3514.82.1.112

McCullough, M. E., Fincham, F. D., & Tsang, J. (2003). Forgiveness, forbearance, and time: The temporal unfolding of transgression-related interpersonal motivations. *Journal of Personality and Social Psychology, 84*, 540–557. doi:10.1037/0022-3514.84.3.540

McCullough, M. E., Kilpatrick, S. D., Emmons, R. A., & Larson, D. B. (2001). Is gratitude a moral affect? *Psychological Bulletin, 127*, 249–266. doi:10.1037/0033-2909.127.2.249

McCullough, M. E., Kimeldorf, M. B., & Cohen, A. D. (2008). An adaptation for altruism? The social causes, social effects, and social evolution of gratitude. *Current Directions in Psychological Science, 17*, 281–285. doi:10.1111/j.1467-8721.2008.00590.x

McCullough, M. E., Rachal, K. C., Sandage, S. J., Worthington, E. L., Jr., Brown, S. W., & Hight, T. L. (1998). Interpersonal forgiving in close relationships: II. Theoretical elaboration and measurement. *Journal of Personality and Social Psychology, 75*, 1586–1603. doi:10.1037/0022-3514.75.6.1586

McCullough, M. E., & Witvliet, C. V. O. (2002). The psychology of forgiveness. In C. R. Snyder and S. J. Lopez (Eds.), *Handbook of positive psychology* (pp. 446–458). New York, NY: Oxford.

McCullough, M. E., & Worthington, E. L., Jr. (1994). Models of interpersonal forgiveness and their applications to counseling: Review and critique. *Counseling and Values, 39*, 2–14. doi:10.1002/j.2161-007X.1994.tb01003.x

McCullough, M. E., Worthington, E. L., Jr., & Rachal, K. C. (1997). Interpersonal forgiving in close relationships. *Journal of Personality and Social Psychology, 73*, 321–336. doi:10.1037/0022-3514.73.2.321

McKinney, J. P., & McKinney, K. G. (1999). Prayer in the lives of late adolescents. *Journal of Adolescence, 22*, 279–290. doi:10.1006/jado.1999.0216

Mullet, E., Neto, F., & Riviere, S. (2005). Personality and its effects on resentment, revenge, and forgiveness and on self-forgiveness. In E. L. Worthington Jr. (Ed.), *Handbook of forgiveness* (pp. 159–182). New York, NY: Brunner-Routledge.

Okamoto, S., & Robinson, W. P. (1997). Determinants of gratitude expressions in England. *Journal of Language and Social Psychology, 16*, 411–433. doi:10.1177/0261927X970164003

Powers, C., Nam, R. K., Rowatt, W. C., & Hill, P. C. (2007). Associations between humility, spiritual transcendence, and forgiveness. *Research in the Social Scientific Study of Religion, 18*, 75–94. doi:10.1163/ej.9789004158511.i-301.32

Rind, B., & Bordia, P. (1995). Effect of server's "Thank you" and personalization on restaurant tipping. *Journal of Applied Social Psychology, 25*, 745–751. doi:10.1111/j.1559-1816.1995.tb01772.x

Roberts, R. C. (2004). The blessings of gratitude: A conceptual analysis. In R. A. Emmons & M. E. McCullough (Eds.), *The psychology of gratitude* (pp. 58–78). New York, NY: Oxford University Press.

Roberts, R. C. (2007). *Spiritual emotions: A psychology of Christian virtues*. Grand Rapids, MI: Eerdmans.

Rye, M. S. (2005). The religious path toward forgiveness. *Mental Health, Religion, and Culture, 8*, 205–215. doi:10.1080/13694670500138882

Rye, M. S., Loiacono, D. M., Folck, C. D., Olszewski, B. T., Heim, T. A., & Madia, B. P. (2001). Evaluation of the psychometric properties of two forgiveness scales. *Current Psychology, 20*, 260–277. doi:10.1007/s12144-001-1011-6

Rye, M. S., Pargament, K. I., Ali, M. A., Beck, G. L., Dorff, E. N., Hallisey, C., . . . Williams, J. G. (2000). Religious perspectives on forgiveness. In M. E. McCullough, K. I. Pargament, & C. E. Thoresen (Eds.), *Forgiveness: Theory, research, and practice* (pp. 17–40). New York, NY: Guilford Press.

Rye, M. S., Pargament, K. I., Pan, W., Yingling, D. W., Shogren, K. A., & Ito, M. (2005). Can group interventions facilitate forgiveness of an ex-spouse? A randomized clinical trial. *Journal of Consulting and Clinical Psychology, 73*, 880–892. doi:10.1037/0022-006X.73.5.880

Samuels, P. A., & Lester, D. (1985). A preliminary investigation of emotions experienced toward God by

Catholic nuns and priests. *Psychological Reports, 56*, 706. doi:10.2466/pr0.1985.56.3.706

Schimmel, S. (2004). Gratitude in Judaism. In R. A. Emmons & M. E. McCullough (Eds.), *The psychology of gratitude* (pp. 37–56). Oxford, England: Oxford University Press. doi:10.1093/acprof:oso/9780195150100.003.0003

Schultz, J. M., Tallman, B. A., & Altmaier, E. M. (2010). Pathways to posttraumatic growth: The contributions of forgiveness and importance of religion and spirituality. *Psychology of Religion and Spirituality, 2*, 104–114. doi:10.1037/a0018454

Schwarz, N. (1990). Feelings as information: Informational and motivational functions of affective states. In E. T. Higgins & R. M. Sorrentino (Eds.), *Handbook of motivation and cognition: Foundations of social behavior* (Vol. 2, pp. 527–561). New York, NY: Guilford Press.

Seligman, M. E. P., Steen, T. A., Park, N., & Peterson, C. (2005). Positive psychology progress: Empirical validation of interventions. *American Psychologist, 60*, 410–421. doi:10.1037/0003-066X.60.5.410

Steindl-Rast, D. (2004). Gratitude as thankfulness and as gratefulness. In R. A. Emmons & M. E. McCullough (Eds.), *The psychology of gratitude* (pp. 282–290). Oxford, England: Oxford University Press. doi:10.1093/acprof:oso/9780195150100.003.0014

Tesser, A., Gatewood, R., & Driver, M. (1968). Some determinants of gratitude. *Journal of Personality and Social Psychology, 9*, 233–236. doi:10.1037/h0025905

Toussaint, L., & Williams, D. (2008). National survey results for Protestant, Catholic, and nonreligious experiences of seeking forgiveness and of forgiveness of self, of others, and by God. *Journal of Psychology and Christianity, 27*, 120–130.

Toussaint, L., Williams, D., Musick, M., & Everson-Rose, S. (2008). The association of forgiveness and 12-month prevalence of major depressive episode: Gender differences in a probability sample of U.S. adults. *Mental Health, Religion, and Culture, 11*, 485–500. doi:10.1080/13674670701564989

Tsang, J. (2006). Gratitude and prosocial behavior: An experimental test of gratitude. *Cognition and Emotion, 20*, 138–148. doi:10.1080/02699930500172341

Tsang, J. (2007). Gratitude for small and large favors: A behavioral test. *Journal of Positive Psychology, 2*, 157–167. doi:10.1080/17439760701229019

Tsang, J., McCullough, M. E., & Fincham, F. D. (2006). The longitudinal association between forgiveness and relationship closeness and commitment. *Journal of Social and Clinical Psychology, 25*, 448–472. doi:10.1521/jscp.2006.25.4.448

Tsang, J., McCullough, M. E., & Hoyt, W. T. (2005). Psychometric and rationalization accounts of the religion-forgiveness discrepancy. *Journal of Social Issues, 61*, 785–805. doi:10.1111/j.1540-4560.2005.00432.x

Tsang, J., Schulwitz, A., & Carlisle, R. D. (2012). An experimental test of the relationship between religion and gratitude. *Psychology of Religion and Spirituality, 4*, 40–55. doi:10.1037/a0025632

Watkins, P. C., Woodward, K., Stone, T., & Kolts, R. L. (2003). Gratitude and happiness: Development of a measure of gratitude, and relationships with subjective wellbeing. *Social Behavior and Personality, 31*, 431–452. doi:10.2224/sbp.2003.31.5.431

Weiner, B., Graham, S., Peter, O., & Zmuidinas, M. (1991).Public confession and forgiveness. *Journal of Personality, 59*, 281–312. doi:10.1111/j.1467-6494.1991.tb00777.x

Weiner, B., Russell, D., & Lerman, D. (1978). Affective consequences of causal ascriptions. In J. H. Harvey, W. J. Ickes, & R. F. Kidd (Eds.), *New directions in attribution research* (Vol. 2, pp. 59–90). Hillsdale, NJ: Erlbaum.

Witvliet, C. V. O., Hinze, S. R., & Worthington, E. L., Jr. (2008). Unresolved justice: Christian religious commitment, forgiveness, revenge, and cardiovascular responding. *Journal of Psychology and Christianity, 27*, 110–119.

Witvliet, C. V. O., Ludwig, T., & Vander Laan, K. (2001). Granting forgiveness or harboring grudges: Implications for emotion, physiology, and health. *Psychological Science, 12*, 117–123. doi:10.1111/1467-9280.00320

Witvliet, C. V. O., Phipps, K. A., Feldman, M. E., & Beckham, J. C. (2004). Posttraumatic mental and physical health correlates of forgiveness and religious coping in military veterans. *Journal of Traumatic Stress, 17*, 269–273. doi:10.1023/B:JOTS.0000029270.47848.e5

Witvliet, C. V. O., Worthington, E. L., Jr., Root, L. M., Sato, A. F., Ludwig, T. E., & Exline, J. J. (2008). Retributive justice, restorative justice, and forgiveness: An experimental psychophysiology analysis. *Journal of Experimental Psychology, 44*, 10–25. doi:10.1016/j.jesp.2007.01.009

Wood, A. M., Froh, J. J., & Geraghty, A. W. A. (2010). Gratitude and well-being: A review and theoretical integration. *Clinical Psychology Review, 30*, 890–905. doi:10.1016/j.cpr.2010.03.005

CHAPTER 24

RELIGION, SPIRITUALITY, AND ALTRUISM

Vassilis Saroglou

The world religions proclaim prosocial values (Habito & Inaba, 2006), but it is still unclear whether these values translate into behaviors (Ellens, 2007) and whether they are really altruistic (Neusner & Chilton, 2005). Religious and atheist individuals have diverging opinions regarding whether or not religion promotes altruism. Historical and contemporary evidence seems to provide testimony in favor of both sides: Religious charity and religious violence have coexisted, in parallel or intertwined.

Asking the same question from a psychological perspective implies the need to focus on people's specific cognitions, emotions, and behaviors relating to altruism and the way these are influenced by, or possibly influence, religion. Interestingly, almost all classic theorists (James, Freud, Skinner, Erikson, and Allport) and contemporary evolutionary scholars underline the positive connection between religion and altruism, although each approaches this issue from a different theoretical perspective (for a review, see Saroglou, 2006a).

Yet, religious beliefs, psychological theory, and empirical research are different, sometimes conflicting, things. In the present chapter, a brief overview of the psychology of altruism and prosocial behavior (concepts, models, and research traditions) is first provided. Afterward, the chapter presents a synthesis of the empirical research on religion (including spirituality) and prosociality, with an emphasis on the past 15 years (for an earlier review, see Batson, Schoenrade, & Ventis, 1993). Consistent with the integrative paradigm of this handbook (see Chapter 1 in this volume), distinctions are made between different levels of analysis (personality, behavior, and underlying processes), dimensions of religion, and types of prosocial behavior. When possible, information is provided on group-level factors and cross-religious differences, and questions for future research arise. The conclusion provides a synthesis of the main lines of knowledge and considers the implications for scholars and practitioners.

MAPPING THE PROSOCIALITY-RELATED CONCEPTS AND PROCESSES

Psychological research from different fields (social, personality, developmental, and moral psychology) has developed many terms that beyond some common overlap, denote distinct aspects and processes involved in altruism (Dovidio, Piliavin, Schroeder, & Penner, 2006; Mikulincer & Shaver, 2010b). To examine how religion relates to altruism, it is useful to briefly review these concepts and corresponding processes.

A key distinction is made between prosocial behavior and altruism. *Prosocial behavior* is a descriptive, neutral, term denoting an act that benefits others (e.g., help, donation). *Altruism* refers to the subtler evaluative qualification of the motivation of prosocial behavior as being other-oriented rather than egotistic or self-oriented. People may help others to get personal or social benefits and not because they care about the person in need. It is, however, a debatable issue in psychology and other fields whether it is possible to distinguish between altruistic and egotistic motivations when people

DOI: 10.1037/14045-024
APA Handbook of Psychology, Religion, and Spirituality: Vol. 1. Context, Theory, and Research, K. I. Pargament (Editor-in-Chief)
Copyright © 2013 by the American Psychological Association. All rights reserved.

behave prosocially: When we help others so that we feel good about having done the right thing, or at least not guilty for omitting the action, are our motives egotistic or altruistic? The present chapter focuses on *prosocial behavior* and *prosociality* in general. The term *altruism* is used as an equivalent only because of the familiarity with this term in everyday language. The term *altruistic motivation* is used when referring specifically to the qualification of prosocial behavior as other oriented.

Social psychologists have focused on prosocial behavior as a function of different contexts (Dovidio et al., 2006; Mikulincer & Shaver, 2010b). Different types of prosocial behavior vary in many ways, including their costs and rewards (nonaggression, cooperation, help, donating, volunteering, forgiving, sacrifice), duration (one-shot help in a lab experiment vs. long-term volunteering), the urgency of the situation and the spontaneity of the reaction, and the duplicable (e.g., blood donation) or nonduplicable (e.g., organ donation) character of the prosocial act. Distinctions can also be made as a function of the type of target, the degree of proximity and familiarity with that target, and the corresponding chance for reciprocity: Kin-based, extended reciprocity-based, and universal altruism imply distinct psychological processes. In addition, prosocial behavior occurs not only at the individual level but also at the group and organizational levels (Stürmer & Snyder, 2010).

Personality psychologists are interested in individual differences that are stable across situations and throughout the life span. Indeed, some individuals are higher overall than others in the broad personality dimension of *agreeableness*, which entails a prosocial and communal orientation in interacting with others (Graziano & Tobin, 2009). Some are also more likely than others to highly endorse the values of *benevolence* and *universalism*. Benevolence involves preservation and enhancement of the welfare of people with whom one is in frequent contact, whereas universalism involves appreciation, tolerance, and protection of the welfare of all people as well as nature (Schwartz, 1992).

Across the many psychological fields that are interested in the interplay of emotions and cognitions or reasoning, a major distinction is made between (a) prosociality based on feelings of *empathy* and similar other-focused *moral emotions* such as moral outrage (anger, contempt, and disgust), elevation, and gratitude (Bartlett & DeSteno, 2006; Batson, 2010; Haidt, 2003); and (b) prosociality based on moral judgments that follow other-oriented moral principles (i.e., *principlism*; Batson, 2010). Various conceptual models of the latter exist, with the principles of *care* (Gilligan, 1982) and *justice* (Kohlberg, 1981) being at the heart of interpersonal morality. These universal principles of interpersonal morality are complemented in traditional societies or among conservatives by other kinds of moral principles that place value on the group or sacred entities: loyalty, authority, and purity (Haidt & Graham, 2007).

Developmental psychologists are interested in the origin and development of prosociality (empathy, moral principles, and moral judgment or reasoning) from infancy to late adulthood, with a particular emphasis on the environmental factors that, in interaction with age and personality, influence this development (Eisenberg, Fabes, & Spinrad, 2006; Hoffman, 2000). These factors are mainly educational styles emphasizing warmth, modeling, socialization, formation of moral identity, and security in parent–child relations that facilitate *trust*. Adulthood brings a key developmental task, *generativity* for others and the world, which adds a proactive and prospective dimension to prosociality (de St. Aubin, McAdams, & Kim, 2004). Contrary to previous theorizations or common assumptions, research in developmental psychology has established that basic moral principles such as justice and care emerge in early childhood in a universal way. Furthermore, these principles seem to be autonomous with respect to religious teachings and socialization by parents (Turiel, 2006).

Following developments in positive psychology, other researchers have recently operationalized prosocial constructs that are highly ideal and moral and, to some extent, inspired by religious and spiritual traditions. These include *compassion* (Cassell, 2009) and *compassionate love* (Fehr, Sprecher, & Underwood, 2009; Underwood, 2002). Compassionate love refers to altruistic tendencies (other-oriented feelings, beliefs, and acts) that are conscious, well motivated, and deliberate. Compassionate love includes (a) compassion for those who are suffering and (b) passionate attachment to the flourishing of other, possibly all people.

In conclusion, if one wants to understand how religion relates to, influences, or is influenced by prosociality, one actually needs to examine how religion is connected with various prosocial personality traits, values, principles, emotions, behaviors, and motivations. These elements of prosociality, in turn, may vary considerably on the basis of contextual factors.

RELIGION AND PROSOCIAL PERSONALITY: TRAITS, VALUES, AND EMOTIONS

In recent decades, a growing body of evidence has demonstrated that people who are religious (intrinsic religion, beliefs, or practice) perceive themselves as being prosocial. The global personality dimensions of agreeableness (in the five-factor model; for a meta-analysis, see Saroglou, 2010) and low psychoticism (in Eysenck's model; for a review, see Francis, 2009) are typical among religious individuals. These broad prosocial traits translate into more focused traits or dispositions, such as helping (Batson et al., 1993), honesty (e.g., Saroglou, Pichon, Trompette, Verschueren, & Dernelle, 2005), forgiveness (McCullough & Worthington, 1999), gratitude (see Chapter 23 in this volume), and generativity (Dillon, Wink, & Fay, 2003). Both prosocial principles and emotions seem to be implicated. Indeed, religious people tend to attribute high importance to the value of benevolence (for a meta-analysis, see Saroglou, Delpierre, & Dernelle, 2004) and the moral principles of care and justice (Graham & Haidt, 2010). They also report high feelings of empathy (e.g., Markstrom, Huey, Stiles, & Krause, 2010; Saroglou et al., 2005), compassion, and love (e.g., Smith, 2009). Interestingly, these prosocial traits, values, or emotional dispositions are typical of religiosity not only among Christians (from which the majority of studies in psychology of religion derive) but also among Buddhists, Jews, and Muslims; and they are present in both genders, in different ages, and in various cohorts from the World War II into the early 21st century (see Saroglou, 2010; Saroglou et al., 2004, for meta-analyses; see also Francis, 2009).

The associations between religious and prosocial measures, however, are typically modest in size, as if the prosociality of religious people was not as important as one might suspect on the basis of theological traditions and classic psychological theories. Examining then the "real" prosocial behavior of religious people, as the next section of this chapter does, is a way to test the accuracy of such a link—although behavior is, of course, not a simple mirror of personality. Behavior varies importantly as a function of situational features, whereas personality characteristics reflect tendencies shown across situations. The associations between religiousness and prosocial personality traits become greater when one focuses on specific traits rather than global dimensions. In addition, the association between religiousness and prosocial constructs becomes clearer when one moves from adolescence and early adulthood to middle and late adulthood (for a review, see Saroglou, 2010).

A modest but consistent link also exists between religion and social desirability (for a meta-analysis, see Sedikides & Gebauer, 2010). This finding raises questions about whether the results linking religion and prosocial tendencies reflect nothing more than conformity to social standards and expectations—or whether they might simply reflect the concern to relay a positive image to oneself or the researcher. When social desirability is controlled for, the strength of the link between religion and prosocial self-perception decreases; importantly, however, the link does not disappear. More important, several kinds of "others" (parents, teachers, siblings, friends, and colleagues) provide peer validation: They also perceive religious targets as being high in agreeableness, honesty, forgiveness, gratitude, and generativity (for a review, see Saroglou, 2010). Moreover, the idea that religious people are prosocial—and, in parallel, that atheists are low in prosociality—seems to be intrinsic to the stereotypes regarding religious and atheist people (Harper, 2007; Lewis, 2001). Such perceptions are also part of both believers' and nonbelievers' *metastereotypes*—that is, their estimations of how they are perceived by the other group (nonbelievers and believers, respectively; Saroglou, Yzerbyt, & Kaschten, 2011).

In sum, although modest in size, the association between individual religiousness and prosocial dispositions emerges consistently across studies, contexts (countries, religions, ages, genders), and the psychological dimensions concerned (traits, values, emotions). Prosociality seems to be a key characteristic of religious personality, possibly one of its universals. Religious people perceive themselves, are perceived by others, feel, think and value things in a way that emphasizes the importance of others' interests and needs as well as social cohesion.

RELIGION AND LIMITED PROSOCIAL BEHAVIOR AS A FUNCTION OF CONTEXTUAL FACTORS

There is some correspondence between religious personality (and related values and emotions) and prosocial behavior. The picture, however, is complex. As will be detailed in the following section, religious prosociality, like prosocial behavior in general, varies as a function of several factors: nature of the behavior, type of target, costs and benefits, competing principles, salience of religious norms, and type of motivation. Moreover, beyond general, personal religiosity (intrinsic religion, religious beliefs and practices), specific dimensions, such as fundamentalism, spirituality, and religion-as-quest, have been tied to significant variations in the extent and nature of prosocial behavior.

Limited and Minimal Religious Prosociality: Targets and Costs

According to Saroglou et al. (2005; see also Saroglou, 2006a), one reason why the link between religiosity and prosocial personality is modest is that religious prosociality is not unconditional; instead, it seems to be limited in several ways. First, religious prosociality is limited as a function of contextual features, which include proximity and familiarity with the target. Religious people value cohesion in interpersonal relationships, need social approval, and support the existence of in-group versus out-group barriers. Religious people should thus show prosociality toward relatives, acquaintances, and people with whom they are in close interaction and whose judgment is valued. They should be less likely to behave prosocially toward unknown people with whom there is little or no chance for reciprocity—and certainly not toward individuals who, like out-group members, threaten their religious values. Second, with the exception of sacrificial acts made at critical moments in life (especially by heroic figures and saints), religiosity in everyday life should predict *minimal prosociality*. This term refers to behaviors that are not necessarily of high cost but hold at least some importance if one wants to perceive oneself and be perceived by others as moral (see also Batson et al., 1993).

Several studies confirm that religious prosociality is limited to personally known targets and does not extend to unknown people and those who threaten religious values. These studies used the strategy of presenting the same series of hypothetical situations with versions (conditions) in which the target in need varied in proximity. Among Belgian students, religiosity was positively related to the willingness to help acquaintances and relatives ($r = .38$) but was totally unrelated to the willingness to help unknown targets in the exact same situations ($r = -.01$) (Saroglou et al., 2005, Study 2). Similarly, among Polish students, religiosity predicted willingness to help friends in need ($r = .46$) but was unrelated to willingness to help unknown targets with the same needs ($r = .03$; Blogowska & Saroglou, 2011, Study 2). Another study showed that Polish religious students were willing to help a confederate pass an exam ($r = .36$) but not if the confederate was a feminist ($r = -.02$; Blogowska & Saroglou, 2011, Study 1). In the United States, Batson et al. (1993) reviewed studies suggesting that (intrinsic) religiosity predicts prosocial behavior; however, the target was always an in-group member such as another student, a blind student, or a coreligionist.

Intentions may indicate real behavior. In another study, the more religious students were, the more likely they were to help an older student with her master's thesis by immediately dedicating 30 min to filling out a questionnaire (Blogowska, Lambert, & Saroglou, 2012). Other studies confirm the idea of at least minimal (in standards, extent, and resources to invest) religious prosociality, such as nonaggression.

For instance, using a projective measure (the Rosenzweig Frustration Test), Saroglou et al. (2005, Study 1) found that religious participants tended to spontaneously provide few aggressive responses when hypothetically interacting with frustrating others. Similarly, analyses of large international data sets from European countries show that individual religiosity is neither positively nor negatively related to attitudes toward immigrants (Strabac & Listhaug, 2008). It protects religious people, however, who have the tendency to vote in favor of conservative right-wing parties, from voting for extreme right-wing parties, which are prone to violence and anti-immigrant hostility (Arzheimer & Carter, 2009). In another study, religious Israeli children were evaluated by their peers as using less aggressive behavior and victimization than their secular counterparts (Landau, Björkqvist, Lagerspetz, Österman, & Gideon, 2002). Religious people also seem to be immune to the aggressive consequences of the activation of mortality salience (Norenzayan, Dar-Nimrod, Hansen, & Proulx, 2009). Finally, the link between religion and low aggression is also supported at the community and institutional level. Analyzing violent crime rates in rural areas in the United States, Lee (2006) found that rates of rural violence are lower where there are more churches per capita, after accounting for the effects of several important control variables.

Although aggression is not the mere opposite of prosociality, nonaggression can be seen as minimal prosociality. Forgiving an offender, in contrast, may demand greater personal effort and the investment of more psychological resources than simply helping or not aggressing. In line with the idea of religious minimal and no-high-cost prosociality, the existing evidence suggests that religious people, who constantly value and report practicing forgiveness, do not really differ from their nonreligious counterparts when it comes to real behavior (McCullough & Worthington, 1999). In several recent studies, participants' religiosity turned out to be unrelated to behavioral forgiveness, measured as low retaliation. This was the case when participants (a) administered questions varying in difficulty to a confederate who allegedly had given them a negative evaluation (Saroglou, Corneille, & Van Cappellen, 2009), (b) allocated money to a disruptive confederate (Greer, Berman, Varan, Bobrycki, & Watson, 2005), or (c) administered "shocks" to a provocative (but fictitious) opponent (Greer et al., 2005; Leach, Berman, & Eubanks, 2008).

Religious Prosociality Limited by Competing Principles

There may be another explanation, besides that of the high cost, for this scarcity of behavioral confirmation of religious forgiveness. In fact, together with prosocial ideals, religion also promotes other aspects of moral integrity (Graham & Haidt, 2010). It can provide a sense of personal coherence, which seems to correspond to religious people's need for order and closure instead of uncertainty and ambiguity (Saroglou, 2002). Thus, not surprisingly, in some religions, effective forgiveness seems to depend on other principles. For instance, for Jews, some offenses are unforgivable (Cohen, Malka, Rozin, & Cherfas, 2006). Muslims are particularly sensitive to the offender's apologies and demonstrations of repentance, and they thus tend to endorse less unconditional forgiveness than Christians (Mullet & Azar, 2009).

More generally, acting prosocially with regard to several targets in need may be in conflict with other principles and beliefs that religious people endorse. For instance, people who held orthodox religious beliefs were found to be unwilling to help homeless or illegal immigrants, and this finding was partially explained by participants' just-world beliefs—beliefs that "they deserve what they got" (Pichon & Saroglou, 2009; for similar findings on fundamentalists' low helping of unemployed people who are gay or single mothers, see also Jackson & Esses, 1997). In another study focusing on the moral conflict between abstract, impersonal deontology (e.g., honesty, loyalty) and interpersonal care (e.g., helping, saving another person's life), religious priming made people high in authoritarianism led to a preference for the respect of abstract deontology despite the detrimental consequences for the other person (Van Pachterbeke, Freyer, & Saroglou, 2011).

We can interpret in a similar way (i.e., abstract deontology limits care) several studies showing religious people's uneasiness to apply the sinner–sin distinction: "Love the sinner, hate the sin." Not only were intrinsically religious people less willing to help a gay confederate participate in a gay rally, but also they were less willing to help this target visit his or her grandparents (Batson, Floyd, Meyer, & Winner, 1999). And although religiosity relates to the endorsement of the sinner–sin distinction, it predicts negative attitudes toward both homosexual behavior and homosexual persons (Veenvliet, 2008).

In a more fundamental way, as argued elsewhere (Saroglou, 2010), the religious personality disposition for prosociality (high Agreeableness) is not unlimited but restricted by another important personality dimension that is also systematically related to religion: conscientiousness. Conscientiousness implies order, self-control, and dutifulness. In fact, altruism, care, and justice, which are aspects of interpersonal morality, are not the only moral concerns of religion. Religion is also concerned with principles of authority, loyalty, and purity that imply duties and obligations to oneself, to society, or to transcendent entities (Graham & Haidt, 2010). Morality having to do with purity and sexuality seems even more strongly linked to religious attendance than interpersonal morality (Weeden, Cohen, & Kenrick, 2008). Similarly, organ donation, which is a typical altruistic act and is supported by the major religious institutions, does not follow the general positive religion–donation link (e.g., Cornwall, Perry, Louw, & Stronger, 2012; W. A. Lam & McCullough, 2000; Stephenson et al., 2008), possibly because of conflicting religious views having to do with purity, integrity, and related fears of disgust and contamination. The same could be true for blood donation (Gillum & Masters, 2010).

Average-Level Religious Prosociality: Cooperation, Volunteering, and Donating

Several studies in recent years have examined whether religiousness predicted behaviors of cooperation during lab experiments that used different versions of economic games. When studies provided significant results, religious participants showed higher cooperation or generosity in the United States (Anderson & Mellor, 2009), India (Muslim students; Ahmed, 2009), and Israel (Jewish kibbutzim; Ruffle & Sosis, 2007). Moreover, participants in general (independently of their religiousness) increase trust and cooperation when they interact with a religious partner, as found in Germany (Tan & Vogel, 2008), Belgium (De Dreu, Yzerbyt, & Leyens, 1995), and Bangladesh (Johansson-Stenman, Mahmud, & Martinsson, 2009).

Cooperation, helping, forgiveness, and other interpersonal prosocial behaviors have been the main focus of psychological research on prosociality. More often, sociologists have studied volunteering and charitable donations. On the basis of multilevel analyses of the World Values Survey data from 53 countries (mostly Christian populations), Ruiter and De Graaf (2006; see also Ruiter & De Graaf, 2010) found that religious attendance at the individual level predicts higher rates of volunteering for both religious and secular organizations. The (higher) level of religiousness of the country has an additive positive effect on volunteering. Interestingly, the greater volunteering of religious compared with nonreligious participants becomes clearer in secular national contexts. Protestantism implies stronger effects on volunteering. Analyzing data from 29 nations, P.-Y. Lam (2006) found that Protestants, more oriented to the extrafamilial social world, are more likely than Catholics, who are more family oriented, to be members of voluntary associations; this difference was found at both the individual and the country levels. Furthermore, across dozens of countries from all continents, it is institutional, broad societal collectivism and not familism (in-group collectivism) that predicts participation in voluntary organizations, including religious organizations, an effect that is more typical of countries of Protestant tradition (Realo, Allik, & Greenfield, 2008).

Bekkers and Wiepking (2007; see also Lincoln, Morrissey, & Mundey, 2008) made an extensive review of studies on charitable donations. Among other results, they found that individual religiosity (affiliation and especially church attendance) and parents' religiosity predicted both religious and secular philanthropy. Contexts implying solicitation (e.g., religious congregations) heightened the generosity of religious individuals. Differences in solicitation strategies may explain why, in several countries,

Protestants seem to give more than Catholics. (Again, note that most studies sampled Christian populations.) People holding strongly orthodox beliefs were high in religious charity, an effect due to church attendance rather than the orthodox beliefs themselves, but they were not necessarily high in nonreligious charity. Interestingly, the role of religious attendance and related solicitation on increased donations has been confirmed among adherents of Eastern religions in Asia (Chang, 2006).

To some extent, religious giving may be a relatively easy way to fulfill one's own religious obligations. Interesting findings, diverging from those of many other studies, have emerged from an economist's study (Gruber, 2004). This study found that greater levels of religious giving led to lower levels of religious participation, suggesting that religious giving and participation may be substitutes for one another.

From Coalitional Fundamentalism to Universal Spirituality

An important body of research has demonstrated that some religious dimensions, but not others, are associated with prejudice and violence. For instance, in a survey of six religions in six nations as well as two surveys of Palestinians, regular attendance at religious services positively predicted support of religious suicide and out-group hostility, but regular prayer did not (Ginges, Hansen, & Norenzayan, 2009). Other work has demonstrated that religious fundamentalism—rather than personal, intrinsic religiosity—predicts greater prejudice toward people who differ on ethnicity, race, gender, sexual orientation, religious affiliation, or convictions (Hunsberger & Jackson, 2005).

Nevertheless, the religious dimension of fundamentalism or orthodoxy seems to attenuate the aggressive character of the authoritarian structure typical of conservative (orthodox) and dogmatic (fundamentalist) religiosity. Indeed, the links between fundamentalism (or orthodoxy) and derogation, discrimination, and prejudice repeatedly have been found to be mediated by right-wing authoritarianism (Rowatt, Johnson, LaBouff, & Gonzalez, in press). An exception may be homophobia, which may depend rather directly on religious morality (for a meta-analysis, see Whitley, 2009). Going a step further, Blogowska and Saroglou (2011, 2012) hypothesized that fundamentalism may show some prosocial tendencies that are typical of mere religiosity. Across four studies in two European countries, these authors found that people scoring high on fundamentalism showed negative attitudes toward value-threatening individuals and were not necessarily willing to help unknown targets; fundamentalism thus paralleled authoritarianism. Yet the same high scorers on fundamentalism were also prone to help and show prosocial tendencies toward acquaintances (friends and colleagues) or even toward unknown and threatening (e.g., atheist) targets after exposure to a positive religious text; in this context, fundamentalists were behaving similarly to other people with high personal religiosity scores—and unlike authoritarians.

Taken as a whole, these studies suggest that fundamentalists' authoritarianism is, to some extent, responsible—statistically speaking—for prejudice and violence. Fundamentalists' religiosity is also responsible for in-group prosociality, however. Fundamentalism would seem to accentuate the general coalitional aspect of religious attitudes, beliefs, and practices. More precisely, fundamentalism combines in-group favoritism and prosociality, typical of common religiosity, and out-group derogation, typical of authoritarianism.

Attitudes toward out-group members may vary from negative (e.g., derogation, discrimination, and prejudice) to positive (e.g., tolerance, equal treatment, and preferential over in-group treatment). On the positive pole of the continuum, one can find open-minded religious and spiritual dimensions. This is the case with spirituality, which Piedmont (2007) has framed in terms of *connectedness* (a sense of connection and commitment to others and humanity as a whole) and *universalism* (a belief in the unity and purpose of life), be it within or outside a context of a specific religious tradition. Open-minded thinking also characterizes *religion-as-quest*, which is the religious attitude defined by valuing doubt, self-criticism, and openness to the possibility of change (Batson et al., 1993).

The importance attributed to spirituality in one's personal life reflects several features contrary to traditional religiosity, including (a) universalism and not only benevolence in value hierarchies (Saroglou & Muñoz-García, 2008), (b) willingness to help unknown rather than only known people (Saroglou et al., 2005, Study 2), and (c) citizen-of-the-world identity and not only ethnic and national identities (Saroglou & Cohen, in press). People characterized by relativism in their beliefs express willingness to help individuals in need, such as immigrants and homeless people—a tendency partially mediated by a belief in ultimate justice (Pichon & Saroglou, 2009). In some studies, spirituality relates even more clearly to compassionate love of strangers and humanity than to compassionate love of close others (Sprecher & Fehr, 2005).

Moreover, experiments by Batson and collaborators have shown that religious people with high scores on quest orientation do not discriminate between those who violate norms (gay, antigay, fundamentalists) and "neutral" individuals in general helping contexts. They are, however, less willing to help an intolerant individual (e.g., an antigay, a fundamentalist) if it involves participation in activities promoting intolerance (Batson, Denton, & Vollmecke, 2008; Batson et al., 1999; Batson, Eidelman, Higley, & Russell, 2001). In addition, when they act prosocially, people high in quest seem to be more intrinsically motivated by altruism than by self-concerns. They tend to be sensitive to the needs expressed by the suffering individual, and they are willing to help even if the cost is high and the social pressure low (Batson et al., 1993).

In sum, religion seems to be drawn by two oppositional forces coming from two distinct components. Its coalitional dimension (community and shared normative beliefs and practices) emphasizes the in-group versus out-group barriers, thereby limiting the extent of prosociality apparently inherent in the very nature of religion. Yet, its spiritual (devotional, mystical) dimension, reflected in the connection with the divine or transcendence in general, points to a universal altruistic prosociality. Prayer, beliefs, or measures of personal, intrinsic religiousness often seem to predominate over measures of religious attendance and affiliation in terms of predicting compassionate values, feelings, and behaviors (e.g., Markstrom et al., 2010; Smith, 2009). Religious donation seems to be an exception to this pattern, however, because religious attendance plays an important role in this context.

CAUSAL DIRECTIONS AND PROCESSES

Is there a causal relationship between religion and prosociality? What may be the explanatory psychological processes beside this relationship? The following sections will address these questions.

Causal Directions

Until now, the reviewed studies have measured religion as an individual-difference construct and investigated correlational links of religiousness and its different forms with prosocial attitudes or behaviors, alone or as a function of contexts varying across experimental conditions. Yet the question remains as to whether there are causal links between religion (not only individual religiousness) and prosociality, and what the directions of these links may be.

Promising experiments in recent years have provided evidence in favor of the more intuitive causal direction that goes from religion to prosociality. Most of these experiments used priming techniques. Many priming studies have established the powerfulness of mental representations, which, even when activated outside participants' conscious awareness, increase the odds of related behaviors. For instance, briefly holding a cup of hot coffee (vs. a cup of ice-cold coffee) increases the perception of a target as being warm, generous, or caring (Williams & Bargh, 2008). Being exposed for milliseconds—thus, nonconsciously—to words related to the elderly stereotype causes participants to subsequently walk slower (Bargh, Chen, & Burrows, 1996).

Introducing religious words in a scrambled test increased people's accessibility of prosocial concepts (Pichon, Boccato, & Saroglou, 2007, Study 2) as well as the tendency to be more generous, as measured by the allocation of more money to a hypothetical confederate in a one-shot anonymous dictator game (Shariff & Norenzayan, 2007; see also Ahmed & Salas, 2011). Depicting a target in need (homeless) in front of a church instead of a secular building increased participants' willingness to help this target (Pichon & Saroglou, 2009).

Subliminal exposure to religious words has been shown to increase (a) participants' willingness to volunteer to distribute pamphlets for a charity (Pichon et al., 2007, Study 1); (b) "forgiveness," as indicated by participants being more prone to ask easy rather than difficult questions to a hypothetical confederate who had allegedly provided negative feedback (Saroglou et al., 2009, Study 2); and (c) cooperation, measured in a one-trial dictator game (Preston & Ritter, 2010, Study 1). Finally, in a series of three experiments, prayer reduced anger and aggression after a provocation (Bremner, Koole, & Bushman, 2011).

Interestingly, in those studies, religious concepts worked to activate prosocial concepts, intentions, and behaviors for all participants, both religious and nonreligious. The extent of prosociality activated by religious concepts is not unlimited, however. In all of these experiments, the targets were people in need or anonymous confederates. But when the targets are out-group members (other ethnicity or race), religious priming is not found to increase prosociality (Pichon & Saroglou, 2009, willingness to help; Preston & Ritter, 2010, Study 1, cooperation). In fact, religious priming can actually lead to in-group over out-group preference (Preston & Ritter, 2010, Study 2, charity donation) or even increase covert racial prejudice (M. K. Johnson, Rowatt, & LaBouff, 2010) and negative attitudes toward various outgroups (LaBouff, Rowatt, Johnson, & Finkle, 2012). It may also be that not all religious primes have the same effects (Preston, Ritter, & Hermandez, 2010). For instance, priming "synagogue" was found to increase Israeli settlers' endorsement of a suicide attack against Palestinians, whereas priming "prayer" decreased endorsement of such an attack (Ginges et al., 2009, Study 3). Similarly, priming "God" instead of "religion" was found to enhance cooperation with and charity toward an out-group in another set of studies (Preston & Ritter, 2010, Studies 1 and 2).

Yet the opposite causal direction that goes from prosociality to religion is not to be excluded. At the moment, there is only indirect evidence in favor of this alternative and possibly complementary pathway—one that concerns religion as a whole as well as individual religiousness. In a recent experiment, Van Cappellen and Saroglou (2010) found that watching a video praising charity increased participants' reported spirituality in comparison with a humor-inducing video or a neutral video. Moreover, as argued elsewhere (Saroglou, 2010), studies on personality and individual religiousness suggest that people with basic personality tendencies to be agreeable (and also conscientious) are more prone to remain or become religious throughout the life span. Several longitudinal studies (e.g., McCullough, Tsang, & Brion, 2003; Wink, Ciciolla, Dillon, & Tracy, 2007) show that both baseline personality and personality changes influence religiousness and changes in religiousness years, if not decades, later. People with dispositions to be agreeable—across situations and time—may be more attracted by cultural systems, like religion, that promote altruistic values, beliefs, and rituals corresponding to and reinforcing agreeableness (Saroglou, 2010).

A complementary perspective is that individual differences on religiousness and prosocial or antisocial behavior, in part, may be outcomes of the same causes. In a study on adult male twins, Koenig, McGue, Krueger, and Bouchard (2007) found that the variance shared between (retrospective and current) religiousness and the adult antisocial or prosocial behavior (self-reported) was due to both genetic and shared environmental influences. Finally, personality and genetic dispositions may moderate the role of religion on altruism (Sasaki et al., 2011).

Processes

What are the psychological mechanisms explaining how religion relates to and influences prosociality? Unfortunately, there is almost no research on the psychological mediators of the religion–prosociality relation. There is indirect evidence suggesting multiple possible processes, however, as religion relates or leads to most of the psychological factors known to play a role in building and promoting prosociality.

Other-oriented emotions, principles, and relational experiences. As mentioned in this chapter, religion relates to both emotional (empathy and other moral emotions) and cognitive–appreciative dimensions (prosocial values, reasoning, and social norms) related to prosocial behavior, especially when the latter is altruistically motivated. This implies that one motivation of religious prosociality can be other-oriented concerns and, possibly, internalization of prosocial values and teachings. These values are likely to come from parental education and broader socialization. There is evidence for the intergenerational transmission of volunteering and charity by religious parents (Caputo, 2009; Wilhelm, Brown, Rooney, & Steinberg, 2008) and of religion by generous parents (Peterson, 2006). The religion–empathy link may explain why religiousness is found only occasionally to predict cooperation in prisoner's dilemma and dictator games (in cases in which the partner is not in need), whereas it quite consistently predicts volunteering and donating for targets in need.

Imitation of prosocial parents and peers—and, more generally, role modeling—is another important mechanism that contributes to the development of empathy and altruism (Eisenberg et al., 2006). Religion's exemplary figures are saints and holy figures who, like heroes, show other-oriented, often sacrificial altruism. Such altruism is a major characteristic of the personalities of heroes and saints, as evidenced by self-reported, peer-reported, archival, and interview-based data (Saroglou, 2006b; Walker, Frimer, & Dunlop, 2010). Saints demonstrate to others that altruism, an a priori risky behavior in interpersonal relations, is an ideal that can be realistic (James, 1902/1985). More generally, religious texts and institutions provide moral exemplars that may serve for role identification (Sundén, 1959) and spiritual modeling at many levels, including interpersonally oriented virtues (see Chapter 10 in this volume). This may be particularly important in adolescence for reasons focused on moral development and identity.

A specific ingredient of religious prosociality, when motivated by other-oriented concerns, may be the emotion of gratitude (see Chapter 23 in this volume). In many religions, compassion and love are conceptualized as a way to pass on to others the compassion and love received from the divine. Moreover, as previously suggested (Saroglou et al., 2005, Study 2), secure attachment may be an additional mechanism that contributes to a religious prosociality. Secure attachment is known to relate to both prosocial concerns and behaviors (Mikulincer & Shaver, 2010a) and to religiosity through the life span, especially a socialization-based religiosity (see Chapter 7 in this volume). Secure attachment has been found to consolidate the effects of gratitude on prosocial behavior, whereas insecure attachment undermines these effects (Mikulincer & Shaver, 2010a).

Self-control and self-enhancement. A series of other processes that may underlie the religion–prosociality link can be classified as self-oriented, or at least as aiming to increase self-control or self-enhancement. This may be egoistic in the case that one chooses the self at the detriment of the others; but in some cases, self-control and self-enhancement concerns also serve other-oriented goals. Religion aims to satisfy needs for self-control at the emotional, cognitive, and motivational levels (see Chapter 6 in this volume). Religion may help to meet needs for self-enhancement, which is the motivation to see oneself favorably in terms of culturally valued characteristics (Sedikides & Gebauer, 2010). Compassionate and self-image goals seem to coexist within religion and spirituality (Crocker & Canevello, 2008).

In addition, low impulsivity as a function of religiosity, which seems to be a consistent finding across studies (Saroglou, 2010), may be responsible for the role of religion in reducing antisocial behavior. More generally, prosocial behavior demands effort, self-regulation, and energy (Gailliot, 2010). Religion's enhancement of self-control may thus facilitate prosociality. Similar self-control-related concerns, centering on the need for social cohesion, may at least partly explain why religion primarily leads to minimal prosociality (e.g., low aggression) and philanthropy toward those in need, but it may not necessarily lead to universal and unlimited love, especially toward out-groups and people perceived as threats to religious values. The latter forms of prosociality introduce complexity, disorder, and uncertainty.

Self-enhancement covers psychological processes having to do with (a) self-esteem and positive self-image, (b) positive reputation and social approval, and (c) symbolic rewards. Each of these dimensions is related to general religiosity and seems to contribute to a prosociality limited by concerns for positive self-image (Batson et al., 1993), social reputation (Norenzayan & Shariff, 2008), or afterlife-related rewards (Tao & Yeh, 2007).

Theorists who adopt an evolutionary approach to religious prosociality point out the role religion has played in human evolution in enhancing reputation, trust, and cooperation within extended social groups (e.g., Norenzayan & Shariff, 2008). A reputation-based religious prosociality has been facilitated by the belief in an omniscient supernatural being that controls human actions and thoughts and punishes the cheaters of the reciprocity norms (D. D. P. Johnson & Bering, 2006; D. D. P. Johnson & Kruger, 2004). It has been facilitated by religious collective rituals that, although costly, constitute opportunities to experience emotions of connectedness (Wiltermuth & Heath, 2009). Rituals may also provide opportunities to present oneself and be perceived by others as worthy of trust and cooperation (Sosis & Alcorta, 2003) or to enhance followers' commitment to the group's ideology and in-group cooperation (Henrich, 2009). Such mechanisms obviously have facilitated the extension from a kinship-based altruism to altruism at the level of culture. Cultural altruism, which is found in large and complex human societies, involves reciprocity between unrelated partners that can be reinforced by beliefs, symbols, moral gods, and norms of fairness of the world religions (Batson, 1983; Henrich et al., 2010; Roes & Raymond, 2003; Stark, 2001).

Moral identity. Prosocial behavior also can be based on principlism, which is the motivation to act in order to be moral and to conform with one's own moral identity and principles (Batson, 2010). It is unclear whether principlistic prosociality should be considered other oriented or self oriented: Is doing the right thing primarily important and beneficial for others or the self? Nevertheless, the role of principlism may be important to understand religious prosociality. For instance, priming people with the Ten Commandments activates moral self-schemas, which increase one's willingness to behave in a prosocial manner (Aquino, Freeman, Reed, Lim, & Felps, 2009). More generally, religious priming has been found to activate moral integrity by increasing honesty (Randolph-Seng & Nielsen, 2007) and decreasing hypocrisy (Carpenter & Marshall, 2009).

Following sources of authority. Finally, moral decisions and behaviors, including those that are prosocial, may result from either an autonomous internalization of moral values or from a mere conformity to social standards and submission to various sources of authority. People with individual dispositions for submissiveness may be particularly sensitive to religion's power to induce behaviors, moral or immoral, through submission. In a series of three experiments, Saroglou and collaborators found that among people with dispositional submissiveness, religious words (indeed, the same that previously were found to activate volunteering; Pichon et al., 2007) also (a) activated submission-related concepts, (b) increased the odds of showing behavioral retaliation when requested by the experimenter, and (c) increased conformity to informational influence exerted by anonymous others (Saroglou et al., 2009, Studies 1 and 2; Van Cappellen, Corneille, Cols, & Saroglou, 2011).

Religious texts are highly authoritative for religious people. Depending on the compassionate versus violent nature of the religious text to which participants were exposed, religious fundamentalists showed prosocial (or decreased antisocial) tendencies versus antisocial attitudes, respectively (Blogowska & Saroglou, 2012; Rothschild, Abdollahib, & Pyszczynski, 2009). Aggression after exposure to a violent religious text was also found to occur for participants in general, and more strongly for the religious (Bushman, Ridge, Das, Key, & Busath, 2007). Responsiveness to an appeal for charity was found to be higher among religious, compared with nonreligious, people—but only on Sundays after worship, not during the weekdays (Malhotra, 2010). Religious teachings and rituals may serve as an arousal of prosociality. Experimental induction of awe was found to lead religious people to express feelings of oneness with others (Van Cappellen & Saroglou, 2011).

CONCLUSION

Religious prosociality is not a myth. The partial discrepancy, in religious people, between self-perceptions as being prosocial and real behavior seems to reflect complex underlying psychological processes rather than simple moral hypocrisy (as suspected in the past). Prosociality exists—not only in religious people's minds—as an important key part of religious people's personality and related aspirations, values, moral principles, and emotions. Yet, common religious prosocial behavior does seem to be largely limited to known people and in-group members. It does not appear to be universal in terms of being extended to unknown people and those who threaten religious values. Religious prosociality also seems to be conditional rather than unconditional, depending on other possibly conflicting principles, beliefs, and concerns. It tends to be minimal and of low or average cost (e.g., nonaggression, volunteering, cooperation, conditional help) rather than highly costly (e.g., forgiveness, sacrifice), and it may need some arousal (i.e., activation of religious concepts, norms, and emotions) to be better manifested. Religious prosociality often appears to be motivated by concerns for positive self-perception, social reputation, and reciprocity; however, other-oriented emotions, values, and family and socialization experiences seem to also play a role.

In terms of a link between religion and prosociality, evidence exists for both causal directions. People with prosocial personality predispositions, for which both genetic and environmental influences are responsible, are attracted by religion's norms, symbols, and rituals emphasizing altruism and harmony. In turn, religion can activate—even subliminally—prosocial ideas, and it enhances altruism in a rather universal way (i.e., among both the religious and nonreligious). There is also evidence to suggest that sacrificial altruistic behaviors are present in the lives of saints and heroes and are motivated, among others, by religious reasons.

In fact, religion seems to operate in the middle of two tendencies exerting opposite influences. Its coalitional dimension pushes for strong in- versus out-group barriers, which, in the context of fundamentalism and conservative religion, can facilitate out-group prejudice and derogation. On the contrary, religion's spiritual, devotional, and self-reflective dimension pushes for an extended altruism, which possibly may be universal and motivated by other-oriented concerns. Several differences in prosociality between religions or religious denominations can be explained as reflecting the way religiosity, as experienced in a specific context, is more focused on spiritual (self-transcendent) concerns versus those that are more coalitional. Charity for those in need, helping in-group members, and reciprocity between people worthy of trust are prosocial tendencies that are present across religions (e.g., Buddhists, Christians, Hindus, Jews, and Muslims). Competing principles having to do with other norms, conservative morality, just-world beliefs, or out-group avoidance may limit prosociality in traditional religious contexts. Trust in cooperation and social collectivism is more evident among Protestant individuals and nations. In sum, different aspects of religion are linked with different levels of the process going from a kinship-based altruism to an extended cultural altruism, both at the individual and the collective levels.

Galen (2012) conducted a critical review of the empirical research and concluded that religious prosociality is simply a stereotype, mere ingroup favoritism, and possibly even a myth; in his view, no real, causal effects of religion on prosociality exist. Although Galen's review addressed very interesting issues, his conclusion seems excessive and more provocative than well justified (Saroglou, 2012).

Understanding the complex ways in which religion, spirituality, and altruism are interconnected has several important implications. These implications are relevant not only for scholars of different fields but also for different kinds of practitioners working, for instance, in counseling, psychotherapy, training of ministers, and interfaith dialogue. Three issues that seem the most intriguing or important will be discussed in this section.

A broad question that arises is how altruism works in a nonreligious, including atheist, context. This is an area for which studies are needed. The following are just a few ideas that may be worth investigating. On average, nonbelievers seem to score lower than believers on prosocial personality dispositions (at least if the reported correlations between religiosity and prosocial traits are linear). This does not mean, however, that nonbelievers should necessarily show low levels of empathy, prosocial moral reasoning, and prosocial behavior. Probably, the role of environment, socialization, and personal effort is stronger among nonbelievers when acting prosocially, because they may be less "naturally" agreeable (in terms of genetic predisposition). Moreover, prosociality within religion presents the advantage of a powerful combination of nonreligious (secular) and religious sources (beliefs, practices, community). Furthermore, the mutual reinforcement between emotional, role-modeling, principlistic, and social components integrated into a coherent religious set can reasonably be expected to increase the motivational force to act prosocially.

On the other hand, there are two limitations in religious prosociality that may constitute advantages within a nonreligious context. First, religious and conservative moral concerns for principles such as authority, loyalty, and purity do not only extend the sphere of morality beyond the interpersonal principles of care and justice, as initially argued (Haidt & Graham, 2007). They also limit care, when in conflict with it (Van Pachterbeke et al., 2011). Care and justice among nonconservatives and the nonreligious thus may be "freer" from other constraints. Not surprisingly, therefore, feelings of compassion seem more powerful among less religious people in leading to generosity (Saslow et al., 2012). Second, although religiousness may be compatible with internalization of values and autonomous thinking, it presents an overall discomfort with the value of autonomy, even among young generations (for a meta-analysis, see Saroglou et al., 2004). Also, as detailed in this chapter, religion can activate conformity among people with dispositional submissiveness. Nonreligious prosociality thus may be, as far as it exists, more autonomous and intrinsic than religious prosociality.

Experts and practitioners may be interested in some good news: Religious fundamentalism is not a mere manifestation of authoritarianism. The religious dimension of fundamentalism provides tools (e.g., altruistic values, rituals, theology, and texts; recategorization of different groups under a superordinate broader in-group, such as "we are all children of God") that can be selectively used to encourage prosociality and tolerance. Religious authorities' or psychotherapists' selection of altruistic and encompassing out-group material may have beneficial effects for interpersonal, intergroup, and interreligious relations. Recategorization under a broader in-group membership not only reduces intergroup prejudice but also enhances intergroup altruism (Dovidio, Gaertner, Shnabel, Saguy, & Johnson, 2010).

Finally, an important psychological implication of altruism in a religious context is that prosocial attitudes and behaviors contribute to the agent's well-being (Krause, 2007; Post, 2007). Volunteering across the life span improves psychological well-being because it leads people to develop other-oriented values, motives, and a sense of self that leads them to believe that they matter to others in the social world (Piliavin, 2010). There is suggestive, cross-sectional, evidence that compassionate attitudes mediate the link between religiosity and indicators of well-being, an effect found to be stronger than that of social support (Steffen & Masters, 2005; for a nonlaboratory intervention study, see also Oman, Thoresen, & Hedberg, 2010).

In conclusion, altruism is an important, but obviously not unique, psychological dimension of religion. Well-being, moral integrity, and both social cohesion and individuation are also important dimensions of religion. Understanding how these dimensions are affected by or shape religious prosociality is still an issue to be fully investigated and of great interest for both theory and practice.

References

Ahmed, A. M. (2009). Are religious people more prosocial? A quasi-experimental study with *Madrasah* pupils in a rural community in India. *Journal for the Scientific Study of Religion, 48*, 368–374. doi:10.1111/j.1468-5906.2009.01452.x

Ahmed, A. M., & Salas, O. (2011). Implicit influences of Christian religious representations on dictator and prisoner's dilemma game decisions. *Journal of Socio-Economics, 40*, 242–246. doi:10.1016/j.socec.2010.12.013

Anderson, L. R., & Mellor, J. M. (2009). Religion and cooperation in a public goods experiment.

Economics Letters, 105, 58–60. doi:10.1016/j.econlet.2009.05.016

Aquino, K., Freeman, D., Reed, A., Lim, V. K. G., & Felps, W. (2009). Testing a social–cognitive model of moral behavior: The interactive influence of situations and moral identity centrality. *Journal of Personality and Social Psychology, 97*, 123–141. doi:10.1037/a0015406

Arzheimer, K., & Carter, E. (2009). Christian religiosity and voting for West European radical right parties. *West European Politics, 32*, 985–1011. doi:10.1080/01402380903065058

Bargh, J. A., Chen, M., & Burrows, L. (1996). Automaticity of social behavior: Direct effects of trait construct and stereotype activation on action. *Journal of Personality and Social Psychology, 71*, 230–244. doi:10.1037/0022-3514.71.2.230

Bartlett, M. Y., & DeSteno, D. (2006). Gratitude and prosocial behavior: Helping when it costs you. *Psychological Science, 17*, 319–325. doi:10.1111/j.1467-9280.2006.01705.x

Batson, C. D. (1983). Sociobiology and the role of religion in promoting prosocial behavior. *Journal of Personality and Social Psychology, 45*, 1380–1385. doi:10.1037/0022-3514.45.6.1380

Batson, C. D. (2010). Empathy-induced altruistic motivation. In M. Mikulincer & P. R. Shaver (Eds.), *Prosocial motives, emotions, and behaviors: The better angels of our nature* (pp. 15–34). Washington, DC: American Psychological Association. doi:10.1037/12061-001

Batson, C. D., Denton, D. M., & Vollmecke, J. T. (2008). Quest religion, anti-fundamentalism, and limited versus universal compassion. *Journal for the Scientific Study of Religion, 47*, 135–145. doi:10.1111/j.1468-5906.2008.00397.x

Batson, C. D., Eidelman, S. H., Higley, S. L., & Russell, S. A. (2001). "And who is my neighbor?" II: Quest religion as a source of universal compassion. *Journal for the Scientific Study of Religion, 40*, 39–50. doi:10.1111/0021-8294.00036

Batson, C. D., Floyd, R. B., Meyer, J. M., & Winner, A. L. (1999). "And who is my neighbor?": Intrinsic religion as a source of universal compassion. *Journal for the Scientific Study of Religion, 38*, 445–457. doi:10.2307/1387605

Batson, C. D., Schoenrade, P., & Ventis, W. L. (1993). *Religion and the individual: A social–psychological perspective.* New York, NY: Oxford University Press.

Bekkers, R., & Wiepking, P. (2007). *Generosity and philanthropy: A literature review.* Report commissioned by the John Templeton Foundation, Social Sciences Research Network. Retrieved from http://ssrn.com/abstract=1015507

Blogowska, J., Lambert, C., & Saroglou, V. (2012). *Religious prosociality and aggression: It's real.* Manuscript submitted for publication.

Blogowska, J., & Saroglou, V. (2011). Religious fundamentalism and limited prosociality as a function of the target. *Journal for the Scientific Study of Religion, 50*, 44–60. doi:10.1111/j.1468-5906.2010.01551.x

Blogowska, J., & Saroglou, V. (2012). For better or worse: Fundamentalists' attitudes toward outgroups as a function of exposure to authoritative religious texts. *The International Journal for the Psychology of Religion.* Advance online publication. doi:10.1080/87567555.2012.687991

Bremner, R. H., Koole, S. L., & Bushman, B. J. (2011). "Pray for those who mistreat you": Effects of prayer on anger and aggression. *Personality and Social Psychology Bulletin, 37*, 830-837. doi:10.1177/0146167211402215

Bushman, B. J., Ridge, R. D., Das, E., Key, C. W., & Busath, G. L. (2007). When God sanctions killing: Effect of scriptural violence on aggression. *Psychological Science, 18*, 204–207. doi:10.1111/j.1467-9280.2007.01873.x

Caputo, R. K. (2009). Religious capital and intergenerational transmission of volunteering as correlates of civic engagement. *Nonprofit and Voluntary Sector Quarterly, 38*, 983–1002. doi:10.1177/0899764008323990

Carpenter, T. P., & Marshall, M. A. (2009). An examination of religious priming and intrinsic religious motivation in the moral hypocrisy paradigm. *Journal for the Scientific Study of Religion, 48*, 386–393. doi:10.1111/j.1468-5906.2009.01454.x

Cassell, E. J. (2009). Compassion. In C. R. Snyder & S. J. Lopez (Eds.), *Oxford handbook of positive psychology* (2nd ed., pp. 393–403). New York, NY: Oxford University Press.

Chang, W.-C. (2006). Determinants of religious giving in an Eastern-culture economy: Empirical evidence from Taiwan. *Review of Religious Research, 47*, 363–379.

Cohen, A. B., Malka, A., Rozin, P., & Cherfas, L. (2006). Religion and unforgivable offenses. *Journal of Personality, 74*, 85–117. doi:10.1111/j.1467-6494.2005.00370.x

Cornwall, J., Perry, G. F., Louw, G., & Stringer, M. D. (2012). Who donates their body to science? An international, multicenter, prospective study. *Anatomical Sciences Education.* Advance online publication. doi:10.1002/ase.1278

Crocker, J., & Canevello, A. (2008). Creating and undermining social support in communal relationships: The role of compassionate and self-image goals. *Journal of Personality and Social Psychology, 95*, 555–575. doi:10.1037/0022-3514.95.3.555

De Dreu, C. K. W., Yzerbyt, V., & Leyens, J.-Ph. (1995). Dilution of stereotype-based cooperation in mixed-motive interdependence. *Journal of Experimental Social Psychology, 31*, 575–593. doi:10.1006/jesp.1995.1026

de St. Aubin, E., McAdams, D. P., & Kim, T.-C. (Eds.). (2004). *The generative society: Caring for future generations.* Washington, DC: American Psychological Association. doi:10.1037/10622-000

Dillon, M., Wink, P., & Fay, K. (2003). Is spirituality detrimental to generativity? *Journal for the Scientific Study of Religion, 42*, 427–442. doi:10.1111/1468-5906.00192

Dovidio, J. F., Gaertner, S. L., Shnabel, N., Saguy, T., & Johnson, J. (2010). Recategorization and prosocial behavior: Common in-group identity and a dual identity. In S. Stürmer & M. Snyder (Eds.), *The psychology of prosocial behavior: Group processes, intergroup relations, and helping* (pp. 191–207). Chichester, England: Wiley-Blackwell.

Dovidio, J. F., Piliavin, J. A., Schroeder, D. A., & Penner, L. A. (2006). *The social psychology of prosocial behavior.* Mahwah, NJ: Erlbaum.

Eisenberg, N., Fabes, R. A., & Spinrad, T. L. (2006). Prosocial development. In W. Damon, R. M. Lerner (Series Eds.) & N. Eisenberg (Vol. Ed.), *Handbook of child psychology: Vol. 3. Social, emotional, and personality development* (6th ed., pp. 646–718). Hoboken, NJ: Wiley.

Ellens, J. H. (Ed.). (2007). *The destructive power of religion: Violence in Judaism, Christianity, and Islam.* Westport, CT: Praeger.

Fehr, B., Sprecher, S., & Underwood, L. G. (Eds.). (2009). *The science of compassionate love: Theory, research, and applications.* Chichester, England: Wiley-Blackwell.

Francis, L. J. (2009). Comparative empirical research in religion: Conceptual and operational challenges within empirical theology. In L. J. Francis, M. Robbins, & J. Astley (Eds.), *Empirical theology in texts and tables* (pp. 127–152). Leiden, The Netherlands: Brill. doi:10.1163/ej.9789004168886.i-408.48

Gailliot, M. T. (2010). The effortful and energy-demanding nature of prosocial behavior. In M. Mikulincer & P. R. Shaver (Eds.), *Prosocial motives, emotions, and behaviors: The better angels of our nature* (pp. 169–180). Washington, DC: American Psychological Association. doi:10.1037/12061-009

Galen, L. W. (2012). Does religious belief promote prosociality? A critical examination. *Psychological Bulletin.* Advance online publication. doi:10.1037/a0028251

Gilligan, C. (1982). *In a different voice: Psychological theory and women's development.* Cambridge, MA: Harvard University Press.

Gillum, R. F., & Masters, K. S. (2010). Religiousness and blood donation: Findings from a national survey. *Journal of Health Psychology, 15*, 163–172. doi:10.1177/1359105309345171

Ginges, J., Hansen, I., & Norenzayan, A. (2009). Religion and support for suicide attacks. *Psychological Science, 20*, 224–230. doi:10.1111/j.1467-9280.2009.02270.x

Graham, J., & Haidt, J. (2010). Beyond beliefs: Religions bind individuals into moral communities. *Personality and Social Psychology Review, 14*, 140–150. doi:10.1177/1088868309353415

Graziano, W. C., & Tobin, R. M. (2009). Agreeableness. In M. R. Leary & R. H. Hoyle (Eds.), *Handbook of individual differences in social behavior* (pp. 46–61). New York, NY: Guilford Press.

Greer, T., Berman, M., Varan, V., Bobrycki, L., & Watson, S. (2005). We are a religious people, we are a vengeful people. *Journal for the Scientific Study of Religion, 44*, 45–57. doi:10.1111/j.1468-5906.2005.00264.x

Gruber, J. (2004). Pay or pray? The impact of charitable subsidies on religious attendance. *Journal of Public Economics, 88*, 2635–2655. doi:10.1016/j.jpubeco.2004.03.006

Habito, R. L. F., & Inaba, K. (Eds.). (2006). *The practice of altruism: Caring and religion in global perspective.* Cambridge: Cambridge Scholars Press.

Haidt, J. (2003). The moral emotions. In R. J. Davidson, K. R. Scherer, & H. H. Goldsmith (Eds.), *Handbook of affective sciences* (pp. 852–870). Oxford: Oxford University Press.

Haidt, J., & Graham, J. (2007). When morality opposes justice: Conservatives have moral intuitions that liberals may not recognize. *Social Justice Research, 20*, 98–116. doi:10.1007/s11211-007-0034-z

Harper, M. (2007). The stereotyping of nonreligious people by religious students: Contents and subtypes. *Journal for the Scientific Study of Religion, 46*, 539–552. doi:10.1111/j.1468-5906.2007.00376.x

Henrich, J. (2009). The evolution of costly displays, cooperation and religion: Credibility enhancing displays and their implications for cultural evolution. *Evolution and Human Behavior, 30*, 244–260. doi:10.1016/j.evolhumbehav.2009.03.005

Henrich, J., Ensminger, J., McElreath, R., Barr, A., Barrett, C., Bolyanatz, A., . . . Ziker, J. (2010). Markets, religion, community size, and the evolution of fairness and punishment. *Science, 327*, 1480–1484. doi:10.1126/science.1182238

Hoffman, M. L. (2000). *Empathy and moral development: Implications for caring and justice.* New York, NY: Cambridge University Press.

Hunsberger, B., & Jackson, L. M. (2005). Religion, meaning, and prejudice. *Journal of Social Issues, 61*, 807–826. doi:10.1111/j.1540-4560.2005.00433.x

Jackson, L. M., & Esses, V. M. (1997). Of scripture and ascription: The relation between religious fundamentalism and intergroup helping. *Personality and Social Psychology Bulletin, 23*, 893–906. doi:10.1177/0146167297238009

James, W. (1985). *The varieties of religious experience: A study in human nature*. Cambridge, MA: Harvard University Press. (Original work published 1902)

Johansson-Stenman, O., Mahmud, M., & Martinsson, P. (2009). Trust and religion: Experimental evidence from rural Bangladesh. *Economica, 76*, 462–485. doi:10.1111/j.1468-0335.2008.00689.x

Johnson, D. D. P., & Bering, J. M. (2006). Hand of God, mind of man: Punishment and cognition in the evolution of cooperation. *Evolutionary Psychology, 4*, 219–233.

Johnson, D. D. P., & Kruger, O. (2004). The good of wrath: Supernatural punishment and the evolution of cooperation. *Political Theology, 5*, 159–176. doi:10.1558/poth.2004.5.2.159

Johnson, M. K., Rowatt, W. C., & LaBouff, J. P. (2010). Priming Christian religious concepts increases racial prejudice. *Social Psychological and Personality Science, 1*, 119–126.

Koenig, L. B., McGue, M., Krueger, R. F., & Bouchard, T. J., Jr. (2007). Religiousness, antisocial behavior, and altruism: Genetic and environmental mediation. *Journal of Personality, 75*, 265–290. doi:10.1111/j.1467-6494.2007.00439.x

Kohlberg, L. (1981). *The philosophy of moral development: Moral stages and the idea of justice* (Vol. 1). San Francisco, CA: Harper & Row.

Krause, N. (2007). Altruism, religion, and health: Exploring the ways in which helping others benefits support providers. In S. G. Post (Ed.), *Altruism and health: Perspectives from empirical research* (pp. 410–421). New York, NY: Oxford University Press.

LaBouff, J. P., Rowatt, W. C., Johnson, M. K., & Finkle, C. (2012). Differences in attitudes toward outgroups in religious and nonreligious contexts in a multinational sample: A situational context priming study. *The International Journal for the Psychology of Religion, 22*, 1–9. doi:10.1080/10508619.2012.634778

Lam, P.-Y. (2006). Religion and civic culture: A cross-national study of voluntary association membership. *Journal for the Scientific Study of Religion, 45*, 177–193. doi:10.1111/j.1468-5906.2006.00300.x

Lam, W. A., & McCullough, L. B. (2000). Influence of religious and spiritual values on the willingness of Chinese–Americans to donate organs for transplantation. *Clinical Transplantation, 14*, 449–456. doi:10.1034/j.1399-0012.2000.140502.x

Landau, S. F., Björkqvist, K., Lagerspetz, K. M. J., Österman, K., & Gideon, L. (2002). The effect of religiosity and ethnic origin on direct and indirect aggression among males and females: Some Israeli findings. *Aggressive Behavior, 28*, 281–298. doi:10.1002/ab.80006

Leach, M. M., Berman, M. E., & Eubanks, L. (2008). Religious activities, religious orientation, and aggressive behavior. *Journal for the Scientific Study of Religion, 47*, 311–319. doi:10.1111/j.1468-5906.2008.00409.x

Lee, M. R. (2006). The religious institutional base and violent crime in rural areas. *Journal for the Scientific Study of Religion, 45*, 309–324. doi:10.1111/j.1468-5906.2006.00309.x

Lewis, C. A. (2001). Cultural stereotype of the effects of religion on mental health. *British Journal of Medical Psychology, 74*, 359–367. doi:10.1348/000711201161037

Lincoln, R., Morrissey, C. A., & Mundey, P. (2008). *Religious giving: A literature review*. Report for the John Templeton Foundation Generosity Planning Project. Retrieved from http://generosityresearch.nd.edu/assets/20447/religious_giving_final.pdf

Malhotra, D. (2010). (When) are religious people nicer? Religious salience and the "Sunday effect" on prosocial behavior. *Judgment and Decision Making, 5*, 138–143.

Markstrom, C. A., Huey, E., Stiles, B. M., & Krause, A. L. (2010). Frameworks of caring and helping in adolescence: Are empathy, religiosity, and spirituality related constructs? *Youth and Society, 42*, 59–80. doi:10.1177/0044118X09333644

McCullough, M. E., Tsang, J.-A., & Brion, S. (2003). Personality traits in adolescence as predictors of religiousness in early adulthood: Findings from the Terman Longitudinal Study. *Personality and Social Psychology Bulletin, 29*, 980–991. doi:10.1177/0146167203253210

McCullough, M. E., & Worthington, E. L., Jr. (1999). Religion and the forgiving personality. *Journal of Personality, 67*, 1141–1164. doi:10.1111/1467-6494.00085

Mikulincer, M., & Shaver, P. R. (2010a). Does gratitude promote prosocial behavior? The moderating role of attachment security. In M. Mikulincer & P. R. Shaver (Eds.), *Prosocial motives, emotions, and behaviors: The better angels of our nature* (pp. 267–283). Washington, DC: American Psychological Association. doi:10.1037/12061-014

Mikulincer, M., & Shaver, P. R. (Eds.). (2010b). *Prosocial motives, emotions, and behaviors: The better angels of our nature*. Washington, DC: American Psychological Association. doi:10.1037/12061-000

Mullet, E., & Azar, F. (2009). Apologies, repentance, and forgiveness: A Muslim-Christian comparison. *The*

International Journal for the Psychology of Religion, 19, 275–285. doi:10.1080/10508610903146274

Neusner, J., & Chilton, B. D. (Eds.). (2005). *Altruism in world religions*. Washington, DC: Georgetown University Press.

Norenzayan, A., Dar-Nimrod, I., Hansen, I. G., & Proulx, T. (2009). Mortality salience and religion: Divergent effects on the defense of cultural values for the religious and the non-religious. *European Journal of Social Psychology, 39*, 101–113. doi:10.1002/ejsp.482

Norenzayan, A., & Shariff, A. (2008). The origin and evolution of religious prosociality. *Science, 322*, 58–62. doi:10.1126/science.1158757

Oman, D., Thoresen, C. E., & Hedberg, J. (2010). Does passage meditation foster compassionate love among health professionals? A randomized trial. *Mental Health, Religion, and Culture, 13*, 129–154. doi:10.1080/13674670903261954

Peterson, B. E. (2006). Generativity and successful parenting: An analysis of young adult outcomes. *Journal of Personality, 74*, 847–870. doi:10.1111/j.1467-6494.2006.00394.x

Pichon, I., Boccato, G., & Saroglou, V. (2007). Nonconscious influences of religion on prosociality: A priming study. *European Journal of Social Psychology, 37*, 1032–1045. doi:10.1002/ejsp.416

Pichon, I., & Saroglou, V. (2009). Religion and helping: Impact of target, thinking styles and just-world beliefs. *Archive for the Psychology of Religion, 31*, 215–236.

Piedmont, R. L. (2007). Cross-cultural generalizability of the Spiritual Transcendence Scale to the Philippines: Spirituality as a human universal. *Mental Health, Religion, and Culture, 10*, 89–107. doi:10.1080/13694670500275494

Piliavin, J. A. (2010). Volunteering across the life span. In S. Stürmer & M. Snyder (Eds.), *The psychology of prosocial behavior: Group processes, intergroup relations, and helping* (pp. 157–172). Chichester, England: Wiley-Blackwell.

Post, S. G. (Ed.). (2007). *Altruism and health: Perspectives from empirical research*. New York, NY: Oxford University Press.

Preston, J. L., & Ritter, R. S. (2010, January). *What do God and religion prime? Effects on helping ingroup vs. outgroup members*. Paper presented at the Second SPSP Preconference on the Psychology of Religion and Spirituality, Las Vegas, NV.

Preston, J. L., Ritter, R. S., & Hermandez, J. I. (2010). Principles of religious prosociality: A review and reformulation. *Social and Personality Psychology Compass, 4*, 574–590. doi:10.1111/j.1751-9004.2010.00286.x

Randolph-Seng, B., & Nielsen, M. E. (2007). Honesty: One effect of primed religious representations. *The International Journal for the Psychology of Religion, 17*, 303–315. doi:10.1080/10508610701572812

Realo, A., Allik, J., & Greenfield, B. (2008). Radius of trust: Social capital in relation to familism and institutional collectivism. *Journal of Cross-Cultural Psychology, 39*, 447–462. doi:10.1177/0022022108318096

Roes, F. L., & Raymond, M. (2003). Belief in moralizing gods. *Evolution and Human Behavior, 24*, 126–135. doi:10.1016/S1090-5138(02)00134-4

Rothschild, Z. K., Abdollahib, A., & Pyszczynski, T. (2009). Does peace have a prayer? The effect of mortality salience, compassionate values, and religious fundamentalism on hostility toward out-groups. *Journal of Experimental Social Psychology, 45*, 816–827. doi:10.1016/j.jesp.2009.05.016

Rowatt, W. C. Johnson, M. K., LaBouff, J. P., & Gonzalez, A. (in press). Religious fundamentalism, right-wing authoritarianism, and prejudice: Insights from meta-analyses, implicit social cognition, and social neuroscience. In R. F. Paloutzian & C. L. Park (Eds.), *Handbook of the psychology of religion and spirituality* (2nd ed.). New York, NY: Guilford Press.

Ruffle, B. J., & Sosis, R. (2007). Does it pay to pray? Costly ritual and cooperation. *BE Journal of Economic Analysis and Policy, 7* (Contributions), Article 18. Retrieved from http://www.bepress.com/bejeap/vol7/iss1/art18

Ruiter, S., & De Graaf, N. D. (2006). National context, religiosity, and volunteering: Results from 53 countries. *American Sociological Review, 71*, 191–210. doi:10.1177/000312240607100202

Ruiter, S., & De Graaf, N. D. (2010). National religious context and volunteering: More rigorous tests supporting the association. *American Sociological Review, 75*, 179–184. doi:10.1177/0003122409359168

Saroglou, V. (2002). Beyond dogmatism: The need for closure as related to religion. *Mental Health, Religion, and Culture, 5*, 183–194. doi:10.1080/13674670210144130

Saroglou, V. (2006a). Religion's role in prosocial behavior: Myth or reality? *Psychology of Religion Newsletter: American Psychological Association Division* 36, 31, 1–8. Retrieved from http://www.division36.org/Newsletters/v31n2.pdf

Saroglou, V. (2006b). Saints et héros: Vies parallèles et psychologies spécifiques [Saints and heroes: Parallel lives and distinct psychologies]. *Revue Théologique de Louvain, 37*, 313–341. doi:10.2143/RTL.37.3.2018929

Saroglou, V. (2010). Religiousness as a cultural adaptation of basic traits: A five-factor model perspective.

Personality and Social Psychology Review, 14, 108–125. doi:10.1177/1088868309352322

Saroglou, V. (2012). Is religion not prosocial at all? Comment on Galen (2012). *Psychological Bulletin*. Advance online publication. doi:10.1037/a0028927

Saroglou, V., & Cohen, A. B. (in press). Cultural and cross-cultural psychology of religion. In R. F. Paloutzian & C. L. Park (Eds.), *Handbook of the psychology of religion and spirituality* (2nd ed.). New York, NY: Guilford Press.

Saroglou, V., Corneille, O., & Van Cappellen, P. (2009). "Speak, Lord, your servant is listening": Religious priming activates submissive thoughts and behaviors. *The International Journal for the Psychology of Religion, 19*, 143–154. doi:10.1080/10508610902880063

Saroglou, V., Delpierre, V., & Dernelle, R. (2004). Values and religiosity: A meta-analysis of studies using Schwartz's model. *Personality and Individual Differences, 37*, 721–734. doi:10.1016/j.paid.2003.10.005

Saroglou, V., & Muñoz-García, A. (2008). Individual differences in religion and spirituality: An issue of personality traits and/or values. *Journal for the Scientific Study of Religion, 47*, 83–101. doi:10.1111/j.1468-5906.2008.00393.x

Saroglou, V., Pichon, I., Trompette, L., Verschueren, M., & Dernelle, R. (2005). Prosocial behavior and religion: New evidence based on projective measures and peer ratings. *Journal for the Scientific Study of Religion, 44*, 323–348. doi:10.1111/j.1468-5906.2005.00289.x

Saroglou, V., Yzerbyt, V., & Kaschten, C. (2011). Metastereotypes of groups with opposite religious views: Believers and nonbelievers. *Journal of Community and Applied Social Psychology, 21*, 484–498.

Sasaki, J. Y., Kim, H. S., Mojaverian, T., Kelley, L. D., Park, I., & Janušonis, S. (2011). Religion priming differentially increases prosociality among variants of Dopamine D4 Receptor (DRD4) gene. *Social Cognitive and Affective Neuroscience*. Advance online publication. doi:10.1093/scan/nsr089

Saslow, L. R., Willer, R., Feinberg, M., Piff, P. K., Clark, K., Keltner, D., & Saturn, S. R. (2012). My brother's keeper? Compassion predicts generosity more among less religious individuals. *Social Psychological and Personality Science*. Advance online publication. doi:10.1177/1948550612444137

Schwartz, S. H. (1992). Universals in the content and structure of values: Theory and empirical tests in 20 countries. In M. Zanna (Ed.), *Advances in experimental social psychology* (Vol. 25, pp. 1–65). New York, NY: Academic Press.

Sedikides, C., & Gebauer, J. E. (2010). Religiosity as self-enhancement: A meta-analysis of the relation between socially desirable responding and religiosity. *Personality and Social Psychology Review, 14*, 17–36. doi:10.1177/1088868309351002

Shariff, A. F., & Norenzayan, A. (2007). God is watching you: Priming God concepts increases prosocial behavior in an anonymous economic game. *Psychological Science, 18*, 803–809. doi:10.1111/j.1467-9280.2007.01983.x

Smith, T. W. (2009). Loving and caring in the United States: Trends and correlates of empathy, altruism, and related constructs. In B. Fehr, S. Sprecher, & L. G. Underwood (Eds.), *The science of compassionate love: Theory, research, and applications* (pp. 81–119). Chichester, England: Wiley-Backwell.

Sosis, R., & Alcorta, C. (2003). Signaling, solidarity, and the sacred: The evolution of religious behavior. *Evolutionary Anthropology, 12*, 264–274. doi:10.1002/evan.10120

Sprecher, S., & Fehr, B. (2005). Compassionate love for close others and humanity. *Journal of Social and Personal Relationships, 22*, 629–651. doi:10.1177/0265407505056439

Stark, R. (2001). Gods, rituals, and the moral order. *Journal for the Scientific Study of Religion, 40*, 619–636. doi:10.1111/0021-8294.00081

Steffen, P. R., & Masters, K. S. (2005). Does compassion mediate the intrinsic religion–health relationship? *Annals of Behavioral Medicine, 30*, 217–224. doi:10.1207/s15324796abm3003_6

Stephenson, M. T., Morgan, S. E., Roberts-Perez, S. D., Harrison, T., Afifi, W., & Long, S. D. (2008). The role of religiosity, religious norms, subjective norms, and bodily integrity in signing an organ donor card. *Health Communication, 23*, 436–447. doi:10.1080/10410230802342119

Strabac, Z., & Listhaug, O. (2008). Anti-Muslim prejudice in Europe: A multilevel analysis of survey data from 30 countries. *Social Science Research, 37*, 268–286. doi:10.1016/j.ssresearch.2007.02.004

Stürmer, S., & Snyder, M. (Eds.). (2010). *The psychology of prosocial behavior: Group processes, intergroup relations, and helping*. Chichester, England: Wiley-Blackwell.

Sundén, H. (1959). *Religionen och rollerna* [Religion and roles]. Stockholm, Sweden: Diakonistyrelsen.

Tan, J. H. W., & Vogel, C. (2008). Religion and trust: An experimental study. *Journal of Economic Psychology, 29*, 832–848. doi:10.1016/j.joep.2008.03.002

Tao, H. L., & Yeh, P. (2007). Religion as an investment: Comparing the contributions and volunteer frequency among Christians, Buddhists, and folk religionists. *Southern Economic Journal, 73*, 770–790.

Turiel, E. (2006). The development of morality. In W. Damon & R. M. Lerner (Series Eds.) & N. Eisenberg

(Vol. Ed.), *Handbook of child psychology: Vol. 3. Social, emotional, and personality development* (6th ed., pp. 789–857). Hoboken, NJ: Wiley.

Underwood, L. G. (2002). The human experience of compassionate love: Conceptual mapping and data from selected studies. In S. Post, L. G. Underwood, J. P. Schloss, & W. B. Hurlbut (Eds.), *Altruism and altruistic love: Science, philosophy and religion in dialogue* (pp. 72–88). New York, NY: Oxford University Press. doi:10.1093/acprof:oso/9780195143584.003.0009

Van Cappellen, P., Corneille, O., Cols, S., & Saroglou, V. (2011). Beyond mere compliance to authoritative figures: Religious priming increases conformity to informational influence among submissive people. *The International Journal for the Psychology of Religion, 21*, 97–105.

Van Cappellen, P., & Saroglou, V. (2010, June). *Induction of positive emotions leads to spirituality through changes in basic beliefs: An experimental study.* Paper presented at the Fifth European Conference on Positive Psychology, Copenhagen, Denmark.

Van Cappellen, P., & Saroglou, V. (2011). Awe activates religious and spiritual feelings and behavioral intentions. *Psychology of Religion and Spirituality*. Advance online publication. doi:10.1037/a0025986

Van Pachterbeke, M., Freyer, C., & Saroglou, V. (2011). When authoritarianism meets religion: Sacrificing others in the name of abstract deontology. *European Journal of Social Psychology, 41*, 898–903. doi:10.1002/ejsp.834

Veenvliet, S. G. (2008). Intrinsic religious orientation and religious teaching: Differential judgments toward same-gender sexual behavior and gay men and lesbians. *The International Journal for the Psychology of Religion, 18*, 53–65. doi:10.1080/10508610701719348

Walker, L. J., Frimer, J. A., & Dunlop, W. L. (2010). Varieties of moral personality: Beyond the banality of heroism. *Journal of Personality, 78*, 907–942. doi:10.1111/j.1467-6494.2010.00637.x

Weeden, J., Cohen, A. B., & Kenrick, D. T. (2008). Religious attendance as reproductive support. *Evolution and Human Behavior, 29*, 327–334. doi:10.1016/j.evolhumbehav.2008.03.004

Whitley, B. E., Jr. (2009). Religiosity and attitudes toward lesbians and gay men: A meta-analysis. *The International Journal for the Psychology of Religion, 19*, 21–38. doi:10.1080/10508610802471104

Wilhelm, M. O., Brown, E., Rooney, P. M., & Steinberg, R. (2008). The intergenerational transmission of generosity. *Journal of Public Economics, 92*, 2146–2156. doi:10.1016/j.jpubeco.2008.04.004

Williams, L. E., & Bargh, J. A. (2008). Experiences of physical warmth influence interpersonal warmth. *Science, 322*, 606–607. doi:10.1126/science.1162548

Wiltermuth, S. S., & Heath, C. (2009). Synchrony and cooperation. *Psychological Science, 20*, 1–5. doi:10.1111/j.1467-9280.2008.02253.x

Wink, P., Ciciolla, L., Dillon, M., & Tracy, A. (2007). Religiousness, spiritual seeking, and personality: Findings from a longitudinal study. *Journal of Personality, 75*, 1051–1070. doi:10.1111/j.1467-6494.2007.00466.x

CHAPTER 25

RELIGIOUS AND SPIRITUAL STRUGGLES

Julie J. Exline

For many people, religion and spirituality constitute a major domain of life, one that may influence other domains (e.g., work, relationships, self-regulation). As with any dimension of human experience, religion and spirituality hold the potential for both joys and struggles. Religion and spirituality can help to meet human needs for meaning (e.g., Park, 2005; see also Chapter 8 in this volume), comfort (e.g., Exline, Yali, & Sanderson, 2000), and attachment (e.g., Beck & McDonald, 2004; Kirkpatrick, 2004; Rowatt & Kirkpatrick, 2002; see also Chapter 7 in this volume). Yet these benefits do not rule out the possibility of strain and difficulty in religious and spiritual life.

The past decade has witnessed a veritable tidal wave of empirical research on religious and spiritual struggle. Although several literature reviews were published in the first part of the decade (e.g., Exline, 2002; Exline & Rose, 2005; Pargament, 2002; Pargament, Murray-Swank, Magyar, & Ano, 2005), along with a meta-analysis (Ano & Vasconcelles, 2005), the literature has more than doubled since these reviews were completed. There are now several hundred relevant entries in the PsycINFO database alone. Many of the articles to date have focused on links between struggle and other indexes of emotional and physical well-being.

Although space constraints do not permit an exhaustive review, the aim of this chapter is to orient readers to this burgeoning area of research. The first section describes what religious and spiritual struggles are and how they have been assessed. The second section briefly describes some situational and personal factors that might precipitate struggle. The third section reviews research on the broad concept of religious and spiritual struggle and how it relates to well-being, with an emphasis on studies from the past decade. This section also discusses the controversial question of whether struggle can lead to growth or other benefits. The fourth section briefly describes several types of specific struggles, highlighting select studies and suggesting topics for future research. (For additional recent reviews of specific struggles, see Exline & Rose, in press; Pargament, 2007; for reviews of literature relevant to management settings, see also Exline & Bright, 2011.)

RELIGIOUS AND SPIRITUAL STRUGGLE: DEFINITIONS AND ASSESSMENT TECHNIQUES

The notion of struggle implies that something in a person's current belief, practice, or experience is causing or perpetuating distress. This distress might take the form of a single, primary negative emotion (e.g., sadness; anger; guilt), or it might represent an internal conflict in which people experience thoughts or feelings that they cannot easily reconcile. Religious and spiritual struggle can focus on several domains, categorized by Pargament (2007) as divine (e.g., feeling angry at God), intrapersonal (e.g., being unable to forgive oneself for a transgression), and interpersonal (e.g., feeling betrayed by a religious leader). Struggles with supernatural evil will be briefly mentioned in this chapter. Following

DOI: 10.1037/14045-025
APA Handbook of Psychology, Religion, and Spirituality: Vol. 1. Context, Theory, and Research, K. I. Pargament (Editor-in-Chief)
Copyright © 2013 by the American Psychological Association. All rights reserved.

the definitions of religion and spirituality for this handbook, some struggles are clearly *spiritual* in nature—that is, they focus on people's relationships with God or with a transcendent or sacred realm. Other struggles are clearly *religious*—that is, they center on teachings, practices, or group dynamics of an organized religious group. Yet because the two types of struggle often overlap, the general term *religious or spiritual struggle* (or the shorthand term *struggle*) is often used in this chapter.

This chapter frames religious or spiritual struggle as a form of distress or conflict in the religious or spiritual realm. Struggle can be understood in the context of several broader theoretical frameworks, however. For instance, religious or spiritual struggle has been conceptualized and operationalized as a specific, negative form of religious coping elicited by various life stressors (Pargament, Murray-Swank, et al., 2005). Religious or spiritual struggle could be viewed as a relational variable, a stable dispositional variable, or an indicator of more general psychological distress and disorder. Indeed, as we will see, there is support for each of these perspectives. Because religious or spiritual struggle can be conceptualized from different theoretical vantage points, there will be some overlap of this chapter with material in other chapters in this volume (e.g., for information on religious coping, see Chapter 19 in this volume). This chapter, however, devotes only passing attention to forms of struggle that can be clearly traced to specific psychological disorders because this material is covered in the second volume of this handbook. This chapter also does not focus heavily on interventions for spiritual struggle, which are covered in the chapter on spiritual problems (see Volume 2, Chapter 4, this handbook).

What about problematic aspects of religion or spirituality that are not linked with internal struggle? Pargament (2007) described various problems associated with pathways to the sacred, including problems of breadth and depth, fit, and continuity and change (see also Pargament, 1997, 2002). For example, a person might hold an immature, self-centered form of spirituality, one that others see as problematic but that is not causing any internal struggle for the person. Alternatively, members of a religious sect might share beliefs that diverge sharply from those of society at large. Although such situations could set the stage for struggle, they would not meet criteria for inclusion here unless the beliefs were causing distress or conflict.

ASSESSMENT OF RELIGIOUS AND SPIRITUAL STRUGGLE

Although interest in spiritual struggle has grown dramatically in the past decade, several scholars did earlier work on the topic. For example, Funk (1958) developed a 22-item measure of religious conflict, which was later divided by Trenholm, Trent, and Compton (1998) into positive and negative domains. Berg (1994) developed an eight-item measure of spiritual risk for use in hospital settings. The Quest scale by Batson and Schoenrade (1991a, 1991b) assesses religious doubts and questioning as part of an ongoing existential dialogue. In a related vein, Altemeyer and Hunsberger (1997) developed a measure assessing the extent to which various issues (e.g., evil and suffering, hypocrisy, specific doctrines) prompt religious questions and doubts.

As reviewed in the following section, most studies have framed religious or spiritual struggle in terms of coping with specific stressors (Pargament, 1997). Many have used the full Religious Coping Inventory (RCOPE; Pargament, Koenig, & Perez, 2000) or the 14-item Brief RCOPE (Pargament, Smith, Koenig, & Perez, 1998). The 16-item Suffering With God Scale (M. Webb, Sink, McCann, Chickering, & Scallon, 2010) focuses specifically on divine struggles. Specialized religious coping scales have been made for the faiths of Judaism (Rosmarin, Pargament, Krumrei, & Flannelly, 2009), Islam (Raiya, Pargament, Mahoney, & Stein, 2008), and Hinduism (Tarakeshwar, Pargament, & Mahoney, 2003), and qualitative work has been done in a U.S. Buddhist sample (Phillips et al., in press). Other measures have been designed for use in medical settings (for reviews, see Fitchett, 1999a, 1999b; Fitchett & Risk, 2009). Two of these measures are used to assess reactions to cancer diagnoses: The Spiritual Transformation Scale (Cole, Hopkins, Tisak, Steel, & Carr, 2008) asks about positive and negative spiritual changes, and the Cancer and Deity Questionnaire (Bowman, Beitman, Palesh, Prez, &

Koopman, 2009) focuses on perceived relationships with God.

Some measures frame spiritual struggle in non-coping terms, so that participants focus on their general perceptions, feelings, or attitudes rather than their coping responses to a specific stressor. For example, the Religious Comfort and Strain Scale (Exline et al., 2000) assesses the degree to which participants are experiencing feelings of comfort and three types of strain (alienation from God, fear and guilt, and social rifts) associated with religion. In terms of social aspects of religious struggle, Krause and colleagues (e.g., Krause, Chatters, Meltzer, & Morgan, 2000) have developed specific items to tap negative social interactions in religious organizations. Also noteworthy is the Spiritual History Scale (Hays, Meador, Branch, & George, 2001), which includes items on the costs of religiousness in one's earlier life.

Measures of how people perceive their relationships with God often include subscales related to struggle. For example, the object-relations-based Spiritual Assessment Inventory (SAI; T. W. Hall & Edwards, 1996, 2002) addresses how people respond to disappointments or other conflicts in their relationships with God. The nine-item Attitudes Toward God Scale (Wood et al., 2010) taps current positive feelings and anger or disappointment toward God. Exline, Park, Smyth, and Carey (2011) have developed items to assess situation-specific anger and negative attributions regarding God. Measures of attachment to God (e.g., Beck & McDonald, 2004; Rowatt & Kirkpatrick, 2002) also include negative or conflicted feelings associated with God, as do many measures of God image (for reviews, see Moriarty & Hoffman, 2007; see also Chapter 15 in this volume).

WHEN AND FOR WHOM DOES STRUGGLE ARISE?

Although struggle can be framed as a natural part of spiritual or religious development (Pargament, 2007), it can be useful to reflect on when—and for whom—struggles tend to arise. As described in the following section, many studies have assessed struggle in response to negative life events such as illness, and this seems appropriate, particularly given that negative life events often elicit negative religious coping (e.g., Bjorck & Thurman, 2007). Yet, as we will see, there are many types of religious and spiritual struggle, and some might occur even in the absence of serious negative events.

A large-scale study of college students (Bryant & Astin, 2008) identified several religious and spiritual correlates of struggle. For example, greater struggle was associated with being part of a religious minority group, a quest orientation toward religion (see also Sandage, Jankowski, & Link, 2010), and seeing God as elusive (i.e., mysterious, "universal spirit") as opposed to beloved or protective. Religious and spiritual predictors also may vary on the basis of the type of struggle. Concerns related to desecration, for example, are more likely among religious persons who perceive violations to their sacred beliefs (e.g., Pargament, Magyar, Benore, & Mahoney, 2005). Anger and disappointment toward God, in contrast, are more likely among those lower in religious commitment (e.g., Exline et al., 2011) and intrinsic religiosity (e.g., T. W. Hall & Edwards, 2002) but higher in extrinsic religiosity (e.g., T. W. Hall & Edwards, 2002). Anger toward God is also more likely when people see God's intentions as cruel (Exline et al., 2011) and when they see such anger as morally acceptable (Exline, Kaplan, & Grubbs, 2012).

Several studies have identified individual-difference predictors of religious or spiritual struggle. Struggle has been associated with demographic factors such as being young (Exline et al., 2011; McConnell et al., 2006), female (Bryant & Astin, 2008), and unmarried (McConnell et al., 2006). In terms of personality, struggle has been linked with insecure and anxious or ambivalent attachment (Ano & Pargament, 2003; Belavich & Pargament, 2002; T. W. Hall & Edwards, 2002) and negative affectivity (e.g. Ano & Pargament, 2003; Schottenbauer, Rodriguez, Glass, & Arnkoff, 2006; Wood et al., 2010). Anger and disappointment with God have also been linked to narcissistic qualities (Sandage & Moe, 2011), such as tendencies to exploit others (T. W. Hall & Edwards, 2002) and a sense of entitlement (e.g., Wood et al., 2010). Religious or spiritual struggles are also more likely for those who report poor social support (McConnell et al., 2006) and family-of-origin stressors such as alcoholism (Szewczyk & Weinmuller, 2006) and childhood physical or sexual abuse (Fallot & Heckman, 2005).

LINKS WITH INDICATORS OF WELL-BEING, DISTRESS, AND GROWTH

Because religious and spiritual struggle connotes some degree of discomfort, it seems reasonable to predict that measures of struggle would be associated with other measures of emotional distress. Emotional distress may, in turn, translate into physical symptoms. To date, the vast majority of the literature on religious and spiritual struggle has focused on these types of associations with emotional and physical well-being. Such studies are important in terms of clarifying the psychological and medical importance of religious and spiritual struggle. This section provides a brief (and admittedly not exhaustive) overview of this large literature. Many studies have a strong emphasis on *divine struggles*—struggles related to God or a Higher Power. The following section will give more detail on specific types of religious and spiritual struggles, including not only divine struggles but also those that are intrapersonal and interpersonal.

Mental Health

Studies to date have shown strong support for a link between religious or spiritual struggle and emotional distress. Results come from several types of studies, including meta-analyses and surveys of both nonclinical and clinical samples. A brief review follows.

Meta-analyses. Ano and Vasconcelles (2005) consolidated much of the early research on religious coping and adjustment in a meta-analysis of 49 studies. Twenty-two of the effect sizes focused on links between spiritual struggle and negative psychological adjustment (e.g., anxiety, depression, anger, negative mood, guilt, social dysfunction). Results revealed a modest but significant association (effect size of .22) between spiritual struggle and indicators of poor adjustment. Similarly, in a major meta-analysis on the link between religiosity and depression, T. B. Smith, McCullough, and Poll (2003) found that negative religious coping was linked with greater depression (weighted mean $r = .136$, $N = 1,999$ participants across eight studies).

Nonclinical samples. Surveys using nonclinical samples have also shown consistent links between spiritual struggle and emotional distress. In one large study, McConnell and colleagues (2006) surveyed a random sample of 1,629 respondents from the United States. Spiritual struggle showed positive links with all of the study's distress measures: depression, paranoid ideation, somatization, and several indicators of anxiety. Another recent study using a large sample from the 1998 General Social Survey (Ellison & Lee, 2010) also showed connections between distress and spiritual struggle (intrapsychic, divine, and interpersonal). Similar links between spiritual struggle and emotional distress have been found in nonclinical samples of Jews (e.g., Rosmarin, Krumrei, & Andersson, 2009; Rosmarin, Pargament, & Flannelly, 2009; Rosmarin, Pargament, Krumrei, & Flannelly, 2009; Rosmarin, Pirutinsky, Pargament, & Krumrei, 2009), Muslims (Raiya et al., 2008), and Christians (e.g., Krause, Ingersoll-Dayton, Ellison, & Wulff, 1999; Pargament, Zinnbauer, et al., 1998; Rosmarin, Krumrei, & Andersson, 2009; Strelan, Acton, & Patrick, 2009). Studies of undergraduates have yielded comparable patterns (e.g., Exline, Yali, & Lobel, 1999; Exline et al., 2000, 2011; Pargament, Smith, et al., 1998; Pargament, Zinnbauer, et al., 1998), and spiritual struggles have been shown to be common among undergraduates (Bryant & Astin, 2008; C. V. Johnson & Hayes, 2003).

Psychiatric and interpersonal stressors. Many studies have evaluated whether spiritual struggle is linked with poorer adaptation to major stressors. Some of these studies have focused on psychiatric populations. Studies have shown the struggle–distress link in individuals coping with anxiety and depression (e.g., Bosworth, Park, McQuoid, Hays, & Steffens, 2003; Dew et al., 2010; Exline et al., 2000; Trenholm et al., 1998), chemical dependency (Conners, Whiteside-Mansell, & Sherman, 2006; Fallot & Heckman, 2005), schizophrenia (Duarte, 2010; Phillips & Stein, 2007), and bipolar disorder

(Phillips & Stein, 2007). Struggle has also been tied to more distress, including posttraumatic stress disorder (PTSD) symptoms, in the wake of trauma (e.g., Bradley, Schwartz, & Kaslow, 2005; Fallot & Heckman, 2005; Harris et al., 2008; Pargament, Smith, et al., 1998; B. W. Smith, Pargament, Brant, & Oliver, 2000; Witvliet, Phipps, Feldman, & Beckham, 2004). Furthermore, struggle has been linked with poorer adaptation to interpersonal stressors such as divorce (e.g., Krumrei, Mahoney, & Pargament, 2009; Krumrei, Mahoney, & Pargament, 2011; Warner, Mahoney, & Krumrei, 2009; A. P. Webb, 2009), childhood sexual abuse (e.g., Gall, 2006; Murray-Swank & Pargament, 2008), intimate partner violence (Bradley et al., 2005), caregiving (e.g., Herrera, Lee, Nanyonjo, Laufman, & Torres-Vigil, 2009; Pearce, Singer, & Prigerson, 2006), bereavement (e.g., Exline et al., 2011, Study 4), and parenting (Butter, 2004; Dumas & Nissley-Tsiopinis, 2006). Although most of these studies were cross-sectional, longitudinal work is beginning to suggest that spiritual struggles may perpetuate distress. For example, in a study of 145 depressed adolescents (Dew et al., 2010), loss of faith predicted less improvement in depression scores over 6 months.

Medical samples. Without question, the most-studied stressors in the struggle literature have involved medical conditions. For example, struggle has been associated with greater emotional distress for patients facing cardiovascular problems (e.g., Abel, 2009; Ai, Pargament, Kronfol, Tice, & Appel, 2010; Ai, Park, Huang, Rodgers, & Tice, 2007; Ai, Seymour, Tice, Qatar, & Bolling, 2009; Edmondson, Park, Chaudoir, & Wortmann, 2008; Fitchett et al., 2004), cancer (e.g., Boscaglia, Clarke, Jobling, & Quinn, 2005; Cole, Hopkins, Tisak, Steel, & Carr, 2008; Exline et al., 2011; Fitchett et al., 2004; Gall, de Renart, & Boonstra, 2000; Gall, Kristjansson, Charbonneau, & Florack, 2009; Hebert, Zdaniuk, Schulz, & Scheier, 2009; Khan, Sultana, & Watson, 2009; Manning-Walsh, 2005; Sherman, Plante, Simonton, Latif, & Anaissie, 2009; Sherman, Simonton, Latif, Spohn, & Tricot, 2005; Tarakeshwar et al., 2006; Zwingmann, Müller, Körber, & Murken, 2008; Zwingmann, Wirtz, Müller, Körber, & Murken, 2006; for a review and critique, see Thuné-Boyle, Stygall, Keshtgar, & Newman, 2006), HIV/AIDS (e.g., Cotton et al., 2006; Kudel et al., 2006; Trevino et al., 2010; Yi et al., 2006), chronic pain (e.g., Parenteau, 2009; Rippentrop, Altmaier, Chen, Found, & Keffala, 2005), lung disease (e.g., Burker, Evon, Sedway, & Egan, 2005), end-of-life issues (e.g., Edmondson et al., 2008; Hills, Paice, Cameron, & Shott, 2005), diabetes (Fitchett et al., 2004), and child and adolescent asthma (Benore, Pargament, & Pendleton, 2008). Religious and spiritual struggles have been linked with negative health-related outcomes, including greater substance use (e.g., T. J. Johnson, Sheets, & Kristeller, 2008; Raiya et al., 2008) as well as more negative body images and increased dieting (Kim, 2006).

Several of the health-related studies have used longitudinal designs to disentangle the links between religious or spiritual struggle and emotional distress. For example, a study of children hospitalized for asthma symptoms (Benore et al., 2008) showed that baseline struggle predicted greater anxiety at a 1-month follow-up. A longitudinal study of patients with congestive heart failure (Park, Brooks, & Sussman, 2009) revealed that spiritual struggle at baseline predicted positive shifts in depression and negative shifts in self-efficacy and growth 6 months later. Another study among Orthodox Jews showed that spiritual struggle (in the form of negative religious coping) predicted increases in depression over 2 weeks (Pirutinsky, Rosmarin, Pargament, & Midlarsky, in press). Most recently, a longitudinal study of cancer patients (Exline et al., 2011, Study 5) revealed that at the 1-year follow-up, positive shifts in anger toward God were linked with negative shifts in adjustment. Anger that was chronic or recurrent, rather than transient, seems to have been the issue: At follow-up, the highest levels of distress were reported by patients who reported anger at God at both time points (rather than just at one time point).

Physical Health

Although most of the studies on physical illness have emphasized links between spiritual struggle and emotional distress, spiritual struggle has also been linked with variables related to health status, disease process, and biomarkers of illness. Early studies revealed cross-sectional links between spiritual struggles and poorer health status (e.g., Koenig, Pargament, & Nielsen, 1998). More recently, studies have gone a step further by using longitudinal designs. For example, in a 2-year longitudinal study of 596 older adults who were hospitalized for medical conditions, Pargament, Koenig, Tarakeshwar, and Hahn (2001) found that spiritual struggle (feeling abandoned by God, questioning God's love, and demonic reappraisal) predicted higher mortality rates. In another 2-year longitudinal study from the same site (Pargament et al., 2004), spiritual struggle at baseline predicted declines in functional status 2 years later.

Other researchers have found similar results in studies of a variety of illness conditions. For example, in a study of 96 medical rehabilitation inpatients, Fitchett, Rybarczyk, DeMarco, and Nicholas (1999) found that spiritual struggle at admission—and, in particular, anger toward God—was associated with poorer rehabilitation outcomes at a 4-month follow-up. Sherman et al. (2009), in a longitudinal study of 94 myeloma patients undergoing stem cell transplants, found that patients who showed increases in negative religious coping reported lower functional and physical well-being after their transplants. Trevino et al. (2010) found that negative religious coping among HIV/AIDS patients predicted worsening of symptoms 12 to 18 months later. New work on biomarkers comes from several studies by Ai and colleagues (Ai et al., 2009, 2010), who have shown links between spiritual struggle and higher levels of inteleukin-1, an inflammatory cytokine, in patients facing cardiac surgery.

Possible Benefits From Struggle

Taken together, the studies reviewed so far have painted a grim picture of religious and spiritual struggles: Not only are these struggles painful, but they may even suggest a poor prognosis for future health and well-being. Yet intuitively, it seems that struggle should hold the potential for benefits (Exline, 2012), even if such benefits take time to unfold. After all, human development requires learning how to face new challenges, and stress can provide opportunities for growth (e.g., Calhoun & Tedeschi, 2006). When faith is tested, it seems reasonable to believe that it could become stronger—at least if a person turns to faith-building responses when faced with spiritual choice points (Pargament, 2007). Some may even begin to embrace questioning as a valued part of their spiritual identity (e.g., Batson & Schoenrade, 1991a, 1991b).

But what evidence is there, if any, to support the idea that spiritual struggles can promote growth or other benefits? This issue has been understudied, especially in comparison to the simpler question of whether religious and spiritual struggle are linked with distress. The few studies that have examined potential benefits from struggle have yielded mixed findings. Some have found no relationship between religious or spiritual struggle and growth (e.g., Krumrei et al., 2009; for a review, see Ano & Vasconcelles, 2005). Yet as reviewed by Pargament, Desai, and McConnell (2006), several cross-sectional studies do suggest positive connections between spiritual struggles and posttraumatic growth (e.g., Pargament, Smith, et al., 1998; Pargament et al., 2000). How can these results be squared with the studies described thus far, which typically suggested that struggle was a risk factor for prolonged distress? In fact, one of the longitudinal studies (Park, 2008) looked at stress-related growth specifically, revealing that spiritual struggles actually predicted negative shifts in stress-related growth over time.

To date, there is no definitive explanation for why some studies suggest positive links between struggle and growth, whereas others suggest nonassociations and even negative associations. One possible explanation is that when compared with trivial problems, serious problems create not only more distress but also more opportunities for growth (Pargament et al., 2006). Major stressors can encourage people to cultivate new skills or sources of social support, for example, which can promote growth. Yet not all people will respond by building their resources; some instead will become mired in chronic struggles. To date, at least two longitudinal studies have identified chronic struggle as a problem. In their 2-year study of elderly, medically ill individuals, Pargament et al. (2004) identified four groups: nonstrugglers, transitory strugglers (struggle at baseline only), acute strugglers (follow-up only), and chronic struggles (both time points). Chronic strugglers were the only ones who showed declines in physical and mental health over 2 years. Similar patterns emerged from a 1-year longitudinal study of cancer patients (Exline et al., 2011, Study 5): Those who reported anger toward God at both time points showed the worst outcomes in terms of mental and physical well-being.

Another relevant idea is that some people may protest or complain to God while remaining closely engaged in the relationship (e.g., Zornow, 2001). These people might be said to have a "winter" form of faith as opposed to a sunny, optimistic, "summery" variety (Beck, 2006, 2007; Marty, 1997). In fact, recent research suggests that positive, resilient relationships with God often entail some tolerance for negative emotions, questioning, and complaint, just so long as exiting the relationship is not seen as a viable option (Exline et al., 2012). This type of flexibility might be seen as a sign of spiritual maturity or integration (e.g., Pargament, 2007).

Yet most studies that emphasize struggle only assess negative thoughts and emotions; they usually do not take the extra step of seeing how people handle their negative emotions once they arise. The SAI (T. W. Hall & Edwards, 1996, 2002) is one notable exception: In addition to evaluating whether participants experience negative feelings such as disappointment or anger with God, the SAI includes additional questions focusing on how people handle such feelings in the context of the relationship. Being able to express negative feelings while staying engaged in the relationship is framed as realistic acceptance, which is seen as a mature spiritual response. Another good option for assessing growth from struggle may be to supplement self-report measures (which may be prone to retrospective reporting biases) with behavioral measures related to the virtues. For example, studies might provide participants with opportunities to demonstrate such behaviors as generosity, forgiveness, or self-regulation.

Social support may also moderate the link between religious or spiritual struggles and outcomes. For example, Exline and Grubbs (2011) assessed responses that people received when they told others that they felt angry at God. To the extent that people reported supportive responses, they reported more spiritual engagement (i.e., approach behaviors toward God; strengthened faith). In contrast, reports of nonsupportive responses were associated with continued anger toward God, attempts to suppress such anger, use of substances to cope, and spiritual disengagement via exit behaviors (e.g., rebellion, withdrawal, deciding that God did not exist). Although based on retrospective reports, these findings suggest the potential importance of interpersonal responses to disclosures of religious or spiritual struggle.

SPECIFIC TYPES OF STRUGGLE

Many studies have framed religious and spiritual struggles as broad constructs, which makes sense when the purpose is to examine links with mental and physical health. Yet use of such broad categories could limit conceptual and theoretical development because many distinct problems can fit under the umbrella category of struggle. To provide some sense of this diversity, this section will describe several specific types of struggle using the categories outlined by Pargament (2007): divine, interpersonal, and intrapersonal. Because of space constraints, these overviews are brief and selective. For more elaboration on the specific struggles described in this section as well as discussion of demonic aspects of struggle, see Exline and Rose (2005, in press).

Struggles With the Divine

Many spiritual struggles involve seeing God in a negative light—as uncaring, punitive, or unworthy of trust. Research on negative religious coping has placed a heavy emphasis on these struggles with the divine: In fact, five of the seven negative items on the Brief RCOPE (Pargament, Smith, et al., 1998) focus on God (e.g., "wondered whether God had abandoned me"; "felt punished by God for my lack of devotion"). Research on God images (see Chapter 15 in this volume) and attachment to God (see Chapter 7 in this volume) are also of obvious relevance here.

Existing studies make it clear that divine struggles are linked with mental and physical health. Two facets of struggle with the divine are described in this section: anger toward God and concern about punishment from God. More broadly speaking, the study of divine struggles could make important conceptual contributions to the larger field of psychology. After all, God is a relational partner with unique qualities: In contrast to human beings, God is often seen as all powerful, all knowing, and holy. In addition, most people do not report that they can see or hear God with their physical senses. This lack of unambiguous sensory evidence, in turn, can prompt many questions about God's qualities, communication, and very existence.

Anger toward God. The topic of anger toward God has begun to receive some focused attention (see Exline & Martin, 2005), as highlighted in a recent article describing five recent studies of undergraduates, a national sample, and individuals coping with bereavement and cancer (Exline et al., 2011). Results from these studies suggest that anger toward God seems to be common, albeit at low levels of intensity, and it shows correlates with emotional distress and physical symptoms that parallel those for other religious and spiritual struggles. In general, people seem to become angry at God for the same reasons they get angry at other people: when they see God as responsible for serious harm, when God's intentions are seen as cruel, and when there is no sense of a close, committed relationship with God before the incident.

Many people see anger toward God as morally wrong, particularly those who are devout and hold positive images of God (Exline et al., 2012). As with human relationships, the domains of closeness and anger regarding God are largely independent (Beck, 2006), suggesting that positive and negative feelings can coexist. As described earlier, staying engaged while being willing to express questions or negative feelings to God may be part of a healthy spiritual process (Beck, 2007; Exline et al., 2012; T. W. Hall & Edwards, 1996, 2002). Yet the fact that many people see anger toward God as wrong raises practical questions about whether people will admit to such feelings. This potential problem highlights the need for alternate means of assessment, such as psychophysiological or implicit measures, to complement self-report instruments.

How do people resolve anger toward God? In one study of undergraduates (see Exline & Martin, 2005), 80% of participants who reported some anger toward God in response to a past event said that their anger had decreased over time. Common reasons included finding a sense of meaning, benign reappraisals about God's intentions, and the simple passage of time. A vital next step will be the development of interventions focused specifically on anger toward God.

Concern about divine punishment. Some people also worry that God feels punitive or disapproving toward them, as captured on the RCOPE (Pargament, Koenig, & Perez, 2000) and Brief RCOPE (Pargament, Smith et al., 1998). They may envision God as a stern judge, for example, or as a parent who offers only conditional acceptance. Regardless of theological beliefs, depression or low self-esteem might make people assume that God disapproves of them (e.g., Greenway, Milne, & Clarke, 2003). Some people might also find it difficult to experience God's love or forgiveness at an emotional level, even if they believe intellectually that God is loving and merciful. For example, some might agree with a statement about God being forgiving because their tradition endorses such a belief, even though their internal experiences suggest fear or unresolved guilt. Although perhaps difficult to tap with self-report measures, such a division between "head and heart" (e.g., Tallon, 2008) would be an interesting topic for future work.

In terms of intervention, any type of struggle with the divine may warrant a close inspection of one's God image and its possible sources (e.g., doctrine, socialization, experiences with parents). Sensitivity to theological differences is important here. For example, some faiths portray God (or some facets of God) as punitive, and to challenge such beliefs could be seen as misinformed or disrespectful. In future research, it will be important to examine how people from varied traditions seek and perceive God's forgiveness (e.g., Toussaint & Williams, 2008).

Intrapersonal Struggles

Other spiritual struggles have an inward focus, even though they center on beliefs associated with the divine realm. The boundaries here quickly become fuzzy, because any religious or spiritual struggle could cause personal distress. In intrapersonal struggles, however, the primary emphasis is on one's own thoughts or actions rather than on God or others. Two areas of intrapersonal struggles are briefly highlighted in the next sections: moral imperfection and questioning or doubt.

Facing moral imperfection. Even if they do not fear God's punishment, people may struggle when they confront their own imperfections of morality or character (e.g., "I'm too weak to stop drinking" or "I'm too selfish"). At some level, these types of struggles can be framed in general psychological terms as experiences of personal failure or limitation. However, specific religious beliefs or practices might increase anxiety or guilt about moral failings. For example, a negative view of human nature could lead to shame and self-loathing, whereas perfectionistic approaches to religious rules could feed into scrupulosity (e.g., Abramowitz, Huppert, Cohen, Tolin, & Cahill, 2002), with its associated excesses of guilt and anxiety. Such preoccupation with sin may be linked in important ways with frightening beliefs about the afterlife, such as fears of hell (e.g., Exline & Yali, 2006) or, in Eastern traditions, bad karma.

In severe forms, extreme scrupulosity may be a sign of obsessive–compulsive disorder (OCD), which would require specialized treatment. In milder cases, resolving religious shame or guilt might entail working toward acceptance of human imperfection, perhaps by fostering self-forgiveness, humility, or self-compassion. Although there is some research on these topics (for reviews, see J. H. Hall & Fincham, 2005; Wayment & Bauer, 2008), more work is needed on ways to foster these qualities across various belief systems. Within Christianity, for example, it may be appropriate to infuse discussions about sin with attention to the topic of grace (e.g., McMinn, Ruiz, Marx, Wright, & Gilbert, 2006), as shown in a recent intervention study (Ano, 2006).

Spiritual questions and doubts. Struggles can also arise when people try to reconcile their thoughts and beliefs about God or about religious doctrines. Attempts to conserve cherished or long-held beliefs might fail as people are exposed to new ideas or contradictory information. In the wake of negative life events, people may find themselves on an attributional search, asking, "Why?" and finding that their existing meaning systems cannot provide satisfying answers.

Altemeyer and Hunsberger (1997) developed a tool to assess sources of questions or doubts about religion, such as religious teachings (e.g., sex, evolution) and offenses by religious people (e.g., hypocrisy, intolerance). Their work has suggested that religious doubt is a mixed experience in psychological terms: On the bright side, doubt is linked with potentially positive qualities such as openness to experience, complex thinking, and ego identity development. These findings parallel Batson and Schoenrade's (1991a, 1991b) quest orientation to religion, in which doubt and questioning are framed positively. Yet doubt, like other struggles, has been associated with distress (e.g., Krause, Ingersoll-Dayton, Ellison, & Wulff, 1999) and does predict religious disengagement for some individuals (Hunsberger, Pratt, & Pancer, 2002).

One compelling topic for future work involves the interface between cognitive and emotional aspects of doubt. For example, one recent study showed that anger-related struggles with God were greatest for participants who were uncertain about whether God exists (as opposed to being sure about God's existence or nonexistence; M. Webb et al., 2010). More broadly speaking, anger toward God tends to correlate with doubts about God's existence (Exline & Park, 2010). It may be that doubt creates a tenuous relational foundation, which, in turn, makes anger more likely. Anger might promote doubt ("I can't believe that a loving God would do this") or lead to nonbelief as a way to exit the relationship, as captured in Novotni and Petersen's (2001) concept of *emotional atheism*. Consistent with this logic, some atheists and agnostics do report anger focused on the idea of God, especially in reference to past events or hypothetical images of God (e.g., Exline et al., 1999, 2011; see also M. Webb et al., 2010).

Interpersonal Struggles

Some religious struggles focus specifically on interpersonal issues. Many problems fall into this category, ranging from family conflicts to religious wars. Social psychological research on social influence, prejudice, and intergroup dynamics can be helpful in understanding these types of struggles. This section focuses on two broad categories of interpersonal struggle: disagreements about religious issues and offenses committed by members of religious groups.

Disagreements about religious issues. Even when people agree on general beliefs such as the existence of God, they can diverge in many of their specific beliefs. These disagreements can cause stress within families (e.g., Curtis & Ellison, 2002), as when devout members of two faiths try to marry or when a teenager breaks away from the faith of her parents. People who hold minority religious beliefs within a larger group or culture can also face difficulties ranging from teasing and social exclusion to aggression. These can be seen not only as serious social problems but also as sources of personal distress for minority group members, who may experience anxiety, shame, or a sense of stigma. Such issues have been documented among Jews, for example (e.g., Dubow, Pargament, Boxer, & Tarakeshwar, 2000), and among individuals who identify as gay, lesbian, bisexual, and transgender (e.g., Halkitis et al., 2009).

Given that almost any disagreement could cause struggle, how are disagreements about religion unique? One possibility is that because religious beliefs are often central to how people make sense of the world (Park, 2005), clashes on these meaning-laden issues will carry special significance. Also, to the extent that people associate religion with the sacred, they may see all beliefs and practices associated with their religion as sacrosanct. Those who seem to disrespect these sanctified beliefs or practices may thus be seen as committing sacrilege (e.g., Pargament, Magyar, et al., 2005; Pargament, Trevino, Mahoney, & Silberman, 2007). Another factor that could fuel conflict and aggression is the belief that violence has been sanctioned by God—an idea that has received support in laboratory experiments (e.g., Bushman, Ridge, Das, Key, & Busath, 2007). Given the potential volatility of religious disagreements, more research is needed on how individuals and groups can navigate religious disagreements in constructive ways.

Offenses by members of religious groups. Some religious struggles center on offenses committed by religious persons or groups. For example, people may note atrocities that have been committed in God's name or the intolerance shown by certain religious groups. Others report direct harm by religious group members, which can range from negative social interactions within congregations (e.g., Ellison, Krause, Shepherd, & Chaves, 2009; Krause et al., 2000; Krause, Ellison, & Wulff, 1998) to sexual abuse by clergy (e.g., Pargament, Murray-Swank, & Mahoney, 2008; Plante, 2004). These offenses not only cause strife within congregations, but they may also be a reason for people to disengage from religion or to doubt its value (Altemeyer & Hunsberger, 1997). Offenses by religious leaders might be particularly damaging: Not only do these individuals hold positions of authority, but also some are seen as appointed by God or even as representatives of God. Thus, moral offenses by religious leaders might seem to reflect on God.

How can people and religious communities heal from the damage caused by these offenses? Resolution strategies would need to be tailored to the specific problem (e.g., trauma work in abuse cases, conflict resolution, pastoral restoration, forgiveness). Regardless of the exact offense, some people may benefit from focusing on the idea of universal human limitation: No matter how devout and well-intentioned people might be, the inevitable flaws and shortcomings of human nature may prevent us from being perfect representatives of the sacred.

Struggles Related to Perceptions of Supernatural Evil

Some people also experience struggles related to belief in supernatural evil forces, such as the devil or evil spirits (for details, see Exline & Rose, 2005, in press). Studies have shown that demonic appraisals for negative events such as divorce are quite common (Krumrei et al., 2011). Such appraisals typically correlate with other struggle indicators and adjustment difficulties (e.g., Pargament et al., 2000, 2001; Pargament, Smith, et al., 1998). Yet attributing negative events to the devil could serve a defensive function by helping individuals to preserve a positive view of God (e.g., Beck & Taylor, 2008). Some people might find a personification of evil to be preferable to the idea of a completely capricious, impersonal universe in which negative events are attributed entirely to chance or natural laws.

CONCLUSIONS AND FUTURE DIRECTIONS

This chapter has provided an overview of empirical research on religious and spiritual struggle, a literature that has more than doubled since the last reviews were written (Ano & Vasconcelles, 2005; Exline & Rose, 2005; Pargament, Murray-Swank, et al., 2005). Most of this literature has focused on associations between struggle (often framed as negative religious coping), distress, and health. Many studies now document links between struggle and distress, and a growing number show links with physical outcomes. Several longitudinal studies also clarify that struggles—particularly chronic ones—predict later declines in emotional and physical health.

Where might the field go from here? In terms of the religion–health link, it now seems prudent to move beyond cross-sectional, correlational studies to continue the trends toward more sophisticated measures: longitudinal designs, use of biomarkers, and evaluation of psychological mediators. It would be useful to learn more about whether certain types of religious and spiritual struggles are especially strong predictors of distress or illness. In addition, the possibility that religious and spiritual struggle might lead to growth under some conditions is a compelling but difficult question, one that has received little attention to date. Complex and sometimes contradictory findings on this topic point to the need for more research to clarify the conditions under which struggles lead to growth versus decline (Pargament et al., 2006).

Although research linking religious or spiritual struggle with mental and physical health has been fruitful, a narrow focus on health outcomes runs the risk of diverting attention from other important facets of struggle. To provide precise conceptualization and better integration with other theoretical work, a useful next step may be to focus more attention on specific types of struggles: what they entail, how they develop, and how they can be resolved. While digging more deeply into conceptual questions about struggles and their resolution (see Volume 2, Chapters 4 and 17, this handbook), social scientists should try to glean from the wisdom of others who wrestle with these issues on a regular basis: theologians, philosophers, clergy, educators, pastoral counselors, chaplains, and spiritual directors, to name a few. Although psychologists have much to contribute, we also have much to learn, particularly given our status as relative newcomers to this conversation. Over the long term, our ability to make meaningful and lasting contributions to science and society may depend on our ability to step outside the confines of our profession and see ourselves as part of a bigger picture—both historically and in terms of interdisciplinary dialogue.

References

Abel, E. A. (2009). *Religious coping and nonreligious coping in Jewish adults who have had cardiac surgery.* Unpublished doctoral dissertation, Adelphi University, Garden City, NY.

Abramowitz, J. S., Huppert, J. D., Cohen, A. B., Tolin, D. F., & Cahill, S. P. (2002). Religious obsessions and compulsions in a non-clinical sample: The Penn Inventory of Scrupulosity (PIOS). *Behaviour Research and Therapy, 40,* 825–838. doi:10.1016/S0005-7967(01)00070-5

Ai, A. L., Pargament, K., Kronfol, Z., Tice, T. N., & Appel, H. (2010). Pathways to postoperative hostility in cardiac patients: Mediation of coping, spiritual struggle and interleukin-6. *Journal of Health Psychology, 15,* 186–195. doi:10.1177/1359105309345556

Ai, A. L., Park, C. L., Huang, B., Rodgers, W., & Tice, T. N. (2007). Psychosocial mediation of religious coping styles: A study of short-term psychological distress following cardiac surgery. *Personality and Social Psychology Bulletin, 33,* 867–882. doi:10.1177/0146167207301008

Ai, A. L., Seymour, E. M., Tice, T. N., Qatar, K. Z., & Bolling, S. F. (2009). Spiritual struggle related to plasma interleukin-6 prior to cardiac surgery. *Psychology of Religion and Spirituality, 1,* 112–128. doi:10.1037/a0015775

Altemeyer, B., & Hunsberger, B. (1997). *Amazing conversions: Why some turn to faith and others abandon religion.* Amherst, NY: Prometheus.

Ano, G. G. (2006). *Spiritual struggles between vice and virtue: A brief psychospiritual intervention.* Unpublished doctoral dissertation, Bowling Green State University, Bowling Green, OH.

Ano, G. G., & Pargament, K. I. (2003). *Predictors of spiritual struggles: An exploratory study.* Unpublished manuscript, Bowling Green State University, Bowling Green, OH.

Ano, G. G., & Vasconcelles, E. B. (2005). Religious coping and psychological adjustment to stress: A meta-analysis. *Journal of Clinical Psychology, 61,* 461–480. doi:10.1002/jclp.20049

Batson, C. D., & Schoenrade, P. A. (1991a). Measuring religion as Quest: I. Validity concerns. *Journal for the Scientific Study of Religion, 30,* 416–429. doi:10.2307/1387277

Batson, C. D., & Schoenrade, P. A. (1991b). Measuring religion as Quest: II. Reliability concerns. *Journal for the Scientific Study of Religion, 30,* 430–447. doi:10.2307/1387278

Beck, R. (2006). Communion and complaint: Attachment, object-relations, and triangular love perspectives on relationship with God. *Journal of Psychology and Theology, 34,* 43–52.

Beck, R. (2007). The winter experience of faith: Empirical, theological, and theoretical perspectives. *Journal of Psychology and Christianity, 26,* 68–78.

Beck, R., & McDonald, A. (2004). Attachment to God: The Attachment to God Inventory, tests of working model correspondence, and an exploration of faith group differences. *Journal of Psychology and Theology, 32,* 92–103.

Beck, R., & Taylor, S. (2008). The emotional burden of monotheism: Satan, theodicy, and relationship with God. *Journal of Psychology and Theology, 36,* 151–160.

Belavich, T. G., & Pargament, K. I. (2002). The role of attachment in predicting spiritual coping with a loved one in surgery. *Journal of Adult Development, 9,* 13–29. doi:10.1023/A:1013873100466

Benore, E., Pargament, K. I., & Pendleton, S. (2008). An initial examination of religious coping in children with asthma. *The International Journal for the Psychology of Religion, 18,* 267–290. doi:10.1080/10508610802229197

Berg, G. E. (1994). The use of the computer as a tool for assessment and research in pastoral care. *Journal of Health Care Chaplaincy, 6,* 11–25. doi:10.1300/J080v06n01_03

Bjorck, J. P., & Thurman, J. W. (2007). Negative life events, patterns of positive and negative religious coping, and psychological functioning. *Journal for the Scientific Study of Religion, 46,* 159–167. doi:10.1111/j.1468-5906.2007.00348.x

Boscaglia, N., Clarke, D. M., Jobling, T. W., & Quinn, M. A. (2005). The contribution of spirituality and spiritual coping to anxiety and depression in women with a recent diagnosis of gynecological cancer. *International Journal of Gynecological Cancer, 15,* 755–761. doi:10.1111/j.1525-1438.2005.00248.x

Bosworth, H. B., Park, K-S., McQuoid, D. R., Hays, J. C., & Steffens, D. C. (2003). The impact of religious practice and religious coping on geriatric depression. *International Journal of Geriatric Psychiatry, 18,* 905–914. doi:10.1002/gps.945

Bowman, E. S., Beitman, J. A., Palesh, O., Prez, J. E., & Koopman, C. (2009). The Cancer and Deity Questionnaire: A new religion and cancer measure. *Journal of Psychosocial Oncology, 27,* 435–453. doi:10.1080/07347330903181913

Bradley, R., Schwartz, A. C., & Kaslow, N. J. (2005). Posttraumatic stress disorder symptoms among low-income, African American women with a history of intimate partner violence and suicidal behaviors: Self-esteem, social support, and religious coping. *Journal of Traumatic Stress, 18,* 685–696. doi:10.1002/jts.20077

Bryant, A. N., & Astin, H. S. (2008). The correlates of spiritual struggle during the college years. *Journal of Higher Education, 79,* 1–27. doi:10.1353/jhe.2008.0000

Burker, E. J., Evon, D. M., Sedway, J. A., & Egan, T. (2005). Religious and non-religious coping in lung transplant candidates: Does adding God to the picture tell us more? *Journal of Behavioral Medicine, 28,* 513–526. doi:10.1007/s10865-005-9025-4

Bushman, B. J., Ridge, R. D., Das, E., Key, C. W., & Busath, G. L. (2007). When God sanctions killing: Effects of scriptural violence on aggression. *Psychological Science, 18,* 204–207. doi:10.1111/j.1467-9280.2007.01873.x

Butter, E. M. (2004). *Emotion as a mediator between religious coping and adjustment among parents of children with autistic disorder.* Unpublished doctoral dissertation, Bowling Green State University, Bowling Green, OH.

Calhoun, L. G., & Tedeschi, R. G. (Eds.). (2006). *Handbook of posttraumatic growth: Research and practice.* Mahwah, NJ: Erlbaum.

Cole, B. S., Hopkins, C. M., Tisak, J., Steel, J. L., & Carr, B. I. (2008). Assessing spiritual growth and spiritual decline following a diagnosis of cancer: Reliability and validity of the Spiritual Transformation Scale. *Psycho-Oncology, 17,* 112–121. doi:10.1002/pon.1207

Conners, N. A., Whiteside-Mansell, L., & Sherman, A. C. (2006). Dimensions of religious involvement and mental health outcomes among alcohol- and drug-dependent women. *Alcoholism Treatment Quarterly, 24,* 89–108. doi:10.1300/J020v24n01_06

Cotton, S., Puchalski, C. M., Sherman, S. N., Mrus, J. M., Peterman, A. H., Feinberg, J., . . . Tsevat, J. (2006). Spirituality and religion in patients with HIV/AIDS.

Journal of General Internal Medicine, 21(Suppl. 5), S5–S13. doi:10.1111/j.1525-1497.2006.00642.x

Curtis, K. T., & Ellison, C. G. (2002). Religious heterogamy and marital conflict: Findings from the national survey of families and households. *Journal of Family Issues, 23*, 551–576. doi:10.1177/0192513X02023004005

Dew, R. E., Daniel, S. S., Goldston, D. B., McCall, W. V., Kuchibhatla, M., Schleifer, C., . . . Koenig, H. G. (2010). A prospective study of religion/spirituality and depressive symptoms among adolescent psychiatric patients. *Journal of Affective Disorders, 120*, 149–157. doi:10.1016/j.jad.2009.04.029

Duarte, E. A. (2010). *General religiosity and use of religious coping as predictors of treatment gains for patients with schizophrenia and their relatives.* Unpublished doctoral dissertation, University of Miami, FL.

Dubow, E. F., Pargament, K. I., Boxer, P., & Tarakeshwar, N. (2000). Initial investigation of Jewish early adolescents' ethnic identity, stress, and coping. *Journal of Early Adolescence, 20*, 418–441. doi:10.1177/0272431600020004003

Dumas, J. E., & Nissley-Tsiopinis, J. (2006). Parental global religiousness, sanctification of parenting, and positive and negative religious coping as predictors of parental and child functioning. *The International Journal for the Psychology of Religion, 16*, 289–310. doi:10.1207/s15327582ijpr1604_4

Edmondson, D., Park, C. L., Chaudoir, S. R., & Wortmann, J. H. (2008). Death without God: Religious struggle, death concerns, and depression in the terminally ill. *Psychological Science, 19*, 754–758. doi:10.1111/j.1467-9280.2008.02152.x

Ellison, C. G., Krause, N. M., Shepherd, B. C., & Chaves, M. A. (2009). Size, conflict, and opportunities for interaction: Congregational effects on members' anticipated support and negative interaction. *Journal for the Scientific Study of Religion, 48*, 1–15. doi:10.1111/j.1468-5906.2009.01426.x

Ellison, C. G., & Lee, J. (2010). Spiritual struggles and psychological distress: Is there a dark side of religion? *Social Indicators Research, 98*, 501–517. doi:10.1007/s11205-009-9553-3

Exline, J. J. (2002). Stumbling blocks on the religious road: Fractured relationships, nagging vices, and the inner struggle to believe. *Psychological Inquiry, 13*, 182–189. doi:10.1207/S15327965PLI1303_03

Exline, J. J. (2012) The flame of love as a refining fire: Gifts of spiritual struggle. In M. T. Lee & A. Yong (Eds.) *Godly love: Impediments and possibilities* (pp. 57–74). Lanham, MD: Lexington Books.

Exline, J. J., & Bright, D. S. (2011). Spiritual struggles in the workplace. *Journal of Management, Spirituality, and Religion, 8*, 123–142. doi:10.1080/14766086.2011.581812

Exline, J. J., & Grubbs, J. (2011). *"If I tell others about my anger toward God, how will they respond?" Predictors, associated behaviors, and outcomes in an adult sample.* Manuscript submitted for publication.

Exline, J. J., Kaplan, K. J., & Grubbs, J. B. (2012, March 19). Anger, exit, and assertion: Do people see protest toward God as morally acceptable? *Psychology of Religion and Spirituality*. Advance online publication. doi: 10.1037/a0027667

Exline, J. J., & Martin, A. (2005). Anger toward God: A new frontier in forgiveness research. In E. L. Worthington Jr. (Ed.), *Handbook of forgiveness* (pp. 73–88). New York, NY: Routledge.

Exline, J. J., & Park, C. L. (2010). *Anger toward God and doubts about God's existence.* Manuscript in preparation.

Exline, J. J., Park, C. L., Smyth, J. M., & Carey, M. P. (2011). Anger toward God: Social–cognitive predictors, prevalence, and links with adjustment to bereavement and cancer. *Journal of Personality and Social Psychology, 100*, 129–148. doi:10.1037/a0021716

Exline, J. J., & Rose, E. (2005). Religious and spiritual struggles. In R. F. Paloutzian & C. L. Park (Eds.), *Handbook of the psychology of religion and spirituality* (pp. 315–330). New York, NY: Guilford Press.

Exline, J. J., & Rose, E. D. (in press). Religious and spiritual struggles. In R. F. Paloutzian & C. L. Park (Eds.), *Handbook of the psychology of religion and spirituality* (2nd ed.). New York, NY: Guilford Press.

Exline, J. J., Yali, A. M., & Lobel, M. (1999). When God disappoints: Difficulty forgiving God and its role in negative emotion. *Journal of Health Psychology, 4*, 365–379. doi:10.1177/135910539900400306

Exline, J. J., Yali, A. M., & Sanderson, W. C. (2000). Guilt, discord, and alienation: The role of religious strain in depression and suicidality. *Journal of Clinical Psychology, 56*, 1481–1496. doi:10.1002/1097-4679(200012)56:12<1481::AID-1>3.0.CO;2-A

Exline, J. J., & Yali, A. Y. (2006). Heaven's gates and hell's flames: Afterlife beliefs of Catholic and Protestant undergraduates. *Research in the Social Scientific Study of Religion, 17*, 235–260.

Fallot, R. D., & Heckman, J. P. (2005). Religious/spiritual coping among women trauma survivors with mental health and substance use disorders. *Journal of Behavioral Health Sciences and Research, 32*, 215–226. doi:10.1007/BF02287268

Fitchett, G. (1999a). Screening for spiritual risk. *Chaplaincy Today, 15*(1), 2–12.

Fitchett, G. (1999b). Selected resources for screening for spiritual risk. *Chaplaincy Today, 15*(1), 13–26.

Fitchett, G., Murphy, P. E., Kim, J., Gibbons, J. L., Cameron, J. R., & Davis, J. A. (2004). Religious struggle: Prevalence, correlates and mental health risks in diabetic, congestive heart failure, and oncology patients. *International Journal of Psychiatry in Medicine, 34*, 179–196. doi:10.2190/UCJ9-DP4M-9C0X-835M

Fitchett, G., & Risk, J. L. (2009). Screening for spiritual struggle. *Journal of Pastoral Care and Counseling, 63*(1–2). Retrieved from http://journals.sfu.ca/jpcp/index.php/jpcp/article/view/71/57

Fitchett, G., Rybarczyk, B. D., DeMarco, G. A., & Nicholas, J. J. (1999). The role of religion in medical rehabilitation outcomes: A longitudinal study. *Rehabilitation Psychology, 44*, 333–353. doi:10.1037/0090-5550.44.4.333

Funk, R. A. (1958). Experimental scales used in a study of religious attitudes as related to manifest anxiety. *Psychological Newsletter, New York University, 9*, 238–244.

Gall, T. L. (2006). Spirituality and coping with life stress among adult survivors of childhood sexual abuse. *Child Abuse and Neglect, 30*, 829–844. doi:10.1016/j.chiabu.2006.01.003

Gall, T. L., de Renart, M., & Boonstra, B. (2000). Religious resources in long-term adjustment to breast cancer. *Journal of Psychosocial Oncology, 18*, 21–37. doi:10.1300/J077v18n02_02

Gall, T. L., Kristjansson, E., Charbonneau, C., & Florack, P. (2009). A longitudinal study on the role of spirituality in response to the diagnosis and treatment of breast cancer. *Journal of Behavioral Medicine, 32*, 174–186. doi:10.1007/s10865-008-9182-3

Greenway, A. P., Milne, L. C., & Clarke, V. (2003). Personality variables, self-esteem and depression in an individual's perception of God. *Mental Health, Religion, and Culture, 6*, 45–58. doi:10.1080/1867467021000029381

Halkitis, P. N., Mattis, J. S., Sahadath, J. K., Massie, D., Ladyzhenskaya, L., Pitrelli, K., . . . Cowie, S. E. (2009). The meanings and manifestations of religion and spirituality among lesbian, gay, bisexual, and transgender adults. *Journal of Adult Development, 16*, 250–262. doi:10.1007/s10804-009-9071-1

Hall, J. H., & Fincham, F. D. (2005). Self-forgiveness: The stepchild of forgiveness research. *Journal of Social and Clinical Psychology, 24*, 621–637. doi:10.1521/jscp.2005.24.5.621

Hall, T. W., & Edwards, K. J. (1996). The initial development and factor analysis of the spiritual assessment inventory. *Journal of Psychology and Theology, 24*, 233–246.

Hall, T. W., & Edwards, K. J. (2002). The spiritual assessment inventory: A theistic model and measure for assessing spiritual development. *Journal for the Scientific Study of Religion, 41*, 341–357. doi:10.1111/1468-5906.00121

Harris, J. I., Erbes, C. R., Engdahl, B. E., Olson, R. H. A., Winskowski, A. M., & McMahill, J. (2008). Christian religious functioning and trauma outcomes. *Journal of Clinical Psychology, 64*, 17–29. doi:10.1002/jclp.20427

Hays, J. C., Meador, K. G., Branch, P. S., & George, L. K. (2001). The Spiritual History Scale in four dimensions (SHS-4): Validity and reliability. *The Gerontologist, 41*, 239–249. doi:10.1093/geront/41.2.239

Hebert, R., Zdaniuk, B., Schulz, R., & Scheier, M. (2009). Positive and negative religious coping and well-being in women with breast cancer. *Journal of Palliative Medicine, 12*, 537–545. doi:10.1089/jpm.2008.0250

Herrera, A. P., Lee, J. W., Nanyonjo, R. D., Laufman, L. E., & Torres-Vigil, I. (2009). Religious coping and caregiver well-being in Mexican-American families. *Aging and Mental Health, 13*, 84–91. doi:10.1080/13607860802154507

Hills, J., Paice, J. A., Cameron, J. R., & Shott, S. (2005). Spirituality and distress in palliative care consultation. *Journal of Palliative Medicine, 8*, 782–788. doi:10.1089/jpm.2005.8.782

Hunsberger, B., Pratt, M., & Pancer, S. M. (2002). A longitudinal study of religious doubts in high school and beyond: Relationships, stability, and searching for answers. *Journal for the Scientific Study of Religion, 41*, 255–266. doi:10.1111/1468-5906.00115

Johnson, C. V., & Hayes, J. A. (2003). Troubled spirits: Prevalence and predictors of religious and spiritual concerns among university students and counseling center clients. *Journal of Counseling Psychology, 50*, 409–419. doi:10.1037/0022-0167.50.4.409

Johnson, T. J., Sheets, V. L., & Kristeller, J. L. (2008). Identifying mediators of the relationship between religiousness/spirituality and alcohol use. *Journal of Studies on Alcohol and Drugs, 69*, 160–170.

Khan, Z. H., Sultana, S., & Watson, P. J. (2009). Pakistani Muslims dealing with cancer: Relationships with religious coping, religious orientation, and psychological distress. *Research in the Social Scientific Study of Religion, 20*, 218–237.

Kim, K. H. (2006). Religion, body satisfaction, and dieting. *Appetite, 46*, 285–296. doi:10.1016/j.appet.2006.01.006

Kirkpatrick, L. A. (2004). *Attachment, evolution, and the psychology of religion.* New York, NY: Guilford Press.

Koenig, H. G., Pargament, K. I., & Nielsen, J. (1998). Religious coping and health status in medically ill hospitalized older adults. *Journal of Nervous and Mental Disease, 186*, 513–521. doi:10.1097/00005053-199809000-00001

Krause, N., Chatters, L. M., Meltzer, T., & Morgan, D. L. (2000). Negative interaction in the church: Insights from focus groups with older adults. *Review of Religious Research, 41*, 510–533. doi:10.2307/3512318

Krause, N., Ellison, C. G., & Wulff, K. M. (1998). Church-based support, negative interaction, and psychological well-being: Findings from a national sample of Presbyterians. *Journal for the Scientific Study of Religion, 37*, 725–741. doi:10.2307/1388153

Krause, N., Ingersoll-Dayton, B., Ellison, C. G., & Wulff, K. M. (1999). Aging, religious doubt, and psychological well-being. *The Gerontologist, 39*, 525–533. doi:10.1093/geront/39.5.525

Krumrei, E. J., Mahoney, A., & Pargament, K. I. (2009). Divorce and the divine: The role of spiritual appraisals, coping, and struggles for adults' post-divorce adjustment. *Journal of Marriage and Family, 71*, 373–383. doi:10.1111/j.1741-3737.2009.00605.x

Krumrei, E. J., Mahoney, A., & Pargament, K. I. (2011). Demonization as a spiritual struggle with divorce: Prevalence rates and links to post-divorce adjustment. *Family Relations, 60*, 90–103.

Kudel, I., Farber, S. L., Mrus, J. M., Leonard, A. C., Sherman, S. N., & Tsevat, J. (2006). Patterns of responses on health-related quality of life questionnaires among patients with HIV/AIDS. *Journal of General Internal Medicine, 21*, S48–S55. doi:10.1111/j.1525-1497.2006.00645.x

Manning-Walsh, J. (2005). Spiritual struggle: Effect on quality of life and life satisfaction in women with breast cancer. *Journal of Holistic Nursing, 23*, 120–140. doi:10.1177/0898010104272019

Marty, M. E. (1997). *A cry of absence: Reflections for the winter of the heart.* Grand Rapids, MI: Eerdmans.

McConnell, K. M., Pargament, K. I., Ellison, C. G., & Flannelly, K. J. (2006). Examining the links between spiritual struggles and symptoms of psychopathology in a national sample. *Journal of Clinical Psychology, 62*, 1469–1484. doi:10.1002/jclp.20325

McMinn, M. R., Ruiz, J. N., Marx, D., Wright, J. B., & Gilbert, N. (2006). Professional psychology and doctrines of sin and grace: Christian leaders' perspectives. *Professional Psychology: Research and Practice, 37*, 295–302. doi:10.1037/0735-7028.37.3.295

Moriarty, G., & Hoffman, M. (Eds.). (2007). *God image handbook for spiritual counseling and psychotherapy: Research, theory, and practice.* Philadelphia, PA: Haworth Press.

Murray-Swank, N. A., & Pargament, K. I. (2008). Solace for the soul: Evaluating a spiritually-integrated counseling intervention for sexual abuse. *Counselling and Spirituality, 27*, 157–174.

Novotni, M., & Petersen, R. (2001). *Angry with God.* Colorado Springs, CO: Piñon.

Parenteau, S. C. (2009). *The mediating role of secular coping strategies in the relationship between religious beliefs and adjustment to chronic pain: The middle road to Damascus.* Unpublished doctoral dissertation, University of Kansas, Lawrence.

Pargament, K. I. (1997). *The psychology of religion and coping.* New York, NY: Guilford Press.

Pargament, K. I. (2002). The bitter and the sweet: An evaluation of the costs and benefits of religiousness. *Psychological Inquiry, 13*, 168–181. doi:10.1207/S15327965PLI1303_02

Pargament, K. I. (2007). *Spiritually integrated psychotherapy: Understanding and addressing the sacred.* New York, NY: Guilford Press.

Pargament, K. I., Desai, K. M., & McConnell, K. M. (2006). Spirituality: A pathway to posttraumatic growth or decline? In L. G. Calhoun & R. G. Tedeschi (Eds.), *Handbook of posttraumatic growth: Research and practice* (pp. 121–137). Mahwah, NJ: Erlbaum.

Pargament, K. I., Koenig, H. G., & Perez, L. M. (2000). The many methods of religious coping: Development and initial validation of the RCOPE. *Journal of Clinical Psychology, 56*, 519–543. doi:10.1002/(SICI)1097-4679(200004)56:4<519::AID-JCLP6>3.0.CO;2-1

Pargament, K. I., Koenig, H. G., Tarakeshwar, N., & Hahn, J. (2001). Religious struggle as a predictor of mortality among medically ill elderly patients: A two-year longitudinal study. *Archives of Internal Medicine, 161*, 1881–1885. doi:10.1001/archinte.161.15.1881

Pargament, K. I., Koenig, H. G., Tarakeshwar, N., & Hahn, J. (2004). Religious coping methods as predictors of psychological, physical and spiritual outcomes among medically ill elderly patients: A two-year longitudinal study. *Journal of Health Psychology, 9*, 713–730. doi:10.1177/1359105304045366

Pargament, K. I., Magyar, G. M., Benore, E., & Mahoney, A. (2005). Sacrilege: A study of sacred loss and desecration and their implications for health and well-being in a community sample. *Journal for the Scientific Study of Religion, 44*, 59–78. doi:10.1111/j.1468-5906.2005.00265.x

Pargament, K. I., Murray-Swank, N., Magyar, G. M., & Ano, G. G. (2005). Spiritual struggle: A phenomenon of interest to psychology and religion. In W. R. Miller & H. Delaney (Eds.), *Judeo-Christian perspectives on psychology: Human nature, motivation, and change* (pp. 245–268). Washington, DC: American Psychological Association. doi:10.1037/10859-013

Pargament, K. I., Murray-Swank, N., & Mahoney, A. (2008). Problem and solution: The spiritual dimension of clergy sexual abuse and its impact on survivors. *Journal of Child Sexual Abuse, 17*, 397–420. doi:10.1080/10538710802330187

Pargament, K. I., Smith, B. W., Koenig, H. G., & Perez, L. (1998). Patterns of positive and negative religious coping with major life stressors. *Journal for the Scientific Study of Religion, 37*, 710–724. doi:10.2307/1388152

Pargament, K. I., Trevino, K., Mahoney, A., & Silberman, I. (2007). They killed our Lord: The perception of Jews as desecrators of Christianity as a predictor of anti-Semitism. *Journal for the Scientific Study of Religion, 46*, 143–158. doi:10.1111/j.1468-5906.2007.00347.x

Pargament, K. I., Zinnbauer, B. J., Scott, A. B., Butter, E. M., Zerowin, J., & Stanik, P. (1998). Red flags and religious coping: Identifying some religious warning signs among people in crisis. *Journal of Clinical Psychology, 54*, 77–89. doi:10.1002/(SICI)1097-4679(199801)54:1<77::AID-JCLP9>3.0.CO;2-R

Park, C. L. (2005). Religion and meaning. In R. F. Paloutzian & C. L. Park (Eds.), *Handbook of the psychology of religion and spirituality* (pp. 295–314). New York, NY: Guilford Press.

Park, C. L. (2008). Estimated longevity and changes in spirituality in the context of advanced congestive heart failure. *Palliative and Supportive Care, 6*, 3–11. doi:10.1017/S1478951508000023

Park, C. L., Brooks, M. A., & Sussman, J. (2009). Dimensions of religion and spirituality in psychological adjustment of older adults living with congestive heart failure. In A. L. Ai & M. Ardelt (Eds.), *Faith and well-being in later life* (pp. 41–58). Hauppauge, NY: Nova Science.

Pearce, M. J., Singer, J. L., & Prigerson, H. G. (2006). Religious coping among caregivers of terminally ill cancer patients: Main effects and psychosocial mediators. *Journal of Health Psychology, 11*, 743–759. doi:10.1177/1359105306066629

Phillips, R. E., III, Cheng, C. M., Pargament, K. I., Oemig, C., Colvin, S. D., Abarr, A. N., . . . Reed, A. S. (in press). Spiritual coping in American Buddhists: An exploratory study. *The International Journal for the Psychology of Religion.*

Phillips, R. E., III, & Stein, C. H. (2007). God's will, God's punishment, or God's limitations? Religious coping strategies reported by young adults living with serious mental illness. *Journal of Clinical Psychology, 63*, 529–540. doi:10.1002/jclp.20364

Pirutinsky, S., Rosmarin, D. H., Pargament, K. I., & Midlarsky, E. (in press). Does negative religious coping accompany, precede, or follow depression among Orthodox Jews? *Journal of Affective Disorders.*

Plante, T. G. (Ed.). (2004). *Sin against the innocents: Sexual abuse by priests and the role of the Catholic Church.* Westport, CT: Praeger.

Raiya, H. A., Pargament, K. I., Mahoney, A., & Stein, C. (2008). A psychological measure of Islamic religiousness: Development and evidence for reliability and validity. *The International Journal for the Psychology of Religion, 18*, 291–315. doi:10.1080/10508610802229270

Rippentrop, A. E., Altmaier, E. M., Chen, J. J., Found, E. M., & Keffala, V. J. (2005). The relationship between religion/spirituality and physical health, mental health, and pain in a chronic pain population. *Pain, 116*, 311–321. doi:10.1016/j.pain.2005.05.008

Rosmarin, D. H., Krumrei, E. J., & Andersson, G. (2009). Religion as a predictor of psychological distress in two religious communities. *Cognitive Behaviour Therapy, 38*, 54–64. doi:10.1080/16506070802477222

Rosmarin, D. H., Pargament, K. I., & Flannelly, K. J. (2009). Do spiritual struggles predict poorer physical/mental health among Jews? *The International Journal for the Psychology of Religion, 19*, 244–258. doi:10.1080/10508610903143503

Rosmarin, D. H., Pargament, K. I., Krumrei, E. J., & Flannelly, K. J. (2009). Religious coping among Jews: Development and initial validation of the JCOPE. *Journal of Clinical Psychology, 65*, 670–683. doi:10.1002/jclp.20574

Rosmarin, D. H., Pirutinsky, S., Pargament, K. I., & Krumrei, E. J. (2009). Are religious beliefs relevant to mental health among Jews? *Psychology of Religion and Spirituality, 1*, 180–190. doi:10.1037/a0016728

Rowatt, W. C., & Kirkpatrick, L. A. (2002). Two dimensions of attachment to God and their relation to affect, religiosity, and personality constructs. *Journal for the Scientific Study of Religion, 41*, 637–651. doi:10.1111/1468-5906.00143

Sandage, S. J., Jankowski, P. J., & Link, D. C. (2010). Quest and spiritual development moderated by spiritual transformation. *Journal of Psychology and Theology, 38*, 15–31.

Sandage, S. J., & Moe, S. P. (2011). Narcissism and spirituality. In W. K. Campbell & J. Miller (Eds.), *The handbook of narcissism and narcissistic personality disorder: Theoretical approaches, empirical findings, and treatment* (pp. 410–419). New York, NY: Wiley.

Schottenbauer, M. A., Rodriguez, B. F., Glass, C. R., & Arnkoff, D. B. (2006). Religious coping research and contemporary personality theory: An exploration of Endler's (1997). integrative personality theory. *British Journal of Social Psychology, 97*, 499–519. doi:10.1348/000712606X97840

Sherman, A. C., Plante, T. G., Simonton, S., Latif, U., & Anaissie, E. J. (2009). Prospective study of religious coping among patients undergoing autologous stem cell transplantation. *Journal of Behavioral Medicine, 32*, 118–128. doi:10.1007/s10865-008-9179-y

Sherman, A. C., Simonton, S., Latif, U., Spohn, R., & Tricot, G. (2005). Religious struggle and religious comfort in response to illness: Health outcomes among stem cell transplant patients. *Journal of Behavioral Medicine, 28*, 359–367. doi:10.1007/s10865-005-9006-7

Smith, B. W., Pargament, K. I., Brant, C., & Oliver, J. M. (2000). Noah revisited: Religious coping by church members and the impact of the 1993 Midwest flood. *Journal of Community Psychology, 28*, 169–186. doi:10.1002/(SICI)1520-6629(200003)28:2<169::AID-JCOP5>3.0.CO;2-I

Smith, T. B., McCullough, M. E., & Poll, J. (2003). Religiousness and depression: Evidence for a main effect and the moderating influence of stressful life events. *Psychological Bulletin, 129*, 614–636. doi:10.1037/0033-2909.129.4.614

Strelan, P., Acton, C., & Patrick, K. (2009). Disappointment with God and well-being: The mediating influence of relationship quality and dispositional forgiveness. *Counseling and Values, 53*, 202–213. doi:10.1002/j.2161-007X.2009.tb00126.x

Szewczyk, L. S., & Weinmuller, E. B. (2006). Religious aspects of coping with stress among adolescents from families with alcohol problems. *Mental Health, Religion, and Culture, 9*, 389–400. doi:10.1080/13694670500212182

Tallon, A. (2008). Christianity. In J. Corrigan (Ed.), *The Oxford handbook of religion and emotion* (pp. 111–124). New York, NY: Oxford University Press.

Tarakeshwar, N., Pargament, K. I., & Mahoney, A. (2003). Initial development of a measure of religious coping among Hindus. *Journal of Community Psychology, 31*, 607–628. doi:10.1002/jcop.10071

Tarakeshwar, N., Vanderwerker, L. C., Paulk, E., Pearce, M. J., Kasl, S. V., & Prigerson, H. G. (2006). Religious coping is associated with the quality of life of patients with advanced cancer. *Journal of Palliative Medicine, 9*, 646–657. doi:10.1089/jpm.2006.9.646

Thuné-Boyle, I. C., Stygall, J. A., Keshtgar, M. R., & Newman, S. P. (2006). Do religious/spiritual coping strategies affect illness adjustment in patients with cancer? A systematic review of the literature. *Social Science and Medicine, 63*, 151–164. doi:10.1016/j.socscimed.2005.11.055

Toussaint, L. L., & Williams, D. R. (2008). National survey results for Protestant, Catholic, and nonreligious experiences of seeking forgiveness and of forgiveness of self, of others, and by God. *Journal of Psychology and Christianity, 27*, 120–130.

Trenholm, P., Trent, J., & Compton, W. C. (1998). Negative religious conflict as a predictor of panic disorder. *Journal of Clinical Psychology, 54*, 59–65. doi:10.1002/(SICI)1097-4679(199801)54:1<59::AID-JCLP7>3.0.CO;2-P

Trevino, K. M., Pargament, K. I., Cotton, S., Leonard, A. C., Hahn, J., Caprini-Faigin, C. A., & Tsevat, J. (2010). Religious coping and physiological, psychological, social, and spiritual outcomes in patients with HIV/AIDS: Cross-sectional and longitudinal findings. *AIDS and Behavior, 14*, 379–389. doi:10.1007/s10461-007-9332-6

Warner, H. L., Mahoney, A., & Krumrei, E. J. (2009). When parents break sacred vows: The role of spiritual appraisals, coping, and struggles in young adults' adjustment to parental divorce. *Psychology of Religion and Spirituality, 1*, 233–248. doi:10.1037/a0016787

Wayment, H. A., & Bauer, J. A. (Eds.). (2008). *Transcending self-interest: Psychological explorations of the quiet ego*. Washington, DC: American Psychological Association. doi:10.1037/11771-000

Webb, A. P. (2009). *A religious coping model of divorce adjustment*. Unpublished doctoral dissertation, University of Texas at Austin.

Webb, M., Sink, C. A., McCann, R. A., Chickering, S. A., & Scallon, M. J. (2010). The Suffering With God Scale: Theoretical development, psychometric analyses, and relationships with indices of religiosity. *Research in the Social Scientific Study of Religion, 21*, 71–94.

Witvliet, C. V. O., Phipps, K. A., Feldman, M. E., & Beckham, J. C. (2004). Posttraumatic mental and physical health correlates of forgiveness and religious coping in military veterans. *Journal of Traumatic Stress, 17*, 269–273. doi:10.1023/B:JOTS.0000029270.47848.e5

Wood, B. T., Worthington, E. L., Jr., Exline, J. J., Yali, A. M., Aten, J. D., & McMinn, M. R. (2010). Development, refinement, and psychometric properties of the Attitudes Toward God Scale (ATGS-9). *Psychology of Religion and Spirituality, 2*, 148–167. doi:10.1037/a0018753

Yi, M. S., Mrus, J. M., Wade, T. J., Ho, M. L., Hornung, R. W., Cotton, S., . . . Tsevat, J. (2006). Religion, spirituality, and depressive symptoms in patients with HIV/AIDS. *Journal of General Internal Medicine, 21*(Suppl. 5), S21–S27. doi:10.1111/j.1525-1497.2006.00643.x

Zornow, G. B. (2001). *Crying out to God: Prayer in the midst of suffering*. Unpublished manuscript, Evangelical Lutheran Church in America.

Zwingmann, C., Müller, C., Körber, J., & Murken, S. (2008). Religious commitment, religious coping and anxiety: A study in German patients with breast cancer. *European Journal of Cancer Care, 17*, 361–370. doi:10.1111/j.1365-2354.2007.00867.x

Zwingmann, C., Wirtz, M., Müller, C., Körber, J., & Murken, S. (2006). Positive and negative religious coping in German breast cancer patients. *Journal of Behavioral Medicine, 29*, 533–547. doi:10.1007/s10865-006-9074-3

CHAPTER 26

RELIGION AND EVIL IN THE CONTEXT OF GENOCIDE

James E. Waller

Despite predictions of its demise, religion continues to exert strong influence on a wide range of political, social, and individual phenomena (Fox & Sandler, 2003). Osiander (2000) has argued that religion is a political and psychological cement that binds society together. Similarly, Eisenstadt (1993) maintains that religion is and always has been one of the "premises" of civilization, making it an essential element in political processes and social change. As such, religion is potentially a major source of legitimacy for both the establishment and those who oppose it. At the individual level, Myers (1992) is among many who have demonstrated that people active in faith communities report greater-than-average happiness and often cope well with crisis. Religion is clearly a significant source of cultural meaning, security, and individual and group identity.

Religion, however, also can, in some instances, be the source of the divisions between factions and a major influence on political and social behaviors of exclusion, persecution, conflict, destruction, and terrorism (Juergensmeyer, 1997). As Johnston and Sampson (1994) suggested, since the end of the Cold War, intergroup conflicts have become rooted less in political ideology and more in communal identity—race, ethnicity, nationality, or religion. So, contrary to many predictions (and certainly contrary to the U.S. notion of the rigorous separation of church and state), the role of religion and religious institutions in the life of states and in international affairs is becoming more, rather than less, important in understanding contemporary world politics (for information on religion and terrorism, see Volume 2, Chapter 18, this handbook).

This chapter focuses on religion and evil in the context of a specific form of intergroup conflict—genocide—by exploring three specific interfaces: religion and culture, religion and the "other," and religion and the institutional church. Consistent with this handbook's vision of an "integrative paradigm," this chapter addresses several of the guiding themes underlying the handbook—approaching religion as a multidimensional phenomenon with myriad beliefs, practices, relationships and experiences; analyzing religion at multiple levels (individual, familial, community, and cultural phenomena); and treating religion as a multivalent phenomenon with varying meanings and values. In so doing, and complementing other contributor's chapters, this chapter affirms the volume's "integrative paradigm" of religion as a rich and complex process that can impact people in diverse ways.

DEFINITIONAL CONTEXT

Religion

Reflecting this handbook's commitment to working from a shared perspective on the meanings of religion and spirituality, this chapter uses *religion* or *religiousness* to refer to (a) the beliefs, practices, relationships, or experiences having to do with the sacred that are explicitly and historically rooted in established institutionalized systems and (b) the psychological, social, or physical functions of beliefs, practices, relationships, or experiences

DOI: 10.1037/14045-026
APA Handbook of Psychology, Religion, and Spirituality: Vol. 1. Context, Theory, and Research, K. I. Pargament (Editor-in-Chief)
Copyright © 2013 by the American Psychological Association. All rights reserved.

having to do with the sacred (refer to Chapter 1 in this volume for a more extended discussion about the meaning of these concepts as they are being used in the handbook).

This chapter primarily looks at religion from an institutional rather than theological framework. It approaches religious institutions as real, formal organizations; worldly (as opposed to divine) social structures that govern the behavior of individuals within them. As institutionalized systems, they have a mission and purpose; they shape individual human lives and intentions just as they are, in turn, shaped by human lives and intentions. Religious institutions are birthed by individuals, and it is inappropriate to separate the two. I do not regard religious institutions as an instance of emergence in which they arise beyond, or are transcendent of, the conscious intentions of the individuals involved. Rather, I regard religious institutions as social constructions whose combined effect, in a synergistic relationship, is greater than the sum of their individual effects.

In such an analysis, we cannot, of course, artificially separate religious institutions from their underlying theological frameworks and, in fact, those frameworks (encompassing beliefs, practices, relationships, and experiences) play a significant role in institutional direction and decision making—just as they play a significant role in meeting the psychological, social, or physical needs of individuals. Neither can we disentangle religious institutions from the cultures in which they have been shaped and that they have, in turn, shaped (see Chapter 13 in this volume).

Evil

In virtually every human culture, there has existed some word for "evil," a linguistic acknowledgment of its reality in everyday human affairs. For millennia, the concept of evil was central to religious and much secular thought. Events in the 20th century, particularly two world wars and the horrors of the Holocaust, kept the universal reality of evil on the front pages. Indeed, it was a time in history that led philosopher Hannah Arendt to declare, "The problem of evil will be the fundamental question of postwar intellectual life in Europe" (Kohn, 1994, p. 134). Her prediction, though, was not quite right. For most of the 20th century, evil remained an unpopular concept among intellectuals in Europe—as well as others around the world. As Neiman (2002) pointed out, "No major philosophical work but Arendt's own appeared on the subject [of evil] in English, and German and French texts were remarkably oblique" (p. 2).

Until recently, the concept of evil had almost completely disappeared from the vocabulary of the social sciences that seek to understand the human situation. In 1969, the eminent sociologist Kurt Wolff wrote,

> To my knowledge, no social scientist, as a social scientist, has asked what evil is. "What is evil?" is a question that rather has been raised (both in the West and in the East) by philosophers and theologians, as well as by uncounted, unclassified, unrecorded people since time immemorial. (p. 111)

More than 3 decades later, it appeared that little had changed; a survey of psychology articles written in the previous 10 years found only nine that were pertinent to the concept of evil (Malony, 1998). The prevailing normative picture of humankind held up by the social sciences still portrayed, for the most part, rational creatures who could be expected to relate to and treat fellow humans with basic empathy, kindness, respect, and decency.

More recently, however, there have been signs that the social scientific neglect of evil is beginning to be rectified. For instance, an entire 1999 issue of the *Personality and Social Psychology Review*, the official journal of the Society for Personality and Social Psychology, was devoted to social scientific perspectives on evil and violence. Baumeister's (1999) *Evil: Inside Human Violence and Cruelty* addressed a broad spectrum of interpersonal and intergroup violence, from everyday evil to mass atrocity. A. G. Miller's (2004) edited volume, *The Social Psychology of Good and Evil*, included contributions from prominent social psychologists examining conceptions of good and evil in contemporary social psychology. Zimbardo's (2007) *The Lucifer Effect: Understanding How Good People Turn Evil*, while primarily an exhaustive synopsis of the Stanford Prison Experiment (the first written form in which Zimbardo has revisited the experiment in such detail), extends our understanding of the "power of the situation" to Abu Ghraib while also turning our attention to our abilities to act heroically.

Although "evil" certainly has become a more oft-studied construct, it still presents a definitional and operational challenge. Most would agree that—in its broadest sense—evil is anything detrimental to the well-being of living things. Following that, we can then distinguish between the two most common categories of evil: natural and human (sometimes called *moral*) evil. Natural evil is a function of natural processes of change. It is the evil that originates independently of human actions—events such as earthquakes, tornadoes, floods, fires, pestilence, droughts, and diseases. Human evil, in contrast, is evil that we originate. It refers to the destructive things that we do to each other and ourselves.

This chapter focuses on the specific question of *human evil*—defined as the deliberate harming of humans by other humans (Waller, 2007). This is a behavioral definition that focuses on how people act toward one another. This definition judges as evil any human *actions* leading to the deliberate harming of other humans. In short, harm is the most salient characteristic of human evil, and it is the deliberate intentionality of harm, inflicted with reasonable foreseeable consequences, that is the focus of this chapter.

Believing that there is much to learn about everyday evil from looking at the extremes of human behavior, this chapter specifically focuses on the harm we perpetrate on each other under the sanction of political, social, or religious groups—in other words, the malevolent human evil perpetrated in times of collective social unrest; war; mass killings; and, at its most extreme, genocide. The 20th century saw an unmatched scale of systematic and intentional mass murder coupled with an unprecedented efficiency in the mechanisms and techniques of state-sponsored terrorism, or genocide. All told, it is estimated that 60 million men, women, and children were victims of genocide in the past century alone, and the dawn of the 21st century brings little light to that darkness. A 2009 empirically based risk assessment by the Genocide Prevention Advisory Network, for instance, found highest risks of genocide in Sudan and Burma followed by Somalia. Risks also remain high in Zimbabwe and Rwanda and are greater than previously estimated for Iran, Saudi Arabia, and China (Harff & Gurr, 2009).

RELIGION AND EVIL IN THE CONTEXT OF GENOCIDE: THREE INTERFACES

Myriad historical, social, and cultural influences must be considered in understanding genocidal societies and, although often marginalized in existing scholarship, the role of religion is one such factor in that broad and interconnected array of contextual forces. With that in mind, this chapter will focus on the interface of religion with culture, the "other," and the institutional church in episodes of genocidal violence.

Religion and Culture

All cultures leave their fingerprints on the members within them—most often through the transmission of a worldview. A worldview includes the presuppositions, intentions, meanings, rules, norms, values, principles, practices, and activities through which people live their lives. It is a fundamental orientation that includes the core cultural ideas of what is good, what is moral, and what is the self. As Oyserman and Lauffer (2002) explained, "as cultural beings, we see what it makes sense to see in our local worlds; we make sense of things using a culture-specific scaffolding" (p. 163). In short, a worldview is a cultural construction that frames an individual's perception of his or her social world and, subsequently, influences their actions within that social world.

Psychologists understand the ultimate importance of worldview as deriving from an awareness of our own finitude and mortality. Given our capacity for self-consciousness and abstract symbolic thought, humans are the only animals that know they are to die. The existential concerns (conscious and unconscious) arising from this awareness motivate us to transcend vulnerability, and even death, by investing ourselves in a worldview that gives the world and ourselves larger meaning and value. As conceptualized by *terror management theory* (TMT), and originally articulated by Ernest Becker, the symbolic identities and self-esteem that are secured by identification with a worldview transcend natural physical decay and allow us a measure of control over our own existential terror (see Becker, 1973; Greenberg, Landau, Kosloff, & Solomon, 2009; Pyszczynski, Greenberg, Solomon, Arndt, & Schimel, 2004; Pyszczynski, Rothschild, & Abdollahi, 2008). Understood from this perspective, allegiance to a worldview is one answer to the human problem of mortality. As Routledge, Arndt, and Goldenberg (2004) stated, "Worldviews related to religious and political ideologies, ethics, romance, and a variety of other domains transform a chaotic and unpredictable world of inevitable death into a meaningful world of order and predictability" (p. 1348). In short, TMT theorizes that the ultimate function of any worldview is to serve as a protective anxiety buffer against existential fears inherent exclusively to human beings.

On a more proximal level, cognitive anthropology understands worldview in the rich theoretical context of *cultural models*. As Hinton (1998) described, "cultural models are largely tacit knowledge structures that are both widely shared by and mediate the understanding of the members of a social group" (p. 96). In other words, cultural models give us the background, or lens, through which we interpret our social world and make judgments about appropriate responses. Cultural models are the constituent elements of an encompassing worldview in which culture-specific thoughts, norms, values, codes, and principles become part of an individual's perceptual frame and, in certain situations, may enable the commission of extraordinary evil. Although such models influence, and are influenced by, ecological, economic, and sociopolitical factors, they often persevere despite drastic historical and structural change and are not always confined to prescribed national or territorial boundaries.

Hinton (1998), for example, has explored the contributing role played by cultural models of face, honor, shame, revenge, patronage, paranoia, detachment, and obedience during the Cambodian genocide. He has argued that the vertical structuring of Cambodian society—where people are differentiated in terms of power, status, and patronage—lays the groundwork for a cultural model of obedience to, and respect for, authority. Enculturation to this cultural model of obedience and respect begins at an early age and is reinforced by a wide range of social, political, linguistic, behavioral, and religious conventions. As Hinton pointed out, even though the Khmer Rouge destroyed much of this traditional hierarchical system in Cambodian society, status differences continued to be structured vertically—and with more fixity—in the Communist regime. In this way, the Khmer Rouge was able to tap into a preexisting—and, for many Cambodians, highly salient—cultural model of hierarchically based authority orientation to legitimate their power, goals, social structures of inequality, and even mass murder.

For all of their influence, however, cultural models do not deterministically dictate human thoughts, feelings, and behaviors. For the social group, cultural models vary in their salience and importance between situations and through time. Moreover, people are not always successful at deciphering the prevailing cultural models in a social group. Social psychologists refer to this as *pluralistic ignorance*, the recognition that the beliefs that people perceive and conform to might not accurately reflect the social group's actual beliefs (D. T. Miller & Prentice, 1994). Finally, individuals vary substantially in their motivation to embrace certain cultural models—a model that is highly relevant for some may be regarded with only passing indifference by others. As a result of all of these factors, the cultural construction of a worldview is differentially internalized across individuals within a social group.

Cultural models remain, however, the associative network, or system, underlying the cultural construction of worldview. For many, religion is the part of culture that offers the most explicit answer to the meaning of life and, in so doing, affords us the greatest salve to the anxieties that beset life. At times, religion, in its institutional manifestation, motivates an impulse to heal—as evidenced by its role in the origins of some of our most humane and caring social institutions, its application in liberation theology as seen in the civil rights movement and struggles for human rights in Latin America, and its provision of security to oppose potentially destructive ideas and practices throughout wide swaths of society. At other times, however, institutionalized religion can be a motivating element in the impulse to kill. There is a dark side of religious belief systems that often are fused with ethnic and national identities. In this sense, religion is epiphenomenal—attached to and living off other phenomena.

One of the phenomena to which religion is often attached to, and lives off of, are cultural models of authority orientation. Blass (1991) reviewed research demonstrating that subjects who scored high on a multidimensional measure of Christian religious orientation were more accepting of the commands of an authority than were those who scored lower or were indiscriminately antireligious. Similarly, Altemeyer and Hunsberger (1992) found that children who grow up in fundamentalist families do tend to obey the authorities and follow the rules, but they also tend to be self-righteous, prejudicial, and condemnatory toward people outside their groups.

The trends of this research suggest that religious belief systems emphasizing divine influence and authority may be particularly relevant in shaping our responses to worldly influence and authority. Although the teachings of most religious belief systems are replete with affirmations of the dignity of human life and the responsibilities of human beings to respect and preserve that dignity, there is a wealth of social psychological research suggesting that religious belief systems influence individuals' proneness to prejudice (see Chapter 24 in this volume). Allport and Ross (1967) found that indiscriminately proreligious persons—those who report being both intrinsically and extrinsically religious—"are the most prejudiced of all" (p. 432). More recently, Rowatt, LaBouff, Johnson, Froese, and Tsang (2009), utilizing a large national random sample, found that general religiousness is not associated with universal acceptance of others, but, rather, is associated with a selective intolerance toward those persons perceived to behave in a manner inconsistent with some traditional religious teachings. This more nuanced understanding of the relationship between religious belief systems and prejudice suggests the existence of proscribed (explicitly opposed by an individual's religious group) and nonproscribed (either endorsed or implicitly encouraged) prejudices (see Batson & Stocks, 2009).

The general finding, however, that enduring religious belief systems make us more amenable to the commands of authority also is affirmed by the historical realities surrounding many cases of mass killing and genocide. It was in Rwanda, for instance, that many of the worst massacres occurred in churches and mission compounds where Tutsis had sought refuge. It is very likely that more people were killed in church buildings than anywhere else in Rwanda. From the beginning of the genocide, human rights groups charged that some church leaders from various denominations used their authority to encourage the massacres and join in the killing.

Unfortunately, the reality of such charges are now undisputed as we have a sad litany of well-documented cases. For example, in June 2001, a Belgian court convicted two Benedictine nuns, Sisters Gertrude Mukangango and Julienne Kisito, who were found guilty of having participated in the massacre of more than 7,600 people at the Sovu convent in Butare. Despite the convictions, the Vatican has taken no steps toward excommunicating the nuns and, indeed, a Vatican spokesperson could not understand why the court singled out the two nuns "seeing the grave responsibility of so many [other] people and groups involved" (Hennig, 2001). Rwanda also saw the head of its Roman Catholic Church, Archbishop Thaddee Ntihinyurwa, accused of abetting the murder of Tutsis by ordering at least 600 people out of the Nyamasheke Cathedral in which they sought to seek refuge and into a local stadium, where they were killed. Ntihinyurwa appeared before the Gacaca court in Nyamasheke district in July 2005 and was questioned intensively but has remained as Archbishop of the Kigali Diocese in Rwanda.

An Anglican Bishop, Samuel Musabyimana, was indicted by the International Criminal Tribunal for Rwanda (ICTR) for the crime of genocide, specifically "for killing or causing serious bodily or mental harm to members of the Tutsi population with intent to destroy, in whole or in part, a racial or ethnic group" (a copy of indictment can be found on the ICTR website at http://ictr-archive09.library.cornell.edu/ENGLISH/cases/Musabyimana/indictment/indictment.html). The indictment claims that although Musabyimana publicly stated that he did not oppose the killing of Tutsis, he did not want killings at the diocese and that the Tutsis should be taken to Kabgayi to be killed. The indictment further alleges that Musabyimana participated in, or facilitated, the killings by specifically instructing subordinates to assist soldiers and militias, and by directly or indirectly providing firearms to civilians, under circumstances in which he knew, or should have known, that Tutsi civilians would be killed. Samuel Musabyimana died in detention on January 24, 2003, before the start of his trial.

Religion and the "Other"

The psychological construction of the "other" is pivotal to understanding the development of moral sanctions, or exclusions, that excommunicate "them" from our common social or moral community. The roots of us–them thinking run deep in our human psyche. Human minds are compelled to define the limits of the tribe. Kinship, however defined, remains an important organizing principle for most societies in the world. Knowing who is kin, and knowing who is in our social group, has a deep importance to species like ours. We construct this knowledge by categorizing others as "us" or "them," a tendency that many scholars have called one of the few true human universals. Once these boundaries are established, we tend to be partial toward "us" and label "them"—those with whom "we" share the fewest genes and least culture—as enemies. We have an evolved capacity to see our group as superior to all others and even to be reluctant to recognize members of other groups as deserving of equal respect.

Ethnocentrism and xenophobia are two complementary psychological adaptations that are central to understanding this process. First, *ethnocentrism* refers to the tendency to focus on one's own group as the "right" one. Sumner (1906) first coined this term and defined it as

> a differentiation that arises between ourselves, the we-group, or in-group, and everybody else, or the others-group, out-groups. The insiders in a we-group are in a relation of peace, order, law, government, and industry to each other. . . . Ethnocentrism is the technical name for this view of things in which one's own group is the center of everything, and all others are scaled and rated with reference to it. . . . Each group nourishes its own pride and vanity, boasts itself superior, exalts its own divinities, and looks with contempt on outsiders. (pp. 12–13)

Ethnocentrism is a universal characteristic of human social life and, as often as not, it is fairly harmless. From an evolutionary perspective, there is an advantageous reinforcement of communal identity and "we-ness" when groups consider their ideas, their cultures, their religions, or their aesthetic standards to be either superior to others, or at least in certain ways to be preferential or noteworthy in comparison to other groups. As Hinde (1989) wrote, "It is not unreasonable to entertain the possibility that natural selection acted on individuals to enhance this identification with groups and to augment the (real or perceived) superiority of the group with which they identified" (p. 60).

Ethnocentric loyalties show themselves early in life. The importance of both the caretaker–infant bonds and stranger anxiety reactions of the first year of life demonstrate a universality of the us–them differentiation process. Experimental social psychologists have even demonstrated that classifying individuals into *arbitrary* groups in the laboratory (for example, forming groups on the basis of a coin toss or musical preferences) can elicit ethnocentric reactions (see Tajfel & Turner, 1979). Other recent social psychological experimental evidence suggests that the concepts "us" and "them" carry positive emotional significance that is activated automatically and unconsciously (Leyens et al., 2000). Once identified with a group—even in the complete *absence* of any links, kinship or otherwise, among individuals in that group—individuals find it easy to exaggerate differences between their group and others.

Included with ethnocentrism is a second universal adaptation—*xenophobia*, the complementary tendency to fear outsiders or strangers. It can even be said that in forming bonds we deepen fissures. In other words, defining what the in-group is also requires defining what it is *not*. As Tajfel and Forgas put it, "We are what we are because *they* are not what we are" (cited in Brewer & Miller, 1996, pp. 47–48).

Ridley (1996) argued that humans have evolved natures with a host of social instincts. On the positive side, these social instincts equip us "with predispositions to learn how to cooperate, to discriminate the trustworthy from the treacherous, to commit [ourselves] to be trustworthy, to earn good reputations, to exchange goods and information, and to divide labour" (p. 249). On the negative side, however, these social instincts also promote ethnocentric conflict by providing a critical building block for in-group alliance and out-group hostility. In other words, the evolution of sociability, altruism, and cooperation goes hand in hand with the evolution of animosity to outsiders, or what Ridley referred to as "xenophobic group loyalty" (p. 167). We cooperate to compete. There is no "us" without a corresponding "them" to oppose.

On a broader societal level, governments, propaganda, and militaries can easily evoke our evolved capacities for ethnocentrism and xenophobia. At the extreme, these capacities may even translate into a genocidal imperative as they are used to forge in-group solidarity and undermine the normal inhibitions against killing out-group strangers. As Ghiglieri (1999) wrote,

> Xenophobia and ethnocentrism are not just essential ingredients to war. Because they instinctively tell men precisely whom to bond with versus whom to fight against, they are the most dangerously manipulable facets of war psychology that promote genocide. Indeed, genocide itself has become a potent force in human evolution. (p. 211)

Although social exclusion, let alone genocide and mass killing, is not an inevitable consequence of these adaptations, we are reminded that—once identified with a group—we find it easy to exaggerate differences between our group and others, enhancing in-group cooperation and effectiveness, and, frequently intensifying antagonism toward other groups. Most religious belief systems, by their very nature, play on ethnocentrism and xenophobia and, in the extreme, may even foster a devaluing effect on the human life that falls outside the veil of the faithful. They distinguish all too clearly between "us" and "them," between the committed and the nonbelievers, between those whom the gods love and those whom they hate. In this way, religion can define the "other" in forms perverted to justify and reward the most horrendous of human deeds. Carroll (2001), for instance, traced how Christianity's early self-definition in opposition to Judaism devolved, over the centuries, into often vitriolic forms of anti-Semitism as revealed in the foundational texts and practices of Christianity—and as culminating in the churches' silence, and complicity, in the attempted extermination of European Jewry under Nazism (1939–1945). Recent research by Pargament, Trevino, Mahoney, and Silberman (2007) confirmed that continuing perceptions of Jews as desecrators remains central to understanding contemporary anti-Semitic attitudes (see also Pargament, Magyar, Benore, & Mahoney, 2005, for an investigation of the relationship between desecration and physical health).

Religion may even justify a moral imperative for mobilizing a collectivity for extraordinary actions and, frequently, does so through ritualizing conduct. *Ritual conduct* refers to behaviors that are apparently excessive or unproductive but that nonetheless are persistent. In other words, ritual conduct is persistent indulgence in apparently noninstrumental exercises—exercises that consume radically limited energies and resources but that also cement a moral imperative for social exclusion and even mass murder. During the Yugoslav Wars (1991–1995), for instance, Serbian Orthodox and Croatian Catholic priests offered ritualized blessings for soldiers embarking on sacred missions to exterminate Bosnian Muslims. A 1992 article in a popular Croatian Catholic magazine rejoiced that the cross of Christ stood next to the Croatian flag, a Croatian bishop next to the Croatian minister of state, and "guardsmen wore rosaries around their necks" (cited in Sells, 1996, p. 103).

Recent experimental research by Bushman, Ridge, Das, Key, and Busath (2007) found that scriptural violence, sanctioned by God, can increase aggression—especially in believers. As they have concluded, "To the extent religious extremists engage in prolonged, selective reading of the scriptures, focusing on violent retribution toward unbelievers instead of the overall message of acceptance and understanding, one might expect to see increased brutality" (Bushman et al., 2007, p. 204).

Conversely, religion can widen our circle of moral commitment to alter who is a "we" and who is a "they." In so doing, group membership can be redefined along the boundaries of an interdependent or superordinate group. For example, the identity of Hutu Muslims in Rwanda centered more on religion than ethnicity. For them, religion was not fused with or co-opted by ethnic or national identities. Rather, religion was the primary identity and other allegiances fell secondary to it. During the Rwandan genocide, Hutu Muslims—living together in the Biryogo neighborhood of Kigali—stood up to the militias and most Muslim Tutsi were spared. The fact that mosques never became the killing sites that many Christian churches and compounds became, helps explain why Islam currently is the fastest growing religion in Rwanda—already claiming about 15% of the population (Lacey, 2004).

Religion and the Institutional Church

There have been notable cases in which religious institutions stood and resisted the power of state-sponsored terrorism. For example, German Roman Catholic and Lutheran leaders' opposition to the "T4" program, Hitler's systematic program of state-sanctioned murder disguised as "euthanasia," is well chronicled (e.g., see Burleigh, 1997). It was such institutionally led opposition that led to the official termination of the T4 program on August 24, 1941.

Such cases, however, have been the scattered exceptions to the more general rule of recent history in which religious institutions have been notoriously silent, or even complicit, in the face of genocidal violence. This section of the chapter specifically focuses on the role of indigenous Christian institutions in contexts of genocidal violence. How do such institutions shape a culture in which genocidal violence may occur and how do they respond to such a culture both during and after the genocidal violence? The following section of the chapter will analyze three stages of institutional Christian response to genocide—pregenocidal, genocidal, and postgenocidal.

Pregenocidal responses include the fusion of religious belief systems with ethnic, national, and political identities that provide theological justifications for us–them thinking by constricting the churches' universe of moral obligation. Most often, this fusion is not a joining of equals; generally, the ethnic, national, or political identities co-opt religion and, eventually, neutralize it. The church loses its critical role as a prophetic voice of the voiceless and becomes, instead, married to other social identities that privilege it among powerholders and mobilize the church to preserve, rather than challenge, the status quo. It is, as Volf (2000) described, an "idolatrous shift of loyalty" in which faith is "employed" as a weapon in an ethnic, national, or political struggle.

A consequence of this fusion is the churches' role in providing a theological justification for us–them thinking. In Christian institutions, us–them thinking constricts the churches' universe of moral obligation and leaves the church unwilling to curb the ethnic and national ethnocentrisms, or political divisions, to which it has become fused. In this way, Christian institutions help build the scaffolding for moral sanctions, or exclusions, that heighten intergroup tensions and may, ultimately, "excommunicate" the victims of genocidal violence from the perpetrators' moral community. The danger, and historical reality, of such exclusions makes Freud's famous dictum seem more true than exaggerated: "Cruelty and intolerance to those who do not belong to it are natural to every religion" (cited in Atran, 2002, p. 115).

During the Holocaust, the institutional identities of the Catholic Church and Protestant churches were compromised by their decision, motivated by self-interest to retain their prominent place in society, to maintain some degree of independence by entering into various "agreements" with the Nazi regime. Although it could be argued that such arrangements ensured institutional independence from Nazi control, it is equally clear that there was a fusion of identity that neutralized the churches' voice and negated most forms of public institutional criticism of Nazi policies and practices (for an overview, see the edited volume by Spicer, 2007).

Moreover, the groundwork for the moral exclusion of Jewish victims was laid in the centuries preceding the Holocaust as Jews were regarded as aliens who were on the remote fringes of Christian Europe's universe of moral obligation. The historical stigmatization and exclusion of the Jews meant that the traditions, habits, images, and vocabularies for extreme dehumanization were already well established. The centuries-old image of the vile and diabolical Jew was woven into the fabric of German, and European, culture. The deluge of racist and anti-Semitic propaganda ribboning throughout Germany society during the rise of Nazism was thus profoundly effective in placing, and keeping, the Jews entirely outside the realm of moral obligation for perpetrators.

In Rwanda, the churches, especially the Roman Catholic Church, had historically reinforced us–them thinking and behavior both in public life and in the church itself. As early as 1957 (although an even more accurate analysis would go back to the introduction of Christianity during the colonization of Rwanda), the Catholic Church in Rwanda had supported the creation of a Hutu identity and nationalism. As radical Hutus gained power after the social revolution of 1959–1962, the Catholic Church found itself with well-placed connections at all levels of government and with unimpeded access to the centers of power. Similarly, many within the hierarchy of the Protestant churches in Rwanda had developed intimate ties with the Hutu regime over the years. Although several Rwandan bishops made statements urging unity, justice, peace, and harmony between 1990 and the start of the genocide in 1994, such admonitions came too late to reverse decades of religion-entrenched us–them thinking in Rwandan society.

So, in 1994, as Hutu extremists began to dominate the government and plan the genocide, it was easy for the church—both Catholic and Protestant—to fuse its identity, and interests, with the ethnic, national, and political identities, and interests, of the genocidal regime. As Scheer (1995) wrote of the church in Rwanda, "Staying on the good side of the local mayor became as important as staying on the good side of God (sometimes more so)" (p. 326). As early as August 1994, within weeks after the end of the genocide, a World Council of Churches team that had visited Rwanda concluded that both Catholic and Protestant churches alike had "betrayed their beliefs by aligning themselves far too closely with the former Hutu-dominated regime and its tribal politics" ("Rwandan Churches Culpable," 1994, p. 778). Clearly, the blood of tribal ethnic ties ran deeper than the waters of baptism in Rwanda.

Similarly, Sells (1996) explored the role of Christian mythology in the fusion of religion and ethnicity in Bosnia that makes the two identities virtually indistinguishable—one "ethnoreligious" identity. Central to the ethnoreligious identity of Bosnian Christians was the historical construction of Bosnian Muslims as "the other." Sells traced centuries of religious-based Serb ideology in which Muslims are portrayed as Christ killers, heretics, perverts, and sadists. He labeled the ideology as *Christoslavism*, meaning the notion that Slavs are Christian by nature and conversion to another religion is ethnic or racial betrayal. Sells argued that such Serbian mythology provided the ideological fuel to motivate and justify the genocide of the Bosnian Muslims in pursuit of an ethnoreligiously pure state.

In this vein, the Serbian Orthodox Church has been particularly criticized for its role in the Bosnian genocide. The church's episcopate is dominated by hardline nationalists with visions of a traditional, patriarchal society. As Sells (2003a) pointed out, there was a close relationship of Serb bishops to war criminals, massive Serb funeral processions of war criminals, and repeated church attacks on the International Criminal Tribunal for the Former Yugoslavia (ICTY) as an anti-Serb plot. In 1995, Konrad Raiser, general secretary of the World Council of Churches, said he personally believed that "much of what we are seeing in the Serbian Orthodox Church" could be criticized in terms similar to those in which the ecumenical movement criticized pro-Hitler Christians in Germany (Paul, 1995, p. 881).

Although Bosnian Serb extremists were responsible for about 90% of the war crimes committed during the conflict, Bosnian Croats also were affected by a similar religious-based ideology that fostered anti-Muslim stereotypes and depicted them as enemies of Christianity. The role of Catholicism in the Bosnian genocide has been less acknowledged, and the crimes of Bosnian Croat extremists were fewer, but they were no less in intensity. Sells (2003b) has chronicled, for instance, the activities of Bishop Ratko Peric and Franciscan friars in the Mostar region of Bosnia in supporting Catholic militias' involvements in mass killings, expulsions, annihilation of the sacral heritage of other traditions ("triumphal shrines of exclusion"), and imprisonment of Muslims in concentration camps where prisoners were starved and tortured regularly.

Ultimately, the product of such mythologies and ideologies that define "us" and "them" is an excommunication of victims from the perpetrators' moral universe. In Sells's (2003a) words, "Religions in their ideological manifestations have traditionally been strong at promoting an interior identity in opposition to the religious other than in affirming identity in affirmation of the other" (p. 329). This is a moral exclusion, with theological backing, that can have disastrous consequences. As Fein (1979) wrote,

> A church holding out the possibility of conversion to all must assume a common humanity, and therefore may not sanction unlimited violence. But a doctrine that assumes people do not belong to a common species knows no limits inhibiting the magnitude of permissible crime. (p. 30)

Genocidal responses include sins of omission (silence and denial) as well as sins of commission (active participation in killings). In the former, there is a resignation of institutional agency in the face of mass murder and, in the latter, a functional involvement in the process of destruction.

During a genocide, institutional responses most often center around silence. In the Holocaust, as pointed out, church hierarchies followed their own narrowly defined best interests, particularly that of protecting their own institutional autonomy within a totalitarian state. Such interests were best advanced by silence, rather than by protest or heroism. In Rwanda, church hierarchies also remained mostly silent. When churches spoke, their words were seldom direct calls for institutional action but were most often public displays of "theologically correct" hand-wringing. In May 1994, for instance, in the midst of the Rwandan genocide, Catholic and Protestant leaders issued a joint letter calling for an end to the killing; yet they failed to condemn the atrocities or to describe the mass murder as genocide. Likewise, Pope John Paul II called for a general end to the violence, but made no specific, overt plea to Rwandan Catholic Church leaders to use their authority to do so (for an overview, see the edited volume by Rittner, Roth, & Whitworth, 2004). Similarly, the Pope's numerous pronouncements to end the violence in Bosnia unfailing called for international intervention but seldom called for institutional leadership from the Catholic churches in the region.

Although it borders even more on a sin of commission, we also often see silence take the form of active denial as an institutional response during genocide. For instance, even after the revelation of Serb-initiated atrocities at the beginning of the Bosnian genocide, the Holy Episcopal Synod of the Serbian Orthodox church distributed a document in response to the "false accusations against the Serbian people" in which they denied the existence of such atrocities. "In the name of God's truth," the document read, "and on the testimony from our brother bishops from Bosnia-Herzegovina and from other trustworthy witnesses, we declare, taking full moral responsibility, that such camps [concentration and killing camps] neither have existed nor exist in the Serbian Republic of Bosnia-Herzegovina" (Sells, 1996, p. 84). Unfortunately, at the time this document was composed in May 1992, thousands of non-Serbs were being raped, driven from their homes, and killed—all before the eyes of local Serbian Orthodox priests and bishops.

Perhaps the most chilling are the sins of commission in which individual actors, laity, and clergy of Christian institutions, actively participate in—even organize—the killings. Although present in the

Holocaust (clergy members were even found in the membership of the Einsatzgruppen killing units) and Bosnian genocide, these sins of commission, as we have read in this chapter, are most extensively documented in Rwanda. In addition to examples discussed in this chapter, there are also clear accusations of active participation by clergy of the Free Methodist, Presbyterian, Baptist, and Seventh-Day Adventist Churches in the Rwandan genocide. According to an August 2001 report by afrol News, Bishop Aaron Ruhumuliza, head of the Free Methodist Church in Gikondo, Kigali, helped the militia carry out a massacre in his own church on April 9, 1994. Michel Twagirayesu, the president of the Presbyterian Church in Rwanda and a former vice president of the World Council of Churches, is alleged to have betrayed parishioners and fellow clergy alike in Kirinda, Kibuye (Hennig, 2001). Seventh-Day Adventist pastor Elizaphan Ntakirutimana was the first church leader to be brought to trial at the ICTR. In February 2003, the ICTR found it proven beyond reasonable doubt that Ntakirutimana had transported armed Hutu killers to a church and hospital in the Kibuye region of western Rwanda, where they killed hundreds of Tutsi refugees who had been encouraged by Ntakirutimana to seek refuge there. At his trial, a British prosecutor stated, "Dressed in his customary suit and tie, Pastor Ntakirutimana watched as people were shot and beaten to death, encouraging the killers to ensure no one survived" (Reuters, 2001).

Finally, although Christian institutions should be credited with decisive humanitarian efforts that provide physical, emotional, and spiritual sustenance following genocidal violence, *postgenocidal responses* also include (a) the accentuation of the church's persecution and resistance (marked by the appropriation of the victim groups' suffering as well as the glorification of individual heroes and martyrs) and (b) official declarations of contrition that avoid direct acknowledgment of institutional guilt.

Following genocide, Christian institutions often will accentuate their own persecution by appropriating the victim group's suffering. Such appropriation is a deliberate act of acquisition in which the victim group's suffering is borrowed, or co-opted, by Christian institutions to accentuate their own persecution. In this way, Christian institutions, and their actors, distract attention from the victim groups' suffering by reallocating that attention to their own suffering.

For example, we see an appropriation of the Jews' suffering in the Catholic Church's response following the Holocaust. Rather than engage in self-critical analysis of their institutional response (which many have described as complicity; e.g., see Cornwell, 1999) to the Nazi process of destruction, the Vatican's primary response was to appropriate the Jewish victims' suffering by taking quick steps to ensure that the Nuremberg Trials also included the persecution of the Christian church, particularly the Catholic Church in Germany and the Nazi-occupied territories. While choosing, on the grounds that the "universal religious mission of Church would be compromised," not to cooperate with the Nuremberg Tribunal in preparing a list of war criminals (and even advocating that war criminals be given clemency), the Vatican readily supplied the tribunal with "an important collection of documents dealing with the persecution of the Church [Catholic] by the Nazi regime" (Gallagher, 1962, p. 169).

This appropriation of the victim group's suffering is complemented by a tendency to inordinately, and sometimes inaccurately, accentuate the exceptional individual actions of Christian heroes and martyrs in the face of mass destruction. Alongside the continued pursuit of the beatification of Pope Pius XII and the glorification of Christian martyrs, such as Dietrich Bonhoeffer, Bernhard Lichtenberg, Kurt Gerstein, Martin Niemoller, or Corrie ten Boom, there is a misdirection of attention away from the complicity of the dominant social structure of an *institution* (the Church) and to the exceptional actions of *individuals*. At issue here is not necessarily the veracity of their lives and witness. Rather, at issue here is how the Christian church has used the lives and witness of exceptional individuals to deflect attention from a self-critical analysis of the churches' institutional response during genocide. Rather than focusing on the silence and neglect of the many and, particularly, the institution, there is a glorification of the individual actions of the few.

This most recently was seen in Pope Benedict XVI's May 2006 visit to Auschwitz. Visiting

Auschwitz as "a son of the German people," Benedict was silent on the collective guilt of the German people, the biblical and Catholic roots of anti-Semitism, the role of the Catholic church under Pius's leadership during the Holocaust, and his own personal experiences during the war as a member (involuntarily conscripted) of the Hitler Youth. He was not silent, however, in continuing a Papal tradition of extolling the virtues of the exceptional Catholic individuals who stood up in the face of Nazi tyranny. Benedict's address at Auschwitz highlighted the lives of two Auschwitz victims—both now Catholic saints—who have become a source of tension between Catholics and Jewish groups: Maximilian Kolbe, a Polish priest accused of editing anti-Semitic tracts; and Edith Stein, a convert from Judaism who entered a convent in a failed bid to escape Nazi persecution. In this example, the accentuation of exceptional individual actions is coupled with a gross appropriation of the victim group's suffering. As Abraham Foxham, national director of the Anti-Defamation League pointed out, Benedict did not make "one explicit acknowledgment of Jewish lives vanquished simply because they were Jews" (Meichtry, 2006).

Following the Holocaust, the initial work on statements of contrition came from individual Christian theologians, not institutional leaders. Such individual statements of contrition, however admirable, avoided directly shining a spotlight on the dark recesses of Christian institutional actions before and during genocidal violence.

So, it was with much anticipation that the world received the post-Holocaust statement, *Nostra Aetate* (Latin for *In Our Time*), issued by the Catholic Church in 1965. Although the Vatican heralded the document as a significant change in Jewish–Christian relations, critics assailed it for its brevity ("much too little and much too late") and its lack of acknowledgment of the Holocaust as a reference point. In response, this Conciliar declaration was followed in 1975 by the *Guidelines for Implementing Nostra Aetate* and in 1986 by the *Notes on the Correct Ways to Present Jews and Judaism in Preaching and Catechesis in the Roman Catholic Church*. Despite the Catholic Church's efforts, however, many still expressed dissatisfaction. So, in 1998, the church issued *We Remember: A Reflection on the Shoah* as yet another addition to the ongoing dialogue in Jewish–Christian relations. Like the declaration and implementing documents that preceded it, *We Remember* found its critics. Many took the document to task for the continuing failure of the Catholic church to acknowledge its complicity in the Holocaust; others expressed concern that the conciliatory tone in the document was weaker than many of Pope John Paul II's public statements; still others criticized the footnoted tributes to Pope Pius XII and the document's attempt to defend the dubious validity of a distinction between theological anti-Judaism (opposition to Judaism by people who accept a competing system of beliefs and practices; see Langmuir, 1990) and social anti-Semitism (powered by nationalist and racist myths that castigate Jews as an alien and dangerous race threatening the survival of the nation; see Perry & Schweitzer, 2002).

Over the next several decades, post-Holocaust declarations of contrition emerged from a wide range of Protestant denominations around the world. As Obrecht (2000) pointed out, most of these statements shared two important similarities. First, they affirmed God's continuing covenantal relationship with, or election of, the Jewish people as the people of God. Such affirmations, often couched in dual covenantal or "partners in waiting" language, were meant to reverse centuries of theological supersessionism as Christian doctrine. Second, most of the statements affirmed the responsibility of the church to teach about Judaism from Judaism's own texts. In so doing, it was hoped that the misleading stereotypes that lay at the root of us–them thinking in Jewish–Christian relations would be ameliorated.

In Rwanda, reactions of contrition, although varying in degrees of accountability, came from many Christian churches. In May 1995, the archbishop of Canterbury, speaking for the Anglican Church, went to Rwanda himself and apologized. In December 1996, Protestant and Catholic Christians—laity and clergy, Rwandan and European—came together in Detmold, Germany, to "confess their own offense and to humbly ask forgiveness of their victims" (Ntezimana, 2002, p. 1). That same month, the Presbyterian Church of Rwanda became the first denomination to confess the failure of its leaders to provide the moral and spiritual strength to denounce and oppose the genocide. Other Protestant congregations asked pardon for the atrocities committed by their members and even excommunicated members alleged to be organizers of the genocide.

An official denominational response from the Seventh-Day Adventists did not come until 2 years after the genocide, and even then, the response, given by General Conference president Robert S. Folkenberg during a sermon in Kigali, only addressed broad issues of Christians' responsibility for forgiveness and reconciliation with no clear mention of a need for accountability. The Catholic response has been no more concrete. In May 1996, Pope John Paul II wrote in a letter to the Rwandan people,

> The Church . . . cannot be held responsible for the guilt of its members that have acted against the evangelic law; they will be called to render account of their own actions. All Church members that have sinned during the genocide must have the courage to assume the consequences of their deeds they have done against God and fellow men. (Hennig, 2001)

Browne (2010) offered a stinging summary of the church's response:

> And what did the Roman Catholic and Apostolic Church do in the wake of this mass murder? It gave aid and assistance to the genocidal priests in escaping retribution in Rwanda and elsewhere. . . . There was no church inquiry into its own culpability for what happened. I suspect there were few if any canonical trials. There was no Pastoral Letter expressing shame for the involvement of the functions of the Catholic Church in that terrible crime. No apology. No papal visitation to identify with the victims. No papal audiences for the survivors. Nothing.

In Bosnia, stopping short of directly acknowledging institutional responsibility, Catholic bishops haltingly asked "for forgiveness from all those who feel in some way hit by the injustices of sons of the Catholic Church" in a February 1996 pastoral letter. In the same letter, they also were quick to pledge to "forgive all who have done injustice and evil to us" (Malcolm, 1996, p. 8). Responses from the Serbian Orthodox Church have even more fully evaded responsibility and, instead, have stressed that all sides and religious factions in the region—including Catholic Croats and Bosniak Muslims—are guilty. In addition, the Serbian Orthodox Church expressed "deep concern" about the 1995 Dayton Peace Agreement between the Serbian, Croatian, and Bosnian governments ("Peace Terms Worry Serbian Orthodox," 1996, p. 8).

On one hand, there is great reason to applaud these profound, and sometimes courageously introspective, statements of contrition offered by the churches. Public confession of actions, or inaction, before or during genocidal violence that humbly recognize the failure of the church, as an institution, and of church leaders, as individuals, to be a prophetic voice for the voiceless must not be discounted. On the other hand, what is missing from nearly all of the official declarations of contrition following each of these genocides is full acknowledgment of the guilt of the churches as institutions. Only passive complacency has been admitted, rather than active complicity. At the institutional level, there has been little confrontation with their own sin, a gaping void where there should be a call for sincere repentance. Where guilt has been confessed, it has been inevitably confessed at either the level of individuals or with a global abstractness that offers no concrete hope that such an event will not be repeated.

IMPLICATIONS AND CONCLUSION

The chapter has reviewed the interface of religion with culture, the "other," and the institutional church in episodes of genocidal violence. We have seen the ways in which religion becomes conflated with cultures of authority, is used as a tool of exclusion to justify moral indifference, and is institutionalized in ways that shape a culture in which genocidal violence may occur and respond to such a culture both during and after the genocidal violence. This is a bleak picture of religion, the sacred, and the abuses of religion in established institutionalized systems that should cause pause even amongst the most ardent of believers.

We also, however, have touched on how religion can challenge cultures of illegitimate or immoral authority, can be used to foster inclusion and moral sensitivity, and can be institutionalized in humane and caring ways that give voice to the voiceless and demand power for the powerless. There are striking moral moments when religious institutions are active in reconstructing their societies torn by conflict. Religious actors have, for instance, had a significant influence on transitional justice in Guatemala, Chile, Brazil, South Africa, Peru, Sierra Leone, and East Timor (Philpott, 2009). Following the Holocaust, Jewish–Christian organizations, with significant Christian institutional leadership, are operating around the world to foster interfaith dialogue. In Rwanda, Christian clergy and laypeople have joined Kagame's "Government of National Unity" in preaching and fostering unity among the Rwandan people. In Bosnia, Sarajevo's Cardinal Vinko Puljic has become one of the most prominent, and active, spokespersons for tolerance and multicultural coexistence.

What remains necessary is an examination of the capacity for religious institutions to redeem themselves—and the world—by being involved in postgenocidal transitional justice. Religious institutions, particularly those that remain independent in their policies and practices from the state, can be powerful forces of mobilization for political activism. As was seen in Nazi Germany, genocidal regimes are often more reluctant to restrict the activities of religious institutions and organizations. Religious institutions and organizations are ready-made networks that also have good access to the media, offer places to meet, provide membership lists, maintain educational institutions, and train leaders (Tuckwood, 2008). Religious institution can act as "superconnector" social networks, so well-linked as to exert an outsize influence in a genocidal society (see Christakis & Fowler, 2010). Many religious institutions and organizations have far-reaching international support and connections, and may, in states with weak or unstable governments, even be the strongest institutions (Fox & Sandler, 2003). All of these factors point to the promise of religion and religious institutions to offer resistance in the face of genocidal intent and violence.

Several vital questions must be addressed in future research. How can religious institutions prepare themselves to foster cultures that encourage voices of defiance and resistance in the face of mass murder and still protect the integrity of religious identity? How can these institutions overcome the inertia inherent in organizational structures, people, and processes—particularly in those institutions feeling the "divine" weight of ecclesiastical hierarchies?

More important are the questions from which we must draw practical applications of education, prevention, intervention, consultation, and social change for the structure, policies, and procedures of religious institutions. Here we are asking questions regarding both the nature of organizational change and the magnitude of change (Robbins, 2001). The nature of change relevant to religious institutions involves both changing *structure* (alterations in authority relations, coordination mechanisms, etc.) as well as changing *people* (changes in attitudes, expectations, perceptions, behavior, etc.). Structural changes require overcoming the built-in mechanisms, often centuries in the making, that have evolved to produce stability in religious institutions. This structural inertia is compounded by a group inertia founded in strong, both explicitly and implicitly, group norms. Changes in structure also often involve changes in long-held power relationships, particularly in religious institutions with strong ecclesiastical hierarchies. Similarly, changing people must confront resistance stemming from habit, security, and fear of uncertainty.

Even if religious institutions can overcome the challenges to structural and people changes, they are still faced with issues of the magnitude of change. The magnitude of change is determined by the implications of change for individuals and organizations. First-order changes that are an extension of the past—that is, consistent with prevailing values and norms, linear, incremental, continuous, marginal, and requiring no fundamental shifts in assumptions—are too often the default in the self-reflective responses of religious institutions to genocide. For many, however, the changes necessary for religious institutions to redeem themselves and become fully involved in postgenocidal transitional justice are even more drastic—second-order changes that represent an emergent and unbounded break with the past born through multidimensional, multilevel, discontinuous, and radical change involving reframing of assumptions about the nature of religious institutions and the world in which they operate. Such second-order change could include concrete restructuring of doctrine, ecclesiology, or church hierarchy—that is, changes fundamental to the nature of religious institutions and also central to reclaiming the integrity of religious identity in the aftermath of mass atrocity.

As Volf (2000) pointed out, too often the social agenda of the church is isolated from the message of reconciliation. To do reconciliation most effectively, however, we can no longer avoid asking tough questions of why religion so easily becomes conflated with cultures of authority. We can no longer avoid asking why, in the name of their chosen sacred deity, religion has been at the front of defining the "other" throughout human history. We can no longer ignore the deep analysis necessary to understand why religious institutions can be silent, or complicit, in the face of mass destruction. It is only in facing such questions that religious institutions can begin to fulfill their promise and foster periods of peace and tolerance in a pluralistic society.

References

Allport, G. W., & Ross, J. M. (1967). Personal religious orientation and prejudice. *Journal of Personality and Social Psychology, 5*, 432–443. doi:10.1037/h0021212

Altemeyer, B., & Hunsberger, B. (1992). Authoritarianism, religious fundamentalism, quest, and prejudice. *The International Journal for the Psychology of Religion, 2*, 113–133. doi:10.1207/s15327582ijpr0202_5

Atran, S. (2002). *In gods we trust: The evolutionary landscape of religion.* New York, NY: Oxford University Press.

Batson, C. D., & Stocks, E. L. (2009). Religion and prejudice. In J. F. Dovidio, P. Glick, & L. A. Budman (Eds.), *On the nature of prejudice: Fifty years after Allport* (pp. 413–427). Malden, MA: Blackwell.

Baumeister, R. F. (1999). *Evil: Inside human violence and cruelty.* New York, NY: Freeman.

Becker, E. (1973). *The denial of death.* New York, NY: Simon & Schuster.

Blass, T. (1991). Understanding behavior in the Milgram obedience experiment: The role of personality, situations, and their interactions. *Journal of Personality and Social Psychology, 60*, 398–413. doi:10.1037/0022-3514.60.3.398

Brewer, M. B., & Miller, N. (1996). *Intergroup relations.* Pacific Grove, CA: Brooks/Cole.

Browne, V. (2010, March 31). Pope should say sorry for Rwanda genocide. *Irish Times.* Retrieved from http://www.irishtimes.com/newspaper/opinion/2010/0331/12242 67400781_pf.html

Burleigh, M. (1997). *Ethics and extermination: Reflections on Nazi genocide.* New York, NY: Cambridge University Press.

Bushman, B. J., Ridge, R. D., Das, E., Key, C. W., & Busath, G. L. (2007). When God sanctions killing: Effect of scriptural violence on aggression. *Psychological Science, 18*, 204–207. doi:10.1111/j.1467-9280.2007.01873.x

Carroll, J. (2001). *Constantine's sword: The church and the Jews.* Boston, MA: Houghton Mifflin.

Christakis, N. A., & Fowler, J. H. (2010). Social network sensors for early detection of contagious outbreaks. *PLoS ONE, 5*(9), e12948. doi:10.1371/journal.pone.0012948

Cornwell, J. (1999). *Hitler's pope: The secret history of Pius XII.* New York, NY: Viking.

Eisenstadt, S. N. (1993). Religion and the civilizational dimensions of politics. In S. A. Arjomand (Ed.), *The political dimensions of religion* (pp. 13–41). New York: State University of New York Press.

Fein, H. (1979). *Accounting for genocide.* New York, NY: Free Press.

Fox, J., & Sandler, S. (2003). Quantifying religion: Toward building more effective ways of measuring religious influence on state-level behavior. *Journal of Church and State, 45*, 559–588. doi:10.1093/jcs/45.3.559

Gallagher, L. J. (1962). *Edmund A. Walsh, S. J.: A biography.* New York, NY: Benziger Brothers.

Ghiglieri, M. (1999). *The dark side of man: Tracing the origins of male violence.* Reading, MA: Perseus Books.

Greenberg, J., Landau, M. J., Kosloff, S., & Solomon, S. (2009). How our dreams of death transcendence breed prejudice, stereotyping, and conflict. In T. Nelson (Ed.), *The handbook of prejudice, stereotyping, and discrimination* (pp. 309–332). New York, NY: Psychology Press.

Harff, B., & Gurr, T. R. (2009). Assessing country risks of genocide and politicide in 2009 [Data set]. Available from http://gpanet.org

Hennig, R. C. (2001, August 8). The cross and the genocide. *Afrol News.* Retrieved from http://www.afrol.com/features/10600

Hinde, R. A. (1989). Patriotism: Is kin selection both necessary and sufficient? *Politics and the Life Sciences, 9,* 58–61.

Hinton, A. L. (1998). Why did you kill? The Cambodian genocide and the dark side of face and honor. *Journal of Asian Studies, 57,* 93–122. doi:10.2307/2659025

Johnston, D., & Sampson, C. (1994). *Religion: The missing dimension of statecraft.* New York, NY: Oxford University Press.

Juergensmeyer, M. (1997). Terror mandated by God. *Terrorism and Political Violence, 9,* 16–23. doi:10.1080/09546559708427400

Kohn, J. (Ed.). (1994). *Hannah Arendt: Essays in understanding, 1930–1954.* New York, NY: Harcourt Brace.

Lacey, M. (2004, April 7). Since '94 horror, Rwandans turn toward Islam. *New York Times.* Retrieved from http://www.nytimes.com/2004/04/07/world/since-94-horror-rwandans-turn-toward-islam.html

Langmuir, G. I. (1990). *Toward a definition of anti-Semitism.* Berkeley: University of California Press.

Leyens, J. P., Paladino, P. M., Vaes, R., Rodriguez-Torres, S., Demoulin, S., Rodriguez-Perez, A., & Gaunt, R. (2000). The emotional side of prejudice: The attribution of secondary emotions to ingroups and outgroups. *Personality and Social Psychology Review, 4,* 186–197. doi:10.1207/S15327957PSPR0402_06

Malcolm, T. (1996, February 23). Bishops ask forgiveness. *National Catholic Reporter,* p. 8.

Malony, H. N. (1998). The question of evil in psychology. *Catalyst, 24.*

Meichtry, S. (2006, May 31). Pope under fire for Auschwitz remarks, urges end to "racial hatred." *Associated Press.* Retrieved from http://www.beliefnet.com/story/192/story_19206.html

Miller, A. G. (Ed.). (2004). *The social psychology of good and evil.* New York, NY: Guilford Press.

Miller, D. T., & Prentice, D. A. (1994). Collective errors and errors about the collective. *Personality and Social Psychology Bulletin, 20,* 541–550. doi:10.1177/0146167294205011

Myers, D. G. (1992). *The pursuit of happiness: Who is happy and why?* New York, NY: Morrow.

Neiman, S. (2002). *Evil in modern thought: An alternative history of philosophy.* Princeton, NJ: Princeton University Press.

Ntezimana, L. (2002). *The confession of Detmold.* Retrieved from http://rwandahope.com/confession.pdf

Obrecht, P. (2000). After the Shoah: Christian statements of contrition. In C. Rittner, S. D. Smith, & I. Steinfeldt (Eds.), *The Holocaust and the Christian world: Reflections on the past, challenges for the future* (pp. 174–178). London, England: Kuperard.

Osiander, A. (2000). Religion and politics in western civilization: The ancient world as matrix and mirror of the modern. *Millennium, 29,* 761–790. doi:10.1177/03058298000290030201

Oyserman, D., & Lauffer, A. (2002). Examining the implications of cultural frames on social movements and group action. In L. S. Newman & R. Erber (Eds.), *Understanding genocide: The social psychology of the Holocaust* (pp. 162–187). New York, NY: Oxford University Press. doi:10.1093/acprof:oso/9780195133622.003.0008

Pargament, K. I., Magyar, G. M., Benore, E., & Mahoney, A. (2005). Sacrilege: A study of sacred loss and desecration and their implications for health and well-being in a community sample. *Journal for the Scientific Study of Religion, 44,* 59–78. doi:10.1111/j.1468-5906.2005.00265.x

Pargament, K. I., Trevino, K., Mahoney, A., & Silberman, I. (2007). They killed our lord: The perception of Jews as desecrators of Christianity as a predictor of anti-Semitism. *Journal for the Scientific Study of Religion, 46,* 143–158. doi:10.1111/j.1468-5906.2007.00347.x

Paul, D. (1995, September 27). A cry for human rights in a "cleansed" Banja Luka. *Christian Century, 881.*

Peace terms worry Serbian Orthodox. (1996, January 3). *Christian Century, 8.*

Perry, M., & Schweitzer, F. M. (2002). *Anti-Semitism: Myth and hate from antiquity to the present.* New York, NY: Palgrave Macmillan.

Philpott, D. (2009). When faith meets history: The influence of religion on transitional justice. In T. Brudholm & T. Cushman (Eds.), *The religious in responses to mass atrocity: Interdisciplinary perspectives* (pp. 174–212). New York, NY: Cambridge University Press. doi:10.1017/CBO9780511575730.009

Pyszczynski, T., Greenberg, J., Solomon, S., Arndt, J., & Schimel, J. (2004). Why do people need self-esteem?: A theoretical and empirical review. *Psychological Bulletin, 130,* 435–468. doi:10.1037/0033-2909.130.3.435

Pyszczynski, T., Rothschild, Z., & Abdollahi, A. (2008). Terrorism, violence, and hope for peace: A terror management perspective. *Current Directions in Psychological Science, 17,* 318–322. doi:10.1111/j.1467-8721.2008.00598.x

Reuters. (2001, September 19). *News report.* Retrieved from http://www.cnn.com/2001/WORLD/africa/09/19/crime.rwanda.pastor.reut

Ridley, M. (1996). *The origins of virtue: Human instincts and the evolution of cooperation.* New York, NY: Viking.

Rittner, C., Roth, J. K., & Whitworth, W. (Eds.). (2004). *Genocide in Rwanda: Complicity of the churches?* Minneapolis, MN: Paragon.

Robbins, S. P. (2001). *Organizational behavior* (9th ed.). Upper Saddle River, NJ: Prentice-Hall.

Routledge, C., Arndt, J., & Goldenberg, J. L. (2004). A time to tan: Proximal and distal effects of mortality salience on sun exposure intentions. *Personality and Social Psychology Bulletin, 30,* 1347–1358. doi:10.1177/0146167204264056

Rowatt, W. D., LaBouff, J., Johnson, M., Froese, P., and Tsang, J. A. (2009). Associations among religiousness, social attitudes, and prejudice in a national random sample of American adults. *Psychology of Religion and Spirituality, 1,* 14–24. doi:10.1037/a0014989

Rwandan churches culpable, says WCC. (1994, August 24). *Christian Century, 778.*

Scheer, G. (1995). Rwanda: Where was the church? *Evangelical Missions Quarterly, 31,* 324–328.

Sells, M. A. (1996). *The bridge betrayed: Religion and genocide in Bosnia.* Berkeley: University of California Press.

Sells, M. A. (2003a). Crosses of blood: Sacred space, religion, and violence in Bosnia- Hercegovina. *Sociology of Religion, 64,* 309–331. doi:10.2307/3712487

Sells, M. A. (2003b, October 27). [Personal correspondence to Pope John Paul II]. Held by Michael Sells, Haverford College, Haverford, PA.

Spicer, K. (Ed.). (2007). *Antisemitism, Christian ambivalence, and the Holocaust.* Bloomington: Indiana University Press.

Sumner, W. G. (1906). *Folkways.* New York, NY: Ginn.

Tajfel, H., & Turner, J. C. (1979). An integrative theory of intergroup conflict. In W. G. Austin & S. Worchel (Eds.), *The social psychology of intergroup relations* (pp. 33–47). Monterey, CA: Brooks/Cole.

Tuckwood, C. (2008). Religion and genocide studies. *The Ecumenist: A Journal of Theology, Culture, and Society, 45*(1). Available at http://thesentinelproject.org/wp-content/uploads/religion-and-genocide-prevention-christopher-tuckwood-for-the-ecumenist.pdf

Volf, M. (2000). The social meaning of reconciliation. *Interpretation: A Journal of Bible and Theology, 54,* 158–172. doi:10.1177/002096430005400205

Waller, J. E. (2007). *Becoming evil: How ordinary people commit genocide and mass killing* (2nd ed.). New York, NY: Oxford University Press.

Wolff, K. H. (1969). For a sociology of evil. *Journal of Social Issues, 25,* 111–126. doi:10.1111/j.1540-4560.1969.tb02581.x

Zimbardo, P. (2007). *The Lucifer effect: Understanding how good people turn evil.* New York, NY: Random House.

Part IV

WHO IS RELIGIOUS AND SPIRITUAL: SPECIFIC POPULATIONS

CHAPTER 27

THE NATURE AND FUNCTIONS OF RELIGION AND SPIRITUALITY IN CHILDREN

Chris J. Boyatzis

Historically, religious and spiritual development has been a neglected domain within the broader area of developmental studies, but now these topics are receiving burgeoning attention. Dissertations on children and spirituality have surged, with most of the dissertations on this topic appearing since 2000. Recently, many major volumes have appeared, including *The Handbook of Spiritual Development in Childhood and Adolescence* (Roehlkepartain, King, Wagener, & Benson, 2006), edited books (e.g., Bunge, 2001; Dowling & Scarlett, 2006; Ratcliff, 2004), and special journal issues (Boyatzis, 2003, 2006; King & Boyatzis, 2004). The most recent edition of the prestigious *Handbook of Child Psychology* had for the first time a chapter on religious and spiritual development (Oser, Scarlett, & Bucher, 2006).

This chapter focuses on major topics on religion and spirituality that have been studied in children. A much larger literature exists on adolescents. The review is organized around several areas of inquiry: children's religious cognition, studied primarily from a cognitive–developmental framework; family dynamics and parent–child interaction; and children's well-being. Throughout this review, recent research is highlighted: Fully 73% of the work cited has been published since 2000 and 40% since 2006. The chapter closes with suggested new directions for the field. Before beginning, it will be useful to define some key terms.

CHALLENGES AND PROGRESS IN DEFINING KEY TERMS

This volume attempts to clarify conceptual confusion around religion and spirituality. In this chapter, *religion* or *religiousness* refer to institutional practices, beliefs, and experiences centering around the sacred and to the psychological functions of such practices, beliefs, and experiences. *Spiritual* and *spirituality* are used to refer to feelings, experiences, practices, and relationships with what one considers self-transcendent and sacred, which may or may not be grounded in institutional religion. The constructs are separated here because most of the relevant literature on children allows such a distinction. Nevertheless, defining spirituality in children is especially challenging (see Scarlett, 2006).

Some leading scholars have concluded that "there is no consensus about what 'this domain' really is" (Roehlkepartain, Benson, King, & Wagener, 2006, p. 4). If children develop spiritually, *what* develops? Scholars at the Center for Spiritual Development have defined spiritual development as growth in "the intrinsic capacity for self-transcendence, in which the self is embedded in something greater than the self, including the sacred . . . shaped both within and outside of religious traditions, beliefs, and practices" (Benson, Roehlkepartain, & Rude, 2003, pp. 205–206). This definition depicts spirituality as a natural human propensity, shaped by multiple experiences within and without religion, and characterized by connectedness and relationality to what is beyond the self. In their rich qualitative work, Hay and Nye (1998) labeled this latter quality *relational consciousness*. Spirituality, then, is not confined to a religious doctrine or sacred entity; God or a divinity is not a priori the only

DOI: 10.1037/14045-027
APA Handbook of Psychology, Religion, and Spirituality: Vol. 1. Context, Theory, and Research, K. I. Pargament (Editor-in-Chief)
Copyright © 2013 by the American Psychological Association. All rights reserved.

transcendent entity with which a child could be in relation. Hence, children's spirituality precedes religious socialization, although children's spirituality is subject to many religious influences. These definitions and approaches are consistent with the definitional and integrative–paradigm approach of this volume.

But if "the sacred" is essential to these definitions and approaches, a conceptual and methodological challenge arises: What does "sacred" mean to a child, and how could we find out? The construct of sanctification (Pargament & Mahoney, 2005) may help, although it is not clear how this construct would apply, theoretically or methodologically, to children; the empirical work and operationalization have not yet been done. Rich qualitative inquiry by such scholars as Hay and Nye (1998) and Coles (1990), using lengthy interviews, has suggested that it is possible to assess older children's relational consciousness with what is significant and beyond the self. Nevertheless, children's transcendent relationships and feelings toward the sacred remain an open issue needing systematic inquiry. In addition, there may be novel ways to think about children's self-expression, agency, and maturity in realms of religion and spirituality (Boyatzis, 2011). For now, we commence our inquiry with humility in the face of these conceptual challenges.

COGNITIVE–DEVELOPMENTAL APPROACHES TO RELIGIOUS COGNITION

Recently, Johnson and Boyatzis (2006) proposed that spiritual development proceeds from intuitive understanding to increasingly reflective thought. This cognitive approach may illuminate children's relationships with the sacred. Young children use inference mechanisms to intuitively sort out reality and the supernatural. Such intuition becomes increasingly reflective and is buttressed by cultural practices that orient the child to cultural modes of spiritual being. Spiritual development arises not from mere acquisition of knowledge about the transcendent—which may be the outcome of religious education—but from increasingly meaningful experiential connections of the self to the "something more."

Within developmental psychology, cognitive–developmentalism has long been a dominant theoretical framework guiding scholars' inquiry into children's religious and spiritual development. This framework has been deeply influenced by a Piagetian approach that posits the following: (a) distinct stages of thinking that yoke a particular quality and structure of thought to a specific age range; (b) a progression from concrete to abstract understanding; (c) the march from immature thought to more mature abstract, rational thought; and (d) clear distinctions between children's (immature) and adults' (mature) religious cognition. Within this approach, a major theme has been *religious cognition*, or children's thinking about religious concepts (see reviews and critiques by Boyatzis, 2005, 2009). Elkind (1970) was a major figure in this area. Through his many studies in the 1960s, Elkind introduced U.S. psychologists to Piagetian cognitive–developmental models of religious cognition. One conclusion from that era of research was that structural qualities of children's thinking about religious concepts parallel their thinking about other *non*religious concepts. For example, children's descriptions of God were akin to their descriptions of (older adult male) people. Religious cognition was a specific case of a generic conceptual process.

A second wave of cognitive–developmentalism brought revisions to the traditional Piagetian model. One change was the rejection of the idea of global stages of children's thinking. In the 1980s, developmentalists endorsed models of domain specificity, depicting the child as creating naïve cognitive theories in specific domains rather than being governed by age-yoked cognitive processes that crossed all domains. By the 1990s, domain specificity and research on theory of mind had become so central in the field that scientists viewed children's concepts of God and prayer, for example, as part of the general growth of understanding of the mind, agency, and mental–physical causality. Children's religious cognitions were understood to operate under the same principles and tendencies of children's everyday cognition but within specific domains of thought (Boyer, 1994; Boyer & Walker, 2000). For example, the anthropomorphic God images common to children (and adults) arise from the natural extension of an intuitive folk psychology used to understand people and other agents to supernatural figures. Cognitive–developmentalists now emphasize *religious ontologies*, mental representations about the existence and powers of supernatural entities. These ontologies possess key features. First, they are counterintuitive beliefs (i.e., they violate ordinary expectations, as in the case of spiritual entities who are immortal or omniscient). Second, counterintuitive religious beliefs operate above the foundational processes of theory of mind that equip children with a prepared set of qualities to extend to religious agents (e.g., "My supernatural God has wishes and thoughts and worries [just like all beings with minds do]"). Third, the combination of these agents' counterintuitiveness with the judgment that such agents are *real* makes the belief more salient to the believers.

CHILDREN'S CONCEPTS OF GOD

The most studied topic in religious cognition is children's concepts of God—not surprising, given that most research has been done by Westerners in monotheistic cultures. Children's ideas of God are typically anthropomorphic. In his large collection of schoolchildren's drawings, Coles (1990) found that 87% depicted God's face. Studies on religiously diverse samples have found widespread anthropomorphism but with some denominational variation. Among 6- to 10-year-olds, the most anthropomorphic God drawings were by Mormon, Mennonite, and Lutheran children and the least by Jewish children (Pitts, 1976). Heller (1986) found that Hindu children, more than Jewish, Baptist, or Catholic ones, described a multifaceted God who feels close and like a person yet also has abstract and intangible qualities. Hindu children's accounts reflected their religion's doctrine about different Gods with different natures. These studies suggest the influence of religious background on children's God images and show that children extend a folk psychology to their God images but also conceptualize God as considerably more than human.

In the latest wave of cognitive–developmental work, research by Barrett has challenged this view of the child's God as a personified God (see Chapter 12 in this volume). Barrett and colleagues (Barrett & Keil, 1996; Barrett & Richert, 2003) have studied young children to test whether they equate God's capabilities with humans' capabilities (i.e., think about God anthropomorphically). Barrett has offered an alternative, the "preparedness" hypothesis, which posits that children are prepared conceptually at young ages to think about God's *unique qualities—not only those shared with humans.* In one study (Barrett, Newman, & Richert, 2003), 5-year-olds claimed that God, but not their mothers, would immediately understand ambiguous drawings. In another (Barrett, Richert, & Driesenga, 2001), 3- to 7-year-old children claimed that God, but not their mother, would know the contents of a cracker box that actually contained rocks. Akin to this finding is the report that most children 5 years and older felt that God "just knows" what people are praying without needing to hear them (Woolley & Phelps, 2001). Barrett asserted that children are prepared conceptually at early ages to view God as unique, which helps explain why children easily distinguish God's special status. Barrett and Richert (2003) stated that although cultural contributions help create God concepts, children need "little direct training or tuition to acquire fairly rich theological concepts" (p. 310).

An excellent study by Lane, Wellman, and Evans (2010) interrogated the preparedness argument and offered new evidence for the anthropomorphism hypothesis. They tested young children's beliefs about ordinary characters (mom, a girl) and extraordinary ones (God) by using a false belief task in which children were asked if the character, on looking at a closed crayon box, would say the box held crayons or marbles (when the character did not have the opportunity to look in the box to see that marbles were actually inside). To say the character would think "marbles" shows the child can attribute false beliefs to another character. The basic question is whether children think God possesses false beliefs or will merely think the crayon box holds crayons—like mere mortals would assume. The methods and findings are simplified here because of space limits. In short, their young preschoolers, from 40 to 52 months, failed to attribute false beliefs to any characters (all characters including God would know the crayon box had marbles, and hence God was not special in this knowledge). The middle age-group, 53 to 59 months, said that ordinary characters and God would have false beliefs, and hence God was not omniscient. In the oldest group, more than 59 months, children said that ordinary characters would mistakenly think the box held crayons, but God would know it held marbles.

Lane et al. (2010) concluded that young children's understanding of extraordinary minds—such as God's—arises from their intuitive psychology of ordinary minds. Young children are cognitively prepared to first think about God in anthropomorphic terms and only later, starting around age 5, must adapt and overcome those propensities to appreciate God's counterintuitive, special abilities. Lane et al. noted that their interpretation is supported by other studies. For example, in one study of Greek Orthodox children, 3- and 4-year-olds claimed that both a young girl *and* God would be ignorant of the hidden contents in a box; only at age 5 did children believe that God would have unique knowledge of the box's contents (Makris & Pnevmatikos, 2007). It is certain, then, that cognitive–developmentalists continue to be intrigued by children's thoughts about God, and they continue to situate such concepts within a framework of children's domain-specific cognitive development. The chapter now turns to other domains of religious cognition.

CHILDREN'S CONCEPTS OF THE SOUL OR AFTERLIFE

In contrast to children's God concepts, their thoughts about the soul have received less attention. Children's beliefs about the afterlife are connected with an early distinction between minds and bodies (Bering & Bjorklund, 2004; Richert & Harris, 2006). Children know that, at death, physical and biological functions cease; however, children do not clearly see that death terminates all mental and emotional processes. Bering, Blasi, and Bjorklund (2005) used a clever task about a mouse (a puppet) eaten by a hungry alligator to study afterlife beliefs in 5- to 12-year-old secular and Catholic children in Spain. Results supported the biological cessation and psychological continuity pattern in the afterlife, especially in younger children and children who attended a secular school. If children hold early intuitions about the afterlife, there are surrounding familial and cultural practices that provide ample testimony and rituals to reify and scaffold them. As Bering et al. (2005, p. 600) stated, in a socialization milieu that espouses the continued spiritual life of the deceased, "biological reasoning about the psychological status of dead agents may be set aside in favour of explicit religious ideas that defy naturalistic principles" (Bering et al., 2005, p. 600). These conceptual accounts await confirmation and clarification from scholars in other cultures and religious groups, and additional methodologies should assess children's views of the afterlife with tasks that rely on materials more germane to humans than Bering's task focusing on a mouse puppet eaten by an alligator.

CHILDREN'S UNDERSTANDING OF PRAYER

Cognitive–developmentalists have examined how children think about and understand prayer. An early study of prayer approached the topic from a Piagetian perspective. Long, Elkind, and Spilka (1967) interviewed 5- to 12-year-olds about prayer and found developmental trends. Younger children (5- to 7-year-olds) described prayer as an emotionally neutral, formulaic act associated with specific times and locations, with little sense of the function of prayer. Prayers were said by all children in this age-group who believed that prayers came from heaven and God, and God had to process prayers one at a time. In the early elementary school years (7 to 9 years of age), prayer was seen as a specific act usually motivated by a desire (often to ask God for material objects such as toys). Prayers were not done by all children in this group because some were too sleepy to pray and some children simply did not "want anything"; prayers were communicated to God by messengers or God would descend to retrieve them. In later elementary school years (9 to 12 years of age), prayer became a mental, covert, private activity in the child to communicate with God. Prayer was no longer yoked to ritual events, and beliefs motivated prayer: Those who did not believe in God did not pray. Older children saw prayer as a means to ask God to respond to more abstract, humanitarian needs such as peace, and a coping function was evident as children said negative emotions could lead to prayer. At this age, God did not need messengers but could hear prayers directly and was able to attend to all people's prayers simultaneously.

More recent research has corroborated these patterns but with some refinements. One study found that even young children (4 to 6 years) believe that one can pray anywhere and must be able to think and know about God to pray, and from ages 4 to 8 years children increasingly believe that prayer helps people feel better (Woolley & Phelps, 2001). An excellent study by Bamford and Lagattuta (2010) is situated within the analysis of children's religious concepts as related to specific domains of cognition (e.g., theory of mind, causality). This work was cross- sectional, testing 4-, 6-, and 8-year-olds and adults on a rich variety of measures. Interview questions included, "Can prayer be done in the head or do you have to say words?" and "Is prayer the same thing as talking to God?" On other story and vignette tasks with characters feeling different emotions in various situations, children were asked how the characters' feelings might inspire praying and how praying might help their feelings.

Bamford and Lagattuta (2010) found that with increasing age, children better understood that prayer is a mental activity done in one's head (endorsed by only 45% of 4-year-olds but 84% of older children) and that prayer and talking to God is the same thing (endorsed by only 43% of 4-year-olds but 90% and 94% of 6- and 8-year-olds). With age, children also came to better appreciate the role of emotions in prayers. Four- and 6-year-olds believed that positive emotions more than negative ones would cause people to pray, whereas 8-year-olds believed that both kinds of emotions would inspire prayer similarly. From 6 to 8 years of age, there were significant increases in believing that negative emotions would lead to prayer and declines in believing that positive emotions would. As children got older they also realized that prayers of thanksgiving were more likely in positive, rather than negative, situations. As for the emotional benefits from praying, children felt that people would feel better after praying. The younger age-groups felt that story characters would feel better after praying if they had enjoyed positive emotions in the story, whereas from 6 to 8 years of age, there was a significant increase in reporting that a character would feel better from praying in a sad or scary situation.

In addition to collecting cross-sectional data, Bamford and Lagattuta (2010) tested two alternative hypotheses: a *religious socialization model* in which children's knowledge of prayer (tapped by the questions described in the previous paragraphs) would be associated with their level of religious experience and education, and a *cognitive maturation model* in which children's prayer concepts would reflect age-related cognitive constraints. Parents provided data on a variety of children's religious activities (e.g., frequency of prayer alone, prayer with others, discussion about religion with parents, involvement in religious activities, worship attendance, etc.). Although children's understanding of prayer was positively correlated with religious activity in the two younger ages, on most measures there were no relationships between children's religious activity and their prayer knowledge. The only group showing a link between religious activity and prayer knowledge was 4-year-olds, but this association emerged on a minority of measures. Thus, this study does not support the socialization hypothesis, consistent with the lack of such evidence in another study on parents' religiosity and their young children's comprehension of prayer (Woolley & Phelps, 2001). Bamford and Lagattuta have suggested that religious socialization may promote some prayer knowledge in children too young to have generated more mature prayer concepts on their own, and they wisely noted that there may be other ways, not tapped in their study, that socialization could influence children's prayer sophistication. In contrast to the weak role for socialization, the study's evidence gives strong support to the cognitive maturation model—children's understanding of many psychological and spiritual aspects of prayer became increasingly sophisticated from age 4 to 8.

In sum, in their thinking about God, the soul, and prayer, children's cognitions follow inherent developmental trends; the data in these domains support a cognitive–maturation model. This is not to say that socialization does not matter—indeed, the next sections describe many ways in which it does, although in children's behavior and well-being rather than children's thinking. It is likely that socialization may influence other kinds of religious knowing beyond the ontological domains studied by cognitive–developmentalists (e.g., gods, the afterlife). Children may revise their implicit religious theories and beliefs when exposed to conflicting evidence in parental testimony or experiences that support alternate accounts (Harris & Koenig, 2006).

One of the premiere studies to shed light on children's processing of family input comes from Evans (2000), who studied children in secular and Fundamentalist Christian families to learn whether the children endorsed creationist or evolutionary accounts. At all ages, Fundamentalist children—who attended religious schools or were home-schooled—strongly accepted creationist views. However, 7- to 9-years-old children from secular homes also endorsed creationist accounts, and not until early adolescence did secular-home children accept their families' evolutionist explanations. This and prior work reviewed demonstrates that parents' beliefs may affect children's notions about origins and other concepts, but children will filter such beliefs through their own intuitive cognitive systems. Given the venerable assumption in other bodies of research that parents shape children's religious and spiritual development through parent–child "transmission," the key point from cognitive–developmental work is that children are anything but blank slates, and instead—as Piaget taught us long ago—they actively construct their own knowledge. With this in mind, let us consider children's socialization.

SOCIALIZATION FACTORS AND A SOCIAL–ECOLOGY APPROACH

Several frameworks help organize our thinking about the myriad social influences on children's religious and spiritual development. A social–ecology model (Bronfenbrenner, 1979) posits multiple interrelated contexts of influence on children's development. These contexts range from the most proximal *microsystems* (e.g., family, school, peer group, or religious community) to more distal *macrosystems* (e.g., dominant cultural values and ideologies). In this chapter, the focus is on the family because this is the context that has received the most empirical attention (see also Chapter 20, this volume, and Volume 2, Chapter 9, this handbook). A thorough treatment of other social contexts, from peers to culture, is available in Roehlkepartain, King, Wagener, and Benson (2006).

A sociocultural model emphasizes the influence of knowledgeable adults and peers who use guided participation in culturally meaningful practices to help the child apprentice move to higher competence (Vygotsky, 1978). Hence, parents, relatives, clergy, educators, older siblings, and knowledgeable friends can act as mentors. Any of these mentors can guide children to more advanced levels of spiritual connectedness to the sacred and, in more religious contexts, greater understanding and engagement in rituals, creeds, and communal worship.

A third framework (Kuczynski, 2003) is a transactional model that posits children and parents influence each other in reciprocal exchanges, with parent–child interaction possessing a bidirectional influence. This departs from the traditional view that parents shape children in a unilateral Parent → Child fashion. That "transmission" model long dominated socialization research, but scholars now endorse a more dynamic conceptualization of bidirectional and multidirectional influence (see Boyatzis, 2005; Boyatzis, Dollahite, & Marks, 2006). Social control theory is often used (e.g., Bartkowski, Xu, & Levin, 2008) to explain how parents use church settings and faith communities to reinforce the parents' own values and expose children to other adults with faith beliefs.

Another approach that is central in psychology though less common in the psychology of religion involves behavioral genetics. The few such analyses have shown that for religiosity in childhood and adolescence, genetic relatedness explains little variance, whereas shared family environment explains religious similarity between parents and children. This evidence, however, comes from studies of adolescents, not younger children, and the outcomes are religious rather than spiritual in nature (Koenig, McGue, & Iacono, 2009).

THE FAMILY AS A CONTEXT OF SPIRITUAL AND RELIGIOUS DEVELOPMENT

Although social–ecology models posit that it takes a village to raise a child, the family is "the first village" of religious and spiritual development (Boyatzis et al., 2006). The scholarly literature is only slowly studying the interplay between socialization factors and the child's own endogenous cognitive processes and temperamental variables; these latter variables could act as filters that determine the degree to which exogenous socialization attempts influence the child. Little work has investigated children's religious and spiritual development from this integrated perspective. In the family, whatever input children receive from their parents must be processed through the child's inherent cognitive structures and may also be mediated through external processes such as sibling relationships. Thus, children may modify or jettison some beliefs because of parent input (Harris & Koenig, 2006) and may also make *secondary adjustments* through "third-party discussions" (Kuczynski, 2003, p. 10) with siblings and family members. Our field knows little about these complex multidirectional dynamics (see Boyatzis, 2005).

Within parental socialization research, there is the assumption that parents shape their children through socialization methods found in nonreligious domains, including induction or explaining and reasoning with children to help them internalize the parent's values and beliefs, modeling, and reinforcement. Unfortunately, little research provides evidence on these specific mechanisms (but see Silberman, 2003). There is some evidence, however, that parental modeling is a key influence on the prayer behavior of children in England (Francis & Brown, 1990). Although progress has been made to understand such processes, more refined studies are needed of proximal processes through which religion operates in the family (Mahoney, 2010; Mahoney et al., 2001).

PARENT–CHILD CONVERSATION ABOUT RELIGION AND SPIRITUALITY

Parent–child conversation about religion may be an important mechanism through which parents and children coconstruct religious and spiritual meaning (Boyatzis, 2004). Unfortunately, there is a paucity of empirical data on this process regarding children, especially when compared with the extant data on parent–adolescent communication. One study of Christian families with children ages 3 to 12 asked parents to complete a religious-conversation diary for 2 weeks and to complete surveys on the content and process in such conversations (Boyatzis & Janicki, 2003). Both measures indicated that parents and children had about three conversations per week about religion and spirituality. Analyses of diaries revealed that children were active participants: They initiated and terminated about half of conversations, spoke as much as parents did, and frequently asked questions and offered their own views. These data support the view that children are active participants rather than passive recipients of ideas "transmitted" by parents, and that a bidirectional reciprocal style is more prominent in many families.

This characterization is supported by other studies of adolescents in Christian families in the South (Flor & Knapp, 2001) and religious Jewish, Muslim, and Christian families (Dollahite & Thatcher, 2008). In this latter study, many families had a youth-centered milieu in which conversations focused on the adolescents' spiritual needs. Youth-centered conversations were described by adolescents and parents as positive experiences, which may explain why Flor and Knapp (2001) found that higher parent–child communication predicted higher religiosity in youth: Such conversations are positive experiences reflecting a healthy relationship in which youth will be more likely to internalize parents' religious values and attitudes.

We need more data on the frequency, content, and structure of parent–child communication about religious and spiritual issues. We also need to learn how such discussion contributes uniquely to children's religious and spiritual development above and beyond parent–child communication in general (see Brelsford & Mahoney, 2008, on adolescents). In addition, longitudinal data from multiple informants will determine whether communication variables at Time 1 are causally related to youth religiosity at Time 2. Many issues must be settled for a genuine understanding of how religion and spirituality work in the family.

THE NEED TO ANALYZE MULTIPLE VARIABLES AND THEIR INTERACTIONS IN PARENTING AND RELIGION

Many researchers have used limited assessments of religiosity, as reviews of research from the past three decades found that more than three quarters of studies on religion and family measured religiosity with only one or two items (Mahoney, 2010; Mahoney, Pargament, Swank, & Tarakeshwar, 2001). This is problematic given the multidimensional nature of both religiosity and parenting. Fortunately, some studies have analyzed multiple dimensions of religiosity to better understand parenting behavior and attitudes.

Parents with conservative Protestant affiliations endorse and use spanking as a disciplinary technique more than other parents do (Gershoff, Miller, & Holden, 1999). Perhaps paradoxically, conservative Protestant parents are less likely to yell at their children (Bartkowski & Wilcox, 2000) and use a warm, expressive style in nondisciplinary situations (Bartkowski & Xu, 2000). Although parents' denomination is related to discipline, a stronger predictor of spanking is parents' theological conservatism (Gershoff, Miller, & Holden, 1999). On this and other variables, researchers should move away from simple categorical variables to continuous dimensions. Let us review recent studies that assessed multiple dimensions of parent religiosity to learn how religion plays a role in parenting and young children's development.

Murray-Swank, Mahoney, and Pargament (2006) measured indexes of mothers' religious belief including theological conservatism and sanctification of their roles as parents, or how much the mothers imbued their role with sacred and divine qualities and saw parenting as "God's work." Conservatism and sanctification were not related independently to mothers' use of spanking, but spanking was predicted by the interaction between mothers' conservatism and sanctification. Specifically, mothers who were theologically conservative were more likely than other conservative mothers to spank their children if they also viewed their parent role as sacred and holy; in contrast, mothers who were theologically liberal were less likely than other liberal mothers to spank their children if they also viewed their role as sacred and holy.

Volling, Mahoney, and Rauer (2009) measured parental disciplinary strategies and sanctification of parenting in relation to their preschool children's moral conduct. The more mothers and fathers sanctified their role, the more they used induction (e.g., focusing on consequences of children's wrongdoing) and positive socialization techniques (e.g., approving good behavior, recognizing when child was nice). A key finding was that parents' positive techniques combined with sanctification of parenting to predict children's conscience development. Children were most mature morally when fathers used induction and sanctified their role. A similar interaction obtained for children's affective discomfort: After misbehaving, children's apologizing and concern for others was highest when parents used positive socialization techniques *and* were high in sanctification of parenting.

Another study (Dumas & Nissley-Tsiopinis, 2006) analyzed a diverse sample of families with preschoolers. Parents reported on sanctification of parenting and style of religious coping in response to children's defiant behavior. Sanctification did not predict children's behavior, but oppositional behavior increased when parents' religiousness was low and when mothers used negative religious coping (e.g., expressing anger at God, feeling abandoned by God). Thus, children's defiant behavior was most evident at the interplay of different facets of religiosity.

In sum, various socialization frameworks are helpful in thinking about how children develop religiously and spiritually. The studies reviewed in this section confirm the value of measuring multiple variables of religiosity and assessing interactions between them and between parenting and family variables. Surely other questions remain. We can study how parent and child personality variables affect religious dynamics in the child's upbringing. We know that children's temperament interacts with parents' disciplinary styles to shape different outcomes. For example, anxious or fearful children internalize parents' rules more when their mothers use gentle persuasion techniques (Kochanska, 1995). There may be similar interactions of child personality and parenting style at play in children's religious and spiritual development. More research should address how parents' religiosity interacts with their parenting styles and goals to affect their young children (see Desrosiers, Kelley, & Miller, 2011; Duriez, Soenens, Neyrinck, & Vansteenkiste, 2009, on adolescents). We now turn to work on other dimensions of well-being in various populations of children.

CHILDREN'S RELIGION, SPIRITUALITY, AND WELL-BEING

Researchers have assessed the links between religion and spirituality among children with outcome variables from academic to psychosocial to emotional well-being. Other studies have explored religious and spiritual elements in children's coping and outcomes in a variety of challenging circumstances, from family dysfunction to medical problems.

Davis and Epkins (2009) examined whether 11- to 12-year-olds' private religious practices, such as prayer, scripture reading, and listening to religious programs, would buffer them against the impact of family conflict. The children's religious practices showed no direct association with their depressive and anxiety symptoms, but they did moderate relations between family conflict and their own anxiety and depression. Specifically, family conflict was more related to youths' depression and anxiety when youth were low (as opposed to high) in private religious practices. Similarly, school-age children who prayed frequently were significantly higher in protective resources, such as social connectedness and sense of humor (Rew, Wong, & Sternglanz, 2004).

Some scholars have investigated religion in sick children. A qualitative study examined how children with cystic fibrosis used religion to cope with their illness (Pendleton, Cavalli, Pargament, & Nasr, 2002). On the basis of their interview responses, children described 11 different religious coping strategies. Sample strategies included petitioning God to intercede, working with God to cope with their struggles, and expressing discontent with God or their congregation. On the basis of their comments, children felt that most of these coping strategies helped them with their illness.

Another study addressed how children with asthma used religion to cope with their illness. Benore, Pargament, and Pendleton (2008) tested a sample of children, most African American and Baptist. Many predictors of child well-being were assessed to learn whether children's religious coping enhanced well-being uniquely. Religious coping was assessed on an existing measure adapted to make it age-appropriate, which is a genuine methodological contribution to the study of children. This scale generated two forms of coping, positive and negative, parallel to these forms used by adults. A sample positive coping item was "I think God is watching over me," whereas "I think God cannot help me" was a sample negative item. Children's quality of life, asthma severity, and psychosocial well-being were largely uncorrelated with children's importance of religion and religious activities reported by parents (e.g., children's prayer or attendance frequency, religious education). In contrast, children's well-being was clearly related to religious coping. In regressions that controlled for secular coping and importance of religion, positive religious coping did not predict unique variance in most outcomes, although it did predict—paradoxically—higher worrying by children when hospitalized, which may have triggered greater use of positive religious coping In contrast, negative religious coping predicted poor outcomes while hospitalized: lower quality of life related to asthma, higher depression, and higher anxiety. At 1-month follow-up, negative coping predicted higher anxiety whereas positive coping predicted greater spiritual growth; children who used more positive coping came to feel closer to God and their faith community.

Kim, McCullough, and Cicchetti (2009) examined parents' and children's religiosity in normal and maltreated children from low-income families. This study was the first, the authors claimed, to examine how parental religiosity is related to adjustment in maltreated children. Maltreated children placed less importance on religion than did nonmaltreated children, although the two groups did not differ on worship attendance, parents' attendance, or importance of religion. Other results show that parent religiosity was more protective for children who were not maltreated (than for those who were) and who were not religious. Parents' worship attendance predicted fewer internalizing symptoms (e.g., anxiety) in nonmaltreated children who did not attend worship frequently (but not in children who attended frequently). Also, the more importance parents placed on their faith, the lower the internalizing and externalizing problems in nonmaltreated children who were low in faith. In contrast, in families with maltreated children, neither parent and child attendance nor their interaction predicted children's functioning.

The evidence demonstrates the value of measuring different dimensions of religiosity and well-being (Pargament, 1997). Different child outcomes are associated with positive versus negative religious coping, with worship attendance versus importance of religion, and in children low versus high in religiosity.

Two recent ambitious studies deserve elaboration. Both studies examined the role of religion and spirituality in the well-being of children who were not suffering from any kind of acute or chronic malady or life circumstance. In the first study, Holder, Coleman, and Wallace (2010) assessed happiness in a sample of 320 children, ages 8 to 12 years, from public and private religious schools. It was posited that religion and spirituality could enhance children's (as adults') happiness through the provision of social support, relationship with the divine, and a sense of meaning. Holder et al. claimed to be the first to study these issues in children. Children's happiness was assessed on four different but similar measures (e.g., a smiley-face task in which children chose the facial expression that matched how they felt). Children also completed a survey of a variety of religious practices (e.g., worship attendance, prayer frequency) and beliefs (e.g., desire to be closer to a higher power). A key predictor was the Spiritual Well-Being Questionnaire that tapped four dimensions of children's (self-reported) spirituality: *personal,* or the value and meaning in one's life; *communal,* or quality and depth of relationships with others; *environmental*, or a sense of awe for nature; and *transcendental*, or faith in and relationship with something or someone beyond the human level (Holder et al., 2010, p. 136).

Holder et al. (2010) found that children's happiness was not related to religiosity but had widespread correlations across measures of children's spirituality, albeit with low *r*s (.12–.21). In subsequent regressions that controlled for children's gender, school type, and temperament, only two spirituality dimensions—personal and communal spirituality—predicted significant variance in children's happiness. That is, children were happier the more they had a positive sense of self and better relationships with others. In contrast, children's sense of awe for the environment did not predict any happiness outcomes, and a sense of transcendental connection predicted happiness on only one of four outcomes (and on that only about 1% of variance).

Holder et al. (2010) can be lauded for studying these constructs with multiple measures and computing regressions that controlled for many variables (most noteworthy was children's temperament). Unfortunately, the authors did not present evidence for the internal reliability of the religiosity and spirituality surveys. Although their data confirm that a greater sense of personal meaning is related to happiness, the major finding from their study may be a null one, that transcendental spirituality was largely *not* related to 8- to 12-year-olds' happiness. This point is important to emphasize because transcendence was their one spirituality dimension that seems *most* consistent with how psychologists define spirituality. When combined with the finding that children's religiosity did not predict happiness, this study offers little evidence that religion and spirituality play a positive role in happiness in this age range of children.

Another recent study illuminates the role of religion in children's lives. Bartkowski et al. (2008) used data from one wave (*N* = approximately 17,000 children) of a large, nationally representative sample of kindergarten and first-grade children and their parents and teachers. This study measured several aspects of family religiosity—mothers' and fathers' worship attendance (separately and together), frequency of discussion with the child about religion, and frequency of spousal arguing about religion. Many forms of children's psychological and psychosocial functioning served as outcomes, some rated by parents and teachers and others by only one group. Regression analyses with many demographic variables as controls showed that frequency of worship attendance by mothers and fathers separately, and by parents together, was widely associated with children's higher levels of positive outcomes (self-control, social skills) and lower levels of undesirable outcomes (internalizing and externalizing problems), as rated by both parents and teachers. These findings illustrate the potential benefits of involvement in organized religion on many different types of psychological and psychosocial outcomes in children; furthermore, these benefits seem to be apparent to parents and teachers alike.

Bartkowski et al. (2008) claimed that their findings support a social control theory, which states that parents bring their children into a context of religious capital in which nonparent adults reinforce the parents' values; as a result, benefits of religious involvement are apparent across contexts and raters (see Chapter 6 in this volume). A weaker pattern emerged from the predictor variable of how often parents discussed religion with the child. Of the 10 possible outcomes, this measure was significantly linked to only three (better self-control, approaches to learning, and interaction with peers). Interestingly, these significant findings emerged only from parents' reports of children's outcomes; none of the teacher-reported child outcomes was significant. This pattern recurred with the other communication variable, as spousal disagreement about religion predicted poorer functioning in children on five of five outcomes rated by parents but on zero of five outcomes rated by teachers. This discrepancy, according to the authors, could mean that any impact of family discussion is limited to the family context or that religious parents are biased in reports of their children's behavior in ways that would inflate the benefit of religion.

Although the Bartkowski et al. (2008) study is significant for offering a major data set with multiple measures and outcomes, some measures had low alpha values, and religiosity predictors often yielded small effects in regression analyses. Although the study tapped the interesting variable of parent–child discussion about religion, such findings would be clearer (in this study and others like it) if the study included a measure of more generic parent–child conversation about other, secular topics to serve as a control in testing the unique value of communication about *religion*. Their finding that conflict about religion predicts poorer outcomes when rated by parents only is constrained by the nature of their predictor, which assessed spousal, not parent–child, disagreement. In future work, it would be helpful to assess verbal religious disagreement between parents and children.

A deeper problem in the study is less methodological than hermeneutic: the authors' overdrawn interpretations of data. Despite their nonexperimental design, Bartkowski et al. (2008) used causal language throughout their article. For example, they wrote that parents' religious attendance has a "positive effect on child development," parent–child discussion about faith "produces a positive effect on interaction skills" (pp. 27–28), and family arguments over religion are "deleterious" (p. 33). Although this problem is surely not unique to this study, such statements are inappropriate in light of the study's design, and although at the end of the article the authors expressed caution regarding such presumptions, they nevertheless made them throughout their article. Similarly, although the authors stated that their findings were "robust and quite clear" (Bartkowski et al., 2008, p. 31), this conclusion seems limited to the positive outcomes associated with parents' worship attendance. As for the other findings, the low alphas on some predictor variables, the modest variance explained, and the inconsistent patterns between parent and teacher findings indicate that the findings are neither robust nor clear. Finally, Bartkowski et al. offered the sweeping conclusion that "speculation and limitations aside, religion does seem to be good for young children" (p. 34). Good science requires that speculation and limitations be duly noted and *not* swept aside.

These problems are highlighted to use this otherwise informative Bartkowski et al. (2008) article to caution against premature or simplistic conclusions. At this point in the field—given its definitional challenges, complexity of variables, relatively small database, limitations of research designs, and charged nature of topics—it is important to strive for more modest and nuanced interpretations. Rather than asking, "Is religion good for children?" we might ask a more differentiated question consistent with the integrative paradigm espoused in this handbook (see Chapter 1 in this volume), such as "Under what conditions and on what indexes and in what samples is religion good (and bad) for children?" The many studies reviewed in this chapter reveal that this more refined and complex approach is called for.

CONCLUSION AND FUTURE DIRECTIONS

Interest in children's religious and spiritual development has exploded, with most of the attention surrounding the several themes reviewed in this chapter. Progress is being made in clarifying the semantic and conceptual issues in religiosity and spirituality, but much work remains to determine just what these terms mean to children. Children's thinking about religion and religious concepts is a main thematic focus, especially from cognitive–developmentalists who view children's religious cognition as a special case of more generic age-appropriate thinking in which children recruit their inherent cognitive processes to understand God, prayer, the soul, and so on. The social ecology that surrounds children and ostensibly shapes their religious and spiritual development is a major focus of other scholars. In this work, the antiquated view of the child as a tabula rasa and of the parent–child relationship as a one-sided flow of influence have been replaced with a depiction of the child as actively processing external inputs and as engaging in dynamic bidirectional interaction with parents. Another focus is the association between children's psychological, medical, and psychosocial functioning and various dimensions of religiosity in the child and in the family.

The existing literature suggests that certain facets of religiosity are linked with positive outcomes for children. In this conclusion, however, it is important to emphasize many qualifications and caveats in the current literature: The particular positive associations vary by measure, population, and level of child religiosity; the vast majority of studies are correlational in nature, and even powerful statistical approaches (multiple regression, structural equation modeling) that are common in recent work cannot confirm causality; and many studies obtain numerous nonsignificant results amidst their positive findings. Given the number of variables and statistical tests in many studies that increase the risk of Type II errors, it would behoove researchers to set stringent probability levels and report effect sizes. In light of these concerns, scholars must resist the temptation to force complex results into a simple conclusion that religion is all good (or all bad) all the time. On some outcome variables, in some families, religiosity is not linked to better functioning in children, and we should strive to identify more precisely what dimensions of religion and spirituality matter for which outcomes in which children in which circumstances.

The field is ripe for growth in many other directions. First, the literature on children is still relatively small (compared with that on adolescents, for example). Second, many studies on children have no developmental design (microgenetic or longitudinal), which limits inferences about how religion and spirituality relate to child outcomes and maturity at different ages. Although some cognitive studies have had cross-sectional designs, longitudinal ones are needed to deepen understanding of how religious beliefs and concepts evolve over time. Longitudinal work is also needed to build an integrative paradigm across subdisciplines of psychology and to achieve a richer understanding of the roles of religion and spirituality in children's lives. Longitudinal research will tell us how childhood forms of religiosity or family religiosity predict adult religiosity, and it can also inform us about whether certain childhood psychological profiles set the stage for particular religious or spiritual outcomes later in life.

Another growth opportunity is that the reigning quantitative paradigm should be complemented by a more meaning-centered qualitative analysis. The limits of quantitative approaches were captured eloquently by the religion scholar Smith (1991), who compared researchers to "flies crawling on the outside of a goldfish bowl," carefully measuring the fish inside but never asking "how it feels to be a goldfish" (p. 7). To do so requires greater respect for and use of qualitative methodology, illustrated in rich sources (e.g., Coles, 1990; Hay & Nye, 1998; Reimer & Furrow, 2001). In a related vein, we will benefit from using more ethnographic approaches, a superb example being Bales's (2005) ethnographic account of Roman Catholic children's First Communion. Given that children's religiosity and spirituality are influenced within organized faith traditions, scholars should do more focused study of the rituals and sacraments that are essential mechanisms in faith communities, such as a Christian child's confirmation, a Jewish child's Bar or Bat Mitzvah, a Muslim child's first *hajj*, and so on (see Chapter 18 in this volume). Organized religions prioritize these events as milestones, but do children feel transformed by them? Some scholars have wisely suggested that researchers could go further than quantitative data to "ask preadolescents to describe the meaning behind their religious behaviors" (Davis & Epkins, 2009, p. 712). Scholars should heed this stunningly simple but smart suggestion.

Many qualitative methods could provide eclectic and creative means to study different modes of children's spiritual consciousness and experience, including the intuitional marked by nonverbal, nonlinear processes. Children may experience transcendental feelings while dancing (Bond & Stinson, 2000) and engage in spiritual reflection while reading picture books (Kendall, 1999); they also may reflect on religious themes in their personal writing (Van Dyke & Elias, 2008). Thus, social scientists may benefit from moving beyond their comfort zones and reach out to artists, dancers, and musicians to discover novel ways to explore, assess, and enhance children's religiosity and spirituality. Finally, beyond methodological advances, the field requires richer theory. With the exception of some grand stage-development theories (e.g., Fowler, 1981, on faith development), there is little theory offering an integrative synthesis specifically with respect to the topic of religious and spiritual growth. In sum, amid the exciting growth of knowledge regarding the roles of religion and spirituality in childhood, there remains much to learn.

References

Bales, S. R. (2005). *When I was a child: Children's interpretation of First Communion.* Chapel Hill: University of North Carolina Press.

Bamford, C., & Lagattuta, K. H. (2010). A new look at children's understanding of mind and emotion: The case of prayer. *Developmental Psychology, 46*, 78–92. doi:10.1037/a0016694

Barrett, J. L., & Keil, F. C. (1996). Conceptualizing a natural entity: Anthropomorphism in God concepts. *Cognitive Psychology, 31*, 219–247. doi:10.1006/cogp.1996.0017

Barrett, J. L., Newman, R., & Richert, R. A. (2003). When seeing is not believing: Children's understanding of humans' and non-humans' use of background knowledge in interpreting visual displays. *Journal of Cognition and Culture, 3*, 91–108. doi:10.1163/156853703321598590

Barrett, J. L., & Richert, R. A. (2003). Anthropomorphism or preparedness? Exploring children's God concepts. *Review of Religious Research, 44*, 300–312. doi:10.2307/3512389

Barrett, J. L., Richert, R. A., & Driesenga, A. (2001). God's beliefs versus mother's: The development of nonhuman agent concepts. *Child Development, 72*, 50–65. doi:10.1111/1467-8624.00265

Bartkowski, J. P., & Wilcox, W. B. (2000). Conservative Protestant child discipline: The case of parental yelling. *Social Forces, 79*, 263–290.

Bartkowski, J. P., & Xu, X. (2000). Distant patriarchs or expressive dads? The discourse and practice of fathering in conservative Protestant families. *Sociological Quarterly, 41*, 465–485. doi:10.1111/j.1533-8525.2000.tb00088.x

Bartkowski, J. P., Xu, X., & Levin, M. L. (2008). Religion and child development: Evidence from the Early Childhood Longitudinal Study. *Social Science Research, 37*, 18–36. doi:10.1016/j.ssresearch.2007.02.001

Benore, E., Pargament, K. I., & Pendleton, S. (2008). An initial examination of religious coping in children with asthma. *The International Journal for the Psychology of Religion, 18*, 267–290. doi:10.1080/10508610802229197

Benson, P. L., Roehlkepartain, E. C., & Rude, S. P. (2003). Spiritual development in childhood and adolescence: Toward a field of inquiry. *Applied Developmental Science, 7*, 205–212. doi:10.1207/S1532480XADS0703_12

Bering, J. L., & Bjorklund, D. F. (2004). The natural emergence of reasoning about the afterlife as a developmental regularity. *Developmental Psychology, 40*, 217–233. doi:10.1037/0012-1649.40.2.217

Bering, J. M., Blasi, C. H., & Bjorklund, D. F. (2005). The development of "afterlife" beliefs in religiously and secularly schooled children. *British Journal of Developmental Psychology, 23*, 587–607. doi:10.1348/026151005X36498

Bond, K. E., & Stinson, S. W. (2000). "I feel like I'm going to take off!": Young people's experiences of the superordinary in dance. *Dance Research Journal, 32*, 52–87. doi:10.2307/1477981

Boyatzis, C. J. (Ed.). (2003). Religious and spiritual development [Special issue]. *Review of Religious Research, 44*(3).

Boyatzis, C. J. (2004). The co-construction of spiritual meaning in parent-child communication. In D. Ratcliff (Ed.), *Children's spirituality: Christian perspectives, research, and applications* (pp. 182–200). Eugene, OR: Cascade Books.

Boyatzis, C. J. (2005). Children's religious and spiritual development. In R. F. Paloutzian & C. L. Park (Eds.), *Handbook of the psychology of religion and spirituality* (pp. 123–143). New York: Guilford Press.

Boyatzis, C. J. (Ed.). (2006). Unraveling the dynamics of religion in the family and parent-child relationships [Special issue]. *The International Journal for the Psychology of Religion, 16*(4).

Boyatzis, C. J. (2009). Examining religious and spiritual development during childhood and adolescence. In L. Francis (Ed.), *The international handbook of education for spirituality, care, and well-being* (pp. 51–67). New York, NY: Springer. doi:10.1007/978-1-4020-9018-9_4

Boyatzis, C. J. (2011). Agency, voice, and maturity in children's religious and spiritual development. In S. R. Bales (Ed.), *Children and religion: A methods handbook* (pp. 19–32). New York: New York University Press.

Boyatzis, C. J., Dollahite, D. C., & Marks, L. D. (2006). The family as a context for religious and spiritual development in children and youth. In E. C. Roehlkepartain, P. E. King, L. Wagener, & P. L. Benson (Eds.), *The handbook of spiritual development in childhood and adolescence* (pp. 297–309). Thousand Oaks, CA: Sage.

Boyatzis, C. J., & Janicki, D. (2003). Parent–child communication about religion: Survey and diary data on unilateral transmission and bi-directional reciprocity styles. *Review of Religious Research, 44*, 252–270. doi:10.2307/3512386

Boyer, P. (1994). *The naturalness of religious ideas: A cognitive theory of religion.* Berkeley: University of California Press.

Boyer, P., & Walker, S. (2000). Intuitive ontology and cultural input in the acquisition of religious concepts. In K. S. Rosengren, C. N. Johnson, & P. L. Harris (Eds.), *Imagining the impossible: Magical, scientific, and religious thinking in children* (pp. 130–156). Cambridge, England: Cambridge University Press. doi:10.1017/CBO9780511571381.006

Brelsford, G. M., & Mahoney, A. (2008). Spiritual disclosure between older adolescents and their mothers. *Journal of Family Psychology, 22*, 62–70. doi:10.1037/0893-3200.22.1.62

Bronfenbrenner, U. (1979). *The ecology of human development.* Cambridge, MA: Harvard University Press.

Bunge, M. (Ed.). (2001). *The child in Christian thought.* Grand Rapids, MI: Eerdmans.

Coles, R. (1990). *The spiritual life of children.* Boston, MA: Houghton Mifflin.

Davis, K. A., & Epkins, C. C. (2009). Do private religious practices moderate the relation between family conflict and preadolescents' depression and anxiety symptoms? *Journal of Early Adolescence, 29*, 693–717. doi:10.1177/0272431608325503

Desrosiers, A., Kelley, B., & Miller, L. (2011). Parent and peer relationships and relational spirituality in adolescents and young adults. *Psychology of Religion and Spirituality, 3*, 39–54. doi:10.1037/a0020037

Dollahite, D. C., & Thatcher, J. Y. (2008). Talking about religion: How religious youth and parents discuss their faith. *Journal of Adolescent Research, 23*, 611–641. doi:10.1177/0743558408322141

Dowling, E., & Scarlett, W. G. (Eds.). (2006). *Encyclopedia of spiritual development in childhood and adolescence.* Thousand Oaks, CA: Sage.

Dumas, J. E., & Nissley-Tsiopinis, J. (2006). Parental global religiousness, sanctification of parenting, and positive and negative religious coping as predictors of parental and child functioning. *The International Journal for the Psychology of Religion, 16*, 289–310. doi:10.1207/s15327582ijpr1604_4

Duriez, B., Soenens, B., Neyrinck, B., & Vansteenkiste, M. (2009). Is religiosity related to better parenting? Disentangling religiosity from religious cognitive style. *Journal of Family Issues, 30*, 1287–1307. doi:10.1177/0192513X09334168

Elkind, D. (1970). The origins of religion in the child. *Review of Religious Research, 12*, 35–42. doi:10.2307/3510932

Evans, E. M. (2000). Beyond Scopes: Why creationism is here to stay. In K. S. Rosengren, C. N. Johnson, & P. L. Harris (Eds.), *Imagining the impossible: Magical, scientific, and religious thinking in children* (pp. 305–333). New York, NY: Cambridge University Press. doi:10.1017/CBO9780511571381.012

Flor, D. L., & Knapp, N. F. (2001). Transmission and transaction: Predicting adolescents' internalization of parental religious values. *Journal of Family Psychology, 15*, 627–645. doi:10.1037/0893-3200.15.4.627

Fowler, J. (1981). *Stages of faith*. San Francisco, CA: Jossey-Bass.

Francis, L. J., & Brown, L. B. (1990). The predisposition to pray: A study of the social influence on the predisposition to pray among 11-year-old children in England. *Journal of Empirical Theology, 3*, 23–34. doi:10.1163/157092590X00101

Gershoff, E. T., Miller, P. C., & Holden, G. W. (1999). Parenting influences from the pulpit: Religious affiliation as a determinant of corporal punishment. *Journal of Family Psychology, 13*, 307–320. doi:10.1037/0893-3200.13.3.307

Harris, P. L., & Koenig, M. A. (2006). Truth in testimony: How children learn about science and religion. *Child Development, 77*, 505–524. doi:10.1111/j.1467-8624.2006.00886.x

Hay, D., & Nye, R. (1998). *The spirit in the child*. London, England: Fount.

Heller, D. (1986). *The children's God*. Chicago, IL: University of Chicago Press.

Holder, M. D., Coleman, B., & Wallace, J. M. (2010). Spirituality, religiousness, and happiness in children aged 8–12 years. *Journal of Happiness Studies, 11*, 131–150. doi:10.1007/s10902-008-9126-1

Johnson, C. N., & Boyatzis, C. J. (2006). Cognitive-cultural foundations of spiritual development. In E. C. Roehlkepartain, P. E. King, L. Wagener, & P. L. Benson (Eds.), *The handbook of spiritual development in childhood and adolescence* (pp. 211–223). Thousand Oaks, CA: Sage.

Kendall, S. (1999). The role of picture books in children's spiritual development and meaning making. *International Journal of Children's Spirituality, 4*, 61–76. doi:10.1080/1364436990040106

Kim, J., McCullough, M. E., & Cicchetti, D. (2009). Parents' and children's religiosity and child behavioral adjustment among maltreated and nonmaltreated children. *Journal of Child and Family Studies, 18*, 594–605. doi:10.1007/s10826-009-9262-1

King, P. E., & Boyatzis, C. J. (Eds.). (2004). Exploring adolescent spiritual and religious development [Special issue]. *Applied Developmental Science, 8*(1).

Kochanska, G. (1995). Children's temperament, mothers' discipline, and security of attachment: Multiple pathways to emerging internalization. *Child Development, 66*, 597–615. doi:10.2307/1131937

Koenig, L. B., McGue, M., & Iacono, W. G. (2009). Rearing environmental influences on religiousness: An investigation of adolescent adoptees. *Personality and Individual Differences, 47*, 652–656. doi:10.1016/j.paid.2009.06.003

Kuczynski, L. (2003). Beyond bidirectionality: Bilateral conceptual frameworks for understanding dynamics in parent-child relations. In L. Kuczynski (Ed.), *Handbook of dynamics in parent–child relations* (pp. 3–24). Thousand Oaks, CA: Sage.

Lane, J. D., Wellman, H. M., & Evans, E. M. (2010). Children's understanding of ordinary and extraordinary minds. *Child Development, 81*, 1475–1489. doi:10.1111/j.1467-8624.2010.01486.x

Long, D., Elkind, D., & Spilka, B. (1967). The child's conception of prayer. *Journal for the Scientific Study of Religion, 6*, 101–109. doi:10.2307/1384202

Mahoney, A. (2010). Religion in families, 1999–2009: A relational spirituality framework. *Journal of Marriage and Family, 72*, 805–827. doi:10.1111/j.1741-3737.2010.00732.x

Mahoney, A., Pargament, K. I., Swank, A., & Tarakeshwar, N. (2001). Religion in the home in the 1980s and 90s: A meta-analytic review and conceptual analysis of religion. *Journal of Family Psychology, 15*, 559–596. doi:10.1037/0893-3200.15.4.559

Makris, N., & Pnevmatikos, D. (2007). Children's understanding of human and super-natural minds. *Cognitive Development, 22*, 365–375. doi:10.1016/j.cogdev.2006.12.003

Murray-Swank, A., Mahoney, A., & Pargament, K. I. (2006). Sanctification of parenting: Links to corporal punishment and parental warmth among Biblically conservative and liberal mothers. *The International Journal for the Psychology of Religion, 16*, 271–287. doi:10.1207/s15327582ijpr1604_3

Oser, F., Scarlett, G. W., & Bucher, A. (2006). Religious and spiritual development throughout the life span. In W. Damon & R. M. Lerner (Eds.), *Handbook of child psychology: Vol. 1. Theoretical models of development* (6th ed., pp. 942–997). New York, NY: Wiley.

Pargament, K. I. (1997). *The psychology of religion and coping*. New York, NY: Guilford Press.

Pargament, K. I., & Mahoney, A. (Eds.). (2005). Sanctification: Seeing life through a sacred lens [Special issue]. *The International Journal for the Psychology of Religion, 15*(3).

Pendleton, S. M., Cavalli, K. S., Pargament, K. I., & Nasr, S. Z. (2002). Religious/spiritual coping in childhood cystic fibrosis: A qualitative study. *Pediatrics, 109*, e8. doi:10.1542/peds.109.1.e8

Pitts, V. P. (1976). Drawing the invisible: Children's conceptualization of God. *Character Potential: A Record of Research, 8*, 12–24.

Ratcliff, D. (Ed.). (2004). *Children's spirituality: Christian perspectives, research, and applications*. Eugene, OR: Cascade.

Reimer, K. S., & Furrow, J. L. (2001). A qualitative exploration of relational consciousness in Christian children. *International Journal of Children's Spirituality, 6*, 7–23. doi:10.1080/13644360124074

Rew, L., Wong, Y. J., & Sternglanz, R. W. (2004). The relationship between prayer, health behaviors, and protective resources in school-age children. *Issues in Comprehensive Pediatric Nursing, 27*, 245–255. doi:10.1080/01460860490884156

Richert, R. A., & Harris, P. L. (2006). The ghost in my body: Children's developing concept of the soul. *Journal of Cognition and Culture, 6*, 409–427. doi:10.1163/156853706778554913

Roehlkepartain, E. C., Benson, P. L., King, P. E., & Wagener, L. (2006). Spiritual development in childhood and adolescence: Moving to the scientific mainstream. In E. C. Roehlkepartain, P. E. King, L. Wagener, & P. L. Benson (Eds.), *The handbook of spiritual development in childhood and adolescence* (pp. 1–15). Thousand Oaks, CA: Sage.

Roehlkepartain, E. C., King, P. E., Wagener, L., & Benson, P. L. (Eds.). (2006). *The handbook of spiritual development in childhood and adolescence.* Thousand Oaks, CA: Sage.

Scarlett, G. (2006). Toward a developmental analysis of religious and spiritual development. In E. C. Roehlkepartain, P. E. King, L. Wagener, & P. L. Benson (Eds.), *The handbook of spiritual development in childhood and adolescence* (pp. 21–33). Thousand Oaks, CA: Sage.

Silberman, I. (2003). Spiritual role modeling: The teaching of meaning systems. *The International Journal for the Psychology of Religion, 13*, 175–195. doi:10.1207/S15327582IJPR1303_03

Smith, W. C. (1991). *The meaning and end of religion.* Minneapolis, MN: Fortress Press.

Van Dyke, C. J., & Elias, M. J. (2008). How expressions of forgiveness, purpose, and religiosity relate to emotional intelligence and self-concept in urban fifth-grade students. *American Journal of Orthopsychiatry, 78*, 481–493. doi:10.1037/a0014451

Volling, B. L., Mahoney, A., & Rauer, A. J. (2009). Sanctification of parenting, moral socialization, and young children's conscience development. *Psychology of Religion and Spirituality, 1*, 53–68. doi:10.1037/a0014958

Vygotsky, L. S. (1978). *Mind in society.* Cambridge, MA: Harvard University Press.

Woolley, J. D., & Phelps, K. E. (2001). The development of children's beliefs about prayer. *Journal of Cognition and Culture, 1*, 139–166. doi:10.1163/156853701316931380

CHAPTER 28

SEARCHING FOR THE SACRED: RELIGION, SPIRITUALITY, AND ADOLESCENT DEVELOPMENT

Pamela Ebstyne King, Jenel Sánchez Ramos, and Casey Erin Clardy

Adolescence has always been recognized as an especially dynamic stage of the life cycle. Although often thought of as a turbulent time of growth characterized by storm and stress, scholars now emphasize that this rich period of development is not predominantly defined by developmental crisis but rather by mutual interactions between young people and their contexts that may promote thriving and flourishing (Benson, Scales, Hamilton, & Sesma, 2006; Damon, 2004; Lerner, 2006). Sometimes these interactions go awry, but more often than not, they lead to positive, healthy development. Religion and spirituality are relevant to this positive developmental journey. The biological, psychological, and social changes that take place during adolescence naturally propel youth to engage in religious and spiritual tasks, such as questioning worldviews and values, seeking meaning and purpose, making lifestyle choices, experiencing transcendence, and searching for the sacred. Additionally, in many cases, religion and spirituality may provide rich and fertile environments in which young people have access to ideological, social, and transcendent resources. As such, this chapter provides an overview of the nature and function of religion and spirituality in the lives of diverse adolescents.

The chapter addresses religion and spirituality from two perspectives. First, religious and spiritual development (RSD) are described as unique domains of human development; we explore how young people grow and develop in both religiousness and spirituality. Second, we discuss how religion and spirituality may serve as developmental systems that distinctively contribute to and shape adolescent development overall. One of the aims of this chapter is to elucidate the uniqueness of religion and spirituality as two overlapping, but distinct concepts. Consequently, religion and spirituality will be addressed individually whenever possible.

The chapter provides an overview of the existing literature on religion and spirituality in the lives of adolescents by drawing on the integrative paradigm of the psychology of religion and spirituality (see Chapter 1 in this volume). First, we describe current sociological trends that elucidate the known demographics of adolescent RSD. After examining the prevalence of religion and spirituality among adolescents, we discuss its developmental pertinence during adolescence. Following, we review the literature and offer conceptualizations of key terms related to religion and spirituality. We conclude this section by offering an overview of a developmental systems perspective as a helpful framework for understanding diverse expressions and experiences of adolescent religiousness and spirituality. Next, we look at how religion and spirituality have the potential to affect adolescent development overall. Through a review of empirical literature, the chapter then examines how religion and spirituality might make a difference in the lives of youth, promoting indicators of thriving, buffering against risk behaviors, and assisting in coping with life struggles. To give a full representation, we examine religion and spirituality's potential negative influence on adolescents as well. Finally, we consider implications of work in this area for practice and future directions for research.

DOI: 10.1037/14045-028
APA Handbook of Psychology, Religion, and Spirituality: Vol. 1. Context, Theory, and Research, K. I. Pargament (Editor-in-Chief)
Copyright © 2013 by the American Psychological Association. All rights reserved.

DEMOGRAPHICS OF ADOLESCENT RELIGIOUSNESS AND SPIRITUALITY

Of the industrial nations, the United States reports the highest rates of adolescent religious and spiritual affiliation. Two nationally representative studies of American youth have documented that 84% to 87% of U.S. adolescents are affiliated with a specific religious group (Smith & Denton, 2005; Wallace, Forman, Caldwell, & Willis, 2003). The remaining 13% to 16% of religiously unaffiliated youth are a significant minority, but the number appears to be rising, with 10% identifying as "just not religious," 3% as "unexplored or uncertain," 1.5% as "atheist," and 1.5% as "agnostic." Although still relatively religious in comparison with other industrial nations, U.S. adolescents show a high degree of diversity in affiliation, including a growing number who self-identity as spiritual but not religious. For example, 8% of the sample responded "very true" when asked if they considered themselves as "spiritual but not religious," and 46% said "somewhat true" (Smith & Denton, 2005).

Apart from affiliation, religious attendance is another mechanism by which adolescent religiousness and spirituality are often measured. It is unclear to what extent the world's youth attend religious services or participate in such institutions as mosques, synagogues, temples, or churches. A study of 14-year-olds across 28 countries showed that on average, 41.9% of youth participate in an organization sponsored by a religious group in the United States, 14.4% in Western Europe, 27.6% in Southern Europe, 19.9% in Asia and Pacific regions, 13.1% in Northern Europe, and 10.3% in Eastern Europe (Lippmann & Keith, 2006). Although there is minimal youth participation in religious organizations in nations apart from America, these findings may not necessarily indicate a lack of religious importance or belief. One possibility is that youth of more industrial nations may have greater access to opportunities for participation in organized religious groups than youth of developing nations (Brown, Larson, & Saraswathi, 2002).

Despite the idiosyncratic differences that emerge in an examination of trends of adolescent religiousness and spirituality, it is clear that a disparity often exists between religious affiliation and importance in the lives of youth. For example, 84% to 87% of U.S. teens reported an affiliation with a particular religious group; however, only 47% of U.S. youth endorsed the importance of religion in their lives (Smith & Denton, 2005). Although there is no set trend among adolescents around the globe, it is clear that an important number of young people are engaged in various religions and forms of spirituality (for a review, see the World Values Survey in Lippman & Keith, 2006). The next section of this chapter provides a conceptual framework to gain insight into the diversity of adolescent religiousness and spirituality.

ADOLESCENT RELIGIOUSNESS AND SPIRITUALITY

Despite the prevalence of research suggesting that spirituality and religion are significant factors in the lives of diverse young people, only a few attempts have been made to understand adolescent religiousness and spirituality and related constructs such as faith development (i.e., Fowler, 1981; Rizzuto, 1979; Wilbur, 2006). Furthermore, few of these attempts have a prominent place in contemporary developmental psychology. A thorough review of the history of the study of religiousness and spirituality in adolescence is beyond the scope of this chapter and can be found in several comprehensive reviews of the literature (King & Roeser, 2009; Oser, Scarlett, & Bucher, 2006). To provide a conceptual understanding of adolescent religiousness and spirituality, we delineate our conceptualization of key terms. Drawing on the integrative paradigm put forth in the introductory chapter (see Chapter 1 in this volume), we emphasize that religion and spirituality are unique but overlapping constructs. In addition, they are relevant to multiple levels of the developmental system (i.e., individual, institutional, cultural) and may either help or hinder development. To understand how these concepts pertain to adolescence, we review existing definitions within the literature and offer a framework for understanding diverse religiousness and spirituality on the basis of developmental systems theory.

Initially, in the field of psychology, the terms *religion* and *spirituality* were used synonymously (see Chapter 1 in this volume). As the field evolved, however, the concepts of religion and spirituality began to diverge both in scholarship and in culture (Koenig, McCullough, & Larson, 2001; Zinnbauer & Pargament, 2005). For example, sociologists suggest that youth are increasingly identifying as "spiritual, but not religious" (Smith & Denton, 2005). In the literature, religion is increasingly conceptualized at the level of an organized socio-cultural-historical system, and spirituality is conceptualized at the level of an individual's personal quest for meaning, satisfaction, and wisdom. For instance, a well-accepted definition defines *religion* as follows:

> An organized system of beliefs, practices, rituals, and symbols that serve (a) to facilitate individuals' closeness to the sacred or transcendent other (i.e., God, higher power, ultimate truth) and (b) to bring about an understanding of an individual's relationship and responsibility to others living together in community. (Koenig et al., 2001, p. 18)

From this perspective, *religiousness* refers to the extent to which an individual has a relationship with a particular institutionalized doctrine about ultimate reality. This relationship occurs through affiliation with an organized religion, participation in its prescribed rituals and practices, and assent to its espoused beliefs (Benson & Roehlkepartain, 2008).

In contrast, Koenig et al. (2001) defined *spirituality* as "a personal quest for understanding answers to ultimate questions about life, about meaning, and about relationship to the sacred or transcendent, which may (or may not) lead to or arise from the development of religious rituals and the formation of community" (p. 18). This aligns with Pargament's (2007) view of personal religiousness or spirituality as a "search for the sacred" in which the sacred is defined in terms of an individual's concept of God, the divine and transcendent reality, as well as other aspects of life that take on divine character or are imbued with divinelike qualities, such as transcendence, immanence, boundlessness, and ultimacy (Pargament & Mahoney, 2005; see Chapter 1 in this volume). It is also consistent with definitions stemming from the field of youth development that emphasize the intrinsic capacity for self-transcendence and the goals of connectedness, meaning, purpose, and contribution (Benson, Roehlkepartain, & Rude, 2003; Benson, Roehlkepartain, & Scales, 2010).

Although an emphasis on personal and institutional levels may illuminate potential distinctions between religion and spirituality, to overemphasize this point and dichotomize the constructs is shortsighted and would limit an understanding of the complexity of both religion and spirituality. As the editors of this volume point out, religion cannot be viewed as purely institutional, as important individual-level processes such as selecting, interpreting, and constructing religious worldviews could be missed. Conversely, when spirituality is treated as a strictly individual phenomenon, the rich and varied ways that spirituality expresses itself in intimate relationships, families, congregations, organizations, and cultures may be overlooked. Personal spiritual expressions are often embedded in larger religious, social, and cultural contexts. Religion and spirituality are multidimensional constructs that consist of diverse cognitions, feelings, behaviors, experiences, and relationships and must be considered multilevel from both theoretical and methodological perspectives (see Chapter 1 in this volume).

According to this perspective, spirituality involves seeking transcendence and connecting to something bigger than one's self and may occur within or outside of a religious context. At the same time, although religion entails participation in prescribed beliefs, practices, and rituals of specific traditions, it often includes spirituality. Koenig et al. (2001) acknowledged that some people, search for meaning to ultimate questions through religion and some through "unmoored" sources of spirituality, such as humanism and vocation, in which the focal concerns center on the cultivation of humanity and universal ethics.

Although these definitions bring clarity, they do not address the ontogeny of religiousness and spirituality among adolescence, whether moored or unmoored to a religion. Consistent with Mahoney's (2010; see also Chapter 20 in this volume) presentation of a relational spirituality framework that incorporates the "search for the sacred and the search for relationships," (Mahoney, 2010, p. 810) we turn to developmental systems theory to understand a relational spirituality that emphasizes the development of religiousness and spirituality across the multiple contexts in which they occur, as unique contributions to adolescent development. Such a perspective aims to answer such questions as, How does a person grow in religiousness and spirituality? What psychological processes are involved? Why is this relevant to adolescent development? How do we understand diverse expressions of religious and spiritual development?

Developmental systems theory focuses on transactions between individuals and their various embedded sociocultural contexts of development (Bronfenbrenner, 1979; Lerner, 2006). Using this framework, development occurs through adaptive developmental regulation, or the mutual interactions between individuals and the contexts in which they live over time (Lerner, 2006). Individuals actively process environmental influences and shape their environment rather than being passively molded by their environment. Thus, it is important to consider both the uniqueness of individuals, and the larger systems or contexts in which they are embedded. As such, religious development refers to the systematic changes in how one understands and utilizes the doctrines, practices, and rituals of a religious institution. Religious development generally occurs through affiliation with an organized religion, participation in its prescribed rituals and practices, or assent to its prescribed beliefs.

Spiritual development refers to a broader domain of development that is experienced by all youth, whether or not they are a part of a religious tradition. Spiritual development occurs through a young person's interactions with the contexts in which he or she lives over time.

Specifically, spiritual development involves transactions with "something beyond the self," which may be ideological, social, or supernatural (King, 2008). Although an expression of the divine is not needed to instigate spiritual development, the forces that stimulate spiritual growth are imbued with divine-like qualities, such as transcendence, immanence, boundlessness, and ultimacy (see Chapter 1 in this volume) and informs what is sacred. Transcendence involves a shifting of a young person's cognitive and emotional orientation from one's self to another in such a way that provides ultimate value and meaning beyond the mundane and material and shapes identity (Lerner, Roeser, & Phelps, 2008).

Building on Mahoney (2010; see also Chapter 20 in this volume), we refer to this as *relational spirituality,* because seminal to spiritual development are the relations or interactions between the self and some form of the other, which informs one's beliefs and commitments, and propels young person to live in a manner mindful of others. Erikson (1968) described this as *fidelity*. He argued that youth who successfully resolve the identity crisis gain the virtue of fidelity, which he referred to as loyalty to an ideology that engages youth in a greater world (King & Roeser, 2009; Lerner, Alberts, Anderson, & Dowling, 2006; Lerner et al., 2008).

Spirituality is more than a feeling of transcendence, but a growing sense of identity or awareness that can motivate young people to care for themselves and to contribute to the greater good. As such, spiritual development requires more than simple, positive interactions between a person and his or her context; instead, development results more specifically from transactions that promote transcendence, fidelity, and generative actions.

ADOLESCENT DEVELOPMENT

Religion and spirituality can be relevant to the period of adolescence, which has long been recognized for the marked changes young people go through in body, mind, and relationships (Lerner et al., 2008). Recognizing that youth are malleable and have the potential for change (Lerner, 2006), optimistically, adolescence is a time of potentially profound maturation as youth grow in their sense of self and their place in the world (Damon, 2004). The following section describes how the many changes happening at different levels of the developmental system (i.e., biological, psychological, social) are germane to religion and spirituality during adolescence.

One of the main developmental tasks of adolescence is identity formation, of which adolescent religiousness and spirituality can play a vital role, as youth endeavor to establish self-definition and belonging (Erikson, 1965; Lerner, 2004). In striving toward identity cohesion, young people actively search for a sense of self. In this process of seeking to form a meaningful identity, adolescents are exposed to a variety of beliefs, values and roles, and they begin to ask existential questions and search for purpose (Damon, Menon, & Bronk, 2003; Mariano & Damon, 2008; Markstrom, 1999). They embark on this psychological endeavor to consolidate and understand their experience of self and identify themselves in terms of familial, vocational, and societal roles. The quest for identity in adolescence is marked by yearnings and behaviors that simultaneously bond them to or locate them within something beyond themselves and affirm their sense of uniqueness and independence.

Religious and spiritual communities also may be helpful to adolescents as their relationships begin to shift. As they attempt to establish autonomy and independence from their family, they often renegotiate their relationships and begin to emphasize the importance of peers. Although this is not at the exclusion of parental and sibling relations, peer ties become more salient and influential during the adolescent years. In addition to friendships, adolescents also seek other affiliations outside the family, such as with mentors (i.e., teachers, coaches), organizations, institutions, and ideologies. Congregations can be a meaningful and prosocial place for these new ties and also can serve as safe environments in which youth can experiment and explore new roles and competencies.

Simultaneous to the pursuit of identity, belonging, and contribution, recent research reveals that the adolescent brain undergoes significant changes that may contribute to the psychological and spiritual endeavors of identity formation. Specifically, during adolescence, the frontal and prefrontal cortex develop and neural connections increase, which facilitate the cognitive processes related to reflection, abstract reasoning, decision making, and processing speed (Paus, 2009). These abilities are hypothesized to enable adolescents to engage cognitively with narratives, meaning systems, and moral codes (Lerner et al., 2008). With an increased capacity to grapple with abstract ideologies and concepts of transcendence, adolescents are potentially able to connect meaningfully to something beyond themselves, whether that be God, a belief system, or a group of people.

Consequently, young people have many opportunities and challenges that grow out of their changing bodies, minds, and social worlds. To thrive and be on a pathway to a meaningful and productive future, young people need to consolidate a sense of identity, renegotiate their social ties, and find meaningful ways to contribute to the greater good. Religion and spirituality can facilitate this process by offering youth ideological, social, and transcendent resources in their pursuit of identity consolidation, connection, and contribution.

THE INFLUENCE OF RELIGION AND SPIRITUALITY ON ADOLESCENT DEVELOPMENT

The following section summarizes existing conceptual explanations for why religion and spirituality may be important developmental contexts for young people. In addition to discussing the important role of the ideological and social resources potentially embedded within religion and spirituality, we examine the transcendent resources that may offer unique benefits to youth.

Ideological Context

Young people strive to make sense of the world and to assert their place in it. The beliefs, worldviews, and values of religious and spiritual traditions provide an ideological context in which a young person can generate a sense of meaning, order, and place in the world that is crucial to adolescent development (King, 2003, 2008). Erikson (1965) pointed to religion as an important aspect of the sociohistorical matrix in which identity takes shape. He argued that religion is the oldest and most lasting institution that promotes fidelity. Religion intentionally offers beliefs, moral codes, and values from which a young person can build a personal belief system (Smith, 2003). Spirituality entails the intentional identification and integration of beliefs, narrative, and values in the process of making meaning (see Chapter 8 in this volume). Whether this process is one of personal construction or socialization, the intentional act of relying on personal, religious, or cultural ideology is central to spirituality and crucial to the development of identity, meaning, and purpose (Damon et al., 2003).

Research provides evidence that religion is helpful in enabling youth to internalize a set of beliefs and morals. In studies of individuals nominated for moral excellence, participants frequently reported that religion served as a foundation for their moral action (Colby & Damon, 1992; Hart & Fegley, 1995). In addition, Larson, Hansen, and Moneta (2006) found that youth involved in faith-based youth programs were significantly more likely to be engaged in higher rates of identity work than youth not engaged in faith-based programs. Furthermore, they found that 75% of youth in faith-based programs reported discussing morals and values, in comparison with 24% of youth involved in other types of organized youth programs. King and Furrow (2004) found that higher levels of adolescent religiousness were associated with having significantly more shared beliefs, values, and expectations with parents, friends, and adults. Furthermore, Bertram-Troost, de Roos, and Miedema (2009) studied students at Dutch Christian secondary schools and found that religiously grounded education was associated with espousing a commitment to a particular worldview.

Social Context

Religion and spirituality do more than provide a transcendent worldview and morality. Community members embody religious and spiritual ideological norms in a community setting and thereby act as role models for youth (Erikson, 1968). Although religion and spirituality are not the exclusive providers of these social resources, a significant body of research documents that they may be particularly effective in offering social capital, social support, and mentors. Religious influence might be better understood by the network of relationships, opportunities, and shared values common to religious congregations, and empirical research on the developmental asset framework highlights the resources available to youth through religious and spiritual involvement (Wagener, Furrow, King, Leffert, & Benson, 2003).

Social capital models posit that religion's constructive influence on young people may be accounted for by the nature and number of relationships it provides youth. For instance, young people have access to intergenerational relationships that are recognized as rich sources of social capital through religious involvement (King & Furrow, 2004; Putnam, 2000; Smith, 2003). Few other social institutions afford the opportunity to build trustworthy cross-generational relationships and link youth to sources of helpful information, resources, and opportunities. King and Furrow (2004) found that religiously engaged youth reported significantly higher levels of social capital resources than less active youth. The developmental asset framework provides such an account of the resources available to youth through religious and spiritual involvement. For example, Wagener et al. (2003) found that the positive benefits of adolescent religiousness were partially mediated through developmental resources available to these youth.

Religious institutional involvement may involve social channeling, the conscious process on the part of adults to steer their children toward particular individuals positioned to discourage negative behaviors and promote positive life practices among young people (Smith, 2003). Research shows that social channeling in congregations has helped to promote spiritual development, academic achievement, and general positive development (e.g., Martin, White, & Perlman, 2003; Regnerus & Elder, 2003; Schreck, Burek, & Clark-Miller, 2007). Religious institutions and the relationships they afford also provide forms of social support that are particularly important to adolescent coping, resilience, and well-being. In two studies of adolescents, social support from a religious community emerged as a strong negative predictor of depressive symptoms (Miller & Gur, 2002; Pearce, Little, & Perez, 2003). Specifically, Pearce et al. (2003) found that the expectation of social support from religious congregations in times of need was associated with less depressive symptoms; conversely, expectations that religious congregations were critical of teenagers generally were linked with more depressive symptoms. Thus, religious communities can be sources of social support or socioemotional distress based on the ways adults in those communities perceive and relate to youth.

Spiritual modeling and mentorship are two other means in which adults may socialize young people's religious and spiritual identities to align with the beliefs, norms, and expectations of a particular religious group (Schwartz, Bukowski, & Aoki, 2006). Spiritual modeling refers to emulating another to grow spiritually (Bandura, 2003; Oman, Flinders, & Thoresen, 2008; see also Chapter 10 in this volume). Foundational to this approach is the notion that the people with whom we regularly associate shape the behavioral patterns that will be repeatedly observed and learned most thoroughly. Religious and spiritual groups are often intentional about mentoring younger members. For example, the Hindu tradition has gurus, the Jewish tradition sages, and the Christian tradition disciples. Through these intentional relationships, adults connect youth to a larger whole, enabling them to identify with a community beyond the self. Several studies demonstrate the frequency and efficacy of adult relationships among youth embedded in religious contexts (Ellis et al., 2010; King & Furrow, 2004; Larson, Hansen, & Moneta, 2006).

Transcendent Context

Religion and spirituality provide not only important ideological resources and social relationships that may nurture adolescent development but also valuable opportunities for transcendent experiences. Transcendence, connecting with something beyond the self in ways that bring about deeper awareness of one's self and others, is often intentionally nurtured in religious and spiritual communities. Although the current literature substantiates the relationship between ideology and social support, little empirical research exists on transcendence. Consequently, the following section identifies potential ways to conceptualize how transcendence may promote adolescent development and provides empirical evidence when available (see King, Carr, & Boitor, 2011).

A sense of connecting to something beyond the self is an important resource for identity development and coping. Experiences of transcendence can affirm one's own sense of identity and self-worth through a profound sense of connection to a divine or human other. In a recent qualitative study on spiritually exemplary youth, a boy from Kenya described this sentiment: "Knowing that I'm actually a child of the Most High God, I find that I'm actually a bit special" (King, Clardy, & Ramos, 2010). In an affiliated international quantitative study of youth, initial findings suggest that awareness of one's inherent value and strength is a common aspect of spirituality among youth from eight different countries (Benson et al., 2010). In addition, youth may experience transcendence through connection to a religious community. A U.S. exemplar explained, "Well, we're [the Jews] a people who suffer. That's who we are and what we do. I get my social consciousness, my beliefs, my view of humanity from my Jewish traditions" (King et al., 2010, p. 21). Additionally, the findings by Benson et al. (2010) suggest that a sense that life is interconnected and interdependent is a factor of adolescent spirituality.

The experience of transcendence is not limited to religious traditions; it can occur in nature. Young people may find a strengthened sense of identity from being part of creation. Encountering the majesty of creation or being sensually aroused through the aesthetics of nature may offer experiences of boundlessness and ultimacy (see Chapter 1 in this volume) that can inspire perspective on one's sense of self or one's life. In the study of adolescent spiritual exemplars, a Catholic boy from India described his general connection to God in nature: "Just being in this world, just in that place where there are trees and the beaches, I just feel the presence of God in those places" (King et al., 2010, p. 19). Benson et al. (2010) identified this sense of awareness of the world as one of the four factors of spirituality.

Spirituality also promotes transcendence through ritual, whether through worship, spiritual practices, or rites of passage (see Chapter 18 in this volume). Ongoing worship rituals may promote one's awareness of the divine or human other as well as confirm one's place in a community. In the exemplar study, a Hindu boy from India talked about rituals in this way: "It's because of the ceremonies, which are held, and it makes people come together . . . and then sometimes you get a connection with God, a special time with God" (King et al., 2010, p. 17). Rites of passage are unique events that intentionally celebrate and affirm a young person's sense of identity as a religious or spiritual person, in addition to recognizing his or her place within the faith community, which may contribute to the youth's personal development and commitment to something beyond the self.

Spiritual practices or disciplines also promote experiences of transcendence. In a nationally representative study of religion and spirituality among youth, Smith and Denton (2005) found that 10% of all young people reported practicing religious or spiritual meditation during the prior year. The practice of meditation can promote the realization of higher states of awareness and unity with others. Spiritual practices including service to the poor provide the opportunity to learn the intrinsic value of others, gratitude, and self-sacrifice. In addition to promoting character, these opportunities for service allow youth to explore different competencies and skills. Experiences of answered prayer may also further a youth's sense of commitment or devotion to the practice of spirituality (Smith, 2003). These practices may provide young people with an experience of something beyond themselves, which not only affirms their uniqueness but also may engender their commitment to others.

These experiences of transcendence may promote key facets of positive development. Moving beyond the self provides the opportunity for the search for meaning and belonging that is central to positive youth development. Awareness that stems from this search provides answers and perspective with respect to the larger issues of life that are crucial to the resolution of the adolescent identity crisis (Erikson, 1965). Devotion, responsibility, and commitment inspired by transcendence may play an important role in both motivating and sustaining an altruistic or generative life style. Spirituality provides opportunities to experience a profound sense of connectedness with either supernatural or human others, one that invokes a sense of awareness of self in relation to other. This heightened consciousness of others often triggers an understanding of self and sense of fidelity that are intertwined with and responsible to the other. This attentiveness usually promotes a manner of living that is carried out with the highest regard to the life of self, others, or the divine (King, 2008). Consequently, the transcendent quality of spirituality is especially pertinent to shaping a commitment to contributing to the common good of young people who are thriving.

The various environments in which youth live will foster positive development insofar as they offer clear ideology, social resources, and transcendent spiritual experiences. Whether secular or faith-based, settings can promote spiritual development. They can do so by enabling young people along the quest for self-awareness, meaning, and purpose, helping youth to shape their core identities and to clarify their roles within their families, communities, and the larger world. Perhaps the most unique aspect of spirituality is the potential for transcendence. Many youth programs and organizations offer ideology and rich social environments; however, not many intentionally promote experiences of transcendence, in which young people can acutely experience an entity beyond themselves in such a way that transforms their ideological commitments, inspires devotion, and shapes generative behavior. In particular, those relationships and institutions that provide clear ideology, positive and prosocial modeling, and transcendent experiences tend to nurture young people's religious and spiritual quests. Along these lines, we next discuss some ways in which adolescent religiousness and spirituality can affect adolescent development overall.

CORRELATES OF ADOLESCENT RELIGIOUSNESS AND SPIRITUALITY

A substantial body of literature suggests that religiousness and spirituality can serve as protective factors, potentially buffering young people against health-compromising behaviors and promoting engagement in health-promoting behaviors. Specifically, adolescent religiousness and spirituality have been positively correlated with physical and mental health (Cotton, Zebracki, Rosenthal, Tsevat, & Drotar, 2006) as well as positive youth development (e.g., thriving, meaning and identity, contribution; Benson et al., 2010; King et al., 2011; Lerner et al., 2008). Adolescent religiousness and spirituality also have been negatively correlated with risk-taking behaviors (e.g., substance use, delinquency; see Bridges & Moore, 2002; Smith & Denton, 2005).

Across various domains of physical and mental health, researchers have revealed that religious and spiritual youth are less likely than others to engage in health-compromising behaviors and more likely to engage in health-promoting behaviors. For example, in a 3-year longitudinal study of diverse U.S. adolescents, Jessor, Turbin, and Costa (1998) found religiousness to be a primary factor in promoting healthy diet, sleep, dental hygiene, seatbelt use, and exercise. Similarly, in a 23-year longitudinal study utilizing the Monitoring the Future national probability sample of U.S. adolescents, Wallace and Forman (1998) found that youth who reported greater religiousness also reported healthier patterns of eating, sleeping, and exercise. In addition, Barnes, Johnson, and Treiber (2004) found that the practice of meditation was associated with reduced ambulatory blood pressure among African American adolescents. Overall, studies suggest that religion and spirituality are linked with health-promoting behaviors and positive health outcomes in adolescents.

With respect to adolescent mental health, religiousness and spirituality have been negatively associated with depression and hopelessness (Schapman & Inderbitzen-Nolan, 2002; Sinha, Cnaan, & Gelles, 2007; Wright, Frost, & Wisecarver, 1993) and positively correlated with life satisfaction (Varon & Riley, 1999), happiness (Abdekl-Khalek, 2007), and positive emotions such as vitality and zest (Leak, DeNeve & Greteman, 2007). In a comparison study of adolescent religiousness in Germany, Spain, and the United States, religious attendance and importance were positively correlated with self-esteem (Smith, Weigert, & Thomas, 1979). In a nationally representative sample of U.S. adolescents, youth who reported higher levels of private (but not necessarily public) religiousness experienced less suicidal ideation and fewer suicide attempts (Nonnemaker, McNeely, & Blum, 2003); conversely, a lack of religious affiliation has been linked with higher suicide rates among U.S. adolescents (e.g., Gartner, Larson, & Allen, 1991).

Religiousness and spirituality may serve not only to promote positive physical and mental health outcomes but also to promote what is commonly referred to as *thriving* in adolescence: positive identity development, meaning in life, well-being, competency, contribution, character, morality, academic achievement, and civic engagement (Benson & Scales, 2009; Bundick, Yeager, King, & Damon, 2010; King et al., 2011; Lerner et al., 2006). Dowling et al. (2004) suggested that adolescent religiousness and spirituality are each directly related to thriving outcomes, such as having a sense of purpose, meaning, passion, and identity (e.g., Benson, Roehlkepartain, & Scales, in press; Damon, 2004; Furrow, King, & White, 2004; Markstrom-Adams, Hofstra, & Dougher, 1994) and a sense of responsibility for civic, community, and familial contribution (see Donnelly, Matsuba, Hart, & Atkins, 2006; Kerestes, Youniss, & Metz, 2004).

Adolescent religiousness and spirituality have also been documented as buffers against risk-taking behaviors such as substance use (e.g., marijuana, tobacco, alcohol, steroids, and other illicit drugs), risky sexual activity (i.e., promiscuity, premarital sex), and delinquent and violent behavior (for a review, see King & Roeser, 2009; Regnerus & Elder, 2003). More than participation in school or sports programs, adolescent religiousness is clearly linked to reduced odds of dangerous behaviors, antisocial practices, and witnessing or being a victim of violence (Pearce, 2003). Interestingly, however, it is not that religious or spiritual youth are not taking risks or engaging in dangerous activities; rather, research has suggested that they simply engage in these practices to a lesser extent (Scales & Leffert, 1999).

Existing empirical research strongly supports a beneficial relationship between religion and spirituality and positive adolescent outcomes. Religion and spirituality have the potential to offer ideological, social, and transcendent resources that provide moral direction, relationships, opportunities, and sources of inspiration that enable young people to make healthy decisions, cope with adversity, and develop important competencies. Not only are religion and spirituality relevant during adolescence but also they are pertinent to the next stage of life, emerging adulthood.

RELIGIOUS AND SPIRITUAL DEVELOPMENT IN EMERGING ADULTS

Increasingly, the literature points to a distinctive subset of the population termed *emerging adults* (see

Arnett, 2000). Emerging adulthood is unique from both adolescence and adulthood and is a product of more recent social and technological changes characterized by freedom, exploration, experimentation, discovery, success, failure, life disruption, transition, and globalization as well as philosophical changes (e.g., postmodernism, pluralism, relativism; Smith & Snell, 2009). Emerging adults are those individuals who have moved out of adolescence and into adulthood, which, in primarily industrial societies, is characterized by independent experimentation and exploration in such areas as education, work, love, and worldview (including religious and spiritual frameworks; Arnett, 2004). During this "in-between" time period from ages 18 through 25, emerging adults tend to postpone adult responsibilities while living in temporary, transitory housing. Typically, emerging adults experience diverse life situations that contribute to the individuation and differentiation that has already commenced in their adolescence. Nevertheless, similar to adolescence, the interaction between context and individual continues to be crucial in an emerging adult's development. Emerging adults are incorporating new relationships while sustaining and renegotiating old relationships with family and friends.

Oftentimes, religious and spiritual renegotiation occurs during this time as the emerging adult seeks to answer questions about beliefs, community involvement, and engagement in faith practices. As Smith and Snell (2009) noted, the study of emerging adults' social, cultural, and economic contexts is an essential part of understanding RSD in this life stage. The authors' study of a U.S. sample of emerging adults found they are the least religious group of adults, with older adults being the most religious, although these figures vary slightly on the basis of religious and cultural affiliation. Even though there has not been a significant decline in religiosity in the United States in the past 30 years, church attendance in the Christian tradition for this age group has dropped in recent decades. Yet the authors also discovered that more than 50% of emerging adults they studied demonstrated relatively stable levels of religious commitment and practice (or lack thereof). Furthermore, when it comes to religion, parents and nonparental adults continue to be important influences on emerging adults, often even trumping peer influences. Yet Smith and Snell highlighted that although emerging adults feel comfortable talking about religion, they are not particularly interested in discussing the topic. Emerging adults tend to see the value of religion as a promoter of "good" behavior, but they are also apt to place their trust in science over tradition. Moreover, at least in this U.S. sample, emerging adults viewed religion as a personal matter heavily influenced by pluralism; in other words, most would articulate that no person ultimately knows what is true or right for everyone.

With regard to spirituality, emerging adults continue to explore their spiritual and religious beliefs and identities through a process of questioning and doubting previously held worldviews and self-concepts. The spiritual or religious self seems to be fluid and susceptible to change, as evidenced by decreases or fluctuations in commitments, service attendance, and involvement in religious activities or spiritual practices. Critical thinking regarding one's belief systems and religious affiliation is central to the emerging adult's spiritual development. Arnett's (2004) study on spirituality in emerging adults pointed to a spiritual theme particular to this population—that is, the importance of a personal relationship with God or a higher being that is separate from a religious institution. Specifically, 28% of the participants reported believing in a deistic other (Arnett, 2004). Other themes from the study included an emphasis on self-development in regards to spirituality, the continued quest for beliefs and values considered to be distinct and unique, an increasing capacity for reciprocity through the experience of relational exploration, and the desire to make a difference in the world by showing care or generosity toward others. Essentially, emerging adults' spiritual development appears to be characterized by tolerance, adaptability, openness, community-seeking, and curiosity regarding spiritual matters.

RELIGIOUSNESS AND SPIRITUALITY AS MULTIVALENT PHENOMENA

Up to this point in the chapter, we have focused on the positive aspects of religion and spirituality. To understand religious and spiritual development in their entirety, however, they must be addressed in their full complexity. Just as they have the potential for good, they also have the potential for harm. Religiousness and spirituality are complex and can engender positive results, but they can also be sources of significant distress and struggle (Exline & Rose, 2005; see also Chapter 25 in this volume). A complete picture of adolescent RSD warrants an overview of the negative psychological and social outcomes that arise when religious and spiritual development goes awry (see Oser, Scarlett, & Bucher, 2006; Silberman, Higgins, & Dweck, 2005; Wagener & Malony, 2006). The following section provides an overview of how adolescent religion and spirituality are capable of doing harm to either the developing person or others.

Although most research indicates a positive relationship between religion and spirituality and young people's well-being, not all religious experience is associated with benevolent outcomes. Many youth find religion comforting, whereas others can experience religious life as a potential source of strain. In an undergraduate student sample of 200 participants, Exline, Yali, and Sanderson (2000) found that religious strain was associated with depression. Similarly, Johnson and Hayes (2003) found that in a sample of more than 5,000 university and college students, nearly one third reported some distress related to religious or spiritual concerns. In comparison with their nondistressed religious and spiritual peers, those students who indicated considerable distress with respect to religious or spiritual issues reported greater distress related to relationship losses, confusion about beliefs and values, sexual assault, homesickness, and suicidal ideation or feelings. Additionally, these religiously or spiritually distressed students reported more concomitant distress in terms of confusion about beliefs and values, sexual concerns, relationships, and ideation regarding punishment of sins.

In addition, Pargament, Smith, Koenig, and Perez (1998) described the concept of negative religious coping as "an expression of a less secure relationship with God, a tenuous and ominous view of the world, and a religious struggle in the search for significance" (p. 712). Those who engage in this pattern of religious coping tend to engage in maladaptive appraisals of God and their situations and seem to experience spiritual and interpersonal religious discontent. In a study of 540 college students who experienced a serious negative event, young people who used more negative religious coping methods also reported higher levels of emotional distress, poor physical health, psychosomatic symptoms, and stress-related growth (Pargament et al., 1998). Similarly, in a sample of 145 adolescent psychiatric patients, Dew et al. (2010) discovered that negative religious coping and negative support from a religious community correlated with higher depression scores. Pargament et al. (1998) have observed the presence of "ineffective religious coping" (p. 79) in two groups of college undergraduate students who had undergone at least one serious negative event, such as a death of a significant other. Religious apathy, a view of God as punishing, anger at God, religious doubts, and conflict with church dogma all appeared to be related to poorer mental health and problems in resolving negative life experiences. These characteristics seem to reflect internal tensions between one's self and one's religious world that could contribute to a more fragmented and less effective coping response.

Religion and spirituality are multivalent phenomena that encompass both positive and negative aspects. The studies described in this section indicate that the adolescent experience of religious and spiritual maladaptive forms of coping may result in guilt, isolation, and damaging physical and psychological symptoms. When considering the potential of spirituality and religion, one must consider how they affect both the individual and society.

PRACTICAL IMPLICATIONS OF RELIGIOUSNESS AND SPIRITUALITY FOR ADOLESCENTS

Both religion and spirituality clearly have the capacity for good and for harm. The following section discusses ways to leverage religion and spirituality for positive adolescent development. At their best, religion and spirituality offer explicitly prosocial worldviews, values, and morals; fellow participants as sources of encouragement, teaching, or inspiration; and spiritual experiences and environments that allow people to internalize and integrate a sense of belonging and meaning (King, 2003, 2008). Positive religiousness and spirituality can serve as an ideological framework for youth, a mechanism by which they can explore and construct their personal belief systems. With a greater sense of fidelity to a particular worldview, adolescents are able to gain a greater sense of purpose, hope, and civic engagement in the larger society (e.g., Furrow et al., 2004; King et al., 2011; Lerner et al., 2006).

Within the frameworks of developmental assets, social capital, and coping, religiousness and spirituality have the potential to offer a variety of practical resources for youth. Religiousness and spirituality contribute asset-building resources, such as intergenerational relationships, prosocial norms, leadership opportunities, and adult role models to facilitate positive youth development (Benson et al., 2010; Wagener et al., 2003). Similarly, religiousness and spirituality provide social capital in the form of network closure by allowing parents and other adults the opportunity to contribute to relational networks in which youth are embedded. Through sharing oversight and information about youth, negative behaviors are discouraged and positive practices are promoted among young people (King & Furrow, 2004). Religious and spiritual forms of coping provide youth with resources for seeking comfort, control, transformation, and interpersonal growth in the midst of life stressors (Mahoney, Pendleton, & Ihrke, 2006).

Given the myriad resources that positive religiousness and spirituality afford adolescents, there are several practical implications and clinical interventions to consider. According to National Study of Youth and Religion data, adolescents often struggle to explain their beliefs and the relevance they have for their daily lives. Furthermore, a deeper understanding and embrace of religiousness and spirituality does not appear to be a priority in the lives of many U.S. adolescents (Smith & Denton, 2005). Interventions need to target this gap in education and should incorporate open talks about faith and its practice. It may be that young people are rarely approached by adults who engage them in these types of conversations surrounding matters of belief and how religiousness or spirituality may affect their lives. Consequently, for thriving to occur in this area, adults may need to intentionally and explicitly teach, model, and provide multiple opportunities to practice the language and life of faith.

In addition, although there are many opportunities for young people to engage in religion, at least within North America, they may or may not be developmentally suited and relevant for adolescents. More often than not these environments focus on religious beliefs, practices, and rituals. Although such an emphasis could be beneficial from a developmental perspective, religious contexts or even youth programs may leverage their developmental impact by intentionally nurturing spiritual development as it relates to transcendence, fidelity, and positive actions. Religious contexts that nurture positive identity development, noble purpose, a sense of belonging, leadership and service activities predicated on a prosocial ideology can promote both healthy psychological development as well as positive spiritual and religious development. Although there is a clear link between religiousness or spirituality and indicators of thriving among youth, further research is needed to explore the underlying mechanisms and factors that mediate this process. Longitudinal research is needed to better understand developmental precursors and trajectories of the dynamic, complex process of adolescent religious and spiritual development over time. In addition, more diverse cultural, ethnic, racial, geographic, religious, and spiritual perspectives should be heard in the dialogue on adolescent religiousness and spirituality, given that Western Protestant Christian approaches have dominated the literature.

CONCLUSION

Religion and spirituality are significant factors in the lives of many adolescents. Not only do adolescents grow considerably in their own religious and spiritual development but also religion and spirituality have the potential to significantly affect overall adolescent development. A developmental systems perspective provides a helpful framework to understand how religious and spiritual development can take place through the interactions among young people and the many contexts in which they live. We refer to this as *relational spirituality* to highlight the richness of the transcendence, fidelity, and behaviors that result from young persons' interactions with their contexts. At its best, religious and spiritual development may have the power to facilitate both individual and societal well-being. Religion and spirituality potentially offer youth a host of developmental resources that range from the ideological to the social to the transcendent. When religion and spirituality are fully leveraged, they may serve as a potent milieu in which youth can thrive and flourish.

References

Abdel-Khalek, A. (2007). Religiosity, happiness, health, and psychopathology in a probability sample of Muslim adolescents. *Mental Health, Religion, and Culture, 10*, 571–583. doi:10.1080/13674670601034547

Arnett, J. J. (2000). Emerging adulthood: A theory of development from the late teens through the twenties. *American Psychologist, 55*, 469–480. doi:10.1037/0003-066X.55.5.469

Arnett, J. J. (2004). *Emerging adulthood: The winding road from late teens through the twenties.* Oxford, England: Oxford University Press.

Bandura, A. (2003). On the psychosocial impact and mechanisms of spiritual modeling. *The International Journal for the Psychology of Religion, 13*, 167–173. doi:10.1207/S15327582IJPR1303_02

Barnes, V. A., Johnson, M., & Treiber, F. (2004). Temporal stability of twenty-four-hour ambulatory hemodynamic bioimpedance measures in African American adolescents. *Blood Pressure Monitoring, 9*, 173–177. doi:10.1097/00126097-200408000-00001

Benson, P. L., & Roehlkepartain, E. C. (2008). Spiritual development: A mission priority in youth development. In P. L. Benson, E. C. Roehlkepartain, & K. L. Hong (Eds.), *New directions for youth development: Special issue on spiritual development* (pp. 13–28). San Francisco, CA: Jossey-Bass.

Benson, P. L., Roehlkepartain, E. C., & Rude, S. P. (2003). Spiritual development in childhood and adolescence: Toward a field of inquiry. *Applied Developmental Science, 7*, 205–213. doi:10.1207/S1532480XADS0703_12

Benson, P. L., Roehlkepartain, E. C., & Scales, P. C. (2010). Spirituality and positive youth development. In L. Miller (Ed.), *The Oxford handbook of psychology of spirituality and consciousness* (pp. 468–485). New York, NY: Oxford University Press.

Benson, P. L., & Scales, P. (2009). The definition and preliminary measurement of thriving in adolescence. *Journal of Positive Psychology, 4*, 85–104. doi:10.1080/17439760802399240

Benson, P. L., Scales, P. C., Hamilton, S. F., & Sesma, A. (2006). Positive youth development: Theory, research, and applications. In W. Damon & R. M. Lerner (Eds.), *Handbook of child psychology: Vol. 1. Theoretical models of human development* (6th ed., pp. 894–941). New York, NY: Wiley.

Bertram-Troost, G., de Roos, S., & Miedema, S. (2009). The relationship between religious education and religious commitments and explorations of adolescents on religious identity development in Dutch Christian Secondary Schools. *Journal of Beliefs and Values, 30*, 17–27. doi:10.1080/13617670902784519

Bridges, L. J., & Moore, K. A. (2002). *Religiousness and spirituality in childhood and adolescence.* Washington, DC: Child Trends.

Bronfenbrenner, U. (1979). *The ecology of human development.* Cambridge, MA: Harvard University Press.

Brown, B. B., Larson, R. W., & Saraswathi, T. S. (2002). *The world's youth: Adolescence in eight regions of the globe.* New York, NY: Cambridge University Press.

Bundick, M. J., Yeager, D. Y., King, P. E., & Damon, W. (2010). Thriving across the lifespan. In W. F. Overton & R. M. Lerner (Eds.), *Handbook of lifespan human development* (pp. 882–923). New York, NY: Wiley.

Colby, A., & Damon, W. (1992). *Some do care: Contemporary lives of moral commitment.* New York, NY: Free Press.

Cotton, S., Zebracki, K., Rosenthal, S., Tsevat, J., & Drotar, D. (2006). Religiousness/spirituality and adolescent health outcomes: A review. *Journal of Adolescent Health, 38*, 472–480. doi:10.1016/j.jadohealth.2005.10.005

Damon, W. (2004). What is positive youth development? *Annals of the American Academy of Political and Social Science, 591*, 13–24. doi:10.1177/0002716203260092

Damon, W., Menon, J., & Bronk, K. (2003). The development of purpose during adolescence. *Applied Developmental Science, 7*, 119–128. doi:10.1207/S1532480XADS0703_2

Dew, R. E., Daniel, S., Goldston, D., McCall, W., Kuchibhatia, M., Schleifer, C., . . . Koenig, H. G. (2010). A prospective study of religion/spirituality and depressive symptoms among adolescent psychiatric patients. *Journal of Affective Disorders, 120*, 149–157. doi:10.1016/j.jad.2009.04.029

Donnelly, T., Matsuba, M., Hart, D., & Atkins, R. (2006). The relationship between spiritual development and civic development. In E. C. Roehlkepartain, P. E. King, L. M. Wagener, & P. L. Benson (Eds.), *The handbook of spiritual development in childhood and adolescence* (pp. 239–251). Thousand Oaks, CA: Sage.

Ellis, B. H., Lincoln, A. K., Charney, M. E., Ford-Paz, R., Benson, M., & Strunin, L. (2010). Mental health service utilization of Somali adolescents: Religion, community, and school as gateways to healing. *Transcultural Psychiatry, 47*, 789–811. doi:10.1177/1363461510379933

Erikson, E. H. (1965). Youth: Fidelity and diversity. In E. H. Erikson (Ed.), *The challenges of youth* (pp. 1–28). Garden City, NY: Anchor Books.

Erikson, E. H. (1968). *Identity: Youth and crisis.* New York, NY: Norton.

Exline, J. J., & Rose, E. (2005). Religious and spiritual struggles. In R. F. Paloutzian & C. L. Park (Eds.), *Handbook of the psychology of religiousness* (pp. 315–330). New York, NY: Guilford Press.

Exline, J. J., Yali, A. M., & Sanderson, W. C. (2000). Guilt, discord, and alienation: The role of religious strain in depression and suicidality. *Journal of Clinical Psychology, 56*, 1481–1496. doi:10.1002/1097-4679(200012)56:12<1481::AID-1>3.0.CO;2-A

Fowler, J. (1981). *Stages of faith: The psychological quest for human meaning.* San Francisco, CA: Harper.

Furrow, J., King, P., & White, K. (2004). Religiousness and positive youth development: Identity, meaning, and prosocial concerns. *Applied Developmental Science, 8*, 17–26. doi:10.1207/S1532480XADS0801_3

Gartner, J., Larson, D. B., & Allen, G. D. (1991). Religious commitment and mental health: A review of the empirical literature. *Journal of Psychology and Theology, 19*, 6–25.

Hart, D., & Fegley, S. (1995). Prosocial behavior and caring in adolescence: Relations to self-understanding and social judgment. *Child Development, 66*, 1346–1359. doi:10.2307/1131651

Jessor, R., Turbin, M., & Costa, F. (1998). Risk and protection in successful outcomes among disadvantaged adolescents. *Applied Developmental Science, 2*, 194–208. doi:10.1207/s1532480xads0204_3

Johnson, C., & Hayes, J. (2003). Troubled spirits: Prevalence and predictors of religious and spiritual concerns among university students and counseling center clients. *Journal of Counseling Psychology, 50*, 409–419. doi:10.1037/0022-0167.50.4.409

Kerestes, M., Youniss, J., & Metz, E. (2004). Longitudinal patterns of religious perspective and civic integration. *Applied Developmental Science, 8*, 39–46. doi:10.1207/S1532480XADS0801_5

King, P. E. (2003). Religiousness and identity: The role of ideological, social, and spiritual contexts. *Applied Developmental Science, 7*, 196–203.

King, P. E. (2008). Spirituality as fertile ground for positive youth development. In R. M. Lerner, R. W. Roeser, & E. Phelps (Eds.), *Positive youth development and spirituality: From theory to research* (pp. 55–73). West Conshohocken, PA: Templeton Foundation Press.

King, P. E., Carr, A., & Boiter, C. (2011). Spirituality, religiosity, and youth thriving. In R. M. Lerner, J. V. Lerner, & J. B. Benson (Eds.), *Advances in Child Development and Behavior: Vol. 41. Positive youth development: Research and applications for promoting thriving in adolescence* (pp. 164–197). Amsterdam, the Netherlands: Elsevier.

King, P. E., Clardy, C. E., & Ramos, J. S. (2010, March). *Spiritual exemplars from around the world: An exploratory study of spiritual development in adolescents.* Paper presented at a symposium at the Biennial Meeting of the Society for Research on Adolescence, Philadelphia, PA.

King, P. E., & Furrow, J. L. (2004). Religion as a resource for positive youth development: Religion, social capital, and moral outcomes. *Developmental Psychology, 40*, 703–713. doi:10.1037/0012-1649.40.5.703

King, P. E., & Roeser, R. (2009). Religiousness & spirituality in adolescent development. In R. M. Lerner & L. Steinberg (Eds.), *Handbook of adolescent psychology* (pp. 435–478). Hoboken, NJ: Wiley. doi:10.1002/9780470479193.adlpsy001014

Koenig, H. G., McCullough, M. E., & Larson, D. B. (2001). *Handbook of religiousness and health.* New York, NY: Oxford University Press. doi:10.1093/acprof:oso/9780195118667.001.0001

Larson, R. W., Hansen, D. M., & Moneta, G. (2006). Differing profiles of developmental experiences across types of organized youth activities. *Developmental Psychology, 42*, 849–863. doi:10.1037/0012-1649.42.5.849

Leak, G. K., DeNeve, K. M., & Greteman, A. J. (2007). The relationship between spirituality, assessed through self-transcendent goal strivings, and positive psychological attributes. *Research in the Social Scientific Study of Religion, 18*, 263–280. doi:10.1163/ej.9789004158511.i-301.102

Lerner, R. M. (2004). Diversity in individual context relations as the basis for positive development across the life span: A developmental systems perspective for theory, research, and application. *Research in Human Development, 1*, 327–346. doi:10.1207/s15427617rhd0104_5

Lerner, R. M. (2006). Developmental science, developmental systems, and contemporary theories of human development. In R. M. Lerner (Ed.),

Theoretical models of human development (pp. 1–17). Hoboken, NJ: Wiley.

Lerner, R. M., Alberts, A. E., Anderson, P. M., & Dowling, E. M. (2006). On making humans human: Spirituality and the promotion of positive youth development. In E. Roehlkepartain, P. King, L. Wagener, & P. Benson (Eds.), *The handbook of spiritual development in childhood and adolescence* (pp. 60–72). Thousand Oaks, CA: Sage.

Lerner, R. M., Roeser, R. W., & Phelps, E. (Eds.). (2008). *Positive youth development and spirituality: From theory to research.* West Conshohocken, PA: Templeton Foundation Press.

Lippmann, L. H., & Keith, J. D. (2006). The demographics of spirituality among youth: International perspectives. In E. C. Roehlkepartain, P. E. King, L. M. Wagener, & P. L. Benson (Eds.), *The handbook of spiritual development in childhood and adolescence* (pp. 109–136). Thousand Oaks, CA: Sage.

Mahoney, A. (2010). Religion in families, 1999–2009: A relational spirituality framework. *Journal of Marriage and Family, 72*, 805–827. doi:10.1111/j.1741-3737.2010.00732.x

Mahoney, A., Pendleton, S., & Ihrke, H. (2006). Religious coping by children and adolescents: Unexplored territory in the realm of spiritual development. In E. C. Roehlkepartain, P. E. King, L. M. Wagener, & P. L. Benson (Eds.), *The handbook of spiritual development in childhood and adolescence* (pp. 341–354). Thousand Oaks, CA: Sage.

Mariano, J. M., & Damon, W. (2008). The role of spirituality and religious faith in supporting purpose in adolescence. In R. M. Lerner, R. W. Roeser, & E. Phelps (Eds.), *Positive youth development and spirituality: From theory to research* (pp. 210–230). West Conshohocken, PA: Templeton Foundation Press.

Markstrom, C. A. (1999). Religious involvement and adolescent psychosocial development. *Journal of Adolescence, 22*, 205–221. doi:10.1006/jado.1999.0211

Markstrom-Adams, C., Hofstra, G., & Dougher, K. (1994). The ego virtue of fidelity: A case for the study of religion and identity formation in adolescence. *Journal of Youth and Adolescence, 23*, 453–469. doi:10.1007/BF01538039

Martin, T. F., White, J. M., & Perlman, D. (2003). Religious socialization: A test of the channeling hypothesis of parental influence on adolescent faith maturity. *Journal of Adolescent Research, 18*, 169–187. doi:10.1177/0743558402250349

Miller, L., & Gur, M. (2002). Religiousness and sexual responsibility in adolescent girls. *Journal of Adolescent Health, 31*, 401–406. doi:10.1016/S1054-139X(02)00403-2

Nonnemaker, J. M., McNeely, C. A., & Blum, R. W. (2003). Public and private domains of religiosity and adolescent health risk behaviors: Evidence from the National Longitudinal Study of Adolescent Health. *Social Science and Medicine, 57*, 2049–2054. doi:10.1016/S0277-9536(03)00096-0

Oman, D., Flinders, T., & Thoresen, C. E. (2008). Integrating spiritual modeling into education: A college course for stress management and spiritual growth. *The International Journal for the Psychology of Religion, 18*, 79–107. doi:10.1080/10508610701879316

Oser, F., Scarlett, W., & Bucher, A. (2006). Religious and spiritual development throughout the lifespan. In R. M. Lerner (Ed.), *Handbook of child psychology* (Vol. 1, pp. 942–998). New York, NY: Wiley.

Pargament, K. I. (2007). *Spiritually integrated psychotherapy: Understanding and addressing the sacred.* New York, NY: Guilford Press.

Pargament, K. I., & Mahoney, A. (2005). Sacred matters: Sanctification as a vital topic for the psychology of religion. *The International Journal for the Psychology of Religion, 15*, 179–198. doi:10.1207/s15327582ijpr1503_1

Pargament, K. I., Smith, B., Koenig, H., & Perez, L. (1998). Patterns of positive and negative religious coping with major life stressors. *Journal for the Scientific Study of Religion, 37*, 710–724. doi:10.2307/1388152

Pargament, K. I., Zinnbauer, B., Scott, A., Butter, E., Zerowin, J., & Stanik, P. (1998). Red flags and religious coping: Identifying some religious warning signs among people in crisis. *Journal of Clinical Psychology, 54*, 77–89. doi:10.1002/(SICI)1097-4679(199801)54:1<77::AID-JCLP9>3.0.CO;2-R

Paus, T. (2009). Brain development. In R. M. Lerner & L. Steinberg (Eds.), *Handbook of adolescent psychology: Individual bases of adolescent development* (3rd ed., Vol. 1, pp. 95–115). Hoboken, NJ: Wiley.

Pearce, M. J. (2003). The protective effects of religiousness and parent involvement on the development of conduct problems among youth exposed to violence. *Child Development, 74*, 1682–1696. doi:10.1046/j.1467-8624.2003.00631.x

Pearce, M. J., Little, T. D., & Perez, J. E. (2003). Religiousness and depressive symptoms among adolescents. *Journal of Clinical Child and Adolescent Psychology, 32*, 267–276. doi:10.1207/S15374424JCCP3202_12

Putnam, R. D. (2000). *Bowling alone: The collapse and revival of American community.* New York, NY: Simon & Schuster.

Regnerus, M. D., & Elder, G. H. (2003). Staying on track in school: Religious influences in high- and low-risk settings. *Journal for the Scientific Study of Religion, 42*, 633–649. doi:10.1046/j.1468-5906.2003.00208.x

Rizzuto, A. M. (1979). *The birth of the living God.* Chicago, IL: University of Chicago Press.

Scales, P., & Leffert, N. (1999). *Developmental assets: A synthesis of the scientific research on adolescent development.* Minneapolis, MN: Search Institute.

Schapman, A. M., & Inderbitzen-Nolan, H. M. (2002). The role of religious behaviour in adolescent depressive and anxious symptomatology. *Journal of Adolescence, 25,* 631–643. doi:10.1006/jado.2002.0510

Schreck, C. J., Burek, M. W., & Clark-Miller, J. (2007). He sends rain upon the wicked: A panel study of the influence of religiosity on violent victimization. *Journal of Interpersonal Violence, 22,* 872–893. doi:10.1177/0886260507301233

Schwartz, K. D., Bukowski, W. M., & Aoki, W. T. (2006). Mentors, friends, and gurus: Peer and nonparent influences on spiritual development. In E. Roehlkepartain, P. King, L. Wagener, & P. Benson (Eds.), *The handbook of spiritual development in childhood and adolescence* (pp. 310–323). Thousand Oaks, CA: Sage.

Silberman, I., Higgins, E. T., & Dweck, C. S. (2005). Religiousness and world change: Violence and terrorism versus peace. *Journal of Social Issues, 61,* 761–784. doi:10.1111/j.1540-4560.2005.00431.x

Sinha, J. W., Cnaan, R. A., & Gelles, R. J. (2007). Adolescent risk behaviors and religion: Findings from a national study. *Journal of Adolescence, 30,* 231–249. doi:10.1016/j.adolescence.2006.02.005

Smith, C. B. (2003). Theorizing religious effects among American adolescents. *Journal for the Scientific Study of Religion, 42,* 17–30. doi:10.1111/1468-5906.t01-1-00158

Smith, C. B., & Denton, M. (2005). *Soul searching: The religious and spiritual lives of American teenagers.* Oxford, England: Oxford University Press.

Smith, C. B., & Snell, P. (2009). *Souls in transition: The religious and spiritual lives of emerging adults.* New York, NY: Oxford University Press.

Smith, C. B., Weigert, A. J., & Thomas, D. L. (1979). Self-esteem and religiosity: An analysis of Catholic adolescents from five cultures. *Journal for the Scientific Study of Religion, 18,* 51–60. doi:10.2307/1385378

Varon, S. R., & Riley, A. W. (1999). Relationship between maternal church attendance and adolescent mental health and social functioning. *Psychiatric Services, 50,* 799–805.

Wagener, L., Furrow, J., King, P., Leffert, N., & Benson, P. (2003). Religious involvement and developmental resources in youth. *Review of Religious Research, 44,* 271–284. doi:10.2307/3512387

Wagener, L., & Malony, H. N. (2006). Spiritual and religious pathology in childhood and adolescence. In E. C. Roehlkepartain, P. E. King, L. M. Wagener, & P. L. Benson (Eds.), *The handbook of spiritual development in childhood and adolescence* (pp. 137–149). Thousand Oaks, CA: Sage.

Wallace, J. M., & Forman, T. A. (1998). Religion's role in promoting health and reducing risk among American youth. *Health Education and Behavior, 25,* 721–741. doi:10.1177/109019819802500604

Wallace, J. M., Forman, T. A., Caldwell, C. H., & Willis, D. S. (2003). Religiousness and American youth: Recent patterns, historical trends and sociodemographic correlates. *Youth and Society, 35,* 98–125.

Wilbur, K. (2006). *Integral spirituality: A startling new role for religion in the modern and postmodern world.* Boston, MA: Shambhala.

Wright, L. S., Frost, C. J., & Wisecarver, S. J. (1993). Church attendance, meaningfulness of religion, and depressive symptomatology among adolescents. *Journal of Youth and Adolescence, 22,* 559–568. doi:10.1007/BF01537716

Zinnbauer, B. J., & Pargament, K. I. (2005). Religiousness and spirituality. In R. Paloutzian & C. Park (Eds.), *Handbook for the psychology of religion* (pp. 21–42). New York, NY: Guilford Press.

CHAPTER 29

RELIGIOUS INVOLVEMENT IN THE LATER YEARS OF LIFE

Neal Krause

Demographic projections suggest that by 2030, the number of older adults in the United States will be twice as large as it was in 2000, growing from 35 million to 71.5 million people (Federal Interagency Forum on Aging Related Statistics, 2008). This means that by 2030, nearly one in five Americans will be at 65 years of age or older. These data highlight the pressing need to know more about the factors that shape the health and quality of life of our aging population. There is mounting evidence that involvement in religion may be one such factor (Koenig, McCullough, & Larson, 2001).

The purpose of this chapter is to explore four ways in which religion may be involved in the lives of older people. First, research on age differences in religious beliefs and practices is reviewed and discussed. In the process, an issue that has been largely overlooked in the literature will be examined. Although it is important to compare and contrast differences in religious involvement between younger and older people, researchers need to know more about how involvement in religion may change *within* late life. Second, at the same time that the population of the United States is growing older, it is also becoming more racially diverse. Although non-Hispanic Whites accounted for 81% of the U.S. population in 2006, this number is projected to fall to 61% by the year 2050 (Federal Interagency Forum on Aging Related Statistics, 2008). Consequently, an effort is made to examine religious involvement in different racial groups during late life. Third, research on religion and health is growing exponentially (Koenig, McCullough, & Larson, 2001). This literature shows how one of the most pressing problems facing the nation can be alleviated. Research consistently reveals that older people incur a substantially greater proportion of health care costs than younger individuals. Specifically, the average per capita expenses for health care and prescribed medicine in 2005 for people under age 65 was $3,239, whereas the corresponding figure for adults age 65 and older was nearly three times larger (i.e., $9,074; National Center for Health Statistics, 2008). Fourth, the practical implications of the research in this field are discussed. Interventions that have been implemented in religious settings are reviewed and ways to improve this work are identified.

AGE DIFFERENCES IN RELIGIOUS BELIEFS AND PRACTICES

According to the prevailing view, people are thought to become more deeply involved in religion as they grow older (Levin, 2004). This perspective is supported by two lines of thinking. First, it makes sense to believe that people become more religious with age if for no other reason than they are closer to death (see Chapter 5 in this volume). And the realization that death is approaching for one's self and loved ones inevitably evokes the "ultimate" questions in life, including questions about the purpose

Support for this chapter was provided by Grant Nos. RO1 AG014749 and RO1 AG026259 from the National Institute on Aging, administered through the Duke University Center on Spirituality, and two grants from the John Templeton Foundation awarded directly to the author.

DOI: 10.1037/14045-029
APA Handbook of Psychology, Religion, and Spirituality: Vol. 1. Context, Theory, and Research, K. I. Pargament (Editor-in-Chief)
Copyright © 2013 by the American Psychological Association. All rights reserved.

of life as well as questions about what may lie beyond death. Second, ever since the psychology of religion first emerged, researchers have argued that people become more involved in religion as they grow older. For example, James (1902/1997) maintained that "the religious age *par excellence* [emphasis in original] would seem to be old age" (p. 34). Writing at about the same time, Starbuck (1899) came to the same conclusion: "The belief in God in some form is by far the most central conception, and it grows in importance with advancing years" (p. 320). Although the issue seems relatively straightforward, deeper reflection reveals that conducting research on age differences in religious involvement is fraught with difficulty. The challenges facing the field are discussed in the following section by reviewing empirical findings from research on age differences in religion and the theoretical perspectives that have been developed to explain why people may become more involved in religion as they grown older.

Empirical Research on Aging and Religion

Three survey research designs have been used to assess age differences in religion: cross-sectional studies, longitudinal studies, and studies that rely on the retrospective recall of religious involvement over the life course. Of the three, findings from cross-sectional studies have appeared more frequently. This research suggests, for example, that people who are presently older are more likely than individuals who are currently younger to attend church services, pray, and read the Bible at home (Barna, 2002). Moreover, older adults are more likely than younger people to report that religion is important in their lives (Bruce, 2003), and they are more likely to forgive people for the things they have done (Allemand, 2008).

Recently, Deaton (2009) conducted a cross-sectional study of age differences in religiousness that was based on data provided by 300,000 people in 142 countries. Using a carefully conducted set of analyses, Deaton showed that statistically significant age differences exist in all but four of the 142 nations he studied. These findings suggest that compared with younger adults, people who are presently older attend worship services more often and believe that religion is more important in their lives.

Unfortunately, at least two problems are found in these cross-sectional studies. First, and most important, researchers who conduct cross-sectional studies cannot rule out the possibility that differences in religious involvement reflect the influence of cohort, and not age. Cohort differences are shaped by unique historical forces that are at work at any given time. So, for example, many investigators maintain that the current cohort of older people were uniquely influenced by the Great Depression, whereas other factors, such as the Vietnam War, exerted a greater influence on members of younger cohorts (Meredith & Schewe, 2002). Although cohort effects are likely to be present in many cross-sectional studies on religion and aging, this may be less of a problem in Deaton's (2009) study because it is difficult to believe that people in 142 countries were exposed to the same historical forces. This is especially true because his sample included respondents in Afghanistan, Togo, Belize, and India as well as in Western nations such as the United States and Germany.

The second problem with cross-sectional studies on age differences in religiousness has to do with the way that religion has typically been measured. Researchers have been arguing for decades that religion is a complex, multidimensional phenomenon (Fetzer Institute/National Institute on Aging Working Group, 1999) and as a result, religion should be assessed with a comprehensive battery of measures. Even so, cross-sectional studies on religion typically have been conducted with a limited range of religion measures, such as the frequency of church attendance or the importance of religion in daily life. Because researchers have used a limited range of religion measures, they cannot tell whether age differences are present (or fail to arise) in other, unmeasured aspects of religion. In fact, evidence that supports this concern already exists. Although the wide majority of cross-sectional studies find age differences in religion, Newport (2006) was unable to find age differences in the belief that God exists.

A small group of researchers have conducted studies that employ longitudinal methods to assess change in religious involvement over long periods of time. For example, Shand (2000) analyzed data that were provided by 84 male graduates from Amherst College over a span of 50 years. He found little change in belief that God exists during this time. Wink and Dillon (2001) analyzed data from the well-known Berkeley Growth Studies. They examined change in religiousness when the study participants were ages 30 through 70. Wink and Dillon found that the importance of religion declined during the 30s and 40s, but then increased in the 50s and early 60s. More recently, McCullough and his colleagues analyzed longitudinal data from the widely cited Terman Study that was conducted with bright individuals (i.e., people with IQs of at least 135) from 1940 through 1991 (McCullough et al., 2005). These investigators created a composite measure of religion that consisted of interest in religion and satisfaction with religion. Using sophisticated growth mixture models, they found that instead of one universal pattern of change in religiousness, three distinct trajectories emerged over time. Study participants in the first trajectory (40% of the sample) experienced increases in religiousness in early adult life followed by a decline with advancing age. In contrast, individuals in the second trajectory (41% of study participants) exhibited low levels of religiousness in early adulthood followed by additional age-related decline. Only members of the third trajectory (19% of the subjects) showed that religiousness increases with age.

The findings from longitudinal studies on age differences in religiousness are thought-provoking, but there are at least three shortcomings in this research. First, the samples in these studies have not been selected at random (e.g., people with an IQ of at least 135), and as a result, it is difficult to know whether the findings can be generalized to the wider population. Second, as with the cross-sectional studies, longitudinal studies are based on a limited range of religion measures (e.g., the belief that God exists). Third, even though the data in these longitudinal studies have been provided by the same individuals over time, it is still not possible to rule out the potential influence of cohort effects. For example, McCullough et al. (2005) studied a group of people from 1940 through 1991. If a new group was studied from 2000 through 2051, differences in religiousness may emerge not because of age, but rather they might emerge because people who were first interviewed in 1940 have different worldviews and life experiences than individuals who were first interviewed in 2000.

Investigators who assess age differences in religiousness via retrospective recall typically ask people who are presently older to recall their level of involvement in religion when they were 20 years old, 30 years old, and so on. Following this strategy, George, Hays, Flint, and Meador (2004) presented study participants with a series of questions that were designed to assess change over the life course in four dimensions of religion (the frequency of church attendance, private religious practices such as prayer, religious media use, and the importance of religion). Like McCullough et al. (2005), they found multiple trajectories of religious involvement in the data. For example, some individuals remained highly involved in religion across the life course, other people experienced an increased sense of religiousness with advancing age, some reported a precipitous decline in religion followed by a rebound, and yet other individuals were never deeply involved in religion at any point in their lifetime.

Further support for the notion that there are multiple trajectories of religious involvement over the life course comes from a retrospective qualitative study by Ingersoll-Dayton, Krause, and Morgan (2002). These investigators report four trajectories of change across a range of religious domains, including feelings of closeness to God. These trajectories largely mirror those reported by George et al. (2004).

The findings from these retrospective studies of religious involvement are intriguing because they are similar to the results that emerged from the longitudinal study by McCullough et al. (2005). The fact that similar findings can be found in studies that employ different methods is encouraging. Like the longitudinal studies, however, there are problems with studies that are based on retrospective recall. Perhaps the most significant shortcoming arises from the possibility that as people grow older, they change or reinterpret their level of involvement in religion at earlier points in the life course. Support for this concern may be found in the work of McAdams (2006), who found that people continually reshape the story of their lives in an effort to derive a deeper sense of meaning therein.

Theoretical Issues in Research on Aging and Religiousness

Many of the empirical studies on age differences in religiousness have been conducted without the benefit of a well-developed theoretical framework. Even so, the work of Fowler (1981), Kohlberg (1973), Tornstam (2005), and Erikson (1959) has provided a point of departure for explaining why people may become more involved in religion as they grow older.

Fowler (1981) identified six stages of faith development. Although he did not consistently associate each stage with a specific age or age range, the stages nevertheless roughly map onto the life course. For example, he noted that the first stage of intuitive–projective faith is typically observed in children between the ages of 3 and 7. In contrast, the highest stage of faith development (Stage 6—universal faith) is "exceedingly rare" and attained only by individuals of historic importance, such as Gandhi, Martin Luther King Jr., and Mother Teresa (Fowler, 1981, p. 200). As a result, the highest stage of faith development that is reached by the typical adult is Stage 5—conjunctive faith. Fowler indicated attainment of this stage is "unusual before midlife" (p. 198). Compared with previous stages of faith development, a person who develops conjunctive faith is more reflective and more aware of the paradoxes and contradictions that are inherent in religion. But despite these intellectual challenges, individuals at this stage of development are capable of, and even enjoy, working through these contradictions to attain a deeper and richer understanding.

Kohlberg (1973) is widely known for his theory of moral development. A good deal of attention in his work was devoted to explaining the moral development of children, adolescents, and younger adults. Later in his career, however, he identified a final stage (i.e., Stage 7) that arose in advanced ages. According to Kohlberg, people who attain the seventh stage of moral development take on an increasingly religious or cosmic perspective that focuses on issues involving the infinite and place an emphasis on seeing oneself as part of the larger unified whole of existence.

According to Tornstam's (2005) theory of gerotranscendence, people experience a shift in their worldview as they enter late life. Instead of being preoccupied with material things and other worldly matters, they become increasingly concerned with the cosmic dimension of life, which involves wider existential concerns. More specifically, there is a greater appreciation for the largely inexplicable mystery of life, a diminished fear of death, and a greater sense of connectedness with earlier generations.

Many people are familiar with Erikson's (1959) theory of life course development. He maintained that as people approach late life, they enter the final stage of development that is characterized by the crisis of integrity versus despair. This is a time of deep introspection when older people survey their lives, attempt to reconcile the things they have done, and make sense of the experiences they have had. Ultimately, the goal of this process is to weave the story of one's life into a more coherent whole. Doing so imbues life with a deep sense of meaning and purpose. If people are unable to resolve this developmental challenge successfully, however, they will slip into despair. Notions involving religion are not evident in the discussion of Erikson's work that has been presented so far. Some investigators may not be aware that later in his career, Erikson changed the way he defined integrity by giving this construct a more explicitly religious meaning. Hoare (2002) published a book on insights she gleaned from Erikson's unpublished papers. She pointed out that during the end of his career, Erikson "changed his thinking to build in God . . . by age 80 . . . *faith* then became an alternate term for *integrity*" (Hoare, 2002, p. 90). Cast within the context of the current discussion, this suggests that Erikson believed that people who successfully negotiate the final stage of development experience a deeper faith.

Age Differences in Religiousness Within Late Life

Although some researchers have devoted considerable effort to the study of religious involvement across the life span, far less attention has been given to assessing whether change in religiousness also takes place solely within late life. Even so, justification for expecting change in religiousness is provided by a brief review of some additional demographic data on aging. Earlier it was noted that the number of older adults is growing significantly. A closer examination of these data, however, reveals that the number of years that people spend in late life is also escalating rapidly. Specifically, the oldest–old people (i.e., people who are at least 85 years of age) grew from about 100,000 in 1900 to 5.3 million in 2006. And demographic projections suggest that the number of oldest–old people will grow to approximately 21 million by 2050 (Federal Interagency Forum on Aging Related Statistics, 2008). Moreover, the growth of centenarians is even more remarkable. In 2000, approximately 56,000 individuals lived to age 100. This group is expected to grow to 1 million by 2050 (Hoyer & Roodin, 2009). If one assumes that late life begins around age 65, then the dramatic growth of people who live to age 100 suggests that late life can last 35 years or longer for a growing number of people. It is difficult to believe that a person could live 35 years and not experience further developmental change. This assertion is consistent with the view that human development is marked by continuous change regardless of age. More specifically, as Hoyer and Roodin (2009) pointed out, "One of the most important issues is the idea that development is a lifelong process. . . . The point is that development and change in the form of both gains and losses occur throughout the human life span" (p. 4).

Although change may be an inevitable part of life, it is still not clear whether change occurs specifically in religious involvement over the course of late life. This issue will be addressed in two ways: First, conceptual reasons why religion may change over the course of late life will be presented. Second, two studies that assess change in religiousness after age 65 will be reviewed.

As people move through late life, they encounter a number of challenges that are typically not experienced by younger individuals. Two are especially important. First, research consistently shows that there is a sharp decline in cognitive ability as people go through late life. More specifically, 5.1% of people age 65 to 69 have moderate or severe memory impairment, but by age 85 nearly one out of three individuals (i.e., 32.1%) suffer from this problem (Federal Interagency Forum on Aging Related Statistics, 2004). Although there do not appear to be any studies that assess the relationship between memory decline and religious involvement, it seems likely that people with severe memory impairment will experience a decline in religious involvement, especially with respect to church attendance and reading religious literature. Moreover, severe memory impairment is likely to compromise an older person's ability to develop meaningful relationships with fellow church members. But in contrast, other religious experiences (e.g., feelings of gratitude toward God, awe) may actually increase across late life because they are less likely to be influenced by cognitive functioning. The second factor that may create change in religious involvement over the course of late life is more social in nature. Baltes and Smith (1999) provided an insightful discussion of challenges that arise in the fourth age, which begins around age 80 or so. They maintain that as people enter this period of advanced old age, they encounter a social vacuum that arises because society has not provided a meaningful role for them to occupy. More specifically, Baltes and Smith argued that "relatively speaking, old age is young; therefore neither biological nor cultural evolution has had sufficient opportunity to evolve a full and optimizing scaffolding (architecture) for the later phases of life" (p. 158). If people find there is no place for them in society during advanced old age, then perhaps greater involvement in religion may become an increasingly attractive option.

There appear to be only two studies that empirically evaluate change in religion over the course of late life. Unfortunately, the findings from this research are inconsistent. Krause (2010a) examined the relationship between having a close companion friend at church and rating health and making outpatient physician visits. The data suggest that older people who have a close companion friend in the congregation where they worship tend to rate their health more favorably and make fewer outpatient physician visits than older people who do not have a close friend at church. These findings emerged only among members of the oldest–old cohort (i.e., people 85 years of age and older). This suggests that a close companion friend at church may play an increasingly important role in advanced old age. Unlike Krause, Tornstam (2005) reported that men experience a decline in cosmic transcendence (e.g., being attuned with the universe) around age 90, whereas women experience a steady increase in cosmic transcendence throughout the course of late life.

Summary

It is too early to reach a definitive conclusion about whether people become more religious as they grow older. This unfortunate state of affairs is due primarily to problems with the research designs that investigators employ, the use of limited measures of religion, and the use of samples that are not representative of the wider population. If researchers are to move this literature forward, they must pay attention to two important methodological issues. First, to differentiate between age and cohort effects, investigators must follow multiple cohorts over time. Evidence of age differences would be present if members of different cohorts tend to become more deeply involved in religion as they grow older. In contrast, clear evidence of a cohort effect would be present if members of one cohort grow more religious with age while members of the second cohort do not.

Second, as some of the studies that were reviewed earlier suggest, people may follow different trajectories of religiousness over time. This more complex view of change in religion over the life course is consistent with the basic tenets of Nelson and Dannefer's (1992) aged heterogeneity hypothesis. According to this perspective, differences between people become more pronounced with age. Support for this perspective has been provided by analyses that employ a wide range of outcomes, including feelings of personal control, self-esteem, and social networks (Nelson & Dannefer, 1992). To the extent that this is true, research must utilize statistical procedures, such as individual growth curve analyses, that are capable of capturing different trajectories of religious involvement across multiple cohorts over time.

Third, researchers need to devise better developed theoretical perspectives to explain age differences in religion. Current theoretical models uniformly suggest that there may be a general tendency for all people to become more religious as they reach late life. Some of the empirical studies that were reviewed, however, suggest there may be multiple trajectories of religious involvement over the life course, and although some individuals become more religious with age, other people either remain stable or lose their faith. More finely nuanced theoretical perspectives are needed to explain why multiple trajectories of religious involvement arise over the life course.

It is not possible to determine whether change in religiousness takes place after age 65. This problem arises because there has been far too little research on this issue. And the studies that have been done so far suffer from many of the same limitations that have been identified with research on religion over the life course, especially with respect to the range of religion measures that has been examined.

The conclusions that have been reached with respect to age differences in religion may seem discouraging, but this need not be the case. Instead, the current state of the literature suggests that there is plenty of room for investigators who wish to probe more deeply into one of the most important issues in human development.

RACE AND RELIGIOUS INVOLVEMENT IN LATE LIFE

Research on race differences in religious involvement is, in some respects, better developed and more consistent than studies on age differences in religiousness. The discussion that follows is divided into two main sections. First, religious involvement among older African Americans and older Whites will be examined. Second, research on religious involvement among older Mexican Americans will be reviewed.

Although research on race differences in religion is important for a number of reasons, one figures prominently in the discussion that follows. As C. Wright Mills (1959), a noted social theorist, put it, "Neither the life of an individual nor the history of a society can be understood without understanding both" (p. 3). Cast within the context of the discussion that follows, this means that researchers cannot properly understand race differences in religiousness without taking the history of minority groups into account. This is important because the influence of history has not received sufficient attention in many studies on religion in late life.

Religiousness Among Older African Americans

Because of centuries of prejudice and discrimination, Black people turned to the church for spiritual, social, and material sustenance, as the church was the only institution in their community that they built, funded, and wholly owned (Nelsen & Nelsen, 1975). As a result, the church became a conduit for the delivery of social services, and the first schools for Black children were located in them, as well. Consequently, it is not surprising to find that many of the great political leaders in the Black community have strong ties to the church, and many have been members of the clergy (e.g., Martin Luther King Jr.). The central role of the church in the Black community is perhaps nowhere more evident than in the work of noted Black theologian J. Deotis Roberts (2003), who stated that

> the black church, as a social and religious body, has served as a kind of 'extended family' for blacks. In a real sense then, thousands of blacks who have never known real family life have discovered the meaning in real kinship in the black church. (p. 78)

Given the key historical role that the church has played in the Black community, it is not surprising to find that older Blacks appear to be more deeply involved in religion than older Whites. The scope and consistency of these findings is remarkable. Because it would be difficult to review all the research that has been done in this area, findings from only three representative studies will be discussed here. The first study was conducted by Levin, Taylor, and Chatters (1994). On the basis of data from four nationwide surveys, these investigators found that compared with older Whites, older Blacks attend church services more often, feel that religion is more important in their lives, listen to religious programs on television or the radio more often, read religious books (including the Bible) more often, feel closer to God, and give more money to the church. The second study was conducted by Krause (2002). He studied race differences in a comprehensive set of measures that assess social relationships in the church. He found that compared with older Whites, older Blacks scored higher on 10 of 12 measures of church-based social relationships. The third study on race differences in religiousness was conducted by Krause and Chatters (2005). These investigators examined whether older Whites differ significantly from older African Americans on 17 different measures of prayer. Older Blacks were more deeply involved than Whites in 16 out of the 17 prayer measures.

There is little research on age differences in religion among African Americans. One of the few studies to address this issue was conducted by Barna (1999). He examined age differences in 13 specific religious beliefs (e.g., good people will go to heaven when they die). No clear pattern of findings emerged from the data. Barna (1999), however, compared Black teenagers with Black adults of all ages, which makes it difficult to discern finer gradations of change in religiousness over the life course. In contrast, Holt, Schulz, and Wynn (2009) assessed age differences in nine measures that focus on beliefs about the role that religion might play in promoting health among African Americans. Age differences emerged in three of the nine measures, and in each instance, younger African Americans were less likely to believe that religion plays a role in promoting health than older African Americans. Finally, two additional studies suggest that older Blacks pray more often than younger Blacks (Levin & Taylor, 1997) and older Blacks tend to feel that religion is more important in their lives than younger Blacks (Taylor, Mattis, & Chatters, 1999).

Older Mexican Americans and Religious Involvement

There is dramatically less research on religion among older Mexican Americans. A recent meta-analysis by Lujan and Campbell (2006) provided evidence of this problem. The investigators were able to find only 28 studies on religion, spirituality, and health among Mexican Americans—and the majority of these studies involved people of all ages. This is unfortunate because research indicates that

Blacks currently account for 9% of the population of older adults and Hispanics (of any race) account for only 6%. But by the year 2050, older Hispanics are projected to outnumber older Blacks by a margin of 18% to 12% (Federal Interagency Forum on Aging Related Statistics, 2008). These data are noteworthy because Mexican Americans are the largest Hispanic group.

As with older Blacks, the key to understanding religious involvement among older Mexican Americans lies in their history. And one of the main historical themes that is embedded in the Mexican American ethos has to do with suffering. There are several reasons why this is so. The first reason has to do with the conquest of Mexico by the Spanish. Carrasco (1990) reported the shocking outcome of this era. He indicated that in 1500 there were 25 million indigenous people living in Mexico, but because of such factors as disease and slavery, this population was reduced to 1 million by 1600. This is why Leon (2004) referred to the period of colonization as the "Mexican diaspora" (p. 198). The deleterious consequences of colonization by the Spanish were exacerbated by a number of subsequent historical events. The Mexican American War of 1848 and the Mexican Revolution of 1910 rekindled earlier conditions of subordination that the diaspora encountered during the Spanish colonization.

Given the imprint these broad historical forces left on the psyche of people of Mexican descent, it is not surprising to find that many sought comfort in their faith (Pargament, 1997; see Chapter 19 in this volume).

In 2009 Krause completed the first nationwide survey that was devoted exclusively to religion and health among older Mexican Americans. Because of the lack of data availability, a comprehensive assessment of religious involvement in this important minority group has not yet been conducted. Even so, findings from the first three papers written with these data provide insight that expands the scope of research on race differences in religious involvement beyond the study of African Americans alone.

The first paper dealt with religion, suffering, and health (Krause & Bastida, 2011b). In addition to historical issues, further insight into the role that suffering plays in the lives of older Mexican Americans was provided by extensive qualitative work conducted before the nationwide survey took place (Krause & Bastida, 2009). Consistent with research on benevolent religious reappraisal (Pargament, Koenig, & Perez, 2000), the older participants in this qualitative research indicated that they attempt to handle suffering by trying to find something positive in this otherwise deleterious experience. In addition to looking for something positive in the face of suffering, some of the older participants in the qualitative research indicated that it was important to bear this suffering in silence. Questions were devised for the nationwide survey to assess the extent to which older Mexican Americans try to find something positive in the suffering they encounter as well as the extent to which they feel it is important to suffer in silence. These measures were then embedded in a latent variable model that was designed to show how beliefs about suffering may influence health. The data indicate that only searching for something positive in suffering provides beneficial effects. In contrast, suffering in silence failed to benefit older Mexican Americans in any way.

The second paper written by Krause and Bastida (2011a) is concerned with the vitally important role that a sense of belonging plays in the Mexican American church. Virgil Elizondo is widely considered to be the founder of Latino theology (Matovina, 2000). He identified three key functions that are performed by the church in the Mexican American community (Elizondo & Matovina, 2010). The first function he mentioned involves the deep sense of belonging that is fostered in Mexican American congregations. Krause and Bastida (2011a) devised a measure of belonging in a congregation and embedded it in a larger conceptual model that was designed to see whether a sense of belonging is associated with health. The data provided strong support for the notion that a sense of belonging is related to better health.

One of the culturally unique aspects of religion among Mexican American Catholics involves making *mandas* or *promesas* (i.e., promises). Essentially a manda involves striking a bargain with the Virgin or one of the saints whereby the individual promises to perform a religious act, such as making a pilgrimage to a sacred shrine, if the deity provides something that is requested. For example, a manda is often made to ensure the health of a loved one. A key issue involves the expectations that are associated with making a manda. As Turner (2008) pointed out, a manda is proposed with the presumption that it will certainly be fulfilled. In fact, Turner reported that a manda is a form of "assertive asking," which is thought to empower the individual (2008, p. 199). Krause and Bastida (2010) developed questions to assess the extent to which older Mexican Americans Catholics offer mandas. Consistent with the observations of Turner (2008), subsequent analyses revealed that study participants who offer mandas tend to have a stronger sense of personal control than study participants who do not make mandas.

Summary

With the exception of older African Americans (see Chapter 30 in this volume), empirical research on religious involvement among older minority group members is in its infancy. There are few empirical studies on religious involvement among older Mexican Americans (see Chapter 33 in this volume), and even less is known about religion among older Asian Americans (see Chapter 32 in this volume). Moreover, there is little research on age differences and religion within each race or ethnic group. Even so, the scant research that has been done so far suggests that religion may be an especially important source of resilience among older people of color.

RELIGION, AGING, AND HEALTH

The literature on religion and health is vast. As Koenig, McCullough, and Larson (2001) have reported, more than 1,200 studies appeared on religion and health by the year 2000. Thousands more have been conducted since then. As Levin (2001) noted, a significant number of these studies have been conducted with older adults. The range of health-related outcomes that have been associated with religion is impressive (for reviews of this research, see Krause, 2008; see also Volume 2, Chapters 12 and 14, this handbook). For example, studies utilizing a wide range of religion measures indicate that greater involvement in religion is associated with better self-rated health, fewer functional limitations, and lower odds of developing a number of specific acute and chronic health problems, such as hypertension. In addition, a growing number of studies suggest that greater involvement in religion is associated with key precursors of physical health, including enhanced immune functioning and a broad array of health behaviors, such as diet, exercise, and the avoidance of tobacco and alcohol. An equally large number of studies reveal that greater involvement in religion is associated with fewer symptoms of depression and dementia. Moreover, greater involvement in religion appears to enhance psychological well-being, including life satisfaction and happiness.

It would not be possible to conduct an exhaustive critique of all the research on religion and health in this chapter—this task is best left to a full-length volume. Instead, the discussion that follows explores two key issues. The first involves whether the effects of religious involvement on health in late life are unique, or whether religion merely provides health-related benefits that may be found in a number of secular settings. The second issue has to do with the fact that the wide majority of studies focus solely on the ways in which religion may enhance and maintain the health of older people. A small cluster of studies, however, indicates that there may be a negative side to religion, as well. To provide a more balanced view of the research on religion and health, it is important to discuss the potential dark side of religion, as well.

Are the Effects of Religion on Health Unique?

As research on religion and health continues to mature, it is important for researchers to reflect on whether the relationships they find are due to the unique influence of religion, or whether they are merely observing processes that may be found in the wider secular world as well (for a detailed discussion of this issue, see Pargament, Magyar-Russell, & Murray-Swank, 2005). For example, the classic work of Allport and Ross (1967) suggested that religious beliefs and practices are driven by uniquely religious motivation (i.e., intrinsically motivated individuals). But this is less true for other aspects of religion. For example, even though research indicates that church-based social relationships may exert a beneficial effect on health in late life (Krause, 2008), a considerable number of studies indicate that social ties that are formed outside the context of religion also may have similar health-enhancing effects (Krause, 2006b). Unfortunately, only two studies in the literature appear to evaluate this issue empirically. Both are reviewed in the following paragraphs.

A good deal of research that has been conducted in secular settings suggests that the deleterious effects of stress on health are buffered or offset for older people who have strong social support systems (Krause, 2006b). For this reason, Krause (2006a) assessed whether emotional support from fellow church members or from people outside the church buffered the effects of ongoing financial problems on the health of older adults. The findings revealed that church-based support, but not secular support, successfully moderated the effects of financial strain on self-rated health. But further reflection reveals that this issue can be evaluated only by focusing on older people who receive support at church as well as assistance from their social network members. Consequently, some researchers may challenge these findings by arguing that because this type of analysis deals solely with people who are religious, it is not surprising to find that church-based support is more important to them. Krause (2006a) conducted a set of supplemental analyses that focused solely on the effects of secular social support among older people who were not deeply involved in religion. The data suggest that secular support did not offset the effects of financial problems in this group.

The second study that provided some evidence of the unique effects of religion on health was conducted by Krause, Shaw, and Liang (2011). The purpose of this study was to examine the factors that influence whether older adults adopt healthy lifestyles. The findings from the study by Krause et al. (2011) indicated that encouragement from fellow church members to adopt healthy lifestyles is associated with a greater likelihood of adopting beneficial health behaviors. Encouragement from secular social network members failed to exert a similar effect.

Taken together, this research suggests that the effects of church-based social relationships on health may be unique. These findings should be viewed cautiously for two reasons: First, these results must be replicated in other studies. Second, the findings reflect the influence of only one dimension of religion—that is, social relationships in the church. More research is needed to determine whether other dimensions of religion, such as forgiveness, are also unique and whether forgiving for secular reasons conveys similar health-related benefits (see Chapter 23 in this volume).

Exploring the Dark Side of Religion

Research on the ways that religion may compromise health and well-being in late life is considerably underdeveloped (see Chapter 25, this volume and Volume 2, Chapter 4, this handbook). Most of the work that has been done so far focuses on two problems. The first has to do with negative interaction with fellow church members, and the second involves the negative fallout from having doubts about religion.

Negative interaction involves social encounters with people at church who are characterized by criticism, unwanted advice, prying into personal affairs, and behavior that is thoughtless and inconsiderate. Although a number of studies that have been conducted in the church with people of all ages suggest that negative interaction may exert a deleterious effect on health and well-being (e.g., Krause & Wulff, 2005), there is reason to believe that the effects of unpleasant social encounters may be even more troubling for older people. Support for this notion comes from Carstensen's (1992) emotional selectivity theory. She has maintained that as people enter late life, they realize they have relatively little time left to live. This realization changes social relationship preferences. More specifically, as people grow older, they prefer social relationships that are close emotionally and disengage from more peripheral social network ties. If people place a greater value on emotionally close relationships as they grow older, but encounter negative interaction instead, it follows that they may be more disturbed than younger individuals when interpersonal conflict arises.

There appear to be only two empirical studies in the literature that examine the relationship between negative interaction in the church and well-being in late life. The first study, which was conducted by Krause (2003), focused on negative interaction that rank-and-file church members have with members of the clergy. The findings reveal that negative interaction tends to lower the self-esteem of older people, but only if they fail to rely on positive religious coping responses, such as turning to God for strength and guidance.

The second study on negative interaction in the church in late life was conducted by Krause and Ellison (2009a). This study is noteworthy because it shows that church-based negative interaction in the church exerts a deleterious effect on health because it is linked to the second way in which religion may compromise the health of older people (i.e., religious doubt).

Hunsberger, McKenzie, Pratt, and Pancer (1993) defined *religious doubt* as "a feeling of uncertainty toward, and questioning of, religious teachings and beliefs" (p. 28). Unfortunately, there has been very little research on religious doubt in late life. Instead, most of the work that has been done involves either people of all ages (Krause, Ingersoll-Dayton, Ellison, & Wulff, 1999) or college students (Hunsberger, Pratt, & Pancer, 2002).

Research on religious doubt is challenging because it may have detrimental as well as desirable effects. With respect to the negative aspects of doubt, Krause et al. (1999) pointed out that religious doubt creates an unsettling state of indecision that arises from seeing the validity of two seemingly inconsistent points of view. For example, it may be difficult for some people to believe in a loving and protecting God while at the same time recognizing there is a great deal of pain, suffering, and injustice in the world. Viewed in this way, doubt may be seen as a specific type of cognitive dissonance (Festinger, 1957). In addition to creating cognitive dissonance, religious doubt may carry the added burden of negative sanctions and guilt. Evidence of this may be found in the New Testament, where the book of Romans unequivocally states that "he who has doubts is condemned" (Romans 14:23, King James Version).

In contrast to the view that doubt is detrimental, some theologians and researchers maintain that religious doubt should be embraced because it is the gateway to a deeper and more meaningful faith. This perspective is perhaps nowhere more evident than in the writing of Paul Tillich, who was an important Protestant theologian. Tillich (1957) argued that "doubt is not the opposite of faith; it is an element of faith" (p. 73).

Viewed more broadly the proper question to examine when studying doubt is not whether doubt has positive or negative effects on health. Instead, the key task involves identifying the conditions that determine whether doubt will enhance or compromise health. Krause and Ellison (2009a) recently conducted one of the few studies that explore these finer nuances of religious doubt in late life. The results indicate that some older adults attempt to cope with doubts about their faith by denying them when they arise. The emphasis on the denial of doubt is important because findings suggest that older people who deny religious doubt when it arises rate their health less favorably over time.

Summary

As the research discussed is this section reveals, there has been a good deal of research on the relationship between religion and health with data that have been provided by older people. Far fewer studies have been conducted to see whether there are age differences in the relationship between religion and health. This is unfortunate because a number of intriguing issues have yet to be examined within this context. For example, as discussed, research by Carstensen (1992) and others has indicated that emotionally close relationship become more important as people grow older. To the extent that this is true, the relationship between church-based emotional support and health should become progressively stronger as people grow older. The same issue arises in research on the detrimental aspects of religion. A good deal has been written about death anxiety (e.g., Neimeyer, 1994). Because older people are closer to death than young individuals, one might expect to find greater feelings of death anxiety among older adults who have doubts about religion than among younger people who have doubts about religion.

The research reviewed in this section suggests that both negative interaction in the church and religious doubt may erode health and well-being in late life. This work is important because it helps researchers confront bitter criticisms made about research on religion and health (Sloan & Bagiella, 2002). Recognizing that involvement in religion has both beneficial and detrimental effects on health should go a long way toward assuaging these concerns.

PRACTICAL APPLICATIONS

If older people consume far more health-care resources than younger individuals, and if greater involvement in religion is associated with better health in late life, then it follows that steps should be taken to devise interventions that can be implemented in the church to improve the health of older people. Although a number of interventions (i.e., faith-based initiatives) have been devised (see Campbell et al., 2007), there are at least two limitations in the work that has been done so far. First, most of the interventions have been conducted with people of all ages and not with older adults specifically. Second, many of these interventions have not been evaluated in a methodologically rigorous manner.

Johnson, Tompkins, and Webb (2002) reviewed 800 faith-based programs and found that only 25 were even formally evaluated. Moreover, the few evaluations that were conducted were not based on rigorous methodological procedures. Similar findings are reported in a review of this literature by Ferguson et al. (2007), who wrote that "more specific conclusions regarding faith as a programmatic factor remain outstanding given the lack of apparent theoretical frameworks to guide both the design of previous evaluation studies and the selection of relevant variables" (p. 273). Simply put, studies are needed that bridge the wide chasm between basic and applied research on religion and health (see Volume 2, this handbook). This is especially true when the interventions focus on older people. Baruth, Wilcox, Laken, Bopp, and Saunders (2008) reported the results of a large-scale, faith-based physical activities initiative. Health directors from participating congregations were interviewed. The data suggest that having a high percentage of elderly church members was a significant barrier to successful program implementation.

At least three issues must be addressed so that more effective faith-based programs can be developed for older adults. First, researchers must devise and empirically evaluate conceptual models that identify the specific mechanisms linking religion and health. Second, well-developed measures of religiousness must be used to evaluate faith-based interventions and the models that are used to guide them. Third, researchers must ensure that faith-based interventions are successful with older people.

Although it is not possible to fully address these issues in this chapter, it may be helpful to sketch out some preliminary ideas about how to overcome these problems. DeHaven, Hunter, Wilder, Walton, and Berry (2004) reported that about half of the faith-based programs they reviewed focused on primary prevention (i.e., enhancing health behaviors), so it makes sense to limit the discussion to this type of intervention. Looking more closely at the findings from two studies by Krause provides a point of departure for thinking about how to devise interventions that aim to get older people to adopt beneficial health behaviors. Krause et al. (2011) showed that support from fellow church members is more likely to promote adoption of healthy lifestyles than support from secular social network members. In addition, this study further revealed that encouragement from fellow church members to adopt healthy lifestyles was even more effective than formal church programs that were developed for this purpose. Moreover, the results reveal that older people who felt like they belonged in their congregations were more likely to respond to the health-related requests of their fellow church members.

The insights reported by Krause et al. (2011) are helpful, but they do not provide the level of specificity that is needed to devise effective faith-based programs. The problem arises because Krause et al. evaluated the influence of all church members taken together. It is unlikely, however, that all of the people at church carry the same weight. Fortunately, findings from a second study by Krause (2010a) provided some insight into this issue. Recall that this study suggested that older people who had a close companion friend in their congregation made fewer outpatient physician visits than older adults who did not have a close friend at church.

Taken as a whole, these studies suggest that faith-based initiatives might be developed along the following lines: First, it may be useful to determine the extent to which older study participants identify or feel they belong in their congregations. Separate interventions may be needed to more effectively reach people who are more tightly integrated and less tightly integrated into the places where they worship. Second, some faith-based initiatives have used church members as lay advisors or peer educators to promote intervention messages (Campbell et al., 2007). But it is not clear how to identify lay advisors. These findings indicate that close companion friends at church may be well suited for this task. Third, it may be better to work with dyads than larger support groups because it is unlikely that the same individual serves as a close companion friend for all older people in a congregation.

CONCLUSION

Research on religion in late life is maturing rapidly, but it still has a long way to go. Researchers need to determine whether people become more religious as they grow older, and if they do, then the reasons for greater involvement in religion during late life must be spelled out clearly and evaluated empirically. Much more work is also needed on race and ethnic differences in religion. Although research with older African Americans is shaping up nicely, we know far too little about religious involvement among older Mexican Americans and (especially) older Asian Americans. Identifying the aspects of religion that are common across racial groups, as well as the facets of religion that are unique to each racial group, holds the promise of providing greater insight into the fundamental nature of religion itself. Research is also beginning to provide valuable insights into the factors that bolster and maintain the health of our aging population. It is also time to turn to the identification and empirical evaluation of the intervening constructs that explain how the salubrious effects of religion on health arise in late life. At the same time, more attention must be paid to the ways in which religion may compromise the health of older people. Research in this area has barely scratched the surface of what are likely to be complex processes. Studies on negative interaction in the church and religious doubt were examined in this chapter, but this hardly exhausts all the ways in which the dark side of religion may be manifest. For example, there do not appear to be any studies on how older people cope with hypocrisy in the church even though it is likely to be a constant feature of congregational life. Moreover, as Exline and Rose (2005) have shown, there are other types of spiritual struggles, including feeling angry toward God, facing one's own sins, and attributing misfortunes to evil forces, such as Satan. As Pargament, Koenig, and Hahn (2004) demonstrated, wrestling with these (and other) spiritual struggles may have an adverse effect on health over time.

Although these specific research issues are important, perhaps the greatest need involves devising better developed theories about the role that religion plays in late life. Use of the plural form, "theories," is important because as the research reviewed in this chapter suggests, multiple trajectories of religious involvement over the life course are likely. These theories should explain why some people lose interest in religion as they grow older, whereas others remain committed to their faith. As a qualitative study by Ingersoll-Dayton, Krause, and Morgan (2002) suggested, perhaps major life events that cannot be altered easily may have something to do with it. And at some point, theories about specific facets of religion should be merged to create a higher order theoretical framework that is broad and sweeping in scope. For example, some investigators have developed and tested models that are only concerned with religious coping responses (Koenig, Pargament, & Nielsen, 1998), whereas others focus on the role that is played by the search for a religious sense of meaning in life (Park, 2006). Some scholars highlight the role that church-based social relationships play in late life (Krause, 2008), whereas other investigators have been concerned with God-mediated control (i.e., the notion that God helps people gain control over their lives by working together with Him; Krause, 2005). This problem can be eradicated by identifying an underlying conceptual thread that can pull these diverse lines of research into a more coherent whole.

Although identifying a theme that can unify the literature is a formidable task, it can be accomplished if researchers are willing to make fundamental assumptions about the nature of men and women. One promising approach to this challenge was provided some time ago by Berger and Pullberg (1965) in their insightful discussion of how the social world is created: "*Men together* engage in constructing the world, which then becomes their dwelling. Indeed, since sociality is a necessary element of human being, the process of world production is necessarily a social one" (p. 201). They went on to argue that efforts to develop definitions of social reality are not a one-time effort. Instead, "the world must be confirmed and re-confirmed *by others*" (Berger & Pullberg, 1965, p. 201). Viewed more broadly, these observations speak to building more comprehensive theories of religious involvement based on the social relationships that older people develop at church (Krause, 2008). Krause embarked on a systematic series of studies to assess the merit of this approach. Taken as a whole, this research program suggests that it might be beneficial to use church-based social relationships as the thread that pulls the field together. More specifically, findings from this work reveal that the social relationships that older adults develop at church influence feelings of God-mediated control (Krause, 2007), a sense of religiously oriented meaning in life (Krause, 2008), feelings of gratitude toward God (Krause & Ellison, 2009b), the use of religious coping responses (Krause, 2010b), and self-forgiveness (Krause, 2010c). It is especially important to point out that these findings are all based on longitudinal data.

Some time ago, Jung argued that "everything to do with religion, everything it is and asserts, touches the human soul so closely that psychology least of all can afford to overlook it" (as quoted in Jacobi & Hull, 1953, p. 337). The fact that 74% of older adults strongly agree that their religious faith is a very important part of their lives attests to the validity of Jung's observations (Barna, 2002). And if religion occupies such a central role, it may well be the key to understanding a good deal of human behavior in late life.

References

Allemand, M. (2008). Age differences in forgiveness: The role of future time perspective. *Journal of Research in Personality, 42*, 1137–1147. doi:10.1016/j.jrp.2008.02.009

Allport, G. W., & Ross, J. M. (1967). Personal religious orientation and prejudice. *Journal of Personality and Social Psychology, 5*, 432–443. doi:10.1037/h0021212

Baltes, P. B., & Smith, J. (1999). Multilevel and systemic analysis of old age: Theoretical and empirical evidence for a fourth age. In V. L. Bengston & K. W. Schaie (Eds.), *Handbook of theories of aging* (pp. 153–173). New York, NY: Springer.

Barna, G. (1999). *African Americans and their faith.* Oxnard, CA: Barna Institute.

Barna, G. (2002). *The state of the church, 2002.* Ventura, CA: Issachar Resources.

Baruth, M., Wilcox, S., Laken, M., Bopp, M., & Saunders, R. (2008). Implementation of a faith-based physical activity intervention: Insights from church health directors. *Journal of Community Health, 33*, 304–312. doi:10.1007/s10900-008-9098-4

Berger, P. L., & Pullberg, S. (1965). Reification and sociological critique of consciousness. *History and Theory, 4*, 196–211. doi:10.2307/2504151

Bruce, D. A. (2003, July). *Generational differences in personal religious practices.* Presented at the Annual Meeting of International Society for the Sociology of Religion, Turin, Italy.

Campbell, M. K., Hudson, M. A., Resnicow, K., Blakeney, N., Paxton, A., & Baskin, M. (2007). Church-based health promotion interventions: Evidence and lessons learned. *Annual Review of Public Health, 28*, 213–234. doi:10.1146/annurev.publhealth.28.021406.144016

Carrasco, D. (1990). *Religions of Mesoamerica: Cosmovision and ceremonial centers.* Long Grove, IL: Waveland Press.

Carstensen, L. L. (1992). Social and emotional patterns in adulthood: Support for socioemotional selectivity theory. *Psychology and Aging, 7*, 331–338. doi:10.1037/0882-7974.7.3.331

Deaton, A. (2009). *Aging, religion, and health.* Retrieved from http://www.nber.org/papers/w15271.pdf

DeHaven, M. J., Hunter, I. B., Wilder, J., Walton, J. W., & Berry, J. (2004). Health programs in faith-based organizations: Are they effective? *American Journal of Public Health, 94*, 1030–1036. doi:10.2105/AJPH.94.6.1030

Elizondo, V., & Matovina, T. (2010). *Virgilio Elizondo: Spiritual writings*. Maryknoll, NY: Orbis Books.

Erikson, E. (1959). *Identity and the life cycle*. New York, NY: International University Press.

Exline, J. J., & Rose, E. (2005). Religious and spiritual struggles. In R. F. Paloutzian & C. L. Park (Eds.), *Handbook of the psychology of religion and spirituality* (pp. 315–330). New York, NY: Guilford Press.

Federal Interagency Forum on Aging Related Statistics. (2004). *Older Americans 2004: Key indicators of well-being*. Washington, DC: U.S. Government Printing Office.

Federal Interagency Forum on Aging Related Statistics. (2008). *Older Americans 2008: Key indicators of well-being*. Washington, DC: U.S. Government Printing Office.

Ferguson, K. M., Wu, Q., Spruijt-Metz, D., & Dyrness, G. (2007). Outcomes evaluation in faith-based social services: Are we evaluating faith accurately? *Research on Social Work Practice, 17*, 264–276. doi:10.1177/1049731505283698

Festinger, L. (1957). *A theory of cognitive dissonance*. Palo Alto, CA: Stanford University Press.

Fetzer Institute/National Institute on Aging Working Group. (1999). *Multidimensional measurement of religiousness/spirituality for use in health research*. Kalamazoo, MI: John E. Fetzer Institute.

Fowler, J. W. (1981). *Stages of faith: The psychology of human development and the quest for meaning*. New York, NY: Harper & Row.

George, L. K., Hays, J. C., Flint, E. P., & Meador, K. G. (2004). Religion and health in life course perspective. In K. W. Schaie, N. Krause, & A. Booth (Eds.), *Religious influences on health and well-being in the elderly* (pp. 246–282). New York, NY: Springer.

Hoare, C. H. (2002). *Erikson on development in adulthood: New insights from the unpublished papers*. New York, NY: Oxford University Press.

Holt, C. L., Schulz, E., & Wynn, T. A. (2009). Perceptions of the religion-health connection among African Americans in the southeastern United States: Sex, age, and urban/rural differences. *Health Education and Behavior, 36*, 62–80. doi:10.1177/1090198107303314

Hoyer, W. J., & Roodin, P. A. (2009). *Adult development and aging*. New York, NY: McGraw-Hill.

Hunsberger, B. S., McKenzie, B., Pratt, M., & Pancer, S. M. (1993). Religious doubt: A social psychological analysis. *Research in the Social Scientific Study of Religion, 5*, 27–51.

Hunsberger, B. S., Pratt, M., & Pancer, S. M. (2002). A longitudinal study of religious doubt in high school and beyond: Relationships, stability, and searching for answers. *Journal for the Scientific Study of Religion, 41*, 255–266. doi:10.1111/1468-5906.00115

Ingersoll-Dayton, B., Krause, N., & Morgan, D. L. (2002). Religious trajectories and transitions over the life course. *International Journal of Aging and Human Development, 55*, 51–70. doi:10.2190/297Q-MRMV-27TE-VLFK

Jacobi, Y., & Hull, R. F. C. (1953). *C. G. Jung psychological reflections: A new anthology of his writings 1905–1961*. Princeton, NJ: Princeton University Press.

James, W. (1997). *Selected writings—William James*. New York, NY: Book-of-the-Month Club. (Original work published 1902)

Johnson, B. R., Tompkins, R. B., & Webb, D. (2002). *Objective hope: Assessing the effectiveness of faith-based organizations*. Philadelphia, PA: Manhattan Institute, Center for Research on Religion and Urban Civil Society.

Koenig, H. G., McCullough, M. E., & Larson, D. B. (2001). *Handbook of religion and health*. New York, NY: Oxford University Press. doi:10.1093/acprof:oso/9780195118667.001.0001

Koenig, H. G., Pargament, K. I., & Nielsen, J. (1998). Religious coping and health status in medically ill hospitalized older adults. *Journal of Nervous and Mental Disease, 186*, 513–521. doi:10.1097/00005053-199809000-00001

Kohlberg, L. (1973). Stages and aging in moral development—some speculations. *The Gerontologist, 13*, 497–502. doi:10.1093/geront/13.4.497

Krause, N. (2002). Exploring race differences in a comprehensive battery of church-based social support measures. *Review of Religious Research, 44*, 126–149. doi:10.2307/3512512

Krause, N. (2003). Exploring race differences in the relationship between social interaction with the clergy and feelings of self-worth in late life. *Sociology of Religion, 64*, 183–205. doi:10.2307/3712370

Krause, N. (2005). God-mediated control and psychological well-being in late life. *Research on Aging, 27*, 136–164. doi:10.1177/0164027504270475

Krause, N. (2006a). Exploring the stress-buffering effects of church-based social support and secular social support on health in late life. *The Journals of Gerontology, Series B: Psychological Sciences and Social Sciences, 61*, S35–S43. doi:10.1093/geronb/61.1.S35

Krause, N. (2006b). Social Relationships. In R. H. Binstock & L. K. George (Eds.), *Handbook of aging and the social sciences* (pp. 181–200). San Diego, CA: Academic Press. doi:10.1016/B978-012088388-2/50014-6

Krause, N. (2007). Social involvement in religious institutions and God-mediated control beliefs: A longitudinal investigation. *Journal for the Scientific Study of Religion, 46*, 519–537. doi:10.1111/j.1468-5906.2007.00375.x

Krause, N. (2008). *Aging in the church: How social relationships affect health.* West Conshohocken, PA: Templeton Foundation Press.

Krause, N. (2010a). Close companions at church, health, and health care use in late life. *Journal of Aging and Health, 22*, 434–453. doi:10.1177/0898264309359537

Krause, N. (2010b). The social milieu of the church and religious coping responses. A longitudinal investigation of older whites and older blacks. *The International Journal for the Psychology of Religion, 20*, 109–129. doi:10.1080/10508611003608007

Krause, N. (2010c). Church-based emotional support and self-forgiveness in late life. *Review of Religious Research, 52*, 72–89.

Krause, N., & Bastida, E. (2009). Religion, suffering, and health among older Mexican Americans. *Journal of Aging Studies, 23*, 114–123. doi:10.1016/j.jaging.2008.11.002

Krause, N., & Bastida, E. (2010). Religion and health among older Mexican Americans: Exploring the influence of making mandas. *Journal of Religion and Health.* Advance online publication. doi:10.1007/s10943-010-9389-9

Krause, N., & Bastida, E. (2011a). Church-based social relationships, belonging, and health among older Mexican Americans. *Journal for the Scientific Study of Religion, 30*, 397–409. doi:10.1111/j.1468-5906.2011.01575.x

Krause, N., & Bastida, E. (2011b). Religion, suffering, and self-rated health among older Mexican Americans. *The Journals of Gerontology, Series B: Psychological Sciences and Social Sciences, 66*, 207–216. doi:10.1093/geronb/gbq086

Krause, N., & Chatters, L. M. (2005). Exploring race differences in a multidimensional battery of prayer measures among older adults. *Sociology of Religion, 66*, 23–43. doi:10.2307/4153114

Krause, N., & Ellison, C. G. (2009a). The doubting process: A longitudinal study of the precipitants and consequences of religious doubt. *Journal for the Scientific Study of Religion, 48*, 293–312. doi:10.1111/j.1468-5906.2009.01448.x

Krause, N., & Ellison, C. G. (2009b). The social environment of the church and feelings of gratitude toward God. *Psychology of Religion and Spirituality, 1*, 191–205. doi:10.1037/a0016729

Krause, N., Ingersoll-Dayton, B., Ellison, C. G., & Wulff, K. M. (1999). Aging, religious doubt, and psychological well-being. *The Gerontologist, 39*, 525–533. doi:10.1093/geront/39.5.525

Krause, N., Shaw, B. A., & Liang, J. (2011). Social relationships in religious institutions and healthy lifestyles. *Health Education and Behavior, 38*, 25–38. doi:10.1177/1090198110370281

Krause, N., & Wulff, K. M. (2005). Church-based social ties, a sense of belonging in a congregation, and physical health status. *The International Journal for the Psychology of Religion, 15*, 73–93. doi:10.1207/s15327582ijpr1501_6

Leon, L. (2004). *LaLlorona's children: Religion, life and death on the U.S.–Mexican borderlands.* Berkeley: University of California Press.

Levin, J. S. (2001). *God, faith, and health: Exploring the spirituality-healing connection.* New York, NY: Wiley.

Levin, J. S. (2004). Prayer, love, and transcendence: An epidemiologic perspective. In K. W. Schaie, N. Krause, & A. Booth (Eds.), *Religious influences on health and well-being in the elderly* (pp. 69–95). New York, NY: Springer.

Levin, J. S., & Taylor, R. J. (1997). Age differences in patterns and correlates of the frequency of prayer. *The Gerontologist, 37*, 75–88. doi:10.1093/geront/37.1.75

Levin, J. S., Taylor, R. J., & Chatters, L. M. (1994). Race and gender differences in religiosity among older adults: Findings from four national surveys. *The Journals of Gerontology, Series B: Psychological Sciences and Social Sciences, 49*, S137–S145.

Lujan, J., & Campbell, H. B. (2006). The role of religion on the health practices of Mexican Americans. *Journal of Religion and Health, 45*, 183–195. doi:10.1007/s10943-006-9019-8

Matovina, T. (2000). *Beyond borders: Writings of Virgilio Elizondo and his friends.* Maryknoll, NY: Orbis Books.

McAdams, D. P. (2006). *The redemptive self: Stories Americans live by.* New York, NY: Oxford University Press.

McCullough, M. E., Enders, C. K., Brion, S. L., & Jain, A. R. (2005). The varieties of religious development in adulthood: A longitudinal investigation of religion and rational choice. *Journal of Personality and Social Psychology, 89*, 78–89. doi:10.1037/0022-3514.89.1.78

Meredith, G. E., & Schewe, C. D. (2002). *Defining markets defining moments: America's 7 generational cohorts, their shared experiences, and why business should care.* New York, NY: Hungry Minds.

Mills, C. W. (1959). *The sociological imagination.* New York, NY: Oxford University Press.

National Center for Health Statistics. (2008). *Health, United States, 2008.* Hyattsville, MD: U.S. Government Printing Office.

Neimeyer, R. A. (1994). *Death anxiety handbook: Research, instrumentation, and application.* Washington, DC: Taylor & Francis.

Nelsen, H. M., & Nelsen, A. K. (1975). *Black church in the sixties.* Lexington: University of Kentucky Press.

Nelson, E. A., & Dannefer, D. (1992). Aged heterogeneity: Fact or fiction? The fate and diversity in gerontological research. *The Gerontologist, 32,* 17–23. doi:10.1093/geront/32.1.17

Newport, F. (2006). *Who believes in God and who doesn't?* Retrieved from http://www.gallup.com/poll/23470/Who-Believes-God-Who-Doesn't

Pargament, K. I. (1997). *The psychology of religion and coping: Theory, research, practice.* New York, NY: Guilford Press.

Pargament, K. I., Koenig, H. G., & Hahn, J. (2004). Religious coping methods as predictors of psychological, physical and spiritual outcomes among medically ill elderly patients: A two-year longitudinal study. *Journal of Health Psychology, 9,* 713–730. doi:10.1177/1359105304045366

Pargament, K. I., Koenig, H. G., & Perez, L. M. (2000). The many methods of religious coping: Development and initial validation of the RCOPE. *Journal of Clinical Psychology, 56,* 519–543. doi:10.1002/(SICI)1097-4679(200004)56:4<519::AID-JCLP6>3.0.CO;2-1

Pargament, K. I., Magyar-Russell, G. M., & Murray-Swank, N. A. (2005). The sacred and the search for significance: Religion as a unique process. *Journal of Social Issues, 61,* 665–687. doi:10.1111/j.1540-4560.2005.00426.x

Park, C. L. (2006). Exploring relations among religiousness, meaning, and adjustment to lifetime and current stressful encounters in late life. *Anxiety, Stress, and Coping: An International Journal, 19,* 33–45.

Roberts, J. D. (2003). Black ecclesiology of involvement. In E. M. Goatley (Ed.), *Black religion, black theology* (pp. 73–86). Harrisburg, PA: Trinity Press International.

Shand, J. D. (2000). The effects of life experiences over a 50-year period on the certainty of belief and disbelief in God. *The International Journal for the Psychology of Religion, 10,* 85–100. doi:10.1207/S15327582IJPR1002_02

Sloan, R. P., & Bagiella, E. (2002). Claims about religious involvement and health outcomes. *Annals of Behavioral Medicine, 24,* 14–21. doi:10.1207/S15324796ABM2401_03

Starbuck, D. E. (1899). *The psychology of religion.* New York, NY: Charles Scribner's Sons.

Taylor, R. J., Mattis, J., & Chatters, L. M. (1999). Subjective religiosity among African Americans: A synthesis of findings from five national samples. *Journal of Black Psychology, 25,* 524–543. doi:10.1177/0095798499025004004

Tillich, P. (1957). *The dynamics of faith.* New York, NY: Harper & Brothers.

Tornstam, L. (2005). *Gerotranscendence: A developmental theory of positive aging.* New York, NY: Springer.

Turner, K. (2008). Voces de Fe: Mexican American altaristas in Texas. In G. Espinosa & M. T. Garcia (Eds.), *Mexican American religions: Spirituality, activism, and culture* (pp. 180–205). Durham, NC: Duke University Press.

Wink, P., & Dillon, M. (2001). Religious involvement and health outcomes in late adulthood: Findings from a longitudinal study of women and men. In T. G. Plante & A. C. Sherman (Eds.), *Faith and health: Psychological perspectives* (pp. 75–106). New York, NY: Guilford Press.

Chapter 30

FAITH AND THE SACRED IN AFRICAN AMERICAN LIFE

Jacqueline S. Mattis and Nyasha A. Grayman-Simpson

Eighty-nine percent of African American adults self-identify as religious; 78% attend religious services regularly; and 90% pray, meditate, or use religious materials (Taylor, Chatters, & Levin, 2004). Data on African American youth indicate that 51% of eighth graders, 55% of 10th graders, and 55% of 12th graders report that religion plays a "very important" role in their lives (Taylor et al., 2004). Consistent with these data, 46% of African American 10th graders and 40% of 12th graders report that they attend religious services weekly (Taylor et al., 2004). In fact, African American eighth through 12th graders are significantly more likely to attend religious services, and significantly more likely to belong to a religious youth group than U.S. adolescents of other ethnic groups (Smith, Denton, Faris, & Regnerus, 2002). Taken together, these data illustrate the centrality of religion for African Americans and the relevance of faith life across the life span (Taylor et al., 2004; Taylor, Mattis, & Chatters, 1999). The pivotal role of religion and spirituality in the lives of African Americans marks this ethnoracial group as a particularly important target for attention in research on the psychology and sociology of religion. In this chapter we endeavor to achieve three ends: First, we briefly review literature on the meanings of religiosity and spirituality among African Americans. Second, we review the literature on the link between religiosity, spirituality, and health among African Americans. Finally, we examine findings regarding the pathways by which religion and spirituality may achieve its ends.

ON THE MEANING OF RELIGION AND SPIRITUALITY

Jagers (1997) defined *spirituality* as a belief in a sacred, transcendent force that permeates all things and influences all aspects of lived experience. When invited to provide subjectively meaningful definitions of religiosity and spirituality, African American adults define *religion* or *religiosity* as one's adherence to the prescribed beliefs and devotional practices associated with the worship of God (Mattis, 2000). In contrast, African Americans define *spirituality* as individuals' recognition of the sacredness of all things, a relationship between humans and sacred or transcendent forces (e.g., God, spirits, ancestors), and as the consequent conscious commitment made by individuals to live a life of virtue (Mattis, 2000).

Although these definitions are rich, sociological and anthropological evidence points to a conceptual gap that plagues psychology research on religion and spirituality. Missing from the psychology literature is systematic attention to secular cultural beliefs in the transcendent, noncorporeal (i.e., spiritual) dimensions of life. Indeed, from a cultural perspective, "spirituality" references rituals, symbols, and patterns of cognition that we refer to as *intuition*, *prophetic vision*, and *wisdom*. Spirituality also refers, in part, to secular, cultural, and theologically grounded beliefs about the nature of life and the nature of reality (e.g., belief in transcendence and an afterlife, purpose, and in the existence of spirits

DOI: 10.1037/14045-030
APA Handbook of Psychology, Religion, and Spirituality: Vol. 1. Context, Theory, and Research, K. I. Pargament (Editor-in-Chief)
Copyright © 2013 by the American Psychological Association. All rights reserved.

including angels and ancestral spirits); to a complex web of experiences with the transcendent dimensions of life; and to understandings about how those transcendent dimensions manifest in and influence numerous aspects of life, including (but not limited to) fate, health, and healing. Although the cultural aspects of spiritual life are deeply intertwined with religiosity, empirical research on the devotional life of African Americans consistently fails to embrace the broad meanings and manifestations of spirituality and religiosity as cultural phenomena.

The need for critical attention to culture in our studies of African American religiosity and spirituality is all the more evident when we consider that the label African American is a homogenizing term that highlights biological similarities but obscures cultural differences (i.e., differences in national histories, language, beliefs, and practices) between multigenerational Black Americans and first- and second-generation Black immigrants (e.g., from the Caribbean and Africa) living in the United States. Recent work on religiosity and spirituality emerging out of the National Survey of American Life (NSAL) has begun to explore similarities and differences in the religious and spiritual lives of African Americans and Caribbean Americans living in the United States (Chatters et al., 2008; Neighbors et al., 2007). The findings of this body of research indicate that African Americans and Caribbean Americans are similar with respect to their tendency to self-define as both religious and spiritual (as opposed to only religious or only spiritual; Chatters et al., 2008). Research is needed, however, that critically examines differences in the religious histories and identities of African Americans and Afri-Caribbean peoples and that explores how cultural identities inform their beliefs, practices, and life outcomes.

The differences in religiosity and spirituality among multigenerational African Americans and Blacks of Caribbean and African descent (i.e., Blacks who immigrate to the United States from Anglophone, Francophone, Hispanophone, Dutch West Indian/Caribbean, and West African nations) is not well documented because of the tendency of social scientists to conceive of Blacks in the United States as a homogenous group. Scholars in sociology, religious studies, and history have highlighted a number of cultural differences related to religion that are noteworthy. First, R. Stewart (1999) aptly noted that in Caribbean contexts, Christian deities and beliefs often are synthesized with African culture symbols to produce creolized forms of Christian ideology and creolized patterns of worship. Second, although Christianity is dominant in both African American and Caribbean contexts, scholars assert that there are a number of religious and spiritual traditions that have deep roots among Blacks in the Caribbean (e.g., Rastafarianism, Obeah, Vodou) that may be unfamiliar to, or may be stigmatized by, African Americans or may be understood only marginally in U.S. contexts (Chatters et al., 2008; R. Stewart, 1999). Finally, despite the substantial Christian bias in much of the psychology of religion, historians have demonstrated that intercultural contact over the course of the histories of African and Caribbean nations, as well as patterns of immigration, have led to the involvement of Afri-Caribbeans and Africans in Abrahamic as well as non-Abrahamic religions. The substantial pattern of intermarriage and everyday cultural contact between Blacks and South and East Asians in Trinidad and Guyana, for example, means that Black Americans who are of Trinidadian and Guyanese descent may identify as Muslim or Hindu (Khan, 1999). Thus, the lack of attention to non-Christians in psychology research on African American religiosity is noteworthy.

Abdullah (2009) documented the rapid rise in the number of West African Muslims in major U.S. cities, including New York, Atlanta, Boston, Chicago, and Los Angeles, and the ways in which the presence of these Muslim communities have challenged ideas of what it means to be African, Black, and Muslim. Using Harlem as a context for analysis, Abdullah noted that decades of immigration have brought West African Sufi Muslims, including the Murids of Senegal, and West African Sunni Muslims, into the same neighborhoods as African American Sunni Muslims, and the subset of African Americans who are members of the Nation of Islam (NOI). This contact has highlighted crucial inter- and intracultural, ethnic, and sociopolitical differences between these groups (e.g., differences in languages of origin, customs) as well as important differences in their religious ideologies and religious histories. The extent to which beliefs, practices, and identities are retained by Africans and Caribbeans who immigrate to the United States deserves empirical attention. The ways that these beliefs, practices, and identities shape behavior and psychosocial outcomes among Black immigrant youth and adults also deserves attention.

RELIGION, SPIRITUALITY, AND HEALTH AMONG AFRICAN AMERICANS

In this section, we provide an overview of findings related to the role of religion and spirituality in several domains of health: religious and spiritual health, mental health, physical health, relational health, and community health. We conclude by integrating the findings into a conceptual model of religiosity, spirituality, and health in the African American context.

Religious and Spiritual Health

Few studies have explored the meaning of spiritual or religious health among African Americans. The work conducted by Ravenell and colleagues and by Russell and colleagues are notable exceptions. Findings from these studies demonstrate that African American men think of spiritual health (e.g., being "spiritually fit") as a component of overall health (Ravenell, Johnson, & Whitaker, 2006). Similarly, Russell, Swenson, and Skelton (2003) found that African American women conceive of spirituality as important in global health (e.g., they view health as a balance between body, mind, and spirit). Russell found that for these women, "spiritual health" involves having a personal relationship with God, talking to God about health concerns, being blessed with good health, and being wise about health decisions (Russell et al., 2003). The extent to which spiritual health may be synonymous with or distinct from religious and spiritual maturity is a matter for exploration.

Religion, Spirituality, and Psychological and Mental Health

Much of the empirical research in the social sciences focuses on the link between religion, spirituality, and mental health. Within that context, there are four streams of work: The first centers on the ties between religion, spirituality, and identity. The second centers on the associations between religion, spirituality, and self-esteem. The third focuses on the link between religion, spirituality, and coping. The final stream attends to the relationship between religion and internalizing and externalizing behaviors among youth and adults.

The literature indicates that religious identity, gender identity, and gender construction are integrally related among African American adults. One line of work demonstrates that religiosity is critical to gender identity. In particular, Hunter and Davis (1992) found that being religious and spiritual are central in African American men's definitions of masculinity. In a more recent qualitative study, when asked to describe "what it means to be a man," African American men asserted that being a "man" means, in part, "being Godly in word and deed" and "turning to God and faith for guidance in everyday life" (Hammond & Mattis, 2005). That is to say that men believed that being an authentic and mature man meant being a person of principles, being a person who has the willingness and courage to pray and submit to God's will, and being someone who behaves in accordance with the virtues that are identified with faith (e.g., forgiveness, love, compassion). In the same way that religiosity influences gender identity construction, research demonstrates that gender also informs religious identity formation. More specifically, pointing to the powerful role of women in the process of religious socialization, empirical findings demonstrate that maternal religious affiliation among African Americans robustly predicts religious affiliation of adults (Taylor & Chatters, 1991).

Religion and religious institutions influence mental health by shaping other social identities—particularly racial, political, and sexual identity. African American religious institutions (particularly religious institutions that espouse liberationist social justice themes) promote a strong sense of racial identity in their members (Reese & Brown, 1995). African Americans who attend church frequently, and those who score higher on indexes of subjective religiosity, tend to express pride in being members of their racial and religious groups and to believe that others regard their racial and religious groups positively (Brega & Coleman, 1999). Individuals who attend social justice–oriented religious institutions (i.e., churches and mosques that highlight the importance of faith as a tool for liberation and for achieving social transformation) also tend to explain the challenges facing African Americans in terms of sociological and political forces rather than in terms of individual factors such as personality (Calhoun-Brown, 1996). Furthermore, members of these churches are more likely to respond to unjust social arrangements and unjust events by attending political and protest rallies, voting, political fundraising, participating in boycotts, and contacting public officials to insist on change (Calhoun-Brown, 1996).

The relationship between religiosity and political identity and political engagement is a complex one. Indeed, contrary to expectations, findings suggest that African American adults who are otherworldly oriented may tend to endorse radical nationalist political approaches, including institutional separatism and racial and institutional autonomy (Calhoun-Brown, 1996). Calhoun-Brown's (1996) findings may suggest that even among those African Americans who have an otherworldly orientation, the hope that is placed in heaven and in life after death do not obscure the everyday realities of race and class discrimination. Otherworldly African Americans who live with the realities of racism and classism and with the ways in which these "-isms" compromise their safety, well-being, and life conditions, may see value in separatism as a path to survival while on Earth. The tendency of religious African Americans (including otherworldly oriented African Americans) to take a systems-level rather than individual-level focus on explaining social problems, along with the tendency to hold other Blacks in positive regard, may buffer against the deleterious mental and physical health consequences of race-related stress. That is to say, these tendencies may prevent feelings of powerlessness and hopelessness and may buffer against assaults on a personal sense of esteem and efficacy. Importantly, the relationship between religiosity and race appears to be dynamic rather than unidirectional. Indeed, youth who are raised on a diet of positive racial socialization messages (e.g., messages that encourage pride in being Black) tend to place greater value and emphasis on using religious and spiritual strategies to cope with the challenges of life (Stevenson et al., 2002).

Although faith life appears to shape racial identity positively, the link between religiosity, mental health and other social identities (e.g., sexual identity) may be less positive. Miller (2007) aptly noted that historically, churches, including Black churches, have taken a hostile and sometimes punitive stance towards lesbian, gay, bisexual, and transgender (LGBT) individuals (see Chapter 34 in this volume). Certainly, some LGBT African Americans are members of faith communities that are explicitly welcoming and affirming of their identities. Those who remain in religious institutions that are hostile to LGBT identities, however, often are exposed to homophobic messages that can undermine their well-being and self-worth. Homophobia in the church may also negatively affect individuals' efforts to seek emotional, social, or instrumental supports from religious leaders, coreligionists, and religious institutions as a whole. Finally, homophobia may limit individuals' ability to coherently integrate their sexual, racial, and spiritual identities (e.g., individuals may be unable to reconcile their identities as Black, gay, and Christian or Muslim with their understandings of God and of faith life).

As noted, religion's influence in the mental health of African Americans is not limited to issues of identity. Indeed, empirical findings indicate that, a second pathway through which religiosity and spirituality influences mental health is by promoting positive self-esteem for African Americans. Blaine and Crocker (1995) noted that the belief that they are loved by God may be particularly important in promoting the self-esteem of African Americans—especially African Americans who may experience psychic assaults in other areas of life. In addition to personal religious and spiritual beliefs, religious institutions are vital contexts for bolstering the self-esteem and self-efficacy of African Americans. These institutions serve as milieu in which individuals can build and demonstrate competencies, talents, and qualities (e.g., intellectual gifts, musical talents, oratorical skills, leadership skills) that may be invisible or actively denigrated in secular settings. African American religious institutions also routinely and publicly celebrate the personal achievements of members of their congregations (e.g., ministers may announce the names of those who made the honor roll or who are accepted into college). The enthusiastic and authentic public support that youth and adults in these settings receive from religious leaders, congregations, and their peers can bolster pride, create a psychological sense of purpose and connectedness, and buffer against perceived isolation, hopelessness, and despair.

A third line of work in the area of religion and mental health attends to religion's role in coping (i.e., in buffering against negative mental health outcomes for African Americans; see Chapter 19 in this volume). To negotiate stress, African Americans often seek religious (i.e., divine or ministerial) support. Indeed, data indicate that African Americans turn to God and to religious leaders for support with a wide array of stressors (e.g., racial discrimination, chronic and acute financial problems, grief, and illness; see Ali, Milstein, & Marzuk, 2005; Byng, 1998; Mattis et al., 2007; Neighbors, Musick, & Williams, 1998). Although the overwhelming majority of work on religion and coping among African Americans focuses on Christians, Byng (1998) and Wyche (2004) noted that faith and the support of the religious community are central in African American Muslim women's efforts to cope with discrimination. Indeed, the Qur'an provides a context for reifying African American women's faith in their own humanity, for claiming their power to define themselves (as opposed to being defined by others), and for making meaning of unjust events (Byng, 1998).

Although religious support is important in coping with stress, for African Americans the effort to cope with life's challenges may be informed by religion's impact on expectancies. Recent research suggests that religious African Americans (i.e., those who attend church more frequently, and those who view God as a benevolent figure) are more optimistic about the future and are less likely to be pessimistic (Mattis, Fontenot, Hatcher-Kay, Grayman, & Beale, 2004). The extent to which African Americans' expectations about future outcomes influences behaviors (e.g., task perseverance, decision making) remains unstudied.

The protective effects of religion and spirituality are evident across the developmental span. Indeed, for African American adolescents experiencing a high level of stress, religiosity serves as a buffer against depression, anxiety, and social withdrawal (Grant et al., 2000). Religiosity also appears to buffer against suicide by minimizing the extent to which African American youth perceive themselves to be at risk of dying by suicide (Greening & Stoppelbein, 2002). Some African American youth may be less likely to attempt suicide because they hold the attitude that suicide is not a choice that African Americans make (i.e., they believe that suicide is not "a Black thing"). Importantly, styles of religious coping also appear to be relevant to the relationship between religiosity and suicidality among African American youth. Those youth who rely on themselves as well as on God in times of stress (i.e., those who use collaborative strategies of religious coping) report a greater number of reasons for living (Molock, Puri, Matlin, & Barksdale, 2006). In contrast, youth who rely principally on themselves rather than on God to cope in times of stress (i.e., those who used self-directed forms of coping) report greater depression, a greater sense of hopelessness, and a greater number of suicide attempts (Molock et al., 2006). Adults also experience the prophylactic effects of religion. For example, African American men and women who regularly attend religious services report fewer family, work, and financial stresses than do their less religiously involved counterparts (Ellison et al., 2001). Adults who attend formal religious services more frequently and those who report strong religious beliefs also report lower levels of psychological distress, such as depression and anxiety (Blaine & Crocker, 1995; Jang & Johnson, 2004; Neighbors et al., 1998).

Research demonstrates that direct and intercessory prayers are vital and primary coping resources for most African Americans (see Chapter 16 in this volume). Prayer serves as a vehicle through which individuals experience emotional support, information, and moral guidance (El-Khoury et al., 2004; Mattis, 2002; Neighbors et al., 1998). Importantly, although we are accustomed to viewing prayer as a coping strategy employed by adults, data indicate that African American children pray independently and that they pray for comfort and about concerns that are developmentally relevant (e.g., school-related goals such as performance on exams;

see Humphrey, Hughes, & Holmes, 2008; Norton, 2006; see also Volume 2, Chapter 21, this handbook). As is the case with the prayers of adults, the prayers of African American children reveal a strong belief in God as a causal agent who has the ability and the will to intervene in important domains of life (Humphrey et al., 2008; Norton, 2006). To date, there is no body of work that systematically examines the prayer life of African American youth. The few studies on youth prayer life, however do reveal that religious youth and college students (i.e., those who pray and attend services more frequently) perform better academically than less religious youngsters (Jeynes, 2002; Walker & Dixon, 2007).

The fourth and final stream of research on the link between religiosity, spirituality, and mental health examines the impact of religion on internalizing (e.g., depression and anxiety) and externalizing symptoms and behaviors (e.g., drug use). Using data from a national probability sample of African Americans, Ellison and Flannelly (2009) found that adults who use religion to guide their everyday decisions reported significantly lower depression levels than their less religious counterparts. Interestingly, Ellison and Flannelly found no relationship between religious service attendance or church support and depressive symptomatology. Chatters et al. (2008), however, found that for adults over the age of 55, religious service attendance was negatively related to the likelihood of experiencing a mood disorder in one's lifetime. Religious values, formal religious involvement (e.g., service attendance), and the subjective importance of religion in one's life also are associated with a lower likelihood of engaging in such externalizing behaviors as alcohol, cigarette, and marijuana use among African Americans (Brody, Stoneman, & Flor, 1996; Steinman & Zimmerman, 2004).

Ministers and coreligionists may influence psychological health in these domains by fostering trust in, a healthy mistrust of, or skepticism about secular interventions (e.g., professional psychology, psychiatry, medical help). Importantly, given the well-documented history of medical abuse experienced by African Americans from slavery through the recent present (e.g., the Tuskeegee syphilis experiments, forced sterilization of African American women; see Jones, 1981; Roberts, 1997) a healthy mistrust of medical and professional recommendations often serves as a precursor to the questioning and research needed to ensure effective and trustworthy care by mental health and medical (e.g., psychiatric) professionals.

Although religious African Americans are especially likely to turn to religious leaders for support with physical, emotional, relational, and general concerns (Neighbors et al., 1998), recent evidence suggests that greater involvement in the public aspects of faith life (e.g., religious attendance) is associated with a greater willingness to seek mental health care from someone other than a minister (Morse et al., 2000). Adults attribute the decision not to seek emotional or instrumental support from ministers to a number of factors. Some individuals choose to take their concerns to God directly. Others reported that they would not seek ministerial support because of concerns about the minister's character (e.g., indiscreet, uncompassionate ministers) and competence, access to alternative sources of support (e.g., friends, therapists), and shame and guilt (Mattis et al., 2007).

Religion, Spirituality, and Physical Health

Scholars have identified a range of factors that serve as barriers to health care access and health care utilization among African Americans. Some scholars note that disrespectful and sometimes dehumanizing treatment at the hands of medical professionals, incompetent medical treatment, and medical abuse have contributed to an entrenched sense of medical mistrust among many African Americans (Giger, Appel, Davidhizar, & Davis, 2008; Hammond, Matthews, Mohottige, Agyemangm, & Corbie-Smith, 2010). Furthermore, poorly equipped medical care settings, lack of transportation, and lack of medical insurance all have contributed to health care underutilization and to disparities in health care for African Americans (Giger et al., 2008). Against the landscape of disparities in access to quality care, Black religious institutions have emerged as contexts through which health information and health care services are provided (Giger et al., 2008; Lincoln & Mamiya, 1990).

Historically, religious and African American medical professionals have used the pulpit as a space from which to admonish risky behaviors, to encourage positive health practices, and to disseminate health information to congregations. More recently, researchers have begun in earnest to use religious institutions as crucial platforms through which to provide health education and deliver health care interventions to African Americans (e.g., see Dodani & Fields, 2010; Molock, Matlin, Barksdale, Puri, & Lyles, 2008).

Religiosity and spirituality are associated with lower mortality risk (Ellison et al., 2000) and with better management of symptoms (Harrison et al., 2005) among African Americans. Scholars have suggested that these positive health outcomes are the results of religion and spirituality's impact in shaping health practices, coping, and health beliefs. For Muslims, for example, the core tenets of faith have been identified as factors that reinforce the importance of a healthy diet, exercise, moderation, and the avoidance of any substances that might compromise health (Ohm, 2003).

Among African Americans, religiosity and spirituality appear to be inversely associated with risky behaviors. Marks et al. (2005) found that a low level of religious involvement is associated with greater risk-taking and greater use of unhealthy coping strategies, such as alcohol and drug (ab)use. Greater reported religiosity also is associated with abstinence from substance use (C. Stewart, Koeske, & Pringle, 2008) and premature sexual intercourse (Lewis, Mellins, & Brackis-Cott, 2006). The inverse relationship between religion and risky behaviors may be especially pronounced among African American Muslims. Central to Islam is the belief that the body is God's gift to humans. Because the body is viewed as a divine gift, Islam expressly forbids the consumption of alcohol or of any food or substance that is intoxicating or that harms the body (Rajaram & Rashidi, 2003). Furthermore, Muslims engage in ritual fasting to purify the body (Rajaram & Rashidi, 2003). Religiously adherent Muslims are, therefore, less likely than others to engage in such risky behaviors as alcohol or drug (ab)use and more likely to engage in behaviors that promote healthy outcomes.

Marks et al. (2005) noted that religion helps African Americans to cope with health concerns. African Americans pray to God and ask for divine support in managing their diets, managing smoking, and engaging in regular exercise (King et al., 2005). Indeed, for African Americans, prayer provides a mechanism for meaning making and for fostering a feeling of hope, solace, and posttraumatic growth related to significant health problems among African Americans (Marks et al., 2005).

Although coping is an important function of religiosity and spirituality, religiosity also is associated with a complex set of health beliefs and health decisions among African Americans. Empirical research has demonstrated a link between religious beliefs and negative health decision making (e.g., with the failure to seek medical treatment and the failure to adhere to medication protocols). Religious African Americans often report that prayer can heal, that God has the capacity to cure any illness, and that health outcomes reflect God's will (Holt, Schulz, & Wynn, 2006). These beliefs can inspire a tendency to turn health outcomes over to God and a tendency to adopt a passive and fatalistic stance with regard to health. An emerging body of research suggests that religion's influence on the health beliefs and health practices of African Americans is quite complex. Wittig (2001) found, for example, that although religiosity was associated with African Americans' reluctance to donate organs to strangers (i.e., people often insisted that God is in charge of health and therefore donations were not necessary), religious sensibilities were associated with a willingness to donate organs to family members (i.e., respondents believed that donating to a family member was an index of authentic faith). Similarly, Holt et al. (2006) found that although Africans Americans may believe that God is in control of their health outcomes, they do acknowledge that misinterpretations of the Bible and extreme religious beliefs can lead people to make poor or inaccurate health decisions. King et al. (2005) advanced the view of a "combined agency" approach in their effort to explain the way that religion shapes the health decision making and health behavior of African Americans. King et al. suggested that although African Americans regard God as in ultimate control with regard to health outcomes, they still exercise agency over their health by seeking medical care and by electing to behave in ways that promote health (e.g., managing their diet, exercising).

Religious involvement gives people access to supportive social networks that may promote positive health outcomes by ameliorating the negative effects of stress. Mattis et al. (2007) noted that African American believers often include ministers in their support networks and turn to ministers for help and solace in the face of health problems (see also Neighbors et al., 1998). Importantly, other researchers have noted that religion may work in tandem with network support to influence the amount of time that individuals take before seeking medical care. Indeed, Gullatte et al. (2010) found that religious African American women who disclosed their physical health symptoms to friends and female family members were more likely to seek medical care than nondisclosers. In contrast, women who did not share their symptoms with loved ones and who turned only to God were more likely to postpone seeking medical care. These findings suggest that the relationship between religion and health may be informed by personality factors (e.g., tendency toward self-disclosure), by social network factors, and perhaps by the real or perceived severity of health concerns.

Religion, Spirituality, and Relational Health

In addition to their roles in mental health, religiosity and spirituality may play crucial roles in shaping the relational health and well-being of African Americans. Sacred texts, notably the Bible and Qur'an, provide clear expectations regarding the respect due to parents, elders in communities, siblings, and those who are viewed as vulnerable (e.g., children, the poor, the ill). Religions may highlight the importance of a host of moral emotions (e.g., compassion, shame, guilt) that can lead individuals to forgive others, care for others, and fulfill obligations to those around them.

Religious institutions may serve as important contexts for supporting relational health. African American youth and adults who are involved in organized faith life may be enveloped in an enduring and supportive web of relationships that include religious leaders (e.g., ministers, youth ministers) and fellow worshippers who hold common beliefs and values and who comprise a family (e.g., church brothers and sisters; Townsend Gilkes, 2001). Religious institutions may also affect the relational health of believers by sponsoring family outreach programs, including family and couples counseling initiatives and activities (e.g., couples retreats) that provide opportunities for couples and families to understand and enact their relationship and their family life as extensions of their faith experience (Caldwell et al., 1995; Jang & Johnson, 2004). Finally, religious beliefs and devotional practices such as prayer appear to play positive roles in relational life by shaping the efforts of grandparents, parents, and male caregivers to cope with the social, emotional, and financial responsibilities associated with family life and with the demands of care giving (Brodsky, 2000; Gibson, 2002).

Research on relational quality points to a possible impact of organized religion, prayer, and subjective religiosity on relationships. Indeed, religiously involved adults report fewer family problems than those with less active religious involvement (Ellison et al., 2001). More specifically, among African American fathers, greater religiosity is associated with reports of more supportive relationships with spouses and less conflict in roles as cocaregivers (Brody et al., 1994). African American families that score higher on indexes of religiosity also tend to extend greater levels of emotional and social support to husbands and fathers who are unemployed or underemployed; this heightened support appears to be crucial to men's efforts to cope with the challenges of fulfilling their roles as providers (Bowman, 1990). Support, whether perceived or received, may help couples and families to cope effectively with life's challenges generally, and with the challenges of marriage specifically (Chadiha, Veroff, & Leber, 1998). Furthermore, Jang and Johnson (2004) have found that not only do religious African Americans report receiving more levels of social support from friends and family relative to their less religious counterparts but also that this reported support mediates the relationship between religiosity and psychological distress.

Religion's influence on family life seems to resonate through the spousal relationship to affect the level of warmth, harmony, and the quality of communication and discipline in the relationship between African American parents and their children (Simons, Simons, & Conger, 2004). Mothers who are more religious report more consistent parenting and less conflictual relationships with their children (Brody et al., 1994). There also is evidence that religion's effects filter downward from parents to siblings. African American parents who are more religious have children who tend to report more positive sibling relationships (McHale, Whiteman, Kim, & Crouter, 2007).

Religion's impact on family life is not necessarily or uniformly positive. Religious involvement and religious identification may affect the ways in which believers, religious leaders, and religious institutions understand and respond to interpersonal (e.g., partner) violence as well as their tendencies to commit such acts of violence (Watlington & Murphy, 2006). In some religious communities, theology is used to justify patriarchal domination and control of women. Skewed and uncritical discourses about the need for female submission and about men's rights to exercise power over women and children may be used to rationalize the use of violence to control women. Such readings, when combined with religious mandates against divorce, may encourage victims of interpersonal violence to remain in relationships that leave them (and sometimes their children) vulnerable to emotional control, physical injury, or death (see Volume 2, Chapters 17 and 20, this handbook). Although research on interpersonal violence among African American Muslims is sparse, Kiely-Froude and Abdul-Karim (2009) suggested that mandates against divorce, fears of exposing spouses and children to shame and unwanted public scrutiny, and fears of losing the support of their faith community may leave African American Muslim women especially vulnerable to spousal violence.

On the positive side, religiosity and spirituality can inform African American women's efforts at meaning making and coping when they become victims of violence, and they also may help women to extricate themselves from violent situations (Watlington & Murphy, 2006) or from those involving other forms of abuse, such as incest (Robinson, 2000).

For some women, empowerment may result from a general belief that a forgiving and loving God would not require them to submit to or endure the violence of others. For other women, empowerment may be rooted in specific readings of the Bible and Qur'an. For example, the following passage of New Testament text from the Christian Bible often has been used (acontextually) as evidence of men's right to insist on the submission of their wives:

> [22]Wives, submit to your own husbands, as to the Lord. [23]For the husband is the head of the wife even as Christ is the head of the church, his body, and is himself its Savior. [24]Now as the church submits to Christ, so also wives should submit in everything to their husbands. (Ephesians 5, v. 22–24, New American Standard Bible)

Women, however, may find the subsequent verses of the same chapter of Ephesians to be empowering:

> [25]Husbands, love your wives, as Christ loved the church and gave himself up for her, [26]that he might sanctify her, having cleansed her by the washing of water with the word, [27]so that he might present the church to himself in splendor, without spot or wrinkle or any such thing, that she might be holy and without blemish. [28]In the same way husbands should love their wives as their own bodies. He who loves his wife loves himself. [29]For no one ever hated his own flesh, but nourishes and cherishes it, just as Christ does the church, [30]because we are members of his body. [31]Therefore a man shall leave his father and mother and hold fast to his wife, and the two shall become one flesh. [32]This mystery is profound, and I am saying that it refers to Christ and the church. [33]However, let each one of you love his wife as himself, and let the wife see that she respects her husband. (Ephesians 5, v. 25–33, New American Standard Bible)

In sum, many Christian women may take solace in the fact that the Bible does not equate a wife's "submission" with a husband's violence and that the Bible explicitly identifies hurting one's wife as sinful. The extent to which, and the ways in which, African American women reread the Bible and Qur'an in the service of empowering themselves against, and to cope with the consequences of, spousal violence deserves empirical attention.

Religion's impact on relational life extends beyond the family to peer and more distal (i.e., community) relationships. For African American boys, for example, religiosity and spirituality are associated with feeling more valued by and more popular with others (Spencer et al., 2003). Research on the link between religiosity, spirituality, and friendship suggests that spirituality also positively affects the friendships of men. Indeed, African American men who are more subjectively spiritual report a greater level of emotional sharing with their male friends and a tendency to experience their friendships with other men as more supportive (Mattis et al., 2001). Mattis et al. (2001) speculated that African American men who view themselves as more spiritual may be more willing to make themselves emotionally vulnerable in their friendships with other men—a fact that may lead to a deepened level of support in these friendships. These findings suggest that spirituality, with its explicit focus on interconnectedness, intimacy, and the sacredness of life (Mattis, 2000; Zinnbauer et al., 1997), may push men to challenge traditional scripts of restrictive masculinity that prohibit emotional expressiveness. The extent to which religion and spirituality inform women's same-sex or cross-sex (i.e., male–female) friendships among African Americans is not clear.

With respect to relationships, religiosity also appears to influence beliefs about such relationally relevant topics as sexual abstinence and abortion, attitudes toward contraceptives, and the timing of sexual intimacy (see Brewster et al., 1998). African Americans who hail from families that pray frequently are less likely to be sexually active than youth from less religious families (Lewis et al., 2006). African American youth who are personally religious are also less likely to be sexually active than their less religious counterparts (Ball et al., 2003; Childs, Moneyham, & Felton, 2008). Importantly, the lower level of sexual activity among religious youth may owe, in part, to the fact that these youth are less likely to spend time in situations that increase the risk of sexual acting out (e.g., they spend less unsupervised time in private settings with the opposite sex; see Lewis, Mellins, & Brackis-Cott, 2006). When they do engage in sexual activity, religious youth may be particularly able to exercise sexual agency. In fact, religious African American adolescent girls report greater self-efficacy than their less religious counterparts in rejecting unsafe sexual activities and in discussing sex, sexual health, and sexual safety (e.g., preventing sexually transmitted disease, using condoms) with their partners (McCree, Wingood, DiClemente, Davies, & Harrington, 2003).

Finally, the literature on the link between faith and relationship outcomes indicates that religiosity and spirituality are associated with efforts to negotiate relationship violations. Religiosity and spirituality are associated, for example, with African American men's efforts to forgive race-related transgressions (Powell Hammond, Hudson-Banks, & Mattis, 2006). More specifically, African American men who are subjectively religious, and those who rely more heavily on religious coping (i.e., the search for spiritual guidance, meaning and support in times of crisis) are significantly more likely to embrace positive affect, cognitions, and behaviors toward transgressors ("positive forgiveness") and to relinquish negative affect, cognitions, and behaviors toward perpetrators of aggression ("negative forgiveness"). This greater capacity to forgive has implications for the ability of religious or spiritual men and women to reconcile after a transgression and to sustain relationships with others over time.

Religion, Spirituality, and Community and Political Health

In addition to their roles at the individual level, religion and spirituality are central in mitigating negative outcomes and promoting positive outcomes at the group level. Relative to those who are less religious, urban-residing African American and Afri-Caribbean adolescents who are religiously involved are less likely to engage in risky or antisocial activities that compromise the quality of community life (Cook, 2000; Wallace & Forman, 1998). Pearce et al. (2003) have demonstrated that African American youth who engage in private religious activities (e.g., prayer, listening to religious music) and those who are more subjectively religious tend to report fewer conduct problems (e.g., lower number of incidents of lying, destroying property, fighting) than their less involved peers. Youth who attend religious services also are significantly less likely to commit non-drug-related crimes and are less likely to engage in drug dealing than children who do not attend religious services (Johnson, Larson, Li, & Jang, 2000). In fact, religiously involved youth tend to withdraw from social interactions with individuals who are engaged in antisocial behaviors (Jagers, 1997).

Religiosity and spirituality are negatively associated with antisocial acting out. Religiosity and spirituality, however, are also associated with prosocial action (Jagers, Smith, Mock, & Dill, 1997). Religious and spiritual youth and adults (particularly those who are involved in organized faith life) are more likely to volunteer, to be involved in civic life, and to spend more hours involved in volunteer activities (Mattis et al., 2000; Musick, Wilson, & Bynum, 2000). Church involvement is also strongly linked to formal prosocial involvement among men. Religiously involved African American men (e.g., those who attend church more frequently) are significantly more likely than their less involved counterparts to engage in volunteer work, and they spend more time volunteering (Mattis et al., 2000; Mattis, Beckham, et al., 2004). Furthermore, men who report that religion is important to their identity (i.e., those who are subjectively religious) are more likely to belong to a political or social justice organization (Mattis, Beckham, et al., 2004).

Historically, despite the visible presence of men in positions of leadership in Black churches, church-based outreach ministries in African American communities have been catalyzed and sustained largely through the work of women (Townsend Gilkes, 2001). Through their involvement in church ministries, African American women have served several vital roles: They have launched protest activities and been actively engaged in political education and political organizing; they have provided spiritual as well as secular educational opportunities for youth and adults; and they have created opportunities for economic relief, assisted in providing housing, and led efforts in health education and in providing medical care and psychological counseling to those who are most in need.

The institutional context in which African Americans worship powerfully shapes their political identities and the specific ways that they enact commitment to social justice and social change. Although limited in scope, the extant work on the lives of African American Muslims demonstrates that whereas Orthodox African American Muslims (i.e., Sunnis) of immigrant origins are more likely to hold broadly humanistic political stances, those native-born African American Sunnis who worship as a part of the NOI are more likely to endorse specifically pro-Black, social justice–oriented political views (Lumumba, 2003). As is the case with members of the NOI, African Americans Christians who attend "political Black churches" (i.e., churches that view theology and faith as inextricably linked to social justice, liberation, and political activism) are more likely to engage in conventional forms of activism, including voting and seeking public office (Calhoun-Brown, 1996). Individuals who attend church frequently and those who attend politicized churches, however, are not more likely to attend political or protest rallies, and are actually less likely than those who do not attend church to sign a petition and picket and boycott (Swain, 2010). Swain has suggested that these findings point to the increasing depoliticization of the Black church. It is equally feasible, however, that these findings simply reflect the complex relationship between the various domains of religiosity and spirituality and the various forms of activism and civic engagement.

Social scientists have paid significant attention to religion's role in formal acts of prosocial engagement (e.g., volunteerism; see Mattis et al., 2000; Mattis, Beckham, et al., 2004). Far less attention has been paid to religion and spirituality's role in motivating informal acts of selfless (i.e., altruistic) giving (see Chapter 24 in this volume). Mattis et al. (2009) found that in spite of the dire social and economic contexts in which they live, low-income, inner-city-residing African American adults reported being motivated by religion and spirituality to behave altruistically. Participants in this study indicated that they behave altruistically because doing so is (a) a way of honoring God's command to be good to each other; (b) a way of seeing and respecting both the divinity in others and their belief in the fundamental interconnectedness of all life; and (c) a manifestation of individuals' awareness of, and gratitude for, God's grace.

Pathways

The mechanisms by which religiosity and spirituality inform the various domains of health are myriad. A review of the literature, however, suggests that the core pathways of influence include emotions, cognitions, and behaviors. Youth and adults who, as a consequence of their religious or spiritual leanings, are able to better manage their emotions may be more likely to develop and maintain supportive relationships (e.g., friendships, healthy family relationships) and may reduce their risk of being exposed to depressogenic stressors (e.g., social stigma and retaliation). For these youth and adults, religion and spirituality may provide subjectively and culturally meaningful and authoritative moral codes from which to draw as they make life choices and as they negotiate the challenges of everyday life. This moral code may be especially meaningful for individuals who are embedded in high-risk environments.

Theologians argue that for African Americans, love, humility, compassion, empathy, and forgiveness even in the face of overwhelming suffering come from the tradition of linking their plight to the plight of prominent figures from sacred texts including the Bible (Cone, 1997). Sacred texts and other religious materials (e.g., music, art, literature) provide believers with portrayals of life's most overwhelming dramas and dilemmas (e.g., grief, catastrophic loss, relational conflict, infidelity, illness) and give guidance about how to make meaning of, respond to, and transcend life's most extraordinary difficulties (see Chapter 10 in this volume). The guidance that sacred texts (and religious leaders) provide regarding how to address life's joys and challenges exists alongside the subjective meanings that individuals ascribe to events.

Religion and spirituality inform various domains of health by establishing an authoritative set of beliefs, norms, attitudes, and values (Wills et al., 2003) to which individuals will adhere. Individuals who internalize the norms, attitudes, and values of their faith community are likely to behave in ways that are consistent with these norms, attitudes, and values (Lumumba, 2003; Ohm, 2003). Those who violate the moral codes and norms established by religion are likely to suffer distress-inducing public and private emotional consequences, including guilt and shame (Hardy & Raffaelli, 2003). The extent to which particular emotions, norms, and practices are implicated in the various domains of health deserves greater attention.

IMPLICATIONS

Directions for Future Research

Taken together, the current literature demonstrates that the effort to examine the role of religion and spirituality in African American life and health is a complex enterprise. Figure 30.1 presents a model that we hope will guide future empirical research on the role of religiosity and spirituality in African American health. Several key elements of this model are highlighted in the following paragraphs.

First, the model highlights the notion that at the heart of any discussion about the role of religion and spirituality in African American health must be a focus on the question of who is African American. In that regard, we must attend to the ways in which the religiosity–spirituality–health link is informed by such factors as the ethnic and cultural origins, immigrant status, gender, sexual identity, educational level, socioeconomic status, area of residence (e.g., region, neighborhood), and degree of enculturation and acculturation.

Second, we must seek to delineate the domains of religious and spiritual life in which we are interested. Here, the model compels us to understand the ways in which African American people's intersecting identities complicate myriad aspects of religiosity and spirituality, including religious affiliation, readings and interpretations of sacred texts, access to religious institutions, public and private devotional practices, subjective beliefs about the sacred and about faith, and subjective religious or spiritual identity. People's social identities (e.g., gender, education, urbanicity) both inform the kinds of risk

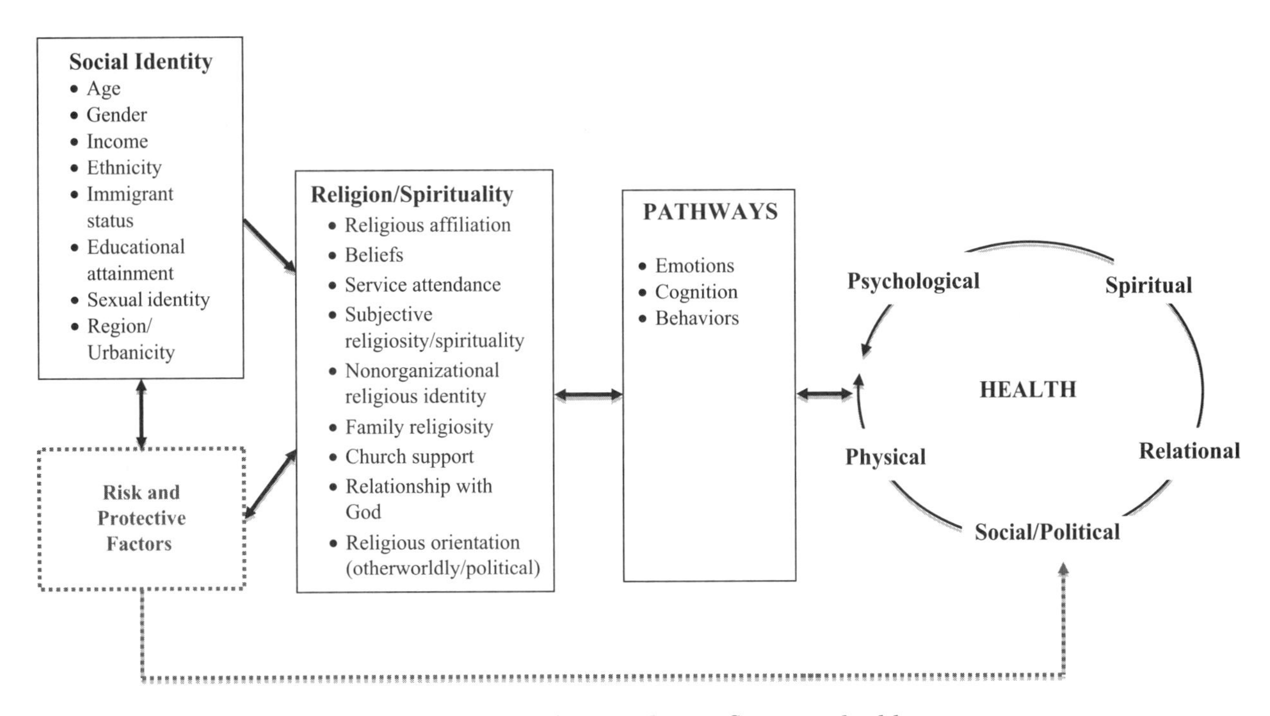

FIGURE 30.1. Conceptual model of religion and spirituality's influence on health.

factors to which they are exposed and the kinds of protective factors that are available to them.

With respect to risks and protections, there is a need for empirical attention to individual-level risks and protections (e.g., temperament) as well as to risks and protections within the broader ecologies in which people live. Importantly, the tendency in social science literatures is to examine religiosity and spirituality as protective factors that buffer against the potentially deleterious impact of *either* individual-level *or* broader ecological-level stressors on health. However, people routinely negotiate both individual-level and ecological-level stresses (e.g., genetic vulnerability to illness and exposure to crime or toxins). Furthermore, the effort to negotiate both levels of stress is affected by individual-level as well as broader ecological-level protections (e.g., temperament and access to health care). The field is in dire need of studies that take a nuanced view of the ways in which religiosity and spirituality work together with individual-level and broader contextual-level stressors and protections to inform health outcomes. Studies of this kind will provide us with a more complex (and perhaps more ecologically valid) view of the way that religion and spirituality operate in the lives of individuals.

Third, this model suggests the need for attention to the mechanisms through which religion and spirituality operate. In the face of particular background as well as risks and protective factors, religious beliefs influence health by shaping emotions (e.g., the emergence of love, guilt), cognitions (e.g., values), and behavior (e.g., decision making, risk-taking). Here again, it will be useful to explore how emotions, cognitions, and behavior operate together with ecological risks and protections to inform health outcomes for people who define themselves as religious or spiritual. More specifically, it might be useful to explore the ways in which religiosity, spirituality, fear of being incapacitated by illness (emotion), and optimism about health outcome (cognition) shape health outcomes for people who have limited access to health insurance and live in high-stress contexts.

Fourth, the model recognizes the interdependence of all domains of health (e.g., physical health is inextricably tied to psychological health and both are tied to relational health). Furthermore, consistent with the integrative paradigm of this handbook (see Chapter 1 in this volume), the model recognizes that the religion-spirituality-health relationship is dynamic, multidirectional, multilevel, and multivalent. In sum, religiosity and spirituality influence emotions, beliefs, and behaviors, which, in turn, inform health outcomes. Health reciprocally, however, influences our thoughts, emotions, actions, and the quality and direction of our religious and spiritual lives. The recognition of the dynamic relationship between these factors highlights the need for longitudinal quantitative as well as qualitative data on the religiosity-spirituality-health link for African Americans. Importantly, although this model points us toward a nuanced approach to the study of the religiosity–spirituality–health link among African Americans, extant research is varied in the extent to which it explores the various components of this complex set of relationships.

Clinical Implications

Religion and spirituality are topics that are rarely explored in depth in mental health training programs—even in programs that attend to multicultural competence. As such, practitioners often struggle to determine how (if at all) to address issues of faith in their work with clients. Clinicians working with African American clients must be aware of the heterogeneity in the ethnic, cultural, religious, and spiritual identities of African American people. Tools such as spiritual eco-maps (Hodge, 2000) can be quite useful in capturing the social ecology of clients' spiritual life (i.e., the role of family, friends, institutions, rituals in faith life). Furthermore, spiritual life maps (Hodge, 2005) can point to hallmark experiences in the spiritual life and development of individuals. These tools can help mental health practitioners to identify core themes in African American clients' spiritual journeys (e.g., themes of loss, guilt, and growth) and can serve as means to elucidate how those themes have emerged in relation to the full spectrum of health outcomes (e.g., mental health, physical health challenges, relational health). Mental health practitioners who are able to elicit African American clients' spiritual life histories, and to explore the beliefs, values, emotions, and behaviors associated with high and low points in their clients' lives may be well situated to support effective change work with their clients.

References

Abdullah, Z. (2009). African "Soul Brothers" in the 'Hood: Immigration, Islam, and the Black encounter. *Anthropological Quarterly, 82*, 37–62. doi:10.1353/anq.0.0054

Ali, O. M., Milstein, G., & Marzuk, P. (2005). The Imam's role in meeting the counseling needs of Muslim communities in the United States. *Psychiatric Services, 56*, 202–205. doi:10.1176/appi.ps.56.2.202

Ball, J., Armistead, L., & Austin, B. (2003). The relationship between religiosity and adjustment among African American, female, urban adolescents. *Journal of Adolescence, 26*, 431–446. doi:10.1016/S0140-1971(03)00037-X

Blaine, B., & Crocker, J. (1995). Religiousness, race, and psychological well-being: Exploring social psychological mediators. *Personality and Social Psychology Bulletin, 21*, 1031–1041. doi:10.1177/01461672952110004

Bowman, P. (1990). Coping with provider role strain: Adaptive cultural resources among Black husband-fathers. *Journal of Black Psychology, 16*, 1–21. doi:10.1177/00957984900162002

Brega, A. G., & Coleman, L. (1999). Effects of religiosity and racial socialization on subjective stigmatization in African American adolescents. *Journal of Adolescence, 22*, 223–242. doi:10.1006/jado.1999.0213

Brewster, K., Cooksey, E., Guilkey, D., & Rindfuss, R. (1998). The changing impact of religion on the sexual and contraceptive behavior of adolescent women in the United States. *Journal of Marriage and the Family, 60*, 493–504. doi:10.2307/353864

Brodsky, A. (2000). The role of religion in the lives of resilient, urban, African American single mothers. *Journal of Community Psychology, 28*, 199–219. doi:10.1002/(sici)1520-6629(200003)28:2<199::aid-jcop7>3.0.co;2-3

Brody, G., Stoneman, Z., & Flor, D. (1996). Parental religiosity, family processes, and youth competence in rural, two-parent African American families. *Developmental Psychology, 32*, 696–706. doi:10.1037/0012-1649.32.4.696

Brody, G., Stoneman, Z., Flor, D., & McCrary, C. (1994). Religion's role in organizing family relationships: Family process in rural, two-parent African American families. *Journal of Marriage and the Family, 56*, 878–888. doi:10.2307/353600

Byng, M. D. (1998). Mediating discrimination: Resisting oppression among African-American Muslim women. *Social Problems, 45*, 473–487. doi:10.1525/sp.1998.45.4.03x0176t

Caldwell, C., Chatters, L., Billingsley, A., & Taylor, R. (1995). Church-based support programs for elderly Black adults: Congregational and clergy characteristics. In M. Kimble, S. McFadden, J. Ellor, & J. Seeber (Eds.), *Aging, spirituality and religion* (pp. 306–324). Minneapolis, MN: Fortress Press.

Calhoun-Brown, A. (1996). African American churches and political mobilization: The psychological impact of organizational resources. *Journal of Politics, 58*, 935–953. doi:10.2307/2960144

Chadiha, L., Veroff, J., & Leber, D. (1998). Newlywed's narrative themes: Meaning in the first year of marriage for African American and White couples. *Journal of Comparative Family Studies, 29*, 115–130.

Chatters, L. M., Bullard, K., Taylor, R., Woodward, A., Neighbors, H., & Jackson, J. (2008). Religious participation and DSM-IV disorders among older African Americans: Findings from the National Survey of American Life. *American Journal of Geriatric Psychiatry, 16*, 957–965. doi:10.1097/JGP.0b013e3181898081

Childs, G., Moneyham, L., & Felton, G. (2008). Correlates of sexual abstinence and sexual activity of low-income African American adolescent females. *Journal of the Association of Nurses in AIDS Care, 19*, 432–442. doi:10.1016/j.jana.2008.04.013

Cone, J. (1997). *God of the oppressed.* New York, NY: Orbis Press.

Cook, K. V. (2000). "You have to have somebody watching your back, and if that's God, then that's mighty big": The church's role in the resilience of inner-city youth. *Adolescence, 35*, 717–730.

Dodani, S., & Fields, J. (2010). Implementation of the Fit Body and Soul, church-based lifestyle program for diabetes prevention in high-risk African Americans: A feasibility study. *The Diabetes Educator, 36*, 465–472. doi:10.1177/0145721710366756

El-Khoury, M. Y., Dutton, M., Goodman, L., Engel, L., Belamaric, R., & Murphy, M. (2004). Ethnic differences in battered women's formal help-seeking strategies: A focus on health, mental health, and spirituality. *Cultural Diversity and Ethnic Minority Psychology, 10*, 383–393. doi:10.1037/1099-9809.10.4.383

Ellison, C., Boardman, J., Williams, D., & Jackson, J. (2001). Religious involvement, stress, and mental health: Findings from the 1995 Detroit Area Study. *Social Forces, 80*, 215–249. doi:10.1353/sof.2001.0063

Ellison, C., & Flannelly, K. (2009). Religious involvement and risk of major depression in a prospective nationwide study of African American adults. *Journal of Nervous and Mental Disease, 197*, 568–573. doi:10.1097/NMD.0b013e3181b08f45

Ellison, C., Hummer, R., Cormier, S., & Rogers, R. (2000). Religious involvement and mortality risk among African American adults. *Research on Aging, 22*, 630–667. doi:10.1177/0164027500226003

Gibson, P. (2002). African American grandmothers as caregivers: Answering the call to help their grandchildren. *Families in Society, 83*, 35–43. doi:10.1111/j.1752-0606.2002.tb01191.x

Giger, J. N., Appel, S., Davidhizar, R., & Davis, C. (2008). Church and spirituality in the lives of the African American community. *Journal of Transcultural Nursing, 19*, 375–383. doi:10.1177/1043659608322502

Grant, K., O'Koon, J., Davis, T., Roache, N., Poindexter, L., Armstrong, M., . . . McIntosh, J. (2000). Protective factors affecting low-income urban African American youth exposed to stress. *Journal of Early Adolescence, 20*, 388–417. doi:10.1177/0272431600020004002

Greening, L., & Stoppelbein, L. (2002). Religiosity, attributional style, and social support as psychosocial buffers for African American and White adolescents' perceived risk for suicide. *Suicide and Life-Threatening Behavior, 32*, 404–417. doi:10.1521/suli.32.4.404.22333

Gullatte, M. M., Brawley, O., Kinney, A., Powe, B., & Mooney, K. (2010). Religiosity, spirituality, and cancer fatalism beliefs on delay in breast cancer diagnosis in African American women. *Journal of Religion and Health, 49*, 62–72. doi:10.1007/s10943-008-9232-8

Hammond, W. P., Hudson-Banks, K., & Mattis, J. (2006). Masculinity ideology and forgiveness of racial discrimination among African American men: Direct and interactive relationships. *Sex Roles, 55*, 679–692. doi:10.1007/s11199-006-9123-y

Hammond, W. P., Matthews, D., Mohottige, D., Agyemangm, A., & Corbie-Smith, G. (2010). Masculinity, medical mistrust, and preventive health services delays among community-dwelling African-American men. *Journal of General Internal Medicine, 25*, 1300–1308. doi:10.1007/s11606-010-1481-z

Hammond, W. P., & Mattis, J. S. (2005). Being a man about it: Constructions of masculinity among African American men. *Psychology of Men and Masculinity, 6*, 114–126. doi:10.1037/1524-9220.6.2.114

Hardy, S. A., & Raffaelli, M. (2003). Adolescent religiosity and sexuality: An investigation of reciprocal influences. *Journal of Adolescence, 26*, 731–739. doi:10.1016/j.adolescence.2003.09.003

Harrison, M. O., Edwards, C., Koenig, H., Bosworth, H., Decastro, L., & Wood, M. (2005). Religiosity/spirituality and pain in patients with sickle cell disease. *Journal of Nervous and Mental Disease, 193*, 250–257. doi:10.1097/01.nmd.0000158375.73779.50

Hodge, D. R. (2000). Spiritual eco-maps: A new diagrammatic tool for assessing marital and family spirituality. *Journal of Marital and Family Therapy, 26*, 217–228. doi:10.1111/j.1752-0606.2000.tb00291.x

Hodge, D. R. (2005). Spiritual lifemaps: A client-centered pictorial instrument for spiritual assessment, planning, and intervention. *Social Work, 50*, 77–87. doi:10.1093/sw/50.1.77

Holt, C. L., Schulz, E., & Wynn, T. (2006). Perceptions of the religion-health Connection Among African Americans in the Southeastern United States: Sex, Age, and Urban/Rural Differences. *Health Education and Behavior, 36*, 62–80. doi:10.1177/1090198107303314

Humphrey, N., Hughes, H., & Holmes, D. (2008). Understanding of prayer among African American children: Preliminary themes. *Journal of Black Psychology, 34*, 309–330. doi:10.1177/00957984 08319885

Hunter, A. G., & Davis, J. E. (1992). Constructing Gender: An exploration of African American men's conceptualization of manhood. *Gender and Society, 6*, 464–479. doi:10.1177/089124392006003007

Jagers, R. (1997). Afrocultural integrity and the social development of African American children: Some conceptual, empirical and practical considerations. *Journal of Prevention and Intervention in the Community, 16*, 7–34. doi:10.1300/J005v16n01_02

Jagers, R., Smith, P., Mock, L., & Dill, E. (1997). An Afrocultural social ethos: Component orientations and some social implications. *Journal of Black Psychology, 23*, 328–343. doi:10.1177/00957984970234002

Jang, S., & Johnson, B. (2004). Explaining religious effects on distress among African Americans. *Journal for the Scientific Study of Religion, 43*, 239–260. doi:10.1111/j.1468-5906.2004.00230.x

Jeynes, W. H. (2002). Attending a religious school on the academic achievement of children. *Educational Policy, 16*, 406–424. doi:10.1177/0890480201 6003003

Johnson, B., Larson, D., Li, S., & Jang, S. (2000). Escaping from the crime of inner cities: Church attendance and religious salience among disadvantaged youth. *Justice Quarterly, 17*, 377–391. doi:10.1080/07418820000096371

Jones, J. (1981). *Bad blood: The Tuskegee syphilis experiment.* New York, NY: Free Press.

Khan, A. (1999). On the "right path": Interpolating religion in Trinidad. In J. Pulis (Ed.), *Religion, diaspora, and cultural identity: A reader in the Anglophone Caribbean* (pp. 247–275). Amsterdam, The Netherlands: Gordon & Breach.

Kiely-Froude, C., & Abdul-Karim, S. (2009). Providing culturally conscious mental health treatment for African American Muslim women living with spousal abuse. *Journal of Muslim Mental Health, 4*, 175–186. doi:10.1080/15564900903245824

King, S., Burgess, E., Akinyela, M., Counts-Spriggs, M., & Parker, N. (2005). "Your body is God's temple": The spiritualization of health beliefs in multigenerational African American families. *Research on Aging, 27*, 420–446. doi:10.1177/0164027505276315

Lewis, L., Mellins, C., & Brackis-Cott, E. (2006). Developmental, ethnic, and social influences on participation in sexual possibility situations for youth with HIV-positive and HIV-negative mothers. *Journal of Early Adolescence, 26*, 160–185. doi:10.1177/0272431605285716

Lincoln, C., & Mamiya, L. (1990). *The Black church in the African-American experience.* Durham, NC: Duke University Press.

Lumumba, H. (2003). The impact of Al-Islam on the African American population. *Counseling and Values, 47*, 210–219. doi:10.1002/j.2161-007X.2003.tb00267.x

Marks, L., Nesteruk, O., Swanson, M., Garrison, B., & Davis, T. (2005). Religion and health among African Americans: A qualitative examination. *Research on Aging, 27*, 447–474. doi:10.1177/0164027505276252

Mattis, J. S. (2000). African American women's definitions of spirituality: A qualitative analysis. *Journal of Black Psychology, 26*, 101–122. doi:10.1177/009579 8400026001006

Mattis, J. S. (2002). The role of religion and spirituality in the coping experience of African American women: A qualitative analysis. *Psychology of Women Quarterly, 26*, 309–321. doi:10.1111/1471-6402.t01-2-00070

Mattis, J. S., Beckham, W., Saunders, B., Williams, J., McAllister, D., Myers, V., . . . Dixon, C. (2004). Who will volunteer? Religiosity, everyday racism and social participation among African American men. *Journal of Adult Development, 11*, 261–272. doi:10.1023/B:JADE.0000044529.92580.6d

Mattis, J. S., Fontenot, D., Hatcher-Kay, C., Grayman, N., & Beale, R. (2004). Religiosity, optimism and pessimism among African Americans. *Journal of Black Psychology, 30*, 187–207. doi:10.1177/0095798403260730

Mattis, J. S., Hammond, W. P., Grayman, N., Bonacci, M., Brennan, W., Cowie, S.-A., . . . So, S. (2009). The social production of altruism: Motivations for caring action in a low-income urban community. *American Journal of Community Psychology, 43*, 71–84.

Mattis, J. S., Jagers, R., Hatcher, C., Lawhon, G., Murphy, E., & Murray, Y. (2000). Religiosity, communalism and volunteerism among African American men: An exploratory analysis. *Journal of Community Psychology, 28*, 391–406. doi:10.1002/1520-6629(200007)28:4<391::AID-JCOP2>3.0.CO;2-A

Mattis, J. S., Mitchell, N., Zapata, A., Grayman, N., Taylor, R., Chatters, L., & Neighbors, H. (2007). Uses of ministerial support by African Americans: A focus group study. *American Journal of Orthopsychiatry, 77*, 249–258. doi:10.1037/0002-9432.77.2.249

Mattis, J. S., Murray, Y., Hatcher, C., Hearn, K., Lawhon, G., Murphy, E., & Washington, T. (2001). Religiosity and the subjective quality of African American men's friendships: An exploratory study. *Journal of Adult Development, 8*, 221–230. doi:10.1023/A:1011338511989

McCree, D. H., Wingood, G., DiClemente, R., Davies, S., & Harrington, K. (2003). Religiosity and risky sexual behavior in African American adolescent females. *Journal of Adolescent Health, 33*, 2–8. doi:10.1016/S1054-139X(02)00460-3

McHale, S. M., Whiteman, S., Kim, J., & Crouter, A. (2007). Characteristics and correlates of sibling relationships in two-parent African American families. *Journal of Family Psychology, 21*, 227–235. doi:10.1037/0893-3200.21.2.227

Miller, R. L. (2007). Legacy denied: African American gay men, AIDS, and the Black church. *Social Work, 52*, 51–61. doi:10.1093/sw/52.1.51

Molock, S. D., Matlin, S., Barksdale, C., Puri, R., & Lyles, J. (2008). Developing suicide prevention programs for African American youth in African American churches. *Suicide and Life-Threatening Behavior, 38*, 323–333. doi:10.1521/suli.2008.38.3.323

Molock, S. D., Puri, R., Matlin, S., & Barksdale, C. (2006). Relationship between religious coping and suicidal behaviors among African American adolescents. *Journal of Black Psychology, 32*, 366–389. doi:10.1177/0095798406290466

Morse, E., Morse, P., Klebba, K., Stock, M., Forehand, R., & Panayotova, E. (2000). The use of religion among HIV-infected African American women. *Journal of Religion and Health, 39*, 261–276. doi:10.1023/A:10 10314724910

Musick, M., Wilson, J., & Bynum, W. (2000). Race and formal volunteering: The differential effects of class and religion. *Social Forces, 78*, 1539–1571. doi:10.2307/3006184

Neighbors, H. W., Caldwell, C., Williams, D., Nesse, R., Taylor, R., Bullard, K., . . . Jackson, J. S. (2007). Race, ethnicity, and use of services for mental disorders: Results from the National Survey of American Life. *Archives of General Psychiatry, 64*, 485–494. doi:10.1001/archpsyc.64.4.485

Neighbors, H. W., Musick, M., & Williams, D. (1998). The African American minister as a source of help for serious personal crises: Bridge or barrier to mental health care. *Health Education and Behavior, 25*, 759–777. doi:10.1177/109019819802500606

Norton, N. (2006). Talking spirituality with family members: Black and Latina/o children co-researcher methodologies. *Urban Review, 38*, 313–334. doi:10.1007/s11256-006-0036-4

Ohm, R. (2003). The African American experience in the Islamic faith. *Public Health Nursing, 20*, 478–486. doi:10.1046/j.1525-1446.2003.20608.x

Pearce, M. J., Jones, S., Schwab-Stone, M., & Ruchkin, V. (2003). The protective effects of religiousness and parent involvement on the development of conduct problems among youth exposed to violence. *Child Development, 74*, 1682–1696. doi:10.1046/j.1467-8624.2003.00631.x

Rajaram, S. S., & Rashidi, A. (2003). African-American Muslim Women and Health Care. *Women and Health, 37*, 81–96. doi:10.1300/J013v37n03_06

Ravenell, J. L., Johnson, W., Jr., & Whitaker, E. (2006). African-American men's perceptions of health: A focus group study. *Journal of the National Medical Association, 98*, 544–560.

Reese, L., & Brown, R. (1995). The effects of religious messages on racial identity and system blame among African Americans. *Journal of Politics, 57*, 24–43. doi:10.2307/2960269

Richey Wittig, D. (2001). Organ donation beliefs of African American women residing in a small Southern community. *Journal of Transcultural Nursing, 12*, 203–210. doi:10.1177/104365960101200304

Roberts, D. E. (1997). *Killing the Black body: Race, reproduction, and the meaning of liberty*. New York, NY: Pantheon Books.

Robinson, T. (2000). Making the hurt go away: Psychological and spiritual healing for African American women survivors of childhood incest. *Journal of Multicultural Counseling and Development, 28*, 160–176. doi:10.1002/j.2161-1912.2000.tb00343.x

Russell, K. M., Swenson, M., & Skelton, A. (2003). The meaning of health in mammography screening for African American women. *Health Care for Women International, 24*, 2–39. doi:10.1080/07399330304022

Simons, L., Simons, R., & Conger, R. (2004). Identifying mechanisms whereby family religiosity influences the probability of adolescent anti-social behavior. *Journal of Comparative Family Studies, 35*, 547–563.

Smith, C., Denton, M., Faris, R., & Regnerus, M. (2002). Mapping American adolescent religious participation. *Journal for the Scientific Study of Religion, 41*, 597–612. doi:10.1111/1468-5906.00148

Spencer, M., Fegley, S., & Harpalani, V. (2003). A Theoretical and empirical examination of identity as coping: Linking coping resources to the self-processes of African American youth. *Applied Developmental Science, 7*, 181–188. doi:10.1207/S1532480XADS0703_9

Steinman, K. J., & Zimmerman, M. (2004). Religious activity and risk behavior among African American adolescents: Concurrent and developmental effects. *American Journal of Community Psychology, 33*, 151–161. doi:10.1023/B:AJCP.0000027002.93526.bb

Stevenson, H., Jr., Cameron, R., Herrero-Taylor, T., & Davis, Y. (2002). Development of the teenager Experience of Racial Socialization Scale: Correlates of race-related socialization frequency from the perspective of Black Youth. *Journal of Black Psychology, 28*, 84–106. doi:10.1177/0095798402028002002

Stewart, C., Koeske, G., & Pringle, J. (2008). Religiosity as a predictor of successful post-treatment abstinence for African American clients. *Journal of Social Work Practice in the Addictions, 7*, 75–92. doi:10.1300/J160v07n04_05

Stewart, R. (1999). Religion in the Anglophone Caribbean: Historical overview. In J. Pulis (Ed.), *Religion, diaspora, and cultural identity: A reader in the Anglophone Caribbean* (pp. 13–35). Amsterdam, The Netherlands: Gordon & Breach.

Swain, R. (2010). Shall we march on? An analysis of non-electoral participation in the Black community in the post-civil rights era. *Journal of Black Studies, 40*, 566–582. doi:10.1177/0021934708315156

Taylor, R. J., & Chatters, L. M. (1991). Religious life. In J. S. Jackson (Ed.), *Life in Black America* (pp. 105–123). Newbury Park, CA: Sage.

Taylor, R. J., Chatters, L. M., & Levin, J. S. (2004). *Religion in the lives of African Americans: Social, psychological, and health perspectives*. Thousand Oaks, CA: Sage.

Taylor, R. J., Mattis, J., & Chatters, L. (1999). Subjective religiosity among African Americans: A synthesis of findings from five national samples. *Journal of Black Psychology, 25*, 524–543. doi:10.1177/009579849 9025004004

Townsend Gilkes, C. (2001). *If it wasn't for the women: Black women's experience and Womanist culture in church and community*. Maryknoll, NY: Orbis Books.

Wallace, J. M., Jr., & Forman, T. A. (1998). Religion's role in promoting health and reducing risk among American youth. *Health Education and Behavior, 25*, 721–741. doi:10.1177/109019819802500604

Watlington, C. G., & Murphy, C. (2006). The roles of religion and spirituality among African American survivors of domestic violence. *Journal of Clinical Psychology, 62*, 837–857. doi:10.1002/jclp.20268

Wills, T. A., Gibbons, F., Gerrard, M., Murry, V., & Brody, G. (2003). Family communication and religiosity related to substance use and sexual behavior in early adolescence: A test for pathways through self-control and prototype perceptions. *Psychology of Addictive Behaviors, 17*, 312–323. doi:10.1037/0893-164X.17.4.312

Wyche, K. (2004). African American Muslim women: An invisible group. *Sex Roles, 51*, 319–328. doi:10.1023/B:SERS.0000046615.22900.b2

Zinnbauer, B. J., Pargament, K. I., Cole, B., Rye, M. S., Butter, E. M., Belavich, T. G., . . . Kadar, J. L. (1997). Religion and spirituality: Unfuzzying the fuzzy. *Journal for the Scientific Study of Religion, 36*, 549–564. doi:10.2307/1387689

Chapter 31

THE SPIRITUAL AND SACRED AMONG NORTH AMERICAN INDIANS AND ALASKA NATIVES: MYSTERY, WHOLENESS, AND CONNECTEDNESS IN A RELATIONAL WORLD

Jeff King and Joseph E. Trimble

There are a great many spirits. They control everything; and they know everything. They can make a man do anything they wish. They can make animals and trees and grass do as they wish. They can talk with animals and can make animals talk with men. The spirits go about the world all the time and they make everything do as they please. Some spirits may want things done one way and others may want them done [in another way]. Then the stronger spirits will overcome the weaker. Any spirit is more powerful than a man.

—Ringing Shield (Walker, 1980, p. 113)

The words of the Lakota elder and "old shaman" Ringing Shield (*Wahacanka hotun*) capture the core theme of this chapter—a theme exemplified in the worldviews of North American indigenous populations concerning spirit and spirituality. At the crux of the core motif is the belief that spirit and spirituality is omniscient, omnipresent, and omnipotent. For most North American Indians and Natives the belief is indisputable and unassailable; for most individuals, the belief and conviction is woven so tightly within the fabric of their belief systems that they are rarely given any open consideration. Yet the deeply held and abiding beliefs are not without those who criticize them for their seeming animalistic qualities, their ethereal fundamentals, and their seeming lack of demonstrable evidence (Gray, 2005; Grover, 2008; Norder, 2007; Warber & Irvine, 2008). Most Natives and Indians scoff at the accusations and ignore them as those born from people who do not take the time and interest in learning the lifeways and thoughtways of others from their perspective. The prominent anthropologist Margaret Mead (1959) with the assistance of her mentor, William Fielding Ogburn, stated it effectively with the words, "Never look for a psychological explanation unless every effort to find a cultural one has been exhausted" (p. 16). This is more fitting within most Native American perspectives in that the aforementioned tribal values and understandings have typically and historically been overlooked, dismissed, or discredited by Western science. To explain Native tribal spirituality, an approach to these views must be authentically respectful of the cultural ceremonies, visions, spirit songs, dances, and, in general, the living connection to the spirit world. Psychological explanations up to this point have failed to capture this. Thus, a psychology that overlooks the cultural context of any people is incomplete and misleading.

Let an illustration assist in emphasizing the main point. An old Crow (Apsáalooke) American Indian leader from Montana was asked once to describe the difference between Native people and Whites (Euro-Americans). He replied that "the White man has ideas; the Indian has visions" (Deloria, 1999). In a succinct manner, the Crow leader captures the strong possibility that there are fundamental differences between North American Indigenous worldviews and those held by most Western Europeans or Euro-Americans, including its scientists and the

DOI: 10.1037/14045-031
APA Handbook of Psychology, Religion, and Spirituality: Vol. 1. Context, Theory, and Research, K. I. Pargament (Editor-in-Chief)
Copyright © 2013 by the American Psychological Association. All rights reserved.

science it has developed and continues to pursue. Thus, to discuss what is spiritual and sacred among North American Indigenous people, the reader must be willing to set aside the Western worldview that divides the world into physical and spiritual and separates the subject from the object. Separation of the elements from one another would be seen as an anomaly to a traditional Indian or Native. To a traditional Native person, there is no divide or separation, but all are an integral part of life. Jung (1931/1971; see also Volume 2, Chapter 7, this handbook) recognized this difference in worldview as it applied to Native people and Western science when he wrote,

> Thanks to our one-sided emphasis on so-called natural causes, we have learned to differentiate what is subjective and psychic from what is objective and "natural." For primitive man, on the contrary, the psychic and the objective coalesce in the external world. In the face of something extraordinary it is not he who is astonished, but rather the thing that is astonishing. (p. 93)

As the editors of the volume point out, Western science has limited itself within a system that values objectivity, scientific method, skepticism, and expectations that phenomena occur in a causal and relational manner. The present claims of psychology as objective, value free, and universal are in reality deeply enmeshed with Euro-American values that champion rational, liberal, individualistic, and materialistic (as opposed to spiritual) ideals (Kim, Park, & Park, 2000). Furthermore, it elevates its epistemology above other epistemologies, attributing these other ways of knowing as inferior, primitive, and unsophisticated. In reality, North American Indigenous people have been just as systematic and philosophical as their Western scientist counterparts in their attempts to understand the world and its phenomena. They, however, have used and continue to use different methodologies to understand how lives are lived and the realities that surround them (Fixico, 2003). For example, within the Seneca spiritual worldview, they recognized that corn, squash, and beans were the three Sisters of the Earth. Because they were compatible spirits and inhabited a certain place and order in this world, they were always planted together. Only recently has Western scientific method discovered that the three plants together produce a natural nitrogen cycle that keeps the land fertile and productive (Deloria & Wildcat, 2001). Certainly, appreciating the sacred and spiritual allows for a breadth of perspective that the conventional scientific model does not. There are countless examples in which solutions to a multitude of problems were discovered and woven into the fabric of the village or tribes' lifeways and thoughtways (O'Brien, 2008).

Many contemporary scientists continue to think that Native (and other non-Western) cultures have not been sophisticated enough in scientific inquiry regarding the specific problems they encounter and thus have not been able to make effective strides to address those problems or that the traditional, religious, or spiritual approaches are inferior (Warber & Irvine, 2008). The notions of scientific supremacy within conventional science are displayed when psychologists suggest that *they* must go into these communities and conduct research to determine what are being referred to in modern medicine and treatment as "best practices." In fact, this is what has been happening over the decades with little to show in terms of improving psychological services to Native communities (President's New Freedom Commission on Mental Health, 2003).

The first part of this chapter has strongly emphasized the limitations of the *zeitgeist* of Western science and psychology. This was done purposely. In fact, from the experience of many North American Indigenous scholars, it has been observed that the ability to understand North American Indigenous perspectives on spirituality, religion, healing, and psychology begins with a deep acknowledgment of these limitations. Staying within the contemporary and conventional scientific grid actually hinders one's capacity to see or understand Native American spiritual perspectives. Yet, allowing ourselves to move outside this perspective can open up dimensions of knowing and relating that previously have been hidden from the scientific mind. As the editors of this volume have noted, "The field continues to be marked by mystery" (see Chapter 1 in this volume, p. 17).

This chapter focuses primarily on traditional Native beliefs as opposed to the beliefs held by many

North American Indigenous people who have adopted, to one degree or another, beliefs not original to tribal views. Additionally, the chapter provides a general purview of what this essence contains for North American indigenous peoples. We discuss selected lifeways and thoughtways of Indians and Natives that are influenced by the spiritual and the sacred and how they are woven into the framework of traditions, customs, ceremonies, rituals, and everyday life. Literature on the topic is organized and summarized following prominent themes. Beliefs and practices are compared and contrasted for a select number of tribes and villages to illustrate their commonalities and differences. Additional sections show how spirituality and the sacred have become integral components of healing and in the emerging fields of multicultural counseling and psychotherapy. Although the research literature on Indian and Native spirituality is thin at best, there is ample testimony that the gentle blend of the spirit and the sacred in the health professions is effective and helpful. A section of the chapter focuses on the need for greater understanding of Indian and Native spirituality in the helping professions and how they can be best coordinated with conventional practitioners. Also addressed are problems associated with the blending of Native and mainstream Western perspectives and practices.

Throughout this chapter, we use different terms to refer to the indigenous peoples of North America; these terms include *American Indians, Alaska Natives, First Nations peoples, Native American Indians, Native Americans, Indians,* and *Natives.* We use the briefest of these terms frequently for ease of reading and to make the best use of our limited space. Although all these terms have historical and sociopolitical value, the indigenous peoples of the Americas generally prefer to be referred to by the names of their tribes or village affiliations.

THE HETEROGENEITY OF TRIBAL AND VILLAGE SPIRITUAL BELIEFS AND PRACTICES

Much of Indian country, a general euphemism for describing where Native people live, has become Christianized with multiple variations in how this has played out both between and within tribes. For example, among the Cherokee (as well as other tribes), there are the "traditional" and the "church-goers." Among the church-goers, there is further divide: those who still practice the traditional ways along with their Christianity and those who practice Christianity exclusive of their tribal beliefs. One Cherokee elder stated, "Oh, yeah! They [Cherokee Christians] believe in the little people (spirit entities) and in the Bible. They believe just as strongly in both" (D. Stewart, personal communication May 23, 1987). Traditional medicine men and women and Native Christians disagree among each other as to whether these beliefs are compatible. There are no data that describe the degree to which Christianity has affected the more than 550 federally recognized tribes. In fact, delving into these multifaceted iterations of acculturation and one's acculturative status is overwhelming and tends to miss the more central dynamics that have preserved tribal identities over time and in spite of multiple efforts and levels of historical hostilities, atrocities, and genocide. What is more remarkable is the resilience and strength to survive and retain cultural identities in spite of hundreds of years of oppression.

For example, the Muscogee Nation of Oklahoma possesses a "sacred fire," which was given to them at the beginning of their existence and has been kept and rekindled periodically (Chaudhuri & Chaudhuri, 2001). The fire was and is seen as an essential part of all life. The fire supplied heat and light for both the households and the community ceremonies, just as the sun supplied the same so that all living things might flourish. For the Muscogee, the sun and the sacred fire within the ceremonial ring (*paskofv*, where stomp dances are held) are the same. The fire, like an ancestor or tribal elder, must be treated with respect. When the U.S. government forced their removal from the eastern part of the United States, their homeland for centuries, the Muscogee brought the embers of the sacred fire all along the way of the Trail of Tears into their new settlements in what is now Oklahoma. They used these embers to light the fire of their new *paskofv*. This story metaphorically highlights what many or most tribes have done over the centuries. They have maintained their spiritual and cultural essence as a people in spite of forced relocations, invasions, betrayal, separation of children from families, death, poverty, disease, and genocidal attempts. The fire still burns.

We do not want to stereotype North American indigenous peoples in a manner that locks them into a certain time frame, for this has never been the case. Native people have always been cultivating change and adaptation. Interestingly, time is typically not viewed in the same manner as mainstream society views it. Rather, time is seen in a more circular fashion, where things of the past and the future have life and meaning in the present as well. Native people embrace ancient wisdom and teachings as well as contemporary approaches to life. It should come as no surprise that a medicine woman would not only have knowledge of her tribal ways but also perhaps acupuncture or Ayurvedic medicine. A Dakota medicine man told one of the authors of this chapter that in his visits with various African healers there was a shared understanding of the spirit world and the visits were full of exchanges of knowledge. Furthermore, tribal people who have been cured of disease in ceremony will often go to allopathic doctors for confirmation of the healing (Schwarz, 2008).

Furthermore, the heterogeneity of tribal and village spiritual beliefs and practices requires attention. It is essential to understand the extraordinarily diverse demographic and individual identity characteristics of the groups that make up North America's indigenous populations. These populations are no doubt more diverse than those that make up the rich tapestry of national and ethnic groups in European countries (more than 550 federally recognized tribes and 150 language groups within the United States). Native American Indians reside in all of Canada's provinces and in all of the United States (Trimble & Gonzalez, 2008). Unknown numbers follow traditional lifestyles, and countless others embrace the values and lifestyles of mainstream North American culture. The extraordinary variation in lifestyle orientations and physical appearance among the Native populations presents a daunting challenge for anyone who tends to view American Indians as a homogeneous group. Indeed, the tendency of non-Natives to view American Indians and Alaska Natives in a collective manner has been a source of considerable concern among scholars. It may well be the major reason so many non-Natives experience difficulty in understanding the complexity of the varied lifeways and thoughtways of Native American Indians. Yet with all of the cultural variability, a common theme runs through the core of spiritual belief and practices; it is the common conviction that all things have spirit (see Sullivan, 2000).

THE SPIRITUAL AND THE SACRED

The English language has numerous synonyms for *spirit* that suggest the concept or term is not that well understood. For example, *New Webster's Dictionary and Roget's Thesaurus* lists the following for the construct:

> breath of life, consciousness, soul, psyche, mind, understanding, immateriality, intangibility, apparition, ghost, motivational force, essence, embodiment, truth, disposition, mood, animus, genius, valor, courage, dauntlessness, enthusiasm, zeal, warmth, togetherness, communality, oneness, unity, allegiance, devotion, inspire, invigorate, devoted, religious, humble reverential, righteous, clean-minded, pure of heart, heavenly, shadowliness, imponderability, sacred, devotional, and piousness. (Spirit, 1991, p. 205)

Extending the theme inherent in the various synonyms, May (1982) emphasized, "Spirit, like mystery, is a concept easily confused and distorted" (p. 32). He added that the soul is the fundamental essence of a person and spirit is "the aspect of that essence that gives it power. Thus, spirit and soul are not 'things' which one may choose to believe or not to believe" (p. 32). Mystery, according to May, can involve and embrace a spiritual experience, but it may not always involve the spiritual; on the contrary, he argued, spirituality is always mysterious.

Religion, as it is conventionally expressed and understood, can exist without spirituality especially if the religious expression is mired down in dogma, ritual, and strict adherences to laws and tenets by its followers and worshipers. In this vein, Shults and Sandage (2006) defined *spirituality* as "ways of relating to the sacred" (p. 161). This relational definition of spirituality builds on the psychological work of

Hill and Pargament (2003), who defined both spirituality and religion as arising from the "search for the sacred" (p. 65), with *sacred* referring to persons and objects of ultimate truth and devotion. Hill and Pargament argued that the "polarization of religion and spirituality into institutional and individual domains ignores the fact that all forms of spiritual expression unfold in a social context" (p. 64), and they make spirituality the broader construct that can sometimes be expressed through religious or other social contexts. According to Pargament (2007), "We cannot decontextualize spirituality. This dimension of life does not unfold in a vacuum, but rather in a larger religious context, even if it is a context that has been rejected" (p. 31). In Pargament's view, "the critical function of religion is spiritual in nature" (p. 31). Thus, for most people influenced by religious traditions, spiritual and religious development are best understood as interactive and overlapping even if the developmental process includes questioning or distancing from one's religious tradition (Hay, Reich, & Utsch, 2006).

At a much broader level, Canda (1994) outlined spirituality as having both broad and narrow meanings:

> In a narrow sense, spirituality involves the basic human need to strive for a sense of meaning purpose, and moral relatedness with self, other and ultimate reality, whether or not that reality is viewed in materialist, theistic, animistic, monistic, or in other terms. (p. 34)

In this definition, spirituality is one part of the person, along with the biological, psychological, and social dimensions. He continued,

> The broad meaning of spirituality, however, is not limited to any one aspect of the person. Spirituality is the wholeness of what it is to be human and is not reducible to any one aspect. Spirituality in this sense is a striving to actualize in awareness and behavior the wholeness of each person. (p. 34)

Yet, "spirit is the aspect of reality," reasoned Lerner (2000), "that cannot be quantified or subjected to repeated observations. It is, rather, the realm of ultimate freedom" (p. 7). Spirit and spirituality are not objects to be set apart from life and treated as though they are specimens for detailed investigation and scientific validation. Spirituality and all that it represents is not exclusive—spirituality and the sacred are inclusive of all that is and can be. No one owns it.

Although these definitions capture the essence of spirituality, it appears that scholars are wont to elaborate on the concept rather than rely on the principle of parsimony—the principle attributed to William of Occam that in explaining a thing no more assumptions should be made than are necessary. Consistent with the parsimonious principle, most Indian and Natives capture "spirit" with one or two words. Thus, what is commonly known as spirit in the English language the Lakota call *wakan. Wakan* means both mystery and holiness and is used by the Lakota to designate all that is sacred, mysterious, spiritual, or supernatural. The Supreme Being or Creator of the Lakota is called *Wakan-Tanka.* In the 19th century, a Lakota elder, Good Seat, stated that

> *wakan* was anything that was hard to understand. A rock was sometimes *wakan*. Anything might be *wakan*. When anyone did something that no one understood, that was *wakan*. If the thing done was what no one could understand it was *wakan tanka*. How the world was made was *wakan tanka*. How the sun was made was *wakan tanka*. How men used to talk to animals and birds was *wakan*. Where the spirits and ghosts are is *wakan tanka*. How the spirits act is *wakan tanka*. A spirit is *wakan*. (Walker, 1980, p. 70)

In the English language, this name is commonly rendered as the "The Great Spirit," but it would be translated more correctly as "The Great Holy-Mystery" (Curtis, 1968, p. 32). The Muscogee Creek Nation use the term *boea fikcha/puyvfekcv*, which encompasses "all my relations"—male, female, human and nonhuman, known and unknown, all part of a continuum of energy that is at the heart of the universe (Chaudhuri & Chaudhuri, 2001). Numerous tribes have similar words to convey spirit, such as the Diné, Hopi, Tlingit, Ojibwa, Cheyenne, Arapahoe, Kiowa, and Osage. The closest

Christian, Jewish, or Islamic concept for this comes from the scripture that describes God as "too mysterious to understand" (Judges 13:18, New International Version).

Indian and Native spirituality is centered on the Creator and human beings' unique, personal relationship with the Creator. By definition, spirituality is everywhere, imbued in all of life (Earth's beings, rocks, trees, animals, wind). Historically, this view has been seen as primitive and animistic; however, simply by substituting the word *spirit* with *energy*, we have quantum physics' definition of energy or matter. This definition encompasses human relationships with all beings. The sacred teachings come from oral traditions, some more than 8,000 years old. The symbols for life include the circle (representing the cycles of life), the Medicine Wheel, and the Sacred Tree.

Contrasted with the dominant Western European view that humans are *superior to* the rest of creation, Native people see themselves as *part of* creation. Many terms of spirituality (encompassing health, well-being, and social responsibility) embrace this idea. *Mitakea Oyasin* is Lakota for "All my relations," implying a responsibility to all of life. People, animals, and nature are regarded as relatives. *Hózhó* is Diné (Navajo) for the responsibility to live in balance with all of life. Thus, the central purpose in life is for people to take care of the Earth and to serve others. Peace and wholeness come through living in balance. Personal well-being cannot be separate from one's connectedness to this purpose. The afterlife is a continuation of physical life on an energetic plane and includes a continual process of teaching and learning lessons (Fukuyama, Siahpoush, & Sevig, 2005). In this context of all things related, Native people's spirituality also encompasses healing from and overcoming the effects of colonization (O'Brien, 2008).

In many North American tribes, this way of life is often symbolized by a circle but contains the same meaning. The Diné emphasize harmony and beauty in relationships and connections with others and nature; the Apache call this "living in the pollen way"; for the Lakota, one can choose to follow the Red Road or the Black Road, each of which presents unique challenges for the proper way to live; for the Inupiat Eskimo, *ahregah*, or "well-being," is a state of being in which one experiences a healthy body, inner harmony, and "a good feeling within" oneself; and for the Ojibwe, the Seven Council Fires of Life mark significant transitions through life stages. Locust (1990) pointed out that

> Native American Indians believe that each individual chooses to make himself well or to make himself unwell. If one stays in harmony, keeps all the tribal laws and the sacred laws, one's spirit will be so strong that negativity will be unable to affect it. Once harmony is broken, however, the spiritual self is weakened and one becomes vulnerable to physical illness, mental and/or emotional upsets, and the disharmony projected by others. (p. 4)

This "path" or "way of living" provides the individual with traditionally grounded directions and guidelines for living a life free of emotional turmoil, confusion, animosity, unhappiness, poor health, and conflict-ridden interpersonal and intergroup relations. The goal of traditional spiritual beliefs and practices is to provide assistance for the individual or community to once again find the "straight path" or way back to the circle and balance. This is illustrated by Diné distrust of Western medicine because it does not concern itself with whether the patient's life is in balance or whether their own life is in balance when they intervene with pills or surgery (Schwarz, 2008).

PSYCHOLOGY AND NORTH AMERICAN INDIAN SPIRITUALITY

Considerable discussion has taken place concerning counseling paradigm shifts and the manner in which counseling and mental health services are offered to Indian and Native individuals and communities. Rather than focusing exclusively on how to use or adapt Western perspectives of healing, many are describing and proposing models of healing from a Native American Indian perspective. A few authors have recommended that counselors establish working relationships with traditional healers (BigFoot & Schmidt, 2009; Duran, 2006; Gone, 2010; King, 2008; Mills, 2004; Nebelkopf & King, 2004). Such collaboration with an indigenous healing system can take several forms: The counselor may (a) support the viability of traditional healing as an effective treatment system, (b) actively refer clients to indigenous healers, or (c) actively work together with indigenous healers. Increasingly, numerous examples have been proposed concerning the worth of introducing Indian and Native beliefs and ceremonies within the conventional counseling setting. In general, the recommendations and examples follow the wisdom and advice offered by several counselors and clinicians concerning the importance of blending culturally unique and conventional psychological interventions to advance the goal of Native American Indian empowerment.

Interest in the spiritual and the sacred is accelerating within Indian and Native communities. Previously suppressed tribal ceremonies and rituals are resurfacing in great numbers across North America (DeMaillie & Parks, 1987; McGaa, 1992; Mohatt & Eagle Elk, 2000; Sullivan, 2000). This ecumenical resurgence in spirituality represents "the realm of ultimate freedom" and a different way of "orienting to reality, a way that is based on awe, reverence, and a deep appreciation of the Unity of All Being" (Lerner, 2000, pp. 7, 31).

Counseling psychologists and social workers, too, are expressing and advocating the importance of including spiritual perspectives within treatment modalities and clinical sessions with Native clients (Fukuyama & Sevig, 1999; Hodge & Limb, 2010; Nadeau & Young, 2008; Voss, Douville, Little Soldier, & Twiss, 1999). The interest is more widespread than one might imagine, given that spirituality is not a formal part of counseling or social work education programs. Canda and Furman (2010, p. 9) surveyed members of the National Association of Social Workers and found that 81.9% of respondents said they "help clients consider the spiritual meaning and purpose of their current life situation," 77.1% "help clients develop religious/spiritual rituals as a clinical intervention," and 22.3% have physically touched clients for "healing" purposes.

Counselors with an interest in as well as respect and appreciation for spirituality are in an advantageous position to work effectively with Indian and Native clients (Dufrene & Coleman, 1992; Trujillo, 2000). Spirituality and holism are synonymous constructs that are essential elements within the traditional belief systems of many Indians and Natives (Roberts, Harper, Tuttle-Eagle Bull, & Heideman-Provost, 1998). Although the deep meanings of spirituality may vary from one individual or tribe to another, for most, the sacred encompasses harmony, balance, vision, relationships, transcendence, and connectedness (M. Garrett & Wilbur, 1999; McCormick, 1996). Of course, these very elements are at the core of the establishment of trusting, long-term relationships between people. Openness to and respect for these values can promote a healthier and more stable world for all.

A good number of counselors working with Indian and Native clients have incorporated spirituality in counseling sessions and have achieved relatively good outcomes. J. Garrett and Garrett (1998) described the use of the "sacred circle" and its related symbolism in an "inner/outer circle" form of group therapy and how the Native perspective can facilitate client progress (see Exhibit 31.1 for a description of this and other Native healing methods). Using a variant of process-oriented training that is grounded in spirituality, Lewis, Duran, and Woodis (1999) have found that the technique can allow therapists to enter into a non-Western-based reality with their clients, thus enhancing their sensitivity to and respect for Native worldviews. Heilbron and Guttman (2000) used a traditional aboriginal "healing circle" with nonaboriginal and First Nations women who were survivors of child sexual abuse and found that both groups responded favorably to the approach. Whitbeck, McMorris, Hoyt, Stubben, and LaFromboise (2002) found that engagement in traditional practices serves as a buffer to depression as well as the effects of discrimination. The use of sweat lodges and talking circles to promote client participation and retention is receiving some attention in the multicultural counseling literature (M. Garrett & Osborne, 1995). Specifically, Colmant and Merta (1999) described the effectiveness of incorporating a sweat lodge ceremony in the treatment of Navajo youth who were diagnosed with behavioral disruptive disorders. They showed how the ceremony has considerable

Exhibit 31.1
Native American Spiritual Traditions

Sweat Lodges: The Native American sweat lodge has been used for many purposes. It is typically a small, dome-like structure in the center of which are placed heated stones. The leader of the sweat lodge pours water on the stones to create an intense steamy atmosphere, that when followed with the proper mind-set can lead to acute focus and openness on the part of the participants. It has been used for purification, healing, blessing, renewal, personal growth, and intense prayer. The ritual cleans and heals the body, mind, and spirit. It can also bring in entities from the spirit world responding to the specific needs of the participants.

Prayer Ties: Prayer ties are offered to the Spirit in exchange for blessings. They are small bags of cloth that contain tobacco or other herbs that are tied with ribbon, sinew, or string, oftentimes attached to branches (if in the outdoors) or to the frames of sweat lodges. One's prayers are contained in these ties. Prayer ties are not seen in isolation, rather, the process of making the ties, how many ties are made, the music heard while making the ties, plus who is involved in helping are all important parts of this process.

Smudging: The smoke from burning sweet grass, cedar, or sage (other elements, such as white copal are also used) is used for purification is part of many Native American traditions. It can allow the individual or group to feel purified and a sense of being part of the sacred. Smudging can be used by itself for entering into sacred discussion or a sense of being centered. It can also be a first step for other ceremonial or healing activities as cleansing is necessary for involvement in these practices. Smudging is also used to cleanse objects and rooms and to rid places of negative energy or spirits.

Ceremonial Peace Pipes: The Native American pipe is smoked in a ceremonial or ritual to call on the four elements and give an offering to the Great Spirit. The parts of the pipe all have spiritual meaning and the smoking of the pipe is not to be taken lightly. Those "who take up the pipe" are committing themselves to lives of spiritual integrity and balance.

Medicine Wheel: The medicine wheel is used among many tribes for numerous purposes. Although tribes vary on the colors and dimensions, the core lesson of the wheel is harmony with all the elements of the universe. The medicine wheel is a circle divided into quadrants, most often corresponding to the four directions, and each direction representing life dimensions (e.g., east represents renewal). These are further broken down into various areas of life issues that correspond with the central meaning within the quadrant. The colors are also associated with these core meanings.

Talking Circle: The talking circle is a group process that involves passing the talking stick (or feather) from speaker to speaker is a respectful way to communicate and share opinions. Often this involves smudging with sweet grass, cedar, or sage; the group leader opens the discussion by sharing a personal experience and then the group members talk about their own experiences and feelings. Only one person speaks at a time, and there is no cross-talk or questioning.

Vision Quest: The vision quest has been part of many tribal practices for centuries. The core of the vision quest is receiving a vision from the spirit world. Some tribes have used this as a rite of passage for youth, whereas others have used it as part of a journey toward maturity. The vision quest is a bit of a misnomer in that it is not in the seeking that the vision comes. Rather, the individual makes him- or herself available through the ritual, but the vision comes from the spiritual world.

overlap with conventional forms of group therapy and thus merits consideration in the treatment of Native youth.

Wilson (2007) reported significant symptom reduction for Native American Vietnam veterans who participated in Lakota sweat lodge ceremony and discussed the psychological dimensions involved in this type of approach. Johnson, Feldman, Lubin, and Southwick (1995) also found that the use of traditional North American Indian ceremonies such as sweat lodge and honoring powwows were effective in treating posttraumatic stress disorder among veterans (see also Gross, 2007). Holm (1996) specifically addressed the effectiveness of Native traditional approaches to addressing psychological difficulties experienced by Native American veterans of the Vietnam War.

For the Inupiat people from Northern Alaska, spirituality is inseparably intertwined with the concept of personal well-being (Reimer, 1996, 1999, 2002). To be well grounded in their spirituality includes a strong belief in a personal God and to be in harmony with their surroundings, their community, and their environment. Personal well-being has to be meshed with one's way of being and living; it protects them from illness and negative spiritual forces.

According to Reimer (2002),

> spirits or ghosts are said to make their appearance to many people. Some of

> these spirits appeared in order to comfort people such as in the case of an elderly Village #3 woman whose friends appeared at her deathbed or when a grandmother would often make her appearance to her beloved grandchild in a friendly non-threatening way. (p. 25)

To illustrate her point, Reimer summarized three instances in which spirits or ghosts appear in their lives to provide them guidance and support. With an elder in Village 1, she described the experience as follows: "As a young girl, she was walking on the beach and she saw someone who wore Khaki clothes and she did not know it was a ghost until she came face to face with him and he suddenly disappeared" (p. 25). In the case incident of Village 2,

> elders and a middle age male had convincing stories about young people who asked for prayer, even though they were not practicing Christians, because something or someone was bothering and frightening them. These young people described in detail the identities of these people. (p. 25)

Continuing, she added that a Village 1 elder "believed one male killed himself after his brother drowned after being haunted, and now his brother was haunting him" (p. 25).

A family asked a Village 2 middle-aged man to pray for the removal of a spirit haunting his family's children's bedroom because the children were having difficulty sleeping. Some of these spirits exhibited extraordinary strength as described by a Village 2 man who entered the haunted bedroom. Feeling this powerful force that dropped him to his knees, he said, "When I started praying and we were able to get rid of it. I prayed until that feeling left and it was gone," and in an informal meeting in Village 4, "a young Village 1 woman told how two threatening spirits held her down and tried to smother her when she was young. She said she cried out the name of Jesus and they vanished" (p. 25). Additionally, seven participants mentioned they experienced spirit visitations frequently when alone.

Spirituality and Alcohol and Drug Abuse Recovery Programs

Indian clients with alcohol and drug abuse problems also may require unique attention (Oetting & Beauvais, 1990; Trimble & Beauvais, 2000). Intervention and treatment techniques that follow the recommendations made earlier in this chapter may be effective in many cases, but because of the complexity of the problem of substance abuse among Native populations, treatment effectiveness may be compromised. An example of the unique attention this problem may require is that substance abuse counselors may need to develop a respect and appreciation for the spirituality that is strongly entrenched in indigenous communities. Research has shown that infusing traditional spirituality in alcohol recovery programs for Natives, coupled with a multicultural counseling perspective, can enhance outcome effectiveness (M. Garrett & Carroll, 2000; Navarro, Wilson, Berger, & Taylor, 1997).

Thus, the influence of spirituality in promoting recovery from alcoholism in Indian Country is slowly gaining support from tribal, community, state, and federal programs (Abbott, 1998; Garroutte, Goldberg, Beals, Herrell, & Manson, 2003; Grant, 1995; Kelly, 2008). For example, The People Awakening Project is a collaborative relationship between community members and university scientists that emphasized the role of traditional beliefs and spirituality in advancing sobriety. The project developed over several years into an effort to identify protective and resiliency factors among Alaska Natives who recover from or do not abuse alcohol; the project heavily relied on the traditional knowledge and wisdom of the Alaska Native communities involved in the long-term project (Hazel & Mohatt, 2001). The approach drew from community psychology, specifically community-based participatory research perspectives that attend to the context of community, empowerment, and an emphasis on the culturally resonant ethical conduct of the research team. This effort required the team from the University of Alaska Fairbanks to build relationships in which community members were equal partners who shaped and constructed the research questions, methods, interpretations, and conclusions. The collaborative approach imbues knowledge with the meaning of the participants and promotes and encourages "conscientization," wherein knowledge is emancipatory and is generated in a process of empowering communities.

A Muscogee (Creek) medicine man who also worked in an American Indian substance abuse treatment center reported that those who chose a more Native traditional approach did not relapse. He said that the spiritual connection made through the traditional approach filled the empty or wounded place inside that they were trying to fix by using alcohol (George Coser, personal communication, July 5, 2005). Duran (2006) spoke of alcohol addiction as a spiritual problem, more specifically stating that there is a "spirit of alcohol" (p. 61) that needs a spiritual intervention for recovery to occur. Although Duran received this understanding from a medicine man, he noted that this thinking was shared by Jung:

> Jung continues by making the point that the Latin word for spirit, "spiritus," by which alcohol is also known, is the word for religious experience. In addition, Jung tells Bill W. that there is an evil principle that prevails in the world that an ordinary individual cannot resist unless there is some protection from a higher source of power. (p. 63)

In a unique study involving spirituality and alcohol use, Stone, Whitbeck, Chen, Johnson, and Olson (2006) emphasized the influence of enculturation and related constructs that included traditional practices, traditional spirituality, and cultural identity to identify the mechanisms through which traditional culture affects alcohol cessation. The study consisted of a sample of 980 American Indians from four reservations in the upper Midwest and five Canadian First Nation reserves. Overall, the findings provide supportive empirical evidence that traditional Native and Indian practices and traditional spirituality positively influence alcohol cessation; however, the researchers caution that the data are cross-sectional and therefore do not indicate the direction of effects. They suggest that future studies on the topic should take on a longitudinal format.

Local and regional organizations are cropping up that encourage and promote the infusion of Native healing practices and spiritual beliefs in addiction recovery programs. Coyhis and Simonelli (2008) described the importance of the Wellbriety Movement, a Native value-based empowerment group that has demonstrated that recovery from alcohol and drug addiction can more effectively occur with the assistance of culture-specific traditions and spiritual practices in American Indian and Alaska Native communities. Native community treatment programs do not ignore the field's best practices research. Rather, they infuse cultural, spiritual, and ethnic strengths into their addictions recovery programs. Reflecting on a long-term commitment to research on American Indian alcohol use and spirituality, Spicer, Bezdek, Manson, and Beals (2007) concluded that many people find that traditional healing systems will strongly contribute to ending lifetimes of alcohol use and abuse. The healing systems are deeply embedded in tribal religious and spiritual practices and, more generally, in religious and spiritual practices and orientations.

An American Indian Psychology?

The practice of an "American Indian" psychology is not simply the application of ritual or ceremony to psychotherapy. Native practitioners acknowledge that there is a spiritual force that guides the healing process (Duran, 2006; King, 2008). There is a strong conviction derived from experience—that this spiritual force pervades all of life and works toward moving us toward wholeness and well-being. Some scholars have called this power *mana* following Polynesian beliefs. Native American tribes have various names for this power. Jung made similar observations about this healing process: "The mana theory maintains that there is something like a widely distributed power in the external world that produces all those extraordinary effects" (1931/1971, p. 69) and that this belief does not arise out of "thin air . . . but is grounded in experience. The groupings of chance occurrences justify what we call his superstition, for there is a real measure of probability that unusual events will coincide in time and place" (p. 60). Many practitioners in Indian Country who trust this power have reported countless "remarkable events" that occur beyond the scope of their own therapeutic plans or ideas. Place, ritual, and ceremony, among other tribally recognized valences, are powerful avenues through which healing manifests itself. Among these rituals and ceremonies are sweat lodge, smudging (purification), vision quest, trance states, and journeys to places of power. Narcisse Blood, a Blackfoot elder from Canada, once addressed a group of American Indian psychologists with this statement: "Psychologists talk about identity crises. I'll tell you what an identity crisis is: it is when you do not know the land and the land does not know you" (Narcisse Blood, personal communication, June, 18, 2007). Many clients benefit from connection to the land, especially places that hold power or significance for them (Deloria & Wildcat, 2001).

For non-Native practitioners who will be working with Native people, it is of central importance to understand and acknowledge the spiritual realm, ceremony, and sacred quality of places, persons, and life. Although traditional healing has been passed down through the generations, not all choose or have an opportunity for participation. Individuals may be active participants in these activities but look to traditional healers—not counselors—for this knowledge. Choice of a mental health provider apart from traditional healers is a decision potentially associated with distrust, misunderstanding, apprehension, and the possibility that mental health practitioners may be ignorant or insensitive to the cultural backgrounds, worldviews, and historical experiences of Indian and Native clients. Clients' presenting problems may be distorted by Western protocol or diagnoses may be guided by a different cultural worldview. The mere placement of therapy in a therapy room may be difficult as may be the expectation that credentials or degrees, so valued by Western psychology, mean very little to Native people compared with the genuineness and quality of the relationship. Traditional Native people are likely to be assessing the counselor in light of whether they can connect spiritually. It is not necessary for the counselor to embrace the specific beliefs of the tribal person. It is extremely important, however, that the counselor hold the sacred and spiritual in highest regard. Anything less will hinder the therapeutic relationship.

Psychology, in its attempts to demonstrate itself as a legitimate science, has embraced the scientific model, following the medical practice's approach to science. In this pursuit, it has all but abandoned spirituality, albeit with some important exceptions. Consequently, it has developed training programs for which little to no attention is given this domain. Thus, counselors are ill equipped to address the spiritual and sacred among their clientele. It is quite puzzling that this has happened because most of the world's populations have the spiritual domain as central to their cultures and psychologies. This is true for traditional Native communities. Sensitivity to the history of the tribe, as well as to its relative openness to disclosure of these domains to outsiders, is paramount. As mentioned, some tribes forbid the communication of sacred beliefs to the outside world. In fact, a number of tribes hold the belief that if you do so, it will bring harm to the community as well as to the person receiving the information. There is controversy among tribal peoples over whether to share sacred knowledge with nontribal members, especially Euro-Americans. Anyone with a cursory knowledge of Indian–White relations can understand why this might the case. Some tribal members, however, believe that they were given this knowledge to share with others, not to keep it only for themselves. What is critical in this process is that the knowledge be preserved intact. That is, if the knowledge is shared, it must be shared with nothing lost from the full meaning and context. To do so without retaining the full meaning is to pollute the "power" or "medicine." Within tribes, words contain power and thus must be used respectfully. Words can bring into being both good and evil.

Careful Use of Spirituality in Mental Health Programs

Although incorporating traditional spiritual and healing methods such as the sweat lodge and talking circles can facilitate counselor effectiveness, client retention, and progress under controlled circumstances, decisions to use such techniques must be made with a strong degree of caution. LaDue (1994) strongly recommended that non-Indian counselors abstain from participating in and using such practices, asserting that they should not promote or condone the stealing and inappropriate use of Native spiritual activities. Doing so may invoke ethical considerations, as Native spiritual activities and practices are the sole responsibility of recognized and respected Native healers and elders. Indeed, there is currently high interest in spirituality worldwide, and part of this growing interest involves the exploitation and appropriation of traditional Indian and Native ceremonies without the consent of indigenous healers. Matheson (1986) maintained that non-Native individuals who use traditional Native American Indian spiritual healing practices are under mistaken, even dangerous impressions and, as a consequence, are showing grave disrespect for the indigenous origins, contexts, and practices of these traditions by Native peoples. Furthermore, many tribes believe that using sacred medicine or teachings without full knowledge will bring harm to the individuals and to the tribe. If the essence of a counseling relationship is built on trust, rapport, and respect, then the exploitation and appropriation of indigenous traditional healing ceremonies and practices for use in counseling sessions undoubtedly will undermine a counselor's efforts to gain acceptance from the Indian community and the client.

The essence of the healing relationship is best captured with the words of Joseph Eagle Elk, a 20th-century Lakota healer, who said,

> The medicine man is not the only expert. Everyone has a purpose. Everyone is born to a family and a community for a reason. Like I explained about the tobacco, or the tree, or the animals. We are all alive, all have a purpose, and we all help each other. So each of us must learn to pay attention to what we learn from our dreams, what the animals tell us, and what nature says. (Mohatt & Eagle Elk, 2000, p. 42)

It is with these thoughts in mind that we conclude the chapter.

SUMMARY AND CONCLUSION

This chapter presented major elements and dynamics related to American Indian spirituality and religion. Spirituality is at the heart of traditional North American Indian culture. It is the "organizing principle" by which all community activities, knowledge, identification, relationships, practices, and religions are derived. In traditional Native cultures, spirituality is not just seen as at the core but also is infused throughout all ways of life.

Knowledge of these traditional ways cannot be obtained through the current scientific grid. Although scientists have produced important studies that come more closely to capturing an accurate view of tribal lifeways, these are typically descriptive of behaviors, cognitions, relationship patterns, and "outcomes" from scientific studies. The experience of the connection to "spirit" requires a deep respect, an ability to set aside previously held judgments, and an openness to a different way of living life. A different attitude and mind-set toward the universe in which we live, including living and nonliving entities, and toward one's position in life, power, space, and time is necessary before one can begin to grasp Native American Indian traditional knowledge. Native spirituality and religion are not static, but rather they are continually evolving. Tribal or community understanding may deepen or change over time and religious practices may undergo transformation. Yet, the essence of tribal spirituality remains the same—that is, the essence containing that of change and transformation.

Native traditional ways and spirituality can be unique to an individual, but it must be understood that the individual is not construed in the same way as Western European culture construes the individual. Rather, the individual is seen as part of the community and his or her purposes and gifts are directly tied to community functioning. An individual spiritual experience (such as a vision during a vision quest) is not solely for the person but for the whole community. In light of this, tribal religious practices are recognized as an outward ritual of the communally shared essence of spirituality. This, too, is not person-centric, as many of the religious practices honor the animals, plants, and land that share and contribute to our life together.

We have acknowledged that there is tremendous diversity among tribes and communities in terms of both spirituality and religion. Yet common themes exist across these groups. Tied into the cosmology of most, if not all, North American Indian tribes is the importance of harmony, balance, vision, relationship, transcendence, connectedness, humility, respect, and mystery. Although there is no denying the schisms and conflicts that exists within and between tribes regarding spirituality and religious practices, it is remarkable that these values have endured. Further complications have been introduced by colonization, oppression, disease, relocation, the maintenance of tribal language, acculturation, and the degree to which and way that Christianity has had its impact on Native peoples.

It cannot be underscored enough how remarkable it is that the essence of tribal spirituality has survived holocaust conditions and assimilation policies. Not only has there been survival but also a growing momentum among Native peoples to reclaim and allow this essence to flourish and inform its tribes and communities. It is now recognized that the introduction of traditional teachings and spirituality serve to improve treatment strategies in the areas of both mental health and substance abuse. Furthermore, traditional teachings and spirituality have been demonstrated to serve as protective factors in these same areas.

Psychotherapy is now being reshaped within American Indian cultures. There is a strong sense among practitioners and researchers that the inclusion of spirituality and collaboration with traditional healers and elders in the counseling process and intervention programs can create better outcomes. Furthermore, it is recognized that the counselor mind-set must be open and flexible to accept and respect the local tribal beliefs and lifeways. When therapy is offered in a manner that is congruent with the tribal values and spirituality, it actually reverses the historical trend of Native people having to "become White" (adapting strategies derived from Western European values) to get better. Now, with counseling aligning with culture, there is the possibility of receiving treatment that is congruent with one's own culture, beliefs, and spirituality. As can be seen, this process includes that part of spirituality within Native culture that seeks to reclaim its identity and establishes a greater sense of social justice. Native people would see this as restoring balance.

Although these are exciting and promising trends, there are also pitfalls or dangers associated with these endeavors. Caution is encouraged, and the development of keen sensitivity and respect is required when attempting to move into these areas.

This chapter has implied that our science and psychology programs do not offer training that can equip the scientist or practitioner to effectively negotiate this territory. As the editors of this volume have noted, psychology gives scant attention to spirituality and its importance in the lives of individuals and communities. Research has shown that Western European approaches in behavioral health have not reduced disparities in care nor improved treatment outcomes in the past 25 years (President's New Freedom Commission on Mental Health, 2003; U.S. Department of Health and Human Services, 2001, 2010). Recent research, however, suggests that the inclusion of within-group spiritual and religious practices into intervention and treatment produce better outcomes (see Volume 2, Chapter 34, this handbook). The challenge is clear. Science and psychology must examine its historic Eurocentric views, recognize its limitations, seek to expand and transcend its knowledge, and thus restore balance to its original purpose, the pursuit of truth for the common good. Advances in cross-cultural psychology are accumulating the pieces of a mosaic that are giving us a much broader outlook on spirituality, culture, and psychology. The scant research studies combined with clinical observations from those who have ventured beyond their own cultural milieu all indicate that culture in psychotherapy matters. This implies spirituality and religion, as these include the cultural outlook for all North American indigenous cultures. Scientists must seek out the wisdom holders within other cultures and meet on equal ground for the exchange of knowledge. As Draguns (2004) has stated, "the efforts of theoreticians, researchers and clinicians should be directed at this ambitious issue, a both fascinating and urgently needed endeavor in the new millennium" (p. 385). This is not without precedent, but it is rare. The Dalai Lama, beginning in 1987, coinitiated ongoing meetings between Buddhist scholars and top Western scientists in what is now called Mind and Science Dialogue (Dalai Lama, 2005). Similar meetings could be established among North American Indian tribal elders and healers and Western scientists and educators. Although this may be a difficult and trying endeavor, it is worth every effort. This may work toward restoring harmony to our world, and we will all benefit.

References

Abbott, P. J. (1998). Traditional and Western healing practices for alcoholism in American Indians and Alaska Natives. *Substance Use and Misuse, 33*, 2605–2646. doi:10.3109/10826089809059342

BigFoot, D. S., & Schmidt, S. R. (2009). Science-to-practice: Adapting an evidence-based child trauma treatment for American Indian and Alaska Native populations. *International Journal of Child Health and Human Development*, 2, 33–44.

Canda, E. R. (1994). Spiritually sensitive social work. In C. H. Simpkinson, D. A. Wengell, & M. J. Casavant (Eds.), *The common boundary graduate education guide: Holistic programs and resources integrating spirituality and psychology* (2nd ed., pp. 31–34). Bethesda, MD: Common Boundary.

Canda, E. R., & Furman, L. D. (2010). *Spiritual diversity in social work practice: The heart of helping* (2nd ed.). New York, NY: Oxford University Press.

Chaudhuri, J., & Chaudhuri, J. (2001). *A sacred path: The way of the Muscogee Creeks*. Los Angeles: University of California–Los Angeles, American Indian Studies Center.

Colmant, S., & Merta, R. (1999). Using the sweat lodge ceremony as group therapy for Navajo youth. *Journal for Specialists in Group Work, 24*, 55–73. doi:10.1080/01933929908411419

Coyhis, D., & Simonelli, R. (2008). The Native American healing experience. *Substance Use and Misuse, 43*, 1927–1949. doi:10.1080/10826080802292584

Curtis, N. (1968). *The Indian's book*. New York, NY: Dover.

Dalai Lama. (2005). *The universe in a single atom*. New York, NY: Doubleday.

Deloria, V. (1999). *Spirit and reason: The Vine Deloria Jr. reader*. Golden, CO: Fulcrum.

Deloria, V., & Wildcat, D. R. (2001). *Power and place: Indian education in America*. Golden, CO: Fulcrum Resources.

DeMaillie, R. J., & Parks, D. R. (Eds.). (1987). *Sioux Indian religion: Tradition and innovation*. Norman: University of Oklahoma Press.

Draguns, J. G. (2004). From speculation through description toward investigation: A prospective glimpse at cultural research in psychotherapy. In U. P. Gielen, J. M. Fish, & J. G. Draguns (Eds.), *Handbook of culture, therapy, and healing* (pp. 369–387). Mahwah, NJ: Erlbaum.

Dufrene, P., & Coleman, V. (1992). Counseling Native Americans: Guidelines for group process. *Journal for Specialists in Group Work, 17*, 229–234. doi:10.1080/01933929208414354

Duran, E. (2006). *Healing the soul wound: Counseling with American Indians and other Native peoples*. New York, NY: Teachers College Press.

Fixico, D. L. (2003). *The American Indian mind in a linear world: American Indian studies and traditional knowledge*. New York, NY: Routledge.

Fukuyama, M. A., & Sevig, T. D. (1999). *Integrating spirituality into multicultural counseling*. Thousand Oaks, CA: Sage.

Fukuyama, M. A., Siahpoush, F., & Sevig, T. D. (2005). Religion and spirituality in a cultural context. In C. Cashwell & J. S. Young (Eds.), *Integrating spirituality and religion into counseling: A guide to competent practice* (pp. 123–142). Alexandria, VA: American Counseling Association.

Garrett, J., & Garrett, M. (1998). The path of good medicine: Understanding and counseling Native American Indians. In D. R. Atkinson, G. Morten, & D. W. Sue (Eds.), *Counseling American minorities* (5th ed., pp. 183–192). New York, NY: McGraw-Hill.

Garrett, M., & Carroll, J. (2000). Mending the broken circle: Treatment of substance dependence among Native Americans. *Journal of Counseling and Development, 78*, 379–388. doi:10.1002/j.1556-6676.2000.tb01921.x

Garrett, M., & Osborne, W. (1995). The Native American sweat lodge as a metaphor for group work. *Journal for Specialists in Group Work, 20*, 33–39. doi:10.1080/01933929508411323

Garrett, M., & Wilbur, M. (1999). Does the worm live in the ground? Reflections on Native American spirituality. *Journal of Multicultural Counseling and Development, 27*, 193–206. doi:10.1002/j.2161-1912.1999.tb00335.x

Garroutte, E. M., Goldberg, J., Beals, J., Herrell, R., & Manson, S. M. (2003). Spirituality and attempted suicide among American Indians. *Social Science and Medicine, 56*, 1571–1579. doi:10.1016/S0277-9536(02)00157-0

Gone, J. P. (2010). Psychotherapy and traditional healing for American Indians: Exploring the prospects for therapeutic integration. *The Counseling Psychologist, 38*, 166–235. doi:10.1177/0011000008330831

Grant, B. H. (1995). Spirituality and sobriety: The experience of alcohol use and abuse among the Menominee Indians of Wisconsin. *Dissertation Abstracts International, 55*(12), 3897A.

Gray, M. (2005). Geodiversity and geoconservation: What, why, and how? *Geodiversity and Conservation*, *22*(3), 4–12.

Gross, L. W. (2007). Assisting American Indian veterans of Iraq and Afghanistan cope with posttraumatic stress disorder: Lessons from Vietnam veterans and the writings of Jim Northrup. *American Indian Quarterly*, *31*, 373–409. doi:10.1353/aiq.2007.0033

Grover, J. G. (2008). Challenges in applying indigenous evaluation practices in mainstream grant programs to indigenous communities. *Canadian Journal of Program Evaluation*, *23*(2), 33–50.

Hay, D., Reich, K. H., & Utsch, M. (2006). Spiritual development: Intersections and divergence with religious development. In E. C. Roehlkepartain, P. E. King, L. Wagener, & P. L. Benson (Eds.), *The handbook of spiritual development in childhood and adolescence* (pp. 46–59). Thousand Oaks, CA: Sage.

Hazel, K. L., & Mohatt, G. V. (2001). Cultural and spiritual coping in sobriety: Informing substance abuse prevention for Alaska Native communities. *Journal of Community Psychology*, *29*, 541–562. doi:10.1002/jcop.1035

Heilbron, C., & Guttman, M. (2000). Traditional healing methods with First Nations women in group counseling. *Canadian Journal of Counselling*, *34*, 3–13.

Hill, P. C., & Pargament, K. I. (2003). Advances in the conceptualization and measurement of religion and spirituality: Implications for physical and mental health research. *American Psychologist*, *58*, 64–74. doi:10.1037/0003-066X.58.1.64

Hodge, D. R., & Limb, G. E. (2010). Native Americans and brief spiritual assessment: Examining and operationalizing the joint commission's assessment framework. *Social Work*, *55*, 297–307. doi:10.1093/sw/55.4.297

Holm, T. (1996). *Strong hearts, wounded souls: Native American veterans of the Vietnam War.* Austin: University of Texas Press.

Johnson, D. R., Feldman, S. C., Lubin, H., & Southwick, S. M. (1995). The therapeutic use of ritual and ceremony in the treatment of post-traumatic stress disorder. *Journal of Traumatic Stress*, *8*, 283–298. doi:10.1002/jts.2490080209

Jung, C. G. (1971). *Civilization in transition: Collected works* (Vol. 10; R. F. C. Hull, Trans.). Princeton, NJ: Princeton University Press. (Original work published 1931)

Kelly, D. F. (2008). Alcohol abuse recovery and prevention as spiritual practice. In S. J. C. O'Brien (Ed.), *Religion and healing in Native America: Pathways for renewal* (pp. 65–90). Westport, CT: Praeger.

Kim, U., Park, Y.-S., & Park, D. (2000). The challenge of cross-cultural psychology: The role of indigenous psychologies. *Journal of Cross-Cultural Psychology*, *31*, 63–75. doi:10.1177/0022022100031001006

King, J. (2008). Psychotherapy within an American Indian perspective. In M. Gallardo & B. McNeill (Eds.), *Casebook for multicultural counseling* (pp. 113–136). Mahwah, NJ: Erlbaum.

LaDue, R. (1994). Coyote returns: Twenty sweats does not an Indian expert make. *Women and Therapy*, *15*, 93–111. doi:10.1300/J015v15n01_09

Lerner, M. (2000). *Spirit matters.* Charlottesville, VA: Hampton Roads.

Lewis, E. W., Duran, E., & Woodis, W. (1999). Psychotherapy in the American Indian population. *Psychiatric Annals*, *29*, 477–479.

Locust, C. (1990). Wounding the spirit: Discrimination and traditional American Indian belief systems. In G. Thomas (Ed.), *U.S. race relations in the 1980s and 1990s: Challenges and alternatives* (pp. 219–232). New York, NY: Hemisphere.

Matheson, L. (1986). If you are not an Indian, how do you treat an Indian? In H. P. Lefley & P. B. Pedersen (Eds.), *Cross-cultural training for mental health professionals* (pp. 115–130). Springfield, IL: Charles C Thomas.

May, G. G. (1982). *Will and spirit.* San Francisco, CA: Harper & Row.

McCormick, R. (1996). Culturally appropriate means and ends of counseling as described by the First Nations people of British Columbia. *International Journal for the Advancement of Counselling*, *18*, 163–172. doi:10.1007/BF01407960

McGaa, E. (1992). *Rainbow tribe: Ordinary people journeying on the red road.* San Francisco, CA: Harper.

Mead, M. (1959). *An anthropologist at work: Writings of Ruth Benedict.* Boston, MA: Houghton Mifflin.

Mills, P. A. (2004). Joining and sustaining Yup'ik and Cup'ik healing with behavioral health treatment. In E. Nebelkopf & M. Phillips (Eds.), *Healing and mental health for Native Americans: Speaking in red* (pp. 57–63). Walnut Creek, CA: Altamira Press.

Mohatt, G., & Eagle Elk, J. (2000). *The price of a gift: A Lakota healer's story.* Lincoln: University of Nebraska Press.

Nadeau, D., & Young, E. Y. (2008). Restoring the sacred connection with Native women in the inner city. In S. J. C. O'Brien (Ed.), *Religion and healing in Native America: Pathways for renewal* (pp. 115–134). Westport, CT: Praeger.

Navarro, J., Wilson, S., Berger, L., & Taylor, T. (1997). Substance abuse and spirituality: A program for Native American students. *American Journal of Health Behavior*, *21*, 3–11.

Nebelkopf, E., & King, J. (2004). Urban trails: A holistic system of care for Native Americans in the San Francisco Bay area. In E. Nebelkopf & M. Phillips (Eds.), *Healing and mental health for Native*

Americans: *Speaking in red* (pp. 45–55). Walnut Creek, CA: Altamira Press.

Norder, J. W. (2007). Iktomi in the land of the Maymaygwayshi: Understanding lived experience in the practice of archaeology among American Indians/First Nations. *Archaeologies, 3*, 230–248. doi:10.1007/s11759-007-9044-6

O'Brien, S. J. C. (2008). *Religion and healing in Native America: Pathways for renewal*. Westport, CT: Praeger.

Oetting, E. R., & Beauvais, F. (1990). Adolescent drug use: Findings of national and local surveys. *Journal of Consulting and Clinical Psychology, 58*, 385–394. doi:10.1037/0022-006X.58.4.385

Pargament, K. I. (2007). *Spiritually integrated psychotherapy: Understanding and addressing the sacred*. New York, NY: Guilford Press.

President's New Freedom Commission on Mental Health. (2003). *Achieving the promise: Transforming mental health care in America* (Publication No. SMA 03-3831). Rockville, MD: Substance Abuse and Mental Health Administration.

Reimer, C. S. (1996). *The concept of personal well-being in the Inupiat worldview and their view of counselor effectiveness*. Unpublished doctoral dissertation, George Washington University, Washington, DC.

Reimer, C. S. (1999). *Counseling the Inupiat Eskimo*. Westport, CT: Greenwood Press.

Reimer, C. S. (2002). *What is the relationship to suicide, alcohol abuse, and spirituality among the Inupiat?* Retrieved from http://www.swancircle.com

Roberts, R., Harper, R., Tuttle-Eagle Bull, D., & Heideman-Provost, L. (1998). The Native American medicine wheel and individual psychology. *Journal of Individual Psychology, 54*, 135–145.

Schwarz, M. T. (2008). "Lightening followed me": Contemporary Navajo therapeutic strategies for cancer. In S. J. C. O'Brien (Ed.), *Religion and healing in Native America: Pathways for renewal* (pp. 19–42). Westport, CT: Praeger.

Shults, F. L., & Sandage, S. J. (2006). *Transforming spirituality: Integrating theology and psychology*. Grand Rapids, MI: Baker Academic.

Spicer, P., Bezdek, M., Manson, S. M., & Beals, J. (2007). A program of research on spirituality and American Indian alcohol use. *Southern Medical Journal, 100*, 430–432. doi:10.1097/SMJ.0b013e318031715c

Spirit. (1991). In *New Webster's dictionary and Roget's thesaurus*. Miami, FL: PSI & Associates.

Stone, R. A. T., Whitbeck, L. B., Chen, X., Johnson, K., & Olson, D. (2006). Traditional practices, traditional spirituality, and alcohol cessation. *Journal of Studies on Alcohol, 67*, 236–244.

Sullivan, L. E. (Ed.). (2000). *Native religions and cultures in North America: Anthropology and the sacred*. New York, NY: Continuum.

Trimble, J. E., & Beauvais, F. (Eds.). (2000). *Health promotion and substance abuse prevention among American Indians and Alaska Natives: Issues in cultural competence* (CSAP Cultural Competence Series, No. 9). Rockville, MD: U.S. Department of Health and Human Services, Substance Abuse and Mental Services Administration, Center for Substance Abuse Prevention, and Office of Minority Health, Health Resources and Service Administration, Bureau of Primary Health.

Trimble, J. E., & Gonzalez, J. (2008). Cultural considerations and perspectives for providing psychological counseling for Native American Indians. In P. Pedersen, J. Draguns, W. Lonner, & J. Trimble (Eds.), *Counseling across cultures* (6th ed., pp. 93–111). Thousand Oaks, CA: Sage.

Trujillo, A. (2000). Psychotherapy with Native Americans: A view into the role of religion and spirituality. In P. Richards & E. Allen (Eds.), *Handbook of psychotherapy and religious diversity* (pp. 445–466). Washington, DC: American Psychological Association. doi:10.1037/10347-018

U.S. Department of Health and Human Services. (2001). *Mental health: Culture, race, and ethnicity—A supplement to mental health: A report of the Surgeon General*. Rockville, MD: U.S. Department of Health and Human Services, Substance Abuse and Mental Health Services Administration, Center for Mental Health Services.

U.S. Department of Health and Human Services. (2010). *2010 national healthcare disparities report* (Publication No. 11–0005). Rockville, MD: Agency for Healthcare Research and Quality.

Voss, R. W., Douville, V., Little Soldier, A., & Twiss, G. (1999). Tribal and shamanic-based social work practice: A Lakota perspective. *Social Work, 44*, 228–241. doi:10.1093/sw/44.3.228

Walker, J. R. (1980). *Lakota belief and ritual*. Lincoln: University of Nebraska Press.

Warber, S. L., & Irvine, K. N. (2008). Nature and spirit. In D. Goleman and Associates (Ed.), *Measuring the immeasurable: The scientific case for spirituality* (pp. 135–182). Boulder, CO: Sounds True.

Whitbeck, L. B., McMorris, B. A., Hoyt, D. R., Stubben, J. D., & LaFromboise, T. (2002). Perceived discrimination, traditional practices, and depressive symptoms among American Indians in the upper Midwest. *Journal of Health and Social Behavior, 43*, 400–418. doi:10.2307/3090234

Wilson, J. P. (2007). Reversing cultures: The wounded teaching the healers. In B. Drožđek & J. P. Wilson (Eds.), *Voices of trauma: Treating psychological trauma across cultures* (pp. 87–103). New York, NY: Springer Science.

Chapter 32

ASIAN AMERICAN SPIRITUALITY AND RELIGION: INHERENT DIVERSITY, UNIQUENESS, AND LONG-LASTING PSYCHOLOGICAL INFLUENCES

Amy L. Ai, Jeffrey P. Bjorck, Hoa B. Appel, and Bu Huang

Asian Americans are immigrant descendants or immigrants themselves. They represent legacies of diverse nations that constitute a major proportion of the world population. In the early to mid-19th century, European Americans experienced the first major influx of Asians to the United States. A large cohort of farmers emigrated from Canton and Fujian (southeastern provinces in China) to seek work building major railways in the United States, during a time when their homeland experienced a number of natural disasters, uprisings among poor farmers, and invasion by foreign troops (Chen, 1940). Now, less than 200 years later, Asian Americans, labeled the "model minority" (Sue & Sue, 2003), account for 5.6% of the U.S. population. This figure is projected to triple by the year 2050 (U.S. Census Bureau, 2012). Research, however, has not yet provided an in-depth look at the role of religion and spirituality in the lives of these individuals.

This chapter aims to clarify the roles played by religion and spirituality in the lives of Asian Americans. The first section describes the diverse religious and spiritual backgrounds found in this group, alongside the diversity of ethnicities constituting the group. The second section describes empirical evidence on the diverse roots of faith and practice in Asian American culture. The third section summarizes the few available studies that provide solid data on the role of religion and spirituality in the lives of Asian Americans. These findings are also discussed in reference to existing and emerging social science theories on religion. The fourth section focuses on Asian-specific religions, particularly East Asian Daoism (Taoism) and Confucianism, and expressions of spirituality among Asian descendants in the United States. This section also addresses the influence and specific challenges of Asian-born faiths and practices on conceptualization in the psychology of religion and spirituality. The final section provides directions for research and implications for clinical practice. Particular attention is given to the need for culturally sensitive practice for psychologists and others who serve Americans influenced by Asian legacies.

In this chapter, we use the collective language of *religiousness and spirituality* and do not distinguish the two, given the great diversity regarding both concepts among Asian Americans. (For an explanation of how these two concepts are used in this handbook, see Chapter 1 in this volume.) For example, some might see belief systems such as Confucianism and Daoism as religions, whereas others might see them as philosophical worldviews with spiritual overtones. Given the tremendous diversity of Asian American cultural roots (including approximately 100 languages), comprehensive coverage of the beliefs of each subgroup is not possible. Rather, this chapter is intended as a stimulus for discussion and research in this understudied but major area.

CULTURAL AND FAITH-BASED DIVERSE ROOTS AMONG ASIAN AMERICANS

The paucity of research on religion and spirituality among Asian Americans is partly due to their cultural, linguistic, socioeconomic, and ideological

DOI: 10.1037/14045-032
APA Handbook of Psychology, Religion, and Spirituality: Vol. 1. Context, Theory, and Research, K. I. Pargament (Editor-in-Chief)
Copyright © 2013 by the American Psychological Association. All rights reserved.

diversity (Ai, Bjorck, Huang, & Appel, 2012; Furuto & Murase, 1992). According to the U.S. Census Bureau (2012), there are almost 17.3 million Asian Americans: 4.1 million Chinese Americans, 3.4 million Filipino Americans, 3.2 million East Indian Americans, 1.7 million Vietnamese Americans, 1.7 million Korean Americans, 1.3 million Japanese Americans, and 232,000 Laotian Americans. Although Asian Americans constitute a small proportion of the U.S. population, the group reflects a wide variety of Asian-born religions and spiritual practices (e.g., Buddhism, Confucianism, Daoism) and adopted faiths (e.g., Christianity, Islam, Judaism). This diverse religious landscape is inevitably related to the widespread cultural diversity within this ethnic group. The scarcity of attention to Asian American ethnocultural differences underlying religious and spiritual diversity is a major limitation of current research. Even in a national study specifically focusing on religion and spirituality (Emerson, Sikkink, & James, 2010) with 2,610 respondents, only 202 were Asian American, which limited any meaningful subgroup analysis because of underrepresentation.

Asian Americans constitute a multiethnic subpopulation with varied ancestries from the vast land of Asia. Classifying them as one racial group can be artificial and misleading. Regarding racial identity, for example, descendants from South Asia may see themselves as quite distinct from those of East Asian origin. In fact, South Asia and East Asia are each considered to be the birthplace of a unique major world culture with distinct religious and spiritual roots (Ai & McCormick, 2010). Smart (1999) proposed that these two cultures—along with Western culture—comprised the Great Three origins, which collectively embodied the world's seven dominant philosophical and cultural legacies, including spiritual and religious beliefs. The seven religions with roots stemming from the Great Three include (a) Daoism and Confucianism from East Asia; (b) Judaism, Christianity, and Islam, which began in Middle East Asia but came to dominate the West; and (c) Hinduism and Buddhism, rooted in South Asia. Even though two of the Great Three originated in East and South Asia, respectively, they differ fundamentally from one another and from Western monotheist religions and cultures originating in Middle East Asia. The influence of both Eastern and Western religions on Asian Americans can be traced to origins that precede the initial immigration of Asians to America.

Whereas monotheist belief systems did not originate in South or East Asia, many Asians who came to the United States already were adherents to one of them, particularly Christianity, because of the influence of missionaries since the 19th century (Fong, 2000). Among the earliest Chinese farmer immigrants, many were followers of *Hong Xiuquan*, a religious prophet and Christian leader who led the *Taiping Rebellion* against the Manchu (Qing) dynasty (Chen, 1940; Fong, 2000; Spence, 1996). The civil war spread from Canton to southern China (1850–1864) and was won by the *Qing* army and Westerners. Many other Asian Americans converted to Christianity before or after immigrating to the United States, with acculturation being one major motivation. The number of converts has continued to grow to the present day. For example, Yang (1999) noted that one third of Chinese Americans are Christians, in contrast to a much smaller number of their counterparts in Asia. The United States also has thousands of Korean American churches (Hurh, 2011; Hurh & Kim, 1990).

Islam is another monotheistic religion originating outside Eastern and Southern Asia, but it spread widely beyond the Middle East to Asia, including countries in Central, South, and Southeast Asia, and vast areas in China (Reid & Gilsenan, 2007). As such, some Asian Americans cite Islam as part of their religious heritage or current practice. In addition, Jews entered China in the 10th century (Humphrey, 1982), possibly as early as in the Han dynasty (206 B.C.E. to 220 C.E.), bringing the Hebrew Bible, the *Tanach*, and cultural practices (Neubauer, 1895). Their impact was extended through interracial marriage and building synagogues in the central part of China. During the two world wars, Jews from Europe and the former Soviet Union moved to other regions in China, and some mingled with Chinese. Their descendants, along with Asian Americans who converted through marriage, constitute a small but significant part of the American Jewish community.

Although many Asian Americans have adopted one of the monotheistic religions prevalent in the Western Hemisphere, they may retain cultural and spiritual influences of the four Asian-born faiths practiced for generations by their ancestors. Such intercultural integration may result in expressions of the monotheistic faiths that are uniquely Asian American (Bjorck, Lee, & Cohen, 1997; Bjorck, Cuthbertson, Thurman, & Lee, 2001). This integration fits with the tendency of East Asian traditions to embrace diverse faiths as compatible. Indeed, Ai et al. (2012) have argued that Asian American religious and spiritual practices tend to be intertwined with the Asian-born legacies of Confucianism, Daoism, Buddhism, or Hinduism, with their roots tracing back roughly 2.5 millennia. Moreover, these belief systems have expanded beyond their Asian regions. In particular, Buddhism has spread considerably in the United States and in Europe and is practiced by persons of many ethnocultural groups in addition to Asian Americans (Ai, 2000). Hinduism is still common in South Asian American populations from India and elsewhere. Both Confucianism and Daoism, on the other hand, remain influential among East Asian Americans with ancestry in China, Japan, Korea, Vietnam, Singapore, and other Asian communities.

Given the cultural and spiritual diversity of Asian Americans, no single faith-based category or general pattern can encompass them all. A comprehensive coverage of Asian spiritual and religious practices is thus beyond the scope of this chapter. Such a discussion would require precise information about each unique conceptual system in major Asian-born faiths. It would also require descriptions of lesser known groups, such as some Pacific Islander and Southeast Asian cultures that still practice shamanism and worship spirits, including nature spirits, demons, or ghosts (Gehlert, 2006). Given the space constraints, we will not detail folk religions or spirituality in this chapter. Conversely, whereas other chapters in the handbook focus on the monotheistic faiths, we provide a few ideas from Confucianism and Daoism. We also briefly address Buddhism (which is detailed in Chapter 35 in this volume), specifically with respect to its integration with Confucianism and Daoism. These latter two faiths collectively comprise the one group among the Great Three that is least known by psychologists and by laity.

Empirical Evidence for Faith Diversity Among Asian Americans

As a step toward describing spirituality and religion among Asian Americans, we have elsewhere (Ai et al., 2012) reported findings from the first nationally representative data set of Asian Americans (the National Latino and Asian American Study [NLAAS]; Alegría et al., 2004). The NLAAS, which used telephone interviews, was part of the National Institute of Mental Health's Collaborative Psychiatric Epidemiology Surveys (CPES; Kessler et al., 2004). Adapting the research design of the CPES (Wang et al., Lane, Olfson, Pincus, Wells, & Kessler, 2005) with variables more relevant to Latino and Asian Americans (Alegría et al., 2004), the NLAAS is the first national psychiatric epidemiologic study to assess psychiatric disorders and mental health service use among Asian Americans, with 2,095 Asian descendants in the sample (Alegría et al., 2004). As described elsewhere (Ai et al., 2012), one limitation of the NLAAS is that it included representative samples from only three Asian American subgroups: Chinese (29%), Filipino (24%), and Vietnamese (25%). All remaining subgroups (22%) were classified as "other," including three major subgroups (e.g., South Asian, Japanese, Korean).

A second limitation was the fact that the NLAAS obtained only a few single-item measures of spirituality or religion. Asian American religious affiliations included Protestant (21%), Catholic (25%), other religion (32%), and no religion (21%). The NLAAS did not specify other faiths (e.g., Buddhism, Hinduism, Islam, or Judaism). Given the problematic sampling and assessment issues, especially the lack of precision regarding Asian-born religions, the inter-subgroup differences reported in this chapter should be considered preliminary. Table 32.1 shows that whereas the vast majority of the Vietnamese, Filipino, and "other" subgroups reported a religious affiliation, almost half of the Chinese indicated a preference for no religion. Among those Asian Americans who did self-identify as religious, Filipinos were overwhelmingly Catholic, whereas more

TABLE 32.1

Religious Affiliation, Attendance, and Coping Among Major Asian American Ethnic Subgroups

Variable	Chinese	Filipino	Vietnamese	Other Asians	Overall
	Ethnic subgroup				
Religious affiliation					
Protestant	20.4%	15.3%	5.5%	31.2%	21.3%
Catholic	7.8%	71.0%	32.8%	8.1%	24.8%
Other religion	22.7%	7.9%	54.9%	46.8%	32.5%
None	49.1%	5.7%	6.8%	13.9%	21.3%
Attendance frequency					
Never	60.6%	17.5%	24.0%	27.8%	34.5%
Less than once a month	19.0%	19.1%	36.2%	22.4%	22.5%
One to three times a month	6.9%	15.0%	8.3%	14.1%	11.5%
Once a week	9.0%	38.0%	23.1%	25.3%	23.1%
More than once a week	4.5%	10.3%	8.4%	10.5%	8.5%
Religious coping					
Never	52.0%	18.6%	42.2%	26.7%	34.2%
Rarely	19.3%	13.0%	17.0%	19.1%	17.6%
Sometimes	13.3%	24.0%	18.8%	24.2%	20.3%
Often	15.4%	44.5%	21.9%	30.0%	27.9%

than half of religious Vietnamese and almost half of religious Chinese reported an "other" religion. Even with the limitations of this data set, the important finding emerged that roughly 62% of Vietnamese Americans and 72% of Chinese Americans did not identify with any mainstream religion—percentages higher than those reported in prior literature (Yang, 1999).

The NLAAS included two variables to assess religious involvement, the first of which was religious attendance. Attendance patterns among Asian Americans were as diverse as affiliation (Table 32.1). Filipino Americans attended services more often than Vietnamese Americans, who in turn attended more often than Chinese Americans. Given study limitations, subgroup differences should be interpreted with caution, especially because several groups were not well represented. Observed differences may have been confounded by differences in prescribed attendance between faiths. For example, Catholicism (predominant among Filipinos) encourages more-than-weekly attendance, whereas the "other religion" category (cited often by Chinese Americans) is not often associated with regular attendance. There are also more religious services available for mainstream faiths than for nonmainstream faiths.

The second religious involvement variable was religious coping. Results showed that 28% of the sample used religious coping often, 20% used it sometimes, and 18% used it rarely, whereas 34% never used religious coping. Once again there were subgroup differences (see Table 32.1), with Filipinos reporting more religious coping than Vietnamese or Chinese Americans. The language of single-item measures might have been culturally biased toward Christian faiths; the item tapped a tendency to seek religious comfort, whereas some Asian traditions may not use religion in this way. For example, Buddhism might be used to help a person accept the dark nature of one's present life (Ai, 2000), rather than providing comfort per se.

Clearly, subgroup sampling as well as cultural and psychometric sensitivity should be improved in future waves of this national study. For now, however, the significant subgroup differences discussed thus far regarding religious affiliation, religious attendance, and religious coping all suggest considerable diversity and point to the need for in-depth analyses of Asian Americans' many different faith traditions (Ai et al., 2012).

The Role of Religion and Spirituality in Asian Americans' Lives

Whereas religious views and practices among Asian Americans are too varied to examine as one construct, it is vital to ask how religion and spirituality function in this diverse multiethnic group. Research with other groups (e.g., African Americans and Caucasian Americans) suggests that religion and spirituality can benefit mental health (e.g., Ai, Park, Huang, Rodgers, & Tice, 2007; Gorsuch, 1988; Mattis & Watson, 2009; Pargament, 1997; Willoughby, Cadigan, Burchinal, & Skinner, 2008). Few studies, however, have explored links between religion, spirituality, and mental health in Asian Americans. Diwan, Jonnalagadda, and Balaswamy (2004) surveyed 226 older Asian Indian immigrants and found that greater religiousness (a sum of items on meditation, prayer, reading holy books, participating in spiritual discourses, and attending religious functions) was linked to better mood. Other studies have assessed ties between faith and mental health in Asian American Christian samples. Findings from these studies reflect a complex intersection of religion and culture.

Bjorck et al. (1997) assessed locus of control attributions (including those to God, self, powerful others, and chance), negative events, and psychological distress in 93 Korean American and 80 Caucasian American Protestants. They found that even when ethnoculturally diverse groups hold the same specific beliefs, religiousness can have different associations with outcomes. Whereas Caucasians' God control was related to less anxiety, Koreans' God control was related to more anxiety. Koreans might perceive God less as a helper or rescuer and more as authoritarian or stern, causing anxiety. A three-way interaction (ethnicity vs. God control vs. negative events) supported this hypothesis. Caucasians' God Control beliefs buffered the effect of negative events on depression, but Koreans' God control exacerbated the effect. Bjorck et al. suggested that

> Protestant Koreans' Christian perspective on God Control might be mixed with an Eastern view of fatalism and submission to authority. Their God concepts (e.g., God as ultimate authoritative judge) might also differ from Caucasians' (e.g., God as deliverer and problem solver). (1997, p. 70)

These findings might also imply different norms that underlie this cross-cultural variation in God control beliefs (see Chapter 13 in this volume). Along these lines, Weisz, Rothbaum, and Blackburn (1984) noted that Christianity in the United States emphasized individualism and primary control (e.g., action), whereas Zen Buddhism in Japan focused on collectivism and secondary control (e.g., accommodation). This contrast illustrates how Asian cultural traditions might result in uniquely Asian American expressions of Western faiths such as Christianity.

Furthermore, Bjorck et al. (2001) examined appraisal and coping in 93 Korean American, 49 Filipino American, and 86 Caucasian American Protestants. Both Korean and Filipino Americans reported more reliance on passive coping methods, including distancing, escape-avoidance, and religious coping, compared with Caucasians. This finding might reflect Asian norms regarding Confucianist social obedience and group harmony. Such norms, in turn, may be partly related to the emphasis within Daoism on passivity as a positive coping approach. More recently, Yi and Bjorck (2012) examined religious support in 295 Korean-speaking Christians in America. Support perceived from God and from religious institutions (leaders and fellow believers) were both related to more life satisfaction and less depression. These positive correlates of support from specifically religious sources remained significant even after controlling for general support from one's ethnic community. This finding, which suggests that religious support is not simply a facet of general social support, may be particularly significant in Koreans, whose community and religious support tend to come from ethnically homogeneous and perhaps overlapping groups. Yi (2007) also found that the combination of God Support and Religious Institution Support was linked with more life satisfaction, whereas experiencing only one or the other was not. These findings may reflect a longstanding belief with pre-Christian East Asian roots: Harmony comes from a unity of heaven and humans in which God may be seen as a part of heaven. Conversely, for Caucasian Christians, support from God and the religious community can function independently as resources (Fiala, Bjorck, & Gorsuch, 2002).

Together, these studies imply that even for Asian Americans who adopt monotheist faiths such as Christianity, Asian culture still can have a significant effect on how such beliefs are related to functioning. As another example, Guest (2003) argued that Chinese churches have become a major source of support, bridging cross-cultural gaps and offering a sense of ethnic community for Chinese Americans in New York. In this case, the ethnic church may act both to enhance the members' collectivist cultural identity and to serve as a resource of acculturation. Not all studies have found such beneficial effects, however. The National Longitudinal Study of Adolescent Health found that religious participation and religious importance among Asian adolescents predicted greater depression (Petts & Joliff, 2008). Although Asian ethnic churches are usually characterized as traditional and patriarchal, younger Asian American Christians who joined ethnic religious services might have experienced more cross-cultural conflicts between Asian cultural norms and the Western faith context with its individualistic focus. Indeed, a number of cultural theories attempt to explain East–West differences in psychological constructs, including primary–secondary control (Weisz et al., 1984), individualism–collectivism (Oyserman, Coon, & Kemmelmeier, 2002), and independent–interdependent self-concepts (Heine & Lehman, 1997). The influence of Confucianism on such social norms is delineated later in this chapter.

The studies discussed thus far all assessed relatively small samples, limiting generalizability. Clearly, research using national samples is needed. To this end, our recent studies with a national data set (the NLAAS; Ai et al., 2012; Appel, Ai, Huang, & Nicdao, 2012) represent initial attempts to examine links between religion, spirituality, and emotional functioning in Asian Americans. We used religious involvement as a predictor, on the basis of the measures of attendance and religious coping described earlier. For criteria, we used depression, anxiety, and a self-report measure of mental health (Ai et al., 2012; Appel et al., 2012).

As Durkheim (1915/1965) stated, one function of religion is to promote social coherence, a sense of belonging, and social solidarity. Because most Asian cultures emphasize a communal outlook that outweighs individual interests (Fischer, Ai, Aydin, Haslam, & Frey, 2010), we proposed that religious attendance (and therefore religious support) would predict better functioning for Asian Americans (Guest, 2003; Yi & Bjorck, 2012). Results supported this prediction. After controlling for demographics, socioeconomic status, and acculturation, religious attendance still predicted less depression and anxiety and better mental health (Ai et al., 2012; Appel et al., 2012). After social support was controlled, the role of religious attendance vanished, indicating that the role of religious involvement was mediated by faith-based social networking. These findings suggest that the potentially protective role of religious involvement identified in African and Caucasian American populations (e.g., Gorsuch, 1988; Mattis & Watson, 2009; Pargament, 1997; Willoughby et al., 2008) may generalize to Asian Americans as well. Our findings reinforced the vital role of social aspects of religious involvement in Asian American mental health, in line with the collective nature of Asian cultural norms (Fischer et al., 2010; Heine & Lehman, 1997; Oyserman et al., 2002).

Our second set of analyses focused on individuals' connection with the sacred, a core idea in Pargament's definition of spirituality (Chapter 14 in this volume). We used the single-item religious coping measure as a proxy for this connection with the sacred. Results revealed that religious coping was unrelated to emotional functioning (Ai et al., 2012; Appel et al., 2012). Although this result counters most prior findings using mainstream populations (e.g., Pargament, 1997; Pargament et al., 2000), it is consistent with earlier findings that failed to show any link between religious coping and emotional functioning in Filipino Americans and only revealed several zero-order correlations in Korean Americans (Bjorck et al., 2001). These findings raise questions about whether the concept of religious coping (an intrapersonal aspect) in religious involvement may fit better in individualist Western culture than in the collectivist Asian American culture. By contrast, the concept of religious attendance (an interpersonal aspect) could more adequately reflect a social function of religious involvement (e.g., Krause, 2006a, 2006b; Durkheim, 1915/1965) among Asian descendants in the United States. Interpersonal expressions of religiousness and spirituality might feel more culturally appropriate for them as a part of their acculturation experiences, especially among non-U.S.-born Asian Americans who reported higher attendance rates (Ai et al., 2012).

The relative absence of individualistic expressions of religion and spirituality might also be explained by a different cultural interpretation. Positive correlations were found between religious coping, discrimination, and years in the United States. These associations raise the possibility that the longer Asian Americans stay in the United States, the more likely it is that they experience discrimination, feel isolated from the mainstream, and use individualistic means (e.g., prayer) to cope. Yet, the picture of religious coping is complicated by its correlation with a protective factor, English proficiency (Ai et al., 2012). All these hypotheses are tentative and await future testing with longitudinal data.

In future work, it will be necessary to expand the concepts of religion and spirituality to include a deeper understanding of Asian-born faiths with their distinctive cultural and historical traditions. This inclusion will have implications for other Americans as well, particularly given that Asian-born religions have spread widely in the United States. Indeed, the Pew Forum (2008, 2009) showed that the U.S. religious landscape is becoming more diverse and complex, and Eastern religion and spirituality are growing in influence. A new survey indicates that roughly one quarter of adults in the United States hold beliefs connected with certain Eastern religions (Pew Forum, 2009). This increasing influence of Eastern faiths shows a new trend toward "spirituality globalization," alongside the globalization of capitalist economy, labor, and culture. This spiritual globalization also involves the rapid growing impact of Western religions in Asia, but that topic is beyond the scope of this chapter.

ASIAN-BORN SPIRITUAL TRADITIONS

To advance the psychology of religion and spirituality, it is crucial to consider some core ideas in Asian-born religious and spiritual beliefs. Buddhism and Hinduism have been addressed to some extent and are covered in Chapters 35 and 36 in this handbook. Confucianism and Daoism have received far less attention. This is particularly significant, given their influences on East Asian cultures and their roles in the development of Zen Buddhism (Ai, 2000, 2010; Munro, 1969, 1985; Weber, 1922, 1959). According to Weber (1959), Eastern religions involve delineated systems of belief and practice, and they have sacred texts that serve as guides for their adherents, similar to Western monotheist religions.

Asian-born religions differ in major ways from their Western counterparts and do not fit readily into Western theoretical models. For example, to distinguish conceptual differences between religion and spirituality, researchers often dichotomize the former as organizational and the latter as personal (Koenig, McCullough, & Larson, 2001; Pargament, 1997; see also Chapter 1 in this volume). This distinction, however, does not fit noninstitutionalized Asian-born faiths well. To better understand these lesser-known faiths, it is helpful to begin with Pargament's (1997; see also Chapter 1 in this volume) notion that religion offers significance, whereas spirituality represents the core functions of religious life, such as yearning for a connection with the sacred. The sense of connection has been highlighted in various definitions for spirituality (Lewis, 2001; Myers, Sweeney, & Witmer, 2000). Perhaps some of the primary distinctions between West and East (or between various Eastern faiths) hinge on divergence regarding the particular nature of the sacred or the various ways of connectedness in faith.

Asian-born spirituality allows for the sacred beyond the personalized god or spirit. Asians' sense of deep connection can take approaches that differ from those familiar in the West. These dissimilarities can be traced to differences in *worldview*, a term corned by Dilthey (1991). Worldview refers to the embracing of stable ontological and epistemological perspectives on the human perception of reality (Ai, Tice, & Kelsey, 2009). To illustrate cross-cultural differences, it is necessary to attend to the multidimensionality of both the sacred and the connection to it, as Smart (1999) did when describing the Great Three. Much earlier, Durkheim (1915/1965) extended the sacred beyond God or spirit, noting that "a word or anything can be sacred" (p. 52). As for connections to the sacred, Buber (1923/1958) proposed a triad composed of society, spirit, and nature. All three aspects can offer meaning or significance via connection to the sacred as a perceived reality, whether natural or supernatural (Ai & McCormick, 2010). Likewise, Pargament and Mahoney (2005) defined *sanctification*, which may or may not include theistic elements (e.g., god, spirit, a tree, crystals), as a process "through which aspects of life are perceived as having divine character and significance" (p. 183).

To allow for the diverse use of the term *sacred* in conceptualizing spirituality cross-culturally, Ai and colleagues defined the sense of deep interconnectedness (or connection) to be consistent with Pargament's (1997) notion as the profound human interaction with a significant entity or context, religious or secular, which bestows grand purpose and inspiration in life (Ai et al., 2009; Ai, Wink, & Shearer, 2011). On the basis of Smart's (1999) categories and Buber's (1923/1958) triad, Ai, Kastenmüller, et al. (2011) argued that at the core of spirituality, deep connection can be presented at both the physical level (relating to nature and society) and the nonphysical level (relating to spirit). To demonstrate cross-cultural differences in this sense of interconnectedness, Ai and colleagues (Ai, Kastenmüller, et al., 2011; Ai & McCormick, 2010) developed a three-dimensional scale, the Connection of Soul (COS) scale. The COS scale has three dimensions: (a) secular view (i.e., one with physical nature or society), corresponding to Eastern Asian faiths (e.g., Confucianism and Daoism); (b) God-centered view, corresponding to Western faiths (e.g., Christianity, Judaism, Islam); and (c) cosmic–spiritual view, corresponding to South Asian faiths (e.g., Buddhism and Hinduism; Ai, Kastenmüller, et al., 2011; Ai & McCormick, 2010).

Whereas Pargament (1997; see also Chapter 14 in this volume) offers a platform to understand overarching spirituality cross-culturally, the COS provides one way to show the dimensionality of this latent concept, the connection with the sacred, by operationally defining God-centered, cosmic, and secular spirituality, respectively. Another way to formulate this dimensionality can be to further divide the secular factor of the COS, resulting in a four-dimensional model (Worthington, 2010). Although both Daoism and Confucianism both represent secular spirituality, they do so by portraying the sacred via two different belief systems or dimensions. Specifically, whereas they both depersonalize the concept of supreme deity, they do so by representing the sacred via naturalistic spirituality and humanistic spirituality, respectively.

An exception to the depersonalized view of the sacred in the East Asian tradition did occur in Moism, established by Mo Tzu (479–438 B.C.E.) in China. He endorsed nonviolence and a personalized sacred god or heaven that universally loved all humans (Munro, 1969). The Moist faith shared some similarities with Christianity; both were practiced by either Chinese or Middle Eastern migrants (e.g., merchants or herdsman) in ancient times rather than by mainly land-bound farmers (Ai, 1990). Moism survived only 200 to 300 years in early China, however, in part because of the establishment of the agriculturally centered economy and related kingdoms in Asia, which adopted the dominant Confucianism to flourish and maintain civic stability for a large, centralized hierarchical society.

To illustrate cultural differences in the nature of sacred connection, it is also necessary to describe how lasting Eastern spiritual faiths differ from their Western counterparts. Briefly stated, the connection with the sacred in the West is a personalized object relation with the set-apart God. In contrast, the connection with the sacred in non-god-centered terms within certain Eastern faiths emphasizes the complete integration of humans as parts of a coherent whole (e.g., a sacred natural environment or the energy-based universe; Ai, 2010; Munro, 1969). With respect to Asians' integration of the part to the whole, deep connections are built with nature, within society, or through practice to prepare for the afterlife (Ai, Kastenmüller, et al., 2011). Such relations do not involve a personified tie to the sacred One (God), which in the West can involve such terms as *love*, *hate*, or *collaboration with that One* (Ai, Tice, Peterson, & Huang, 2005). This difference may explain the absence of a link between religious coping and emotional functioning in the East. In the West, the faithful may pursue God's help through this coping strategy, whereas in the East, people integrate with the sacred through their own practices (e.g., mindfulness, behaviors).

One way that East Asian spirituality expresses deep connection is reflected in the ancient phrase, "the unity of Heaven and humans." This core idea was described 4,000 to 5,000 years ago in *Huang Di Nei Jing* (*Yellow Emperor's Inner Classic*), even before the faiths in Smart's (1999) categories developed their bodies of sacred literature (Liao, 1992). The *Inner Classic* system espoused universal principles that synchronize what are seen as primary phenomena: heaven, Earth, and humanity. This system describes the human body in both cosmic and geographic terms and relates each organ with multiple natural phenomena, including time and space, to illustrate *Unity* (Ai, 2010). The true integration of these principles manifests itself in the key concept of *Qi (Chi)*, which is inherent in all three primary phenomena. This term means "flow of air," in a more literal sense in Chinese characters, or "vital energy," in a more symbolic sense (Ai, 2003, 2010). In fact, the idea of flowing energy or vital breath is shared by many non-Western legacies, including indigenous African culture (*num*), certain Native American cultures (*holy wind*), Eastern Indian culture (*prana*), and the shamanic tradition in Western culture, including the ancient Egyptians and Greeks (Ai, 2010). The uniqueness of the Asian version of this concept, *Qi*, lies in a complex coding system, registered in rhythmic changing patterns in many levels of nature and the universe. It is described in an ancient book, *I Ching* or *Yi Jing* (*Book of Changes*), traditionally dated to the 3rd millennium B.C.E. (Ai, 2010; Capra, 1991). Even with a common origin in *Qi*, the nature of *Unity* also varies among Asian traditions.

Historically, the core idea of *Unity* is reflected in all three major faiths in East Asia: Daoism, indicating naturalistic spirituality; Confucianism, centering on humanistic–moralistic spirituality; and Zen Buddhism, focusing on cosmic spirituality. In all three faiths, *heaven* is a symbol of the sacred without any focus on a central God as creator. This depersonalization of the sacred is one of the relatively unique features of East Asian faiths (Munro, 1969). In Zen Buddhism, unity is achieved through spiritually disciplined mind–body practice, detachment from the materialistic world, and, eventually, the soul's literal union with the cosmic divine force (Ai, 2000; Groth-Marnat, 1992). In Confucianism, unity is achieved through the virtuous correspondence between heavenly and humanistic consciousness, termed as *Dao mind* in heaven and *human mind* in humans (Munro, 1969, 1988, 1996). In Daoism, a spiritual worldview that also profoundly affects the holistic view in the philosophy and practice of Asian medicine, unity is achieved through the integrative balance among constantly changing energy patterns in both the nature and humans, or among heaven, Earth, and humans (Ai, 2003, 2010).

The idea of unity has influenced interfaith relationships in the East, resulting in a positive attitude toward the compatibility of diverse beliefs. This positive view is expressed in an East Asian slogan, "three teachings (i.e., Buddhism, Confucianism, and Daoism, in China, or Shintoism, in Japan) are one," and an ancient painting in which Confucius, Buddha, and Lao Zi each saw life (indicated as the taste of vinegar) as sour (rules for correction), bitter (pain and suffering), and sweet (fundamentally good in its natural state), respectively. This unity perspective has led to totalism or holism (Munro, 1969) and spiritual flexibility, allowing East Asian descendants to unite various faiths on the basis of developmental needs (e.g., moving up the social ladder in Confucianism, adapting to retirement in Daoism, and transforming from death to an afterlife in Buddhism). Indeed, it can be argued that this unique positive attitude toward unity of faiths has long prepared some Asian Americans to integrate Asian-born faiths with Western religions in the United States. (Bjorck et al., 2001). Similarly, this inclusive perspective has likely facilitated the coexistence of both Muslim and Jewish communities in central China over thousands of years (Neubauer, 1895; Reid & Gilsenan, 2007).

The inclusiveness of the Asian perspective also facilitated religious exchange between East Asia and

South Asia for millennia, especially as promoted through an imperial invitation of Buddhism to China by *Emperor Xuanzong* (712–756 C.E.) *of the Tang* Dynasty, which was to be practiced side by side with the exalted Daoism (Ebrey, 1999). The resulting adaptation may help to address spiritual topics not fully covered in Confucianism and Daoism, such as suffering (e.g., death, illness, disability, aging; Ai, 2000). In Buddhism, the Great Vehicle (*Mahayana*) has intertwined with ideas of Confucianism and Daoism and influenced descendants from China, Japan, Korea, Singapore, Tibet, and Vietnam (Epstein, 2003). Encouraging the ultimate achievement of Buddhahood (Bodhisattva) in humans (Epstein, 2003), these Buddhists (e.g., practitioners of Zen or Tibetian Buddhism) pursue enlightenment through human companionship and awakening from the materialistic life to pursue the eternal (Ai, 2000). In contrast, the Small Vehicle (*Hinayana*), influencing descendants from Burma, Cambodia, Lao, and Thailand, is less affected by East Asian faiths. Despite the fact that it focuses less on the ultimate achievement of Buddhahood, this branch tends to request temple-based practice, especially in men's early lives, to reach enlightenment and the next stage of reincarnation. In the tradition of many East Asian Americans, Buddhist cosmic spirituality and Daoist naturalistic spirituality both focus on mindful practice and harmony with the natural and cosmic environment (Ai, 2000, 2010).

Daoism

Unlike either Western religions or Buddhism, the original Daoism did not address concepts of the divine and afterlife but rather fundamental principles in a cosmic nature, *Dao*, the sacred law that governs the universe to which humans are tied (Ai, 2003, 2010; Peterson & Seligman, 2004). Daoism pays great attention to the harmonizing energetic patterns with nature, with respect to Daoist principles beyond the physical world, for health or longevity (Ai, 2003). In his legendary book *Dao De Jing* (*Tao Te Jing, Book of Way and Virtue*), the father of Daoism, Lao Zi (Lao-tzu; 571–471 B.C.E.), encouraged individuals to follow the *Dao*, referring to the formless and timeless nonbeing ("the nonexistence"; see Ai, 2006; Rosenthal, 2007). Nonbeing gives birth to all being or "existence," meaning everything with a certain space–time form in the universe. Nonbeing and being thus manifest energetic and substantive dimensions of all things in the universe. Unity in Daoism, therefore, is not merely expressed symbolically but reflects a systematic worldview, with humans and the universe sharing the identical essence. As Lao-tzu stated, "the universe is the center of his world" (Rosenthal, 2007). Zhuang Zi (Chuang-tzu; 369–286 B.C.E.), a Daoist precursor of *relativism* whose dialectic philosophy helped to catalyze the development of Zen, said, "Heaven, Earth, and I are simultaneously produced, and the myriad of creatures and I are one" (1968). He believed that humans are subject to the process of transforming to more complex forms because humans are part of nature (Chan, 1963). This Eastern idea (human evolving into higher beings) counters Western faiths that posit humans as already being in the image of God.

Daoist ideology resembles worldviews based on European objective idealism, espoused by Spinoza, Hegel, and Bruno, in which humans can be conscious of harmony with nature (Dilthey, 1991). It also can be compared with perspectives from quantum physics (Capra, 1991). The Daoist view, however, does not center on material aspects of the world. In Daoism, the universe is viewed in a dynamically continuous flow with constant changes in energy, shown as ordering patterns manifested in the movement of *Qi* (Ai, 2003, 2010). It represents a spiritual and intellectual tradition quite different from any Western counterparts (Ai, 2010). *The Book of Changes*, devoted to the basic principles and patterns of universal changes, used 64 hexagrams to present all possible combinations of yin and yang aspects in six lines (Capra, 1991). Enhanced by the five-element theory (Wu Xing) during the Han dynasty, the dialectic yin and yang theory became the primary code system for a complex web of space-and-time principles for understanding the nature–human unity. The system also led to the theoretical framework underlying traditional Chinese medicine (TCM; see Ai, 2003; Cheng, 2000; Hammer, 1990).

The ancient TCM perspective organized health phenomena in a system of vital energy movement. In this view, which still influences East Asian descendants, physical and mental health are framed in terms of multilevel Qi patterns, and spiritual, emotional, and behavioral components are seen as central to holistic health and prevention of illness. For example, the energetic concept of heart, where a person's spirit resides, is often referred to as *heart Qi* in TCM (Ai, 1996). It signifies a functional organ that governs both circulation and the mind, including cognition and joyful emotion. This brain-mind-heart framework is echoed in modern psychoneuroimmunology (PNI) research, as shown in a recent study with cardiac patients that offered support for Daoist views (Ai, Pargament, Appel, & Kronfol, 2010). Daoism, along with Confucianism, thus influenced East Asians' emphasis on unity, holism, and harmony, a view that also may help to explain higher rates of somatic symptoms for psychological conditions in Asian Americans (Herrick & Brown, 1999; McCarthy, 2001; Takeuchi, Chun, Gong, & Shen, 2002).

Confucianism

Whereas Daoism helped to shape TCM and informed philosophical views of humanity's place in the universe, Confucianism provided humanistic views that shaped social norms underlying traditional East Asian society (Munro, 1969, 1985). Confucian spirituality cultivates positive characteristics such as benevolence, reverent concentration, social obligation, and wisdom through education (Munro, 1985, 2005). Its founding father, Confucius (Kong Tzu, or Kung-tzu, 551–478 B.C.E.) believed that humans are naturally good and have the potential to love others; humans are thus teachable, improvable, and perfectible through the cultivation of heavenly virtues and the development of moral perfection (Lo, 1999). Han Yu (768–824 C.E.) was an essayist and poet in the Tang Dynasty and a precursor of neo-Confucianism, which merged elements of Confucianism, Daoism, and Buddhism in the Song (960–1279 C.E.) and Ming Dynasties (1368–1644 C.E.). According to Han Yu, unity as conceptualized by Confucianism can be fulfilled when individuals devote their lives, if necessary, to the goal of upholding cardinal moral values. These include *ren* (Humanity) and *yi* (Righteousness) as well as *li* (Ritual), *zhi* (Knowledge), and *xin* (Integrity) (Lo, 1999). Furthermore, other Confucian virtues involve *zhong* (loyalty), *xiao* (filial piety), *jie* (continence), *cheng* (honesty), *shu* (forgiveness), *lian* (honesty and cleanliness), *chi* (shame, judgment, and the sense of right and wrong), *yong* (bravery), *wen* (kindness and gentleness), *liang* (goodness, kindness), *gong* (respect, reverence), *jian* (frugality), and *rang* (modesty, humility). The social emphasis of Confucianism is evident in the fact that many of these virtues are defined in social contexts, whereby they are viewed interpersonally, intergenerationally, intersocial classes, and between one and the state.

In a Confucian framework, moral emotions and conduct, such as humaneness, mutual altruism, and social responsibility, among citizens are seen as imperative to maintain a spiritual, moral, and social relationship with the self, the family, and the noble state (Munro, 2005; Taylor, 1998). For example, the *Analects*, an early Confucian text, promotes reverence or deep mutual respect as an appropriate interpersonal feeling and attitude among fellow humans. Following this attitude, appropriate interpersonal behaviors were organized to a cluster of ritualistic actions, *li* (Munro, 1985; Woodruff, 2001). Confucian virtues set up behavioral norms among people (e.g., respect the elderly) within a state-centered social hierarchy. This hierarchy was ultimately spiritually linked because the person in the highest position, the emperor, was seen as the son or commander of heaven. In contrast to the emperor, gods and ghosts are often respectfully acknowledged but viewed as relatively distant rather than at the center of human discourse (Ai & McCormick, 2010). For example, ancestral spirits are believed to affect descendants' lives in various ways (e.g., a source of inspiration for pursuing education and family honor), which organizes individuals in family chains and keeps such spirits "alive" in the memory of generations to come (Ai & McCormick, 2010). In the absence of theology on personalized gods, humanistic spiritual connections and practices have been most salient in Confucianism. These are seen to promote transcendence through the integration of heaven and humans by means of participation in *li* (i.e., ritual; Woodruff, 2001).

The historical and cultural influence of Confucianism may help to explain the authoritarian God image apparently held by some Korean Americans, which in turn can be linked with their anxiety in Western society (Bjorck et al., 1997). Indeed, such anxiety might be partly due to the possibility that the prosocial solidarity ideology in Confucianism can be at odds with the proindividual autonomy spirit of Protestantism (Weber, 1922). This might also serve as a cross-cultural interpretation for Petts and Joliff's (2008) study linking religious involvement in ethnic churches with greater depression among Asian American adolescents. Specifically, there may be a cultural clash for these teens between the collectivist Asian social norms and the individualist ones that characterize worship settings in the United States.

IMPLICATIONS FOR RESEARCH AND CLINICAL PRACTICE

The Asian-born legacies—Buddhism, Confucianism, Hinduism, and Daoism—have been cited by positive psychologists to enhance their global perspective in conceptualization of human virtues and strengths (Peterson & Seligman, 2004). Yet psychologists have underestimated cross-cultural differences with respect to West, East, and South Asian faith perspectives. A full description of the many distinct features in Asian-born religion and spirituality, such as the dialectic worldview in Daoism (Ai, 2010), are beyond the scope of this chapter. Hopefully, however, this review begins to illustrate that the god-centered perspective of most psychology of religion and spirituality literature does not adequately address the broadly varied systems within Asian faith traditions. By studying similarities and distinctions among different faiths, the psychology of religion and spirituality can begin to encompass a more global perspective.

Whereas Western theology does address the nature of God (an unconditional reality), the psychology of religion and spirituality does not because science could only examine the conditional reality (Ai, 2006). Similarly, whereas Asian philosophies and TCM address the various ideological structures in Asian-born beliefs, the psychology of religion and spirituality likely will not reach this level of meticulous detail (Ai, 2010). Nevertheless, if Asian Americans are to be given the increasing empirical and theoretical attention that is clearly warranted, it will be crucial to investigate the role of different culture-based conceptualizations of the sacred and the sense of deep connection or connectedness.

For Asian Americans, both Western and Asian-born worldviews are important and both must be integrated into overarching theories of the psychology of religion and spirituality. A preliminary example of such integration was discussed here regarding development of the COS scale (Ai, Kastenmüller, et al., 2011; Ai & McCormick, 2010). Findings with this scale suggest the possible dimensionality of spirituality in relation to different sacred and spiritual connections dating back to the world's major cultural origins. Similar to Pargament and Mahoney's (2005) notion about diverse objects of sanctification, Ai and colleagues (2008, 2009, 2010, 2012) have shown this in a sacred feeling, *reverence*, for which secular and religious forms predicted health and other outcomes. Secular reverence reflects a similar worldview to those influencing certain Asian-born faiths, in which significance may be derived from a sense of attachment to sources other than personalized divine forces.

Our summary indicates that within their varied subcultural roots, Asian-born spirituality and religion may have diverse impacts on the values, meaning systems, behavioral guidelines, and emotional health of Asian Americans. Studying the effects of these faith factors will enhance theories and interventions for populations influenced by Asian traditions. Research on Asian Americans' faith-related involvement—be it Western, Asian-born, or combined—remains in its infancy, even though Asian Americans have contributed to American economic prosperity for nearly 200 years (Chen, 1940). There is a clear need for research with representative Asian American samples from a more diverse pool of ethnic and religious or spiritual backgrounds.

Even our research with the NLAAS data set falls short as a comprehensive first step, particularly given problems in the study design. Nevertheless, our pilot findings do suggest that culture-based worldview differences between Asian-born and Western-rooted religions may have important implications for the mental health of Asian Americans. At this point, there is a clear need for more precise investigation on the roles of religion and spirituality in the lives of Asian Americans. This will be a daunting task, given the huge diversity within this ethnic group. For example, almost no research has been done on spirituality in many smaller subgroups that may hold diverse faiths involving beliefs in ghosts and spirits, as is the case for some South Asians and Pacific Islanders (Gehlert, 2006). This fact underscores the need for psychological studies of Asian American religion and spirituality with a multifaceted picture in mind. Such studies must also consider the cultural and historical context of each subgroup, rather than simply treating this ethnic mosaic as if it were monotone. Following are some suggestions for future research:

- Conceptualize spirituality as a multifaceted construct, including perspectives both with and without a central focus on a personal god concept.
- Develop valid measures to assess spiritual constructs specific to Asian-born faiths.
- Establish national databases on Asian American religion and spirituality or enhance existing national surveys with culturally sensitive faith measures.
- Investigate cross-cultural differences in original versus Americanized Asian faiths.
- Compare differential roles of various faiths, West versus East, among Asian Americans.
- Assess how acculturation transforms Asian Americans' religious beliefs and practices.
- Develop a special issue of a major journal on the concepts and roles of Asian-born faiths.

One other area for new research may be the assessment of Buddhist and Daoist mindful practices and their effects on behavioral health. Indeed, Newberg and Iversen (2003), using advanced brain imaging, have offered a model to explain the brain mechanisms underlying the experience of certain Asian-based mindful practices. Other researchers have also speculated on their biological correlates (Herzog et al., 1990–1991; Infante et al., 2001; Ingvar, 1994). These preliminary studies suggest the potential benefit of investigating how such Asian-born practices might promote mental and behavioral health in Asian descendants and others. Mindfulness has been gaining increasing popularity among psychologists (Grossman, Niemann, Schmidt, & Walach, 2004). The perspectives and practices on mindfulness are more complex in Asian-born faiths. As such, despite potential benefits, these practices also could carry some risks if not provided appropriately (see Ai, 2010). Mindfulness represents a potentially fruitful yet challenging area for future research.

Deepened understanding of Asian American faiths will have implications for clinical intervention and behavioral health. Asian Americans often hesitate to seek services for emotional needs (Cheung & Snowden, 1990; Ying & Hu, 1994). Their low utilization is partly attributable to the lack of appropriate mental health services with culturally competent providers (Huang, Appel, & Ai, 2011; Okazaki, 2000; Takeuchi & Kramer, 1995; Takeuchi et al., 1998). Although it could be argued that Asian Americans simply have low levels of mental health problems, low levels of reported problems may be partly due to the lack of sensitivity in psychological instruments to the influence of Daoist mind-body-spirit holism on mental health (Ai, 2010). Also, there may be high rates of somatization in Asian Americans, as noted earlier. This Asian American perspective should be considered by those developing the fifth edition of the *Diagnostic and Statistical Manual of Mental Disorders*, especially regarding diagnoses including psychosomatic and other psychological symptoms (Kessler et al., 1994).

To improve provider–client relationships, clinical psychologists and health providers need to better understand Asian models of physical and mental health. For example, in Daoist spirituality and dialectics, yin-yang and five-element systems are used to map changing patterns of energetic movement in natural phenomena and human health (Ai, 2010; Huang et al., 2011). Cultural sensitivity will require a basic grasp of these concepts, given their prevalence in many Asian Americans' understandings of health. In TCM, for example, the five elements are paired with five vital organs expressing specific emotions: *Wood*/Liver-Anger, *Fire*/Heart-Joy, *Earth*/Spleen-Contemplation/Concentration, *Metal*/Lung/Grief, and *Water*/Kidney-Fear/Sadness (Ai, 2003). The health of each hosting organ thus becomes inseparable from its paired emotion, and illness conditions may be improved through mindful practice for emotional balance and healing (Ai, 1996, 2003, 2010). The circulating effects among the five systems also provide major guidance for health- and emotion-related interventions in the Eastern perspective. Seemingly irrational in terms of anatomy from a Western perspective, these symbolically interactive patterns fit within the combined system-view of ancient TCM and modern PNI (Hammer, 1990; Temkin, 1991). As with Buddhism, the Daoist perspective on emotional health does not simply reflect different nomenclature; it reflects a different worldview. Further description of Daoist interventions is beyond the scope of this chapter (see Ai, 2010).

As another example, the role of virtues and character strengths in Confucianism seems particularly relevant to positive psychology (Peterson & Seligman, 2004). Confucian teaching encourages moral self-enhancement to reach the higher stage of the *noble gentleman*, compared with the lower stage of *layman* (Munro, 1985). Within a collectivist family-oriented culture, in-group harmony is a major focus of such spirituality. The influence of Confucian education on East Asian descendants (e.g., academic excellence among Asian American students) was noted by the developmental psychologist Harold Stevenson more than a decade ago (Stevenson & Stigler, 1994). Focusing on these positive aspects may enhance cross-cultural counseling and clinical intervention related to motivation and psychological well-being of Asian Americans, especially youth. Compared with positive psychology, however, the cultural difference in Confucian ethics lies in its emphasis on social relations and interpersonal support, rather than on individual traits.

Clinicians should remember that such a collective emphasis can be beneficial. For example, Asian American women born outside the United States (who presumably have more ties to traditional social networks and support) were less likely to experience a mental disorder than their more individualistic U.S.-born counterparts (Abe-Kim et al., 2007). Conversely, for some Asian Americans, behavioral health might be negatively affected by cross-cultural conflicts between the collectivist Confucianism of older adults and the individualistic orientation in U.S. society—a problem that could be particularly relevant for those who are younger or those transitioning between cultures.

References

Abe-Kim, J., Takeuchi, D. T., Hong, S., Zane, N., Sue, S., Spencer, M. S., . . . Alegría, M. (2007). Use of mental health-related services among immigrant and US-born Asian Americans: Results from the National Latino Asian American Study. *American Journal of Public Health, 97*, 91–98. doi:10.2105/AJPH.2006.098541

Ai, A. L. (1990). *Ancient thinkers (Plato, Aristotle, and Christian thinkers) in the Western tradition meet ancient thinkers (Confucius, Lao Zi, and Mo Zi) in the Eastern tradition*. Unpublished manuscript.

Ai, A. L. (1996). Psychosocial adjustment and health care practices following coronary artery bypass surgery (CABG). *Dissertation Abstracts International, Section B: The Sciences and Engineering, 57*(6), 4078.

Ai, A. L. (2000). Spiritual well-being, spiritual growth, and spiritual care for the aged: A cross-faith and interdisciplinary effort. *Journal of Religious Gerontology, 11*, 3–28. doi:10.1300/J078v11n02_02

Ai, A. L. (2003). Assessing mental health in clinical study on Qigong: Between scientific investigation and holistic perspectives. *Seminars in Integrative Medicine, 1*, 112–121. doi:10.1016/S1543-1150(03)00022-X

Ai, A. L. (2006). Faith matters, empirical research, and professional practice: Current gaps and future steps. *Arête, 30*, 30–41.

Ai, A. L. (2010). Qigong. In M. S. Micozzi (Ed.), *Fundamentals of complementary and integrative medicine* (pp. 438–454). St. Louis, MO: Elsevier Health Sciences.

Ai, A. L., Bjorck, J. P., Huang, B., & Appel, H. B. (2012). *Religious attendance and major depression among Asian Americans in the national database: The mediation of social support*. Manuscript submitted for publication.

Ai, A. L., Kastenmüller, A., Wink, P., Tice, T. N., Fischer, P., & Frey, D. (2011). *The connection of soul (COS) with a transcendental world: A cross-cultural assessment tool*. Manuscript submitted for publication.

Ai, A. L., & McCormick, T. R. (2010). Increasing diversity of Americans' faiths alongside baby boomers' aging: Implications for health chaplains, intervention. *Journal of Health Care Chaplaincy, 16*, 24–41. doi:10.1080/08854720903496126

Ai, A. L., Pargament, K., Appel, H., & Kronfol, Z. (2010). Depression following open-heart surgery: A path model involving interleukin-6, spiritual struggle, and hope under pre-operative distress. *Journal of Clinical Psychology, 66*, 1057–1075. doi:10.1002/jclp.20716

Ai, A. L., Park, C., Huang, B., Rodgers, W., & Tice, T. N. (2007). Psychosocial mediation of religious coping: A prospective study of short-term psychological distress after cardiac surgery. *Personality and Social Psychology Bulletin, 33*, 867–882. doi:10.1177/0146167207301008

Ai, A. L., Park, C., & Shearer, M. (2008). Spiritual or religious involvement related to end-of-life decision in patients undergoing coronary artery bypass surgery. *International Journal of Psychiatry in Medicine, 38*, 113–132. doi:10.2190/PM.38.1.k

Ai, A. L., Tice, N., & Kelsey, C. L. (2009). Coping after 9/11: Deep interconnectedness and struggle in posttraumatic stress and growth. In M. Morgan (Ed.), *The impact of 9/11 on psychology and education. The day that changed everything* (pp. 115–138). New York, NY: Palgrave Macmillan.

Ai, A. L., Tice, T. N., Peterson, C., & Huang, B. (2005). Prayers, spiritual support, and positive attitudes in coping with the 9–11 national crisis. *Journal of Personality, 73*, 763–791. doi:10.1111/j.1467-6494.2005.00328.x

Ai, A. L., Wink, P., & Shearer, M. (2011). Secular reverence predicts shorter hospital length of stay among middle-aged and older patients following open-heart surgery. *Journal of Behavioral Medicine, 34*, 532–541. doi:10.1007/s10865-011-9334-8

Ai, A. L., Wink, P., Tice, T. N., Bolling, S. F., Wasin, A., & Shearer, M. (2009). Prayer and reverence in naturalistic, aesthetic, and socio-moral contexts predicted fewer complications following coronary artery bypass. *Journal of Behavioral Medicine, 32*, 570–581. doi:10.1007/s10865-009-9228-1

Alegría, M., Takeuchi, D., Canino, G., Duan, N., Shrout, P., Meng, X. L., . . . Gong, F. (2004). Considering context, place and culture: The National Latino and Asian American Study. *International Journal of Methods in Psychiatric Research, 13*, 208–220. doi:10.1002/mpr.178

Appel, H. B., Ai, A. L., Huang, B., & Nicdao, E. G. (2012). *Detrimental effects of discrimination on mental health in Asian Americans: Counteracting roles of religious involvement.* Manuscript submitted for publication.

Bjorck, J. P., Cuthbertson, W., Thurman, J., & Lee, Y. S. (2001). Ethnicity, coping, and distress among Korean-, Filipino-, and Caucasian-Americans. *Journal of Social Psychology, 141*, 421–442. doi:10.1080/00224540109600563

Bjorck, J. P., Lee, Y. S., & Cohen, L. H. (1997). Control beliefs and faith as stress moderators for Korean- versus Caucasian-American Protestants. *American Journal of Community Psychology, 25*, 61–72. doi:10.1023/A:1024645824829

Buber, M. (1958). *I and thou (Ich und Du)*. New York, NY: Charles Scribner's Sons. (Original work published 1923)

Capra, F. (1991). *The Tao of physics: An exploration of the parallels between modern physics and Eastern mysticism.* Boston, MA: Shambhala.

Chan, W. T. (1963). *A source book in Chinese philosophy* (p. 204). Princeton, NJ: Princeton University Press.

Chen, T. (1940). *Emigrant communities in South China.* New York, NY: Institute of Pacific Relations.

Cheng, J. T. (2000). Review: Drug therapy in Chinese traditional medicine. *Journal of Clinical Pharmacology, 40*, 445–450. doi:10.1177/00912700022009198

Cheung, F. K., & Snowden, L. (1990). Community mental health and ethnic minority populations. *Community Mental Health Journal, 26*, 277–291. doi:10.1007/BF00752778

Dilthey, W. (1991). Introduction to the human sciences. In R. A. Makkreel & F. Rodi (Eds.), *The formation of the historical world in the human sciences* (pp. 101–159). Princeton, NJ: Princeton University Press.

Diwan, S., Jonnalagadda, S., & Balaswamy, S. (2004). Resources predicting positive and negative affect during the experience of stress: A study of older Asian Indian immigrants in the United States. *The Gerontologist, 44*, 605–614. doi:10.1093/geront/44.5.605

Durkheim, E. (1965). *The elementary forms of the religious life.* New York, NY: Free Press. (Original work published 1915)

Ebrey, P. B. (1999). *The Cambridge illustrated history of China.* Cambridge, MA: Cambridge University Press.

Emerson, M. O., Sikkink, D., & James, A. D. (2010). The Panel study on American religion and ethnicity: Background, methods, and selected results. *Journal for the Scientific Study of Religion, 49*, 162–171. doi:10.1111/j.1468-5906.2009.01498.x

Epstein, R. B. (2003). *Buddhist Text Translation Society's Buddhism A to Z.* Burlingame, CA: Buddhist Text Translation Society.

Fiala, W. E., Bjorck, J. P., & Gorsuch, R. (2002). The Religious Support Scale: Construction, validation and cross-validation. *American Journal of Community Psychology, 30*, 761–786. doi:10.1023/A:1020264718397

Fischer, P., Ai, A. L., Aydin, N., Haslam, A., & Frey, D. (2010). The relationship between religious identity and preferred coping strategies: An examination of the relative importance of interpersonal and intrapersonal coping in Muslim and Christian faiths. *Review of General Psychology, 14*, 365–381. doi:10.1037/a0021624

Fong, R. (2000). A history of Asian Americans. In S. M. Furuto, R. Biswas, D. Chung, K. Murase, & F. Ross-Sheriff (Eds.), *Social work practice with Asian Americans* (pp. 3–26). Newbury Park, CA: Sage.

Furuto, S. M., & Murase, K. (1992). Asian Americans in the future. In S. M. Furuto, R. Biswas, D. K. Chung, K. Murase, & F. Ross-Sheriff (Eds.), *Social work practice with Asian Americans* (pp. 240–253). Newbury Park, CA: Sage.

Gehlert, S. (2006). Communication in health care. In S. Gehlert & T. A. Brown (Eds.), *Handbook of health and social work* (pp. 252–281). Hoboken, NJ: Wiley.

Gorsuch, R. L. (1988). Psychology of religion. *Annual Review of Psychology, 39*, 201–221. doi:10.1146/annurev.ps.39.020188.001221

Grossman, P., Niemann, L., Schmidt, S., & Walach, H. (2004). Mindfulness-based stress reduction and health benefits: A meta-analysis. *Journal of Psychosomatic Research, 57*, 35–43. doi:10.1016/S0022-3999(03)00573-7

Groth-Marnat, G. (1992). Buddhism and mental health: A comparative analysis. In J. F. Schumaker (Ed.), *Religion and mental health* (pp. 270–280). New York, NY: Oxford University Press.

Guest, K. J. (2003). *God in Chinatown: Religion and survival in New York's evolving immigrant community*. New York, NY: New York University Press.

Hammer, L. (1990). *Dragon rises, red bird flies: Psychology, energy, and Chinese medicine*. Barrytown, NY: Station Hill Press.

Heine, S. J., & Lehman, D. (1997). The cultural construction of self-enhancement: An examination of group self-enhancement and group-serving bias. *Journal of Personality and Social Psychology, 72*, 1268–1283. doi:10.1037/0022-3514.72.6.1268

Herrick, C., & Brown, H. N. (1999). Mental disorders and syndromes found among Asians residing in the United States. *Issues in Mental Health Nursing, 20*, 275–296.

Herzog, H., Lele, T., Kuwert, T., Langen, K. J., Kops, E. R., & Feinendegen, L. E. (1990–1991). Changed pattern of regional glucose metabolism during yoga meditative relaxation. *Neuropsychobiology, 23*, 182–187. doi:10.1159/000119450

Huang, B., Appel, H., & Ai, A. L. (2011). The effects of discrimination and acculturation on service seeking satisfaction for Latina and Asian American women: Implications for mental health professions. *Social Work in Public Health, 26*, 46–59. doi:10.1080/10911350903341077

Humphrey, P. (1982). Jewish in China. *Religion, state, and society, 10*, 330–331.

Hurh, W. M. (2011). Korean immigrants. In R. Bayor (Ed.), *Multicultural America: An encyclopedia of the newest Americans* (pp. 1329–1396). Santa Barbara, CA: Greenwood Press.

Hurh, W. M., & Kim, K. C. (1990). Religious participation of Korean immigrants in the United States. *Journal for the Scientific Study of Religion, 29*, 19–34. doi:10.2307/1387028

Infante, J. R., Torres-Avisbal, M., Pinel, P., Vallejo, J. A., Peran, F., Gonzales, F., . . . Latre, J. M. (2001). Catecholamine levels in practitioners of the transcendental meditation technique. *Physiology and Behavior, 72*, 141–146. doi:10.1016/S0031-9384(00)00386-3

Ingvar, D. H. (1994). The will of the brain: Cerebral correlates of willful acts. *Journal of Theoretical Biology, 171*, 7–12. doi:10.1006/jtbi.1994.1206

Kessler, R. C., Berglund, P., Chiu, W. T., Demler, O., Heeringa, S., Hiripi, E., . . . Zheng, H. (2004). The U.S. National Comorbidity Survey Replication (NCS-R): An overview of designing and field procedures. *International Journal of Methods in Psychiatric Research, 13*, 69–92. doi:10.1002/mpr.167

Kessler, R. C., McGonagle, K. A., Zhao, S., Nelson, C. B., Hughes, M., Eshleman, S., . . . Kendler, K. S. (1994). Lifetime and 12-month prevalence of DSM-III-R psychiatric disorders in the U.S. Results from the National Comorbidity Survey. *Archives of General Psychiatry, 51*, 8–19. doi:10.1001/archpsyc.1994.03950010008002

Koenig, H. G., McCullough, M., & Larson, D. B. (2001). *Handbook of religion and health*. New York, NY: Oxford University Press. doi:10.1093/acprof:oso/9780195118667.001.0001

Krause, N. (2006a). Church-based social support and mortality. *The Journals of Gerontology, Series B: Psychological Sciences and Social Sciences, 61*, S140–S146. doi:10.1093/geronb/61.3.S140

Krause, N. (2006b). Exploring the stress-buffering effects of church-based social support and secular social support on health in late life. *The Journals of Gerontology, Series B: Psychological Sciences and Social Sciences, 61*, S35–S43. doi:10.1093/geronb/61.1.S35

Lewis, M. M. (2001). Spirituality, counseling, and elderly: An introduction to the spiritual life review. *Journal of Adult Development, 8*, 231–240. doi:10.1023/A:1011390528828

Liao, S. J. (1992). Acupuncture for low back pain in *Huang Di Nei Jing Su Wen* (Yellow emperor's classic of internal medicine book of common questions). *Acupuncture and Electro-Therapeutics Research, 17*, 249–258.

Lo, P. C. (1999). *Confucian ethics of death with dignity and its contemporary relevance*. Society of Christian Ethics. Retrieved from http://arts.hkbu.edu.hk/~pclo/e5.pdf

Mattis, J. S., & Watson, C. R. (2009). Religion and spirituality. In B. M. Tynes, S. O. Utsey, & H. A. Neville (Eds.), *Handbook of African American psychology* (pp. 91–102). Thousand Oaks, CA: Sage.

McCarthy, M. (2001). U.S. mental-health system fails to serve minorities, says U.S. Surgeon General. *Lancet, 358*, 733. doi:10.1016/S0140-6736(01)05940-2

Munro, D. J. (1969). *Concept of man in early China.* Ann Arbor: Center for Chinese Studies, University of Michigan.

Munro, D. J. (1985). *Individualism and Holism: Studies in Confucian and Taoist values.* Ann Arbor: Center for Chinese Studies, University of Michigan.

Munro, D. J. (1988). *Images of human nature: A Sung portrait.* Princeton, NJ: Princeton University Press.

Munro, D. J. (1996). *The imperial style of inquiry: Twentieth-century Chinese.* Ann Arbor: Center for Chinese Studies, University of Michigan.

Munro, D. J. (2005). *A Chinese ethics for the new century: The Ch'ien Mu Lecture on History and Culture and other essays on science and Confucian ethics.* Hong Kong: Chinese University Press.

Myers, J. E., Sweeney, T. J., & Witmer, J. M. (2000). The wheel of wellness counseling for wellness: A holistic model for treatment planning. *Journal of Counseling and Development, 78,* 251–266. doi:10.1002/j.1556-6676.2000.tb01906.x

Neubauer, A. (1895). Jewish in China. *Jewish Quarterly Review, 7,* 398–417. doi:10.2307/1449924

Newberg, A. B., & Iversen, J. (2003). The neural basis of the complex mental task of meditation: Neurotransmitter and neurochemical considerations. *Medical Hypotheses, 61,* 282–292. doi:10.1016/S0306-9877(03)00175-0

Okazaki, S. (2000). Treatment delay among Asian American patients with severe mental illness. *American Journal of Orthopsychiatry, 70,* 58–64. doi:10.1037/h0087751

Oyserman, D., Coon, H., & Kemmelmeier, M. (2002). Rethinking individualism and collectivism: Evaluations of theoretical assumptions and meta-analysis. *Psychological Bulletin, 128,* 3–72. doi:10.1037/0033-2909.128.1.3

Pargament, K. I. (1997). *The psychology of religion and coping: Theory, research, and practice.* New York, NY: Guilford Press.

Pargament, K. I., Koenig, H. G., & Perez, L. M. (2000). The many methods of religious coping: Development and initial validation of the RCOPE. *Journal of Clinical Psychology, 56,* 519–543. doi:10.1002/(SICI)1097-4679(200004)56:4<519::AID-JCLP6>3.0.CO;2-1

Pargament, K. I., & Mahoney, A. (2005). Sacred matters: Sanctification as a vital topic for the psychology of religion and spirituality. *The International Journal for the Psychology of Religion, 15,* 179–198. doi:10.1207/s15327582ijpr1503_1

Peterson, C., & Seligman, M. E. P. (2004). *Character strengths and virtues: A handbook and classification.* New York, NY: American Psychological Association & Oxford University Press.

Petts, R. J., & Joliff, A. (2008). Religion and adolescent depression: The impact of race and gender. *Review of Religious Research, 49,* 395–414.

Pew Forum. (2008). *U.S. Religious Landscape Survey.* Retrieved from http://religions.pewforum.org

Pew Forum. (2009). *Many Americans mix multiple faiths: Eastern, new age beliefs widespread.* Retrieved from http://pewforum.org/docs/?DocID=490

Reid, A., & Gilsenan, M. (2007). Islam and cultural modernity: In pursuit of democratic pluralis in Asia. In A. Reid & M. Gilsenan (Eds.), *Islamic legitimacy in a plural Asia* (pp. 28–52). New York, NY: Routledge.

Rosenthal, S. (Trans.). (2007). *Tao Te Ching. Resource document. Taoism virtual library.* Retrieved from http://www.v1-site.org/taoism/ttcstan3.html

Smart, N. (1999). *World philosophies.* New York, NY: Macmillan.

Spence, J. D. (1996). *God's Chinese son.* New York, NY: Norton.

Stevenson, H. W., & Stigler, H. (1994). *The learning gap.* New York, NY: Simon & Schuster.

Sue, D. W., & Sue, D. (2003). *Counseling the culturally diverse: Theory and practice* (4th ed.). New York, NY: Wiley.

Takeuchi, D. T., Chun, C. A., Gong, F., & Shen, H. (2002). Cultural expressions of distress. *Health: An Interdisciplinary Journal for the Social Study of Health, Illness, and Medicine, 6,* 221–235.

Takeuchi, D. T., Chung, R. C., Lin, K. M., Shen, H., Kurasaki, K., Chun, C., & Sue, S. (1998). Lifetime and twelve-month prevalence rates of major depressive episodes and dysthymia among Chinese Americans in Los Angeles. *American Journal of Psychiatry, 155,* 1407–1414.

Takeuchi, D. T., & Kramer, E. J. (1995). Mental health services research in Asian Americans. What do we know and where are we going? *Western Journal of Medicine, 176,* 225–228.

Takeuchi, D. T., Zane, N., Hong, S., Chae, D. H., Gong, F., Gee, G. C., & Sue, S. (2007). Immigration-related factors and mental disorders among Asian Americans. *American Journal of Public Health, 97,* 84–90. doi:10.2105/AJPH.2006.088401

Taylor, R. L. (1998). The religious character of the Confucian tradition. *Philosophy East and West, 48,* 80–107. doi:10.2307/1399926

Temkin, O. (1991). *Hippocrates in a world of pagans and Christians.* Baltimore, MD: John Hopkins University Press.

U.S. Census Bureau. (2012). *The Asian population, 2012.* Retrieved from http://www.census.gov/prod/cen2010/briefs/c2010br-11.pdf

Wang, P. S., Lane, M., Olfson, M., Pincus, H. A., Wells, K. B., & Kessler, R. C. (2005). Twelve-month use of mental health services in the United States: Results from the National Comorbidity Survey Replication. *Archives of General Psychiatry, 62*, 629–640. doi:10.1001/archpsyc.62.6.629

Weber, M. (1922).*The sociology of religion*. Boston, MA: Beacon Press.

Weber, M. (1959). *The religion of China* (H. Gerth, Ed.). New York, NY: Free Press.

Weisz, J. R., Rothbaum, F. M., & Blackburn, T. C. (1984). Standing out and standing in: The psychology of control in America and Japan. *American Psychologist, 39*, 955–969. doi:10.1037/0003-066X.39.9.955

Willoughby, M. T., Cadigan, R. J., Burchinal, M., & Skinner, D. (2008). An evaluation of the psychometric properties and criterion validity of the Religious Social [sic] Support Scale. *Journal for the Scientific Study of Religion, 47*, 147–159. doi:10.1111/j.1468-5906.2008.00398.x

Woodruff, P. (2001). *Reverence: Renewing a forgotten virtue*. New York, NY: Oxford University Press.

Worthington, E. L., Jr. (2010, August). *Positive psychology and the psychology of religion and spirituality: A match made in heaven?* Paper presented at the 118th Annual Convention of the American Psychological Association, San Diego, CA.

Yang, F. (1999). *Chinese Christians in America: Conversion, assimilation, and adhesive identities*. University Park, PA: Penn State Press.

Yi, G. H. (2007). Ethnic support, religious support, gratitude, and psychological functioning in Korean American Christians. *Dissertation Abstracts International: Section B: The Sciences and Engineering, 68*(4-B), 2678.

Yi, G. H., & Bjorck, J. P. (2012). *Religious support and psychological functioning in Korean American Protestant Christians*. Manuscript submitted for publication.

Ying, Y. W., & Hu, L. (1994). Public outpatient mental health services: Use and outcome among Asian Americans. *American Journal of Orthopsychiatry, 64*, 448–455. doi:10.1037/h0079549

Zhuang Zi. (1968). Qi wu lun. In B. Watson (Trans.), *The complete works of Chuang Tzu*. New York, NY: Columbia University Press.

Chapter 33

RELIGION AND SPIRITUALITY IN LATINO LIFE IN THE UNITED STATES

Joan Koss-Chioino

> The story, belief, image and cultural memory of our Lady of Guadalupe . . . helps Mexican Americans envision a different world. . . . the marginalized have a special relation with God, one that is especially meaningful for the people who have no other relationship with anything powerful in this world. (Rodriguez, 1994, p. 131)

This chapter summarizes information on religion and spirituality in the lives of Latinos. *Latino* is a label for the Spanish-speaking population of the United States, either born in the United States or descendants of persons from Latin America or the Hispanic Caribbean; they are also referred to as *Hispanics*. Some authors reserve the term *Latino* for persons of Latin American descent born in the United States, which fails to account for immigrants and mixed immigrant and first-generation families. This chapter reviews literature and selected studies on religiousness and spirituality among Latinos. The aim will be to construct an integrative, descriptive paradigm to identify what is known and what is important to know in terms of the implications of religiousness and spirituality for the health and well-being of Latinos.

Latinos are the largest and fastest growing ethnic minority group in the United States. As reported by the U.S. Census Bureau (2004), about 44 million persons identify as Hispanic. Although Latinos have high rates of some emotional disorders, they show low utilization of mental health services (Vega et al., 1998). The situation is complex, in part, because of two factors: First, there is great cultural diversity among Latinos, who are (or descend from) Puerto Rican, Mexican, Cuban, Dominican, Central American, and Latin American origins. Adaptation, education, geographic regional clusters and processes of acculturation and ethnic identification differ significantly among persons from these varied countries of origin, and within and across generations born in the United States. Moreover, stresses surrounding immigration are very different for undocumented Latinos compared with those who are citizens (Puerto Ricans) or who hold valid work permits (mostly Mexicans). The concept of race, as defined by U.S. social norms, can divide cultural groups and create more issues, such as identification with African Americans because of skin color. Yet these cultures share important similarities. For example, they share similar colonial histories in their countries of origin, and they may share similar problems in adapting to the U.S. environment. The related phenomena of ethnic identity formation and acculturation often mediate the role of religion or spirituality in Latino lives, in part by creating stressors that lead to the use of spiritual healing practices or affiliation with churches.

Cultural patterns (with *culture* defined as shared concepts and traditions leading to shared experiences) influence spiritual practices in the United States (see Chapter 13 in this volume). Cultural patterns also shape religious preferences and behavior in ways that are different from what has been described for most "middle" Americans (e.g., Pargament, 2007; Zinnbauer & Pargament, 2005).

DOI: 10.1037/14045-033
APA Handbook of Psychology, Religion, and Spirituality: Vol. 1. Context, Theory, and Research, K. I. Pargament (Editor-in-Chief)
Copyright © 2013 by the American Psychological Association. All rights reserved.

Warner (1993) has suggested that life in the United States, especially for second and third generations, transmutes ethnicity into religion, which in turn can reaffirm the ethnic identity of group members. This process may not be evident for all Latino Catholics, Protestants, or Evangelicals, but it does apply to what has been termed *communitarian spirituality* (Díaz-Stevens, 1996). Communitarian spirituality can refer to events, such as community and family celebrations of the Day of the Dead by Mexicans and Mexican Americans. The term also can refer to neighborhood-oriented healing "cults," such as Spiritism (identified as Puerto Rican or Brazilian but has other Latino adherents, especially of Venezuelan descent; Harwood, 1977; Koss-Chioino, 1992), Mesa Blanca (mostly among NiyorRicans and other Latinos in New York and Chicago; Pérez y Mena, 1991), and Santería (identified as Cuban but includes Puerto Ricans and other Latinos; Gonzalez-Wippler, 1989). Some Mexican Americans utilize the healing practices of curers (Curanderas), who use herbs, massage, card reading (for diagnostic and prognostic purposes), and prayer (Trotter & Chavira, 1981).

The definitions of religiousness and spirituality in the introductory chapter of this handbook are used here as general guidelines. Discussions of the literature reviewed in this chapter are based on author understandings and definitions of these terms, which are described where necessary to facilitate understanding of Latino perspectives. Despite carefully constructed guidelines for approaching the topics of religiousness and spirituality, a review of the literature suggests that relatively little research has responded to the mandate of a cultural perspective.

PRACTICING RELIGION AND SPIRITUALITY

Religious behavior among Latinos includes participation and dedicated involvement in Catholic, Protestant, and Evangelical churches (e.g., Pentecostal, Baptist) by subgroups that can differ by gender, age, or culture of origin. (Note, however, that mixed groups of Spanish speakers often share churches where Spanish-speaking priests or ministers are present.) Popular individual, familial, and community religiousness and spirituality are also integral to Latino life.

This prompts discussion first of home- and community-based religious and spiritual practices, the latter geared toward satisfying individual needs (especially by women) to maintain contact with God and certain spirits (e.g., saints, dead relatives) as part of daily life. Such rituals, described further in the following sections, are often used to cope with distress (see Chapters 18 and 19 in this volume). Common stresses include accommodation to a *frio* (cold) environment along with denigrating and difficult social and economic conditions in which family and community patterns are radically altered; worse, dark skin can attract blatant racial prejudice (Koss-Chioino & Vargas, 1999). Yet Latino immigrants (both adults and youth) suffer less from emotional disorders and substance abuse than do second- and third-generation Latinos (Comas-Diaz, 2006; Rios-Ellis et al., 2005; Vega et al., 1998), which may partly reflect the prevalence and significance of home-based and community ritual practices. In this regard, there is a need for well-designed studies of familial and community religious coping.

Catholic churches maintained a missionary attitude toward Latino immigrants in Southwestern urban areas and Latino communities for much of the 20th century, providing social services and an assimilatory policy. In the latter half of the century, these churches made strides toward cultural relevance through such means as Spanish-speaking priests and Spanish language masses (Stevens-Arroyo, 1998). Catholic, Protestant, and some Pentecostal churches provide material assistance and counseling. Furthermore, immigrants who adapt well may have greater resilience based on frequent spiritual practices (inside or outside of established churches), which in turn may promote constructive responses to difficult social and economic environments.

Formal Religion

The Hispanic Churches in American Public Life Survey found that 93% of Latinos identify as Christians, 6% have no religious preference, and fewer than 1% are agnostic or atheist. Of the 93% who identify as

Christians, 70% self-identify as Catholic and 23% as Protestant. Among Protestants, almost 8% identify with Evangelical and Pentecostal–Charismatic traditions, 4.5% with mainline Protestant traditions, and 3% with alternative traditions such as Jehovah's Witnesses and Mormonism (Espinosa, 2008). The survey found that 26% of Latino Catholics reported a "born-again" experience with Jesus Christ, 86% of these through participation in the Pentecostal–Charismatic movement. In another survey, 37% of Latinos self-identified as born again, which is of interest if this phenomenon is viewed as an attempt to create a new way of life, either as part of adaptation to the United States or as a panacea for life stress (Espinosa, 2004). Espinosa (2008) stated that despite the "rich tradition of Catholic spirituality. . . and spiritual formation in the parochial schools, Latino Protestants were significantly more likely to affirm and engage in spiritual practices than their Catholic counterparts" (p. 212). The prevalence of individual or church-based spiritual practices may be significant only in the context of observations or personal accounts of how they are used as coping mechanisms. It is important to consider the personal meanings of such practices as well as the circumstances that prompt their use.

Other functions of religion include its effects on education and marriage. One survey (Espinosa, 2008) found that Latino Protestants showed greater education achievement than Latino Catholics, including higher high school graduation rates and college involvement. This disparity may reflect the fact that Latino Catholics are more likely to be immigrants (54% vs. 33%). About 50% of Latinos reported being married, and the survey showed a positive link between religiousness and marriage. Latino Protestants were more likely to be married than Latino Catholics, suggesting greater family stability. It has been widely reported that, within the United States and Latin America, conversion to Evangelical sects favors stable marriages mediated by mandated behavior changes, such as abstinence from drugs and alcohol among men (Brusco, 1995). More studies of diverse subgroups of U.S. Latinos, including those emphasizing conversion, would add to scientific understanding of religion as a means of coping with stress.

Intertwining of Religious and Spiritual Practices

Religion and spirituality are intertwined in Latino life. Both are found at four social levels in which many persons participate regularly: churches, communities and families, individuals (in groups or alone), and small groups or dyads in which popular healing takes place. At each level, rituals and practices stem from a worldview that may include diverse spiritual elements: the Holy Spirit as an active presence, spirits of deceased relatives, mythic personages, saints, or famous deceased historical beings, any of whom may respond to supplicants asking for help or protection. Frequent appeals are made to God the Father, the Virgin Mary, and Jesus Christ. A host of popular saints (including some not canonized by the Catholic Church) occupy important niches (literally and figuratively) in Mexican lives, not only for the sacraments and as objects of prayer during distress, but also for dangerous undertakings such as U.S. border crossings (Borden, 2003). For Mexicans and Mexican Americans, the Virgin of Guadalupe is the most popular religious and cultural image. She is a Catholic symbol with rays of sun surrounding her, the moon under her feet, and a crown of 12 stars. She is said to have appeared miraculously on the cloak of a poor peasant, Juan Diego, in 1531, and was noted to have Nahuatl symbols by indigenous peoples: a blue-green cape for the divine couple, a pregnancy belt with a cross-shaped image below to symbolize the universe, and maguey spines (instead of sun rays). In addition, pilgrimages to places where saints have appeared (*sanctuarios*) are a widespread individual, family, or church-group practice. Although inherited from Spanish folk and formal religious traditions as well as indigenous traditions, they find their own expressions in the United States. One example is an old *sanctuario* (from the time of the early Spanish settlements) dedicated to healing in Chimayo, New Mexico. It is visited on Good Friday by hundreds of the faithful, who often walk for days from many parts of the state, and who offer promises to El Niño Atocha if he provides the cures they seek.

For young children, spirituality frequently begins with their leave-taking from home, a process that is initiated by asking for and receiving God's blessings

(*Dios te bendiga*) from a maternal or paternal figure. Most children learn about the Catholic sacraments when they are 7 or 8 years old and when they are confirmed. Adults go to church when in distress, but most also engage in a ritual of daily prayer, often to the Mother of God (or another saintly being) at a home altar containing statues of the Virgin and the saints. In the case of Spiritists or Santeros, healer icons, such as Native American medicine men, are the altar occupants.

Community involvement is evident in small stores (*botanicas*) in Latino markets or shopping areas, such as those of East Los Angeles, which sell iconic statues and prints as well as healing herbs, oils, candles, perfumed alcohols, and prayer sheets; the *botanica* owners often give advice as well (Viladrich, 2006). These stores also sell the materials for the important family rituals, such as the Mexican Day of the Dead celebrations that memorialize dead relatives.

DEFINING AND ASSESSING LATINO SPIRITUALITY

Defining Latino spirituality is challenging given the diverse practices and ideas among different groups. Studies require carefully constructed methods that are culturally responsive, but few to date have attained this level of understanding. A positive example is a recent study of Latina nurses from the three main Latino cultural streams by Campesino and Schwartz (2006). These researchers used systematic methods to develop a new instrument, the Latino Spiritual Perspectives Scale (LSPS). They framed religion in terms of behavioral activities, whereas spirituality was framed as an exploration of "meanings ascribed to events, self-transcendence, and the intimate relationship of an individual's particular conception of a universal being or consciousness" (p.70). The nurses scored high on the LSPS, suggesting a "strong spiritual perspective in their lives." Church attendance was related to total LSPS scores, but the strongest relationship to total scores was with personal prayer. The sample, however, was weighted toward Puerto Rican female nurses (47%) and women with higher education, making it hard to generalize to larger, more diverse groups in Puerto Rico or the United States.

The LSPS and the Spiritual Perspectives Scale were also given to Latino and non-Latino college students in Arizona (84% Mexican Americans and smaller numbers of Central Americans, Puerto Ricans, South Americans, and Cubans); non-Latinos were not identified ethnically (Campesino & Schwartz, 2009). When compared with non-Latino students, Latino students scored higher on both measures of spirituality (one "theologically" Latino and reflective of Latino cultural values; the other more "universal"), especially on items assessing the frequency of church attendance and personal prayer addressing God. These studies offer innovative methods to confirm the hypothesis that spirituality is a basic Latino value.

Popular Spiritual Practices

The term *popular spiritual practices* refers here to independent spirit healing systems (Espiritismo, Santería, Curanderismo) established in many Latino communities, partly as a way of coping in the U.S. social environment. These groups are sometimes referred to as healing "cults," for lack of a better term for independent spiritual groups that disavow "religion" as a label. Ritual processes differ among these spiritual groups, as do the entities believed to appear in healing sessions. Anecdotal and research accounts suggest that such groups help Latinos cope with stress and also may help to treat preclinical and diagnosed emotional disorders (Comas-Diaz, 2006; Garrison, 1977; Harwood, 1981; Koss-Chioino, 1992; Moreira-Almeida & Koss-Chioino, 2009). A later section briefly describes the types of spiritual groups found in most Latino communities, their rituals and beliefs, use with clients, and cultural variations.

My research has focused on Spiritism in the United States and Puerto Rico and has explored its recognition and treatment of mental illness. In the late 1970s, data from Spiritist groups and mental health programs in Puerto Rico revealed that about 55% of those seeking help at 40 Spiritist centers in three Department of Health regions presented with problems that did not meet diagnostic criteria. The rest of the clients had diagnosable emotional disorders, some of whom were seeing (or had seen) mental health professionals (Koss, 1987; Koss-Chioino,

1992). Earlier, Rogler and Hollingshead (1965) documented how Spiritist healers in Puerto Rico supported families of persons diagnosed as schizophrenic. The healers offered respite care and acted as community caregivers for many ambulatory persons living with severe mental disorders. As described for Brazil and Puerto Rico (Moreira Almeida & Koss-Chioino, 2009), Spiritists take a perspective on psychotic symptoms that shifts agency and blame from the patient to illness-causing spirits, which can help to reduce criticism and distress in the family.

Significance of Religion and Spirituality in Latino Life

How do religious behavior and spirituality affect Latino life? This section first considers how religious practices affect social roles structured by gender or developmental stage. It then explores how religion and spirituality affect the experience and treatment of addictions, serious physical illness, and mental illness. Religious views on pain and suffering are discussed, along with ideas about death among older Mexican Americans. Overall, there is a need to consider how aspects of worldview, expressed through religious or spiritual behavior, shape ideas about suffering and illness as well as issues such as abortion and the care of ill or elderly family members.

Religion and Gender

Several descriptive studies have discussed how women, especially immigrant Latinas, can be empowered to change from subordinate familial roles to leadership roles through active participation in church groups. One study described the transformation of a Mexican woman within a Catholic Charismatic prayer group that fostered spirituality and encouraged leadership. In the same area (an Atlanta, Georgia, suburb), Mexican immigrant women have been reported to undergo similar transformations in the context of religious conversions (Marquardt, 2005). These were conversion experiences of a special kind, preparing women for more independent social roles within the family and community and providing tools for participation in U.S. civic life. Other studies have shown increased literacy and oral proficiency among women who became active in fundamentalist churches or the Catholic Charismatic movement, both of which require extensive Bible reading and interpretation (Farr, 2005). Women in Pentecostal churches may benefit from

> increased participation of men in the home, public roles for women, challenges in conceptual dualisms, harsh criticisms of U.S. consumerism and hyper-individualism, and help with child care—have we stumbled on a feminist utopia? . . . Church constitutes a space where women find security, moral support and spiritual and material aid. (Lorentzen & Mira, 2005, p. 69)

Regarding popular religious and spiritual practices, men usually fulfill leadership roles in communitywide activities that are sponsored by the church. Women more often lead church-sponsored rituals that are family-based, such as maintaining and transferring saints' images from one household to the next, or leading prayers at home-centered wakes. One example is the *novenario*, traditionally a 9-day prayer vigil, now often truncated in the United States. In popular healing groups (e.g., Espiritismo or Curanderismo), female mediums and curers may work independently or in groups, but they often outnumber men by three or four to one (Koss, 1977; Koss-Chioino, 1992). Men most often have leadership roles in such groups when the groups are organized beyond the community. In Spiritist groups studied in the United States and Puerto Rico (Koss-Chioino, 1992), older women dominated as medium-healers. Typically, if they worked outside the home, they had retired. Their interest in spirituality and altruism was at a high level.

Religion and Spirituality Among Latino Youth

A recent study of a large, nationally representative sample of eighth-, 10th-, and 12th-grade students found religiousness to be increasing among youth, especially among younger students, girls, Black and Latino youth, and rural and Southern youth

(Wallace, Forman, Caldwell, & Willis, 2003). A number of studies have described the role of religion in the lives of Latino youth through youth ministries and programs for at-risk youth. There is little information on the outcomes of these programs, however, and only a few studies have described religious and spiritual socialization of Latino children (Cervantes & Ramirez, 1992; Koss-Chioino & Vargas, 1999) or the effect of religiosity on well-being among youth (Milevsky & Levitt, 2004). Of interest is the role of religious symbolism in gang behavior as a way to express solidarity, Latino membership and identity (Koss-Chioino & Vargas, 1999). For example, Mexican American gang members may adopt the image of the Virgin of Guadalupe as a logo for shirts or jackets or the bleeding heart of Jesus as a hand or body tattoo. Obviously, such behavior contrasts with membership in a Pentecostal church or other church programs, which would provide routes to escape gang lifestyles and foster upward social mobility (Flores, 2009); however, the use of religious symbols also indicates a perceived need for religion or spirituality among some who have chosen a gang lifestyle. This perspective on gangs, which suggests that Latino youth have unfulfilled spiritual needs, clearly merits more empirical attention (e.g., Koss-Chioino & Vargas, 1999; Milevsky & Levitt, 2004).

As shown in a recent study (Goldston et al., 2008), attention to religion and spirituality among Latino (and other) youth and families is vital for mental health interventions involving partnerships with faith communities. Cook (2000) found that among Latino male and female inner-city teenagers (ages 12–20), Protestant church members who saw the church as central to their lives were less stressed, more likely to be living with both biological parents, less likely to have a family member on welfare, and more likely to have a job when compared with those who were not church members. However, a contrasting perspective comes from a description of teen and college-age Latino women in Protestant evangelical ministries in Chicago, which revealed that their experiences in religious groups and activities were often socially marginalized; for example, female participants were not permitted to take leadership roles (Armitage & Dugan, 2006). These findings raise the possibility that when religious groups promote traditional gender roles, they may lead to a sense of oppression even while offering ways to help young at-risk women. More research is needed on this question as well as the broader effects of church-based programs on male and female Latino youth.

LATINO RELIGION AND SPIRITUALITY IN RELATION TO MENTAL AND PHYSICAL HEALTH

This section briefly reviews studies that explore how religious behavior relates to emotional and physical health among Latinos. These studies typically frame religious behavior as a contributor to prevention, an element in treatment success or adherence, or an aspect of the treatment protocol. The studies reviewed focus on substance abuse, gambling, alcohol addiction, HIV, cancer, and schizophrenia. In addition, several studies have examined the role of religion among caretakers of aging or chronically ill persons. Studies that have explored spirituality in relation to chronic illness or problem behaviors are much fewer, although several key studies will be mentioned. Unfortunately, there is little agreement across the studies on definitions of religiousness or spirituality, making comparisons between Latinos and other ethnic groups rather suspect. A few studies of the effect of religion or spirituality on health, in which Latinos are compared with other ethnic groups, are included because they offer interesting perspectives.

Chronic and Life-Threatening Illness

In several studies of HIV-positive men, expressed spirituality (e.g., prayer) was linked with positive mood. In one study, this finding was greater for gay African Americans than for gay Latinos—a difference attributed to Latino men's greater physical symptoms and the homonegative attitudes of religious leaders (Domanico & Crawford, 2000). Sunil and McGehee (2007) explored treatment adherence among HIV patients. For African Americans and Hispanics compared with Whites, religious and social support variables were more influential, but the strategies somewhat different. For Whites, education level and age predicted adherence; among Hispanics, church involvement and social support were key predictors. These researchers suggested that religious organizations should be involved in efforts to increase support for Latino HIV-positive groups. Yet this process may be a difficult one, given the antipathy toward HIV-infected persons in many Evangelical and Pentecostal churches.

Simoni and colleagues (Simoni et al., 2002; Simoni & Ortiz, 2003) reported high levels of spirituality, mastery, and non-HIV-related social support as strengths of Latina HIV-positive women in their New York City sample; these resources were associated with less depressive symptomatology. In a separate analysis of 142 Puerto Rican HIV-positive women, mastery and self-esteem were shown to mediate the negative relationship between spirituality and depression.

Several studies of Latina breast cancer survivors suggest that spirituality is often central to their recovery and coping (Ashing-Giwa et al., 2004). Women who were optimistic about their health used more cultural and religious recovery practices than those who were less optimistic. Another study (Culver et al., 2004) revealed that when coping with early stage breast cancer, African American women and Latinas used humor less and religious coping more in comparison with White women (Culver et al., 2004). In a study by Alferi, Culver, Carver, Arena, and Antoni (1999), 49 indigent Hispanic women with early stage breast cancer were divided into two cohorts of practicing Catholics and Evangelicals. Religious coping was assessed before and after surgery with follow-ups at 3, 6, and 12 months. In Catholic women, religiosity was linked with more distress throughout the year; in contrast, for Evangelical women, religiosity was linked with less distress. The authors explained the difference in terms of ideological factors. They proposed that whereas Catholic confession and absolution may better prepare adherents to deal with controllable stressors, the Protestant emphasis on faith and acceptance may better prepare adherents to cope with uncontrollable stressors. The authors also considered availability of social support as a mediating factor. Although the idea that religious foci may have different effects on coping is intriguing, it is important to first develop a better understanding of how different individuals interpret such concepts as "faith," "absolution," and "acceptance."

Coping With Addictions

In a community study of 249 Hispanics in New Mexico, spiritual or religious lifestyles emerged as protective influences against high levels of tobacco and alcohol use as well as gambling (Hodge et al., 2007). Also relevant is a study of a Protestant Evangelical church's effect on alcohol consumption, which proposed two mechanisms leading to control or abstention: (a) Variations in drinking are due to doctrinal prohibitive norms proposed by the church; and (b) the church provides close-knit membership in a valued community along with social support (Ford, 2006). These mechanisms may act alone or in tandem. The first is common to some Protestant denominations, and social integration is also found in the Catholic Church. When viewed through the lens of women's interests, the "doctrinally specific norms" against alcohol and other drugs were more powerful in maintaining family life (Ford, 2006, p. 260).

A study by De La Rosa and White (2001) explored the hypothesis that religiosity may buffer the impact of life stress on Hispanic adolescents who use substances. A total of 1,182 youths from seventh to 10th grade were surveyed on four occasions. Results showed that religiosity was inversely related to the use of alcohol, tobacco, and marijuana, both in terms of baseline associations and shifts in substance use over time. Although it seems worthwhile to deal with the stressors that youth experience as a way to reduce substance use, such programs for Latino youth are likely to be complex given the many persistent social stressors that Latino youth encounter, especially as members of immigrant families or families of single mothers.

Coping With Mental Disorders

Only recently have researchers begun to examine religion and spirituality in relation to psychiatric illness in Latinos, including coping mechanisms and approaches to intervention. In a study of family caretakers of Latino patients diagnosed with schizophrenia in Miami, Weisman et al. (2004) found that families who implicated God in their causal attributions of the illness and used religion for comfort showed less blame and expressed less shame toward the ill family member. In addition, Moreira-Almeida and Koss-Chioino (200) have described how Spiritism recognizes and treats persons diagnosed with schizophrenia compared with treatment in the mental health care system in Puerto Rico and Brazil. In Spiritism, the overall perspective on the treatment of the individual with psychotic symptoms consists of a focus on the lack of agency and fault on the part of the sufferer of psychotic symptoms. It provides a cultural category (a meaning) that negates the involvement of the sufferer's self and identity. There are relatively few studies of religion or spirituality in relation to Latinos diagnosed with mental illness in the United States Yet there are some examples, such as work by Aranda (2008), who studied a clinical sample of 230 older U.S.-born and immigrant Latinos. Aranda found that greater religious attendance was linked with lower risk for depressive illness, after adjusting for physical functioning, stress exposure, and social support. Of interest, private prayer was not associated with depression. Several studies have focused specifically on depression among women. For example, Latinas in the United States are at greater risk for mood disorders compared with non-Latinas (Muñoz, Mrazek, & Haggerty, 1996), and Puerto Rican women have been found to have the highest prevalence of depression among Latinas (Koss-Chioino, 1999). Exploring the association between religious activities and suicidal ideation in a sample of adult Latino immigrants, Hovey (1999) found no relationship between religious affiliation and suicidal ideation; however, church attendance and self-perceived religiosity were negatively associated with suicidal ideation.

A number of studies, now considered "classic," show that religious involvement predicts better mental health outcomes (see George et al., 2000). Of particular interest is one by Tabak and Mickelson (2009), who suggested that the impact of religiosity on mental health is mediated by race or ethnicity, levels of service attendance, and life events. These researchers showed that when compared with Whites, Hispanics and African Americans showed a stronger negative relationship between attendance at religious services and distress. Yet few studies have specified the ethnicity of their participants or the cultural contexts of the religious behavior they study. (For example, cultural context was not mentioned in the Tabak and Mickelson study.) Religious coping could vary in important ways on the basis of cultural and situational differences within and between faiths. It is important to ask, Which religious or spiritual groups or practices need to be considered to make a valid assessment of the relationship between religious coping and illness or distress?

Family Matters: Caregivers, Elders

One study of dementia caregiving in Florida and California provides a useful illustration of ethnically diverse family caregivers (Coon et al., 2004). The study showed that when compared with Caucasian women who were caregivers, Latina caregivers reported lower appraisals of distress, greater perceived benefits of caregiving, and greater use of religious coping. A parallel study (Mausbach, Coon, Cardenas, & Thompson, 2003) compared Latina and Caucasian caregivers on measures of religiosity and religious coping and found a similar pattern: Compared with their Caucasian counterparts, Latina caregivers prayed and attended religious services more often, and they rated religion as more important in their lives. A higher degree of acculturation, however, was related to less frequent use of religious coping, suggesting that acculturation may bring important shifts in religious values and behavior.

In a study of Mexican American, Catholic family caregivers located near the U.S. border, Pargament's spiritual coping scale and the Duke Religiosity Index were used to explore the association between religiosity and caregivers' physical and mental health, including depressive symptoms and perceived burden (Herrea, Lee, Nanyonjo, Torres-Vigil, & Laufman, 2009). Controlling for familism, acculturation, and social support outside of religious activity, intrinsic and organizational religiosity were associated with lower perceived burden, and nonorganizational religiosity was associated with poorer mental health. It is not clear whether these labels for religious or spiritual behavior match those of participants, nor is the role of acculturation clear, because its effect was controlled in the analysis. In addition, a novel study of Dominican immigrant elderly persons, using a focus group methodology, revealed "a strong sense of spirituality as a way of coping with stressful events," especially family illness (Paulino, 1998, p. 69). Several participants testified that they found strength in helping others. Most Latin Americans consider their community to be an organic extension of their families (which often is the case in rural barrios), although this pattern often changes in the second generation after immigration (Koss-Chioino & Vargas, 1999).

Religion, Suffering, and the Elderly

In a study that explored views on illness and health with a focus on the role of religion, Krause and Bastida (2009) conducted in-depth qualitative interviews with 52 elderly Mexican Americans. Results revealed that "pain and suffering are deeply embedded in many facets of Mexican American life, including religion (p. 114). The belief that people suffer because of Jesus' suffering was reported by a majority of participants, most of whom were Catholic. Such beliefs may function to deepen faith, empower those who suffer, and help people to identify with others who suffer. Participants also reported a belief that people should suffer in silence, both to follow the examples of Jesus and the saints and also to avoid causing distress for family members. These views on suffering were not found among Evangelical or Protestant participants. Similar studies of suffering in other Latino cultures could help to develop culturally responsive clinical practices for both physical and mental illness.

SPIRIT HEALING AND POPULAR RELIGION AND SPIRITUALITY

As described earlier, there are several informally organized, autonomous, popular small-group healing practices. There are also dramatic healing rituals in some churches, such as those found in Pentecostal, Baptist, and other Evangelical sects as well as the Catholic Charismatic movement. The latter will be briefly described later in this chapter. Fernández Olmos and Paravisini-Gebert (2003) provided very good descriptions of Spiritism and Santería as practiced in the Caribbean and recreated in the United States (with some variations such as the Mesa Blanca, which combines elements of both spirit-healing practices). Regarding Latinos in the United States, the authors commented (based on Harwood, 1981) that "the Spiritist centro contributed to the psychological and social well being of its adherents by serving as a voluntary community organization, a religion and a cultural identity" (p. 191). Affiliation of healer-mediums in a center is voluntary. The center is not an organization or a religion; instead, it is a scheduled meeting for spirit-based ritual healing practices. Santería is similar in this way. However, Santería focuses on interactions with gods/saints (*orishas*) by priests (*babalaos*) and initiated adherents (*santeros*), whereas Spiritism centers on experiences of an invisible spirit world that interacts with incarnate persons (i.e., medium-healers) on behalf of petitioners. In contrast to Spiritism, adherents of Santería are organized into pseudo-family groups who offer material and emotional support and demand explicit loyalty. A third major variant on autonomous healing practices is Curanderismo, a one-on-one healer–client relationship that calls on God and the Holy Trinity to enhance the effectiveness of a variety of healing techniques: herbs and massages, incense, candles, and the ritual of the *limpia* (cleansing) of the body and its auras to treat physical and emotional distress.

Various syndromes have been described in the literature. *Susto* (soul loss) is seen as a widespread ancient condition in Latin America in which the soul must be coaxed back into the body. *Mal aire* (bad air) is blamed for a number of illnesses related to what modern medicine sees as infections and viruses. Two other syndromes include *mal de ojo* (evil eye) and witchcraft. The evil eye often affects small children who are viewed with envy by a passerby or neighbor. Witchcraft can be ordered from persons who claim to work evil spells. These illnesses have their own symbolism within the eclectic, integrated mind-body-spirit (and emotion) perspectives typical of Curanderismo. Apart from ethnographic studies, such as those of Trotter and Chavira (1981) and de la Portilla (2009), a wonderful description can be found in the quasi-autobiographic novel *Bless Me Ultima* (Anaya, 1972).

Santería (including the widespread Regla de Ocha as well as Regla de Palo, Abakua Secret Society, and Sarabando) developed in Cuba in the 17th century from a syncretic mix of Catholicism and African religions, mainly from West Africa–especially Yoruba, although one variant is based on religious beliefs from the Congo. The development of Santería was a response to the institution of slavery by seeking a way to recapture and continue contact with the superior forces of the gods (*orishas*) who rule the natural forces of the universe and personal fates. This spiritual practice functioned to recover traditions that marked African identity and African worldviews of *aché*, or "growth, the force for completeness and divinity" (Fernández Olmos & Paravisini-Gebert, 2003, p. 33). A complex divination system, Ifá, is based on West African models of life paths; it preserves and accesses naturalist, medicinal, mythological, and spiritual knowledge. The enslaved received the rudiments of Catholicism and, when freed to urban centers, entered into *cabildos* (church-based brotherhoods for mutual support and mortuary expenses). These groups exhibited African songs and dances (and costumes) on special days of the religious calendar and shared African rituals in their separate houses. These activities were outlawed when slavery was abolished in Cuba in 1886.

Spiritism has a more recent history. This philosophical and ethical system grew out of the mid-19th-century experiments and writings of Allan Kardec (1804–1869), the pseudonym of a French scholar (Leon Hippolyte Denizarth Rivail). The movement spread first to Spain and then to Latin America, carried by scholars who studied in France or Spain. In the 19th century, the ideas and moral philosophy of Kardec led to the Latin elites' view of Spiritism as a special psychological science. This is still the view of educated Spiritists in the 21st century; however, less educated people in the rural and urban barrios, early in the movement, syncretized Spiritism with their indigenous systems of folk healing, consisting mainly of folk Catholicism and a few Afro-Caribbean beliefs and practices. Spiritism includes ethical and moral regulations about spirit behavior (both incarnate and disincarnate) and a complex explanation of the cycle of disincarnation and reincarnation based on the evolution of the individual spirit. Disincarnated spirits reside in a world apart from living beings but usually contact that world through mediums who have developed their faculties. Uneducated or troubled spirits who do not rise to the throne of God are seen as causes of bodily and emotional distress. They are invoked through visions and possession trances of a small group of mediums. These mediums are led by a president of the *centro* and meet regularly in rooms attached to a home or in larger churchlike temples.

Persons who attend sessions for advice or healing most often report satisfaction with their treatment (Koss-Chioino, 1992). The medium-healers are sometimes suspected of using their powers to harm as well as heal and are branded as witches (*brujas* or *brujos*). Over many years of observation and interviews, not one of more than 100 mediums ever admitted to doing harm; nonetheless, the accusations persist, and the possibility of witchcraft is reflected in the ostensibly protective but some potentially harmful ritual paraphernalia sold in the *botanicas*.

THE HEALING PROCESS

Over several decades of ethnographic research among Spiritists in Puerto Rico and the United States as well as observations in evangelical and charismatic Catholic church settings, a picture of the healing process has emerged. What is presented here is based on the broader literature as well as the author's observations, and these ideas are hypothesized to apply to other popular spirit healing cults among Latinos (Koss-Chioino, 2006). The proposed formulation of core components of ritual healing process, using spirit healing in Spiritism as a prototype, focuses on the client-turned-nascent-healer's experience of spiritual transformation, associated with a life-threatening illness or period of distress. This leads to an emergent ability to commune with the sacred (however conceived—as spirits, gods, saints or God, or a numinous being). From this spiritual transformation emerges the capacity for what has been termed *radical empathy* in the developing spirit healer. Radical empathy involves the embodiment of the client's pain and distress. New medium-healers often undergo ongoing experiences of visions and spirit possession, which thread through their healing work for the rest of their lives.

Following are the three basic components of a model of ritual healing process:

1. *Primary spiritual transformation* has been defined very generally as "fundamental changes in the

place or character of the sacred as a goal or destination that guides the individual's life" (Pargament, 2006, p. 20). It might be defined more specifically as "dramatic changes in world and self views, purposes, religious beliefs, attitudes or behavior" (S. H. Katz, 2004, p. 1). As the hallmark of spirit healer initiation, spiritual transformation is reported by many ritual healers across cultures and also by some of their clients. (For a few examples, see Csordas & Lewton, 1998; R. Katz, 1993.) Furthermore, the facility to experience bodily or psychic incorporation of spirits, God(s), or other extraordinary beings as outcomes of a spiritual transformation is associated with being healed, whether or not the sufferer's symptoms remain (Csordas, 1994).

2. The *wounded healer* is the second component. The anthropological literature contains many examples of how indigenous healers and shamans are initiated into their healing roles via a serious, often life-threatening illness, one that is resolved when one or more extraordinary beings are introduced into their consciousness and life world. Behavioral and attitudinal changes ensue once the spirit becomes an integral part of the novitiate's life and being. Initiation into the healer role is both preceded and accompanied by changes in self and worldviews (i.e., spiritual transformation). Descriptions of healer initiation via life-threatening illness have led to the formulation of the "wounded healer," whose source of power and authority as a healer is a continuous relationship to her or his own wounding, exemplified by the healer's willingness to maintain consciousness of those parts of herself that are perpetually wounded (Kirmayer, 2003).
3. *Communion with the sacred* is the third component. It may take three main forms: visions of the spirit world, journeys to that world, and voluntary (involuntary for persons who are not "developed") embodiment, called *obsession* (i.e., possession–trance) by spirit beings or gods or the Holy Spirit. In Spiritism, for example, both protector–guide spirits and intrusive, harmful spirits may possess mediums; the harmful spirits displace the medium's own spirit. Novitiate healers learn how to control communication with spirits or gods through the tutelage of other healers. They then experience protector–guide spirits in ways that are both personally and cosmically meaningful. Given widespread belief in the special qualities of extraordinary beings across many cultures, experience of sacred beings during a life-threatening illness can make a significant impression on the sufferer (who is in a state of high emotional arousal—confused, fearful, desperate, socially withdrawn, etc.). As Frankl (1959) observed long ago (and many others have observed since), there are many reports of transcendence in the context of suffering, which are facilitated by both psychological and physical factors.

These basic components of the process of development and healing in clients-cum-healers, like Alcoholics Anonymous' continually "recovering alcoholics," have been identified in popular healing rituals with diverse, culturally patterned symbol systems across the world; they are characteristic of popular spirit healing cults among Latinos. Studies of these popular healing practices are mainly descriptive and experiential. Many self-reports, however, verify the effectiveness of these healing ritual practices within Spiritism (for which there are a number of studies in the United States and Puerto Rico), Santería and Curanderismo (which have fewer studies; e.g., see Fernández Olmos & Paravisini-Gebert, 2003). To date, persons who study popular healing have not been able to construct an "empirical" study of effectiveness that meets scientific canons because of the complexity of the treatments, the outcome measures, and the mediating factors.

EVANGELICAL–PENTECOSTAL CHURCHES, ORIENTATIONS, AND RITUAL PRACTICES

The conversion from Catholicism to Evangelical Christianity (mainly Pentecostalism), which began at the start of the 20th century, has grown rapidly ("a seismic shift" according to Espinosa, 1999, p. 598) since the midcentury in the Southwestern United States and California as well as the Northeast and Midwest. Much of this growth can be attributed to the "multiple roles this (latter) religious tradition plays in negotiating the challenges of everyday life for Latino immigrants" (Vazquez, 1999, p. 617). To cite a few resources in the literature, Vazquez (1999) and Menjívar (1999) wrote about Salvadoran and Peruvian immigrants, Ramirez (1999) focused on Southern California and the U.S. Mexican Border, and Espinosa (1999) provided a postcolonial account of religion as viewed through the life story of a Latino Pentecostal charismatic faith healer, Francisco Olazábal. Vazquez (1999) studied two independent churches in Paterson, New Jersey and Washington, DC, which he compared with bureaucratized churches, such as the Assemblies of God. He stated that the founding pastors of the former are charismatic, which augments their flexibility in doctrine and ritual in bringing the personal relevance of the Holy Spirit to their congregations. The "Holy Spirit is at once the sign and the vehicle of charismata (gifts like glossolalia [*speaking in tongues*], divine healing, prophesying and exorcism . . .) and of the imminent second coming of Jesus Christ" (p. 619). The pastors teach a one-world, one-family message ("we are all brothers in Christ") yet promulgate a Latin accent in the church. Apart from practical issues of adaptation to the U.S. social milieu, Vasquez showed how the benefits of affiliation differ for rural immigrants, who reestablish a sense of belonging to a community, and better educated immigrants, who are forced into a lower social echelon but acquire a sense of optimism and progress (through spiritual progress) and the possibility of upward mobility in the context of a foreign society. In becoming a Pentecostal, one escapes the "fatalistic traditionalism of Catholicism" and acquires a personal God (Vazquez, 1999, p. 630).

Menjívar (1999) focused on the transnational and U.S. characteristics of one all-Salvadoran church she studied, in comparison with a mixed-ethnic Latino church that did not emphasize individual nationalities. But here, too, the emphasis was on born-again Christianity, which focuses on a conversion experience (a genre of spiritual transformation) to bring about deep spiritual and personal change. In contrast, Ramirez (1999, p. 574) explored the history from 1906 of what he called "Borderland Pentecostalism" in Southern California among Mexicans and Mexican Americans, noting that Pentecostalism has played a "valid role against the dislocation, anomie and despair of (post) modern Latin American societies" (p. 590). The churches in the United States are "harbors of secure and effective refuge on the margins—yet in the shadowy heart—of a society that refuses to accord the immigrant his/her worth" (p. 591). Thus Pentecostalism offers more than the healing of the person through the conversion of individuals who are born again in Jesus; it also offers healing of the social fabric through religious congregation of culturally compatible people. One might speculate that the "shadowy heart" remains to the present time, raising the possibility that Pentecostalism will continue to grow in popularity.

Espinosa (1999) provided another view of the start of Latino Pentecostalism through the biography of Francisco Olazábal. Olazábal, an early 20th-century Methodist minister of Mexican birth, was converted to Pentecostalism through baptism in the Holy Spirit, coupled with a demonstration of divine healing of his wife, who was physically ill. These experiences alienated him from the Methodist church. After being ordained as a Pentecostal, he started his own evangelical healing ministry. His campaigns took him to Mexico and later to Chicago, New York, and Puerto Rico, where he attracted large crowds and thousands of converts. He is credited with 20,000 conversions in one 1934 crusade in Puerto Rico, leading to the organization of an ecumenical Latin American Council of Christian churches. Successful beyond expectations in a racially prejudiced U.S. society, Olazábal was characterized by Espinosa as a Latin American prophetic leader credited with the widespread popularity of his denomination (150 churches by the time of his death in 1957) and contributions to at least 10 other denominations. Much of his attraction was the widespread belief that he possessed extraordinary powers to heal. This is very much within the pattern of the popular communitarian healing groups described in this chapter and includes some of the basic components of the healing process proposed earlier. In Latino popular healing systems, the experience of emotional distress is often converted into a meaningful opportunity for development of one's own spirit (and life change) and frequently initiates or activates a process of personal and spiritual transformation (Koss-Chioino, 2006). Espinosa (1999, p. 598) characterized Olazábal as a classic Weberian prophet, charismatically leading the change from priestly religion to a personal religion that conveys a direct link to God. Thousands of Latinos were receptive to his messages because he incorporated a worldview and notions about the reality of spirits (including the Holy Spirit and dead ancestors) that developed over four centuries from intimate contacts among the indigenous inhabitants of Latin America, neo-Caribbean peoples from Africa, and folk Spanish religiousness and spirituality.

PSYCHOTHERAPEUTIC INTERVENTIONS AND RELIGIOUSNESS AND SPIRITUALITY

An important question raised by this review is as follows: Should spirituality or religion be incorporated as aspects of culturally responsive (or sensitive or competent) psychotherapy for Latinos? If so, what components are called for? As Griner and Smith (2006) showed in a meta-analysis of 76 studies of culturally adapted mental health interventions, such interventions show moderately strong benefits. Interventions targeting a particular cultural group were four times more effective than interventions directed at clients from diverse cultural groups. Twenty-eight (including nine dissertations) of the 76 studies focused on children and youth. Adaptations of the interventions included incorporation of cultural content and values, racial–ethnic matching of therapist and client, use of the native language, an explicit paradigm of the agency or clinic, special recruitment efforts, professionals trained in cultural content and sensitivity, and consultation with persons knowledgeable about the culture. The inclusion of cultural content as an adaptation (in 64 studies) did not yield a high effect size. And only two of 76 studies included religion or spirituality as foci for intervention. Regarding children and youth, a literature search yielded similar findings: The inclusion of religion or spirituality as aspects of the treatment of culturally diverse children and youth has yielded few studies; it does not parallel the growing interest and continuing use of these approaches for adult interventions. A key question, then, is as follows: Would inclusion of spirituality or religion referenced to a specific cultural context of Latinos, both adults and children, yield more effective interventions?

Comas-Diaz (2006) and Baez and Hernandez (2001) provided cogent arguments to integrate "ethnic psychology" into psychotherapy with Latinos. Their view of ethnic psychology entails adding traditional healing practices to contemporary counseling and therapy modalities (McNeill & Cervantes, 2008). Ethnic psychology, according to Comas-Diaz (2006, 2008) includes popular healing processes and concepts; it also "promotes emotional and spiritual redemption" through "calling back the spirit" (Comas-Diaz, 2006, p. 440) as a process of reformulating cultural identity. Some years ago Cervantes and Ramirez (1992) argued that family therapy with Mexican Americans must be concerned with "mestizo spirituality" (p. 103) as expressed in family lifeways. In the book containing that chapter, Vargas and Koss-Chioino (1992) outlined a model of how to incorporate culture as content and context when treating minority youth. They framed religion and spirituality as key aspects of cultural context, essential to understanding the development of Latino children and youth as well as family dynamics (Koss-Chioino & Vargas, 1999).

Several interesting culturally adapted interventions have been proposed. As one example, Bermudez and Bermudez (2002) combined art and narrative family therapy by having families construct shrines or altars so that clients could "co-create an experience . . . (to) relive, reinvent, or experience for the first time an event or relationship that does not pertain to their dominant story" (p. 334). The idea is to experience a unique outcome pertaining to one's "preferred self."

These approaches bring with them complex issues relating to the question of which elements of psychotherapy or counseling are actually effective and in what way. Baez and Hernandez (2001) stated unequivocally that "the successful provision of culturally sensitive . . . mental health services depends in large part on the level of congruence between the client's and the mental health practitioner's respective views of mental illness and its treatment" (p. 408). They asserted that the belief systems of

Santería and Espiritismo represent "highly relevant cultural knowledge that can contribute to the quality of understanding between clinicians and Latino clients" (Baez & Hernandez, 2001, p. 408). But they also showed that these beliefs are not uniformly subscribed to by Latinos; they offer a spectrum of individual positions regarding these beliefs. Moreover, Santería and Espiritismo are strongly rejected by Latinos who are deeply involved in Catholicism or Pentecostalism; the priests and pastors consistently assert that the popular spirit healing traditions are diabolic. Despite bad press from these churches, the spirit healing cults are very available and utilized in times of high stress, when cures in the orthodox medical system are unavailable or lacking, or when psychotherapeutic modalities fail to provide relief. A companion question would be, If we hypothesize that spirituality or religiousness can be therapeutically advantageous if included in interventions for some Latino individuals or groups, which types of spirituality or religiousness work best for particular persons or groups?

CONCLUSION AND FUTURE DIRECTIONS

This chapter began with an acceptance of the perspective on religiousness and spirituality given in the Introduction to this handbook (see Chapter 1 in this volume), qualified by the observation that we must also assess these definitions from a cultural perspective. In defining and discussing spirituality as a "search for the sacred," Pargament (2007) framed it as a universal "dimension of human motivation" (p. 60). He then acknowledge the dual aspect of spirituality as more than personal but also contextual, including "life events, family, community, institutions and culture" (p. 64). I suggest that we augment Pargament's definitional approach and explore what specific cultures consider sacred. For many Latinos, the sacred includes intense and often frequent experiences that psychologists have labeled as anomalous (and at times as pathological): communication and intense experiences involving spirits of the dead or sacred beings such as gods, relating to saints as living beings who communicate and support in times of need, and experiencing God as an intimate and present life force (e.g., see Krause & Bastida, 2009, who discussed how experiences of dead relatives affect the well-being of the elderly). Although the physical and mental health associations of these experiences of the sacred are little researched, the possibility that they confer some adaptive advantages is not untenable.

New avenues of research and practice can help to clarify the relationships between religiousness, spirituality, and physical or mental health. An adaptation to the cultural context of popular healing systems has been to work with the folk healers in a collaborative way (Cavazos & Faver, 2007; Koss-Chioino, 2008). The experiment and study bridging Spiritist healers and mental health professionals by Koss-Chioino (2008) was sponsored by the Department of Health of Puerto Rico and funded by the National Institute of Mental Health. Other studies have been individually carried out by Latino health care professionals in collaboration with various health care institutions.

My research project in Puerto Rico that is currently in progress is exploring how medical doctors are spiritual or religious (some self-identify as Spiritists) and how this affects their clinical work and relationships with patients. Other avenues might explore the relationship of spirituality or religion to thoughts and experiences around death, dying, and bereavement, using perspectives of both caregivers and patients as suggested by Krause and Bastida (2009). Such research would be especially relevant given the widespread belief in life after death and reincarnation by Spiritists and most other Latinos.

References

Alferi, S. M., Culver, J. L., Carver, C. S., Arena, P. L., & Antoni, M. H. (1999). Religiosity, religious coping, and distress. *Journal of Health Psychology*, 4, 343–356. doi:10.1177/135910539900400304

Anaya, R. (1972). *Bless me Ultima.* Berkeley, CA: Quinto del Sol.

Aranda, M. P. (2008). Relationship between religious involvement and psychological wellbeing: A social justice perspective. *Health and Social Work*, *33*, 9–21. doi:10.1093/hsw/33.1.9

Armitage, J. S., & Dugan, R. E. (2006). Marginalized experiences of Hispanic females in youth-based religious groups. *Journal for the Scientific Study of Religion*, *45*, 217–231. doi:10.1111/j.1468-5906.2006.00302.x

Ashing-Giwa, K. T., Padilla, G. V., & Tejero, J. S. (2004). Breast cancer survivorship in a multiethnic sample. *Cancer, 101*, 450–465. doi:10.1002/cncr.20370

Baez, A., & Hernandez, D. (2001). Complementary spiritual beliefs in Latinos: The interface with psychotherapy. *American Journal of Orthopsychiatry, 71*, 408–415. doi:10.1037/0002-9432.71.4.408

Bermudez, J. M., & Bermudez, S. (2002). Altar-making with Latino families. *Journal of Family Psychotherapy, 13*, 329–347. doi:10.1300/J085v13n03_06

Borden, T. (2003). Border saints. *Hispanic, April,* 64–66.

Brusco, E. E. (1995). *The reformation of Machismo: Evangelical conversion and gender in Colombia.* Austin: University of Texas Press.

Campesino, M., & Schwartz, G. E. (2006). Spirituality among Latinas/os: Implications of culture in conceptualization and measurement. *Advances in Nursing Science, 29*, 69–81.

Campesino, M., & Schwartz, G. E. (2009). Spirituality and cultural identification among Latino and non-Latino College students. *Hispanic Health Care International, 7*, 72–79. doi:10.1891/1540-4153.7.2.72

Cavazos, A., Jr., & Faver, C. A. (2007). Social work and spiritual healing: Partnering with a Curandero. *Reflections: The SoL Journal, 13*(1), 16–29.

Cervantes, J., & Ramirez, O. (1992). Spirituality and family dynamics in psychotherapy with Latino children. In L. Vargas & J. D. Koss-Chioino (Eds.), *Working with culture* (pp. 103–128). San Francisco, CA: Jossey-Bass.

Comas-Diaz, L. (2006). Latino healing: The integration of ethnic psychology into psychotherapy. *Psychotherapy: Theory, Research, Practice, Training, 43*, 436–453. doi:10.1037/0033-3204.43.4.436

Comas-Diaz, L. (2008). Latino psychospirituality. In K. J. Schneider (Ed.), *Existential-integrative psychotherapy: Guideposts to the core of practice* (pp. 100–109). New York, NY: Routledge.

Cook, K. V. (2000). "You have to have somebody watching your back, and if thats God, then thats mighty big": The church's role in the resilience of inner city youth. *Adolescence, 35*, 717–730.

Coon, D. W., Rupert, M., Solano, N., Mausbach, B., Kraemer, H., Arguëlles, T., . . . Gallagher-Thompson, D. (2004). Wellbeing, appraisal and coping in a Latina and Caucasian female dementia caregivers; Findings from the REACH study. *Aging and Mental Health, 8*, 330–345. doi:10.1080/13607860410001709683

Csordas, T. (1994). *The sacred self: A cultural phenomenology of charismatic healing.* Berkeley: University of California Press.

Csordas, T., & Lewton, E. (1998). Practice, performance, and experience in ritual healing. *Transcultural Psychiatry, 35*, 435–512. doi:10.1177/136346159803500401

Culver, J. L., Arena, P. L., Wimberly, S. R., Antoni, M. H., & Carver, C. S. (2004). Coping among African American, Hispanic, and non-Hispanic White women recently treated for early stage breast cancer. *Psychology and Health, 19*, 157–166. doi:10.1080/08870440310001652669

de la Portilla, E. (2009). *They all want magic: Curanderas and folk healers.* College Station: Texas A&M University Press.

De La Rosa, M. R., & White, M. (2001). A review of the role of social support systems in the drug use behavior of Hispanics. *Journal of Psychoactive Drugs, 33*, 233–240. doi:10.1080/02791072.2001.10400570

Díaz Stevens, A. M. (1996). *Latino popular religiosity and communitarian spirituality.* Brooklyn, NY: Program for the Analysis of Religion Among Latinos.

Domanico, R., & Crawford, I. (2000). Psychological distress among HIV-impacted African American and Latino males. *Journal of Prevention and Intervention in the Community, 19*, 55–78. doi:10.1300/J005v19n01_04

Espinosa, G. (1999). "El Azteca": Francisco Olazábal and Latino Pentecostal charisma. *Journal of the American Academy of Religion, 67*, 597–616.

Espinosa, G. (2004). The Pentecostalization of Latin American and U.S. Latino Christianity. *Pneuma: Journal of the Society for Pentecostal Studies, 26*, 262–292.

Espinosa, G. (2008). The influence of religion on Latino education, marriage, and social views in the United States. *Marriage and Family Review, 43*, 205–225. doi:10.1080/01494920802072439

Farr, M. (2005). Literacy and religion: Reading, writing, and gender among Mexican women in Chicago. In M. Farr (Ed.), *Latino language and literacy in ethnolinguistic Chicago* (pp. 305–321). Mahwah, NJ: Erlbaum.

Fernández Olmos, M., & Paravisini-Gebert, L. (2003). *Creole religions of the Caribbean.* New York: New York University Press.

Flores, E. (2009). "I am somebody": Barrio Pentecostalism and gendered acculturation among Chicano ex-gang members. *Ethnic and Racial Studies, 32*, 996–1016. doi:10.1080/01419870802485507

Ford, J. (2006). Some implications of denominational heterogeneity and church attendance for alcohol consumption among Hispanics. *Journal for the Scientific Study of Religion, 45*, 253–267. doi:10.1111/j.1468-5906.2006.00304.x

Frankl, V. E. (1959). *Man's search for meaning*. Boston, MA: Beacon Press.

Garrison, V. (1977). The Puerto Rican syndrome in psychiatry and espiritismo. In V. Crapanzano & V. Garrison (Eds.), *Case studies in spirit possession* (pp. 383–449). New York, NY: Wiley.

George, L. K., Larson, D. B., Koenig, H. G., & McCullough, M. E. (2000). Spirituality and health: What we know, what we need to know. *Journal of Social and Clinical Psychology, 19*, 102–116. doi:10.1521/jscp.2000.19.1.102

Goldston, D. B., Davis Molock, S., Whitbeck, L. B., Murakami, J. L., Zayas, L. H., & Nagayama Hall, G. C. (2008). Cultural considerations in adolescent suicide prevention and psychosocial treatment. *American Psychologist, 63*, 14–31. doi:10.1037/0003-066X.63.1.14

Gonzalez-Wippler, M. (1989). *Santería: The religion*. New York, NY: Harmony Books.

Griner, D., & Smith, T. B. (2006). Culturally adapted mental health intervention: A meta-analytic review. *Psychotherapy: Theory, Research, Practice, Training, 43*, 531–548. doi:10.1037/0033-3204.43.4.531

Harwood, A. (1977). *Rx: Spiritist as needed*. New York, NY: Wiley.

Harwood, A. (1981). *Ethnicity and medical care*. Cambridge, MA: Harvard University Press.

Herrera, A. P., Lee, J. W., Nanyonjo, R. D., Torres-Vigil, I., & Laufman, L. E. (2009). Religious coping and caretaker wellbeing in Mexican American families. *Aging and Mental Health, 13*, 84–91.

Hodge, D., Andereck, K., & Montoya, H. (2007). The protective influence of spiritual-religious lifestyle profiles on tobacco use, alcohol use and gambling. *Social Work Research, 31*, 211–219. doi:10.1093/swr/31.4.211

Hovey, J. D. (1999). Religion and suicidal ideation in a sample of Latin American immigrants. *Psychological Reports, 85*, 171–177. doi:10.2466/PR0.85.5.171-177

Katz, R. (1993). *The straight path: A story of healing and transformation in Fiji*. Reading, MA: Addison-Wesley.

Katz, S. H. (2004). *The spiritual transformation research program*. Philadelphia, PA: Metanexus.

Kirmayer, L. J. (2003). Asklepian dreams: The ethos of the wounded-healer in the clinical encounter. *Transcultural Psychiatry, 40*, 248–277. doi:10.1177/1363461503402007

Koss, J. (1977). Social process, healing, and self-defeat among Puerto Rican Spiritists. *American Ethnologist, 4*, 453–469. doi:10.1525/ae.1977.4.3.02a00040

Koss, J. (1987). Expectations and outcomes for patients given mental health care or Spiritist healing in Puerto Rico. *American Journal of Psychiatry, 144*, 56–61.

Koss-Chioino, J. D. (1992). *Women as healers, women as patients: Mental health and traditional healing in Puerto Rico*. Boulder, CO: Westview Press.

Koss-Chioino, J. D. (1999). Depression among Puerto Rican women: Culture, etiology and diagnosis. *Hispanic Journal of Behavioral Sciences, 21*, 330–350. doi:10.1177/0739986399213008

Koss-Chioino, J. D. (2006). Spiritual transformation, relation, and radical empathy: Core components of ritual healing process. *Transcultural Psychiatry, 43*, 652–670. doi:10.1177/1363461506070789

Koss-Chioino, J. D. (2008). Bridges between mental health care and religious healing in Puerto Rico. In R. A. Hahn & M. C. Inhorn (Eds.), *Anthropology and public health: Bridging differences in culture and society* (pp. 221–244). New York, NY: Oxford University Press.

Koss-Chioino, J. D., & Vargas, L. A. (1999). *Working with Latino youth: Culture, context, and development*. New York, NY: Wiley.

Krause, N., & Bastida, E. (2008). Exploring the interface between religion and contact with the dead among older Mexican Americans. *Review of Religious Research, 51*, 5–20.

Krause, N., & Bastida, E. (2009). Religion, suffering, and health among older Mexican Americans. *Journal of Aging Studies, 23*, 114–123. doi:10.1016/j.jaging.2008.11.002

Lorentzen, L. A., & Mira, R. (2005). El milagro está en casa: Gender and private/public empowerment in a migrant Pentecostal church. *Latin American Perspectives, 32*, 57–71. doi:10.1177/0094582X04271852

Marquardt, M. F. (2005). From shame to confidence: Gender, religious conversion, and civic engagement of Mexicans in the U.S. South. *Latin American Perspectives, 32*, 27–56. doi:10.1177/0094582X04271850

Mausbach, B. T., Coon, D. W., Cardenas, V., & Thompson, L. W. (2003). Religious coping among Caucasian and Latino dementia caregivers. *Journal of Mental Health and Aging, 9*, 97–110.

McNeill, B. W., & Cervantes, J. M. (Eds.). (2008). *Latina/o healing practices: Mestizo and indigenous perspectives*. New York, NY: Routledge/Taylor & Francis.

Menjívar, C. (1999). Religious institutions and transnationalism: A case study of Catholic and Evangelical Salvadoran immigrants. *International Journal of Politics Culture and Society, 12*, 589–612. doi:10.1023/A:1025990209941

Milevsky, A., & Levitt, M. J. (2004). Intrinsic and extrinsic religiosity in preadolescence and adolescence: Effect on psychological adjustment. *Mental Health, Religion, and Culture, 7*, 307–321. doi:10.1080/13674670410001702380

Moreira-Almeida, A., & Koss-Chioino, J. D. (2009). Recognition and treatment of psychotic symptoms: Spiritists compared to mental health professionals in Brazil and Puerto Rico. *Psychiatry: Interpersonal and Biological Processes, 72*, 268–283.

Muñoz, R. F., Mrazek, P. J., & Haggerty, R. J. (1996). Institute of Medicine report on prevention of mental disorders: Summary and commentary. *American Psychologist, 51*, 1116–1122. doi:10.1037/0003-066X.51.11.1116

Pargament, K. I. (2006). The meaning of spiritual transformation. In J. D. Koss-Chioino & P. Hefner (Eds.), *Spiritual transformation and healing: Anthropological, theological, neuroscientific and clinical perspectives* (pp. 10–24). Lanham, MD: AltaMira Press.

Pargament, K. I. (2007). *Spiritually integrated psychotherapy*. New York, NY: Guilford Press.

Paulino, A. (1998). Dominican immigrant elders: Social service needs, utilization patterns, and challenges. *Journal of Gerontological Social Work, 30*, 61–74. doi:10.1300/J083v30n01_05

Pérez y Mena, A. I. (1991). *Speaking with the dead: Development of Afro-Caribbean religion among Puerto Ricans in the United States*. New York, NY: AMS Press.

Ramirez, D. (1999). Borderlands praxis: The immigrant experience in Latino Pentecostal churches. *Journal of the American Academy of Religion, 67*, 573–596.

Rios-Ellis, B., Chandler, L. R., & Arroya, L. E. (2005). *Critical disparities in Latino mental health: Transforming research into action*. Washington, DC: Institute for Hispanic Health, National Council of La Raza.

Rodriguez, J. (1994). *Our Lady of Guadalupe: Faith and empowerment among Mexican American women*. Austin: University of Texas Press.

Rogler, L. H., & Hollingshead, A. B. (1965). *Trapped: Families and schizophrenia*. New York, NY: Wiley.

Simoni, J. M., Martone, M. G., & Kerwin, J. F. (2002). Spirituality and psychological adaptation among women with HIV/AIDS: Implications for counseling. *Journal of Counseling Psychology, 49*, 139–147. doi:10.1037/0022-0167.49.2.139

Simoni, J. M., & Ortiz, M. Z. (2003). Mediational models of spirituality and depressive symptomatology among HIV-positive Puerto Rican women. *Cultural Diversity and Ethnic Minority Psychology, 9*, 3–15. doi:10.1037/1099-9809.9.1.3

Stevens-Arroyo, A. (1998). The Americans and religions in the twenty-first century. *Annals of the American Academy of Political and Social Science, 558*, 163–177.

Sunil, T. S., & McGehee, M. A. (2007). Social and religious support on treatment adherence among HIV patients by race/ethnicity. *Journal of HIV/AIDS and Social Services, 6*, 83–99. doi:10.1300/J187v06n01_06

Tabak, M. A., & Mickelson, K. D. (2009). Religious service attendance and distress: The moderating role of stressful life events and race/ethnicity. *Sociology of Religion, 70*, 49–64. doi:10.1093/socrel/srp001

Trotter, R. T., II, & Chavira, J. A. (1981). *Curanderismo: The gift of healing*. Athens: University of Georgia.

U.S. Census Bureau. (2004). *U.S. interim projections by age, sex, race, and Hispanic origin*. Retrieved from http://www.census.gov/ipc/www/usinterimproj

Vargas, L., & Koss-Chioino, J. (Eds.). (1992). *Working with culture: Psychotherapeutic interventions with minority children and adolescents*. San Francisco, CA: Jossey-Bass.

Vazquez, M. A. (1999). Pentecostalism, collective identity, and transnationalism among Salvadorans and Peruvians in the U.S. *Journal of the American Academy of Religion, 67*, 617–636.

Vega, W. A., Kolody, B., Agilar-Gaxiola, S., Alderete, E., Catalano, R., & Caraveo-Anduaga, J. (1998). Lifetime prevalence of DSM-III-R psychiatric disorders among urban and rural Mexican Americans in California. *Archives of General Psychiatry, 55*, 771–778. doi:10.1001/archpsyc.55.9.771

Viladrich, A. (2006). Botánicas in America's backyard: Uncovering the world of Latino healers' herb healing practices in New York City. *Human Organization, 65*, 407–420.

Wallace, J. M., Forman, T. A., Caldwell, C. H., & Willis, D. S. (2003). Religion and U.S. secondary school students: Current patterns, recent trends, and sociodemographic correlates. *Youth and Society, 35*, 98–125. doi:10.1177/0044118X03254564

Warner, R. S. (1993). Work in progress toward a new paradigm for the sociological study of religion in the United States. *American Journal of Sociology, 98*, 1044–1093. doi:10.1086/230139

Weisman, A. G., Feldman, G., Gruman, C., Rosenberg, R., Chamorro, R., & Belozersky, I. (2005). Improving mental health services for Latino and Asian immigrant elders. *Professional Psychology: Research and Practice, 36*, 642–648. doi:10.1037/0735-7028.36.6.642

Zinnbauer, B. J., & Pargament, K. I. (2005). Religiousness and spirituality. In R. L. Paloutzian & C. L. Park (Eds.), *Handbook of the psychology of religion and spirituality* (pp. 21–42). New York, NY: Guilford Press.

CHAPTER 34

UNLIKELY CONGREGATION: GAY AND LESBIAN PERSONS OF FAITH IN CONTEMPORARY U.S. CULTURE

Edouard Fontenot

Nonheterosexual men and women are increasingly visible in American culture, giving both research and clinical psychologists unprecedented access to the diversity of gay and lesbian lives. Although many gay men and lesbians reject religion, others continue to be religiously or spiritually identified. Just as no scholarly consideration of sexual minority persons can proceed without attention to their religious and spiritual lives, no comprehensive analysis of the U.S. religious landscape can ignore millions of nonheterosexual people of faith.

In recent years, psychology has turned its attention away from the etiology and cure of homosexuality toward an improved understanding of the complexity of gay and lesbian experience and to supporting the well-being of this population. The American Psychiatric Association removed homosexuality per se from its catalog of mental illness in 1973 (American Psychiatric Association, 1980). In 1975 the American Psychological Association (APA) supported this shift and urged psychologists to lead the mental health field in depathologizing homosexual orientation. Since the 1970s, same-sex sexual desire and behavior increasingly have been seen as a naturally occurring variation in human sexuality both by scholars and clinicians in psychology, and by an increasing number of Americans. A similar shift has occurred with regard to the psychological study of religion and spirituality as humanistic–existential and multicultural trends in psychology have depathologized religiosity (Bartoli, 2007). Psychologists generally understand both religious and sexual identity as two among many competing social "meaning-threads" from which persons weave a composite sense of self (Berger & Luckman, 1967; Goffman, 1959; Morris, 1967). This intellectual shift makes the present a unique opportunity for researchers and practitioners to explore two dimensions of identity that until quite recently seemed implacably at odds.

This chapter will provide an overview of current psychological research on the religious and spiritual lives of gay men and lesbians. First the chapter will note the historical context shaping contemporary gay and lesbian religiosity and spirituality. Next, it will review demographic data on religiosity and spirituality among gay men and lesbians. The focus of the chapter will then shift to a consideration of current data on associations between religion and spirituality and well-being among nonheterosexual populations. Finally the chapter will address clinical and practical perspectives and directions for further research

For the purposes of this chapter, the term *sexual minority person* will refer to a gay or lesbian person. *Gay* and *lesbian* refer to men and women respectively who are characterized by an enduring emotional, romantic, sexual, or affectionate attraction for persons of the same sex (APA, 2000). This attraction may exist on many levels including erotic desire, affection, fantasy, and sexual activity. Most research on nonheterosexuals has focused on gay men and lesbians—indeed primarily on gay Caucasian men. Bisexual and transgender persons, particularly with regard to religious and spiritual issues, have not received much research attention. This chapter, therefore, reviews primarily research on the

DOI: 10.1037/14045-034
APA Handbook of Psychology, Religion, and Spirituality: Vol. 1. Context, Theory, and Research, K. I. Pargament (Editor-in-Chief)
Copyright © 2013 by the American Psychological Association. All rights reserved.

lives of gay men and lesbians. For a discussion of these and other conceptual and methodological challenges to psychological research on sexual minority populations, see Moradi, Mohr, Worthington, and Fassinger (2009).

Religion and *spirituality* (or *religious* and *spiritual*) are most often used in tandem in this chapter to indicate and encompass the fullest range of human experiences related to the sacred (see Chapter 1 in this volume). This usage refers to practices and beliefs, both traditional and nontraditional, and includes institutional and individualized manifestations. The conjunction of the terms religious and spiritual also refers to the full range of potential functions (psychological, social, physical and spiritual) linked to human beliefs, practices, relationships, and experiences related to the search for significance and for the sacred (Pargament, 1997).

Finally, in this chapter, *heterosexism* refers to an ideological system that stigmatizes and punishes any nonheterosexual behavior, identity, relationship, or community (Herek, 1992). Heterosexism may range from passive prejudice, to inequity in social, political, and economic contexts, to overt verbal and physical violence. *Homophobia* is the affective dimension of heterosexism (an emotional revulsion for homosexuality). *Religious heterosexism* and *religious homophobia* are antigay and lesbian attitudes, behaviors, and feelings that are explicitly rooted in religious ideas and symbols and that may have a particularly powerful impact because of their religious dimension (Fontenot, 2002).

UNLIKELY CONGREGATION: RELIGION AND SEXUAL MINORITY PERSONS IN HISTORICAL CONTEXT

The historical conflict between religious institutions, persons, and ideas and nonnormative sexualities has been well-documented (e.g., Bailey, 1955; Barret & Barzan, 1996; Boswell, 1980; Mixner, 1997). Contemporary gay men and lesbians have a uniquely problematic relationship with religion and spirituality because same-sex desire, behavior, and identity have historically been understood from the religious frame not simply as wrong but as something much worse. Homosexuality has historically been construed as the defilement of the most foundational dimension of existence, the sacred (see Pargament, 1997). Same-sex desire and behavior have been perceived as violating fundamental moral precepts that are associated with transcendently ordained values about the proper expression of human life: sexual practices, gender norms, and the organization of the family and human society (Lynch, 1996). Sexual minority persons are the ultimate religious out-group (Sherkat, 2002) because their most significant defining characteristic has often been understood as antithetical to fundamental, sacred truths (Heermann, Wiggins, & Rutter, 2007; M. Warner, 1999). In light of this historical reality, it has been difficult for gay and lesbian persons to find a home in religious communities, and it is for this reason that the religious dimension of heterosexism is so powerful and so potentially damaging to gay and lesbian people.

Transhistorical conceptualizations of same-sex desire, behavior, and identity are complex and intertwined with conceptions of gender and gender variance. Historical evidence of nonheterosexual (often conceptualized as gender-variant) persons of faith across many cultures and religious traditions is increasingly noted by scholars (Boswell, 1980; Connor, 1993; Herdt, 1994). A nuanced reading of history suggests that the relationship between persons experiencing same-sex desire and religious persons and communities has itself been complex and evolving. In spite of strong antihomosexual impulses across religious traditions, nonheterosexual persons have long been found within religious communities, often living quietly at the margins or in more visible roles while concealing this aspect of themselves. This is the historical paradox of sexual minority religiosity—explicitly condemned and simultaneously present at the edges and interstices of religion.

The complexities of sexual minority faith and the reasons for which nonheterosexual persons remain religiously or spiritually observant in spite of the pervasive heterosexist context are not well understood. When challenged for his decision to remain a Christian in spite of pervasive religious heterosexism in his tradition, the priest and activist Malcolm Boyd articulated the reason quite simply: "The Church belongs to me" (Thompson, 1995, p. 234).

Anecdotal data and spiritual autobiography suggest that whatever the costs of religious heterosexism to gay men and lesbians, some aspects of religion or spirituality also provide spiritual benefits (see Comstock & Henking, 1997; Lake, 1999; Thompson, 1995). Data suggest that just as religion or spirituality remains resonant for the majority of Americans, so too does it among sexual minority populations.

Social psychologists and scholars of religion have noted that within the contemporary U.S. pluralistic religious environment, all persons of faith are increasingly free to create composite identities outside of formal religious contexts (Davidman, 2003). The simultaneous decline in formal religious practices and maintenance of a steady level of religious or spiritual belief has resulted in growing numbers of idiosyncratic identities based on seemingly incongruous socioreligious pairings (Ammerman, 2003), not the least of which is the identity of sexual minority persons of faith. Cultural shifts have been accompanied by technological innovations that make it possible for persons to access vast amounts of information about sexuality and religion. Sexual minority persons of faith can safely locate others like themselves, enabling them to cobble together new kinds of identities and communities.

The rapid evolution of a discrete gay and lesbian identity in the post–World War II period has created a new and serious conflict (Stein, 1992). For religious communities, the new reality is that no longer is homosexuality merely a set of feelings or behaviors that may be reformed or repudiated, but rather it is a cohesive and defining identity, one very often in competition with religious identity (Ammerman, 2003; Sherkat, 2002; Wilcox, 2002). Shifts in the culture have also created spaces in which religious identity is not necessarily at odds with sexual minority identity. The composite category "openly gay person of faith" is a living reality.

STAYING AND GOING: THE DEMOGRAPHICS OF SEXUAL MINORITY RELIGIOSITY

A 2002 study using data from the General Social Surveys identified that there are more nonheterosexuals in the United States than persons identifying as Episcopalians, Evangelical Lutherans, or Jews, and than the combination of Muslims, Buddhists, and Hindus—that is, about 3.6% of the population (between 10.5 and 11 million people; Sherkat, 2002). In recent decades, psychologists have begun to collect both quantitative and qualitative data focused specifically on religious and spiritual dimensions of the lives of this population (Neitz, 2000; Rodriguez & Ouellette, 2000; Sherkat, 2002; Thumma, 1991; R. S. Warner, 1995; Wilcox, 2002; Yip, 1997).

Beginning in the 1960s, a few studies found an overall tendency among gay and lesbian persons to reject religious communities and ideas at rates higher than the general population (Comstock, 1996; Kenyon, 1968; Sagir & Robins, 1973; Schofield, 1965; Sherkat, 2002). For example, Franks, Templer, Cappelletty, and Kaufman (1990–1991) found 49% of respondents endorsing "no affiliation" or "other affiliation" (a group other than Christian or Jewish) among a gay and lesbian population. Forty percent of the members of a similar sample indicated "no affiliation" or "other affiliation" (Partners Task Force for Gay and Lesbian Couples, 1990). By contrast, only 12% of Kosmin and Lachman's 1993 sample of the general population endorsed "no affiliation" or "other affiliation." Although the percentages of adult sexual minority persons reared in religious traditions are roughly the same as the general population, affiliation shifts significantly over time as sexual minority persons become less religiously observant at higher rates than the general population, whether measured by attendance at religious services, salience of religion, or endorsement of specific beliefs (Bell & Weinberg, 1978; Comstock, 1996; Ellis & Wagemann, 1993; Greenberg, 1973; Jay & Young, 1979; Laumann, Gagnon, Michael, & Michaels, 1994; Remafedi, French, Story, Resnick, & Blum, 1998; Ross, 1990; Sherkat, 2002).

Researchers have found that those gay men and lesbians who do remain religiously observant tend to switch religious affiliations more frequently than heterosexuals and are more likely than the general population to belong to a religious group different from the one in which they were reared (Ellis & Wagemann, 1993; Franks et al., 1990–1991;

Kosmin & Lachman, 1993; Partners Task Force for Gay and Lesbian Couples, 1990). In these studies, gay men consistently show a higher rate of religious participation on all measures than lesbians. Indeed, studies have shown that gay men and heterosexual women tend to score similarly on various measures of religiosity, followed by heterosexual men and, finally, lesbians (Miller & Stark, 2000; Sherkat, 2002). Theories of risk preference have been proposed to explain these findings. Briefly, men have been found to tolerate risk more readily, including the risk of not receiving the benefits of religious belief (e.g., salvation). According to the empirical research of Miller and Hoffman (1995), gay men and lesbians exhibit many characteristics of the opposite gender (e.g., with regard to traits traditionally conceived of as "masculine" or "feminine"). Their work suggests that gay men, like heterosexual women, may be less tolerant of the risk of not believing, although lesbians are more like heterosexual men in supernatural risk tolerance (Miller & Stark, 2000; Stark, 2000).

The overall tendency of gay and lesbian people to be less religious than heterosexuals is likely related to a number of factors. As noted, the association between heterosexism and religion is often vivid in the minds of gay and lesbian people, often through personal experiences of religious heterosexism (Fontenot, 2002). In addition to the impact of negative religious attitudes, many of the social advantages that are associated with greater religiosity in general populations have not historically affected gay and lesbian persons in the same way. For example, in comparison to heterosexuals, sexual minority persons are less likely to be positively influenced by their families' religious choices (indeed, research suggests they are more likely to be alienated from them), less likely to have children to draw them to religion, and less likely to have religious partners than heterosexual persons. Nor do they reap the social rewards heterosexuals do by being religiously identified. Indeed, many sexual minority affinity groups with which gay men and lesbians may affiliate have tended to hold distinctly negative opinions about religion, and ironically, some gay and lesbian persons have felt compelled to keep their religiosity secret (Sherkat, 2002). It remains to be seen whether the greater assimilation of openly gay men and lesbians into U.S. culture, reduced conflict with families of origin, increasing numbers of marriage and marriage-like relationships, the growing trend toward parenting by same-sex couples, and the moderation of religious heterosexism by some religious communities will bring the religious demographics of gay and lesbian persons into alignment with the larger population.

For those gay men and lesbians who are religiously or spiritually identified, the scope of their belief and practice reflects the religiously plural culture in which they live. The range of their affiliation spans religious communities from those most hostile to homosexuality to those that are the most affirming. As with the general population, gay and lesbian religiosity and spirituality mirror the growing heterogeneity of individualized religious or spiritual expression in the United States (Wilcox, 2002). Maher, in his 2006 survey of gay and lesbian religious groups in the Western United States, found a surprisingly rich array:

> While one might expect to find gay and lesbian Christian congregations in San Francisco and Los Angeles, readers might be surprised with a few of these examples of gay and lesbian religious groups in the study: New Hope Christian Faith Church in Flat River Missouri; The Women's Minyan (Jewish) in Minneapolis; Mennonites and Brethren for Gay and Lesbian Concerns in Ames, Iowa; The Society of Western Buddhism in Kansas City; Pagan Ritual Group in Grand Rapids, Minnesota; and Axios, a gay and lesbian Greek Orthodox group in Denver. Thirty-five groups and congregations out of the Mormon tradition [and] Unity Fellowship of Christ, a 500-member gay and lesbian African-American Church in Los Angeles [are] worth noting. (Maher, 2006, p. 95)

Scholars have compiled the narratives of sexual minority persons of faith, stories that document the experiences of gay and lesbian Mormons, Seventh-Day Adventists, Evangelical Christians, Buddhists, Pagan and Wiccan practitioners, Orthodox Jews, Santeria practitioners, Buddhists, Roman Catholics, mainstream Protestants, Muslims, Pentecostals, and others (e.g., Comstock & Henking, 1997; Thumma & Gray, 2005).

RELIGION, SPIRITUALITY, AND WELL-BEING

The impact of religious or spiritual identity and practice on well-being within gay and lesbian populations is not well understood. Historically, most psychologists have attended to the consequences (mostly documented as negative) for gay men and lesbians who participate in (nonaffirming) religious congregations. More recently, the religious landscape has changed and increasing numbers of nonhostile religious environments are to be found. Dedicated ministries, specialized churches and synagogues, splinter organizations, and new religious movements have all made new kinds of gay and lesbian religious and spiritual experience possible.

Although early research on religion and health in the general population has found a positive correlation between the two variables, research on the lives of gay men and lesbians has told a different story. Participation in religious communities by gay and lesbian persons has been associated with negative self-views and internalized homonegativity (negative attitudes toward one's own homosexual desire; Herek, 1987; Shidlo, 1994), with shame about same-sex sexual desire (Allen & Oleson, 1999), and with low self-esteem and social isolation (Ritter & Terndrup, 2002). Internalized homonegativity, in turn, has been shown to correlate negatively with measures of psychological health (Nicholson & Long, 1990; Ross & Rosser, 1996).

Some researchers have attributed the negative relationship between religiosity and measures of well-being to religiously validated shame and self-hatred that undermines self-esteem and leads to depressive symptoms (Ritter & O'Neill, 1996). Lease, Horne, and Noffsinger-Frazier (2005) have argued that the negative associations between well-being and religion are attributable to negative religious teachings about homosexuality, failure of religious communities to honor and support gay and lesbian partnerships and families, the lack of gay and lesbian leadership models, and the absence of welcome for gay men and lesbians (see also Ritter & Terndrup, 2002). Although empirical psychological research in this area is relatively new, there does exist a literature of spiritual narrative and memoir filled with personal accounts that illustrate the ways nonheterosexual persons have grappled with religiosity and sexuality (e.g., Hay, 1996; Sears, 1991; M. Warner, 1997). Psychologists and others have begun to catalog this data.

A 2001 study by Schuck and Liddle found that among persons who experienced conflict between religious and sexual identities, 53% became more spiritual than religious, 40% reinterpreted religious teachings, 33% changed religious affiliation, 33% left organized religion altogether, 23% observed religious beliefs privately, and 16% remained in their religious communities and attempted to effect change. Many study participants engaged in more than one strategy. Fontenot (2002) documented four styles used by gay men and lesbians in response to religious heterosexism. The conserving, reconstructing, replacing, and rejecting styles are each a particular attempt to cope with specifically religious antigay experiences; these styles will be discussed further in the section Well-Being and the Special Significance of Religious Symbols later in this chapter. Minwalla, Rosser, Feldman, and Varga (2005) found that among gay North American Muslim men, a deepened relationship with Allah and a reinterpretation of the Qu'ran were necessary adaptations to maintain a religious identity. Rodriguez and Ouellette (2000) and Yip (2003) noted a variety of solutions for persons who identify as both religious (in the former case, Christian, in the latter Christian and Muslim) and gay or lesbian: (a) she or he may reject a religious identity altogether and prioritize sexual identity; (b) she or he may reject sexual minority identity and attempt to either transform her or his same-sex sexual desire or to control behavior; (c) she or he may keep identities separate and switch between the two; and, finally (d) she or he may find ways to integrate identities and thus to be simultaneously religious or spiritual and gay or lesbian, often by switching to a more welcoming religion or by constructing an idiosyncratic spirituality.

WELL-BEING AND THE SPECIAL SIGNIFICANCE OF RELIGIOUS SYMBOLS

Although gay men and lesbians experience various kinds of antihomosexual prejudice throughout their lives, some research suggests that religiously based prejudice is unique and may have an especially pernicious impact, particularly for those for whom religion is a significant aspect of history or identity. Because religion is composed of "foundational" symbols, symbols that purport to reveal aspects of fundamental or sacred reality, religiously based antigay prejudice may undermine sexual minority persons' sense of fundamental goodness—one's own sexual desire and behavior may be associated with a violation of dimensions of reality held sacred. Indirect support for this idea comes from McCarthy (2008) who noted that religiously based child abuse is more strongly associated with negative psychological symptoms than nonreligiously based abuse (e.g., Bottoms, Nielsen, Murray, & Filipas, 2003). McLaughlin (1994) and Rossetti (1995) have discussed the unique impact of religious victimization manifested in clergy sexual abuse and its effect on the spiritual lives of the abused.

It has been documented that persons who view certain events as violations of foundational truth, that is, as "desecrations," tend to endorse more negative views as well as retaliatory actions toward the perceived desecrators. When Jews (Pargament, Trevino, Mahoney, & Silberman, 2007), Muslims (Abu Raiya, Pargament, Mahoney, & Trevino, 2008), and gay and lesbian persons (McCarthy, Trevino, Desai, Pargament, & Mahoney, 2007) are perceived to be at odds with sacred or foundational truth, they are subject to particularly significant hostility. Sexual minority persons also may experience themselves and their desires as "desecrations." In a 2002 study of sexual minority religiosity, of 34 possible heterosexist religious stressors, "Felt Unloved by God" (a measure of alienation from the divine) was the most frequently endorsed stressor. As one participant reported,

> I just didn't know where to turn. All I could hear was how much God condemned me, and I couldn't figure out why He made me and then condemned me. There wasn't anywhere for me to go in the Church. I just wanted to die. (Fontenot, 2002, p. 298)

Religious heterosexism may impede access to religious ideas, symbols, rituals, texts, communities, and identities, rendering them inefficacious as tools for coping and meaning-construction, and turning them into instruments of harm (Fontenot, 2002; Pargament, 1997).

At the same time, increasingly nuanced research suggests that as in the general population, religion is not universally harmful to gay men and lesbians (Yakushko, 2005). For example, Tan (2005) reported high levels of spiritual and existential well-being among a sample of lesbian and gay adults. Fontenot (2002) found that heterosexist religious stress was positively correlated not with depression but rather with stress-related growth. Davidson (2000) cataloged the possible positive aspects of religion and spirituality for gay and lesbian persons: the affirmation of goodness, the creation of community, and a connection with the transcendent or divine dimension of life. These benefits are not different from those afforded heterosexuals and apparently may occur even in hostile religious environments.

Indeed, the religious and spiritual struggles and strains of gay men and lesbians may lead to a deepened religious or spiritual connection: Exline and Rose (2005) have noted that spiritual suffering such as that experienced by gay and lesbian people "can act as turning points, places in which faith can wither or bloom afresh" (Exline & Rose, 2005, p. 315). Some empirical research has shown positive correlations between the experience of negative religious experiences and religious growth/satisfaction (Fontenot, 2002). O'Neill and Ritter (1992) and others have characterized *coming out*, the often painful process of coming to terms with nonnormative sexual desire, as a spiritual journey (Fortunato 1982; Helminiak 1996). This struggle and its process of self-examination, mourning, and liberation can create a deep sense of spiritual well-being and connection with the divine.

RELIGION, SPIRITUALITY, AND SEXUAL IDENTITY DEVELOPMENT

Psychologists have studied sexual identity development among lesbians and gay men to clarify how same-sex-attracted men and women come to understand the relationship between sexual desire and other aspects of the self as well as how different self-understandings are associated with aspects of well-being. Troiden (1989) and Cass (1979) have outlined classic stage-oriented identity development theories that end with identity synthesis, a stage in which various aspects of the self are integrated into a comprehensive whole. Although integrating nonnormative sexuality and religious identity may be a difficult process, D'Augelli (1994) has argued that as for heterosexual persons, religion may nevertheless aid in identity development by providing a connection to history and offering ways to ground the meaning and purpose of the self within a larger meaning-context. Although some empirical research has found associations between attempts to reconcile nonheterosexual sexual identities and religious identities and depression, guilt, shame, and suicidal ideation (Bartoli & Gillem, 2008; Khan, 2008; Levy, 2008; Mahaffy, 1996; Schuck & Liddle, 2001), anecdotal data and religious and spiritual narratives suggest that gay men and lesbians do find ways to render religious symbols useful. For example, research has investigated the ways in which nonheterosexual men and women, rather than resigning themselves to heterosexist religious symbols or radically rejecting religion altogether, may maintain a connection with the divine by using religious symbols in novel ways or with new meanings attached (the symbols are critically assessed and reconstructed). Alternately they may discard traditional religious symbols and meanings and substitute other, unconventional symbols as paths to the sacred (traditional symbols are replaced). In his research, Fontenot (2002) found that the former reconstructing style was overall much more positively correlated with well-being than the latter replacing style.

In their analysis of gay-positive religious communities, Rodriguez and Ouellette (2000) found that participation in a supportive religious congregation helped gay and lesbian people to integrate their sexual and religious identities. As more and more gay-positive religious or spiritual possibilities appear, it may be that the automatic coupling of religious symbols and heterosexist attitudes will lessen in the minds of sexual minority populations, allowing them to more easily access religious or spiritual identities.

Troiden (1989) argued that sexual identity formation is shaped primarily by support or its lack from family and friends. He maintained that supportive environments facilitate healthy sexual identity formation, whereas hostile environments impede it. It is likely that supportive and unsupportive religious environments, especially for those for whom religion is particularly important (either personally or for one's family), affect identity development and well-being. If, as many psychologists suggest, an integration of salient dimensions of identity—including religious identity—is optimal for successful identity formation (Cass, 1979; Rosser, 1990; Troiden, 1989), it may be that gay men and lesbians from unsupportive families or religious communities will struggle to consolidate sexual and religious identities more than persons from more supportive environments (Lease et al., 2005; Newman & Muzzonigro, 1993). Ultimately, not all persons resolve the tension between dimensions of identity.

RACE AND ETHNICITY

A significant methodological problem that plagues research on sexual minority issues is the failure to recognize the diversity within sexual minority populations and the ways in which gender, race, class, age, regional location, religious affiliation, and other contextual factors shape sexual minority experience. Psychological research on gay and lesbian persons has been primarily confined to the experiences of middle-class white men, a fact that limits the generalizability of these findings (Greene, 1994; for exceptions, see Brown, 2005; Conerly, 2001; Crawford, Allison, Zamboni, & Soto 2002; Crisp, Priest, & Torgenson, 1998; Harris, 2003). Sexual minority persons in the United States come from diverse cultural groups and have multiple racial and ethnic identities

(Black, Gates, Sanders, & Taylor, 2000). The race–ethnicity lens is significant given the powerful impact of race and ethnicity in U.S. culture. Racial and ethnic minorities have a yet more complex task in navigating multiple sociocultural identities.

It is clear that religion, spirituality, and religious community are often significant resources for racial–ethnic minorities in the United States. The historic role of both African American Christianity and Islam in helping individuals of color to navigate racism in U.S. culture is well-documented (Lincoln & Mamiya, 1990). Similarly, recent immigrants of color to the United States often use religious identity and community as a means of coping with dislocation and finding emotional and material support (Khan, 2008). As a result, the implications of religiosity for racial and ethnic minorities—whether heterosexual or nonheterosexual—will likely be different than for Whites (see Chapters 30, 32, and 33 in this volume). In spite of this reality, in a 2010 article entitled "Content Analysis of Literature About LGB People of Color: 1998–2007" (Huang et al., 2010), topics such as religion, spirituality, and religious affiliation are not mentioned. Similarly, in the same journal, Nancy Boyd-Franklin's 2010 article "Incorporating Spirituality and Religion Into the Treatment of African-American Clients" does not mention sexuality or offer any resources for nonheterosexual African Americans.

Gay and lesbian racial minorities bear the burden of being too visible in the larger gay and lesbian culture—and so subject to racism—and largely invisible in their own religious communities. Conerly (2001) has argued that the essential difficulty facing nonheterosexual African Americans is finding a space in which sexual orientation and racial identity can coexist. Because of racism in gay and lesbian communities and negative attitudes about homosexuality among African Americans, particularly those who are religious, gay and lesbian persons of color often feel the necessity of choosing between communities and identities. Indeed, because of perceived racism among sexual minority communities, some nonheterosexual African Americans reject the terms gay and lesbian altogether and chose either not to identify their same-sex desire in any public way or identify themselves with alternative concepts (e.g. same-gender-loving or men-who-have-sex-with-men.

Nonheterosexual African Americans are in a painful bind. African Americans disclose same-sex desire and gay or lesbian identity at much lower rates than Caucasians and at a somewhat lower rate than Latinos (Edwards, 1996). Feeling unsafe in disclosing one's sexual orientation is thought to contribute to greater internalized heterosexism and negative psychological outcomes, such as depression, lower self-esteem, and shame (Good-Cross & Good, 2009; Williams, Wyatt, Resell, Peterson, & Asuan-O'Brien, 2004). Good-Cross and Good (2009) found that among a sample of male African American college students who had sex with other men, race, gender, and religious belief were rated as much more salient aspects of identity than sexual minority status.

Gay and lesbian African Americans experience both racial and heterosexist prejudice; some research suggests that heterosexist prejudice is uniquely significant. Szymanski and Gupta (2009) found that within a sample of nonheterosexual African-Americans, internalized racism and internalized heterosexism were both significant predictors of lower self-esteem; however, only internalized heterosexism was a unique predictor of psychological distress. They speculated that the religious designation of homosexuality as sinful and morally unacceptable may undergird the relationship between internalized heterosexism and distress, and points, again, to the unique impact of the religious dimensions of heterosexism.

Other research has shown that in spite of conservative and heterosexist religious values among much of the African American religious community, lesbian and gay people of color may have access to certain resources and strengths that may buffer the consequences of heterosexist stigma (Moradi, DeBlaere, & Huang, 2010). A "resilience perspective" includes religion as a significant resource for gay and lesbian people of color. Some aspects of religiosity (e.g., a relationship with God or with a community) may serve as a buffer against religious heterosexism (Moradi et al., 2010, p. 401). Indeed this "double valence" of religion as both source of prejudice and source of strength may also be at play in the larger gay and lesbian population and may account for ongoing gay and lesbian religiosity or spirituality (Fontenot, 2002).

CLINICAL AND PRACTICAL PERSPECTIVES

Gay men and lesbians access psychological services more frequently than the general population (Bieschke, McClanahan, Tozer, Grzegorek, & Park, 2000). This suggests that psychologists are uniquely positioned to work with gay and lesbian persons struggling with issues related to sexuality and religious or spiritual meaning. As psychologists find themselves increasingly working with gay and lesbian clients who are grappling with a clash of identities, they must find ways to offer professional opinions regarding optimal outcomes for emotional health and psychological well-being. Clinicians should understand their own biases toward sexual minorities and explore their own religious and secular meaning system for messages regarding homosexuality (Reynolds, 2003). Similarly, psychologists should examine whether they are able to take a nonpathologizing stance toward religion and spirituality. An "informed but not knowing" perspective maintains an awareness of religiousness or spirituality, of sexuality, and of their intersection and avoids presuming a complete understanding of clients' perspectives. Similarly, clinicians should not preemptively force a focus toward or away from religion or sexuality but should express curiosity regarding the place of each in clients' lives. Clinicians can listen for implicit and explicit expressions of religious and spiritual life and inquire as appropriate to normalize the discussion of religious and spiritual histories, beliefs, practices, and struggles. Similarly, sexual history, desire, and behavior should evoke the curiosity of the clinician. Minimizing prejudice requires self-awareness and education as well as humility (Pargament, 2007) in the face of the mystery of the complexity of both human sexuality and the human yearning for the sacred.

Recent data confirm a trend among therapists toward affirmative attitudes and treatments for lesbian and gay persons (for a summary, see Bieschke, Paul, & Blasko, 2007). At the same time Phillips and Fischer (1998) have documented ongoing heterosexist bias in the field, from training to practice to research. To practice ethically, psychologists should familiarize themselves with the APA's *Ethical Principles of Psychologists and Code of Conduct*. These principles require psychologists to avoid bias and prejudice toward both religion and sexual orientation (APA, 2010, p. 118). They should also consult the *Guidelines for Psychotherapy With Lesbian, Gay and Bisexual Clients* (APA, Division 44/Committee on Lesbian, Gay and Bisexual Concerns, Joint Task Force on Guidelines for Psychotherapy With Lesbian, Gay, and Bisexual Clients, 2000) and take the following steps:

1. Be familiar with theories of sexual minority identity development, while maintaining an awareness that existing models were crystallized in the 1970s and may not represent contemporary developmental experience (Fassinger, 2000).
2. Become comfortable with discussing religious or spiritual concepts in a nonpathologizing or judgmental way.
3. Be aware of one's own inevitable bias toward heterosexuality as normative.
4. Be willing to develop an understanding of the complexities of the religious or spiritual histories of clients.
5. Attend to within-group differences and contextual factors associated with gender, race and ethnicity, socioeconomic status, age, religious history or affiliation, and so on.
6. Understand that, like all clients, gay and lesbian persons will resolve conflicts between aspects of identity in a variety of ways and in concert with the relative salience of each.

Becoming competent with regard to sexuality or religion is no different from any other area of cultural competence. With regard to the sixth guideline, many psychologists may struggle to accept client decisions to prioritize religious identity and to constrict or conceal sexual identity, particularly if the clinician holds negative or pathologizing views of religion. But full disclosure of sexuality and the use of gay or lesbian as a primary orienting identity is not always optimal (e.g., for adolescents in nonsupportive homes, for persons in hostile environments, for ethnic minorities or immigrants). To build a consolidated sense of self, some clients may privilege religious identity, including antihomosexual beliefs. They may request interventions to change their desires from homosexual to heterosexual, placing psychologists in an ethical quandary.

For others, sexual identity will be the most salient identity, and they will abandon religious identity. Psychologists should not be surprised, however, if clients turn to previously rejected religious resources in the midst of life transitions or crises. Persons who consciously abandon religion can nevertheless be strongly bound to it, and so clinicians should pay attention to the ongoing fingerprints of religion in an otherwise secular life (Doehring, 1996). The task is neither to advocate for religion nor to dissuade persons from abandoning it, but rather to remain curious and to provide the widest range of options—including the possibility of being both gay or lesbian and a person of authentic religious or spiritual faith.

Affirmative psychological care includes a supportive and accepting stance (of both sexual desire and religious belief), psychoeducation reflecting the latest psychological research on sexuality and same-sex attraction, balancing one-sided and prejudicial antihomosexual religious beliefs, promoting and supporting stalled emotional and identity development, provision of gay-positive religious resources, provision of the opportunity to name the ways in which religion has injured persons, and exploration of the ongoing significance of religious beliefs and practices. Supportive, affirmative psychological care may develop out of many different theoretical orientations: insight oriented, humanistic, cognitive–behavioral, or any other school of thought. Buchanan, Dzelme, Harris, and Hecker (2001) have articulated a narrative therapeutic approach to working with gay and lesbian clients. This method objectifies and externalizes the "problem" (of being same-sex attracted), separating it from a person's identity ("I'm sick, flawed, sinful") and locating it instead in the dynamic interplay between an individual and the systems in which she or he participates: "Why do some say homosexuality is sick? What is the evidence for that?" And it introduces alternative narrative possibilities to those that present gay people as unhappy, condemned, alone, or morally bankrupt. Instead, gay men and lesbians can live in stable, happy relationships, have children, and attend religious services. Responsibility for the "problem" is no longer an individual's alone (for a description of clinical interventions, see Buchanan et al., 2001).

Pargament's (2007) spiritually integrated psychotherapy is a perspective fully compatible with gay and lesbian affirmative treatment. Although he himself is not focused on this population, his approach understands religiousness and spirituality as "a set of pathways that people follow in search of the sacred" (p. 196) and spiritually integrated psychotherapy as attuned to the ways religious and spiritual meanings and experiences (whether positive or negative) are part of the process of change. This perspective, with its attention to the ways spiritual problems can cause psychological problems, and the understanding that spirituality can be a source of solutions or a source of resistance, seems particularly useful for gay and lesbian persons of faith as well as those who have lost or rejected faith but continue to be burdened by hurt or grief. Regardless of the method employed, psychologists should take a religious history and ask gay men and lesbians what their religion means to them (both positively and negatively). They should assess for religious conflict or struggle and normalize those struggles. Finally psychologists, as appropriate, should help sexual minority persons of faith find religious symbols and ideas, from their tradition or perhaps outside of it to help them in their struggle (Abu Raiya & Pargament, 2010).

THE DILEMMA OF NONAFFIRMATIVE TREATMENTS

Psychologists may encounter some persons who experience same-sex desire and who seek not integration but rather to alter or at least constrain those desires. Interventions that seek to alter the object of sexual or affectional desire are sometimes referred to as *conversion treatment* (also called *reparative* or *reorientation treatment*). For some persons, particularly those for whom conservative religious identities are especially salient, a reorientation to heterosexuality is highly desirable. Conversion treatment is controversial (see Beckstead & Morrow, 2004, for an analysis of factors predisposing persons to seek conversion therapy). Morrow and Beckstead (2004) and Bieschke et al. (2007) have reviewed the literature on treatment by both paraprofessional (usually Christian ministry-based organizations) and professional therapists (licensed mental health care providers), noting the biological, surgical, and psychotherapeutic iterations of this kind of treatment. The basic assumption of this type of treatment is that same-sex attractions are chosen and amenable to change and that this change is desirable for either religious and moral or mental health reasons. The most common interventions include education, discussion, religious worship, prayer, psychoanalysis, hypnosis, cognitive restructuring, abstinence coaching, aversion treatment, and so-called gender training (among some practitioners, same-sex desire is often thought to be related to underdeveloped gender identity; Morrow & Beckstead, 2004).

An ever-growing body of research has shown that conversion treatment lacks a solid empirical base and poses significant ethical questions. Cramer, Golom, LoPresto, and Kirkley (2008), in an extensive review article, noted that the conversion therapy efficacy literature is, at best, scant, anecdotal, and retrospective, and fails to meet conventional standards of evidenced-based treatment. Beckstead and Morrow (2004), in their review of empirical studies of conversion therapy, report that such interventions have little long-lasting influence on same-sex attraction and that any perceived benefits reported by research participants were the result of other factors—relief at the knowledge that same-sex attraction can be separated from behavior, an increased sense of fitting in, improved gender identity—rather than any significant diminishment of same-sex desire (see also Schaeffer, Hyde, Kroencke, McCormick, & Nottebaum, 2000; Shidlo & Schroeder, 2002).

At the same time, research documents that conversion therapy techniques decreased sexual arousal of all kinds and created persons who were more "shamed, conflicted and fearful" than persons not treated with such techniques (Beckstead & Morrow, 2004; Haldeman, 1994, p. 225). Other negative outcomes include long-term sexual dysfunction, lowered self-esteem, loss of family affiliation, loss of religious beliefs or sense of spirituality, increased self-hatred, and symptoms of depression and anxiety (Cramer et al., 2008). In short, the perceived benefits of conversion therapy were short term and greatly outweighed by the long-term negative effects.

A minority of psychologists have argued that the refusal to provide services demanded by clients seeking transformation of same-sex desire denies the client's autonomy and her or his right to self-determination, and is disrespectful of her or his religious beliefs. It is, however, unethical for a psychologist to provide interventions known to cause harm (see Fischer & Debord, 2007). Indeed, psychologists are not obliged to meet every demand of a client; rather they are ethically obligated to make available to clients the latest and most accurate clinical and research data. They also make recommendations on the basis of these data so that clients may realistically assess the increasingly conclusive evidence that change of sexual orientation is doubtful and that attempts to do so have been found to be harmful. Psychologists can help clients to explore the reasons for which change of orientation seems desirable. They can balance negative stereotypes, and offer community, religious, and other resources. They can also explore the losses associated with non-normative sexuality, neither denying the reality of the loss nor failing to challenge assumptions about them. The goal of these interventions is not to convince clients of what they should do but to inform them of the real dangers and possibilities, while respecting the client's right to disagree or reject these recommendations.

DIRECTIONS FOR FUTURE RESEARCH

Although psychologists have turned a nonpathologizing eye to nonheterosexuals as never before, the available data about gay and lesbian lives are as yet sparse. Much work remains to be done. The continued collection of descriptive statistics on the evolving demographics of gay and lesbian religiosity and spirituality will help researchers to track and compare majority and minority religiosity and to respond to such questions as, "Will gay and lesbian persons of faith become more like heterosexuals as acceptance and assimilation continues or will their religious and spiritual paths and identities remain distinct?"

Longitudinal studies and random sampling are difficult even under the best of circumstances and difficult to the point of impossibility within a stigmatized population. Nevertheless, only these research methods can track the changing relationships between religious or spiritual identity and sexual identity over the life span and allow for meaningful generalization of findings. As it stands the preponderance of research, however interesting, is limited by cross-sectional research design and convenience sampling. A related methodological problem is the significant overrepresentation of White, educated males in the research. Expanded research on ethnic minorities, persons of varied socioeconomic status, persons belonging to nontraditional religious groups, and so on is needed. Attention to multiple intersecting minority identities provides data on within-group differences and avoids reifying the identities "gay" or "lesbian" outside of the contexts in which they develop. In the same way that the term *Christian* is expansive to the point of meaninglessness outside of context, the terms *gay* and *lesbian* increasingly fail to describe the complexities of the lives of persons to whom they are applied in any meaningful way without the larger context of coexisting dimensions of identity. Furthermore, a more nuanced perspective on nonnormative sexual identities should increasingly draw attention to other, largely marginalized sexual minority identities, such as bisexual, transgender, and queer.

Finally, as U.S. culture continues to shift, whole sets of research questions related to evolving family structure ("How has the expansion of openly gay couples and families affected gay and lesbian religiosity and spirituality?"), religious community ("What is the impact of being reared in a gay-positive religious environment on gay and lesbian religiosity and spirituality?"), and clinical care ("Are new models of 'Spiritually Conscious Psychological Care' useful to gay and lesbian persons of faith?" Saunders, Miller, & Bright, 2010) are significant areas of inquiry.

References

Abu Raiya, H., & Pargament, K. I. (2010). Religiously integrated psychotherapy with Muslim clients: From research to practice. *Professional Psychology: Research and Practice, 41*, 181–188. doi:10.1037/a0017988

Abu Raiya, H., Pargament, K. I., Mahoney, A., & Trevino, K. (2008). When Muslims are perceived as a religious threat: Examining the connection between desecration, religious coping and anti-Muslim attitudes. *Basic and Applied Social Psychology, 30*, 311–325. doi:10.1080/01973530802502234

Allen, D. J., & Oleson, T. (1999). Shame and internalized homophobia in gay men. *Journal of Homosexuality, 37*, 33–43. doi:10.1300/J082v37n03_03

American Psychological Association. (2010). *Ethical principles of psychologists and code of conduct (2002, Amended June 1, 2010)*. Washington, DC: Author. Retrieved from http://www.apa.org/ethics/code/index

American Psychological Association, Division 44/ Committee on Lesbian, Gay and Bisexual Concerns, Joint Task Force on Guidelines for Psychotherapy With Lesbian, Gay, and Bisexual Clients. (2000). Guidelines for psychotherapy with lesbian, gay, and bisexual clients. *American Psychologist, 55*, 1440–1451. doi:10.1037/0003-066X.55.12.1440

American Psychiatric Association. (1980). *Diagnostic and statistical manual of mental disorders* (3rd ed.). Washington, DC: Author.

Ammerman, N. (2003). Religious identities and religious institutions. In M. Dillon (Ed.), *Handbook of the sociology of religion* (pp. 207–224). Cambridge, England: Cambridge University Press.

Bailey, S. (1955). *Homosexuality and the western Christian tradition*. London, England: Mowbray.

Barret, R., & Barzan, R. (1996). Spiritual experiences of gay men and lesbians. *Counseling and Values, 41*, 4–15. doi:10.1002/j.2161-007X.1996.tb00858.x

Bartoli, E. (2007). Religious and spiritual issues in psychotherapy practice: Training the trainer. *Psychotherapy: Theory, Research, Practice, Training, 44*, 54–65. doi:10.1037/0033-3204.44.1.54

Bartoli, E., & Gillem, A. R. (2008). Continuing to depolarize the debate on sexual orientation and religion: Identity and the therapeutic process. *Professional Psychology: Research and Practice, 39*, 202–209. doi:10.1037/0735-7028.39.2.202

Beckstead, A. L., & Morrow, S. L. (2004). Mormon clients' experiences of conversion therapy: The need for a new treatment approach. *Counseling Psychologist, 32*, 651–690. doi:10.1177/0011000004267555

Bell, A., & Weinberg, M. (1978). *Homosexualities: A study of diversity among men and women*. New York, NY: Simon & Schuster.

Berger, P., & Luckman, T. (1967). *The social construction of reality: A treatise in the sociology of knowledge*. New York, NY: Anchor Books.

Bieschke, K. J., McClanahan, M., Tozer, E., Grzegorek, J. L., & Park, J. (2000). Programmatic research on the treatment of lesbian, gay and bisexual clients: The past, the present, and the course for the future. In R. M. Perez, K. A. DeBord, & K. J. Bieschke (Eds.), *Handbook of counseling and psychotherapy with lesbian, gay, and bisexual clients* (pp. 309–335). Washington, DC: American Psychological Association. doi:10.1037/10339-013

Bieschke, K. J., Paul, P. L., & Blasko, K. A. (2007). Review of empirical research focused on the experiences of lesbian, gay, bisexual clients in counseling and psychotherapy. In K. J. Bieschke, R. M. Perez, & K. A. Debord (Eds.), *Handbook of counseling and psychotherapy with lesbian, gay, bisexual, and transgender clients* (2nd ed., pp. 293–315). Washington, DC: American Psychological Association. doi:10.1037/11482-012

Black, D., Gates, G., Sanders, S., & Taylor, L. (2000). Demographics of the gay and lesbian population in the United States: Evidence from available systematic data sources. *Demography, 37*, 139–154. doi:10.2307/2648117

Boswell, J. (1980). *Christianity, social tolerance and homosexuality*. Chicago, IL: University of Chicago Press.

Bottoms, B. L., Nielsen, M., Murray, R., & Filipas, H. (2003). Religion-related child physical abuse: Characteristics and psychological outcomes. *Journal of Aggression, Maltreatment, and Trauma, 8*, 87–114.

Boyd-Franklin, N. (2010). Incorporating spirituality and religion into the treatment of African American clients. *The Counseling Psychologist, 38*, 976–1000. doi:10.1177/0011000010374881

Brown, E. (2005). We wear the mask: African American contemporary gay male identities. *Journal of African American Studies, 9*, 29–38. doi:10.1007/s12111-005-1020-x

Buchanan, M., Dzelme, K., Harris, D., & Hecker, L. (2001). Challenge of being simultaneously gay or lesbian and spiritual and/or religious: A narrative perspective. *American Journal of Family Therapy, 29*, 435–449. doi:10.1080/01926180127629

Cass, V. C. (1979). Homosexual identity formation: A theoretical model. *Journal of Homosexuality, 4*, 219–235. doi:10.1300/J082v04n03_01

Comstock, G. (1996). *Unrepentant, self-affirming, practicing: Lesbian/bisexual/ gay people within organized religion*. New York, NY: Continuum.

Comstock, G. D., & Henking, S. E. (Eds.). (1997). *Que(e)rying religion: A critical analysis*. New York, NY: Continuum.

Conerly, G. (2001). Are you black first or queer? In D. Constantine-Simms (Ed.), *The greatest taboo: Homosexuality in black communities* (pp. 7–23). Los Angeles, CA: Alyson.

Connor, R. (1993). *Blossom of bone: Reclaiming the connection between homoeroticism and the sacred*. San Francisco, CA: HarperSanFrancisco.

Cramer, R. J., Golom, F. D., LoPresto, C. T., & Kirkley, S. M. (2008). Weighing the evidence: Empirical assessment and ethical implications of conversion therapy. *Ethics and Behavior, 18*, 93–114. doi:10.1080/10508420701713014

Crawford, I., Allison, K. W., Zamboni, B. D., & Soto, T. (2002). The influence of dual-identity development on the psychosocial functioning of African American gay and bisexual men. *Journal of Sex Research, 39*, 179–189. doi:10.1080/00224490209552140

Crisp, D., Priest, R., & Torgenson, A. (1998). African American gay men: Developmental issues, choices and self-concept. *Family Therapy, 25*, 161–168.

D'Augelli, A. R. (1994). Identity development and sexual orientation: Toward a model of lesbian, gay, and bisexual development. In E. J. Trickeett, R. J. Watts, & D. Birman (Eds.), *Human diversity: Perspectives on people in context* (pp. 312–333). San Francisco, CA: Jossey-Bass.

Davidman, L. (2003). Beyond the synagogue walls. In M. Dillon (Ed.), *Handbook of the sociology of religion* (pp. 261–275). Cambridge, England: Cambridge University Press.

Davidson, M. G. (2000). Religion and spirituality. In R. M. Perez, K. A. DeBord, & K. J. Bieschke (Eds.), *Handbook of counseling and psychotherapy with lesbian, gay, and bisexual clients* (pp. 409–433). Washington, DC: American Psychological Association. doi:10.1037/10339-017

Doehring, C. (1996). *The practice of pastoral care: A postmodern approach*. Louisville, KY: John Knox.

Edwards, W. J. (1996). A sociological analysis of an in/visible minority group: Male adolescent homosexuals. *Youth and Society, 27*, 334–355. doi:10.1177/0044118X96027003004

Ellis, L., & Wagemann, B. M. (1993). The religiosity of mothers and their offspring as related to the offspring as sex and sexual orientation. *Adolescence, 28*, 227–234.

Exline, J. J., & Rose, E. (2005). Religious and spiritual struggles. In R. F. Paloutzian & C. L. Park (Eds.), *Handbook of the psychology of religion and spirituality* (pp. 315–330). New York, NY: Guilford Press.

Fassinger, R. E. (2000). Applying counseling theories to lesbian, gay, and bisexual clients: Possibilities and pitfalls. In R. M. Perez, K. DeBord, & K. Bieschke (Eds.), *Handbook of counseling and psychotherapy with lesbian, gay, and bisexual clients* (pp. 107–131). Washington, DC: American Psychological Association. doi:10.1037/10339-005

Fischer, A., & Debord, K. (2007). Perceived conflicts between affirmation of religious diversity and affirmation of sexual diversity: That's perceived. In K. J. Bieschke, R. M. Perez, & K. A. DeBord (Eds.), *Handbook of counseling and psychotherapy with lesbian, gay, bisexual, and transgender clients* (2nd ed., pp. 317–339). Washington, DC: American Psychological Association. doi:10.1037/11482-013

Fontenot, E. (2002). *The use of religious resources in response to anti-homosexual religious attitudes and behaviors.* Unpublished doctoral dissertation, Boston University, MA.

Fortunato, J. (1982). *Embracing the exile.* New York, NY: Seabury.

Franks, K., Templer, D., Cappelletty, G., & Kaufman, I. (1990–1991). Exploration of death anxiety as a function of religious variables in gay men with AIDS. *Omega: Journal of Death and Dying, 22,* 43–50. doi:10.2190/KPB8-UP81-N3BH-1PTJ

Goffman, E. (1959). *The presentation of self in everyday life.* Garden City, NY: Doubleday.

Good-Cross, D., & Good, G. E. (2009). Managing multiple-minority identities: African American men who have sex with men at predominately white universities. *Journal of Diversity in Higher Education, 2,* 103–112. doi:10.1037/a0015780

Greenberg, J. S. (1973). A study of male homosexuals (predominately college students). *Journal of Psychology: Interdisciplinary and Applied, 83,* 137–143. doi:10.1080/00223980.1973.9915601

Greene, B. (1994). Ethnic minority lesbians and gay men: Mental health and treatment issues. *Journal of Consulting and Clinical Psychology, 62,* 243–251. doi:10.1037/0022-006X.62.2.243

Haldeman, D. C. (1994). The practice and ethics of sexual orientation conversion therapy. *Journal of Consulting and Clinical Psychology, 62,* 221–227. doi:10.1037/0022-006X.62.2.221

Harris, W. G. (2003). African American homosexual males on predominately White college and university campuses. *Journal of African American Studies, 7,* 47–56. doi:10.1007/s12111-003-1002-9

Hay, H. (1996). *Radically gay: Gay liberation in the words of its founder* (W. Roscoe, Ed.). Boston, MA: Beacon Press.

Heermann, M., Wiggins, M. I., & Rutter, P. A. (2007). Creating a space for spiritual practice: Pastoral possibilities with sexual minorities. *Pastoral Psychology, 55,* 711–721. doi:10.1007/s11089-007-0085-y

Helminiak, D. (1996). *The human core of spirituality: The mind as psyche and spirit.* Albany: State University of New York.

Herdt, G. M. (1994). *Third sex, third gender: Beyond sexual dimorphism in culture and history.* New York, NY: Zone Books.

Herek, G. M. (1987). Religious orientation and prejudice: A comparison of racial and sexual attitudes. *Personality and Social Psychology Bulletin, 13,* 34–44. doi:10.1177/0146167287131003

Herek, G. M. (1992). The social context of hate crimes: Notes on cultural heterosexism. In G. M. Herek & K. T. Berrill (Eds.), *Hate crimes: Confronting violence against lesbians and gay men* (pp. 89–104). Newbury Park, CA: Sage.

Huang, Y., Brewster, M. E., Moradi, B., Goodman, M. B., Wiseman, M. C., & Martin, A. (2010). Content analysis of literature about LGB people of color: 1998–2007. *Counseling Psychologist, 38,* 363–396. doi:10.1177/0011000009335255

Jay, K., & Young, Y. (1979). *The gay report: Lesbians and gay men speak out about sexual experiences and lifestyles.* New York, NY: Summit Books.

Kenyon, F. (1968). Studies in female homosexuality: Social and psychiatric aspects, sexual development, attitudes, and experience. *British Journal of Psychiatry, 27,* 107–115.

Khan, M. F. (2008). *Feminist and queer Muslims in America: The struggle to reconstruct religious identity and practice.* Unpublished dissertation.

Kosmin, B., & Lachman, S. (1993). *One nation under God: Religion in contemporary American society.* New York, NY: Harmony.

Lake, C. (1999). *Recreations: Religion and spirituality in the lives of queer people.* Toronto, Ontario, Canada: Queer Press.

Laumann, E. O., Gagnon, J. H., Michael, R. T., & Michaels, S. (1994). *The social organization of sexuality: Sexual practices in the United States.* Chicago, IL: University of Chicago Press.

Lease, S. H., Horne, S. G., & Noffsinger-Frazier, N. (2005). Affirming faith experiences and psychological health for Caucasian lesbian, gay, and bisexual individuals. *Journal of Counseling Psychology, 52,* 378–388. doi:10.1037/0022-0167.52.3.378

Levy, D. (2008). *Gay, lesbian, and queer individuals with a Christian upbringing: Exploring the process of resolving conflict between sexual identity and religious beliefs.* Unpublished doctoral dissertation, University of Georgia, Athens.

Lincoln, C., & Mamiya, L. (1990). *The Black church in the American experience.* Raleigh, NC: Duke University Press.

Lynch, B. (1996). Religious and spirituality conflicts. In D. Davies & C. Neal (Eds.), *Pink therapy: A guide for counselors and therapists working with lesbian, gay and bisexual clients* (pp. 199–207). Buckingham, England: Open University Press.

Mahaffy, K. A. (1996). Cognitive dissonance and its resolution: A study of lesbian Christians. *Journal for the Scientific Study of Religion, 35,* 392–402. doi:10.2307/1386414

Maher, M. J. (2006). A voice in the wilderness: Gay and lesbian religious groups in the western United States. *Journal of Homosexuality, 51,* 91–117. doi:10.1300/J082v51n04_05

McCarthy, S., Trevino, K., Desai, K., Pargament, K., & Mahoney, A. (2007, August). *Is homosexuality an abomination? How perceptions of desecration relate to anti-homosexual prejudice.* 115th Annual Convention of the American Psychological Association, San Francisco, CA.

McCarthy, S. K. (2008). *The adjustment of lesbian, gay, and bisexual (LGB) older adolescents who experience minority stress: The role of religious coping, struggle, and forgiveness.* Unpublished doctoral dissertation, Bowling Green State University, Bowling Green, OH.

McLaughlin, B. R. (1994). Devastated spiritually: The impact of childhood sexual abuse on the survivor's relationship with God and the church. *Sexual Addiction and Compulsivity: The Journal of Treatment and Prevention, 1,* 145–158.

Morris, C. (Ed.). (1967). *The works of George Herbert Mead: Vol. 1. Mind, self, and society: From the standpoint of a social behaviorist.* Chicago, IL: University of Chicago Press.

Miller, A., & Hoffman, J. (1995). Risk and religion: An explanation of gender differences in religiosity. *Journal for the Scientific Study of Religion, 34,* 63–75. doi:10.2307/1386523

Miller, A. S., & Stark, R. (2000, November). *Gender and religiousness: Can socialization explanations be saved?* Paper presented at the Annual Meeting of the Religious Research Association, Houston, TX.

Minwalla, O., Rosser, B. R. S., Feldman, J., & Varga, C. (2005). Identity experience among progressive gay Muslims in North America: A qualitative study within al-Fatiha. *Culture, Health, and Sexuality, 7,* 113–128. doi:10.1080/13691050412331321294

Mixner, R. (1997). Pastoral care of gay men. In C. Neuger & J. Poling (Eds.), *The care of men* (pp. 163–183). Nashville, TN: Abingdon Press.

Moradi, B., DeBlaere, C., & Huang, Y. (2010). Centralizing the experiences of LGB people of color in counseling psychology. *Counseling Psychologist, 38,* 322–330. doi:10.1177/0011000008330832

Moradi, B., Mohr, J. J., Worthington, R. L., & Fassinger, R. E. (2009). Counseling psychology research on sexual (orientation) minority issues: Conceptual and methodological challenges and opportunities. *Journal of Counseling Psychology, 56,* 5–22. doi:10.1037/a0014572

Morrow, S., & Beckstead, A. (2004). Conversion therapies for same-sex attracted clients in religious conflict: Context, predisposing factors, experiences, and implications for therapy. *Counseling Psychologist, 32,* 641–650. doi:10.1177/0011000004268877

Neitz, M. J. (2000). Queering the dragonfest: Changing sexualities in a post-patriarchal religion. *Sociology of Religion, 61,* 369–391. doi:10.2307/3712521

Newman, B. S., & Muzzonigro, P. (1993). The effects of traditional family values on the coming out process of gay male adolescents. *Adolescence, 28,* 213–226.

Nicholson, W. D., & Long, B. (1990). Self-esteem, social support, internalized homophobia and coping strategies of HIV+ gay men. *Journal of Consulting and Clinical Psychology, 58,* 873–876. doi:10.1037/0022-006X.58.6.873

O'Neill, C., & Ritter, K. (1992). *Coming-out within: Stages of spiritual awakening for lesbians and gay men.* San Francisco, CA: Harper-Collins.

Pargament, K. I. (1997). *The psychology of religion and coping: Theory, research, practice.* New York, NY: Guilford Press.

Pargament, K. I. (2007). *Spiritually integrated psychotherapy: Understanding and addressing the sacred.* New York, NY: Guilford Press.

Pargament, K. I., Trevino, K., Mahoney, A., & Silberman, I. (2007). They killed our Lord: The perception of Jews as desecrators of Christianity as a predictor of anti-Semitism. *Journal for the Scientific Study of Religion, 46,* 143–158. doi:10.1111/j.1468-5906.2007.00347.x

Partners Task Force for Gay and Lesbian Couples. (1990, May/June). Partners' national survey of lesbian and gay couples. *Partners: Newsletter for Gay and Lesbian Couples.*

Phillips, J. C., & Fischer, A. R. (1998). Graduate students' training experiences with lesbian, gay and bisexual issues. *Counseling Psychologist, 26,* 712–734. doi:10.1177/0011000098265002

Remafedi, G., French, S., Story, M., Resnick, M., & Blum, R. (1998). The relationship between suicide risk and sexual orientation: Results of a population-based study. *American Journal of Public Health, 88*, 57–60. doi:10.2105/AJPH.88.1.57

Reynolds, A. L. (2003). Counseling issues for lesbian and bisexual women. In M. Kopala & M. Keitel (Eds.), *Handbook of counseling women* (pp. 53–73). Thousand Oaks, CA: Sage.

Ritter, K. Y., & O'Neill, C. W. (1996). *Righteous religion: Unmasking the illusions of fundamentalism and authoritarian Catholicism.* New York, NY: Haworth Pastoral Press.

Ritter, K. Y., & Terndrup, A. I. (2002). *Handbook of affirmative psychotherapy with lesbians and gay men.* New York, NY: Guilford Press.

Rodriguez, E. M., & Ouellette, S. C. (2000). Gay and lesbian Christians: Homosexual and religious identity integration in the members and participants of a gay-positive church. *Journal for the Scientific Study of Religion, 39*, 333–347. doi:10.1111/0021-8294.00028

Ross, M. W. (1990). The relationship between life events and mental health in homosexual men. *Journal of Clinical Psychology, 46*, 402–411. doi:10.1002/1097-4679(199007)46:4<402::AID-JCLP2270460405>3.0.CO;2-Q

Ross, M. W., & Rosser, B. R. S. (1996). Measurement and correlates of internalized homophobia: A factor analytic study. *Journal of Clinical Psychology, 52*, 15–21. doi:10.1002/(SICI)1097-4679(199601)52:1<15::AID-JCLP2>3.0.CO;2-V

Rossetti, S. J. (1995). The impact of child sexual abuse on attitudes towards God and the Catholic Church. *Child Abuse and Neglect, 19*, 1469–1481. doi:10.1016/0145-2134(95)00100-1

Sagir, M., & Robins, E. (1973). *Male and female homosexuality: A comprehensive investigation.* Baltimore, MD: Williams & Wilkins.

Saunders, S., Miller, M., & Bright, M. (2010). Spiritually conscious psychological care. *Professional Psychology: Research and Practice, 41*, 355–362. doi:10.1037/a0020953

Schaeffer, K. W., Hyde, R. A., Kroencke, T., McCormick, R., & Nottebaum, L. (2000). Religiously-motivated sexual orientation change. *Journal of Psychology and Christianity, 19*, 61–70.

Schofield, M. (1965). *Sociological aspects of homosexuality: A comparative study of three types of homosexuals.* Boston, MA: Little, Brown.

Schuck, K. D., & Liddle, B. J. (2001). Religious conflicts experienced by lesbian, gay, and bisexual individuals. *Journal of Gay and Lesbian Psychotherapy, 5*, 63–82. doi:10.1300/J236v05n02_07

Sears, J. T. (Ed.). (1991). *Growing up gay in the south: Race, gender and the journey of the spirit.* New York, NY: Harrington Park Press.

Sherkat, D. E. (2002). Sexuality and religious commitment in the United States: An empirical examination. *Journal for the Scientific Study of Religion, 41*, 313–323. doi:10.1111/1468-5906.00119

Shidlo, A. (1994). Internalized homophobia: Conceptual and empirical issues in measurement. In B. Green & G. Herek (Eds.), *Lesbian and gay psychology: Theory, research and clinical applications* (pp. 176–205). Thousand Oaks, CA: Sage.

Shidlo, A., & Schroeder, M. (2002). Ethical issues in sexual orientation conversion therapies: An empirical study of consumers. *Professional Psychology: Research and Practice, 33*, 249–259. doi:10.1037/0735-7028.33.3.249

Stark, R. (2000, November). *Physiology and faith: Addressing the universal gender differences in religious commitment.* Paper presented at the Annual Meeting of the Religious Research Association, Houston, TX.

Stein, E. (1992). *Forms of desire: Sexual orientation and the social constructionist controversy.* New York, NY: Routledge.

Szymanski, D. M., & Gupta, A. (2009). Examining the relationship between multiple internalized oppressions and African American lesbian, gay, bisexual and questioning persons' self-esteem and psychological distress. *Journal of Counseling Psychology, 56*, 110–118. doi:10.1037/a0013317

Tan, P. P. (2005). The importance of spirituality among gay and lesbian individuals. *Journal of Homosexuality, 49*, 135–144. doi:10.1300/J082v49n02_08

Thompson, M. (1995). *Gay soul.* San Francisco, CA: HarperSanFrancisco.

Thumma, S. (1991). Negotiating a religious identity: The case of the gay evangelical. *Sociological Analysis, 52*, 333–347. doi:10.2307/3710850

Thumma, S., & Gray, E. R. (2005). *Gay religion.* Walnut Creek, CA: AltaMira Press.

Troiden, R. R. (1989). The formation of homosexual identities. *Journal of Homosexuality, 17*, 43–74. doi:10.1300/J082v17n01_02

Warner, M. (1997). Tongues untied: Memories of a Pentecostal boyhood. In G. D. Comstock & S. E. Henking (Eds.), *Que(e)rying religion: A critical anthology* (pp. 223–231). New York, NY: Continuum.

Warner, M. (1999). *The trouble with normal: Sex, politics, and the ethics of queer life.* Minneapolis, MN: University of Minnesota Press.

Warner, R. S. (1995). The metropolitan community churches and the gay agenda: The power of

Pentecostalism and essentialism. *Religion and the Social Order, 5*, 67–94.

Wilcox, M. M. (2002). When Sheila's a lesbian: Religious individualism among lesbian, gay, bisexual, and transgender Christians. *Sociology of Religion, 63*, 497–513. doi:10.2307/3712304

Williams, J. K., Wyatt, G. E., Resell, J., Peterson, J., & Asuan-O'Brien, A. (2004). Psychosocial issues among gay and non-gay-identifying HIV-seropositive African American and Latino MSM. *Cultural Diversity and Ethnic Minority Psychology, 10*, 268–286. doi:10.1037/1099-9809.10.3.268

Yakushko, O. (2005). Influence of social support, existential well-being, and stress over sexual orientation and self esteem of gay, lesbian, and bisexual individuals. *International Journal for the Advancement of Counselling, 27*, 131–143. doi:10.1007/s10447-005-2259-6

Yip, A. K. T. (1997). Attacking the attacker: Gay Christians talk back. *British Journal of Sociology, 48*, 113–127. doi:10.2307/591913

Yip, A. K. T. (2003). The self as the basis of religious faith: Spirituality of gay, lesbian, and bisexual Christians. In G. Davie, P. Heelas, & L. Woodhead (Eds.), *Predicting religion* (pp. 135–146). Burlington, VT: Ashgate.

CHAPTER 35

BUDDHISM: A BLEND OF RELIGION, SPIRITUALITY, AND PSYCHOLOGY

Jean Kristeller and Lobsang Rapgay

In addition to providing an overview of Buddhism, the primary focus of this chapter is on the expression of Buddhism within the United States. At the same time that Buddhism has a presence in the United States, it remains a vibrant religion and cultural force in many parts of Asia, and consideration is given to these traditions and to related immigrant groups in the United States. This chapter reviews some of the major tenets of Buddhism; the background and expression of key variants of Buddhism; and the interface of Buddhism with psychology, both conceptually and in regard to the research evidence that exists. Although meditation as a core Buddhist practice is primarily addressed in Chapter 17 in this volume, some reference to it as a spiritual and therapeutic practice central to Buddhism is explored here as well.

HISTORICAL BACKGROUND OF BUDDHISM

Siddhartha Gautama, who became known as Shakyamuni, the sage of the Shakyas, and finally the Buddha, the Awakened One, was born about 486 B.C.E. in northern India into a wealthy Hindu family (Buswell, 2004). He left the folds of the family as a young man to pursue the life of an ascetic after encountering the suffering of poverty, illness, and death. After 6 years of studying and meditation, he reached a state of enlightenment in which the truth of human existence in relation to both the reality of suffering (*dukkha*) and the path to release from that suffering became clear to him. Over the next 45 years he taught the principles of what was to become Buddhism to an increasing group of followers (Amore & Ching, 2002; Smith & Novak, 2003).

Buddhism first spread east into Sri Lanka, Thailand, Burma, and other Southeast Asian countries, including Indonesia. Around the 1st century C.E., with the development of Mahayana Buddhism, it began moving north through China, then east into Korea and Japan, and south into Vietnam. Vajrayana Buddhism, drawing on the esoteric and Yogic aspects of Hinduism, also began developing around the 1st century C.E. and was brought into Tibet by Padmasambhava in the 700s, where it began blending with indigenous religious traditions. In India, after being spread throughout the Indian empire by King Asoka (ca. 272–232 B.C.E.), Buddhism largely melded back into Hinduism or was supplanted by Islam, as was also true in Indonesia. The three primary schools of Buddhism remain vibrant in the 21st century in Asia: Theravada, Mahayana, and Vajrayana or Tantric Buddhism (Fischer-Schreiber, Ehrhard, & Diener, 1991; Smith & Novak, 2003).

Theravadan Buddhism (sometimes referred to as *Hinayana*, the "lesser vehicle," in somewhat derogatory contrast to *Mahayana*, the "greater vehicle") is dominant in Sri Lanka and Southeast Asia, particularly in Thailand and Burma, and remains the closest to the original teachings of the Buddha as laid out in the Pali *sutras* and the texts of the *Abhidharma*. *Vipassana*, insight or mindfulness meditation, associated with Theravadan traditions, was codified by Buddhaghosa, an Indian Buddhist monk trained in Sri Lanka, in the treatise *Visuddhimagga*

DOI: 10.1037/14045-035
APA Handbook of Psychology, Religion, and Spirituality: Vol. 1. Context, Theory, and Research, K. I. Pargament (Editor-in-Chief)
Copyright © 2013 by the American Psychological Association. All rights reserved.

(Goleman, 1988), in the 5th century. In Theravadan Buddhism, the emphasis is on liberation of the individual and attainment of wisdom. For the most part Theravada Buddhism recognizes Shakyamuni as the only Buddha or consummately enlightened being, whereas Mahayana and Vajrayana recognize numerous Buddhas as incarnated beings who represent enlightenment. Buddhas, however, are not transcendent gods in the Judeo-Christian sense of God.

Historically, within Theravadan Buddhism, importance has been placed on the meditative discipline of the monastic life. In contemporary Thailand, most young men are expected to attend at least brief retreat experiences, with symbolic ordination. This supports the continuity of a vibrant, active religious and spiritual tradition in Thailand, along with the plethora of temples often containing spectacular gold godlike images of the Buddha.

Mahayana Buddhism began to develop around the 1st century C.E., emphasizing the availability of liberation to all, with the Buddha as a savior and with more emphasis on the divine; at the same time, the focus was on the ability of all to find enlightenment. The primary virtue emphasized in Mahayana Buddhism is compassion for others, and a major concept introduced was that of the existence of *bodhisattvas*, or reincarnated figures who decline freedom from rebirth to assist others spiritually. Unlike Theravada, which has held to the primacy of the original teachings, Mahayana has produced elaborated texts or *sutras* of substantial variation. Mahayana, as it spread into China, and then into east Asia, developed various sects that continue to the present day, including Ch'an, T'ien-t'ai, and Pure Land in China, and their equivalent, Zen, Tendai, and Amidism (or Jōdo Shinshū/Shin Buddhism [True Pure Land]) in Japan, respectively. Shinran, the founder of Shin Buddhism in the 1200s, was substantially responsible for breaking the tradition of celibacy among priests in Japan, leading in the 21st century to a largely hereditary succession within most Japanese Buddhist temples. Shin Buddhism remains the most prominent sect in Japan (Andreasen, 1998; Bloom, 2004). Within Zen, two branches were transmitted to Japan from China in the 1200s and survive in the 21st century: *Rinzai*, associated with use of the *kōan* in meditation practice, and *Soto* Zen, emphasizing *shikantaza*, "just sitting," which is more similar to mindfulness meditation of Vipassana traditions. Unique to Japan is *Nichiren* Buddhism, also developing in the 1200s, and intended to simplify access to enlightenment for all through recitation of the mantra *Namu myōhō renge-kyō*, the Lotus Sutra (Amore & Ching, 2002; Causton, 1989). In China and Japan, Buddhism has blended synergistically with other major religious, philosophical, and spiritual traditions, including Taoism and Confucianism in China, and Confucianism and Shinto in Japan (Ching, 2002), while maintaining its own identity.

Vajrayana or Tantric Buddhism, although identified primarily with Tibetan Buddhism, refers to the power of enlightened awareness, originally depicted as a thunderbolt (*vajra*) in Hinduism and *dorje* (the indestructible strength of a "diamond") in Tibetan (Amore & Ching, 2002; Fischer-Schreiber et al., 1991). Originally linked with early Mahayana teachings, Vajrayana originated in northern India, with elements from Tantric Hinduism, drawing on Indian texts referred to as the *Tantras*. It was brought from northern India into Tibet by Padmasambhava in the 700s and into China in the 800s and carried onward from China through Korea and to Japan, where it continues to be represented in Shingon Buddhism (not to be confused with Japanese Shinran or Shin Buddhism). Vajrayana contains many esoteric elements, with complex meditative practices that include evocative use of symbolic mantras and visualization of *mandalas* that depict elaborate depictions of Buddha figures. In India, there was a limited resurgence beginning in the late 1800s and expanding more recently with the influx of Tibetan refugees.

Estimates of the number of practitioners of Buddhism within Asia vary considerably. One reason is that among the major religions, Buddhism may be unique in supporting individuals who blend a reverence for the teachings of the Buddha with observance of other religious traditions. Even up-to-date sources vary tremendously in their estimates (Buddhism by Country, 2011; World Factbook, 2011). In Mongolia and the Southeast Asian countries of Thailand, Burma, and Cambodia, about 90% of individuals are identified as practicing Buddhists, with about 65% to 75% in Sri Lanka and Burma. In India, estimates range from 1% to 3%, with the higher number suggesting a recent upswing in identification with Buddhism. Elsewhere, secularization has had a major impact. Numbers in Vietnam and China range from less than 10% (reflecting the Communist prohibitions against religion) to more than 80% if traditional identity, along with more recent trends toward lifting the political restrictions, are taken into account. In both countries, with the shift in state Communism toward more openness, temples are being reopened and reinvigorated. In Korea, percentages range from 23% to 38%, about the same as for Christianity. In Japan, estimates vary hugely, from 20% to more than 90%; the lower number reflects that fewer and fewer individuals identify as active practitioners, whereas the higher number reflects a more general cultural identity. Traditional engagement primarily has focused on death rituals and funerals, and there is little sense of community around identity with local temples. The hereditary aspect of Buddhist temples is increasingly challenging to maintain in a modern society. For many, Buddhism may serve primarily as a cultural vehicle to engage in religious practices marking birth, coming of age, and death (Ando, 2008). Japanese psychologists have invested considerable scholarly and research interest in meditation practice, particularly in Zen Buddhism (e.g., Haruki & Takase, 2001; Kasamatsu & Hirai, 1963), have actively promoted international dialogue in these areas (cf. Kwee, Gergen, & Koshikawa, 2006), and in the case of psychologist Hayao Kawai (1996), hugely popularized a link between Buddhism and Jungian psychology in Japan.

CORE BUDDHIST CONCEPTS

The three core elements of Buddhism are the *Buddha*, the *Dharma*, and the *Sangha* (Smith & Novak, 2003). The *Buddha* is the person of Siddhartha Gautama, who laid out, over a course of 45 years, the principles of what was to become Buddhism. But to take refuge in the Buddha means to commit to looking for the Buddha within, guided by his teachings, rather than by worshiping him as a historical figure or savior. The *Dharma*, or the "way," consists of these teachings, in content and spirit, as communicated and translated into practice. Regardless of the branch of Buddhism, the core teachings consist of the Four Noble Truths and the Noble Eightfold Path. The *Sangha* is the collective of individuals providing both spiritual leadership and support within a Buddhist community.

Four Noble Truths

The First Noble Truth states that all life and existence contain suffering or *dukkha,* which may also be translated as pain, dissatisfaction, or, in contemporary language, stress. Dukkha is not to be escaped or avoided, but rather it is to be engaged and understood. It is not framed as a punishment from God—or from the Devil—but rather as an inherent aspect of life. It encompasses the mild aversions, tensions, or frustrations that may show up repeatedly during the day as well as the traumas of illness, accidents, or catastrophes. That all life contains suffering is not intended as a pessimistic perspective on life, but rather as a statement of reality, which if not understood and dealt with, leads to pervasive unhappiness, greed, and further distress.

The Second Noble Truth addresses the origin of such suffering: that much of suffering is the result of our attachment to pleasure and craving, to our desire to avoid discomfort, and to our need to maintain an identity with a created sense of "self" that in reality is fluid and ephemeral. Suffering is therefore proportional to the attachments to these states.

The Third Noble Truth is that release from suffering comes from understanding the reality of these principles, understanding the insubstantial quality of both pleasure and discomfort, and understanding the illusionary nature of the concrete self.

The Fourth Noble Truth contains the instructions for learning how to experience a release from suffering: the Noble Eightfold Path.

The Noble Eightfold Path

Smith and Novak (2003) have referred to the Eightfold Path as a "course of treatment," containing explicit guidelines for "curing" the "dis-*ease*" of life. The elements of the Eightfold Path overlap with but go beyond the Judeo–Christian Ten Commandments and are intended to be guidelines for training in pursuit of a better life not only in relation to the spiritual but also more broadly. The eight components

(Das, 1997; Keown, 1996; Smith & Novak, 2003) are laid out not as a ladder but as a wheel or a multipetaled flower, with each linked to another. Together they constitute the "middle way" of Buddhism, in contrast to the extreme denial of the Hindu ascetic or the indulgence and ignorance of the everyday life. These eight are divided into three sets: wisdom (understanding and intent), morality (speech, action, and livelihood), and meditation (effort, mindfulness, and concentration; Keown, 1996). Exercise of them is designed to allow the *three* poisons—ignorance, craving, and aversion—to diminish their hold on one's life. Lama Surya Das (1997) has built his entire book *Awakening the Buddha Within* around exploring these eight steps—or spokes of a wheel—in highly approachable language that links the growth of the spiritual with the sensitivity of the personal. In following the Noble Eightfold Path, one is committing to working for the enlightenment of both oneself and all other living beings (Amore & Ching, 2002; Das, 1997; Smith & Novak, 2003).

The components of the Noble Eightfold Path classically are divided into three parts addressing wisdom, ethics, and meditation training.

Wisdom Training:

1. Right view or understanding: acceptance of Buddhist teachings, both intellectually and experientially.
2. Right intent or resolve: a commitment to developing right attitudes.

Ethics Training:

1. Right speech: telling the truth and speaking in a thoughtful and sensitive way.
2. Right conduct or action (the Five Precepts): abstaining from killing any living creature, stealing, sexual misconduct, false speech, and intoxication.
3. Right livelihood: not engaging in an occupation that causes harm to others.

Meditation Training:

1. Right effort: exerting the effort required to meet goals; gaining control of one's thoughts and cultivating positive states of mind.
2. Right mindfulness (*sati/smrti*): cultivating constant awareness; witnessing all thoughts, feelings, actions, and bodily sensations without reactivity.
3. Right concentration (*samadhi*): cultivating mental calm through concentrative training/meditation practices.

Other Core Concepts

Contained in the voluminous Pali Canon and the scholarly Abhidhamma are other core Buddhist concepts, including several of particular interest from a psychological and practice perspective. These include the concepts of "store or storehouse consciousness" (*ālaya-vijñāna*), interdependent arising or co-origination (*pratitya samutpada*), no-self (*anatta*), and states of meditative absorption (the *jhanas*; Amore & Ching, 2002; Fischer-Schreiber et al., 1991). The first two concepts are noteworthy because of their compelling links to contemporary psychological constructs. Within the framework of this book, these concepts of psychological well-being are also of interest because they meld into spiritual growth and enlightenment.

Storehouse consciousness. Buddhism developed complex models of mind to explain both the experience of "knowing" and the development of attachment and aversion, projection of meaning, and distortion of reality that keep one bound up in *dukkha*, delusion, and self-absorption. Functionally, these models map surprisingly well onto developing models of the complexity of neuronal systems, the challenge of relearning entrenched habit patterns, particularly those sustained by long-hidden or unconscious attachments and aversions, and the extended impact of symbolic learning and trauma. The path to spiritual growth and enlightenment is viewed as lying within the gradual loosening of these interconnections, through the use of meditative practices (Sharp, 2011), first by bringing them into awareness, and then by practicing nonattachment.

Interdependent arising or co-origination. Every effect has a cause; everything is related to something else in a dynamic process. The significance of this is core to understanding other essential elements of Buddhism: impermanence, a lack of stable "self-identity," karma, and that happiness or satisfaction comes from letting go of desire or aversion. This core concept of fluid interdependency can be viewed as the original statement of conditioning theory—that the quality of our experience lies entirely in our relation to that experience, and that release from the power of experience is also more under conscious control than it is generally experienced as being.

No-self. Often misinterpreted as self-denying, this actually speaks to the risk and pain associated with searching for a single identity of self, rather than embracing the flexible, fluid nature of who we each are. "You are *not* your thoughts" is an expression of this aspect of Buddhism on an everyday level of understanding and experience; a corollary is that there is no single part of our experience that can—or should—drive how we see ourselves. This is a very powerful message to convey in a therapeutic context. This concept also speaks to the neurologically grounded experience of losing all sense of "self" during certain stages of meditation practice. Experiencing this can be disturbing or profoundly life changing. At a milder level, it may be the spiritual experience of sensing a profound connection with something "outside" the self, an element described in virtually all religious and spiritual traditions.

Compassion. Opening the heart, suspending negative judgment, both of the self and of others, is an element common to most religious traditions. More strongly identified with Mahayana and Vajrayana practices than with Theravada, it is an aspect of Buddhism that has garnered more recognition over the past 20 years, both because of the influence of teachings from the Dalai Lama and his associates and through the work of Thich Nhat Hanh, in communicating the simplicity and profound value of loving kindness meditations. Understanding the centrality of compassion also counters the perception of meditative practice as self-absorbed "navel gazing." Although meditation is certainly a privately engaged process, evidence is growing that the suspension of self-engaged conditioning may open awareness to the needs of others, regardless of whether guided or directed meditations related to cultivating compassion are being utilized (Gilbert, 2009; Kristeller & Johnson, 2005).

Deep meditative states. As a spiritual practice, regardless of the Buddhist tradition, meditation is recognized as potentially producing profound levels of experience often identified as mystical or even as altered states. These altered states are identified as enlightenment experiences, such as kensho or *satori* in Zen practice, that signal increasingly attuned levels of "knowing" (*prajna*). Sophisticated neurological modeling has been applied to exploring such experiences (Austin, 1998, 2006, 2009; Lutz, Greischar, Rawlings, Ricard, & Davidson, 2004; Newberg, 2010). Traditional Buddhist texts acknowledge the development of such states, particularly within Tibetan Buddhist practices, identifying multiple levels of *jhanas* or levels of training in awareness and attention (Wallace, 2006), while at the same time cautioning that experiencing deeper states is more of a marker of cultivating the capacity for following the Noble Eightfold Path, rather than as goals in themselves. Much of the therapeutic value that has been identified with use of both meditation practice and engagement of other aspects of Buddhist teaching neither presumes the experience of such states nor suggests that such experiences are needed to gain value from practice.

Wisdom. The concept of wisdom from a psychological perspective, as informed by Buddhism, deserves further consideration. Wisdom has been examined as a psychological construct (Baltes & Staudinger, 2000; Sternberg, 1990) that extends beyond intellectual knowledge but still in a more limited way than within Buddhist psychology. In keeping with the notion of inherent wisdom found in Buddhism (Das, 1997; Gethin, 1998), the experiencing of "wisdom" can be considered an emergent process that occurs when conditioned habitual reactions are suspended, allowing integration of more complex processing, parallel to the traditional categories of "stillness" and "insight." Stillness involves suspending the mind's habitual patterns; insight refers to the more complex, creative, and "deeper" levels of processing that emerge. This type of "wisdom" need not entail intellectual processing, but it can occur within any capacity, experienced as a sense of "knowing"—that is, a sense of realizing a true or wise perspective. Such insight involves disengagement from habitual patterns and preoccupation with self, while seeing a problem, whether simpler or more profound, in a larger perspective;

thus, it is in continuity with the Buddhist concepts of insight, wisdom, and spiritual growth (Austin, 2009; Kornfield, 2000; Kristeller & Jones, 2006).

Many other core concepts associated with Buddhism are important to understanding religious beliefs, such as *samsara*, *nirvana*, and reincarnation. Those discussed earlier in this section are coming to play a more substantial role in understanding the interface of Buddhism with psychology. The concept of mindfulness (*sati* in Pali, *smrti* in Sanskrit), from the Eightfold Path, and clearly one of the most important concepts from a psychological perspective, are discussed further in the section Key Buddhist Concepts Entering Psychological Discourse later in this chapter.

BUDDHISM WITHIN THE UNITED STATES

Buddhism has entered the United States through a number of paths beginning in the late 1800s. Those practicing Buddhism in the United States have included both individuals with Asian backgrounds in Buddhism and non-Asian Americans who have found their way to Buddhism both through personal travels in Buddhist cultures and through the dissemination of Buddhist teachings within the United States.

Traditions of Buddhism Within the United States

Each of the schools of Buddhism has a presence within the United States, with remarkable growth over the past 2 decades (Amore & Ching, 2002; Coleman, 2001; Fields, 1992; Keown, 1996; Morgan, 2004; Smith & Novak, 2003). The distinction between Mahayana and Theravada Buddhism, however, particularly among non–Asian Americans, has blurred considerably over the past 20 to 30 years. At the same time, well-established Buddhist centers within these denominations (some founded in the late 1800s) that primarily serve Asian Americans continue to flourish.

Chinese Buddhist temples were well established on the West Coast by the late 1800s, but they served only the Chinese communities (Fields, 1992). Buddhist Churches of America (the BCA) grew out of Japanese efforts to provide services to immigrants beginning in the late 1890s in the San Francisco, California, area. The BCA represents Pure Land or Shin Buddhism (Bloom, 2004) and has developed services into a form similar to those of the Protestant church in structure; there are more than 60 temples in the United States, with about 20,000 members. Priests are trained at the Institute for Buddhist Studies in Berkeley, California. Membership in the BCA appears to be declining as acculturation increases, however (Morgan, 2004). Smaller groups from Cambodia, Thailand, and Laos exist but are less well established.

Buddhism first came to the attention of the Euro-American public in the late 1800s, largely via England and other parts of Europe, through the efforts of the transcendentalists. The first American English translation (from French) of a Buddhist text was completed in 1844 by Elizabeth Palmer Peabody, the editor of the transcendentalist journal, the *Dial* (although this translation is often credited to Henry David Thoreau; Sutin, 2006). Far more interest in Buddhism grew out of the World Congress of Religion in 1894, particularly because of a presentation by Roshi Soyen Shaku, a Rinzai Zen monk. This presentation was notable as it provided a primary link to the development of Zen in the United States through his disciples, D. T. Suzuki, who first traveled to the United States in 1897, and Nyogen Sensaki, who founded Zen groups on the West Coast (Coleman, 2001; Fields, 1992; Morgan, 2004). There continue to be clear links from this Congress to contemporary interest in Zen Buddhism, fostered through Suzuki's direct influence on prominent scholars, such as Erich Fromm (Fromm, Suzuki, & DeMartino, 1970), Karen Horney (DeMartino, 1991), and Alan Watts (1957) following World War II, and their students, such as Jeffrey Rubin (1996). Other Zen monks came from Japan and from Korea, both to the West Coast and the East Coast, founding retreat centers and monasteries (Fields, 1992; Prebish & Tanaka, 1998). Among the more notable of these are the San Francisco Zen Center, founded in 1962 by Shunryu Suzuki (1973) in the Soto Zen tradition; the Zen Meditation Center of Rochester, New York, founded by Philip Kapleau (1970) in 1966; and the Cambridge Zen Center in Massachusetts, founded in 1973 by students of the Korean Zen Master Seung Sahn (Coleman, 2001; Sahn, 1997).

Contemporary interest in the Vipassana traditions can be traced primarily to individuals traveling to Southeast Asia during and following the Vietnam War, and as part of the Peace Corps, studying particularly in the Thai Forest tradition (Swearer, 1970) and in Burma. In 1974, the Insight Meditation Society was founded in Barre, Massachusetts, by Jack Kornfield, Joseph Goldstein, and Sharon Salzberg, who had studied Vipassana Buddhism in northern India, Burma, and Thailand and were ordained as monks. They then had returned to the United States to disseminate this wisdom more widely. Contemporary use of Vipassana (or insight) meditation has become one of the more accessible practices both within the United States and elsewhere through the teachings of Jack Kornfield, who later became a clinical psychologist, and his associates (Goldstein & Kornfield, 1987; Kornfield, 1993; Salzberg, 1999). On the West Coast, Kornfield, Goldstein, and Salzberg founded another center, Spirit Rock, just north of San Francisco, which also serves as a center for extended meditation retreats. Numerous other Vipassana centers exist. Some are monastic centers, such as the Metta Forest Monastery near San Diego, founded by Thanissaro Bhikku, an American who follows the Thai Forest tradition closely (Thanissaro, 2006). Others are in the community, such as the Cambridge Insight Meditation Center (Cadge, 2005). These centers have made the practices more accessible and somewhat less esoteric. Teachers within these communities have elucidated the value of mindfulness meditation training as a means to cultivating nonreactive attention in the service of becoming aware of—and managing—inner experience, an approach that has resonated widely within both Buddhist and, increasingly, secular circles.

Also in the Vipassana tradition are the teachings of S. S. Goenka (Hart, 1987), a Burmese teacher of Indian background, who, with his followers, has been leading traditional 10-day silent retreats for many years in India, in the United States, and throughout the world. He is particularly noted for bringing his work into prison environments, as documented in the film *Doing Time, Doing Vipassana* (1997), reflecting his work in India, and the film *Changing From Inside* (1998), of transformation in a woman's prison in Seattle, Washington. Related research by Marlatt and his associates has also been carried out in Seattle (Bowen et al., 2006). The impact of Goenka's work has been documented in a book of published letters written by prison inmates after their retreat experience (J. Phillips, 2008).

Exposure to Vajrayana traditions is largely a function of the flight of Tibetan monks, including the Dalai Lama, to Dharamsala, India, and Kathmandu, Nepal, after the invasion of Tibet by the Chinese in 1950. In 1974, Chogyam Trungpa Rinpoche (Trungpa, 1973) founded the Naropa Institute in Boulder, Colorado, which has since become an accredited full-service university. Although Naropa still maintains a Buddhist orientation, it is officially nondenominational, with a particular focus on programs in applied psychology. In addition, Americans who lived in Asia, including Robert Thurman, who became the first American to be ordained a Tibetan Buddhist monk (Thurman, 1998), Lama Surya Das (born Jeffrey Miller; Das, 1997), and Alan Wallace (Wallace, 2006; Wallace & Shapiro, 2006) have contributed in substantial ways to transmitting the value of Tibetan Buddhist teachings. The Dalai Lama has expanded awareness of the value of Buddhism and is a world leader in cultivating dialogue between religion and science, particularly in regard to psychological and neuroscience research (cf. Dalai Lama & Goleman, 2003).

Other Expressions of Buddhism Within the United States

One notable group of nondenominational Buddhists that emphasizes the importance of community, is Friends of the Western Buddhist Order (FWBO; now the Triatina Buddhist Community), originally founded in England by Sangharakshita (born Dennis Lingwood), now with affiliated groups in the United States (Coleman, 2001; Subhuti, 1995). Sangharakshita, a prolific scholar and teacher, was exposed to Buddhism as a young man and then converted after being stationed in northern India. After being ordained, he became involved with the movement to extend Buddhism to the untouchable (*dalits*) caste of Hindus, and he has been powerfully successful in his work both in India in that regard and in revitalizing interest in Buddhism in England.

Another relatively recent development is the Engaged Buddhism movement, committed to the manifestation of compassion through social action and transformation. Although often identified as representing the influence of Western thought on Buddhism, the early beginnings are also associated with Thich Nhat Hanh's social and political actions during the Vietnam War. Engaged Buddhism has expanded substantially to frame a wide range of socially committed activities across Buddhist groups and denominations, both within the United States. and throughout Asia (King, 2005; Queen, 2000).

Scholarly interest in Buddhism continues to grow; Buddhist studies programs are increasingly available at major U.S. universities. Many of the newer programs explicitly address Buddhist psychology, including those at Harvard University, Emory University, Brown University, the University of Wisconsin, University of California (UC)–Santa Barbara, UC–San Diego, UC–Berkeley, UC–Los Angeles, UC–Davis, and the University of Michigan. The recent influence of the Dalai Lama on intellectual discourse is particularly striking. Several centers for study of Tibetan Buddhism have been established. Prominent among them are the Stanford University Center for Compassion and Altruism Research and Education and the Tibetan Studies Program at Emory. At the Massachusetts Institute of Technology, the Dalai Lama Center for Ethics and Transformative Values primarily provides education in Buddhism and western sciences. Under the auspices of the Dalai Lama, the Mind & Life Institute has successfully facilitated annual exchanges between leading scientists in various fields and Buddhist scholars. They also provide research grant support related to the study of various Buddhist practices.

Numbers of Buddhists in the United States

As in Asia, it is very challenging to identify how many individuals in the United States identify as Buddhist, much less within each of the Buddhist traditions. The 2008 Pew Forum report, the U.S. Religious Landscape Survey, based on random telephone sampling, identified 0.7% of the population as Buddhist, or about 2 million people, slightly more than self-identified as Muslim. Yet this survey did not report on the variant of Buddhism identified by the individual. Furthermore, specifying such numbers is complicated because three distinct categories of individuals must be considered: immigrant Buddhists (whether first generation or later) who come from traditionally Buddhist countries; "new Buddhists" who have been drawn to Buddhism, both through Buddhist teachers from these same traditions and through Americans or other Westerners who have spent substantial time studying in these countries; and uncountable numbers who might not label themselves as Buddhist but who are strongly influenced by Buddhist perspectives on understanding human wisdom, spirituality, and psychological well-being.

Of identified Buddhists in America, approximately 30% are immigrants or from an immigrant background (Pew Forum, 2008) and are associated with established temples within Zen, Nichiren Buddhism, Theravadan, or Tibetan/Vajrajana traditions that are important sources of support for those individuals. They have relatively little interaction with Western Buddhist groups. Therefore, Buddhism is notable in the degree to which practice communities have been established in the United States that primarily serve nonimmigrant groups separate from immigrant groups.

Non–Asian Americans have tended to associate with or be drawn to meditation centers, both local *sanghas* (Buddhist religious groups) and regional retreat centers. Morreale (1998), in his comprehensive overview of Buddhist practice in the United States, pointed to the explosion of Buddhist meditation centers. Before 1965, only 21 Buddhist meditation centers had been founded in North America, in contrast to more than 1,000 between 1965 and 1995 (each of which is briefly described in his book). Of these centers, about 40% are in the Mahayana tradition, 33% Vajrayana, 14% Theravadan, and the remainder are transdenominational (sometimes referred to as *Buddhayana*). In his terms, Morreale also noted that an increasing proportion of individuals practice primarily in the context of their daily lives, rather than focusing on extended retreat experiences or Buddhist living environments. The growing number of *sanghas* throughout the United States, within each of the traditions, provide community support, often along with residential and retreat opportunities.

BUDDHISM AND PSYCHOLOGY

It can be argued that Buddhism is as much a psychology as a religion. The Eastern traditions of which it is a part did not, for the most part, deem it necessary to clearly separate religion from philosophy and psychology, as has occurred in Western traditions. It is therefore somewhat artificial to draw such distinctions here, but nevertheless it is useful to identify ways in which Buddhist thought and practices are making substantial contributions to contemporary psychological science and practice.

Key Buddhist Concepts Entering Psychological Discourse

It can be argued that no religious tradition has had as much impact on contemporary psychology as has Buddhism. Buddhism contains within it an explicit psychology or understanding of the mind, which is seamlessly interwoven within the religious traditions of Buddhism. The primary interface with psychology is generally identified as the growing interest in, and acceptance of, meditation-based practices in therapy (see Chapter 17, this volume, and Volume 2, Chapter 10, this handbook). Interest in meditation, although practiced in various forms within virtually all world religions, has entered American culture almost entirely from Asia, both from Hinduism and as an influence of Japanese Zen Mahayana Buddhism, Thai and Burmese Vipassana Buddhism, and Tibetan Vajrayana Buddhism (Morreale, 1998; Seager, 2000; Smith & Novak, 2003).

Somewhat more subtle is the evolving recognition that Buddhist constructs such as mindfulness (*sati/smirti*), nonattachment, and *dukkha* (suffering) mesh extraordinarily well with current understanding of learning processes, emotional regulation, and the neuroscience of attention and awareness, indeed contributing over the past decade to scholarly thinking and research in these areas. Interest in the mind–body interface has been informed for a number of decades by Buddhist psychology; more recently, the role of spiritual well-being has become recognized as important to the psychological modulation of health and illness in ways that also link to Buddhist tenets. Much of the research in the area for the past 40 years has focused on the multiple domains in which meditation practices affect the mind and the body (Didonna, 2009; Kristeller, 2007; Shapiro & Walsh, 1984). It is important to consider broader ways that Buddhist concepts relate to psychology in general and the psychology of spirituality more specifically (Austin, 1998, 2006; Newberg & D'Aquili, 1998; Walsh, 1999) and to identify areas of congruence with contemporary psychological theory (Aronson, 2004; Wallace & Shapiro, 2006; Walsh & Shapiro, 2006).

Of particular significance is the concept of mindfulness, associated traditionally with Theravadan/Vipassana Buddhism, but also recognized as an aspect of Zen or Ch'an meditation. By learning to cultivate mindfulness as a means to observe and experience mental experiences as they are, rather than reacting to them automatically, one can learn to observe the busy mind, gaining a sense of choice and increasing a sense of internalized control. This contrasts with other contemporary psychological approaches in which one tries to replace maladaptive thoughts, feelings, and behavior with adaptive approaches even before establishing a working relationship with anxious thoughts and feelings as they arise.

The concept of mindfulness has been hugely popularized by Jon Kabat-Zinn who, although not a psychologist, created a meditation-based intervention, the mindfulness-based stress reduction (MBSR) program within a mind–body model originally designed to help chronic pain patients (Kabat-Zinn, 1990, 2005; Kabat-Zinn, Lipworth, & Burney, 1985). The program has been investigated in numerous empirical studies with individuals dealing with a wide range of clinical issues, including anxiety disorders and cancer (e.g., Carlson, Speca, Patel, & Goodey, 2003; Carmody, Reed, Kristeller, & Merriam, 2008; Kabat-Zinn et al., 1992) and currently is offered within more than 100 settings, primarily hospitals, in the United States and elsewhere. Furthermore, mindfulness is rapidly gaining credence as a viable psychological construct within the science of mind, contributing to understanding how certain qualities of attention and awareness may modulate emotional and behavioral self-regulation (Bishop et al., 2004; Rapgay & Bystrisky, 2009). Publications addressing the construct of mindfulness have been increasing exponentially over the past 10 years, with more than 1,000 publications in English referencing this term between 2005 and 2010 (Williams & Kabat-Zinn, 2011). Although considerable debate remains regarding the original meaning of the term *mindfulness* (*smrti*) and the mapping of this onto its use as a construct in contemporary psychology, there is little debate regarding the value of the underlying processes from a therapeutic perspective. For extended discussion of the issues as they relate to Buddhism, see the core article by K. W. Brown, Ryan, and Creswell (2007) in a special issue of *Psychological Inquiry* and the related set of responses (e.g., Baer, 2007; Hayes & Plumb, 2007; Rosch, 2007). Also see a more recent set of articles by individuals from a range of disciplines, including philosophy of mind and Buddhist studies, in *Contemporary Buddhism* (e.g., Dreyfus, 2011; Dunne, 2011; Williams & Kabat-Zinn, 2011).

Other arenas of influence, such as the recognition of the inherent interaction between mind and body, are not unique to Buddhism. But along with influences from Hinduism, concepts regarding mind–body interaction have had substantial impact on research on biofeedback and psychophysiology, continuing to influence the development of 21st-century mind–body medicine. Cutting-edge research on the neurophysiology of emotion, particularly Davidson's research with Buddhist monks (Davidson & Harrington, 2002; Lutz, Brefczynski-Lewis, Johnstone, & Davidson, 2008), has been informed by recognizing the unusual focus of Tibetan Buddhism on cultivating compassion and positive emotional states. The concept of self-acceptance is linked with cultivating compassion for oneself, but extends beyond it by engaging awareness of the pernicious effects of critical self-judgment, reflecting both explicitly Buddhist perspectives (Brach, 2003; Germer, 2009; Neff, 2004; Neff & Vonk, 2009) and implicit influences, as in Hayes's Acceptance and Commitment Therapy (Hayes, Strosahl, & Wilson, 1999).

The central value to Buddhism of cultivating intentional awareness and attention on capacity for self-regulation (Wallace, 2006) is influencing contemporary thinking in areas of neurological processing of emotion and behavioral regulation (Goleman, 2003). Although these do not necessarily fall within what are considered spiritual or religious domains of experience, such capacities are generally framed within Buddhism as potentiating a capacity for spiritual growth and well-being. According to traditional Buddhism, these capacities are cultivated within the context of religious practice, much as other religions also address the value of ethical action and emotional well-being.

Often viewed as more esoteric and challenging to conceptualize within contemporary psychology are the rich traditions of Tibetan Vajrayana Buddhism. The complex mandala images of this tradition are visually engaging, with elaborate colorful images of various deities seated on stylized lotus blossoms, surrounded by richly colored smaller figures, swirls of patterns and figures, and spikes of fire. These images are easy to compartmentalize as primarily "religious" in nature. Therefore, in the context of the present discussion, it is useful to consider further how these images, and the practices related to them, are intended to engage both the psychological and spiritual aspects of human functioning and struggle. For example, each deity is intended to express an aspect of self, with the rich imagery of the mandala expressing the constant dialogue between these aspects of self and the complexity of the surrounding world, both inner and outer, which has been effectively tied to Jungian psychology (Jung, 1958/1970; Preece, 2006). For example, among the more prominent deities, Chenrezig represents enlightened compassion, Manjushri represents wisdom and clear intellect, and Vajrapani represents the power of enlightened activity. Each tantric deity "occupies a central position" on the threshold of the interface between the sacred and the relative, or in Jung's terms, between the archetypal collective unconscious and the swirls of daily life, both conscious and unconscious (Jung, 1959/1981). Specific mantras associated with each deity are intended to evoke related capacities. *Om mani padme hum,* "O the Jewel in the Lotus," one of the best known mantras, is intended to evoke compassion associated with Chenrezig, whereas the wisdom mantra of Manjushri is *om ah ra pa tsa na dhih.* The purpose of repeating the mantra is psychological and physical healing, associated not with the meaning of the words or sounds per se but with imputed shifts in internal "energy winds" associated with the distinct sounds of the mantra, when appropriately practiced. Far less esoteric, but also exploring the potential interface of Vajrayana Buddhism with psychology, are the eloquent dialogues between the Dalai Lama and prominent psychologists, including Daniel Goleman, Richard Davidson, and others, that engage more accessible psychological themes, such as emotional intelligence and neuroplasticity (Goleman, 2003; Sharp, 2011).

Influence on Contemporary Psychotherapeutic Traditions

Buddhists tenets are compatible with various theoretical perspectives within both basic and applied psychology (Didonna, 2009; Mruk & Hartzell, 2003). Within clinical psychology, each of the major theoretical clinical traditions—psychodynamic, humanistic, and cognitive–behavioral—have identified fruitful ways to draw on the traditions of Buddhism to inform and engage productive dialogue. Within psychodynamic theory, the dialogue could be argued to have begun with Jung's interest in Buddhism (Daniel, 2007). Interest then expanded in the United States, with Karen Horney's and Erich Fromm's involvement with Japanese Zen Buddhism in the 1950s, and continues through the work of Rubin (1996, 1999), Epstein (Epstein, 1990, 1995, 2001), D. Brown and Engler (1984), Germer and his associates (Germer, Siegel, & Fulton, 2005), and others, influenced broadly by Zen, Vipassana, and Tibetan traditions.

Humanistic–transpersonal psychology has embraced each of the traditions—including Zen (e.g., Mathers, Miller, & Ando, 2009; Rosenbaum, 1998), Vipassana (e.g., Kornfield & Walsh, 1993), and Vajrayana—at Naropa University (e.g., Wegela, 2009) and elsewhere, informing approaches to both individual and group psychotherapy. Within this arena, issues of spiritual engagement have been particularly salient and are consistently respected as core to individual growth and well-being (Brach, 2003; Marlatt & Kristeller, 1999; Walsh, 1999).

Mindfulness meditation practice has been particularly influential within cognitive–behavioral perspectives, as melded into the MBSR, mindfulness-based cognitive therapy (MBCT; Segal, Williams, & Teasdale, 2002), mindfulness-based relapse prevention (MBRP; Bowen et al., 2009; Marlatt et al., 2004), and mindfulness-based eating awareness therapy (MB-EAT; Kristeller & Wolever, 2011) programs, among others (for clinical overview, see Sears, Tirch, & Denton, 2011) and as an explicit contributor to dialectical behavior therapy (Linehan, 1993). Moving outside these three traditional schools and drawing on other directions for therapeutic change are a number of other programs informed by Buddhist perspectives and practices. These include spiritual self-schema therapy (Avants & Margolin, 2004) for individuals struggling with drug addictions and vulnerable to HIV, the melding of Buddhism with the Twelve Step approach to treating alcohol and drug addiction developed by Kevin Griffin (Griffin, 2004), and the link that Daniel Siegel has created between attachment theory and mindfulness approaches (Siegel, 2010; see also Volume 2, Chapter 10, this handbook), among others

The question also needs to be considered as to why Buddhism would have so much continuing, and even deepening, influence on psychology and in the broader community. It can be argued that (a) Buddhist perspectives are consistent with a complex view of human functioning yet one that remains compatible with, and respectful of, the process of science; (b) Buddhism presents a framework that is compatible with a nondualistic approach to understanding the interaction of the mind and body; (c) Buddhism provides a framework within which spirituality and related processes are respected, yet one that does not necessarily entail belief in particular religious structures or emanations of God or gods; and (d) Buddhism supports community in the form of *sanghas* and retreat environments, yet it also provides structure for meaningful individual practice in the form of meditation practice, reading, and clear ethical guidelines.

One powerful dimension that is being integrated increasingly into therapeutic approaches is the concept of cultivating nonjudgmental acceptance of both self and others as reflected in acceptance and commitment therapy (Hayes et al., 1999) and dialectical behavior therapy (Linehan et al., 1999). Loving-kindness meditations, simple guided practices introduced through the writings of Thich Nhat Hanh (Hanh, 1975, 1991) and others (Chodran, 1996; Kornfield, 1993), have been increasingly integrated into other mindfulness-based interventions, such as MBSR, MBRP, MBCT, and Mindfulness-Based Eating Awareness Training (MB-EAT). They reflect the compassion perspective of Mahayana Buddhism and are spiritually engaging yet secular in content. Thich Nhat Hanh is also notable for having actively engaged a dialogue between the meditative and spiritual traditions of Buddhism and Christianity in his book *Living Buddha, Living Christ* (1995), as has J. W. Jones (2003) in his reflections on the commonalities between Christianity and Buddhism when applied more holistically to the purposes of psychotherapy.

The fact that Buddhism can be considered a well-developed psychological system, distinct from the religious tenets, is essential not only to understanding the influence of Buddhist perspectives on current psychological models but also in representing Buddhism to the general public. In particular, the interweaving of psychology, philosophy, and religious belief within Buddhism can lead to confusion in the course of application of Buddhist principles psychotherapeutically. Part of the difficulty lies in the marked efforts within Western intellectual traditions over the past 500 years to draw sharp lines between religion and philosophy, and more recently, psychology. Clients, upon hearing of meditation-based treatments, may feel that engaging in them somehow confuses their therapeutic efforts with their allegiance to their own religious beliefs. One common approach to this quandary is to secularize the practices as much as possible, avoiding any mention of Buddhism or even spirituality. An alternative approach is to acknowledge the linkage with Buddhism, but to note that meditation (and related practices) are drawn from Buddhist perspectives on psychology and on ways to promote general well-being, while at the same time acknowledging that meditation practices are used within all religions as a means to engage "inner wisdom" and cultivate spiritual well-being.

Impact of Buddhist Practice on Well-Being: Empirical Evidence

Despite the explicit engagement of fundamental spiritual issues in much of the Buddhist-informed literature on psychotherapy, a paradox exists regarding research on Buddhist practice and psychological well-being. Research on the psychological and physical effects of meditation practice has exploded over the past 20 years, much of it drawn from Buddhist traditions (see Chapter 17 in this volume), yet much of this work also has explicitly disengaged itself from any religious context. Conversely, spiritual or religious-based coping has been investigated within the context of other traditions, yet rarely within Buddhism. Researchers are beginning to call for this obvious gap to be addressed (Dimidjian & Linehan, 2003; Kristeller, 2007). Only a modest amount of research has explored the impact of Buddhism on psychological adjustment and well-being outside of research on meditation as an intervention component. Leaving the review of that literature to Chapter 17 in this volume, the following summary focuses on research that more explicitly explores Buddhist experience or spiritual effects within Buddhist-related practices.

One creative study (Cook, Sandage, Hill, & Strawn, 2010) compared Cambodian immigrants in the United States who self-identified as Buddhists with those who had converted to Christianity. A Euro-American Christian group was also included for further comparison. The study combined qualitative and quantitative methods to explore the interaction of culture and religion on understanding of everyday virtues. There were a number of themes similar for both Cambodian groups: the importance of duty and responsibility as distinctive motivations, the interrelatedness of the virtues, and the domains of their influence (societal in collectivist perspectives, narrower in individualist perspectives). Warmth-based virtues, such as compassion and forgiveness, generally were described in religious terms and were ranked relatively high by all groups. In contrast, conscientiousness-based virtues, such as self-control and justice, were described in religious terms by the Buddhists but as cultural by Cambodian Christians. The Buddhists also more highly valued conscientiousness-based virtues than did the Euro-American Christians, with the Cambodian Christians at an intermediate level.

Another study investigated the noted resilience of Tibetans in the face of persecution by the Chinese. Informed by the presumption that Buddhist beliefs and practices would serve to modulate and protect against posttraumatic stress, 102 Tibetans who had survived torture and imprisonment by the Chinese before fleeing to India were interviewed using qualitative approaches (Elsass & Phuntsok, 2009). In general, they identified both their political beliefs and engagement and their Buddhism as important coping strategies.

A recent exploratory study (R. E. Phillips et al., 2009) utilized qualitative interviews, informed by grounded theory methodology, with 24 practicing Buddhists (all but one were American Buddhists who converted as adults) to investigate how they drew on their understanding of Buddhism to help cope with stress. The most common theme was "right understanding," drawing on the principle that experience of stress and related suffering often was due to inaccurate perceptions of the world; Buddhist concepts of impermanence, compassion, karma, interbeing, dharma, and "not-self" were mentioned. The second primary theme (21 of 24 participants) was use of meditative techniques to deal with stress; the way meditation was used varied from tension reduction, to distraction, to engaging the spiritual value of a particular mantra (such as a loving kindness meditation). The third domain (20 of 24) was use of mindfulness, separate from meditation practice, as an active way to observe, rather than react to, distressful thoughts and emotions, and to cultivate acceptance of things as they are. In addition, most made explicit reference to Buddhist precepts and the Eightfold Path for guidance to act in helpful, rather than self-centered, ways. Less frequently (seven out of 24), individuals reported drawing on Buddhist friends, mentors, or a *sangha* (Buddhist community) for emotional or instrumental support. The low frequency was hypothesized to be both a function of sociocultural isolation in this group of primarily converts and of the low density of Buddhists in the United States. In truth, the Buddhist community within the United States places far less emphasis on the social support of a faith congregation than do most Judeo-Christian groups. Interestingly, the equivalent of negative religious coping or religious struggle (see Chapter 25 in this volume) was voiced by 14 of 24, taking the form of self-blame ("if I practiced more/better, then I wouldn't be as distressed"), or as experiencing the burden of staying true to Buddhist precepts in the face of misfortune.

As noted earlier, a number of treatment programs that incorporate mindfulness-based meditation, generally modeled on Kabat-Zinn's MBSR program (Kabat-Zinn, 1990), draw on Buddhist principles of mindfulness, loving kindness, and cultivating non-reactive observation of thoughts, emotions, body feelings, and behavior. The aim of these programs is to help individuals cultivate a higher level of functioning and inner wisdom in the face of a variety of issues. Although each of these programs is informed by Buddhist theory and practice, they are neither explicitly Buddhist nor spiritual in their content (for more details on meditation, see Chapter 17 in this volume) except in limited ways. For example, in the MB-EAT program (Kristeller & Wolever, 2011), participants are encouraged to cultivate both "inner wisdom" and "outer wisdom," drawing on higher capacities to inform their intentions and choices in relation to food, consistent with the conative or motivational element of Wallace and Shapiro's model of meditative processes (2006). Spirituality is not explicitly mentioned until late in the MB-EAT program, and then in the context of a guided wisdom meditation. At that point, participants often reflect that they realize they have been increasingly drawing on their spiritual selves in rebalancing their relationship to eating and food. The MBSR program, without explicitly engaging spirituality, has been shown to increase scores on a measure of spiritual well-being; furthermore, this increase showed a strong relationship to improvement on measures of physical health (Carmody et al., 2008).

Spiritual self-schema therapy (often referred to as 3-S+; Avants & Margolin, 2004), developed at Yale University School of Medicine for the treatment of HIV-positive individuals or those at risk for drug addiction, was designed explicitly to engage the "spiritual self." Although it is tailored to each participant's own spiritual and religious beliefs, it draws systematically on Buddhist principles. As noted, a Buddhist framework was chosen because of its compatibility with cognitive–behavioral principles and the appropriateness of drawing on the Noble Eightfold Path for individuals struggling with drug addiction and those at high risk for HIV infection.

A randomized study of chronic heroin and cocaine abusers (Margolin, Beitel, Schuman-Olivier, & Avants, 2006) found substantially stronger effects for those enrolled in the spiritual self-schema therapy than in standard care on decreases in drug use, and in a shift in personal identification from "addict self" to "spiritual self." In a randomized study with individuals who were HIV positive (Margolin et al., 2007), there was a decrease in impulsivity and intoxicant use; greater use of spiritual practices; and higher levels of motivation for HIV prevention, drug abstinence, and medication adherence. This research, therefore, supports the value of explicitly drawing on spiritual expression, and the value of a framework for informing therapy that blends a cognitive–behavioral approach with Buddhist principles while respecting and supporting individual's own religious beliefs.

SUMMARY AND CONCLUSION

The range and depth of the influence of Buddhism on U.S. religious culture and on the psychology of spirituality and well-being has been reviewed. Buddhism has been a significant world religion for more than 2,000 years. It first came to the attention of the U.S. public through the efforts of the transcendentalists of the mid- to late 1800s, who perceived the unique value of a religious tradition that also spoke to the psychological validity of the spiritual experience. Buddhism has continued to influence psychology in increasingly substantive ways, since the early development of psychology as a discipline. It can be argued that Buddhism has uniquely and in many identifiable ways enriched psychological thinking and practice in this country. Buddhism also has, and will continue, to enrich the dialogue regarding the distinctions and complex interactions between psychological well-being, religion, and spirituality.

References

Amore, R. C., & Ching, J. (2002). The Buddhist traditions. In W. G. Oxtoby (Ed.), *World religions: Eastern traditions* (2nd ed., pp. 198–315). Don Mills, Ontario, Canada: Oxford University Press Canada.

Ando, O. (2008). Psychotherapy and Buddhism: Spirituality underneath psychotherapies in East Asia. *International Medical Journal, 15*(2), 115–118.

Andreasen, E. (1998). *Popular Buddhism in Japan: Shin Buddhist religion and culture.* Honolulu: University of Hawaii Press.

Aronson, H. B. (2004). *Buddhist practice on Western ground: Reconciling Eastern ideals and Western psychology.* Boston, MA: Shambala.

Austin, J. H. (1998). *Zen and the brain: Toward an understanding of meditation and consciousness.* Cambridge, MA: MIT Press.

Austin, J. H. (2006). *Zen-brain reflections.* Cambridge, MA: MIT Press.

Austin, J. H. (2009). *Selfless insight.* Cambridge, MA: MIT Press.

Avants, S. K., & Margolin, A. (2004). Development of spiritual self-schema therapy for the treatment of addictive and HIV risk behavior: A convergence of cognitive and Buddhist psychology. *Journal of Psychotherapy Integration, 14,* 253–289. doi:10.1037/1053-0479.14.3.253

Baer, R. A. (2007). Mindfulness, assessment, and transdiagnostic processes. *Psychological Inquiry, 18,* 238–242. doi:10.1080/10478400701598306

Baltes, P. B., & Staudinger, U. M. (2000). Wisdom: A metaheuristic (pragmatic) to orchestrate mind and virtue toward excellence. *American Psychologist, 55,* 122–136. doi:10.1037/0003-066X.55.1.122

Bishop, S. R., Lau, M., Shapiro, S., Carlson, L., Anderson, N. D., Carmody, J., . . . Devins, G. (2004). Mindfulness: A proposed operational definition. *Clinical Psychology: Science and Practice, 11,* 230–241. doi:10.1093/clipsy.bph077

Bloom, A. (Ed.). (2004). *Living in Amida's universal vow: Essays on Shin Buddhism.* Bloomington, IN: World Wisdom.

Bowen, S., Chawla, N., Collins, S. E., Witkiewitz, K., Hsu, S., Grow, J., . . . Marlatt, G. A. (2009). Mindfulness-based relapse prevention for substance use disorders: A pilot efficacy trial. *Substance Abuse, 30,* 295–305. doi:10.1080/08897070903250084

Bowen, S., Witkiewitz, K., Dillworth, T. M., Chawla, N., Simpson, T. L., Ostafin, B. D., . . . Marlatt, G. A. (2006). Mindfulness meditation and substance use in an incarcerated population. *Psychology of Addictive Behaviors, 20,* 343–347. doi:10.1037/0893-164X.20.3.343

Brach, T. (2003). *Radical acceptance: Embracing your life with the heart of a Buddha.* New York, NY: Bantam Books.

Brown, D., & Engler, J. (1984). A Rorschach study of the stages of mindfulness meditation. In D. Shapiro & R. N. Walsh (Eds.), *Meditation: Classic and contemporary perspectives* (pp. 232–262). New York, NY: Aldine.

Brown, K. W., Ryan, R. M., & Creswell, J. D. (2007). Mindfulness: Theoretical foundations and evidence for its salutary effects. *Psychological Inquiry*, *18*, 211–237. doi:10.1080/10478400701598298

Buddhism by country. (2011). Retrieved from http://en.wikipedia.org/wiki/Buddhism_by_country

Buswell, R. E., Jr., (Ed.). (2004). *The encyclopedia of Buddhism*. New York, NY: Thomson Gale.

Cadge, W. (2005). *Heartwood: The first generation of Theravada Buddhism in America*. Chicago, IL: University of Chicago Press.

Carlson, L. E., Speca, M., Patel, K. D., & Goodey, E. (2003). Mindfulness-based stress reduction in relation to quality of life, mood, symptoms of stress, and immune parameters in breast and prostate cancer outpatients. *Psychosomatic Medicine*, *65*, 571–581. doi:10.1097/01.PSY.0000074003.35911.41

Carmody, J., Reed, G., Kristeller, J. L., & Merriam, P. (2008). Mindfulness, spirituality, and health-related symptoms. *Journal of Psychosomatic Research, 64*, 393–403. doi:10.1016/j.jpsychores.2007.06.015

Causton, R. (1989). *Nichiren Shoshu Buddhism*. New York, NY: Harper & Row.

Ching, J. (2002). East Asian religions. In W. G. Oxtoby (Ed.), *World religions: Eastern traditions* (2nd ed., pp. 316–429). Don Mills, Ontario, Canada: Oxford University Press Canada.

Chodran, P. (1996). *Awakening loving-kindness* (abridged ed.). Boston, MA: Shambala.

Coleman, J. W. (2001). *The new Buddhism*. New York, NY: Oxford University Press.

Cook, K. V., Sandage, S. J., Hill, P. C., & Strawn, B. D. (2010). Folk conceptions of virtue among Cambodian American Buddhists and Christians: A hermeneutic analysis. *Psychology of Religion and Spirituality*, 2, 83–103. doi:10.1037/a0018754

Dalai Lama & Goleman, D. (2003). *Destructive emotions: How can we overcome them?* New York, NY: Bantam Books.

Daniel, M. (2007). Jung's affinity for Buddhism: Misunderstandings and clarifications. *Psychological Perspectives*, *50*, 220–234. doi:10.1080/00332920701681718

Das, S. (1997). *Awakening the Buddha within*. New York, NY: Broadway Books.

Davidson, R. J., & Harrington, A. (Eds.). (2002). *Visions of compassion: Western scientists and Tibetan Buddhists examine human nature*. New York, NY: Oxford University Press. doi:10.1093/acprof:oso/9780195130430.001.0001

DeMartino, R. J. (1991). Karen Horney, Daisetz T. Suzuki, and Zen Buddhism. *American Journal of Psychoanalysis*, *51*, 267–283. doi:10.1007/BF01249250

Didonna, F. (Ed.). (2009). *Clinical handbook of mindfulness*. New York, NY: Springer. doi:10.1007/978-0-387-09593-6

Dimidjian, S., & Linehan, M. M., (2003). Defining an agenda for future research on the clinical application of mindfulness practice. *Clinical Psychology: Research and Practice, 10,* 166–171

Dreyfus, G. (2011). Is mindfulness present-centred and non-judgmental? A discussion of the cognitive dimensions of mindfulness. *Contemporary Buddhism*, *12*, 41–54. doi:10.1080/14639947.2011.564815

Dunne, J. (2011). Toward an understanding of non-dual mindfulness. *Contemporary Buddhism*, *12*, 71–88. doi:10.1080/14639947.2011.564820

Elsass, P., & Phuntsok, K. (2009). Tibetans' coping mechanisms following torture: An interview study of Tibetan torture survivors' use of coping mechanisms and how these were supported by Western counseling. *Traumatology*, *15*, 3–10. doi:10.1177/1534765608325120

Epstein, M. (1990). Beyond the oceanic feeling: Psychoanalytic study of Buddhist meditation. *International Journal of Psychoanalysis*, *17*(2), 159–166.

Epstein, M. (1995). *Thoughts without a thinker: Psychotherapy from a Buddhist perspective*. New York, NY: Basic Books.

Epstein, M. (2001). *Going on being: Buddhism and the way of change, a positive psychology for the West*. New York, NY: Broadway Books.

Fields, R. (1992). *How the swans came to the lake. A narrative history of Buddhism in America* (3rd ed.). Boston, MA: Shambala.

Fischer-Schreiber, I., Ehrhard, F.-K., & Diener, M. S. (1991). *The Shambala dictionary of Buddhism and Zen* (M. H. Kohn, Trans.). Boston, MA: Shambala.

Fromm, E., Suzuki, D. T., & DeMartino, R. J. (1970). *Zen Buddhism and psychoanalysis*. New York, NY: Harper & Row.

Germer, C. K. (2009). *The mindful path to self-compassion: Freeing yourself from destructive thoughts and emotions*. New York, NY: Guilford Press.

Germer, C. K., Siegel, R. D., & Fulton, P. R. (Eds.). (2005). *Mindfulness and psychotherapy*. New York, NY: Guilford Press.

Gethin, R. (1998). *The foundations of Buddhism*. New York, NY: Oxford University Press.

Gilbert, P. (2009). *The compassionate mind*. London, England: Constable & Robinson.

Goldstein, J., & Kornfield, J. (1987). *Seeking the heart of wisdom: The path of insight meditation*. Boston, MA: Shambala.

Goleman, D. (1988). *The meditative mind: The varieties of meditative experience*. New York, NY: Putnam.

Goleman, D. (2003). *Destructive emotions: How can we overcome them? A scientific dialogue with the Dalai Lama.* New York, NY: Bantam Books.

Griffin, K. (2004). *One breath at a time: Buddhism and the twelve steps.* Emmaus, PA: Rodale.

Hanh, T. N. (1975). *The miracle of mindfulness.* Boston, MA: Beacon Press.

Hanh, T. N. (1991). *Peace is every step: The path of mindfulness in everyday life.* New York, NY: Bantam Books.

Hanh, T. N. (1995). *Living Buddha, living Christ.* New York, NY: Riverhead Books.

Hart, W. (1987). *The art of living: Vipassana meditation as taught by S. N. Goenka.* San Francisco, CA: HarperCollins.

Haruki, Y., & Takase, H. (2001). Effects of the Eastern art of breathing. In Y. Haruki, I. Homma, A. Umezawa, & Y. Masaoka (Eds.), *Respiration and emotion* (pp. 101–111). Tokyo, Japan: Springer-Verlag. doi:10.1007/978-4-431-67901-1_10

Hayes, S. C., & Plumb, J. C. (2007). Mindfulness from the bottom up: Providing an inductive framework for understanding mindfulness processes and their application to human suffering. *Psychological Inquiry, 18*, 242–248. doi:10.1080/10478400701598314

Hayes, S. C., Strosahl, K. D., & Wilson, K. G. (1999). *Acceptance and commitment therapy: An experiential approach to behavior change.* New York, NY: Guilford Press.

Jones, J. W. (2003). *The mirror of God: Christian faith as spiritual practice—lessons from Buddhism and psychotherapy.* New York, NY: Palgrave Macmillan.

Jung, C. G. (1970). *The collected works of C. G. Jung: Vol. 11. Psychology and religion: West and east* (G. Adler & R. F. C. Hull, Eds. & Trans.). Princeton, NJ: Princeton University Press/Bollingen Foundation. (Original work published 1958)

Jung, C. G. (1981). *The collected works of C. G. Jung: Vol. 9. Archetypes and the collective unconscious* (G. Adler & R. F. C. Hull, Eds. & Trans.). Princeton, NJ: Princeton University Press/Bollingen Foundation. (Original work published 1959)

Kabat-Zinn, J. (1990). *Full catastrophe living.* New York, NY: Delacorte Press.

Kabat-Zinn, J. (2005). *Coming to our senses: Healing ourselves and the world through mindfulness.* New York, NY: Hyperion.

Kabat-Zinn, J., Lipworth, L., & Burney, R. (1985). The clinical use of mindfulness meditation for the self-regulation of chronic pain. *Journal of Behavioral Medicine, 8*, 163–190. doi:10.1007/BF00845519

Kabat-Zinn, J., Massion, A. O., Kristeller, J. L., Peterson, L. G., Fletcher, K. E., Pbert, L., . . . Santorelli, S. F. (1992). Effectiveness of a meditation-based stress reduction program in the treatment of anxiety disorders. *American Journal of Psychiatry, 149*, 936–943.

Kapleau, P. (1970). *The three pillars of Zen: Teaching, practice, and enlightenment.* Tokyo, Japan: Weatherhill.

Kasamatsu, A., & Hirai, T. (1963). Science of *Zazen. Psychologia, 6*, 86–91.

Kawai, H. (1996). *Buddhism and the art of psychotherapy.* College Station: Texas A & M Press.

Keown, D. (1996). *Buddhism: A very short introduction.* Oxford, England: Oxford University Press.

King, S. B. (2005). *Being benevolence: The social ethics of engaged Buddhism.* Honolulu: University of Hawaii Press.

Kornfield, J. (1993). *A path with heart.* New York, NY: Bantam Books.

Kornfield, J. (2000). *After the ecstasy, the laundry.* New York, NY: Bantam Books.

Kornfield, J., & Walsh, R. (1993). Meditation: Royal road to the transpersonal. In R. Walsh & F. Vaughan (Eds.), *Paths beyond ego: The transpersonal vision* (pp. 56–69). New York, NY: Perigee Books.

Kristeller, J. L. (2007). Mindfulness meditation. In P. Lehrer, R. Wookfolk, & W. E. Simes (Eds.), *Principles and practices of stress management* (3rd ed., pp. 393–427). New York, NY: Guilford Press.

Kristeller, J. L., & Johnson, T. J. (2005). Cultivating loving kindness: A two-stage model of the effects of meditation on empathy, compassion, and altruism. *Zygon: Journal of Religion and Science, 40*, 391–407.

Kristeller, J. L., & Jones, J. W. (2006). Mindfulness and wisdom in the Buddhist tradition: Lessons for the treatment of compulsive eating. In D. K. Nauriyal, M. S. Drummond, & Y. B. Lal (Eds.), *Buddhist thought and applied psychological research: Transcending the boundaries* (pp. 374–392). London, England: Routledge.

Kristeller, J. L., & Wolever, R. Q. (2011). Mindfulness-based eating awareness training for treating binge eating disorder: The conceptual foundation. *Eating Disorders, 19*, 49–61. doi:10.1080/10640266.2011.533605

Kwee, M., Gergen, K. J., & Koshikawa, F. (Eds.). (2006). *Horizons in Buddhist psychology: Practice, research, and therapy.* Chagrin Falls, OH: Taos Institute Publications.

Linehan, M. M. (1993). *Skills training manual for treating borderline personality disorder.* New York, NY: Guilford Press.

Linehan, M. M., Schmidt, H. I., Dimeff, L. A., Craft, J. C., Kanter, J., & Comtois, K. A. (1999). Dialectical behavior therapy for patients with borderline personality disorder and drug-dependence. *American Journal on Addictions, 8*, 279–292. doi:10.1080/105504999305686

Lutz, A., Brefczynski-Lewis, J., Johnstone, T., & Davidson, R. J. (2008). Regulation of the neural circuitry of emotion by compassion meditation: Effects of meditative expertise. *Plos ONE, 3*(3), e1897.

Lutz, A., Greischar, L. L., Rawlings, N. B., Ricard, M., & Davidson, R. J. (2004). Long-term meditators self-induce high-amplitude gamma synchrony during mental practice. *Proceedings of the National Academy of Sciences of the United States of America, 101*, 16369–16373. doi:10.1073/pnas.0407401101

Margolin, A., Beitel, M., Schuman-Olivier, Z., & Avants, S. K. (2006). A controlled study of a spiritually-focused intervention for increasing motivation for HIV prevention among drug users. *AIDS Education and Prevention, 18*, 311–322. doi:10.1521/aeap.2006.18.4.311

Margolin, A., Schuman-Olivier, Z., Beitel, M., Arnold, R. M., Fulwiler, C. E., & Avants, S. K. (2007). A preliminary study of spiritual self-schema (3-S+) therapy for reducing impulsivity in HIV-positive drug users. *Journal of Clinical Psychology, 63*, 979–999. doi:10.1002/jclp.20407

Marlatt, G. A., & Kristeller, J. L. (1999). Mindfulness and meditation. In W. R. Miller (Ed.), *Integrating spirituality into treatment: Resources for practitioners* (pp. 67–84). Washington, DC: American Psychological Association. doi:10.1037/10327-004

Marlatt, G. A., Witkiewitz, K., Dillworth, T. M., Bowen, S. W., Parks, G. A., Macpherson, L. M., . . . Crutcher, R. (2004). Vipassana meditation as a treatment for alcohol and drug use disorders. In S. C. Hayes, V. M. Follette, & M. M. Linehan (Eds.), *Mindfulness and acceptance: Expanding the cognitive–behavioral tradition* (pp. 261–287). New York, NY: Guilford Press.

Mathers, D., Miller, M. E., & Ando, O. (Eds.). (2009). *Self and no-self: Continuing the dialogue between Buddhism and psychotherapy*. New York, NY: Routledge/Taylor & Francis.

Morgan, D. (2004). *The Buddhist experience in America.* Westport, CT: Greenwood Press.

Morreale, D. (Ed.). (1998). *The complete guide to Buddhist America.* Boston, MA: Shambala.

Mruk, C. J., & Hartzell, J. (2003). *Zen and psychotherapy: Integrating traditional and nontraditional approaches.* New York, NY: Springer.

Neff, K. D. (2004). Self-compassion and psychological well-being. *Constructivism in the Human Sciences, 9*(2), 27–37.

Neff, K. D., & Vonk, R. (2009). Self-compassion versus global self-esteem: Two different ways of relating to oneself. *Journal of Personality, 77*, 23–50. doi:10.1111/j.1467-6494.2008.00537.x

Newberg, A. B. (2010). *Principles of neurotheology.* Burlington, VT: Ashgate.

Newberg, A. B., & D'Aquili, E. G. (1998). The neuropsychology of spiritual experience. In H. G. Koenig (Ed.), *Handbook of religion and mental health* (pp. 75–94). San Diego, CA: Academic Press.

Pew Forum. (2008). *U.S. religious landscape survey.* Washington, DC: Pew Research Forum.

Phillips, J. (2008). *Letters from the Dhamma brothers.* Onalaska, WA: Pariyatti Press.

Phillips, R. E., III, Cheng, C. M., Pargament, K. I., Oemig, C., Colvin, S. D., Abarr, A. N., . . . Reed, A. S. (2009). Spiritual coping in American Buddhists: An exploratory study. *The International Journal for the Psychology of Religion, 19*, 231–243. doi:10.1080/10508610903143263

Prebish, C. S., & Tanaka, K. K. (Eds.). (1998). *The faces of Buddhism in America.* Berkeley: University of California Press.

Preece, R. (2006). *The wisdom of imperfection: The challenge of individuation in Buddhist life.* Ithaca, NY: Snow Lion.

Queen, C. S. (Ed.). (2000). *Engaged Buddhism in the West.* Boston, MA: Wisdom Publications.

Rapgay, L., & Bystrisky, A. (2009). Classical mindfulness: An introduction to its theory and practice for clinical application. *Annals of the New York Academy of Sciences, 1172*, 148–162. doi:10.1111/j.1749-6632.2009.04405.x

Rosch, E. (2007). More than mindfulness: When you have a tiger by the tail, let it eat you. *Psychological Inquiry, 18*, 258–264. doi:10.1080/10478400701598371

Rosenbaum, R. (1998). *Zen and the heart of psychotherapy.* Boston, MA: Brunner/Mazel.

Rubin, J. B. (1996). *Psychotherapy and Buddhism: Toward an integration.* New York, NY: Plenum Press.

Rubin, J. B. (1999). Close encounters of a new kind: Toward an integration of psychoanalysis and Buddhism. In R. Segall (Ed.), *Encountering Buddhism* (pp. 31–60). Albany: State University of New York Press.

Sahn, S. (1997). *The compass of Zen.* Boston, MA: Shambhala.

Salzberg, S. (1999). *Voices of insight.* Boston, MA: Shambhala.

Seager, R. H. (2000). *Buddhism in America.* New York, NY: Columbia University Press.

Sears, R., Tirch, D., & Denton, R. (2011). *Mindfulness in clinical practice.* Sarasota, FL: Professional Resource Press.

Segal, Z. V., Williams, J. M. G., & Teasdale, J. D. (2002). *Mindfulness-based cognitive therapy for depression: A new approach to preventing relapse.* New York, NY: Guilford Press.

Shapiro, D. H., & Walsh, R. N. (Eds.). (1984). *Meditation: Classic and contemporary perspectives.* New York, NY: Aldine.

Sharp, P. E. (2011). Buddhist enlightenment and the destruction of attractor networks: A neuroscientific speculation on the Buddhist path from everyday consciousness to Buddha-awakening. *Journal of Consciousness Studies, 18*(3–4), 137–169.

Siegel, D. J. (2010). *Mindsight.* New York, NY: Bantam Books.

Smith, H., & Novak, P. (2003). *Buddhism: A concise introduction.* New York, NY: HarperCollins.

Sternberg, R. J. (1990). *Wisdom: Its nature, origins, and development.* Cambridge, England: Cambridge University Press.

Subhuti. (1995). *Bringing Buddhism to the West: A life of Sangharakshita.* Birmingham, England: Windhorse.

Sutin, L. (2006). *All is change: The two-thousand year journey of Buddhism to the west.* New York, NY: Little, Brown.

Suzuki, S. (1973). *Zen mind, beginner's mind.* New York, NY: Weatherhill.

Swearer, D. (1970). *Buddhism in transition.* Philadelphia, PA: Westminster Press.

Thanissaro, B. (2006). *Meditations 3: Dhamma talks.* Valley Center, CA: Metta Forest Monastery.

Thurman, H. (1998). *Inner revolution: Life, liberty and the pursuit of real happiness.* New York, NY: Riverhead Books.

Trungpa, C. (1973). *Cutting through spiritual materialism.* Berkeley, CA: Shambala.

Wallace, B. A. (2006). *The attention revolution: Unlocking the power of the focused mind.* Ithaca, NY: Snow Lion.

Wallace, B. A., & Shapiro, S. L. (2006). Mental balance and well-being: Building bridges between Buddhism and western psychology. *American Psychologist, 61,* 690–701. doi:10.1037/0003-066X.61.7.690

Walsh, R. (1999). *Essential spirituality: The seven central practices to awaken heart and mind.* New York, NY: Wiley.

Walsh, R., & Shapiro, S. L. (2006). The meeting of meditative disciplines and Western psychology: A mutually enriching dialogue. *American Psychologist, 61,* 227–239. doi:10.1037/0003-066X.61.3.227

Watts, A. (1957). *The way of Zen.* New York, NY: Vintage Books.

Wegela, K. K. (2009). *The courage to be present: Buddhism, psychotherapy, and the awakening of natural wisdom.* Boston, MA: Shambala.

Williams, J. M. G., & Kabat-Zinn, J. (2011). Mindfulness: Diverse perspectives on its meaning, origins, and multiple applications at the intersection of science and dharma. *Contemporary Buddhism, 12,* 1–18. doi:10.1080/14639947.2011.564811

World factbook. (2011). Retrieved from https://www.cia.gov/library/publications/the-world-factbook/fields/2122.html

CHAPTER 36

WHAT DOES IT MEAN TO BE A HINDU? A REVIEW OF COMMON HINDU BELIEFS AND PRACTICES AND THEIR IMPLICATIONS FOR HEALTH

Nalini Tarakeshwar

There are more than 850 million Hindus in the world in the 21st century, most of whom live in India (World Almanac, 2010). Nevertheless, there is a significant Hindu population outside of India, including about 1 million in the United States (Gaustad & Barlow, 2001). The term *Hindu* originated from *Sindu*, the term the early Vedic-Indians used to describe the great river in the northwest part of India (present-day Punjab) as well as themselves (Brockington, 1996). Hinduism is regarded as a philosophy of life (Radhakrishnan, 1975) and is characterized by the drive to achieve unity of one's spirit (*atman*) with the Supreme Being (*Brahman*). It is a quest to fathom the nature of reality, the ideal of life, and the way for realizing it.

The purpose of this chapter is to enlighten the reader on four things: (a) key facets within Hinduism that are relevant to psychological research and practice, (b) published evidence on beliefs and practices of Hindus, (c) links between these beliefs and practices and mental and physical health, and (d) recommendations for practitioners who are engaged in work with the Hindu population and for researchers interested in filling the gap on what more needs to be understood or established on this topic.

Certain limitations in the scope of the chapter must be acknowledged at the start. This chapter is not designed to provide readers with a comprehensive history of Hindu philosophy, nor will it review every piece of existing research on Hinduism. Moreover, given that most readers of this handbook likely live in the United States, an attempt has been made to target recommendations for U.S. practitioners (although they probably could be applied to Hindus in other countries, outside of India). Hence, there is a bias toward studies conducted in the United States, with a smattering of studies from India and the United Kingdom. Furthermore, reference to Hindus in this chapter focuses on those who are Indian immigrants. Of note, one is Hindu by birth, and there is no religious conversion.

KEY FACETS OF HINDUISM

Hindu religious thought is derived from the Vedas that were written during the period between the 10th and 6th centuries B.C.E., known as the *Vedic* period. The Vedas are four in number: *Rigveda*, *Samaveda*, *Yajurveda*, and *Atharvaveda*, and were each composed by different persons at different places and times. The post-Vedic period provided a transition to the nine systems of Indian thought, six of which accepted the Vedas. These six include (a) Nyaya, school of logic and epistemology started by Gautama; (b) Vaisesika, developed by Kanada, who endorsed the belief that nature is made up of atoms distinct from the soul and that this knowledge can lead one to *moksha* or spiritual liberation; (c) Sankhya, founded by Kapila, who believed that liberation consists of recovering the soul's original purity in isolation from matter; (d) Yoga, founded by Patanjali, who advocated practice of physical postures, meditation, and control of breath to achieve *moksha*; (e) Purva-Mimamsa, by Jaimini, which focuses on sacrificialism derived from the first two

DOI: 10.1037/14045-036
APA Handbook of Psychology, Religion, and Spirituality: Vol. 1. Context, Theory, and Research, K. I. Pargament (Editor-in-Chief)
Copyright © 2013 by the American Psychological Association. All rights reserved.

parts of the Veda; and (f) Vedanta, originated by Badrayana, that emphasizes the latter sections of the Veda, the Upanishads. The three that explicitly rejected the authority of the Vedas were Carvaka or materialistic philosophy, Buddhism (founded by Siddhartha Gautama), and Jainism (established by Vardhamana Mahavira).

Apart from the Vedas, Hindu auxiliary literature includes such epics as the Ramayana and Mahabharata (both written between 400 B.C.E. and 400 C.E.) and sectarian scriptures that each gives prominence to different deities (such as Vishnu and Siva). Over the centuries, on the basis of the interpretation of the Upanishads, subschools of Vedanta emerged, such as the traditions of Sankara (788–820 C.E.), Ramanuja (1017–1137 C.E.), Madhva (1238–1317 C.E.), and Vallabha (1473-1531 C.E.), among others.

References to more comprehensive and thorough reviews of Hindu philosophy and its origins are provided at the end of this chapter. These references form the background for this section, which summarizes key facets of Hinduism. These elements of Hinduism bear significant implications for the health and well-being of Hindus through their influence on interpretation of events and organization of day-to-day routines. Despite theological differences between the Vedanta subschools, the features described in this section are applicable to all. It is unknown whether these theological differences within Hinduism have different effects on Hindus.

Ideals of Moral Life

The Hindu manuals of moral conduct and social law require every Hindu to strive toward achieving the ideals of wealth, pleasure, ethical merit, and spiritual liberation, in that order. Although wealth, earned through ethical ways, and pleasure may dominate one's life at a point, they lead to an endless cycle of experience and have to be transcended. Thus, spiritual liberation or achieving unity of one's *atman* with the Supreme Being, *Brahman*, is the ultimate purpose of life on Earth. All deeds are to be enacted with this goal in mind.

Paths to Spiritual Liberation

Four paths are defined for Hindus to achieve the ultimate union with the *Brahman*. In the *path of devotion*, through practices such as prayer, rituals, and maintaining physical and mental purity, the emotion of love is directed toward becoming one with God. The *path of ethical action* advocates detachment from the fruits of one's deeds—performing work not out of any personal desire but purely for God's pleasure. Through the *path of knowledge*, a Hindu can remove the bondage to ignorance by dedicating him- or herself to learning that will reveal the ephemeral nature of worldly things and the permanence of spiritual bliss attained by uniting with the *Brahman*. Finally, the *path of mental concentration* prescribes disciplinary measures involving physiological controls and psychological restraints to gain mastery over one's mind and thereby achieve spiritual liberation. Each of these paths is designed to suit different temperaments: The path of devotion is ideal for individuals with a more emotional orientation, the path of ethical action is suited to those who are more driven by action, the path of knowledge is tailored to persons with a philosophical and intellectual bent of mind, and the path of mental concentration appeals to those more scientifically inclined.

Caste System

Although there are several thousand castes in existence in India in the 21st century, four are most important: *Brahmins, Kshatriyas, Vaisyas*, and *Sudras*. Notably, membership to a caste is determined by birth. The duty of Brahmins, who occupy the highest status, was to serve the *Veda* by reciting, practicing and teaching it. They also serve the community by performing rituals for which they are allowed to receive donations. The *Kshatriyas*, who are next in the hierarchy, were required to protect the community, ensure that justice prevailed, and provide an environment for Hindus to practice their ethical merit. The *Vaisya* caste members were expected to engage in trade and commerce to ensure that the society would be structured on a sound and ethical economic basis. These three castes were regarded as "twice born," with the first birth being physical and the second being spiritual (the result of formal initiation into Vedic study). The lowest in the hierarchy were the *Sudras*, who were not eligible to be initiated in the rights and responsibilities of a life based on the Vedas; they were expected to serve the members of the other three castes.

Stages of Life

Hinduism divides the life of a twice-born Hindu into four stages. The first stage is that of a student between the age of 6 and 8 years, followed by that of a householder when duties of sacrifices to gods and alms giving, along with familial responsibilities, play a central role. This stage of a householder is followed by that of an anchorite, when a Hindu begins the process of self-reflection and self-examination. When no longer drawn by worldly pleasures, in the last stage, a Hindu spends the rest of his life as an ascetic. Only the first two stages are considered obligatory. Even if these stages were prescribed with Hindu males in mind, in ancient times, women had the right to be initiated into Vedic study. As time went on, however, marriage came to be regarded as the chief responsibility of women, making emancipation of women one of the important issues for 19th-century reformers.

Doctrine of Karma

The karmic doctrine extends the notion of cause and effect in the physical universe to the moral realm. According to this doctrine, people are reflections of their past deeds and furthermore, present actions will shape their future. The future can span more than one lifetime; thus, the theory of reincarnation of the same soul in different bodies is a corollary of this doctrine. Although karma may appear to be a deterministic doctrine, there is a place for free will. Even if a Hindu has to experience the results of past actions in the present life, she or he can develop tendencies and dispositions to act in a righteous manner. She or he can invoke the grace of God to prevent or mitigate effects of bad actions. In addition, by performing actions without a selfish motive, a Hindu can be freed of karmic effects. After a Hindu has exhausted him- or herself of all of the accumulated karma through accumulation of good deeds and is freed of ignorance, desire, and self-interest, the soul becomes one with the *Brahman*. Thus, karma offers a preliminary route to spiritual liberation.

Hindu Rituals

The Hindu manuals of moral conduct and social law prescribe 16 rituals that mark key life transitions: birth of child, naming of baby, giving baby first solid food, baby's first haircut, introduction to studies, sacred thread ceremony for upper-caste boys, returning home after studies, attainment of puberty for girls, marriage, consummation of marriage, prayers for pregnant woman, funeral for the departed, postfuneral honoring of the departed, building a new home, entering a new home, and spiritual initiation. In addition to these rituals, Hindus are expected to adhere to daily duties, such as rising before sunrise, chanting mantras, having a bath, saying the morning prayer, and reading sacred texts, which are followed by rituals in the noon and evening. There are also rituals tied to the various Hindu festivals, such as *Diwali* and *Holi*, although these have regional variations.

Health-Related Beliefs (Ayurveda and Yogasutra)

Hindu concepts of health and disease follow the thought patterns during the Vedic period, ritualistic beliefs followed by monistic practices. As such, the original hymns of the earlier works of the *Vedic* period (before 6th century B.C.E.) provide descriptions of charms and other rituals to "cure" mental disorders that are attributed to the influence of demons and sorcerers. During the *Upanishadic* period (between 6th and 3rd century B.C.E.), the *Ayurveda*, or the science of life, was developed, in which health is conceived as the proper balance of the five elements (water, air, fire, Earth, sky) and three humors (phlegm, bile, wind). This system of medicine insists that treatment should be centered on the individual rather than the disease. The goal is to achieve tranquility through the balance of physical, physiological, psychological, and spiritual levels, reflecting the monistic Indian worldview that all that is part of the cosmos has its homologue within the person. Recommended treatment could be classified into three categories: (a) faith healing through incantation, herbs, sacrifices, and propitiatory rites; (b) rational therapy through cleaning nasal passage, vomiting, purgation, enema, and nutrition; and (c) psychotherapy with emphasis on restraint of impulses.

Around the same time (3rd century B.C.E.), a system of yoga was formed called *yogasutra* that attributed the root cause of human suffering to the attraction we feel toward pleasurable things and the repulsion to things that give us unhappiness. To free the consciousness from these qualities, the yoga system advocated practice of physical postures, meditation, and controlled breathing to regulate the mind and attain liberation.

COMMON RELIGIOUS PRACTICES AND BELIEFS AMONG HINDUS

A lot has been written about Hindu philosophy, but it is only recently that the use of these philosophical concepts by Hindus has been subjected to empirical scrutiny. The studies, although clearly increasing in number, are limited to small samples and anecdotal observations. Following is a summary of key findings.

First, Hinduism is multifaceted in its manifestation, and it would indeed be a futile effort to describe a single, specific way in which it is practiced. An in-depth study conducted in the United States that used both qualitative and quantitative methods provides substantive evidence in this regard (Tarakeshwar, Pargament, & Mahoney, 2003b). This study was divided into three phases. Phase I was a qualitative study based on detailed interviews with 15 Hindus (seven male, eight female), who had immigrated to the United States from India, to understand the religious dimensions that influenced their life. These interviews revealed four pathways to spiritual liberation, characterized by specific behaviors (see Table 36.1): devotion, ethical action, knowledge, and physical restraint/yoga. A Hindu may choose to place greater emphasis on one path or to adopt a specific set of behaviors across the various paths. Thus, an indicator such as "attendance at religious services" could not be a proxy indicator of the importance of religion to Hindus because visiting temples or performing rituals represents only one of the four paths of Hinduism. In fact, there may be Hindus who do not adopt any of the devotional behaviors but adopt the path of ethical action, which could still make them "religious" Hindus.

TABLE 36.1

Behaviors Characterizing Each of the Four Hindu Pathways

Hindu pathways	Behaviors
Path of devotion	Prayer Going to temple Performing *puja* at home Listening to devotional music Singing devotional songs or *bhajans* Observing festivals Going on a religious pilgrimage Observing Hindu rituals marking key life transitions
Path of ethical action	Following duties in the various roles: ■ Parent ■ Student ■ Son/daughter ■ Daily habits (eating, work) ■ Spouse
Path of knowledge	Reading religious texts Attending religious talks Teaching others, including their children, about Hinduism
Path of physical restraint/yoga	Observing vegetarian diet Avoiding alcohol and smoking Yoga practice Meditation

Second, the social context influences the practice of these behaviors. Unsurprisingly, the interviews showed that how a Hindu follows religious practices in India, where Hinduism was born and is practiced by the majority population, is different from how she or he would apply the same practices when living as a religious minority in a foreign land. Given that it is one of the oldest religions in India, Hinduism has gone through several transformations to absorb other perspectives (e.g., Buddhism, Jainism), such that it is difficult to separate what is religious from cultural norms and practices or other factors.

On the other hand, it can be said that for Hindus living outside of India, religion can become a source of cultural identity, thereby blending religion and culture for different reasons. Yet practicing one's religion within a dissonant religious context can also pose challenges for Hindus. First and foremost, temples have to be constructed. In the United States, to date there are more than 200 Hindu temples (Anand, 2004). Hindus in the United States have had to modify some of their practices to suit their environmental context. For example, Hindu festivals are celebrated over weekends, Sunday classes are held in the temples to help children learn about their religion, and the Hindu temple serves as a gathering place for both religious and social events (Eck, 2000; Tarakeshwar et al., 2003b). Moreover, Hindus may be faced with situations in which they have to provide explanations of their beliefs and rituals. Such modifications can be dissatisfying for the religious if they have strictly observed their practices in India, but the situation may be different for second-generation Indians. In sum, the practice of Hinduism serves as an illustration of how religion and the sociocultural context can shape each other (see Tarakeshwar, Stanton, & Pargament, 2003; Chapter 13 in this volume).

Third, specific mention needs to be made about Hindu rituals. Phase II of the Tarakeshwar et al. (2003b) study involved piloting a scale on the Hindu pathways among 42 Hindus in the U.S. Midwest. Three Hindu scholars reviewed the items on the scale that were derived from the Phase I interviews. The responses were subjected to descriptive and standard reliability analyses, and in Phase III, a revised measure of Hindu religious pathways was mailed to Hindus in different parts of the United States, along with physical and mental health measures. Participant names were obtained from the telephone directory and Indian associations on the Internet. Of the 367 surveys that were mailed, responses were obtained from 182 (106 male, 76 female). Table 36.2 shows the scale that is the result of further reliability and validity analyses conducted as part of Phase III.

Findings from Phase III indicated that the vast majority of Hindus practice rituals, including those that are performed on a daily basis as well as those that mark key life transitions. (As described earlier, there are 16 in total.) The study further found that prayer and performing *puja* (i.e., religious rituals performed as an offering to different Hindu deities) at home were common daily practices. Among the 16 life transition rituals, rituals associated with marriage, entering a new home, and funeral ceremonies for the departed were moderately practiced. Many Hindus felt that they did not possess sufficient knowledge about the significance of Hindu rituals, which made it difficult to practice them, especially outside of India.

Fourth, similar to other religions, age and marital status play a role in the intensity and choice of religious practices. Intensity of religious practice increases with age (Kumar, 2000) and is also tied to marital status, with married individuals more likely to be religious (Tarakeshwar et al., 2003b). Interestingly, Hindus who may not have been religious when they immigrated to another country subsequently may turn to religion to provide their children with a sense of cultural identity. This is another example of the cultural context's influence on religious practice (Kurien, 2005).

Fifth, in regard to religious beliefs that are commonly acknowledged by Hindus, the dominant one is their belief in karma, which pervades the interpretation of illness and death (Firth, 2005) and serves as an important coping mechanism (Pargament, Poloma, & Tarakeshwar, 2001). When faced with an inexplicable event, such as the death of a child, the cause can be attributed to the individual's sins committed in the past life. Such stoic acceptance of the past can help in conserving the notion of a benevolent or just God. At the same time, a Hindu can try to influence the future through current actions, the fruits of which may be manifested in the current or future lifetime. Thus the notion of hope and control over one's destiny is also conserved. Interviews with Hindus also underscore a sense of duty, especially toward families (Mullatti, 1995). As addressed later in this chapter, the significance of the family for Hindus has important implications for how practitioners approach psychotherapy with these families (Sharma, 2000).

Finally, there is scant research on the religious development of Hindu children and adolescents, be it in India or outside. But qualitative research and case studies highlight the notion that although religion can be important to them, how it is practiced is not just a product of age or cognitive differences but also can be influenced by the familial and social context in which they are raised (Takriti, Barrett, & Buchanan-Barrow, 2006). On the basis of interviews among Hindu parents living in India, Saraswathi and Ganapathy (2002) concluded that the majority

TABLE 36.2

Items on the Hindu Religious Pathways Scale

Hindu pathways	Behaviors
Path of devotion	1. How often do you pray?[a]
	2. How often do you go to the temple?[a]
	3. How often do you perform *puja* in honor of your deity?[b]
	4. How often do you sing classical music as a form of worship?[b]
	5. In the past 5 years how often have you celebrated the following religious festivals: *Diwali, Dussehra, Ganesh Chaturthi, Saraswati puja*[c]
	6. Have you performed or intend to perform the following religious rituals (16 indicated in the text)[d]
Path of ethical action	How closely do the following statements reflect what you do in your daily life?[e]
	1. I organize my life according to the ethical guidelines prescribed by my religion (e.g., honesty, respect).
	2. At work (or school), I do my job and treat my colleagues in accordance with my religious principles (e.g., respect, selfless work).
	3. I perform (or have performed) my religious duties as a son/daughter according to the ethical guidelines prescribed by my religion (e.g., honesty, respect, obedience).
	4. My daily habits (e.g., eating, exercise, conduct) reflect the ethical guidelines of my religion.
Path of knowledge	How often do you read/listen to the following religious scriptures?[f]
	1. *Bhagavad Gita*
	2. Tales of Ramayana and Mahabharata
	3. Advanced Hindu literature, such as the Vedas and Upanishads
	4. Books on Hindu Gods and Goddesses and by religious leaders
	5. Attend meetings to discuss Hindu philosophy
Path of physical restraint/yoga[g]	1. How strictly do you observe a vegetarian diet?
	2. How often do you smoke cigarettes?
	3. How often do you have alcoholic drinks?
	4. How often do you practice yoga/meditate?

[a]Participants responded on a scale from 0 (*never*) to 5 (*more than once a day*). [b]Participants responded on a scale from 0 (*never*) to 6 (*daily*). [c]Participants responded on a scale from 0 (*never*)) to 4 (*every year*). [d]Participants responded on a scale from 1 (*have performed*) to 4 (*no and no intention to perform*). [e]Responses were scored on a scale from 0 (*never*) to 4 (*always*). [f]For Items 1 to 4, participants indicated their frequency of reading/listening to the religious scriptures on a scale from 0 (*never*) to 5 (*daily*). For Item 5, responses were on a scale from 0 (*never*) to 3 (*once a week*). [g]For Item 1, responses were scored on a scale from 0 (*never*) to 4 (*all the time*); for Item 2, on a scale from 0 (*few times a day*) to 4 (*never*); for Item 3, on a scale from 0 (*few times a week*) to 4 (*never*); and for Item 4, on a scale from 0 (*never*) to 6 (*daily*). Items 2 and 3 were reverse coded.

expressed a distinct preference for a child who was obedient, respectful of elders, and socially conforming. This is consistent with tales from Hindu myths that value social embeddedness, as opposed to an emphasis on self-maximization (i.e., self-reliance, self-confidence) often expressed by U.S. parents (Harwood, Miller, & Irizarry, 1995).

Links Between Hindu Beliefs and Practices and Mental and Physical Health

As with other religions (Koenig, 1998), there is an association between specific religious beliefs and practices of Hindus and mental health. Tarakeshwar et al. (2003b) used Phase III of the study to examine whether and how the Hindu pathways to spiritual liberation were linked to mental health outcomes, both positive and negative. Hierarchical regression analyses of the Hindu Religious Pathways scale (see Table 36.2) showed that the path of ethical action was linked to positive outcomes (better life satisfaction, marital satisfaction, and less depressed mood), whereas the path of devotion was tied to poorer outcomes (greater depressed mood and lower marital satisfaction). Perhaps poorer outcomes are markers of distress that trigger the use of this path in particular. Even if the study's cross-sectional design precludes drawing conclusions about the directionality of these links, it is notable that the pathways are associated with mental health outcomes in a distinct manner.

Findings from a qualitative study among Indian men and women who were infected with HIV that explored the role of religion, among other factors, indicated that belief in a benevolent God, acts of faith (daily prayers), familial support, and access to HIV treatment all contributed to a positive self-concept manifested through self-efficacy and self-esteem (Tarakeshwar et al., 2007). The importance of fulfilling their duties, especially toward their families, is often a source of motivation for Hindus to focus their activities such that they contribute to their family's well-being. For instance, the same study (Tarakeshwar et al., 2007) showed that for many patients, a major reason for living is to ensure that their families remain unaffected by the impact of the disease. This influenced their desire to seek treatment and to adopt good health habits. This is an interesting contrast to the perspective of the psychology of religion in the United States, where extrinsic religious motivations often have been considered dysfunctional (e.g., linked to prejudice; Allport & Ross, 1967). The lack of family support, however, can then negatively affect individuals with HIV. Moreover, in the case of HIV infection in India, where heterosexual transmission is the predominant cause, patients with HIV often report a sense of guilt in having brought shame to their family.

Interpreting events through the lens of the karmic doctrine plays a vital role in helping Hindus cope with stressful events in their lives, especially those that do not have an obvious cause. In a study conducted among permanently and temporarily disabled accident patients in India, 1 week and 3 weeks after the accident, psychological recovery in both groups of patients was correlated with causal attribution to karma (Dalal & Pande, 1988). Patients with a permanent disability made higher attributions to karma than those with a temporary disability. The former were more likely to ask their doctors about the duration and degree of recovery—implying that they sought to control their future by actively seeking treatment. The attribution of their injury to the past may have helped them cope with its permanency, providing them a sense of external control. Belief in karma, however, could lead to a sense of fatalism, such that Hindus may perceive that they have no choice but to accept their lot in life—reasoning that sociologists argue has perpetuated the caste system in India (Omprakash, 1989). In short, these findings highlight that the use of karma cannot be simply dismissed as passive submission to an external locus of control, as it can also drive individuals to adopt healthy behaviors.

Nevertheless, using karma to interpret events is only one way that Hindus cope. There are indeed other beliefs that Hindus draw on when dealing with specific situations. A few studies of Hindus from India and elsewhere report the use of overt religious practices, such as physical torture (e.g., striking the body against hard objects) and expiatory rites (e.g., not drinking water, standing on one leg) in dealing with psychological illnesses. Such practices are linked to the causal beliefs of supernatural powers (e.g., evil eye, ghost) in illnesses and have been observed not just among the rural population in India (Balodhi, 1989) but also among Indians living in Britain (Spiro, 2005).

A more comprehensive study on religious coping among Hindus in the United States (Tarakeshwar, Pargament, & Mahoney, 2003a) yielded strategies that fell along three dimensions: (a) *God-focused coping* (e.g., do what I can and put the rest in God's hands; seek God's love and care); (b) *spirituality-focused coping* that did not reference any deity (e.g., look for a total spiritual awakening; offer spiritual support to family and friends); and (c) *religious guilt, anger, and passivity* (e.g., feel punished by God for lack of devotion; voice anger that God did not answer my prayers). Interestingly, the God-focused coping methods were tied to greater life satisfaction, whereas methods that focused on guilt, anger, and passivity were associated with lower life satisfaction, depressed mood, and lower marital satisfaction. Although these are not causal relationships, it seems that religious coping and mental health are closely linked. Moreover, these findings are consistent with literature on religious struggles among other religious groups (Exline, 2009; Exline & Rose, 2005; Pargament et al., 2005; see also Chapter 25 in this volume).

Although the Hindu religion views health as encompassing both physical–physiological and psychological–spiritual levels, documentation of the link between Hinduism and physical health is scarce. A few studies using small samples of volunteers (e.g., Udupa, Singh, & Settawar, 1971) have shown the physical health benefits of a rigorous and systematic training in yoga, including reduction in body weight and improvement in respiratory functions. Such studies are few and far between, however. There is some evidence that belonging to the Hindu religion can predict sexual behavior and decisions related to pregnancy (e.g., prenatal genetic screening) and fertility (Ahmed, Atkin, Hewison, & Green, 2006; Dharmalingam & Morgan, 2004). Although religious leaders did not have a role in the decision, it is unclear what about being a Hindu accounts for these links. Perhaps specific beliefs within Hinduism serve as a guiding force in helping Hindus make these choices.

IMPLICATIONS FOR PRACTITIONERS

With this background theory and available empirical evidence, following are some concrete recommendations for professionals providing psychological services to Hindus, especially to those living in the United States

Understanding the Religious Background of Hindus

Given the multifaceted nature of Hinduism, it is essential to delve individually and qualitatively into how each individual applies the beliefs and practices (and which ones) to suit his or her daily life. Moreover, how a person's Hindu practices are perceived by his or her immediate and extended family might also be important. For recent immigrants, it is important to understand the ways in which their beliefs and practices have been affected since coming to the United States. For second-generation Hindus, their experiences and perceptions of being raised in a dissonant religious context and how it has influenced their own religious development and practice will be a significant factor in psychological treatment. Williams (1996) has highlighted five adaptive strategies, on the basis of length of stay and strategy of acculturation, that Asian Indian immigrants use to preserve their tradition in the United States: (a) individual, where in their early years, they are likely to observe their religion within their homes; (b) national, where they may join organizations that are secular but incorporate religious activities; (c) ecumenical, where ethnic, denominational, and sectarian differences are brushed aside to create an "American" form of Hinduism; (d) ethnic, where the individuals are divided by their regional–linguistic identities; and (e) hierarchical, illustrated by organizations and individuals who pledge loyalty to a living religious leader.

Along with a grasp of the client's acculturation status, it may be useful for the practitioner to map a client's practices along the pathways listed in Table 36.1 to develop a better understanding of the individual. It should not be assumed that all Hindu clients are aware of these pathways and consciously classify their practices in such a manner. But for a practitioner, such classification can help to develop a further understanding of how a Hindu client fits within a traditional framework of the Hindu religion.

Importance of Hindu Rituals

In general, rituals play an important role in the practice of Hinduism. Moreover, the discipline of following rituals on a daily basis can serve as a source of comfort for many Hindus. Hence, it is useful to know which rituals a Hindu observes and on what occasions, how rituals affect his or her life, and what challenges she or he faces related to their observance. Such knowledge can contribute to conceptualizing the problems (religious or otherwise) faced by Hindu clients and finding applicable solutions. On the other hand, because of the multiple pathways to spiritual liberation, it would be wrong to assume that a Hindu who does not observe rituals is not religious.

Using Belief in Karma

As discussed earlier, the karmic doctrine can serve as a useful framework to interpret life events. On the one hand, it can be therapeutically useful in helping Hindu clients cope with events or circumstances that are beyond their personal control—such as the diagnosis of certain terminal illnesses or the loss of a loved one—by attributing the cause of such events to a past life. In a way, it can enable a Hindu client to "get on with it" (Sharma, 2000). And they can do so by acting responsibly so that positive karma is accumulated for a better future, either in this lifetime or next. Hence not looking for an immediate reward is also important in applying this doctrine. A recent article on end-of-life issues in *The Lancet* (Firth, 2005) elaborated on how belief in an afterlife associated with the karmic doctrine can affect not only conduct in the current life but also one's attitude toward death. Cited in this article is a verse from the *Bhagavad Gita*: "And whoever, at the time of death, gives up his body and departs, thinking of Me alone, he comes to Me; of that there is no doubt" (Firth, 2005, p. 683).

As per scripture, a good death should be prepared for throughout life and should be entered into consciously and willingly. Preparation for death involves fulfillment of all familial duties, resolution of conflicts, and gifting of money and land.

Overall, karmic belief can be a useful tool when helping Hindu clients cope with difficult events. It is important, however, to first acknowledge the client's interpretation of the event (whether they view it as controllable or not) and then to determine the relevance of the doctrine.

Family Involvement and Influence

Family, both immediate and extended, plays a significant role in the lives of most Hindus. Hence, it is recommended that psychological assessment of Hindus include an understanding of the extent to which his or her life is influenced by family members and in what way. Many Hindus are likely to feel a sense of duty toward their family, so an appreciation of whether and how their goals fit with their sense of familial duties is important. In the case of therapy, it may be helpful if some sessions are held with family members not only to maximize support for the Hindu client outside of therapy but also to help the family feel that they have a voice in the process. This may be particularly important when working with children and adolescents.

Hindu Religion and Cultural Identity

In the United States and other contexts in which Hindus are a minority religious population, religion can become an important source of cultural identity. How a Hindu client views religion—whether as inextricable from culture or distinct from it—can be an important factor when working with Hindus in the United States. For Hindu parents for whom religion is important, their ability to impart religious education to their children can play a role in their well-being. Access to Hindu temples and opportunities to mingle with other Hindus can be a major influence for such families. For second-generation Hindus, whether they see religion as a facilitator or hindrance to the process of fitting in with the majority culture is essential to understand, and any resulting conflict needs to be addressed.

FUTURE RESEARCH AGENDA

The theory and available empirical evidence on the practice of Hinduism points to similarities and differences with other religions (or cultural context). For instance, the religious coping findings of Tarakeshwar et al. (2003a) are similar to those from other religions that show that religious struggles relate to poorer outcomes (Pargament et al., 2005). On the other hand, the finding from the study of Tarakeshwar et al. (2007) offered an interesting contrast to the United States. In India, religious motivation to fulfill family duties helps sustain those with HIV, whereas in the United States this might be construed as extrinsic religious motivation that is tied to negative outcomes (Allport & Ross, 1967). There are important differences on what Hindu parents might value in their children—for example, social embeddedness as opposed to the self-maximization that is often valued by parents in the United States. Along similar lines, Western psychologists might tend to be critical of the notion of karma as a belief that fosters an external locus of control, whereas the findings noted in this chapter suggest it can foster a greater sense of understanding, meaning, and control.

Clearly, far more research is needed to understand the application of Hindu concepts, beliefs, and practices in daily life and their links with mental and physical health. There are perhaps several reasons for this lack of evidence. It is possible that the lack of a framework of study has been an impediment to research, resulting in Hinduism being reflected in nothing more than an affiliation. Or it is likely that the inextricable nature of Hinduism with Indian culture (Tarakeshwar, Stanton, & Pargament, 2003) has obstructed researchers in defining what Hinduism (separate from culture) means to its followers. Finally, to be worthy of study, the issue must be relevant to more than the minority. Unfortunately, the lack of funding for social science research in general in India, where most Hindus reside, has contributed to the scarcity of evidence on the issue of religion and its links to physical health and mental health, particularly outside the realm of psychiatry. With more than a million Hindus in the United States and with Indians now beginning to occupy positions of power, the study of the manifestation of Hinduism may be seen as increasingly important and relevant.

Below are some recommendations that could markedly enhance the evidence that has formed the basis of this chapter. First and foremost, when studying Hindus, use of a few indicators as a proxy for religion should be avoided. It is recommended that researchers use the items discussed in Table 36.2 (or any additional items) that are grounded in the theoretical framework of Hinduism and thereby illuminate its unique aspects, such as belief in karma and Hindu rituals, and how these influence the health of Hindus. To make the findings meaningful, it is important that the study address *in what way* the beliefs and practices are linked to health, not just *whether* such links exist. When studying Hindus outside of India, length of stay and acculturation status should be included as variables, aside from others considered important to any religious study, such as gender, age, and marital status.

Second, studies are needed that shed light on whether Hindus experience conflict with other religious traditions, to what degree and why. How does this conflict affect Hindu religious practice and health, both physical and mental?

Third, although causal links are often hard to establish, studies among Hindus should attempt to gather longitudinal data to test hypotheses regarding the impact of Hindu beliefs and practices on health and to see whether and how time influences these beliefs and practices. For instance, is there a change in the significance, interpretation and practice of Hinduism over time? How do factors such as gender, age, and marital status affect this process?

Fourth, an important but severely neglected area of study is the intergenerational transmission of religious practice in the United States. This issue would be best examined through longitudinal studies, especially if these include both immigrant Hindus and their children. How do the different expectations or values of Hindu parents (as opposed to the social context in the United States) affect their own well-being and that of their children? What are the most effective coping methods in this situation, for both parents and children?

On the topic of children, the religious development of second-generation Hindus needs special study, using a combination of both qualitative and quantitative methods. For example, it would be useful to examine how members of this group view their religious and cultural identities and how their religion might facilitate or hinder their adjustment to the social context.

Sixth, the physical health impact of Hindu beliefs and practices is especially worthy of empirical scrutiny. The reference here is not just to practices, such as meditation and yoga that are used more universally and are inherently physical practices, but also those that are applicable to the other paths to spiritual liberation, such as rituals and belief in karma. To generate robust evidence, studies should use both biological measures and self-report of perceptions as outcomes.

Finally, although recommendations have been provided for practitioners working with (or likely to work with) Hindu clients, documentation of how these are applied and how they affect the therapeutic process is needed. For instance, what issues seem to be most relevant for Hindu clients seeking therapy? What works and under what circumstances? Are there practices that are to be avoided in therapy? How does an understanding of Hinduism facilitate the process (or not)?

CONCLUSION

This chapter has examined what it means to be a Hindu and summarized research on the implications of Hinduism for mental health and physical health. Although empirical evidence on how Hinduism is observed in daily life and its significance for health and well-being is gradually growing out of its infancy, questions continue to far outnumber answers. Several of these questions have been identified in this chapter. The Hindu Religious Pathways scale provides researchers and practitioners with a preliminary framework and tool for studying what aspects may be important to Hindus and how these can be incorporated into work with Hindu clients or research participants. Hopefully further research of this kind will enrich our theoretical and practical understanding of how Hinduism affects the life of Hindus.

Suggested Reading for Comprehensive Reviews of Hindu Philosophy

Balodhi, J. P., & Chowdhary, B. C. (1986). Psychiatric concepts in Atharvaveda: A review. *Indian Journal of Psychiatry, 28*, 63–68.

Bhaskarananda, S. (1994). *The essentials of Hinduism.* Seattle, WA: Viveka Press.

Hiriyanna, M. (1996). *Essentials of Indian philosophy* (2nd ed.). London, England: Diamond Books.

Kitagawa (1960). *Religions of the East* (pp. 99–154). Philadelphia, PA: Westminster Press.

Klostermaier, K. K. (1994). *A survey of Hinduism* (2nd ed.). Albany: State University of New York Press.

Lipner, J. (1994). *Hindus: Their religious beliefs and practices.* New York, NY: Routledge.

Mahadevan, T. M. P. (1946). Indian ethics and social practice. In C. A. Moore (Ed.), *Philosophy and culture east and west: East-West philosophy in practical perspective* (pp. 476–495). Honolulu: University of Hawaii Press.

Parinder, G. (Ed.). (1984). *World religions: From ancient history to the present* (pp. 192–240). New York, NY: Facts on File.

Raju, P. T. (1985). *Structural depths of Indian thought.* Albany: State University of New York Press.

Reichenbach, B. R. (1990). *The law of karma: A philosophical study.* Honolulu: University of Hawaii Press.

Smith, H. (1991). *The world's religions.* New York, NY: HarperCollins.

Wig, N. N. (1989). Indian concepts of mental health and their impact on care of the mentally ill. *International Journal of Mental Health, 18*, 71–80.

References

Ahmed, S., Atkin, K., Hewison, J., & Green, J. (2006). The influence of faith and religion and the role of religious and community leaders in prenatal decisions for sickle cell disorders and thalassaemia major. *Prenatal Diagnosis, 26*, 801–809. doi:10.1002/pd.1507

Allport, G. W., & Ross, J. M. (1967). Personal religious orientation and prejudice. *Journal of Personality and Social Psychology, 5*, 432–443. doi:10.1037/h0021212

Anand, P. (2004, July). *Hindu diaspora and religious philanthropy in the United States.* Paper presented at the Sixth International Conference of the International Society for Third Sector Research, Toronto, Ontario, Canada.

Balodhi, J. P. (1989). In pursuit of Indian *shastric* sources for community mental health. *NIMHANS Journal, 7*, 49–54.

Brockington, J. L. (1996). *The sacred thread: Hinduism in its continuity and diversity* (2nd ed.). Edinburgh, Scotland: University Press.

Dalal, A. K., & Pande, N. (1988). Psychological recovery of accident victims with temporary and permanent disability. *International Journal of Psychology, 23*, 25–40. doi:10.1080/00207598808247750

Dharmalingam, A., & Morgan, S. P. (2004). Pervasive Muslim-Hindu fertility differences in India. *Demography, 41*, 529–545. doi:10.1353/dem.2004.0020

Eck, D. L. (2000). Negotiating Hindu identities in America. In H. Coward, J. R. Hinnells, & R. B. Williams (Eds.), *The South Asian diaspora in Britain, Canada, and the United States* (pp. 219–237). New York: State University of New York Press.

Exline, J. J. (2009). Relationships with God. In H. Reis & S. Sprecher (Eds.), *Encyclopedia of human relationships* (Vol. 1, pp. 767–768). Thousand Oaks, CA: Sage.

Exline, J. J., & Rose, E. (2005). Religious and spiritual struggles. In R. F. Paloutzian & C. L. Park (Eds.), *Handbook of the psychology of religion* (pp. 315–330). New York, NY: Guilford Press.

Firth, S. (2005). End-of-life: A Hindu view. *Lancet, 366*, 682–686. doi:10.1016/S0140-6736(05)67141-3

Gaustad, E. S., & Barlow, P. L. (2001). *New historical atlas of religion in America.* New York, NY: Oxford University Press.

Harwood, R. L., Miller, J. G., & Irizarry, N. L. (1995). *Culture and attachment: Perceptions of the child in context.* New York, NY: Guilford Press.

Koenig, H. G. (1998). *Handbook of religion and mental health.* New York, NY: Academic Press.

Kumar, P. P. (2000). *Hindus in South Africa: Their traditions and beliefs.* Park Rynie, South Africa: Majestic Printers.

Kurien, P. A. (2005). Being young, brown and Hindu: The identity struggles of second-generation Indian Americans. *Journal of Contemporary Ethnography, 34*, 434–469. doi:10.1177/0891241605275575

Mullatti, L. (1995). Families in India: Beliefs and realities. *Journal of Comparative Family Studies, 26*, 11–25.

Omprakash, S. (1989). The doctrine of karma: Its psycho-social consequences. *American Journal of Community Psychology, 17*, 133–145. doi:10.1007/BF00931209

Pargament, K. I., Murray-Swank, N., Magyar, G., & Ano, G. (2005). Spiritual struggle: A phenomenon of interest to psychology and religion. In W. R. Miller & H. Delaney (Eds.), *Judeo-Christian perspectives on psychology: Human nature, motivation, and change* (pp. 245–268). Washington, DC: American Psychological Association.

Pargament, K. I., Poloma, M. M., & Tarakeshwar, N. (2001). Methods of coping from the religions of the world: Spiritual healing, Karma, and the Bar Mitzvah. In C. R. Snyder (Ed.), *Coping and copers: Adaptive processes and people* (pp. 259–284). New York, NY: Oxford University Press.

Radhakrishnan, S. (1975). *The Hindu view of life*. New York, NY: Macmillan.

Saraswathi, T. S., & Ganapathy, H. (2002). Indian parents' ethnotheories as reflections of the Hindu scheme of child and human development. In H. Keller, Y. H. Poortinga, & A. Scholmerich (Eds.), *Between culture and biology: Perspectives on ontogenetic development* (pp. 79–88). Cambridge, England: Cambridge University Press. doi:10.1017/CBO9780511489853.005

Sharma, A. (2000). Psychotherapy with Hindus. In P. S. Richards & A. E. Bergin (Eds.), *Handbook of psychotherapy and religious diversity* (pp. 341–365). Washington, DC: American Psychological Association. doi:10.1037/10347-014

Spiro, A. M. (2005). Najar or Bhut-Evil eye or ghost affliction: Gujarati views about illness causation. *Anthropology and Medicine, 12*, 61–73. doi:10.1080/13648470500049867

Takriti, R. A., Barrett, M., & Buchanan-Barrow, E. (2006). Children's understanding of religion: Interviews with Arab-Muslim, Asian-Muslim, Christian and Hindu children aged 5–11 years. *Mental Health, Religion, and Culture, 9*, 29–42. doi:10.1080/13674670512331335677

Tarakeshwar, N., Krishnan, A. K., Johnson, S., Vasu, C., Solomon, S., Merson, M., & Sikkema, K. J. (2007). A social cognitive model of health for HIV-positive adults in India. *AIDS and Behavior, 11*, 491–504. doi:10.1007/s10461-006-9161-z

Tarakeshwar, N., Pargament, K. I., & Mahoney, A. (2003a). Initial development of a measure of religious coping among Hindus. *Journal of Community Psychology, 31*, 607–628. doi:10.1002/jcop.10071

Tarakeshwar, N., Pargament, K. I., & Mahoney, A. (2003b). Measures of Hindu pathways: Development and preliminary evidence of reliability and validity. *Cultural Diversity and Ethnic Minority Psychology, 9*, 316–332. doi:10.1037/1099-9809.9.4.316

Tarakeshwar, N., Stanton, J., & Pargament, K. I. (2003). Religion: An overlooked dimension in cross-cultural psychology. *Journal of Cross-Cultural Psychology, 34*, 377–394. doi:10.1177/0022022103034004001

Udupa, K. N., Singh, R. H., & Settawar, R. (1971). Studies on physiological, endocrine, and metabolic response to the practice of yoga in young normal volunteers. *Journal of Research in Indian Medicine, 6*, 345–353.

Williams, R. B. (Ed.). (1996). *A sacred thread: Modern transmission of Hindu traditions in India and abroad* (pp. 228–257). New York, NY: Columbia University Press.

World Almanac. (2010). Ethnologue: Languages of the world. In *World almanac and book of facts* (16th ed.). New York, NY: Infobase.

CHAPTER 37

THE RELIGION, SPIRITUALITY, AND PSYCHOLOGY OF JEWS

Adam B. Cohen, Benjamin J. Gorvine, and Harold Gorvine

In this chapter, we discuss the religion and spirituality of Jews. We focus on four main areas of research, which suggest similarities and differences between Jews and members of other religious groups: religiousness, moral judgment, forgiveness, and health and well-being. We suggest throughout the chapter important directions for future research, particularly paying more attention to important distinctions among Jews of different denominations. Throughout this chapter, we also briefly provide historical context. We hope that this chapter will promote understanding of the psychology, religion, and spirituality of Jews and that it will have some broader messages for a psychology of religion and spirituality.

WHO IS A JEW?

Critical to any discussion of the religion, spirituality, and psychology of Jewish people is the question of who is a Jew. This is a question not only of psychological interest, but it has enormous historical and political importance as well. In the 20th century, defining who is a Jew has determined who would be sent to death camps in Nazi Germany and who has a claim under the Right of Return to Israeli citizenship. No doubt the psychology of who is a Jew has been influenced by these considerations as well as by theological and cultural notions that reach back hundreds and even thousands of years of Jewish history. Scholars and lay people have long debated whether Judaism is best defined as a religion, a spiritual system, a blueprint for living, a culture, an ethnicity, or an ethical civilization. Do certain beliefs or practices make someone a Jew? Is one a Jew by birthright? Can one choose to cease to be Jewish?

One feature of Judaism that distinguishes it from many other religions (at least in the United States) is that membership in the Jewish religion is largely determined by birth. For those adhering to traditional interpretations of Judaism, a person is irrevocably Jewish if he or she was born to a Jewish mother. For more liberal strains of Judaism (e.g., Reform Judaism), a person is Jewish if he or she has a Jewish mother or father. Put in Morris's (1996) terms, Judaism is a descent religion—one to which a person belongs on the basis of their biological descent. Morris distinguished such religions (of which Hinduism is also a good example) from assent religions—religions to which a person belongs depending on beliefs. In empirical work, Jews, on average, endorse descent rather than assent as a criterion for being Jewish, whereas Protestants do the opposite (Cohen & Hill, 2007). A person born Jewish who does not practice any of the requirements of the religion or believe in any of its teachings is still Jewish. Jewish ethnic and religious identities are hard to distinguish but are dissociable (Saroglou & Hanique, 2006).

This is a difference between Judaism and many other religions with far-reaching psychological implications. This brings us to the first area of research we want to review: what religiousness and spirituality mean to Jews.

We thank David Rosmarin and Jedidiah Siev for comments on the chapter.

DOI: 10.1037/14045-037
APA Handbook of Psychology, Religion, and Spirituality: Vol. 1. Context, Theory, and Research, K. I. Pargament (Editor-in-Chief)
Copyright © 2013 by the American Psychological Association. All rights reserved.

JEWISH RELIGIOUSNESS AND SPIRITUALITY

In this handbook (see Chapter 14 in this volume), religiousness refers to beliefs, practices, relationships, or experiences having to do with the sacred that are explicitly and historically rooted in established institutionalized systems. Spirituality refers to beliefs, practices, relationships, or experiences having to do with the sacred that are not necessarily linked to established institutionalized systems. How do Jews relate to the terms religiousness and spirituality? What is sacred in Judaism?

Most Jewish movements see God as sacred, and the Jewish concept of God is monotheistic. Historical and modern Jewish movements differ, however, in their basic conceptions of the nature of God (some, such as Reconstructionist Judaism, even reject a supernatural view of God). Another candidate for the sacred is the Torah, which is the textual basis for all of Jewish religion and practice, and includes the first five books of the Hebrew bible. More closely linked to actual Jewish practice are the Talmud, the collection of rabbinical explanations, interpretations, and allegories building on the Torah and the Shulchan Aruch, the code of Jewish law that more specifically guides daily practice. In Orthodox Judaism, they form the basis for religious authority, whereas other movements view the writings as important but not necessarily binding. Additional traditions are viewed by some (especially the Orthodox) as sacred, although they tend to be seen as less important than the Talmud and Torah. The Jewish State and land of Israel are often viewed as sacred (Rozin & Wolf, 2008), but the notion that Israel is sacred is often held separately from the modern state (i.e., the land promised by God to the people of Israel). The concept of the Jewish people is also held sacred, with the more traditional Jewish movements expressing this notion of the sacred by emphasizing the "chosenness" of the Jews in contrast to other peoples.

In many Protestant Christian faith systems, one can equate internal faith with what it means to have a religion (Cohen, Hall, Koenig, & Meador, 2005). In Judaism, the emphasis is quite different. In fact, some have argued that there is much less of an emphasis on internal faith in Judaism than in some other religions. At the very least, it seems fair to say that there is an enormous amount of latitude in terms of what it is acceptable for Jews to believe, and in what Jews actually do believe (Cohen, Siegel, & Rozin, 2003; Gilman, 1990). Instead, most Jewish commandments (*mitzvot*) are concerned with prescriptions or proscriptions for behavior. Fewer specify what one must believe or not believe, think or not think (Cohen & Rozin, 2001), although there are exceptions, one famous example being the 11th-century treatise *Duties of the Heart*.

In contrast, there have been many attempts throughout Jewish history to specify obligatory beliefs among Jews. The most famous is from the preeminent Jewish philosopher, physician, and rabbi, Maimonides (Rambam). Rambam argued there is an obligation to believe in God and indeed in 13 articles of faith. Nevertheless, there has never been an accepted taxonomy of required Jewish beliefs (Cohen, 2002). Even Maimonides's assertion that the first of the Ten Commandments commands Jews to believe in God has been disputed on logical grounds. Nachmonides (Ramban), for example, criticized the apparently circular logic of such a commandment. Only if one already believes in God does a commandment to believe in God have the force of divine law. Nevertheless some Jews (particularly Orthodox Jews) do understand the first of the Ten Commandments to be an obligation to believe in God.

On the basis of this viewpoint, one would hypothesize that for Jews what it means to be religious is not what one internally believes, but rather what one does. Much Jewish practice is rooted in traditions that are hundreds and thousands of years old, and religious practice can for some Jews be less about expressing one's personal religious feelings than it is about participating in and continuing the arc of Jewish history, defined by the community's relationship with God (Cohen, Hall, et al., 2005; Cohen et al., 2003; Cohen & Hill, 2007). Rituals bind the community together and signal commitment, and as a consequence, more religious *kibbutzim* show greater longevity (Sosis & Alcorta, 2003).

Consistent with the complex relationship of Judaism and belief, there are some differences in the ways that Jews (as a group) and Protestants (as a group) and Roman Catholics consider what it means to be religious. Two empirical articles have addressed these issues (Cohen et al., 2003; Cohen & Hill, 2007). In Cohen et al. (2003), Jews and Protestant Christians were asked to indicate how important a variety of beliefs and practices are in being religious or a good member of religion. These were carefully chosen (at least on the bases of theology and face validity) to be appropriate in both groups (e.g., not belief in Jesus but belief in God; not keeping kosher but attending religious services). An interaction emerged such that Jews and Protestants rated practice equally important, but Protestants rated belief more important than practice. Another way of decomposing that same interaction was that Jews rated practice more important than belief, but Protestants rated belief more important than practice. In this study, no attention was paid to subgroups. If Orthodox Jews are in some sense the most religious and fundamentalist of Jews, are they more concerned with practice and not belief than other kinds of Jews? Or, are they more likely to be focused on belief than other kinds of Jews?

A second article (Cohen & Hill, 2007) followed in the theoretical tradition of intrinsic and extrinsic religiosity (Allport & Ross, 1967). Allport proposed that intrinsic religiosity is mature, internalized, and a master motive. Extrinsic religiosity is instrumental and is used for other purposes, like social integration, economic benefits, or comfort. Allport theorized extrinsic religiosity to be immature and less sincere than intrinsic religiosity. Cohen, Hall, et al. (2005), however, proposed that community-oriented religion is common and appropriate in Judaism, and not just as a side effect but rather as a legitimate, meaningful way of being religious. For Jews, intrinsic and extrinsic religiosity were positively correlated, which was the opposite found among Protestants (Cohen & Hill, 2007).

Thus, Judaism is a religion concerned with ritual boundaries—kosher versus not kosher, Chosen versus Gentile, Sabbath versus not. Many aspects of Jewish law first given in the Torah (the five books of Moses) have been extended to be more general so that one does not accidentally transgress a commandment. This is called "building a fence around the Torah" (Talmud, Avot, Chapter 1). For example, a commandment not to cook a kid in its mother's milk (Exodus 23:19, 34:26; Deuteronomy 14:21) has been extended to prohibit eating any sort of dairy with certain kinds of meat. A religious Jew will not eat dairy products with fowl, even though this is not specifically prohibited in the Torah. How do Jews feel about somewhat arbitrary practices? These questions may apply most to Orthodox Judaism as it contains rules, in exquisite detail, for how to fulfill *mitzvoth* (Keller, 2000; Telushkin, 1991).

Nemeroff and Rozin (1992) noted that there is a rule in *kashrut* (Jewish dietary system) that one may eat an otherwise *kosher* (ritually acceptable) food if it has been accidentally contaminated by something nonkosher so long as the contaminant is less than one 60th of the total volume. Do kosher Jews feel fine about foods they know are technically kosher but do not seem so? The answer is, some do and some do not, but this is not apparently predictable by any obvious variable like level of religiousness.

The previous discussion has focused on religion. There is also a growing empirical base of research on Jewish spirituality. Sands, Marcus, and Danzig (2008) used data from the 2000–2001 National Jewish Population Survey, which is a large, national sample, to examine religiousness and spirituality among U.S. Jews. Some demographic and other psychological variables predicted greater religiousness and spirituality: lower education, being younger, the experience of anti-Semitism in the past year, and greater ethnic and Jewish social identity. Women and people who lived outside of the Northeastern United States were more spiritual. Predictors of considering oneself to be highly religious but not spiritual included being married, having children, living in the Northeast, and having a Jewish background. This is a particularly interesting finding in the context of a growing literature on what it means to be spiritual but not religious in the United States (e.g., Zinnbauer, Pargament, & Scott, 1999); the converse pattern does not seem so common on the basis of the current literature.

Jewish Diversity

Most of the existing literatures on Jews can be criticized because of the lack of attention to meaningful subgroups within Judaism. How do religiousness and spirituality, belief and practice, and notions of the sacred vary among Orthodox, Conservative, Reform, and Reconstructionist Jews? We now briefly review the historical development of these denominations in modern history. This is important not only to understand the distinctions between these denominations but also because historical forces may be represented in some way in the psychologies of members of these denominations.

Judaism has tremendous diversity of practices and beliefs. The major denominations in the United States include the Orthodox, Conservative, Reform, and Reconstructionist movements. There are also smaller denominations of importance, such as the ultra-Orthodox sects (*Charedi*) and the Secular Humanists. In Israel, religious denominations as well as ethnic origin (e.g., Eastern-European Ashkenazi Jewish vs. Spanish–Moroccan–African Sephardic Jewish) are important. There are distinctly different religious and other cultural traditions for each group, and a modern history of certain contention and competition between the groups. To the extent that there are religious denominations in Israel historically, they have tended to collapse into Orthodox or traditional (*dati*) versus secular as well as *Charedi* versus non-*Charedi*. Recent trends have led to an even more nuanced set of distinctions among Israeli Jews, with denominations emerging in identities and levels of practice more parallel to those in the United States.

The key event in modern Jewish history was the 1791 political emancipation of the Jews by the French National Assembly. Other emancipation measures ensued in Western Europe during subsequent decades in the 19th century. The Russian Empire did not follow suit. In 1740, the British Parliament passed a law permitting the naturalization of Jews in the British colonies. Historian Nathan Glazer (1972) noted that "by this time, the Jews enjoyed more freedom, legally and in fact, in the British colonies in America than anywhere else in the world" (p. 17; see also Mendes-Flohr & Reinharz, 1995). The American Constitution of 1789 provided that "no religious Test shall ever be required as a Qualification to any Office or public Trust under the United States." Two years later Article I of the Bill of Rights stipulated that "Congress shall make no law respecting an establishment of religion, or prohibiting the free exercise thereof." Some of the 13 original states still had legal restrictions concerning Jewish political participation. In 1868, North Carolina's state legislature renounced the last of these (Sachar, 1992). Emancipation opened the way for a flood of change in the ways Jews viewed themselves and the non-Jewish world in which they lived. Were Jews a people or a religion? Both? Did Jewish belief and practice need modification? Would adaptation to the forces of modernity lead to the disappearance of the Jews through assimilation into the non-Jewish world?

The Reform Movement in Germany and the United States took the lead in advocating major changes in Jewish belief and practice. These changes were epitomized in the 1885 Pittsburgh Platform adopted by a conference of German American rabbis. The platform recognized "in every religion an attempt to grasp the infinite one" (Mendes-Flohr & Reinharz, 1995, p. 468). It accepted as binding only the moral laws of the Mosaic legislation and retained only those ceremonies that "elevate and sanctify lives, but reject[ed] those that are not adapted to the views and habits of modern civilization" (Mendes-Flohr & Reinharz, 1995, p. 468). *Kashrut*, laws concerning priestly purity, and laws concerning dress were specifically mentioned as obstructions "to further modern spiritual elevation" (Mendes-Flohr & Reinharz, 1995, p. 469). The rabbis wrote that Reform Jews no longer considered themselves a nation; they were a religious community that did not expect to return to Palestine. Judaism, they insisted, was "a progressive religion" whose mission, with the aid of Christianity and Islam, was to spread "monotheistic and moral truth" (Mendes-Flohr & Reinharz, 1995, p. 469). They accepted the Jewish doctrine of the immortality of the soul, but rejected as "ideas not rooted in Judaism, the belief . . . in bodily resurrection, Gehenna, and Eden (Hell and Paradise)" (Mendes-Flohr & Reinharz, 1995, p. 469). Finally, they embraced as the duty of Jews the obligation to pursue social justice for the poor. The American Reform movement, reacting to Hitler's persecution of the Jews, accepted Zionism during the 1930s. More recently Reform has become more traditional, reinstating rituals that it had abandoned during the 19th century, such as observance of the Sabbath and of *kashrut*.

In both Germany and the United States, Orthodox Jews broke with Reform. In Germany, Rabbi Samson Raphael Hirsch (1808–1888) rejected Reform Judaism's negation of Jewish *halachah* (Jewish law as developed over the centuries in the Talmud). He was, however, willing to "revise certain 'external aspects' of Judaism"—for example, "aesthetic forms of the public worship service—to facilitate the Jew's adjustment to the modern sensibility." In addition, he endorsed secular education and loyalty to the country of which Jews were citizens. The movement that Hirsch founded is known as neo-Orthodoxy (Mendes-Flohr & Reinharz, 1995, p. 202). By contrast, Akiba Joseph Schlesinger (1837–1922), who lived in Germany and later moved to Palestine, was one of the founders of ultra-Orthodox Judaism. Not only did he reject all "innovations within Judaism," but he called on Torah-true Jews to separate themselves from Jews who were drawn to the modern world (Mendes-Flohr & Reinharz, 1995, p. 204). Modern Orthodoxy, on the other hand, has become more separatist, perhaps in response to the rising intermarriage rate and the pressure from the ultra-Orthodox.

An earlier rift within Judaism had occurred in Poland during the 18th century when a revolt against the rabbinical domination of Jewish life took place. Led by Israel Baal Shem Tov, Hasidism emphasized "good deeds and pious living over the intellectual attainments of rabbinism." Hasidism attracted the support of the "half-learned or illiterate masses" (Baron, 1956). The Besht's "learning was emotional rather than intellectual" (Baron, 1956). During prayers Hasidim felt themselves enveloped in states of ecstasy (Katz, 1961). For Hasidim what mattered most about observance of rituals and *Halachic* precepts was religious experience. Opponents of Hasidism, called *Mitnagdim* ["those who oppose"], were appalled by this challenge to their authority and by its anti-intellectualism (Baron, 1956, p. 372; Ettinger, 1976, pp. 772–774). Over time, the rift between the two camps healed, and Hasidic rabbis became as learned as their non-Hasidic contemporaries. There are now many active Hasidic groups in Israel, the United States, and elsewhere.

The Conservative Movement in both Germany and the United States tried to steer a middle course between Orthodoxy and Reform, attempting to honor and observe biblical and rabbinical Judaism while reconciling such aims with living in modernity (Baron, 1956). Conservative Jews are likely to keep kosher (Jewish dietary laws) at least to some extent and observe other commandments, but they often do this in a way that balances the demands of modern life with those of Jewish tradition and law. A Conservative Jew might drive on the Sabbath, for example, but only to synagogue. This distinction between Orthodox and Conservative Judaism is a bit of a gloss because Orthodox Judaism, too, constantly needs to find how to apply traditional Jewish law to modern times; rabbinical "responsa" do just this. This may be particularly true for Modern Orthodoxy. Conservatism has often found itself under attack from both Reform and Orthodoxy. Internally, too, it has been bitterly divided when confronting issues of accepting women as rabbis and welcoming gay men and lesbians as full members.

Theologically speaking, the most radical modern Jewish approach was articulated by Rabbi Mordecai Kaplan in the 20th century, founding Reconstructionist Judaism. Reconstructionist Judaism is the newest branch of Judaism and is mostly an American movement. In comparison with the other three, it is a relatively small movement. It sees Jews as an evolving religious civilization, but it also rejects the notion of God as understood in traditional Judaism. At its center stands Jewish peoplehood. Kaplan denied the existence of a supernatural God, and he dismissed the idea of the chosenness of the Jewish people. He thought of God as *godhood*, "the divine quality of universal being, all the relationships, tendencies and agencies which in their totality go to make human life worthwhile in the deepest and most abiding sense" (Kaplan, 1995, p. 25). In short, the divine is a "quality," not "an entity or being" (Kaplan, 1995, p. xv). All in all, the American Jewish religious scene at present offers a variety of options. It can be argued that this is one of the most creative periods in American Jewish religious history.

Jewish Moral Judgment

Moral judgment is the second area of research we wish to review. There are several perspectives one could potentially have on religion and moral judgment, and we will mention three—each one having some empirical backing for it. The first is that religion has nothing to do with moral judgment. People of different religions, and people who are religious or not, might show the same moral judgments. In fact, in Jewish philosophy and theology, there is a class of commandments called *mishpatim*—commandments that are so self-evident that had God not given them, we still would have come up with them (e.g., commandments against murder and stealing). Indeed, in all cultures, there are certain consistencies in moral codes (Brown, 1991).

A second possible perspective on religion and moral judgment is that it is not the religion people belong to, but rather it is how religious they are that determines their moral judgments. Under this view, religious Jews, Christians, and Muslims would all have similar moral judgments, but these would be different from the moral judgments of people who are not religious. Schwartz and Huismans (1995) examined religious and nonreligious Jews, Orthodox Christians, Protestant Christians, and Catholics in several European countries. They found that religious members of all these religions had conservative values (such as valuing tradition, benevolence, and conformity), whereas nonreligious people of all these religions similarly valued things like self-direction and hedonism (cf. Saroglou, Delpierre, & Dernelle, 2004).

A third perspective on religion and moral judgment is that different religions consider different things to be moral or immoral. In Judaism, there is a category of laws classified as *chukim*, which are commandments that seem arbitrary to people but are adhered to because God has commanded them not because of their self-evident nature. A good example of a commandment in this category is the prohibition against eating pork. Often people imagine that the biblical commandment prohibiting Jews from eating pork has its roots in the desert climate, where eating pork was a health risk. In fact this is one justification some modern Jews give for not abiding by this commandment, seeing it as no longer necessary. But there actually is a Talmudic discussion about what one's attitude should be in observing this commandment. One should not think to oneself that pork is disgusting—where is the virtue in not committing a sin one never wanted to do anyway? Instead, there is the viewpoint that one very much should want to eat pork but avoid it only out of obedience to God's will (Talmud, Sifra, Kedoshim, Parasha 10).

One program of research to fall under this category has examined the moral status of thoughts about moral or immoral actions for Jews and Christians. In terms of moral judgment, Christianity focuses as much on internal as external states. Thinking about an immoral action, according to Jesus' Sermon on the Mount, is the exact moral equivalent of doing it. This is a radically different view than is contained within Judaism, which largely considers thoughts about immoral actions to be normal, and even necessary. Empirical research shows that to a Christian, a married man thinking about having an affair with an attractive colleague is an adulterer (famously illustrated in Jimmy Carter's *Playboy* magazine interview), but Jews consider such thoughts to be much less morally diagnostic, and this difference is fully mediated by large Jewish–Christian differences in endorsement of the notion that thoughts are as important as actions (Cohen, 2003; Cohen & Rozin, 2001). Jews and Christians, however, give equal moral credit to thoughts about highly virtuous actions (Cohen & Rankin, 2004). This is important because it strongly suggests that relevant theological differences drive these group differences because Jewish sacred texts (the Talmud) say God does not penalize for immoral thoughts that are not enacted, but God does give credit for positive thoughts that are not enacted. As a result, one can make a strong case that religious theology drives religious cultural differences (represented in people's lived psychologies of moral judgment), even if people are not especially religiously identified.

One interesting but unknown question regarding the moral status of thoughts is whether people of different denominations show the same patterns. For Orthodox Jews, for example, one could imagine two very different possibilities. On the one hand, Orthodox Jews are so immersed in the correct practice of Judaism that they may be even more likely to look only at actions. On the other hand, Orthodox Jews may be especially likely to believe that God knows their thoughts (one of Maimonides's 13 articles of faith). And there is the notion of *hirhur*—

avoiding thoughts that could lead the individual to commit a sin, so the thoughts take on some moral import—but again in this case perhaps because it could lead to certain *behaviors*.

Another interesting but unexplored issue concerning the morality of thoughts is how religion and country may interact. Jews in the United States are a minority, living in a Christian culture. Is their moral judgment unaffected by this, which would mean that Jews in various countries would show the same patterns? If this is the case, it would be a piece of evidence that moral judgment is so protected a part of religious culture that it is unaffected by the overall cultural context (e.g., country). Another possibility is that Jews in the United States are similar to the overall Christian culture, so that Jews in another country—Israel, for example—would look even more "Jewish" in this sense than would American Jews. A third possibility is that Jews in the United States develop their moral judgments to dissociate themselves from the overall Christian culture; as a result, their moral judgments are even more different from Christians than they would be otherwise. Future work on religion and culture should examine how religion and nationality–ethnicity interact (Cohen et al. 2009; Saroglou & Cohen, in press; Sasaki & Kim, 2010; see also Chapter 13 in this volume).

Next we turn to a closely linked issue that is perhaps best understood as a subarea within the study of morality: forgiveness. The Jewish perspective on forgiveness is particularly relevant and fascinating in light of some of the formative events in Jewish history.

Jewish Forgiveness and Unforgiveness

Much of the work on forgiveness has fallen squarely within the realm of the psychology of religion and spirituality. Given the close links between this work and the more general topic of morality, we next discuss Jewish notions of forgiveness and unforgiveness. Christian theology specifies that Jesus died to atone for the sins of others (see Chapter 39 in this volume). In this sense, forgiveness is not contingent on a perpetrator's repentance toward the victim, and few if any sins are too severe to forgive (Marty, 1998). Perhaps not coincidentally, there are many arguments in the forgiveness literature in psychology espousing forgiveness as a moral imperative and as a healthy process (e.g., Witvliet, Ludwig, & Vander Laan, 2001; see also Chapter 23 in this volume).

Jewish theology considers forgiveness to be highly virtuous but not for all offenses. In Jewish theology, forgiveness cannot be extended by someone who was not the direct victim of an offense, some offenses are too severe to be forgiven, and offenders must repent to be offered forgiveness (Dorff, 1998). Moreover, for Christians, forgiveness is a personal process (an internal change in emotions), but for Jews, forgiveness is an interpersonal process involving reconciliation between the victim and offender (Cohen, Malka, Rozin, & Cherfas, 2006).

In one of the few sets of studies to examine religious group differences on forgiveness, Cohen et al. (2006) compared Jews and Protestants on dispositional forgiveness (forgiving everyday, interpersonal offenses) and forgiveness for extreme offenses, such as the Holocaust. Jews agreed much more than did Protestants that certain offenses were unforgivable. This was not explained by differences in dispositional forgiveness. Salience of religious identity was much more negatively correlated with belief in unforgivable offenses among Protestants ($r = -.76$) than Jews ($r = -.02$). This research did not look for denominational differences, and it may be that sampling from more highly religiously identified Jews may uncover a correlation between religiousness and endorsement of unforgivable offenses.

In an additional study, Cohen et al. (2006) presented participants with two scenarios. The first concerned a severe plagiarism offense that a person committed against a friend of the participant, and the offender did not repent to the actual victim. The second offense was a true story described by Simon Wiesenthal (1997). While in a Nazi concentration camp, Wiesenthal was asked by a dying *Schutzstaffel* (SS) soldier for forgiveness for having murdered Jews. Jews were much less willing to forgive both of these offenses, and Jews also agreed much more than did Protestants with theological reasons for not forgiving (some offenses are too severe to forgive, only victims have the right to forgive, and offenders must repent). Group differences in forgiveness for both offenses were fully mediated by the theological reasons for nonforgiveness.

These differences have important implications for how groups interact—and how well they get along—following conflict. Jews and Germans in the wake of the Holocaust would be one example here. Jews may persist in finding Germans, even those not alive during World War II, to be appropriate targets of blame and aversion (Cherfas et al., 2006). Holocaust survivors vary widely in this respect, and a small study suggested that the best account for differences between survivors in their feelings about modern Germans is whether they were born in Germany—and presumably knew Germans before the Holocaust (Cherfas et al., 2006).

An interesting area for future exploration here is how specifically the Jewish ideas of forgiveness have been affected by the Holocaust. Although the basic theology around forgiveness appears to be constant both pre- and post-Holocaust, it is not entirely clear what the specific impact of the Holocaust may have been. Are Jewish ideas about forgiveness essentially unchanged? Or have such ideas somehow become amplified in Jewish consciousness because of the Holocaust? Would the theology we reviewed in this section (e.g., some offenses are too severe to forgive) be less salient in Jewish consciousness had the Holocaust not occurred?

This brings us to a final set of research that has examined the particular interface between religion and well-being. The literature examining this topic has been especially rich and diverse.

Jewish Health and Well-Being

Much attention has been paid to the ways that religion may be correlated with and promote or detract from health and well-being (Koenig, McCullough, & Larson, 2001). It could be instructive to study Jews in this regard because the ways in which Jewish religion relates to health outcomes can be similar to or different from such relations in other religious communities, or some mechanisms may be stronger or weaker (Cohen & Koenig, 2003). An understanding of how Jewish religious and spiritual variables relate to health and well-being should be of general interest.

We first summarize the (not very easy to synthesize) work on health and well-being. Coming to grips with the literature is going to potentially involve different explanations for mental versus physical health, studies comparing Jews with other religious groups, studies on subgroups within Judaism such as Orthodox versus non Orthodox, and relationships between dimensions of religiousness and spirituality within Judaism.

Some evidence suggests greater religiousness and spirituality among Jews is protective. Rosmarin, Pargament, and Mahoney (2009) found that more trust in God was correlated with less anxiety and depression and more happiness, and the opposite was true for people who showed mistrust in God, and similar results were obtained by Rosmarin, Krumrei, and Andersson (2009). Shkolnik, Weiner, Malik, and Festinger (2001) studied elderly Jewish men in religious neighborhoods in Israel and found that those who were more traditionally religious showed higher life satisfaction. Nevertheless, Iecovich (2001) found religiosity and well-being to be uncorrelated in elderly Jewish women in Israel after controlling for possible confounds.

In comparison with other groups, Jews tend to show less well-being and more depression. In older adults in the United States, Kennedy, Kelman, Thomas, and Chen (1996) found that Jews were more likely to be depressed at baseline as well as were more likely to develop depressive symptoms over 2 years. Cohen and Hall (2009) also found lower rates of well being in Jewish older adults, compared with Catholics or Protestants in North Carolina.

When it comes to physical health, Jews may have some advantages and disadvantages. For example, Jews may manifest longer life spans, reduced family history of stroke, and lower rates of penile cancer. There is, however, also some evidence of higher rates of breast cancer among Jews (Friedman & Hellerstein, 1968; Koenig, McCullough, & Larson, 2001).

Explanations

These different effects, some positive, some negative, will require a variety of potential explanations. Various possibilities have been proposed, and we propose several more.

Biology. One intriguing but underexplored possibility is that there are particular genetic predispositions that are more common among Jews than other groups. For example, Tay Sachs disease is much more common among Ashkenazi Jews than among other ethnoreligious groups. There is an increasing interest in combining genetic and cultural approaches to understanding health outcomes. Cultural groups can differ in proportions of genetic alleles that may promote or reflect differences in cultural norms (Chiao & Blizinsky, 2010; Sasaki, Kim, & Xu, 2010). Jewish culture strongly favors endogamy, and marrying outside the faith is strongly discouraged. Members of a Jewish community are as closely genetically related to each other as fourth or fifth cousins, much more than people chosen at random in a large population (Atzmon et al., 2010; Behar et al., 2010). Perhaps because of such a focus on genetic relatedness, providing a biological explanation for mental illness relates to *increased* stigmatization among Jews, relative to a psychological explanation. This is contrary to the usual finding that people consider biological disorders to be less stigmatizing than psychological disorders (Pirutinsky, Rosen, Safran, & Rosmarin, 2010).

Reporting differences. A second reason that may predispose Jews in some ways to showing poorer health or well-being is that Jews could be more willing to report mental health problems, or label issues as mental health problems (e.g., Guttmacher & Ellinson, 1971). This could result from several processes. The culture and norms of psychotherapy may also be particularly compatible with those of Judaism or Jewish culture (Langman, 1997). Jews may also be less stoic than other groups. Wex (2005) proposed that Jews are prone to complaining because Eastern European Jewish language and culture emphasize a feeling of being a persecuted minority in the Diaspora.

We want to make two qualifications to this idea. First, we speculate that this may be different among Israeli Jews, who have adopted instead a no-nonsense and practical approach to life. Second, there is also a pervasive optimism contained in Jewish culture and theology, which could explain why religious Jews are apt to report better well-being. Jewish prayers are more optimistic than those of certain other religions (Sethi & Seligman, 1993). One example is the *shir hamaalot* prayer, taken from the Psalms, which is sung as a prelude to Grace after meals on holidays. The optimism is apparent in lines such as "Those who sow in tears, in joy will reap." (Other prayers are not so optimistic, like those from *Lamentations* [*Eicha*]).

Models of health and illness. Another factor that needs to be considered is models of health or illness. Jews may be particularly likely to subscribe to materialist, medical models of health and disease. For Protestants, estimates of health and well-being ratings may be affected by a person's perceived spiritual health to a large extent (e.g., Idler, 1995). Jews may not do this because of lower levels of certain kinds of spirituality, particularly belief in a soul or afterlife (Cohen & Hall, 2009), and hence they may be more likely to endorse biological or medical explanations of disease. It would be important to discover whether such tendencies vary across Jewish denominations.

Death. All religions deal in some way with death, but religions deal with death in different ways. Thoughts, feelings, and concerns about death could affect health and well-being. Beliefs in the afterlife could reduce death anxiety (see Chapter 5 in this volume), but such beliefs have been claimed to be much less salient in Jews than in Christians (Cohen, Pierce, et al., 2005). For Cohen and Hall (2009), less well-being in Jewish older adults in comparison with Catholics and Protestants could partly be explained by differing levels of satisfaction with social relationships and existential concerns. Some work has even gone so far as to suggest that Jews and non-Jews may differ in their capacity to cope with grief around the loss of a child, although the particular evidence here is preliminary (Goodman, Rubinstein, Alexander, & Luborsky, 1991). It is possible that Jewish rituals around death (like sitting *shiva*) can be helpful in terms of helping people cope.

Here, too, subgroup differences are poorly understood; Orthodox Jews probably have greater belief in life after death than more secular Jews. These beliefs could take various forms (Cohen & Hall, 2009), including belief in resurrection when the messiah comes, or belief in *olam habah* (i.e., the world to come), or living on through the Jewish people or through one's children.

Protective Factors

There are several aspects of Jewish culture and religion that could be protective of health and well-being. Jews could have lower cervical cancer rates or penile cancer rates, perhaps because of practices like circumcision (Koenig et al., 2001). Speaking more sociologically, Durkheim (1951/1997) found that Jews were particularly less likely to commit suicide, less than Catholics and much less than Protestants, which he attributed to the great emphasis on social integration and support found in Jewish culture. We now discuss two other factors: coping and self-regulation.

Coping. Like many religions, religiousness and spirituality among Jews could promote some kinds of effective coping. Rosmarin, Pargament, Krumrei, and Flannelly (2009) suggested that the religious coping of Jews may differ from that of other religious groups, and they pointed out that the current literature on coping has focused on Christians. They developed a two-factor (positive and negative) scale for religious coping among Jews, using a diverse sample in terms of the denominations of the Jewish participants. An example of positive religious coping was, "I do the best I can and know the rest is G-d's will," and an example of negative religious coping was, "I get mad at G-d." (Many Jews, in order to not violate the commandment against taking God's name in vain, will write G [dash] d; this is also why many Jews will say the word *Hashem,* "the Name," when referring to God in casual conversation). Religious beliefs and practices and cultural practices correlated positively with positive coping and negatively with negative religious coping. Positive religious coping predicted less psychological distress (i.e., worry, anxiety, depression), whereas negative religious coping predicted more distress.In related work, Lazar and Bjorck (2008) found that for a community of Orthodox Jews living in Israel, perceptions of support from religious leaders and God were related to lower levels of emotional distress, perceptions of support from the Jewish community and from God predicted higher levels of perceived health, and perceptions of religious leader and religious community support were associated with reports of greater life satisfaction.

Self-regulation. Judaism encourages effective self-control and self-regulation. Recently, it has been shown that religious people could be higher in self-control than nonreligious people (McCullough & Willoughby, 2009; see also Chapter 6 in this volume). Having better self-control clearly could have health benefits from resisting eating those potato chips to exercising regularly to drinking less. We propose that Jews could be especially high in self-control and self-regulation, for two reasons. First, many Jewish practices can be understood theologically as exercises in self-regulation (Klein, 1979). Judaism rarely forbids an activity outright (such as sex), but it instead regulates the contexts under which the activity is acceptable (within marriage), prohibited (outside of marriage), and especially virtuous (on the Sabbath). Second, as discussed, Judaism considers it especially virtuous to want to commit certain sins (such as eating pork) but to override that temptation—a viewpoint tailor-made to cultivate self-regulation. This culture of self-regulation (Yeung & Greenwald, 1992) is sometimes proposed as an explanation for the lower rates of alcohol abuse among Jews.

Illness Versus Normative Practice

We now turn to another issue, the difficulty in identifying excessive religion. The strictures of religious practice could promote or be expressed through scrupulosity, a need to perform religious rituals in exactly the right way that could lead to anxiety (Greenberg & Witztum, 2001). Is an observant Jew showing signs of obsessive–compulsive disorder (OCD) or adherence to Jewish dietary laws if he refuses to eat a meat soup into which a drop of milk has accidentally fallen—and if he further wonders whether the contamination is more or less than one 60th of the total volume (Nemeroff & Rozin, 1992)? It can be difficult to distinguish scrupulosity from appropriate or even virtuous religious practice (Pirutinsky, Rosmarin, & Pargament, 2009; Rosmarin, Pirutinsky, & Siev, 2010). Distinguishing appropriate practices and beliefs from problematic ones is a concern that has been expressed about Jews as well as other religious groups (Greenberg & Witztum, 2001; Loewenthal, 2007; O'Connor & Vanbenberg, 2005).

Siev and Cohen (2007) examined the thought–action fusion of Orthodox, Conservative, and Reform Jews (as well as of Christians). *Thought–action fusion* is the tendency to consider a thought (a) the moral equivalent of an action and (b) as making an event more likely to actually occur (which was not particularly relevant in this study). On the basis of Jewish–Christian differences in the moral status of thoughts, Siev and Cohen theorized that Christians might score in the clinical range of a scale measuring thought–action fusion. They found that Jews of different denominations were similarly low on the moral component of thought–action fusion, whereas Christians were much higher—higher even than the clinical norms for the scale. At least in this case, Jews of different denominations showed similar effects. Siev and Cohen stressed the difficulty of distinguishing religious beliefs from pathology.

Criticisms and Future Directions

Socioeconomic status. One criticism of research on religion and health is that much existing work may confound religious identification with socioeconomic status (SES). Jewish Americans are overwhelmingly college educated, at a much higher rate than the general population (e.g., Cohen et al., 2002). Differences characterized as Jewish–Christian may, to some degree, reflect differences in SES (cf. Graham, 1992). Subgroups within Judaism also may differ. Although education is perhaps highly valued across the Jewish spectrum, different kinds of education may be valued. Secular medical and law degrees may be prized among non-Orthodox Jews, whereas *yeshiva* and *kollel* learning may be most valuable in ultra-Orthodox communities.

Culturally and religiously contextualized treatment. How to integrate religious and cultural sensitivity into clinical practice is always a challenge, and no less so in the case of Judaism. Some work has been done on the intersection between Judaism and clinical practice with an attempt to define how psychotherapeutic approaches can both be sensitive to and incorporate Jewish cultural and religious practice (Miller & Lovinger, 2000; Rabinowitz, 2000). Spiritually integrated treatments may be effective among Jews for treating anxiety (Rosmarin, Pargament, Pirutinsky, & Mahoney, 2010; see also Volume 2, Chapter 4, this handbook and cf. Volume 2, Chapter 5, this handbook).

Huppert and Siev (2010), using a case study, suggested that there may be particular principles for treating religious individuals with scrupulosity by using the patient's own values and language, and focusing on helping the individual to have better and healthier religious functioning (see also Volume 2, Chapter 12, this handbook). Recent work has also explored the possibility that exposure and response-prevention (the current first-line treatment for OCD) can be adapted to be consistent with the values of the ultra-Orthodox community (Huppert, Siev, & Kushner, 2007).

The broadly defined literature on diversity and clinical practice must grapple with the tricky issue of how one integrates cultural and religious considerations into interventions without overly stereotyping groups (i.e., ignoring within-group difference). A common hazard for clinicians is making assumptions about an individual client's beliefs based on knowledge of group membership (see Volume 2, Chapter 34, this handbook); this hazard can be magnified when a clinician belongs to the same group as the client with whom they are working (i.e., a Jewish therapist working with a Jewish client).

Subgroups. As noted in prior sections, one of the most pressing criticisms of existing work on health and well-being among Jews has been the insufficient attention to subgroups. Fortunately, there are signs that this picture is starting to change. Cohen (2002) claimed that measures of spirituality that correlate with well-being among Christians are irrelevant to the well-being of Jews. Rosmarin, Pirutinsky, Pargament, and Krumrei (2009) showed that although this pattern held true for non-Orthodox Jews, for Orthodox Jews, measures of religious beliefs were correlated with greater well-being.

Similarly, Rosmarin, Pargament, and Flannelly (2009) showed that spiritual struggle was associated with lower levels of physical and mental health in a Jewish sample as a whole, but Orthodox Jews with the highest level of spiritual struggle showed *higher* physical and mental health. This was in contrast to the observation that non-Orthodox Jews with the highest levels of spiritual struggle were still worse off. Pirutinsky (2009) also demonstrated subtleties depending on fine-grained denominational differences in priming death and religiousness. For people whose religiosity had changed substantially in their life (including *baalei tshuvah*, people who have become Orthodox), priming death resulted in higher religiosity. The opposite was true for people whose religiosity had remained constant across their lives.

CONCLUSION

We have identified some important ways in which the religion and spirituality of Jews may differ from those of other groups. Psychology, it seems to us, has been slow to recognize this point perhaps because it does not consider religious groups to be cultural groups (Cohen, 2009a, 2009b). Some of these differences are, for example, that Jews tend to define their religion on the basis of ethnicity (descent) rather than specific beliefs (assent). In contrast to other groups such as Protestant Christians, Jews seem to focus much more on practice than on belief. Perhaps as a consequence, Jews consider thoughts about immoral actions to be much less morally diagnostic than do Christians. In addition, Jews may have particular health benefits and risks that are not characteristic of other groups. One limitation we highlighted was the lack of attention in much (but not all) of the literature to denominational differences.

With all of those things said, we do not want to overstate the argument for Jewish uniqueness. Terms like *Judeo-Christian* and *Abrahamic* accurately imply much commonality among Judaism, Christianity, and Islam in religion, spirituality, and culture. All consider themselves monotheistic and include great moral systems. Jews, Muslims, and Christians alike consider it immoral to commit adultery, even if Jews are unlikely to consider thoughts about adultery to be a sin (see Chapters 38 and 39 in this volume). All consider religious practice to be a defining element of religious community participation, and all consider forgiveness in general to be a great virtue, even if Jews are unwilling to forgive egregious offenses. All three groups encourage self-regulation and coping in ways that have implications for health outcomes.

To leave this chapter then, we want to stress that all religious and spiritual systems have important similarities as well as differences. To develop the richest possible psychology of religion and spirituality, it will be important to gain a deeper understanding of the generalities as well as the particularities of the world's varied religious traditions (Moberg, 2002).

References

Allport, G. W., & Ross, J. M. (1967). Personal religious orientation and prejudice. *Journal of Personality and Social Psychology, 5*, 432–443. doi:10.1037/h0021212

Atzmon, G., Hao, L., Pe'er, I., Velez, C., Pearlman, A., Palamara, P. F., . . . Ostrer, H. (2010). Abraham's children in the genome era: Major Jewish diaspora populations comprise distinct genetic clusters with shared Middle Eastern ancestry. *American Journal of Human Genetics, 86*, 850–859. doi:10.1016/j.ajhg.2010.04.015

Baron, S. W. (1956). The enduring heritage. In L. W. Schwarz (Ed.), *Great ages and ideas of the Jewish people* (pp. 360–390). New York, NY: Random House.

Behar, D. M., Yunusbayev, B., Metspalu, M., Metspalu, E., Rosset, S., Parik, J., . . . Villems, R. (2010). The genome-wide structure of the Jewish people. *Nature, 466*, 238–242. doi:10.1038/nature09103

Brown, D. (1991). *Human universals.* San Francisco, CA: McGraw-Hill.

Cherfas, L., Rozin, P., Cohen, A. B., Davidson, A., & McCauley, C. (2006). The framing of atrocities: Documenting and exploring wide variation in aversion to Germans and German-related activities among Holocaust survivors. *Peace and Conflict, 12*, 65–80. doi:10.1207/s15327949pac1201_5

Chiao, J. Y., & Blizinsky, K. D. (2010). Culture–gene coevolution of individualism– collectivism and the serotonin transporter gene. *Proceedings of the Royal Society, Series B: Biological Sciences, 277*, 529–537. doi:10.1098/rspb.2009.1650

Cohen, A. B. (2002). The importance of spirituality in well-being for Jews and Christians. *Journal of Happiness Studies, 3*, 287–310. doi:10.1023/A:1020656823365

Cohen, A. B. (2003). Religion, likelihood of action, and the morality of mentality. *The International Journal for the Psychology of Religion, 13*, 273–285. doi:10.1207/S15327582IJPR1304_4

Cohen, A. B. (2009a). Many forms of culture. *American Psychologist, 64*, 194–204. doi:10.1037/a0015308

Cohen, A. B. (2009b, August). *There are many forms of culture, including religion*. Invited address presented at the 117th Annual Convention of the American Psychological Association, Toronto, Ontario, Canada.

Cohen, A. B., & Hall, D. E. (2009). Existential beliefs, social satisfaction, and well-being among Catholic, Jewish, and Protestant older adults. *The International Journal for the Psychology of Religion, 19*, 39–54. doi:10.1080/10508610802471088

Cohen, A. B., Hall, D. E., Koenig, H. G., & Meador, K. G. (2005). Social versus individual motivation: Implications for normative definitions of religious orientation. *Personality and Social Psychology Review, 9*, 48–61. doi:10.1207/s15327957pspr0901_4

Cohen, A. B., & Hill, P. C. (2007). Religion as culture: Religious individualism and collectivism among American Catholics, Jews, and Protestants. *Journal of Personality, 75*, 709–742. doi:10.1111/j.1467-6494.2007.00454.x

Cohen, A. B., & Koenig, H. G. (2003). Religion, religiosity and spirituality in the biopsychosocial model of health and ageing. *Ageing International, 28*, 215–241. doi:10.1007/s12126-002-1005-1

Cohen, A. B., Malka, A., Hill, E. D., Thoemmes, F., Hill, P. C., & Sundie, J. M. (2009). Race as a moderator of the relationship between religiosity and political alignment. *Personality and Social Psychology Bulletin, 35*, 271–282. doi:10.1177/0146167208328064

Cohen, A. B., Malka, A., Rozin, P., & Cherfas, L. (2006). Religion and unforgivable offenses. *Journal of Personality, 74*, 85–117. doi:10.1111/j.1467-6494.2005.00370.x

Cohen, A. B., Pierce, J. D., Jr., Meade, R., Chambers, J., Gorvine, B. J., & Koenig, H. G. (2005). Intrinsic and extrinsic religiosity, belief in the afterlife, death anxiety, and life satisfaction in young Catholic and Protestant adults. *Journal of Research in Personality, 39*, 307–324.

Cohen, A. B., & Rankin, A. (2004). Religion and the morality of positive mentality. *Basic and Applied Social Psychology, 26*, 45–57. doi:10.1207/s15324834basp2601_5

Cohen, A. B., & Rozin, P. (2001). Religion and the morality of mentality. *Journal of Personality and Social Psychology, 81*, 697–710. doi:10.1037/0022-3514.81.4.697

Cohen, A. B., Siegel, J. I., & Rozin, P. (2003). Faith versus practice: Different bases for religiosity judgments by Jews and Protestants. *European Journal of Social Psychology, 33*, 287–295. doi:10.1002/ejsp.148

Dorff, E. N. (1998). The elements of forgiveness: A Jewish approach. In E. L. Worthington Jr., (Ed.), *Dimensions of forgiveness: Psychological research and theological perspectives* (pp. 29–55). Philadelphia, PA: Templeton.

Durkheim, E. (1997). *Suicide: A study in sociology*. New York, NY: Free Press. (Original work published 1951)

Ettinger, S. (1976). The internal struggle in Eastern European Jewry. In H. H. Ben-Sasson (Ed.), *A history of the Jewish people* (pp. 764–776). Cambridge, MA: Harvard University Press.

Friedman, E. H., & Hellerstein, H. K. (1968). Occupational stress, law school hierarchy, and coronary artery disease in Cleveland attorneys. *Psychosomatic Medicine, 30*, 72–86.

Gilman, N. (1990). *Sacred fragments: Recovering theology for the modern Jew*. Philadelphia, PA: Jewish Publication Society.

Glazer, N. (1972). *American Judaism* (2nd ed.). Chicago, IL: University of Chicago Press.

Goodman, M., Rubinstein, R. L., Alexander, B. B., & Luborsky, M. (1991). Cultural differences among elderly women in coping with the death of an adult child. *The Journals of Gerontology, Series B: Psychological Sciences and Social Sciences, 46*, S321–S329.

Graham, S. (1992). "Most of the subjects were White and middle class": Trends in published research on African Americans in selected APA journals, 1970–1989. *American Psychologist, 47*, 629–639. doi:10.1037/0003-066X.47.5.629

Greenberg, D., & Witztum, E. (2001). *Sanity and sanctity: Mental health work among the ultra-Orthodox in Jerusalem*. New Haven, CT: Yale.

Guttmacher, S., & Ellinson, J. (1971). Ethno-religious variation in perceptions of illness: The use of illness as an explanation for deviant behavior. *Social Science and Medicine, 5*, 117–125. doi:10.1016/0037-7856(71)90092-8

Huppert, J. D., & Siev, J. (2010). Treating scrupulosity in religious individuals using cognitive–behavioral therapy. *Cognitive and Behavioral Practice, 17*, 382–392. doi:10.1016/j.cbpra.2009.07.003

Huppert, J. D., Siev, J., & Kushner, E. S. (2007). When religion and obsessive–compulsive disorder collide: Treating scrupulosity in Orthodox Jews. *Journal of Clinical Psychology, 63*, 925–941. doi:10.1002/jclp.20404

Idler, E. L. (1995). Religion, health, and nonphysical senses of self. *Social Forces, 74*, 683–704. doi:10.2307/2580497

Iecovich, E. (2001). Religiousness and subjective well-being among Jewish female residents of old age homes in Israel. *Journal of Religious Gerontology, 13*, 31–46. doi:10.1300/J078v13n01_04

Kaplan, M. M. (1995). *The meaning of God in modern Jewish religion.* Detroit, MI: Wayne State University Press.

Katz, J. (1961). *Tradition and crisis: Jewish society at the end of the Middle Ages.* New York, NY: Schocken Books.

Keller, R. R. (2000). Religious diversity in North America. In P. S. Richards & A. E. Bergin (Eds.), *Handbook of psychotherapy and religious diversity* (pp. 27–55). Washington, DC: American Psychological Association. doi:10.1037/10347-002

Kennedy, G. J., Kelman, H. R., Thomas, C., & Chen, J. (1996). The relation of religious preference and practice to depressive symptoms among 1,855 older adults. *The Journals of Gerontology, Series B: Psychological Sciences and Social Sciences, 51*, 301–308. doi:10.1093/geronb/51B.6.P301

Klein, I. (1979). *Guide to Jewish religious practice.* New York, NY: Jewish Theological Seminary.

Koenig, H. G., McCullough, M. E., & Larson, D. B. (2001). *Handbook of religion and health.* Oxford, England: Oxford University Press. doi:10.1093/acprof:oso/9780195118667.001.0001

Langman, P. (1997). White culture, Jewish culture, and the origins of psychotherapy. *Psychotherapy: Theory, Research, Practice, Training, 34*, 207–218. doi:10.1037/h0087640

Lazar, A., & Bjorck, J. P. (2008). Religious support and psychosocial well-being among a religious Jewish population. *Mental Health, Religion, and Culture, 11*, 403–421. doi:10.1080/13674670701486142

Loewenthal, K. M. (2007). *Religion, culture, and mental health.* Cambridge, England: Cambridge University Press.

Marty, M. E. (1998). The ethos of Christian forgiveness. In E. L. Worthington Jr. (Ed.), *Dimensions of forgiveness: Psychological research and theological perspectives* (pp. 9–28). Philadelphia, PA: Templeton.

McCullough, M. E., & Willoughby, B. L. (2009). Religion, self-regulation, and self-control: Associations, explanations, and implications. *Psychological Bulletin, 135*, 69–93. doi:10.1037/a0014213

Mendes-Flohr, P., & Reinharz, J. (Eds.). (1995). *The Jew in the modern world: A documentary history* (2nd ed.). New York, NY: Oxford University Press.

Miller, L., & Lovinger, R. J. (2000). Psychotherapy with Conservative and Reform Jews. In P. S. Richards & A. E. Bergin (Eds.), *Handbook of psychotherapy and religious diversity* (pp. 259–286). Washington, DC: American Psychological Association. doi:10.1037/10347-011

Moberg, D. O. (2002). Assessing and measuring spirituality: Confronting dilemmas of universal and particular evaluative criteria. *Journal of Adult Development, 9*, 47–60. doi:10.1023/A:1013877201375

Morris, P. (1996). Community beyond tradition. In P. Heelas, S. Lash, & P. Morris (Eds.), *Detraditionalization: Critical reflections on authority and identity* (pp. 222–249). Cambridge, England: Blackwell.

Nemeroff, C., & Rozin, P. (1992). Sympathetic magical beliefs and kosher dietary practice: The interaction of rules and feelings. *Ethos, 20*, 96–115. doi:10.1525/eth.1992.20.1.02a00040

O'Connor, S., & Vandenberg, B. (2005). Psychosis or faith? Clinicians' assessment of religious beliefs. *Journal of Consulting and Clinical Psychology, 73*, 610–616. doi:10.1037/0022-006X.73.4.610

Pirutinsky, S. (2009). The terror management function of Orthodox Jewish religiosity: A religious culture approach. *Mental Health, Religion, and Culture, 12*, 247–256. doi:10.1080/13674670802455756

Pirutinsky, S., Rosen, D. D., Safran, R. S., & Rosmarin, D. H. (2010). Do medical models of mental illness relate to increased or decreased stigmatization of mental illness among Orthodox Jews? *Journal of Mental and Nervous Disease, 198*, 508–512. doi:10.1097/NMD.0b013e3181e07d99

Pirutinsky, S., Rosmarin, D. H., & Pargament, K. I. (2009). Community attitudes toward culture-influenced mental illness: Scrupulosity vs. non-religious OCD among Orthodox Jews. *Journal of Community Psychology, 37*, 949–958. doi:10.1002/jcop.20341

Rabinowitz, A. (2000). Psychotherapy with Orthodox Jews. In P. S. Richards & A. E. Bergin (Eds.), *Handbook of psychotherapy and religious diversity* (pp. 237–258). Washington, DC: American Psychological Association. doi:10.1037/10347-010

Rosmarin, D. H., Krumrei, E. J., & Andersson, G. (2009). Religion as a predictor of psychological distress in two religious communities. *Cognitive Behaviour Therapy, 38*, 54–64. doi:10.1080/16506070802477222

Rosmarin, D. H., Pargament, K. I., & Flannelly, K. J. (2009). Do spiritual struggles predict poorer physical/mental health among Jews? *The International Journal for the Psychology of Religion, 19*, 244–258. doi:10.1080/10508610903143503

Rosmarin, D. H., Pargament, K. I., Krumrei, E. J., & Flannelly, K. J. (2009). Religious coping among Jews: Development and initial validation of the JCOPE. *Journal of Clinical Psychology, 65*, 670–683. doi:10.1002/jclp.20574

Rosmarin, D. H., Pargament, K. I., & Mahoney, A. (2009). The role of religiousness in anxiety, depression and happiness in a Jewish community sample: A preliminary investigation. *Mental Health, Religion, and Culture, 12*, 97–113. doi:10.1080/13674670802321933

Rosmarin, D. H., Pargament, K. I., Pirutinsky, S., & Mahoney, A. (2010). A randomized controlled evaluation of a spiritually integrated treatment for subclinical anxiety in the Jewish community, delivered via the Internet. *Journal of Anxiety Disorders, 24*, 799–808. doi:10.1016/j.janxdis.2010.05.014

Rosmarin, D. H., Pirutinsky, S., Pargament, K. I., & Krumrei, E. J. (2009). Are religious beliefs relevant to mental health among Jews? *Psychology of Religion and Spirituality, 1*, 180–190. doi:10.1037/a0016728

Rosmarin, D. H., Pirutinsky, S., & Siev, J. (2010). Are Orthodox and non-Orthodox Jews equally likely to recognize scrupulosity as OCD and recommend professional treatment? *Journal of Social and Clinical Psychology, 29*, 931–945.

Rozin, P., & Wolf, S. (2008). Attachment to land: The case of the land of Israel for American and Israeli Jews and the role of contagion. *Judgment and Decision Making, 3*, 325–334.

Sachar, H. M. (1992). *History of the Jews in America.* New York, NY: Knopf.

Sands, R. G., Marcus, S. C., & Danzig, R. A. (2008). Spirituality and religiousness among American Jews. *The International Journal for the Psychology of Religion, 18*, 238–255. doi:10.1080/10508610802115974

Saroglou, V., & Cohen, A. B. (in press). Cultural and cross-cultural psychology of religion. In R. F. Paloutzian & C. Park (Eds.), *Handbook of psychology and religion.* New York, NY: Guilford Press.

Saroglou, V., Delpierre, V., & Dernelle, R. (2004). Values and religiosity: A meta-analysis of studies using Schwartz's model. *Personality and Individual Differences, 37*, 721–734. doi:10.1016/j.paid.2003.10.005

Saroglou, V., & Hanique, B. (2006). Jewish identity, values, and religion in a globalized world: A study of late adolescents. *Identity: An International Journal of Theory and Research, 6*, 231–249. doi:10.1207/s1532706xid0603_2

Sasaki, J. Y., & Kim, H. S. (2010, January). *The origins, predictors, and moderators of religious beliefs and involvement.* Symposium conducted at the convention of Society of Personality and Social Psychology, Las Vegas.

Sasaki, J. Y., Kim, H. S., & Xu, J. (2010). *Religion and well-being: An analysis of an oxytocin receptor polymorphism (OXTR) and culture.* Manuscript submitted for publication.

Schwartz, S. H., & Huismans, S. (1995). Value priorities and religiosity in four Western religions. *Social Psychology Quarterly, 58*, 88–107. doi:10.2307/2787148

Sethi, S., & Seligman, M. E. P. (1993). Optimism and fundamentalism. *Psychological Science, 4*, 256–259. doi:10.1111/j.1467-9280.1993.tb00271.x

Shkolnik, T., Weiner, C., Malik, L., & Festinger, Y. (2001). The effect of Jewish religiosity of elderly Israelis on their life satisfaction, health, function and activity. *Journal of Cross-Cultural Gerontology, 16*, 201–219. doi:10.1023/A:1011917825551

Siev, J., & Cohen, A. B. (2007). Is thought-action fusion related to religiosity? Group differences between Jews and Christians. *Behaviour Research and Therapy, 45*, 829–837. doi:10.1016/j.brat.2006.05.001

Sosis, R., & Alcorta, C. (2003). Signaling, solidarity, and the sacred: The evolution of religious behavior. *Evolutionary Anthropology, 12*, 264–274. doi:10.1002/evan.10120

Telushkin, J. (1991). *Jewish literacy: The most important things to know about the Jewish religion, its people, and its history.* New York, NY: William Morrow.

Wex, M. (2005). *Born to kvetch: Yiddish language and culture in all its moods.* New York, NY: St. Martin's Press.

Wiesenthal, S. (1997). *Sunflower: On the possibilities and limits of forgiveness.* New York, NY: Schocken.

Witvliet, C. V. O., Ludwig, T. E., & Vander Laan, K. L. (2001). Granting forgiveness or harboring grudges: Implications for emotion, physiology, and health. *Psychological Science, 12*, 117–123. doi:10.1111/1467-9280.00320

Yeung, P. P., & Greenwald, S. (1992). Jewish Americans and mental health: Results of the NIMH epidemiologic catchment area study. *Social Psychiatry and Psychiatric Epidemiology, 27*, 292–297.

Zinnbauer, B. J., Pargament, K. I., & Scott, A. B. (1999). The emerging meanings of religiousness and spirituality: Problems and prospects. *Journal of Personality, 67*, 889–919. doi:10.1111/1467-6494.00077

Chapter 38

THE PSYCHOLOGY OF ISLAM: CURRENT EMPIRICALLY BASED KNOWLEDGE, POTENTIAL CHALLENGES, AND DIRECTIONS FOR FUTURE RESEARCH

Hisham Abu-Raiya

Research in the psychology of religion has grown dramatically in the past 2 decades, and researchers and practitioners have gained some important insights into the impact of religious beliefs and practices on the psychological well-being of the individual (Hood, Hill, & Spilka, 2009; Paloutzian & Park, 2005; Pargament & Abu-Raiya, 2007). This field of inquiry, however, has focused almost exclusively on Christian populations and largely neglected people from other traditional faiths, Islam in particular. Systematic, rigorous, and large-scale scientific psychological research on Muslims has been particularly sparse (Abu-Raiya, Pargament, Stein, & Mahoney, 2007). This oversight is striking given the fact that Islam represents the fastest-growing religion in the United States and the world. An estimated 1 billion to 1.8 billion Muslims live in the world, and 6 to 7 million of them reside in the United States (U.S. State Department, 2001).

Historically, the psychology of Islam has relied almost entirely on theological speculation, clinical observations, and anthropological methods of inquiry (e.g., Carter & Rashidi, 2003; Dwairy, 2006; MacPhere, 2003). Recently, this picture has begun to change as empirical studies on the psychology of Islam have grown in number. Collectively, this emerging body of empirical research has underscored the centrality of Islam to the lives of Muslims and has identified clear connections between Islamic beliefs and practices and the well-being of Muslims.

In this chapter, I summarize the major findings of the emerging empirically based psychology of Islam, point to the challenges that researchers in this area might potentially face, and suggest future directions for research in this field of inquiry. To help the reader who is unfamiliar with Islam, I start with a summary of the basic tenets of this religion.

SUMMARY OF ISLAM

Islam is the last major monotheistic traditions to emerge in history. From the Islamic viewpoint, however, instead of being the youngest of the major monotheistic world religions, it is the oldest. Islam, according to this view, represents the "original" as the final revelation of God to Abraham, Moses, Jesus, and Muhammad (Esposito, 1998). According to Gordon (2002), the word *Islam*, often translated as "submission" or "surrender," reflects the decision by the *Muslim* ("one who submits or surrenders") to abide in mind and body by the will of the one and the true God (*Allah*). The word *Islam* also has a linguistic connection to the word *salam* (peace). To surrender to Allah's will then is to bring about a harmonious and peaceful order to the universe.

Islamic tradition started in the early 7th century C.E. in the town of *Mecca* in the Arabian Peninsula. According to this tradition, a 40-year-old reflective and trusted merchant, *Muhammad*—commonly referred to as the prophet, or messenger

DOI: 10.1037/14045-038
APA Handbook of Psychology, Religion, and Spirituality: Vol. 1. Context, Theory, and Research, K. I. Pargament (Editor-in-Chief)
Copyright © 2013 by the American Psychological Association. All rights reserved.

of Allah—received a series of revelations, collectively known as the *Qura'n,* from Allah beginning in the 610 C.E. and ending soon before his death in 632 C.E. In the eyes of Muslims, the Qura'n is considered Allah's direct and unchangeable word (Gordon, 2002). Allah, in the Qura'n, describes His unique and intimate relationship with humankind as follows: "This book, without doubt, is a guide to those of awe and fear (of Allah)" (The Qura'n, 2:2).

In what follows, I briefly describe the basic beliefs, practices, and ethical conduct common to all Muslims. For a detailed description of these Islamic components and for a general introduction to Islam, the reader is referred to Abu-Raiya (2006), Esposito (1998), and Gordon (2002).

Major Islamic Beliefs

Belief in God (Allah). According to Islamic beliefs there is

> one, unique, unmatched God, Who has neither son nor partner, and none has the right to be worshipped but Him alone. He is the true God, and every other deity is false. He has the most significant names and sublime perfect attributes. No one shares His divinity or His attributes. (Ibrahim, 1997, p. 45)

Belief in the day of judgment (*Yawm al-Hisab*). One of the basic Islamic beliefs is the belief in the Day of Judgment (the Day of Resurrection). According to Islamic belief, in that time, all people will be resurrected for Allah's judgment based on their beliefs and deeds. On the basis of Allah's judgment, people will be either rewarded (heaven, *al-Jana*) or punished (hell, *al-Nar*; Farah, 1987; Ibrahim, 1997).

Belief in divine predestination (*al-Qadar*). Another tenet of Islam is the belief in *al-Qadar,* which is divine predestination. This belief in divine predestination, however, does not mean that human beings do not have free will. Rather, the latter is believed to be given to human beings by Allah. This implies that people can choose right or wrong and are responsible for their choices (Ibrahim, 1997).

The Five Pillars of Islam

In the domain of human relationship with Allah, five acts of devotion (*ibadat*, singular *ibada*) are required practices for Muslims: shahada, salah, zakah, sawm, and hajj. These actions are considered to be the "building blocks" of the Islamic religion. They are very often referred to as the "five pillars" of Islam and constitute the Islamic ritual system and the ceremonial duties (Farah, 1987; Gordon, 2002).

The testimony of faith (shahada). The pivotal and often-repeated act among the Muslims' ritual duties is the testimony of faith (*shahada*). The testimony of faith is to say with conviction, "There is no true god but Allah, and Muhammad is the messenger of Allah." Shahada is the only prerequisite for becoming a Muslim, and its words are the first words that should be spoken in the ears of a newborn babe and the last on the lips of the dying (Farah, 1987).

Prayer (salah). Of the five pillars of Islam, *salah*, or the ritual prayer, is the essential obligation of Muslim worship and is considered the supreme act of righteousness. Therefore, greater importance is placed on prayer than on any other duty in Islam (Farah, 1987). It is believed that Muhammad said, "When each of you performs his prayer, he is in intimate communication with his Lord" (cited in Gordon, 2002, p. 63).

Prayer is considered the foundation of the Islamic religion. According to the Qura'n and the *hadith* (the sayings and deeds of the prophet Muhammad), any Muslim who fails to pray without a justifiable reason is committing a grave sin (Abdalati, 1970). Many virtues are attributed to prayer in the Islamic tradition, such as discipline, willpower, and moral soundness.

Almsgiving (zakah). Invariably referred to as the "poor tax" or "poor-due" and "almsgiving," *zakah* literally means purification. In practical terms, zakah designates the annual amount in kind, coin, or any material possessions that a Muslim with means must distribute among the rightful beneficiaries (Abdalati, 1970). According to the Islamic faith, the zakah is a means of avoiding the sufferings of the next life, and is an "expiation" or "purification" of the Muslim's soul (Farah, 1987).

Fasting (*sawm*) the month of Ramadan. *Sawm*, or fasting in the month of Ramadan, is another requirement of the Islamic faith. During Ramadan, the Muslim cannot eat or drink, smoke, or have sexual intercourse from sunrise until sunset. To be accepted by Allah, the fast must be accompanied by *niyah* (intention) of the Muslim. The fast is broken immediately after sunset with *futur* (light mail). During this month, Muslims increase their prayer and the mosques are well attended (Farah, 1987; Gordon, 2002; Ibrahim, 1997).

Pilgrimage (*al-Hajj*). The fifth ritual duty of the Muslim is pilgrimage to Mecca, an obligation once in a lifetime for those who are physically and financially able to perform it. The rites of the hajj include circling the *ka'aba* (a building in Mecca that according to the Islamic belief stores the Black Stone that Adam brought with him from the Garden of Eden) seven times and going seven times between the hillocks of *Safa* and *Marwa*, as Hagar (Abraham's wife) did during her search for water for her son Ishmael. Then the pilgrims stand together on the mount of *Arafat* (15 miles from Mecca) and ask Allah for what they wish and for His forgiveness (Ibrahim, 1997).

The Ethical Conduct of Islam

Because ethical guidelines of Islam are not specifically spelled out in any one document, the "dos" and "don'ts" of Islam must be adduced from the contents of the Qura'n. Reviewing these contents, Farah (1987) has identified the 10 major ethical guidelines of Islam: (a) acknowledge there is no god whatsoever but Allah, (b) honor and respect parents, (c) respect the rights of others, (d) be generous but do not squander, (e) avoid killing except for a justifiable reason, (f) commit no adultery, (g) safeguard the possessions of the orphans, (h) deal justly and equitably, (i) be pure in heart and mind, and (j) be humble and unpretentious.

THE EMPIRICALLY BASED PSYCHOLOGY OF ISLAM: WHAT HAVE WE LEARNED?

Recently, Abu-Raiya and Pargament (2011) systematically and comprehensively reviewed what they referred to as the "empirically based psychology of Islam." In this section, I summarize the substantial knowledge on the relationship between Islam and the health and well-being of Muslims that has been generated on the basis of this review.

Islam Is a Multidimensional Religion

The findings of the empirically based psychology of Islam lend support to the multidimensionality of Islam (e.g., Abu-Raiya, Pargament, Mahoney, & Stein, 2008; Aguilar-Vafaie & Moghanloo, 2008; AlMarri, Oei, & Al-Adawi, 2009; Ghorbani, Watson, Ghramaleki, Morris, & Hood, 2000; Jana-Masri & Priester, 2007; Krauss, Azimi, Rumaya, & Jamaliah, 2006; Tiliouine, Cummins, & Davern, 2009; Wilde & Joseph, 1997). For example, factor analysis of the Psychological Measure of Islamic Religiousness (PMIR), developed by Abu-Raiya et al. (2007, 2008), yielded seven distinct, highly reliable factors. Ghorbani et al. (2000) factor analyzed an Iranian version of the Muslim Attitudes Towards Religion (MARS) scale using a sample of 178 Iranian university students. They found that the scale is composed of three reliable factors (Personal Help, Muslim Worldview, Muslims' Practices), which were identical to what Wilde and Joseph (1997), the constructers of the scale, hypothesized. The most recurrent factors identified in empirical studies with Muslims were *beliefs* and *practices* testifying to the centrality of these two dimensions to the lives of Muslims (Abu-Raiya & Pargament, 2011).

In its multidimensionality, Islam is not unique; previous research has shown that other religions, such as Christianity (Glock & Stark, 1966), Judaism (Lazar, Kravetz, & Frederich-Kedem, 2002), and Hinduism (Tarakeshwar, Pargament, & Mahoney, 2003) are multidimensional as well (see Chapter 3 in this volume).

The multidimensional nature of Islam highlights the need to view Islam from a broad perspective; Islam might mean different things to different people, and some people might adhere to some of its elements but not to others. Therefore, although economical and efficient, studies using a few items (i.e., global religiousness, prayer, mosque attendance) to measure Islamic religiousness do not capture the depth, richness, and multifaceted nature of Islam. The multidimensionality of Islam also has practical clinical implications, which are described later.

Islam Is Similar to Yet Different From Other Religions

Although Islam is similar to other religious traditions in many ways, it is distinctive in other ways. Most Islamic religious domains and dimensions that emerged from empirical research with Muslims (beliefs, practices, ethical conduct, struggle, intrinsicness, extrinsicness, positive religious coping, exclusivism, punishing God) characterize other religious traditions as well. Nonetheless, there are dimensions, configurations, and nuances of religiousness that seem unique to Islam, such as believing in all messengers sent by Allah to humankind, the importance of pilgrimage to Mecca and wearing hijab (headscarf). Furthermore, the sense of universality (i.e., the degree to which a Muslim perceives him- or herself as belonging to the larger Islamic nation) is strongly endorsed by Muslim believers and was found to be related to desirable outcomes, such as positive relations with others and purpose in life (Abu-Raiya et al., 2008). To my best knowledge, no similar phenomenon was observed in empirical studies with samples from other religious traditions. Consider also the Islamic Religious Duty, Obligation, and Exclusivism dimension of the PMIR (Abu-Raiya et al., 2008). Each of the components that make up this dimension can be found in different religious traditions. In empirical studies of non-Muslim samples, however, these components have not loaded on one dimension.

Islam Is Central to the Lives of Muslims

Islam is deeply embedded in the lives of many Muslims; the majority of Muslims view life through "sacred lenses." For example, Abu-Raiya et al. (2008) found that most of their study's participants reportedly adhered to different Islamic beliefs and ethical conduct, adopted various Islamic religious attitudes, and observed a diverse array of Islamic religious practices. Furthermore, Islam's role in the lives of Muslims seems mostly positive. Similar to other faiths (Pargament, 1997), Islam is linked to a variety of functions, such as the provision of comfort, meaning, identity, spirituality, and community. Although several factors identified in research with Muslims (global religiousness, beliefs, practices, altruism, ethical conduct, universality) were positively correlated with measures of greater well-being, two seemed especially salient in this domain: positive religious coping (e.g., Abu-Raiya et al., 2008; Aflakseir & Coleman, 2009; Ai, Peterson, & Huang, 2003; Khan & Watson, 2006a) and intrinsic religiousness (e.g., Ghorbani & Watson, 2006; Khan & Watson, 2004; Watson et al., 2002). These two factors were strongly, consistently, and positively linked to indicators of well-being among Muslims (e.g., hope, satisfaction in life, positive relationships with others, self-esteem), on the one hand, and robustly, persistently, and negatively associated with indicators of distress (e.g., depression, anxiety, poor physical health, angry feelings) on the other. This finding is similar to those obtained from Christian samples; among these samples, positive religious coping (e.g., Ano & Vasconcelles, 2005; Pargament, Koenig, & Perez, 2000) and intrinsic religiousness (e.g., Allport & Ross, 1967; Donahue, 1985; Ryan, Rigby, & King, 1993) were found to be linked to better health and well-being.

In contrast, some types of Islamic religiousness can be associated with poorer health and well-being. The empirically based psychology of Islam has revealed a few forms of Islamic religiousness that have potential negative implications for the well-being of Muslims: negative religious coping (Abu-Raiya et al., 2008; Aflakseir & Coleman, 2009), extrinsic–social religiousness (Ghorbani & Watson, 2006; Watson et al., 2002), and afterlife motivation (i.e., the desires of Muslims to reach heaven and avoid hell; Ghorbani, Watson, & Shahmohamdi, 2008). Again, these findings are consistent with those obtained from Christian samples. In those samples, negative religious coping methods (e.g., punishing God reappraisal, questioning God's power) were related to negative outcomes, such as poorer physical health and emotional distress (e.g., Pargament et al., 2000; Sherman, Simonton, Latif, Spohn, & Tricot, 2005). Extrinsic religiousness was linked to negative outcomes as well (Bergin, Masters, & Richards, 1987; Donahue, 1985).

These points underscore the relevance of Islam to Muslims' lives and well-being and therefore highlight the need for greater attention to the Islamic religion when dealing with Muslim populations. Failure to do so could lead to an incomplete and perhaps distorted picture of Muslims. Furthermore, these findings strongly challenge commonplace misconceptions and stereotypes of Islam (e.g., Islam is dangerous to the health and well-being of Muslims). Quite the contrary, most Muslims adopt types of religiousness that enhance their lives and foster their well-being. Except for negative religious coping, afterlife motivation and extrinsic–social religiousness, the other types of religiousness found among Muslim populations were related to indicators of greater well-being. Additional empirical data are needed to clarify misconceptions of the role of Islam in individuals' lives and replace them with scientifically based knowledge.

Some Forms of Religious Psychotherapy Are Effective With Muslim Clients

As stated earlier, historically, the psychology of Islam has relied almost exclusively on clinical observations and anthropological methods of inquiry. Drawing on this base, a few models have been proposed that incorporate Islamic spiritual and religious elements into psychotherapy (e.g., Carter & Rashidi, 2003; Dwairy, 2006; Hamdan, 2008; Mehraby, 2003). For example, on the basis of her clinical experience, Mehraby (2003) developed a model of counseling that might be potentially helpful to Muslim clients coping with loss and grief. Her model combines Islamic practices and beliefs (e.g., prayer, supplications) and Western psychological tools, such as cognitive restructuring.

A few empirical studies have tested the efficacy of religiously integrated psychotherapy for Muslim clients. All these studies found that different forms of religious psychotherapy are effective with Muslim clients who suffer from anxiety, depression, and bereavement (Azhar & Varma, 1995a, 1995b; Azhar, Varma, & Dharap, 1994; Razali, Aminah, & Khan, 2002; Razali, Hasanah, Aminah, & Subramaniam, 1998). For example, Razali et al. (1998) worked with a sample of 203 Malay individuals who suffered from either anxiety or depression. Participants were randomly assigned to either a control or a study group. Both groups received standard treatment (medication, supportive psychotherapy, and relaxation exercises) for their condition, but the study group received additional religious–sociocultural psychotherapy based on Islamic principles (i.e., prayer, expressing repentance and forgiveness, relying on Allah and supplicating to Him in times of needs). Clients in the group receiving additional psychotherapy that included Islamic components responded significantly faster to therapy and manifested better adjustment than those receiving standard treatment.

Promising as these attempts to incorporate Islamic practices and beliefs into psychotherapy may be, they have a major limitation. To my best knowledge, with one exception (Abu-Raiya & Pargament, 2010), there have been thus far no attempts to integrate the empirical findings of the psychology of Islam into treatment. Given the successful outcome of recent attempts to convert the knowledge gained from empirical research into practical applications with clients (Freedman & Enright, 1996; McCullough & Worthington, 1994; Pargament, 2007; Richards & Bergin, 1997), we recommend researchers and mental health professionals develop empirically based psychospiritual interventions that can be used in psychotherapy with Muslim clients.

A few suggestions can clarify what a more empirically based approach to treatment might look like (for more details, see Abu-Raiya & Pargament, 2010). First, given the centrality of Islam to many Muslims, mental health professionals should invite Muslim clients into a "religious conversation" by explicitly inquiring about the place of religion in their lives. Second, because Islam is a multidimensional religion and can mean different things to different people, it is important to ask Muslim clients, "What does Islam mean for you?" Third, given the demonstrated links between positive religious coping and well-being, therapists can encourage their clients to identify and draw on their religious coping resources (e.g., considering stressors as a test from Allah, seeking Allah's love, care and forgiveness, reading the Holy Qura'n to find consolation). Finally, given the potential negative impacts of religious doubts and struggles, therapists should thoroughly assess for the presence of religious struggle and doubts, normalize them, and avoid passing judgment on clients who are struggling. In the process of normalizing spiritual struggles, it might be helpful to refer to individuals from the Islamic tradition (e.g., Muhammad, Moses,

Abraham) as models of esteemed figures who experienced such struggles (see Chapter 10 in this volume).

THE PSYCHOLOGY OF ISLAM: POTENTIAL CHALLENGES, LIMITATIONS, AND DIRECTIONS FOR FUTURE RESEARCH

Clearly, the empirically based psychology of Islam has made important steps toward expanding our understanding of the ways in which this religion affects the well-being of its adherents. This body of research is in its early stages, however, and is limited in some important respects. In this section, I discuss these limitations in detail, point to the challenges that researchers in this area face, offer some suggestions of how to address these challenges, and propose directions for research to advance this field of inquiry.

First, a significant number of empirical studies conducted among Muslims used a single-item index (e.g., "What is your level of religiosity in general?" "How religious are you?" "How important is religion for you?") to measure religiousness among Muslims (e.g., Abdel-Khalek, 2007, 2009; Al-Sabwah & Abdel-Khalek, 2006). There are advantages to using single-item indexes of religiousness (Gorsuch & McPherson, 1989). Studies of this kind can be conducted efficiently and are economical and feasible in large-scale community surveys in which time and space are at a premium (Abdel-Khalek, 2007).

Unfortunately, however, a single-item index to assess such a multidimensional complex phenomenon provides at best a birds-eye view of a faith tradition. Furthermore, this approach to measurement can lead to an incomplete and imprecise understanding of religion in general (Pargament & Abu-Raiya, 2007) and Islam in particular. Even when significant findings are obtained, we are left with some key questions. For instance, what aspects of Islam are people responding to when they assess their own religiousness, and are individuals responding to the same dimensions of Islam when they engage in these self-ratings? Idiographic studies of ratings of religiousness among Christians in the United States suggest that individuals use very different cues in forming their estimates of someone's level of religiousness (see Pargament, Sullivan, Balzer, Van Haitsma, & Raymark, 1995). This may hold true for Muslims as well. Furthermore, what is it about Islam that accounts for the findings that emerge from studies that make use of single-item religious indexes? Does the critical factor have to do with rituals, beliefs, ethical conduct, religious emotions, religious knowledge, religious community, or some combination of these elements? The depth and richness of information obtained from a single-item measure is limited. To gain a clearer picture of the potentially complex relationships between Islam and well-being, multiitem, multidimensional measures are needed.

Second, the lion's share of empirical research conducted among Muslims utilized religiousness measures validated in Christian samples (e.g., Ai et al., 2003; Hood et al., 2001; Rippy & Newman, 2006). Despite the potential value of conceptual frameworks and religiousness scales developed and validated among Christian populations and extended to Muslim populations, this derivative approach to studying Muslims is associated with significant difficulties and challenges. These theorizations and instruments are rooted in a different cultural climate and based on Western Christian assumptions about, and definitions of, religion. The application of existing psychological theories and conceptual frameworks that have been developed mainly within Western cultural contexts to Islam might be biased, may fail to capture the uniqueness of this religion, and may be culturally insensitive (Abu-Raiya et al., 2007; Amer, Hovey, Fox, & Rezcallah 2008; Ghorbani, Watson, & Khan, 2007), even ethnocentric (Sue, 1992). Purely Western measures of religiousness may, for instance, overlook salient aspects of Islam (e.g., pilgrimage, specific ethical conduct). Furthermore, this approach might be problematic for some Muslims. For example, Khan and Watson (2004) reported that some of their Pakistani research participants found items of the extrinsic–social orientation scale to be offensive to their religion (see also Khan, Watson, & Habib, 2005). Finally, some of the items of these measures might be irrelevant to Muslims (e.g., Williamson & Ahmad, 2007).

What can researchers do to address these difficulties and challenges? Clearly, researchers interested in the empirically based psychology of Islam should be well-versed in the particularities and nuances of Islamic faith and culture. I advocate a bottom-up approach of inquiry; research among Muslims should be grounded in Muslims' experiential lives, worldviews, and methods of communication. Using qualitative research methods might be an important first step in this direction as this format of investigation allows Muslim participants to voice their concerns and religious feelings and thoughts in their own ways and in their own words (Abu-Raiya, 2005a). On the other hand, the facts that religion possesses universal aspects and that "Western psychology of religion" has revealed multiple important insights into the relationship between religion and well-being cannot be overlooked. In this vein, Ghorbani et al. (2007) proposed a "dialogical model" to advance research in this area. This model would bring Western social scientific understandings of religion and mental health into dialogue with Muslim perspectives, approaches, and conceptualizations. To illustrate this model, the authors noted studies of Iranian and Pakistani samples that have confirmed the similarities between the three religious orientations identified in Western samples (i.e., intrinsic, extrinsic, quest) and the three types of Muslim religiousness (i.e., experiential, utilitarian, Gnostic) described by the Iranian philosopher Soroush.

Third, there is a scarcity of literature that offers an in-depth perspective on Islam and its links to health and well-being. One of the main reasons for the lack of study in this area may be the unavailability of reliable measures of Islamic religiousness derived from Islamic teachings and validated among Muslim samples (Abu-Raiya et al., 2007). Measures of this kind are needed to build a solid foundation of knowledge and understanding about the impact of Islam on the lives of its adherents.

Fortunately, several recent attempts have been made to develop scales of this nature. Table 38.1 displays the titles of 14 such measures, their developers, and sample items that assess the measures. Overall, most of the scales demonstrated internal consistencies that are adequate or higher than .80, the recommended guideline by Nunnaly (1978).

There are, however, a few limitations of these measures as a group. First, the validity of these instruments has not yet been robustly demonstrated. With a few exceptions (Ghorbani et al., 2008; Ji & Ibrahim, 2007a; Khan & Watson, 2006a; Tiliouine et al., 2009), the studies used one or no outcome measures, which limits the concurrent validity of these instruments. Second, with the exceptions of the MARS (Ghorbani et al., 2000; Khan et al., 2005), the Attitudes Toward Islam (Abu-Rayya & Abu-Rayya, 2009; Francis, Sahin, & Al-Failakawi, 2008; Khan & Watson, 2006b), and Doctrinal Orthodoxy (Ji & Ibrahim, 2007b) scales, these instruments have not been extended to samples beyond the ones used in the initial validation. Third, these scales have not been examined in international Muslim samples. Instead, convenient samples have been used that are drawn from Muslims from one geographic location (e.g., the United States, Iran, Algeria), a specific Islamic sect (e.g., Shiite), or a specific population (e.g., college students). Finally, most of these instruments do not assess the construct of Islamic religiousness comprehensively. By and large, these instruments are composed of a few items and a few factors.

These shortcomings, especially the lack of support for the validity and generalizability of the instruments, can be attributed, in part at least, to their recency. Future research that uses health and well-being measures as well as diverse Muslim samples should shed further light on the validity and generalizability of these scales.

To address some of these limitations, Abu-Raiya et al. (2008; see also Abu-Raiya, 2005a, 2005b, 2006; Abu-Raiya et al., 2007) conducted a three-stage program of research to develop and validate a comprehensive, multidimensional, theoretically based, valid, and reliable measure of Islamic beliefs and practices. The ultimate outcome of Abu-Raiya et al.'s program of research was the PMIR (see Table 38.2 for more detail), which yielded seven factors that demonstrated desirable variability, reliability, and discriminant, convergent, predictive, and incremental validity using multiple mental and physical health criterion variables.

Fourth, there is a particular dearth of empirical research that assesses the prevalence and impact of negative types of religiousness among Muslims. I believe that the main reason behind this lack of

TABLE 38.1

Measures of Islamic Religiousness Found in the Literature

Construct	Developers	Sample items
Muslim Attitudes Towards Religion (MARS)	Wilde & Joseph (1997)	I pray five times a day.
Attitudes Toward Islam Scale (ATIS)	Sahin & Francis (2002)	Allah means a lot to me.
The Religiosity of Islam Scale (RoIS)	Jana-Masri & Priester (2007)	I believe that the final and complete religion is Islam.
Islamic Religiosity Scale (IRS)	Tiliouine, Cummins, & Davern (2009)	Advising others to do good and avoid sin.
Short Muslim Belief and Practice Scale (Short-MBPS)	AlMarri, Oei, & Al-Adawi (2009)	All Muslims should be governed by absolute Shariah law.
Afterlife Motivation Scale (AMS)	Ghorbani, Watson, & Shahmohamdi (2008)	I do my best to avoid sin because I do not want to go to hell.
The Sahin Index of Islamic Moral Values (SIIMV)	Francis, Sahin & Al-Failakawi, (2008)	I believe honesty is always good regardless of the consequences.
Islamic Doctrinal Orthodoxy (IDO)	Ji & Ibrahim (2007a)	I believe that *salat* (prayer) is crucial to the life of the Muslim.
Knowledge-Practice Measure of Islamic Religiosity (KPMIR)[4]	Alghorani (2008)	Do you date?
Islamic Religious Orientation Scale (IROS)	Aguilar-Vafaie & Moghanloo (2008)	I fast during the month of Ramadan if am not sick or traveling.
Islamic Reflection Scale (IRS)	Dover, Miner, & Dowson (2007)	Studying nature and the universe would reveal treasures of knowledge and truth.
Muslim Religiosity-Personality Inventory (MRPI)	Krauss, Azimi, Rumaya, & Jamaliah (2006)	All Islamic laws can be modified to fulfill contemporary needs.
Pakistani Religious Coping Practices Scale	Khan & Watson (2006a)	Read special *daus* (supplications) for the solution of the problem.
Brief Arab Religious Coping Scale (BARCS)	Amer, Hovey, Fox, & Rezcallah (2008)	Prayed to get mind off problems.

Note. From "Empirically Based Psychology of Islam: Summary and Critique of the Literature," by H. Abu-Raiya and K. I. Pargament, 2011, *Mental Health, Religion, and Culture, 14*, pp. 100–101. Copyright 2010 by Taylor and Francis. Adapted with permission.

research is the unwillingness of many Muslims to admit negative consequences of Islam (Abu-Raiya et al., 2007). This unwillingness can be attributed to three reasons. First, rather than trying to present themselves in a favorable light, some Muslims might be motivated to present Islam in such a manner. Perceptions that Islam is under attack may lead many Muslims to defend Islam by minimizing or even denying its potential negative impact. Second, admitting religious struggles and doubts might be considered by some Muslims as an offense to Allah who presumably provided Muslims with the perfect solution and cure (i.e., Islam) to all their problems and concerns. Third, expressions of religious struggles, especially doubts about the existence of Allah or the afterlife, may be taboo (see also Amer et al., 2008) or particularly socially unacceptable in the Islamic culture given the potential lack of models of individuals who acknowledge and work through their religious struggles. As a result, Muslims who experience religious struggles may be especially vulnerable to stigma, strong reactions from fellow Muslims, and loneliness.

Regardless of the cause, it seems that researchers, acknowledging the potential sensitivity of this sphere, largely avoid studying negative types of religiousness among Muslims. Sidestepping or overlooking these topics in research may lead to a partial picture of the lives of Muslims. What can researchers in the field do to increase the willingness of Muslim participants to report undesirable aspects of their religiousness? I propose three suggestions. (a) When conducting a study that requires divulging information regarding any type of negative religiousness, we recommend including a statement that encourages participants to disclose their actual

TABLE 38.2

The Psychological Measure of Islamic Religiousness (PMIR)

Factor	Definition of constructs	Reliability estimate (Cronbach's Alpha)	Sample items
Islamic Beliefs	Basic Islamic beliefs about the world	.97	I believe in the existence of Allah.
Islamic Ethical Principles and Universality	1. Basic ethical guidelines that are encouraged or discouraged among Muslims.	.96	Islam is the major reason why I do not drink alcohol.
	2. The degree to which a Muslim perceives him- or herself as belonging to the larger Islamic nation.		I consider every Muslim as my brother or sister.
Islamic Religious Struggle	Difficulties, doubts, and conflicts that the Muslim experiences when adhering to a Islam	.90	I doubt the existence of Allah.
Islamic Positive Religious Coping and Identification	1. Coping methods that reflect a secure relationship with God, a belief that there is a greater meaning to be found, and a sense of spiritual connectedness with others (Pargament, Koenig, & Perez, 2000).	.88	When I face a problem in life, I consider that a test from Allah to deepen my belief.
	2. An adoption of religious beliefs as personal values (Ryan, Rigby, &, King, 1993).		I pray because I enjoy it.
Islamic Religious Duty, Obligation, and Exclusivism	1. Basic practices to demonstrate adherence to religion	.77	How often do you pray?
	2. The sense of obligation associated with performing religious duties		I fast in Ramadan because I would feel bad if I did not.
	3. The assumption that there is an absolute reality and a single way to approach it (Pargament, 1997).		Islam is Allah's complete, unfailing guide to happiness and salvation, which must be totally followed.
Punishing Allah Reappraisal	Reappraising a stressor as a punishment from God (Pargament et al., 2000).	.77	When I face a problem in life, I wonder what I did for Allah to punish me.
Islamic Religious Conversion	A process during which the individual moves from being a nonreligious person to a religious one.	.89	Islam has moved from the outside to the very center of my life.

Note. From "Empirically Based Psychology of Islam: Summary and Critique of the Literature," by H. Abu-Raiya and K. I. Pargament, 2011, *Mental Health, Religion, and Culture, 14*, p. 103. Copyright 2010 by Taylor and Francis. Adapted with permission.

personal behaviors and not how they should behave according to Islam. Normalizing negative types of religiousness in this process might be helpful as well. (b) It might be helpful to include two sets of items to assess religiousness. The first set of items would refer to the ideals of Islam. These items would be followed by a second set of items that assess how individuals personally think, feel, or behave in relationship to these ideals. The contrast between these two sets of items might motivate some participants to respond more openly and honestly about undesirable aspects of their religious lives. (c) Rather than assessing attitudes, we recommend asking research participants about the frequency of *concrete behaviors* that potentially represent negative types of religiousness.

A fifth area of challenge in the psychology of Islam (to continue the enumeration at the beginning of this section) is the antipathy, mistrust, and suspicion characterize the attitudes of many Muslims toward the field of psychology. For example, Abu-Raiya (2005a) found that many Muslims view psychology as a "Western," "antireligious" endeavor and consequently "improper" to understanding Muslims' religious lives and ways of thinking. Amer et al. (2008) reported that many of their Muslim participants expressed discomfort and uneasiness with being associated with what they perceived to be a "psychology project." The root of these suspicions is unclear. Psychology may have contributed in its own way to these attitudes by the antireligious stance of some of the founding fathers of the field (e.g., Freud, Skinner). On the other hand, these attitudes may be fostered by the fears of some Muslims that psychological research contradicts what Muslims hold as the ultimate truth, the Qura'n.

To bridge the gap between Muslims and psychology, I recommend that researchers reach out to Muslims in general and to Muslim religious leaders in particular. This outreach can be achieved through workshops, presentations, and dissemination of written materials in settings that are most familiar and comfortable to Muslims, such as mosques and Islamic centers. Increasing contact, collaboration, and respectful partnerships could reduce suspicion among Muslims toward the field of psychology and increase their willingness to participate in psychological research.

Sixth, some nuances in language and communication style are worth mentioning. For example, Abu-Raiya (2005a) found that most of the participants in his qualitative study used the pronoun *you* rather than *I*, although they were asked clearly about their feelings, thoughts, and experiences. Moreover, a few participants preferred to talk about Muslims in general, even though they appeared to be referring to themselves. There are a few possible interpretations of this phenomenon. First, it could reflect a cultural way of communication; Arabs (the vast majority of the respondents in this study) prefer an indirect style when communicating, especially feelings (McLaren, 1998), and the reluctance to use the pronoun "I" may be a manifestation of this style. Second, avoiding the use of "I" may reflect the humility with which Muslims approach their religious life. Humility is considered one of the virtues within Islamic teachings. This tendency to humility manifested itself strongly in the religious realm when the participants were asked to self-rate their religiousness. Most of them used "moderate" terms to describe their religiousness, although they endorsed all of the beliefs that constitute the Islamic belief system, reported adhering to all ethical conducts, and reported performing most of the rituals of Islam. Finally, as mentioned earlier, it is possible that some interviewees used the interview as an opportunity to praise the Islamic doctrine in an attempt to prove its multiple benefits and applicability to modern life and, as a result, talked about how Muslims in general should approach life rather than the ways in which Islam affected them personally.

Therefore, it is important to pay special attention to the subtleties of language. Some important nuances might be lost in translation. I propose that each research team interested in the scientific investigation of Islam should include members who are fluent in the language spoken by the majority of the participants in their study. This might increase the validity of the findings of their research.

Seventh, most of the empirical studies conducted among Muslims utilized relatively small, convenience samples. Furthermore, although empirical research on the psychology of Islam has been carried out in many Muslim (e.g., Kuwait, Pakistan, Algeria, Indonesia, Malaysia, Egypt) and non-Muslim (e.g., Britain, Australia) countries, the majority of research in this field has utilized American and Iranian samples. Given the significant cultural, geographic, ethnic, and socioeconomic differences found among Muslims in different places in the world, future studies with larger, more diverse, and representative samples of Muslims could further distinguish among the "bitter" and the "sweet" of Islam.

Eighth, several important as yet unstudied topics with respect to the relationship between Islam and the health and well-being of Muslims deserve further consideration: the links between Islam and mortality, marital functioning, parenting practices, and spiritual well-being; the prevalence and ramifications of religious conversion among Muslims; the relationship between different types of Islamic religiousness and attitudes of Muslims toward people from different faiths (e.g., Christians, Jews,

Hindus) as well as attitudes of people from different faiths toward Muslims; and the impacts of recent and global events on the psychological well-being of Muslims (e.g., the September 11, 2001, attacks; the invasion of Iraq and Afghanistan; the Palestinian–Israeli conflict). In particular, it seems that the September 11 attacks left many Muslims in the United States concerned about their survival, suspicious about the motives of others, and consequently reluctant to disclose information regarding their religious lives (Abu-Raiya et al., 2008; Jana-Masri & Priester, 2007). With a few exceptions (Abu-Raiya et al., in press; Abu-Ras & Abu-Bader, 2008), research conducted to test the influence of September 11 has focused exclusively on Christians, with Muslims "left behind." Important questions remain. What stressors did Muslims experience and do they continue to experience following the September 11 attacks? What methods of coping—religious and nonreligious—do they use to understand and deal with these stressors? What kinds of religious struggles and concerns have been elicited by the September 11 attacks among Muslims? Studies that shed light on these questions could be quite informative.

Finally, there is a need for more varied research methods in studies of Muslim populations (see Chapter 4 in this volume). Most of the research in the field has utilized survey designs to the exclusion of other methods. For example, only a few studies (e.g., Abu-Raiya, 2005a; Ali et al., 2008; Hassouneh-Phillips, 2003; Kamal & Loewenthal, 2002; Odoms-Young, 2008) used qualitative methods of investigation. Qualitative studies in this area would be particularly helpful in this early state of the field. Additionally, future studies utilizing observer reports and direct observations would provide an important check on the findings of self-report studies. Moreover, experimental studies that test how Muslims interact with people from other faiths can shed light on how Islamic beliefs and attitudes affect Muslims' well-being in interpersonal and interfaith contexts. Last, to our best knowledge, all studies conducted with Muslim samples have been cross-sectional. Longitudinal studies are needed to provide a clearer understanding of the causal connections between Islamic religiousness and well-being.

CONCLUSION

This chapter has summarized the main lessons we have learned from the growing empirically based psychology of Islam, has referred to the major challenges researchers in this field might face, has pointed to some limitations of this field of inquiry, and has suggested a few directions of research that might advance the empirically based psychology of Islam.

To conclude, stereotypes and misinformation, especially in the Western world, are highly prevalent about Islam in the 21st century (Pew Research Center, 2005; Strabac & Listhaug, 2008). This undoubtedly makes research on Muslims and Islam a sensitive area of study. The empirically based psychology of Islam opens the door to more systematic psychological study and greater understanding of perhaps the most neglected and misunderstood of all religious traditions. Researchers in the field have made important progress in expanding our understanding of the impact of Islam on the health and well-being of Muslims, on the one hand, and in combating deep-seated negative views of Islam, on the other. Nonetheless, additional empirical data are sorely needed to clarify misconceptions of the role of Islam in individuals' lives and replace these misconceptions with scientific knowledge.

References

Abdalati, H. (1970). *Islam in focus.* Alriyad, Saudi Arabia: World Assembly of Muslim Youth.

Abdel-Khalek, A. M. (2007). Assessment of intrinsic religiosity with a single item measure in a sample of Arab Muslims. *Journal of Muslim Mental Health, 2,* 211–215. doi:10.1080/15564900701614874

Abdel-Khalek, A. M. (2009). Religiosity, subjective well-being, and depression in Saudi children and adolescents. *Mental Health, Religion, and Culture, 12,* 803–815. doi:10.1080/13674670903006755

Abu-Raiya, H. (2005a). *Identifying dimensions of Islam relevant to physical and mental health.* Unpublished master's thesis, Bowling Green State University, Bowling Green, OH.

Abu-Raiya, H. (2005b). *An initial psychological measure of Islamic beliefs and practices: A pilot testing.* Unpublished manuscript, Bowling Green State University, Bowling Green, OH.

Abu-Raiya, H. (2006). *A psychological measure of Islamic religiousness: Evidence for relevance, reliability, and validity*. Unpublished doctoral dissertation, Bowling Green State University, Bowling Green, OH.

Abu-Raiya, H., & Pargament, K. I. (2010). Religiously integrated psychotherapy with Muslim clients: From research to practice. *Professional Psychology: Research and Practice*, *41*, 181–188. doi:10.1037/a0017988

Abu-Raiya, H., & Pargament, K. I. (2011). Empirically based psychology of Islam: Summary and critique of the literature. *Mental Health, Religion, and Culture*, *14*, 93–115. doi:10.1080/13674670903426482

Abu-Raiya, H., Pargament, K. I., & Mahoney, A. (2011). Examining coping methods with stressful interpersonal events experienced by Muslims living the U.S. following the 9/11 attacks. *Psychology of Religion and Spirituality*, *3*, 1–14. doi:10.1037/a0020034

Abu-Raiya, H., Pargament, K. I., Mahoney, A., & Stein, C. (2008). A psychological measure of Islamic religiousness: Development and evidence of reliability and validity. *The International Journal for the Psychology of Religion*, *18*, 291–315. doi:10.1080/10508610802229270

Abu-Raiya, H., Pargament, K. I., Stein, C., & Mahoney, A. (2007). Lessons learned and challenges faced in developing the Psychological Measure of Islamic Religiousness. *Journal of Muslim Mental Health*, *2*, 133–154. doi:10.1080/15564900701613058

Abu-Ras, W., & Abu-Bader, S. H. (2008). The impact of September 11, 2001, attacks on the well-being of Arab Americans in New York City. *Journal of Muslim Mental Health*, *3*, 217–239. doi:10.1080/15564900802487634

Abu-Rayya, H. M., & Abu-Rayya, M. H. (2009). Attitude towards Islam: Adaptation and initial validation of the Francis Scale of Attitude towards Christianity in a sample of Israeli-Arab Muslims. *Archive for the Psychology of Religion*, *31*, 115–122.

Aflakseir, A., & Coleman, P. G. (2009). The influence of religious coping on mental health of disabled Iranian war veterans. *Mental Health, Religion, and Culture*, *12*, 175–190. doi:10.1080/13674670802428563

Aguilar-Vafaie, M. E., & Moghanloo, M. (2008). Domain and facet personality correlates of religiosity among Iranian college students. *Mental Health, Religion, and Culture*, *11*, 461–483. doi:10.1080/13674670701539114

Ai, A. L., Peterson, C., & Huang, B. (2003). The effects of religious-spiritual coping on positive attitudes of adult Muslim refugees from Kosovo and Bosnia. *The International Journal for the Psychology of Religion*, *13*, 29–47. doi:10.1207/S15327582IJPR1301_04

Alghorani, M. A. (2008). Knowledge-Practice Measure of Islamic Religiosity (KPMIR): A case of high school Muslim students in the United States. *Journal of Muslim Mental Health*, *3*, 25–36. doi:10.1080/15564900802035169

Ali, S. R., Mahmood, A., Moel, J., Hudson, C., & Leathers, L. (2008). A qualitative investigation of Muslim and Christian women's view of religion and feminism in their lives. *Cultural Diversity and Ethnic Minority Psychology*, *14*, 38–46. doi:10.1037/1099-9809.14.1.38

Allport, G. W., & Ross, J. M. (1967). Personal religious orientation and prejudice. *Journal of Personality and Social Psychology*, *5*, 432–443. doi:10.1037/h0021212

AlMarri, T. S. K., Oei, T. P. S., & Al-Adawi, S. (2009). The development of the short Muslim Practice and Belief Scale. *Mental Health, Religion, and Culture*, *12*, 415–426. doi:10.1080/13674670802637643

Al-Sabwah, M. N., & Abdel-Khalek, A. M. (2006). Religiosity and death distress in Arabic college students. *Death Studies*, *30*, 365–375. doi:10.1080/07481180600553435

Amer, M. M., Hovey, J. D., Fox, C. M., & Rezcallah, A. (2008). Initial development of the Brief Arab Religious Coping Scale (BARCS). *Journal of Muslim Mental Health*, *3*, 69–88. doi:10.1080/15564900802156676

Ano, G. G., & Vasconcelles, E. B. (2005). Religious coping and psychological adjustment to stress: A meta-analysis. *Journal of Clinical Psychology*, *61*, 461–480. doi:10.1002/jclp.20049

Azhar, M. Z., & Varma, S. L. (1995a). Religious psychotherapy with depressive patients. *Psychotherapy and Psychosomatics*, *63*, 165–173. doi:10.1159/000288954

Azhar, M. Z., & Varma, S. L. (1995b). Religious psychotherapy as management of bereavement. *Acta Psychiatrica Scandinavica*, *91*, 233–235. doi:10.1111/j.1600-0447.1995.tb09774.x

Azhar, M. Z., Varma, S. L., & Dharap, A. S. (1994). Religious psychotherapy in anxiety disorder patients. *Acta Psychiatrica Scandinavica*, *90*, 1–3. doi:10.1111/j.1600-0447.1994.tb01545.x

Bergin, A. E., Masters, K. S., & Richards, P. S. (1987). Religiousness and mental health reconsidered: A study of an intrinsically religious sample. *Journal of Counseling Psychology*, *34*, 197–204. doi:10.1037/0022-0167.34.2.197

Carter, D. J., & Rashidi, A. (2003). Theoretical model of psychotherapy: Eastern Asian-Islamic women with mental illness. *Health Care for Women International*, *24*, 399–413.

Donahue, M. J. (1985). Intrinsic and extrinsic religiousness: Review and meta-analysis. *Journal of Personality and Social Psychology*, *48*, 400–419. doi:10.1037/0022-3514.48.2.400

Dover, H., Miner, M., & Dowson, M. (2007). The nature and structure of Muslim religious reflection. *Journal of Muslim Mental Health*, *2*, 189–210. doi:10.1080/15564900701614858

Dwairy, M. (2006). *Counseling and psychotherapy with Arabs and Muslims: A culturally sensitive approach.* New York, NY: Teachers College Press.

Esposito, J. L. (1998). *Islam: The straight path.* New York, NY: Oxford University press.

Farah, C. E. (1987). *Islam.* New York, NY: Barron's.

Francis, J. F., Sahin, A., & Al-Failakawi, F. (2008). Psychometric properties of two Islamic measures among young adults in Kuwait: The Sahin-Francis scale of attitudes toward Islam and the Sahin Index of Islamic Moral Values. *Journal of Muslim Mental Health, 3,* 9–24. doi:10.1080/15564900802035201

Freedman, S. R., & Enright, R. D. (1996). Forgiveness as an intervention goal with incest survivors. *Journal of Consulting and Clinical Psychology, 64,* 983–992. doi:10.1037/0022-006X.64.5.983

Ghorbani, N., & Watson, P. J. (2006). Religious orientation types in Iranian Muslims: Differences in alexithymia, emotional intelligence, self-consciousness and psychological adjustment. *Review of Religious Research, 47,* 303–310.

Ghorbani, N., Watson, P. J., Ghramaleki, A. F., Morris, R. J., & Hood, R. W. (2000). Muslim Attitudes towards Religion scale: Factors, validity, and complexity of relationships with mental health in Iran. *Mental Health, Religion, and Culture, 3,* 125–132. doi:10.1080/713685603

Ghorbani, N., Watson, P. J., & Khan, Z. H. (2007). Theoretical, empirical and potential ideological dimensions of using Western conceptualizations to measure Muslim religious commitment. *Journal of Muslim Mental Health, 2,* 113–131. doi:10.1080/15564900701613041

Ghorbani, N., Watson, P. J., & Shahmohamdi, K. (2008). Afterlife Motivation Scale: Correlations with maladjustment and incremental validity in Iranian Muslims. *The International Journal for the Psychology of Religion, 18,* 22–35. doi:10.1080/10508610701719314

Glock, C. Y., & Stark, R. (1966). *Christian beliefs and anti-Semitism.* New York, NY: Harper & Row.

Gordon, M. S. (2002). *Islam: Origins, practices, holy texts, sacred persons, and sacred places.* New York, NY: Oxford University Press.

Gorsuch, R. L., & McPherson, S. E. (1989). Intrinsic/extrinsic scales: I/E-revised and single item scales. *Journal for the Scientific Study of Religion, 28,* 348–354. doi:10.2307/1386745

Hamdan, A. (2008). Cognitive restructuring: An Islamic perspective. *Journal of Muslim Mental Health, 3,* 99–116. doi:10.1080/15564900802035268

Hassouneh-Phillips, D. (2003). Strength and vulnerability: Spirituality in abused American Muslim women's lives. *Issues in Mental Health Nursing, 24,* 681–694. doi:10.1080/01612840305324

Hood, R. W., Jr., Ghorbani, N., Watson, P. J., Ghrarmaleki, A. F., Bing, M. N., & Davison, H. K. (2001). Dimensions of mysticism scale: Confirming the three- factor structure in the United States and Iran. *Journal for the Scientific Study of Religion, 40,* 691–705. doi:10.1111/0021-8294.00085

Hood, R. W., Jr., Hill, P. C., & Spilka, B. (2009). *The psychology of religion: An empirical approach* (5th ed.). New York, NY: Guilford Press.

Ibrahim, I. A. (1997). *A brief illustrated guide to understanding Islam.* Houston, TX.

Jana-Masri, A., & Priester, P. E. (2007). The development and validation of a Qura'n- based instrument to assess Islamic religiosity: The Religiosity of Islam Scale. *Journal of Muslim Mental Health, 2,* 177–188. doi:10.1080/15564900701624436

Ji, C-H. C., & Ibrahim, Y. (2007a). Islamic doctrinal orthodoxy and religious orientations: Scale development and validation. *The International Journal for the Psychology of Religion, 17,* 189–208. doi:10.1080/10508610701402192

Ji, C-H. C., & Ibrahim, Y. (2007b). Islamic religiosity in right-wing authoritarian personality: The case of Indonesian Muslims. *Review of Religious Research, 49,* 128–146.

Kamal, Z., & Loewenthal, K. M. (2002). Suicide beliefs and behavior among young Muslims and Hindus in the UK. *Mental Health, Religion, and Culture, 5,* 111–118. doi:10.1080/13674670210141052

Khan, Z. H., & Watson, P. J. (2004). Religious orientations and the experience of Eid-ul-Azha among Pakistani Muslims. *Journal for the Scientific Study of Religion, 43,* 537–545. doi:10.1111/j.1468-5906.2004.00254.x

Khan, Z. H., & Watson, P. J. (2006a). Construction of the Pakistani Religious Coping Practices Scale: Correlations with religious coping, religious orientation, and reactions to stress among Muslim university students. *The International Journal for the Psychology of Religion, 16,* 101–112. doi:10.1207/s15327582ijpr1602_2

Khan, Z. H., & Watson, P. J. (2006b). Factorial complexity and validity of the Sahin–Francis Attitude Toward Islam Scale among Pakistani University students. *Journal of Beliefs and Values, 27,* 231–235.

Khan, Z. H., Watson, P. J., & Habib, F. (2005). Muslim attitudes toward religion, religious orientation and empathy among Pakistanis. *Mental Health, Religion, and Culture, 8,* 49–61. doi:10.1080/13674670410001666606

Krauss, S. E., Azimi, H., Rumaya, J., & Jamaliah, A. H. (2006). The Muslim Religiosity-Personality

Inventory (MRPI): Towards understanding differences in the Islamic religiosity among Malaysian youth. *Pertanika Journal of Social Science and Humanities, 13*, 173–186.

Lazar, A., Kravetz, S., & Frederich-Kedem, P. (2002). The multidimensionality of motivation for Jewish religious behavior: Content, structure, and relationship to religious identity. *Journal for the Scientific Study of Religion, 41*, 509–519. doi:10.1111/1468-5906.00134

MacPhere, M. (2003). Medicine of the heart: The embodiment of faith in Morocco. *Medical Anthropology, 22*, 53–83. doi:10.1080/01459740306766

McCullough, M. E., & Worthington, E. L., Jr. (1994). Encouraging clients to forgive people who hurt them: Review, critique, and research prospectus. *Journal of Psychology and Theology, 22*, 3–20.

McLaren, M. C. (1998). *Interpreting cultural differences: The challenge of intercultural communication.* London, England: Peter Francis.

Mehraby, N. (2003). Psychotherapy with Islamic clients facing loss and grief. *Psychotherapy in Australia, 2*, 30–34.

Nunnaly, J. (1978). *Psychometric theory.* New York, NY: McGraw-Hill.

Odoms-Young, A. (2008). Factors that influence body image representations of Black Muslim women. *Social Science and Medicine, 66*, 2573–2584. doi:10.1016/j.socscimed.2008.02.008

Paloutzian, R. F., & Park, C. L. (2005). Integrative themes in the current science of the psychology of religion. In R. F. Paloutzian & C. L. Park (Eds.), *Handbook of the psychology of religion and spirituality* (pp. 3–20). New York, NY: Guilford Press.

Pargament, K. I. (1997). *The psychology of religion and coping: Theory, research, practice.* New York, NY: Guilford Press.

Pargament, K. I. (2007). *Spirituality integrated psychotherapy: Understanding and addressing the sacred.* New York, NY: Guilford Press.

Pargament, K. I., & Abu-Raiya, H. (2007). A decade of research on the psychology of religion and coping: Things we assumed and lessons we learned. *Psyke and Logos, 28*, 742–766.

Pargament, K. I., Koenig, H. G., & Perez, L. M. (2000). The many methods of religious coping: Development and initial validation of the RCOPE. *Journal of Clinical Psychology, 56*, 519–543. doi:10.1002/(SICI)1097-4679(200004)56:4<519::AID-JCLP6>3.0.CO;2-1

Pargament, K. I., Sullivan, M. S., Balzer, W. K., Van Haitsma, K. S., & Raymark, P. (1995). The many meanings of religiousness: A policy capturing approach. *Journal of Personality, 63*, 953–983. doi:10.1111/j.1467-6494.1995.tb00322.x

Pew Research Center. (2005). *Islamic extremism: Common concern for Muslim and Western publics.* Retrieved from http://pewglobal.org/reports/display.php?ReportID=248

The Qura'n. (1985). Brattleboro, VT: Amana Books.

Razali, S. M., Aminah, K., & Khan, U. A. (2002). Religious-cultural psychotherapy in the management of anxiety patients. *Transcultural Psychiatry, 39*, 130–136. doi:10.1177/136346150203900106

Razali, S. M., Hasanah, C. I., Aminah, K., & Subramaniam, M. (1998). Religious socio-cultrual psychotherapy in patients with anxiety and depression. *Australian and New Zealand Journal of Psychiatry, 32*, 867–872. doi:10.3109/00048679809073877

Richards, P. S., & Bergin, A. E. (1997). *A spiritual strategy for counseling and psychotherapy.* Washington, DC: American Psychological Association. doi:10.1037/10241-000

Rippy, E. R., & Newman, E. (2006). Perceived religious discrimination and its relationship to anxiety and paranoia among Muslim Americans. *Journal of Muslim Mental Health, 1*, 5–20. doi:10.1080/15564900600654351

Ryan, R. M., Rigby, S., & King, K. (1993). Two types of religious internalization and their relations to religious orientations and mental health. *Journal of Personality and Social Psychology, 65*, 586–596. doi:10.1037/0022-3514.65.3.586

Sahin, A., & Francis, L. J. (2002). Assessing attitude toward Islam among Muslim adolescents: The psychometric properties of the Sahin-Francis Scale. *Muslim Education Quarterly, 19*(4), 35–47.

Sherman, A. C., Simonton, S., Latif, U., Spohn, R., & Tricot, G. (2005). Religious struggle and religious comfort in response to illness: Health outcomes among stem cell transplant patients. *Journal of Behavioral Medicine, 28*, 359–367. doi:10.1007/s10865-005-9006-7

Strabac, Z., & Listhaug, O. (2008). Anti-Muslim prejudice in Europe: A multilevel analysis of survey data from 30 countries. *Social Science Research, 37*, 268–286. doi:10.1016/j.ssresearch.2007.02.004

Sue, S. (1992). Ethnicity and mental health: Research and policy issues. *Journal of Social Issues, 48*, 187–205. doi:10.1111/j.1540-4560.1992.tb00893.x

Tarakeshwar, N., Pargament, K. I., & Mahoney, A. (2003). Measures of Hindu pathways: Development and preliminary evidence of reliability and validity. *Cultural Diversity and Ethnic Minority Psychology, 9*, 316–332. doi:10.1037/1099-9809.9.4.316

Tiliouine, H., Cummins, R. A., & Davern, M. (2009). Islamic religiosity, subjective well-being and health.

Mental Health, Religion, and Culture, 12, 55–74. doi:10.1080/13674670802118099

U.S. State Department. (2001). *Fact sheet: Islam in the United States.* Retrieved from http://usinfo.state.gov/usa/islam/fact2.htm

Watson, P. J., Ghorbani, N., Davison, H. K., Bing, M. N., Hood, R. W., Jr., & Ghrarmaleki, A. F. (2002). Negatively reinforcing personal extrinsic motivations: Religious orientation, inner awareness, and mental health in Iran and the United States. *The International Journal for the Psychology of Religion*, 12, 255–276. doi:10.1207/S15327582IJPR1204_04

Wilde, A., & Joseph, S. (1997). Religiosity and personality in a Muslim context. *Personality and Individual Differences, 23*, 899–900. doi:10.1016/S0191-8869(97)00098-6

Williamson, W. P., & Ahmad, A. (2007). Survey research and Islamic Fundamentalism: A question about validity. *Journal of Muslim Mental Health, 2*, 155–176. doi:10.1080/15564900701614809

Chapter 39

THE CHRISTIAN RELIGION: A THEOLOGICAL AND PSYCHOLOGICAL REVIEW

Richard Beck and Andrea D. Haugen

Recent figures place the number of Christians worldwide from 1.9 to 2.1 billion, or 32% to 33% of the world's population (*World Almanac and Book of Facts*, 2004, p. 612). The largest number of Christians are found in Europe (531 million), with those in Latin America numbering 511 million; North America, 381 million; and Asia, 269 million (Barrett, Johnson, & Crossing, 2005; *World Factbook*, 2009). Christian growth in Africa is especially pronounced, with current numbers at 389 million, although Asia (2.64% growth per year) is the fastest-growing continent of the Christian world (*World Factbook*, 2009). The four major traditional branches of Christianity are Catholic (1.1 billion adherents, or 52.4% of Christians), Protestant (375 million, or 17.9%), Orthodox (219 million, or 10.4%), and Anglican (79 million, or 3.8%; *World Factbook*, 2009).

OVERVIEW OF THE CHAPTER

This chapter introduces the core tenets of the Christian faith and reviews the empirical psychological literature related to those beliefs. This poses some difficulties given the diversity of Christian belief and practice. The strategy employed in this chapter to survey Christian belief is to use the Apostles' Creed, one of the oldest and most universal statements of the core doctrinal commitments of the Christian faith. Given the diversity of the Christian faith, however, our use of the Apostles' Creed should be seen simply as a reference point, a means of entry, into Christian doctrine. For example, a recent survey by Elliott and Hayward (2007) of 142 noncreedal (Unitarian–Universalist) Christians suggested that the Christian religious experience might not differ significantly between orthodox (creedal) and heterodox (noncreedal) Christian traditions. Elliott and Hayward, however, did not explicitly make this contrast; thus, a direct comparison of creedal versus noncreedal traditions exists as an outstanding research question.

Moreover, there may be deep and significant sociological and theological differences between liberal and more conservative faith traditions (and among liberals and conservatives within those faith traditions). For example, using an experiencing sampling method, Storm and Wilson (2009) compared adolescents from liberal mainline Protestant traditions (Methodist, Presbyterian, Episcopalian) with teens from more conservative Christian groups (Pentecostal, Mormon). The results suggested that liberal and conservative Christian groups socialize their members in different ways. Conservative Christians tend to rely on external controls, making them socially dependent, more sociable, family-oriented, and less anxious. By contrast, liberal Christians tend to stress internal controls, making them more autonomous but prone to anxiety in decision making. This observation is supported by cross-cultural comparisons that suggest that the differences between liberals and conservatives may be a constant across world religions. For example, in a comparison of liberal versus conservative Christians and Hindus, Jensen (1998) noted that liberal

DOI: 10.1037/14045-039
APA Handbook of Psychology, Religion, and Spirituality: Vol. 1. Context, Theory, and Research, K. I. Pargament (Editor-in-Chief)
Copyright © 2013 by the American Psychological Association. All rights reserved.

Christians and Hindus were similar in their likelihood to consult an ethic of autonomy (Shweder, Much, Mahapatra, & Park, 1997) when compared with their conservative counterparts. Such a finding suggests that the liberal–conservative divide is not particular to the Christian religious experience but rather is a more general religious–cultural worldview phenomenon (see Haidt & Graham, 2007; Rozin, Lowery, Imada, & Haidt, 1999). In light of these findings, it is difficult, if not impossible, to describe the "Christian faith" in any generic sense. Still, we have to start somewhere.

These clarifications duly noted, the text of the Apostles' Creed (*Book of Common Prayer*, 2007) is as follows:

> I believe in God, the Father Almighty,
> creator of heaven and earth.
> I believe in Jesus Christ, his only Son, our Lord.
> He was conceived by the power of Holy Spirit
> and born of the Virgin Mary.
> He suffered under Pontius Pilate,
> was crucified, died, and was buried.
> He descended to the dead.
> On the third day he rose again.
> He ascended into heaven,
> and is seated at the right hand of the Father.
> He will come again to judge the living and the dead.
> I believe in the Holy Spirit,
> the holy catholic Church;
> the communion of saints;
> the forgiveness of sins;
> the resurrection of the body,
> and the life everlasting.
> Amen.

Throughout this chapter, the various statements of the Apostles' Creed are taken up and used to gather, topically and doctrinally, the empirical research related to the Christian faith. For those unfamiliar with the Christian faith, at the start of each section a short theological discussion is provided to "unpack" the creedal assertions.

"I BELIEVE IN GOD THE FATHER ALMIGHTY": THE EXPERIENCE OF GOD

The Apostles' Creed uses a three-part structure addressing, in turn, the three persons of the Trinity. The first section speaks of "the Father."

Interlude: The Trinity

One of the theological distinctive traits within the Christian faith, in sharp contrast to the other monotheistic Abrahamic faiths—Islam and Judaism—is the doctrine of the Trinity: the belief that God is "composed" of three divine "persons"—Father, Son, and Holy Spirit—who are, in fact, an ontological unity ("three in one"). Interestingly, although many Christian traditions place great weight on the doctrine of the Trinity, suggesting that Christian identity, community, and ethics must be grounded in Trinitarian theology, there is (researchers take note here) no empirical literature examining the social–psychological correlates of Trinitarian belief. Although not containing an explicit Trinitarian assertion, the Apostles' Creed uses a Trinitarian structure with three sections of "I believe" associated, in turn, with God the Father, Jesus Christ, and the Holy Spirit. Consequently, we will follow the structure of the Apostles' Creed and take up the three persons of the Christian Trinity starting, in this section, with the doctrine of "God the Father."

God the Father?

As the anthropomorphic descriptor "Father" indicates, Christians believe that the Creator God is also a personal God, a God with whom they are in a relationship. Readers will have noted that the Apostles' Creed uses a masculine image for God: Father. God is often, contentiously so, gendered within the Christian tradition, as Father is the dominant image of God in both the Old and New Testaments. Imagery of God as Mother, however, is also found in the Bible (cf. Isaiah 49:15, 66:13).

Surrounding these gendered images of God, there is a vast array of adjectives used to describe the character or "personality" of God. Generally, these adjectives cluster around the communion (*loving, caring, nurturing, patient*) and agency (*strong, powerful, dominant, harsh, wrathful*) dimensions.

A great deal of empirical work has been devoted to examining how these adjectives are applied to God, for better or for worse (e.g., Benson & Spilka, 1973; Bradshaw, Ellison, & Flannelly, 2008; Dickie, Ajega, Kobylak, & Nixon, 2006; Gorsuch, 1968; Spilka, Armatas, & Nussbaum, 1964). God imagery seems to vary across Christian traditions. For example, Noffke and McFadden (2001) observed that Evangelical Christians experience God as more vindictive and stern relative to Catholics and more liberal Protestants (Methodists). The important point, particularly for clinicians, is that God imagery varies, individually and across Christian traditions, and needs to be assessed on a case-by-case basis.

In one interesting study regarding God's providential role as "Father," Norenzayan and Lee (2010) observed across a variety of samples that Christians have higher fate attributions than do the nonreligious. That is, Christians are more likely to believe that life events were "meant to happen," a belief likely due to a conviction that God is providentially in control of the world. An open question is how this "fatalism" might positively or negatively affect Christians coping in the face of negative life events.

Relationship With God

Given the anthropomorphic metaphors used to describe God, it is not surprising that Christian believers tend to describe their relationship with God in the idiom of human relationality, generally as a parental or marital relationship. This has led some researchers to suggest that Christian believers are importing relational schemas shaped in human love relationships into the God experience. For example, Kirkpatrick (1999) has argued that religious believers experience their relationship with God as an attachment bond. Studies with Christian samples have shown this to be a viable model for describing the God relationship within Christianity (e.g., Rowatt & Kirkpatrick, 2002) as well as being robust across Christian denominations. For example, Beck and McDonald (2004) observed no differences in attachment to God between Catholics and conservative Pentecostals.

The attachment to God model highlights that relationship with God can be as dynamic and conflicted as any human love relationship. For example, in a factor analytic study with a conservative Christian sample (Southern nondenominational, Baptist, Church of Christ), Beck (2006a) observed that experiences of communion and intimacy with God are often mixed with experiences of compliant, negativity, protest, anger, and lament. To date, most of the empirical literature has framed complaint within the Christian faith experience as pathological, which does not jibe with either the biblical witness (e.g., the Psalms) or the Christian tradition (e.g., St. John of the Cross' Dark Night of the Soul or the recent revelations about the spiritual journey of Mother Teresa). Consequently, an important area for future research is the development of models, both theoretical and operational, that can discriminate between healthy and unhealthy forms of lament in the relationship with God.

"I BELIEVE IN JESUS CHRIST": THE CHRISTOLOGICAL EXPERIENCE

The second part of the Apostles' Creed turns to the second person of the Trinity, "the Son." These beliefs focus on the life and career of Jesus of Nazareth.

Father and Son

Christians understand themselves to be in relationship with Jesus Christ in ways similar to their relationship with God. According to the New Testament, however, Jesus functions beyond his role as Savior as an empathic mediator between God the Father and humankind (cf. Heb. 4:15). Given this function, we might expect that God imagery and Jesus imagery could diverge. For example, Howell (2004) observed in a predominantly Baptist sample that the majority of participants tended to see Jesus as sociable and feeling oriented, as assessed by the Jungian personality typology. Piedmont, Williams, and Ciarrocchi (1997) also observed, using an adjective rating, that Christians tend to see Jesus as empathic, compassionate, and similar in personality to themselves. To date, however, there is no empirical literature that directly compares and contrasts the imagery related to God the Father versus Jesus Christ.

"Born of the Virgin Mary": The Incarnation

A central claim of the Christian creeds is the doctrine of the Incarnation, the confession that in the man Jesus, God "became flesh and dwelt among us" (John 1:4). This simple claim hides vast amounts of theological controversy and ecclesial dispute from the earliest days of the church to the present. Much, if not most, of this controversy has swirled around the struggle to embrace the "full divinity" of Jesus (the Trinitarian claim that Jesus was fully God) and the "full humanity" of Jesus (the Incarnational claim that Jesus was fully human). Historically, Christians have been sharply divided in how they reconcile these two seemingly irreconcilable notions. Interestingly, in light of these theological and philosophical tensions there has been little empirical attention devoted to the psychological dissonances that might be inherent in the doctrine of the Incarnation. In one study directly concerning the subject of the Incarnation, Beck (2008) observed in a conservative Protestant sample that death anxiety was positively correlated with discomfort in imagining Jesus affected by physical vulnerability (e.g., illness, injury). This finding suggests that, theology aside, existential anxieties may be unconsciously affecting how Christians wrestle with the full humanity of Jesus.

"Was Crucified" and "The Forgiveness of Sins": The Atonement

As recounted in the four gospels of the New Testament, at the end of 3 years of public ministry, Jesus was arrested, put on trial, and sentenced to death by crucifixion. The early followers of Jesus eventually came to view his death in sacrificial terms in which the death and blood of Jesus was believed to have sacrificially atoned for the sins of humankind (past, present, and future). Metaphorically, then, many Christians believe that the blood of Jesus, shed during his crucifixion, cleanses them and "washes their sins away." Through the death of Jesus, Christians receive forgiveness for their sins. (There is, however, a great deal of theological debate about the exact function of the death and bloodshed of Jesus in effecting Christian "salvation." For an introductory review about the variety of ways Christian think about the death of Jesus, see McKnight, 2007.)

And yet, the Christian experience of forgiveness can be a complex mixture of gratitude and love as well as guilt and fear. For example, in a survey of Evangelical seminarians McConahay and Hough (1973) noted that although Christians believe that God loves and desires to save the world, much of the world stands under God's wrath and judgment. Consequently, Christians can be motivated by gratitude and love for God as well as from a sense of guilt or fear regarding one's sinfulness and God's associated judgment. It is important for clinicians to attend to these motivational differences when working with Christian populations. For example, across a variety of Catholic and Protestant samples, Ryan, Rigby, and King (1993) observed that Christians motivated by guilt report lower self-esteem, increased anxiety and depression, and greater social dysfunction than those motivated by personal feelings of commitment and valuing of religious practices.

Along with the Christian experience of divine forgiveness comes the imperative to "forgive others as you have been forgiven" (cf. Eph. 4.32). For example, Exline (2008) observed in a congregational Baptist sample that a belief in God's forgiveness was associated with feeling mandated to forgive others. Interestingly, in a study of practicing Christians, Krause and Ellison (2003) found that the horizontal act of forgiving others (human-to-human) predicted greater well-being when compared to the vertical (God-to-human) experience of being forgiven by God. Overall, although the literature on interpersonal forgiveness is robust and growing, researchers are only just beginning to wrestle with the associations between the experiences of divine versus interpersonal forgiveness (see Davis et al., 2009, for research in this direction with religiously mixed but greater than 65% Christian samples).

"Lord" and "Judge": The Imitation of Christ

Beyond the salvific effects associated with his death and resurrection, the life and teachings of Jesus are considered normative for Christian life and practice because Christians describe themselves as disciples (followers) of Jesus. In this, Jesus is considered by Christians to be Lord and Master and eventually the moral Judge of all of humanity. The imperatives to conform one's life to the example of Jesus fill the New Testament. This is what is known in the Christian tradition as the *Imitatio Christi*, the "imitation of Christ."

The Christian moral experience (the attempt to be "Christ-like") can be examined in two different ways. First, Christians compare themselves with behavioral norms that are held up as standards within their faith communities. These norms vary across Christian communities, but most tend to cluster around issues related to self-control and hedonic excess (e.g., extramarital sexual activity, drug use). And it is important to note that these norms vary across Christian groups. For example, in a survey of Christian denominations, Engs, Hanson, Gliksman, and Smythe (1990) noted that Catholics tend to consume more alcohol than liberal (mainline) Protestants, who in turn consume more than conservative Protestants. In a correlated way, a survey by Petersen and Donnenwerth (1997) noted that a liberalization of views regarding premarital sexual activity has been occurring among Catholics and mainline Protestants. By contrast, the sexual mores of fundamentalist Protestants have remained consistently conservative over the past few decades.

A second approach into the Christian moral experience is associated less with behavioral norms than with character formation and the acquisition of virtue. That is, Christians seek to acquire the behavioral, affective, and cognitive habits that conform to the example and teachings of Jesus in the New Testament (Wright, 2010). Historically, this transformation was guided by a variety of virtue and vice lists in the New Testament. The two most famous virtue lists in the New Testament come from the Apostle Paul: his list of "faith, hope, and love" (I Cor. 13:13) and his list of the "fruits of the Spirit" (Gal. 5:22–23a): "The fruit of the Spirit is love, joy, peace, patience, kindness, goodness, faithfulness, gentleness and self-control." In addition to these virtues, the early church also recognized four cardinal virtues shared with or borrowed from the Greeks: prudence, justice, temperance, and courage.

The Christian virtue tradition (along with other virtue traditions) is receiving greater theoretical and empirical attention because of a resurgence of interest in the ancient virtue traditions in both moral philosophy (Hursthouse, 1999) and psychology (Peterson & Seligman, 2004). Explicitly following these virtue traditions (in both the West and the East), research in positive psychology has attempted to create a science of *eudaimonia* to facilitate investigation into the associations between virtue and subjective well-being. As a part of this effort, an influential taxonomy of virtue has been offered by Peterson and Seligman's (2004) identification of six "core virtues" with 24 associated "character strengths." Table 39.1 compares Peterson and Seligman's list of virtues and character strengths with virtue lists from the Christian tradition.

As seen in Table 39.1, there is significant overlap between the Christian virtue tradition and the growing literature of positive psychology. In many ways, however, Table 39.1 is misleading. Many of the Christian virtues are robust. For example, biblical notions of joy encompass feelings of peace, happiness, contentment, well-being, optimism, and gratitude. In a similar way, the Christian notion of love (*agape*) involves notions of mercy, peace-making, forgiveness, kindness, justice, fairness, and self-sacrificing courage. In addition, the biblical witness has a great deal of material devoted to virtues that seem absent from Table 39.1 (e.g., wisdom). In short, given the narrative and ethical richness of the biblical narrative, Christians can easily locate all six core virtues (with their associated character strengths) within their faith tradition.

From these observations we can make two important contrasts between the Christian virtue tradition and the literature emerging from positive psychology. (For other perspectives on the relationship between the Christian virtue tradition and positive psychology, see Gubbins, 2008; Hackney, 2007; Tan, 2006.) First, as noted, Christians tend to use thicker descriptions of their virtues compared with Peterson and Seligman's (2004) more atomistic trait-like approach. Christian notions of joy, peace, and love are rich and interrelated, blended, and reinforcing composites of the character strengths found in Table 39.1. This observation is related to the second contrast. Positive psychology research, as we have noted, tends to examine the virtues in isolation. From an assessment and research perspective this is perfectly understandable. The virtue tradition within Christianity,

TABLE 39.1

Comparison of Virtues in Positive Psychology and the Christian Tradition

Positive psychology	The Christian tradition		
Core virtues and associated character strengths (Peterson & Seligman, 2004)	The Three Theological Virtues (1 Cor. 13:13)	The Fruits of the Spirit (Gal. 5:22–23)	The Four Cardinal Virtues
Wisdom and knowledge (creativity, curiosity, open-mindedness, love of learning, perspective/wisdom)			
Courage (bravery/valor, persistence/perseverance, integrity/honesty, vitality/enthusiasm)	Faith	Faithfulness	Courage
Humanity (love, kindness, social intelligence)	Love	Love, kindness, gentleness	
Justice (citizenship/loyalty, fairness, leadership)			Justice
Temperance (forgiveness/mercy, humility/modesty, prudence, self-regulation/self-control)		Peace, self-control, goodness, patience	Prudence, temperance
Transcendence (appreciation of beauty/excellence, gratitude, hope/optimism, humor, spirituality/faith)	Hope	Joy	

however, both prioritizes the virtues (e.g., Christian *agape* or love is considered to be the greatest Christian virtue, the virtue the Christian should devote the most effort toward acquiring) and expects the Christian to train in acquiring and exemplifying the entire suite of virtues (e.g., Christians should display, as faith matures, all the fruits of the Spirit). These notions contrast with the individual differences approach used by researchers who suggest that people identify their "signature strengths"—the virtues that come easily and naturally to the person, similar to a Big Five personality assessment (e.g., Seligman, 2004). Although the Christian virtue tradition recognizes individual differences and that individual Christians will begin the project of virtue acquisition at different starting places (being more or less, let's say, patient or kind by nature), it also expects a Christian, in taking up one virtue, to take up all of them. They are of a piece. With these contrasts in hand, we note that there is a growing empirical literature associated with positive psychology examining many virtues important to the Christian virtue tradition. (For more on gratitude and forgiveness, see Chapter 23 in this volume; for more on altruism, see Chapter 24 in this volume; for more on positive psychology, see Volume 2, Chapter 25, this handbook.)

"I BELIEVE IN THE HOLY SPIRIT": THE PNEUMALOGICAL EXPERIENCE

The third person of the Trinity is the Holy Spirit. Jesus promised his followers, after his death, burial, resurrection, and ascension into heaven, that he would not leave them alone, that he would send to them God's Spirit to be a *paraclete* (comforter, advisor, or helper) for the church (cf. John 14:16, 26; 15:26; 16:7). Many Christian traditions believe that the fulfillment of this promise occurred on the day of Pentecost as recounted in Acts 2. In the wake of the Pentecost, the early Christians confessed to experiencing an "indwelling of the Holy Spirit." Consequently, many Christian traditions believe that the Holy Spirit dwells within each believer. There the Holy Spirit fulfills its role as *paraclete*: guiding, empowering, revealing, prompting, assisting, convicting, helping, gifting, and transforming the Christian during her day-to-day spiritual journey.

Theologically and phenomenologically, then, Christians experience their relationship with the Holy Spirit as a kind of spiritual and moral partnership, a partnership very much mediated by prayer. Consequently, it is with the Holy Spirit where we can explore how Christians partner with God in day-to-day experience.

Religious Coping

One way the Christian believer may experience her partnership with the Holy Spirit is in relying or calling on the divine to face challenges, obstacles, and stressors. In the psychology of religion literature, these attempts typically have been studied under the constructs of religious coping and religious problem solving, a reliance and turning toward God in the face of life struggles. (It should be reiterated that these measures do not explicitly specify the Holy Spirit; however, because there is a dearth of research on the Christian's experience with the Holy Spirit, we are assuming that many Christians understand their reliance on God in religious coping as being mediated by the Holy Spirit. But research assessing Holy Spirit attributions in religious coping is needed to test this assumption.) For an example of this research with a Christian population, Pargament, Tarakeshwar, Ellison, and Wulff (2001) observed, in a large national survey of Presbyterians, that positive religious coping was associated with beneficial outcomes, such as increased positive affect, reduced depressive affect, and higher ratings of religious satisfaction. For comparisons within and outside the Christian faith, Cohen (2002) surveyed the religious coping of Catholic, Protestant, and Jewish participants. Cohen observed minimal differences in the overall use of religious coping between Protestants and Catholics. And for both groups, religious coping was an important predictor of happiness and life satisfaction. By contrast, Jewish participants were less likely to use religious coping and, consequently, religious coping was not a significant predictor of subjective well-being among the Jewish sample.

The Experience of Prayer

As noted, one way Christians seek guidance from God and the Holy Spirit is through prayer. In the Christian experience, prayer is one of the primary means of coping identified by the New Testament writers (cf. Mark 11:24; Rom. 8:26; Eph. 6:18; 1 Thess. 5:17; James 5:13, 15–16; Jude 1:20). With the expectation that the Holy Spirit will intercede on their behalf, Christians are exhorted to pray with the Spirit and through the Spirit with all kinds of requests, particularly during times of moral, psychological, and physical struggle and weakness.

In the psychology of religion literature, prayer has been associated with a variety of physical and psychological benefits (see Chapter 16 in this volume). For example, prayer has been associated with tension reduction (Elkins, Anchor, & Sandler, 1979), attenuating depressive affect (Parker & Brown, 1982), effective coping with the stress of surgical procedures (Saudia, Kinney, Brown, & Young-Ward, 1991; Sutton & Murphy, 1989), and long-term coping of the elderly (Koenig, George, & Siegler, 1988; Manfredi & Pickett, 1987; Shaw, 1992). Most prayer research, such as the studies just cited, has utilized religiously mixed samples. But these trends have been observed when Christians are studied in isolation. For example, in a large survey ($N = 1,412$) of Presbyterian pastors, Meisenhelder and Chandler (2001) noted that greater prayer frequency was predictive of higher general health, vitality, and mental health. Interestingly, given the size of the prayer literature, little work has been done comparing the uses and influences of prayer between the Christian traditions or between Christians and other religious groups.

Ecstatic Experience

In certain Christian traditions, Pentecostalism in particular, the Holy Spirit is implicated in certain ecstatic religious experiences, such as prophecy, supernatural healing, deliverance from evil spirits, and glossolalia (speaking in tongues). Biblically, glossolalia served as an outward indication that believers had received the Holy Spirit (Acts 2:4, 19:6). Much of the early research on glossolalia focused on whether or not it occurs in a trance state or if it is associated with psychopathology. Although there is some ambiguity in the literature, current findings suggest that trance is not a necessary state for glossolalia to occur (for a review, see Hood, Hill, & Spilka, 2009, Chapter 10). Regarding personality and psychopathology, a recent survey of 991 Evangelical clergy in the United Kingdom, conducted by Francis and Robbins (2003), noted that the experience of glossolalia was unrelated to psychopathology.

Spiritual Conflict

Before leaving our discussion of the Holy Spirit, we should also mention that many Christians consider a part of their day-to-day existence to be a struggle against malevolent supernatural forces (e.g., Satan, demons). In many places, the New Testament exhorts believers to take note of their true enemy: The Satanic forces arrayed against them and tempting them into immorality. How this spiritual conflict is experienced and understood can vary significantly across faith traditions. For example, Wesselmann and Graziano (2010) compared a nondenominational–Protestant sample with a Catholic–Orthodox sample regarding their attitudes toward mental illness and treatment. Overall, compared with the Catholic–Orthodox sample, the Protestant sample was more likely to believe that mental illness was caused by spiritual affliction (e.g., demonic attacks) or moral failures (e.g., sin) and that spiritual forms of treatment (such as prayer) are effective remedies for mental illness.

A common way Christians understand the experience of Satan (literally or metaphorically) is as tempter, the allure of immorality. And yet how Christians understand the mechanics of temptation remain unclear. For example, in a comparison of Christian and Jewish participants, Cohen and Rozin (2001) observed that Christian participants tended to moralize mental states more than their Jewish counterparts. That is, Christians believed that they could sin with their thoughts. For example, many Christians, in light of teachings such as Matthew 5:22, 28, feel that mental states such as lust or anger are immoral and sinful. By contrast, Jewish participants tended to see mental states as morally neutral (neither good nor bad) and focused their moralization on resultant actions and behaviors. In light of this finding, it is unclear how Christians parse their mental states. When is a mental state understood to be a temptation (potentially immoral) versus a sin (actually immoral)?

"I BELIEVE": THE BIBLICAL EXPERIENCE

Similar to the other Abrahamic faiths, Christianity has a sacred text, the Bible. How Christians interact with the Bible dramatically affects their faith experience.

The Christian Scriptures

Before coming to the end of the Apostles' Creed, we should stop and consider something not explicitly stated in the Creed but implied throughout. Specifically, where do Christians find the assertions found within the Creed? What is the source of the repeated refrain "I believe"?

For those familiar with the Christian faith the answer is obvious: the Bible. Christianity, similar to the other Abrahamic faiths, is a religion of "the book," a divinely inspired and sacred text at the heart of the faith. For Jews it is the Tanakh, for Muslims it is the Qura'n, and for Christians it is the 27 books of the New Testament. Christians also consider the 39 books of the Jewish Tanakh to be a part of their Bible and generally call these books the Old Testament. (Some Christian communities also recognize a variety of "Deuterocanonical books" written in the interlude between the composition of the Old and New Testaments.) Although Christians do not consider the Old Testament to be authoritative, they consider the Old Testament to be crucial to understanding the human predicament, the nature of God, the role of Jesus, and the mission of church in salvation history. Christians, however, do consider the New Testament to be normative for their life and practice. And although exegetical and hermeneutical disagreements abound, Christians generally believe that the New Testament specifies the core theological commitments of the faith (as summarized in the Christian creeds), articulates the moral vision of the Christian life, and offers guidance on the formation, organization, common life, and shared mission of the Christian *ecclesia* ("assembly"), the basic unit of Christian community generally referred to as "the church."

The Biblical Experience: Literalism, Fundamentalism, and Quest

Despite wide agreement on the centrality and authority of the Bible, Christians are sharply divided on the exact meaning and interpretation of a variety of biblical teachings and parts of the biblical narrative. Simplifying greatly, liberal Christians tend to make significant accommodations to modern scientific worldviews by interpreting the biblical stories mythically, symbolically, existentially, and moralistically. In contrast, conservative Christians resist making accommodations to modernity, choosing to treat the events recounted within the biblical narrative as literal, historical facts. This hermeneutical stance is generally called "biblical literalism." Again, this is an oversimplification, creating the appearance of two dichotomies in a relationship probably closer to a continuum.

A keen focus in the psychological literature has been the attempt to tease apart the relationship between biblical literalism and what is known as "fundamentalism," particularly among conservative Protestants. Although biblical literalism is associated with fundamentalism, they are not to be equated, prompting researchers to make distinctions among conservative Christian groups. For example, in their analysis of a survey of conservative Protestants, Kellstedt and Smidt (1991) observed that Evangelical Protestants and fundamentalist Protestants both endorsed biblical literalism. Fundamentalists, however, in contrast to Evangelicals, were more likely to be antagonistic toward the surrounding culture. This finding suggests that fundamentalism has less to do with the *contents* of belief than the way the believer *holds* those beliefs. This assessment fits with more general observations that fundamentalism, of whatever stripe, is strongly associated with dogmatism: the degree to which beliefs (whatever they are) are considered to be unassailable and held with fervent certainty (Altemeyer & Hunsberger, 2005).

In contrast to a fundamentalist and even literalist stance, liberal Christians tend to view the Christian creeds and the biblical stories existentially and moralistically. An influential attempt to assess a more existential mode of belief is Batson's construct of religion as quest (Batson, 1976; Batson, Schoenrade, & Ventis, 1993; Batson & Ventis, 1982). As operationalized by Batson, religious believers high on quest view religious doubt as healthy and are open to changing their beliefs in the face of life experience. Although quest is not unique to the Christian tradition, the construct has been used to explore faith orientations within Christian samples. In one interesting longitudinal study by Williamson and Sandage (2009), with graduate seminary students at an Evangelical Protestant seminary, it was observed that quest ratings increased across 2 years of seminary education, a finding that suggests a link between education and how people hold their religious beliefs. Williamson and Sandage also observed, however, that increased quest ratings were associated with a decrease in spiritual well-being among the seminary students. This trend is not surprising in that a movement into doubt or a willingness to change previously held convictions is likely to be associated with emotional turmoil or upheaval. How this process unfolds over time, toward either the reconfiguration of faith or the disintegration of faith, remains an outstanding research question. More longitudinal work is needed.

"THE RESURRECTION OF THE BODY, AND THE LIFE EVERLASTING": THE EXPERIENCE OF DEATH

Central to Christians' experience is their understanding of death and life after death in light of their belief that Jesus of Nazareth was resurrected from the dead.

"The Third Day He Rose Again": Christian Resurrection

For Orthodox Christians, the defining event in world history was the resurrection of Jesus of Nazareth 3 days after his death and burial. According to the gospel accounts, after his resurrection, Jesus appeared multiple times to his followers and, ultimately, ascended into heaven to reign with God. For many Christians, the resurrection of Jesus is a sign of God's promise that death has been defeated and that faithful believers will experience their own resurrection to enjoy eternal life in communion with God and the multitude of other faithful saints. Regarding faith group difference concerning belief in the afterlife, Cohen and Hall (2008) observed no difference between Catholics and Protestants in belief in the afterlife. Additionally, both Catholics and Protestants were more likely to endorse belief in the afterlife than Jewish participants.

Christian Faith and Death Anxiety

Metaphysics aside, a psychological impact of a Christian's belief in the resurrection could be that secure in Christ's victory over death, death holds no terrors for the believer. In fact, this is a regular theme in the New Testament, the claim that Christ's resurrection has, in the words of Hebrews 2:15, set free those who "were held in slavery by their fear of death." In light of these claims we might ask, Is there any evidence that Christians live, relatively speaking, free from the fear of death? Generally speaking, although the psychology of religion data are mixed, Hood et al. (2009) concluded that religious belief does attenuate death anxiety. More specifically, in a study of military personnel in the Korean army, Jeon (1997) observed that Christian solders reported significantly less death anxiety when compared with their non-Christian counterparts. In light of such general and specific findings, it seems that the Christian belief in the resurrection may attenuate death anxiety, an observation that is psychologically consistent with the promise of Hebrews 2:15 (being set free from "the fear of death").

Ever since Freud's *The Future of an Illusion* (1927/1989), many existential psychologists have wondered whether this reduced death anxiety among Christians (and religious persons generally) might be symptomatic of existential repression, what Ernest Becker (1973) called "the denial of death." Recent work in terror management theory (TMT; Greenberg, Solomon, & Pyszczynski, 1997) has offered some support for this assessment. Specifically, in an experimental study conducted by Greenberg et al. (1990), Christian participants denigrated out-group (Jewish) targets in the face of a death-awareness prime. This reactivity in the face of a death is symptomatic of what TMT researchers call "worldview defense," and it suggests that the Christian participants in the Greenberg et al., study were deploying their beliefs in a defensive manner, as a form of death repression (a fear-induced psychic avoidance). A study by Beck (2006b), prompted by Greenberg et al., found that the Christian response in the face of death is a bit more complex. Specifically, following William James (1902/2009), Beck argued that a particular constellation of Christian belief (e.g., denial of randomness, divine solicitousness, specialness) might be adopted and deployed for the sake of existential solace (believers James called "healthy minded"). Consequently, in procedures (similar Greenberg et al., 1990), Christian participants in Beck's study who displayed these beliefs did denigrate the non-Christian out-group member in the face of the death-awareness prime. The Christian participants who tended to eschew existentially comforting beliefs (believers James called "sick souls") did not denigrate the out-group member in the death prime condition. This difference suggests that some Christians do not appear to adopt or deploy their beliefs to achieve or maintain existential equanimity, contrary to what Freud might have suggested in *The Future of an Illusion*.

CONCLUSION

Having reached the end of our brief and selective survey of the Christian faith, we conclude with some reflections for both clinicians and researchers.

Clinical Reflections

For clinicians working with Christian clients, perhaps the most important takeaway from this overview is the recognition of the heterogeneity of the Christian faith. Christians are a diverse lot. Throughout this review, we have noted differences among faith traditions and between liberals and conservatives within those traditions. In short, knowing that your client is "Christian" will tell you very little. She may be, to deploy some stereotypes, a nominal Catholic, a liberal Episcopalian, a conservative Evangelical, or a charismatic Pentecostal. But it is just as possible that she is a conservative Catholic or a charismatic Baptist, or any other combination. Additionally, even these broad labels will lack critical information. Individual Christians frequently dissent from their traditions on a doctrine-by-doctrine basis, creating a personal (and often private) bricolage of belief. There are Episcopalians who are against same-sex marriage, Evangelicals who are prochoice, and Catholics who do not believe in papal infallibility. Very often, these locations of dissent are the result of life history, particular life experiences that prompted the believer to go against the grain of her faith tradition. As the saying goes, there is no theology, only biography. In sum, the diversity of the Christian faith and the theological idiosyncrasies of individual Christian clients need to be noted and treated as a location for clinical inquiry and attention.

Given this diversity, can the present review offer any guidance for clinicians working with Christian clients (see Volume 2, Chapters 8 and 34, this handbook)? This overview has been too brief and selective to offer any comprehensive clinical guidance, so caution is warranted (for more comprehensive treatments, consider Pargament, 2007; Richards & Bergin, 2005). This review, however, has suggested a variety of questions (among many others) worth considering when working with Christian populations. Following the order of our précis:

1. What is the dominant God-image the client is working with? Is the client responding positively or negatively to gendered God-images?
2. Is the client expressing anger, disappointment, or disillusionment with God? How is the "dark night of the soul" being coped with?
3. How does the client's imagery of Jesus compare and contrast with her God imagery?
4. Is the client's faith experience being motivated by guilt and a fear of God's judgment?
5. How does the client compare herself, for good or ill, to the behavioral norms and virtue ideals of her faith community?
6. How does the client use religious coping strategies (such as prayer) in handling life experiences?
7. How does the client understand her spiritual and moral struggles? Is the conflict with Satan understood to be literal demonic attack, the mere experience of temptation, or something more symbolic and metaphorical?
8. Does the client hold her beliefs dogmatically or is she "questing" and open to change?
9. Finally, does the client deploy her beliefs to deny or repress existential anxiety?

This list is only meant to be suggestive, a preliminary attempt to get the theology and research of this chapter "off the page" and into the clinical setting.

Research Reflections

When we set about writing this chapter we adopted a top-down approach. We laid out a theological map of the Christian faith (i.e., the Apostles' Creed) and went in search of empirical literature related to the major theological landmarks. What we discovered surprised us. Enormous swaths of the Christian experience have virtually no associated empirical literature. Moreover, many of these unexplored areas are central and fundamental to the Christian faith. For example, as noted, although there is an enormous literature associated with the God experience (e.g., God imagery, God attachment, spiritual well-being) there is virtually no literature on the Christological aspects of the Christian faith, the psychological correlates associated with the Christ-experience or the doctrines related to the Incarnation, the crucifixion, and the resurrection. And as we have noted, there is great diversity within the Christian tradition regarding these beliefs, and we can expect distinctive psychological and sociological correlates associated with these diverse understandings. Yet, here at the core of the Christian faith, we face an empirical void.

Our suspicion is that this void is largely due to the long shadow cast by William James and *The Varieties of Religious Experience* (1902/2009). In *The Varieties* James explicitly eschewed a consideration of metaphysics, theology, and religious doctrine. James's approach was experiential and phenomenological. The power of this approach was in its universality. It allowed James to gather experiences from every world religion under broad phenomenological categories (e.g., mysticism, conversion), categories that continue to dominate psychology of religion research. What has been lost in this approach is a sustained and fine-grained empirical consideration of the theological distinctive traits that exist among the world religions, Christian denominations, and individual believers (e.g., liberals vs. conservatives). Simply put, these diverse theologies (be they Buddhist vs. Christian or Evangelical vs. Catholic) are worldviews that shape how individuals apprehend and make meaning of life experience. By focusing on the commonalities of religious experience, James's approach misses what is unique, distinctive, and particular to a religious tradition. Consequently, perhaps because of the influence of *The Varieties*, little attention has been devoted to assessing the psychosocial correlates associated with the theological distinctive traits within faith traditions. It may be time for researchers to address this imbalance. Beliefs matter as much as experience.

Two examples might help to illustrate this point. First, consider again the study by Cohen and Rozin (2001) contrasting how Jewish persons and Christians moralize mental states. In the Jewish anthropological tradition, the mind is a location of moral struggle, a battleground where our innate inclination for the good (what Jewish teaching calls the *yetzer tov*) struggles against our equally innate evil impulses (the *yezter ra*). This struggle back and forth is considered to be the natural state of human existence, an innate moral seesaw within the mind that cannot be overcome and, thus, should not be moralized. Only the behavioral outcomes of this struggle, the resultant actions, are to be moralized. Christians, by contrast, in light of Jesus' teachings in Matthew 5:22, 28, do moralize mental states. Christians, in contrast to Judaism, feel they can sin with their thoughts. Recall Jimmy Carter's infamous *Playboy* interview: "I've committed adultery in my heart many times" (Scheer, 2006, p. 98). The point is, theology affects psychology: In this case, the experience of shame and guilt in reaction to how a particular faith tradition construes (or does not construe) moral failure.

As a second example, consider a study by Beck and Taylor (2008) regarding how beliefs about Satan, the spiritual enemy of the Christian believer, affect the God experience. Recall from our survey that Christian faith traditions differ in how active or influential they believe Satan to be in the world. In their study with conservative Christian participants, Beck and Taylor observed that individuals with robust beliefs about Satan's activity in the world (e.g., that Satan was actively affecting events in their lives) tended to report more positive experiences with God, presumably because some negative life events were being attributed to Satanic "attack" rather than to God. By contrast, Christian participants who tended to dismiss the role of Satan in daily life reported more conflicted experiences with God, presumably because, with their attenuated views of Satan, these Christian believers were attributing both positive *and* negative life events to the actions (or inaction) of God, infusing the God-experience with ambivalence. In all this, we see again how theological differences (in this case, beliefs about Satan and his role in life events) affect religious experience.

In sum, one takeaway for researchers is the suggestion that future research bracket the experiential and the phenomenological facets of Christianity (experiences, per *The Varieties*, likely shared with other world religions and, thus, nonspecific to Christianity) to take up fine-grained psychosocial examinations of the theological distinctive traits within the Christian faith. Borrowing from the growing field of experimental philosophy (for a review, see Knobe & Nichols, 2008), in which empirical methods are used to explore the philosophical assumptions of ordinary people (across a range of topics from free will to causality to ethics), we suggest future research move toward an "experimental theology": investigations into how Christians of all stripes reason about God, temptation, sin, grace, repentance, prayer, heaven, hell, angels, Satan, death, the Bible, the body, the soul, miracles, love, hate, evil, and the end of the world—to name but a few of the topics awaiting empirical attention.

At the very least, researchers should begin to consciously attend to and report faith group differences. It has become common practice for researchers to routinely examine gender and ethnicity as potential covariates in their research designs. Religious affiliation and Christian denomination should be added to that list. Quick progress could be made if researchers begin to consistently examine and report any faith group differences they uncover while exploring covariates within their data sets.

"Amen"

So concludes our theological and psychological survey of the Christian faith. The Apostles' Creed ends with the affirmation "Amen," an ancient and common ending to Jewish and Christian prayers and statements of faith. With roots in the Hebrew language, "Amen" means "so be it" and thus seems a fitting conclusion for this chapter.

References

Altemeyer, B., & Hunsberger, B. E. (2005). Fundamentalism and authoritarianism. In R. F. Paloutzian & C. L. Park (Eds.), *Handbook of the psychology of religion and spirituality* (pp. 378–393). New York, NY: Guilford Press.

Barrett, D. B., Johnson, T. M., & Crossing, P. F. (2005). Missiometrics 2005: A global survey of world mission. *International Bulletin of Missionary Research, 29,* 27–30.

Batson, C. D. (1976). Religion as prosocial: Agent or double agent? *Journal for the Scientific Study of Religion, 15,* 29–45. doi:10.2307/1384312

Batson, C. D., Schoenrade, P. A., & Ventis, W. L. (1993). *Religion and the individual: A social–psychological perspective.* New York, NY: Oxford University Press.

Batson, C. D., & Ventis, W. L. (1982). *The religious experience: A social–psychological perspective.* New York, NY: Oxford University Press.

Beck, R. (2006a). Communion and complaint: Attachment, object-relations, and triangular love perspectives on relationship with God. *Journal of Psychology and Theology, 34,* 43–52.

Beck, R. (2006b). Defensive versus existential religion: Is religious defensiveness predictive of worldview defense? *Journal of Psychology and Theology, 34,* 143–153.

Beck, R. (2008). Feeling queasy about the Incarnation: Terror management theory, death, and the body of Jesus. *Journal of Psychology and Theology, 36,* 303–313.

Beck, R., & McDonald, A. (2004). Attachment to God: The Attachment to God Inventory, tests of working model correspondence, and an exploration of faith group differences. *Journal of Psychology and Theology, 32,* 92–103.

Beck, R., & Taylor, S. (2008). The emotional burden of monotheism: Satan, theodicy, and relationship with God. *Journal of Psychology and Theology, 36,* 151–160.

Becker, E. (1973). *The denial of death.* New York, NY: Simon & Schuster.

Benson, P., & Spilka, B. (1973). God image as a function of self esteem and locus of control. *Journal for the Scientific Study of Religion, 12,* 297–310. doi:10.2307/1384430

Book of common prayer. (2007). New York, NY: Oxford University Press.

Bradshaw, M., Ellison, C. G., & Flannelly, K. J. (2008). Prayer, God imagery, and symptoms of psychopathology. *Journal for the Scientific Study of Religion, 47,* 644–659. doi:10.1111/j.1468-5906.2008.00432.x

Cohen, A. B. (2002). The importance of spirituality in well-being for Jews and Christians. *Journal of Happiness Studies, 3,* 287–310. doi:10.1023/A:1020656823365

Cohen, A. B., & Hall, D. E. (2008). Existential beliefs, social satisfaction, and well-being among Catholic, Jewish, and Protestant older adults. *The International Journal for the Psychology of Religion, 19,* 39–54. doi:10.1080/10508610802471088

Cohen, A. B., & Rozin, P. (2001). Religion and the morality of mentality. *Journal of Personality and Social Psychology, 81,* 697–710. doi:10.1037/0022-3514.81.4.697

Davis, D. E., Worthington, E. L., Jr., Hook, J. N., Van Tongeren, D. R., Green, J. D., & Jennings, D. J. (2009). Relational spirituality and the development of the similarity of the offender's spirituality scale. *Psychology of Religion and Spirituality, 1,* 249–262. doi:10.1037/a0017581

Dickie, J. R., Ajega, L. V., Kobylak, J. R., & Nixon, K. M. (2006). Mother, father, and self: Sources of young adults' God concepts. *Journal for the Scientific Study of Religion, 45,* 57–71. doi:10.1111/j.1468-5906.2006.00005.x

Elkins, D., Anchor, K. N., & Sandler, H. M. (1979). Relaxation training and prayer behavior as tension reduction techniques. *Behavioral Engineering, 5,* 81–87.

Elliott, M., & Hayward, D. (2007). Religion and well-being in a church without a creed. *Mental Health, Religion, and Culture, 10,* 109–126. doi:10.1080/13694670500386069

Engs, R. C., Hanson, D. J., Gliksman, L., & Smythe, C. (1990). Influence of religion and culture on drinking behaviours: A test of hypotheses between Canada and the USA. *British Journal of Addiction, 85,* 1475–1482. doi:10.1111/j.1360-0443.1990.tb01631.x

Exline, J. J. (2008). Beliefs about God and forgiveness in a Baptist church sample. *Journal of Psychology and Christianity, 27,* 131–139.

Francis, L. J., & Robbins, M. (2003). Personality and glossolalia: A study among male evangelical clergy. *Pastoral Psychology, 51,* 391–396. doi:10.1023/A:1023618715407

Freud, S. (1989). *The future of an illusion* (J. Strachey, Ed.). New York, NY: Norton. (Original work published 1927)

Gorsuch, R. L. (1968). The conceptualization of God as seen in adjective ratings. *Journal for the Scientific Study of Religion, 7,* 56–64. doi:10.2307/1385110

Greenberg, J., Pyszczynski, T., Solomon, S., Rosenblatt, A., Veeder, M., & Kirkland, S. (1990). Evidence for terror management theory II: The effects of mortality salience on reactions to those who threaten or bolster the cultural worldview. *Journal of Personality and Social Psychology, 58,* 308–318. doi:10.1037/0022-3514.58.2.308

Greenberg, J., Solomon, S., & Pyszczynski, T. (1997). Terror management theory of self-esteem and cultural worldviews: Empirical assessments and conceptual refinements. In M. Zanna (Ed.), *Advances in experimental social psychology* (Vol. 29, pp. 61–139). San Diego, CA: Academic Press.

Gubbins, J. P. (2008). Positive psychology: Friend or foe of religious virtue ethics? *Journal of the Society of Christian Ethics, 28*, 181–203.

Hackney, C. H. (2007). Possibilities for a Christian positive psychology. *Journal of Psychology and Theology, 35*, 211–221.

Haidt, J., & Graham, J. (2007). When morality opposes justice: Conservatives have moral intuitions that liberals may not recognize. *Social Justice Research, 20*, 98–116. doi:10.1007/s11211-007-0034-z

Hood, R. W., Hill, P. C., & Spilka, B. (2009). *The psychology of religion: An empirical approach*. New York, NY: Guilford Press.

Howell, S. H. (2004). Students' perceptions of Jesus' personality as assessed by Jungian-type inventories. *Journal of Psychology and Theology, 32*, 50–58.

Hursthouse, R. (1999). *On virtue ethics*. New York, NY: Oxford University Press.

James, W. (2009). *The varieties of religious experience* (J. Pelikan, Ed.). New York, NY: Library of America. (Original work published 1902)

Jensen, L. (1998). Moral divisions within countries between orthodoxy and progressivism: India and the United States. *Journal for the Scientific Study of Religion, 37*, 90–107. doi:10.2307/1388031

Jeon, J. (1997, February). Death anxiety and religious affiliation: A comparative study of military personnel. *Dissertation Abstracts International, 57*(8A), 3534.

Kellstedt, L., & Smidt, C. (1991). Measuring fundamentalism: An analysis of different operational strategies. *Journal for the Scientific Study of Religion, 30*, 259–278. doi:10.2307/1386972

Kirkpatrick, L. A. (1999). Attachment and religious representations and behavior. In J. Cassidy & P. R. Shaver (Eds.), *Handbook of attachment: Theory, research, and clinical applications* (pp. 803–822). New York, NY: Guilford Press.

Knobe, J. M., & Nichols, S. (2008). *Experimental philosophy*. Oxford, England: Oxford University Press.

Koenig, H. G., George, L. K., & Siegler, I. C. (1988). The use of religion and other emotion-regulating coping strategies among older adults. *The Gerontologist, 28*, 303–310. doi:10.1093/geront/28.3.303

Krause, N., & Ellison, C. G. (2003). Forgiveness by God, forgiveness of others, and psychological well-being in late life. *Journal for the Scientific Study of Religion, 42*, 77–94. doi:10.1111/1468-5906.00162

Manfredi, C., & Pickett, M. (1987). Perceived stressful situations and coping strategies utilized by the elderly. *Journal of Community Health Nursing, 4*, 99–110. doi:10.1207/s15327655jchn0402_7

McConahay, J. B., & Hough, J. C. (1973). Love and guilt-oriented dimensions of Christian belief. *Journal for the Scientific Study of Religion, 12*, 53–64. doi:10.2307/1384954

McKnight, S. (2007). *A community called atonement*. Nashville, TN: Abingdon Press.

Meisenhelder, J. B., & Chandler, E. N. (2001). Frequency of prayer and functional health in Presbyterian pastors. *Journal for the Scientific Study of Religion, 40*, 323–330. doi:10.1111/0021-8294.00059

Noffke, J. L., & McFadden, S. H. (2001). Denominational and age comparisons of God concepts. *Journal for the Scientific Study of Religion, 40*, 747–756. doi:10.1111/0021-8294.00089

Norenzayan, A., & Lee, A. (2010). It was meant to happen: Explaining cultural variations in fate attributions. *Journal of Personality and Social Psychology, 98*, 702–720. doi:10.1037/a0019141

Pargament, K. I. (2007). *Spiritually integrated psychotherapy: Understanding and addressing the sacred*. New York, NY: Guilford Press.

Pargament, K. I., Tarakeshwar, N., Ellison, C. G., & Wulff, K. M. (2001). Religious coping among the religious: The relationships between religious coping and well-being in a national sample of Presbyterian clergy, elders, and members. *Journal for the Scientific Study of Religion, 40*, 497–513. doi:10.1111/0021-8294.00073

Parker, G. B., & Brown, L. B. (1982). Coping behaviors that mediate between life events and depression. *Archives of General Psychiatry, 39*, 1386–1391. doi:10.1001/archpsyc.1982.04290120022004

Petersen, L. R., & Donnenwerth, G. V. (1997). Secularization and the influence of religion on beliefs about premarital sex. *Social Forces, 75*, 1071–1088.

Peterson, C., & Seligman, M. (2004). *Character strengths and virtues: A handbook and classification*. New York, NY: Oxford University Press.

Piedmont, R. L., Williams, J. E. G., & Ciarrocchi, J. W. (1997). Personality correlates of one's image of Jesus: Historiographic analysis using the five-factor model of personality. *Journal of Psychology and Theology, 25*, 364–373.

Richards, P. S., & Bergin, A. E. (2005). *A spiritual strategy for counseling and psychotherapy* (2nd ed.). Washington, DC: American Psychological Association. doi:10.1037/11214-000

Rowatt, W. C., & Kirkpatrick, L. A. (2002). Two dimensions of attachment to God and their relation to affect, religiosity, and personality constructs. *Journal for the Scientific Study of Religion, 41*, 637–651. doi:10.1111/1468-5906.00143

Rozin, P., Lowery, L., Imada, S., & Haidt, J. (1999). The CAD hypothesis: A mapping between three moral emotions (contempt, anger, disgust) and three moral codes (community, autonomy, divinity). *Journal of Personality and Social Psychology, 76*, 574–586. doi:10.1037/0022-3514.76.4.574

Ryan, R. M., Rigby, S., & King, K. (1993). Two types of religious internalization and their relations to religious orientations and mental health. *Journal of Personality and Social Psychology, 65*, 586–596. doi:10.1037/0022-3514.65.3.586

Saudia, T. L., Kinney, M. R., Brown, K. C., & Young-Ward, L. (1991). Health locus of control and helpfulness of prayer. *Heart and Lung, 20*, 60–65.

Scheer, R. (2006). *Playing president: Up close with Nixon, Carter, Reagan, Bush, and Clinton—and how they did not prepare me for George W. Bush*. New York, NY: Akashic Books.

Seligman, M. (2004). *Authentic happiness*. New York, NY: Simon & Schuster.

Shaw, R. J. (1992). Coping effectiveness in nursing home residents. *Journal of Aging and Health, 4*, 551–563. doi:10.1177/089826439200400406

Shweder, R., Much, N., Mahapatra, M., & Park, L. (1997). The "big three" of morality (autonomy, community, divinity) and the "big three" explanations of suffering. In A. Brandt & P. Rozin (Eds.), *Morality and health* (pp. 119–169). New York, NY: Routledge.

Spilka, B., Armatas, P., & Nussbaum, J. (1964). The concept of God: A factor-analytic approach. *Review of Religious Research, 6*, 28–36. doi:10.2307/3510880

Storm, I., & Wilson, D. (2009). Liberal and conservative Protestant denominations as different socioecological strategies. *Human Nature, 20*, 1–24. doi:10.1007/s12110-008-9055-z

Sutton, T. D., & Murphy, S. P. (1989). Stressors and patterns of coping in renal transplant patients. *Nursing Research, 38*, 46–49. doi:10.1097/00006199-198901000-00010

Tan, S. (2006). Applied positive psychology: Putting positive psychology into practice. *Journal of Psychology and Christianity, 25*, 68–73.

Wesselmann, E. D., & Graziano, W. G. (2010). Sinful and/or possessed? Religious beliefs and mental illness stigma. *Journal of Social and Clinical Psychology, 29*, 402–437. doi:10.1521/jscp.2010.29.4.402

Williamson, I. T., & Sandage, S. J. (2009). Longitudinal analyses of religious and spiritual development among seminary students. *Mental Health, Religion, and Culture, 12*, 787–801. doi:10.1080/1367467090 2956604

World almanac and book of facts. (2004). New York, NY: World Almanac Books.

World factbook. (2009). Retrieved from https://www.cia.gov/library/publications/the-world-factbook/index.html

Wright, N. T. (2010). *After you believe: Why Christian character matters*. New York, NY: HarperOne.

Chapter 40

ATHEISTS, AGNOSTICS, AND APOSTATES

Heinz Streib and Constantin Klein

In the scientific study of religion in general and the psychology of religion in particular, atheists and agnostics have received limited attention, whereas believers and converts have stood in the center of interest. More recently, however, more attention has been given to atheists and agnostics, and several researchers have recommended studying atheists and agnostics in their own right (Hood, Hill, & Spilka, 2009; Hunsberger & Altemeyer, 2006; Keysar, 2007; Kosmin & Keysar, 2007). This new interest may in part be due to indications of a considerable increase in the probability of religious nonaffiliation in the United States. According to one recent study, this probability has risen "from between .06 and .08 in the 1970s and 1980s to almost .16 in 2006" (Schwadel, 2010, p. 318). Although the question of who the "nones" are (cf. Pasquale, 2007) should be approached with care, these groups of unaffiliates and disaffiliates likely include a number of atheists and agnostics.

Most of the research in this area takes a static and synchronic approach, contrasting belief versus unbelief or religiosity versus atheism or agnosticism. We believe that a more dynamic approach is called for, one that views atheism and agnosticism as processes. From the perspective of a dynamic approach, it is also necessary to include apostasy in this discussion, because people who leave their faith are in the process of a developmental change, a migration in the religious field that eventually may lead to exiting the religious domain altogether. Therefore, the three terms *atheist*, *agnostic*, and *apostasy* are interrelated and need to be studied together.

For a deeper understanding of atheists, agnostics, and people who deconvert eventually to atheist and agnostic beliefs, it is imperative to know their motivations, the predictors of their stance toward religion, and the effects of their religious approach on various outcomes. There are a number of particularly interesting questions about outcomes: Are the shifts to atheism, agnosticism, and apostasy associated with an increase or a decrease in psychological well-being? How do these religious positions affect physical health? Do they lead to differences in preferences in the ways of coping with major life stressors? In this chapter, we address these questions, discuss the results from extant research, and suggest directions for future research.

DEFINITIONS AND MODELS FOR UNDERSTANDING ATHEISTS, AGNOSTICS, AND APOSTATES

We begin with a discussion of concepts and models. Some important questions have been raised or reopened on the theoretical level, questions that relate to the conceptualization of religion and spirituality in general.

The Substantive Definition

The most widely accepted definition of atheism is substantive in nature: Atheism is characterized by the denial of the existence of God, whereas agnosticism is characterized by skepticism about, or bracketing of, the existence of God, the construction of worldview and identity without any assumption that there is

DOI: 10.1037/14045-040
APA Handbook of Psychology, Religion, and Spirituality: Vol. 1. Context, Theory, and Research, K. I. Pargament (Editor-in-Chief)
Copyright © 2013 by the American Psychological Association. All rights reserved.

a God (Baggini, 2003; Mackie, 1982). Here atheism and agnosticism are understood as interrelated but nevertheless different constructs. Both signify a turn away from specific images of God, but atheism is more resolute than agnosticism, less open to a religious or spiritual sentiment and quest. From this substantive perspective, atheism and agnosticism can be understood as *beliefs* (Hood et al., 2009; Martin, 2007), although many atheists and agnostics do not see their views as "faith based" (Saeed & Grant, 2004). Nevertheless, atheism and agnosticism are based on (even though refusing or bracketing) a culturally dominant and specifically theistic image of God.

In atheism, however, there is more at work than simply substantive concepts of religion, such as theoretical, philosophical questions of whether God exists; atheism also involves hostility toward organized religion in the name of reason, freedom, and autonomy. Although "popular" atheism certainly draws on the opposition against, and falsification of, theistic beliefs, it is also accompanied by vigorous claims about the irrationality and vanity of all religion and every belief in gods, spirits, or transcendental entities (e.g., Dawkins, 2006; Hitchens, 2007). As C. Taylor (2007) maintained, modern atheism emerged as a consequence of the Enlightenment and the ethical fight for freedom in matters of religion that gained most of its popularity in the 19th century.

Our understanding of atheism and agnosticism is more comprehensive and not confined to the substantive paradigm. It draws on functional and structural perspectives on religion and includes such dimensions as experience, meaning making, ritual, or participation. On the basis of this broader concept of religion, atheism and agnosticism can be understood as disbelief in, hostility toward, or ignorance of a specific established religion. From this point of view, atheism represents the hard core of an antireligious sentiment, whereas agnosticism constitutes a rather mild position of religious abstinence (Hunsberger & Altemeyer, 2006).

The Varieties of Atheisms and Agnosticisms and the Dynamics of Change

The association of *atheism* and *agnosticism* with *unbelief* is also problematic, for it is plausible only in a monoreligious environment or a culture with one dominant and unchanging religion. If, however, understandings of God vary and change, then understandings of atheism will vary and change as well. This means that there will be as many varieties of atheism as there are varieties of belief in God (Hyman, 2007). It follows that in multireligious cultures, we must be even more specific and explicate which God is called into question, what kind of religious experiences or rituals have become empty, and which religious establishment is opposed. And occasionally, atheist or agnostic developments in regard to one religion go hand in hand with an appreciation for another religion or spirituality.

What has been said about the conceptualization of atheism and agnosticism also applies generally to the conceptualization of apostasy. To respond to some terminological uncertainty (cf. the discussion about definitions in Hood et al., 2009, pp. 132–133), we suggest a broad understanding of apostasy as disidentification and eventually disaffiliation from a religious tradition. Thus, the term *apostate* is similar to *deconvert*, as Streib and colleagues (Streib, Hood, Keller, Csöff, & Silver, 2009; Streib & Keller, 2004) have defined it with reference to Barbour (1994), and includes core criteria, such as the loss of religious experiences, intellectual doubt and denial, moral criticism, and disaffiliation from a religious community. From our point of view, all three concepts—atheism, agnosticism, and apostasy—are interrelated. Each construct is dynamic and includes experiential, moral, ritual, and participatory dimensions.

The Beliefs of the Nones

Atheism, agnosticism, and apostasy must not be lumped together with the unspecified group of the unaffiliated or "nones"—who might include nonattending believers and private practitioners who still feel attached to their (former) religious traditions (Albrecht, Cornwall, & Cunningham, 1988; Fuller, 2001; Hunsberger & Altemeyer, 2006). Pasquale (2007) asked unchurched persons from the U.S. Northwest about their worldviews. Although most described themselves as humanists, others viewed themselves as atheistic, secular, skeptical, or scientific. Smaller groups in Pasquale's (2007) study called themselves naturalists, agnostics, or antireligious. All of them had very low scores in personal religiosity and spirituality, but all rated their spirituality as slightly higher than their religiosity. Other studies in the past decade have identified individuals who define themselves "more spiritual than religious" or "spiritual, but not religious," including those who decline in their belief in a theistic God and those who oppose religion and disaffiliate from religious organizations (Hood, 2003; Marler & Hadaway, 2002; Streib, 2008; Zinnbauer et al., 1997). Apparently, the description of being more spiritual than religious can also be used by atheists, agnostics, or apostates, and it may reflect what has been identified as "post-Christian spirituality" (cf. Houtman & Aupers, 2007) or "holistic subjective-life spirituality" (cf. Heelas, Woodhead, Seel, Szerszynski, & Tusting, 2005).

To understand atheism and agnosticism, it is important to realize that the symbolization of experiences of transcendence can occur in terms of vertical or of horizontal transcendence (cf. Hood et al., 2009): Vertical transcendence involves the symbolization of a heaven above with person-like beings; in horizontal transcendence, experiences of transcendence are symbolized as experience of the holy or something of ultimate concern, but *within this world*, such as Mother Earth in green spirituality (Kalton, 2000). The concept of horizontal transcendence helps prevent the misunderstanding of "nones" who self-identify as nontheists but who nevertheless experience transcendence and ultimate concern in this world—which also may be interpreted as "implicit religion" (Bailey, 2001; Schnell, 2003). There is some parallel between horizontal transcendence and what C. Taylor (2007) called "immanent" transcendence. This latter construct refers to those who stand outside of organized religion but nevertheless have a sense of spirituality and of relation to something transcendent or sacred (Fuller, 2001; Heelas et al., 2005; Hood, 2003; Marler & Hadaway, 2002; Streib, 2008; Zinnbauer et al., 1997; Zinnbauer & Pargament, 2005). On the basis of this conceptualization, it is no surprise that among atheists and agnostics, we find versions of spirituality or religiosity that may be primarily associated with horizontal transcendence.

RESEARCH ON ATHEISTS, AGNOSTICS, AND APOSTATES

The sections that follow pay special attention to the psychological issues that are, and should be, discussed in research on atheists, agnostics, and apostates. The discussion is based on summaries of the most important extant research.

Survey Results on Atheists, Agnostics, and Apostates

A number of surveys have documented changes in religious preferences in the United States, including atheism and agnosticism. These include the studies of Fuller (2001), the Pew Religious Landscape Survey (Pew Forum on Religion & Public Life, 2009), Roof (1999), and Sherkat (2001). A few studies have devoted special attention to atheists and agnostics, including Hunsberger and Altemeyer (2006) and the American Religious Identification Survey (ARIS; Kosmin & Keysar, 2009). The documentation of the past and the probability of future religious nonaffiliation and disaffiliation in the United States has been presented by Schwadel (2010) on the basis of General Social Survey (GSS) data. Cross-cultural comparison of religiosity data, including atheist tendencies, can be gleaned from the recent Religion Monitor survey (Bertelsmann Foundation, 2009; Meulemann, 2009). A cross-cultural *and* longitudinal perspective can be generated from the World Value Survey, which Houtman and Aupers (2007) have used to demonstrate a trend toward "post-Christian spirituality" in 14 Western countries. Special attention should also be given to the survey results of the International Social Survey Programme (ISSP) as collected in the third round on religion in 2008. The ARIS and ISSP data are of particular interest for our theme.

Belief in God. The ARIS data allow for an assessment of atheistic and agnostic milieus in the United States (Keysar, 2007; Kosmin & Keysar, 2006, 2009). Results from 2008 identify atheists and agnostics on the basis of a set of items probing beliefs about God: 2.3% agreed that "there is no such thing"; 4.3% said "there is no way to know"; 5.7% were "not sure," and 12.1% believed that "there is a higher power but no personal God."

Similar results in the United States emerged out of the ISSP 2008 survey: 2.8% said "I don't believe in God"; 5.0% agreed to the statement, "I don't know whether there is a God and I don't believe that there is a way to find out"; and 10.3% agreed with "I don't believe in a personal God, but I do believe in a Higher Power of some kind."

Of special interest for our topic are the data that yield a perspective on biographical–diachronic change and cross-cultural comparison at the same time. In the ISSP data, a set of items asked about changes in beliefs in God. Results demonstrated huge cross-cultural differences. Specifically, eastern Germany appears to be the most secular region of the world with only 14.5% permanent believers in God and 65.3% who said that they did not believe in God and never had (cf. also Froese & Pfaff, 2005; Schmidt & Wohlrab-Sahr, 2003; Zuckerman, 2007). On the other end of the spectrum, in Turkey, 96.6% said that they had always believed in God. Similar to Turkey, in the United States, 83.1% indicated that they were permanent believers in God, and 4.2% said they never believed in God.

Survey findings also point to cross-cultural differences in the loss of belief in God. Although only 5.4% in the United States reported a loss of belief in God, between 15% and 20% in Western Germany or other European countries indicated a similar loss of belief.

Disaffiliation and nonaffiliation. A similar picture of cross-cultural diversity emerges from surveys on disaffiliation and nonaffiliation. In the ISSP data (for calculations and some more details, see Streib, in press), disaffiliation can be separated from nonaffiliation by two variables, one asking for present religious affiliation and the other asking in which religion, if any, the respondent has been raised. Here again, East Germans reported the highest proportion of those nonaffiliated (52.1%); people from Great Britain reported the highest disaffiliation rates (31.2%). In the United States, fewer than 50% reported a stable religious affiliation. This, however, reflects a large number of religious switchers (33.1%) rather than a large number of nonaffiliates. Only 16% of people in the United States indicated no religious preference.

Atheist and agnostic worldviews. For a deeper understanding of apostates, we have to go into more detail and estimate the portions of atheists and agnostics in the disaffiliate group. Atheist and agnostic worldviews can be estimated when we include one item from the ISSP questionnaire, which rates the statement: "I don't believe in God" and another item that rates the statement: "I don't know whether there is a God, I don't believe there is a way to find out." On this basis, we calculate rather small portions of atheists and agnostics in the groups of nonaffiliates and disaffiliates in the United States: Only 10% to 15% of nonaffiliates and disaffiliates reported disbelief in God's existence, and only 20% of nonaffiliates and disaffiliates self-identified as agnostics. Interestingly, a fourth of the nonaffiliates and disaffiliates in the United States had no doubt about God's existence. Thus, in contrast to most European countries, nonaffiliates and disaffiliates in the United States include smaller portions of atheists and agnostics than people who are convinced of God's existence.

Taken together (and referring to ISSP results), survey data allow, for the United States, some estimation of the—globally rather low—quantity of nonaffiliates (4.6%) and disaffiliates (11.4%), of nonbelievers in God (4.2% permanent and 5.5% who lost believe in God), and of atheistic (2.9%) and agnostic (4.6%) preferences. These survey findings, however, are limited in some important respects. Most of the surveys relied on one-item measures that did not assess the broader variety of atheistic beliefs (e.g., in evolution, science, rationality, care for humanity) or distinctions between different nonreligious orientations. Furthermore, those scales that have been developed to measure atheism and agnosticism focus on what people do *not* do or believe, the extent of their religious doubts (Altemeyer, 1988; Hunsberger & Altemeyer, 2006), rejection of religious beliefs (Greer & Francis, 1992), or spiritual disengagement (Cole, Hopkins, Tisak, Steel, & Carr, 2008). Only a few attempts have been made to assess atheistic beliefs more comprehensively, such as the Post-Critical Belief Scale (PCBS; Fontaine et al., 2003) and a scale by Gibson (2010). The major limitation of survey data, however, involves the lack of information on psychological factors that are relevant to atheism, agnosticism, and apostasy. For that information, we turn to other research findings.

Psychological Research on Predispositions of Atheist or Agnostic Orientation and Apostasy

Religious socialization. Some research has focused on religious socialization and its relation to apostasy, atheism, and agnosticism. Developmentally, apostasy appears to be more common in adolescence and young adulthood than in other phases of life. This is reflected, for example, in the results of the Pew study (Forum on Religion & Public Life, 2009), which document that for the 44% respondents who do not belong to their childhood faith, most changes of religious affiliation occurred in or before early adulthood. The figures are even more striking for the "secular exiters," those who disaffiliate with no reaffiliations: 79% of the former Catholics and 85% of the former Protestants reported disaffiliation under the age of 25.

Does apostasy indicate a lack of parental emphasis on religion or is it a form of rebellion against religion and a radical demand for autonomy? This is an unanswered question (for a review, see Hood et al., 2009). There is some support for the assumption that apostasy is the result of socialization processes in families where religion is of low importance (Hunsberger et al., 1993; Nelsen, 1981). On the other hand, Altemeyer and Hunsberger's (1997; Hunsberger, 2000) comprehensive study of extreme groups of "amazing apostates" and "amazing believers" who were identified through a major questionnaire study suggests the opposite explanation. "Amazing apostates" came from highly religious backgrounds but rejected their family's religious beliefs and scored very low on a measure of religious orthodoxy; "amazing believers" came from families with little emphasis on religion while growing up but turned to religion and faith as adolescents or adults. In the interviews, many "amazing apostates" confirmed that because of their dedication to truth, they had rejected the religious teachings of their family. Despite strong pressure from their families to hold on to their religious beliefs, "they gave up their faith because they could not make themselves believe what they had been taught" (Hunsberger & Altemeyer, 2006, p. 42).

In their study of atheists in the San Francisco Bay area, Hunsberger and Altemeyer (2006) found that more than 70% of the atheists said they believed in God before they found the teachings of their religion "unbelievable" and became atheists. Similarly, in the Bielefeld-Based Cross-Cultural Study on Deconversion (Streib et al., 2009), a typology of four types of deconverts could be identified on the basis of the analysis of narrative interviews: "pursuit of autonomy" (long-term gradual process of stepping away from the previous religious environment), "debarred from paradise" (deconversion from a religious tradition, mostly high-tension organizations, which was once chosen because it was supposed to solve all problems), "finding a new frame of reference" (leaving one's childhood religious tradition in search of a more structured religious environment), and "lifelong quests—late revisions" (leaving a religious environment because it does not sufficiently meet religious needs and expectations). The "pursuit of autonomy" type is of special interest here because it reflects a process of deconversion from the individual's established religious milieu. It is a search for individuation and the critical development of new perspectives that mostly leads to secular exits. Secular exiters make up 30% of the deconverts, another 30% leave organized religion for privatized or heretical forms of religiosity, and the rest remain within some kind of organized religion.

Moving beyond issues associated with religious upbringing, the relationship between children and their parents in general may be of relevance to atheism, agnosticism, and apostasy. In their psychohistorical studies of the impact of "defective fathering," Koster (1989) and Vitz (2000) argued that many famous atheists (like Darwin, Nietzsche, or Freud) suffered in their childhoods under the demands of their dominant and bigoted fathers who failed to express feelings of love and esteem to their sons. The sons became apathetic, unhappy, and melancholic and tried to flee from their family situations. In later life, they rebelled against the demanding beliefs of their fathers, calling into question the complete worldview in which they were raised. The denial of their own roots, however, caused psychopathological symptoms, including depression or self-hatred, so that their fight for autonomy resulted in what Lepp (1963) called a "neurotic denial of God."

Hood et al. (2009) have criticized the theories of neurotic atheism because of their exclusive focus on males and their fathers and the lack of broader empirical support. More solid empirical data come from research on religion and attachment (Granqvist & Kirkpatrick, 2008; for an overview, see Chapter 7 in this volume), which shows that in religious families, closer parent–child attachments in childhood correspond with closer attachment to God and more positive images of God in adulthood. Secure parent–child attachments can thus lead to more stable religiosity, whereas distant or avoidant relationships between parent and child increase the likelihood of sudden conversions and religious switching or of secular exits (Granqvist & Hagekull, 2003; Granqvist & Kirkpatrick, 2004; Kirkpatrick, 1997, 1998).

Motives and developmental factors. A body of research has focused on motives and biographical factors associated with the development of atheism, agnosticism, and apostasy. This research includes studies about religious doubts (Brinkerhoff & Mackie, 1993; Hunsberger & Altemeyer, 2006) and personal experiences of disappointment with religious professionals, communities, or God or anger against God (Exline, 2002; Exline & Rose, 2005).

In a comprehensive content analysis of 1,226 statements that atheistic and agnostic Internet users had posted on a Catholic webpage (http://www.ohne-gott.de; "without God"), Murken (2008) identified five clusters of statements that articulated doubts, disappointments, and frustrations with respect to religious beliefs and institutions: (a) an opposition against Christianity because of faults of the Catholic Church (e.g., the crusades or witch-hunting, clergy sexual abuse) and its rigid sexual morals regarding contraception, premarital sex, and homosexuality; (b) experiences of religious hurt and disappointment, in particular the feeling of being abandoned by God in times of burden and loss; (c) negative and critical images of God (e.g., the feeling of incapacity to meet God's demands and of being supervised and punished by God); (d) the question of theodicy (if God is just, loving, and all-powerful, why does he allow evil and suffering to exist?); and (e) the yearning for God and for faith to find meaning and comfort. These factors may support the emergence of skepticism against religious beliefs, groups, and institutions and, as a consequence, raise serious questions about religion in general.

In particular, experiences of personal suffering can throw an individual's fundamental system of religious beliefs into question, producing religious and spiritual struggles marked by feelings of abandonment and punishment by God as well as questions about whether God really exists and is truly loving and almighty (Pargament et al., 1998; Pargament, Koenig & Perez, 2000; see Chapter 25 in this volume). Research shows that such experiences as severe illness; the loss of a loved person; physical, emotional, and sexual abuse; and other traumata can provoke spiritual struggle that can transform former beliefs and lead to spiritual disengagement, apostasy, and atheism or agnosticism but potentially to spiritual growth, too (Pargament, 2007). Pargament (2007) and Pargament and Mahoney (2005) argued that the experience of a desecration, the perception that things that have been perceived as sacred (e.g., my body, my integrity, my beliefs, my relationships) have been violated, is particularly likely to shake the individual to the core. In a similar way, Novotni and Petersen (2001) described "emotional atheism" as the result of a process of repression and emotional distancing from God. They view the conflict between the need to blame God in difficult situations and the recognition that God must not be blamed as a trigger for the onset of emotional distancing. Thus, "emotional atheism" emerges from the stepwise loss of an unsatisfying faith. In short, experiences of spiritual struggles (Exline & Rose, 2005; McConnell, Pargament, Ellison, & Flannelly, 2006; Pargament, 2007) represent important developmental factors that may generate atheism or agnosticism.

Predictors of (dis)belief in God. Some scholars have tried to identify sociodemographic predictors of apostasy (Hadaway, 1989) and atheism or agnosticism (Sherkat, 2008). Sherkat (2008) used data from the 1988–2000 GSS to analyze the effects of sociodemographic variables on (dis)belief in God as measured by the single GSS item Belief in God. Sherkat found that (dis)belief was predicted by being younger, male, White, and more highly educated. These results are in line with findings that the elderly (cf. Hout & Fischer, 2002), women (cf. Francis, 1997), and Blacks (cf. Batson, Schoenrade, & Ventis, 1993) display higher levels of religiosity. The effect of age has been explained in terms of a rebellion against established authorities and beliefs during younger phases of life or in terms of generational and cohort effects (Hood et al., 2009; Levenson, Aldwin, & D'Mello, 2005; see Chapter 29 in this volume). The gender difference has been explained by the structural location of men and women in society (working vs. staying at home and caring for the children, including religious instruction); by gender roles and personality factors (Francis, 1997); and recently, as a consequence of lower risk aversion (calling religion into question) among men (Collett & Lizardo, 2009; Miller & Hoffmann, 1995). The effects of gender and race have been understood in terms of the comfort and self-esteem religion offers to members of socially disadvantaged groups (Maselko et al., 2007; R. J. Taylor, Chatters, & Levin, 2004; see Chapter 30 in this volume). In addition, familial factors play a role because those who have never been married and have no children are more likely to have an atheistic orientation (Sherkat, 2008). This result coincides with findings that atheists and agnostics report slightly higher levels of introversion (Bainbridge, 2005) and more feelings of loneliness (Lauder, Mummery, & Sharkey, 2006) in comparison with religious persons. Living in rural areas and in the southern states (the Bible Belt) of the United States—where being nonreligious can even appear to be "deviant" (Heiner, 1992)—decreases the likelihood of being atheist. Finally, religious affiliation has predictive power, even after controlling for the effects of other sociodemographic factors. Compared with mainline Protestants or Jews, belonging to a sect or to the Catholic Church decreases the probability of atheism. Furthermore, being unaffiliated is associated with a considerable higher tendency toward atheism (Sherkat, 2008).

Psychological Correlates of Atheism, Agnosticism, and Apostasy

Education and intelligence. The link between higher education and atheism or agnosticism is a classic finding within the psychology of religion (Beit-Hallahmi, 2007; Hood et al., 2009): In 1916 and 1934, Leuba (an agnostic himself) found that eminent scientists (mathematicians, physicists, biologists) showed higher rates of unbelief in God and immortality (Leuba, 1916, 1934). Some 80 years after Leuba's first study, Larson and Witham (1998) tried to replicate these findings. They surveyed members of the U.S. National Academy of Sciences and found that this generation of scientists had become even more strongly atheistic: Whereas 53% (1916) and 68% (1934) of the respondents in Leuba's studies said that they did not believe in any God and 25% (1916) and 53% (1936) reported no personal belief in immortality, in the study by Larson and Witham (1998), 72% reported no personal belief in God and 77% no belief in immortality. The beliefs of U.S. scientists appear to differ strongly from those of the U.S. public.

Such findings have led some researchers to hypothesize that higher intelligence leads to an atheistic orientation. For instance, Nyborg and colleagues (Nyborg, 2009; Lynn, Harvey, & Nyborg, 2009) argued that mean IQ scores show a declining line, with atheists having the highest IQ scores, dogmatic persons the lowest IQ scores, and agnostics and liberals in the middle, and a similar line from more atheistic nations to more religious countries because intelligence leads toward a worldview that best fits cognitive complexity and brain efficiency. Kanazawa (2009, 2010) postulated an evolutionary principle that more intelligent individuals are more likely to acquire and espouse novel values, including atheism, liberalism, and—for men—sexual exclusivity and monogamy. Kanazawa claimed to have found a number of results supporting this hypothesis; however, the theories of Nyborg and Kanazawa about intelligence and atheism neglect a number of factors. The most important is that a substantial number of well-educated, highly intelligent people are still religious. Also, it is not clear why an atheistic worldview is necessarily more cognitively complex than a theological system. Furthermore, Kanazawa's evolutionary argument that more intelligent persons tend toward atheism, liberalism, and sexual exclusivity is plausible only if it is assumed that evolution leads inevitably toward atheism. Finally, most of the findings to which Nyborg, Kanazawa, and their colleagues referred are based on measures of school achievement and education rather than intelligence. Although education, school achievement, and intelligence are highly correlated, they are not identical. As an alternative to evolutionary explanations, the tendency of higher education and better school achievement to be associated with atheism could be understood in terms of a particular "social inheritance" within better educated families and institutions of higher education, which transmit a scientific worldview challenging religious beliefs. The findings could then be interpreted as an indication that it is difficult and challenging to integrate a religious worldview and scientific education.

Personality factors and values. Some reviews and meta-analyses (Piedmont, 2005; Saroglou 2002, 2010; Saroglou, Delpierre, & Dernelle, 2004) are relevant to the personality and value characteristics of less religious and nondenominational people. These studies, however, have not focused on atheists or agnostics explicitly. It would be inappropriate to conclude that atheists and agnostics are less conscientious and less agreeable (Saroglou, 2010) because high scores on several religiosity measures are significantly correlated with conscientiousness and agreeableness. What is needed are studies that compare the personalities of atheists, agnostics, and apostates to those of religious people.

In the Bielefeld-Based Cross-Cultural Study of Deconversion (Streib et al., 2009), the NEO Five-Factor Inventory personality measure (Costa & McCrae, 1985), the Ryff Scale on Psychological Well-Being and Growth (Ryff & Singer, 1996), the Religious Fundamentalism Scale (Altemeyer & Hunsberger, 1992), and the Right-Wing Authoritarianism Scale (RWA; Altemeyer, 1981) were included for both members of religious communities and for deconverts in the United States and in Germany. Across both cultures, deconverts scored significantly higher on openness to experience and, interestingly, somewhat higher on neuroticism. Compared with members of religious communities, deconverts also manifested considerably lower scores on religious fundamentalism and RWA. Finally, deconverts reported a significantly higher sense of personal growth and autonomy (Ryff Scale) than members of religious traditions.

In their comprehensive study of U.S. and Canadian atheists, Hunsberger and Altemeyer (2006) found similar results. Atheists indicated less prejudice against ethnic minorities and homosexuals than did highly religious people. In general, compared with the highly religious group, atheists were found to be less dogmatic and zealous in their worldviews, with little need to proselytize, although they regarded religious fundamentalists as enemies. Hunsberger and Altemeyer attributed the lower dogmatism and zealotry of atheists to their lower scores on RWA. Comparing atheists and agnostics, Hunsberger and Altemeyer found agnostics to be even less dogmatic and zealous than atheists, although they had slightly higher levels of prejudice and RWA. Maybe this result is due to the more cohesive and resolved worldview of the atheists.

Similarly, according to the findings of Baker and Smith (2009), atheists are more strongly opposed to religious teachings and the public presence of the church than are agnostics. Unchurched believers were found to be as opposed to religion in the public sphere as atheists, but they displayed higher levels of spirituality and personal religiosity than atheists or agnostics. Findings from both the United States and the United Kingdom illustrate that atheists, agnostics, and unchurched believers hold patterns of individualistic values and very liberal political stances concerning abortion, divorce, drug use, euthanasia, stem cell research, or gay marriage (Baker & Smith, 2009; Farias & Lalljee, 2008).

Research on values in Belgium using the PCBS gives further insight into the dynamics of atheism or agnosticism and value orientations. The scale distinguishes between an exclusion and an inclusion of transcendence in combination with a distinction between a literal and a symbolic understanding of these different beliefs (Fontaine et al., 2003; see also Wulff, 1997). Hence, the PCBS assesses two alternative atheistic orientations, the literal *external critique* (denial of transcendence because the stories told in sacred scriptures cannot be literally true) and the symbolic *relativism* (denial of transcendence while accepting an existential truth of sacred scriptures as an expression of human wisdom). Although nonreligious orientations in general were found to correlate with self-enhancing values, such as hedonism or stimulation, external critique was associated with conservative values, such as security and power, and relativism showed significant associations with universalism and benevolence (Fontaine et al., 2005)—values that indicate an openness to change (Schwartz, 1992, 1994). Other findings with the PCBS elaborate on these results: External critique is positively correlated with more cultural conservatism (Duriez, 2003), more racism (even after controlling for RWA; Duriez, 2004), and lower agreement with moral attitudes (Duriez & Soenens, 2006). Interestingly then, it appears to be the case that the correlates of a literal understanding of atheism resemble those of literal religious beliefs. Research with the PCBS makes the crucial point that to understand value orientations, we must consider not only whether someone is religious or atheist but also the way in which religious or atheistic contents are processed.

Although there seem to be at least some characteristic patterns of atheists' and agnostics' personality and value orientations, we conclude that the existing data do not allow causal interpretations: Whether an agnostic or atheistic position is the result of more openness and more tolerant and self-enhancing values, or whether an agnostic or atheist worldview leads to such values, is answerable only through future longitudinal studies.

ATHEISM, AGNOSTICISM, AND APOSTASY, AND THEIR RELATION TO HEALTH AND WELL-BEING

A large body of research has demonstrated relationships between religion, coping, health, and well-being. On the psychological level, many findings illustrate associations between higher religiosity and less depression (see Smith, McCullough, & Poll, 2003; see also Volume 2, Chapter 12, this handbook), less addiction (Geppert, Bogenschutz, & Miller, 2007; see also Volume 2, Chapter 15, this handbook), higher life satisfaction and well-being (Hackney & Sanders, 2003), and differential effects of religious coping (Ano & Vasconcelles, 2005; Pargament, 1997; see also Chapter 19 in this volume). Higher religiosity has been related to better physical health, perhaps as a result of lifestyle factors and psychoneuroimmunological processes (Chida, Steptoe, & Powell, 2009; Koenig, McCullough, & Larson, 2001; see also Chapter 11, this volume and Volume 2, Chapter 14, this handbook). It could be tempting to reason that the converse would be true—that is, atheism and agnosticism would be associated with poorer health.

Low scores on religious measures should not be equated with atheism, agnosticism, or apostasy. Indexes of organizational and individual religiosity (e.g., church attendance, prayer, intrinsic and extrinsic orientation, religious affiliation) are poor indictors of atheism or agnosticism. According to Hall, Koenig, and Meador (2008), these measures of religiousness can be understood as reverse-scored indexes of "secularism." Doubts persist, however, whether the concept of secularism fully captures the characteristics of atheism, agnosticism, and apostasy as described in this chapter. Thus, although there is strong evidence for an overall positive correlation between religiosity and mental and physical health, this does not automatically imply that lower religiosity or secularism is identical with high atheism or apostasy. Neither does it indicate that atheism, agnosticism, and apostasy are associated with poorer health, coping and well-being. It therefore would be helpful and challenging to study mental health and well-being of atheists and agnostics in their own right with comprehensive measures of these dynamic processes (Hwang, Hammer, & Cragun, 2009; Whitley, 2010).

Comparative research on atheists, agnostics, apostates, and religious people might help clarify those studies that do not support the assumption that religiosity is generally associated with better health and well-being. In this vein, Baker and Cruickshank (2009) compared the depressive symptoms of atheists, agnostics, and religious groups and found that their health scores did not differ. Similarly, O'Connell and Skevington (2009) found no differences between atheists, agnostics, and religious persons with respect to their quality of life except between their scores on spiritual well-being.
Also, although apostasy is often accompanied by

emotional suffering, the process of becoming an apostate does not necessarily end in a "neurotic denial of God." Recall too that deconverts in the United States reported higher scores on the autonomy and personal growth subscales than the members in religious organizations (Streib et al., 2009). Taken together, firm conclusions about the relationships between health and atheism, agnosticism, or apostasy cannot yet be drawn (Stefanek, McDonald, & Hess, 2005).

Some studies in which atheists and agnostics have been explicitly identified have detected a U-shaped relationship in which the most and least religious groups report fewer symptoms of mental illness or better well-being scores than the moderately religious group (Donahue, 1985; Riley, Best, & Charlton, 2005; Shaver, Lenauer, & Sadd, 1980). These findings are in line with the classical assumption of William James (1902/1985) that the certitude of an individual's beliefs might be of more importance for his or her well-being than specific belief contents. It seems that these curvilinear effects are easier to find in more secular contexts than the United States, such as the United Kingdom (Baker & Cruickshank, 2009; Riley, Best, & Charlton, 2005) or Germany (Klein, 2010; Zwingmann et al., 2006) where religious and existential beliefs have become increasingly personalized, detached, and heterogeneous (Jagodzinski & Dobbelaere, 1995). Conversely, clear associations between religion and mental health seem to be more difficult to detect in these more secularized contexts. Additionally, research in more secular European contexts shows that scales for the study of religious coping from the United States demonstrate effects primarily within specific, highly religious subsamples (Pieper, 2004); however, other forms of existential or spiritual coping are more common and perhaps more predictive of health-related outcomes in European populations, including the Netherlands (van Uden, Pieper, & Alma, 2004) and Sweden (Ahmadi, 2006).

To make sense of this complex pattern of findings, it may be helpful to recognize that each study of the religion–health nexus offers insights only into one particular sociocultural context. The results of each study might therefore best be understood as one part of a U-curve describing the complete relation between (non)religious orientation and mental health. Given the differences in religiosity levels between the United States and the more secular parts of Europe—for instance, although 62% of the U.S. population can be rated as highly religious, only 19% of the U.K. population or 18% of the German population can be labeled as highly religious (Bertelsmann Foundation, 2009; Huber & Klein, 2007)—U.S. samples are likely to include more religious persons and less likely to include those who are agnostics or atheists. Such samples, however, capture the middle to the right part of the U-curve, and findings from these studies would typically reveal a positive linear relationship between religion and health or well-being (see Figure 40.1).

Samples from more secular contexts, however, are more likely to cover the middle and the left part of the U-curve, including not only some religious persons, but also a substantial number of doubting, agnostic, and atheistic persons. Hence, such samples might yield contradictory findings, including negative relationships between religion and health and well-being. The curvilinear character of relationships between religion and health may emerge only if the full range of beliefs and nonbeliefs is represented in the research. Of course, this explanation is only hypothetical, but it highlights the need for cross-cultural studies of the religion–health nexus in ways that might reveal the interactions among the sample, the larger cultural context, and the local salience of diverse beliefs.

Although the relations between atheistic and agnostic orientations and well-being have not been studied in detail yet, a growing number of reports from physicians, therapists, and nurses both from the United States (Josephson & Peteet, 2007; Moadel et al., 1999; Peteet, 2001) and Europe (O'Connell & Skevington, 2005) indicate that nonreligious patients in hospitals and psychotherapy express as much need as religious people to talk about existential issues, such as the meaning of life. We would caution against interpreting this interest in existential issues per se as a "spiritual" interest (as some authors do): Such an inflationary usage might be terminologically misleading because it camouflages existing differences between exclusively immanent existential issues and "spiritual"

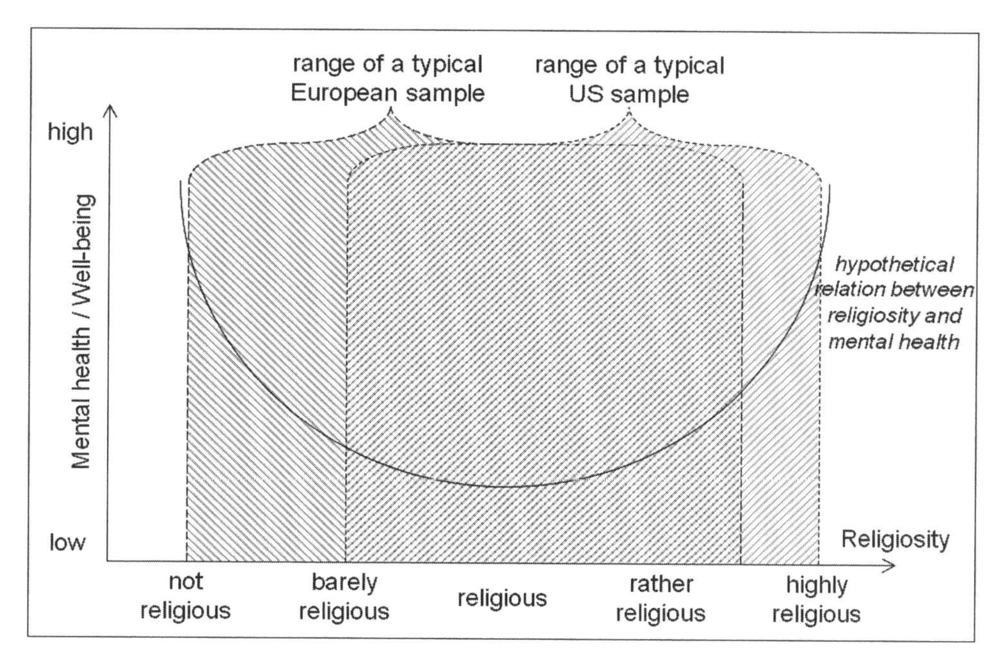

FIGURE 40.1. Hypothetical U-shaped relation between religiosity, mental health, and well-being, and sampling effects resulting from cultural context.

interests—for example, there are patients with completely secular, neither religious nor spiritual interests, too (Koenig, 2008; Pargament, 1999). It nevertheless should be clear that atheists, agnostics, and apostates deserve attention as substantial groups in their own right and should be treated with respect and appreciation for their distinctive beliefs (D'Andrea & Sprenger, 2007; Saeed & Grant, 2004).

OUTLOOK ON FUTURE RESEARCH

We conclude with four suggestions for future research. First, with some exceptions, only a few studies have compared atheists, agnostics, and apostates with religious people in terms of classical psychological constructs such as personality factors, coping, well-being, and health. Thus, we need not only studies that focus specifically on atheists and agnostics but also studies of classical psychological constructs among actively committed atheists using measures that delve more deeply and comprehensively into atheists' and agnostics' worldviews. Second, longitudinal studies of atheism, agnosticism, and apostasy are also needed to shed light on the dynamic, evolving character of these processes. Third, cross-cultural comparisons of religious, atheistic, and agnostic milieus in the United States and other cultures around the globe are needed to clarify the religion–health nexus. Tests of the hypothesis of a cross-culturally U-shaped relation between (non)religiousness and health might be particularly illuminating. Finally, it is important to pay special attention to the "spiritual" self-identification of some atheists, agnostics, and apostates: Echoing Hood et al.'s (2009) recommendation, we encourage closer investigations of the reasons why a considerable portion of atheists and agnostics self-identify as "spiritual, but not religious." Perhaps this group understands "spirituality" as a process of searching for and finding meaning—and perhaps a sense of the sacred—in domains that are not traditionally "religious," such as the ecological movement and the concern for the preservation of Mother Earth.

References

Ahmadi, F. (2006). *Culture, religion and spirituality in coping: The example of cancer patients in Sweden.* Uppsala, Sweden: Acta Universitatis Upsaliensis.

Albrecht, S. L., Cornwall, M., & Cunningham, P. H. (1988). Religious leave-taking. In D. G. Bromley (Ed.), *Falling from the faith* (pp. 62–80). Newbury Park, CA: Sage.

Altemeyer, B. (1981). *Right-wing authoritarianism.* Winnipeg, Manitoba, Canada: University of Manitoba Press.

Altemeyer, B. (1988). *Enemies of freedom: Understanding right-wing authoritarianism.* San Francisco, CA: Jossey-Bass.

Altemeyer, B., & Hunsberger, B. (1992). Authoritarianism, religious fundamentalism, quest and prejudice. *The International Journal for the Psychology of Religion, 2,* 113–133. doi:10.1207/s15327582ijpr0202_5

Altemeyer, B., & Hunsberger, B. (1997). *Amazing conversions. Why some turn to faith and others abandon religion.* New York, NY: Prometheus Books.

Ano, G. G., & Vasconcelles, E. B. (2005). Religious coping and psychological adjustment to stress: A meta-analysis. *Journal of Clinical Psychology, 61,* 461–480. doi:10.1002/jclp.20049

Baggini, J. (2003). *Atheism: A very short introduction.* Oxford, England: Oxford University Press.

Bailey, E. (2001). *Implicit religion in contemporary society.* Leuven, Belgium: Peeters.

Bainbridge, W. S. (2005). Atheism. *Interdisciplinary Journal of Research on Religion, 1,* 1–26.

Baker, J. O., & Smith, B. (2009). None too simple: Examining issues of religious nonbelief and nonbelonging in the United States. *Journal for the Scientific Study of Religion, 48,* 719–733. doi:10.1111/j.1468-5906.2009.01475.x

Baker, P., & Cruickshank, J. (2009). I am happy in my faith: The influence of religious affiliation, saliency, and practice on depressive symptoms and treatment preference. *Mental Health, Religion, and Culture, 12,* 339–357. doi:10.1080/13674670902725108

Barbour, J. D. (1994). *Versions of deconversion. Autobiography and the loss of faith.* Charlottesville: University Press of Virginia.

Batson, C. D., Schoenrade, P., & Ventis, W. L. (1993). *Religion and the individual: A social-psychological perspective.* New York, NY: Oxford University Press.

Beit-Hallahmi, B. (2007). Atheists: A psychological profile. In M. Martin (Ed.), *The Cambridge companion to atheism* (pp. 300–318). New York, NY: Cambridge University Press. doi:10.1017/CCOL0521842700.019

Bertelsmann Foundation. (Ed.). (2009). *What the world believes: Analysis and commentary on the Religion Monitor 2008.* Gütersloh, Germany: Verlag Bertelsmann Stiftung.

Brinkerhoff, M. B., & Mackie, M. M. (1993). Casting off the bounds of organized religion: A religious-careers approach to the study of apostasy. *Review of Religious Research, 34,* 235–258. doi:10.2307/3700597

Chida, Y., Steptoe, A., & Powell, L. H. (2009). Religiosity/spirituality and mortality. *Psychotherapy and Psychosomatics, 78,* 81–90. doi:10.1159/000190791

Cole, B. S., Hopkins, C. M., Tisak, J., Steel, J. L., & Carr, B. I. (2008). Assessing spiritual growth and spiritual decline following a diagnosis of cancer: Reliability and validity of the Spiritual Transformation Scale. *Psycho-Oncology, 17,* 112–121. doi:10.1002/pon.1207

Collett, J. L., & Lizardo, O. (2009). A power-control theory of gender and religiosity. *Journal for the Scientific Study of Religion, 48,* 213–231. doi:10.1111/j.1468-5906.2009.01441.x

Costa, P. T., & McCrae, R. R. (1985). *Revised NEO Personality Inventory (NEO PI–R) and NEO Five-Factor Inventory (NEO–FFI): Professional manual.* Odessa, Ukraine: Psychological Assessment Resources.

D'Andrea, L., & Sprenger, J. (2007). Atheism and nonspirituality as diversity issues in counseling. *Counseling and Values, 51,* 149–158. doi:10.1002/j.2161-007X.2007.tb00072.x

Dawkins, R. (2006). *The God delusion.* Boston, MA: Houghton Mifflin.

Donahue, M. J. (1985). Intrinsic and extrinsic religiousness: Review and meta-analysis. *Journal of Personality and Social Psychology, 48,* 400–419. doi:10.1037/0022-3514.48.2.400

Duriez, B. (2003). Religiosity and conservatism revisited: Relating a new religiosity measure to the two main conservative political ideologies. *Psychological Reports, 92,* 533–539. doi:10.2466/pr0.2003.92.2.533

Duriez, B. (2004). A research note on the relation between religiosity and racism: The importance of the way in which religious contents are being processed. *The International Journal for the Psychology of Religion, 14,* 177–191. doi:10.1207/s15327582ijpr1403_3

Duriez, B., & Soenens, B. (2006). Religiosity, moral attitudes and moral competence: A critical investigation of the religiosity–morality relation. *International Journal of Behavioral Development, 30,* 76–83. doi:10.1177/0165025406062127

Exline, J. J. (2002). Stumbling blocks on the religious road: Fractured relationships, nagging vices, and the inner struggle to believe. *Psychological Inquiry, 13,* 182–189. doi:10.1207/S15327965PLI1303_03

Exline, J. J., & Rose, E. (2005). Religious and spiritual struggles. In R. F. Paloutzian & C. L. Park (Eds.), *Handbook of the psychology of religion and spirituality* (pp. 315–330). New York, NY: Guilford Press.

Farias, M., & Lalljee, M. (2008). Holistic individualism in the age of Aquarius: Measuring individualism/collectivism in New Age, Catholic, and atheist/agnostic groups. *Journal for the Scientific Study of Religion, 47,* 277–289. doi:10.1111/j.1468-5906.2008.00407.x

Fontaine, J. R. J., Duriez, B., Luyten, P., Corveleyn, J., & Hutsebaut, D. (2005). Consequences of a multidimensional approach to religion for the relationship between religiosity and value priorities. *The International Journal for the Psychology of Religion, 15,* 123–143. doi:10.1207/s15327582ijpr1502_2

Fontaine, J. R. J., Duriez, B., Luyten, P., & Hutsebaut, D. (2003). The internal structure of the Post-Critical Belief Scale. *Personality and Individual Differences, 35*, 501–518. doi:10.1016/S0191-8869(02)00213-1

Francis, L. J. (1997). The psychology of gender differences in religion: A review of empirical research. *Religion, 27*, 81–96. doi:10.1006/reli.1996.0066

Froese, P., & Pfaff, S. (2005). Explaining a religious anomaly: A historical analysis of secularization in Eastern Germany. *Journal for the Scientific Study of Religion, 44*, 397–422. doi:10.1111/j.1468-5906.2005.00294.x

Fuller, R. C. (2001). *Spiritual, but not religious: Understanding unchurched America*. Oxford, England; New York, NY: Oxford University Press. doi:10.1093/0195146808.001.0001

Geppert, C., Bogenschutz, M. P., & Miller, W. R. (2007). Development of a bibliography on religion, spirituality and addictions. *Drug and Alcohol Review, 26*, 389–395. doi:10.1080/09595230701373826

Gibson, N. J. S. (2010, October). *Dimensions and types of non-religiosity: Scale development in progress*. Paper presented at the Annual Meeting of the Society for the Scientific Study of Religion and the Religious Research Association, Baltimore, MD.

Granqvist, P., & Hagekull, B. (2003). Longitudinal predictions of religious change in adolescence: Contributions from the interaction of attachment and relationship status. *Journal of Social and Personal Relationships, 20*, 793–817. doi:10.1177/0265407503206005

Granqvist, P., & Kirkpatrick, L. A. (2004). Religious conversion and perceived childhood attachment: A meta-analysis. *The International Journal for the Psychology of Religion, 14*, 223–250. doi:10.1207/s15327582ijpr1404_1

Granqvist, P., & Kirkpatrick, L. A. (2008). Attachment and religious representations and behavior. In J. Cassidy & P. R. Shaver (Eds.), *Handbook of attachment: Theory, research, and clinical applications* (2nd ed., pp. 906–933). New York, NY: Guilford Press.

Greer, J. E., & Francis, L. J. (1992). Measuring rejection of Christianity among 14–16-year-old adolescents in Catholic and Protestant schools in Northern-Ireland. *Personality and Individual Differences, 13*, 1345–1348. doi:10.1016/0191-8869(92)90178-R

Hackney, C. H., & Sanders, G. S. (2003). Religiosity and mental health: A meta-analysis of recent studies. *Journal for the Scientific Study of Religion, 42*, 43–55. doi:10.1111/1468-5906.t01-1-00160

Hadaway, C. K. (1989). Identifying American apostates: A cluster analysis. *Journal for the Scientific Study of Religion, 28*, 201–215. doi:10.2307/1387059

Hall, D. E., Koenig, H. G., & Meador, K. G. (2008). Hitting the target: Why existing measures of "religiousness" are really reverse-scored measures of "secularism." *Explore: The Journal of Science and Healing, 4*, 368–373. doi:10.1016/j.explore.2008.08.002

Heelas, P., Woodhead, L., Seel, B., Szerszynski, B., & Tusting, K. (2005). *The spiritual revolution: Why religion is giving way to spirituality*. Oxford, England: Blackwell.

Heiner, R. (1992). Evangelical heathens: The deviant status of freethinkers in Southland. *Deviant Behavior, 13*, 1–20. doi:10.1080/01639625.1992.9967895

Hitchens, C. (2007). *God is not great: How religion poisons everything*. New York, NY: Twelve.

Hood, R. W. (2003). Spirituality and religion. In A. L. Greil & D. G. Bromley (Eds.), *Religion: Critical approaches to drawing boundaries between sacred and secular* (pp. 241–264). Amsterdam, the Netherlands: Elsevier. doi:10.1016/S1061-5210(03)10014-X

Hood, R. W., Hill, P. C., & Spilka, B. (2009). *The psychology of religion: An empirical approach* (4th ed.). New York, NY: Guilford Press.

Hout, M., & Fischer, C. S. (2002). Why more Americans have no religious preference: Politics and generations. *American Sociological Review, 67*, 165–190. doi:10.2307/3088891

Houtman, D., & Aupers, S. (2007). The spiritual turn and the decline of tradition: The spread of post-Christian spirituality in 14 Western countries, 1981–2000. *Journal for the Scientific Study of Religion, 46*, 305–320. doi:10.1111/j.1468-5906.2007.00360.x

Huber, S., & Klein, C. (2007). *Kurzbericht zu einzelnen Ergebnissen der internationalen Durchführung des Religionsmonitors der Bertelsmann-Stiftung* [Brief report on selected findings of the international Religion Monitor survey of the Bertelsmann Foundation]. Retrieved from http://www.bertelsmann-stiftung.de

Hunsberger, B. (2000). Swimming against the current: Exceptional cases of apostates and converts. In L. J. Francis & Y. J. Katz (Eds.), *Joining and leaving religion: Research perspectives* (pp. 233–248). Leominster, England: Gracewing.

Hunsberger, B., & Altemeyer, B. (2006). *Atheists: A groundbreaking study of America's nonbelievers*. Amherst, NY: Prometheus Books.

Hunsberger, B., McKenzie, B., Pancer, S. M., & Pratt, M. W. (1993). Religious doubt: A social psychological analysis. *Research in the Social Scientific Study of Religion, 5*, 27–51.

Hwang, K., Hammer, J. H., & Cragun, R. T. (2009). Extending religion-health research to secular minorities: Issues and concerns. *Journal of Religion and Health*. Online first: DOI 10.1007/s10943-009–9296-0

Hyman, G. (2007). Atheism in modern history. In M. Martin (Ed.), *The Cambridge companion to atheism* (pp. 27–46). New York, NY: Cambridge University Press. doi:10.1017/CCOL0521842700.003

Jagodzinski, W., & Dobbelaere, K. (1995). Secularization and church religiosity. In J. W. van Deth & E. Scarbrough (Eds.), *The impact of values* (pp. 76–119). Oxford, England: Oxford University Press.

James, W. (1985). *The varieties of religious experience: A study in human nature*. Cambridge, MA: Harvard University Press. (Original work published 1902)

Josephson, A. M., & Peteet, J. R. (2007). Talking with patients about spirituality and worldview: Practical interviewing techniques and strategies. *Psychiatric Clinics of North America, 30*, 181–197. doi:10.1016/j.psc.2007.01.005

Kalton, M. C. (2000). Green spirituality: Horizontal transcendence. In P. Young-Eisendrath & M. E. Miller (Eds.), *The psychology of mature spirituality: Integrity, wisdom, transcendence* (pp. 187–200). London, England: Routledge.

Kanazawa, S. (2009). IQ and the values of nations. *Journal of Biosocial Science, 41*, 537–556. doi:10.1017/S0021932009003368

Kanazawa, S. (2010). Why liberals and atheists are more intelligent. *Social Psychology Quarterly, 73*, 33–57.

Keysar, A. (2007). Who are America's atheists and agnostics? In B. A. Kosmin & A. Keysar (Eds.), *Secularism and secularity. Contemporary international perspectives* (pp. 33–39). Hartford, CT: Institute for the Study of Secularism in Society and Culture, Trinity College.

Kirkpatrick, L. A. (1997). A longitudinal study of changes in religious belief and behavior as a function of individual differences in adult attachment style. *Journal for the Scientific Study of Religion, 36*, 207–217. doi:10.2307/1387553

Kirkpatrick, L. A. (1998). God as a substitute attachment figure: A longitudinal study of adult attachment style and religious change in college students. *Personality and Social Psychology Bulletin, 24*, 961–973. doi:10.1177/0146167298249004

Klein, C. (2010, October). *Beyond the religion-spirituality antagonism: Measuring interest in existential questions.* Paper presented at the Annual Meeting of the Society for the Scientific Study of Religion and the Religious Research Association, Baltimore, MD.

Koenig, H. G. (2008). Concerns about measuring "spirituality" in research. *Journal of Nervous and Mental Disease, 196*, 349–355. doi:10.1097/NMD.0b013e31816ff796

Koenig, H. G., McCullough, M. E., & Larson, D. B. (2001). *Handbook of religion and health*. New York, NY: Oxford University Press. doi:10.1093/acprof:oso/9780195118667.001.0001

Kosmin, B. A., & Keysar, A. (2006). *Religion in a free market: Religious and non-religious Americans*. Ithaca, NY: Paramount.

Kosmin, B. A., & Keysar, A. (Eds.). (2007). *Secularism and secularity: Contemporary international perspectives*. Hartford, CT: Institute for the Study of Secularism in Society and Culture.

Kosmin, B. A., & Keysar, A. (2009). *American Religious Identification Survey (ARIS 2008)*. Summary report. Retrieved from http://www.trincoll.edu

Koster, J. P. (1989). *The atheist syndrome*. Brentwood, TN: Wolgemuth & Hyatt.

Larson, E. J., & Witham, L. (1998). Correspondence: Leading scientists still reject God. *Nature, 394*, 313. doi:10.1038/28478

Lauder, W., Mummery, K., & Sharkey, S. (2006). Social capital, age and religiosity in people who are lonely. *Journal of Clinical Nursing, 15*, 334–339. doi:10.1111/j.1365-2702.2006.01192.x

Lepp, I. (1963). *Atheism in our time*. New York, NY: Macmillan.

Leuba, J. H. (1916). *Belief in God and immortality: An anthropological and statistical study*. Boston, MA: Sherman & French.

Leuba, J. H. (1934). Religious beliefs of American scientists. *Harper's Magazine, 169*, 291–300.

Levenson, M. R., Aldwin, C. M., & D'Mello, M. (2005). Religious development from adolescence to middle adulthood. In R. F. Paloutzian & C. L. Park (Eds.), *Handbook of the psychology of religion and spirituality* (pp. 144–161). New York, NY: Guilford Press.

Lynn, R., Harvey, J., & Nyborg, H. (2009). Average intelligence predicts atheism rates across 137 nations. *Intelligence, 37*, 11–15. doi:10.1016/j.intell.2008.03.004

Mackie, J. L. (1982). *The miracle of theism: Arguments for and against the existence of God*. Oxford, England: Oxford University Press.

Marler, P. L., & Hadaway, C. K. (2002). "Being religious" or "being spiritual" in America: A zero-sum proposition? *Journal for the Scientific Study of Religion, 41*, 289–300. doi:10.1111/1468-5906.00117

Martin, M. (2007). Atheism and religion. In M. Martin (Ed.), *The Cambridge companion to atheism* (pp. 217–232). New York, NY: Cambridge University Press. doi:10.1017/CCOL0521842700.014

Maselko, J., Kubzansky, L., Kawachi, I., Seeman, T., & Berkman, L. (2007). Religious service attendance and allostatic load among high-functioning elderly. *Psychosomatic Medicine, 69*, 464–472. doi:10.1097/PSY.0b013e31806c7c57

McConnell, K. M., Pargament, K. I., Ellison, C. G., & Flannelly, K. J. (2006). Examining the links between spiritual struggles and symptoms of psychopathology in a national sample. *Journal of Clinical Psychology, 62*, 1469–1484. doi:10.1002/jclp.20325

Meulemann, H. (2009). Secularization or religious renewal? Worldviews in 22 societies: Findings and indications of a cross-sectional survey. In Bertelsmann Foundation (Ed.), *What the world believes: Analysis and commentary on the Religion Monitor* 2008 (pp. 691–723). Gütersloh, Germany: Verlag Bertelsmann Stiftung.

Miller, A. S., & Hoffmann, J. P. (1995). Risk and religion: An explanation of gender differences in religiosity. *Journal for the Scientific Study of Religion, 34*, 63–75. doi:10.2307/1386523

Moadel, A., Morgan, C., Fatone, A., Grennan, J., Carter, J., Laruffa, G., . . . Dutcher, J. (1999). Seeking meaning and hope: Self-reported spiritual needs among an ethnically-diverse cancer patient population. *Psycho-Oncology, 8*, 378–385. doi:10.1002/(SICI)1099-1611(199909/10)8:5<378::AID-PON406>3.0.CO;2-A

Murken, S. (Ed.). (2008). *Ohne Gott leben. Religionspsychologische Aspekte des "Unglaubens."* [Living without God: Aspects of "unbelief" from a psychology of religion perspective]. Marburg, Germany: Diagonal.

Nelsen, H. M. (1981). Religious conformity in an age of disbelief—contextual effects of time, denomination, and family processes upon church decline and apostasy. *American Sociological Review, 46*, 632–640. doi:10.2307/2094944

Novotni, M., & Petersen, R. (2001). *Angry with God.* Colorado Springs, CO: Pinon Press.

Nyborg, H. (2009). The intelligence–religiosity nexus: A representative study of white adolescent Americans. *Intelligence, 37*, 81–93. doi:10.1016/j.intell.2008.08.003

O'Connell, K. A., & Skevington, S. M. (2005). The relevance of spirituality, religion and personal beliefs to health-related quality of life: Themes from focus groups in Britain. *British Journal of Health Psychology, 10*, 379–398. doi:10.1348/135910705X25471

O'Connell, K. A., & Skevington, S. M. (2009). Spiritual, religious, and personal beliefs are important and distinctive to assessing quality of life in health: A comparison of theoretical models. *British Journal of Health Psychology*. Online first DOI:10.1348/135910709X479799

Pargament, K. I. (1997). *The psychology of religion and coping: Theory, research, practice.* New York, NY: Guilford Press.

Pargament, K. I. (1999). The psychology of religion and spirituality? Yes and no. *The International Journal for the Psychology of Religion, 9*, 3–16. doi:10.1207/s15327582ijpr0901_2

Pargament, K. I. (2007). *Spiritually integrated psychotherapy. Understanding and addressing the sacred.* New York, NY: Guilford Press.

Pargament, K. I., Koenig, H. G., & Perez, L. M. (2000). The many methods of religious coping: Development and initial validation of the RCOPE. *Journal of Clinical Psychology, 56*, 519–543. doi:10.1002/(SICI)1097-4679(200004)56:4<519::AID-JCLP6>3.0.CO;2-1

Pargament, K. I., & Mahoney, A. (2005). Sacred matters: Sanctification as a vital topic for the psychology of religion. *The International Journal for the Psychology of Religion, 15*, 179–198. doi:10.1207/s15327582ijpr1503_1

Pargament, K. I., Smith, B. W., Koenig, H. G., & Perez, L. M. (1998). Patterns of positive and negative religious coping with major life stressors. *Journal for the Scientific Study of Religion, 37*, 710–724. doi:10.2307/1388152

Pasquale, F. L. (2007). The "nonreligious" in the American northwest. In B. A. Kosmin & A. Keysar (Eds.), *Secularism and secularity: Contemporary international perspectives* (pp. 41–58). Hartford, CT: Institute for the Study of Secularism in Society and Culture.

Peteet, J. R. (2001). Putting suffering into perspective: Implications of the patient's world view. *Journal of Psychotherapy Practice and Research, 10*, 187–192.

Pew Forum on Religion and Public Life. (2009). *Faith in flux: Changes in religious affiliation in the U.S.* Retrieved from http://pewforum.org/newassets/images/reports/flux/fullreport.pdf

Piedmont, R. L. (2005). The role of personality in understanding religious and spiritual constructs. In R. F. Paloutzian & C. L. Park (Eds.), *The handbook of the psychology of religion and spirituality* (pp. 253–273). New York, NY: Guilford Press.

Pieper, J. Z. T. (2004). Religious resources of psychiatric inpatients: Religious coping in highly religious inpatients. *Mental Health, Religion, and Culture, 7*, 349–363. doi:10.1080/13674670410001719805

Riley, J., Best, S., & Charlton, B. G. (2005). Religious believers and strong atheists may both be less depressed than existentially-uncertain people. *QJM: Monthly Journal of the Association of Physicians, 98*, 840. doi:10.1093/qjmed/hci132

Roof, W. C. (1999). *Spiritual marketplace. Baby boomers and the remaking of American religion.* Princeton, NJ: Princeton University Press.

Ryff, C. D., & Singer, B. H. (1996). Psychological well-being: Meaning, measurement, and implications for psychotherapy research. *Psychotherapy and Psychosomatics, 65*, 14–23. doi:10.1159/000289026

Saeed, S. A., & Grant, R. L. (2004). Atheists and agnostics. In A. M. Josephson & J. R. Peteet (Eds.), *Handbook of spirituality and worldview in clinical practice* (pp. 139–153). Arlington, VA: American Psychiatric Publishing.

Saroglou, V. (2002). Religion and the five factors of personality: A meta-analytic review. *Personality and Individual Differences, 32,* 15–25. doi:10.1016/S0191-8869(00)00233-6

Saroglou, V. (2010). Religiousness as a cultural adaptation of basic traits: A five-factor model perspective. *Personality and Social Psychology Review, 14,* 108–125. doi:10.1177/1088868309352322

Saroglou, V., Delpierre, V., & Dernelle, R. (2004). Values and religiosity: A meta-analysis of studies using Schwartz's model. *Personality and Individual Differences, 37,* 721–734. doi:10.1016/j.paid.2003.10.005

Schmidt, T., & Wohlrab-Sahr, M. (2003). Still the most areligious part of the world: Developments in the religious field in Eastern Germany since 1990. *International Journal of Practical Theology, 7,* 86–100.

Schnell, T. (2003). A framework for the study of implicit religion: The psychological theory of implicit religiosity. *Implicit Religion, 6,* 86–104.

Schwadel, P. (2010). Period and cohort effects on religious nonaffiliation and religious disaffiliation: A research note. *Journal for the Scientific Study of Religion, 49,* 311–319. doi:10.1111/j.1468-5906.2010.01511.x

Schwartz, S. H. (1992). Universals in the content and structure of values: Theoretical advances and empirical tests in 20 countries. In M. P. Zanna (Ed.), *Advances in experimental social psychology* (Vol. 25, pp. 1–65). Orlando, FL: Academic Press.

Schwartz, S. H. (1994). Are there universal aspects in the content and structure of values? *Journal of Social Issues, 50,* 19–45. doi:10.1111/j.1540-4560.1994.tb01196.x

Shaver, P., Lenauer, M., & Sadd, S. (1980). Religiousness, conversion and subjective well-being: The "healthy-minded" religion of modern American women. *American Journal of Psychiatry, 137,* 1563–1568.

Sherkat, D. E. (2001). Tracking the restructuring of American religion: Religious affiliation and patterns of religious mobility, 1973–1998. *Social Forces, 79,* 1459–1493. doi:10.1353/sof.2001.0052

Sherkat, D. E. (2008). Beyond belief: Atheism, agnosticism, and theistic certainty in the United States. *Sociological Spectrum, 28,* 438–459. doi:10.1080/02732170802205932

Smith, T. B., McCullough, M. E., & Poll, J. (2003). Religiousness and depression: Evidence for a main effect and the moderating influence of stressful life events. *Psychological Bulletin, 129,* 614–636. doi:10.1037/0033-2909.129.4.614

Stefanek, M., McDonald, P. G., & Hess, S. A. (2005). Religion, spirituality, and cancer: Current status and methodological challenges. *Psycho-Oncology, 14,* 450–463. doi:10.1002/pon.861

Streib, H. (2008). More spiritual than religious: Changes in the religious field require new approaches. In H. Streib, A. Dinter, & K. Söderblom (Eds.), *Lived religion—conceptual, empirical and practical-theological approaches* (pp. 53–67). Leiden, the Netherlands: Brill. doi:10.1163/ej.9789004163775.i-404.30

Streib, H. (in press). Deconversion. In L. R. Rambo & C. E. Farhadian (Eds.), *Oxford handbook of religious conversion.* Oxford, England: Oxford University Press.

Streib, H., Hood, R. W., Jr., Keller, B., Csöff, R.-M., & Silver, C. (2009). Deconversion: Qualitative and quantitative results from cross-cultural research in Germany and the United States of America. *The International Journal for the Psychology of Religion, 20,* 303–305. doi:10.1080/10508619.2010.507701

Streib, H., & Keller, B. (2004). The variety of deconversion experiences: Contours of a concept in respect to empirical research. *Archive for the Psychology of Religion. Archiv für Religionspsychologie, 26,* 181–200. doi:10.1163/0084672053598030

Taylor, C. (2007). *A secular age.* Cambridge, MA: Harvard University Press.

Taylor, R. J., Chatters, L. M., & Levin, J. (2004). *Religion in the lives of African Americans: Social, psychological, and health perspectives.* Thousand Oaks, CA: Sage.

van Uden, M. H. F., Pieper, J. Z. T., & Alma, H. A. (2004). "Bridge over troubled water": Further results regarding the Receptive Coping Scale. *Journal of Empirical Theology, 17,* 101–114. doi:10.1163/1570925041208916

Vitz, P. C. (2000). *Faith of the fatherless: The psychology of atheism.* Dallas, TX: Spence.

Whitley, R. (2010). Atheism and mental health. *Harvard Review of Psychiatry, 18,* 190–194. doi:10.3109/10673221003747674

Wulff, D. M. (1997). *Psychology of religion: Classic and contemporary.* New York, NY: Wiley.

Zinnbauer, B. J., & Pargament, K. I. (2005). Religiousness and spirituality. In R. F. Paloutzian & C. L. Park (Eds.), *Handbook of the psychology of religion and spirituality* (pp. 21–42). New York, NY: Guilford Press.

Zinnbauer, B. J., Pargament, K. I., Cole, B., Rye, M. S., Butter, E. M., Belavich, T. G., . . . Kadar, J. L. (1997). Religion and spirituality: Unfuzzying the fuzzy. *Journal for the Scientific Study of Religion, 36,* 549–564. doi:10.2307/1387689

Zuckerman, P. (2007). Atheism: Contemporary numbers and patterns. In M. Martin (Ed.), *The Cambridge companion to atheism* (pp. 47–66). New York, NY: Cambridge University Press. doi:10.1017/CCOL0521842700.004

Zwingmann, C., Wirtz, M., Müller, C., Körber, J., & Murken, S. (2006). Positive and negative religious coping in German breast cancer patients. *Journal of Behavioral Medicine, 29,* 533–547. doi:10.1007/s10865-006-9074-3

Chapter 41

CHARISMATIC GROUPS AND CULTS: A PSYCHOLOGICAL AND SOCIAL ANALYSIS

Marc Galanter

The term *charismatic group*, as discussed here, applies to a variety of social phenomena characterized by intense cohesiveness with an ideological commitment associated with a view of transcendence. *Cults*, on the other hand, can be considered a subgroup of this latter phenomenon, defined by the common culture as alien and deviant on the basis of values within that culture. The number of such groups, both of the former and latter type, vary greatly from one geographic setting to the next, and from one era to another, but they are more likely to arise during periods of relative anomie, or ones during which the established values of the society come into question. Such groups may either be large or small in the number of their members as well. Additionally, many such groups operate without attracting notice of the general society. For these reasons, it is not possible to ascertain the number of these groups in a particular national setting, such as contemporary in the United States, or the number of members overall.

It is not uncommon to think of cultlike new religious movements as anomalies. A cult is often portrayed as a sort of oddity, with little attention to the psychology and social structure that most such groups have in common. The beliefs and behaviors of their members become more understandable, however, when the patterns underlying these organizations are viewed within the context of their psychology. Drawing on my professional research and experience, this chapter provides a psychological and social analysis of cults within the context of charismatic groups.

THE CHARISMATIC GROUP

A cultlike new religious movement is one of several types of charismatic groups. A charismatic group consists of a dozen or more members, even hundreds of thousands. It is characterized by the following psychological elements: Members (a) have a shared belief system, (b) sustain a high level of social cohesiveness, (c) are strongly influenced by the group's behavioral norms, and (d) impute charismatic (or sometimes divine) power to the group or its leadership. In a charismatic group, commitments can be elicited by relative strangers in a way rarely seen in other groups (Galanter, 1990). Even Freud, who championed the compelling nature of individual motives, addressed this impressive capacity at length in his book *Group Psychology and the Analysis of the Ego*. He discussed these forces in terms of the "primitive sympathetic response of the group," and said that "something is unmistakably at work in the nature of a compulsion to do the same as others, to remain in harmony with the many" (Freud, 1922/1955, p. 84).

The cognitive basis for this conformity is a shared belief system. The beliefs held in common by members of charismatic groups are a vital force in the group's operation. They bind members together, shape their attitudes, and motivate them to act in self-sacrifice. When these groups are religious in

This chapter was funded in part by the John Templeton Foundation.

DOI: 10.1037/14045-041
APA Handbook of Psychology, Religion, and Spirituality: Vol. 1. Context, Theory, and Research, K. I. Pargament (Editor-in-Chief)
Copyright © 2013 by the American Psychological Association. All rights reserved.

nature, their beliefs are often codified, but some groups have no more than an ill-defined ideological orientation. In some religious cults, converts are introduced to the group's ideology only after they have affiliated. Once they have identified with the group's general orientation, though, they tend to accept their beliefs quite readily when these are spelled out. Members of these groups tend to be intensely concerned about each other's well-being and are deeply committed to joint activities. Their social cohesiveness, essential to the group's integrity, is reflected in the close intertwining of the individual's life circumstances with those of all group members. Meetings are frequent; they serve as a focus for group functions and articulate their cohesiveness. Members often express their need to associate regularly with each other by developing joint activities such as minor group tasks and rituals, which in turn justify such meetings. Group members are always aware of when their next group meeting will be held and look to them as a means of instilling commitment and a sense of purpose. A member's emotional state may be highly vulnerable to disruptions of this routine, and a group gathering missed can become a source of distress.

All charismatic groups engage the emotional needs of their members in an intensely cohesive social system. Group cohesiveness may be defined as the result of all the forces acting on members to keep them engaged in the group. When cohesiveness is strong, participants work to retain the commitment of their fellow members, protect them from threat, and ensure the safety of shared resources. With weak cohesiveness, there is less concern over the group's potential dissolution or the loss of its distinctive identity, and joint action is less likely.

Our understanding of group cohesiveness—particularly as applied to charismatic groups—is informed by studies of family relationships. The concept of "differentiation of self," developed by family theorists such as Bowen (1978) and Wynne (e.g., Wynne, Ryckoff, Day, & Hirsch, 1958), helps explain the interaction between the individual and his or her family and can be assessed independently of a person's diagnosis, social class, and cultural background. At one end of this scale lies the highly differentiated individual, characterized by autonomy and even rugged individualism. At the other end, family relationships exhibit emotional fusion and an inability to make critical judgments because of a need to ensure harmony with others.

Emotional fusion in families is akin to group cohesiveness in its merging of identity and decision-making functions. It occurs in large charismatic groups as well as in families because members of both may be highly dependent on each other and rely excessively on their compatriots for emotional support and decision making (Reiss, 1971). This is also seen among certain families who are unable to tolerate disruptions in the balance of their members' relationships. For example, if a clinician attempts to change an apparently harmful pattern of interaction within a family, one way or another, that pattern will soon reestablish itself; this takes place without any formal understanding among family members, as if a governing structure existed outside their awareness.

Preserving intense interrelatedness is also essential to a charismatic group (Galanter, 1999). Because of the need to preserve cohesiveness and interdependency, close-knit and religious cults employ strategies to maintain stability in the face of internal or external threat. A distorted consensus emerges, a mutually held point of view that allows the perception of equilibrium to be maintained. This consensus is often achieved by denying reality and rationalizing a shared perspective. In essence, reality becomes less important to certain groups than the preservation of their ties.

The norms for behavior in a charismatic group also play an important role in determining how its members conduct themselves. Members typically look to group norms for learning ways to behave in new situations. They may respond in a similar fashion to strangers perceived as threatening—in some groups, with a blunted and distant stare. Often they are implicitly aware of their style of behavior in an unexpected situation, whereas at other times, it emerges without conscious appreciation of how they act. Behavioral change may extend to mimicking the symptoms of mental illness. In these groups, transcendental experiences—often hallucinatory—are quite common. A deceased comrade "literally" stands by a member or a historical figure, bringing divinely inspired advice. Intense emotional experiences are reported, such as profound euphoria or malaise. Such phenomena, which often are seen among the mentally ill, occur among individuals who give no evidence of psychiatric disorder.

Finally, charismatic powers are typically imputed to leaders of these groups, but they also can be ascribed to the group or its mission. Some such groups are viewed by their members as heralding an inevitable new world order. The leaders of some religious-oriented groups are believed by their followers to have a uniquely close relationship with God, giving a virtually uncontestable authority for that leader's decisions. These four psychological elements—shared belief system, social cohesiveness, behavioral norms, and charismatic power—are common to most charismatic groups. Furthermore, they reinforce each other through series of interactions that are similar in virtually any social system.

THE EXPERIENCE

The Attraction of Entry Into the Group

Charismatic groups are likely to emerge at a time when the values of a society are felt to be inadequate for addressing major social issues. Individuals are more prone to join if they are unhappy because of situational problems or chronic distress and if they have limited affiliate ties to family and friends. Groups generally engage new members by creating an atmosphere of unconditional acceptance and support and offering a worldview that promises a solution for all existential problems. Engagement (or conversion) entails experiences of intensely felt emotion or perceptual change. It also provides a relief of neurotic distress and a feeling of well-being. For newly recruited members of the group, these experiences validate the group's mission.

The Transformative Experience of Group Membership

The group's leader is reputed to have the potential of bringing a resolution to the problems of humanity. In interacting with followers, the leader is also drawn into believing the grandiose role accorded him or her and justifies his or her behavior by referring to the transcendent mission suggested by the group's philosophy. This can cause him or her to make demands on his or her followers that outsiders would see as petulant and abusive. The group attributes special meaning, colored by its philosophy, to everyday language and events; this meaning is usually related to dogma or written code attributed to the group's leader or progenitor. Recruits experience a relief effect with membership. That is, the closer they feel to their fellow members and the group's values, the greater the relief in their emotional distress; the more they become emotionally distanced from the group, the greater their experience of distress. This relief effect serves as the basis for reinforcing compliance with the group's norms, as it implicitly rewards conformity with enhanced well-being and punishes alienation with feelings of distress. It also keeps members from leaving the group because they are conditioned to avoid the distress that results from relinquishing the benefits of the relief effect.

Group behavioral norms generally structure all areas of members' lives, including their work, sexuality, socialization, and intellectual pursuits. Activities in these areas are preferentially carried out with other members, so that colleagues are generally shunned as outsiders. Membership is characterized by levels of "sanctity," so that a member is continually striving to achieve a higher level of acceptance by conforming all the more with the group's expectations. Such conformity generally results in members' experiencing considerable hardship.

Through a mix of psychological and social dimensions observed in this discussion, the charismatic group and the individual form a symbiotic relationship, serving each other's needs. When joining a charismatic group, an individual is transformed by powerful forces into a personal extension of the group's identity, which compels him or her to carry out activities that were unthinkable before group membership. Even if a terrorist attack is the goal, this act can be justified as serving the needs of the group, needs that take primacy over the individual's basic desire for a longer life.

SOME ILLUSTRATIONS

The impact of group cohesiveness on the psychological status of members was evident in a study of a modern charismatic sect, the Divine Light Mission (Galanter, 1978). Young adult members of the group reported appreciable psychiatric problems before joining. For example, 30% had sought professional help and 9% had been hospitalized for emotional disorders. Furthermore, their self-reports reflected a considerable relief in neurotic distress after they became affiliated with the Divine Light Mission. Their responses also demonstrated an intense social cohesiveness in the group that was highly correlated with the degree of symptom relief evidenced by individual members. Cohesive forces based on family and community ties operate in a similar fashion in a wide variety of indigenous mental healing rituals, both in preindustrial societies, as in Zar ceremonies of Northeast Africa (Kennedy, 1967), and in the United States, as in Espiritismo among Puerto Rican immigrants (Singer & Borrero, 1984).

Shared belief, a second force in the charismatic group, was evident in studies on the psychological well-being of longstanding Unification Church members (Galanter, Rabkin, Rabkin, & Deutsch, 1979). Measures of social cohesiveness and religious belief accounted for a large portion of the variance in well-being, and items that measured religious belief were the highest ranking predictors of well-being. This suggests the additional role of belief as a force in charismatic groups. It also reflects the importance of a set of beliefs held by healers and their patients about illness and treatment. Kleinman (1980) found this explanatory model to be an important component of the effectiveness of indigenous healing in his cross-cultural studies of shamanistic treatment.

In the charismatic group, the forces of group cohesiveness, shared belief, and altered consciousness operate to compel behavioral conformity and modulate affect without overt coercion. To understand this process of social control, it is useful to contrast it with the influence of brainwashing. Brainwashing was described by Lifton (1961) among prisoners of the Korean War who were forcibly confined by the Communist Chinese. In both brainwashing and charismatic groups, those directing the process maintain control over the "context of communication" to prevent the expression of perspectives contrary to their own. In the brainwashing setting, however, participants are imprisoned and physically coerced. There is no physical coercion in charismatic groups. Instead, the psychological forces allow members to attribute new meaning and values to their experiences by means of social reinforcement of compliance.

How does this reinforcement take place? Findings on the role of these forces (Galanter, 1978) suggest the operation of a "relief effect" in the psychiatric impact of charismatic groups. That is to say, both recruits and long-term members experience a relief from emotional distress when they feel more closely affiliated with the group; a decline in affiliate feelings, on the other hand, can result in greater distress. Such an effect, sociobiologically grounded and mediated by the social context, can serve as an operant reinforcer for regulating behavior. Members who act in accordance with the group's expectations are reinforced by enhanced well-being; when they reject the group's behavioral norms, they experience the negative reinforcement of increased distress. This also serves to enhance the likelihood of members' maintaining affiliation with the group and compliance with its expectations for behavior. It takes place both informally and in structured rituals. Because the operant reinforcement of approved behaviors can engage members into compliance with the group and restructure their perceptions of the world around them as well, it can also serve as the basis for a remission in recruits' pathological perceptions. The enhanced well-being inherent in the affiliation process can then contribute to the relief of major psychopathology, as illustrated by the following case history.

A 24-year-old technician with no history of psychiatric illness became increasingly isolated over the course of a year after beginning to smoke marijuana. He felt that his coworkers were conspiring to have him arrested for drug possession. He then moved into a secluded rural setting, where he soon came to believe that his "soul was moving out" of him and that he saw flying saucers nearby. Soon he felt he was going out of his mind. At this point, he met several members of the Divine Light Mission, an Eastern cultic group, who invited him to spend time at their communal residence. After 2 months of meditation and daily attendance at their religious services, he was no longer anxious or delusional, reporting that he was "at peace with himself." A year later, he had had no recurrence in symptoms and was still involved in the group's activities. His diagnosis was delusional disorder, persecutory type.

The intense cohesiveness of the charismatic group in combination with its ability to influence members' beliefs can yield relief in psychopathology. It also can generate psychiatric syndromes, however. This is particularly true when an individual becomes alienated from a cohesive group but still accepts its belief system. The potent impact of such estrangement, even to the point of inducing psychotic symptoms, is illustrated in the next example.

A 16-year-old boy whose family belonged to a neo-Christian cult was admitted to the hospital because he was hearing voices. Both the patient and others reported that he had never experienced psychiatric difficulties until fellow members caught him smoking marijuana; the members insisted that he was tainted by the devil because he had violated the group's religious injunction against smoking marijuana. Very soon after this experience, the boy became alienated from the group and ran off to stay at the home of a relative not affiliated with the cult. Over the course of a month, he became increasingly guilty and anxious about having left the group and then began to hallucinate the voice of the devil telling him he had betrayed the cult. His symptoms remitted during a 1-month hospitalization that provided supportive milieu treatment only. His diagnosis was brief reactive psychosis.

The impact of group forces is felt at each stage of membership in a charismatic group, from induction to stabilization to departure. Members' commitment to a charismatic group is remarkably persistent, even after they leave the group. For example, 3 years after their departure from the Unification Church, ex-members still maintained a considerable fidelity toward the group, although most of them were well adjusted in the general community (Galanter, 1983). A sizable majority still cared strongly for the members they knew best and reported that they "got some positive things" out of their involvement with the group. This fidelity is evidence of the potential of a charismatic group for continuing its influence even after a member departs, as we shall see among self-help groups that operate along similar lines.

THE CHARISMATIC GROUP AS A SOCIAL SYSTEM

At the interface between charismatic group and society at large, strange things happen. Many people have noted the glazed look of members of such cults as the Unification Church when they venture outside the fold and mix with nonmembers. It has been suggested that such behavior is symptomatic of psychopathology, specifically a detached state. Others who have studied cults and other charismatic groups, however, have not made such observations. This discrepancy represents different aspects of behavior at the boundary of a social system. All social systems have certain functions that act to protect their integrity and implement their goals. To view cultic groups more clearly in the broad social context, and to understand their interactions with society better, it is useful to draw on systems theory. Four functions characteristic of systems are transformation, monitoring, feedback, and boundary control (Galanter, 1997).

Transformation in the Social System of the Charismatic Group

Systems have been likened to factories; they take input from the outside, which can be raw material, energy, or information, and process it into output, a product. This function, called *transformation*, allows the system to carry out operations essential to its own continuity or to the needs of a larger suprasystem to which it belongs. In a given system, the most important transformation—the one that typically defines its identity—is its primary task; most components of the system are geared toward either carrying out this primary task or preventing its disruption. The primary task of many religious cults is to prepare for the messianic end they envision.

An unstable system, such as a cult in its earlier stages, is particularly susceptible to dissolution. Members may disaffiliate at any time, because the ties that bind them together have yet to be woven into the stable network of a social structure. In this regard, the concept of transformation can be used as a mode for the persistent attempts of certain charismatic groups to stabilize themselves by acquiring new members. This may be why members can become so deeply involved in conversion activities; they are motivated not only by an inherent need to become engaged in the charismatic group, but they also begin conforming to the group's needs as a system. Members would not on their own be inclined to go out and recruit for the group, but as part of its system, they come to act in accordance with its goals.

At some point in their evolution, most charismatic groups focus on recruitment as a primary task. The process may ensure a larger and stronger group and, when successful, can confer legitimacy to the group's own ideology, thereby consolidating the commitment of its long-standing members.

Another important aspect of the transformation function is how it disrupts the psychological stability of potential recruits—the "input" to this process. Because an intensive mobilization of a charismatic group's psychological and material resources may be directed at the conversion of new members, they can create deep turmoil in the individual convert. On the one hand, the group is intensely seductive in its attempt to attract new members; on the other, it demands a disruption of antecedent social ties and a metamorphosis in the new member's worldview. Thus, when the full resources of the group are focused on a recruit, the potential for tearing the fabric of that individual's psychological stability is considerable. The result may be psychiatric symptoms in people with no history of mental disorder or psychological instability. The genesis of these symptoms may lie more in the conflict between the recruit's needs and the group's demands than in an underlying psychological impairment of the individual. In essence, an effective cult is able to engage and transform individuals in ways that disrupt an otherwise-stable psychological condition, in many cases causing significant guilt and resulting in a severe psychiatric reaction.

A variety of devices are employed in this group to intensify the forces operating on potential recruits. The "training" is carried out in protracted sessions where disagreement with the trainer is actively discouraged, often by harsh verbal abuse. Little respite is afforded from the intensity of the group experience, and the training setting includes as many as 200 potential recruits herded together, with their behavior tightly controlled. The dynamism of the experience further heightens the potential for energetic group influence and emotional contagion, and altered consciousness is promoted by a variety of contextual cues and behavioral controls.

Casualties incurred during the difficult training regimen may have to be ignored, and the problematic issues they raise, repressed. This reinforces the "shared beliefs" of other followers, those who see "getting it" as more important than attention to specific personal conflicts or day-to-day relationships. Suppression of concerns that might detract from the primary task of an intensely committed social system is actually quite common. In the time of battle, for example, an army may be mobilized to achieve its immediate military objectives, and its primary task is therefore the transformation of all personnel and material into a fighting force. The psychology of the troops is bent to this mission to the exclusion of all else because victory in battle is paramount. Concern for the needs of the wounded may be secondary because this could detract from the thrust into battle. In a similar way, mobilization for the transformation process in the terrorist group cannot be deflected by the difficulties experienced by individual recruits because the usual constraints on exerting social pressure are suppressed.

Monitoring of Members

To operate effectively, a system must transform input from the environment into a form that meets its needs, but must also observe and regulate the actions of its component parts, thereby ensuring that their respective activities are properly carried out and coordinated. This constitutes its monitoring function. Such monitoring is essential to any system to ensure the effective implementation of its primary task, whether that system is a living organism, a social organization, or a factory. The system must have an apparatus for monitoring its components. In the living organism, its nervous system serves this function, and in social organizations and factories, it is some form of management structure.

In an effective system, the monitoring function will operate without undue need for communication or conflict resolution. The system's components—the group members—will respond automatically to the suggestions of the leadership. Whether consciously controlled or not, compliance with the group's announced perspective is expected.

To understand the means by which the charismatic group rapidly and effectively monitors the thinking and behavioral norms of its members, one must consider the psychological defense mechanisms employed by the group as a whole, which are unlike those operating in individuals. These defenses are employed for the unconscious management of conflicting motives so that the group can function smoothly in the face of conflict. Although similar defenses may be observed in other social systems, the charismatic group responds in particular ways that distinguish it from less tightly knit groups, because the forces of group cohesiveness and shared beliefs in the charismatic group facilitate its operation as a functional whole. These psychological defenses protect the group culture from unacceptable ideas, often "realities" produced by outdated initiatives or outside influences. Such realities may be ignored outright, by means of denial; forgotten through repression; or distorted through rationalization.

In a social system, monitoring is most easily implemented when a voluntary collaboration exists between those in control and those being managed, as outright coercion necessitates undue expenditure of resources and detracts from cooperative efforts to carry out the system's primary task. It is best, in fact, if those monitored accept the leadership without conscious deliberation, and because the defense mechanism of identification operates in an unconscious fashion, those who adopt the attitudes of their leaders do so without deliberating over the wisdom of their actions.

Members nonetheless have their own psychological need for maintaining affiliation with the leader and the group, because they are captives by virtue of a pincer effect, which makes their emotional well-being dependent on their involvement in the group that inflicts distress. In a sense, they have no choice but to unconsciously make peace with the potentially threatening agenda of the leadership and comply with its expectations to achieve emotional relief.

A subcomponent of identification in certain cults and terrorist groups involves the suppression of autonomy. For a social system to regulate its functioning effectively, it must have the capacity to suppress members' deviation from its implicit or explicit goals. In charismatic groups, the penalty for those who deviate from norms is psychological distress; overt coercion usually is not necessary to induce compliance. From this, it can be inferred that attempts at achieving independence from such groups become rare and would tend to be easily extinguished by the groups' leaders.

Feedback Within the Social System

Feedback is one way for a system to obtain information about how well it is carrying out its primary task. Analysis of results is fed back into the system, and this provides information for planning future operations. For example, if a cult is trying to recruit, information on the relative response of potential members can be fed back to the cult leaders and can guide them in improving the group's recruitment techniques. Feedback may be positive or negative. Positive feedback gives the system information that will increase the effectiveness in achieving desired results. When negative feedback ceases to be available, the organization loses an important aspect of its ability to self-correct for actions that may be detrimental to the group's members. Transformation activities may go unmoderated, and the system's boundaries can be disrupted (Miller, 1965). Consequently, the system must have unrestrained access to negative feedback to exercise a proper degree of self-regulation and not dissipate its energies.

This latter function is important in charismatic groups because they are prone to suppress negative feedback when it runs contrary to the group's internal stability. It is a special risk because of the highly effective monitoring function that allows the cult system to control the information made available to its members. Means of avoiding undue negative feedback are essential to charismatic groups because their ideology and practices often elicit hostility from the general society. If allowed to enter the system unobstructed, such negative feedback leads to suppression of the group's transcendent vision and a decline in members' morale.

Certain charismatic groups try to isolate their members from all negative feedback, but this can be dangerous because the group may lose information valuable to its own self-regulation. These groups usually are no longer actively recruiting and have little need for protracted contact with outsiders. Other groups, however, rely on the successful recruitment of new members to provide them with positive feedback. Such successes are used to reinforce the merit of the group's own ideology and promote new initiatives that validate the group's chosen course. New recruits give legitimacy to a group in the face of a hostile world and encourage members to carry the group's mission forward. Such feedback can be a useful tool for social regulation.

The Group's Boundary Control

An open system must carry out its transformation functions while maintaining internal stability by monitoring its own components and responding to feedback. These functions, however, can be disrupted by intrusions from outside. For this reason, boundary control is a vital function of any social system.

Boundary control protects social systems against dangerous outsiders. It includes not only the screening of people but also of information, because information is a potent determinant of behavior. If a charismatic group is to maintain a system of shared beliefs markedly at variance with that of the culture, members must sometimes be rigidly isolated from consensual information from the general society that would unsettle this belief system. During the initial phases of conversion to charismatic groups, novices may be regarded as vulnerable and discouraged from establishing contact with their families. Similar processes of individual isolation from family, friends, and society often takes place in the setting of terrorist training camps. After their integration into the group, when their beliefs have been consolidated, these new members may be encouraged to reestablish ties with their families so as to promote a benign public image and perhaps help recruit other new members.

Any group that coalesces around a cause or function must soon establish a boundary to differentiate those who are participating from those who are not. Two important facets of activity form the boundary of charismatic groups, each mirroring the other. The first is a set of behaviors and attitudes of members, often deviant, that is directed at outsiders. It reflects how the system focuses its social forces to protect its boundaries. The second is a reciprocal set of behaviors and attitudes of the surrounding society, often an aggressive response of outsiders to the group's members.

The boundary of behavior of cult members that has made the deepest impression on outsiders involves the glazed, withdrawn look and trance-like state that some find most unsettling. Although this may appear pathologic, it can help group membership by reducing the possibility of direct exchanges with outsiders—it has an insulating effect. Thus, the trancelike appearance protects the group's boundary. It would be more likely to develop in settings that threaten the group's integrity, so that an observer who is perceived as an antagonist is more likely to see the behavior than one who is not.

Fearfulness of outsiders, or xenophobia—a common characteristic of cults—is another important manifestation of boundary control (see Chapters 24 and 26, this volume and Volume 2, Chapter 18, this handbook). It holds groups together, but it can reach the dimensions of outright paranoia. It represents a boundary control function carried to the extreme and is seen among those group members pressed by family or strangers to give up their ties to the group. It is also evident in the way outsiders are often treated with a different standard of openness or honesty.

Defensiveness and paranoia associated with the boundary function of a charismatic group elicit a complementary reaction from the surrounding community. This is seen in the animosity between family members of converts and the sects, in the breakdown in communication between sects and some religious groups, and in the hostility toward sects voiced by some former members.

Attempts at communication between parents and their children who have joined contemporary groups are often rife with misunderstanding and hostility. The new recruit often becomes an agent of the group's boundary control function and regards the relatives who make contact as attempting to disengage the person from the movement, whereas the parents, operating at the boundary of a highly cohesive group, frequently become preoccupied with the effort to dislodge the new member. Communications are often frozen at this level.

Overall, members of a cult may be driven to behave as they do by forces that act within the social system to ensure its stability and implement its primary task. On the other hand, the openness of each member to such influence can only be understood by recourse to one's biologically grounded responsiveness to group influence. In the world of the terrorist organization, then, an individual is transformed by group forces as well as by their personal willingness to be transformed by these forces.

A PROBLEMATIC CASE STUDY

The following extreme example illustrates the behavioral deviancy that can arise in a charismatic group. During a morning rush hour, in March 1995, two five-man teams converged on the Kasumigaseki station, the hub of Tokyo's underground transit system and a short walk from the Japanese Parliament. They carried plastic bags of sarin, a liquefied poison gas, along with their umbrellas. Already protected by antidotes to the poison, they punctured the bags with the umbrellas, releasing vapors from the liquefied gas, and fled quickly. The attack killed 12 subway riders, and many others were temporarily blinded and collapsed on sidewalks as they tried to run for safety.

Aum Shinrikyo was a religious sect that claimed to have 10,000 members in Japan and 20,000 abroad, mostly in Russia. It had been previously suspected of wrongdoing by the Japanese police and was now presumed to be responsible for the subway poisonings. After the subway attack, more than 2,500 officers raided Aum's various offices, while hundreds of Aum priests continued to meditate and pray at its headquarters. The public's anxiety was only heightened when statements of the group's leader, Shoko Asahara, were beamed to Japan by radio from Vladivostok and Sakhalin in Russia—statements such as "Let us face death without regret."

Aum leaders had even considered releasing nerve gas in the United States, a country thought by Asahara to be hostile to his group (Kristof, 1997). Ikuo Hayashi, who had served as medical director of Aum, said that the U.S. attacks were planned for June 1994 but were suspended. The intelligence director of the group had even instructed him to go to the United States to pick up a package of sarin that was to arrive in a shipment of ornaments. Hayashi, by the way, a respected cardiologist who had worked in a U.S. hospital before joining the cult, is illustrative of the talent that was inducted into the group.

In his pamphlets, Shoko Asahara urged people to join his program of "Death and Rebirth," pointing out that "as we move toward the year 2000 there will be a series of events of inexpressible ferocity and terror," that "Japan has been unjustly deprived of the concept of death and life after death," and that "he would teach people about both" (Sayle, 1997). Japanese newspapers estimated that Asahara's chemical stockpile could have created enough nerve gas to kill between 4.2 million and 10 million people.

By 1987, Asahara had acquired a small following and had founded Aum Shinrikyo as a religious sect. It was a time when a number of similar Buddhist- or Shinto-oriented sects were emerging in Japan and attracting young people who were disenchanted with the country's materialist orientation. Aum appeared to offer a clear alternative. As though to prove its special power, it promised its members the ability to levitate and would present recruits with photographs of Asahara poised inches above the ground in a yogic position. It also provided recruits with headgear containing batteries and electrodes designed to align their brain waves with those of their leader. Asahara had a knack for recruitment, and Aum began to attract many bright, discontented university students, particularly those trained in the sciences. As his sect grew richer, he developed a paunch and began to drive around in a Rolls Royce.

Intense cohesiveness, bolstered by physical isolation, was a vehicle for sustaining members' involvement. Asahara demanded that many of his followers live in communes, cut off from relatives and family. There was a striking inconsistency between the activities of Aum's leadership and the Buddhist-derived philosophy maintained by the large majority of its members. Most members knew nothing about the criminal activities of the group's leaders, a fact that reflects the profound discrepancy between the means employed by the core leadership and the pacific attitudes shown by members.

As is typical of many charismatic sects, recruits were often told to sign over their property to the group, and Aum went so far as to murder one person who opposed the expropriation. The relative of a recruit was kidnapped in the street after protesting that his sister had been required to give away all her assets, and police later unearthed evidence that the man had been murdered by Aum members.

Surprisingly, the Tokyo disaster made only a modest impression on most members of the cult. A few weeks after the event, one graduate student reported that he was urged by his family and friends to leave the group. He insisted on staying, and said,

> I've got to do this, and that's all I can say. I'm sorry, Mom. Sorry Dad . . . if I were head of the public security commission in Japan, and I were thinking of what group is the most dangerous for the present social system in Japan, it would be Aum . . . because Aum has such potential for the future. (Kristof, 1995)

The sustained commitment of members after the attack reflected a need to retain fidelity to a failed movement even when it was proven unworthy. This is very much aligned with what other research has discovered about doomsday cults. Members of such groups remain committed even after their leaders' predictions of the world's end came to naught; many simply rationalized this failure and retained their fidelity to the movement (Festinger, Riecken, & Schacter, 1956).

The case of Aum Shinrikyo offers a useful example of how some cults engage the minds of their recruits, how they generate their unique psychological and social forces, and how they acquire structure as a social system. There are four elements in particular by which Aum exemplifies the transformative process of other charismatic groups: isolation, paranoia, grandiosity, and absolute dominion. Regarding isolation, a group can remove or distance itself from the values of our common culture, even the importance of preserving life. This can take the form of geographic isolation, such as Aum's training facilities. For example, Shoko Asahara established an isolated compound in rural Japan; he also maintained a gulf in communication between his inner circle and his widely dispersed adherents, thus isolating the decision makers from the flock of followers.

An isolated cultic group provides fertile soil for the emergence of paranoia and grandiosity in its leader, and will aggravate these traits in the leader who already sees himself as espousing a philosophy of absolute truth. Paranoia and grandiosity are interdependent—a person who needs to sustain full control over his flock, to maintain the appearance of divinity that most charismatic group leaders enjoy, inevitably will begin to suspect others of trying to take it away. He fears that the government, or even parties inside his own sect, will envy his powers and try to obstruct his mission. This sets up a siege mentality and leaves the leader awaiting the moment of assault. The interweaving of grandiosity and paranoia sets the stage for thinking that a fight to the death—or in some cases, mass suicide or martyrdom—following a confrontation with the government is legitimate. Isolation, grandiosity, and paranoia all set the stage for a leader to establish absolute domain over his followers. This can be achieved through the intensification of the system's monitoring of members' behavior—that is, observation and regulation of members to ensure that the group's tasks are carried out as the leader's control continues.

Preserving intense interrelatedness is also essential to a religious cult. Because of the need to preserve cohesiveness and interdependency, close-knit families and religious cults employ adaptive strategies to maintain stability in the face of internal or external threat. As illustrated by the case of Aum Shinrikyo, a distorted consensus emerges, a mutually held point of view that allows the perception of equilibrium to be maintained. This consensus is often achieved by denying reality and rationalizing a shared perspective. In essence, reality becomes less important to certain groups than the preservation of their ties.

Members of Aum had a shared belief in a vision for the future, which served as a vital force in the group's operation. These beliefs bound Aum's members together, shaped their attitudes, and motivated them to act in self-sacrifice. Members of Aum tended to be intensely concerned about each other's well-being as well as that of their leader Asahara. Such shared belief systems are particularly powerful when they include religious dimensions. From Islamic fundamentalist groups in Saudi Arabia or Indonesia to Christian militia groups in the United States, the belief that God endorses the values and objectives of the group is a particularly powerful motivator for group cohesion.

Members of Aum displayed the attributes of other cults—namely, the need to belong to the group, from which psychological well-being is drawn. Often, group membership can replace an individual's psychological distress (which can be the product of any number of personal or social traumas) with an enhanced sense of self-being. This, in turn, helps explain the lengths to which group members will go to protect the group from outside forces, even when presented with evidence that the group is engaged in activities that society deems unacceptable.

As noted, boundary setting plays a critical role in determining patterns of communication between and those deemed "outsiders." In the case of Aum Shinrikyo, members were cordoned off from contact with the outside world, and Asahara maintained a gulf in communication between his inner circle and his widely dispersed adherents, thus isolating the decision makers from the flock of followers. Monitoring and controlling communication, and restricting any form of dissent, enabled Aum Shinrikyo's leaders to ensure that new members of the group accepted the beliefs and values of the group.

PRACTICAL IMPLICATIONS

Empirical data on charismatic groups and cults are often limited and, as a result, clinicians may be asked to consult on members of groups that are not well known and ones whose normative structure is obscure. Nonetheless, a few clinical points can be made.

One point is that the intensity of commitment of a member of such a group needs to be appreciated and members should not be directly confronted in a negative way, as this may only enhance a member's sense of alienation. Second, a nonjudgmental exploration of the views of the member may be helpful in understanding how and why that person became involved and may then be useful in counseling, not only the member him- or herself but also the family members whose concern has been aroused. Third, although cult members may appear to be highly deviant and even delusional in the nature of their commitments, most are not typically pathologically disturbed (Ungerleider & Wellisch, 1979). Careful attention should be given to distinguishing the deviant commitment of group members from the phenomenology of pathologic delusion. The latter usually appears in conjunction with other evidences of mental illness and poor social adjustment.

A final issue that can be of considerable interest to the clinician is the nature of spiritual recovery movements (Galanter, 1997), which may be beneficial in terms of their impact on the adjustment of their members to illness and in aiding them on the path toward recovery from emotional and behavioral problems. Such movements are typically cohesive and oriented toward transcendent commitments above and beyond those of conventional medical care. Nonetheless, the clinician should understand their value, and affiliation with them may be beneficial—or at least not harmful—if they do not contradict involvement in conventional medical or psychological care. Alcoholics Anonymous is a prime example of such a movement, but there are a variety of alternative approaches that although not substantiated by empirical research may be helpful in a person's dealing with the emotional burden of medical or psychological illness.

Because of this, clinicians must be attentive both to the potential benefits and harmful aspects of cultic and charismatic movements. They should consider the impact of membership on the overall adjustment of an adherent and be respectful of the potency of affiliation and the need for care in discussing members' respective commitments and beliefs.

References

Bowen, M. (1978). *Family therapy in clinical practice.* New York, NY: Jason Aronson.

Festinger, L., Riecken, H., & Schacter, S. (1956). *When prophecy fails.* Minneapolis: University of Minnesota Press. doi:10.1037/10030-000

Freud, S. (1955). *The standard edition of the complete psychological works: Vol. 18. Group psychology and the analysis of the ego* (J. Strachey, Ed.). London, England: Hogarth. (Original work published 1922)

Galanter, M. (1978). The "relief effect": A sociobiological model for neurotic distress and large-group therapy. *American Journal of Psychiatry, 135*, 588–591.

Galanter, M. (1983). Unification Church ("Moonie") dropouts: Psychological readjustment after leaving a charismatic religious group. *American Journal of Psychiatry, 140*, 984–989.

Galanter, M. (1990). Cults and zealous self-help movements: A psychiatric perspective. *American Journal of Psychiatry, 147*, 543–551.

Galanter, M. (1997). Spiritual recovery movements and contemporary medical care. *Psychiatry: Interpersonal and Biological Processes, 60*, 211–223.

Galanter, M. (1999). *Cults: Faith, healing, and coercion* (2nd ed., pp. 18–33). New York, NY: Oxford University Press.

Galanter, M., Rabkin, R., Rabkin, J. G., & Deutsch, A. (1979). The "Moonies": A psychological study of conversion and membership in a contemporary religious sect. *American Journal of Psychiatry, 136*, 165–170.

Kennedy, J. G. (1967). Nubian Zar ceremonies and psychotherapy. *Human Organization, 4*, 185–192.

Kleinman, A. (1980). *Patients and healers in the context of culture*. Berkeley: University of California Press.

Kristof, N. D. (1995, April 14). Tokyo journal; with cult under cloud, it's still his guiding stor. *New York Times*. Retrieved from http://www.nytimes.com/1995/04/04/world/tokyo-journal-with-cult-under-cloud-it-s-still-his-guiding-star.html

Kristof, N. D. (1997, March 23). Japanese cult said to have planned nerve gas attacks in U. S. *New York Times*. Retrieved from http://www.nytimes.com/1997/03/23/world/Japanese-cult-said-to-have-planned-nerve-gas-attacks-in-us.html

Lifton, R. J. (1961). *Thought reform and the psychology of totalism*. New York, NY: Norton.

Miller, J. G. (1965). Living systems: Basic concepts. *Behavioral Science, 10*, 193–237. doi:10.1002/bs.3830100302

Reiss, D. (1971). Variety of consensual experience. *Family Process, 10*, 1–28. doi:10.1111/j.1545-5300.1971.00001.x

Sayle, M. (1997, April). *The Buddha bites back* (Japan Policy Research Institute Working Paper No. 32). Retrieved from http://www.jpri.org/publications/workingpapers/wp32.html

Singer, M., & Borrero, M. G. (1984). Indigenous treatment for alcoholism: The case of Puerto Rican spiritualism. *Medical Anthropology: Cross-Cultural Studies in Health and Illness, 8*, 246–273.

Ungerleider, J. T., & Wellisch, D. K. (1979). Coercive persuasion (brainwashing), religious cults, and deprogramming. *American Journal of Psychiatry, 136*, 279–282.

Wynne, L. C., Ryckoff, I. M., Day, J., & Hirsch, S. I. (1958). Pseudomutuality in the family relations of schizophrenics. *Psychiatry, 21*, 205–220.